ANSI FORTRAN IV
with FORTRAN 77 Extensions

DEC VAX-11/780 minicomputer. (Courtesy of Digital Equipment Corporation)

ANSI FORTRAN IV
with FORTRAN 77 Extensions

A Structured Programming Approach

Second Edition

J. W. Perry Cole
University of Colorado
Colorado Springs

wcb

Wm. C. Brown Company Publishers
Dubuque, Iowa

Cover photo: Phillip A. Harrington/Peter Arnold, Inc.

Copyright © 1978, 1983 by Wm. C. Brown Company Publishers

Library of Congress Catalog Card Number: 82-71779

ISBN 0-697-08172-9
2-08172-01

Printed in the United States of America

Contents

Appendixes

Preface

This book is an introductory text for the student with little or no knowledge of computers or programming. It uses a building-block approach to teach FORTRAN, presenting the basic elements and language statements in the early chapters to allow the student to start writing programs quickly. Advanced subjects, such as literal (string) constants, arrays, subroutines, and the like are presented in the later chapters. This prevents the beginning student from becoming bogged down in advanced terminology and concepts. The text covers all the statements and features in many FORTRAN compilers, and may serve as the basis for a two-semester course or as a professional programmer's reference book.

While the text is designed for use by business and social science students, it is also suitable as an introductory text for math and engineering students. It assumes no extensive knowledge of advanced mathematics—a familiarity with first-year high school algebra should be sufficient. The emphasis is on the FORTRAN language and various programming techniques, such as looping, control breaks, use of arrays, subprograms, and others. I believe that the student who masters FORTRAN and programming techniques with low-level mathematics should later be able to apply this knowledge to advanced mathematics and other disciplines without difficulty.

Improvements in the Second Edition

FORTRAN and the development of FORTRAN programs have changed since the first edition of this book was written in the middle-to-late 1970s. Structured and top-down programming methodologies have proved to be a superior means of software development, and the wide-spread use of economical but powerful timesharing minicomputers provides more efficient program development. The revised text reflects these changes. The description of batch-card processing, however, has been retained, since it is still in wide use as a program entry medium.

Eight primary changes have been made to this second edition of the text.

1. While retaining a detailed description of ANSI FORTRAN 66, the text now also describes almost all features of FORTRAN 77, which provides for more structured, reliable, and readable programs.
2. Two new chapters (3 and 14) have been added to discuss general problem solving and the use of top down structured design methodologies in developing problem solutions. The material on general problem solving has been expanded to emphasize the importance of developing a well-planned problem solution *before* writing the program. Pseudocode and structure charts are introduced as tools for the creation of better-structured problem solutions, programs, and logic design.
3. A new chapter and seven appendixes are included on timesharing for various computer systems. Chapter 2 discusses basic concepts of timesharing and general procedures for developing and running a program. Appendixes E through K discuss timesharing options on various specific systems.
4. Debugging syntax and logic errors is discussed in five sections in chapter 7, with many suggestions for preventing and locating such errors. Several other chapters include guidelines for developing reliable, readable, and maintainable programs.
5. This edition goes into more depth on format-free Input/Output statements for those institutions preferring this approach to FORTRAN. Chapter 2 and the new timesharing appendixes include programs with the format-free READ and PRINT statements. Chapter 5 discusses the format-free Input/Output statements and gives the general form used on most systems.
6. There is more emphasis on structured programming. Restricted control-flow structures are discussed in the appropriate chapters. The modern structured programming statements (IF-ENDIF and DO WHILE) are discussed for those organizations having FORTRAN compilers to employ them. Differences between FORTRAN 77 and FORTRAN 66, however, are explicitly noted, with techniques for implementing these structures in FORTRAN 66 given in the appropriate chapters.

7. The first half of the book has been completely reorganized. Chapter 1 explains the fundamentals of FORTRAN programming to get the students into programming more quickly. Chapter 2 provides "canned" programs that students can enter and run in a timesharing environment. Chapter 3 explains in great detail the procedure for developing a computer solution to a problem and the use of flow charts and pseudocode to depict the solution. Complete coverage of the Assignment statement is included in chapter 4—Introduction to the FORTRAN Language. Chapter 5 expands on developing and processing a FORTRAN program. The control statements and program loops are discussed in detail in chapter 6. The built-in functions (intrinsics) have been moved up to chapter 7. Manipulation of alphanumeric (character) data has been moved up to chapter 9.

8. The revised text includes additional statements, techniques, and material. Statements such as CHARACTER Type and ENCODE/DECODE are covered. A new section explains single-level control breaks. New appendixes are included for students desiring additional information, and a glossary is included. A new chapter 20 is included that contains two case studies to provide more advanced problems for term projects. With these new changes, the text should better suit the needs of those teaching and learning FORTRAN today.

Chapter Structure

Most chapters begin with an introduction explaining the overall concept, importance, and use of the statements to be covered. The individual statements are explained, short routines are given to illustrate their coding, and a problem is presented to show their use in an operational program.

Many chapters include a section entitled "Language Extensions in FORTRAN Dialects", that discusses additional features found in other FORTRAN compilers, such as IBM, Honeywell, CDC, Burroughs, UNIVAC, and DEC. Instructors should review these sections for applications to their machines; students should skip them if they do not apply to the FORTRAN compiler used in class.

Pedagogy

Each chapter now has a summary that provides a quick condensation of the information covered. Most chapters also include a section that lists the key terms and concepts a student should gain familiarity with in the chapter. Review questions and exercises are included at the end of each chapter. Answers to review questions and the odd-numbered exercises are given in the back of the book; even-numbered exercises, which are extensions of the odd-numbered ones, may be assigned as homework. Answers to these even-numbered exercises are given in the Instructor's Manual. Programming problems that include business as well as scientific applications are given at the end of most chapters.

Approach to Programming

The text is organized so that most students can start writing FORTRAN programs as soon as possible. The first chapter deals with algorithm development and gives examples and explanations of FORTRAN programs in its latter sections. Chapter 2 describes the timesharing mode of developing programs and presents seven "canned" programs for the student to use in becoming familiar with FORTRAN and timesharing. Chapter 3 details the steps in the problem-solving, expressing an algorithm in a flow chart, pseudocode, and structured programming. Chapter 4 covers the basic elements of the FORTRAN language and Assignment statements. Chapter 5 presents a step-by-step explanation of developing, coding, and running a FORTRAN program. It also gives explanations of the seven basic statements used in nearly all FORTRAN programs.

Structured Programming

Structured programming techniques are illustrated and stressed throughout the text. A detailed discussion of top-down design, structured programming, and basic control-flow structures is presented. Students who properly approach the development of problem solutions and program writing will discover the computer to be a helpful and interesting problem-solving tool.

Coded Routines

Many coded routines are included to illustrate the construction of FORTRAN statements and their application to problem solving. Many programming techniques—such as looping, sentinel record logic, counter and accumulator logic, control breaks, table searching, sorting, and file maintenance—are also explained. Learning these techniques is, in my estimation, just as important as learning FORTRAN itself, since they may be used with any programming language. Purposely simple examples are chosen so that novice programmers will encounter little problem in following the text.

Student Oriented

The detailed explanation of FORTRAN in this book makes it useful for self-paced instruction and work. Most instructors are so busy that they cannot attend to all student problems, which leaves the student to search for help elsewhere. The great detail about FORTRAN found in this text, especially the more complex subjects, such as Input/Output operations and formatting, DO loops, arrays, subprograms, magnetic tape, and magnetic disk, allows the student to glean more than enough information to answer questions and to approach the professor on only the "impossible-to-find" errors. Most introductory programming courses rely heavily on this type of text.

FORTRAN Dialects

This text teaches the standard FORTRAN dialect. The language used is ANSI FORTRAN 66 as described in the ANSI X3.9—1966 specifications. The text also includes features of FORTRAN 77 (ANSI X3.9—1978 specifications), which is a revision of FORTRAN 66. Many language extensions found in WATFOR, WATFIV, and other FORTRAN IV compilers are also covered. Specification distinctions among standard FORTRAN 66, FORTRAN 77, and FORTRAN IV are explicitly noted. The text is well suited to academic institutions using a variety of FORTRAN dialects.

Standard FORTRAN is used because most computer systems include the Standard FORTRAN specifications in their FORTRAN compiler. This version of FORTRAN is also easily transferable to other computer systems in the job market. The additional features found in the IBM FORTRAN IV compilers, WATFOR and WATFIV compilers, the Honeywell 6000, Burroughs 6000, Control Data 6000/7000/Cyber, Univac 1100, PDP-11 FORTRAN IV PLUS, and VAX-11 FORTRAN compilers are discussed in a separate section at the ends of most chapters. Appendix A deals exclusively with the features of the WATFIV and WATFIV-S compilers. Educational institutions using ANSI FORTRAN 77, ANSI FORTRAN 66, FORTRAN IV, WATFOR, WATFIV, or other FORTRAN compilers should have no difficulty using this text.

At this point I would like to make a small disclaimer about the use of the word *data* in this text. Standard English makes the distinction between *data,* as the plural form of the word for facts, statistics, and other information, and *datum* as the singular form. Among data processing and computer professionals, however, the term *data* covers both the singular and plural forms. The same holds true in this text.

I have used the basic information in this book in my FORTRAN programming course for many years. Handouts with condensed subject information and extensive program examples were readily accepted by my students. Their encouragement persuaded me to develop this text from that material. I sincerely hope that you, as both instructors and students, will benefit from it. Areas that students found difficult to master have been given special consideration. Any suggestions for improving this text are welcomed. Letters may be sent to the publisher for my attention.

This book is dedicated to my loving family, my wife Judy and my sons Jeff and Jarrett, whose sacrifices have made my work possible.

Acknowledgments

The author is greatly indebted to so many people who have helped make this FORTRAN text possible. I want to repeat here the acknowledgments to those who contributed to the first edition, which is the basis for this new edition. First of all, I would like to thank the students at San Antonio College who encouraged me to put my class notes into a published text, and who also made teaching a pleasure. I wish to extend my personal thanks to Alvin J. Stehling, Head of Data Processing, San Antonio College, and to other SAC professors, John R. Friedrich and Merle Vogt, each of whom were helpful in many ways and assisted me in the development of this text. Second, I extend a hearty thanks to Mrs. Kay V. Tracy and my wife, Judy, who so diligently typed the manuscript.

Third, I am deeply grateful to the many people who reviewed portions or all of the manuscript and made constructive suggestions. The quality of this text is a direct result of the outstanding efforts of these people who diligently made so many invaluable recommendations. The list is long and includes Professor Dennis M. Anderson, Purdue University at Fort Wayne; Professor Norman Wright, Brigham Young University; Professor E. G. Aseltine, University of Toronto; Dr. Charles Butler, Mississippi State University; Professor Mary C. Durkin, St. Petersburg Community College; Professor Gary Gleason, Pensacola; Professor C. B. Millhaam, Washington State University; Professor Martin Stacy, Tarrant County College; Professor Greg Ulferts, University of South Colorado; Professor Howard D. Weiner, North Virginia Community College; Captain James D. O'Rourke, United States Air Force; Major James H. Nolen, United States Air Force; Major Kenneth C. Hovis, United States Air Force; Mrs. Jan Powell and Mr. Robert Lay, San Antonio College; Mr. Fred Keopping, Ford Aerospace Corporation; Captain Larry Jones, United States Air Force Academy; Lt. Col. Jerry B. Smith, United States Air Force Academy; Captain Ronald E. Joy, United States Air Force Academy; Major Kenneth L. Krause, United States Air Force Academy; and Lt. Col. Clifford J. Trimble, United States Air Force Academy.

There are special acknowledgments I would like to make to those who contributed to this second edition of this text: I want to thank Mrs. Janel Ball and my wife Judy, who performed a superior job in typing the manuscript for this second edition. I cannot thank the reviewers enough for their outstanding suggestions for improving the text. Many reviewers supplied detailed examples, for which I am indeed grateful. The many people who performed invaluable critiques and contributed to the revised text include: Bryan Alvey, University of Colorado; Colonel Willis H. Ball, United States Air Force; Janel Ball, Colorado Springs, CO; Captain Mike Bush, United States Air Force Academy; Major John Case, United States Air Force; Dr. Mel Colter, University of Colorado; Mark May, University of Colorado; Joan Seyer, University of Colorado; Professor Michael Clancy, University of California—Berkeley; Professor Robert H. Dourson, California Polytechnic State University; Professor Michael B. Feldman, George Washington University; Major Michael L. Morgillo, United States Military Academy; Professor Linda T. Moulton, Montgomery County Community College; Professor Charles E. Moulton, Beaver College; Professor Richard M. Reese, Texas A&M University; Professor Peter Richetta, Slippery Rock State College; Professor Gwen Hall Rippey, Austin Community College—Rio Grande Campus; Dwayne Roberts, Digital Equipment Corporation; Frank Holmes, System Development Corporation; Donna Ray, University of Colorado; Faye Bright, University of Colorado; and Professor Charles Shubra, Indiana University of Pennsylvania.

I would again like to thank the staff at Wm. C. Brown Company Publishers for another outstanding job. I thank IBM Corporation, Digital Equipment Corporation, CRAY, and Radio Shack for supplying photographs and illustrations for this revised edition.

Introduction to Computers and Programming

1

1.1 INTRODUCTION TO THE USE AND APPLICATIONS OF COMPUTERS

The use of computers for processing information and solving problems has steadily increased since their introduction in the mid-1940s. Each moment of our day thousands of computers manipulate data that touches lives in a multitude of ways. Wherever we turn, we find computer-related products. Our utility, gas, medical, dental, and credit accounts bills have been calculated and neatly printed by a computer. Our paychecks, saving account statements, and dividend checks are efficiently prepared by computers. We can call our bank or other companies concerning our account balance and receive an immediate reply. A clerk enters our account number into the computer, and the requested data items are immediately available. Managers query the computer concerning status information and are provided the latest data upon which to base their decisions.

The computer is capable of solving many different types of problems. Complex calculations, which would take hours, days, or even weeks to perform by hand, can be done on a computer in seconds. A computer can read data from hundreds of punched cards in a minute and print out information at the rate of thousands of lines per minute. The computer can store millions of numbers and letters and provide almost instantaneous retrieval of this information.

A computer can perform simple-to-complex mathematical tasks, draw pictures, plot graphs, and even play games. It can sort data, search tables of information, and update files of data. It can make comparisons between data values and perform various actions based on the resulting decision.

But the computer cannot solve problems by itself. The thought of a computer's being a "brain" is far from the truth. **It is only a machine—a tool used to extend man's capabilities.** It cannot make any decisions on its own—it must be told explicitly what operations to perform. The computer is limited to applications having predetermined goals that can be defined by a series of explicit logical operations. If a person cannot define all the steps involved in solving a problem, then neither can the computer.

The speed and accuracy of operations in the computer are tremendous. The computer will malfunction only if some component within it fails, and it can perform operations endlessly without getting tired. This is not to say that the products of the computer are always perfect; errors are often found in output listings, reports, and billings. But the errors really originate in the program that instructed the computer, or in the data that was given to it. The acronym **GIGO** (garbage in, garbage out), implies that you get valid results only if the computer is given correct data and is instructed correctly.

To some people, the computer is a wonderful machine that has eliminated the drudgery of their work; to others, it is a brain that never makes a mistake and can perform almost as though it were human. Some consider it a stranger that has overcharged their account; others think that it is an idiot that always gets things mixed up and has no regard for personal feelings. Even with the widespread acceptance of the computer's advantages, some people still consider the computer a threat. People's fear of the computer is often referred to as **computerphobia.**

The widespread and increasing application of computers to all phases of our lives has created professional opportunities that were nonexistent thirty years ago. The job market for students having a computer-related degree is enhanced by the clear trend toward continued growth in the industry. Myriad job opportunities exist for computer science, data processing, and information system majors, and more applications have yet to be discovered.

The number of applications for computers has mushroomed since their introduction. These applications are found in three general categories: business, science, and the humanities.

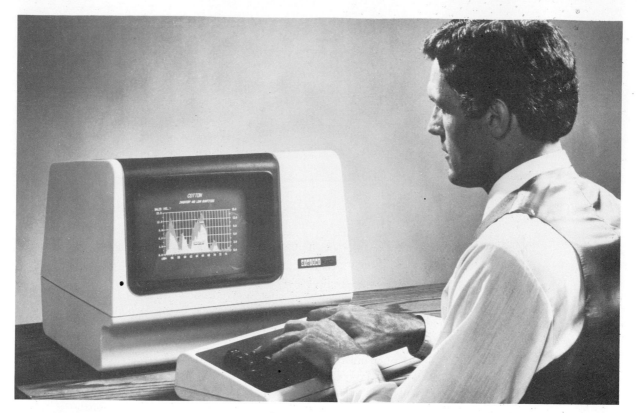

Figure 1.1 Display of graphical information for a business application. (Courtesy of Digital Equipment Corporation)

Business applications are involved mainly with record processing and operational and managerial reports (see figure 1.1). These applications include: payroll, accounting, inventory control, economic forecasting, publishing and printing, farming, and many, many more. Currently there are nearly 2,000 different business computer applications. Figure 1.1 shows a video terminal displaying graphical information for use in a business application.

Scientific applications are primarily involved with numeric processing and include: airplane stress analysis, statistics, matrix manipulation, complex equations, space, engineering, oceanography, meteorology, physics, aeronautics, and many others. There are over 1,000 scientific computer applications today.

Humanities applications are involved mainly with non-numeric processing and include: computer art, music composition, archaeology, psychology, languages, map reproduction, poetry, concordance construction, artifact classification, historical research, culture analysis, architecture, and others.

We are indeed affected by computers in almost every part of our lives—educational, business, social, governmental, religious, and recreational. Computers are here to stay. Our society cannot go back to older manual methods of processing information. Computer applications will become even more widespread. It is up to you to learn to deal with them effectively.

1.2 THE BASIC COMPONENTS OF A COMPUTER

A **COMPUTER** is a data-processing machine consisting of a system of integrated electronic units that accept and store data, perform specified arithmetic (calculating) and logical (decision making) operations on the data, and produce output results (information) from these operations. Basically the computer, therefore, performs the functions of data **input, processing,** and **output.** A computer system manipulates data and solves problems automatically, without human intervention, under the direction of a program stored in its memory unit. The **program** is a sequence of instructions that directs the computer in solving a specific problem by using the computer's various units.

Does the idea of wrestling with computer complexities scare you? Relax—you have already been closer to a personalized computer than you suspect. The automatic washing machine and the telephone share the same fundamentals of operation—**input, processing,** and **output**—that a computer performs. In a washing machine the input is soiled clothes plus detergent. The processing is their washing, which has been selected by choosing one of several different types of cycles (programs). The output is clean clothes. For the telephone, the input is

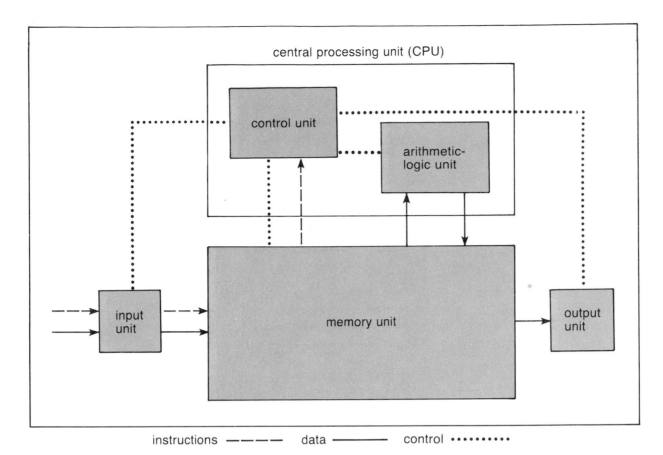

central processing unit (CPU)

control unit

arithmetic-logic unit

input unit

memory unit

output unit

instructions ———— data ——— control •••••••••

Figure 1.2 Five basic components of a computer

the number you are calling. Processing is the telephone system's ability to open and close switches to find that number. The output is the completed connection to the person you called.

Let's look at the components of a computer that allow it to perform its basic functions of input, processing, and output.

A computer, in its simplest form, is composed of five basic units. Each unit is constructed from integrated circuits, various electronic parts, wires and/or switches. These parts are used to form the **central processing unit (CPU),** which controls the processing of information. The CPU consists of two units:

1. The **Control Unit**—for coordinating and directing the operations of the computer.
2. The **Arithmetic-logic Unit**—for performing the calculations and decision-making operations.

Program instructions and the current data being processed must be available to the CPU for execution and manipulation, respectively. They are stored in another unit known as:

3. The **Memory Unit**—for storing computer instructions and data.

Auxiliary devices such as visual display terminals, typewriter-like terminals, line printers, card readers, card punches, magnetic tape drives, and magnetic disk units are connected to the CPU. These auxiliary devices form the last two of the five basic components of a computer and are known as:

4. **Input Units**—to read data on some input medium and transfer it to the memory unit.
5. **Output Units**—to take data from memory and display it on some output medium.

These input and output units are connected to the CPU to form a group of machines called a **computer system** or simply a computer. The collection of the various physical units and equipment is referred to as **hardware.** The auxiliary input/output units are also known as **peripheral equipment,** since they are usually placed peripherally around the computer operator console.

The relationship among these components is illustrated in figure 1.2. The solid lines with arrows represent the flow of data through the computer system. The hashed lines show the units involved with the program instructions. The dotted lines show the relationship of control between the control unit and the other units.

Each of these basic components will now be discussed in more detail.

Control Unit

The control unit serves two main purposes. First, it is the control hub of operations and directs the operations of all the other units. It informs the input devices when to transfer data to memory, and the output devices when to take data from memory and display it to their respective mediums. It directs the arithmetic-logic unit in all of its operations. The second function of the control unit is to "fetch" (obtain), decode, and execute each of the instructions supplied for a problem solution. This unit might be compared to the cop who directs the flow of traffic along a busy intersection.

Arithmetic-logic Unit

The arithmetic-logic unit (ALU) performs the basic arithmetic operations of adding, subtracting, multiplying, and dividing. This unit also performs the logical and decision-making operations, such as comparing two values and determining the resulting condition—e.g., equal to, less than, or greater than. The values to be manipulated in this unit are brought in from memory, and the result of the manipulation is sent back to the memory unit or control unit.

Memory Unit

One of the advantages of a computer is its ability to store information and retrieve it for later use. The memory unit allows the computer to store the data read by the input devices or items calculated in a program. Input data must be transferred to the memory unit before it can be processed by the computer. The memory unit is often referred to as **primary** or **internal storage,** since the data is immediately accessible to the control unit. The memory unit also holds the program instructions used by the control unit to determine the required operations.

The memory unit is broken down into many individual locations that may be thought of as mail boxes. Each location, however, can store only one piece of information at a time. The value stored at a particular memory location is called the **contents** of that location. A new data item may be stored at a location, but doing this will destroy the data value previously contained there.

Each storage location in memory has an **address** by which the location may be referenced. A programmer simply refers to a location by a name (symbolic address), such as X, HOLD, NUMBER, and so forth. Of course, the computer uses machine (numeric) addresses, but suffice it to say that the computer can always obtain the proper address when a **symbolic name** (called a **variable**) is used to refer to an item of data stored in memory.

The first electronic computers (1946) used vacuum tubes as memory components to represent stored information. Later computers (1950s and 1960s) used small magnetic circles referred to as **magnetic cores** to store information. Today's computers use **integrated circuit (IC)** and **magnetic oxide semiconductor (MOS)** memories, which can store thousands of characters on very small components. Figure 1.3 compares various types of computer memories and components used through four generations of computers.

Input Units (Devices)

An input unit reads program instructions and places them in the memory unit for the computer to execute. These devices also accept or read the data items used by the program. A READ command in a program directs the computer to accept the data recorded on some input medium and to transfer that data into the memory unit. There are many types of input devices available today. Each has its own advantages and disadvantages, such as cost, speed, volume of data storage, flexibility, ease in use, and so forth. The devices chosen depend largely upon the application and processing environment.

A computer terminal is a widely used input device. A terminal may be a typewriter-like device that provides a "hard copy" (paper) of all the information sent to or received from the computer. Visual display terminals have a cathode-ray tube (CRT), much like the common TV screen, to display input information and output results. (Visual display terminals are often referred to as CRT terminals.) A terminal is really a combination of an input device (keyboard) and an output device (printer or CRT). Figure 1.4 illustrates these two types of terminals.

first generation

second generation

third generation

fourth generation

Figure 1.3 Four generations of computer components. (Courtesy of IBM)

Figure 1.4 Two types of computer terminals: (left) an IBM 2741 teleprinter terminal, and (right) an IBM 3270 CRT display station. (Courtesy of IBM)

Figure 1.5 An IBM 3505 card reader. (Courtesy of IBM)

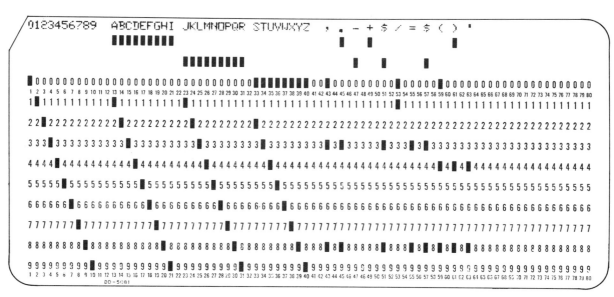

Figure 1.6 An 80-column punched card

The card reader is also a commonly used input device. It reads data on punched cards. If a terminal is not available, a student may enter his or her program and data items into the computer by means of punched cards. Figure 1.5 illustrates a card reader. The speed of card readers varies from several hundred to over a thousand cards per minute.

The type of punched card most commonly used today is the 80-column Hollerith card (named after its inventor, Dr. Herman Hollerith). The Hollerith card is a rectangular, high-quality pasteboard card. It is divided into 80 vertical columns, each capable of containing one character, as shown in figure 1.6. A character may be an alphabetic letter, a numeric digit, or a special character, such as a semicolon, asterisk, comma, or other punctuation mark. If you use punched cards and are unfamiliar with this input medium, see Appendix B for a complete description of the 80-column punched card.

Cards are punched on a machine called a **keypunch,** which has a keyboard similar to that of a typewriter. Depressing a key causes the corresponding character to be punched into the current column of the card. Appendix C describes the operation of the keypunch machine.

Many other devices exist today to provide input to the computer. Magnetic tape units read data recorded as magnetized spots on a long ribbon of tape, in a manner similar to that of a home tape recorder. Magnetic disk units read data also recorded as magnetized spots on a thin metal platter (covered with magnetic oxide) similar to long-playing phonograph records. Other input devices include magnetic drums, paper-tape readers, magnetic ink character readers, optical character readers, cassette tape readers, and floppy disk (diskette) units.

Figure 1.7 IBM 1403 line printer.
(Courtesy of IBM)

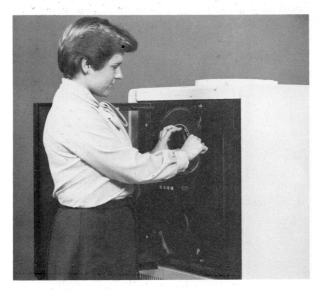

Figure 1.8 DEC TU77 magnetic tape drive.
(Courtesy of Digital Equipment Corporation)

Figure 1.9 DEC RM05 magnetic disk unit.
(Courtesy of Digital Equipment Corporation)

Output Units (Devices)

After data has been manipulated in various ways, such as computing, arranging, or summarizing, the results are displayed in some form. An output command (normally a PRINT or WRITE) causes the computer to transfer data from the memory unit to an output device that records or displays the data on its respective medium.

If a terminal is used as the input device, it is very likely that it can also be used as the output device. Terminals may be used as both input and output devices, since most are capable of transmitting information *to* the computer and also displaying the results output *by* the computer; thus, terminals are very popular input/output devices in a student environment.

The line printer is a well known and frequently used output device. This device prints program listings and output results on a paper sheet in readable form. The line printer uses a continuous flow of perforated sheets. Most printers have the ability to print 132 characters of data per line and sixty or more lines per page. On many computers you can enter your program and data over a terminal, yet direct your program listing and results to be output on the line printer. Figure 1.7 shows an example of a line printer. The speed of many commonly used impact (chain or drum) printers range from 300 to 2,000 lines per minute. The speed of non-impact laser printers may range from 9,000 to 18,000 lines per minute.

Many other types of devices exist to record output data. Output results may be recorded on punched cards or a strip of paper tape by a card punch or a paper-tape punch, respectively. Magnetic tape, disk, and drum devices may record output data. Graphic terminals and plotters are used to provide output results in a graphical form. Figures 1.8 and 1.9 show pictures of a tape drive and a disk unit, respectively.

Magnetic tape, disk, and drum storage units are referred to as **secondary or external storage.** The access to data from these units is much slower than from primary storage (memory), since the data must be transferred from the storage units external to the CPU and brought into memory for processing. The time difference in primary storage (memory) versus secondary storage (tape, disk, and drum) access speed is analogous to a department store item's being available on the shelf or having an employee obtain it from the stockroom. These secondary storage devices are invaluable in storing large quantities of data, since memory has a smaller, limited storage capacity and is much more expensive. The secondary storage units can store billions of characters economically. More information concerning the operation of magnetic tape and magnetic disk storage is presented in chapters 17 and 18, respectively.

Additional Computer System Units

Modern computers have become more complex in their design and operations. Computer architects have designed systems to provide faster transfer of data between the units in order to achieve more efficient processing. Some computers allow the input/output (I/O) devices to access memory directly, without interrupting (communicating with) the CPU. This computer architecture is called **DMA** (direct memory access).

Two additional units in modern computer systems provide faster and more efficient operations:

6. **I/O Control Unit**—to buffer data to and from the I/O devices.
7. **Channel**—to buffer data to and from the I/O control units.

A **buffer** is a temporary, high-speed storage component that allows more data to be transferred at a time between units.

An **I/O control unit** (or **I/O controller**) collects bits (binary digits, the smallest representation of data) and forms a character. This allows a larger unit of data to be collected from an I/O device before transferring it (in the length of characters) to or from a channel connected to the CPU. Thus, I/O control units provide the interface between the I/O devices and channels.

A channel collects the characters transferred to (or from) a control unit into specific groups of characters (referred to as words). It can, therefore, send (or receive) a larger unit of data to (from) the CPU. A channel is in many respects a small computer that receives commands from the CPU. There are two basic types of channels. A high-speed channel (called Selector channels on IBM machines) handles the high-speed I/O devices, such as tape and disk drives. A slow-speed channel (often called a multiplexor) handles the slow speed I/O devices, such as card readers, punches, line printers, terminals, and the operator console. The main difference between a high-speed and low-speed channel is the way that each transfers data—burst mode (without interruption) or byte (character) mode, respectively. A diagram of modern computer systems with I/O control units and channels is shown in figure 1.10.

The input/output devices attached to a computer vary from one installation or computer center to another. Figure 1.11 (p.10) shows a diagram of a model computer system. The number and type of each input and output unit is normally dictated by the processing needs of an installation. There is usually at least one card reader, several printers, one magnetic tape unit, one or more disk units, and varying numbers and types of terminals.

Figure 1.12 (p. 11) illustrates the hardware components found in a large IBM data processing installation. A large computer center may have several card readers, several printers, a dozen tape drives, many disk units, a card punch, and dozens of terminals. Some installations even have several types of computers. The computer and peripheral devices in your college data processing center, may not be as elaborate as those shown in figure 1.12, because of their high cost.

Computers and their related input/output units are very expensive. Large computer systems with a wide array of peripheral equipment may cost millions of dollars. Minicomputers cost a hundred thousand dollars or more, depending upon the number of input/output devices connected to them. Your college, therefore, may rent time (timeshare) on a computer located away from the campus; thus, the only components of a computer system you may see are the terminals, card reader, and line printer to provide the input and output operations. If you have never seen a complete computer system with all its elaborate hardware components, I suggest that you ask your instructor to arrange a tour of a computer center.

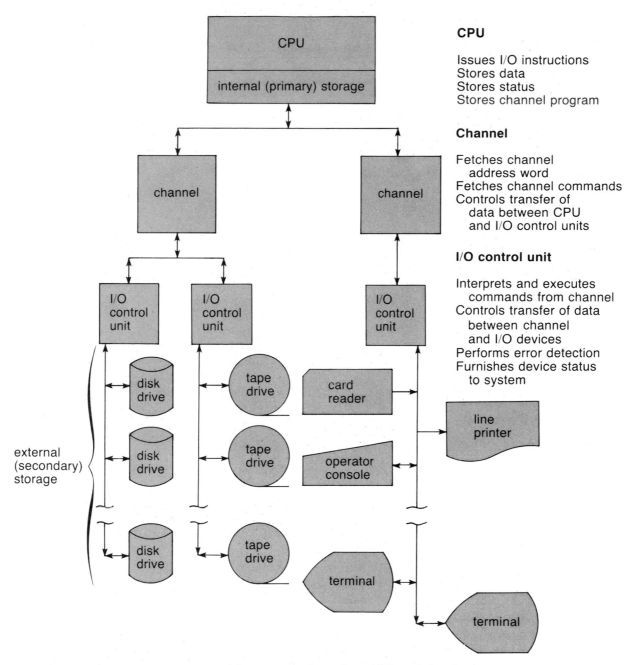

CPU

Issues I/O instructions
Stores data
Stores status
Stores channel program

Channel

Fetches channel
   address word
Fetches channel commands
Controls transfer of
   data between CPU
   and I/O control units

I/O control unit

Interprets and executes
   commands from channel
Controls transfer of data
   between channel
   and I/O devices
Performs error detection
Furnishes device status
   to system

Figure 1.10 Modern computer architecture with channels and I/O control units

The computer is indeed a marvelous machine that synchronizes its operations with great precision. But remember, a person must instruct it in every operation it performs, whether it be an input operation, a calculation, a logical evaluation, or an output operation. A computer must be told to read or accept the desired input values. Just because the computer has two values placed into memory does not cause it to calculate their sum. A command must be given to add the two numbers, and the sum will not be displayed unless the computer receives a command to do so. The computer does not "think," but merely obeys the commands in the sequence of instructions of a program developed by a person. This, then, is your goal in learning FORTRAN—to be able to supply the commands needed to instruct the computer to solve a problem.

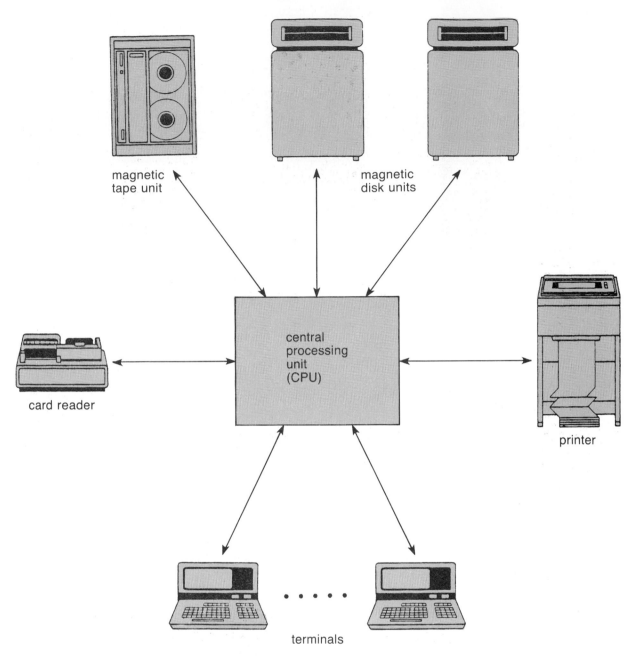

Figure 1.11 Diagram of a model computer system

1.3 TYPES AND CHARACTERISTICS OF COMPUTERS

Some computers are **special-purpose,** designed to solve one particular kind of problem, such as controlling air traffic or metalworking machines. Other computers are **general-purpose** and are used to solve a wide variety of problems. The general-purpose computer is used for the many applications in business and science.

There are two basic types of computers relative to the form of the data being processed. **Analog** computers process data that occurs in a continuous flow, such as temperature, voltage, or pressure. The output from analog computers is often displayed on a cathode-ray tube or plotting device to help monitor the results. Analog computers are frequently used in engineering and scientific applications, where the form of input data is a continuous signal. Common forms of analog devices are the thermometer, the speedometer and gas gauge in a car, a thermostat, a gasoline pump meter, and the pressure gauge on a pressure cooker—each is a measuring device.

CPU

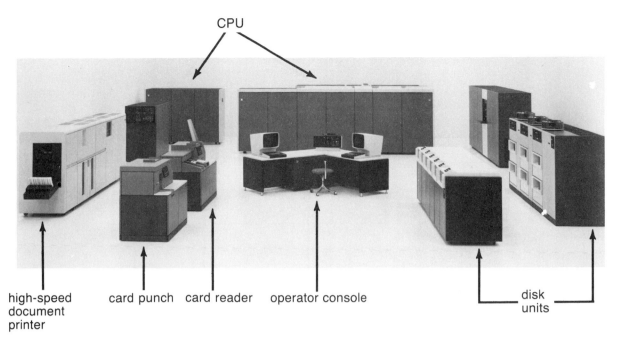

high-speed
document
printer card punch card reader operator console disk
units

Figure 1.12 An IBM system/3033 with various hardware components of a computer system. (Courtesy of IBM)

Digital computers operate on discrete (individual) quantities represented by numbers or letters. **Digital** computers are useful in business applications where separate quantities, such as an account number, payment, receipt, and so forth, are processed. The scientific, engineering, and mathematical fields use digital computers for numerical manipulations. The hand calculator is an excellent example of a digital computer on a very small scale. The abacus and cash register are examples of digital devices. This text devotes its attention exclusively to general-purpose digital computers.

You will run your programs on a general-purpose digital computer. The main advantages of this type of computer in processing data are these:

1. **A high speed of operation** due to its electronic construction.
2. **Accuracy** from the use of individual numbers and other symbols in digital form.
3. **Reliability,** since it is not affected by boredom or fatigue.
4. **Economy** from its efficiency in storing and processing data.

Computers do have limitations. The three main limitations are these:

1. **Limited intelligence,** since it must be told explicitly every step to perform.
2. **Limited language capability,** since it understands only certain programming languages and cannot communicate in ordinary English.
3. **Subject to failure,** since components can burn out or fail.

You must remember these limitations and never assume the computer to be an infallible tool. Do not fall into the trap of thinking that "since the computer produced the output results, they must be correct." Human beings cause the output results to be produced. People program the computer and create and enter the input data.

Since the 1950s, tremendous human and physical resources have been directed towards the design and development of faster and cheaper computers. The impact of semiconductor electronics on these efforts in the last few years has resulted in a variety of computers ranging from multimillion dollar super computers to minicomputers costing several hundred thousand dollars to microcomputers costing only a few hundred dollars.

We are now in the fourth generation of computers. Table 1.1 shows the dates of the four computer generations along with their type of electronic components and speed.

Table 1.1 The Four Generations of Computers

Generation	Period	Circuit Elements	Access Time
First	1946–1956	Vacuum tubes	Milliseconds $(10^{-3}$ second)
Second	1957–1964	Transistors	Microseconds $(10^{-6}$ second)
Third	1965–1970	Integrated chips (IC)	Nanoseconds $(10^{-9}$ second)
Fourth	1971–present	Large scale integration (LSI) and Very large scale integration (VLSI)	Nanoseconds

Circuit elements refer to the main components used for memory and the CPU. Access time refers to the speed at which a data item can be obtained from memory.

Computers are generally placed in three categories according to capability and throughput:

1. Super and mainframe computers
2. Minicomputers
3. Microcomputers

Super computers are used to support engineering and scientific work that is not feasible for humans to attempt. Super computer applications may include performance simulation for nuclear reactors or aircraft, the damage assessment of an atomic explosion, or the vibration response of a building to an earthquake. Large mainframe computers are used in business to read and process millions of data records each day. Super and mainframe computers support applications that require millions upon millions of numeric calculations or maintain and process vast amounts of data. Figure 1.12 in Section 1.2 showed a large IBM mainframe computer. Figure 1.13 shows a super computer.

Minicomputers, or "Minis," have become very popular because of their size (less than 100 pounds in weight), cost (from $10,000 to $200,000), and reliability (in extreme environmental conditions). Small businesses today can now afford minicomputers in their daily operation, whereas large mainframe computers would be cost-prohibitive. Figure 1.14 shows a minicomputer.

Microcomputers (μc), known as **home or personal computers (PC),** have gained wide acceptance in our homes and schools, as well as in very small business organizations. Most people refer to these computers simply as "Micros." Many people confuse the term *microprocessor* with *microcomputer*. A microprocessor is usually the chip around which a microcomputer is based. Probably the three most popular personal microcomputers are the Apple, the IBM, and the TRS-80 (by Radio Shack). There are dozens of other microcomputers used for hobbies or business applications. Close to 750,000 microcomputers have been introduced into homes and small business organizations. Figure 1.15 shows a microcomputer.

If the computer sounds like a super calculator, you are on the right track. You can add, subtract, multiply, and divide with it. But a computer can also do lengthy sequences of additions, subtractions, multiplications, and divisions in complex combinations. So don't be afraid of the computer; there is no magic about it. The computer is only a powerful calculating tool, and any person with an average intelligence and desire to learn can master the ability to communicate with it.

A general-purpose digital computer, regardless of its size or cost, manipulates information under the direction of a written program stored in its memory unit. The next section explains the stored program concept and how a computer executes a program.

1.4 THE STORED PROGRAM CONCEPT

A computer manipulates information under the direction of a program stored in memory. The **stored program** is simply a set of instructions provided by the **programmer** (one who writes the program). It is stored in the memory unit and directs the computer in all its operations. In short, a **program** is a set of commands to the computer. Instructions in the program tell the computer when to read or accept data, when to perform required computations and logical operations, and when to display the output results. The programs that direct the computer in its operations and in the solution of application problems are commonly referred to as **software.**

Figure 1.13 A super computer. (Courtesy of CRAY)

Figure 1.14 A minicomputer. (Courtesy of Digital Equipment Corporation)

Figure 1.15 A microcomputer with external storage devices. (Courtesy of Radio Shack)

When the instructions for a computer program have been entered into the computer and the computer is instructed to RUN (execute) the program, the control unit takes over. The control unit takes the first instruction, analyzes it, determines what is to be done, and then directs the proper hardware unit to perform the required functions. After the first instruction has been properly executed, the control unit fetches (gets) the second instruction and executes it. This cyclic process of fetching an instruction and executing it normally continues until an instruction is executed that commands the computer to stop (terminate) execution of the program.

All computer instructions can be placed into one of five categories, depending on the functions to be performed:

1. Input operations of data (carried out by the input units)
2. Output operations of data (carried out by output units)
3. Calculations and memory assignment of items (carried out by the arithmetic-logic unit)
4. Control for decision making, branching, and looping (carried out by the control and arithmetic-logic units)
5. Specifications to the language translator

By knowing which of the above functions you want performed, you can select the proper FORTRAN statement to command the computer to carry it out. The selected statements indicate which of the five basic computer units is needed to perform the function.

Let us examine a short program—calculating gross pay by multiplying the number of hours worked by the pay rate—to see how a program is written. First, let's look at the relationship between some of the types of commands available and the categories of instructions.

Input Operation

An input unit reads (accepts) values on some input medium (terminal input, punched cards, or others) and stores those values at designated symbolic memory locations. The READ statement is normally the FORTRAN command used to accomplish this task. If the READ command is used in a program run at a terminal, the computer asks the same terminal for the data. If the READ command is used in a program run with punched cards, the computer knows that the input data will also be on punched cards (unless an input disk file is specified). You can, of course, specify other input devices in the READ statement. For example, the statement

READ *, HOURS, RATE

tells the computer to read two values and store them in the memory locations symbolized by the names HOURS and RATE, respectively. The asterisk in this statement indicates format-free input data (which you will learn about later). This form of the READ statement is found in FORTRAN 77 and many computers using terminals as input devices; this form is not available in FORTRAN 66 or on all computers.

The choice of the variable names, HOURS and RATE, is based solely on readability. There is no magical, intrinsic meaning to variable names; the variable names X and Y would work just as well. The statement

READ *, X, Y

would perform the same function, but is not self-explanatory as to the intended use of the variables, while HOURS and RATE provide a clear indication of the intended meaning or purpose of the variables. Variable names are limited to six characters, however, in most FORTRAN dialects.

Calculations

The arithmetic portion of the arithmetic-logic unit performs calculations as indicated in an arithmetic Assignment statement and stores the one resulting value at the designated symbolic name (memory location). For example, the arithmetic Assignment statement

GRSPAY = HOURS * RATE

would cause the arithmetic-logic unit to obtain the values of HOURS and RATE from their memory location, multiply the two values together (indicated by the asterisk [*]), and store the resulting value at the memory location named GRSPAY, which is the variable name immediately to the left of the '' = '' assignment symbol in the statement.

Output Operation

An output unit displays the values from the specified memory locations on some output medium. The PRINT or WRITE statement tells the computer to direct an output unit in this operation. If a PRINT statement is used in a program run at a terminal, the computer will display the values at the terminal. In a program run with punched cards, the computer outputs the values on a printer sheet at the line printer. For example, the instruction

PRINT *, GRSPAY

tells the computer to print the value from the memory location named GRSPAY. The statement

PRINT *, HOURS, RATE, GRSPAY

tells the computer to print the three values taken from the memory locations named HOURS, RATE, and GRSPAY, respectively. The asterisk (*) in the PRINT statement specifies format-free output. This form of the PRINT statement is available in FORTRAN 77, but it is not part of FORTRAN 66.

Control

Control commands instruct the computer in the sequence of program execution. Some statements will be executed only if a specified condition is true. The IF statement is the FORTRAN command to tell the computer to evaluate a condition (using the logic part of the arithmetic-logic unit) and to perform a command only if the statement is true. For example, the statement

IF (HOURS .EQ. 0.0) PRINT *, 'HOURS = 0'

would test the value at the memory location HOURS to see if it is equal to zero. If the condition is true, the message "HOURS = 0" is printed, and control proceeds to the next statement. If the condition is false, the computer proceeds to the next instruction without displaying the message "HOURS = 0."

The FORTRAN control statement

STOP

tells the computer to terminate execution of instructions for a program. No more instructions are processed in the program.

Specification

This type of statement does not direct the computer in any operation. In fact it does not get stored as a program instruction that is executed. It is used to give the language translator information when a program is translated into machine language. A **language translator** is a software program used to convert a programming language into machine language, which is the only language the computer really "understands". The specification statement

END

simply tells the computer that this is the end of the set of instructions, or program. This statement is called a **nonexecutable** statement, but it must be included as the last statement in a FORTRAN program.

These are only a few of the commands available in the FORTRAN language. These commands, however, will be used in nearly all FORTRAN programs that you write. The symbolic memory locations are variable names that you make up according to certain general rules. (Note: the statements discussed using **format-free input/output** are not available in ANSI FORTRAN 66, which uses formatted input/output statements to read and write data.)

A complete FORTRAN program to read the values for hours worked and pay rate from an input medium, compute gross pay, and print the calculated gross pay might look like this:

```
READ *, HOURS, RATE
GRSPAY = HOURS * RATE
PRINT *, GRSPAY
STOP
END
```

The FORTRAN program is given to the computer to be translated into the machine language that it understands; then the program is loaded (placed into memory) for execution. Execution will start at the first instruction and continue in a sequential manner unless a control statement is encountered that may cause it to jump (branch) over some statements. A control statement may cause a branch back up to some previous statement in order to repeat a group of statements, an action called a **loop.** Thus, a loop is a programming technique used to repeat a group of instructions.

In an interactive timesharing environment, you would execute the program from your terminal with the RUN command. When the computer executes the READ instruction, it would stop and print a question mark (?) as a signal or "prompt" for you to enter the data items. After receiving the entered items, it would resume processing. In a batch card environment, you would supply the data items on punched cards.

At some place in your program the computer should encounter a STOP statement, telling it to end the processing for the program. If a STOP statement (or CALL EXIT statement, which will be discussed later) is not reached, the computer will continue processing until an allotted time is reached or a computer operator "kills" the program. A **computer operator** is the person who runs the computer.

In the example program the computer first recognizes a statement that commands it to read and place two data items in the memory cells symbolically named HOURS and RATE, respectively. The next (second) instruction is fetched (obtained) and causes the computer to obtain the values from the memory cells HOURS and RATE, multiply them together, and store the result at the cell GRSPAY. The next instruction in sequence is fetched and decoded. The third statement tells the computer to print the contents of the memory cell named GRSPAY. Then the control unit proceeds to the next (fourth) instruction, which tells the computer to halt processing. The fifth statement—END—is used to tell the FORTRAN language translator that this is the end of the program.

A program must be available for each problem to be solved by the computer. The program may be a new one written by you for a particular problem, or it may be an old one written by you or someone else to solve a recurring problem that has been supplied with a new set of data. The data is comprised of all the related items (values) required to solve the problem. The data varies as to the activity, such as student registration, grade calculation, engineering computations, payroll, accounts receivable, inventory control, and so forth. A different program is needed, therefore, to process the data for different applications and problems.

This explanation of how the computer goes through the process of executing a stored program might be an oversimplification of how the computer solves a problem. However, this is a high-level explanation of how the computer works. It is the stored program that makes a computer "tick." Let us now turn our attention to the fundamentals of writing a computer program. The next section discusses the basic concepts of a program and how to go about developing a program to solve a problem with the computer.

1.5 FUNDAMENTALS OF WRITING A COMPUTER PROGRAM

The computer can solve any type of problem, provided it is given a set of commands that it understands. Such a set of commands is called an **algorithm,** which is defined as a complete, unambiguous procedure for solving a problem in a finite number of steps. For example, a cake recipe is an algorithm for baking a cake; a checklist is an algorithm for assembling a specified piece of equipment; a mathematical formula is an algorithm for computing a desired quantity. To be useful, an algorithm must be:

1. **Complete and finite.** If you cannot define all the steps to a solution, the computer cannot be instructed to solve the problem. The number of steps must be finite.
2. **Unambiguous.** Each step must be clearly and precisely defined. There must be no doubt as to what course of action to take under various conditions. For example, you cannot say: Add some numbers together and get their sum. You must know precisely how many numbers to add and what they are (or at least the name they are stored at in memory).
3. **Correct and effective.** The algorithm must solve the problem correctly and effectively in an acceptable time frame.

Consider the following recipe to make Brownies:

Brownies Recipe

Melt together over hot water .... $\begin{cases} \text{2 sq. unsweetened chocolate—2 oz.} \\ \text{⅓ cup shortening} \end{cases}$

Beat in .... $\begin{cases} \text{1 cup sugar} \\ \text{2 eggs} \end{cases}$

Sift together and stir in .... $\begin{cases} \text{⅔ cup sifted flour} \\ \text{½ teaspoon baking powder} \\ \text{½ teaspoon salt} \end{cases}$

Add .... $\begin{cases} \text{½ cup broken nuts} \\ \text{1 teaspoon vanilla} \end{cases}$

Spread mixture into well greased 8″ pan. Bake until top has dull crust. A slight imprint will be left when top is touched. Bake at 350°F for 30 minutes.

This recipe may not be easily understood by someone who has never followed a recipe. If you were to instruct someone—someone who has never baked brownies following the algorithm above—your steps of instruction might be:

Step 1: Obtain mixing bowl, pans, and necessary ingredients.
Step 2: Melt two squares of unsweetened chocolate (2 oz.) and one-third cup of shortening together over hot water.
Step 3: Beat in one cup of sugar and two eggs for thirty seconds.
Step 4: Sift together two-thirds cup of sifted flour, one-half teaspoon of baking powder, and one-half teaspoon of salt; stir into mix.
Step 5: Mix in one-half cup of broken nuts and one teaspoon of vanilla.
Step 6: Grease an eight-inch pan well.
Step 7: Spread mix into pan.
Step 8: Place pan into a preheated oven (350°F).
Step 9: Bake for thirty minutes at 350°F or until the top has a dull crust.
Step 10: Check for a slight imprint, left when the top is touched lightly with finger, to determine if done.
Step 11: Remove pan from oven and allow to cool slightly. Then cut into two-inch squares for serving.

These instructions are more precisely defined as to order and steps required. They consist of a complete and finite number of steps and should provide a properly baked pan of delicious brownies.

Now, let us see how a developed algorithm is used to produce a computer program to solve a given problem.

Developing a Computer Program

An algorithm to produce the average of three test scores by the computer might be described by the following narrative.

1.   Provide the computer three test scores.
2.   Add the three test scores to produce their sum.
3.   Divide their sum by 3.
4.   Display the resulting average.
5.   Terminate the processing.

The computer doesn't care what the three test scores are as long as you give it the correct numbers properly. Knowing that you gave the correct test scores to the computer and that you instructed it correctly in the operations to find their average, you can be confident that you will receive the correct output results.

In a procedure-oriented, programming language like FORTRAN, you develop an algorithm and write the instructions in much the same way as in a problem solved by hand. For example, if you computed the average of your test scores manually, the algorithm is: first, obtain the scores; second, add the scores together to obtain their sum; third, divide the sum by the number of test scores to obtain their average.

These steps in a hand-calculated average might be represented in a block diagram form this way:

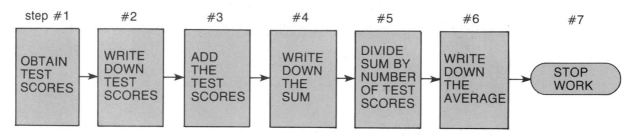

This diagram represents the algorithm or logic you must follow to obtain the average. **Logic** consists of performing the correct operations in the proper sequence. For example, you cannot compute an average until you have computed the sum of the test scores; you cannot compute the sum until you have obtained the test scores; thus, you must develop an ordered set of correct steps before you can solve a problem correctly.

You would follow basically the same procedure in instructing the computer to solve the problem with a program. The test scores may be supplied to the computer by assigning them to a memory location (in an Assignment statement) or by reading them into memory (in a READ statement). Next you compute the required sum and average. Finally, the computed values are written to an output device and the program is terminated. A block diagram to illustrate these computer operations/instructions follows:

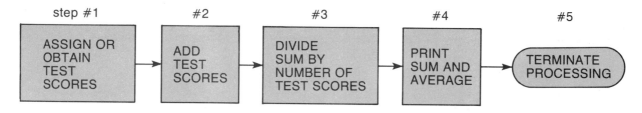

This diagram depicts the same algorithm as the narrative developed earlier for computing the average. Block diagrams help visualize the algorithm. You will learn how to display an algorithm in a block diagram form with specific symbols (called a flowchart) in chapter 3.

Another popular tool for describing the steps in a problem solution is called pseudocode, which is an English-like narrative of an algorithm. For now, it is enough to be able to express an algorithm in a narrative form. Learn what is to be done; decide how to solve the problem with an algorithm; then convert that algorithm into a computer program.

The directions that a computer follows are supplied by a series of instructions called a program. Each instruction is, normally, a command to the control unit to direct the operations of the various units of the computer.

It would be nice if you could simply talk to the computer and tell it how to solve a problem from the algorithm. Basically, that is what you do in writing a program, but the language must be in a form that the computer understands—i.e., in a programming language such as FORTRAN—and must contain only instructions valid in that language. In our example, the operations expressed in the developed algorithm are **coded** into computer instructions in FORTRAN. If the test scores are to be read into memory, you would code a READ statement to read the number of scores used. An Assignment statement is used to sum the scores. The next computer instruction would be another Assignment statement to compute the average of the scores. You could compute the average of the test scores without having a separate statement to compute their sum, but if you wish to print the sum, it must be calculated in a separate statement, in order to be retained in memory. The fourth computer instruction would be a PRINT statement to print the desired results of sum and average. The fifth instruction would be a STOP statement to tell the computer to terminate the processing of the program. The END statement is then included as a required last statement. The completed FORTRAN program (using format-free input/output statements and using the variable names of SCORE1, SCORE2, and SCORE3 for test score 1, test score 2, and test score 3, respectively) would look like this:

```
READ *, SCORE1, SCORE2, SCORE3
SUM = SCORE1 + SCORE2 + SCORE3
AVE = SUM / 3.0
PRINT *, SUM, AVE
STOP
END
```

A slash (/) is used to indicate division in the Assignment statement to calculate the average.

In the case of multiple sets of data, there is no need to write separate READ, Assignment and PRINT statements for each set. Such a technique would require 300 statements to process 100 sets of data. Instead, establish a general procedure for processing one set of data; then use a loop to repeat the instructions until each set has been processed. A **loop** is an iterative process which repeats the execution of a group of statements. FORTRAN contains various control statements that can be used to create loops. The concept of looping is a powerful technique that allows many sets of data to be processed with a very concise program.

In our example (assuming a student number [ID] and three test scores are to be read), the narrative for the algorithm or logic for processing multiple sets of students' test scores and computing their average might be:

1. Read student ID and three test scores.
2. Sum the test scores.
3. Calculate the average by dividing the sum by 3.
4. Print the student ID, computed sum, and average.
5. Repeat steps 1 through 5 until all sets of students' scores have been processed.
6. Terminate processing.

A block diagram representation of this algorithm might look like:

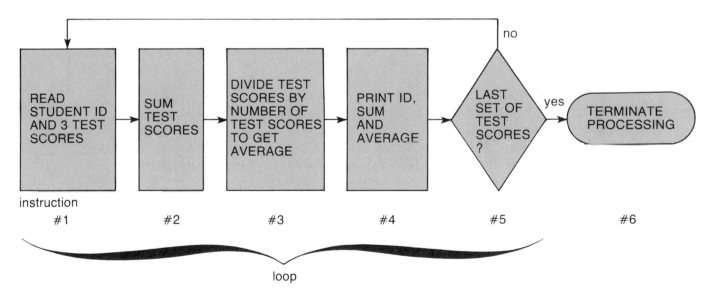

You will learn several techniques and FORTRAN statements to perform looping operations. One such technique is the use of FORTRAN DO and CONTINUE statements to perform a loop a specific number of times. Example: There are thirty students in a class and an instructor wishes to compute the average of three grades of each student (identified by the variable name ID). A FORTRAN program to solve this problem might look like this:

```
        DO  10  NR = 1, 30, 1
            READ *, ID, SCORE1, SCORE2, SCORE3
            SUM = SCORE1 + SCORE2 + SCORE3
            AVE = SUM / 3.0
            PRINT *, ID, SUM, AVE
    10  CONTINUE
        STOP
        END
```

The FORTRAN DO statement tells the computer to do all statements down through statement number 10 thirty times. The counter identified by the variable name NR will start at 1 and be incremented by 1 until it exceeds 30, at which time the loop is exited.

With the DO loop construction and other loop control techniques, many sets of data can be processed with the same series of instructions. Thus, the power of the computer to solve a problem with many sets of data is practically unlimited.

To summarize: The computer processes the instructions in a program by beginning at the first instruction and proceeding in a sequential manner (top to bottom) until it encounters a control instruction that directs it otherwise. For now, we will concern ourselves only with programs that do not contain any control instructions that cause a loop, but contain only instructions executed in a top-to-bottom order.

You should now have a basic idea of what a computer program is and how it directs the hardware units. In the next chapter, you will learn specific techniques for creating and processing programs on a timesharing system.

1.6 SUMMARY

Chapter 1 has exposed you to many terms and concepts related to computers and programming. Computers are widely used in our society. All applications may be grouped into one of three broad categories—business, science, and the humanities.

There are five basic components to any computer system—input units, output units, memory unit, control unit, and arithmetic-logic unit. Modern computers are more sophisticated and include channels and I/O controllers, but all computer systems have at least these five basic components. The input units may consist of terminals (hard-copy and visual-display), card readers, magnetic tape drives, magnetic disk units, magnetic drum units, optical character readers (OCR), magnetic ink character readers (MICR), paper tape units, cassette tape units, floppy disk units, and others. Output units may consist of terminals, printers, card punch, magnetic tape drives, magnetic disk units, magnetic drum units, paper tape punch, graphic terminals, plotters, cassette tape units, floppy disk units, and others. Hardware is the term used to identify the physical components of a computer.

Computers may be classified in terms of their problem-solving characteristics as special-purpose or general-purpose. Special-purpose computers are designed and programmed to perform one specific task, while general-purpose computers can solve a wide range of problems. This type of computer uses stored programs, each of which corresponds to a particular problem to be solved. A second classification of computers is made according to the type of data they process. Analog computers process continuous data such as pressure, voltage, temperature, and so forth. Digital computers process data represented in discrete (separate) quantities. A third classification of computers is by their size and through-put capabilities (amount of data they can process in a period of time). Computers in this classification may be grouped as super and mainframe computers, minicomputers, and microcomputers.

The stored program concept is one of the most important characteristics of the general-purpose computer. A set of instructions in the form of a program is loaded into the memory unit for the computer to execute and solve a problem. A different program can be loaded for each unique problem to make the computer a highly versatile machine. Software is the term to identify the collection of programs that a computer uses to solve various problems.

Writing a program is the process of putting together a set of ordered instructions to direct the computer in the operations needed to solve a problem. The process of writing these instructions is called coding. There are various commands that instruct the computer to read data items into memory, perform calculations on the data items, make decisions regarding the equality or inequality of items, control the flow of execution through the program, and display various output results. The computer starts execution of a program at the first executable instruction and proceeds in a sequential manner in selecting the instructions for execution. A control instruction may be encountered that tells the computer to alter this sequential flow and transfer to a new location to continue execution.

Before writing a program, you must establish the proper order of steps necessary to solve the problem. This procedure or series of steps is called an algorithm. An algorithm must be complete and finite, unambiguous, and correct in order to properly define the solution to a problem by the computer.

A programming language must be used to communicate the algorithm to the computer. You must also use various techniques, such as looping, to use the computer more efficiently for multiple sets of data and complex problems.

You will feel a certain fascination as you solve a problem on the computer—and probably feel a great sense of victory when you finally get the correct output results. It is this exuberant spirit that I wish you to sense in commanding the computer to obey your every instruction.

Programming a computer is a practical skill which requires actual experience. No amount of textbook study will enable you to drive a car, learn to play tennis, or learn to swim. The same is true of computer programming. You gain proficiency through writing programs, not merely reading or studying about them.

This text is designed to present the material in a building-block fashion and provide only the material you actually need to advance your progress in a new area. By fully understanding each new subject as it is explained, you will avoid much frustration in later advanced topics.

Some of you may wonder why you need to know anything about computers in the first place. On a practical level, the answer is clear: the computer is one of the most important technological developments of our age. No matter what field you enter, your work will be affected by it.

Beyond that, though, you should gain an appreciation for the ability of the computer to help solve problems that could not even have been approached a few short years ago. The computer can extend your productive capabilities far beyond what you have ever imagined—if you will only learn to use it.

1.7 TERMS

Terms you should become familiar with in this chapter:

address	general-purpose computer	microcomputer
algorithm	hardware	minicomputer
arithmetic-logic unit	input	output
card reader	input unit	output unit
central processing unit	I/O control unit	primary storage
channel	instruction	program
computer	internal storage	programmer
computer operator	keypunch	punched card
computerphobia	line printer	secondary storage
control unit	logic	software
CPU	magnetic disk	stored program
data	magnetic tape	super computer
digital computer	mainframe computer	terminal
execution	memory unit	variable

1.8 REVIEW QUESTIONS

1. How do people feel and react towards computers?
2. What are some of the tasks or things that a computer can be programmed to do?
3. List the three categories of computer applications.
4. Define the term ''computer'' in your own words.
5. Name the five basic components of a computer.
6. The central processing unit consists of what two units?
7. What are the two basic functions of the control unit?
8. What is the purpose or function of the arithmetic-logic unit?
9. Define a storage address.
10. What is the purpose of input devices?
11. What are the two types of terminals used to enter programs and data?
12. What is the most common type of punched card used today?
13. On what machine are cards punched?
14. What is the purpose of output devices?
15. Name five output devices.
16. What is the normal number of characters that can be printed on a line by a line printer?
17. What type of data do digital computers operate on?
18. List four main advantages of computers?
19. What are three limitations of computers?
20. List the categories of computers as to size, cost, and capability.
21. What is the stored program concept, and why is it so important?
22. List the five categories of instructions found in programming languages.
23. What is an algorithm?
24. A series of FORTRAN statements to instruct the computer how to solve a problem is called a
   _____ .
25. List two tools which may be used to express the algorithm for a problem to be solved by a computer.

Programming with Timesharing Systems

2

2.1 INTRODUCTION TO THE USE OF A TIMESHARING SYSTEM

The purpose of this chapter is to provide an overview of timesharing concepts and operations. Procedures and system commands are discussed in a general manner without regard to a specific system. An explanation of the general procedures followed in developing a FORTRAN program along with warnings of common errors are given. This chapter is intended for those students who have never used a timesharing system. Students who have used a timesharing system may read only sections 2.6 and 2.9 and skip the remainder of the chapter.

Section 2.6 presents seven canned (preprogrammed) FORTRAN programs. The intent of these programs is to get the student on the computer as early as possible—hopefully by the second week or class period. Students can immediately learn their timesharing system and the procedure for developing and running programs without a full understanding of FORTRAN. Thus, any fears and misconceptions a student might have about computers are overcome early in the course.

Timesharing is a sharing of computer time among multiple users that nonetheless gives the impression to each user that he or she has exclusive use of the computer. A timesharing system enables a large number of individuals to make use of a computer system simultaneously. The user has a terminal connected **on-line** (directly or immediately accessible) to the computer. Each user interacts with the computer in a conversational (dialogue) mode. That is, a user seated at a terminal enters his/her program and data and receives prompts and output results displayed on the terminal, directly from the computer. The computer tells the user when a specific action is completed and (with some programming languages) when an **invalid** statement has been entered. Hence, a timesharing system is often referred to as an **interactive, conversational mode** of processing programs.

Terminals may be located in the same or adjacent rooms with the computer; or they can be located a considerable distance (hundreds and even thousands of miles) from the processing computer. They can be scattered across the campus or even around the country to provide an on-line interactive processing capability on a computer system. Figure 2.1 (p. 24) illustrates the general organization of a timesharing system.

A user need not worry about file security, since a timesharing system ensures that any file created belongs exclusively to the person or account creating it, and the system will deny any other user's request to access it.

Timesharing has numerous advantages over batch-card processing mode of running programs. The main advantage is that results are obtained in a matter of seconds or minutes rather than hours or days. This reduction in **turnaround** (time it takes to get the results back from a run) aids the programmer with immediate feedback. This helps the programmer analyze the information he receives and determine more quickly what program error may have caused erroneous results. Programs may thus be finished in a fraction of the time it takes with batch-card operations.

The user "controls" the timesharing system by means of a command language. The command language consists of system commands which are completely different from programming statement instructions. The word "command" in this chapter, therefore, refers to system commands in the timesharing command language.

Even though there are hundreds of different vendor terminals on the market today, there are two basic types. One is the **teleprinter** terminal, which prints the program and its results on paper. The other type has a visual display screen (known as a **cathode ray tube [CRT]**) like a TV screen. Many terminals may have an attached X-Y plotter so that graphical output can be directed to the plotting device.

Computing with a personal microcomputer also provides an on-line, interactive processing environment. You are the sole user of the computer (if the micro has only one terminal attached to it). Therefore, you are not operating in a timesharing environment, since you are not sharing the computer simultaneously with anyone else. The procedures for terminal operations, however, and the system command language to solve problems are very similar to those on timesharing systems. The information in this chapter is thus also pertinent for personal computer users.

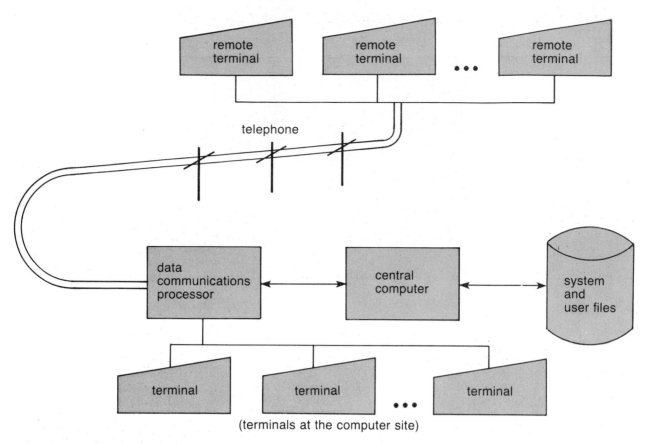

Figure 2.1 A timesharing system with local and remote terminals

This chapter is devoted to the fundamentals of terminal operations and timesharing procedures for creating and processing FORTRAN programs. The system commands required to create, manipulate, execute (run), and save programs in an interactive environment are discussed. There is very little difference between writing a FORTRAN program in an interactive mode and in a batch-card mode. The rules of FORTRAN statement construction and the logical development of a program are the same in either mode. The main difference lies in the means of communicating the program to the computer.

The operations, commands, and capabilities in an interactive mode vary from computer to computer. The concepts and many types of commands, however, are the same for many computer systems. Your instructor will define the commands on your particular system. You may also consult the User's Guide for the specific system you are using to obtain additional detailed information.

Now let us look at the operations of some popular terminals.

2.2 LEARNING TO USE A TERMINAL

Before entering a program, you must first learn to operate your terminal. You must learn how to turn it on, how to use the various functional keys, how to transmit a line of information, and so forth. Both typewriter-like and cathode-ray tube (CRT) terminals have a keyboard similar to that of a typewriter. We shall first look at the teleprinter type of terminal.

Teleprinter Terminals

The typewriter-like terminal is called a **teleprinter** because it is a **tele**communications device which displays a **printed** copy of the information transmitted to and received from the computer. One of the main advantages of this type of terminal is that the user can get a **hard-copy** (paper copy) of the program and output results.

The Digital Equipment Corporation (DEC) Decwriter is a well-known type of teleprinter terminal that comes in several models. The Decwriter II (LA36), an older model with a limited speed of 300 baud (about 30 characters per second), is illustrated in figure 2.2.

Figure 2.2 A Decwriter II (LA36) terminal. (Courtesy of Digital Equipment Corporation)

Figure 2.3 The keyboard layout of a Decwriter II (LA36). (Courtesy of Digital Equipment Corporation)

Figure 2.4 A Decwriter IV (LA34) terminal. (Courtesy of Digital Equipment Corporation)

Figure 2.3 illustrates the keyboard layout of the Decwriter II terminal. (The DEC VT-52 CRT terminal has the same keyboard layout.)

The Decwriter III (LA120) is a modern model with various transmission speeds and a microprocessor. The Decwriter IV (LA34), a smaller, more economical, table-top model with the same capabilities as the Decwriter III, is illustrated in figure 2.4.

You should fully understand the use of several important functional keys on the keyboard. If a terminal has a **CAPS LOCK** key, it should be locked down to cause capital letters to be typed. The **RETURN** key is used to transmit a line of information. If you use a PDP-11 system, the **DELETE** key is used to erase typed character(s). You should depress the DELETE key one time for each character you wish to erase. For example, to erase the last two characters, depress the DELETE key twice. Do not use the BACKSPACE key to erase characters if you are connected to a DEC system. The backspace is a valid character to allow overstriking or underlining. If your terminal is connected to another computer system (such as CDC or Cyber) the BACKSPACE key *is* used to erase characters. You must understand the function of certain keys relative to the computer system to which your terminal is connected.

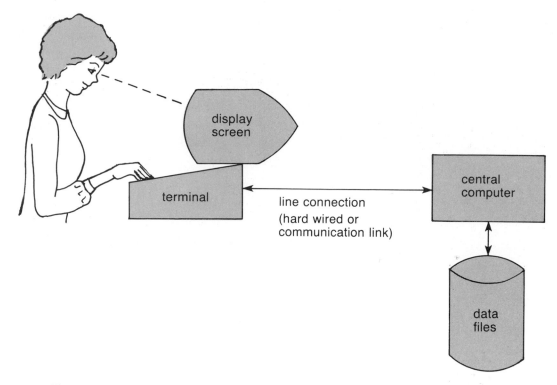

Figure 2.5 CRT type terminal operation

Depressing the combination of the control (CTRL) key and certain other letter keys at the same time provides a special function or control request to a timesharing system. Your instructor should explain those control characters that perform certain operations on your terminal (cancel a line, stop printing, and so forth).

Now let us look at visual display terminals.

Visual Display (CRT) Terminals

The second type of terminal has a **cathode-ray tube (CRT)** to show typed input and to display received output. This type of terminal displays information on a TV-like visual display screen, as illustrated in figure 2.5. Most personal computers also use this type of terminal. Most CRT screens will display 24 lines of data with 80 characters per line.

A built-in **cursor** (location marker) indicates the place on the screen where the next character will be entered. The cursor may be an underline or a block symbol (blinking or steady), and it is usually white or green. As the user enters data, the cursor moves to the right, automatically indicating the current line position. When an entire line has been entered and transmitted, the cursor moves to the leftmost position of the next line.

The CRT keyboard is similar to that of a typewriter, but it usually has additional keys for positioning the cursor. On some CRT terminals there are cursor control keys to move the cursor to the left (←), to the right (→), up to the same position on the previous line (↑), and down to the same position on the next line (↓). On some CRT terminals you must depress two keys, such as the SHIFT key and DEL (delete) key, or the SHIFT key and the RUB (rubout) key, to erase a character and move back one space. On many CRT terminals you cannot return to a previously typed line.

When you have typed your command or line of information to be sent to the computer, depress the **RETURN** key (or NEW LINE, ENTER, or XMT, depending on the terminal), and the line is transmitted. All data from the beginning of the line to the cursor position (where you stopped typing) is sent to the computer to be processed.

After a system command is processed, the computer responds with a control character such as ''#'', ''*'', or a message such as ''Ready'' or ''DONE'' (on the next line) to let you know that it has finished the previous command and is ready for you to enter another one. This character or message is known as a **prompt** and signals you that the computer is ready for a new command.

Figure 2.6 A DEC VT-100 visual-display terminal. (Courtesy of Digital Equipment Corporation)

CRT terminals offer a quieter mode of operation than a teleprinter terminal, since there is no hardcopy printing. CRT's are also faster, since the electronic display of characters on the screen is faster than a printout on a teleprinter. The CRT terminals do not use expensive paper, and they are usually very reliable; thus, you can expect to find many CRT terminals in timesharing environments.

There are dozens of brands of CRT terminals on the market today. Perhaps the more popular CRT terminals in use at academic institutions are the Hazeltine 1500 series, the LSI (Lear Siegler, Inc.) ADM series, and the DEC VT-100 video terminal. Figure 2.6 shows a DEC VT-100 video terminal.

2.3 TIMESHARING SYSTEM COMMAND LANGUAGE

To create and execute programs, save or purge files, or list the contents of files, an interactive computer system must have its own command language. A separate **language,** known as **system commands,** must be used to tell the computer what operations to perform on a program or data file. System commands control the generation, modification, and disposition of program and data files and program execution requests. These commands are usually controlled by the **Timesharing Executive** (part of the operating system for the computer). This set of system commands manipulates programs and data files in an on-line, interactive mode. Before learning about the types of system commands found on a timesharing system, however, you need to understand these terms: file, record, current file, and permanent file.

A **file** is a collection of records (or a set of information). A **record** may be one statement in a program or one line of data. Most computers do not check during file generation or manipulation to see whether a file contains program statements or data records. You, the user, are responsible for distinguishing among your files.

A user may have many permanent programs and/or data files stored on magnetic disk. A **permanent file** is one that is stored on disk (after you sign off) until some later time when it is "purged" (destroyed). However, users in timesharing modes usually work with a **temporary file** (stored in memory) typically known as the **current file.** (The temporary file is also called a workfile, work area, or local file on various computer systems.)

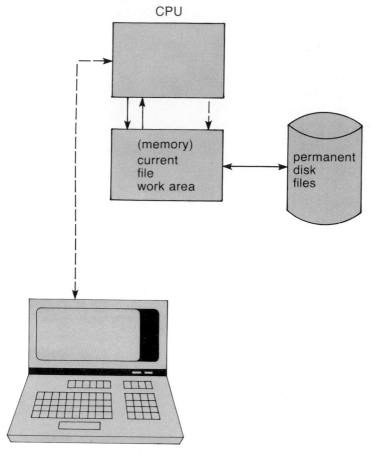

CPU

(memory)
current
file
work area

permanent
disk
files

Figure 2.7 Timesharing environment showing relationship of
a current file and permanent disk files.

For a common name, the term "current file" will be used in this text to denote the temporary file being worked on. The current file is a **temporary work area** assigned to a user to build a new file or to copy a selected permanent file as shown in figure 2.7.

The current file is usually a source program file which the user is creating, modifying, compiling, or executing. It may also be a data file that the user is building. The user is usually allowed to work on only one current file at a given time. To create a new current file, the old current file must either be saved as a permanent file or removed (purged) from the system. A permanent file must normally be loaded as a temporary current file before it is available for use. Thus, commands like OLD, GET, or LOAD must be used to copy a permanent file into the current file. Commands like SAVE, RESAVE, REPLACE, SCRATCH, PURGE, ERASE, or REMOVE tell the system what to do with a current file when you are finished with it. Changes made to a current file affect only the current file; no permanent files are modified.

Timesharing commands and program statements are communicated to the computer by typing the command or statement and then pressing the **RETURN** key, which causes the line of information to be transmitted to the computer. The computer then recognizes the command or statement and takes the proper action. The RETURN key may be labeled ENTER, ENTRY, NEW LINE, or XMT on various terminals.

A timesharing system usually requires that every statement/line in a current file be given a line number to indicate the order in which statements appear in the program. Therefore, line numbers must be in numerical order. You can use the line numbers to identify specific lines, in order to list or correct them, or to delete them from or add them to a program. Line numbers **DO NOT** replace statement numbers in a FORTRAN program. A line number on many timesharing systems may consist of one to five numeric digits, but some timesharing systems allow eight digits.

Your timesharing terminal is both an input and output device. You will transmit the statements of your FORTRAN program and the system commands telling the computer what functions to perform. The computer recognizes the difference between these two types of input information from their beginning character. That is, if you type a **number** as the first part of a line of information, the computer interprets this to be a line number and a FORTRAN statement in your program. If the first character in a line is a **letter,** the computer interprets the line as a system command.

Most timesharing systems require a user to sign on with an account number, password, or some type of identifying user code. One account number may be shared by an entire class, or students may be assigned individual account numbers. In any case, if your timesharing system requires an identification number and a log-on procedure, you must perform these operations before you can use the computer.

Remember, each time you type a command or a statement, you must terminate the line by pressing the RETURN (or appropriate) key. This causes the typed line to be transmitted to the computer. Nothing happens until you press this key.

The following general procedure describes the steps usually followed in processing a FORTRAN program at a terminal:

1. Make sure the terminal is turned on.
2. If your terminal is not directly connected to the computer, dial the computer system's telephone number to connect with it.
3. Complete the log-on (or sign-on) procedure.
4a. On some systems, you must know how to use a text editor to create and modify your FORTRAN program.
4b. If a FORTRAN run-time system is available, you must follow these steps:
    (1) Tell the computer what type of SYSTEM (programming language) you want to use.
    (2) Tell the computer the type of file to use, such as NEW or OLD, to indicate the status of the file.
    (3) Tell the computer the name of the file.
    (4) Type in your program.
5. After your program is complete, follow the correct procedure for the computer to RUN (execute) it. If you do not have a correct program, make the necessary corrections and run the corrected program again.
6. Obtain a printed copy (listing) from the typewriter terminal (or a printer) to study or take back for class.
7. Finally, log off (or sign off) from the system.

These steps are taken on any type of terminal on a timesharing system. Some of the steps in 4b may be performed in a single operation on some systems. The connect and log-on procedures usually differ from one system to another. Section 2.9 presents a detailed discussion of the steps to follow in completing a computer assignment at a terminal. Note: Many systems do not have a subsystem for creating FORTRAN programs. On these systems you must use a text editor to enter a program in FORTRAN.

The next section discusses the log-on procedure for timesharing systems in general. The specific log-on procedure for various timesharing systems may be found in one of the appendixes. These appendixes also explain the timesharing commands by which a user can create, modify, and execute FORTRAN programs. Appendixes are available to explain these timesharing systems:

Appendix	Timesharing System
E	Digital Equipment Corporation (DEC) PDP-11 series computers using RSTS/E
F	Hewlett Packard (HP) 3000
G	International Business Machines Corporation (IBM) S/360,S/370,4300,3030
H	Burroughs 6000
I	Honeywell 60/6000
J	Univac 1100
K	Control Data Corporation (CDC) 6000 and Cyber

2.4 GENERAL LOG-ON PROCEDURE TO A TIMESHARING SYSTEM

The **log-on procedure** connects you to the computer and allows you access to the services it provides. This procedure is also referred to as log-in or sign-on on some systems. This section introduces you to the general procedure and items needed to gain access to a timesharing system.

First, you must make sure the terminal is turned on and connected to the computer. To test whether the terminal is working, depress the RETURN key or type and transmit a few words. A system message or a message instructing you to type the correct log-on command (such as HELLO) will be displayed on most systems (to let you know that you are connected to the computer).

A timesharing user is usually assigned an identification number (or account number) and a password for access to the system. Some systems also require a project number for log-on. You must know these items before starting a timesharing session and attempting to log on. These items must be correctly entered for you to gain access to the computer.

The log-on procedure to a timesharing system usually consists of the following steps:

1. After turning on your terminal, insuring that the necessary switches are set to the correct position, and making connection with the computer, depress the RETURN (or appropriate) key. The computer will respond with a system identification message and a request for your user identification (ID).

2. Type your user ID and depress the RETURN key. The user ID uniquely identifies a particular user, known to the system, for the purposes of charging for the resources used during the timesharing session and locating files in the account.

   If your user ID is not acceptable (invalid because of typing errors or not currently on the system), the computer responds with a message to the effect that you have entered an invalid ID and must try again. If you are unsuccessful in entering a valid user ID several times in succession, the system will issue a message to the effect that you are denied access to the system; it will then terminate the session.

3. After you respond with a valid user ID, the system will request your password. On some teleprinter terminals a "strikeover" mask is printed on the next line after the prompt for your password. The "strikeover" mask is an overstrike (blackout) of characters which ensures that your password, when typed, cannot be read by another person. For example, CDC timesharing systems provide a strikeover mask for hardcopy terminals; DEC does not, since the password is not echoed (printed). On CRT terminals no "strikeover" mask is shown, since the typed password is not normally echoed (displayed) on the screen. After typing the row of blackout characters, the typing position is moved back to the first position in the blackout mask, and the system awaits entry of your password.

4. Type your assigned password and hit the RETURN key. A unique password is assigned to each user as an additional security check. You must protect your password, since other users may sign onto your account if they know it. With the user ID and password the system can verify you as a valid system user.

   If an invalid password is entered (because of typing errors or because it is not on the system), the system will respond with a message to that effect. You must then go back to step 2 and reenter your user ID. On many systems you are allowed only a limited number of log-on attempts before the computer denies you access to the system.

5. After the computer validates the password, it may prompt for a project number. A common project number is usually assigned for an entire class. If the user is not authorized for the given project (usually due to typing an incorrect project number), the system will respond with a message to that effect.

6. Many systems will then print the message "Ready" to let you know that they are ready to accept any of the valid timesharing commands. Some systems will issue a prompt message to ask what system you want to use. This is called the system-selection request. Many timesharing computers have several programming languages in which you can create and run programs in a "run-time" subsystem. A **run-time system** is a sub-monitor in the operating system that provides a command language to manipulate programs. Thus, a run-time system will directly accept statements in a specific programming language, such as FORTRAN or BASIC, and timesharing commands such as NEW, OLD, LIST, SAVE, or RUN. Many timesharing systems do not have a FORTRAN run-time subsystem; therefore, you must use a text editor to create and modify FORTRAN source programs.

If a run-time subsystem is available, the computer may ask you what subsystem you want to use. After you give the run-time subsystem name (such as FORTRAN or BASIC), the computer will ask you what type of file you want to use, by displaying a message such as:

OLD OR NEW FILE:

You would respond with the word "OLD" if you wanted to access an existing program file. You would respond with the word "NEW" if you wanted to create a new file. Then the system will ask for the name of the file.

Let us look at two log-on procedures. The first one is with a minicomputer timesharing system which does not have a FORTRAN run-time subsystem. The second example is with a large mainframe computer which does have a FORTRAN run-time subsystem.

Example of the Log-on Procedure to a Minicomputer Timesharing System Without a FORTRAN Run-time Subsystem

Following is an illustration of a log-on procedure for the PDP-11/70 RSTS/E timesharing system at the University of Colorado at Colorado Springs (UCCS) using the account number [74,3]. The underlined items are entered by the user. The boldface messages are displayed by the system.

①   HELLO
②   **RSTS V7.1-11 UCCS JOB 12<Local>KB6 12-Jul-82 11:26 AM**
③   **User:** 74,3
④   **Password:** XXXX (The X's represent a valid password)
⑤   (a system manager's message is displayed here, if there is one)
⑥   **Ready**

An explanation of the lines is given according to the circled numbers on each line (which are not part of the log-on procedure).

① The word "HELLO" is typed (and transmitted) by the user to gain access to the system and to start a timesharing session.

② The system responds with a message identifying the system, the job number (12), keyboard number (6) and the current date and time (12-Jul-82 11:26 AM).

③ The system first prints the message "User" to let the user know to enter his or her user ID.
   The user enters his or her assigned user ID (account number) to gain access to the system. On a PDP-11 RSTS/E system an account number consists of two parts—a project number and a programmer number (separated by a comma or a slash).

④ Then the system asks for the user password by displaying the message "Password:". The user types and transmits his or her password at this point. The typed password is not printed on the terminal with this system.

⑤ A system manager's message to inform users about the system or computer operations (such as scheduled down times, available hours, and so forth) is printed.

⑥ Then the system prints the "Ready" message to let the user know when to proceed with his or her work.

You must use a text editor to create and modify FORTRAN programs on this timesharing system.

Example of the Log-on Procedure to a Large Mainframe Timesharing System With a FORTRAN Run-time Subsystem

Following is an illustration of a log-on to the Cyber system at the University of Colorado at Boulder from the University of Colorado at Colorado Springs using the user ID S839. A Decwriter II teleprinter is used (notice the overstrike mask). After the log-on procedure is completed, a new FORTRAN source program file named DEMO is specified to be entered.

①   **Cyber system up**
②   **81/12/26. 20.36.44 CYBER USER ID:**S839
③   **PASSWORD**
④   XXXXXXXX (a valid password is entered)
⑤   **PROJECT:**PDJZ
⑥   **TERMINAL: 27, TTY**
⑦   **SYSTEM:** HHAALLFF
⑧   **READY.**
⑨   **READY.**
⑩   FORTRAN
⑪   **OLD OR NEW, FILE:** NEW,DEMO
⑫   **READY.**

The entries which would be typed by a user are underlined. The log-on procedure is explained by the circled numbers corresponding to the typed lines.

1. The message "Cyber system up" is displayed by the system after the user strikes the RETURN key. A system manager's message is also displayed at this time if there is one.
2. The system then displays a message identifying the system and the current date and time. The system identification line also requests entry of the user's account number (USER ID:). The user types his or her user identification number, in this case S839.
3. Then the system asks for the user password by displaying the message "PASSWORD".
4. Since a hardcopy terminal is used, a strikeover mask is displayed on a new line to conceal the typed password. The user types and transmits his or her password at this time.
5. The system next prompts for a project number ("PROJECT:"). The user enters a valid project number at this time (PDJZ).
6. The system prints a message to identify the terminal number (27) and type (TTY).
7. Then the system prompts for the system. Since the terminal is in full-duplex mode, which echoes each typed character, we need to set it at half-duplex to eliminate the redundant character. The command "HALF" is typed, which displays as "HHAALLFF" because the system is in full-duplex mode of message transmission.
8. The system responds with the message "READY".
9. A second system message of "READY" is displayed.
10. Now you enter the system you wish to use, such as FORTRAN, BASIC, EDIT, MANAGE, or any other. The FORTRAN system is requested.
11. The system prompts you for the type of file you want to access; OLD means that you want an existing file; NEW means that you want to create a new file. The file name is also given in the same response as the type of file (NEW,DEMO). A new file with the name of DEMO was requested.
12. Then the system prints the "Ready" message which lets you know when to proceed with your work.

It is not mandatory for you to understand each of these entries. The main point is to illustrate the system messages and requests for items in the order in which they might appear on one timesharing computer with a FORTRAN run-time system. The log-on procedure (commands) for your system may vary slightly from the previously described procedures. Your instructor or computer center staff will assign your user ID (or account number), password, and project number (if needed) and give you the exact log-on procedure for your system. The log-on procedure may be posted next to the terminals or on a bulletin board in the computer center for you to read and follow.

You must also know the correct conventions for naming a file on a system. Most systems limit file names to six or eight characters. Most file-naming conventions require a file name to begin with a letter and be composed of only letters or digits.

2.5 GENERAL TIMESHARING PROCEDURES AND COMMANDS FOR MANIPULATING FORTRAN PROGRAMS

Although the basic concepts and operations for creating, manipulating, and executing FORTRAN are the same, the specific procedures and commands vary from system to system. This section discusses the general operations and procedures for using a timesharing system and developing a FORTRAN program. You should refer to the pertinent appendix for the specific commands and procedures on your system.

Typing (Entering) Your Program

After logging on, you may proceed to use the timesharing commands either to manipulate an existing file or to enter a new FORTRAN program. On a timesharing system with a FORTRAN run-time subsystem, you can enter your statements immediately after you have given the command NEW and your file name. Remember, on most systems you must include a line number before each statement for editing purposes. The system uses these edit line numbers to keep your statements in a specific order. Also, the line numbers are used to delete statements, list portions of your current file (work area in memory), etc. Use some increment—such as 10 or even 100— for the line numbers, to provide flexibility in adding new lines. Do not confuse these edit line numbers with a FORTRAN statement number which is required in positions 1–5 of a statement that is referenced in a program.

If your timesharing system does not have a FORTRAN run-time subsystem, you must use an interactive system program known as a text editor to enter and modify programs. Many programmers, in fact, use a **text editor** even though their system *does* have a FORTRAN run-time subsystem. A **text editor** is a highly versatile program which provides a flexible and easy way to manipulate files.

Suppose you want to enter a program to compute the sum of two numbers and to print the result. The typed program on a FORTRAN run-time system might be:

```
10        X = 10.0
20        Y = 20.5
30        S = X + Y
40        PRINT *, X, Y, ' SUM = ', S
50        STOP
60        END
```

There should be six blank spaces between the end of the line number and the beginning of the FORTRAN statement.

The "PRINT *, variable list" is the form of the FORTRAN format-free output statement. If your timesharing system does not permit the use of the format-free PRINT statement, you must use the standard formatted WRITE and FORMAT statements to display the output results. (The distinction between formatted and format-free statements will be discussed later.) An example of the program with a formatted-output statement is:

```
10        X = 10.0
20        Y = 20.5
30        S = X + Y
40        WRITE (6, 99) X, Y, S
45    99 FORMAT (1X, F5.2, 5X, F5.2, 5X, 6HSUM = , F6.2)
50        STOP
60        END
```

Note the FORTRAN statement number on edit line number 45. The FORTRAN language uses statement numbers (like 99), while the edit function uses edit line numbers (line 45).

Correcting Typing Errors and Cancelling a Line

Everyone makes typing errors when using a terminal. You may correct these errors in one of several ways, depending on how many characters you typed incorrectly.

To correct one or a few incorrect characters while the cursor (location marker on the screen) is still near these errors (or if you have not transmitted the line), you may delete the invalid character(s) and then resume typing. To delete a character, depress the key(s) which move you back one space. This has the effect of deleting the character or space immediately preceding the cursor. Some terminals use the DELETE, BACKSPACE, SHIFT and RUBOUT. You may also use the CTRL (control) key with a proper letter for deletions on some systems. The most common control key combination to delete a character is the CTRL and letter H keys. Continue this process until you have cancelled out the last incorrect character and then continue typing the rest of the line with the correct information. You should consult your instructor or computer center staff for your system's erase sequence.

For example, suppose you typed

40   PIRN

before discovering the misspelled keyword PRINT. You would then depress the ← key, SHIFT/DEL, SHIFT/ RUB, or appropriate key three times to delete the characters N, R, and I. You would then begin typing with the letter R to correctly type the PRINT statement.

You may type a complete or nearly-complete line before discovering a mistake near the beginning of the line. On a run-time subsystem you could transmit the line and retype it correctly, since a new line with the *same* line number replaces a previous statement with the identical line number. You may delete an entire line, however, by depressing the BREAK key or other appropriate keys (CTRL/X, ESCape/X, and others). A message may be printed to the effect that the line is deleted. You must **not** depress the RETURN key before typing the BREAK key (or appropriate key(s)).

Changing or Replacing a Line Using a Run-time Subsystem. When you have syntax or logic errors in a line, you will need to retype it correctly. To replace a line in a program with a new line containing a change, you simply type the same line number with the complete new statement. For example, you may have an error in an assignment statement and need to add parentheses. The current statement in error may be:

$$40 \qquad R = K + 3/M$$

Suppose you wanted to add 3 to K before doing the division by M. You would type the correction with the same line number. For example:

$$40 \qquad R = (K + 3)/M$$

After you type this statement, the computer would delete the old statement with line number 40 and replace it with this new statement.

Thus, the last statement typed with a given line number becomes the current statement with that line number in the program. You must be extremely careful not to type a statement with a line number of a statement already in the program unless you want to change it. If you do, and it is transmitted, say goodbye to the old statement. Students often make this mistake and then wonder why they are not getting the correct output results. It is a good practice to list your program (unless it is quite long) before running it. This procedure can often save valuable time.

Deleting a Line Using a Run-time Subsystem. To delete or remove a line from a program, you simply type and transmit the line number by itself, with no statement. Make sure there are no blanks after the line number; this would replace the line with a blank statement. Transmitting only the line number tells the computer to delete that line from the program. For example, to delete the statement with line number 50 from a current file you would type the command:

$$50$$

To delete a *range* of line numbers from a file you generally use the **DELETE** command. You type the command DELETE followed by the first line number, a comma or a hyphen (depending upon the system), and the last line number in the range you want to delete from the file.

Adding/Inserting a line Using a Run-time Subsystem. To add a line in a program, select a line number between those of the two statements where you want the new line. Suppose you have the statements:

```
20      READ *, X, Y,
30      S = X + Y
```

and wish to print the values of X and Y after they have been read. A PRINT statement is needed between line numbers 20 and 30. You could select a line number of 25 for the PRINT statement and type the new line after line number 30 as follows:

```
20      READ *, X, Y
30      S = X + Y
25      PRINT *, X, Y
```

Since the line number 25 falls between line numbers 20 and 30, the three statements would be arranged in your current file as follows:

```
20      READ *, X, Y
25      PRINT *, X, Y
30      S = X + Y
```

You could have picked any number—21, 22, 23, and so on—that fell between 20 and 30 for the new line number, but if you used 21 for the line number and later needed to add *another* statement between line numbers 20 and 21, there would be no room. In this case you would have to change the line number of either the READ or the PRINT statement to allow another line between them. The best method is to pick a line number that falls halfway between the line numbers at which you are adding a new statement. This will leave room for you to add more statements between the newly added statements later, if the need arises.

Changing, Deleting, and Adding Lines to a Current File with a Text Editor. You follow basically the same procedures in changing, deleting, and adding lines to a program with a text editor. However, a specific command is needed to perform each of these operations. To change a line you must use a command like CHANGE, SUBSTITUTE, MODIFY, or REPLACE. To delete a line or group of contiguous lines, the DELETE command is used. To add new lines you must use a command like INSERT or ADD. You must refer to your related appendix to learn the specific commands for your text editor. In some text editors, commands may be abbreviated to speed up the typing.

Listing the Statements in a Current File

A frequent operation in developing a program is to list part or all of the statements in your current file. The command most frequently used in a FORTRAN run-time subsystem is the **LIST** command. Type LIST, and all statements stored in the current file will be listed in line number order. The following example is given in listing the contents of a current file named DEMO on a large mainframe system.

```
LIST
   12/26/80. 20.37.44
PROGRAM DEMO

10      READ *, X, Y
20      S = X + Y
30      PRINT *, X, Y, S
40      STOP
50      END
READY.
```

On this CDC mainframe system, two header messages are printed after the LIST command. The first message gives the date and time the program is listed. The second message lists the name of the current file (DEMO).

Most systems allow you to list a portion of the lines in a file by using the list command followed by a range of line numbers. The first line number indicates the starting line and the second line number indicates the ending line to be listed. A comma or hyphen is required (depending on the system) to separate the beginning and ending line numbers.

The same type of operations apply to the use of a text editor in listing lines in a file. There is a command to list all of the lines in the file, and there are commands to list portions of the file, beginning with some line number.

Running Your Program under a Run-time Subsystem

After typing all the statements in your program, you are ready for the computer to "run" or execute the program. On a FORTRAN run-time subsystem you simply type the command **RUN**. The computer will proceed to execute the program. A "**RUN COMPLETE**", "**READY**", "**DONE**" or a similar message is displayed after the output, to indicate that the command is completed.

The command **RUN** may cause the program to be run with a date and time header printed before the first line of output. The command **RUNNH, RNH** (run with no header) or similar command will cause the program to be run without such a header. Some instructors require the date and time header on the runs to be submitted for credit. Your instructor should advise you of this requirement.

If a misspelled word or illegally formed statement is found in the attempted execution of the program, an error message will be produced that describes the type of error and the statement in which it occurred. Find the error, correct it, type the correct statement, and type the RUN command to execute the program again.

When your program is free of syntax errors (statement construction errors), it will be executed. The output results will be transmitted to your terminal. Check these results carefully to see that they are what you expected. If the output results are incorrect, there is a logic error in your program. That is, you have not told the computer the correct operations to perform or given the statements in the correct sequence. Review and edit your program and reenter the RUN or appropriate command.

Running Your Program on a System Which Does Not Have a FORTRAN Run-time Subsystem

You must usually go through three steps to obtain output on a system which does not have a FORTRAN run-time subsystem. These will run the FORTRAN compiler and Link Editor system programs to produce the executable machine language from your source program. These three steps are:

1. Compile your source program by running the FORTRAN compiler program.
2. Prepare your object program (converted output from the compiler) for execution. This entails the use of another system program known as a **linkage editor** or **link loader**, to prepare the machine language module to be loaded and executed. This step resolves all unknown addresses, such as calls to subprograms, so that they will all be known at execution time. This step is known as the **preparation step** on some systems (HP) or the **link step** on other systems (DEC). It is usually accomplished by running the linkage editor system program.
3. The final step is to run the prepared **load module** from step two. This is the execution step where the output results are produced and either displayed back to your terminal or written to a file.

Saving the Contents of Current Files

Saving a new current file is a common operation in an interactive programming environment. For many work sessions you will not have time to complete an assignment. You may still save any work you have completed and return later to begin work where you left off. The work will be saved on disk as a permanent file.

To retain a newly built current file for future use, you usually use the **SAVE** command. The SAVE command will store the current file as a permanent file under the assigned name on magnetic disk. Many systems respond with a message to the effect that the file has been stored on disk.

A file created with a text editor is saved as a permanent file upon exiting from the editor program. Once you have saved a file on permanent storage, you will need to retrieve it later to continue work on it.

Retrieving an Existing Permanent File with a Run-time Subsystem

An existing file may be retrieved from permanent storage with the **OLD, LOAD,** or appropriate command. This command causes the system to go out to disk and to bring a copy of the permanent file into the current file area. You may then proceed to execute the program or to make modifications to it. If you already had another file in the current work area, it would be destroyed and replaced with the copy of the permanent file. The name of your current file would be the name of the permanent file which you retrieved from disk.

A text editor will retrieve a permanent file when you execute the editor program. You simply give the command to run the text editor program, followed by the name of the file you wish to edit.

If you do not wish to store the copy of the current file back on disk, you do not have to replace it. But, if you have modified the contents of a current file and wish to save this new version in place of retaining the old version, then you must give the command to save the version in the current file. Otherwise, any changes which you made to a current file are lost.

Replacing Permanent Files with Modified Current Files in a Run-time Subsystem

On most systems the SAVE command can be used only to save a file under a filename that did not previously exist in your user-ID catalog (file directory). What if you recall an old permanent file, modify it, and wish to save it under the same name? You **cannot** normally use the SAVE command, since it is for saving a file under a new, not-yet-existing filename.

You resave a file under its previous file name with the **REPLACE, RESAVE** or appropriate command (depending on the system). Thus, the REPLACE, RESAVE, or appropriate command stores the contents of the current file in the previously existing permanent file. The previous version of the permanent file is destroyed, since it has been replaced with the new version.

Remember, if you recalled a permanent file, ran it, and never made any modifications to the current file, there is no need to replace the permanent file.

Purging a Current File

If you have no further use for a new current file, you should purge (remove or destroy) it from the system. You should never arbitrarily save all current files, since they occupy valuable disk space. On computer systems disk space is highly limited. Most systems automatically purge a current file when you log off. If you retrieve a permanent file, your current file is automatically destroyed and is replaced with the contents from the permanent file.

Purging Existing Permanent Files

As previously mentioned, disk space usually is at a premium on any computer system. Your instructor may plead with you to remove all the unneeded permanent files before the system runs out of disk storage space. When you have finally produced a workable program with the correct solution, you should then remove all related files for that assignment from the system.

You should make sure you wish to delete a permanent file *before* you give the command. Once you have transmitted the command, say good-bye to your file. The only way to get a file back after it has been deleted is to contact a computer center staff member. If they have a "backup" dump of the files for a certain day, then they will be able to load a copy of a file from the backup. This administrative procedure may take several hours or even several days. If you deleted a file on the same day that it was created, there probably will not be a backup copy for that file, so be sure that you do not need a file any longer before deleting it.

Listing the Names of Permanent Files

A common operation performed on a timesharing system is a listing of the names of all your permanent files stored on disk. This operation is often referred to as listing the **file directory** or **file catalog** of your account. You will want to purge all your unneeded files when you are through with a lab problem. You may have several versions of the same program and may have forgotten all their names. The command to list the names of permanent files differs among timesharing systems.

Log-off Procedure

The log-off (or sign-off as it is also called) procedure is quite simple. You type the command **BYE** or a similar command, and the computer terminates your session. The computer responds with an appropriate message saying that it has terminated its session with you. Some accounting messages containing the charges for the session, account balance, and disk blocks of permanent storage in use may be displayed.

On most systems any current file in use when you log off is automatically destroyed. On some systems you will be automatically logged off a terminal if no entry is made during a certain time period (usually 10 minutes).

This section has discussed the various operations you perform to use a timesharing system properly. Not only do you need to know how to create and run a FORTRAN program, but you also need to know how to modify statements in a file, how to save a new file, how to retrieve a permanent file, how to replace a modified permanent file, how to list the file names in your account directory, and so on. The next section provides some short "canned" (already written) programs that you can use to practice the operations and commands of your timesharing system.

2.6 FORTRAN PROGRAM EXAMPLES ON A TIMESHARING SYSTEM

This section presents seven "canned" (prewritten) programs for you to run in your timesharing environment to gain experience entering and running FORTRAN programs. One program is given to illustrate the format of the output results from integer (whole) and real (decimal) numbers on your system. The first five programs use the format-free READ and PRINT statements, which may not be available or may be different on your timesharing system for the input/output of data items. Programs six and seven are revisions of programs one and two to include formatted READ and WRITE statements in place of the format-free READ and PRINT statements. In using these programs, insert six blank spaces on each line, between the line number and the statement (since the FORTRAN statement must begin after position six from the line number, i.e., in position seven or later).

1. FORTRAN program to compute the simple interest earned on $500 invested at 16% interest for 10 years.

```
10      REAL INTRST
20      INTRST = 500. * .16 * 10.
30      PRINT *, INTRST
40      STOP
50      END
```

2. FORTRAN program to read hourly *wage* rate and compute the gross pay for 40 hours worked.

```
10      REAL HRRATE, GRSPAY
20      READ *, HRRATE
30      GRSPAY = HRRATE * 40.0
40      PRINT *, 'GROSS PAY = ', GRSPAY
50      STOP
60      END
```

3. FORTRAN program to compute net pay. The program reads hourly rate, hours worked, and deductions. Gross pay is calculated as regular rate for all hours up to and including 40. All hours over 40 earn time and a half rate (i.e., 1.5 times regular rate).

```
10      REAL RATE, HRS, DEDUC, GRSPAY, NETPAY
20      READ *, RATE, HRS, DEDUC
30      GRSPAY = RATE * HRS
40      IF (HRS .GT. 40.) GRSPAY = GRSPAY + ((HRS − 40.)*RATE*.5)
50      NETPAY = GRSPAY − DEDUC
60      PRINT *, GRSPAY, NETPAY
70      STOP
80      END
```

4. FORTRAN program to compute the area of a circle. The radius is given as 2.3 in an Assignment statement. The formula is $A = \pi r^2$. The value 3.14 is used for π.

```
10      REAL RADIUS, AREA
20      RADIUS = 2.3
30      AREA = 3.14 *RADIUS ** 2.0
40      PRINT *, AREA
50      STOP
60      END
```

5. FORTRAN program to test the printing of real (decimal) numbers on your system.

```
10      REAL N1, N2, N3
20      INTEGER N4, N5
30      N1 = 123.
40      N2 = 456.78
50      N3 = 123456789.
60      N4 = 123
70      N5 = 123456789
80      PRINT *, N1, N2, N3
90      PRINT *, ' '
100     PRINT *, N4, N5
110     STOP
120     END
```

6. FORTRAN program to compute the simple interest earned on $500 invested at 16% interest for 10 years. This is program one rewritten to include formatted I/O.

```
10        REAL INTRST
20        INTRST = 500. * .16 * 10.
30        WRITE (6,299) INTRST
35   299  FORMAT (1X, F7.2)
40        STOP
50        END
```

7. FORTRAN program to read hourly rate and compute the gross pay for 40 hours worked. This program is a rewrite of program two to include formatted I/O.

```
10        REAL HRRATE, GRSPAY
20        READ (5,199) HRRATE
25   199  FORMAT (F5.2)
30        GRSPAY = HRRATE * 40.0
40        WRITE (6,299) GRSPAY
45   299  FORMAT (1X, 12HGROSS PAY = , F7.2)
50        STOP
60        END
```

You should practice the log-on procedure for your timesharing system until you can perform this operation without any trouble. Enter some of the "canned programs" to learn the procedure for creating, manipulating and running FORTRAN programs on your system. Remember, do not be afraid of the computer or a terminal. You cannot do any harm to the timesharing system by entering and running a program.

The next section explains the technique used to stop (kill or terminate) any operation in process or command given on a timesharing system.

2.7 TERMINATING OUTPUT AND ANY OPERATION (COMMAND)

You may sometimes wish to terminate (stop) output or a command on a terminal. You might determine from the first set of answers to a problem that you have a mistake in your program, or that you are caught in an endless loop in which the same answer keeps printing. It is very important for you to know how to "kill" the execution of a program or to terminate a given command in order to get out of an undesired situation.

The action you must take to end a command varies from system to system. Some computers respond to depressing a special key, such as the BREAK key. On other systems, you must hold down the CTRL key and depress another key (such as the letter C). Still other systems require you to type a special command. We will look at some of the procedures used on various systems. You should ask your instructor what procedure you must take to terminate any operation on your system if it is not discussed below.

CDC 6000 and Cyber. The BREAK key is depressed to interrupt processing the current command. The messages *INT* (for interrupt) and *DEL* (for delete) will be printed at the terminal. You then type the command STOP. The system replies with the message *TERM* to let you know that the current operation is terminated. You may then proceed with new work.

DEC PDP-11 Series. To terminate an operation on a PDP-11 series computer, depress the CTRL key and then strike the letter C key. This combination is known as a Control C. The message "Ready" is then displayed to inform you that the operation has been cancelled/terminated and that the computer is ready to accept a new command. The CNTL/C combination prints out a ^C on the terminal.

HP 3000. The BREAK key is depressed to cancel/terminate any operation. The computer responds with a READY message to inform you that you may proceed with a new command.

Honeywell 6000 and Series 66. You must type the command $*$b (the lower case letter b stands for break) to kill the execution of the current command. The computer stops what it is doing; no message is printed. The * prompt character is displayed on a new line to inform you that you may enter a new line or command. On a Honeywell CP-6 system you depress the BREAK and RETURN keys to terminate an operation or command.

Burroughs 6000. You must type the command ?DS (for discontinue). The "?" is a special character which must begin special commands to the operating system. A message is displayed informing you that the current operation has been killed.

Other Systems and Terminals. On IBM 2741 typewriter terminals, the ATTN (attention) key is depressed. On a DATEL terminal, the INT (interrupt) key is typed to terminate processing. On some systems you must type the command STOP. Typing the S key while a program is running is the same as typing the STOP command on some computer systems. Other terminals may have a STOP key for the sole purpose of terminating an operation.

It is of utmost importance for you to know how to get out of a command or instantly terminate an operation. Don't just walk away from your terminal. Ask for assistance if you are unsure of what to do. Do not be afraid to attempt the actions discussed in this section. You cannot harm the computer system (except with a sledge hammer).

2.8 TEXT EDITOR PROGRAMS

A **text editor** is a program that facilitates creation of, and changes to, a file. The file might be a data file containing data records, but it is more often a source program file containing the statement lines of the program. The text editor performs four major functions:

1. Creation of a new file.
2. Adding/inserting new lines in a file.
3. Deleting lines from a file.
4. Modifying the current lines in a file by changing or replacing various portions of one or more lines of text.

Almost all interactive computer systems have some form of editing facility. Some are extremely powerful and sophisticated, while others are rather limited. A text editor is a tool for preparing files for various applications.

An on-line text editor is analogous to the common method of editing a program in a non-timesharing environment, using a punched card deck. The programmer must insert, change, and/or delete cards from a source deck, which then has to be read into the computer through a card reader. An on-line editing system stores programs on disk, eliminates the need for handling clumsy card decks, and enables quick and efficient updates to the source program. When a text editor is used with a timesharing system in which the program can be readily compiled, the time required to develop and debug a program is greatly reduced.

Some timesharing systems have their own subsystem (such as FORTRAN and BASIC) to manipulate source programs. Many timesharing systems such as DEC, Hewlett Packard, and IBM do not have a subsystem for FORTRAN. A text editor, therefore, would be the only way to create and modify FORTRAN source programs on timesharing systems which do not have a FORTRAN subsystem. The text editor—**EDT**—to create and manipulate FORTRAN source programs on the DEC PDP-11 systems is described in Appendix E. The text editor—**EDIT/3000**—to create and manipulate HP 3000 FORTRAN programs is described in Appendix F. The TSO text editor—**EDIT**—to create and manipulate FORTRAN source programs on an IBM system is described in Appendix G. The timesharing system—**CANDE**—to create and manipulate FORTRAN source programs on a Burroughs 6000 system is described in Appendix H. The text editor—**CTS**—to create and manipulate FORTRAN source programs on a Univac 1100 timesharing system is described in Appendix K.

Typical editing commands in text editors include:

INSERT—To insert new lines
DELETE—To delete lines
FIND—To locate lines with a specific pattern of characters
SUBSTITUTE—To replace a pattern of characters with a new pattern of characters
CHANGE—Same as SUBSTITUTE
MOVE—To move one or more lines to a new location in the file
COPY—To duplicate one or more lines in a file at a new location
SEARCH—Same as FIND
REPLACE—Same as SUBSTITUTE

Text editors are indeed a powerful tool in developing source programs. Computer program editors have become increasingly popular in timesharing environments, where a facility for the online modification of programs greatly increases a programmer's productivity.

2.9 SUGGESTIONS FOR ACCOMPLISHING COMPUTER ASSIGNMENTS ON A TERMINAL

The following suggestions describe an orderly procedure to assure that you complete a computer assignment in the most efficient manner. These steps will not only save you time, but they seek to allow maximum terminal usage for you and your fellow students.

A. Before sitting down at a terminal:

1. Read your assignment or problem carefully. Make sure you understand what is required. If there is any doubt about the meaning or requirements, ask your instructor for clarification.
2. Decide what output should be produced and what format it should have. Also identify the input items and processing requirements for the problem solution.
3. Plan your solution and prepare an algorithm (flowchart or other design tool) of the solution logic.
4. Write your program on paper. Start with a clean sheet of paper and skip lines so space will be available for inserting additional lines later. Follow your algorithm when writing the program. Include line numbers and spacing as you will enter them in the program. Include comments/remarks before major routines or parts in the program.
5. Then play computer with your program. That is, take a set of simple numbers and go through the program just as the computer would. Write down the value of variables (from input and calculations) and the printed output results. This process is known as **desk-checking** or **bench-checking**.
6. Make sure you understand the operation of the terminal you will use. Read any handouts and notes or ask for assistance if you need help.
7. After you feel confident that your program will work, and you know how to operate a terminal, proceed to gain access to a terminal.

B. While entering your program at a terminal:

1. Ask anyone who is "just hanging" around or causing disturbance to leave. You need to be able to concentrate during your sessions. Inform the computer center personnel, advisor, or instructor if you have trouble. People using the computer center should always be considerate of the other users.
2. If you cannot understand or correct an error message, ask for help from an advisor or someone you know. If you cannot find someone to help resolve your problem, log off and see your instructor. Always take the listing from the terminal with you, because the instructor will need to see it to analyze the errors.
3. After a successful processing (RUN) of your program, compare the output results with those you expect.
4. If the output results differ from what you expected, list the program and trace through it to find the error(s). You should know simple debugging techniques such as printing the results of calculations and echo printing the input values to help you find the error. If you cannot quickly locate the problem, log off and let someone else use the terminal while you debug.
5. Do not give up too quickly. You learn to debug by staying with a problem until you find the error. Check your text book or notes for possible help. Make sure you have done all you can to find the problem before consulting your instructor. Do not spend days, however, struggling with the problem. If you cannot resolve it after several hours, sleep on it or ask for help.

C. Before turning in an assignment:

1. Reread the assignment and define the solution requirements.
2. Insure that your program does what was required. Double check to make sure your answers are correct. Did you use the required input values? Make sure you check each set of answers and not just the first one or first set.
3. Do you have a clean listing of the source program and output results?
4. Write your name, course and section number, and instructor's name at the top of the listing. Include any explanations or comments if you so desire.

The article titled "A HOPE OF RAY" is reprinted with the permission of the author, Ray Edmonds, a computer center staff member at the University of Colorado at Colorado Springs.[1] This article contains some gems of wisdom which can make your use of the computer center much less painful and more enjoyable.

---

1. Ray Edmonds, "A Hope of Ray," *UCCS Update*, December, 1981.

There comes a time in every student's life when they learn to love or hate their computer. The following is a tale of why this happens.

Many students are in the habit of putting off assignments until the last possible moment. In most classes this doesn't really change the amount of work that you have to do or the time that it takes you to do it. At the Computer Center this is not true. Using the computer is like using the highway. There are rush hours, or more exactly, rush days here at the Center. If you wait until the last possible moment, here is what you will find.

You will enter the Center and you won't find a terminal. All of your classmates will be using them because they waited until the last day also. You will notice a definite foul odor that is evident of people who are under stress, called sweat. The room will be electric with tension and loud noise levels of people yelling at their terminals. The machine, to help things out, will be slow because everyone else is using it. If you can get to an advisor he will answer your question tersely; he has to, as there are five people waiting after you with their questions. You think the advisor is a less than kind person, which probably isn't true. Your frustration level builds and you make more mistakes than you really have to. All in all you learn to truly hate computers and far be it from me not to agree with you. Everyone hates the computer when there is a rush.

Is there hope?

Have you ever wondered how all those people graduate who had to take all those computer courses? You are probably thinking that they are the ones that programming comes easy to. That may be true to an extent, but they were also the ones that always had their programs done early. Just to frustrate you they said that it took them only four hours to do the whole thing and you can't get it done in eight.

Chances are these people aren't really any better at programming than you are. They used the Center at a slow time. They came in and found that they could log on at two or three terminals if they wanted. The fast printer wasn't busy, so they could leave their output on it for twenty minutes and then go get it. The room was still and quiet, great for concentrating. The advisor came over to help them with their program because he was lonely. If the program didn't work, the user didn't feel the sense of urgency to finish. After all he could always come back the next day. He probably also remembered what he was to have learned in class not having time to forget his lessons.

If you talk to this person, he will tell you how easy it is to write the program and you want to punch this person because you know that it wasn't, or more probably won't be. What you don't realize is that it really was that easy to do the assignment. In the future don't punch the person, BE the person. Then you can walk around and act superior to all your classmates who don't have their work done. I know I always do.

This article brings home the importance of starting an assignment early. If you wait to start a problem until the day or even the week before it is due, the computer center will be crowded with all the other people who have put off starting the problem. The computer will certainly be slower in responding to your commands and in producing the output, since it has so many jobs to service. So heed the advice of your instructor when he or she tells you to be sure to start your assignment in plenty of time to allow for problems.

2.10 SUMMARY

A timesharing system provides a powerful computer service by sharing the computer resources among many users simultaneously. It is a more desirable means of developing and processing programs than punched cards. A timesharing system's conversational capabilities permit its users to debug programs much faster than with batch-card processing systems.

There are two types of terminals that you may use. One type, the teleprinter, is like a typewriter with continuous sheets of paper. The second type of terminal contains a visual-display screen and is a CRT. The CRT is a popular terminal, since it does not require paper, is faster, more efficient, and quieter than a teleprinter. Computer terminals have more keys than the common typewriter to provide additional functions. You must learn the functions of these keys in order to use the terminals effectively.

You must be assigned an identification number and a password (and a project number on some systems) to gain access to the timesharing system. This procedure of acquiring use of a timesharing systems is called log-on. Then you may start your work. The procedure to terminate your session is referred to as log-off.

The file you are creating or working on is known as the current file (or work area). Any changes to this file are made in a temporary work area in memory; thus, no changes are made to a permanent file. To save the contents of the current file, you must use the SAVE or an appropriate command if the file does not already exist. To save the current file that already has a file on disk with the same name, you must use the REPLACE, RESAVE, or other appropriate command.

A timesharing system has its own language of commands for instructing the computer what to do with your files. Such system commands on a run-time subsystem include NEW, OLD, LIST, DELETE, RUN, SAVE, and PURGE. You must master these commands to develop and process your programs. A text editor program is used to create and modify your source program if a FORTRAN run-time subsystem is not available.

2.11 TERMS

You should become familiar with the following concepts and terms used in this chapter:

conversational mode	listing a file	purging a file
creating a file	log off	retrieving a file
CRT terminal	log on	running a program
current file	modifying a file	saving a file
cursor	password	teleprinter terminal
file catalog	permanent file	timesharing
file directory	prompt	user ID
hard copy		

This chapter is an overview of the general operations and system commands for a timesharing system. You must consult the user's guide, your instructor, or some other expert to learn the full range of capabilities available on your system. Appendixes are included to provide a detailed explanation of many timesharing systems. Once you succeed in learning how to use a terminal and the many timesharing commands, you should find the direct communication with the computer an enjoyable means to solve computer related problems.

2.12 REVIEW QUESTIONS

1. The sharing of computer time between multiple computer users in an on-line, interactive environment is known as _____ .
2. The term that refers to a continuous dialogue between the user and the computer is _____ processing.
3. The language used in an interactive mode to instruct the computer in what operations to perform is known as _____ .
4. A file retained on disk storage for later retrieval is called a _____ file.
5. A temporary file used to hold the current program for manipulation and processing is called a _____ .
6. To transmit a system command or line of information to the computer, you must usually type the _____ key.
7. The procedure of identifying a user and gaining access to the computer is known as _____ .
8. To identify a valid user and to gain access (log on) to the computer, you must be assigned a _____ and a _____ .
9. On a CRT terminal, the white spot on the screen to indicate your current location is called a _____ .
10. The computer's signal to let you know when to enter a new system command is known as a _____ .
11. Does the computer transmit any response to an entered FORTRAN statement in a run-time subsystem?
12. List two ways to correct a line of information containing an error.
13. How does one add a new line to a FORTRAN program in the current file in a run-time subsystem?
14. How does one delete a line in a program from the current file in a run-time subsystem?
15. What system command do you normally type and transmit to the computer to log-off the system?
16. Most systems allow an abbreviation of system commands to shorten typing. (True/False).
17. What is the purpose of a text editor?

3

Steps in Computer Problem Solving and Structured Program Design

3.1 INTRODUCTION TO THE STEPS IN SOLVING A PROBLEM WITH THE COMPUTER

At this stage in your education you are familiar with calculations. You have undoubtedly done a considerable amount of calculating both at school and at work. Simple calculations can often be performed mentally, but as the computation becomes more lengthy or complex, you may resort to paper and pencil. You have probably used various calculating devices such as desk or hand calculators for lengthy or complicated problem solving.

You may have found it convenient to plan your approach, possibly making all calculations of the same nature before pressing on to the next step, or it may have been necessary to establish definite procedures to arrive at a solution without confusion. You learned and applied various techniques and devices as your problem-solving requirements dictated.

As coursework and problems became more advanced your problem-solving requirements probably became even more time-consuming. Successive calculations of the same problem were performed with different and large amounts of data. Just as you have learned new techniques and devices to serve your needs in the past, so now you are about to learn how to use another, more powerful device—the **COMPUTER**.

When should a problem be solved by a computer? No two people will agree about when a problem is too small for a computer. Three criteria may be used to determine the value of doing an application on a computer—time, expense, and the assurance of accuracy. Developing a computer solution may take more time than a manual solution, but if the problem is a recurring one it may be worthwhile. Implementation of a problem solution on the computer can be expensive. Not only is computer time involved, but operator time, computer supplies, data preparation costs, and so forth. A programmer's time is not inexpensive. If many calculations are made and different reports produced, the computer solution is usually economical. People may get tired and make mistakes, but computers can perform endless and difficult calculations as effortlessly as simple ones, and without error. So, all factors must be considered before using the computer to solve a problem. For your assigned lab problems, the computer is the proper problem-solving tool.

The computer cannot do any calculations that you cannot do by hand, but it can do them much, much faster. The computer can be programmed to solve complicated, time-consuming problems in seconds or less. The important point to remember is that the computer is simply another tool to be *used* in solving problems— it will not solve them for you. You must still solve the problem by programming the computer with instructions for doing calculations and making decisions. Nonetheless, the advantages of using the computer for complex calculations and repetitive work more than make up for the time spent on program development.

Although the computer is a very powerful and versatile problem-solving tool, it is only one part of the problem-solving process. If you are to take full advantage of the computer's capabilities, you must be proficient in all phases of problem solving. You might think that solving a problem on the computer is a simple process, that it simply consists of telling the computer what you want done. After all, isn't the computer a brain? Wrong. Remember, the computer is only a machine—a tool used to extend our mental capacities. While it is often true that simple problems can be solved quickly on the computer, long, complex problems can entail time-consuming and complicated work.

To solve any problem effectively and efficiently, an ordered sequence of steps should be followed. Eight main steps are involved in producing a working computer solution to a problem and supporting documentation

Table 3.1 Problem-solving Procedures

Steps in Computer Problem-solving Procedure	Corresponding Steps in General Problem-solving Procedure
A. Planning the solution	
1. **Analyzing** the problem specifications and **defining** the solution requirements	a. Define the problem requirements (purpose and output results) b. Identify the variables (input items) involved c. Identify the relationship among the variables
2. **Designing** the problem solution	d. Develop a model or formula using the variables e. Analyze the model f. Compute the solution g. Check the results
B. Implementing the solution with a computer	
3. **Writing** the computer program	
4. **Preparing** the program in a computer input medium	
5. **Running** the program and correcting statement errors	
6. **Testing** and debugging the program	
7. **Implementing** the program with operational data	
8. **Documenting** the program and the problem solution.	

for it. These steps are shown in the left-hand column of Table 3.1. They may be divided into two general phases, as shown in the table:

A. Planning the solution

B. Implementing the solution with a computer

Beginning programmers usually spend very little time planning the solution. They feel compelled to write the program as a measure of progress towards a problem solution. Don't do this. You should devote about half the total time to the planning phase. Understanding fully what is needed, what approach to take, and how to organize the problem solution, you should be able to construct a workable program in a reasonably short time (three to six hours).

The amount of time spent in each step varies with problem complexity. Some problems may be so simple that you can readily see the solution; thus, many experienced programmers can start at step 4 and immediately enter the required program at the terminal. Most problems, however, especially for the novice programmer, require careful study and a planned design of the required algorithms.

Some of the steps—especially steps 1 and 2—may overlap. As you begin analyzing the problem, you may simultaneously identify parts of the solution. In addition, program documentation should be done at each step along the way, not delayed until the program has been implemented.

There is a more general problem-solving procedure, often referred to as the scientific approach to problem solving. The steps in this procedure are illustrated in the right-hand column of Table 3.1. As you can see from the table, the first two computer-solving steps correspond to the seven general problem-solving steps. In particular, the first three general problem-solving steps correspond to the first step of the computer procedure and the last four general problem-solving steps correspond to the second step of the computer procedure.

In the first general problem-solving step (a) you analyze the information concerning the problem and determine what needs to be done. The instructor has probably already defined the problem to some extent, but you must study the problem yourself to fully understand what is involved and needed in the solution.

Once the problem has been defined, the variables involved should be identified, general step (b). You need to know those variables that are given, those that must be calculated, and those that must be produced as part of the solution. To sum up, you can develop the calculations and decision-making requirements once you know the output requirements and the initial input values.

In the third general problem-solving step (c), you need to know the relationship among the variables. Certain variables might be used to compute new variables. Is there a formula you can develop to use the variables to progress towards the solution? Once the problem is reduced to its purpose and set of relationships, an analysis can be done. That is, you can apply logical procedures and rules to bring the problem into a more understandable form. When the problem has been defined and you know the relationships among the variables, you can proceed to develop the model for the solution.

The remaining four general problem-solving steps are involved in computer problem-solving step two, for designing a computer solution. (Again, refer to Table 3.1.) In step (d) a model is developed involving the variables you have defined from analyzing the problem. The model may be a single formula or a series of computations to arrive at an answer, such as the computation of an employee's pay. The relationship of the variables and the model may be inherent in the problem requirement—as in a case of computing simple interest on a loan. In step (e) you analyze the model solution design for feasibility and accuracy. In steps (f) and (g) a simple trial run of the model (usually by hand) is performed. If the results are correct, a computer program can be developed in much the same way as this manual solution. If the results are incorrect, the model must be modified, or an entirely new one developed.

Every programming student should force himself or herself to approach the solution of all assigned problems using these steps. A student's conscientious effort in following an organized procedure for problem solving will pay rich dividends later.

Figure 3.1 shows the eight computer problem-solving steps as divided into the planning and implementation phases. This figure also shows the percentages of the time normally spent in each step to produce a computer solution to a problem. While these percentages vary from person to person and problem to problem, they represent the average percentage of time that should be spent in each step.

Each of the eight computer problem-solving steps is briefly explained in the following sections to teach you the proper procedure in computer problem solving. (Chapter 5 will expand on this discussion to take you step-by-step through the solution to a specific problem.) The last sections of this chapter are concerned with a discussion of structured program design techniques.

3.2 ANALYZING THE PROBLEM SPECIFICATIONS AND DEFINING THE SOLUTION REQUIREMENTS (STEP 1)

The first step toward a problem solution is to recognize all the problem requirements and to define the various aspects. The problem must be thoroughly analyzed and fully understood to produce a correct solution. It is also well to remember that, in some cases, a computer solution may be too expensive and time consuming—especially if the problem is simple or non-recurring.

Do not use a sledge hammer to kill a fly. Make sure that the computer is the best tool for the particular job. Figure 3.2 (p. 48) illustrates the analysis step in problem solving.

The set of requirements for a computer problem is generally given in a memo or document known as a **problem specifications** form, which identifies the originator (user), the problem, and the problem solution requirements. Figure 3.3 (p. 48) shows a sample form.

The problem specifications and requirements should be analyzed in the following order: output, input, processing.

Output

First, determine the output results and format. Does the solution require several output values from calculations, a tabular form of computed values, or a complete report generated from detailed input records? If a new report (or a modified report) is requested, a **print layout form** should be used. This form shows the format of the report, with headings and data fields to be printed, summary lines of totals, and so forth. Figure 3.4 (p. 49) shows a blank print layout form.

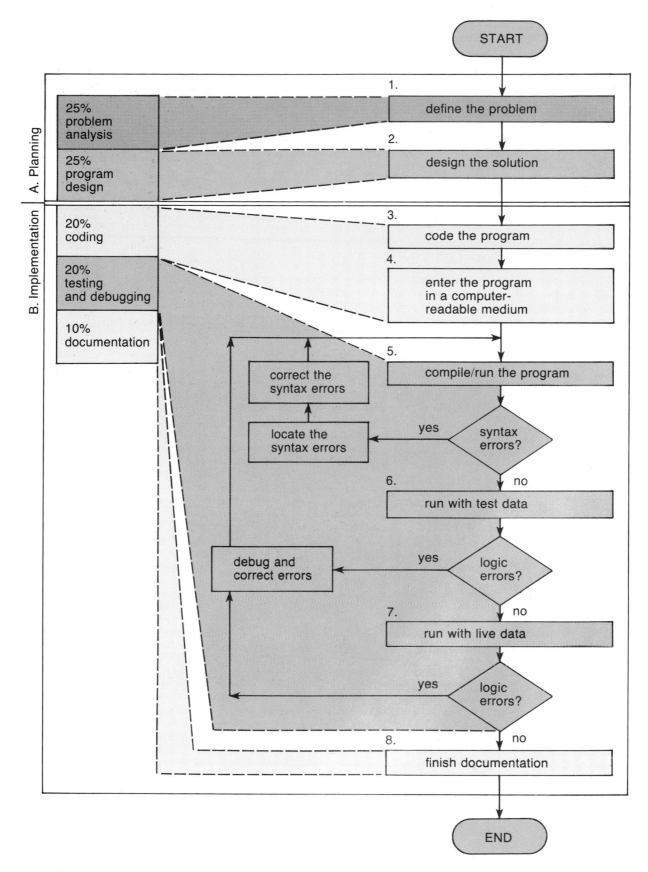

Figure 3.1 Steps in problem solving with the computer

Step 1—Analyzing the problem specifications
and defining the solution requirements

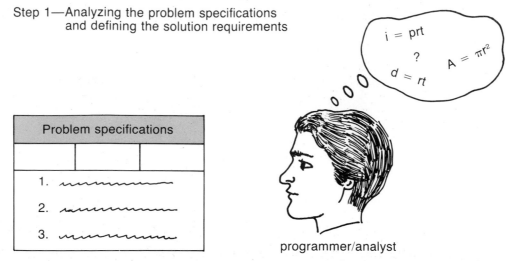

Figure 3.2 Analyzing the problem specifications to determine the user requirements

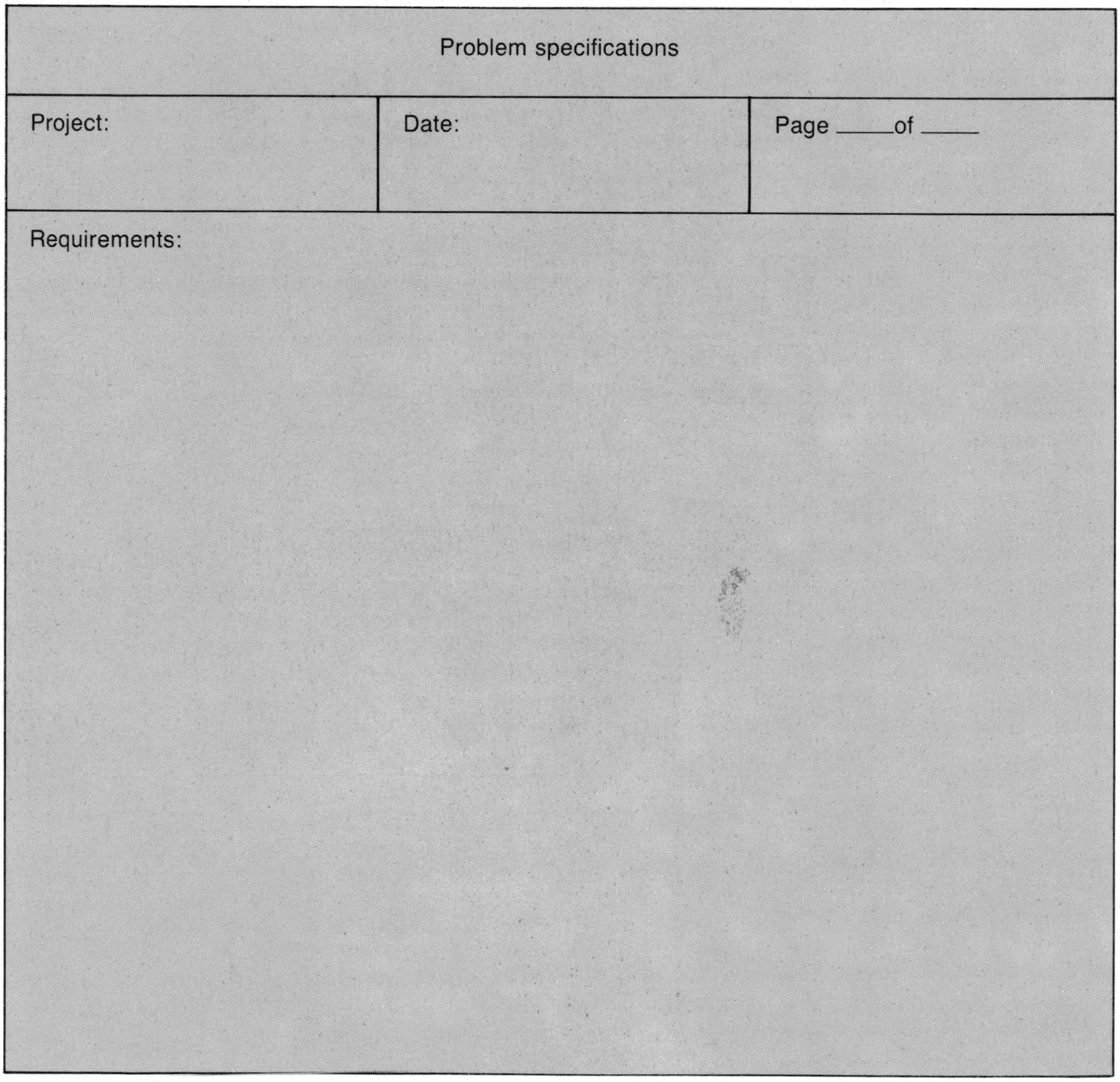

Problem specifications		
Project:	Date:	Page _____ of _____
Requirements:		

Figure 3.3 Problem specification form

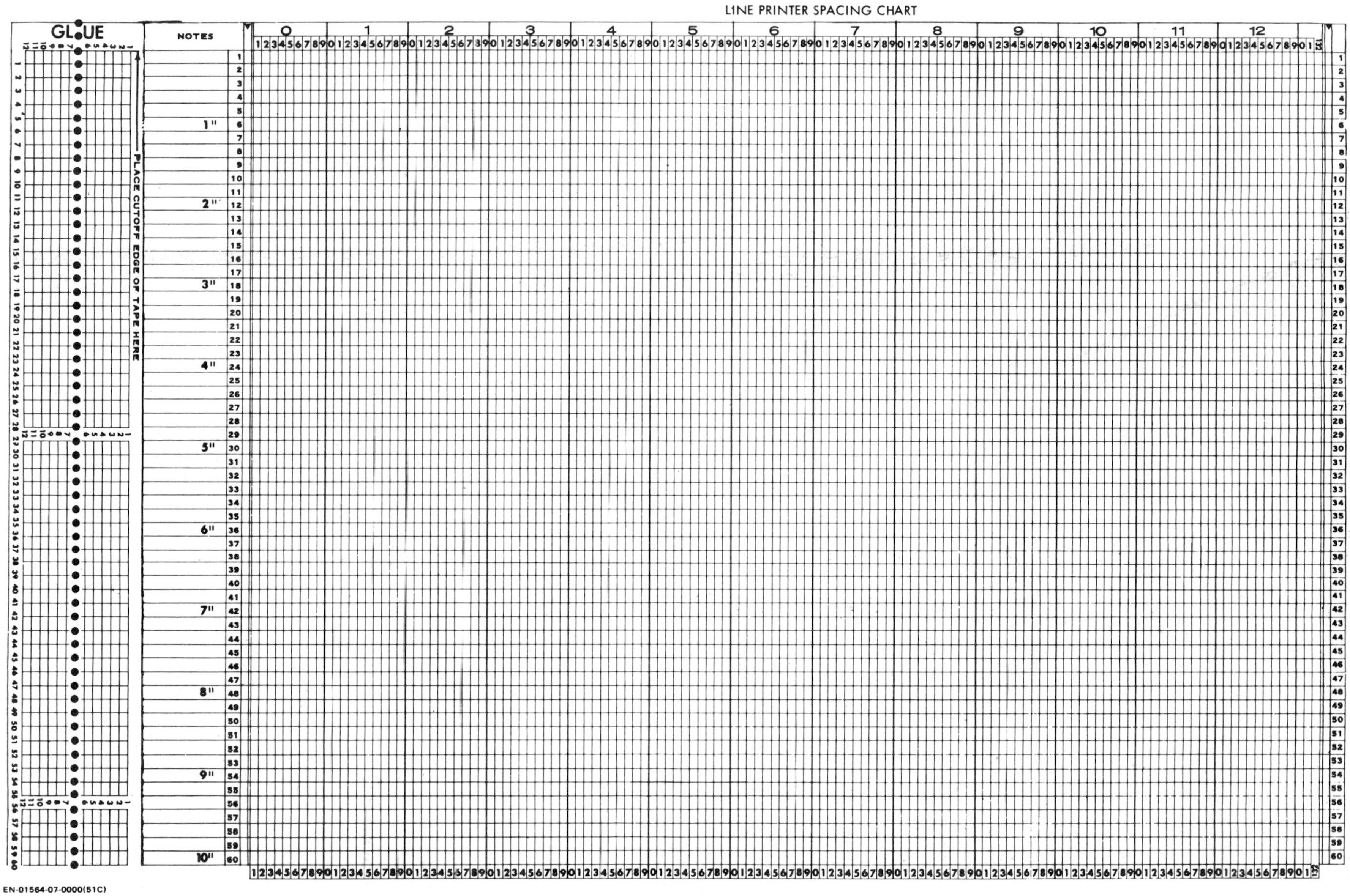

Figure 3.4 Print layout form

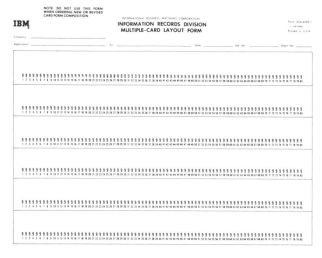

Figure 3.5 Multiple-card layout form

Input

Secondly, identify the input items and the items to be used as input variables. You may list these on a sheet of paper or use a record layout form. A **record layout form** shows the different data fields and their order of placement in a data record. If the input medium is punched cards, use a **multiple-card layout form** to show the data fields. Figure 3.5 illustrates a multiple-card layout form.

Processing

Finally, determine what calculations and manipulations (sorting, summarizing, and so forth) must be performed on the input data to produce the desired output. For your own understanding, you may want to list the various calculations and processing requirements on a sheet of paper. In step two you will use other tools such as flowcharts and pseudocode to illustrate the design solution and processing requirements.

The importance of spending adequate time in defining the problem cannot be overestimated. When you achieve a proper understanding of the problem requirements, you can make rapid progress in the other steps. Without it, you will lose time, become frustrated, and possibly flounder in the later steps.

After the analysis and determination of the problem requirements, you have the necessary information to proceed to the second step—designing the computer solution. In simple problems, many of the required tasks will be almost automatically performed or combined. For complex problems, the steps listed above provide an orderly approach to the problem analysis and solution requirements.

3.3 DESIGNING THE PROBLEM SOLUTION (STEP 2)

After analyzing the problem specifications and determining the output, input, and processing requirements, you must carefully develop a plan for the problem solution. The plan must include the algorithms and logic for the actions and decisions needed; it also requires proper placement of operations necessary to the solution. Figure 3.6 illustrates planning a solution by showing a developed algorithm with flowchart. A flowchart illustrates the developed algorithm in graphic form. The flowchart design tool, by using selected symbols, shows the steps that the computer performs in a program. The program logic is presented by following the connecting lines from symbol to symbol. As each action is performed, the logic proceeds to the next connected symbol.

Using the proposed algorithm, try to "step through" the developed solution to see if it works. This is a way of checking the correctness of your design solution. If your algorithm does not work at this stage, it will not work on the computer. Inspect the entire solution for possible error—programmers should always be skeptical of a proposed problem solution until it has been proven correct by actual program output results.

The checking of "critical values"—such as zero, or negative values—is central to the correctness of a proposed solution. You must also be aware of what will happen if certain "boundary" or "limiting" values are exceeded. Consider **Murphy's Law: Anything that can possibly go wrong, will—and at the most inconvenient time.**

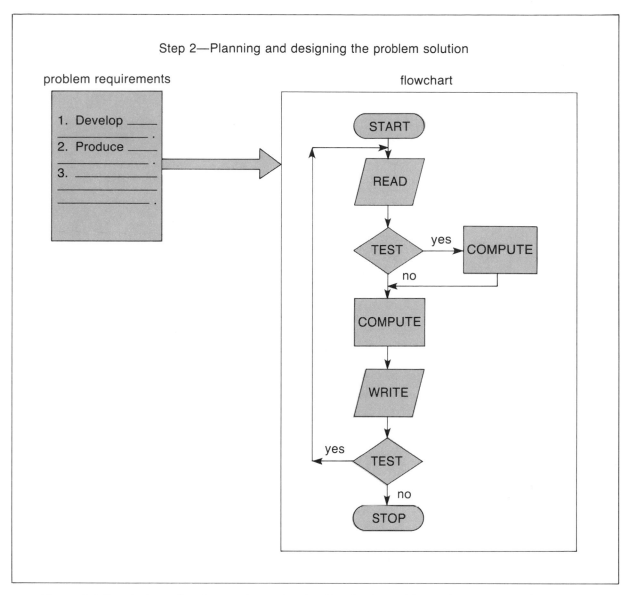

Step 2—Planning and designing the problem solution

problem requirements   flowchart

1. Develop _____
   _____ .
2. Produce _____
   _____ .
3. _____
   _____
   _____ .

START

READ

TEST — yes → COMPUTE

no

COMPUTE

WRITE

TEST — yes

no

STOP

Figure 3.6 Developing a flowchart to depict the algorithm for the problem solution

Many techniques and tools are available to design the required program logic. Some of the more common ones are:

1. Flowcharts
2. Pseudocode
3. Structure and hierarchy charts
4. Decision tables

A program **flowchart**, often called a **program logic chart**, is used to illustrate various actions and their sequence in a problem solution. **Pseudocode** uses an English-like prose to describe the order of solution in a top-down, structured form. A **structure chart** or a **hierarchy chart** divides the problem into sub-parts and displays these sub-parts as modular functions comprising the larger parts of the problem. A **decision table** shows, in pictorial tabular form, the conditions and actions involved in a problem solution. Flowcharts and pseudocode will be discussed in this chapter; structure and hierarchy charts are included in the general discussion of subroutines and modular programming in chapter 14.

Flowcharts

Flowcharts have been used for decades to depict the design of problem solutions. They are often included in the documentation of industrial applications. Many programmers continue to use flowcharts as the primary tool for representing their algorithms. For these reasons you need to understand them.

The program flowchart is a very important tool. It expresses the logical correspondence of your solution to the sequence of operations in a program. Just as a carpenter uses a blueprint to build a house, the programmer constructs a flowchart to ensure that all operations are considered and performed in the correct sequence. A flowchart can also be thought of as a road map used to reach the desired destination in the shortest time. If the logic of the problem is very simple (like adding two numbers together), a flowchart may not be needed. For most problems, however, a flowchart (or other design tool) will prove invaluable.

By definition, a **flowchart** is a pictorial representation of the flow of logical steps in a solution algorithm. It represents the processes and operations that will take place in a computer program, using symbols of different shapes—analogous to road signs—to each step or set of steps. One might do as well by writing a narrative or outline, but, in this case, a picture may well be worth a thousand words. Specifically, the symbols in a flowchart depict the starting point, the reading of data, arithmetic calculations, decision making, the writing of data, and the termination point in the design logic.

Program Flowcharting Symbols. Seven standard symbols are used to construct program flowcharts. Standard symbols are recommended so that all programmers will recognize the type of operation indicated by each symbol and will understand the documentation. Symbols are chosen to represent different computer operations. Their shapes depict the types of desired operations. Size of the symbols has no significance. Short messages are written inside each symbol to provide further meaning concerning the operation, such as the names of input/output files, data to be tested for decisions, arithmetic calculations to be computed, and so on. If a message is too long to fit within a symbol, don't panic. Draw a larger symbol or have a part of the message extend outside the symbol. An annotation symbol also is available for the insertion of long messages. Each symbol is connected by a line with an arrow to show the proper direction of flow in the logic.

The seven standard flowchart symbols are:

1. **TERMINAL.** A flattened oval designates a terminal point such as the start and stop point in flowchart logic. The shape of this symbol is distinctive so that any reader can quickly locate these points. A start symbol will have one flowline leaving it. A stop symbol will have one flowline entering it. Examples are:

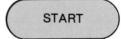

2. **PROCESSING.** A processing function that causes a change in a value or storage location is represented by the rectangle. This symbol is used for all arithmetic calculations and data movement operations. It is probably the most commonly used symbol in any flowchart. A processing symbol will have one flowline into it and one out of it. Examples are:

3. **INPUT/OUTPUT.** The parallelogram depicts a general input/output (I/O) function. All I/O operations, such as the reading and writing of data, are represented by this symbol. An input/output symbol will have one flowline into the symbol and out of it. Examples are:

Some programmers prefer to use system symbols to indicate a specific form of input or output. These are not standard program flowcharting symbols, but your instructor may require you to use them. For example:

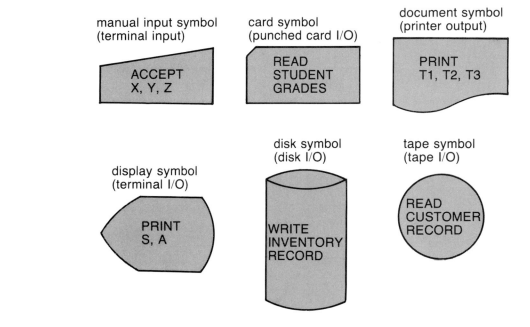

4. **DECISION.** The diamond illustrates a decision function for alternate routes in a program. The decision operation is a test that determines which alternative path of logic to follow. The question to be answered (i.e., the test) is usually written inside the symbol. The possible answers are shown as alternative flowlines proceeding from the diamond. The decision symbol will have one flowline entering it and two flowlines exiting from it. Three examples are:

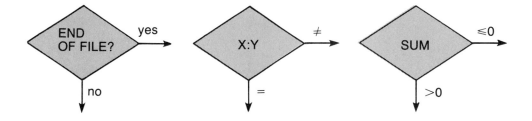

Each exit must be clearly marked to identify the results of the condition for each path. The entire condition may be stated inside the diamond with the results stated on each exit; or, part of the condition may be stated inside the symbol with the remainder given at each exit. The results may be given for each exit in abbreviated form. For example, Y and N may be used for yes and no, respectively. Mathematical operators also may be used. These include the $=$, $\neq$, $<$, $\leq$, $>$, and $\geq$ symbols.

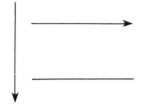

5. **FLOWLINES.** Lines with arrowheads link the symbols together, showing the sequence of operations and direction of control flow. The normal sequence of logic is read from the top of the page to the bottom and from left to right. An example of connecting two symbols is:

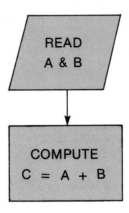

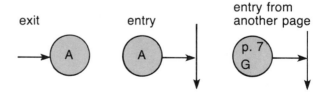

6. **LOGIC CONNECTOR.** A small circle is used as an exit to or entry from another part of the flowchart to indicate the continuation in the flow of logic. This symbol is used: (1) to flow the logic to another page when it is impossible to draw a flowline—the symbol should then be divided in half and the page reference included; (2) to avoid drawing excessively long flowlines (for example, from the bottom of a page to the top of the page); and (3) to keep flowlines from crossing. Put a letter in the exit connector and its corresponding entry connector. One normally starts with the letter A and proceeds through the alphabet, using double letters if the single letters have been used up. Some programmers like to use numbers in place of letters. (In fact, some prefer to put their statement number in the symbol.) Examples are:

A flowline with an arrow pointing *to* the connector means an **exit** is to be made from the logic at this point and a jump made to the location with the matching entry symbol. The **entry symbol** has an arrow pointing *away from* the connector and *into* a flowline.

Some programmers prefer to use the **off-page connector** when the flow of logic continues on a different page. Examples are:

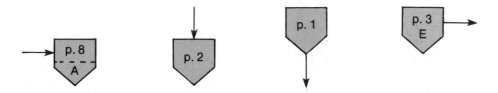

where the page number is included in the symbol. This symbol is especially useful when we wish to continue the logic onto the next page. Here again, we have a symbol *not* recognized as a standard flowcharting symbol. It is widely used, however, and may be required by your instructor.

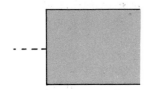

7. **ANNOTATION.** The three-sided rectangle with a connecting broken line is used to add comments to a flowchart. The broken line refers back to the symbol being annotated. For example:

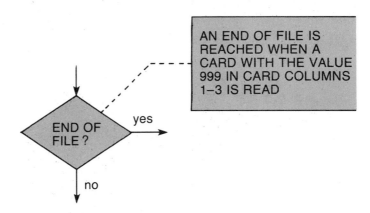

Two additional symbols will be introduced in later chapters when they are needed for more advanced concepts. A tool provided for the programmer's use in drawing flowcharts is the **flowcharting template**, a plastic sheet containing flowcharting symbols as cutout forms for tracing (fig. 3.7).

Now let's review the rules for program flowchart construction:

Rules for Constructing Program Flowcharts

Rule 1: Use a standard set of symbols. This improves readability and interpretation.

Rule 2: The title of the flowchart (program name) should appear on every page. Each page should be numbered sequentially.

Rule 3: The steps constituting a flowchart should start at the top of the page and flow down and towards the right. Several columns of the flowchart logic may be drawn on each page to conserve space.

Rule 4: The messages used to describe each step should be in common English terms insofar as possible, and not in "computer language."

Rule 5: In each step, all the writing should be clearly written within the symbol (to the extent possible). Do not use too many abbreviations. Put yourself in the place of a person not familiar with the problem—would he understand it? Use the annotation symbol, if needed.

Rule 6: Symbols are connected by flowlines with arrows to show the lines of logical flow.

Rule 7: Input/output and process symbols should have exactly one entry line and one exit line.

Rule 8: Decision symbols will have one entry line and two or more exit lines.

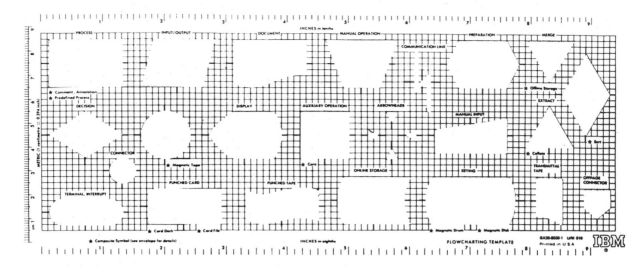

Figure 3.7 IBM flowcharting template. (Courtesy of IBM)

Rule 9: Do not cross over flowlines if avoidable. Use connectors. If a line must be crossed, one line should be ''half-mooned'' over the other to show that no intersection is intended. For example:

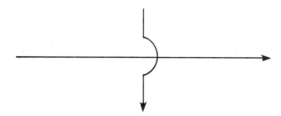

Most programmers do not like to see flowlines of this kind. Connectors are preferable.

Rule 10: Long flowlines (over four inches) should have embedded arrows to clearly delineate the flow of logic. For example:

If this seems likely to cause confusion, use connectors instead.

Rule 11: Try to separate symbols by at least one-half inch.

Rule 12: Allow at least one-inch margin on the left side of the page, in case the pages are bound.

These rules may be too much for you to fully understand at this time, since you have not yet drawn your first flowchart. Digest those you can, for the present, and come back to them after you have had some practice in drawing flowcharts.

The amount of detail to put into a flowchart depends on the intended use. There are three detail-levels in flowcharting: *general, semidetailed,* and *detailed.* The *general level* provides an overview of the problem requirements. Only the main tasks are identified, in the proper sequence. This is a summary level in which you could, for example, give management an overview of a problem solution. They would not be interested in details; so don't get wrapped up in them at this point. For example, a general level flowchart to compute pay might have only three identified operations: (1) compute gross pay, (2) compute deductions, and (3) compute net pay.

The second and third levels of flowcharting are those used by programmers to write their programs. The level used depends upon the complexity of a routine (task) in the problem. When in doubt as to how to accomplish a routine, go into more detail. Too much detail is better than not enough.

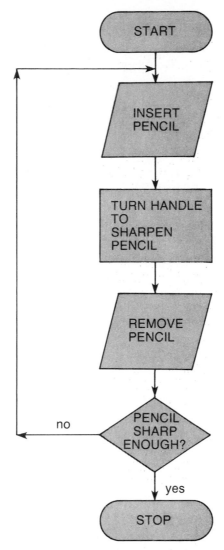

Figure 3.8 Flowchart of how to sharpen a pencil

Your first flowchart should not contain much detail, but show only the main tasks needed in the program. In that way, you will have a better idea of what the problem looks like and not get bogged down in details. Only after determining the main tasks should you draw a more detailed flowchart.

In summary, a flowchart shows *how* to solve a problem. It should be complete, clear, accurate, and neat. Even someone with no knowledge of the problem being solved should be able to prepare a workable computer program from the flowchart.

Flowchart Examples. A flowchart can be used to represent the algorithmic solution to all types of problems, not just computer-related ones. The flowchart for sharpening a pencil is shown in figure 3.8. The insertion of the pencil into the sharpener is shown by the input symbol. Turning the handle to sharpen the pencil is shown by the operation symbol. The removal of the pencil is depicted by the output symbol. The decision symbol shows the test to determine whether the pencil is sharpened sufficiently. If the pencil is not sharp enough, then the flow of processing returns to the input step and the sequence is repeated; thus, a loop is formed. If the pencil is sharpened correctly, the process is terminated.

Some assumptions about the problem are indicated by the flowchart logic. First, it was assumed that the pencil needs sharpening. If we wished to test the sharpness of the pencil before inserting it, the decision symbol which asks if the pencil is sharp enough would be placed at the top of the loop. This is generically known as a *test at the top of the loop.* It was also assumed that only one pencil needed sharpening. If more than one pencil needed to be sharpened, another decision box should be included to test this condition. Thus, another (outer) loop would be formed. It was also assumed that we were at the pencil sharpener. If we wanted to show that we walked to the sharpener and returned to our desk, then another operation symbol would be included after the start and before the stop terminal symbols.

The flowchart to depict the process of how a married person might get up in the morning and get ready to go to work is shown in figure 3.9. Note the decisions involved and their alternative actions.

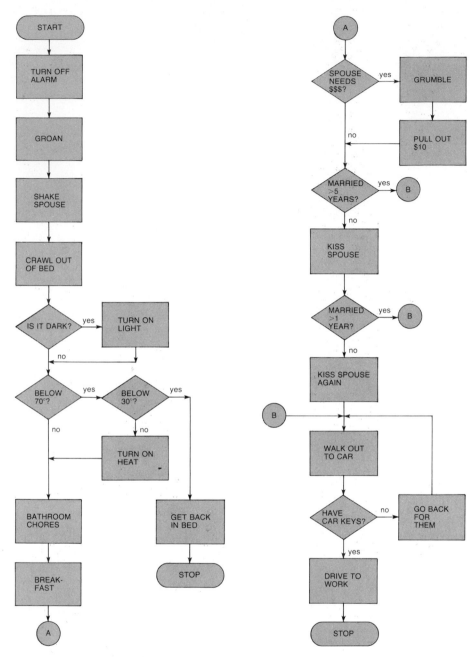

Figure 3.9 Flowchart of how to get up in the morning

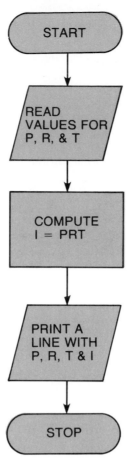

Figure 3.10 Flowchart to compute simple interest

Now let us look at a flowchart depicting the solution for a computer problem. The problem is to read a data record with three values representing principal, rate, and time (in years). The three input values will be used to compute simple interest according to the formula i = prt. The input values and computed interest are then printed. The flowchart might look like figure 3.10.

Our second problem is to calculate grades for a group of students. The first operation prints headings for columns of output values. A student's identification number and five test scores will be read by the computer. The grade average is calculated by adding the test scores and dividing the sum by five. The input values, along with the sum and average, are printed for each student. The same procedure will be done for each student; so a loop must be established to repeat the input, calculation, and output operations until all records have been

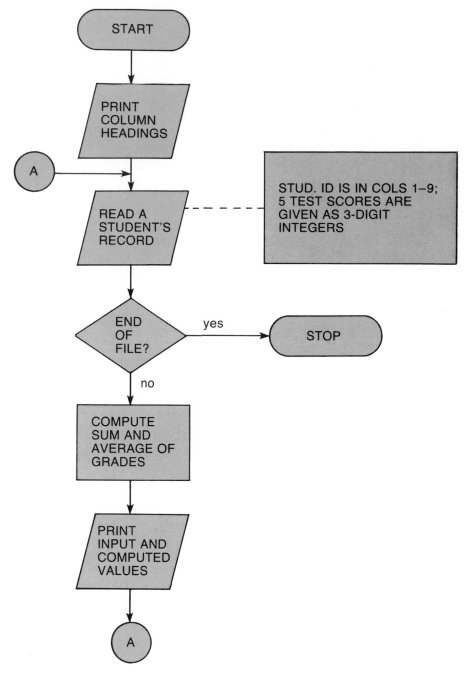

Figure 3.11 Flowchart to compute a group of students' grades

read. When an end-of-file condition is reached (indicating no more data values are present), program execution is terminated. Figure 3.11 illustrates the flowcharted problem.

There are four reasons for using flowcharts to depict algorithms and problem solutions:

1. A flowchart displays the logical solution to the problem in a pictorial fashion, allowing easy checking for correctness.
2. A flowchart is a compact means of communicating the algorithm/solution of a problem to others. A written narrative usually takes more space and does not have the clarity of a flowchart.
3. A flowchart serves as a permanent record of the solution to a problem and can be consulted later by the original programmer or others to gain an understanding of the logic.
4. A flowchart may present the proposed logic for the problem solution in any desired degree of detail. That is, flowcharts may be used to depict the overall parts of the big picture, or may contain such detailed logic that one can readily code the program directly from the flowchart.

Flowcharts do have their disadvantages as design tools. Two disadvantages are:

1. A flowchart allows too much freedom in the flow of control. It is easy, in a flowchart, to draw a connector or line representing a transfer of control, but other design tools force one to eliminate as many branches/transfers as possible. A good structured design shows everything flowing in a top-down manner, rather than as a series of perhaps unexplained branches.

2. A flowchart is a separate document that often does not get updated when the program is finalized or changed. Flowcharts that do not match the solution logic in the actual program are often found in documentation packages. Also, students are often prone to draw flowcharts *after* they have a workable program, in order to save time and draw them only once. In such cases the flowchart is less than useless, since it is a tool specifically designed for use in the *planning* phase of a problem solution.

3.4 WRITING THE COMPUTER PROGRAM (STEP 3)

After the program flowchart (or another design tool) is completed, the next step is writing the computer program. The program specifies the series of operations that must be accomplished in the problem solution by the computer.

Remember that the computer is an extremely stupid machine. It will not do anything on its own. Think of it as a robot whose every action must be programmed. It must be programmed in a limited, but specific set of instructions that it understands. Your robot will not forget anything you have told it and it will not make any mistakes in following your orders; but, it will not do anything unless it is told. Therefore, you must be precise in your instructions, since it will do *exactly* what you say.

Following the sequence of symbols in the flowchart, the programmer **codes** (writes) the computer statements that correspond to the symbols. Usually, you write one FORTRAN statement for each flowchart symbol, as in figure 3.12. Each statement must be written according to the rules of the program language. Some programming languages use a specially designed **coding form** to aid in the later transformation to an input medium because of certain format requirements in coding.

Step 3—Writing the computer program

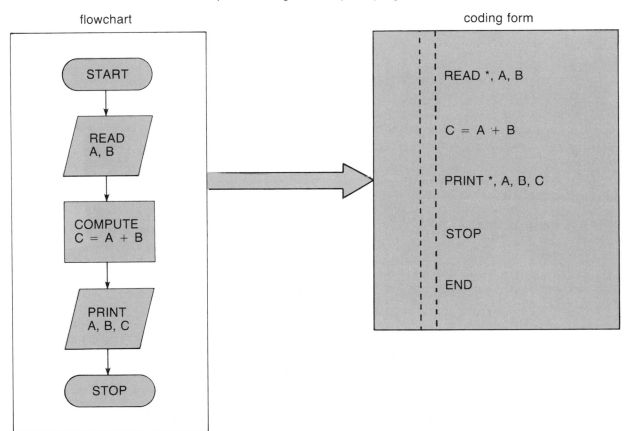

Figure 3.12 Coding a source program from the flowchart

After writing the FORTRAN program, you are ready to have it processed by the computer. The next step is to prepare the coded program on punched cards or to enter it at a terminal so that it can be executed by the computer.

3.5 PREPARING THE PROGRAM IN A COMPUTER INPUT MEDIUM (STEP 4)

Since the computer cannot read a hand-written program, you must put it into an input medium from which the machine can process it. It may be entered either at a terminal or on punched cards. There are generally three modes for entering a program into the computer and running the program. These three modes are:

1. Batch processing (cards or timesharing)
2. Interactive timesharing
3. Single user (personal computers)

Batch processing in a production environment means that the input data for an application is grouped together and processed during a single program execution. Thus, the program and its associated input data may be recorded on punched cards (or built as a disk file) and processed as a batch. Batched card processing provided operating convenience and efficiency on the earlier **first-generation** and **second-generation** computers which processed only one job at a time. Jobs were entered in a sequential manner and each waited its turn before being run.

Timesharing involves the simultaneous sharing of computer time by many users. Since a user takes time to think about an instruction and to type his/her program, the computer can service dozens of users with such efficiency that the user thinks that he alone is using the computer. In fact, timesharing computers may have hundreds of simultaneous users. Figure 3.13 illustrates the process of entering a program over a terminal.

In the mid 1970s microcomputers became a popular way of running programs. The cost of hardware had dropped significantly and computer technology had advanced so that the complete operations of a computer could be contained on a single chip and housed in a stand-alone terminal. The control and arithmetic functions, the memory unit, and even language translators were placed on chips and integrated circuits. Today, a complete computer with all components can be contained in a single small unit such as a CRT terminal. These small, powerful computers are an inexpensive means of providing computer power in small businesses and academic institutions.

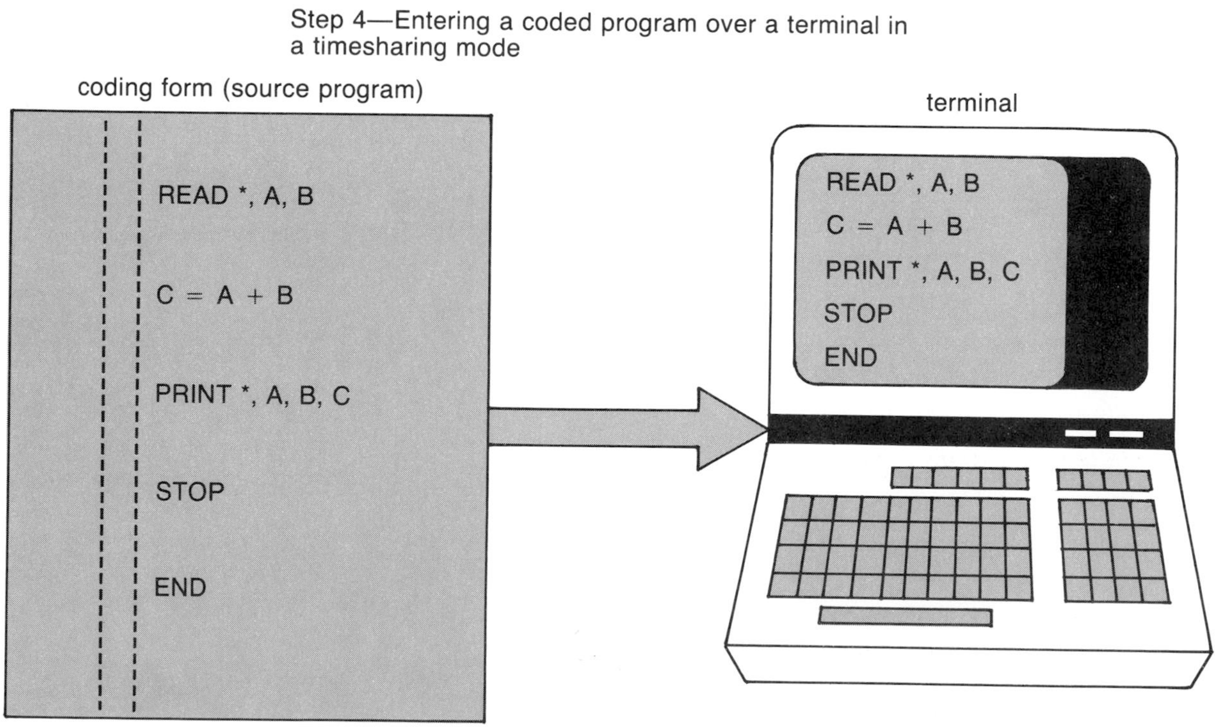

Step 4—Entering a coded program over a terminal in a timesharing mode

Figure 3.13 Using a terminal to enter a program for computer input

Whether you use a timesharing system or a personal computer, a terminal is the common device you will use for entering your program and running it. You log on at a terminal and then type one line for each coded statement. This procedure is continued until all statements in the program have been typed. You are now ready to run your program.

3.6 RUNNING THE PROGRAM AND CORRECTING STATEMENT CONSTRUCTION (SYNTAX) ERRORS (STEP 5)

After your coded program is entered into the computer, it is run (executed) to see if it will work. If your program is on punched cards, you will include job control cards to instruct the computer to execute the program. If your program is entered over a terminal, you must follow the procedure to compile (produce machine language) and run your program in an interactive or remote batch processing mode.

Computer languages have certain rules of composition. If a statement does not conform to these rules, a **syntax** (construction) **error** will occur, and a **diagnostic message** will be displayed to describe the error. A syntax error may be a simple typographical error, or it may mean that the entire statement is incorrectly formed. The programmer uses these error messages to tell him how to correct the statements in error.

The progammer must correct all the syntax errors before the computer can execute the program. The error may be simple to find, e.g., a keyword is misspelled. Sometimes the syntax error may be very difficult to locate, e.g., a missing comma may produce an error message that says that a name is too long. See figure 3.14.

You should expect syntax errors when you first begin writing programs. Even the most experienced programmers occasionally have syntax errors in their work. As you gain more experience in forming statements and writing programs, however, the number of syntax errors should diminish. Chapter 5 provides illustrations of syntax errors from compiling a FORTRAN program.

When all the syntax errors are corrected, you are ready to begin testing your program to ensure it produces the correct results.

Step 5—Correcting statement clerical errors

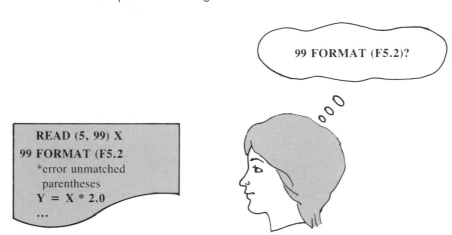

Figure 3.14 Correcting compilation (syntax) errors

3.7 TESTING FOR LOGIC ERRORS AND DEBUGGING THE PROGRAM (STEP 6)

Human errors in programming occur quite frequently and increase as program size and complexity increase. Rarely does the novice programmer develop an error-free program on the first attempt. Even after syntax errors have been removed, logic errors may still exist in the program. **Logic errors** include such things as performing an operation at the wrong place in the program, performing actions out of order, and omitting necessary actions.

During the testing phase all known logic errors in a program are found and corrected. This step is referred to as **testing and debugging. Testing** is the process of executing the program to verify the output results. **Debugging** is the process of locating and correcting program errors. Testing and debugging may be a very time-consuming phase. Generally, larger programs require more time to debug. Valuable time and money may be saved through proper program analysis and design, disciplined program development, and systematic debugging throughout program testing.

Test data is prepared to check each alternative path of logic in a program. If decision making is performed on various input values, you should include a test case for every possible result of each decision. You should also include test data which contains errors, to see if you have properly taken care of all error conditions.

When a programmer locates a discrepancy, a **patch** (change) is made in the program for the determined error. The program is rerun to see if all the bugs (logic errors) have been eliminated. This cycle of testing and debugging recurs until the program produces the correct problem solution. Chapter 5 will present some simple debugging techniques. Chapter 7 discusses more advanced debugging methods.

Once all known errors are removed from the program, you can run the program with live (actual) data to produce desired answers.

3.8   IMPLEMENTING THE PROGRAM WITH OPERATIONAL DATA (STEP 7)

After all known errors have been removed, the program is ready for a production run. In a production run, "**live**" (actual or operational) data is used, data intended for the actual problem solution. Even though the program has been tested, the output results should be carefully checked. If they are not correct, program testing will be resumed and continued until all corrections have been made.

In a production environment an acceptance test is conducted to prove that a new program or system actually works and produces correct output results. A formal procedure is normally conducted where the user signs a letter saying the new program is accepted for operation.

Your instructor (or grader) will act as the user and evaluate your program solution accordingly (figure 3.15). The instructor will require you to use the data or file specified in the lab problem. This way, the instructor knows what the output results should be.

The final step is to complete the documentation of your program and all the aspects of the computer solution to the assigned problem.

Step 7—Implementing the program with live data

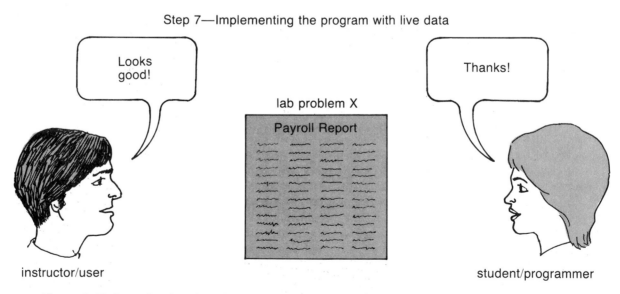

Figure 3.15 Operational testing of the program with live data

3.9 DOCUMENTING THE PROGRAM AND THE PROBLEM SOLUTION (STEP 8)

Program documentation is an important consideration in all steps of developing a workable program. Though listed last, program documentation should be a part of, and accomplished within, each of the preceding seven steps—not delayed until the end. Program documentation is a must in production programming environments with frequent staff turnover. Programmers are promoted, fired, or simply switched to other projects. Program documentation provides continuity in the **maintenance** (upkeep) of operational programs when the original programmer leaves or is moved to another project.

Program documentation consists of all the paperwork which explains how the program works. This paperwork allows one unfamiliar with the program to understand it and make changes—called **program modifications**—in it.

Another type of important program documentation that provides invaluable aid in following program logic is **internal program documentation**—the insertion of comments in the source program itself. Nearly all programming languages allow the programmer to include remarks which explain the function of an instruction (or group of instructions) in the program. You should use internal comments liberally, *as you write the program*, to provide a clear explanation of the program logic for both yourself and your instructor.

The remainder of this chapter discusses other design tools and methodologies which are rapidly becoming popular among programmers. These techniques offer a more structured approach to improve program reliability and maintainability.

3.10 INTRODUCTION TO THE NEED AND IMPORTANCE OF STRUCTURED SOFTWARE DESIGN AND DEVELOPMENT

Designing, writing, and debugging relatively small but important programs should not be a ''major'' or impossible task once you have learned what programming is all about. This is not meant to belittle the effort you will put forth. To the beginning programmer a problem of any size is a complex task and requires much work. Experienced programmers sometimes forget how difficult simple problems can be to someone just learning to program. Until you cross the hurdle of learning how to express the logic of a problem in a straightforward manner, programming is a difficult, frustrating job.

How can you make computer problems easier to solve, with output results known to be correct? Better yet, how can you avoid making logic errors in writing a program? The concepts and techniques employed in top-down structured design and programming can make the task of developing a computer program of any size easier. The programs produced using these techniques are usually more readable, more reliable, and more easily maintained.

Probably the biggest problem facing professional programmers, as well as students, is how to design programs that are easy to understand, relatively error free, and easy to modify and maintain. The sections in the remainder of this chapter introduce you to some of the state-of-the-art concepts, techniques, and design tools which can aid you in developing a computer problem solution. The discussions on problem decomposition, structured programming, and structured design using pseudocode should help you attain the desired program objectives.

Some of the most frequently-used top-down structured techniques and tools are:

1. Structure charts or hierarchy charts to pictorially depict the program structure of functional routines needed in a program.
2. Top-down control-flow structures to represent and implement logic, such as decisions and looping.
3. Pseudocode to present a top-down structured representation of logic.

These relatively new concepts and techniques are rapidly replacing the traditional bottom-up methodologies in developing programs. Before learning to use them, you should understand why a change in software development was needed.

The Software Revolution

In the last decade there has been a dramatic revolution that has established a new discipline within the existing science of computer software development. Its objective is to provide a more organized approach to the analysis, design, coding, testing, implementation, and documentation of computer software. This new discipline is often referred to as **software engineering**, and it focuses on the program development process and the nature of the resulting product.

Top-down structured design and structured programming concepts are dedicated to the production of good programs. What is a good program? Seven desirable qualities include:

1. **The program works.**[1] This is obvious. A program cannot be *useful* if it cannot be *used*. Understandability is very important to assure a correctly working program.

2. **Uncomplicated design to provide readability and understandability.** Programs do not need to be complex to work properly. Your motto should be **KISS—Keep It Simple, Stupid**. Design a program so that someone else can maintain it, since a program is normally maintained over its lifetime by many programmers. The best way to make a program easy to code, test, maintain, and modify is to keep it simple.

3. **Lower development costs.** In top-down structured programming, the modules (functional routines) of a program may be tested and implemented as they are developed, reducing the time and expense of implementation. This top-down modular approach can be achieved only by good functional decomposition and design.

4. **Less testing time and lower testing costs.** In the past nearly fifty percent of the total time in many projects has been devoted to testing and debugging. If you can make a program right to start with, less time and expense are involved in the testing and debugging phase.

5. **Ease of modification.** Changes and modifications to a program will always be required. A system is not static; it must change with its environment and user requirements. Thus, programs should allow flexibility for modifications and later enhancements.

6. **Lower maintenance costs.** The average data processing organization spends fifty percent or more of its entire budget on the maintenance of existing programs.[2] **Program Maintenance** is the activity of keeping operational programs working satisfactorily. Primarily, it involves fixing newly found bugs. Sometimes an existing program has to be completely rewritten because a new programmer could not understand the original programmer's logic or feel comfortable making changes in it.

7. **Efficiency.** This is the last objective in most program development. Too many programmers try to shave microseconds off the execution time, saving perhaps thirty seconds in the weekly running of a program. With the increased speed of modern computers, this is hardly worthwhile. In many programs nearly ninety percent of the execution time is spent in only ten percent of the code. This is often referred to as the 90-10 rule. Therefore, you should:

   a. Write a program/routine in a straightforward manner, emphasizing simplicity, readability, and reliability.
   b. Rewrite and optimize the time-consuming code *after* the program/routine is working. This code is normally found in the iteration logic.

Using this approach, a programmer will invest his or her time in optimizing only those statements which will save an appreciable amount of execution time.

The rising cost of software development (as illustrated in figure 3.16) and maintenance has led to the increasing demand for greater software reliability and productivity. This demand, in turn, led to the development of structured design and programming methodologies. During the first ten to twenty years in the data processing field, computer hardware required the greatest percentage of the budget. The development of solid-state technology and mass production of computers, however, began a downward trend in these costs in the mid-1960s. Meanwhile, the cost of software development continued to grow at a significant rate. By the late 1960s, software cost equalled hardware cost. By the early 1970s, the cost of software development had increased to such an alarming percentage that a **"software crisis"** became apparent. The ratio of current software to hardware cost is roughly 80:20, and it is estimated that this gap will widen even further, becoming 90:10 by 1990, as noted in figure 3.16.

Four major causes of increased software development costs have been identified:

1. Low programmer productivity from excessive program testing.
2. Unreliable software due to unorganized design and development.
3. Software which is difficult to modify and maintain due to poor readability and understandability.
4. Errors in software interface due to poor human communications, interface between program units, and overall design.

---

1. Edward Yourdon, *Techniques of Program Structure and Design* (New Jersey: Prentice-Hall, Inc., 1975), pp. 6–7.
2. Ibid., p. 22.

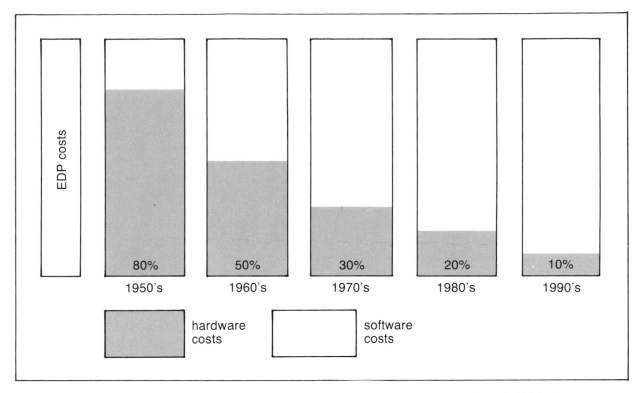

Figure 3.16 Software costs versus hardware costs in an electronic data processing (EDP) budget

Low Programmer Productivity from Excessive Program Testing. The productivity of a programmer is usually measured by the number of debugged (error-free) lines of code written per day. This figure is calculated by dividing the total number of lines of code written (and debugged) for a project by the number of man-days spent on it. Studies of programmer productivity reveal that the average number of debugged lines of code per day is between 10 and 15.[3] This is less than two debugged statements per hour! And this low productivity level has not improved much during the past twenty years. However, the use of structured techniques and tools in program development has produced 35 to 65 lines of debugged lines of code per day![4]

It has been found, however, that some programmers produce as much as ten or twenty *times* as much usable code as others, and this vast difference does not always derive from years of experience. The major difference appears to lie in the way a good programmer plans his/her solution to the problem and develops the code. The production of reliable, efficient, and readable programs in nominal periods of time results from the organized approach and methodologies of the good programmer. One answer to increased programmer productivity, therefore, is using improved techniques and tools to develop programs.

Some programmers spend over half of their time in the testing phase. If the errors can be avoided in the design phase, however, less time is needed for testing and debugging. Errors caught and corrected after the program is in the testing phase are very expensive, while errors caught and corrected in the design phase are cheap. One estimate is that changes to "hard" coded errors may cost as much as 100 *times* more than "paper" changes in program design.

In summary, a poor design effort results in extensive testing and debugging time. Unreliable software is a consequence of not doing adequate planning and proper design in the beginning.

Unreliable Software Due to Unorganized Design and Development. Traditionally, only a small portion of a programmer's time was spent on actual coding. In the past about 25 percent of one's time was spent in program planning and design, 25 percent in coding, and the remaining 50 percent in program checkout (testing and debugging) and other miscellaneous activities. Since structured design and programming require the program to be developed in a more straightforward manner, the resulting code should contain fewer logic errors. The programs are more reliable and require less time in program checkout. More time spent in planning and design produces more reliable and maintainable programs.

3. Ibid., p. 143.
4. Ibid., p. 87.

If the majority of program bugs could be avoided to start with, the programming process would naturally be cheaper. So the current trend is to shift more time back to the analysis and design phase which reduce the time required in the later testing and debugging phase.

Many programmers want to start on the coding to a problem after a minimum effort in design. Besides, how will the supervisor know if a programmer is working if he or she is not turning in decks to the computer center or looking at a listing? So to impress the boss, programmers feel that they must be doing something on the computer.

This approach of "diving" immediately into the coding of the program with very little design effort is known as the **bottom-up approach**. It involves getting into the details as soon as possible and worrying later about how they all fit together. After all, doesn't one simply have to read some data records, do some calculations and then print the results? Wrong, the decision making and ordering of the logic are the tough, complicated aspects of programming. So adequate planning must be done to insure that the solution is well thought out.

Adequate planning of the solution and the use of a good design tool to depict the chosen algorithms before proceeding to the coding phase is known as the **top-down approach**. It starts with the general and then works down into the details. One decomposes a problem from the general to the specific. This allows the programmer to see how the pieces fit together and better understand the decisions which have to be made.

The time spent on planning and designing the solution to a computer problem will be more than repaid over the life of the software product. The real work in developing a computer program is in the design. Once a good design is achieved, it should be an easy task to implement in a program.

Software Which Is Difficult to Modify and Maintain. Program maintenance begins after a program is implemented as an operational system. **Maintenance** is the activity involving the correction of errors to keep a program working satisfactorily. It involves the fixing of program bugs which show up after a program is operational. **Modification** is the programming activity which provides enhancements to an operational program to satisfy new needs of the user. As previously mentioned, approximately fifty percent of all programming effort in a data processing organization is devoted to maintaining, enhancing and troubleshooting existing operational programs. In some organizations software maintenance may reach as high as eighty percent of the overall work load. Programs must be designed and developed with strong emphasis on later maintenance.

The traditional approach to programming was to strive for efficiency. The people who worry about program efficiency are concerned with how much computer time is used in the production runs, and not with how much "people time" is consumed in the extra analysis and debugging required with complex code. "People time" costs much more than machine time, and this disparity will increase even more in the future. With the fast speed and decreasing cost of hardware, it is hardly worthwhile to spend much time on program efficiency with most computer applications.

Today the emphasis is on clear, logical structuring of understandable code. Understandability, reliability, and maintainability take precedence over efficiency. Programmers, therefore, should write their programs in a straightforward manner, emphasizing clarity and reliability. Programs should be "modularized" (developed in functional routines) so that easy maintenance is possible.

Software Interface Errors. **Interface** is the communication between two units of code. These units may be routines within a program, or programs within a system application. The key to a proper software interface is in the communication (passing) of data between the program units. Subprograms usually communicate with a main program by individual data items or records (entire units of related data items). Communication between programs usually is achieved by files (the collection of all related data records).

Different programmers may work on different routines (subprograms) for a large program in order to shorten the overall time required to develop the system; thus there is the human problem of making sure that the interfaces between the program units are correct. Proper program and system design can help avoid many of these interface problems. If a program or system is designed in a top-down way, the interfaces can be worked out as the software is developed. There will be no surprises at the end when it is put together as an integrated unit.

The interface between the user and the programmer/analyst is also highly important. Before starting any design, you must have explicitly communicated with the user regarding desired results. After an agreement is reached, constant user/programmer reviews are required to ensure a proper product. The entire procedure is central to a successful program development.

You should understand now why there is a need for improved software development methodologies and how they have come about. The next section introduces you to a method of "attacking" assigned problems which helps you formulate your solution design in a more organized manner. The additional sections present the more common techniques and tools which can make your task in programming more enjoyable.

3.11 TOP-DOWN PROGRAM DESIGN AND PROBLEM DECOMPOSITION

Programmers using the traditional bottom-up approach try to formulate an algorithm directly in a programming language. Experience has shown that the top-down approach of carefully decomposing a problem into simpler problems produces programs with far fewer mistakes. In the top-down method, you simply decompose the overall problem into precisely defined subproblems. If each subproblem is solved correctly, and these solutions are placed together in the proper logical order, the original problem will be solved correctly. The process of decomposition is then repeated in turn for each of the subproblems until their solutions are simple enough to express in a few lines of code. If each of the subproblems is correctly defined, you can feel confident that you have developed a correct algorithm for your problem solution.

The top-down design method is an orderly approach to the solution of a problem and program design. Take the example of writing a text book on FORTRAN. This is a large, complex task; an author does not sit down and start writing about each of the individual statements and features of the FORTRAN language. He or she first makes a table of contents to identify the information to be included and the sequence in which to cover it. First the chapter topics are selected, then the sections, and finally the detail material. The overall organization of the text is formulated, and the details follow. The same should hold true in programming.

With the top-down approach to design, the first thing to be done is to describe a generalized structure or set of logic modules for the problem solution. A **module** is defined as an independent segment of logically-related code that performs some necessary function. The problem solution is then planned in levels. The statement of the problem is identified at level 0. The major functions of the problem solultion are identified at level 1. These first level modules may then be divided into succeeding lower levels of modules to form an upside-down, treelike pattern for the program development process. The given modules are expanded to as detailed a level of functional definition as is necessary to produce a relatively easy-to-understand and manageable breakdown of the tasks required in the problem solution.

A **structure chart** (or a hierarchy chart) is used to illustrate the major tasks needed in the program and their division into subtasks and even sub-subtasks. Figure 3.17 provides an example of a structure chart used in solving a payroll problem.

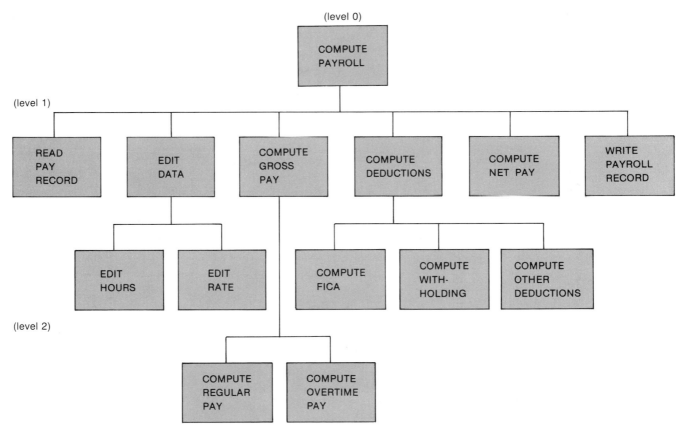

Figure 3.17 Top-down structure chart showing calculation of payroll

The problem definition of computing payroll is included as the program requirement at level 0. The major tasks of reading the input data, editing the data for correctness, calculating gross pay, calculating deductions, calculating net pay, and printing this information are identified at the first level of breakdown. Note that these tasks are stated in abstract terms—they tell what needs to be done and leave the details for later. Some of these tasks are then further subdivided into more detailed parts.

Chapter 14 explains the construction and use of the structure chart in greater detail. This information is delayed until later so that subprograms may be used to implement the functional modules. The programs that you will be assigned at first should not be so complicated as to require structure charts. This brief introduction to them is intended only to emphasize the importance of starting with the general aspects of a problem and breaking these major tasks into more detailed parts. In this section, flowcharts will be used to illustrate the top-down process.

The top-down approach is shown in a flowchart in figure 3.18. Note the decision, which asks whether the modules at the various levels have sufficient logical clarity to fully explain the actions taken in them.

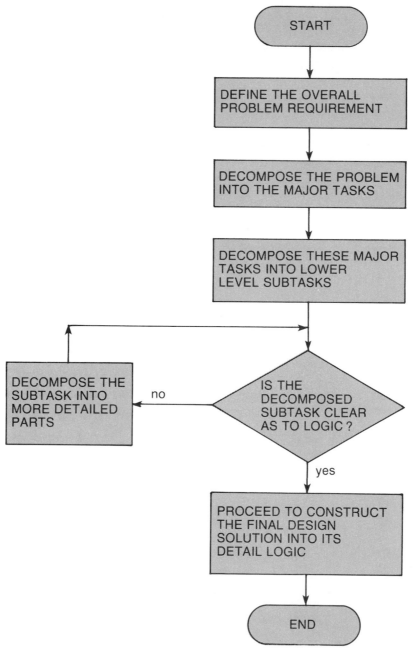

Figure 3.18 The process of decomposing a problem into functional units of subtasks

Now let us take a fairly simple payroll problem and illustrate how one might go about decomposing it into successive levels of detail to produce the final solution design in a flowchart. For simplicity's sake, and to emphasize the decomposing process, the problem is restricted to calculating only gross pay. The specifications of the problem are as follows:

1. Calculate an hourly-wage employee's gross pay, and print the employee name, hours worked, hourly rate, and gross pay.
2. Input items will consist of employee name, hours worked, and hourly rate.
3. Edit the hours worked field to be a positive value no greater than 80.
4. Edit the hourly rate field to be greater than or equal to 3.75 (minimum wage) and less than or equal to 25.
5. Calculate gross pay as the sum of regular and overtime pay.
   a. Regular pay includes the hourly rate times all hours up to and including 40 hours of work.
   b. Overtime pay is one and one-half times the regular hourly rate for all hours over 40.

The definition of the problem requirement is to calculate the gross pay of the employees in a company. An employee gross-pay register might be required by a personnel or plant manager in making budget decisions.

First, decompose the problem into its major tasks. State these tasks in general, abstract terms. Don't worry about the details of decision making or the looping needed to process all the employees' data—postpone these details until you have identified the major parts to the problem solution. These are: reading the employee's data items, editing these data items, calculating gross pay, and printing this information.

If you identified the editing of the individual data items and the calculation of regular and overtime pay as major tasks, you jumped into too much detail at first. Of course, this problem is relatively simple; so you can readily see that these tasks are parts to the solution. The subtasks may not be as obvious in more complex problems.

Just as in developing an algorithm, there is no one correct solution to decomposing a problem. People may look at the problem from different views and levels of decomposition. To keep from getting sidetracked, always make sure that you understand the problem requirement properly. The first-level flowchart showing the major tasks is illustrated in figure 3.19.

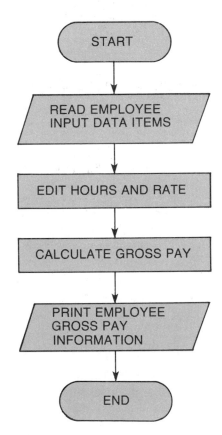

Figure 3.19 Macro flowchart showing the major tasks in calculating gross pay

This level of flowchart is often referred to as a **macro flowchart**. It shows the big picture, a macro view of the parts involved in the problem.

Next, examine each of the major tasks to see if it can be broken down into smaller parts. If you do not understand how to express a major task in one (or a few) instructions in a programming language, you need to decompose it into more detail. Again, postpone the final details until you cannot break the task up any further.

The data input task is detailed enough to understand that a READ command must be used to accomplish this action; so it does not need to be decomposed any more. The individual input items, however, must be identified. The edit task consists of editing the hours and rate data items. This task can be broken into two lower subtasks. The calculation of the gross pay task consists of calculating the regular pay, overtime pay, and the total gross pay; so this major task can be broken up into these three subtasks. The output requirement, consisting of the input and the calculated items for each employee, is detailed enough to understand. The individual items to be printed must be identified. The resulting second-level flowchart is shown in figure 3.20.

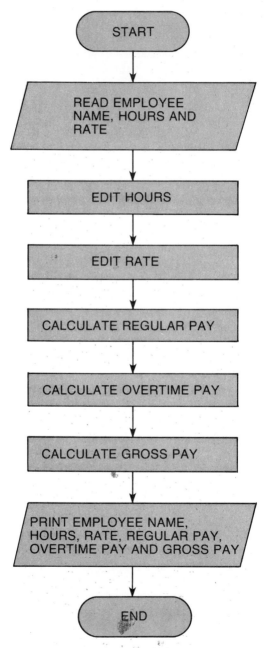

Figure 3.20 Semi-detailed flowchart showing the decomposition of the major tasks in calculating gross pay

This flowchart, showing a fairly detailed level of operations, is referred to as a **semi-detailed flowchart**. It has enough detail to show all the required actions but still doesn't show all the necessary computer commands. This type of flowchart is commonly used because it provides sufficient detail about what must be accomplished but not a list of each specific computer command. A professional programmer would know how to code these operations into a programming language without having to go to the *detailed* level, which has one flowcharting symbol for each needed computer instruction.

You have now shown in sufficient detail *what* must be done and are ready to show the last level of detail— actual computer operations. At this point you put in the decision making and looping. Include a decision symbol after the READ operation to check whether all sets of employee data items have been processed. The decision symbol is also included to show the tests for valid hours, pay rate, and calculation of regular and overtime pay. A connector symbol is included to show a branching operation setting up the loop to process all employees. The final flowchart is shown in figure 3.21.

This is a **detailed flowchart**. All or most computer operations to be expressed in programming language are shown, to provide a clear algorithm of the problem solution. You should construct a detailed-level flowchart to make sure you fully understand the algorithm for the problem's solution. Coding this algorithm into a computer program should then be an easy task. The main difficulty is making sure that the operations are correctly coded, using the proper syntax for the programming language statements.

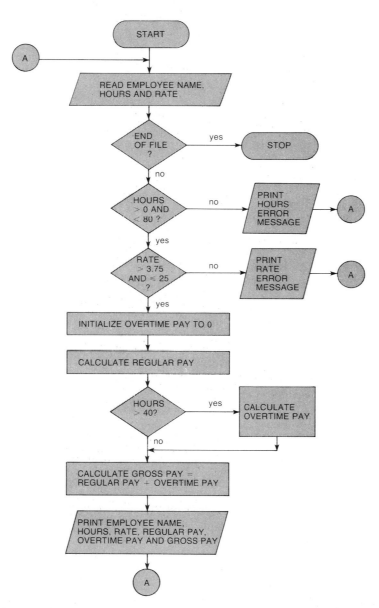

Figure 3.21 Detailed flowchart showing the logic in the solution of calculating gross pay

Suggestions for Developing Programs

The previous sections discussed how to accomplish top-down design for a problem. Several specific suggestions will now be given for implementing your design solution in a computer program:

1. **Build your program in stages.** Don't attempt to put in all the complex logic at the beginning. A good approach is to write the input and output routines first. This way you can make sure that all the sets of data items are being read correctly. Next, put in the parts of another major task, such as calculations. Use test data that contains only valid items; so that the error edits will not yet be needed. Finally, put in the complex decision making. When you build a program in stages, it is much easier to locate and debug the errors. As each new part is included, you can usually depend on the previously debugged routines to be correct; so there is less code to worry about when errors occur.

2. **Build your program small and simple.** Do not put in fancy frills at first. Satisfy the basic requirements instead. A program *working* with the basic requirements is more valuable than a program promised next month with fancy edits and features. If a user changes his or her mind, or if you fail, then you fail quickly with minimum time and expense on the project.

3. **Build your program to be general.** Include flexibility in your program so that it will work for a general problem, not just a specific one. For example, a program to compute the sum of ten numbers should be written with the flexibility to compute the sum of n (where n is variable) numbers. This way the routine can be used again in another program to compute the sum of 100 numbers. The best way to build general routines is to use variables as counters and not be "locked in" with constants. General routines can then be reused in other problems without having to "reinvent the wheel", that is, reuse similar code which is already written and debugged.

4. **Make your program work right, and then make it faster.** As pointed out in an earlier section, the main objective of a program is that it work and do what it is supposed to. Don't spend time worrying about efficiency unless it is really needed. You usually don't get a higher grade based on the efficiency of your program. Your instructor wants to know whether you can program the computer to solve problems. If efficiency is needed, then optimize the code *after* it is working.

5. **Include plenty of internal comments about what each routine is doing—and write them as you are writing the program.** Internal documentation in a program helps a reader—or you yourself—understand what your program is doing and how routines work. A word to the wise—instructors like plenty of internal documentation. Of course, you can overdo it, so use common sense in deciding how much is sufficient.

In summary, there is a great deal more to programming than simply coding. Of equal importance is the ability to break down and organize a problem solution so that a straightforward, easy-to-understand design is developed. The structured coding of the design solution in a programming language is then relatively easy. The next section discusses the principles of restricted control-flow structures to enforce top-down structured design and coding.

3.12 STRUCTURED PROGRAMMING AND TOP-DOWN, RESTRICTED CONTROL-FLOW STRUCTURES

Structured programming is a method of designing and writing programs so that they are easier to code, easier to understand, and less likely to contain logic errors the first time around. By following a set of rules, it aids you in developing the logic and provides a lower probability of error. The basic rules require you to write programs using a restricted set of control-flow structures so that all logic is represented in a top-down fashion. **Structured coding**, therefore, is the process of writing a program using only the recognized top-down, restricted control-flow structures to express logic.

Although a relatively new method of developing programs, structured programming has time and again proven its merit. The use of structured programming methods and techniques by various data processing organizations has resulted in the following benefits:

1. Programs easier to read and comprehend
2. Significant reduction in program logic errors
3. Increased programmer productivity
4. Significant reduction in program maintenance and enhancement costs

A structured program consists of blocks formed from six basic control-flow constructs.[5] These six structures may appear in the *logic* of a program in any language, but *they are not necessarily identical to actual statements or operations in particular languages*. In particular, they do not all occur in FORTRAN dialects; so, for the moment, do not think of them as actual programming language statements.

The idea behind the block structure is that a block of statements may be substituted for a simple statement at any place in a program where an executable statement may appear. A block consists of one or more statements that are combined in some fashion and can be treated as a simple statement. Thus, a block may contain other blocks, or it may be constructed from one or more simple statements. A subroutine is a block. A program is the entire overall block. A structured program becomes a block which contains other blocks built only from the six basic control-flow constructs.[6]

The following paragraphs discuss the six control structures. The symbol **cond** denotes the condition tested in the IF statement. Each of the letters **a, b,** and **s** represents a simple statement or a block of simple statements. A simple statement may be any of the available statements in a programming language. Simple statements include the arithmetic Assignment statement, READ, WRITE, subroutine CALL, and others. They may not include any form of the GO TO statement, since this would cause a transfer of control different from that allowed in the structures. However, it may be necessary to include the GO TO statements in order to implement the control-flow structures in a language, such as ANSI FORTRAN 66 or FORTRAN IV, that is not block structured. Therefore, the GO TO is not considered a simple statement, but an integral part of the control structure in those FORTRAN dialects.

The six control-flow structures are placed into four general categories: sequence, selection, iteration and select case.

Sequence

These statements are executed in the order in which they appear. Control is passed unconditionally from one statement to the next one in sequence. The **Sequence control-flow structure** is so basic to programming that it needs no elaborate explanation. Yet this structure is necessary for the construction of a block from statements that are to be executed sequentially. The logic diagram for this structure is:

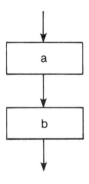

where **a** and **b** represent a simple statement or a block of statements.

Selection

The **selection control-flow structure** provides a top-down structure for decision making. This control-flow structure is also referred to as the **conditional** or **choice** structure, or by the specific name of IF-THEN or IF-THEN-ELSE.

IF cond THEN a: The condition represented by **cond** is tested. If **cond** is true, then statement **a** is executed and control continues at the next statement. If **cond** is not true, **a** is not executed and control is passed to the

---

5. Ted Tenny, "Structured Programming in FORTRAN," *Datamation* 20, no. 7 (July 1974): 110–15.
6. Ibid., p. 110.

next statement. Statement **a** may be a simple statement or a block of statements. The logic diagram for this structure is:

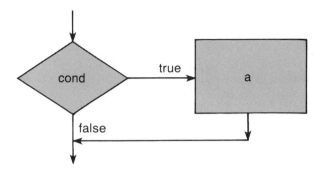

IF cond THEN a ELSE b: The condition represented by **cond** is tested. If **cond** is true, then statement **a** is executed and statement **b** is skipped. Control is resumed at the next statement after **b**. If **cond** is not true, statement **a** is skipped and statement **b** is executed. Control passes to the next statement after **b**. The logic diagram for this structure is:

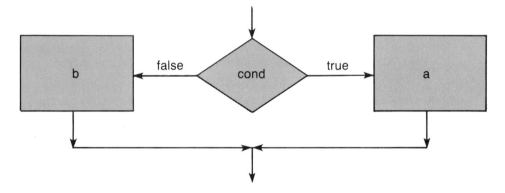

Iteration

The **iteration control-flow structure** provides a top-down structure for looping. This control structure is also referred to as the **repetition** structure or by the specific name of DO WHILE or REPEAT UNTIL. A test must be included in the loop to determine its termination. Loops may be categorized in two ways—test-at-the-top and test-at-the-bottom. The test-at-the-top loop tests a condition *before* a pass of the loop is made. This type of loop is represented by a **DO WHILE** control-flow structure. The test-at-the-bottom loop performs the actions in the loop and *then* makes the test for loop termination. This second type of loop structure is represented by a **REPEAT UNTIL** control-flow structure.

WHILE cond DO a: The condition represented by **cond** is tested. If **cond** is true, the statement **a** is executed and control returns to the beginning of the loop for another test of **cond**. When **cond** is false, statement **a** is skipped and control is passed to the next statement after the end of the loop. The logic diagram for this structure is:

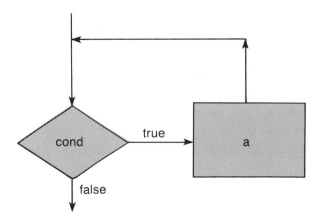

REPEAT a UNTIL cond: Statement **a** is executed and then the condition represented by **cond** is tested. If **cond** is *true*, control continues at the next statement after the end of the loop (since the structure means to repeat statement **a** until the condition **cond** is true). When **cond** is false, controls returns to statement **a** for another iteration. The logic diagram for this structure is:

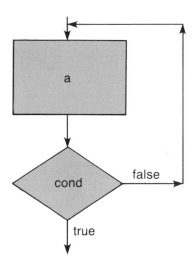

Select Case

The **SELECT CASE control-flow structure** provides a top-down structure for the selection of one set of actions from many possible sets, based on different conditions. For example, you may want to perform a set of actions when a data item is equal to 1, a different set of actions when the same data item is equal to 10, and another set of actions when the same data item is greater than 100. Here is a more formal way of describing this structure:

SELECT CASE i OF $(s_1, s_2, \ldots, s_n)$: The ith statement of the set $(s_1, s_2, \ldots, s_n)$ is executed and all other statements of this set are skipped. That is, the value of **i** determines which statement from among the set is to be executed. Control continues at the next statement after the last one in the set (following s_n). The logic diagram for this structure is:

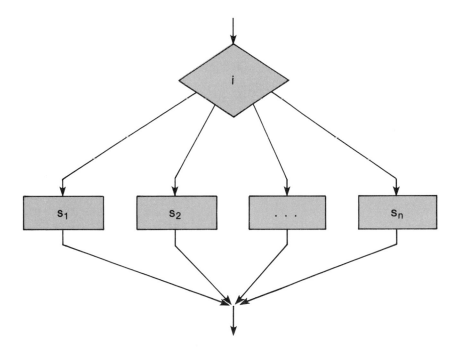

This is equivalent to having multiple IF-THEN structures or nested IF-THEN-ELSE (an IF control structure within another IF) structures. This operation of testing a data item for multiple conditions and performing a different set of actions for the proper condition is frequently found in programming logic. Examples include shift codes, transaction codes, and student class standing.

Each of the mentioned control-flow structures has only one entry and one exit point. When these control structures are put into source code, you have a program that can be read from top to bottom without jumping around in the logic. It is much easier to comprehend what a routine does if all the statements that influence its action are nearby; thus, structured programming uses a group of control structures written with one-entry-point-in and one-exit-point-out.

Nesting of Control-flow Structures

You need not use these six control structures individually or separately from one another. They may be included within one another to achieve the desired logic (see figure 3.22).

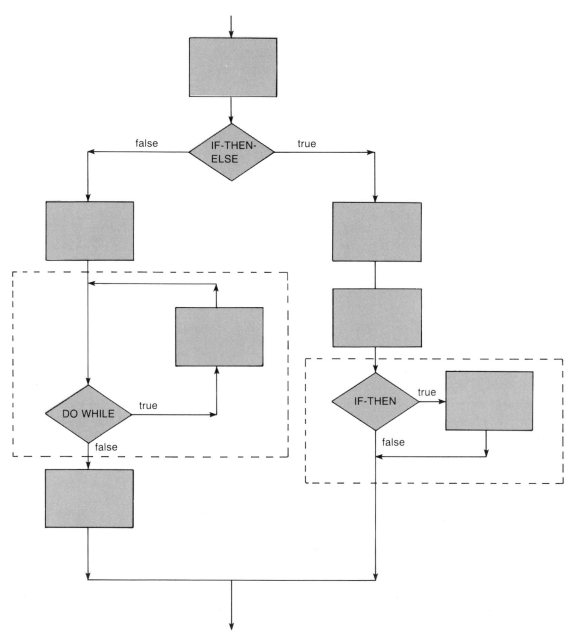

Figure 3.22 A block of statements containing nested control-flow structures

In figure 3.22 the IF-THEN-ELSE control structure is also recognized as a sequence control structure, since control of execution proceeds from the first operation symbol into the IF-THEN-ELSE structure. Inside the IF-THEN-ELSE structure you find an IF-THEN structure down the "true" leg and a DO WHILE structure down the "false" leg. You often need an IF-THEN or IF-THEN-ELSE control structure inside a DO WHILE or REPEAT UNTIL control-flow structure to perform various decision making inside the loop.

Simulation of Restricted Control-flow Structures in ANSI FORTRAN 66 and FORTRAN IV

Top-down readability is one consequence of using only the restricted control-flow structures and avoiding the GO TO statement except in very special cases, such as the simulation of a control-flow structure in a programming language that lacks it. Structured programming is often referred to by some people as "GO TO-less" programming. GO TOs make the logic in a program hard to follow, since the logic is heavily interlocked, rather than being broken down into logically comprehensible blocks. Consider the following segment of code:

```
      IF (N .EQ. 10) GO TO 60
      X = 1.0
      GO TO 70
60    X = 0.0
70    . . .
```

What the routine is trying to achieve is to assign the value of 0.0 to X when N is equal to 10 or to assign the value of 1.0 to X when N is not equal to 10. In a structured FORTRAN dialect which has a block IF-THEN-ELSE statement, this routine could be easily coded as:

```
      IF (N .EQ. 10) THEN
          X = 0.0
      ELSE
          X = 1.0
      END IF
```

The GO TO statements are eliminated and the resulting code is much easier to follow. ANSI FORTRAN 66 and FORTRAN IV do not have the structured block IF-THEN-ELSE statement. With a little thought one can still write this routine using the Logical IF statement and without any GO TO statements. The revised segment of code might be:

```
      X = 1.0
      IF (N .EQ. 10) X = 0.0
```

The value of 1.0 is by default assigned to X. The Logical IF tests the condition for N equal to 10 and assigns the value of 0.0 to X if the condition is true. Forethought and careful planning can help avoid difficult-to-read code resulting from thoughtless jumping with GO TO statements.

It is often very difficult to write a complex program without a single GO TO statement in unstructured FORTRAN dialects! Some people say that GO TO statements should be avoided altogether. Others agree that GO TO statements are all right within each segment of a program, but that these program segments or modules should have one entry point and one exit point in the logic. That is, it is all right to branch within one module of instructions, but you should not jump into the middle of another module and transfer back again to the original. The latter position—using a limited number of GO TOs within an individual program segment—will be our accepted principle.

Some programming languages, such as COBOL, PL/I, Pascal, and ALGOL, are quite adaptable to structured programming. These languages allow a block of instructions to be executed in an IF statement whenever the given condition is met. These languages also have an ELSE option with the IF statement that can provide an instruction or block of instructions to execute whenever the condition in the IF is not met.

ANSI FORTRAN 66 and FORTRAN IV, however, do not have this capability. Only one statement may be executed with the Logical IF statement when the given condition is met. When the condition is not met, control proceeds to the next executable statement. Thus, structured programming is harder to achieve than in some other languages because of the limited capability of the IF statement.

The complete elimination of GO TO's, in a language like ANSI FORTRAN 66 and FORTRAN IV is practically impossible, but their use can be reasonably restricted if the FORTRAN programmer uses them only to build those standard control-flow structures which are not in the language. The techniques for implementing these control-flow structures in ANSI FORTRAN 66 and FORTRAN IV will be presented in the chapters on decision making and looping.

3.13 PSEUDOCODE AS A PROGRAM LOGIC DESIGN TOOL

Pseudocode is a narrative notation for describing the control, logical structure, and general organization of a computer solution to a problem. Essential features of pseudocode are:

1. It is a readable, understandable English-like representation of a computer procedure.
2. It is highly structured, since it uses the restricted control flow structures to display top-down implementation of a solution.
3. Statements within the SELECTION and ITERATION control structures are indented to show relationship to the structure and to improve readability.
4. It uses full words and phrases rather than the graphic symbols of flowcharting. The absence of graphic symbols makes meaningful naming conventions and phrases easier to use; the need for cryptic statements tailored to fit within a small graphic symbol is eliminated.

The basic advantage of pseudocode over flowcharts lies in the easy conversion into programming language. Flowcharts reflect various decision-making alternatives which reflect a transfer of control logic, but such transfers may not correspond to the actual structural logic of a particular programming language. Pseudocode provides a relatively simple transition from its design solution into a structured program. It does not require the programmer to interpret graphic symbols and translate them into code. It uses the restricted control-flow logic structures with indentation conventions to provide an easy translation into a structured programming language. In pseudocode there is usually a one-to-one conversion between the developed solution and statements in a programming language.

The restricted control-flow structures discussed in section 3.12 are used to express logic in pseudocode. These control-flow structures are given in an English narrative form and are not represented by symbols. They are:

1. **Sequence:** shows sequentially executed statements. English-like commands are given for computer operations. For example (no logic is intended in these examples):

    Initialize student counter to zero.
    Set grades accumulator to 0.0.
    Read the variables A and B.
    Compute C = A + B.
    Write the values of A, B and C.
    Input the values for rate and time.
    Calculate distance according to the formula: d = rt.
    Print the values for rate, time and distance.

2. **Selection:** The IF-THEN and IF-THEN-ELSE statements are used to show the actions to be taken with a given condition. Each independent IF statement must end with the keywords END IF to show the termination point of the IF command. The END IF keywords are aligned with the IF keyword. The statements within the IF (after the keywords THEN and ELSE) are indented two to four spaces to show a hierarchical relationship.

    a. **IF-THEN:** causes the execution of a block of statements when the given condition is true. The key word THEN is included after the condition. The form of the IF-THEN pseudocode representation is:

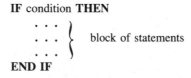

    b. **IF-THEN-ELSE:** causes the execution of one of two functional blocks of statements depending on the result of the test of the given condition. If the evaluated condition is true, the block of statements after the keyword THEN is executed (block a). If the condition is false, the block of statements after the keyword ELSE is executed (block b). The keyword ELSE is placed on a new line and aligned with the IF keyword. The form of the IF-THEN-ELSE pseudocode representation is:

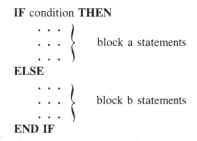

IF condition **THEN**

. . .
. . .   } block a statements
. . .

ELSE

. . .
. . .   } block b statements
. . .

END IF

3. **Iteration:** The DO WHILE and REPEAT UNTIL statements are used to show actions taken within a loop. The DO WHILE statement includes a condition which is tested at the top of the loop. The keywords END DO are used to show the end of the loop. The REPEAT UNTIL structure includes a condition which is tested at the bottom of the loop. The keywords END REPEAT are used to show the end of the loop.

   a. **DO WHILE:** causes a block of statements to be executed within a loop *while* a given condition is *true*. The test for the exit from the loop is checked at the top of the loop. The form of the DO WHILE pseudocode representation is:

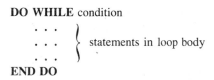

   DO WHILE condition

   . . .
   . . .   } statements in loop body
   . . .

   END DO

   b. **REPEAT UNTIL:** causes the block of statements within a loop to be executed *until* a condition is *true* (i.e., while the condition is false). The form of the REPEAT UNTIL pseudocode representation is:

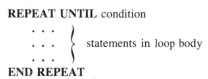

   REPEAT UNTIL condition

   . . .
   . . .   } statements in loop body
   . . .

   END REPEAT

4. **SELECT CASE:** causes control to pass to one of a set of functional blocks of code based on the value of a control variable. A common point in the flow of logic is resumed after the SELECT CASE structure. The SELECT CASE may be implemented with the CASE entry keywords or with nested IF-THEN-ELSE structures. The CASE representation includes the keyword END CASE to show the end of the SELECT CASE control structure. The END CASE keyword is aligned with the CASE ENTRY keyword. Inside the CASE structure are the different cases for the value of the control variable. An ELSE keyword is used to show the case for an error condition (when the value of the control variable is not one of the given cases in the structure). The form of the SELECT CASE pseudocode representation using the CASE entry keywords is:

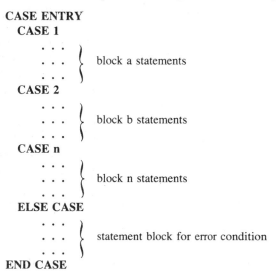

CASE ENTRY
  CASE 1

   . . .
   . . .   } block a statements
   . . .

  CASE 2

   . . .
   . . .   } block b statements
   . . .

  CASE n

   . . .
   . . .   } block n statements
   . . .

  ELSE CASE

   . . .
   . . .   } statement block for error condition
   . . .

END CASE

The form of the SELECT CASE pseudocode representation using nested IF-THEN-ELSE statements is:

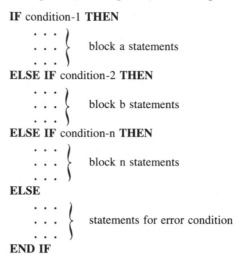

IF condition-1 **THEN**
. . . ⎫
. . . ⎬ block a statements
. . . ⎭
ELSE IF condition-2 **THEN**
. . . ⎫
. . . ⎬ block b statements
. . . ⎭
ELSE IF condition-n **THEN**
. . . ⎫
. . . ⎬ block n statements
. . . ⎭
ELSE
. . . ⎫
. . . ⎬ statements for error condition
. . . ⎭
END IF

Now let us examine several sample problems employing pseudocode.

Examples of a Pseudocode Design Solution

It is recommended that you show the beginning of the pseudocode solution with the phrase—**Start analysis**—and the end with the phrase—**End analysis**. These two phrases correspond to the start and stop terminal symbols in flowcharting.

First, let us develop a short example to illustrate the use of pseudocode for a problem solution without any decision making or loops. The problem is to compute the future value of an investment for a given principal at a certain rate for a given period of time, given in years. The variables for principal, rate, and time will be read as input values. The formula to calculate the future value of an investment (which includes the original principal plus earned interest) is:

$$i = p(1 + r)^n$$

where p is the principal, r is the rate, and n is the number of periods. The input variables and the calculated interest will be printed as output. The pseudocode solution is given in figure 3.23.

Now let us take a more complex example with decision making and looping. The pseudocode will be developed for a salesperson commission problem. The problem is to calculate the weekly commissions earned for a group of salespeople and print a Weekly Sales Commissions report. A salesperson ID and the weekly sales amount are read for each salesperson. A commission of 5 percent is earned for all sales up to and including

> START ANALYSIS.
>   READ THE VALUES FOR PRINCIPAL, RATE, AND TIME.
>   CALCULATE THE EARNED INTEREST ACCORDING TO THE
>   FORMULA: $I = P(1 + R)^N$.
>   PRINT THE VALUES FOR PRINCIPAL, RATE, TIME, AND
>   INTEREST.
> END ANALYSIS.

Figure 3.23 Pseudocode to calculate compound interest

```
START ANALYSIS.
    PRINT REPORT HEADING OF "WEEKLY SALES COMMISSIONS REPORT."
    PRINT COLUMN HEADING FOR "SALESPERSON," "WEEKLY SALES"
                    AND "COMMISSION."
    DO WHILE THERE ARE MORE SALESPERSONS RECORDS
        READ A SALESPERSON RECORD WITH SALESPERSON ID AND SALES.
        IF SALES ARE LESS THAN OR EQUAL TO 5000 THEN
            CALCULATE COMMISSIONS = .05 TIMES SALES.
        END IF
        IF SALES ARE GREATER THAN 5000 AND
                    LESS THAN OR EQUAL TO 10000 THEN
            CALCULATE COMMISSIONS = .07 TIMES SALES.
        END IF
        IF SALES ARE GREATER THAN 10000 THEN
            CALCULATE COMMISSIONS = .10 TIMES SALES.
        END IF
        PRINT SALESPERSON ID, SALES, AND COMMISSIONS,
    END DO
END ANALYSIS.
```

Figure 3.24 Pseudocode example 1 for sales commission report

$5,000. A commission of 7 percent is earned for total sales over $5,000 and up to and including $10,000. A commission of 10 percent is earned for all weekly sales over $10,000. The output report will include:

1. A report heading identifying the report. The title should read: WEEKLY SALES COMMISSION REPORT.
2. Column headings of SALESPERSON, WEEKLY SALES, and COMMISSIONS to be printed over each output field.
3. A detail print line with the salesperson ID, weekly sales amount, and calculated commissions earned.

A DO WHILE loop will be used to process the group of input records. The pseudocode design solution is given in figure 3.24.

You may wonder how we determine when the last record of the salesperson's input records is read. If you wish to be very specific in the design solution, you must provide for this decision making. You must certainly provide for it in a program! A last record is included with a salesperson ID of −999 (since this is an invalid salesperson ID) and sales of 0.00 to signal the end of the input records. This type of trailer record is known as a **sentinel record** since it flags (indicates) the end of input data. Thus, our DO WHILE statement would be:

DO WHILE salesperson ID is not equal to −999

You must include the reading of the first salesperson data before the DO WHILE loop in order that the variable—salesperson ID—will have a valid value. This is known as a **priming read**. Just as a well pump is primed to start the pump working, you must prime the condition in the DO WHILE statement to start the loop working correctly. The READ command in the loop must be moved to the bottom of the loop. If the READ command is placed at the top of the loop, then the first salesperson record, already read in the priming read, would be skipped and not included in the report (imagine how angry that person might be in not getting paid). It is also mandatory to place the READ command at the bottom of the loop to avoid processing the sentinel record with the salesperson ID of −999. We would not want this record to be included on our report. Since the DO WHILE statement tests the condition at the top of the loop, the sentinel value of −999, if read at the bottom of the loop, would terminate the loop, and this sentinel record would not be processed. Another important factor is that a priming read can logically deal with the possibility that there were no salesperson data records present.

The revised pseudocode design to include a priming read for a structured programming solution is given in figure 3.25.

Let us look at one more pseudocode example with counter and accumulation logic. Suppose we modify the same problem to count the number of salesperson records processed and accumulate the total commissions earned. These two new calculations will be printed on a line beneath the last salesperson detail print record. Of course, we must initialize the salesperson counter and commissions accumulator to zero before entering the DO WHILE loop. The pseudocode for this modified problem is given in figure 3.26.

```
START ANALYSIS.
    PRINT REPORT HEADING OF "WEEKLY SALES COMMISSIONS REPORT."
    PRINT COLUMN HEADING FOR "SALESPERSON," "WEEKLY SALES"
                            AND "COMMISSION."
    READ A SALESPERSON RECORD WITH SALESPERSON ID AND SALES.
    DO WHILE SALESPERSON ID IS NOT EQUAL TO -999
        IF SALES ARE LESS THAN OR EQUAL TO 5000 THEN
            CALCULATE COMMISSIONS = .05 TIMES SALES.
        END IF
        IF SALES ARE GREATER THAN 5000 AND
                LESS THAN OR EQUAL TO 10000 THEN
            CALCULATE COMMISSIONS = .07 TIMES SALES.
        END IF
        IF SALES ARE GREATER THAN 10000 THEN
            CALCULATE COMMISSIONS = .10 TIMES SALES.
        END IF
        PRINT SALESPERSON ID, SALES, AND COMMISSIONS.
        READ A SALESPERSON RECORD WITH SALESPERSON ID AND SALES.
    END DO
END ANALYSIS.
```

Figure 3.25 Pseudocode example 2 for sales commission report

```
START ANALYSIS.
    PRINT REPORT HEADING OF "WEEKLY SALES COMMISSIONS REPORT."
    PRINT COLUMN HEADING FOR "SALESPERSON," "WEEKLY SALES"
                            AND "COMMISSION."
    INITIALIZE SALESPERSON COUNTER TO ZERO.
    INITIALIZE COMMISSIONS ACCUMULATOR TO ZERO.
    READ A SALESPERSON RECORD WITH SALESPERSON ID AND SALES.
    DO WHILE SALESPERSON ID IS NOT EQUAL TO -999
        IF SALES ARE LESS THAN OR EQUAL TO 5000 THEN
            CALCULATE COMMISSIONS = .05 TIMES SALES.
        END IF
        IF SALES ARE GREATER THAN 5000 AND
                LESS THAN OR EQUAL TO 10000 THEN
            CALCULATE COMMISSIONS = .07 TIMES SALES.
        END IF
        IF SALES ARE GREATER THAN 10000 THEN
            CALCULATE COMMISSIONS = .10 TIMES SALES.
        END IF
        PRINT SALESPERSON ID, SALES, AND COMMISSIONS.
        INCREMENT SALESPERSON COUNTER BY ONE.
        ADD COMMISSIONS TO COMMISSIONS ACCUMULATOR.
        READ A SALESPERSON RECORD WITH SALESPERSON ID AND SALES.
    END DO
    PRINT THE VALUES FOR SALESPERSON COUNTER AND
                            COMMISSIONS ACCUMULATOR.
END ANALYSIS.
```

Figure 3.26 Pseudocode example 3 for sales commission report

Hopefully, you see from the pseudocode examples just how readable a design solution can be. It is more like English and easier to understand than flowcharts. It would be quite easy to code a workable program from these pseudocode design solutions. Many instructors prefer pseudocode over flowcharts in depicting the logic for a problem solution. Whether you use pseudocode or flowcharts to represent your algorithm design is your choice or your instructor's. Both design tools are used in this text.

3.14 SUMMARY

The most efficient and effective procedure to solve a problem with a computer follows eight basic steps known as the **computer problem-solving process**. These steps provide an ordered methodology for taking the problem specifications, analyzing the problem requirements, designing a computer solution with a specific design tool, and developing a workable program to produce the desired output results. The eight computer problem-solving steps and corresponding computer terms are summarized in the following narrative:

Eight Steps in Solving a Problem with a Computer

General Narrative Description	Computer Terms
1. Analyzing the problem specifications and defining the problem requirements	Problem analysis and definition
2. Designing the computer solution	Solution design (Flowcharts, pseudocode, etc.)
3. Writing the computer program	Coding the source program
4. Preparing the program in a computer input medium	Keypunch or terminal entry of the program
5. Running the program and correcting statement errors	Compiling the source program and correcting syntax errors
6. Testing for logic errors and debugging the program	Testing and debugging the program for logic errors
7. Implementing the program with actual data	Implementing an operational program
8. Documenting the program and the problem solution	Program documentation

The first two steps cover the planning phase—developing an algorithm depicted by a design tool such as a flowchart or pseudocode. The remaining six steps make up the implementation phase. The time devoted to a computer problem should be evenly divided between these two phases. Adequate design will pay large dividends in implementation.

Seven general problem-solving steps were provided to assist the programmer in the analysis and design—the planning phase—of computer problem solving. These are:

1. Define the problem requirements (purpose and output).
2. Identify the pertinent variables involved in the problem.
3. Identify the relationship among the variables.
4. Develop a model (solution) using the variables and developed formulas.
5. Analyze the developed model.
6. Compute output results from some values by using the model (solution).
7. Check the results produced by the model against hand calculated results.

A flowchart, which uses graphic symbols, is a commonly used design tool. Section 3.3 presented the seven basic programming symbols used to illustrate the logic of a computer program. Pseudocode, which uses a narrative description in a top-down manner, is a highly desirable tool. Other design tools such as structure charts, hierarchy charts, and decision tables may also be used.. The computer program is written from the logic expressed in a design tool.

Structured software design and the need for structured programming were introduced to inform the student of the importance of an organized approach to software development. The six restricted control-flow structures used in top-down structured programming and design were presented and discussed. These control-flow structures are simply a means of expressing logic for a function or block of statements so that the block has one entry point and one exit point. Thus, all blocks of code are developed in a complete top-down manner, producing programs which are highly readable and understandable. The six restricted control-flow structures are:

1. **Sequence**—executes statements in a sequential order.
2/3. **Selection**—makes a test or selection of statements to be executed based on the given condition. Two logic structures used in the selection of alternative logic routines are:
   a. **IF-THEN**
   b. **IF-THEN-ELSE**
4/5. **Iteration**—performs loops. A test for the loop exit can be made at the top of the loop or at the bottom of the loop. The two logic structures available to establish loops are:
   a. **DO WHILE**—test at the top of the loop.
   b. **REPEAT UNTIL**—test at the bottom of the loop.
6. **SELECT CASE**—allows selection of a routine from multiple routines, depending upon the given condition.

Section 3.13 further discussed pseudocode as a design tool. Pseudocode is an English narrative notation that incorporates the restricted control-flow structures in expressing logic. Thus, pseudocode is easy to follow and understand. It is relatively easy to convert a pseudocode design solution into a computer program, especially if the structured control-flow constructs are implemented in the programming language. Several examples were given to illustrate the process of using pseudocode to depict a problem design.

This chapter is a very important one for the beginning programming student. The better you understand the techniques and tools of design and how to develop structured design solutions to problems, the easier it will be to write correct programs. Structured design methodologies have already proven their value in developing reliable, readable, understandable, and maintainable software.

3.15 TERMS

Terms and concepts you should become familiar with in this chapter include:

analysis	interface	SELECT CASE control
coding	internal program documentation	structure
compile	iteration control structure	selection control structure
computer problem-solving steps	job control language (JCL)	sentinel (or trailer) record
control-flow structure	language translator	sequence control structure
decision table	live (or operational) data	software engineering
DO WHILE control structure	logic design	source deck
documentation package	Multiple-card layout form	source language
end-of-file condition	Print Layout form	structure chart
flowchart	problem specifications	structured coding
flowcharting symbol	program design	structured design
general problem-solving	program execution	structured programming
procedure	program implementation	syntax error
high-level language	program maintenance	testing and debugging
how to develop a program in	pseudocode	top-down problem
stages	REPEAT UNTIL control	decomposition
IF-THEN-ELSE control	structure	turnaround time
structure		

3.16 REVIEW QUESTIONS

1. When should the computer be chosen for solving an application problem?
2. List the eight computer problem-solving steps.
3. Why is it important to understand and follow these steps in producing a workable computer problem solution?
4. Describe the seven steps in the general problem-solving procedure.
5. The eight computer problem-solving steps may be divided into what two main parts?
6. Why should approximately 50 percent of your time be spent in the planning phase (analysis and design)?
7. Describe the process of analyzing the problem specifications and defining the problem requirements.
8. Why is it important to first identify the output requirements before defining the input and processing requirements?
9. What form is used to identify the items and format for the output requirements?
10. Why is it important to express the solution algorithm with a design tool before writing the program?
11. List two design tools used in depicting program logic.
12. Define a flowchart.
13. Why is the shape of flowcharting symbols important?
14. List the seven standard programming symbols used in flowcharting and their shapes.
15. Describe the difference between batched card processing and interactive timesharing modes of running a program.
16. The errors that occur from the improper construction of a program statement are called _____ .
17. Explain the process of testing a program.
18. What is meant by debugging?
19. What is meant by implementing a program with operational data?
20. Why is program documentation so important?
21. What is internal program documentation, and why is it important?
22. Define software engineering.
23. List five desirable qualities of a program.
24. List the four major problem areas in software development.
25. Describe the difference between the bottom-up and top-down approach to program development.
26. What is meant by software interface?
27. Describe the process of top-down problem decomposition.
28. What is the purpose of a structure chart in top-down design?
29. List the three levels of flowchart detail and explain the difference among them.
30. Why should you build a program in stages?
31. What is the importance of building a general program?
32. Define structured coding and structured programming.
33. List the six restricted control-flow structures and explain their use in representing program logic.
34. Define pseudocode and its importance as a program design tool in contrast to flowcharting.

3.17 FLOWCHARTING AND PSEUDOCODE PROBLEMS

1. Draw a program flowchart to read a single data record with the values RATE and TIME; compute DISTANCE according to the formula $d = rt$; print the two input values and the calculated value for distance.
2. Draw a flowchart to read three records with the values of A, B, and C, respectively. Use these three values to solve the equation: $Y = A + B - C$. Print the three input values and the computed value of Y.
3. Construct a program flowchart to read an inventory file containing the value of unit-cost along with other related values; prepare a printer listing of all input records; accumulate the overall unit-cost of all items; and print the overall unit-cost for all items after listing the file.
4. Develop a program flowchart to read ten values, each on a different record, and compute their average value. (Note: An average is found by dividing the sum of the ten values by 10.) Print the ten values, their sum, and average on different lines.
5. Draw a flowchart to read three values, determine which value is the largest, and print it.

6. Draw a flowchart to compute the square, square root, cube, and cube root of the integers from 1 through 10. Print each integer and its related computed values on double-spaced lines. Print appropriate column headings for each column of values.

7. Draw a flowchart to solve the quadratic equation: $ax^2 + c = 0$. Read the values of A and C. Use these values to solve the equation according to the solution of $X = \pm \sqrt{-c/a}$. If the computed value of $-c/a$ is negative, write an error message to the effect that an imaginary root has been requested. Otherwise, print the positive and negative roots.

8. Draw a flowchart to read and compute the sum of fifty numbers. Print each value as it is read. Print the accumulated sum of the fifty numbers at the end of the program. Establish a counter to keep count of the number of data records read.

9. Draw a flowchart to read the values X, Y, and Z, respectively. Print each input value. Add X and Y. If the result is negative, return to read another set of values. If the result is zero or positive, add Z; print the sum of the three values; return to read another set of values. Terminate processing when a value of -999 is read for X.

10. Draw a flowchart to read the input values A and B, and solve the equation: $C = 2A + 3B$. Write the input values and the computed value of C. Make the program repetitive to handle multiple sets of input records.

11. Draw the flowchart to calculate the volume of a sphere according to the formula:

$$V = \frac{4}{3}\pi r^3$$

Use 3.1416 for π. Assign the value of 10.0 to r (radius). Print the value of radius and the calculated volume.

12. Draw a flowchart to calculate the weekly commissions for a salesperson's weekly sales. Sales commissions are paid on the following basis:

Sales	Commission
Up to $100	zero
Over $100 and up to $500	3% of sales
Over $500 and up to $2000	5% of sales
Over $2000	8% of sales

One value is to be read for the weekly sales amount. Print the weekly sales amount and calculated sales commission.

13. Draw a flowchart to calculate the sales commission for multiple salespersons. Sales commissions are paid on the same basis as problem 12. Read a salesperson number and weekly sales amount from the same data record. Each salesperson's data items will be contained in a separate record. Print the salesperson number, weekly sales amount, and calculated sales commission on a print line. Enter a salesperson number of zero to indicate the end of the valid data records.

14. Draw a flowchart to solve the same sales commission problem given in problem 13 and also include an accumulated total sales amount and total of commissions paid. Print these two calculated items beneath the last salesperson print record.

15. Write the pseudocode to solve problem 1.
16. Write the pseudocode to solve problem 2.
17. Write the pseudocode to solve problem 3.
18. Write the pseudocode to solve problem 4.
19. Write the pseudocode to solve problem 5.
20. Write the pseudocode to solve problem 6.
21. Write the pseudocode to solve problem 7.
22. Write the pseudocode to solve problem 8.
23. Write the pseudocode to solve problem 9.
24. Write the pseudocode to solve problem 10.
25. Write the pseudocode to solve problem 11.
26. Write the pseudocode to solve problem 12.
27. Write the pseudocode to solve problem 13.
28. Write the pseudocode to solve problem 14.

3.18 BIBLIOGRAPHY

The following list of texts is given to provide a more detailed explanation of the modern structured programming methodologies. Numerous articles have been written in the computer magazines on structured programming and design and the related subjects. You should consult your library for additional reference material.

Aron, Joel D. *The Program Development Process*. Reading, Mass.: Addison-Wesley Publishing Company, 1974, 264 pp.

Bohl, Marilyn. *A Guide For Programmers*. Englewood Cliffs, N.J.: Prentice-Hall, Inc., 1978, 216 pp.

_____ . *Tools for Structured Design*. Chicago: Science Research Associates, Inc., 1978, 200 pp.

Couger, J. Daniel; Colter, Mel A.; and Knapp, Robert W. *Advanced System Development/Feasibility Techniques*. New York: John Wiley and Sons, 1982, 506 pp.

De Marco, Tom. *Structured Analysis and System Specification*. New York: Yourdon Inc., 1978, 314 pp.

Dijkstra, Edsger W. *A Discipline of Programming*. Englewood Cliffs, N.J.: Prentice-Hall, Inc., 1976, 217 pp.

Hughes, Joan K., and Michtom, Jay I. *A Structured Approach To Programming*. Englewood Cliffs, N.J.: Prentice-Hall, Inc., 1977, 264 pp.

Jackson, M. A. *Principles of Program Design*. New York: Academic Press, 1975, 299 pp.

Jensen, Randall W., and Tonies, Charles C. *Software Engineering*. Englewood Cliffs, N.J.: Prentice-Hall, Inc., 1979, 580 pp.

Kernighan, Brian W., and Plauger, P. J. *The Elements of Programming Style*. New York: McGraw-Hill Book Company, 1974, 147 pp.

_____ . *Software Tools*. Reading, Mass.: Addison-Wesley Publishing Company, 1976, 338 pp.

Kreitzberg, Charles B., and Shneiderman, Ben. *The Elements of FORTRAN Style: Techniques for Effective Programming*. New York: Harcourt Brace Jovanovich, Inc., 1972, 121 pp.

Ledgard, Henry F., and Chmura, Louis J. *FORTRAN With Style*. Rochelle Park, N.J.: Hayden Book Company, Inc., 1978, 164 pp.

McGowan, Clement L., and Kelly, John R. *Top-Down Structured Programming Techniques*. New York: Petrocelli/Charter, 1975, 288 pp.

Meek, Brian, and Heath, Patricia. *Guide to Good Programming Practice*. London: Ellis Horwood Limited Publishers, 1980, 181 pp.

Myers, Glenford J. *Composite/Structured Design*. New York: Van Nostrand Reinhold Company, 1978, 174 pp.

Orr, Ken. *Structured Requirements Definition*. Topeka, Kansas: Ken Orr and Associates, Inc., 1981, 235 pp.

Page-Jones, Meilir. *The Practical Guide to Structured Systems Design*. New York: Yourdon Press, 1980, 354 pp.

Peters, Lawrence J. *Software Designs: Methods & Techniques*. New York: Yourdon Press, 1981, 234 pp.

Shelly, Gary B., and Cashman, Thomas J. *Introduction to Computer Programming Structured COBOL*. Fullerton, Cal.: Anaheim Publishing Company, 1977.

Shneiderman, Ben. *Software Psychology*. Englewood Cliffs, N.J.: Winthrop Publishing Company, 1980, 320 pp.

Stevens, Wayne P. *Using Structured Design: How to Make Programs Simple, Changeable, Flexible and Reusable*. New York: John Wiley & Sons, Inc., 1981, 213 pp.

Swann, Gloria H. *Top-Down Structured Design Techniques*. New York: Petrocelli Books, Inc., 1978, 140 pp.

Tausworthe, Robert C. *Standardized Development of Computer Software.* Englewood Cliffs, N.J.: Prentice-Hall, Inc., 1977, 379 pp.

Van Tassel, Dennis. *Program Style, Design, Efficiency, Debugging and Testing.* Englewood Cliffs, N.J.: Prentice-Hall, Inc., 1974, 256 pp.

Weinberg, Gerald M. *The Psychology of Computer Programming.* New York: Van Nostrand Reinhold Company, 1971, 288 pp..

Weinberg, Victor. *Structured Analysis.* Englewood Cliffs, N.J.: Prentice-Hall, Inc., 1980, 328 pp.

Yourdon, Edward. *Techniques of Program Structure and Design.* Englewood Cliffs, N.J.: Prentice-Hall, Inc., 1975, 364 pp.

Yourdon, Edward N. *Classics in Software Engineering.* New York: Yourdon Press, 1979, 424 pp.

Yourdon, Edward, and Constantine, Larry L. *Structured Design Fundamentals of a Discipline of Computer Program and System Design.* Englewood Cliffs, N.J.: Prentice-Hall, Inc., 1979, 473 pp.

Zelkowitz, Marvin V.; Shaw, Alan C.; and Gannon, John D. *Principles of Software Engineering and Design.* Englewood Cliffs, N.J.: Prentice-Hall, Inc., 1979, 338 pp.

4 Introduction to the FORTRAN Language

4.1 INTRODUCTION TO THE HISTORY AND PURPOSE OF THE LANGUAGE

For many years people wrote instructions for the computer in **machine language**—the built-in, "native" language of computers. There are hundreds of different machine languages, since each type of computer (vendor and system) has its own. Commands and memory addressess were all specified in numeric digits. Writing programs in machine language proved very time-consuming and lacked the flexibility needed for correcting program errors. Thus, high-level symbolic languages (such as FORTRAN) were developed to shorten the time required to write programs and to provide greater flexibility.

Before the development of high-level languages came what is called assembly language. An **assembly language** is a low-level symbolic language using instructions at the level of the computer (loading registers, shifting registers, storing registers, and others). Each assembly language instruction is translated (by a language translator called an assembler) into one machine language instruction; thus an assembly language instruction is a one-to-one conversion into machine language. A primary disadvantage of assembly language is that, as with machine language, a different instruction set must be used for each type of computer. Programming in an assembly language is also very tedious and slow. Assembly language is rarely used today to code programs, except when extreme efficiency in speed or memory constraints must be met.

High-level symbolic languages such as FORTRAN, or COBOL are widely used today because they are specifically designed to deal with business, scientific, engineering, and other application problems. Many high-level languages have been established in standard versions and can be used on many computer systems. Table 4.1 presents the major programming languages used today.

Table 4.1 Major High-level Programming Languages

Language Name	Year Introduced	Primary Applications
FORTRAN (FORmula TRANslation)	1957	Science and engineering
COBOL (COmmon Business Oriented Language)	1959	Business data processing
ALGOL (ALGOrithmic Language)	1960	Science and engineering
APL (A Programming Language)	1962	Science and engineering (particularly timesharing systems)
PL/I (Programming Language/I)	1964	Business, science and engineering
BASIC (Beginners All-purpose Symbolic Instruction Code)	1965	Business, science and engineering (particularly timesharing systems)
Pascal (named after Blaise Pascal)	1971	Business, science and engineering
Ada (named after Ada Augusta Byron)	1980	Real-time, embedded computer systems

FORTRAN is the name given to a high-level, procedure-oriented language designed primarily to solve problems that can be easily represented by mathematical formulas. The acronym, **FORTRAN**, stands for **FORmula TRANslation** or **FORmula TRANslator**. (Formula translation is the more common expansion.)

Development of the first FORTRAN compiler began in 1954 under the direction of John W. Backus. Mr. Backus, who worked in programming research at IBM, was convinced that a programming language could be constructed to enable computers to produce their own machine code, thereby reducing the errors and time required for programming. During the late 1940s and early 1950s, most programs were written in a machine language that required much coding and debugging time compared to the high-level languages of today.

Three years and 25,000 lines of machine instructions later (1957), the first FORTRAN compiler had been developed so that engineers could easily understand and code their own problems. Today, FORTRAN is solidly established as the language of thousands of programmers. Many improvements have been added as the FORTRAN language has evolved.

FORTRAN compilers have been written for nearly all computer systems of major vendors (manufacturers). Many hardware vendors provide multiple FORTRAN compilers for the same computer system. Wide use of FORTRAN has prompted the adoption of a standard FORTRAN language, the purpose of which is to promote portability of FORTRAN programs for use on a wide variety of computer systems. **Portability** means that a program will run on a different computer with few or no changes. The first standard FORTRAN language specifications are known as ANSI (American National Standard Institute) (Full) FORTRAN, X3.9–1966 and ANSI Basic FORTRAN, X3.10–1966. These standard language specifications are referred to as **ANSI FORTRAN 66**.

Since the original standard FORTRAN specifications, many improvements have been added. IBM introduced FORTRAN IV, a highly flexible, powerful dialect that provides more options for the convenience of the programmer. Univac introduced FORTRAN V, another powerful dialect with even more features.

The introduction of structured programming techniques and language capabilities during the 1970s prompted the development of a new standard FORTRAN language dialect to include statements for structured programming. The latest standard FORTRAN language specifications were approved by the American National Standards Institute on April 3, 1978 and are known as ANSI Programming Language FORTRAN, ANSI X3.9–1978. This standard language is designated and referred to as **FORTRAN 77**, since it was first introduced in 1977. FORTRAN 77 describes two levels of the FORTRAN language, which are referred to as FORTRAN and Subset FORTRAN, respectively.

The University of Waterloo in Ontario, Canada developed an extremely fast FORTRAN "in-memory" compiler, primarily for academic institutions. Their first compiler was called WATFOR (**WAT**erloo **FOR**tran). The University of Waterloo later developed a follow-up to the WATFOR compiler and named it WATFIV (the one after WATFOR). The WATFIV compiler includes the extended features in FORTRAN IV, plus some structured statements. Again, the advantages of a highly structured programming language prompted the introduction of a new, fast FORTRAN compiler known as WATFIV-S (WATFIV Structured). The computer center at the University of Minnesota developed M77 for CDC 6000/7000/Cyber series computers to provide a highly powerful, efficient, and structured FORTRAN compiler that complies with the FORTRAN 77 Standard. Other universities have developed structured FORTRAN compilers to aid in teaching structured programming methodologies.

Each FORTRAN compiler is written for a specific computer and must convert the FORTRAN statements of a program into the machine language code of that machine. FORTRAN programs, however, are generally independent of the computer on which they run. As long as the FORTRAN statements in a program meet all the syntax requirements of a FORTRAN compiler, the program can be compiled into the object language of the specific computer. The FORTRAN programmer, therefore, does not need a detailed knowledge of the computer system on which his or her programs will be run. A general knowledge of the FORTRAN language, along with the proper timesharing commands or job control statements to allow interface with the computer, is sufficient to process most FORTRAN programs.

The ANSI FORTRAN 66 language is taught in this text because programs written under its specifications will run on virtually all modern-day computers. Various extensions in FORTRAN IV and FORTRAN 77 dialects are also included for institutions that use these compilers. FORTRAN 77 is rapidly becoming a primary FORTRAN dialect taught by colleges and universities. These extensions are included in a section at the end of most chapters.

Section 4.2 discusses the categories of statements and identifies the individual FORTRAN statements within each category.

4.2 FORTRAN SOURCE STATEMENTS

Source statements are the instructions written by a programmer. A **FORTRAN source program** consists of a set of source statements from which the FORTRAN compiler generates machine language instructions, establishes storage locations, and supplies information needed to process the program. Each FORTRAN statement is either executable or nonexecutable. An **executable statement** is one that generates machine instructions to be executed by the computer. **Nonexecutable statements** are those which specify instructions to the compiler; they do not generate machine code. They are known as **specification** statements. Nonexecutable statements declare storage requirements for arrays (tables of information) at compile time, specify the type of data belonging to a storage location, and indicate the end of a source program.

Source statements are categorized according to the operations they perform. Five major statement categories are discussed to give you an idea of the type of operations you can perform in a program. The first four categories contain the basic statements you will use in your first few programs. Most of the statements contained in category five (with the exception of the INTEGER and REAL Type statements and the END statement) will not be used until you are further along in the course.

1. **Input/Output Statements (executable):** These statements are used to control input/output devices and to transfer data between memory and an input or output medium. The standard input/output statements are:

    READ—Causes data to be read from external files and placed into memory for use.

    WRITE—Causes data to be transferred from memory and displayed on an output medium with an output device.

    BACKSPACE—Used with sequential disk and tape files to reposition the file to the previous data item.

    REWIND—Used with sequential disk and tape files to reposition the file back to the beginning item.

    END FILE—Used with sequential disk and tape files to cause an end-of-file record to be written.

    The nonstandard PRINT statement is also placed in this category.

2. **Assignment Statement (executable):** This statement simply assigns a value to a storage location or performs calculations and assigns a new value to a variable's storage location. The Assignment statement is not identified by a keyword, but uses the **equal sign** symbol (=) following a variable. The (=) symbol, however, should be thought of as meaning "is assigned the value", not "equals".

3. **Logical and Control Statements (executable):** These statements enable the programmer to control the order of execution of the statements in the program and to terminate program execution. Statements in this category are:

    IF—Performs decision making (includes conditional branching to a new program location to transfer control).

    GO TO—Unconditionally transfers control to a new program location.

    STOP—Terminates program execution.

    DO—Establishes a "counter-type" loop in a program.

    CONTINUE—Provides a numbered statement which can be used as the object of a branch or end of a DO loop.

    CALL—Transfers control to a subroutine subprogram.

    RETURN—Returns control from a subprogram back to the calling program unit.

    Computed GO TO—Allows branching to one of multiple branch points in a program depending on a control variable.

    ASSIGN—Assigns a statement number to a variable for use with the Assigned GO TO statement.

    Assigned GO TO—Transfers control to one of multiple branch points depending upon the statement number assigned to a variable.

    PAUSE—Temporarily stops the computer processing for a manual operation by the computer operator.

4. **FORMAT Specification Statement (nonexecutable):** This statement is used in conjunction with formatted READ and WRITE statements and specifies the location and form in which the data appears in an input or output data record. The FORMAT statement is identified by the keyword FORMAT. It provides format specifications to describe the type and length of individual data fields.

```
       READ (5,990) A, B                          (input statement)
   990 FORMAT (F5.2, F5.2)                         (FORMAT specification statement)
       SUM = A + B                                 (assignment statement)
       WRITE (6,81) A, B, SUM                      (output statement)
    81 FORMAT (1X, F5.2, 3X, F5.2, 3X, F6.2)       (FORMAT specification statement)
       STOP                                        (control statement)
       END                                         (specification statement)
```

Figure 4.1 A FORTRAN program to sum two numbers

5. **Specification Statements (nonexecutable):** These statements provide the FORTRAN compiler with information that is needed at compile time. Some statements initialize storage locations, establish arrays, and supply other pertinent data about the program. The various specification statements are:

    END—Identifies the end of the source program (or subprogram) to the compiler.

    INTEGER—Declares a variable (or array) as being of an integer type.

    REAL—Declares a variable (or array) as being of a real type.

    DATA—Provides initial values to storage locations (variables) during program compilation.

    DIMENSION—Declares the dimension specifications for arrays (tables).

    DOUBLE PRECISION—Declares a variable (or array) as being of a double precision type.

    COMPLEX—Declares a variable (or array) as being of a complex type.

    LOGICAL—Declares a variable (or array) as being of a logical (boolean) type.

    FUNCTION—Identifies a subprogram as a function.

    SUBROUTINE—Identifies a subprogram as a subroutine.

    BLOCK DATA—Declares a special type of subprogram required to initialize items in Blank COMMON.

    COMMON—Declares a list of items assigned to a common (shared) area of memory between program units.

    EQUIVALENCE—Identifies variables (or arrays) which will share the same storage address in memory.

    EXTERNAL—Identifies the name of a subprogram used as an argument to another subprogram.

I realize that this functional list of all FORTRAN 66 statements may be overwhelming at this early stage. This is a complete list of all the operations you can perform with the language. You may want to refer to it later to recall the allowable operations.

Figure 4.1 presents a simple FORTRAN program which reads two values and computes their sum. The category of each source statement is given within parentheses.

See how simple it is to write a FORTRAN program? Don't worry about the construction of each statement now. This will be explained in chapter 5. Now, let's look at the elements in the FORTRAN language and see how they may be used to form statements.

4.3 BASIC ELEMENTS OF THE FORTRAN LANGUAGE

Learning to program in FORTRAN is like learning a foreign language. FORTRAN is similar to English, in that it is not just an arbitrary collection of words and elements. There is a rigid format for constructing FORTRAN statements, just as there is for English sentences. A **character set**, like an alphabet, is available for choosing characters to form elements of the language. Certain **words** (called **keywords**) are used to denote the operations to be performed by the computer, much as verbs are used to denote various actions. **Identifiers** (called **variables**) are established by the programmer from the character set to denote storage locations for various values. **Numbers** or **constants** are formed to represent certain values needed in operations such as calculations and comparisons. **Arithmetic operators** are available in the character set to allow you to perform mathematical computations with values stored in memory and constants. Other operators may be used to compare values of either constants or variables. These keywords, variables, numeric constants, and/or operators are combined to form a FORTRAN statement analogous to a sentence in English. An entire collection of FORTRAN statements comprises a FORTRAN program.

Consider the following FORTRAN source statements:

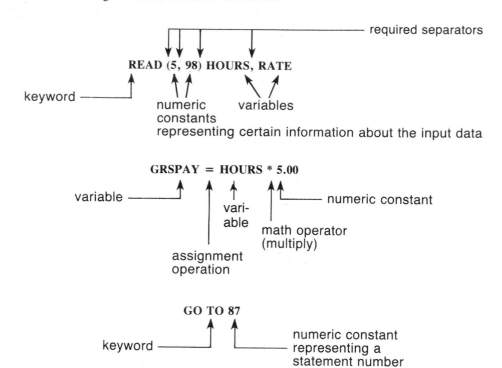

The first statement says to read two values from a data record and transfer them to the storage locations identified by the variable names "HOURS" and "RATE". The second statement calculates a value from the expression ("HOURS" times 5.00) to the right of the equal sign (=) and assigns the result to the memory location of the variable "GRSPAY". The third statement directs the computer to transfer control to the instruction with statement number 87.

Let's take a closer look at these individual elements before forming complete FORTRAN statements.

4.4 FORTRAN CHARACTER SET AND KEYWORDS

Character Set

Forty-seven different characters make up the FORTRAN character set. There are 26 alphabetic characters, 10 numeric digits, and 11 special characters. These characters, grouped with respect to their categories are:

Alphabetic (26)	Numeric (10)	Special (11)
A through Z	0 through 9	.,( ) = + − * / $ ƀ
		(ƀ represents a blank)

The alphabetic letters are used in forming keywords and variables. The numeric digits are used in forming numeric constants and may also be used in variable names. The special characters are used as arithmetic operators and various delimiters (separators) as required by certain FORTRAN statements. See Table 4.2 for a definition of uses for the special characters.

Keywords

Keywords denote what operation is to be performed by the computer with respect to the FORTRAN statement. With the exception of the Assignment statement, the keyword appears as the **first part** of a FORTRAN statement. The various keywords available in FORTRAN are presented in figure 4.2.

A keyword must be spelled exactly as it is given in figure 4.2. Embedded blanks do not matter.

Table 4.2 Special Characters in the FORTRAN Language

Name	Character	Function/Use
Decimal point	.	Decimal point in a real number
Comma	,	To separate variables or elements in a list and subscripts
Left parenthesis	(	To begin the enclosure of expressions, subscripts, and subprogram arguments
Right parenthesis	)	To end the enclosure of expressions, subscripts, and subprogram arguments
Equal sign	=	Assignment operator
Plus sign	+	Addition and unary + ("plus")
Minus sign	−	Subtraction and unary − ("minus")
Asterisk	*	Multiplication (Note: two adjacent asterisks are used for the exponentiation arithmetic operator)
Slash	/	Division
Dollar sign (currency symbol)	$	Special use on different computers
Blank		Readability and a space in literals (character strings)

ASSIGN	END	PAUSE
	END FILE	
BACKSPACE	EQUIVALENCE	READ
BLOCK DATA	EXTERNAL	REAL
		RETURN
	FORMAT	REWIND
CALL	FUNCTION	
COMMON		STOP
COMPLEX		SUBROUTINE
CONTINUE	GO TO	
	IF	WRITE
DATA	INTEGER	
DIMENSION		
DO		
DOUBLE PRECISION	LOGICAL	

Figure 4.2 ANSI FORTRAN 66 keywords

4.5 NUMERIC CONSTANTS IN FORTRAN

A **numeric constant** is a known numeric value that always represents a fixed quantity in a source program. Therefore, numeric constants represent explicit numbers which the programmer wishes to use in his or her program. A numeric constant is composed of one or more decimal digits and may contain a decimal point and a sign. The absence of a decimal point implies a whole number, whereas an included decimal point implies a real (fractional) value. The constant may represent a positive or negative value, depending upon an attached sign. If the sign is a minus sign, then the constant is considered to be negative. A plus sign or the absence of a sign implies a positive quantity. Whenever a sign is used, it must precede the first digit.

Embedded **commas are never** permitted in a numeric constant in FORTRAN. Some examples of FORTRAN constants are:

1	0	$+3.0$
$+12$	0.	$+162.07$
4708296	0.0	$-55.$
-386341	8.569	-10.3875

Numeric constants, however, are specifically recognized in FORTRAN as being either integer-type or real-type (floating-point) constants. These two types of numbers must be handled differently in the computer, and care must be taken to assure that the proper type is used in a FORTRAN statement. It is important, therefore, for you to have a good understanding of these two different types of numbers.

Integer Constants

An integer constant is a **whole number** written without a decimal point. It is formed from the digits 0 through 9. A sign is permitted in the high-order (leftmost) position of the number. A minus sign is mandatory for negative numbers. A zero may be written with a preceding sign, but has no effect on the value zero. That is, zero is always zero; the difference between a positive or negative zero is not usually represented in the computer. (Note: Some computers may represent a negative zero (-0); e.g., Burroughs).

The maximum allowed size of an integer constant varies from computer to computer. The size of the compute word (length of a storage location) on each computer determines the limits of an integer constant. The smallest integer value that may be represented on IBM main frame computers is -2147483648 (i.e., -2^{31}). The largest integer value that may be represented is 2147483647 (i.e., $2^{31}-1$). It is not necessary to memorize these numbers, since few integer numbers in practice exceed this magnitude. It is important to realize that different types of computers have specific magnitude limitations (both positive and negative). You should keep in mind the general limitations and look up the specific limitations only if you write a constant that might approach them.

Integer constants are often referred to as **fixed-point numbers**, because the decimal point is always assumed to be located after the rightmost digit in the number. The assumed position of the decimal point is fixed; thus, only whole numbers are always represented. Both of these terms are used interchangeably. Integer constants should always be used when **counting**, since only whole numbers are involved. For example, the number of students in a class is an integer value; so is the number of cards in a program deck. An integer constant, therefore, always implies that there can be no fractional part associated with the number.

Examples of valid integer constants are:

$$123$$
$$-36$$
$$+4289$$
$$0$$

Examples of invalid integer constants are:

37.5	(not a whole number)
$86-$	(sign must precede number)
1,240	(contains an embedded comma)
3286946175	(exceeds largest value permitted)

Real Constants

A real constant is a string of decimal digits that contains a decimal point. A real quantity may contain an appended sign, as with integer constants. Real constants are more commonly called **floating-point numbers** to reflect the fact that the position of the decimal point may be moved (or floated) in the number. The terms "real" and "floating-point" will be used interchangeably in this text.

Real constants are thought of as **measuring numbers**, since many fractional positions can be included in a floating-point number. When using a measuring number, one is concerned with the **magnitude** (or range) and the **precision** (or accuracy) of the quantity. If we write 1.7 inches, 32.0 inches, and 568.2 inches, we are concerned with successively increasing magnitudes. If we measure the diameter of a shaft, we may come up with 3.0, 3.04, or 3.038 inches, depending upon whether an estimate, a ruler, or a micrometer was used. A micrometer would provide us with a more precise measurement value.

Both larger magnitudes and greater precision are expressed by using more digits in the numbers. There must be a limit, however, to the number of digits in the quantity handled by the computer, since this quantity factor has an important bearing on computer cost. A concept was devised to represent real numbers in the computer with a fractional quantity and an exponential part, the same as with scientific notation for expressing numbers. This, then is why we use the term floating-point: the exponential part actually denotes the placement of the decimal point.

In scientific notation, the precision (number of digits) of the number is expressed in either integer or real form. The magnitude of the number is expressed as a power of ten by which the number is multiplied to obtain the desired value. For example:

$$1.86 \times 10^5 \qquad \text{(value of 186,000)}$$
$$93 \times 10^6 \qquad \text{(value of 93,000,000)}$$
$$.1 \times 10^{-2} \qquad \text{(value of .001)}$$

The precision of most quantities can be expressed in less than six digits. Consequently, some computers have been designed to allow internal floating-point calculations with numbers having a maximum of seven decimal digits and an exponent. Externally, a floating-point number may be constructed with or without the exponent. The exponent, when used, is expressed as a signed or unsigned power of ten by which the number is multiplied to obtain its true value. The exponent can range from a power of -78 to $+75$ on most IBM computers. Thus, extremely small and large numbers can be represented in floating-point form. We will not, for the time being, concern ourselves with expressing a real constant with an exponent. The common decimal form for expressing real numbers will be used.

The use of one to seven digits to represent a real constant is known as **single-precision mode**. A need may occur for a precision of more than seven digits. Thus, some computers also permit an extension of up to roughly sixteen digits for increased precision. This form of extended digits is called **double-precision mode**, which is discussed later in the text.

A single-precision, floating-point number is normally formed as a string of decimal digits with a decimal point similar to a fraction. There is no restriction on the number of digits that may be written with a real constant, but, in some computers, no more than seven (sometimes eight) significant digits may be retained. A whole number may or may not be present with the fraction; a fractional quantity may or may not be present with the whole number portion. A decimal point, however, is *always* included with the number. A real constant must **not** contain embedded commas.

Valid examples of single-precision, floating-point (real) numbers in decimal form are:

$$-12.75 \qquad +4.$$
$$264.8 \qquad -.0029$$
$$.567 \qquad 1.$$
$$-0. \qquad 3481.026$$

Invalid examples of single-precision, floating-point numbers in decimal form are:

57	(no decimal point)
3,860.21	(contains embedded comma)
.589 +	(sign follows number)
26*5.3	(contains a special character)

The next section explains the concept and construction of variables, which are used to store values in the form of constants just discussed.

4.6 VARIABLES IN FORTRAN

The FORTRAN programmer selects symbolic names in accordance with specific rules—primarily to denote quantities in memory. A name, thereby, identifies the value stored at a specific storage location. Since the contents of these locations may vary within the program, these quantities are called variables. A **variable** is, therefore, a symbolic reference to the value that occupies that storage location. A variable can have only one value assigned to it at any given time in program execution. The latest value assigned to a variable at a particular point in program execution is called the **current value** of the variable. Whereas the computer refers to a value at a memory location by a machine address, a FORTRAN programmer refers to the value at a location by its assigned variable, or **variable name**.

The concept of variables and memory may be thought of as residential mailboxes with which we are all familiar. Memory is divided into storage locations as though it were divided into many "boxes," as indicated by the following:

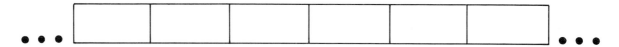

Each box or storage location is capable of storing a single value. Thus, a particular box may contain any value placed in it, such as

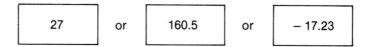

The computer refers to a value in a box by the machine address assigned to it, just as the postman uses a street number to locate your mailbox. In FORTRAN and other programming languages, however, a variable name is associated with a box to refer to its value, just as your mailbox is identified with your name. For example:

	HOURS	RATE	GRSPAY
variable name			
contents	40.0	5.50	220.00

Thus, variable names are a way of telling the computer which box (or value) to use.

Two things can be done with a box or storage location by referring to its assigned variable name.

1. A value can be placed into it by reading an input value with the READ statement and storing it there, or a value can be assigned to the box by means of an Assignment statement. For example:

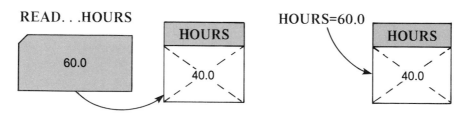

In this example, the old value of 40.0 in the variable HOURS is destroyed and replaced with the new value of 60.0 from the execution of the READ or Assignment statement. When a new value is stored into a box, the value currently stored in the box is destroyed, since a box can contain only one value at any given time. The value in a box is replaced only when the computer is instructed to put a new value into it.

2. The value within a box can be used by a statement to compute other values, to display the value on a terminal, or to print the value on the line printer. For example:

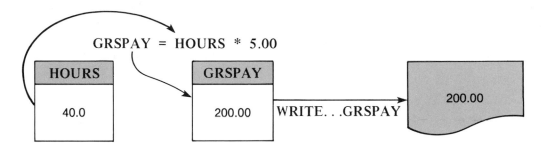

In this example, the value in HOURS is used in the formula to compute GRSPAY. The content of GRSPAY is then printed on the line printer with the WRITE statement. When a value in a box is used, it is not destroyed.

Thus, variable names will be used in all programs to store values at the indicated boxes and to refer to these values for later computations and/or output. The concept of variables, therefore, is fundamental to programming and should be understood before a program is written.

Forming Variable Names

Variable names are formed from alphabetic and numeric characters (A–Z, 0–9). No special characters are allowed. A variable name may be a single alphabetic letter or it may be formed by any combination of alphabetic and numeric characters up to a maximum of **six**. The first character of any variable, however, must always be alphabetic (A–Z). The remaining characters are optional and may be either alphabetic or numeric. Examples of valid variable names are:

INDEX	COUNT	C5R2
RATE2	SUM	MONEY
BASE10	K	N12345

Examples of invalid variable names are:

COUNTER	(exceeds 6 characters)
A*B	(contains a special character)
R2.5	(contains a special character)
5FEET	(first character is not alphabetic)
SUM-2	(contains a special character)

The choice of variable names is entirely up to the programmer. For aid in documentation, the programmer should assign variables with a mnemonic (memory aid) name, that is, with a name that describes the stored value. This gives a better understanding of a variable's meaning and of what action is being accomplished in the program. For example, use:

GRSPAY = HOURS * RATE   (note: the * denotes multiplication)

and not:

A = B * C

to indicate the calculation of one's gross pay.

You may wonder why we use variables and not just constants in a program. The use of variables provides the flexibility needed in programming. Different input values can be read into a variable, yet the same formula is used to calculate the results. For example:

READ (5,99) ID, HOURS, RATE
GRSPAY = HOURS * RATE
WRITE (6,98) ID, GRSPAY

The READ statement reads an employee's identification number, hours worked, and pay rate from the data record. The statement:

GRSPAY = HOURS * RATE

computes the employee's gross pay by multiplying (indicated by *) hours times rate and storing (indicated by the =) the results at the variable named GRSPAY. The WRITE statement will print the employee's ID and computed gross pay on the line printer or user's terminal.

We could have written:

GRSPAY = 80.0 * 4.50

and computed the gross pay for one employee. When you use constants, however, you are "locked in" to these numbers. What if you needed to compute the gross pay for 1,000 employees? Would we have 1,000 such computational statements in which only constants were used? Certainly not! By using variables you can read different values into storage locations and compute a result using the current value in a specific variable; then you can repeat these steps for another employee by reading the hours and rate values from another data record. Now the variables HOURS and RATE contain new values, but the same formula

GRSPAY = HOURS * RATE

is still valid to compute the next employee's gross pay. Thus, what may seem like a gigantic problem to solve on the computer becomes quite simple when variables are used. We are getting ahead of ourselves, but this explanation helps you understand the use and importance of variables.

The FORTRAN language also distinguishes between the types of variables used in a program. FORTRAN variables are identified as being of either type integer or type real, just like constants. Each type relates to the form of the numeric value stored at the memory location.

Integer Variables

Integer variables represent a whole number in memory. For example, the number of statements in a program and the number of courses you are taking are both integer quantities. Integer variables begin with one of the letters I, J, K, L, M, or N to inform the system that it contains an integer value. As a memory aid, remember I–N as in **IN**teger variables. Examples of valid integer variables are:

KTR	KOUNT
N	LOOP
INDEX	M
JSUB	LENGTH

Real Variables

Real variables represent numbers that may include a fractional value. For example, your grade point average and paycheck amount are both real quantities. The fractional value may be zero, but the capability is there for the fractional part to contain any value so desired. Real variables begin with one of the letters A–H and O–Z (all letters other than I–N), to inform the system that it is representing a real (floating-point) value. Examples of real variables are:

RADIUS	COUNT
SUM	X
A90	RANGE
HLD3T	AREASQ

Selecting the first letter of a variable name as a way to declare its type is known as the **FORTRAN predefined naming convention**. The predefined naming convention for declaring integer and real variables may be overridden in FORTRAN by using an **Explicit Type** specification statement. That is, any name, regardless of the beginning letter, may be explicitly declared as an integer or real variable with the INTEGER or REAL Type statements, respectively.

The assignment of names to the integer and real variables appearing in the program is entirely under the control of the programmer. Special care, however, must be taken to observe the rule for distinguishing between the names of integer and real variables, if the predefined naming convention is used. Also, every different combination of letters and digits represents a different name to the compiler. For example, the variable B7 is not the same as BSEVEN. A common error made by beginning programmers is to misspell the name used as a variable, thereby getting incorrect results. To the compiler, each differently spelled name represents a unique variable. For example, the names RATE and RATES represent two different variables to the compiler. If you are getting zeros (or an undefined value) for an answer, check the spelling of your variable. This may be the cause of invalid results.

4.7 ARITHMETIC OPERATORS IN FORTRAN

Arithmetic operations are represented in FORTRAN by symbols. Symbols are used since the use of English words (such as TIMES or PLUS) as operators would be confused with variables. The five arithmetic operators allowed in FORTRAN and their operations are given in figure 4.3.

These operators might be used with variables and numeric constants to compute a value as follows:

$$\text{PAYNET} = \text{HOURS} * 4.50 + \text{BONUS} - \text{DEDUCT}$$

Hours are multiplied by 4.50; the value at BONUS is next added to the product; last, deductions are subtracted from the total. The resulting computed value is stored at the variable PAYNET. Blank spaces are not required to precede or follow an arithmetic operator. However, a space before and after each operator is highly recommended to improve the readability of the statement.

Arithmetic computations that involve more than one operation are performed according to a hierarchy or precedence of the arithmetic operators. This hierarchy is the same as that in algebra, and is as follows:

Precedence	Arithmetic Operator
1st	**
2nd	* and /
3rd	+ and −

For those operators on the same level of precedence, the calculation will be performed in a left-to-right order (except multiple exponentiation, which is performed from right to left).

For example:

$$X = 20 + 10 * 3 / 6$$

Operator	Mathematical operation	FORTRAN example	Algebra
**	exponentiation	X ** Y	X^y
*	multiplication	X * Y	$X \cdot Y$
/	division	X / Y	$X \div Y$
+	addition	X + Y	$X + Y$
−	subtraction	X − Y	$X − Y$

Figure 4.3 Arithmetic operators in FORTRAN

says to first multiply 10 times 3, since multiplication is performed before addition. After the multiplication, the result (30) is divided by 6, which gives an intermediate result of 5. This result (5) is added to 20 to provide a final value of 25 to be stored at the variable X.

The following tree diagram is given to show the precedence (order) of these operations.

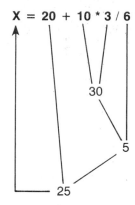

What if you wanted to add 10 to 20 before multiplying by 3? You can enclose the operations you want performed first within a pair of parentheses. For example:

$$X = (20 + 10) * 3 / 6$$

would first add 10 to 20 and multiply the result (30) by 3. Then this result (90) would be divided by 6 to yield a final value of 15, which is stored at X. Parentheses, then, are a means of telling the computer to override the normal order of precedence of the arithmetic operators and to do certain operations first.

The tree diagram to represent the precedence of operations for this calculation, using parenthesis, is:

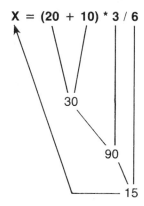

Parentheses may be nested (used inside other sets of parentheses) to specify the needed order of calculations. The calculations in the innermost set of parentheses are evaluated first. For example, the algebraic formula:

$$A = \frac{(B + C) \cdot (D - E)}{8.0}$$

would be written in FORTRAN as:

$$A = ((B + C) * (D - E)) / 8.0$$

The order of calculations for this statement is indicated by circled numbers and illustrated as follows:

⑤ ① ③ ② ④
A = ((B + C) * (D − E)) / 8.0

1. B is added to C because of the first inner set of parentheses.
2. E is subtracted from D because of the second inner set of parentheses.
3. The result of step 1 is multiplied by the result of step 2 because of the outer set of parentheses.
4. The product of step 3 is divided by 8.0.
5. The quotient from step 4 is stored at the variable A.

Next let's look at the importance of the assignment operator.

Assignment Operator

The "equals" sign is used only in the Assignment statement. It is used to assign (store) the single resulting value from the arithmetic expression (given to the right of the [=]) to the variable located on the left side of the (=) symbol. For example:

$$B = 10.5$$
$$A = B + 7.2$$

In the first statement, B is assigned the value of 10.5. In the second statement, A is assigned the value of 17.7 (the sum of 10.5 and 7.2).

To get across the operation performed by the assignment operator, many people use different terms for the (=) symbol. Some people refer to it as a "replacement operator". Thus, the second statement in the preceding paragraph would read: A is replaced by the sum of B + 7.2. An easy-to-understand term used by others for the (=) symbol is "is assigned the value of." Thus, the second statement in the prior paragraph would read: A is assigned the value of B + 7.2.

4.8 ARITHMETIC EXPRESSIONS AND THE ASSIGNMENT STATEMENT

Arithmetic computations play an important role in programming. In putting together the required logic for programs, many calculations are performed, such as computing net pay, grade averages, or the area of a circle. Arithmetic expressions formed in the Assignment statement allow us to perform calculations in FORTRAN. This statement provides the means to store and retrieve calculated values when called for in program execution.

An **arithmetic expression** is used to specify a computation involving two or more operands which may be all numeric constants, all variables, or a combination of the two. An expression may also consist of a single constant or variable. Consider the arithmetic expression in the following statement example.

$$X = 6$$

In this statement the computer is told to assign the value of the expression—6—to the memory cell named X. After execution of this statement, memory cell X would appear as:

X
6

Similarly, if we coded

$$Y = 3$$

the computer is told to assign the value of 3 to the memory cell named Y. The memory cells of X and Y would appear as:

X	Y
6	3

If we wish to add the contents of memory cell X to the contents of memory cell Y and store the results at a new memory cell named Z, we would write the following statement:

$$Z = X + Y$$

This statement tells the computer to compute the expression (X + Y) which would result in the value of 9 and to store the answer at Z. The memory cells named X, Y, and Z would appear as:

X	Y	Z
6	3	9

Suppose we wish to evaluate the algebraic expression

$$2x + 3y - z$$

with the values of X, Y and Z stored in the memory cells. We would select a name for the memory cell at which to store the answer; call it the variable A. The constants 2 and 3 must be expressed as real constants (2.0 and 3.0) to be compatible with the real variables X, Y, and Z in the Assignment statement. Then we would write:

$$A = 2.0 * X + 3.0 * Y - Z$$

This statement tells the computer to evaluate the arithmetic expression 2.0 * X + 3.0 * Y − Z and place the results at a memory cell named A. The computer would calculate the value of the expression by first multiplying 2.0 by X, next multiplying 3.0 by Y, then summing these two products, and finally subtracting Z from the sum. These memory cells would appear as:

X	Y	Z	A
6	3	9	12

The collection of statements put together in a FORTRAN program would appear as:

$$X = 6$$
$$Y = 3$$
$$Z = X + Y$$
$$A = 2.0 * X + 3.0 * Y - Z$$

So you see, forming arithmetic expressions in an Assignment statement is not much different from everyday arithmetic procedures. Generally, arithmetic expressions follow the rules of algebra. However, certain other rules must be followed when writing arithmetic expressions in FORTRAN. These rules follow.

Rule 1. All computations must be explicitly specified by an arithmetic operator. That is, an arithmetic operator must separate all operands if more than one is used. For example:

(X)(Y) must be specified as X * Y
2(K + 3) must be specified as 2 * (K + 3)

Rule 2. No two arithmetic operators may be adjacent to each other in the same expression. Parentheses must be used to enclose the second arithmetic operator. For example:

A / − B must be specified as A / (− B)
Z ** − 3 must be specified as Z ** (− 3)

Rule 3. Computation of arithmetic expressions is performed from left to right according to the precedence or hierarchy of operations. The hierarchy of operations, with the additional parentheses and unary minus sign precedences, is as follows:

Precedence	Arithmetic Operations
1st	Parentheses
2nd	exponentiation (raising to a power)
3rd	evaluation of unary minus sign
4th	multiplication and division
5th	addition and subtraction

A **unary minus sign** is simply the algebraic negation of a value. In the expression $-X + Y$, $-X$ is a unary minus quantity. The value of X is complemented (sign reversed) by the unary minus sign which precedes it, before being added to Y. The expression $-J$ represents the complement (opposite sign) of the value of J. If the contents of J is positive, then $-J$ represents a negative value; if the contents of J is a negative value, then $-J$ represents a positive value. Assuming a value of 7 for the variable J, then the FORTRAN statement

$$R = -J ** 2$$

would produce a value of -49, not $+49$ as some might expect. Since the minus sign before the variable J is considered a unary sign, the complement evaluation is performed after the squaring of J. If you truly wanted to square the complement of J, you must enclose $-J$ in parentheses as follows:

$$R = (-J) ** 2$$

This statement would produce a value of $+49$ for R.

The Assignment statement with the following calculations

$$X = -8 / 2 ** 3 + 5 * 4 - 7$$

would produce a final value of 12 for the variable X. The order of the evaluated arithmetic operations is indicated below using numbered circles.

$$②\ ③\ ①\ ⑤\ ④\ ⑥$$
$$X = -\ 8\ /\ 2\ **\ 3\ +\ 5\ *\ 4\ -\ 7$$

① First, 2 is raised to the power of 3 since exponentiation is performed first. Equals 8.
② Secondly, the value of 8 is complemented to the value of -8 because of the unary minus sign.
③ Then, the result of step 2 is divided by the result of step 1 since the division operator appears before the multiplication operator. Equals -1.
④ Next, the value of 5 is multiplied by 4 since the multiplication is higher precedence of any remaining operator in the expression. Equals 20.
⑤ Fifth, the result of step 3 is added to the result of step 4. Value of 19.
⑥ Finally, 7 is subtracted from the result of step 5 and a value of 12 is stored into X.

Parentheses are used to override the precedence of any operator and to indicate the order of computations as in algebra. Any expressions in parentheses are evaluated first, before continuing with further evaluation. Nested parentheses (use of parentheses within a set of parentheses) may also be used. When nested parentheses are present, calculations proceed from the innermost to the outermost pair. Each left parenthesis must have a corresponding right parenthesis, or a syntax error will occur.

Parentheses should be used to ensure that the calculations are correctly performed in the desired order. Use only as many parentheses as needed, since excessive parentheses make an expression hard to follow. Within parentheses, calculations take place according to the hierarchy of operations.

The following are algebraic expressions, along with their FORTRAN equivalents:

$$\frac{A + B}{X - Y} \text{ would be coded } (A + B) / (X - Y)$$

$$(X - \frac{B + C}{D + E} - 5)^3 \text{ would be coded } (X - (B + C) / (D + E) - 5.) ** 3$$

Let's look at the order of arithmetic operations with some nested parentheses. Given the following FORTRAN Assignment statement, the order of calculations is illustrated by the circled numbers.

$$\textcircled{1} \quad \textcircled{3} \quad \textcircled{2} \quad \textcircled{4} \; \textcircled{5} \; \textcircled{6}$$
$$A = ((5 + 3) / (3 - 1) * 4) ** 2 + 7$$

① First, 3 is added to 5 because of the first innermost pair of parentheses. (Value of 8.)
② Secondly, 1 is subtracted from 3 because of the second inner pair of parentheses. (Value of 2.)
③ The sum from step 1 is divided by the difference from step 2, because the division operator appears before the multiplication within the outer set of parentheses. (Value of 4.)
④ The quotient from step 3 is then multiplied by 4 because of the outer pair of parentheses. (Value of 16.)
⑤ The product from step 4 is raised to a power of 2, since exponentiation is a higher precedence than addition. (Value of 256.)
⑥ Finally, 7 is added to the result of step 5, and a value of 263 is stored into the variable A.

Some calculations such as the previous example can get complex. If you like, you may break long calculations into several shorter ones and save the immediate calculated values in a variable. You could have coded the last example as follows:

$$A = (5 + 3) / (3 - 1)$$
$$A = (A * 4) ** 2$$
$$A = A + 7$$

This method takes more statements but is often less confusing as to the order of calculation and where to properly place the required parentheses. Using this method, errors are more easily detected by printing the results of each intermediate calculation, if the correct answer was not produced originally.

Rule 4. In multiple consecutive exponentiation operations, the calculation is usually intended to be performed from **right** to **left**, as in algebra. The expression X^{2^c} should be coded as X ** (2.0 ** C) which would first raise 2.0 to the power of C and then raise X to the power of the resulting value. In ANSI FORTRAN 66, parentheses *must* be used for multiple consecutive exponentiation. An exponent part of an expression may be a constant, a variable, or an arithmetic expression enclosed within parentheses. The Assignment statement to raise B to the power of C and then raise the variable A to the resulting power of B would be written as

$$X = A ** (B ** C)$$

Some machines allow you to express consecutive raising-to-a-power expressions without using parentheses, such as

$$X = A ** B ** C$$

This is a poor practice but is acceptable to some FORTRAN compilers. You should always use the parentheses to specify the explicit order of consecutive exponentiation operations.

Rule 5. The type and length of the result of an arithmetic operation depend upon the type and length of the two operands involved in the operation. **Type** refers to the **mode** (integer or real) of a value. **Length** refers to the size of the memory location used. Don't worry about the length attribute of a variable for now, since all variables of the same type occupy the same length storage location.

Two basic modes of numeric values used in FORTRAN are integer (fixed point) and real (floating point). Since there are two modes of variables and constants, there are two modes of arithmetic expressions. ANSI FORTRAN 66 requires all variables and constants in an expression to be in the same mode. That is, all operands in an expression must be either type integer or type real. If this rule is violated, a syntax error will occur. To conform to this requirement, you often have to change the mode of a value by assigning the value to the proper type variable. If the value of the variable N is to be added to the constant 5.76, it might be accomplished by the following two Assignment statements:

$$XN = N$$
$$SUM = XN + 5.76$$

Thus, the first statement assigns the value of N to a real variable, so that it can be added to the real constant in the second statement. (Remember, the mode of a variable can usually be determined according to the predefined naming convention.)

If the variable COUNT is to be subtracted from the variable M, this operation might be performed by:

$$K = COUNT$$
$$J = M - K$$

The use of the different modes of expressions are highly important in FORTRAN, since the resulting value may be different from expected.

An **integer mode expression** is one which consists entirely of integer constants and/or variables. **Integer mode arithmetic** is used to evaluate integer mode expressions. Integer mode arithmetic will always produce integer mode results. Any fractional part will always be truncated (chopped off), such as in integer division. Only the integer part of the result will be available. For example: 5 / 3 produces a result of 1. Consider the following examples of integer expressions:

M / 5 - 6 ** K	
N + 4 * KT	
4 / 3	(result is 1)
3 - 5 / 2 + 4 ** 2	(result is 17)
3 ** 2 + 7 - 3 / 6	(result is 16)
2 / 6	(result is 0)

Thus, you must be extremely careful when using integer mode expressions with a division operation.

A **real mode expression** consists of all real constants and/or variables. **Real mode arithmetic** is used to evaluate real mode expressions. Since real mode arithmetic is performed in floating point mode, the fractional part of the computation as well as the integer part is kept. Therefore, 5. / 2. would produce a result of 2.5; 3. / 4. would produce a result of .75. Consider the following examples of real expressions:

S / 6.3 + 4.5 ** D	
A - 5.0 / X ** 3.5	
4. / 3. - 6.	(result is -4.666666)
3. - 5. / 2. + 7.	(result is 7.5)
2. ** 2.0 + 5. * 2. / 4.	(result is 6.5)

Exponentiation is the only arithmetic operation in which the modes may be mixed. Both real variables/constants and integer variables/constants can have integers as exponents. That is, both real and integer values may be raised to an integer power. But, a real exponent can be used only with a real variable or constant. An integer variable/constant **cannot** be raised to a real power. Valid examples are:

$$XSQD = X ** 2$$
$$XSQD = X ** 2.0$$
$$NSQD = N ** 2$$
$$BCSQ = B ** C$$
$$BNSQ = B ** N$$

The following expressions are invalid.

$$NSQD = N ** 2.0$$
$$NBSQ = N ** B$$
$$SQ2B = 2 ** B$$

Rule 6. The type variable to which the resulting value of the expression is assigned in the Assignment statement determines the final mode of the assigned value in memory. No matter what the resulting mode of the value from the evaluation of an expression, it is the variable at which the value is stored that determines the final mode. For example, the expression 2. * 3. / 4.0 yields a real result of 1.5. If this value is assigned to an integer variable, however, the value stored is 1. Real values assigned to integer variables will have any fraction truncated, and only the integer portion of the number is stored in integer form. Integer values assigned to real variables will cause the number to be stored in floating-point form.

The use of integer mode expressions as opposed to real mode expressions, and the choice of integer variables as opposed to real variables, depend on what you are doing. If you are counting or manipulating whole numbers, then integer expressions and variables should be used. If you are working with decimal values which contain a fraction, such as dollars and cents, grade point averages, and so on, then real expressions and variables should be used. Arithmetic operations with integer expressions take far less time than do those with real expressions. So the rule is to use integer expressions and variables unless you need to manipulate real values.

Rule 7. Any variable used in an arithmetic expression must have been previously "defined" (had a value stored at the variable). To obtain a correct result from evaluating an expression, all variables used in the expression must have been given a value prior to the computation. Values may be stored at a variable either by an Assignment or by a READ statement during program execution. (Note: Some computers, such as Honeywell, Univac, and Burroughs initialize all variables to zero by clearing memory to zero before loading the program.)

Consider the Assignment statement:

$$N = N + 1$$

Only if the variable N had been previously given a value would the execution of the statement provide a valid result. Some compilers make no check to see if a variable has been given a value in the program before using it. The student should be extremely careful to ensure that all variables in an expression have a valid value. Failure to observe this rule may result in a very time-consuming debugging effort.

The Assignment Statement

The arithmetic Assignment statement is identified by the equal sign (=) following a variable at the start of a FORTRAN statement. This statement commands the computer to compute the complete expression on the right of the "equal" sign and to assign the one resulting value to the variable on the left of the "equal" sign.

The named variable to the left of the "equal" sign may be a real or integer variable that the programmer has arbitrarily chosen to represent the storage location of the assigned value. The programmer should choose a variable name that conveys some meaning of the stored value and a type variable that stores the data in the proper form (i.e., integer or real). For example, if computed interest is stored in a variable, a likely name chosen might be XNTRST. Even though the variable INTRST is closer to the name "interest," it is undesirable since the computed value would be stored in integer mode and truncated of any cents amount calculated (unless overridden by the REAL Type statement). Remember, an integer variable can store only whole numbers; no fractional part, such as cents, is retained.

The "equal" sign is not used as it is in ordinary mathematical notation. You are not allowed to write statements such as

$$A + X = B - C$$

where X represents an unknown quantity, and A, B, and C are known. Only one variable is permitted to the left of the "equal" sign. The "equal" sign implies that a value is to be **assigned** or **stored** in the left hand variable, and not that it is mathematically equal.

The statement TOTAL = A + B + C means to compute the sum of the values stored at the variables A, B, and C and replace the value of the variable TOTAL with the result. Any previously computed value of TOTAL is lost. A variable always contains the value most recently assigned to it in program execution. The value of any variable in the expression (in the example: A, B, and C) is unchanged.

To sum up, the arithmetic Assignment statement is used to provide four necessary operations in FORTRAN:

1. To calculate a value from a given formula which may be a simple or compound expression. For example:

$$GRSPAY = HOURS * RATE$$
$$AVERGE = SUM / 10.$$

2. To initialize variables. Variables used to represent certain values must first be set to the desired initial value. For example:

$$SUM = 0.$$
$$KTR = 1$$
$$PI = 3.1416$$

A common misunderstanding on the part of beginning students is their assumption that a variable must be assigned as many digits as needed in a maximum value. For example, if a counter may contain a maximum of three digits, the student assumes it necessary to assign that many digits to the variable; "KTR = 000" is an example. This causes no harm, but it is not needed. Simply "KTR = 0" will initialize the variable KTR to zero.

3. To move values from one variable to another. Values may be moved to a different storage location by the Assignment statement. Examples are:

$$HOLD = RESULT$$
$$K2 = K1$$
$$TEMP = KSQD$$

Often the original value in a variable needs to be retained before it is later changed in a calculation. You can assign the variable to a new variable in which either the new variable or the original variable can be used and modified in a calculation. You will still have access to the original value. When a variable is assigned to a new location, the value in the old variable remains unchanged.

4. To change the mode of data. It is often necessary to change the mode of a stored value from integer to real or from real to integer. The arithmetic Assignment statement allows us to accomplish this easily, as illustrated by the following examples:

$$REALN = N$$
$$IRESLT = RESULT$$
$$K = X$$

The assignment of a single constant or another variable to a variable name, as shown in items two, three, and four, is the most frequent usage of the Assignment statement. Now let's examine the results of Assignment statements written in sequence.

Assignment Statements in Sequence. The computer must be informed of the values contained in an expression before the expression is evaluated. A statement such as: $X = A + 5.75$ would be valid only if the variable A had been assigned a previous value (by an Assignment statement or READ statement).

Given the statements:

$$A = 2.3$$
$$X = A + 5.75$$

the computer executes the first statement and assigns a value of 2.3 to the variable A. When the second instruction is executed, the computer supplies 2.3 as the value of A. Therefore, 2.3 is added to 5.75 and a value of 8.05 is stored as the value of X.

You may have many Assignment statements in sequence. For example:

$$T = 3.2$$
$$U = 5.5 - T$$
$$V = 2.0 * U$$
$$X = T + U + V$$

when all four of these statements have been executed, the value of X is 10.1.

If the same variable appears the second time in a sequence of arithmetic Assignment statements, the latest value is assigned to the variable, and the previous value is lost. For example:

$$KNT = 1$$
$$. . .$$
$$. . .$$
$$. . .$$
$$KNT = KNT + 1$$

The value 1 is assigned to KNT in the first statement. In the last statement, the value of 1 is supplied for KNT to the right of the equal sign and 1 is added to 1. The result, 2, is then assigned to KNT; the previous value of KNT is lost. Statements in sequence, such as the above example, occur frequently in computer programs in accumulating totals and counter logic.

Assignment statements are very powerful statements. They are the heart of most FORTRAN programs because of their frequent use. For this reason, you are encouraged to become very familiar with the many capabilities of the arithmetic Assignment statement.

4.9 CODING FORTRAN STATEMENTS

A FORTRAN program may be coded on a special form called a **coding sheet**. (Figure 4.4 shows a sample FORTRAN coding form.) Each line on the coding sheet represents an 80-column punched card. (Figure 4.5 shows the frequently used FORTRAN punched card.) Each designated column on the coding form represents the same relative card column on the punched card. For example, column 7 on the coding sheet represents card column 7 on the punched card. Each FORTRAN statement is coded on one or more lines on the coding form.

If you are using a timesharing system to enter your FORTRAN statements, you do not have to use a FORTRAN coding form to code them. You should, however, have your FORTRAN program already coded before you log on at a terminal, whatever you code it on.

Even though you may be using an interactive system to enter your FORTRAN statements, many timesharing systems require you to enter FORTRAN statements in the same form as if they were punched on cards. This is referred to as **card imagery**. For example, the HP 3000 FORTRAN compiler requires you to build a FORTRAN record that looks like a card image to the text editor. Thus, the following information concerning FORTRAN card format is also pertinent to timesharing systems.

Some timesharing systems, however, allow you to enter FORTRAN statements in a free form without adhering to the prescribed card-column restrictions. Your instructor will tell you whether statements can be entered in a free-form format. Because the recommended alignment of FORTRAN statements improves readability and portability, you are encouraged to follow the prescribed FORTRAN column requirements.

FORTRAN statements are broken down into four different areas, or fields. FORTRAN coding sheets have these specific areas marked off for easy reference. These are:

Positions	FORTRAN statement areas
Columns 1–5	Statement number
Column 6	Continuation
Columns 7–72	FORTRAN statement
Columns 73–80	Program identification and/or sequence number

Statement Number

Columns 1 through 5 are reserved for a statement number. This statement number serves as a statement label or tag that allows you to refer to a FORTRAN statement. This permits the program to skip various statements and to change the execution sequence of statements.

All statement numbers must be one to five numeric digits and may range from 1 to 99999. Statement numbers may be left-justified (begin in column 1), right-justified (end in column 5), or punched anywhere between columns 1 through 5. Embedded blanks and leading zeroes in statement numbers will be ignored.

Statement numbers are not required for all statements. Only those statements which are referenced by other statements need be assigned a statement number. However, you may elect to assign a statement number to all statements as an aid in keeping the statements in the desired order. This is not recommended because it will require longer compile time for the program.

Statement numbers need not be assigned to statements in a program in any specific sequence. All statement numbers assigned within a program, however, must be unique. **No** two statements may be assigned the same number; otherwise, a compile error of duplicate labels will occur.

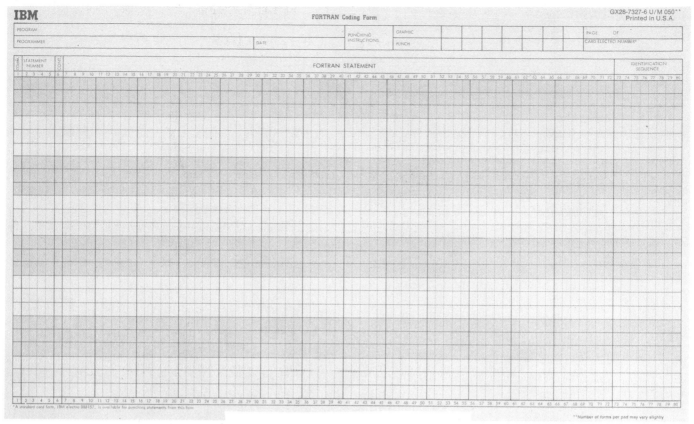

Figure 4.4 FORTRAN coding form

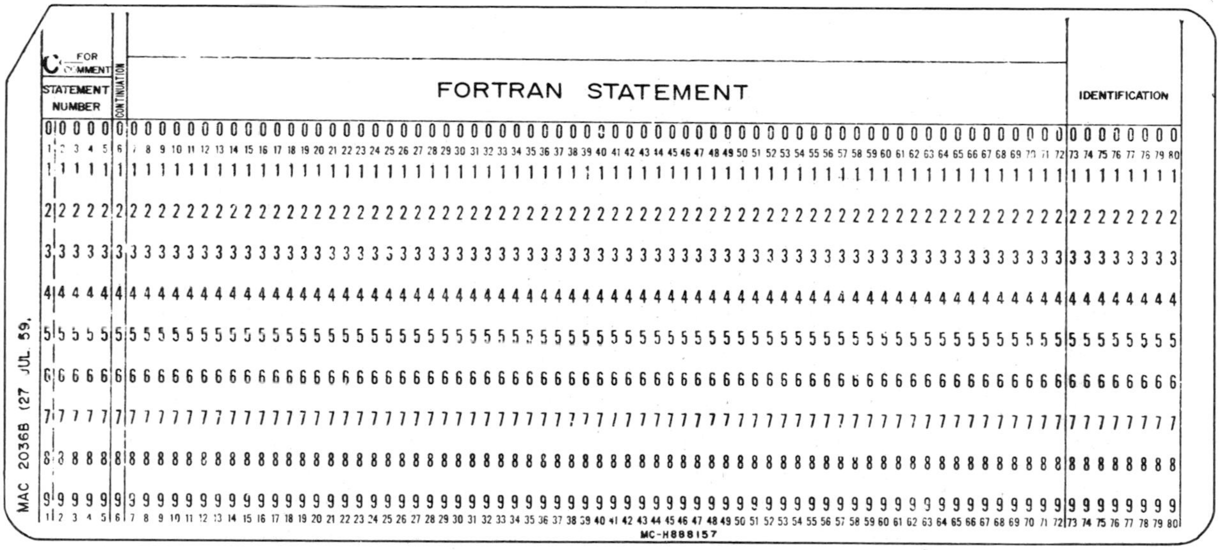

Figure 4.5 FORTRAN program card

Continuation

Column 6 is reserved for the continuation column. The programmer may have the occasion to write a statement that exceeds the length of a single card (i.e., beyond column 72). FORTRAN syntax requires that a program statement fit on one line, unless you explicitly indicate an additional record (line or card) is needed. This continuation of a statement is indicated by a nonblank, nonzero character in column 6. That is, any character other than a **zero** or **blank** in column 6 indicates a continued FORTRAN statement (and the statement is continued after column 6). In the first card of a statement that exceeds one line or card, column 6 must be blank or zero. A blank character (space) in column 6 is the normal practice. Statement numbers are forbidden on continuation cards. Up to nineteen continuation cards are allowed for each FORTRAN statement.

FORTRAN Statement

The FORTRAN statement is punched in columns 7 through 72. A FORTRAN statement must not be coded before column 7; however, it is not mandatory to begin in column 7. Blanks within the FORTRAN statement are ignored completely (except for one special case, which is in literal constants).

Program Identification/Sequence Number

Columns 73 through 80 are reserved for program identification (ID) and/or sequence number. These columns are ignored by the compiler and are primarily for the benefit of the programmer. Any information punched in these columns will be printed on the source listing. If the cards containing the statements in a program were shuffled (from having been dropped, for example), they could easily be rearranged in the correct order by sorting on a mechanical sorter or even by hand. A program ID would prove useful if several FORTRAN programs were shuffled together.

An example of a combination program ID and sequence number would be PAY00100. Sequence numbers should increase by tens or even in increments of 100 to allow for the addition of new statements in the program. This field is usually not used by students, in order to conserve time in typing/punching a program. Production programs, however, because of their large size, are usually coded with a program identification and/or sequence numbers.

In an academic environment you do not usually punch any information in the program ID/sequence number area. Student programs are usually short enough to allow one to rearrange the statements without much difficulty if they become shuffled. A good technique is to draw a diagonal across the top or bottom of the card deck (from a back corner to the opposite front corner) with a felt-marking pen. If the card deck is dropped, the diagonal line provides a rough guide for arranging the cards in their original order. Figure 4.6 illustrates each of the four areas of a FORTRAN statement.

Even though there are specially designed cards to facilitate punching a FORTRAN program, some data processing installations use the regular 80-column punched card for FORTRAN programs. See figure 4.7 for an example of a FORTRAN statement on a punched card.

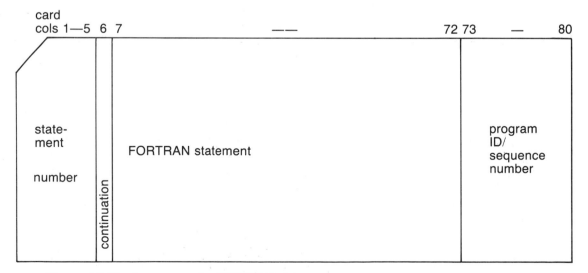

Figure 4.6 The four areas of a FORTRAN statement

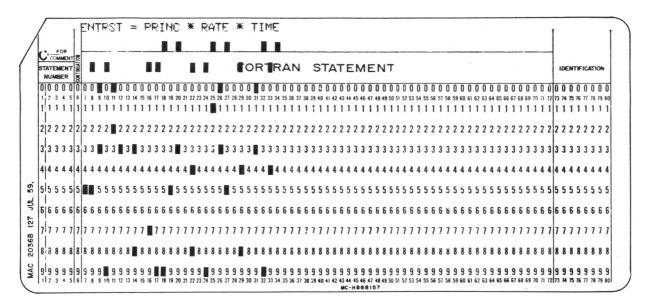

Figure 4.7 An example of a FORTRAN statement on a punched card

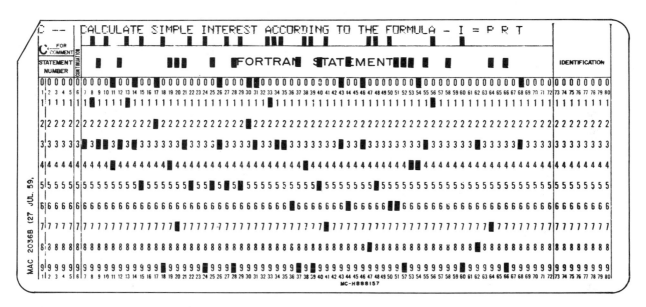

Figure 4.8 An example of a comment card

Comment Card

The character "C" in column 1 indicates a comment card. These cards are used to insert remarks into a program. Any information may be coded in columns 2 through 80. There is no limit to the number of comment cards allowed in a program. If a comment is entered onto more than one consecutive card, each card must have a "C" in column 1. Figure 4.8 gives an example of a comment card.

Comment cards are not processed by the FORTRAN compiler. They are simply printed on the source listings. Any character in the FORTRAN character set may be included in the comment card. They may be placed anywhere in a program, except between continuation cards.

Many timesharing dialects of FORTRAN permit different ways of providing comment lines. For example, CDC, DEC, and FORTRAN 77 dialects also permit the asterisk (*) to be used in position one to indicate a comment line.

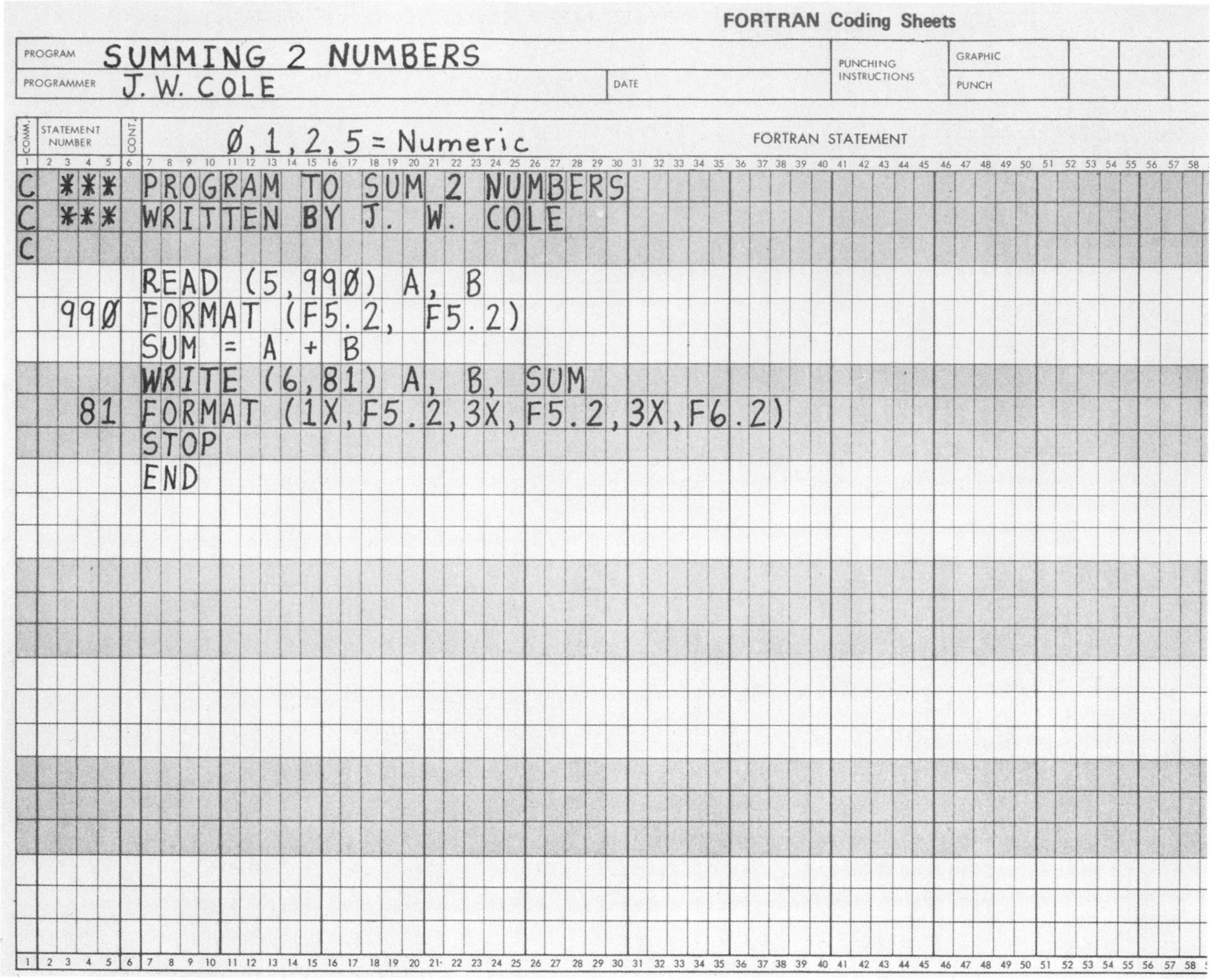
FORTRAN Coding Sheets
PROGRAM SUMMING 2 NUMBERS
PROGRAMMER J.W. COLE
DATE
PUNCHING INSTRUCTIONS
GRAPHIC
PUNCH
COMM.
STATEMENT NUMBER
CONT.
Ø, 1, 2, 5 = Numeric
FORTRAN STATEMENT
C *** PROGRAM TO SUM 2 NUMBERS
C *** WRITTEN BY J. W. COLE
C
READ (5,99Ø) A, B
99Ø FORMAT (F5.2, F5.2)
SUM = A + B
WRITE (6,81) A, B, SUM
81 FORMAT (1X,F5.2,3X,F5.2,3X,F6.2)
STOP
END

Figure 4.9 Example of a coded FORTRAN program

A Coded FORTRAN Program Example

The FORTRAN program presented in figure 4.1 to read and compute the sum of two values is coded on a FORTRAN coding form to illustrate the process of coding FORTRAN statements. Figure 4.9 shows the coded program on a FORTRAN coding sheet. Three comment cards have been added to the program originally shown in figure 4.1.

In coding a FORTRAN program, only capital letters are used. Lower case letters do not exist in FORTRAN. Special care should be made to print each character with maximum legibility on the coding sheet if the program is to be keypunched by someone else. Certain characters are very difficult to distinguish. It is recommended that you use the following coding conventions in order to provide an accurate, easy-to-read program to the keypunch personnel. The same applies for data to be punched.

Numeric Digit	Print	Alphabetic Letter	Print
zero	Ø	O	O
one	1	I	I
two	2	Z	Ƶ
five	5	S	S
eight	8	B	B

When any one of these specific symbols is printed, especially the numeric ones, you should indicate their form in the punching instruction blocks provided on the coding sheet. For example, if you slash your zeroes, you might indicate a note that says: $\emptyset$ = numeric, or $\emptyset$ = zero. Some installations, however, may require the programmer to slash the letter "O" instead of the numeric zero. The zero will be slashed in coded programs on coding sheets within this text.

You may include spaces in FORTRAN statements at any column you wish. The FORTRAN compiler ignores all spaces in FORTRAN statements and reads them as if no blanks were present. However, in literal constants (a special character string), spaces are important and are counted. Spaces should be included in statements whenever it makes them more readable. For example, you might code:

$$\text{GRSPAY} = \text{HOURS} * \text{RATE} + 50.0$$

FORTRAN will read this statement as:

$$\text{GRSPAY} = \text{HOURS*RATE} + 50.0$$

The inserted blanks between the variables, constants, and operators, however, make the statement more readable. It is recommended that blanks be used only as separators after keywords and between variables, constants, operators, and special characters (such as a comma or parentheses) to improve readability. Do not insert blanks in the middle of variables and constants, even though most FORTRAN compilers will ignore them.

4.10 LANGUAGE EXTENSIONS IN FORTRAN DIALECTS

Most computer manufacturers' FORTRAN compilers permit extensions to the features discussed in this chapter. On the other hand, some FORTRAN compilers are more restrictive and limit these features. These extensions and limitations are noted in the following paragraphs for features that may differ.

Character Set. Many FORTRAN dialects include additional characters in their character set. FORTRAN 77 has 49 characters in its character set. The single quote (') and colon (:) are included for format specifications. Two additional characters are included in the IBM S/360 and S/370 G-level FORTRAN IV and WATFIV compilers. The dollar sign ($) is used as an alphabetic letter in addition to A–Z. Thus, twenty-seven alphabetic letters with which to begin variable names are possible. The single quote mark (') represented by a 5/8 punch is used to indicate a "literal string" of characters. The ampersand (&) is also allowed and has a special meaning. The dollar sign ($) and colon (:) are used in DEC PDP-11 FORTRAN for special format specifications. VAX-11 FORTRAN includes additional special characters of single quote ('), double quote ("), underline (___), exclamation point (!), colon (:), left angle bracket (<), right angle bracket (>), percent sign (%), and ampersand (&).

On Honeywell 6000, DEC PDP-11 FORTRAN, and DEC VAX-11 FORTRAN, both the single quote (') and double quote (") may be used to indicate a literal. On the Burroughs 6000 FORTRAN, the double quote (") is used to indicate a literal. The $ is permitted on Honeywell 6000 and CDC 6000 compilers to permit and separate multiple statements on a card/line. The ";" is used on Burroughs and WATFIV compilers to allow and separate multiple statements on a card/line.

Keywords. FORTRAN 77, Honeywell, Univac and VAX-11 FORTRAN compilers have the keywords of CHARACTER, ENCODE, and DECODE for additional language capabilities. The IBM S/360, S/370, G-level, and WATFIV compilers have additional FORTRAN statements denoted by the keywords DEFINE FILE, ENTRY, FIND, IMPLICIT, NAMELIST, PRINT, and PUNCH. Consult **Appendix M** for the statements (keywords) allowed in various compilers.

Variables. Some basic FORTRAN compilers, such as ANSI Basic FORTRAN and IBM Basic FORTRAN IV, limit the number of characters in a variable to five. The CDC 6000 and Cyber compilers permit up to seven characters in their variable names. The Honeywell 6000 compiler permits up to eight characters in a variable name. A maximum of 31 characters are allowed in a symbolic name in VAX-11 FORTRAN. The symbolic names may include the underscore (___) special character to improve understandability. It is recommended that you restrict the length of your variables to six characters in case your program is ever run on a different computer. This helps ensure program transportability to different machines.

Statement Numbers. The ANSI Basic FORTRAN compiler limits its statement numbers to four digits. IBM Basic FORTRAN IV permits five digits, but limits the range to 32767. The Univac 1100 permits statement numbers from 1–32767. In WATFIV, a warning message is issued for all statements that have statement numbers assigned to them but are not referenced in the program.

Continuation Cards. The IBM E level and ANSI Basic FORTRAN compilers limit the number of continuation cards to five. The WATFIV and the Burroughs 6000 compilers permit an unlimited number of continuation cards.

Multiple FORTRAN Statements on a Line/Card. The CDC 6000 and Cyber, Honeywell 6000, Burroughs 6000, and WATFIV compilers permit multiple FORTRAN statements on a line/card. The CDC 6000 and Cyber compilers use a $ symbol to indicate the end of a statement. The Burroughs 6000, Honeywell 6000, and WATFIV compilers use a ; symbol. Although the use of multiple statements per card produces a smaller source deck, their use is strongly discouraged. The loss of portability to another FORTRAN compiler can result in many hours of added hard work caused by having to reconvert the multiple statements back to single statements on a card. The use of multiple statements on a line/card also increases the amount of debugging time and effort that must be given to a program.

Comment Card. The CDC 6000, Cyber, Honeywell 6000, VAX-11, and FORTRAN 77 compilers permit an asterisk (*) in addition to the character "C" to be used in column one to designate a comment card. The character "C" is always recommended to provide comment card compatibility among FORTRAN compilers. Most FORTRAN compilers other than ANSI permit all characters available on a computer to be used in the comment, instead of restricting them to the FORTRAN character set. IBM compilers restrict the number of consecutive comment cards to 49. On most other compilers the number of consecutive comment cards is unlimited. Digital FORTRAN IV Plus and VAX-11 FORTRAN allow an exclamation mark (!) with a following comment to be included after the FORTRAN statement for remarks. For example:

$$\text{LINECT} = \text{LINECT} + 2 \qquad \text{!BUMP LINE COUNTER}$$

Mixed Mode Expressions

Many FORTRAN compilers allow mixed mode expressions. That is, both integer and real constants and/or variables may be included in an expression. A **mixed mode expression** is defined as one in which both integer and real constants and/or variables are used in an arithmetic expression. All internal calculations performed by the computer, however, must be on values in the same mode. Therefore, compilers which allow mixed mode expressions must convert the integer mode operand which is used with a real operand to real mode before doing the calculation. You may wonder then, why have mixed mode expressions at all? They are allowed primarily for the convenience of the programmer—to avoid his having to write additional statements to establish a new mode for a variable. Mixed mode expressions are not recommended, but are explained here, since they are allowed on so many compilers (but not in ANSI FORTRAN 66).

In a mixed mode expression consisting of multiple operations, the arithmetic operation with two integer operands will be performed in integer mode. All other combinations of operands are performed in real mode. It is the type of the two operands involved in each operation that determines the arithmetic mode. Consider the following mixed mode expressions:

$$5 / (A + 3) - X ** 7$$
$$86.3 * K + R / 16.5 ** J$$

$7.5 - 3 / 2$	(result is 6.5)
$4 * 3.5 - 16 ** .5$	(result is 10.0)
$10 / 3. - 1 / 3 + .6$	(result is 3.933333)

Remember, in a single mixed mode expression between two operands, the computer will convert the integer value to real before doing the calculation. The result is, therefore, a real value. The type of the variable to which the calculated value is assigned, however, determines the mode of the stored result. There is no mixed mode across the "equals" sign. An integer variable on the left side of the "equals" sign will cause the resulting value to stored as an integer. A real variable on the left side of the "equals" sign stores the value as a real quantity.

Multiple Assignment Statements

Some compilers, such as WATFIV and CDC 6000, allow the assignment of a value to multiple variables in the same Assignment statement. This form of the Assignment statement is often referred to as multiple replacement. The general form for this type of Assignment statement is:

$$\textbf{variable} = \textbf{variable} = \textbf{variable} = \textbf{expression}$$

where any number of variables may be assigned the value obtained from the expression. For example:

$$X = Y = Z = 0.0$$
$$A = I = V = W = 3.2 * R + X$$

The assignment of the values is from **right** to **left**. That is, the value from the expression is assigned to the rightmost variable, then the value in this variable is assigned to the immediate next left variable, and so on. You must be careful when using this type of Assignment statement, since different types of variables may result in a truncation of fractional digits. Thus, in the latter example, the variable A would contain only the whole number portion of the value since the value in I is assigned to the variable A.

4.11 SUMMARY

Chapter 4 introduced you to the basics of the FORTRAN language. You learned that there are many versions of FORTRAN. The American National Standards Institute has developed several standard versions of FORTRAN so that a FORTRAN program may be run on different computers with few or no changes. ANSI Full FORTRAN 66 is the FORTRAN dialect that is covered in this text, since it is standard on most vendors' computers. FORTRAN 77 and various other FORTRAN compilers (with and without the structured statements) are also discussed in the text to provide a well-rounded knowledge of the capabilities in various FORTRAN dialects.

The commands available in FORTRAN may be grouped into categories which identify the operation you wish the computer to perform. Some FORTRAN commands instruct the FORTRAN compiler to do certain operations. These statements do not get translated into a computer command and thus are known as nonexecutable statements. The instructions such as READ, IF, WRITE, and so on, *do* get translated into computer commands and, thus, are known as executable statements.

FORTRAN is similar to a written language like English. A specific construction format (syntax) exists for each statement, with many rules to follow. Without this structure, you cannot instruct the computer properly as to the statement you wish it to perform. The FORTRAN language can be broken into elements such as keywords, constants, variables, operators, and expressions. You must understand how to form and use each of these elements in composing FORTRAN statements.

A numeric constant represents a fixed number or quantity that never changes during the execution of a program. A variable represents a storage location where the stored value can change during program execution. The last value put into a variable (either by a READ or Assignment statement) is the current value used for that variable. Integer or real constants and variables can represent numeric data in special forms. Therefore, extreme care must be exercised when choosing the name for a variable and using the different forms of constants and variables in developing expressions.

The Assignment statement is a powerful and widely used statement in nearly all FORTRAN programs. You must follow the rules in forming arithmetic expressions, or you will obtain incorrect results in your calculations. Operators are used to denote the mathematical operations for performing calculations. You must be mindful of integer and real mode operations to know what result is being produced by the computer.

A specific location is required in a FORTRAN instruction for coding the statement number, continuation indicator, and FORTRAN statement. If these locations are violated, a syntax error will occur. FORTRAN coding forms are available for coding programs to ensure that you code each part in the proper position. Other rules must be followed to provide proper statement numbers and characters for the continuation indicator.

Comment cards with a "C" in column 1 should be used to contain remarks about the program. This form of internal documentation is invaluable for others reading your programs. Spaces at proper places in the FORTRAN statement also help promote readability.

Many dialects of FORTRAN contain additional features for programmer convenience in writing programs. Additional keywords and special characters are available for greater language capability. Many compilers allow multiple statements to be coded on the same line; additional capabilities are included for internal comments. Appendix M gives the language capabilities and features in various FORTRAN dialects.

With these FORTRAN fundamentals, you can proceed to learn the various statements and their use in developing more complex programs.

4.12 TERMS

Terms you should become familiar with in this chapter are:

arithmetic operation	floating-point number	nonexecutable statement
arithmetic operator	FORTRAN	output statement
assignment statement	identifier	portability
coding form	input statement	real variable
constant	integer arithmetic	single-precision mode
dialect	integer constant	single-precision number
double-precision mode	integer variable	source statement
executable statement	keyword	specification statement

4.13 REVIEW QUESTIONS

1. From what two words is the acronym FORTRAN derived?
2. In what year was the first FORTRAN compiler completed?
3. Name the three categories of executable statements.
4. How many characters are in the FORTRAN character set?
5. What is the purpose of FORTRAN keywords?
6. With the exception of the Assignment statement, where do keywords appear in a FORTRAN statement?
7. Define a numeric constant in FORTRAN.
8. What are the two types of numeric constants that may be formed in FORTRAN?
9. An integer constant represents a _____ number.
10. A real constant is always considered to be in _____ – _____ form.
11. What is the maximum number of decimal digits that can be represented in a single-precision real constant on some computers?
12. Define a variable in FORTRAN.
13. Variables may be formed of from _____ to _____ characters.
14. The first character of a variable must be _____ while the remaining characters (if used) may be _____ or _____.
15. An integer variable begins with one of the letters _____ through _____ in the standard FORTRAN naming convention.
16. A real variable begins with what letters in the standard FORTRAN naming convention?
17. What statement may be used to override the typing of a variable as to its first letter?
18. List three terms that may be used to express the function of the assignment operator.
19. Why is the Assignment statement so important in FORTRAN programs?
20. Name the possible elements of the FORTRAN language that may be used in forming an arithmetic expression.
21. List the five arithmetic operators used in FORTRAN and indicate their order or hierarchy in computations.
22. What is the importance of using parentheses in arithmetic expressions?
23. Why are the following expressions invalid?

   a. $Z / - 3$
   b. $5X + 7Y$
   c. $(A + B * (C - D)$
   d. $6 - X **$

24. The type and length of the result from an arithmetic operation depend on what?
25. The two types of arithmetic expressions are _____ and _____ mode.
26. Describe the general form of the Assignment statement. Give an example.
27. The " = " in the Assignment statement means to S_____ or to R_____ and does not mean algebraic equality.
28. In an Assignment statement, how many values may be assigned to the variable to the left of the equal sign?
29. FORTRAN instructions may be referenced by labels called statement numbers assigned to each instruction. (True or False)
30. Statement numbers used to identify FORTRAN statements are punched in columns _____ through _____ .
31. Statement numbers assigned to a FORTRAN statement for reference purposes may range from _____ to _____ .

32. Statement numbers may be assigned without regard to order or sequence, but no two statements may be assigned the same statement number in the same program. (True or False)

33. Column _____ is reserved for the statement continuation column.

34. Any character other than _____ or _____ may be used to indicate a continuation of a FORTRAN statement.

35. The FORTRAN statement itself begins in column _____ and may extend through column _____ .

36. Columns _____ through _____ are used for statement sequencing and/or program identification and are not checked by the compiler.

37. Comment cards may be entered in a program to insert comments/remarks and are indicated by placing a _____ in column _____ .

38. Comment cards may be placed anywhere in a FORTRAN source program except between continuation cards. (True or False)

39. What are the alphabetic characters that are often confused with the numeric digits 0, 1, 2, 5, and 8?

40. What is the rule regarding spaces in FORTRAN statements?

4.14 EXERCISES

1. Identify the following variables as to type integer or real:

   a. JOE
   b. RATE
   c. PI
   d. SEQNR
   e. TIME
   f. C5A
   g. F16
   h. KEY
   i. LOOP
   j. HOLD

2. Identify the following variables as to type integer or real:

   a. KTR
   b. CTR2
   c. INDX
   d. NSUM
   e. MOUSE
   f. ITEMP
   g. A
   h. X21
   i. JOBNR
   j. TEXT

3. Explain why the following variables are invalid:

   a. COMPUTER
   b. 3B
   c. COST.9
   d. G86R29B
   e. A*B
   f. T5000-

4. Explain why the following variables are invalid:

   a. SUMOFXANDY
   b. NET-PY
   c. A123456
   d. X + 7
   e. 86TYM
   f. UT**2

5. Identify the following constants as to type integer or real:

   a. 12.3
   b. 15
   c. +.56
   d. 0
   e. 0.
   f. −79
   g. −8.7569
   h. +3274
   i. 4296.002
   j. 29036

6. Identify the following constants as to type integer or real:

   a. 0.0
   b. 38.462
   c. 149
   d. 00
   e. −.003
   f. +47.03
   g. +0.
   h. −2
   i. .000001
   j. 29.0

7. Explain why the following constants are invalid:

a. 4,296
b. 25 −
c. 4896102457

d. 4.56.
e. . − 237
f. 2*5

8. Explain why the following constants are invalid:

a. 46**3
b. 0 − 23.4
c. 86,279

d. 5132861004
e. .289 −
f. 2,357 +

9. Evaluate the following arithmetic Assignment statements. Determine the resulting value from each and show whether the result assigned to the variable is in integer or real form.

a. A = 5 / 3 + 8 * (4 − 2)
b. K = 9 − 3 * 2
c. I = 9 − 2 ** 3 + 7

d. R = (6.0 / 3.0 * 2.) ** 3.0 − 15.6
e. J = 8.2 + .8 − 6. ** 2.0

10. Evaluate the following arithmetic Assignment statements. Determine the resulting value from each and show whether the result assigned to the variable is in integer or real form.

a. X = 5. / 2.5 * 6. − 8. ** 2.0
b. L = (3 − 5) * (8 + 3)
c. N = 5.68 − 3.4 + 7.0 / 2.0

d. S = 5 / 2 + 3 ** (2 **2)
e. M = (3 + 2) * (6 − 2) / 4

11. Consider the following arithmetic Assignment statements. If the statement is valid, check the valid column. If invalid, write a correct statement. Mixed mode expressions are not allowed.

Statement		Valid	Rewritten Statement
a.	Q = R − .36 + 7.0		
b.	DISTANCE = RATE*TIME		
c.	SQROOT = X ** .5		
d.	RATE = DIST / TIME		
e.	C**2 = A*A + B*B		
f.	GRSPAY = $210.75		
g.	C = A* −B		
h.	TOTAL = 0.0		
i.	PAGECT = 0001		
j.	A * B / Z = T		

12. Evaluate the validity of the following arithmetic Assignment statements in the same manner as required in exercise 11.

Statement		Valid	Rewritten Statement
a.	RESULT = 8.4 + R / 5.		
b.	AMT = DOL + CENTS		
c.	ADD A TO B GIVING C		
d.	SUM = SUM + CTR.5		
e.	E = 5X**2 + 2Y + Z		
f.	HOLD = 5./3.*(R + S) − B*4.0		
g.	L = (Z + 5.)*((R − 3.2) + V)		
h.	CUBERT = XNUM ** (1./3.)		
i.	AREAT = 1./2. B (H)		
j.	SUM = SUM + VALUEX		

13. List the order (precedence) of calculations in the following Assignment statements.

    a. X = ((3.0 − C) * 7.5) + 8.3

    b. A = X + 5.2 / Y ** Z * 2.0 − 1.0

    c. M = I ** (J ** K) − 3* 7

    d. N = 8 + (4 * M − 1) − ((6 + L) / 10)

    e. Z = (5 * J) ** (3 + L) + 4 ** 2

14. List the order (precedence) of calculations in the following Assignment statements.

    a. B3 = B ** Z + (6.2 − X * 4.1)

    b. X = ((5.0 + C) * (4.0 / D)) ** E + 8.5

    c. Y = (8.0 / A + 2.1) * (B − 4.83) * (C + 2.0)

    d. I = J ** 4 * M ** 5 + (N ** 6 − 1)

    e. J = 3 * M ** 2 + 7 * L / 3 ** 2 + 5

5 Developing and Processing a FORTRAN Program

5.1 INTRODUCTION TO DEVELOPING A BASIC FORTRAN PROGRAM

Chapter 4 introduced you to FORTRAN with its keywords and other language elements. In this chapter a short program will be developed using the seven FORTRAN statements that are used in almost every program you will write. These seven basic statements are:

1. Explicit Type statements—INTEGER and REAL
2. READ statement
3. FORMAT statement
4. Assignment statement
5. WRITE statement
6. STOP statement
7. END statement

Each of the eight steps in solving a computer problem is discussed in developing a workable FORTRAN program. The formatted READ and WRITE statements are used in the program, since they are the ANSI FORTRAN 66 standard input/output statements and will run on virtually all computers. The format-free input/output statements available in FORTRAN 77 and other FORTRAN dialects are discussed at the end of the chapter.

Our work begins with a problem specification to compute the sum and average of three test scores. A planned solution is developed by analyzing the problem requirements and preparing a flowchart and pseudocode to represent the program design. After the FORTRAN program has been written, the construction and use of each of the statements used in the program will be explained. The procedure for preparing the program to run on the computer will be discussed. The compilation phase and the testing and debugging phase for providing a correct computer solution are examined. Finally, the question of what constitutes satisfactory documentation for the problem and program will be discussed.

Now, let's begin work on the problem.

5.2 STEP 1—ANALYZING THE PROBLEM SPECIFICATIONS AND DEFINING THE SOLUTION REQUIREMENTS

The assigned problem is to compute the sum and average of three test scores for one student. The scores are read from an input data record to supply the input values needed in the calculations and to produce the output results. The output should show the three input test scores and the calculated sum and average. The three test scores are printed on a single line. The calculated sum and average are printed on a new line double-spaced below the test scores' line.

The problem requirements may be given in the **problem specifications** document or form. A **systems analyst** (one who analyzes user needs and designs systems and programs) may complete this form for the programmer. Alternatively, the analyst/programmer may complete his or her own document by talking to the users and determining their requirements. Your lab problem handout serves as the problem specifications document in an academic environment.

A problem specifications form to describe the problem requirements is shown in figure 5.1.

Now the analysis phase begins.

Problem specifications		
Project: Student grade average	Date: 2/17/81	Page 1 of 1

Write a program to calculate the sum and average of three student test scores. The format of the input data and printer spacing chart are attached to this document. The processing shall include the following:
1. The program is to be written in FORTRAN.
2. The program will read a student grade record consisting of three integer test scores.
3. The sum and average of the three test scores are to be calculated.
4. The output will consist of:
    a. The three test scores, printed on the same line.
    b. The calculated sum and average, printed on the same line and double-spaced beneath the test scores.

Figure 5.1 Problem specifications form

Analysis of the Problem Requirements

A system or program consists of three main parts—input, processing, and output. This is a good way to break down the analysis of problem specifications and to learn the user requirements.

Get a sheet of paper and write the three parts as headings across the top of the paper. For example:

Inputs   **Processing**   **Outputs**

Next, read the problem specifications (lab problem) carefully to understand the problem requirements and the results you are expected to produce. A good technique is to take a red and blue pencil and identify the verbs (processing required) in red and the nouns (items to be processed) in blue. Try to concentrate on the big picture or main idea of the problem; do not get all wrapped up in details at this point—you will handle them later. Concentrate on the main purpose of the problem and on what is to be done.

Now read through the problem specifications a second time and write the parts of the requirements under their respective heading (Inputs, Processing, and Outputs) on the sheet of paper. Pay close attention to the output requirements, since they will determine what input items are needed and what processing must take place. The second objective, then, is to start understanding the details of the problem requirements by identifying all the output requirements. After this is accomplished, work on the input and processing requirements.

A print layout chart will help show the format of the desired report (or output) to give you a better idea of what the user wants. The record layout or multiple-card layout form will illustrate the location of input fields in a data record. There are also forms for flowcharting, coding, and assisting in most other steps. Let's now look at the problem output requirements in more detail and see how the print layout form is used to display the output information.

Output Requirements

Always start with the output requirements to identify the printed solution. Five data items are to be printed for the output requirements. The three test scores (read as input) will be printed on the first line of the report. The calculated values of sum and average are to be printed on a new line, double-spaced beneath the first.

Many users will describe how they want their report or output to look. You may be required to develop the report format for the user, who will confirm it or make suggestions for change. The output format is illustrated on a **print layout form** (also called a printer spacing chart) by the analyst or programmer.

Print Layout Form. A **print layout chart** is marked off in individual cells. Each cell on the print layout form corresponds to the print positions of a printed line. The numbers across the top of the form represent the actual print positions on the printer output line. The form is used to show where the data fields are to be printed and how the output records (lines) are spaced (single, double, or otherwise).

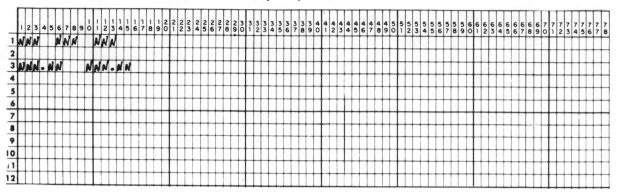

Figure 5.2 Print layout sheet showing output fields

The location and length of each item is indicated on the form. The character **X** is used to show each position that an output field may occupy. For example, if a test score is to occupy three print positions, you would mark three **X**'s (XXX) at the print positions where you want this field to be located. The character N or 9 may also be used to be more specific in designating numeric fields. (N's will be used in the later figure.) A decimal point (.) is shown at the print position at which it is to appear if the output field is to contain a fraction. A comma (,), dollar sign ($), or asterisk (*) is shown if the output fields are to contain these characters.

The three test scores are printed on the first line. They will be printed as a three-digit integer field; so each item will be represented by three N's (NNN). Two spaces are included after the first and second test scores to separate the fields. The first test score will appear in print positions 1–3, the second test score in print positions 6–8, and the third test score in print positions 11–13. The computed sum and average will be printed double-spaced beneath the first line. You drop down to the third line on the form to show that the second line is skipped. Both the sum and average will be printed with two decimal places. Since neither can exceed three integer positions, their output field is designated as NNN.NN. Assuming three spaces between these two items, the sum will be printed in positions 1–6 and the average in positions 10–15. Figure 5.2 shows the selected output formats on the print layout form.

Note that the actual output values are not written on the print layout sheet (unless they are titles, headings, and so forth). There are three reasons for this. First, you are concerned only with the placement of the output field on the print line. Second, you would not want to write the output values for dozens or perhaps hundreds of output values. For repeated fields in an output column, a line with an arrow head is drawn down the column to show that the fields are repeated. Third, the values of some output fields are not known, since they are calculated by the program. From the output requirements and print layout forms, the programmer can develop the output statements in FORTRAN.

After determining the output requirements, look at the input requirements. You must also determine their format. The proper record layout form is selected to illustrate this information.

Input Record Layout Form

Laying out an input data record with its data fields requires you to:

1. identify each item needed;
2. select an order of the items so that each will always appear in the same location on an input record;
3. determine the maximum number of characters or digits to represent the longest/largest value of each item.

The format of punched-card input records is shown on the **multiple-card layout form**. Each line is numbered 1 through 80, to represent the positions in an 80-column punched card. Each numbered column represents a corresponding card position and can contain one character.

IBM.

INTERNATIONAL BUSINESS MACHINES CORPORATION

**INFORMATION RECORDS DIVISION
MULTIPLE–CARD LAYOUT FORM**

Form X24-6599-1
IBM H47090
Printed in U.S.A.

Company _____

Application _Sum and Average of 3 Test Scores_ by _J. W. Cole_ _____ Date _____ Job No. _____ Sheet No. _1_

```
 Test Score 1 | Test Score 2 | Test Score 3 |
 9 9 9 | 9 9 9 | 9 9 9 | 9 9 9 9 9 9 9 9 9 9 9 9 9 9 9 9 9 9 9 9 9 9 9 9 9 9 9 9 9 9 9 9 9 9 9 9 9 9 9 9 9 9 9 9 9 9 9 9 9 9 9 9 9 9 9 9 9 9 9 9 9 9 9 9 9 9 9 9 9 9 9
 1 2 3 | 4 5 6 | 7 8 9 |10 11 12 13 14 15 16 17 18 19 20 21 22 23 24 25 26 27 28 29 30 31 32 33 34 35 36 37 38 39 40 41 42 43 44 45 46 47 48 49 50 51 52 53 54 55 56 57 58 59 60 61 62 63 64 65 66 67 68 69 70 71 72 73 74 75 76 77 78 79 80

 9 9 9 9 9 9 9 9 9 9 9 9 9 9 9 9 9 9 9 9 9 9 9 9 9 9 9 9 9 9 9 9 9 9 9 9 9 9 9 9 9 9 9 9 9 9 9 9 9 9 9 9 9 9 9 9 9 9 9 9 9 9 9 9 9 9 9 9 9 9 9 9 9 9 9 9 9 9 9 9
 1 2 3 4 5 6 7 8 9 10 11 12 13 14 15 16 17 18 19 20 21 22 23 24 25 26 27 28 29 30 31 32 33 34 35 36 37 38 39 40 41 42 43 44 45 46 47 48 49 50 51 52 53 54 55 56 57 58 59 60 61 62 63 64 65 66 67 68 69 70 71 72 73 74 75 76 77 78 79 80
```

Figure 5.3 Multiple-card layout form showing input fields

Other forms are used to illustrate magnetic tape and disk input records, since they may be longer than eighty characters. The multiple-card layout form may also be used for formatted terminal input. An input record layout form is not usually used in academic problems, since few input fields are given. Your instructor often designates the location and format of each input field in the lab problem specifications.

On the multiple-card layout form, you draw vertical lines between the indicated positions to show the location of each input field. Then you write the name of each field within the indicated positions. We will use the first nine columns—three positions for each test score—assuming an integer number from 0 to 100 represents each score. Figure 5.3 shows the multiple-card layout form.

An input field can be punched in any card columns you wish; you do not have to begin in card column 1. The fields do not have to be punched adjacent to each other; there can be blank columns between each field. The computer does not care, since it is already instructed about where to look for the three input values. So, why not start in column 1? To conserve positions on card records, the fields are punched next to each other, with no intervening spaces.

You may wonder why three positions were reserved for each score, since some may be less than 100. The rule is to reserve as many positions (card columns) for an input item as its largest possible value requires. In that way, each field will always be a fixed length and occupy the same positions in all data records. This concept is known as **fixed field layout** or **fixed record layout**. Since similar data records in an application will be in the same format, you will know where to find a data item in any input record.

Figure 5.4 Data card containing three test scores

The Data Card. Assume the values of 100, 76, and 83, respectively, for the three input test scores. Test score one is punched in columns 1 through 3, test score two in columns 4 through 6, and test score three in columns 7 through 9. The input data card would be punched as shown in figure 5.4.

Do not confuse the data cards with FORTRAN statements. In chapter 4 you learned that the FORTRAN statement cards have a fixed location for their various parts. The FORTRAN statement (instruction) is punched in columns 7 through 72. Data cards are different. They contain the input items to be read by an input unit in the READ statement. Thus, all 80 columns of a data card may be used to contain input data. There is no relationship whatsoever between the format of a FORTRAN statement and the format of input items in a data record. They have two completely different types of formats.

The **keypunch machine** is used to punch data cards as well as program instructions. The characters are printed along the top of the card at the same time as the holes are punched. The printing of the characters is for your benefit in reading the punched data; the computer is concerned only with reading the holes. **Appendix C** explains the operation of the keypunch machine for those unfamiliar with its use.

Formats for Timesharing Input/Output Records. For formatted input and output data on timesharing terminals, you follow the same procedure as with card input and printer output. The output results on most CRT screens are limited to 80 positions for each display line. However, you may print up to 132 characters per line with many teleprinter (hard-copy) terminals. For format-free input and output records, you would show the order and output line selection of the individual fields. There are special screen layout forms for formatting terminal input/output records in operational environments. If you are reading disk files, a disk record layout form would be used to show the input record layout.

Processing Requirements

The calculations and processing requirements to produce the output results are quite simple in the problem. The sum of the three test scores is calculated by adding them together. The average is calculated by dividing the sum by three. No decisions are made. No loop is needed, since only one input record is processed. Therefore, the overall algorithm, representing the computer solution, can now be developed.

5.3 STEP 2—DESIGNING THE PROBLEM SOLUTION

The analysis of the problem is easy to visualize, since it is short and straightforward. The three test scores must be read into memory to be available to the computer for the calculations. You must calculate the sum and then the average of the three test scores. Finally, the input values and the two calculated items must be printed.

A narrative describing the steps required to solve this problem might be as follows:

Step 1. Read the three test scores. Use the names TEST1, TEST2, and TEST3 for the memory locations to hold each of the three test scores, respectively.

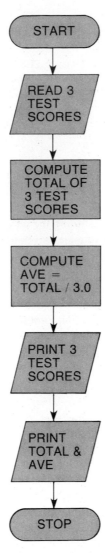

Figure 5.5 Flowchart of problem to compute the sum and average of three test scores

Step 2. Compute the sum of the three test scores by adding them together. Store the computed sum at the memory location given the variable name TOTAL.

Step 3. Compute the average of the test scores by dividing the sum by 3. The computed average will be stored at the variable AVE.

Step 4. Print the three input test scores from the variables TEST1, TEST2, and TEST3 on the first line of a new page.

Step 5. Print the calculated sum from the variable TOTAL and the average from the variable AVE on a double-spaced line.

Step 6. Terminate the program.

Next, express these steps in a flowchart or pseudocode so that you can better visualize the algorithm. Step through the algorithm in your design tool to see if it works. The flowchart of these steps is illustrated in figure 5.5. Note: You do not usually write the English narrative to describe the steps in a problem solution; you go directly to a flowchart or pseudocode. Your first attempt at drawing a correct flowchart does not always provide a correct solution. You may have to redo it several times. Don't worry; this is a natural process for developing the design solution. The flowchart may have to be redrawn several times before all parts of the solution are resolved.

You may be wondering why the test scores are not printed immediately after they are read. Actually, there would be nothing wrong with doing that. Changing the order of these steps will still produce the same correct output results. Programming involves personal choice, which can make it interesting and challenging. There is almost always more than one correct solution to a problem.

```
START ANALYSIS.
    READ THE THREE TEST SCORES INTO THE VARIABLES TEST1,
        TEST2, AND TEST3.
    CALCULATE THE SUM AS TOTAL = TEST1 + TEST2 + TEST3.
    CALCULATE THE AVERAGE AS AVE = TOTAL / 3.
    PRINT THE THREE TEST SCORES TEST1, TEST2, AND TEST3 BEGINNING
        ON A NEW PAGE.
    PRINT TOTAL AND AVE DOUBLESPACED BENEATH THE LAST LINE.
    TERMINATE THE PROGRAM.
END ANALYSIS.
```

Figure 5.6 Pseudocode of problem to compute the sum and average of three test scores

You may prefer to use pseudocode in illustrating the design solution. Pseudocode is often preferred over flowcharts, because it is usually easier to convert into a programming language. You or your instructor must choose the design tool to represent the design logic of the problem solution. The pseudocode for the problem solution is illustrated in figure 5.6.

You might wonder why a flowchart or pseudocode is needed for the problem solution, since it can be easily understood. Later, problems will become more complex and will require decisions and loops. Understanding the procedure in developing a design tool with simple problems, now, provides you with experience that will aid you later in more complex problems. Remember, the time and effort put into *planning* a solution will reduce the time and work required to produce a workable program.

The developed flowchart or pseudocode, along with the input record layout sheet and the print layout form, is used as a guide in writing the program.

5.4 STEP 3—WRITING THE COMPUTER PROGRAM

If you have desk-checked (stepped through the logic) the flowchart or pseudocode and found the logic workable, proceed to write the computer program. Follow the algorithm in your design tool to develop the program. Each step in your design solution is converted into a FORTRAN statement that causes the computer to perform the required operation. More than one FORTRAN statement may be needed for a symbol in the flowchart if the solution has been illustrated in more-general design steps.

When you come to the design step for reading the input values, code the READ statement. The rectangle symbol in the flowchart tells you to assign or compute some value; thus, you write the proper Assignment statement to calculate the required item. The output symbol requires a WRITE statement to print the output items.

The FORTRAN Program and Comment Cards

A FORTRAN program consists of a series of FORTRAN statements, each of which is an instruction to the computer to perform a specified action. You can follow the flowchart and write the FORTRAN program directly from the developed logic. Of course, you must write the actions in FORTRAN and provide additional information such as contained in the multiple-card layout and print layout specifications. Each FORTRAN statement is coded on the FORTRAN coding sheet to facilitate punching the statements onto cards or typing the program at a terminal. The coded FORTRAN program is illustrated in figure 5.7.

Each of the statements in the program will be discussed in turn to determine their construction and use.

Comment Cards

The first six lines represent comment cards to provide remarks about the program. The first two comment cards identify the purpose of the program. The fourth and fifth comment cards provide the name of the person who wrote the program and the date the program was written. The inclusion of remarks at the beginning of a program to identify the program and author (owner) can be very valuable. They help identify the owner of the program in case the beginning job gets lost and/or the job deck gets misplaced in the computer center. For these reasons, it is highly recommended that you include your name and class section in comment cards at the beginning of your program. The third and sixth comment cards, with only the "C" in column 1, are used to separate the initial remarks from the start of the program to improve readability.

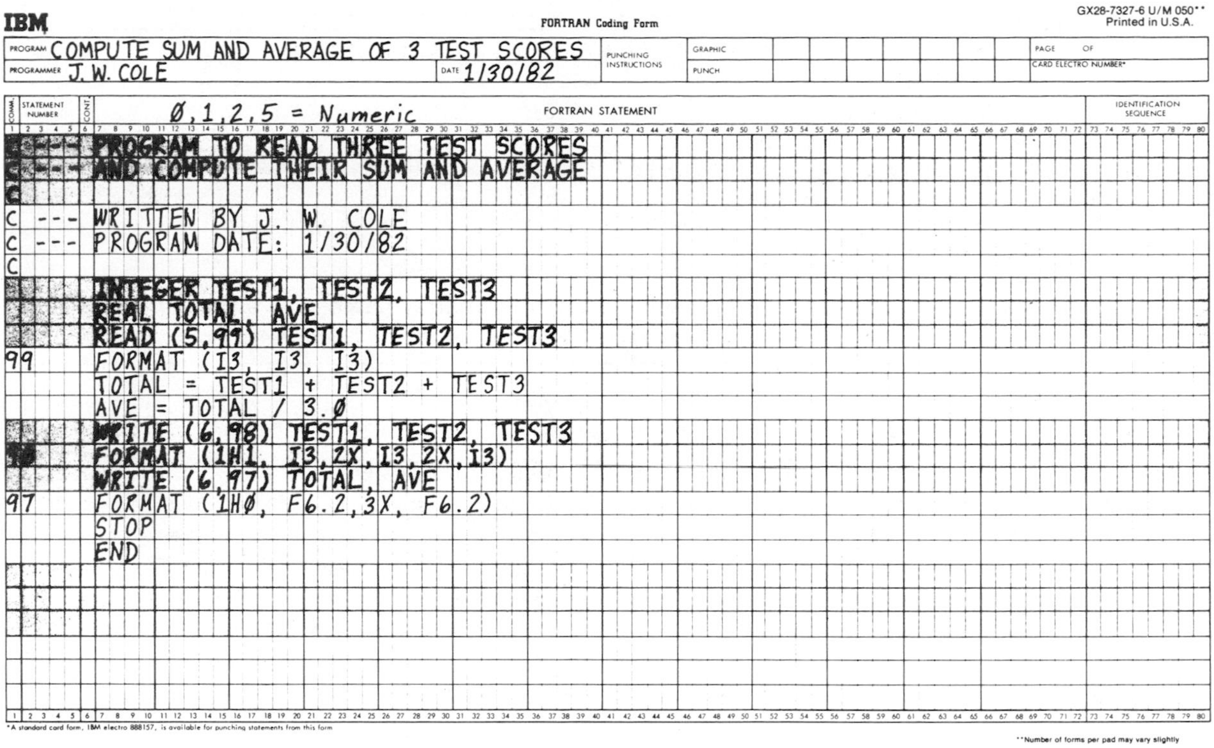

FORTRAN Coding Form

GX28-7327-6 U/M 050**
Printed in U.S.A.

| PROGRAM | COMPUTE SUM AND AVERAGE OF 3 TEST SCORES | PUNCHING INSTRUCTIONS | GRAPHIC | | | | | PAGE OF | |
| PROGRAMMER | J. W. COLE | DATE 1/30/82 | | PUNCH | | | | | CARD ELECTRO NUMBER* | |

```
C***** PROGRAM TO READ THREE TEST SCORES
C***** AND COMPUTE THEIR SUM AND AVERAGE
C
C---    WRITTEN BY J. W. COLE
C---    PROGRAM DATE: 1/30/82
C
       INTEGER TEST1, TEST2, TEST3
       REAL TOTAL, AVE
       READ (5,99) TEST1, TEST2, TEST3
99     FORMAT (I3, I3, I3)
       TOTAL = TEST1 + TEST2 + TEST3
       AVE = TOTAL / 3.0
       WRITE (6,98) TEST1, TEST2, TEST3
98     FORMAT (1H1, I3,2X,I3,2X,I3)
       WRITE (6,97) TOTAL, AVE
97     FORMAT (1H0, F6.2,3X, F6.2)
       STOP
       END
```

0,1,2,5 = Numeric

Figure 5.7 Coded FORTRAN program to compute the sum and average of three test scores

Comment cards are especially useful in programs that include complex logic or a unique way of solving a problem. A routine may take considerable time to understand—even to the person who originally wrote it when he or she comes back later to make a change. Internal remarks are very useful in providing a better understanding of the problem and its logic. You are encouraged to make liberal use of comment cards for this purpose.

5.5 MODE TYPING OF VARIABLES WITH THE EXPLICIT TYPE STATEMENTS

The first statement after the comment cards

INTEGER TEST1, TEST2, TEST3

declares the three variables—TEST1, TEST2, and TEST3—to be integer-type (mode) variables. The variables that represent the storage locations for the three test scores must be integer-type because they are read as integer data fields. You could follow the predefined convention of naming integer variables by starting the variable names with one of the letters I through N. For example, the variables NTEST1, NTEST2, and NTEST3 could have been selected for test scores one, two, and three, respectively. However, the names TEST1, TEST2, and TEST3 are more meaningful.

Since the initial letter T indicates a real-type variable, the predefined FORTRAN naming convention must be overridden by the Explicit Type statement—INTEGER. It is a good idea to express all variables in Explicit Type statements to ensure that a selected variable name is the type required. Some instructors require that you declare all the program variables in the appropriate Type statement. Other instructors prefer that only the variable names be declared that do not agree with the predefined naming convention. Other programming languages such as Pascal, ALGOL, and COBOL require you to declare all variables and identify their type before using them in the program.

The statement after the INTEGER Type statement

REAL TOTAL, AVE

declares the variables TOTAL and AVE to be type real. Of course, their initial letter would establish them as real variables by the FORTRAN predefined naming convention, but the Explicit Type statement—REAL—is used to document this usage.

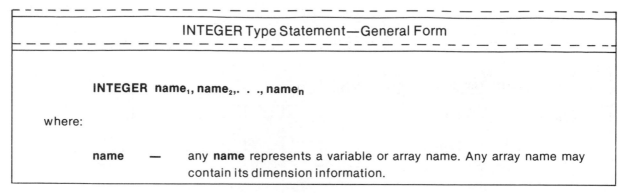

┌───┐
│   INTEGER Type Statement—General Form   │
│   │
│   │
│   INTEGER name₁, name₂,. . ., nameₙ   │
│   │
│   where: │
│   │
│   **name**   —   any **name** represents a variable or array name. Any array name may │
│   contain its dimension information.   │
└───┘

Figure 5.8 General notation of the INTEGER type statement

The Explicit Type statements allow the programmer to declare that specific variables are of a certain type. The Explicit statement is often referred to as the "Type" specification statement, since any variable or array (table) name in FORTRAN can be specified by a particular type. Explicit Type statements are very popular and widely used by FORTRAN programmers. Explicitly typing the variables, rather than using the predefined FORTRAN convention of the initial letter, gives a program more "linguistic" meaning. Names can be used that relate closely to the variables' use in the program, providing greater clarity. For example, the variable QUANTY may be more meaningful than NR to represent an integer quantity of items in an inventory control program.

The Type statements also provide a simple way of correcting the use of illegal variable names in a program. For example, if an integer type name were repeatedly used for a real variable in a program, a single Type statement could tell the compiler to treat the variable as type real instead of type integer. The programmer would avoid having to change each statement containing the illegal variable name.

Type specification statements must appear prior to any executable statement and at the beginning of a program unit. They cannot be assigned a statement number. Multiple Explicit Type statements may be given in a program. Each new Type statement must begin with its specified type, i.e., INTEGER, REAL, and so on.

Two Explicit Type statements—known as the INTEGER and REAL Type statements—are used to declare variables as to type integer and real, respectively. The DOUBLE PRECISION Type statement declares variables to contain double-precision values. Other Type statements must be used to declare the type of variables when other forms of data (logical and complex) are used in FORTRAN. These Type statements will be covered when the additional types of constants and data are used in FORTRAN programs. Let's examine the INTEGER and REAL Type statements in more detail.

INTEGER Type Statement

The INTEGER Type statement tells the compiler to treat all the variables (and arrays) contained in the list as type integer. The general form of the INTEGER Type statement is given in figure 5.8.

Examples are:

> **INTEGER COUNT, SUM**
> **INTEGER TOTAL**
> **INTEGER X1, X2, X3**

The first example declares the variables COUNT and SUM to be type integer. The second example declares the variable TOTAL to be type integer. The third example declares X1, X2, and X3 to be type integer variables.

A language syntax diagram such as figure 5.8 is probably new to you. It is an important technique used to describe the syntax construction of statements in a programming language. FORTRAN uses a general form notation showing the keyword and other language elements permitted in the construction of a statement. The next two paragraphs explain the importance and use of the general notation diagrams presented in this text. It is important that you understand this FORTRAN notation in order to construct error-free statements.

Syntax construction is described by a **general form notation** that is a symbolic representation of the rules for constructing a FORTRAN statement. From the general form of a statement, the programmer determines the keyword and elements of the FORTRAN language required or permitted in writing a specific statement.

```
┌─────────────────────────────────────────────────────────────────────────┐
    REAL Type Statement—General Form
├─────────────────────────────────────────────────────────────────────────┤
│                                                                           │
│         REAL  name₁, name₂, . . ., nameₙ                                  │
│                                                                           │
│   where:                                                                  │
│                                                                           │
│                                                                           │
│         name    —      any name represents a variable or array name. Any array name may │
│                        contain its dimension information.                 │
│                                                                           │
└─────────────────────────────────────────────────────────────────────────┘
```

Figure 5.9 General notation of the REAL type statement

Throughout this text, a general notation diagram is given for each new FORTRAN statement. All words in capital letters and all delimiters must be coded exactly (spelling, location, and so forth) as they appear in the general form notation. All words in lower case letters represent elements which are formed and supplied by the programmer. An explanation of each programmer-supplied element is included in the diagram to explain various aspects of these elements. Optional elements are also indicated. No indication is made as to which statements may be assigned a statement number, since any executable statement may be given a statement number. Each general form notation is enclosed in a boxed diagram to call attention to the statement's general form.

REAL Type Statement

The REAL Type statement tells the compiler to treat all the variables (and arrays) contained in the list as type real. The general form of the REAL Type statement is given in figure 5.9.

Examples are:

> **REAL NTOTAL, INTRST**
> **REAL IPOINT**
> **REAL ISHAPE, KSHAPE, LSHAPE**

The first example declares the variables NTOTAL and INTRST to be type real. The second example declares the variable named IPOINT to be a real-type variable. The third example declares ISHAPE, KSHAPE, and LSHAPE to be real-type variables.

The next section discusses the READ statement and its associated FORMAT statement to provide the input specification for the input data fields.

5.6 THE READ STATEMENT AND ITS ASSOCIATED FORMAT STATEMENT

The next statement in the program is the READ statement. The READ statement begins with the keyword READ; it is a command for the computer to read a data record and store the data items (from the input record) into memory.

The computer needs to know more than that it is supposed to read data. It must be told what input device to use, since you have the choice of reading terminal input, punched cards, magnetic disk and other media. The computer must know how many data items to read and where to store them in memory. The computer must also know where to look for the values on the input record and what form they are in, e.g., integer (whole number), real (decimal number with explicit or implied decimal point), or even alphabetic data. All this information must be provided in the READ statement and its accompanying FORMAT statement.

The first number inside the parentheses on the READ statement denotes the file unit or input device to be used. The number 5 specifies that the data will be read from punched cards by a card reader if a batch-card mode is used. If an interactive timesharing mode is used, the number 5 specifies the terminal as the input device. (Other numbers specify different input devices; don't worry about them for now.) The second number inside the parentheses, the number 99, specifies a related FORMAT statement used in conjunction with the READ statement to provide the format specifications of the input items (data fields).

READ (unit, n) list

where:

unit	—	is an unsigned integer constant or variable used as a file reference number.
n		is the statement number of the associated FORMAT statement which describes the attributes of the input data.
list	—	is an I/O list which may include one or more variables separated by commas.

Figure 5.10 General notation of the formatted READ statement

The names following the closing parenthesis are the variable names given to the data items being read. These variable names are the symbolic addresses of the storage locations at which the input items are placed. When the variable names are used later in the program, the computer will always retrieve the value stored at that location (variable). The first value on a data record is stored at the first variable name, the second value is stored at the second variable name, and so on.

The three names TEST1, TEST2, and TEST3 were chosen for the variable names. They refer to the three test scores that are to be read as input values. You could have used some other names, such as I, J, and K. The computer doesn't care what choices are made for the variable names as long as the FORTRAN rules for forming a variable name are followed and the correct type is chosen to agree with the type of data items read (or you specify the variables' type in the Explicit Type statement). You should always select variable names that provide some meaning to the data items being used.

The parentheses and commas are necessary delimiters (separators). The parentheses are used to enclose the file unit and FORMAT statement number. The commas are used to separate elements. If only one variable is read, then a comma is not used after the variable name. If multiple variables are read, a comma is used between two variable names to separate them. That is, a comma after a variable name says that another variable name follows in the list of variables. Thus, there is no comma after the last variable name in the READ statement.

The general form for the syntax construction of the formatted READ statement is given in figure 5.10.

Examples of the READ statement are:

READ (5, 199) NUMBR
READ (5,98) ITEMNR, QTY, COST
10 READ (5, 187) EMPID, HOURS, RATEPY
READ (INFILE, 88) X, Y

The first example reads one data item and stores it at the memory location NUMBR. The second example reads three data values and stores them in the variables ITEMNR, QTY, and COST. These names imply that inventory data is being read. The third example (with statement number 10) reads three input items and stores them in the memory locations with the variable names EMPID, HOURS, RATEPY. These variable names imply that a payroll record is being read. The fourth example reads two values under the name of X and Y. An integer variable (INFILE) is used to specify the file unit. This can be a valuable technique in a program.

Some FORTRAN compilers (especially those used with timesharing systems) permit the use of format-free input. In such cases, the READ statement does not require an associated FORMAT statement to describe the form and location of the input items. The data items may be entered from a terminal or appear in punched cards in any position as long as they are separated by a comma (or a space on some systems) to indicate the end of the data value. Thus, no FORMAT statement is needed with the READ. Your instructor will tell you about this type of READ statement if it is available on your compiler. (An explanation of format-free input/output statements is included in section 5.14.) Many compilers, such as ANSI FORTRAN 66, however, do not include the format-free input/output statements. In those cases, a FORMAT statement must be used in conjunction with the READ statement to supply the needed information about the input data fields.

The FORMAT Statement for the READ

The FORMAT statement is used in conjunction with a READ or WRITE statement to describe the form and location of the data items being read or written. A FORMAT statement is always assigned a statement number that may be referenced by a READ or WRITE statement to denote which specific FORMAT statement is being used. A program may have many different FORMAT statements to read and write data in different forms, so a unique statement number must be given to each. The keyword FORMAT identifies the FORMAT statement.

It is a good practice to place all the FORMAT statements in a program either at the end of the program or at the beginning of the program to remove them from the executable statements. This practice provides better readability and comprehension of the logic in a program. A FORMAT statement is often placed after the associated READ or WRITE statement for easy reference, such as in the sample program.

Following the FORMAT keyword is a set of parentheses which contain format specifications for the input or output data items. A comma is used to separate multiple format specifications when more than one is given. The format specification relating to each data item is called a format code. A **format code** describes how each individual data field is to be read or written.

A format code provides two pieces of information about the data item—its type and length (size). This information is obtained from the record layout form or multiple-card layout form. Most format codes begin with a letter to indicate the type of data to be read or written. Following the format code letter is a value (called the width part) to specify how many positions are included in the field (its length).

The general construction of a format code is indicated by a notation called its **form**. The three most common format codes used to provide format specifications for a data field, their form, and type-of-field value are given in table 5.1.

Table 5.1 Common Format Codes and Their Notational Form

Format Code	Form	Type of Value
I	Iw	Integer (whole numbers)
F	Fw.d	Floating point (real/decimal numbers)
X	wX	Blank (spaces)

The **I format code** is used to read integer quantities. Following the letter I is the width or size of the data field (in number of positions/card columns). Thus, the form of the I format code is given as Iw. If a three-digit integer field is to be read, you would use an I3 format code, which indicates an integer value of width 3. For example, a seven-digit integer number would be read with the format specifications of I7; a four-digit integer would be read as I4. The width part of a format code must include room for an algebraic sign when given with a numeric quantity. For example, the input value -999 would require an I4 format code.

The FORMAT statement 99 referenced by the READ statement provides three format codes to provide the format specifications for the three input items (TEST1, TEST2, and TEST3). Since each test score is a three-digit integer number, three format codes of I3 were given for the three test scores, respectively.

The **F format code** is used to read decimal values to be stored at a real (or floating point) variable. The notational form of a floating-point format code is:

$$Fw.d$$

where the **F** identifies the type of data field to be read or written. The **w** specifies the width of the decimal number, which includes an algebraic sign (if used) and a decimal point (if present). The "." in the notational form is a required separator. The **d** specifies how many digits follow the decimal point (i.e., fractional positions). The decimal value 24.75 would require an F5.2 format code. The field is 5 positions wide (including the decimal point) and there are two digits following the decimal point. The input field with a value of -3.029 would be specified with a format code of F6.3. The overall field width is 6 characters including the sign and decimal point. There are 3 fractional digits to the right of the decimal point.

The **X format code** is used to indicate blank positions in a record. No variable is associated with this format code since no data items are transferred to memory. This format code may be thought of as skipping so many positions in the input or output record. The notational form of the X format code is:

$$wX$$

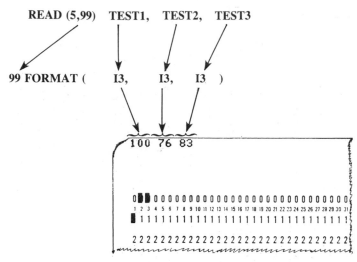

Figure 5.11 Relationship of input data fields, format codes, and variables

Note that the width part precedes the format code. To indicate two blank positions (or to skip two positions) on a data record, you would specify a 2X format code. To indicate 5 blank positions, you would specify a 5X format code.

Each format code in the FORMAT statement (except the X) corresponds to the variables in the READ (or WRITE) statement on a one-to-one, left-to-right basis. The format codes also correspond to the data fields in the input record on a one-to-one, left-to-right basis. See figure 5.11 for an illustration of the association between the variables, format codes, and input data values.

The computer assumes the data fields begin in position 1 (card column 1). The width of a field is added to the first position of that field to provide the starting record position for the next field. For example, if a field has a width of 3 positions and starts in position 1, then the starting position of the next field is 4 (3 + 1).

If input fields are adjacent to each other and use the same type of format code, a repetition factor may be used as a shortcut notation in specifying the format codes. The repetition factor is an unsigned integer number (ranging from 1 through 255) which is placed in front of the format code to indicate how many times it is to be repeated. In the FORMAT statement 99, you could have specified 3I3, which says to repeat the format code I3 three times. Remember, in order for you to use the repetition factor, the input fields must be next to each other, with no blank positions intervening between the fields.

Figure 5.12 gives the general form of the FORMAT statement.

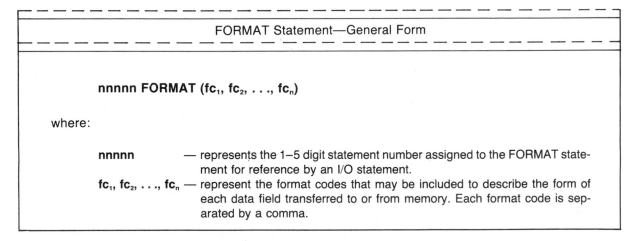

FORMAT Statement—General Form

nnnnn FORMAT (fc₁, fc₂, . . ., fcₙ)

where:

nnnnn — represents the 1–5 digit statement number assigned to the FORMAT statement for reference by an I/O statement.

fc₁, fc₂, . . ., fcₙ — represent the format codes that may be included to describe the form of each data field transferred to or from memory. Each format code is separated by a comma.

Figure 5.12 General notation of the FORMAT statement

Examples of the FORMAT statement for input items are:

96 FORMAT (I4)
198 FORMAT (I2, I5, F6.1)
76 FORMAT (3I3, 2F5.2, 4X, I8)

The first FORMAT statement provides the format specification for one four-digit integer field. The second example provides format specifications for three input fields. The first field is a two-digit integer field; the second field is a five-position integer item; the third field is a six-position decimal value with one fractional position. The third example provides format specifications for six data items. The first three items are three-digit integer values; the next two fields are five-position decimal numbers with two fractional positions; four blank positions are skipped; the sixth field is an eight-digit integer value.

Section 5.7 explains the Assignment statements used in the program and their construction.

5.7 THE ASSIGNMENT STATEMENTS

Now that the input values have been read into memory and stored under the variable names TEST1, TEST2, and TEST3, you can perform various calculations with them. The next two FORTRAN statements are known as Assignment statements. The function of the Assignment statement is to evaluate the expression on the right of the "equal" sign (=) and assign one single value to the variable name on the left of the "equal" sign. If the expression on the right of the "equal" sign is a single constant or variable, this value is simply assigned to the receiving variable. If the expression on the right of the "equal" sign includes arithmetic operators, the required calculating is done and the resulting value is assigned to the variable on the left. Thus, the Assignment statement is used to perform required computations and to assign values to variables.

The most frequent use of the Assignment statement is to assign a single numeric constant to a variable or to assign a variable to a new location (variable). The "equal" sign (=) does not mean "to make equal to," but rather "to assign a value to" or "replace the value of" the variable to the left of the "equal" sign with a new value. The old value is, of course, destroyed.

The first Assignment statement in our program

TOTAL = TEST1 + TEST2 + TEST3

causes the three test scores to be added together and the sum placed in the variable TOTAL. The second Assignment statement

AVE = TOTAL / 3.0

divides the contents of TOTAL (sum of the three test scores) by 3.0, and the quotient is assigned to the variable AVE. The constant 3.0 must be in real form to avoid mixed mode arithmetic. The variables TOTAL and AVE are real variable names; so they can contain fractions.

Figure 5.13 shows the general form of the Assignment statement.

Examples of the Assignment statement are:

20 KOUNT = 0
PI = 3.1416
OLDK = K
31 XSQ = X * X
RESULT = 4. * (R + S) / T − 6.5

Assignment Statement—General Form

variable = expression

where:

variable —— represents any type variable name.
expression —— may be a single constant, variable, or complex combination of arithmetic operations.

Figure 5.13 General notation of the Assignment statement

The first example assigns 0 to the variable KOUNT. The second example assigns the value 3.1416 to the variable PI. The third example assigns the value in K to the variable OLDK. The fourth example (with statement number 31) calculates the square of X and assigns the result to the variable XSQ. The fourth example performs a calculation and assigns the resulting value to the variable RESULT.

The next section discusses the WRITE statements and their associated FORMAT statements.

5.8 THE WRITE STATEMENTS AND THEIR ASSOCIATED FORMAT STATEMENTS

The WRITE statement directs the computer in writing data, stored in memory, to some output device, such as a terminal, line printer, or magnetic disk. In the WRITE statement, a file unit number and associated FORMAT statement number are given within parentheses. These two elements are separated by a comma. Then the list of variables to be written is included in the WRITE. A comma follows each variable except the last one. The comma is a way of saying that another variable follows in the I/O list.

The terminal or printer is designated as file unit 6 in FORTRAN on most computer systems. Thus, the 6, following the open parenthesis, designates the terminal (in an interactive timesharing mode) or the line printer (in batch-card mode) as the output file unit. The second number within the set of parentheses specifies the FORMAT statement used with the WRITE statement. In the first WRITE statement, the number 98 is used to correspond to the FORMAT statement for the first formatted line of output.

The first WRITE statement was:

WRITE (6,98) TEST1, TEST2, TEST3

This statement says to write the three test scores with the variable names TEST1, TEST2, and TEST3. The variable names following the set of parentheses denote the items to be accessed in memory and written on an output line. The items are written in the order in which they are specified in the I/O list. That is, TEST1 is written first, then TEST2, and finally TEST3.

The second WRITE statement

WRITE (6,97) TOTAL, AVE

says to write the calculated values of TOTAL and AVE. The values will be written on a new output line, since a separate WRITE statement is used. Each new WRITE statement indicates a new output record to be written. The format specifications in the FORMAT statement govern the format of the output. FORMAT statement 97 is used to describe the output format from the second WRITE statement.

Figure 5.14 gives the general form of the WRITE statement.

Examples of the WRITE statement are:

WRITE (6,297) EMPNR, HOURS, RATEPY, PAY
30　WRITE (6, 88) X, XSQ, XCUBE
WRITE (6,96) ROOT

The first example uses the format specifications in the FORMAT statement numbered 297 and writes the items EMPNR, HOURS, RATEPY, and PAY. The variable names are descriptive of payroll fields. The second example writes the items X, XSQ, and XCUBE, which are the item X, its square, and its cube. The third example prints one value—ROOT.

The FORMAT statement associated with the WRITE statement is very important in formatting the output properly. It is discussed next.

The FORMAT Statements with the WRITE

A FORMAT statement must be supplied for each WRITE statement to describe the format specifications for an output line. The form of each output field must be described in a format code. In addition, a descriptor must be given to specify how the paper is advanced (called carriage-control operations). This descriptor, a **carriage-control specification,** must be given at the beginning of the output FORMAT statement (before any format codes for the output fields). The carriage-control specification is required for terminal formatted output also. Table 5.2 lists the standard carriage-control characters and their functions in line printer and terminal output line spacing.

WRITE (unit, n) list

where:

unit	—	is an unsigned integer constant or variable used as the file reference number.
n	—	is the statement number of the associated FORMAT statement that describes the attributes of the output data.
list	—	is an optional I/O list which may include one or more variables separated by commas.

Figure 5.14 General notation of the formatted WRITE statement

Table 5.2 Carriage-Control Specifications for Formatted Output

Carriage Control Characters	Paper Movement/ Line Spacing	FORTRAN Specification Examples
1	new page	1H1
ƀ or X	single-space	1Hƀ or 1X
0	double-space	1H0
+	no advance (suppress spacing)	1H+

Note: the ƀ represents a blank character (i.e., a space). The hyphen (-) may be used on some systems for triple spacing.

The carriage-control specification of 1H1 causes the output to begin at the top of a new page (or at the first line on the CRT screen). This operation is called a **page eject** or **form feed operation.** It is a common practice to write the first line of output, such as a heading, beginning on a new page. Some systems automatically start the output results on a new page, but not all systems, such as WATFOR, WATFIV, and others. The specification of 1Hƀ (ƀ represents a blank) or 1X causes the output to be single-spaced (output line printed one line beneath the last line). The 1H0 causes double-spacing (output line printed two lines beneath the previous line). Double-spacing of output lines is the standard practice, since it makes the output lines more readable. Single-spacing may be used for large, voluminous reports to reduce the report size and amount of paper used. The 1H+ causes the paper not to be advanced, i.e., not to be moved. This specification is seldom used, but it is valuable when overprinting is required.

Only the FORMAT statements for the WRITEs need a carriage-control specification; those for READ statements do not. The carriage-control specification is never printed, but is "stripped off" by the output device. The specification provides the output device with the needed descriptor for line spacing on the line printer or a terminal. Remember, only the line printer and terminals require this carriage-control specification for formatted output. When you write formatted data to other devices, such as magnetic disk and tape, you do not include a carriage-control specification in the output format specifications.

The first WRITE statement and its associated FORMAT statement were:

WRITE (6, 98) TEST1, TEST2, TEST3
98 FORMAT (1H1, I3,2X,I3,2X,I3)

The number 98 is given to this FORMAT statement. The first format specification inside the set of parentheses is the carriage-control specification of 1H1, which causes this first line of output to begin at the top of a new page. The first format code of I3 causes the first test score (TEST1) to be printed in the first three print positions.

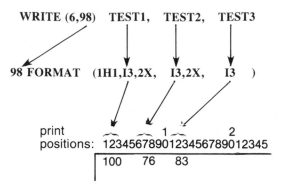

Figure 5.15 Relationship of output data fields, format codes, and variables

The next format code, 2X, represents the **blank format code** used to specify blank positions on an input or output record. This format code does not equate to any variable in memory. It is used to tell the computer to insert spaces (i.e., to skip positions) in the output line. The number before the X format code specifies how many blank positions to skip. Thus, the 2X format code tells the computer to skip two positions from the last position at which it was situated. Since TEST1 is printed in positions 1–3, then positions 4–5 are skipped in the formatted output. The second I3 format code is used to format TEST2 at positions 6–8. The second 2X format code skips positions 9–10. The third I3 format code is used to format TEST3 at positions 11–13. The I/O list of variables is exhausted; therefore, the formatting of the output items terminates, even if there were more format codes remaining in the FORMAT statement.

The same rule for input format codes applies to output format codes. The first variable in the WRITE statement corresponds to the first format code (after the carriage-control specification) in the output FORMAT specifications. It specifies the form and location of the first item (TEST1) to be printed. The second format code is used to format the second variable (TEST2) from the I/O list. The third format code formats the third variable (TEST3) in the I/O list. The relationship of the output variables, format codes, and output results is illustrated in figure 5.15.

The second WRITE statement and its associated FORMAT statement was:

WRITE (6,97) TOTAL, AVE
97 FORMAT (1H0, F6.2,3X, F6.2)

The FORMAT statement numbered 97 is used to provide the format specifications for the second WRITE statement. The values of TOTAL and AVE are to be printed double-spaced below the previous line. The carriage-control character of 1H0 causes the output line to be double-spaced. The value of TOTAL is written as an F6.2 specification. The F format code indicates a decimal field with a decimal point will be written for output. The number following the F specifies the total width of the output field; the digit 6 says the overall field size consists of 6 positions. This field-width specification should be large enough to include an algebraic sign (printed with negative values), the decimal point, and all digits. The decimal point is a necessary separator in the F format code. The last number after the decimal point (in the F format code) tells the number of digits to be printed as fractional digits. Thus the format code F6.2 says to use a six-position output field that includes a decimal point and two fractional digits (which provides for a maximum of three digits to the left of the decimal point).

The second format code 3X causes three positions (7–9) to be skipped so that the second output value is not run together with the first. The third format code F6.2, which includes space for three integer digits, a decimal point, and two fractional digits, is used to print the value of AVE.

The lines of output with their respective values would appear as:

```
print                     1         2
positions:      12345678901234567890
                100   76    83
                259.00    86.33
```

Output fields are always **right-justified** (aligned from the right) in the output-field description (format code). If the output value does not occupy the entire field width, blanks will be inserted in the high-order (left) positions. For example, the value 76 written with an I3 format code would appear on output as Ƅ76 (the Ƅ represents a blank/space). If the output value ever requires more positions than the field width specified in the format code, asterisks will be printed for the output results by most compilers. For example, the value 143 written with an I2 format code would cause two asterisks to be printed as output. The output would not be truncated and printed as 43, as you might expect. The value 259.00 written with a F5.2 format code would cause five asterisks to be printed; as many asterisks are written as are contained in the field width specification. (Note: some compilers may use different symbols, such as ##, to perform the same function as the asterisks.)

Certain rules may be followed in forming format code specifications for formatted output. The input field, of course, determines the format code specifications for formatted input. These rules are discussed for the I, F, and X format codes when used to format output fields.

Integer Field (I Format Code). Always allow room in the width specifications for the maximum number of digits in the integer quantity plus one position for a sign, in case the field has a negative value. Thus, the specification for the minimum integer field should be I2 (one digit plus a sign).

Floating Point (F Format Code). Allow room in the width specification for a sign, the maximum number of integer digits, the decimal point, and the number of fractional digits to be printed. You should always allow room for at least one integer digit, even though the output field consists of all fractional digits. For example, the format code F6.5 is illegal, since the field width of 6 would be consumed by the decimal point and five fractional digits. The minimum field width would be F7.5, with five fractional digits. The minimum field width for a quantity containing only fractional digits would be the number of fractional digits plus two.

A more detailed explanation of the I, F, and other format codes is given in chapter 8. The explicit rules for the formatting of input and output records are also included in chapter 8. The finer points in using complex format specifications take a long time to digest and use correctly. However, complex format specifications are often necessary in various "real-world" applications.

5.9 THE STOP AND END STATEMENTS

The STOP Statement

Once the computer begins the execution of a program, it will continue until (1) the computer or computer operator terminates the job, (2) no more data is available to be read, or (3) an instruction is reached that directs the computer to cease processing the program. The first two types of program termination give us what is called an **abnormal termination**. We can cause a **normal termination** in the program by providing a control statement to signal the computer to stop processing. The control statement most frequently used is the STOP statement.

The STOP statement tells the computer to stop the processing of our program. Program execution is terminated, we are given the output results, and the computer begins processing another person's job. The general form of the STOP statement is given in figure 5.16.

Examples of the STOP statement are:

$$\textbf{76 STOP}$$
$$\textbf{STOP}$$
$$\textbf{STOP 317}$$

The "STOP n" option of the STOP statement consists of the word STOP followed by an integer octal constant of up to five digits, e.g., STOP 266. It has the same effect as the regular STOP statement; but in addition to terminating the program, the word STOP followed by the octal constant is displayed on the computer operator's console typewriter. (An octal constant is a numeric constant in a base-eight number system, with digits ranging from 0 through 7.) If multiple STOP statements have been included in a program, the displayed number provides a record as to the STOP statement which terminated the program. This form of the STOP statement is seldom used.

It is permissible to have multiple STOP statements in a program if conditional testing or branching is used. When a single STOP statement is used in a program, it is normally placed at the end prior to the END statement. This placement, however, is not mandatory. It may be placed anywhere in the program as long as it is the last statement executed in the program logic.

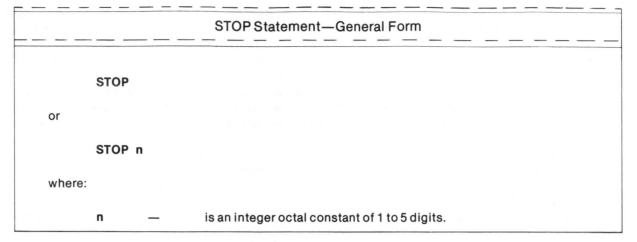

Figure 5.16 General notation of the STOP statement

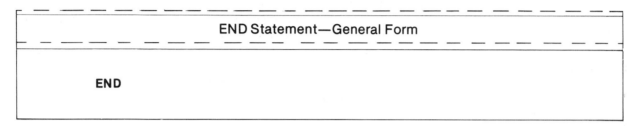

Figure 5.17 General notation of the END statement

In some FORTRAN compilers there is another statement available to terminate program execution: the CALL EXIT. The general form of this statement is simply: CALL EXIT. This statement is actually a call to a system program which performs program wrap-up and termination. It is used in the same manner as the STOP statement. The RETURN statement is used on some systems to terminate a program and return control to the operating system.

THE END STATEMENT

The last statement in every FORTRAN program must be the END statement. This statement simply indicates the end of the program. The END statement does not end processing, as you might be led to believe; the STOP statement causes this action. The END statement is nonexecutable; it is a specification statement used to inform the compiler that no more FORTRAN source statements follow in the program, thus ending program compilation. It is a necessary statement that must be written at the end of all FORTRAN programs.

The END statement consists solely of the word END. It must not have a statement number assigned to it; if it does, a compilation error will occur. Only one END statement is allowed in each FORTRAN program. Figure 5.17 gives the general form of the END statement.

Many beginning students are confused as to the order in which the FORTRAN statements are processed. The computer starts with the first statement and executes the statements in a sequential order. Thus, the order in which the statements are arranged within the program is very important. You cannot place the Assignment statement to compute the average of the test scores before the statement to compute the total. Had you done so, the computed AVE would not have been correct. The computer executes one statement at a time in sequence. When it computes AVE from

$$AVE = TOTAL / 3.0$$

it does not look around or check to see if TOTAL had been calculated already. The computer assumes that you know what you are doing and have already given values to all of the necessary variables for any calculation. If a value has never been defined, the results are, of course, incorrect. Thus, the statements to be executed must be in the proper sequence; otherwise our processing does not match the required logical order of the solution to the problem.

The seven basic statements that we have just discussed are normally used in every FORTRAN program. The discussions in this chapter were intended to give you the basic features of these statements to let you start writing simple FORTRAN programs as soon as possible. Chapters 8 and 9 will present a more detailed explanation, with illustrations and rules on how to use the READ, WRITE, and FORMAT statements for more complicated problems.

The best way to learn to program in FORTRAN is to write FORTRAN programs. You will make mistakes, but so do the most experienced programmers. It is a very rare occurrence for a seasoned programmer to write a lengthy program without a bug (error). The more experience you acquire in writing programs, the easier it becomes to develop and write them.

Programming is partially an art and not a hard science like mathematics. The art of learning to program is analogous to the art of learning to drive a car or to swim. We can talk about driving (or swimming) all day and discuss elaborate techniques to use. But the true test comes when we get behind the wheel (or get into the swimming pool). It is the actual practice that pays off. We may swerve around the road or flounder in a pool at first. Experience is the best teacher. It is with each new attempt that we incorporate the information learned from our previous experiences and become more proficient. So in programming we each apply our own techniques and style learned from ''doing.''

Even though we have written a basic FORTRAN program, there are additional steps that must be completed before one can get results from the computer. In a batch environment you must keypunch the source program statements onto punched cards for entry into the computer. Various control statements must be included with our source deck and data cards to identify your job and specify what you want done. On a timesharing system you type your FORTRAN statements using a terminal and follow the procedure to direct the computer in executing the program.

Once the FORTRAN program has been written, the remaining steps in the computer problem-solving procedure must still be completed. The next step is the preparation of the program for entry on a computer input medium.

5.10   STEP 4—PREPARING THE PROGRAM IN A COMPUTER INPUT MEDIUM

After your FORTRAN source program has been coded, it must be transferred to some input medium to be entered on the computer. In an academic environment the two most common methods used to get a program into a form acceptable to the computer are batch entry and terminal entry. Let us examine these two methods to learn various terms and procedures.

Batch Entry with Punched Cards

FORTRAN statements may be punched into the common 80-column card on the keypunch machine. Each coded line on the coding sheet is punched into one card. Specially designed FORTRAN program cards or any 80-column punched card may be used. The resulting program on punched cards is referred to as a **source deck**, as illustrated in figure 5.18.

You may be required to keypunch your own program. However, many computer centers employ keypunch operators who will punch your program. You simply turn your coded forms in at a designated location and return the next day to pick up the punched deck. From then on, any corrections you make to your program become your responsibility. Thus, keypunch machines are usually available in the computer center for this need. You should read **Appendix C** on the operation of the keypunch if you are not familiar with its use.

After you pick up your punched program (if keypunching is provided by the computer center), you should carefully compare the punched cards with your coded forms. Since keypunch personnel normally have a heavy workload, they do not usually remove any cards they may have punched with an error. For the sake of time they usually leave the error card in the deck and punch the correction in a new card.

The process of checking your punched cards is known as **desk-checking**. You should examine each card to remove any erroneously punched card left by the keypunch operator, to make sure that all statements start in column 7 or later, to make sure that you have not left out a comma or other required punctuation, and to find any other error that may be easily detected. You should desk check your deck even if you punched your own cards. (Note: Desk-checking is also known as **bench checking** by many programmers.)

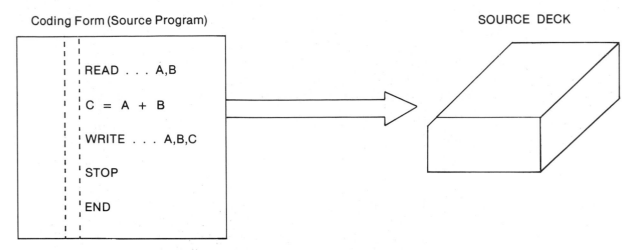

Figure 5.18 Converting a coded program onto punched cards input medium

In preparing a FORTRAN program for the computer, three different types of cards will normally be used. They are:

1. FORTRAN Source Statement cards
2. Job Control Language (JCL) cards
3. Data cards

FORTRAN Source Statements. FORTRAN source statements are the instructions that make up your program. These cards should be arranged in the proper order (as coded) to solve the problem.

Job Control Language (JCL) Cards. **Job control cards,** better known as JCL cards, are needed to communicate various resource needs to the computer. Modern computer systems can process many jobs (tasks) concurrently (this is called *multiprogramming*). A **"JOB" card** is used on most computers to identify the beginning of each new job. The JOB card normally contains the job name, the name of the programmer, and various job accounting information. Additional JCL cards are usually needed to request resources such as a specific compiler, to identify input and output devices, to indicate the beginning of the data cards, and to indicate the end of the data cards. JCL cards to process a FORTRAN job vary by computer and also by installation. Because of the wide variety of JCL cards, the subject of Job Control Language is beyond the scope of this text. The appropriate JCL cards will be explained to you by your instructor for the respective computer system used. **Appendix L** shows the JCL cards in common use on various computer systems.

Data Cards. Data cards are used to contain the data to be read and processed by the program. A data card is distinct from the FORTRAN source statement and is not subject to the same arrangement and rules as the FORTRAN statement. All eighty columns of a data card may be used to contain fields of data. The location of data fields on the data card is unique to each program.

Data cards may contain any of the characters acceptable to the computer system; however, many computers may not be able to print some of these characters, because they are not provided on their printer. Data cards are placed after the end of the FORTRAN program and are preceded by a JCL card to indicate their beginning. The number of data cards and their order are, of course, unique to each execution of a program.

It is possible for a FORTRAN program to generate its own data for processing in the program. To provide much more flexibility and practicality in a program, however, the data to be processed is generally read from some input medium. Data may be read from any input medium, including punched cards, paper tape, magnetic tape, and magnetic disk.

Job Deck. After the three categories of cards have been punched, they are arranged in the proper order to form a **job deck.** Most of the JCL cards will precede your source program. The data cards follow the FORTRAN source deck. The FORTRAN source deck and data cards are separated by a JCL card. A JCL card is normally required after the last data card to mark the end of the job deck. Figure 5.19 illustrates a general job deck setup, showing the placement of the JCL, FORTRAN source statements, and data cards.

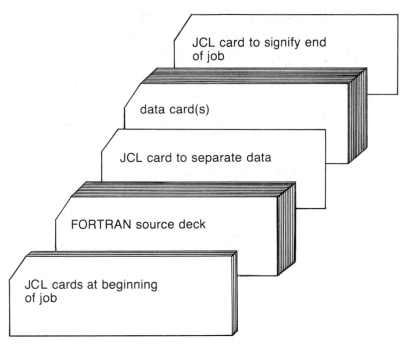

Figure 5.19 Setup for a FORTRAN job deck

Figure 5.20 (p. 146) shows an actual job deck with the three types of cards for a DEC PDP-11 computer using the RSTS/E operating system. The cards with a dollar sign ($) in card column one identify a control card (JCL) to the computer.

Figure 5.21 (p. 147) shows a FORTRAN job deck for an IBM DOS system. The two slashes (//) in card columns 1 and 2 identify a control card to the computer. The first two cards and the last card with an asterisk (*) in column one identify "Power" cards for IBM systems.

The arrangement of the different types of cards and the job deck setup for a NCR 200, Honeywell 60/ 6000, Burroughs 6000, CDC 6000 and Cyber, WATFIV, and IBM DOS computers are shown in **Appendix K**. You must obtain the correct JCL cards and their arrangement from your instructor or the computer center before running your job.

Once you have keypunched your program and arranged the JCL and data cards in your job deck, your FORTRAN job is now ready for submission to the computer facility for entry into the computer. The job deck is loaded into a card reader along with other jobs to be read and stored in the computer system. The start of each job is marked by a job card. You may load your own job deck or turn it in to an operator to load. The mode of operation varies among computer centers.

The use of job decks to be read and processed by the computer is known as **batch processing**. The term batch processing comes from the method of collecting and processing jobs in a batch as the normal mode of operations. When your job deck is read into the computer (by a card reader), it does not get processed immediately unless there are no other jobs in the system. The job deck is actually stored on disk and put in a priority queue. There may be a queue for small jobs arranged in a first-in first-out (FIFO) order of priority. There may be other queues for larger jobs or jobs requiring a tape mount, etc. So don't expect your job to be run immediately after it is read. There is usually a 30-minute wait (**turn around**) to get your results and job deck back, but it may be hours (or even a day) before your job is run, depending on the number of pending jobs. Students usually do not understand why it takes several hours to get their job back at the end of the semester when they received 15-minute turnarounds at the beginning of the semester.

Your job will remain in a queue (holding area) until called for by the computer. When it is identified, the computer determines what is needed from the JCL cards. If a FORTRAN "compile and go" (compile and then execute) job is found, the system calls in the FORTRAN compiler to read the source program and generate the proper machine language instructions for execution. If an error is found in any of the source statements, a syntax error message is produced and printed out along with the source program; no program execution will be attempted. When the source program has no syntax errors, the compiler can generate all the necessary object code.

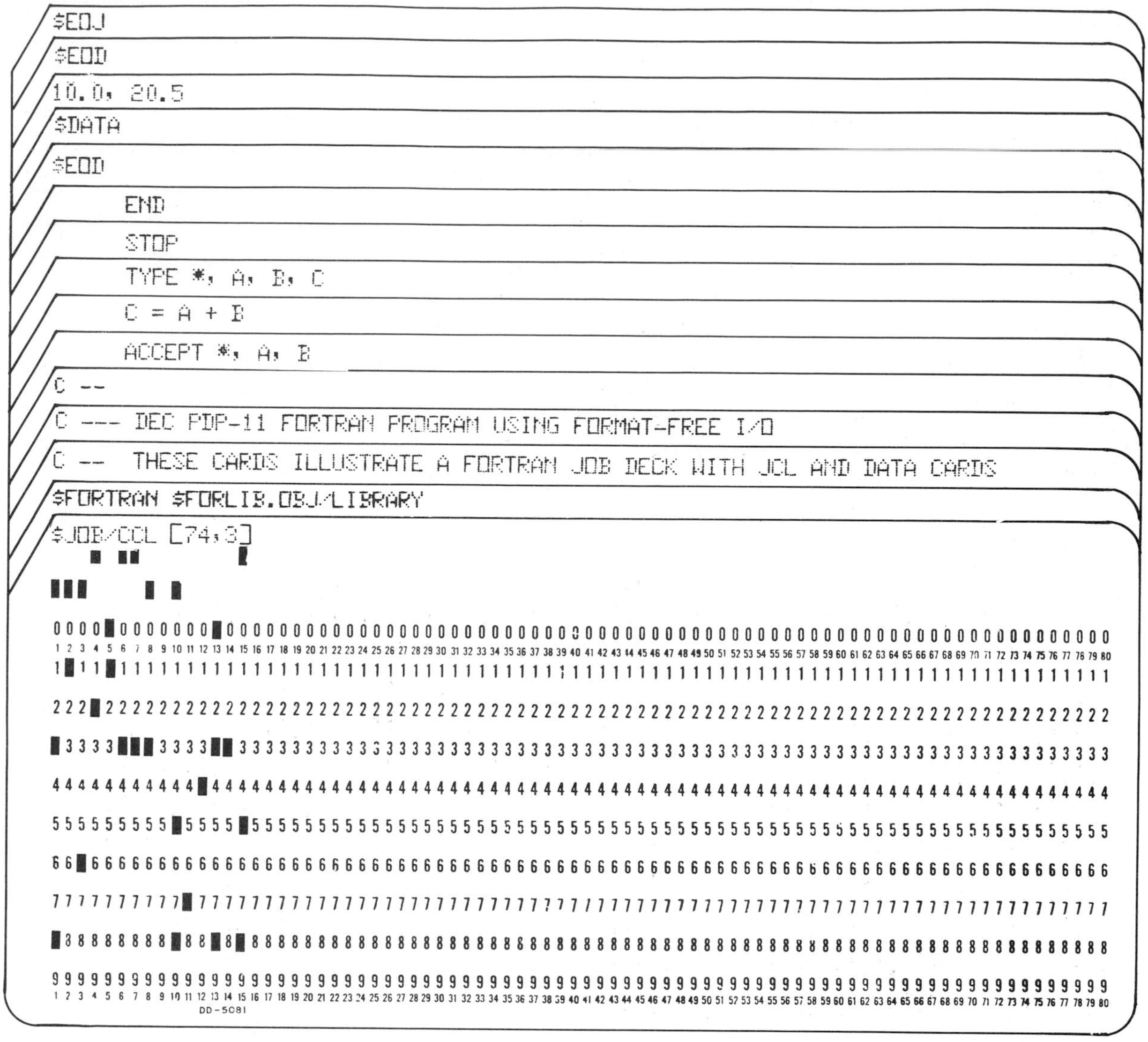

Figure 5.20 FORTRAN job deck for a DEC PDP-11 using RSTS/E

A timesharing system may also be used to perform batch processing. A disk file is built which contains the source program and necessary control statements; then the file is submitted as a job to the operating system. The job is scheduled to run in the same manner as one submitted on punched cards, and output results normally go to the line printer. The results of processing the job may be written to a file (normally a **log file**) which may be reviewed at a terminal to determine the outcome of the processing run.

Entering a FORTRAN Program on a Time Sharing Terminal

FORTRAN programs may also be entered into the computer for compilation and processing by interactive terminals. Terminals such as cathode-ray tubes (CRTs) and typewriters allow the programmer to interact with the computer in a conversational mode. You can create data files on disk and type in your programs over the terminal. The programs may be compiled and executed according to timesharing commands from the terminal, and input data may be entered and output results displayed on the terminal. Chapter 2 discussed programming in a timesharing environment and presented an overview of the concepts involved in this mode of operation. Appendixes E, F, G, H, I, J, and K discuss individual timesharing systems. You must consult your instructor, another experienced user, or obtain the timesharing manual for other systems if you have a timesharing system available for your use.

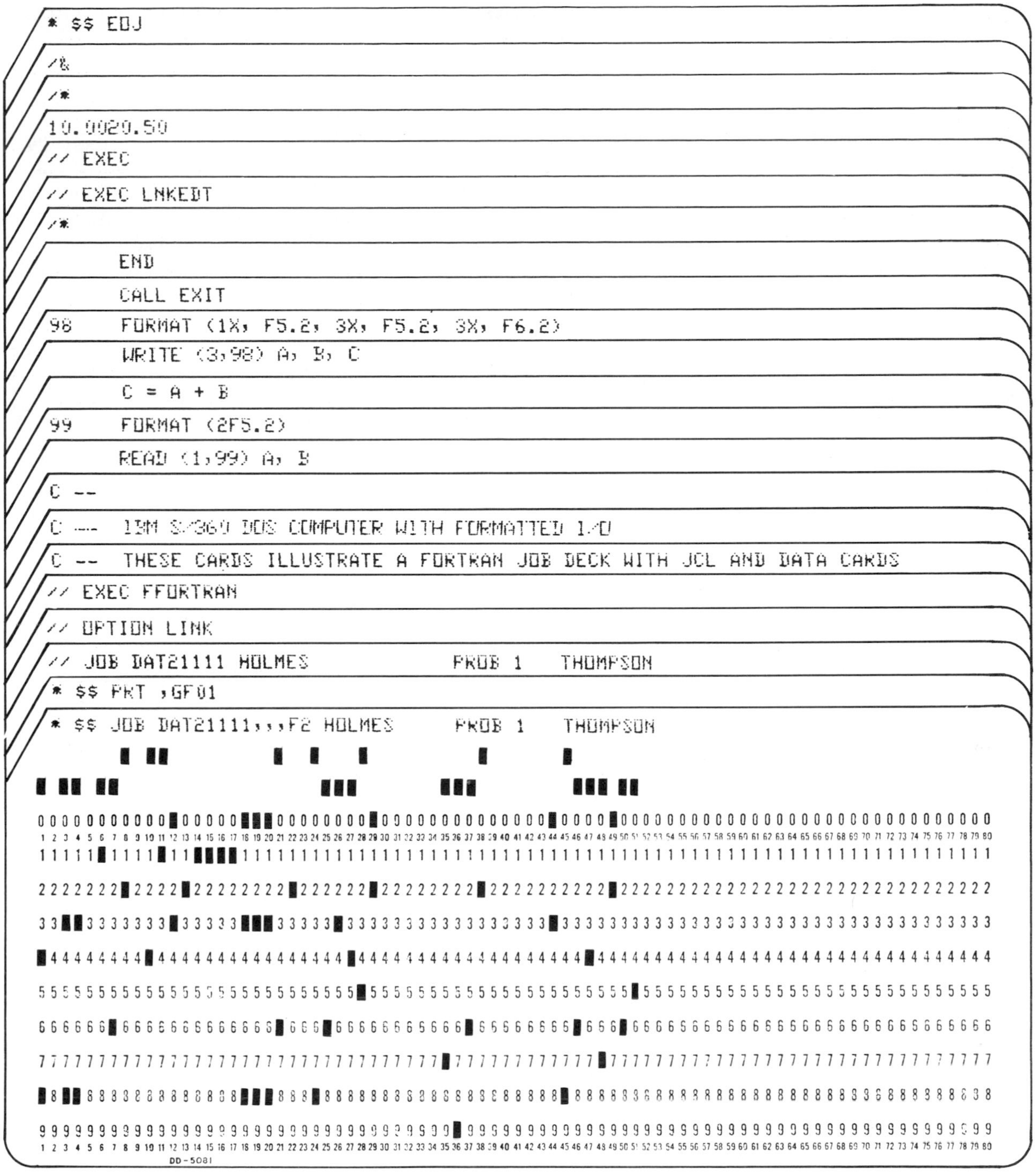

```
* $$ EOJ
/&
/*
10.0020.50
// EXEC
// EXEC LNKEDT
/*
        END
        CALL EXIT
98      FORMAT (1X, F5.2, 3X, F5.2, 3X, F6.2)
        WRITE (3,98) A, B, C
        C = A + B
99      FORMAT (2F5.2)
        READ (1,99) A, B
C --
C --- IBM S/360 DOS COMPUTER WITH FORMATTED I/O
C -- THESE CARDS ILLUSTRATE A FORTRAN JOB DECK WITH JCL AND DATA CARDS
// EXEC FFORTRAN
// OPTION LINK
// JOB DAT21111 HOLMES              PROB 1    THOMPSON
* $$ PRT ,GF01
* $$ JOB DAT21111,,,F2 HOLMES       PROB 1    THOMPSON
```

Figure 5.21 FORTRAN job deck for an IBM S/360 DOS

Once your program is typed for the computer, it may be run and stored on disk for later retrieval. The process of executing your program by the computer is usually the same as if the program had been entered on punched cards. If your program contains syntax errors, you will receive error messages at your terminal or on a special file created by the compiler.

On many computer systems, programs may be processed in both batch and timesharing modes. Normally big programs with large volumes of input data are still run in a batch mode, while short programs with small amounts of input are run under timesharing. Since the FORTRAN programming language can be run over terminals, timesharing is usually the preferred mode of processing.

5.11 STEP 5—RUNNING THE PROGRAM AND CORRECTING STATEMENT CONSTRUCTION (SYNTAX) ERRORS

A program written in a high-level **source language** like FORTRAN must be translated into the **machine language** of the specific computer before execution. Special system programs called **language translators** are available to perform this translation. One such language translator is called a **compiler**, and the process of translating a compiler source language into machine language (or object code) is known as **compiling** or **compilation**. A different compiler must be used for each source language (FORTRAN, COBOL, and so forth). The machine language from a compilation may be saved and rerun later without the time-consuming process of recompiling the source program. Figure 5.22 illustrates the compilation and execution process. The punched card medium of running programs always uses a compiler. Timesharing systems may also use a compiler to translate FORTRAN programs.

An **interpreter** is another type of language translator. It is often used when programs are run in a timesharing mode. The primary advantage of an interpreter is in the speed of program development, since it detects syntax (statement construction) errors *as* each statement is entered at the terminal. An interpreter does not generate any object *program* from a source program, but interprets and executes *each instruction* as it goes through the program.

If a FORTRAN interpreter is used to process programs, the interpreter will syntax-check your statements as each line is entered. If a FORTRAN compiler is used, *all* the statements are entered before the compilation is performed. A compiler reads your source program one statement at a time. The translation of source programs occurs completely independently of the programmer. The conversion and execution of a program is left to the computer. For a few runs, it is very likely that the student will receive a listing that contains a number of error messages instead of the expected answers. These error messages are printed by the compiler during the program compilation. The FORTRAN compiler scans the program one statement at a time, checking for the correct syntax. **Syntax** is the construction or grammatical arrangement according to the rules of the FORTRAN language. If the compiler encounters a misspelled keyword, an extra comma, an incorrectly formed constant or variable, or any statement that is incorrectly formed, a message is printed to flag the error.

These error messages are called **diagnostic or syntax messages** since their purpose is to help you "diagnose" the statement in error. The form of these diagnostic messages varies from compiler to compiler. Some compilers will print only an error message number, which may be found in a manual with a corresponding description of the probable error. Other compilers, like the WATFOR and WATFIV compilers, print a highly descriptive error message that is clearer and more understandable.

There are two types of diagnostic messages that may be produced in the program—error and warning. **Error messages** will cause termination of the program during the compiling phase, and no object code is generated. All errors must be corrected before the program can be processed. **Warning messages** tell us that a violation of some FORTRAN rule occurred but was not severe enough to prevent the compilation of the program. The program, in most cases, may still be executed.

The error message is normally printed immediately below the statement in error. In some cases, however, the error message may actually appear below the statement just *after* the one in error. This happens because the compiler may not detect an error until the statement immediately following the one in error has been read. This is understandable, since statements may be continued on additional cards.

Most compilers attempt to indicate the general area of the error by printing a special symbol such as a $ or * as near the error as possible. In most cases, the "flagging" symbol is printed below the character in error. For example, if you omitted a comma in the I/O list of a READ statement and thus exceeded the maximum length of a variable, the IBM G compiler would print diagnostic messages as follows:

READ (5,99) TEST1, TEST2 TEST3
$

01) IEY003I NAME LENGTH

Note the $ printed beneath the E in the third variable. Since this is the seventh character in forming a variable name, the compiler knows that an error has been made. It doesn't know whether you omitted a comma or tried to use a variable name longer than six characters. So the error message number 01 (the first one found), reading "IEY003I NAME LENGTH," is printed.

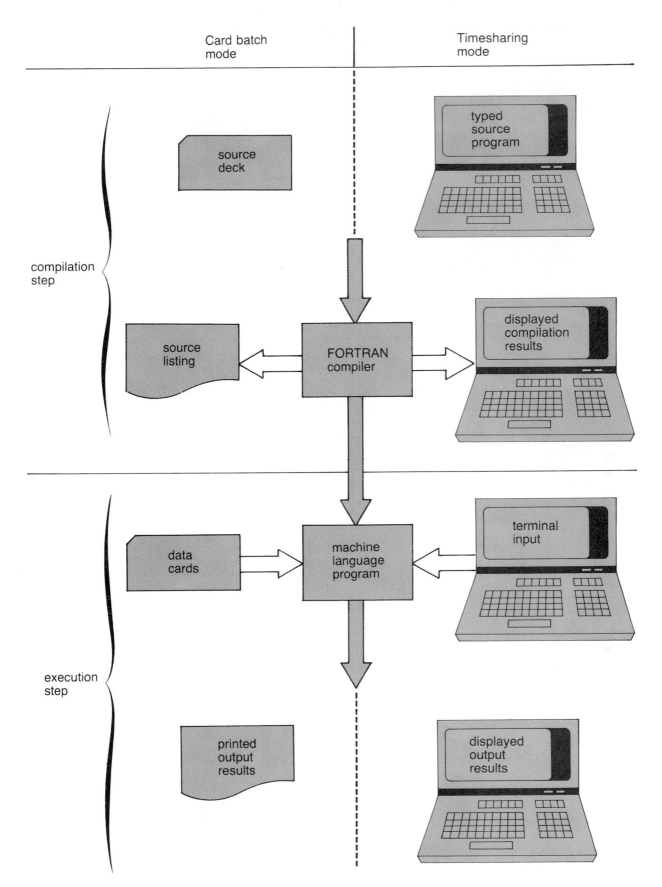

Figure 5.22 The compilation and execution process

As mentioned before, the error message may or may not be descriptive of the error. But you know a syntax error has been found. A manual of error messages, which explains the IEY003I type, may be consulted for a better explanation of what may have caused the error. Some of the more common syntax messages found in IBM compilers follow:

Message	Explanation
IEY001I ILLEGAL TYPE	The type of a constant, a variable, or an expression is not correct for its usage.
IEY002I LABEL	The statement in question is unlabeled.
IEY003I NAME LENGTH	The name of a variable exceeds six characters in length; or two variable names appear in an expression without a separating operation symbol.
IEY004I COMMA	The comma required in the statement has been omitted.
IEY005I ILLEGAL LABEL	Illegal use of a statement label. For example, an attempt is made to branch to the label of a FORMAT statement.
IEY013I SYNTAX	The statement or part of a statement does not conform to the FORTRAN IV syntax.
IEY015I NO END CARD	An END statement is missing.
IEY022I UNDEFINED LABELS	A reference is made to a statement label which does not appear in the problem.

The WATFOR and WATFIV compilers provide much better explanatory messages. Figure 5.23 illustrates some examples of syntax errors that might occur in our basic program to compute the total and average of three test scores.

The first message indicates that we have used too long a variable name, whereas, in reality, we omitted the needed comma. The second message tells us that we forgot to include the closing parenthesis. The third message says that the format code for X is formed incorrectly. There must be a width part even if you really only want to skip one space (1X). The fourth example tells us that statement number 98 is already used and, thus, that we have a duplicate label. The fifth error is the type that appears when we misspell a keyword; the compiler doesn't know what we are trying to tell it. The sixth error refers to a statement number that does not exist in the program. The wrong number is punched on the third FORMAT statement. It should have been labeled 97 instead of 98. The compiler doesn't know this, but it knows that we should have a statement with the label 97, since it is referenced in the second WRITE statement.

The last syntax message brings us to a discussion of the second location of syntax messages in a program. All the source statements may have been formed correctly according to the syntax rules, but if we forget to include a referenced statement in the program or make an error such as punching the wrong label, the compiler will catch it. The statement may have been placed near the end of our program, so the compiler could not have detected a missing statement number until all statements had been scanned. Thus, any unresolved statement numbers are included in error messages that are printed after the end of the program. So make sure you also look for any syntax messages following your program as well as inside the program.

Most compilers provide a count of the number of syntax errors found in your program. This information is usually located after the program listing or on the next page. To make sure you have located all syntax errors, check the printed count with the number you have found. If a program does not contain any syntax errors, the count message will indicate 0 errors found.

Always try to locate and analyze the syntax errors yourself. Don't immediately rush off to find your instructor or someone else to point out the error for you. The trait of a good programmer is the ability to find syntax errors himself. The compiler does the best it can to identify the error and its location in a statement. Use the diagnostic messages to help you find the error. Go to your manual and reread the rules (general notation) for the statements.

```
                  READ (5,99) NTEST1, NTEST2 NTEST3
**WARNING**   NAME NTEST2NTEST3 IS TOO LONG; TRUNCATED TO SIX CHARACTERS
                  99 FORMAT (I3, I3, I3
***ERROR***   NO CLOSING PARENTHESIS
                  TOTAL = NTEST1 + NTEST2 + NTEST3
                  AVE = TOTAL / 3.0
                  WRITE (6,98) NTEST1, NTEST2, NTEST3
                  98 FORMAT (1H1, I3, X, I3, 2X, I3)
***ERROR***   INVALID FIELD OR GROUP COUNT NEAR 3, X
                  WRITE (6,97) TOTAL, AVE
                  98 FORMAT (1H0, F6.2, 3X, F6.2)
**WARNING**   STATEMENT NUMBER 98 HAS ALREADY BEEN DEFINED
                  SOTP
***ERROR***   UNDECODEABLE STATEMENT
                  END
***ERROR***   MISSING STATEMENT NUMBER 97
```

Figure 5.23 Sample program with syntax error messages from WATFOR and WATFIV

Some syntax errors are extremely hard to find. You may have punched the letter ''O'' instead of the digit ''0'' (zero) for a statement number. Both characters look very much alike on the printed page, but to the compiler, they are completely different. The letter ''O'' is normally squared at the corners, while the digit ''0'' has rounded corners. Examine each character very closely. You may also need to examine the preceding statements. The more practice you have in locating compilation errors, the easier it becomes to spot them. Skill in locating errors comes only through experience. Being able to detect and correct syntax errors is a sign that you truly understand the FORTRAN language.

The best thing to do is to correct all the errors you can find and resubmit your program for another run. Fixing one error will, quite often, cause other obscure syntax messages to disappear. But do not resubmit your program simply hoping that all the errors will go away. If the compiler detected errors during the first run, and you did not make any corrections, rest assured that the same errors will be there in the next run.

Sometimes correcting one error may cause new errors to appear, but this is highly infrequent. Don't panic if you can't find all the errors. Take a break and come back to the program later. Your thinking may have fallen into a rut, and looking at the problem later may give you new ideas. When you can't find the error after an intensive search, don't be afraid to ask your fellow students if they can spot the error. Everyone likes to be an expert at finding bugs, so they should be eager to assist you. When all else fails, see your instructor or another expert in the language.

Many types of compilation errors can occur from FORTRAN statements. Every error must be found and corrected in order for the computer to be able to execute your program. However, after the program is clean of all compilation errors, it may still contain logic errors.

5.12 STEP 6—TESTING FOR LOGIC ERRORS AND DEBUGGING THE PROGRAM

After all compilation errors are removed, you enter the cycle of testing and debugging a program. The output must be checked to verify the results. A program may produce answers, but they may be incorrect. Therefore, the program must be modified and rerun for new results. This cycle continues until the correct output results are obtained.

Logic errors result from the programmer's failure to understand the problem requirements or from an oversight in the required logic. They may be caused by performing a calculation incorrectly, reading the input data from the wrong card columns, using the wrong variable, or having the source statements in a sequence that performs the logic incorrectly. Sometimes the input data may be punched wrong; cards may also have been dropped from a source deck or the data deck.

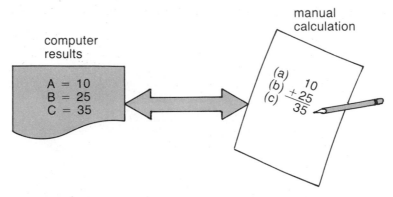

Figure 5.24 Comparing computer output results with manual calculations

The best way for the student to check whether the correct results are produced is to make hand calculations from some of the data used and determine what output results are expected. Output results are compared to manually calculated answers to verify program correctness (see figure 5.24). Simple integer values—1, 2, 10—should be used as test data if complex calculations are made with decimal (fractional) numbers in the actual implementation. They are easier to hand-calculate than decimal numbers to see if a program is correct. Hand calculations for one set of data required for each alternative logic route in the program will usually suffice. That is, if a program reads data from a record, uses that data in various calculations, prints the results, and then returns to read additional reports to do the same operations, it is necessary only to compute the results for the data from one record by hand. If the hand calculations for the data on one record match the computer results, the rest of the data records will probably be correct. One reason for first using test data in program testing (as opposed to live or operational data) is the vast volume of data in live files, which may contain thousands of data records. It is foolish and very time-consuming to begin the initial testing of a program with such a large number of data records. A small number of test records (20 or 100 cases) will require less computer time (and your time) during this phase.

When incorrect output results are produced, **play computer.** Follow the program through manually. You can usually pinpoint a logic error to a particular statement or group of statements. Examine each of these statements carefully and describe verbally what actions the statement is telling the computer to do—not what you want it to do. For example, you might be trying to read data on unit 6, the printer, or write data on unit 5, the card reader. These actions are impossible, but no error message will be issued as a result of these statements. Describing the specified actions orally often helps you detect errors.

To ensure that the data has been read correctly, **echo check** the input values. That is, include a WRITE statement after the READ to make sure that the input values are read and stored correctly. If there are many calculations in your program, write out the intermediate results to determine whether the calculations are right. Many techniques can be used to debug logic errors in your program. Chapter 7 describes the procedures and techniques you can use for complex logic problems. At this stage, follow your simple programs through manually and don't go to the trouble of including extensive trace and debug routines. Again, experience in finding your own logic errors will benefit you in the long run.

Many logical errors can be avoided by spending a bit more time in the planning phase of programming (analyzing the problem, flowcharting the logic, writing the code, and desk-checking the program). The better job you do in these steps, the less time you will have to spend in the testing and debugging phase. The structured approach to programming emphasizes spending more time in the design phase, generally resulting in a more error-free program.

5.13 STEPS 7 AND 8—IMPLEMENTING AND DOCUMENTING THE PROGRAM AND PROBLEM SOLUTION

This section discusses the final two steps in producing a correct and workable program. There are some actions you must take to finally implement your program. You must also wrap up all the documentation needed to accompany the completed program.

Step 7—Implementing the Completed Program with Operational Data

In an operational environment you must schedule a run with "live" data to perform a final test on the new system. A system is considered to be one or more programs which meet some application requirement. An acceptance-test run is scheduled with the computer operations department to allow the user to "buy off" on (accept) the finished product. The user will evaluate the output products and determine if the program meets all the problem specifications and requirements. If the new system passes the user acceptance test, then the system is put into production for operational processing.

You must provide certain documentation to computer operators so that they will know when and how to run the program(s). A schedule is established to reflect the cyclic period in which the system is run. A cycle may occur daily, semiweekly, weekly, bi-weekly, monthly, quarterly, and so on.

In an academic environment you must run the program with the set of data or data file specified by your instructor. Your instructor has checked out the program with specific data and knows the correct answers resulting from a standard set of data used by all students; so he can confirm whether your program works correctly. The instructor may include data that tests your program to see whether you have checked for various errors or have covered all possible alternative routes through the program.

If you have used simple test data to check your program during the testing and debugging step, then you must run the program with the expected data. Don't forget to verify the results produced by this live data. You may have overlooked something in your logic which the live data will catch. After verifying that your output results are correct, complete the necessary documentation to accompany your source program and output answers.

Step 8—Completing the Program and Problem Solution Documentation

Program documentation should be prepared as you progress in a project. In a work environment, there is no guarantee that you will finish a project. You may be switched to a higher priority project because of your expertise; you may get sick or even die. Therefore, protect the continuity of a project by documenting what has happened along the way.

Program documentation is usually kept in a notebook or filing folders in a central location. The final documentation is not kept at a programmer's desk, as some might believe. Other people need access to it, so it must be professionally done and available to them. A programmer may keep rough notes of meetings, problems, and other important facts that happened on the project. The pertinent notes, such as changes to the problem specifications (yes, users do change their minds), should be recorded in the formal program documentation. Other notes such as rough algorithms and detail techniques may be passed on to the person who maintains the programs.

Just because you wrote a program doesn't mean that you will always be responsible for it. There are two types of programming work in a data processing department—new program development and maintenance. At least half of the programmers in most data processing organizations perform maintenance work. **Program maintenance** is the task of eliminating errors and keeping operational programs in satisfactory working condition. Maintenance entails the correction of program bugs that may not show up until weeks or even months after a program is implemented. Some one, not necessarily the person who wrote the program, must be assigned to troubleshoot and correct any errors found in operational programs. The person responsible for maintaining a set of programs (which may range from one to a hundred depending upon their complexity) also performs program modification.

Program modification is the activity of making **enhancements** or new changes to a program. User requirements are dynamic; they are constantly changing due to new procedures or additional needs. A maintenance programmer may be asked to add a new field in a report, provide new totals, sort the report in a new sequence, provide additional control breaks, and so on. Junior programmers may be assigned the task of program maintenance when they first join an organization. This is a good way to learn techniques and how other people solve problems. It is indeed a good education and experience to go through other people's codes. You learn what is good and adopt those techniques; you learn what is bad and avoid those techniques.

In an operational environment you must document every feature of the problem solution that would help someone else understand the program. Remember, someone else will eventually inherit your program. So, consider the documentation as being for others. The author of a program will soon forget the details of the logic and the other aspects of the problem solution. Good documentation is a ''must'' for an organization.

Sufficient documentation in an operational environment consists of the following items:

1. A copy of the project or program specifications as established by the user. Any changes to the original specifications should also be included.
2. A copy of the latest version of the source program, which should include the programmer's name, date written, and date revised.
3. A copy of the Job Control Language (JCL) needed to run the program.
4. A system flowchart to show the input and output files associated with the system.
5. A description of the input and output files, including the print layout form and record layout (multiple-card layout) sheets.
6. A flowchart or other design tool to reflect the logic of the program.
7. A sample output report to show what the results look like.
8. The set of test data used to test and debug the program.
9. The results produced from the test data.
10. A narrative of any complex algorithms or techniques used in the problem solution.
11. Information about the processing of the system, such as what steps to take when a program aborts, how many backup cycles are kept, when the program is to be run, distribution of the output products, and so on.
12. Any other information pertinent to the system.

In an academic environment, such extensive documentation is not needed. In a programming class you normally turn in three or four documents as shown in figure 5.25. These are:

1. A copy of your source program, with your name and the date.
2. The output results produced by the program. These are included in the same listing after the end of the source program in a compile-and-go environment.
3. The design tool used to represent the development of the program. This may include a structure chart, pseudocode, flowchart, or whatever is required by your instructor.
4. A comment sheet reflecting any problems encountered, how much time was spent on the program, any assistance received on the program, how many runs were made, complex algorithms used, and so on.

In addition, internal program documentation is normally recommended at the following locations:

1. At the beginning of the program you should include comments to identify the program, yourself, date written, and revision date (if the program is being revised). A brief overview of the program's purpose and function should also be included. A recommended format is:

```
C – – – PROGRAM TO . . . (provide the program's objective)
C – – – PROGRAMMER: J W COLE
C – – – DATE WRITTEN: 3/3/78
C – – – DATE REVISED: 2/6/82
C
C – – – PURPOSE: THIS PROGRAM . . . (describe its function)
C
```

2. Prior to the input statements to describe the input items.
3. At the beginning of each segment of code (routine) that performs a discrete function (task).
4. At each decision point, to explain the alternative paths.
5. At each subroutine (a type of subprogram) call.
6. At the beginning of each subroutine.
7. Prior to the output statements, to explain the output items.

Obviously, most of the internal documentation will be in the processing procedures of calculations and decision making. Be sure to tell what the routine or statement is *doing*, rather than ''parroting'' the statement itself.

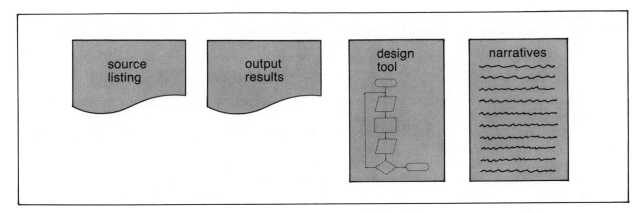

Figure 5.25 Completing the program and problem documentation package

The documentation is usually graded, as well as the program and its output results. Therefore, you should do a professional job on the documentation turned in to your instructor or grader. Quality documentation makes a good impression on the grader and may result in a higher grade for the assigned problem.

5.14 LANGUAGE EXTENSIONS IN FORTRAN DIALECTS (FORMAT-FREE INPUT/OUTPUT STATEMENTS)

Many FORTRAN compilers provide format-free forms of input and output statements that are easy to use in reading and writing data. With format-free I/O statements, you need not worry about the confusing data-field specifications for formatting the input and output records. Instead, you can concentrate on the basic principles of programming.

ANSI FORTRAN 66 allows only the use of the general formatted READ and WRITE statements, which use a corresponding FORMAT statement to describe the form and position of input data fields and output results. Formatted input and output specifications are a complex and difficult capability for the beginning student to master. Nearly one-half of students' program errors occur in FORMAT statements. To eliminate student frustration and avoid many program errors, the ANSI 66 nonstandard format-free I/O statements are now available on WATFOR, WATFIV, WATFIV-S, HP 3000, IBM, CDC, Honeywell, DEC PDP-11, VAX-11, Univac, ANSI FORTRAN 77, and other FORTRAN compilers.

The use of format-free I/O statements is both taught and actively encouraged by many instructors. If your version of FORTRAN does not have the format-free I/O statements, you must, of course, use the general formatted READ and WRITE statements with corresponding FORMAT statements for your input and output operations. This section discusses the forms of the format-free input/output statements available in many FORTRAN compilers.

Format-free Input Statements

The READ statement is the format-free input statement that tells the compiler to read data values from a punched card or terminal and to store them in memory. It tells how many items are to be read and gives the variable names at which the items are to be stored. One value is read for each variable in the I/O list of the READ statement. The first input value goes into the first variable, the second into the second, and so on, until the number of values read agrees with the number of variables given in the READ statement.

The general form for the syntax construction of the format-free READ statement is given in figure 5.26 (p. 156).

Examples of the format-free READ statement are:

$$\textbf{READ *, A, B, C}$$
$$\textbf{20 READ *, HOURS}$$
$$\textbf{READ *, X, Y}$$

The first example tells the computer to read three input values and store them at the variables A, B, and C, respectively. The second example directs the computer to read only one value and place it in the variable HOURS. The third example will cause the computer to read two values and to store them at the variables X and Y, respectively.

```
 ┌────────────────────────────────────────────────────────────────────────┐
 ┊              Format-free READ Statement—General Form                      ┊
 ├────────────────────────────────────────────────────────────────────────┤
 │                                                                          │
 │        READ *, I/O list                                                  │
 │                                                                          │
 │  where:                                                                  │
 │                                                                          │
 │        I/O list—is a list of one or more variable names representing     │
 │           memory locations into which a corresponding number of input    │
 │           values are read.                                               │
 └────────────────────────────────────────────────────────────────────────┘
```

Figure 5.26 General notation of the format-free READ statement for FORTRAN 77

The form of the format-free input statement varies among computers. Some computers require only a comma after the keyword READ (instead of the ''*,'') in their version of FORTRAN. The WATFOR and WATFIV compilers use this simpler form. Other computer systems may use a different keyword instead of READ. The DEC PDP-11 and HP 3000 FORTRAN compilers use the keyword ACCEPT as well as the READ statement. Table 5.3 gives the keyword and syntax for the format-free input statement on different FORTRAN compilers. Your instructor will inform you of the correct form on your system if it is not given in Table 5.3.

Table 5.3 Format-free Input Statements for Various FORTRAN Compilers

FORTRAN Compiler	Syntax Form	Example
ANSI 77	READ *, I/O list	READ *, A, B, C
Burroughs 6000	READ /, I/O list	READ /, A, B, C
CDC (MNF)	READ *, I/O list	READ *, A, B, C
DEC PDP-11	ACCEPT *, I/O list	ACCEPT *, A, B, C
Honeywell 6000	READ, I/O list	READ, A, B, C
HP 3000	ACCEPT I/O list	ACCEPT A, B, C
	or	
	READ (5,*) I/O list	READ (5,*) A, B, C
IBM (G1)	READ *, I/O list	READ *, A, B, C
VAX-11	READ *, I/O list	READ *, A, B, C
	or	
	READ (5,*) I/O list	READ (5,*) A, B, C
	or	
	ACCEPT *, I/O list	ACCEPT *, A, B, C
WATFIV	READ, I/O list	READ, A, B, C
	or	
	READ (5,*) I/O list	READ (5,*) A, B, C
WATFOR	READ, I/O list	READ, A, B, C
	or	
	READ (5,*) I/O list	READ (5,*) A, B, C
UNIVAC 1100	READ *, I/O list	READ *, A, B, C
Your System		

The next topic of discussion is how to keypunch or type values into the data records to be read by the format-free input statements.

Format of Data Values For the Format-free Input Statement

Data values may be punched in any column of a punched card, since the computer will scan the card until it comes to a data value. Generally, however, you punch your data fields starting in column 1. If more than one data value is punched on the same card, the values must be separated from each other by a comma (some systems permit one or more blank columns to be used instead of the comma) to indicate that additional data values

PRINT *, I/O list

where:

I/O list—is an optional list of items which may include one or more variables, numeric constants, arithmetic expressions, and/or literal string constants.

Figure 5.27 General notation of the format-free PRINT statement for FORTRAN 77

follow. The values must be given in the same left-to-right order as the order of the variables in the I/O list of the input statement. That is, if the value 10.5 is to be read for the variable X and the value 35.2 is to be read for the variable Y in the READ statement

READ *, X, Y

then the value 10.5 must be given first in the input record and then the value 35.2.

For terminal input, multiple data values, entered on the same line, are typed with a comma to separate values. The typed line to enter the values 10.5 and 35.2 for the variables X and Y, respectively, in the READ statement

READ *, X, Y

would be typed as:

10.5,35.2

Spaces are normally allowed after a comma and before a new data value. Many timesharing systems will prompt you for input values during program execution by typing a question mark (?) at the beginning of the line on which you are to enter the values. If you have a format-free input statement which reads two variables and you only type in one data value, the system will respond (on a new line) with another question mark to let you know that it is expecting more input values. Good programming technique would include a PRINT (or WRITE) statement before the input statement to describe the type of values to enter.

Now let's look at the format-free output statement used in FORTRAN programs.

The Format-free Output Statement

The PRINT statement is normally the format-free output statement used to communicate the output results to a line printer in a batch card mode or to the terminal in an interactive timesharing mode of operation. The keyword PRINT is followed by an asterisk (*), a comma, and then the I/O list of variables and/or literals to be displayed. The general format notation of the format-free PRINT statement is given in figure 5.27.

Examples of the format-free PRINT statement are:

```
   PRINT *, A, B, C
30 PRINT *, A, B, A+B
   PRINT *, A, B, 'SUM = ', A+B
40 PRINT *, 'STUDENT ID', 'HOURS', 'RATE'
   PRINT *, ' '
```

The first example prints the contents of the three variables A, B, and C. The second example prints the contents of the two variables A and B and the results of calculating the A + B. The third example prints the contents of the two variables A and B, the literal string 'SUM = ', and the results of A + B. The fourth example prints the three literal strings of 'STUDENT ID', 'HOURS', and 'RATE' used for column headings over output fields. The fifth example prints the literal string ' ' which is a way of printing a blank line in case double-spacing is desired between lines of output.

The I/O list of output items, therefore, may be one of the following options:

1. One or more variables.
2. One or more numeric constants.
3. One or more arithmetic expressions.
4. One or more literal strings (literal constants).
5. Any combination of the above four options.

The format-free PRINT statement is formed without the asterisk (*) after the keyword PRINT on some compilers, such as the WATFOR, WATFIV, and WATFIV-S. Other keywords are used in addition to the keyword PRINT on some systems. The DEC PDP-11 FORTRAN compiler uses the keyword TYPE as well as PRINT. The HP 3000 FORTRAN compiler uses the keyword DISPLAY. Table 5.4 shows the keywords and syntax forms that must be used on different computer systems. Your instructor will inform you of the correct form on your system, if it is not included in Table 5.4.

The next question to be answered is how the output values are formatted from the format-free output statements if no format codes are used.

Format of Output Results From the Format-free Output Statements

The form of the output values from the format-free output statements are machine independent and vary from one FORTRAN compiler to another. On some systems, such as WATFOR and WATFIV, all numeric values are displayed in exponential form. (See Appendix D if you are unfamiliar with the scientific or exponential notation for representing numbers.) On most other systems, the output items are printed according to their specific type. That is, integer values are printed as whole numbers without a decimal point. Real (decimal) values are

Table 5.4 Format-free Output Statements for Various FORTRAN Compilers

FORTRAN Compiler	Syntax Form	Example
ANSI 77	PRINT *, I/O list	PRINT *, 'A = ', A
Burroughs 6000	PRINT /, I/O list	PRINT /, "A = ", A
	or	
	PRINT //, I/O list	PRINT //, 'A = ', A
	or	
	PRINT */, I/O list	PRINT */, A
CDC (MNF)	PRINT *, I/O list	PRINT *, 'A = ', A
DEC PDP-11	TYPE *, I/O list	TYPE *, 'A = ', A
Honeywell 6000	PRINT, I/O list	PRINT, "A = ", A
HP 3000	DISPLAY I/O list	DISPLAY "A = ", A
	or	
	WRITE (6, *) I/O list	WRITE (6, *) "A = ", A
IBM (G1)	PRINT *, I/O list	PRINT *, A
	or	
	WRITE (6,*) I/O list	WRITE (6,*) A
VAX-11	PRINT *, I/O list	PRINT *, 'A = ', A
	or	
	WRITE (6,*) I/O list	WRITE (6,*) 'A = ', A
	or	
	TYPE *, I/O list	TYPE *, 'A = ', A
WATFIV	PRINT, I/O list	PRINT, 'A = ', A
	or	
	WRITE (6,*) I/O list	WRITE (6,*)'A = ', A
WATFOR	PRINT, I/O list	PRINT, 'A = ', A
	or	
	WRITE (6,*) I/O list	WRITE (6,*) 'A = ', A
UNIVAC 1100	PRINT *, I/O list	PRINT *, 'A = ', A
Your System		

printed in decimal form if the number is small enough; otherwise the decimal value is printed in exponential form. The number of output items allowed on one line and the horizontal spacing of these values also vary from system to system. A "wrap-around" (fields forced to be printed on the next line) will occur if the line limit is exceeded.

File Unit Numbers

The file unit number (which designates the device a data file is read from or written to with the formatted I/O statements) depends on the computer system and compiler being used. Most FORTRAN compilers use unit number 5 for input from punched cards in a batch mode and from a terminal in an interactive timesharing mode. Most compilers use unit number 6 for output to the line printer in a batch mode and to the terminal in a timesharing mode.

The IBM Disk Operating System (DOS) uses file unit number 1 to indicate the card reader in a batch mode and file unit number 3 to indicate printed output on the line printer. Some Honeywell systems may use unit number 41 for the card reader and unit number 42 for the line printer. Your instructor will tell you the file unit numbers for the standard card reader and line printer files if they are not 5 and 6, respectively.

5.15 SUMMARY

This chapter discussed and implemented (by developing and processing a short FORTRAN program) the eight steps outlined in chapter 3 for solving a problem with a computer. These sections should have provided you with enough background information to understand the procedure of problem solving with a programming language like FORTRAN and how to accomplish a workable program. You should study and understand these eight steps to know the proper procedure to complete your assigned lab problems. The developed program used the seven basic statements that will be included in nearly every FORTRAN program you will write.

The eight computer problem solving steps are summarized here. First, analyze the problem specifications and understand all the problem requirements. Determine what answers and output results are expected from the problem solution.

The second step is one of the most important steps. You must develop the algorithm which depicts the computer solution to the problem. Time and quality effort expended in this step will pay off in later steps. If you do a poor job designing the computer solution, you will experience difficulty in coding the program and may expend much time and effort getting your program to work correctly. You will also avoid much frustration if you desk check your algorithm solution and make sure that it works before attempting to write the FORTRAN program.

Several tools may be used to show the computer solution for a problem. One frequently used tool is a flowchart. Pseudocode is another tool to express the logic for a program. Pseudocode is very beneficial because it requires development of a computer solution in a top-down manner. No jumping around or transfer of control is shown as in flowcharting.

The next six steps constitute the implementation phase of the computer problem-solving procedure:

The third step is writing the algorithm solution in a programming language, in this case, FORTRAN. The example program introduced the basic FORTRAN statements you will use in most programs: the Explicit Type statement to explicitly identify given variables by a specific type such as integer or real; the READ statement, used to obtain input values from a punched card or a terminal (or disk and tape files); the WRITE statement, used to print output lines to the line printer or to a terminal; the FORMAT statement required to provide format specifications on how data is to be read from the input data record and displayed on output; the Assignment statement, to assign a value to a variable or to perform calculations; the STOP statement, to terminate the execution of the program; the END statement, which must be included as the last statement in a FORTRAN program to tell the compiler where the program ends.

The fourth step is to prepare the coded program for entry into the computer for processing. Punched cards are used for the input medium in a batch card environment, while a terminal is used in an interactive or timesharing batch environment. JCL cards and data cards must be included with a FORTRAN source deck to provide a complete job deck to be read by a card reader. The JCL cards tell the computer what resources are needed to process the job. In an interactive, timesharing mode of operation, you may simply give the command RUN on many systems for the computer to execute your program.

The fifth step is to locate and correct any syntax errors detected by the compiler. Diagnostic messages are printed to inform you of any error and the statement in which the error occurred. Fatal errors will prevent your program from executing; a warning message indicates some small error (not severe enough to prevent program execution). After all syntax errors are corrected, rerun your program in hope that it will now execute.

Step six is known as testing and debugging. If the output results from the executed program are not correct, you may have a logic error (bug) in your program. Always check first to make sure the data was correct. Play computer and step through your program, using simple test data to verify the logic. After locating and correcting all logic errors that you can find, rerun the program until the correct results are produced.

In step seven, run the program with the data required by the lab problem specifications—the "live" or actual data against with which the output results are graded. Step eight is the preparation of the documentation required for the problem solution. When completed, the documentation is given to your instructor.

The form of the FORTRAN 77 format-free input statement is the keyword READ followed by an asterisk, a comma, and the I/O list of variables. The form of the FORTRAN 77 format-free output statement is the keyword PRINT followed by an asterisk, a comma, and the I/O list of variables and/or literal constants. Other compilers may use different keywords or variations of the FORTRAN 77 form. The format-free input/output statements greatly reduce syntax errors and the accompanying frustration for beginning programmers.

5.16 TERMS

Terms and concepts you should become familiar with in this chapter are:

abnormal program termination	fixed record layout	predefined naming convention
batch processing	floating-point format code	print layout form
blank format code	format codes	problem specification form
carriage-control specification	format-free I/O	record layout form
comment cards	general form notation	right-justified
compiler	integer format code	source deck
compiling	interpreter	syntax
desk-checking	JCL cards	system
diagnostic message	JOB card	systems analyst
echo-check	job deck	timesharing
error message	multiple-card layout form	warning message
Explicit Type statements	normal program termination	
fixed field layout	output requirements	

5.17 REVIEW QUESTIONS

1. What is the program specification form?
2. What purpose does a print layout form serve?
3. What purpose does a multiple card layout form serve?
4. What does a programmer do during the program design step?
5. Why are comment cards used in a FORTRAN program?
6. What information should be typed in comment cards and placed at the beginning of a source program?
7. Why is internal documentation so important in a source program?
8. What purpose does an Explicit Type statement serve?
9. The Explicit Type statement used to declare variables as type integer is the _____ type statement.
10. The Explicit Type statement used to declare variables as type real is the _____ type statement.
11. The standard FORTRAN statement to read formatted data items on a data record is the _____ statement.
12. The standard FORTRAN statement to write (print or display) formatted data items on an output record is the _____ statement.
13. The FORTRAN statement using the formatted READ and WRITE statements to describe the form and location of data items on a record is the _____ statement.

14. What is the purpose of each format code in the FORMAT statement?
15. What is the purpose of the carriage-control specifications in printer output FORMAT statements?
16. Many calculations can be performed in a single arithmetic Assignment statement. (True/False)
17. If a data item in memory is in integer form, it may be written using an integer variable and the floating-point (F) format code. (True/False)
18. The FORTRAN statement used to terminate execution of the object program is the _____ statement.
19. More than one STOP statement is permitted in a FORTRAN program. (True/False)
20. At least one STOP statement must be placed at the physical end of the program. (True/False)
21. The CALL EXIT statement may be used on some systems to terminate execution of a FORTRAN program. (True/False)
22. The END statement is simply a command to the FORTRAN compiler to mark the end of a source program. (True/False)
23. The END statement may also terminate execution of the object program. (True/False)
24. Only one END statement is allowed in a program, and it must be the last physical statement. (True/False)
25. The process of carefully checking the source deck manually for errors is called _____ _____ .
26. Name the three different types of cards normally associated with a FORTRAN job and give the purpose of each type.
27. You normally place your data cards before your source program in a job deck. (True/False)
28. What is the difference between batch processing and timesharing?
29. What happens to your source program during the compilation phase?
30. The source listing of the compiled program contains an exact image of the information punched in each source statement card. (True/False)
31. What are the two types of error messages that can arise from the compilation of a FORTRAN program?
32. Syntax error messages are usually printed following an erroneous FORTRAN statement. (True/False)
33. What are the two locations where diagnostic messages may be printed by the compiler?
34. List several methods or procedures that can be used to help you in finding syntax errors.
35. What happens to your program during the execution phase?
36. How may one best determine if an execution (logical) error is made in the program?
37. What is probably the best technique you can use to find logic errors in short programs?
38. Name two other techniques that may be used to help you locate logic errors.
39. What is the advantage to beginning students of using the format-free input/output statements?

5.18 EXERCISES

1. Find the syntax errors in the following statements:
   a. READ (5, 10) HOURS RATE
   b. 10 FORMAT (F5.2,3X,F4.1
   c. GPAY = HOURS × RATE
   d. WRITE (5,33 HOURS, RATE, GPAY

2. Find the syntax errors in the following statements:
   a. READ (6;20) HOURS,RATE
   b. 20 FORMAT (F.52;3X;F4.1))
   c. GRSPAY = (HOURS)(PAY)
   d. WRITE (6,88) HOURS, RATE, GRSPAY,

3. Indicate the syntax errors in the following statements.
   a. READ 5,99 X,Y
   b. FORMAT (2F5.2)
   c. WRITE (5,98) X,Y
   d. XYZTOTAL = X + Y + Z
   e. 79 FORMAT (3X,F5.,I2)
   f. STOPTHEPROGRAM
   g. WRITE (6,97,) A,B

4. Indicate the syntax errors in the following statements.
   a. READ (5,95) A,,B,C,
   b. 93 FORMAT 2I3,7XF6.1)
   c. TOTAL = NEWTOTAL
   d. READ (6,97) X,Y
   e. ENDOFPROGRAM
   f. WRITE (6 94) J,M
   g. 96 FORMT (1H0,I3,2X,F6.2)

5. Given the following READ and associated FORMAT statement, indicate what format codes go with which variables.

READ (5,83) A, I, J, B
83 FORMAT (3X,F5.2,I3,2X,I1,1X,F3.1)

6. Given the following READ and associated FORMAT statement, indicate what format codes go with which variables.

$$READ\ (5,\ 13)\ I,\ K,\ L,\ C$$
$$13\ FORMAT\ (1X,I2,3X,2I4,4X,F4.2)$$

7. Given the following READ and associated FORMAT statement, indicate the given error between any variable and listed format codes.

$$READ\ (5,\ 88)\ I,\ A,\ J$$
$$88\ FORMAT\ (I4,3X,2I5)$$

8. Given the following READ and associated FORMAT statement, indicate the given error between any variable and listed format codes.

$$READ\ (5,\ 67)\ PRIN,RATE,TIME$$
$$67\ FORMAT\ (F8.2,3X,F4.3,1X,I2)$$

9. Given the following WRITE and associated FORMAT statement, which format codes go with which variables?

$$WRITE\ (6,18)A,B,C,I$$
$$18\ FORMAT\ (1H0,F4.1,F5.1,3X,F6.2,I3)$$

10. Given the following WRITE and associated FORMAT statement, which format codes go with which variables?

$$WRITE\ (6,97)I,A,J,B,C$$
$$97\ FORMAT\ (1H0,2X,I4,3X,F5.2,I3,5X,2F6.1)$$

5.19 PROGRAMMING PROBLEMS

1. Write a FORTRAN program to compute pay according to the equation:

$$pay\ =\ rate\ times\ hours\ worked$$

Your program should read the values of rate and hours worked as decimal numbers in the following format:

Record Position	Field	Value
1–4	Rate (Form = N.NN)	3.50
5–8	Hours worked (Form = NN.N)	85.0

Write the two input fields and computed pay on a single printer line. (Use a carriage control specification of 1H1.) The output positions are:

Field Description	Print Positions
Rate	1–4
Hours worked	7–10
Computed pay	15–20

2. Write a program to read three 2-digit integer numbers and solve the equation:

$$N\ =\ 2I\ +\ J/3K$$

Use I, J, and K as the integer variables assigned to adjacent input fields beginning in card column 1. Let I = 15, J = 90, and K = 5. Write the three input values and the computed value of N on a single-spaced printer line. Use print positions for the output fields as follows:

Field Description	Print Positions
I	1–2
J	6–7
K	11–12
N	17–20

3. Write a program to compute simple interest according to the formula i = p r t. Read the values of principal, rate, and time from a record as follows.

Record Position	Field	Value
1–8	Principal (Form = NNNNN.NN)	20000.00
10–13	Rate (Form = .NNN)	.075
15–17	Time in years (Form = NN.)	05.

Write output results for the three input values and the computed value of interests on a double-spaced printer line. Use output field positions as follows:

Field Description	Print Positions
Principal	1–8
Rate	11–15
Time	18–20
Computed interest	25–32

4. Write a FORTRAN program to read the values of X and Y and solve the equation $Z = 2X + 3Y$. These values will be read from a record as described below:

Record Position	Field	Value
1–6	X (Form = NNN.NN)	135.63
7–12	Y (Form = NNN.NN)	081.55

Write output results for X, Y, and Z on a double-spaced line with output field positions as follows:

Field Description	Print Positions
X	1–6
Y	10–15
Z	20–27 (Form = NNNNN.NN)

5. Write a program to read the values of length and width from a punched card and solve for the area of a rectangle according to the formula A = l w. The input fields are given as follows:

Record Position	Field	Value
1–5	Length (Form = NN.NN)	20.50
6–10	Width (Form = NN.NN)	08.75

Write the three output fields on a single-spaced line in the following print fields:

Field	Print Positions
Length	5–9
Width	15–19
Area	25–31 (Form = NNNN.NN)

6. Write a program to read the value of radius (15.62) off a punched card in the form NN.NN beginning in record position one. Compute the area of a circle according to the formula a = π r² where π = 3.14. Write output results on a double-spaced line with the value of radius and the computed area in print positions 2–6 and 10–15, respectively.

7. Write a program to read the values of rate and time from a record as follows:

Record Position	Field Description	Value
2–5	Rate (Form = NN.N)	60.5
6–9	Time (Form = NN.N)	03.0

Solve for distance according to the formula d = r t. Write output values for rate, time, and distance beginning at the top of a new page. Each output value will be printed in the following locations:

Field	Print Positions
Rate	10–13
Time	20–23
Distance	30–35 (Form = NNN.NN)

8. Write a program to read an input value for X as the decimal number 26.32 punched in columns 1–5 in the form NN.NN. Compute the square and square root of the value read for X. (The square root of a real number may be obtained by raising the number to the one-half power.) Print output results as a double-spaced print line with the following field positions:

Field	Print Positions
X	5–9
Square	13–19
Square root	23–27 (Form = NN.NN)

9. The XYZ Company pays its night watchman $3.00 an hour for all time up to 40 hours. All hours over 40, he is paid time-and-a-half the normal rate. Last week, the night watchman worked 47 hours. Write a program to compute his gross pay and print his regular time pay, overtime pay, and total gross pay. Print the output results as follows:

Field Description	Print Positions
Regular time pay	5–10
Overtime pay	20–25
Gross pay	35–41

10. Write a program to: (1) read a temperature recorded in Fahrenheit off a card punched in columns 1 through 5 in the form NNN.N, (2) convert the temperature given in Fahrenheit to its corresponding Centigrade temperature according to the formula $C = \frac{5}{9}(F - 32)$, (3) print the Fahrenheit temperature and the converted Centigrade temperature under the format specifications 2F10.1.

11. Write a program to compute the sum and average of four integer values read from a punched card. The four fields are to be referred to as variables N1, N2, N3, and N4, respectively. They are punched in the following record positions.

Record Position	Field	Value
1–3	N1	321
4–6	N2	196
7–9	N3	38
10–12	N4	639

Print the input fields and computed results as follows:

Field Description	Print Positions
N1	3–5
N2	10–12
N3	17–19
N4	24–26
SUM	31–36 (Form NNNN.N)
AVER	41–45 (Form NNN.N)

12. Write a program to find the volume of a cylinder; the radius of its base is 1.75 inches, and its height is 4 inches. The formula is $V = \pi r^2 h$ (use 3.14 as π). Print the radius, height, and computed volume under the format specifications 3F10.2.

13. A salesman earns an 8 percent commission on each item he sells. Read a record with the sales price of each item sold. The sales price is punched in card columns 1–7 in the form NNNN.NN. Compute the commission earned for each sales price in the card file. Print each sales price with its respective earned commission on a new line. Also compute the total of all items sold and the total commission earned. Output each input value and earned commission as double-spaced lines in the following format:

Field Description	Print Positions
Sales price	3–9
Commission	15–20

Output the total sales and total earned commissions on a separate line beneath their respective column values.

6

Control Statements for Decision Making, Branching, and Program Loops

6.1 INTRODUCTION TO THE USE OF CONTROL STATEMENTS

Program execution usually proceeds from one statement to the next in sequence. Control statements are used to alter this sequence of execution. **Control statements** may also provide the programmer with a decision-making capability in the execution of a program. These statements allow you to reexecute a series of statements a desired number of times, to execute a statement only if a certain condition is met, to bypass statements that must not be executed in certain situations, and to terminate the program.

The function of the control and decision-making statements, then, is to allow the programmer to control the sequence in which the instructions will be executed by the computer. Statements are executed in a sequential manner until a control statement is encountered, at which point the computer is usually directed to resume execution at a different location in the program. Using control statements to repeat groups of instructions greatly reduces the size of programs, and using decision-making statements greatly increases program flexibility.

The functions of the control statements may be summed up in these four operations:

1. Program termination
2. Decision making
3. Branching
4. Looping

A control statement may perform any one of these operations separately or it may be used to perform a combination of them. For example, a Logical IF statement may be used in decision making to execute or not to execute a certain statement, such as a calculation. An IF statement may also be used to make a decision whether to terminate the program or branch to another location in the program.

Program Termination

A program automatically starts execution at the first executable statement. The computer must be instructed to **terminate execution**, when processing is finished, to obtain a **normal end of job**. The STOP statement (or CALL EXIT) that you have been using all along in your programs performs this termination.

Decision Making

Decision making is the process of evaluating a certain condition and performing an action based on the result. Decision-making capability is achieved through the use of the IF statements. A branch may be made in some situations; a specific statement (other than a branch) may be executed when a certain condition is met; the Logical IF statement is used with relational operators to evaluate a logical condition. The Arithmetic IF (another type of IF statement, to be covered in chapter 19, may be used to evaluate an arithmetic expression to decide the course of action.) The following Logical IF statements illustrate decision making.

```
      IF (KODE .EQ. 2) GO TO 200
   30 IF (ROOT .EQ. 0.0) WRITE (6,99) ROOT
  110 IF (HOURS .GT. 40.0) OVTPAY = (HOURS – 40.)*RATE*1.5
      IF (ID .EQ. – 9999) STOP
```

The first statement tests the value of the variable KODE to see if it is equal to a value of 2. If the content of KODE is a 2, then the condition is true, and a branch of control is made to statement number 200. If the content of KODE is not equal to a 2, then the condition is false, and the statement after the condition is not executed; instead, control of execution proceeds in sequence to the next executable statement. The second IF statement will write a message (presumably an error message), contained in the FORMAT statement numbered 99, and print the value of ROOT (if it is equal to zero). The third statement compares the variable HOURS to a value of 40.0. If this condition is true—i.e., if HOURS is greater than 40—then overtime pay (OVTPAY) is calculated as time-and-a-half rate for all hours over 40. The last Logical IF statement checks the value of the variable ID to see if it contains the value of -9999. If this condition is true, then the execution of the program is terminated.

Branching

Branching is the process of causing the computer to resume execution at a statement either preceding or following the statement that caused the branch; thus, the computer can transfer control, or "jump," to a statement out of the program sequence. The programmer can control the order in which statements are executed; they do not have to be processed in the actual sequence given in the program.

Branching may be one of two types—unconditional and conditional. An **unconditional branch** always causes a transfer to the indicated statement. A **conditional branch** allows the computer to choose between different courses of transfer. The choice of where to branch and resume execution is usually determined by evaluating a variable or condition.

The Unconditional GO TO statement always causes a branch to the specified statement. The Logical IF may contain an Unconditional GO TO, which will cause a branch to a different location in the program if the evaluated condition is true. A Computed GO TO statement can be used to transfer control to one of several alternative locations, depending on the value contained in an integer variable.

Looping

Looping is the process of repeating a series of instructions in the program. The technique of looping always causes a branch back to a prior program statement. A program loop may be established by using any form of the GO TO or Logical IF statements. Looping is one of the most powerful and widely used techniques in programming. A practically unlimited number of data records can be processed with a precise group of code using a loop. To provide an overview of program looping, let us expand the sample program discussed in chapter 5 to include a loop which calculated the sum and average of three test scores. The revised program will calculate the sum and average for multiple sets of data.

The calculation of the sum and average of three test scores for one student could certainly be done quickly and easily by hand or with a pocket calculator. So, why use the computer? The primary advantage in using a program manifests itself when a large number of the same calculations must be made. Suppose your instructor needs to calculate the sum and average of the test scores for all the students in six sections of a course. The computer can then be used for its primary purpose; it can calculate the values many times faster than we can, and without any mistakes. The program can be used for any class, semester after semester; the creation of new data records would be the only additional requirement.

If there are 30 students in a section, you would **not** write the program logic as

> Read the first student's test scores
> Calculate the sum of the test scores and average
> Print the calculated results
> Read the second student's test scores
> Calculate the sum of the test scores and average
> Print the calculated results
> . . .
> . . .
> . . .
> Read the thirtieth student's test scores
> Calculate the sum of the test scores and average
> Print the calculated results

A program written in this manner would be a time-consuming task. Think of the time it would take to write a program like this to process 2000 employee payroll records.

Notice that the same set of instructions is needed for each student. Therefore, a basic set of instructions is developed to calculate the required values for one student; then a loop can be established to repeat the same operations for every student's test scores. The only change needed in the program given in chapter 5 would be to include a loop so that the same operations are repeated for new student records. To form a program loop, all you need is a control statement to transfer execution back to the READ instruction and a control statement to test when the loop is completed. This type of logic is known as a program loop or looping.

The group of statements repeated in a loop is known as the **loop body**. The loop may consist of a section of a program or even the entire program. The basic logic of a loop is illustrated as:

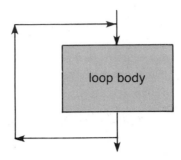

A GO TO statement may be used in FORTRAN to transfer control back to the beginning of the loop. This statement consists of the keyword GO TO followed by a statement number. The statement number is the one assigned to the FORTRAN instruction to which you wish to branch. Of course, the statement to which the branch is made must be an executable statement. The first statement in the loop is assigned a statement number and is referenced by the GO TO to tell the computer where to transfer control. For example:

10 READ (5,99) NR

. . .

. . .

. . .

GO TO 10

You may wonder how to get out of the loop. Another control statement is used to test for a special condition that signals when to end the loop. The control statement most frequently used is the Logical IF. The Logical IF statement tests various values to determine the truth of a condition. If the condition is true, you can branch out of the loop, stop the program, and so forth. If the condition is not met, the loop continues. For example:

10 READ (5,99) NR
IF (NR .EQ. 0) GO TO 20

. . .

. . .

. . .

GO TO 10
20 . . .

The condition is expressed within a set of parentheses. A relational operator .EQ., which means "is equal to," is used to make the test between the specified variables and/or constants. If NR is equal to 0, then the statement GO TO 20 would be executed and the loop exited. Otherwise, the next statement after the IF is executed. The test for the loop exit is made at the top of the loop after the READ statement.

You could have placed the Logical IF statement (with an .NE., for "not equal to") at the bottom of the loop to achieve the same purpose. The example revised to include the test for the loop exit *after* the loop body is:

10 READ (5,99) NR

. . .

. . .

. . .

IF (NR .NE. 0) GO TO 10
20 . . .

This revised example saves one statement (the Unconditional GO TO). However, a test for the exit at the *bottom* of the loop assumes that the loop must be executed at least once.

Now, let's expand the basic program from chapter 5 to compute the sum and averages from the test scores for ten students. To identify the test scores for each student, an extra field is included on the data records to provide a student identification number. The last five digits of one's SSAN (Social Security Account Number) or some other number might be used. The new input record format is shown as follows:

Record Position	Field Description	Variable
1–5	Identification number	ID
10–12	Test score 1	TEST1
13–15	Test score 2	TEST2
16–18	Test score 3	TEST3

The output values for each student will be printed on a line as follows:

Field Description	Print Positions
Identification number	1–5
Test score 1	10–12
Test score 2	17–19
Test score 3	24–26
Total	31–36
Average	41–46

The calculated values of total and average will be printed on the same print as the student ID and test scores.

A loop may be established in one of several ways. You could incorporate counter logic to count the number of students processed, or you could read a sentinel record to indicate the end of the students' records. A sentinel record technique will be used in the revised program. Various other looping techniques will be discussed later. The **sentinel record** technique uses a special value, in a field following the last valid data record, to signal the end of the data. The number used as the last (dummy) record flag must be one that is not a valid value for an input item. Usually a value of 0 or a minus value will insure an invalid data value. In this case, a value of −9999 for the ID field is used to indicate the sentinel record. This sentinel-record technique is known as **sentinel record logic,** an **input-bound loop,** or a **trailer record,** since it trails the valid records. The flowchart of the program logic is given in figure 6.1. Figure 6.2 (p. 170) shows the revised program.

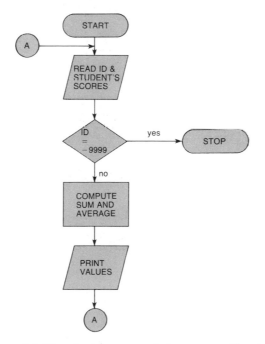

Figure 6.1 Flowchart for expanded program with a loop

```
C --- PROGRAM TO READ THREE TEST SCORES AND
C --- COMPUTE THEIR SUM AND AVERAGE. THIS IS
C --- DONE FOR TEN STUDENTS WITHIN A LOOP.
C
C --- WRITTEN BY J W COLE
C --- PROGRAM DATE: 1/30/82
C
        INTEGER ID, TEST1, TEST2, TEST3
        REAL TOTAL, AVE
C
10      READ (5,99) ID, TEST1, TEST2, TEST3
        IF (ID .EQ. -9999) STOP
        TOTAL = TEST1 + TEST2 + TEST3
        AVE = TOTAL / 3.0
        WRITE (6,98) ID, TEST1, TEST2, TEST3, TOTAL, AVE
        GO TO 10
C
99      FORMAT (I5, 4X, 3I3)
98      FORMAT (1H0, I5,4X, I3,4X, I3,4X, I3,4X, F6.2,4X, F6.2)
        END
```

Figure 6.2 Expanded program to compute ten students grade averages

21234	100	83	76	259.00	86.33
22345	100	100	100	300.00	100.00
43456	90	70	80	240.00	80.00
34567	77	100	93	270.00	90.00
36789	68	79	74	221.00	73.67
67890	74	85	87	246.00	82.00
58901	84	55	76	215.00	71.67
59012	72	70	81	223.00	74.33
31234	82	90	89	261.00	87.00
22405	84	92	100	276.00	92.00

Figure 6.3 Output results from expanded program with a loop

The Logical IF statement after the READ checks for an input value of ID equal to -9999. When this value is read, the condition will be true, the STOP statement on the Logical IF is executed, and the program terminated. If the input value of ID is not equal to -9999, the condition is false, and processing of the test scores continues. The GO TO after the WRITE statement will cause control of execution to be transferred back to the READ statement and the loop entered again.

The output results are shown in figure 6.3.

How the computer selects the record to be read by the READ statement is often a puzzle to the beginning programmer. You must clearly understand one thing about the execution of a READ statement. When the computer executes a READ statement, all the machine can do is read the next data record in the input file (or card deck). The computer cannot recognize that record as being the correct one to read. It must depend on you to arrange the data records in exactly the same order as required by the READ statements. If a standard disk file is read for input, your instructor has created this file with the intended order of the data records. The execution of the first READ statement reads the first record. Execution of this same READ statement again (as in a loop), or of another READ statement, simply reads the next data record. You must always keep this in mind and arrange your data records in the order they are expected to be read.

The next two sections provide a more detailed explanation of the Unconditional GO TO and Logical IF control statements.

GO TO n

where:

   n—is a statement number assigned to an executable statement, to which control is transferred.

Figure 6.4 General notation of the Unconditional GO TO statement

6.2 THE UNCONDITIONAL GO TO STATEMENT FOR UNCONDITIONAL BRANCHING

The Unconditional GO TO statement causes program execution to be transferred to a specified FORTRAN statement, rather than processing the instructions in a continuous sequence. As the statement name indicates, control of execution will **always** (under all conditions) be transferred to the FORTRAN statement with the referenced statement number. The general form of the Unconditional GO TO statement is given in figure 6.4.

The Unconditional GO TO can reference a FORTRAN statement which appears in the program either prior to or after the GO TO. If a branch is made to a previous statement in the program, a loop is formed. If the transfer is to a statement after the GO TO, all the statements between the GO TO and the later referenced statement are skipped in execution. Any statement referenced by the GO TO must be an executable FORTRAN statement; if it is not, a syntax error will occur. The most common usage of the Unconditional GO TO is to send control back "upstream" to a previous statement to form a loop.

The executable statement immediately following an Unconditional GO TO should have a statement number assigned to it. For example:

$$\text{GO TO 37}$$
$$\text{23 C = A + B}$$

Otherwise, the statement following the GO TO could never be executed, since there is no way for the computer to get to this statement. If this mistake is made, a warning (nonfatal error) message will be produced.

Consider a short program with this type of error. The program specifications are to read two input values, calculate their sum, print the input values and sum, loop back to the READ instruction and process more sets of data. The program is as follows:

```
10 READ (5,99) A, B
   SUM = A + B
   GO TO 10
   WRITE (6,98) A, B, SUM
   STOP
99 FORMAT (2F5.2)
98 FORMAT (1H0, F5.2, 3X, F5.2, 3X, F6.2)
   END
```

The GO TO statement is in the wrong place in the program. It should be after the WRITE statement. The WRITE statement is never executed because of the incorrect positioning of the GO TO (since the GO TO always causes an unconditional branch to the READ). A warning message will be printed to alert you that the WRITE statement cannot be reached in the program execution. (A situation like this is suspect for a logic error.) The program also has an endless loop, since there is no test to exit from the loop.

Here is the program written correctly to print the values of A, B, and SUM in the loop and to transfer control back to the READ statement. (A Logical IF statement is also included to test for a value of −9.99 for the variable A, signaling the end of the loop.):

```
10  READ (5,99) A, B
    IF (A .EQ. −9.99) GO TO 20
    SUM = A + B
    WRITE (6,98) A, B, SUM
    GO TO 10
20  STOP
99  FORMAT (2F5.2)
98  FORMAT (1H0, F5.2, 3X, F5.2, 3X, F6.2)
    END
```

6.3 THE LOGICAL IF STATEMENT FOR DECISION MAKING AND BRANCHING

The Logical IF statement is probably the most powerful and widely used decision making statement in FORTRAN. It provides the programmer with the ability to evaluate variables and expressions and to choose one of two possible alternative paths of logic based on the evaluation.

The Logical IF statement is a conditional statement, since it expresses a conditional command. If the condition that is evaluated is met (true), a certain action is taken. If the condition is not met (false), another action is taken. The condition being evaluated is in the form of a logical expression. The expression is referred to as a logical one since only one of two conditions may result—true or false.

The logical expression is enclosed within a set of parentheses following the keyword IF. Following the parentheses is a FORTRAN statement which is executed if the condition is true. The FORTRAN statement can be any executable statement except another Logical IF or a DO statement (another type of control statement to be explained in chapter 10). The general form of the Logical IF statement is presented in figure 6.5.

The relationship between the values in the logical expression is represented by a **relational operator** such as .EQ. to mean "is equal to." The "equal" sign (=) cannot be used, since it has a special meaning in FORTRAN—to assign or replace. Also the relational symbols in math are not in the FORTRAN character set. Therefore, a four-character relational operator is used to denote the respective arithmetic symbols for a logical expression.

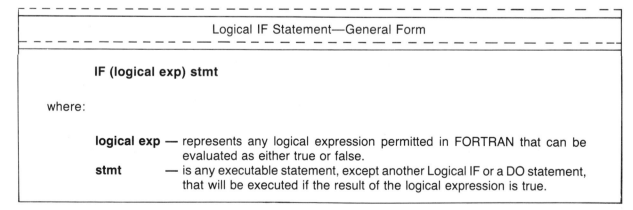

Logical IF Statement—General Form

IF (logical exp) stmt

where:

logical exp — represents any logical expression permitted in FORTRAN that can be evaluated as either true or false.

stmt — is any executable statement, except another Logical IF or a DO statement, that will be executed if the result of the logical expression is true.

Figure 6.5 General notation of the Logical IF statement

The relational operators in FORTRAN equate to the relational symbols in math of $<$, $\leq$, $>$, $\geq$, $=$, and $\neq$, which are used to test the relationship between two values. The six FORTRAN relational operators with their equivalent arithmetic symbols and operations are:

Relational Operator	Arithmetic Symbol	Operation
.LT.	$<$	Less than
.LE.	$\leq$	Less than or equal to
.GT.	$>$	Greater than
.GE.	$\geq$	Greater than or equal to
.EQ.	$=$	Equal to
.NE.	$\neq$	Not equal to

Each relational operator requires a period at both ends to distinguish it from a variable name that could be spelled in the same way. NE, for example, is a variable name, but .NE. is a relational operator.

The expressions before and after the relational operator may each consist of a single constant, a single variable, or an arithmetic expression. All arithmetic computations are performed prior to the relational test. That is, the relational operator has a lower precedence of operation than any arithmetic operator and is performed last.

Examples of Logical IF statements are:

```
     IF (RESULT .LE. 0.0) STOP
     IF (COUNT .LT. 10.0) GO TO 1
  23 IF (X .GE. TEST) TEST = 0.0
     IF (R / S .GT. A * S − B) GO TO 74
     IF (TOTAL .NE. A + B) WRITE (6,91) A,B, TOTAL
```

The first example says that if the value at the variable RESULT is less than or equal to zero, stop execution. The second example tells the computer to transfer control to statement number 1 if the value of COUNT is less than 10.0. The third example (with the assigned statement number 23) says that if X is greater than or equal to the value at the variable TEST, then assign the value of zero to TEST. The fourth example tells the computer to branch to statement number 74 if the quotient of R divided by S is greater than the result of A * S − B. The last example says that if the value of TOTAL is not equal to the sum of A + B, then print the variables A, B and TOTAL.

When the evaluated logical expression is false, the computer proceeds to the next executable statement in sequence. If the statement given on the Logical IF is not a branch statement such as a GO TO, the next sequential instruction will be executed whether the evaluated condition is true or false. Fox example,

```
     ERRORA = 0.0
     ERRORB = 0.0
     IF (A .LE. 0.0) ERRORA = 1.0
     IF (B .GT. 100.0) ERRORB = 1.0
  87 FORMAT (1H0, 2F5.0)
     WRITE (6,87) ERRORA, ERRORB
```

First, the two variables ERRORA and ERRORB are assigned a value of zero. Next, the variable A is tested to see whether it is less than or equal to zero. If it is, the variable ERRORA is assigned the value 1.0. Whether this condition is true or false, control proceeds to the next IF statement. The variable B is tested to see whether it is greater than 100.0. If it is, the variable ERRORB is assigned the value 1.0. Again control continues at the next executable statement, regardless of the logical result. The WRITE statement will be executed whether the conditions are true or false. Remember, the FORMAT statement is not an executable statement, so control proceeds to the WRITE statement after the execution of the second Logical IF.

The execution of the Logical IF is summed up in the following flowchart forms.

Explanation:

Flowchart Form

Flowchart Form

If the logical expression is true, the executable statement (S) is executed. If the logical expression is false, then the executable statement (S) is not executed. In either case, the next statement executed is the one after the Logical IF.

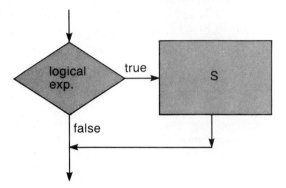

If the executable statement is a GO TO, control is transferred to the statement number specified in the GO TO when the logical expression is true. Otherwise, the next statement after the Logical IF is executed.

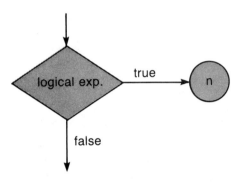

6.4 A SAMPLE PROGRAM TO ILLUSTRATE COUNTING AND ACCUMULATING TOTALS WITHIN A LOOP

A common requirement in many computer programs is to keep a count of a number of items and to accumulate a "running" total of values. These types of operations are often referred to as **counter** and **accumulator logic**, respectively. A **counter** is a variable to which a constant value is added (usually in the form of a numeric constant). For example:

$$KTR = KTR + 1$$

This is illogical in arithmetic, since a value cannot equal itself plus one. In programming, however, this type of instruction tells the computer to add one to a variable and to store this new value back into the same variable. In this way the computer increments (adds to) a variable by a certain quantity. Of course, decrementing (subtracting from) a variable is performed in the same manner. For example:

$$MAX = MAX - 1$$

An **accumulator** is a variable to which various quantities are added (in the form of a variable). For example:

$$SUM = SUM + X$$

The principle is similar to a counter. A variable quantity is added to a variable (called the accumulator), and the sum is stored as the new accumulator value. The value being added is usually a variable which has been read by an input statement. The main difference, then, is that a counter is associated with a constant value, while an accumulator works with a variable quantity.

Counter and accumulator operations are usually accomplished with an Assignment statement in a program loop. At each pass through the loop, the counter is incremented, and the value of an item is added to the accumulator variable. The counter and accumulator variables must, of course, be initialized to some value, usually zero, before entering the loop. Counter logic may be used independently of accumulator logic, or they can both be included in the same loop.

These techniques are illustrated in a program to read an unknown number of test scores and compute their average. Each test score is read from a separate data record under the format specification I3. The last data record (sentinel) contains a value of −99 to indicate the end of the input data. The program is:

```
      INTEGER CNT, TOTAL, SCORE, AVE
      CNT = 0
      TOTAL = 0
   10 READ (5,99) SCORE
      IF (SCORE .EQ. −99) GO TO 20
      CNT = CNT + 1
      TOTAL = TOTAL + SCORE
      GO TO 10
C     COMPUTE AVERAGE OF ALL TEST SCORES
   20 AVE = TOTAL / CNT
      WRITE (6,98) TOTAL, CNT, AVE
      STOP
   99 FORMAT (I3)
   98 FORMAT (1X, I5, 5X, I3, 5X, I3)
      END
```

Each time a valid test score is read in the loop, the counter CNT is incremented by 1, and the test score is added to the variable TOTAL. When the sentinel value of −99 is read, all the test scores have been read, and a branch to statement number 20 is made; then the average of the test scores is computed by dividing the accumulated total by the counter. Finally, the computed values of TOTAL, CNT, and AVE are printed.

6.5 LOGICAL OPERATORS AND COMPOUND CONDITIONS WITH THE LOGICAL IF STATEMENT

Sometimes you need to test multiple conditions to decide whether to perform certain actions. That is, a certain routine may be executed only if several conditions are true, or if any one of several conditions is true. For example, a routine may be executed to calculate electricity consumption by kilowatt hours in the range of 1 to 200. Thus, the conditions would be KWTHRS (kilowatt hours) greater than 0 **and** less than 201. You may want to compute a certain value for a variable only when a certain value exists for one of several variables. For example, you may want to add one to a counter only when X is not equal to 1 **or** Y is less than 0.

Multiple Logical IF statements could be used in succession to test these multiple conditions. However, FORTRAN permits the use of **logical operators** to allow the inclusion of multiple conditions in the same Logical IF statement. For example:

```
      IF (KWTHRS .GT. 0 .AND. KWTHRS .LT. 201) GO TO 20
      IF (X .NE. 1.0 .OR. Y .LT. 0.0) KNT = KNT + 1
```

There are three logical operators in FORTRAN that correspond to these operations in math. Each logical operator is preceded and followed by a period. The **three logical operators**, their order of precedence, and their math functions are:

Logical Operator	Order of Precedence	Meaning	Mathematical Notation
.NOT.	1st	Not (negation)	¬
.AND.	2nd	AND	∧
.OR.	3rd	OR (inclusive or)	∨

The .NOT. operation is performed before any .AND. or .OR. operation. The .AND. operation is performed before the .OR. operation.

The .AND. and .OR. logical operators are known as binary logical operators since two operands (relational expressions) are required in their use. They may be compared to an electrical circuit which connects a power source to a light bulb as follows.

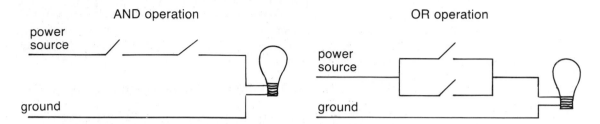

The raised (slanted) lines represent a switch. In order for the light bulb to be lit, both switches must be closed in an "AND" operation. To light the bulb in an "OR" operation, either one of the two switches (or both) may be closed. The .AND. and .OR. logical operators work the same way. All conditions must be met in an .AND. operation for the result to be true. However, only one of the conditions need be met in an .OR. operation for the result to be true.

The .NOT. logical operator is a unary operator, since only one operand is used with it. The .NOT. operator simply reverses the result of the condition. For example:

IF (.NOT. K .EQ. 1) GO TO 40

If K is equal to 1, the condition would be true, but the .NOT. operator changes it to false. If K is not equal to 1, the condition would be false, but the .NOT. operator changes it to true. You may ask why the statement was not written as:

IF (K .NE. 1) GO TO 40

This provides the same result. It is not apparent now, but the .NOT. operator can be highly useful in programming logic, especially in negating compound .AND. or .OR. conditions. For example,

IF (.NOT. (K .EQ. 1 .AND. J .NE. 0)) GO TO 50

The result of the "AND" operation is reversed by the .NOT. operator. The .NOT. operator, however, is generally not used as frequently as the .AND. and .OR. operators.

The .NOT. operator must **never** immediately **precede** the .AND. or .OR. operators. It may immediately **follow** an .AND. or .OR. operator and **must** precede an operand. For example,

IF (K .EQ. 1 .AND. .NOT. J .EQ. 0) GO TO 75
IF (L .EQ. 1 .OR. .NOT. M .EQ. 0) GO TO 77

You have now learned three different types of operators that can be used in a conditional expression. Arithmetic operations are always performed first, then the relational operations. The logical operators are lowest in the precedence of all operators and are performed last. For example:

IF (K .EQ. 1 .AND. J .GT. 3*L + 2) VAL2 = VAL1

The arithmetic expression $(3*L + 2)$ is evaluated first; then each relational expression is evaluated. The logical .AND. operation is evaluated last. However, remember that there are different levels of precedence for the various arithmetic and logical operators within these types. Parentheses must be used to override the precedence of the logical operators when needed, just as is done with arithmetic operators.

If you want the .OR. operation to be performed before the logical .AND. operation (since .AND. takes precedence over .OR.), you must enclose the .OR. operation within parentheses. Suppose you want to branch to a routine when either A or B is equal to 0, and C is equal to 1. The statement is coded as follows:

IF ((A .EQ. 0.0 .OR. B .EQ. 0.0) .AND. C .EQ. 1.0) GO TO 60

If you had not enclosed the .OR. condition within parentheses, the computer would have done the .AND. operation first between the second and third operands and then "ORed" the results with the first operand.

You are not limited to only one .AND. or .OR. operation within a condition. There can be any number of each type. Examples are:

IF (J.EQ.0 .AND. K.EQ.1 .AND. L.NE.0) GO TO 80
IF (J.EQ.0 .OR. K.EQ.0 .OR. L.EQ.0) GO TO 85
IF (J.EQ.1 .AND. .NOT.(K.EQ.0.AND. L.EQ.0)) KOUNT = KOUNT + 1

The condition in the first example would be true only if all the relational expressions are true. The condition in the second example would be true if any of the three relational expressions is true. The condition in the third example would be true when the first relational expression is true and either of the remaining two relational expressions is false.

Whenever the same variable is to be tested for different values, the variable must be repeated in the operands. Suppose you want to test N for a value greater than 0 and less than or equal to 100. You **cannot** code,

IF (N .GT. 0 .AND. .LE. 100) GO TO 90

The variable in each operand must be repeated, and thus coded as

IF (N .GT. 0 .AND. N .LE. 100) GO TO 90

to provide the correct syntax.

The use of logical operators in the Logical IF statement is a complex operation. They can, however, provide flexibility and a short cut in programming.

6.6 LOGICAL CONSTANTS AND VARIABLES

There are only two logical constants. They are expressed in FORTRAN as **.TRUE.** and **.FALSE.**. The period before and after each constant must be used to prevent the constants being taken as variable names.

Logical Variables

A variable which may be assigned a logical value is said to be a logical variable. A logical variable can be any valid symbolic name, but it must be declared in an Explicit Type statement to be type logical. The general form of the LOGICAL statement is given in figure 6.6.

Two examples of the LOGICAL Type statement to declare logical variables are:

LOGICAL FLAG, SWITCH
LOGICAL EOFSWT

The first example declares the variables FLAG and SWITCH to be logical type variables. This means that they can take on only values of either true or false; they cannot be assigned a numeric value. The second example declares the variable EOFSWT to be type logical. Array items and function subprograms (to be covered later) may also be identified as type logical.

LOGICAL Type Statement—General Form

LOGICAL name$_1$,. . ., name$_n$

where:

name$_1$,. . ., name$_n$ — each **name** represents a variable, array, or function subprogram name. If the **name** is an array name, the dimension information may be specified following the array name.

Figure 6.6 General notation of the LOGICAL Type statement

Logical Expressions and Assignment Statements

A logical expression is one that provides a resulting value of "true" or "false" to logical variables or array (table) elements. The three logical operators may be used within logical expressions to form compound expressions. The arithmetic operators must not be used with logical constants and/or variables, since you are not dealing with arithmetic values. Relational operators, however, can be used with numeric constants and/or variables to provide a resulting logical value. Some examples of logical expressions are:

.TRUE.
.FALSE.
X .AND. Y
X .OR. Y
.NOT. X
A .GT. 10.0
B .EQ. C

where the names X and Y are logical variables, and the names A, B, and C are numeric variables. The resulting value of X .AND. Y is true, only if *both* X and Y have true values. The resulting value of X .OR. Y is true, if *either* X or Y has a true value. The .NOT. X produces the opposite value of X. The arithmetic expressions with relational operators produce a true or false value depending on the outcome of the comparison.

The logical Assignment statement is used to assign a logical value to a logical variable. The general form of this type of Assignment statement is:

logical variable = logical expression

The logical expression is evaluated, and the resulting logical value is assigned to the logical variable.

Examples of the logical Assignment statement are:

X = .TRUE.
Y = .NOT. X
L1 = .NOT. (X .AND. Y)
L2 = (X .AND. .NOT. Y) .OR. .FALSE.
L3 = (X .OR. Y) .AND. A .LE. 100.0

In the first example, the logical constant .TRUE. is assigned to the logical variable X. In the second example, a false value results from the expression .NOT. X and is assigned to the logical variable Y. Remember that relational operators take precedence over the logical operators, and the logical operators have a precedence of .NOT., and .AND., and .OR. order. Parentheses are used to override these precedences. Thus, the third example says to produce the logical result of X .AND. Y, which is false, and then to take the opposite of this value, which is true. So a value of true is assigned to the logical variable L1. The fourth example says first to find the value of (X .AND. .NOT. Y), which is true. This value is "ORed" with the constant .FALSE., which produces a true result and is assigned to L2. The fifth example first evaluates the expression (X .OR. Y) to produce a value of true, then A .LE. 100.0 is evaluated. Assuming a value of 10.0 for A, the result is true. Thus, the "ANDing" of the first true result and the second true result assigns a value of true to L3.

Let's look at a short program to illustrate the use of logical variables. The program reads a number and performs a different calculation based on the value of the input item. If the number is between 0–499, we will multiply the number by two and print the result. If the number is between 500 and 999, we will multiply the number by three and print the result. If the number is negative or greater than 999, the program is terminated. The program is shown in figure 6.7.

The variable SWT (for switch) is declared to be a logical-type variable. An input number is read as a three-digit integer. The variable SWT is initalized to .FALSE., thus assuming the number to be between 0 and 499. The logical Assignment statement

SWT = NUMBR .GE. 500

assigns a logical value of ".TRUE." if the input field is greater than or equal to 500. If it is not, the variable retains the previously assigned value of ".FALSE.". The Logical IF statement transfers control to statement number 20 if the value of SWT is true; otherwise, control proceeds to the next assignment statement. The

```
C --- PROGRAM TO ILLUSTRATE THE USE OF LOGICAL VARIABLES
      LOGICAL SWT
10    READ (5,199) NUMBR
      IF (NUMBR .LT. 0 .OR. NUMBR .GT. 999) GO TO 30
      SWT = .FALSE.
C --- SET SWITCH TO TRUE IF THE NUMBER IS BETWEEN 500-999
      SWT = NUMBR .GE. 500
C --- IF SWT IS TRUE (NUMBR IS BETWEEN 500-999), THEN
C --- JUMP TO THE ROUTINE TO MULTIPLY NUMBR BY 3 AND PRINT
C --- THE RESULTS. OTHERWISE, MULTIPLY THE INPUT NUMBER
C --- BY 2 AND PRINT THE RESULTS.
      IF (SWT) GO TO 20
      NUMBR2 = NUMBR * 2
      WRITE (6,299) NUMBR, NUMBR2
      GO TO 10
20    NUMBR3 = NUMBR * 3
      WRITE (6,299) NUMBR, NUMBR3
      GO TO 10
30    STOP
199   FORMAT (I3)
299   FORMAT (1H0, I3,5X, I6)
      END
```

Figure 6.7 Sample program with logical variables

program calculates a different value with NUMBR depending on whether SWT was true or false. Program execution continues until a negative value or a value greater than 999 is read for NUMBR.

Logical values may also be read as input values and printed with output results. The technique of reading and writing logical values is covered in chapter 16.

The newer FORTRAN dialects provide a structured block IF statement to perform decision making. Section 6.7 discusses the block IF-ENDIF statement and its structured use.

6.7 THE STRUCTURED IF-ENDIF STATEMENT

The Logical IF statement is very restrictive, in that you can specify only one statement to be performed when the stated condition is true. The IF-ENDIF statement allows you to specify any number of statements to be executed when the stated condition is true. An ELSE option is also available to specify any number of statements to execute when the given condition is false. The IF-ENDIF statement is not available in ANSI FORTRAN 66. However, many modern FORTRAN compilers (ANSI FORTRAN 77, WATFIV-S, VAX-11 FORTRAN, MNF, M77, and others) include this statement. The statement is explained in this chapter in case your version of FORTRAN supports the IF-ENDIF statement. But remember, it is not implemented in all versions of FORTRAN.

The IF-ENDIF statement provides an IF-THEN-ELSE construct that promotes structured programming. This powerful statement enforces top-down coding and readability. All actions involved with a "true" evaluation of the given condition can be included after the THEN keyword. All actions involved with a "false" evaluation of the given condition can be included after the ELSE option. No GO TO statements are needed. The given condition may be true or false, but the complete set of actions to be performed is presented in a clear, top-down, readable manner. A more understandable and readable code is produced. The end of the IF statement is indicated by the ENDIF keyword.

The IF-ENDIF statement may be used to implement several structured control-flow constructs. The IF-THEN and the IF-THEN-ELSE control structures can be implemented with the block IF-ENDIF statement.

The IF-THEN Control Construct

First, let's look at just the IF-THEN control construct. Remember, in flowcharting and pseudocode this would be represented as:

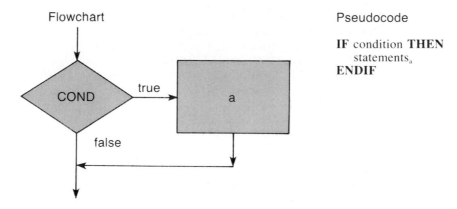

Flowchart

Pseudocode

IF condition **THEN**
    statements$_a$
ENDIF

The structured FORTRAN implementation is the same as pseudocode. The form of the block IF-ENDIF statement, using only the IF-THEN construct, is:

IF (logical-expression) THEN
    . . . ⎫
    . . . ⎬ **group of statements**
    . . . ⎭
ENDIF

For example, suppose you wish to add 1 to K, add X to S and assign S to S2 when the value of the variable A is equal to 10. The statement would be:

IF (A .EQ. 10.0) THEN
    K = K + 1
    S = S + X
    S2 = S
ENDIF

This statement is highly readable about what actions to perform when A is equal to 10. If the logical expression is false, the block of statements is skipped, and control goes to the statement after the ENDIF.

The indentation of the three statements to be executed when the condition is true simply shows that the statements belong to the IF statement. Indentation of four (or several) spaces makes the group of statements more readable and understandable. The ENDIF is aligned with the IF to show the start and end of the IF statement.

The IF-THEN-ELSE Control-flow Construct

The flowchart and pseudocode representation of the IF-THEN-ELSE control-flow construct are:

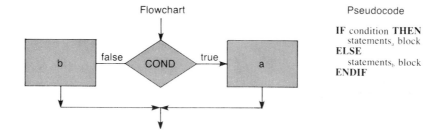

Flowchart

Pseudocode

IF condition **THEN**
    statements$_a$ block
ELSE
    statements$_b$ block
ENDIF

The structured FORTRAN implementation is, again, the same as the pseudocode representation. The ELSE is considered to be a separate statement and must be coded on a line by itself. The group of statements in the ELSE block is like the group of statements in the THEN block. The ELSE keyword is aligned with the IF keyword. The group of statements within each THEN and ELSE blocks is further indented. The general form of the block IF-ENDIF statement with the IF-THEN-ELSE construct is:

IF (logical-expression) THEN

  . . . ⎱
  . . . ⎰ **statements$_a$ block**
  . . .

ELSE

  . . . ⎱
  . . . ⎰ **statements$_b$ block**
  . . .

ENDIF

Suppose you wish to add 1.0 to C and assign X to X2 when the value of A is equal to the value of B, and that if A is not equal to B, you want to subtract 1.0 from C and assign Y to Y2. The coded block IF-ENDIF statement would be:

```
IF (A .EQ. B) THEN
    C = C + 1.0
    X2 = X
ELSE
    C = C - 1.0
    Y2 = Y
ENDIF
```

The IF-THEN-ELSE control-flow structure effectively provides for selecting one of two alternate groups of statements for execution.

Nested Block IF-ENDIF Constructs

There are times when a choice must be made from more than two possible actions. That is, you wish to evaluate more than one condition for a set of actions. There are two choices to make regarding nested IF's. You can evaluate another condition when the first (or previous) condition is true, or you can evaluate another condition when the first (or previous) condition is false. These two choices are identified as "AND IF's" and "OR IF's." That is, with the "AND IF", another condition is tested if the previous condition is true; with the "OR IF", another condition is tested if the previous condition is false. The "OR IF" is used to implement the structured SELECT CASE construct.

    Nested AND IF Control Flow Structure. The form of the nested "AND IF" logic is as follows:

IF (logical-expression-1) **THEN**
    IF (logical-expression-2) **THEN**

      . . .
      . . .   block of statements
      . . .
    ENDIF

This syntax says that execution of the block of statements will occur when both logical-expression-1 and logical-expression-2 are true. You could have used an .AND. logical operator to form a compound condition here. But, what if you wished to add 1 to I when A is equal to X but also add 1 to J when both A and B are equal to X? The coded statements would be:

```
IF (A .EQ. X) THEN
    I = I + 1
    IF (B .EQ. X) THEN
        J = J + 1
ENDIF
```

To accomplish the same thing with the .AND. logical operator you would need to code two statements. They are:

IF (A .EQ. X) I = I + 1
IF (A .EQ. X .AND. B .EQ. X) J = J + 1

The nested "AND IF" logic using the IF-ENDIF statement is much easier to follow.

Nested "OR IF" Control-flow Structure. The ELSEIF option is provided in ANSI FORTRAN 77, WATFIV-S, and M77 dialects to implement "OR IF" logic. The general form of this control construct is:

IF (logical-expression-1) THEN
. . .
. . .
. . .
ELSEIF (logical-expression-2) THEN
. . .
. . .
. . .
ELSE
. . .
. . .
. . .
ENDIF

The ELSEIF condition is evaluated only when the first condition is false. Thus, we generally say "IF condition 1 is true, do certain actions;" or "IF condition 2 is true, do certain actions," and so on. Hence, the term "OR IF" logic. Multiple ELSEIF options may be nested to form the SELECT CASE control-flow construct.

ANSI FORTRAN 66 Implementation of the IF-THEN-ELSE Control-flow Structure

If the structured IF-THEN-ELSE statement is not supported in ANSI FORTRAN 66, then how can this valuable control-flow construct be implemented with ANSI FORTRAN 66 statements? The Logical IF and GO TO statements are used. Even though you want to eliminate the GO TO's in programs, you must use them to implement the IF-THEN and IF-THEN-ELSE constructs.

IF-THEN Control-flow Structure Implementation in ANSI FORTRAN 66

The implementation of this structure is accomplished with the Logical IF statement. If the logical expression is true, the statement given with the Logical IF is executed and control continues at the next statement. If the logical expression is not true, control passes to the next statement. For a simple statement to be executed when the condition is met, the following construct of the Logical IF is used.

C *** THE IF-THEN CONSTRUCT
IF (logical expression) a

For example:

IF (X .GE. 1.) Y = 2. * X

or

IF (SUM .LT. 100.0) CALL SUBRTN

The last statement calls a subroutine named SUBRTN when the value of the variable SUM is less than 100.0.

Whenever *multiple* statements need to be executed for a true condition, you must use a different construction of the Logical IF, since only one statement can be executed if the condition is met. The logical operator .NOT. is placed before the given condition to transfer control *around* the statements for block "**a**", which are placed after the Logical IF. The CONTINUE statement is used as a dummy statement to transfer control. The CONTINUE performs no operation at execution time; it is used only to provide flexibility in creating a statement and a statement number for use in transferring control (branching). The CONTINUE statement will be discussed in more depth in chapter 10 with the DO statement. The construct of the IF-THEN control structure is:

```
C *** THE IF-THEN WITH MULTIPLE STATEMENTS
      IF (.NOT. (logical expression)) GO TO 10
         block a statements
10    CONTINUE
```

For example, to calculate Y as 2 times X and A as B plus C when the variable X is greater than 1, would be coded as follows:

```
IF (.NOT. (X.GE.1.) ) GO TO 10
   Y = 2. * X
   A = B + C
10 CONTINUE
```

To produce the same results, the logic of the relational operators can be reversed, thus eliminating the logical operator ".NOT.". Following is a list of the relational operators, along with their opposite conditions that will provide the same results if the .NOT. operator is omitted.

Relational Operators	Relational Operators for the Opposite Condition
.EQ.	.NE.
.NE.	.EQ.
.GT.	.LE.
.GE.	.LT.
.LT.	.GE.
.LE.	.GT.

The Logical IF equivalent for the given example would be:

```
IF (X .LT. 1.) GO TO 10
   Y = X * 2.0
   A = B + C
10 CONTINUE
```

IF-THEN-ELSE Control-flow Structure Implementation in ANSI FORTRAN 66

This control structure is also implemented with the Logical IF. If the **logical expression** is *true*, the block represented by "**a**" is executed, and control proceeds to the statement following block "**b**." If the **logical expression** is *false*, the block represented by "**b**" is executed, and control continues at the next statement. The logical operator .NOT. is used to provide a true condition when the **logical expression** is false and thus to transfer around **block "a" statements**. A GO TO must be included as the last statement in block "**a**" **statements** to transfer around **block "b" statements** when **block "a" statements** are executed. The construct is:

```
C *** THE IF-THEN-ELSE CONSTRUCT
      IF (.NOT. (logical-expression)) GO TO 10
         block a statements
         GO TO 20
10    CONTINUE
         block b statements
20    CONTINUE
```

For example, if you wish to calculate Y as 2 times X when the variable X is equal to 1.0 and Y as X squared when the value of X is not equal to 1.0, the following segment of code could be written in ANSI FORTRAN 66.

```
        IF (.NOT. (X .EQ. 1.0)) GO TO 10
            Y = X * 2.0
            GO TO 20
    10  CONTINUE
            Y = X ** 2.0
    20  CONTINUE
```

As with the IF-THEN construct, the relational operator may be reversed and the .NOT. omitted.

6.8 TYPES OF PROGRAM LOOPS

Looping is one of the most powerful techniques used in computer problem solving. Programs can be shortened by having the computer perform the same set of operations on a practically unlimited number of data records.

All loops may be classified in two ways: test-at-the-top and test-at-the-bottom. The test-at-the-top type loop includes a condition that is tested *before* the body of the loop is begun and before each repeated pass of the loop is made. This type of loop structure is known as a DO WHILE loop. The test-at-the-bottom loop includes a condition that is tested at the *end* of the loop (after the loop body). The test-at-the-bottom loop structure is known as a REPEAT UNTIL (or a DO UNTIL) loop. At least one pass of the loop is made in a REPEAT UNTIL loop.

There are various techniques for implementing these two types of loops. Three basic techniques for implementing loops with these two types of structures are:

1. Input-bound loops
2. Counter loops
3. General condition loops

The technique chosen to implement a program loop depends on the application of the loop. The following subsections discuss these loop techniques and their application.

Input-bound Loops

An input-bound loop uses the test-at-the-top loop structure. This looping technique is used when a varying (indeterminate) number of records are processed. **Input-bound loops** terminate when some end-of-file record is read. The end-of-file record may be a system JCL card, tape or disk end-of-file record, or a sentinel record (or even a timesharing command such as the ?END on a Burroughs 6000 system). The illustrated logic for an input-bound loop is shown in figure 6.8.

For example, the processing of application files such as payroll, purchase orders, inventory control, accounts receivable, accounts payable, and so forth, are usually programmed as input-bound loops, since the number of records in these types of files changes continually. The number of employees' records varies in a personnel file, since employees quit, retire, or are fired, and new employees are hired. The number of purchase orders and invoices varies from week to week based on needed items. Inventory items continually vary. The number of students in a course varies from semester to semester (or quarter to quarter).

The body of an input-bound loop includes the reading of an input record, the processing of data items, and the writing of results. The loop is terminated when there are no more records to process.

Counter Loops

A counter loop may be implemented with either a test-at-the-top or test-at-the-bottom loop structure. It depends on whether you wish to go through the loop at least once or not at all if a condition is met.

A **counter loop** is used when the number of loop iterations is either exactly known or must meet a prescribed count. An **index variable** is used to keep track of how many times the loop is executed. This index variable must be **initialized** before the loop is started, **modified** (usually incremented) by some value each time through the loop, and then **tested** to see if the loop has been executed the proper number of times. The index variable

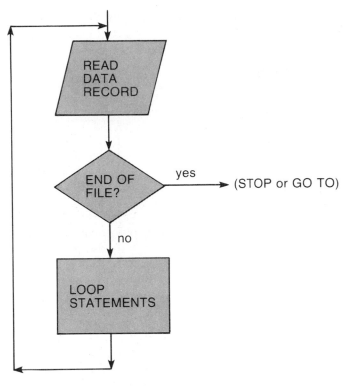

Figure 6.8 Illustrated logic for an input-bound loop

may be tested against some known numeric constant or against a variable that determines the maximum number of loop iterations. The illustrated logic for a counter loop (with the exit test after the loop body) is given in figure 6.9 (p. 186).

Figure 6.9 shows the three operations—initialization, modification, and test—that are always included in a counter loop. The initialization step is performed only one time (before the loop) to set the index variable to a specific value. The index variable is usually incremented after the other instructions in the loop. Finally, the index variable is evaulated to determine whether to repeat the loop or exit from it.

A loan payment schedule, for example, is used to show the payment amounts, interest amounts, and balances during the term of the loan. The payment number is the index variable that is used to determine how many payments are made in the loop. That is, if a loan is taken out for two years and a payment is made every month, then the loop is executed twenty-four times. The loop that computes the interest and balance and prints the appropriate information is executed once for each payment. Tables of values, such as the square of a number, square roots, logarithms, powers of a number base, and others are produced with counter loops. Table or array searching operations use counter loops, since the number of items in the table is known.

Here is a program illustration of counter loop technique: The problem logic is to compute the square and square root of the integers from 1 to 10. A test for the loop exit is made at the top of the loop. The program is:

```
        INTEGR = 1
   10   IF (INTEGR .GT. 10) GO TO 20
        ISQ = INTEGR * INTEGR
        RINTGR = INTEGR
        SQROOT = RINTGR ** .5
        WRITE (6,99) INTEGR, ISQ, SQROOT
   99   FORMAT (1H0,I2,5X,I3,5X,F6.2)
        INTEGR = INTEGR + 1
        GO TO 10
   20   STOP
        END
```

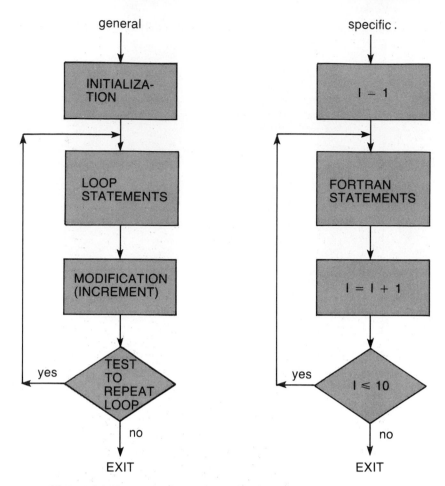

Figure 6.9 Illustrated logic for a counter loop

The variable INTEGR is used as the index variable to control the number of times the loop is executed. Each time the loop is processed, the square and square root are computed. The index variable, representing the integer, and the two computed values are printed. The index variable is incremented by one on each pass of the loop. When the index variable is greater than 10, the loop is terminated. Thus, a table of squares and square roots of the integers from 1 to 10 has been produced.

Many variations of this program loop could be coded. The index variable could have been initialized to 0 and the increment by 1 placed at the top of the loop. The test could have been made at the bottom of the loop to return for another pass in the loop if the index variable was less than 11 (or 10, depending upon whether the test was less than or equal to 10).

Counter loops can be used to process the records in an application file when the exact number of records is known, but the number of records usually varies from one processing to another, because people leave a company, new people are hired, new accounts are added, old accounts are closed out, and so forth. Thus, the variation in the number of records processed prevents effective use of counter loops in many application programs unless the program is modified each time.

You may want to use counter loop logic in your program, but find that the number of times the loop is executed varies from time to time, such as for the number of students in a class. A **header record** is sometimes used with counter loops to supply the count for the number of times the loop is to be executed. This is often referred to as header-record logic. **Header-record logic** is simply the reverse of trailer record logic; an extra data record is included ahead of the data, before the detail data records. The header record is often referred to as a **control record,** since it is used to control the looping process. A value is read from the header record and tested against the counter to see whether the loop has been executed the proper number of times.

Following is a program to illustrate header-record logic. The problem is to read the number of data records, as indicated in the header record, and compute their sum.

```
           INTEGER CNTR
           CNTR = 1
           SUM = 0.0
    C---READ HEADER CARD VALUE
           READ (5,99) NRCRDS
    C
    C ---READ DATA RECORD WITH THE VARIABLE X
    10     READ (5,98) X
           WRITE (6,97) X
           SUM = SUM + X
           CNTR = CNTR + 1
           IF (CNTR .LE. NRCRDS) GO TO 10
           WRITE (6,96) CNTR, SUM
           STOP
    99     FORMAT (I3)
    98     FORMAT (F5.2)
    97     FORMAT (1H0, F5.2)
    96     FORMAT (1H0, I5,5X, F7.2)
           END
```

The first READ statement reads the value, NRCRDS, from the header record, which tells how many detail records to read. The Logical IF statement tests the counter, CNTR, to see if it is still less than or equal to the variable NRCRDS. If the condition is true, the loop is repeated to read and process another data record.

General Condition Loops

The **general condition** loop is really a DO WHILE or REPEAT UNTIL loop structure. This loop is identified as a separate technique because the logic for it is different from that for input-bound and counter loops. In a general condition loop, you want to execute a loop until a certain condition is met. The condition usually involves a test between two variables. It may involve a test with a numeric quantity, such as repeating a loop until some error factor is reached. The logic for implementing a general condition loop is the same as that for the DO WHILE and REPEAT UNTIL loop structures.

A depreciation program, for example, computes the depreciation on a piece of machinery by applying the depreciation formula to the book value of the machine repeatedly until the book value is less than or equal to the scrap value. Periods of interest payments may be determined by knowing how large a payment a person can make on a certain loan. In mathematics, we often want to repeat a loop until a certain error factor is found, such as finding the area under a curve. Counter loop logic could be implemented as a general condition loop that tests for a specific value.

Combination of Looping Techniques

Sometimes the various types of loops will be mixed in a program to accomplish the desired output. For instance, an input-bound loop may be used to read data records. Inside this loop, a counter or general condition type loop might be used to compute various values or to search a table.

6.9 STRUCTURED LOOPS WITH THE ITERATION CONTROL-FLOW STRUCTURE (DO WHILE AND REPEAT UNTIL)

The purpose of the DO WHILE control-flow construct is to provide structured iteration (looping) for top-down structured programming. If branching (GO TO) statements can be eliminated in writing programs loops, more reliable, readable, and understandable programs can be produced.

The DO and REPEAT statements are provided in ANSI FORTRAN 77 to implement structured DO WHILE loops. The WHILE and ENDWHILE statements are provided in WATFIV-S (and other FORTRAN compilers) to implement a DO WHILE loop. These statements are not available in ANSI FORTRAN 66.

The flowchart and pseudocode representation of the DO WHILE control structure are:

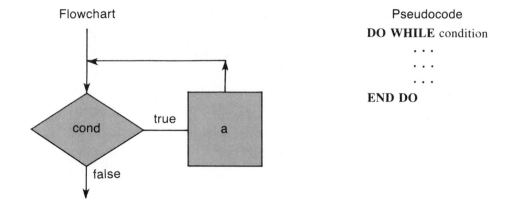

Flowchart

Pseudocode

DO WHILE condition
 . . .
 . . .
 . . .
END DO

This control flow structure makes a test at the top of the loop to see whether a condition is true. If the evaluated condition is true, the block of statements in the body of the loop is executed, and control returns to the condition for re-evaluation. The looping cycle continues as long as the condition is true. When the condition becomes false, control proceeds to the statement after the end of the loop.

ANSI FORTRAN 77 Iteration Implementation

Since so many people disagree on the implementation of the DO WHILE statement, it is not included in FORTRAN 77. The DO WHILE control-flow structure is implemented with indexed DO and CONTINUE statements. The loop is entered from the top at the DO statement, and the end of the loop is identified by the CONTINUE statement. This provides one-entry-in and one-exit-out points for the loop. The body of the loop—between the DO and CONTINUE—may include regular sequence constructs, IF-ENDIF constructs, and nested loops.

The notation for the indexed DO loop is:

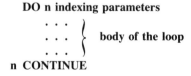

DO n indexing parameters
 . . .
 . . . } **body of the loop**
 . . .
n CONTINUE

"n" represents a statement number. The indexing parameters consist of the initialization, testing, and modification parameters that may be used in the loop. A Logical IF statement may be used to make a test and provide an exit from the loop prior to its completion via the test parameter. The indexed DO is covered in more detail in chapter 10.

Let's look at a sample FORTRAN 77 program using the DO and CONTINUE statements to compute the factorial of N numbers. The factorial of N numbers (N!) is the product of all the numbers in the sequence, e.g., 4! (read as four factorial) yields the value of 24 (1*2*3*4).

```
        READ *, N
        NFACT = N
        DO 10 NR = N − 1, 1, − 1
            NFACT = NFACT * NR
    10 CONTINUE
```

WATFIV-S Iteration Implementation

The DO WHILE control flow construct is implemented in WATFIV with the WHILE and END WHILE statements. The LOOP, QUIT, and ENDLOOP statements may also be used. The general form of the WHILE and END WHILE statements are:

WHILE (logical expression)
. . .
. . . } body of the loop
. . .
END WHILE

A sample program to compute the factorial of N numbers using the WHILE and END WHILE statements in WATFIV-S is:

```
READ, N
NFACT = N
NR = N − 1
WHILE (NR .NE. 0)
      NFACT = NFACT * NR
      NR = NR − 1
END WHILE
```

The LOOP, QUIT, and ENDLOOP Statements. The LOOP, QUIT, and ENDLOOP statements in WATFIV-S may be used to implement a DO WHILE or a REPEAT UNTIL control structure. The general forms of these statements are as follows:

```
LOOP
      . . .
      . . .
      . . .
ENDLOOP
```

A Logical IF statement with the keyword QUIT is used to make a test and to exit the loop. If the Logical IF statement is placed at the top of the loop, a DO WHILE control structure is implemented. For example:

```
LOOP
      IF (logical expression) QUIT
      . . .
      . . .
ENDLOOP
```

The loop is entered at the keyword LOOP. Then a condition is evaluated. If the condition is true, the statement QUIT is executed. The statement QUIT says to terminate the loop. Control resumes after the ENDLOOP statement. ENDLOOP identifies the end of the loop.

If the Logical IF statement is placed at the end of the loop, a REPEAT UNTIL control structure is implemented. For example:

```
LOOP
      . . .
      . . .
      IF (logical expression) QUIT
ENDLOOP
```

The loop is executed at least one time, since the test for the exit is made at the bottom of the loop. If the condition is false, the loop is repeated.

If ANSI FORTRAN 66 does not have the structured repetition statements, how are these control-flow structures implemented?

DO WHILE Control Structure Implementation in ANSI FORTRAN 66

This control structure is implemented by the Logical IF at the head of the loop. The loop is executed *as long as* the **logical expression** is *true*. The construction is:

```
C  *** THE DO WHILE CONSTRUCTION
10      CONTINUE
        IF (.NOT. (logical expression)) GO TO 20
           block of statements
           GO TO 10
20      CONTINUE
```

For example, if you wish to accumulate an input value X and keep a counter to permit 50 iterations of the loop, the program segment might be coded as follows:

```
C —PROGRAM TO ILLUSTRATE THE DO WHILE
C —CONSTRUCT IN ANSI FORTRAN 66
        INTEGER CNT
        CNT = 0
        SUM = 0.0
99   FORMAT (F5.2)
10   CONTINUE
        IF (.NOT. (CNT .LT. 50)) GO TO 20
           READ (5,99) X
           CNT = CNT + 1
           SUM = SUM + X
           GO TO 10
20   CONTINUE
```

Remember, the DO WHILE control structure must perform the exit test at the top of the loop. Now, let's see how the REPEAT UNTIL control structure is implemented.

REPEAT UNTIL Control Structure Implementation in ANSI FORTRAN 66

This construct is implemented with a loop controlled by the Logical IF. The loop is performed *until* the **logical expression** becomes *true*. The construct is:

```
C  *** THE REPEAT UNTIL CONSTRUCT
10      CONTINUE
           block of statements
        IF (.NOT. (logical expression)) GO TO 10
```

To perform the same logic that was coded in the previous DO WHILE loop, but now in a REPEAT UNTIL loop, the following segment of code is presented:

```
C —SEGMENT OF CODE TO ILLUSTRATE THE REPEAT
C —UNTIL CONSTRUCT IN ANSI FORTRAN 66
        INTEGER CNT
        CNT = 0
        SUM = 0.0
99   FORMAT (F5.2)
10   CONTINUE
           READ (5,99) X
           CNT = CNT + 1
           SUM = SUM + X
        IF (.NOT. (CNT .EQ. 50)) GO TO 10
```

The loop performs the same logic as the previous DO WHILE. However, the REPEAT UNTIL structure insures that the statements in the body of the loop are executed at least once.

It is fairly easy to make an error in loop logic, since many things must be considered: initializing, testing for the exit correctly, modifying (incrementing or decrementing) a control variable, ending the loop, and so on. The next section discusses some of the common errors made in single and nested loops, to help you avoid these pitfalls.

6.10 EXAMINING COMMON ERRORS IN WRITING LOOPS

Before proceeding to discuss the additional control statements, let's look at some of the most frequent errors encountered with loops and some of the precautions you should take. When a loop is established within a program, an exit from it is required after so many iterations. If no exit from the loop is provided, an infinite or endless loop results. An **infinite loop** is defined as a set of instructions which have no exit from the loop, but are always repeated. In other words, an **endless** loop exists in the program. For example,

```
        X = 0.0
10 READ (5,99) X
12 SUM = SUM + X
        X = X + 1.0
        GO TO 12
```

No means of exiting from the loop has been provided. The computer repeats the execution of these statements until the allotted amount of computer time has been exhausted. Infinite loops are bad, as you can see, and should be carefully avoided. Student jobs are allocated only a small amount of time, such as 30 seconds, to prevent the computer from running endlessly in case an infinite program loop is encountered.

There are several ways that you can accidentally cause infinite loops. The most frequently encountered causes are:

1. Using a poor loop structure, in which an exit from the loop is not provided. In the previous example of using an Unconditional GO TO, a test or way to exit the loop was not provided. So always include a test or a way to exit from any loop.
2. Not initializing an index variable. You must always set an index variable to some initial value in order to produce the correct results in a loop. The most common mistake is in initializing an index variable in the first loop and completing it correctly, then failing to **reinitialize** the index variable later in a second loop. This always produces a logic error. Say you want two loops—the first one to be for 20 iterations and the second one for 10 iterations. For example:

```
        INDX = 1
10 . . .

        . . .
        INDX = INDX + 1
        IF (INDX .NE. 21) GO TO 10
20 . . .
30 . . .

        . . .
        INDX = INDX + 1
        IF (INDX .NE. 11 ) GO TO 30
```

The first counter loop in which INDX goes from 1–20 is executed properly. But, the second loop in which INDX should go from 1–10 results in an endless loop, because the index variable INDX is not reinitialized back to 1. Another cause of the endless loop is that the .NE. relational operator was used. Always use an .LE. or .GE. operator to prevent exit-test errors. Many endless loop situations can be avoided if the index variable is properly initialized before entering each loop and the "less than" or "greater than" relational test is used with the "equal" relational test.
3. Using two different control variables—incrementing one and testing the other. That is, you may often use two variables in a loop and forget which one is intended to be the index variable. For example,

```
        INDX1 = 1
        INDX2 = 1
        X = 0.0
20 SUM = SUM + X
        X = X + 1.0
        INDX1 = INDX1 + 1
        IF (INDX2 .LE.20) GO TO 20
```

The index variable INDX1 should be tested in the IF statement, since that is the index variable used to control the loop. INDX2 is erroneously tested, resulting in an endless loop.

Any of the above errors can cause an infinite loop. What you really want to establish is a finite loop. A **finite loop** is one that always provides a way to properly exit from the loop and executes the loop only a finite (specific) number of times. The Logical IF statement is used in most loops, either at the beginning or at the end of the loop, to test a certain input or index variable for loop termination. Chapter 7 presents additional considerations in debugging logic errors in loops.

6.11 MULTIPLE BRANCH POINTS WITH THE COMPUTED GO TO STATEMENT

The Computed GO TO statement permits the transfer of control to one of several possible statements, depending on the current value of an integer variable. Thus, the computer can choose the next executable statement from many alternatives, according to a variable evaluated within the statement. The general form of the Computed GO TO statement is illustrated in figure 6.10.

Examples are:

> **GO TO (47, 12), J**
> **GO TO (10, 20, 30, 40, 50, 60), KOUNT**
> **129 GO TO (1804, 37, 456), N**

Control is transferred to the first, second, third, and so on, statement number depending on whether the value of the integer variable is 1, 2, 3, and so forth, respectively. That is, if the value of the variable is 1, control is transferred to the first statement number inside the parentheses. If the value of the variable is 2, control is transferred to the second statement number, and so on.

Let's look at an example of a routine which adds the numbers 1, 2, and 3 to counters with the variable names NROF1S, NROF2S, and NROF3S, respectively, to illustrate the function of the Computed GO TO statement. The routine might be used to count the number of employees on different work shifts, where a 1 represents the day shift, a 2 represents the swing shift, and a 3 represents the graveyard shift. The routine is:

```
      INTEGER EMPNR, SHIFT
      NROF1S = 0
      NROF2S = 0
      NROF3S = 0
   3  READ (5, 199) EMPNR, SHIFT
 199  FORMAT (I5, I2)
      IF (SHIFT .EQ. -9) GO TO 90
      IF (SHIFT.EQ.1 .OR. SHIFT.EQ.2 .OR. SHIFT.EQ.3) GO TO 50
      WRITE (6, 299) SHIFT, EMPNR
```

Computed GO TO Statement—General Form

GO TO (n₁, n₂, . . ., nₙ), ivar

where:

n₁, n₂, . . . , nₙ — are statement numbers of various statements to which transfer of control can be made.

ivar — is an integer variable containing an integer value which determines the specific statement to which control is transferred; ivar must contain a value not greater than the total number of statement labels within the parentheses (i.e., n₁ . . . nₙ).

Figure 6.10 General notation of the Computed GO TO statement

```
299 FORMAT (1H0, 22HERROR IN SHIFT , I2, 13HFOR EMPLOYEE , I5)
    GO TO 3
 50 GO TO (60, 70, 80), SHIFT
 60 NROF1S = NROF1S + 1
    GO TO 3
 70 NROF2S = NROF2S + 1
    GO TO 3
 80 NROF3S = NROF3S + 1
    GO TO 3
 90 . . .
```

An input value of -9 for the variable SHIFT is used to terminate the loop (a transfer is made to the statement numbered 90). An error message is written for an input value that is not a 1, 2, or 3. When the input value of SHIFT is a 1, a branch is made from the Computed GO TO statement to statement number 60, which adds one to the counter NROF1S. When the input value is a 2, a branch is made to statement number 70, which adds one to the counter NROF2S. When the input value for SHIFT is a 3, a branch is made to statement number 80, which adds one to the counter NROF3S. Once control has been transferred by the Computed GO TO statement, the sequence of execution becomes sequential. To avoid error and to skip over undesired code, the Unconditional GO TO statement is often required. Each routine transfers control back to the READ statement to read a new record.

When the value of the integer variable is less than 1 or larger than the number of given statement numbers, different things happen on different computers. Some compilers, such as IBM, WATFIV, and Burroughs, will fall through, that is, continue at the next statement after the Computed GO TO. Other compilers, such as Honeywell, will abort the program and give an error message. Thus, good programming practice would call for an IF statement to check the value of the integer variable to see if it is within the permitted range before executing the Computed GO TO. If it is not, an error message should be printed, and the Computed GO TO should not be performed.

Many compilers place a limit on the quantity of statement numbers within the Computed GO TO. The student need not worry about this limit, since it can be as high as 63.

Note the use of the comma to separate each statement number and also to separate the closing parenthesis from the integer variable outside. You should take special care to remember the comma separating the right parenthesis and the integer variable. The omission of this comma is a frequent mistake made by programmers.

The flowcharting symbol to represent the Computed GO TO statement is a variation of the decision symbol. It may be represented in the following manner:

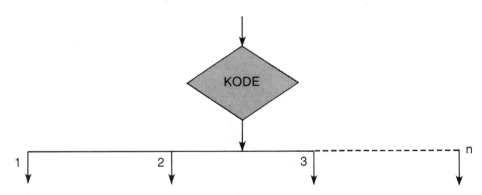

KODE is used in the above example for the integer variable required in the Computed GO TO. The computed GO TO statement is used to implement a restricted version of the generalized SELECT CASE control structure. Let's look at the SELECT CASE control-flow construct and its implementation in FORTRAN.

SELECT CASE Control Structure Implementation With FORTRAN 66 and FORTRAN IV

FORTRAN 77 and WATFIV compilers implement the SELECT CASE restricted control-flow structure with the block IF-ENDIF statement using the ELSEIF option. This statement provides a clear, top-down implementation of the SELECT CASE control structure. Since FORTRAN 66 and FORTRAN IV do not include the block IF-ENDIF statement, the SELECT CASE control-flow structure must be implemented another way.

The SELECT CASE construct is implemented with the Computed GO TO and Unconditional GO TO statements in FORTRAN 66 and FORTRAN IV. An Unconditional GO TO must be included at the end of each statement block to transfer control to the end of the blocks. The construct is:

```
C *** THE SELECT-CASE CONSTRUCT WITH THE COMPUTED GO TO
            GO TO (10, 20, ..., 80), index-variable
10          CONTINUE
               block a statements
               GO TO 100
20          CONTINUE
               block b statements
               GO TO 100
               . . .
               . . .
               . . .
80          CONTINUE
               block n statements
100         CONTINUE
```

The index variable selects which block of statements to transfer control to. If the value of the index-variable is 1, control is transferred to the block of statements beginning with statement number 10; if the value is 2, control is transferred to the block of statements beginning with statement number 20, and so on. Notice that all blocks of statements transfer to statement number 100 to provide a common exit point from the control structure.

For example, assume three possible values of 1, 2, and 3 for the index variable named INDX. The variable INDX is either read as an integer or assigned a value of 1, 2, or 3 from assignment in a Logical IF statement (not shown in the example). If the value for INDX is read as an input field, don't assume a correct value (of 1–3) is read. Always include an error test for the value of the index variable. The example is:

```
C --- CHECK FOR VALID INDEX VARIABLE
        IF (INDX .GE. 1 .AND. INDX .LE. 3) GO TO 5
        WRITE (5,99) INDX
99      FORMAT(1H0, 8HCTL VAR ,INDX, 11H IS INVALID)
        STOP
C --- SELECTION OF BRANCH POINT WIHT COMPUTED GO TO
5       GO TO (10, 20, 30), INDX
10         CONTINUE
              Y = 2.0 * X
              GO TO 40
20         CONTINUE
              Y = X ** 2.0
              GO TO 40
30         CONTINUE
              Y = X −5.0
40         CONTINUE
```

A check is first performed to determine whether the index variable (INDX) contains a correct range of values. If it does, control is transferred to statement number 5 to begin the selection routine. Otherwise, an error message is printed and the program terminated. If the value of INDX is 1, control is transferred to statement number 10; if the value of INDX is 2, control is transferred to statement number 20; if the value of INDX is 3, control is transferred to statement number 30.

6.12 TWO SAMPLE FORTRAN PROGRAMS TO ILLUSTRATE CONTROL STATEMENTS

Two FORTRAN programs will be developed to illustrate the use of control statements for solving more complex problems. The first problem produces a sales commission report. The second problem produces a company gross pay register.

Problem One: Produce a Sales Commission Report

The detailed problem specifications of the first problem, to produce a sales commission report, are:

1. A sales commission report is to be produced to compute the weekly sales commissions for salesmen.
2. A salesperson data record is read containing the fields of salesperson ID and weekly sales amount. An input-bound loop is used to handle a varying number of salesperson records each week. A sentinel record, with salesperson ID of -999, is read to denote the end of the records.
3. The commission for weekly sales is calculated as:

Amount of Sales	Commission Paid
up to and including $5,000	5%
over $5,000 and up to and including $10,000	7%
over $10,000	10%

4. A detail record will be printed that includes the salesperson ID, weekly sales amount, and earned commissions. Each detail print record is to be double-spaced.
5. The number of salesperson records read is to be counted.
6. The total weekly sales amount and earned commissions will be accumulated.
7. The counts of input records, accumulated total sales, and accumulated commissions earned are to be printed double-spaced beneath the last salesperson detail record.

The pseudocode for this example is given in figure 6.11.

```
START ANALYSIS OF SALES COMMISSION REPORT.
    INITIALIZE SALESPERSON COUNTER TO ZERO.
    INITIALIZE TOTAL SALES ACCUMULATOR TO ZERO.
    INITIALIZE TOTAL COMMISSIONS ACCUMULATOR TO ZERO.
    PERFORM PRIMING READ OF FIRST SALES RECORD.
    DO WHILE SALESPERSON ID IS NOT EQUAL TO -999
        IF SALES ARE LESS THAN OR EQUAL TO 5000 THEN
            CALCULATE COMMISSIONS = .05 TIMES SALES.
        END IF.
        IF SALES ARE GREATER THAN 5000 AND LESS THAN OR
                EQUAL TO 10000 THEN
            CALCULATE COMMISSIONS = .07 TIMES SALES.
        END IF.
        IF SALES ARE GREATER THAN 10000 THEN
            CALCULATE COMMISSIONS = .10 TIMES SALES.
        END IF.
        PRINT SALESPERSON ID, SALES AND COMMISSIONS.
        ADD ONE TO SALESPERSON COUNTER.
        ADD SALES TO TOTAL SALES ACCUMULATOR.
        ADD COMMISSIONS TO TOTAL COMMISSIONS ACCUMULATOR.
        READ A NEW SALESPERSON RECORD.
    END DO.
    PRINT THE VALUES FOR SALESPERSON COUNTER, TOTAL SALES
            AND TOTAL COMMISSIONS.
END ANALYSIS.
```

Figure 6.11 Pseudocode for sales commission report

```
C --- PROGRAM TO PRODUCE WEEKLY SALES COMMISSION REPORT
C --- PROGRAM ILLUSTRATES THE USE OF A PRIMING READ AND
C --- THE DO-WHILE CONSTRUCT FOR LOOPING.
C
C --- WRITTEN BY J W COLE
C --- PROGRAM DATE: 1/30/82
C
      INTEGER PERSID, TOTPER
      REAL SALES, COMM, TOTSAL, TOTCOM
C
C --- INITIALIZE SALESPERSON COUNTER AND SALES COMMISSION
C --- ACCUMULATOR. PERFORM PRIMING READ
      TOTPER = 0
      TOTSAL = 0.0
      TOTCOM = 0.0
      READ (5,199) PERSID, SALES
C
C --- DO WHILE LOOP TO PROCESS SALESPERSONS RECORDS
C
100      IF (PERSID .EQ. -999) GO TO 200
         IF (SALES .LE. 5000) COMM = SALES * .05
         IF (SALES .GT. 5000 .AND.
     *       SALES .LE. 10000) COMM = SALES * .07
         IF (SALES .GT. 10000) COMM = SALES * .10
         WRITE (6,299) PERSID, SALES, COMM
         TOTPER = TOTPER + 1
         TOTSAL = TOTSAL + SALES
         TOTCOM = TOTCOM + COMM
         READ (5,199) PERSID, SALES
         GO TO 100
C --- END DO.
C
200      WRITE (6,298) TOTPER, TOTSAL, TOTCOM
         STOP
199      FORMAT (I3, F7.2)
299      FORMAT (1H0, I3,5X, F7.2,5X, F7.2)
298      FORMAT (1H0, I3,4X, F8.2,4X, F8.2)
         END
```

Figure 6.12 Sample FORTRAN program for sales commission report

The FORTRAN program for the problem is shown in figure 6.12.

The variable PERSID represents the salesperson ID; the variable TOTPER is the counter for the number of salespersons' records. The other chosen variable names should be self-explanatory.

Problem Two: Produce a Company Gross Pay Register

The second problem is a little more lengthy and complex. It may be skipped if you feel you have an adequate understanding of control statements. It includes a report and column headings to identify the report and its output fields. Don't worry about understanding these output headings now; chapter 8 explains the development of various report headings.

The detailed problem specifications of the second problem, to produce a company gross pay register, are:

1. A three-shift operation (day, swing, and graveyard) is run in the XYZ Company.
2. Regular pay rate is paid for all hours worked up to and including 40.
3. Overtime pay rate of one and one-half times regular pay rate (regular pay plus 50 percent) is paid for all hours over 40.
4. Personnel on the day shift (8:00 A.M.–4:00 P.M.) earn regular and overtime pay rates.
5. Personnel on the swing shift (4:00 P.M.–12:00 A.M.) earn an extra 10 percent shift differential pay for all hours worked.

6. Personnel on the graveyard or midnight shift (12:00 A.M.–8:00 A.M.) earn an extra 15 percent shift differential pay for all hours worked.

The employee payroll records are laid out as follows:

Card Columns	Field Description
1–9	SSAN (Social Security Account Number) (Integer form)
10–14	Employee number (Integer form)
15–19	Blank
20	Shift code (1 = day, 2 = swing, 3 = graveyard)
21–26	Hours worked (Form = NNN.NN)
27–31	Hourly pay rate (Form = NN.NN)
32–80	Blank

The desired processing is as follows:

a. Read employee's data card.
b. Edit input shift codes to be 1, 2, or 3.
c. Edit hours worked to have a range of 0.00 to 168.00.
d. Edit hourly pay rate to have a range of 3.75 to 25.00.
e. Print error messages for all data records failing their edits.
f. Compute employee's regular, overtime, shift differential, and gross pay.
g. Print input values, computed regular pay, overtime pay, shift differential pay, and total gross pay for all employee records.
h. Compute the total company gross payroll.
i. Print total computed company gross pay after all records have been processed.

Edit processing is simply checking the input data to verify its validity. You may not be able to insure that all input values are correct, but you can check for a range of values if such a variation in data is possible. That is, you can make sure that the shift codes, hours worked, and hourly pay rate are not negative or beyond the maximum value allowed. To process erroneous data would vastly distort the output results. When an error is detected, do not process the data in the normal manner. Write a message identifying the errors found in the data, so that they can be corrected later. Of course, the input values should be printed with the error message to identify the record that is in error.

The output requirements are illustrated in the print layout form shown in figure 6.13.

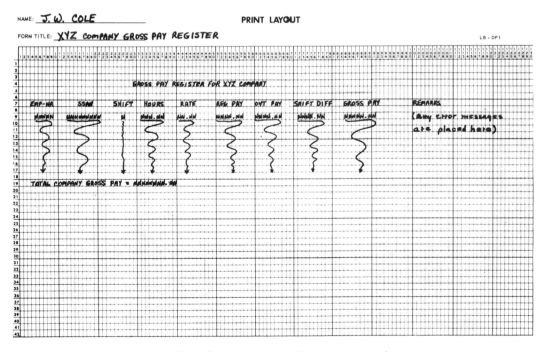

Figure 6.13 Print layout form for gross pay register output requirements

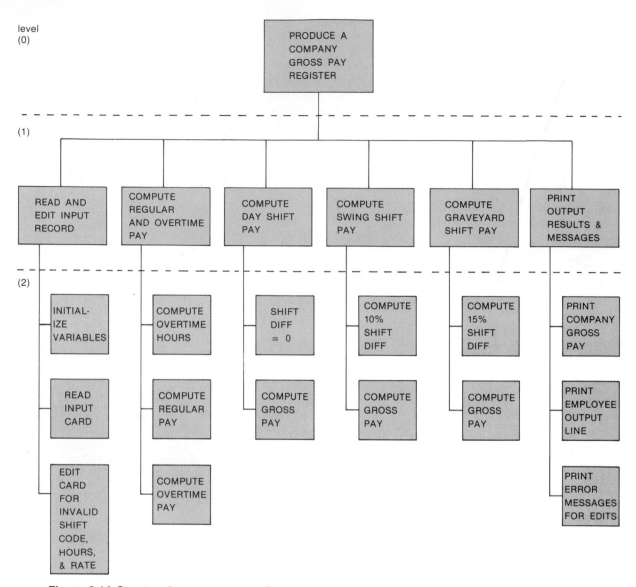

level
(0)

(1)

(2)

Figure 6.14 Structured program approach to company gross pay register (down to two levels)

The problem and the control-logic requirements are illustrated in a structure chart. Figure 6.14 illustrates the structure chart down to two levels.

The control logic is then converted to flowchart form. See figure 6.15 for the developed flowchart.

Now to the coding of the program. The resulting program is presented in figure 6.16 (pp. 200–201).

Assume fifteen data records have been constructed to test the program. The output results are displayed in figure 6.17 (p. 201).

Note that the test records were constructed to check out every logic path in the program. A data record was included for all three shifts, and for overtime hours as well as regular hours. Data records were also included to verify the edit checking in the program. After the program is thoroughly checked with detailed test data, we can be confident of its validity with "live" data files.

The control statements presented in this chapter will allow the programmer to create loops for repetitive execution of statements. The DO statement covered in chapter 10, however, provides a more powerful and flexible capability in program loops. The DO statement also produces a more orderly approach to program logic involving loops, since it eliminates many of the GO TO statements.

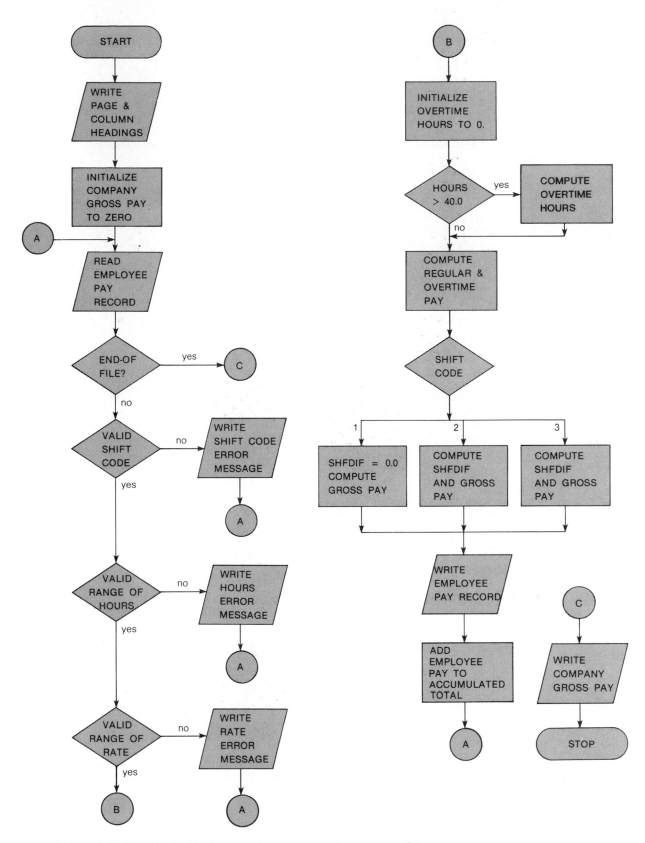

Figure 6.15 Flowchart of logic to produce company gross pay register

```
C ---PROGRAM TO PRODUCE COMPANY GROSS PAY REGISTER
C ---WRITTEN BY J W COLE
C ---PROGRAM DATE: 1/30/82
C
      INTEGER EMPNO, SSAN, SHFCDE
      WRITE (6,299)
      TOTPAY = 0.0
C
C ---TOP OF LOOP FOR READING AND PROCESSING EMPLOYEE RECORDS.
C
100   READ (5,199) SSAN, EMPNO, SHFCDE, HOURS, RATE
      IF (SSAN .EQ. 999999999) GO TO 700
C ---EDIT SHIFT CODE TO BE IN RANGE OF 1-3.
      IF (SHFCDE .GT. 0 .AND. SHFCDE .LT. 4) GO TO 200
         WRITE (6,296) EMPNO, SSAN, SHFCDE, HOURS, RATE
         GO TO 100
C ---EDIT HOURS WORKED TO BE IN RANGE OF 0.00-168.00
200   IF (HOURS .GE. 0.0 .AND. HOURS .LE. 168.0) GO TO 220
         WRITE (6,295) EMPNO, SSAN, SHFCDE, HOURS, RATE
         GO TO 100
C ---EDIT HOURLY RATE TO BE IN RANGE OF 3.75-25.00
220   IF (RATE .GE. 3.75 .AND. RATE .LE. 25.0) GO TO 240
         WRITE (6,294) EMPNO, SSAN, SHFCDE, HOURS, RATE
         GO TO 100
C
C ---COMPUTE REGULAR PAY AND OVERTIME PAY.
C ---BRANCH TO ROUTINE TO COMPUTE SHIFT PAY.
240   OVTHRS = 0.0
      IF (HOURS .GT. 40) OVTHRS = HOURS - 40.0
      REGPAY = HOURS * RATE
      OVTPAY = OVTHRS * (RATE * .50)
      GO TO (300, 400, 500), SHFCDE
C
C ---COMPUTE DAY SHIFT EMPLOYEE GROSS PAY
300   SHFDIF = 0.00
      EMPPAY = REGPAY + OVTPAY
      GO TO 600
C ---COMPUTE SWING SHIFT EMPLOYEE GROSS PAY
400   SHFDIF = (REGPAY + OVTPAY) * .10
      EMPPAY = REGPAY + OVTPAY + SHFDIF
      GO TO 600
C ---COMPUTE GRAVEYARD SHIFT EMPLOYEE GROSS PAY
500   SHFDIF = (REGPAY + OVTPAY) * .15
      EMPPAY = REGPAY + OVTPAY + SHFDIF
C
C ---PRINT EMPLOYEE PAY INFORMATION
600   WRITE (6,298) EMPNO, SSAN, SHFCDE, HOURS, RATE, REGPAY,
     *                OVTPAY, SHFDIF, EMPPAY
      TOTPAY = TOTPAY + EMPPAY
      GO TO 100
C
C ---WRITE SUMMARY TOTAL LINE WITH ACCUMULATED GROSS PAY
700   WRITE (6,297) TOTPAY
      STOP
199   FORMAT (I9, I5, 5X, I1, F6.2, F5.2)
```

Figure 6.16 Sample program to produce company gross pay register
(cont. on next page)

Figure 6.16 (cont.)

```
299   FORMAT (1H1, 29X, 23HGROSS PAY REGISTER FOR,
1        11HXYZ COMPANY//1H0, 3X, 6HEMP NR, 6X, 4HSSAN, 5X, 5HSHIFT,
2        3X, 5HHOURS, 4X, 4HRATE, 5X, 7HREG PAY, 3X, 7HOVT PAY, 3X,
3        10HSHIFT DIFF, 3X, 9HGROSS PAY, 8X, 7HREMARKS)
298   FORMAT (1H0, 4X, I5, 3X, I9, 5X, I1, 4X, F6.2, 3X, F5.2,
1                 5X, F7.2, 3X, F7.2, 4X, F7.2, 5X, F8.2)
297   FORMAT (1H0, 3X, 26HTOTAL COMPANY GROSS PAY = ,F11.2)
296   FORMAT (1H0, 4X, I5, 3X, I9, 5X, I1, 4X, F6.2, 3X, F5.2,
1                 55X, 25H***ERROR IN SHIFT CODE***)
295   FORMAT (1H0, 4X, I5, 3X, I9, 5X, I1, 4X, F6.2, 3X, F5.2,
1                 55X, 26H***ERROR IN HOURS FIELD***)
294   FORMAT (1H0, 4X, I5, 3X, I9, 5X, I1, 4X, F6.2, 3X, F5.2,
1                 55X, 25H***ERROR IN RATE FIELD***)
      END
```

```
                        GROSS PAY REGISTER FOR XYZ COMPANY

EMP NR     SSAN      SHIFT    HOURS   RATE   REG PAY  OVT PAY  SHIFT DIFF  GROSS PAY    REMARKS
12207    456231897    1      40.00   3.50    140.00    0.00      0.00      140.00
12327    503264178    2      40.00   3.00    120.00    0.00     12.00      132.00
12372    482370916    3      40.00   5.00    200.00    0.00     30.00      230.00
12468    123456789    1      30.00   4.00    120.00    0.00      0.00      120.00
12345    245781390    2      30.00   3.00     90.00    0.00      9.00       99.00
12370    341260872    3      35.00   4.00    140.00    0.00     21.00      161.00
12239    464209135    1      60.00   4.00    240.00   40.00      0.00      280.00
12496    522839014    2      45.00   3.00    135.00    7.50     14.25      156.75
12355    582134607    3      70.00   4.00    280.00   60.00     51.00      391.00
12367    502446712    0      40.00   3.00                                            ***ERROR IN SHIFT CODE***
12401    532189264    5      40.00   3.00                                            ***ERROR IN SHIFT CODE***
12357    301258674    1     -40.00   3.00                                            ***ERROR IN HOURS FIELD***
12385    420485261    2     540.00   3.00                                            ***ERROR IN HOURS FIELD***
12265    435126007    3      55.00   0.25                                            ***ERROR IN RATE FIELD***
12461    466320118    3      50.00  33.00                                            ***ERROR IN RATE FIELD***
TOTAL COMPANY GROSS PAY =    1709.75
```

Figure 6.17 Output results of company gross pay register using test data

6.13 LANGUAGE EXTENSIONS IN FORTRAN DIALECTS (DO WHILE CONTROL-FLOW IMPLEMENTATION)

The standard control statements discussed in this chapter are found on nearly all FORTRAN compilers. The CDC 6000 and Cyber compilers, however, also include a two-way branch for their Logical IF statement, in addition to the standard forms.

The general form of the CDC two-way branch on the Logical IF statement is:

IF (logical expression) n_1, n_2

where n_1 and n_2 are statement labels. If the logical expression is true, a branch is made to statement label n_1. If the logical expression is false, the branch is made to statement label n_2. For example,

IF (K .EQ. 10) 50, 60

Thus, if K is equal to 10, control is transferred to statement label 50. If K is not equal to 10, control is transferred to statement label 60.

MNF and M77 FORTRAN

The University of Minnesota Computer Center has developed a powerful FORTRAN dialect for use in batch and timesharing applications on the CDC 6000/7000/Cyber series computers running with the NOS or NOS/BE operating systems. The MNF dialect included many advanced features of FORTRAN and has been used by many universities with CDC computers. The M77 dialect is designed to comply with ANSI FORTRAN 77 standards. Some of the control statement features in M77 are:

The block IF-ENDIF statement with the ELSE IF is available in M77. Its syntax is the same as FOR-TRAN 77.

The WHILE and ENDWHILE statements are included in M77 to provide the DO WHILE control structure. Its general form is:

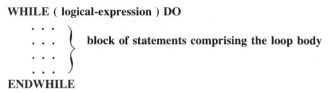

WHILE (logical-expression) DO

   . . .
   . . .   block of statements comprising the loop body
   . . .
   . . .
ENDWHILE

For example, the routine to sum the values of "n" real numbers which are read as input items would be coded as (a value of -999 is read as the sentinel value to terminate the loop):

```
SUM = 0.0
READ *, X
WHILE (X .NE. -999) DO
     SUM = SUM + X
     READ *, X
ENDWHILE
PRINT *, SUM
```

The routine contains a priming read before the WHILE statement to set the condition in the WHILE. The statements in the loop are executed repeatedly while the condition remains true. When the condition becomes false (from X having a value of -999), the loop is terminated, and control passes to the statement following the ENDWHILE.

VAX-11 FORTRAN

DEC VAX-11 FORTRAN is based on ANSI FORTRAN 77 specifications. The block IF-ENDIF statement with the ELSE IF is available in DEC VAX-11 FORTRAN. Its syntax is the same as FORTRAN 77.

VAX-11 FORTRAN also includes enhancements to FORTRAN 77. One enhancement is the DO WHILE and END DO statements to provide the DO WHILE control-flow structure. Its general form is:

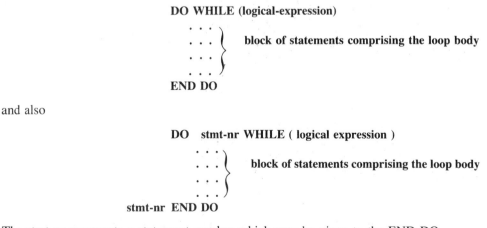

DO WHILE (logical-expression)

   . . .
   . . .   block of statements comprising the loop body
   . . .
   . . .
END DO

and also

DO   stmt-nr WHILE (logical expression)

   . . .
   . . .   block of statements comprising the loop body
   . . .
   . . .
stmt-nr END DO

The stmt-nr represents a statement number which may be given to the END DO.

The routine to sum the values of "n" real numbers which are read as input items would be coded as (a value of −999 is read as the sentinel value to terminate the loop):

```
SUM = 0.0
READ *, X
DO WHILE (X .NE. −999)
    SUM = SUM + X
    READ *, X
END DO
PRINT *, SUM
```

Other FORTRAN dialects may include a version of the DO WHILE statement to provide a way of writing structured loops in FORTRAN.

6.14 SUMMARY

This chapter introduced you to the various control statements used in FORTRAN programs. Program execution usually proceeds from a statement to the one immediately following it in the program. Control statements are used to alter this sequence. The control statements provide four basic operations:

1. Terminating a program
2. Decision making
3. Branching
4. Looping

The STOP (or CALL EXIT) control statement is used to terminate a program in a normal manner. The Logical IF statement is used for decision making, conditional branching, and establishing program loops. The Unconditional GO TO and Computed GO TO statements are used to perform branching to a designated statement, altering the flow of control in program execution. The Logical IF and Unconditional GO TO statements are widely used to set up program loops. Complex problems requiring many decisions can be solved by the computer with the control statements capability; thus, the Logical IF statement is widely used in programming to provide alternate actions under various conditions.

Looping is the process of repeating or re-executing a series of statements in a program, and it is one of the most powerful techniques used in solving problems by the computer. Decision making can be performed on large quantitites of data, and many data records can be processed with a small number of statements executed within a loop. A program is shortened by having one set of instructions repeated to process a practically unlimited set of data records.

The Logical IF statement allows you to use any of six relational operators to form a relational expression comparing data items and/or constants. The three logical operators can establish compound conditions in decision making. Logical variables may be used to provide a more efficient means of testing conditions.

The block IF-ENDIF statement is available in FORTRAN 77, WATFIV, and other modern FORTRAN compilers to provide a structured programming approach to decision making; this statement is not implemented in FORTRAN IV, however. The IF-ENDIF statement allows the implementation of the Selection (IF-THEN-ELSE) restricted control-flow structure programs.

All loops may be classified as one of two types—test-at-the-top and test-at-the-bottom. A test-at-the-top loop includes a condition that is tested before the loop is begun and before it is repeated. This type of loop is known as a DO WHILE loop. The test-at-the-bottom loop includes a condition that is tested at the end of the loop body. Therefore, at least one pass of this type of loop is always made. The test-at-the-bottom loop is known as a REPEAT UNTIL loop.

The test-at-the-top and test-at-the-bottom type loops are used to implement various looping techniques. The **input-bound techniques** uses a test-at-the-top loop to test for an end-of-file condition when reading an unspecified number of input records. The number of records in many application files varies from one processing run to another. For example, the number of employee records varies in a personnel file, the number of inventory items varies in an inventory file, the number of purchase orders varies from week to week, and so on. An end-of-file record or sentinel record must be used to identify the last record in a file, since you do not know in advance the exact number of times the loop will be repeated. A priming read must be performed before the input-bound loop to set the conditions for the tested input item.

Counter loops are used when the exact number of loop iterations is known. An index or control variable must be established to count the number of times the loop is executed. This variable must be initialized to some value—usually zero—before starting the loop. Then a test is made with the counter (index) variable to see if it has reached the value required to exit from the loop. A loop, then involves three operations with the counter variable—initialization (outside or before the loop), modification (normally an increment), and a test within the loop. Counter loops may be implemented as either test-at-the-top or test-at-the-bottom loops.

General condition loops are used to evaluate a condition and repeat the loop while, or until, that condition is met. For example, you may want to produce a depreciation schedule by subtracting the annual depreciation amount from capital cost while the total depreciated value is still more than the salvage value. Perhaps you want to compute an interest schedule for periodic payments until the principal is paid. General condition loops are really the implementation of structured DO WHILE or REPEAT UNTIL loops to handle any type of loop logic or technique without the unstructured GO TO statement.

FORTRAN 77, WATFIV-S, M77, VAX-11, and other structured FORTRAN compilers include a DO or WHILE statement to implement structured looping in programs. FORTRAN 66 and FORTRAN IV do not. A programmer must instead use the Logical IF and GO TO statements to implement the iteration (DO WHILE or REPEAT UNTIL) control-flow structure in a program.

You must be extremely careful when writing loops, since one small mistake may result in an endless loop. Several causes of infinite and incorrect loops were discussed and illustrated.

The Computed GO TO statement allows one to implement a restricted version of the general SELECT CASE construct in FORTRAN programs. This statement is valuable in programming when a selection of multiple branch points must be made based on the value of a data item. One statement can replace multiple Logical IF statements to test for all the possible values of an index or control variable.

Control statements are powerful statements in solving computer applications. They are widely used in nearly all application programs you will write.

6.15 TERMS

You should become familiar with the following terms from this chapter:

abnormal program termination	general condition loop	loop body
accumulator logic	header-record logic	looping
branching	index variable	program loop techniques
control statement	initialization step	relational expression
counter logic	input-bound loop	relational operators
counter loop	logical constants	REPEAT UNTIL loop construct
decision making	logical expression	sentinel or trailer record
DO WHILE loop construct	logical operators	test-at-the-bottom loop
endless or infinite loop	logical variables	test-at-the-top loop
finite loop		

6.16 REVIEW QUESTIONS

1. List the four functions or operations performed by the control statements in a program.
2. What is meant by the term "program termination"?
3. What is meant by the term "decision making"?
4. What is meant by the term "branching"?
5. What is meant by the term "looping"?
6. How do you usually exit from a loop?
7. What is the purpose of the Unconditional GO TO statement?
8. What is the purpose of the Logical IF statement?
9. List the six relational operators that can be used in a Logical IF statement and explain their individual function (i.e., mathematical operation).
10. If the condition (logical expression) in the Logical IF statement is false, what is the location of the next statement to be executed?
11. Name the three logical operators available for forming compound conditions.
12. The logical operator that provides a true condition only if all expressions are true is the _____ .
13. The logical operator that provides a true condition if any of the expressions is true is the _____ .
14. Give the precedence of operation of the three logical operators.
15. Give the precedence of operations between arithmetic expressions, relational operations, and logical operations.
16. What is the difference between an unconditional and a conditional branch?
17. Name the two classifications of loops.
18. Name three looping techniques used with the two classification of loops.
19. How is an input-bound loop terminated?
20. What are the three basic operations that must be performed on the counter (index) variable in a counter loop?
21. When is the loop terminated (exited) in a counter loop?
22. A control item that is read before the detail data records and used in counter loop logic to specify the number of times the loop is to be executed is called a H _____ record.
23. When is a general condition loop implemented in a program?
24. Program loops allow one to perform the same operations on more than one set of data. (True/False)
25. The Computed GO TO statement provides a branching operation to one of multiple statement labels depending on the value of a _____ _____ .
26. The process of checking input values to ensure their validity, such as acceptable range of values, is known as _____ _____ .

6.17 EXERCISES

1. Write an Unconditional GO TO statement to branch to the FORTRAN command with statement number 11 assigned to it.
2. Write an Unconditional GO TO statement to branch to statement number 37.
3. Write Logical IF statements to accomplish the following actions:
   a. If C1 is greater than C2, C3, or C4, then branch to statement label 76.
   b. If R is less than or equal to SUM / 2.0, then read another record with a value of R.
   c. If ROOT is equal to zero, then stop execution of the program.
   d. If A is equal to 10.0 and B is greater than 0.0, then branch to statement label 41.
   e. If X or Y is equal to 0.0 and Z is unequal to 0.0, then add one to KTR.

4. Write Logical IF statements to accomplish the following actions:
   a. If T is not equal to A * B + C, then transfer control to statement number 85.
   b. If LINECT is greater than or equal to 50, then assign to LINECT a value of zero.
   c. If A is less than B or C, then branch to statement label 26.
   d. If 2.0 * A is less than B + C, then assign C a value of zero.
   e. If X and Y are equal to 0.0, or S and T are unequal to 0.0, then branch to statement label 37.

5. Write a Computed GO TO statement to branch to statement numbers 32, 47, 15, 53, or 27 if the value of M is 1, 2, 3, 4, or 5, respectively.

6. Write a Computed GO TO statement to branch to statement numbers 103, 17, 68, or 3 if the value of K is 1, 2, 3, or 4, respectively.

7. Indicate the errors in each of the following statements.
   a. **GO TO (2,18,5,162) KNT**
   b. **IF (J .LT. 2M-3) GO TO 42**
   c. **IF (SUM .LT. 10.0) 13, 14, 15**
   d. **GOTO (3, 1, 16), CODE**

   e. **IF (A EQ B) C = A**
   f. **GO TO 199999**
   g. **IF (N .EQ. 1 AND L .GT. 5) STOP**

8. Indicate the errors in each of the following statements.
   a. **IF (XRESULT .GT.) STOP**
   b. **IF (N = 10) STOP**
   c. **IF (A .GE. C/D) END**
   d. **GO TO 20.**

   e. **GO TO (3,81,5,), L**
   f. **GO TO (1,2) I**
   g. **IF ((X .LT. 0.0ORY .EQ.0.0) AND Z .NE. 0.0)**
      NERR = NERR + 1

6.18 PROGRAMMING PROBLEMS

1. Develop a FORTRAN program to produce a table of simple interest according to the formula $i = prt$. Use a constant of 10000.00 for principal and a constant of .085 for rate. Vary the index variable, ITIME, from value of 1 to 10 to produce a table of simple interest for one to ten years. Write output values for time, principal, rate, and computed interest according to the following output positions.

Field Name	Print Positions
Time	3–4 (Form = NN)
Principal	10–17 (Form = NNNNN.NN)
Rate	23–27 (Form = N.NNN)
Computed interest	33–40 (Form = NNNNN.NN)

2. A salesman earns an 8 percent commission on each item he sells. Read an input file with the sales price of each item sold. The sales price is contained in record positions 1–7 in the form NNNN.NN. Compute the commission earned for each sales price in the input file. Print each sales price with its respective earned commission on a new line. Also compute the total of all items sold and the total commission earned. Output each input value and earned commission as double-spaced lines in the following format:

Field Description	Print Positions
Sales price	3–9
Commission	15–20

   Output the total sales and total earned commissions on a separate line beneath their respective column values. Include an input-bound loop that reads a sentinel record with a value of − 1.00 to terminate the loop.

3. Write a program to compute the sum and average of four integer values read from a punched card. The four fields are to be referred to as variables N1, N2, N3, and N4, respectively. They are punched in the following card columns.

Record Positions	Field	Value
1–3	N1	321
4–6	N2	196
7–9	N3	38
10–12	N4	639

Print the input fields and computed results as follows:

Field Description	Print Positions
N1	3-5
N2	10-12
N3	17-19
N4	24-26
SUM	31-36 (Form NNNN.N)
AVER	41-45 (Form NNN.N)

Include a counter loop to process five data records. Print the results of each set of values on a double-spaced line.

4. Write a program to produce a table of squares, square roots, cubes, and cube roots for the integer numbers 10-25. The square root of a number may be obtained by raising the number to the one-half power. The cube root of a number may be obtained by raising the number to the one-third power. Output each line of computed values as follows:

Field Name	Print Positions
Number	5-6 (I2 format code)
Square	11-13 (I3 format code)
Square root	18-23 (F6.3 format code)
Cube	28-32 (I5 format code)
Cube root	37-42 (F6.3 format code)

5. Write a FORTRAN program to read a student registration file with records containing the following information.

Record Positions	Field Description
1-7	Student number (I7 format code)
8-9	Blank
10	Level of classification (1 = Freshman, 2 = Sophomore, 3 = Junior, 4 = Senior, 5 = Postgraduate)
11-12	Number of courses in which enrolled

Count the number of students within each level of classification. Also accumulate the number of enrolled courses within each classification. Print this computed information on separate lines. A trailer record with a student number of −999999 is used to signal the end of the input file.

6. Write a FORTRAN program to read a student registration file with records containing the following information.

Record Positions	Field Description
1-7	Student number (I7 format code)
8-9	Blank
10	Tuition rate code (1 = resident undergraduate 2 = nonresident undergraduate 3 = resident graduate 4 = nonresident graduate)
11	Blank
12-15	Semester hours enrolled (F4.1 format code)

A sentinel record with a student number −999999 is used to signal the end of the input file.

Compute the required tuition fee for each student according to the following rate code:

Tuition Rate Code	Tuition Fee per Semester Hour
1	20.00
2	50.00
3	30.00
4	75.00

(The required tuition fee is calculated by multiplying the semester hours enrolled by the semester-hour fee.)

Edit semester-hours enrolled to be in the range of 1.00–25.00. Print an appropriate error message if the record fails the edit. Count the number of students registered in each tuition rate code. Also accumulate the total tuition fee for each rate code and the overall tuition fee for all students.

Print a double-spaced detail line of the input values and computed tuition fee for each student who passes the edit check. Suggested output print positions are:

Field Name	Print Positions
Student number	2–8
Tuition rate code	15
Semester hours enrolled	20–23
Tuition fee	30–36

Print the accumulated count of students and total tuition fee within each rate code after the last student output line.

7. Write a program to read three values and determine the largest value. The input values are each two-digit integer numbers punched in adjacent card columns beginning in card column 2. For output results, print the three input integers and the selected largest value.

8. Write a program to perform the same operations as in problem 7, except this time find the smallest of the three integer values.

9. Write a program to read a value for the variable X from an input card in columns 1–4 (format code of F4.1). Evaluate the input value according to the following conditions and compute the respective value of Y. If the value of X is less than zero, then compute $Y = 2X$. If the value of X is equal to zero, compute $Y = 1$. If the value of X is greater than zero, compute $Y = 4X - 1$. For output results, write the values of X and Y.

10. Write a program to perform the same functions as problem 9. Include a loop to read and process multiple sets of data until the input file is exhausted. Terminate the loop with a data card containing a value of 99.9 for X.

11. Write a program which includes counter loop logic to compute the sum and average of five real numbers. Each number is punched in columns 1–5 (form = NN.NN) on a separate card. Print each input value on a new double-spaced line. Write the computed sum and average on separate output lines.

12. Write a program to perform the same operations as in problem 11. Include three sets of five real numbers (total of 15 data cards) to be processed. Print the output results from each set of five numbers on a new page. This problem has two nested counter loops (i.e., a loop within a loop).

Built-in Functions and Debugging Techniques

7

7.1 INTRODUCTION TO FORTRAN BUILT-IN FUNCTIONS

There are operations other than arithmetic that can be performed on numeric quantities, such as obtaining the square root of a number or finding the sine of an angle. Many of these operations require a large number of instructions. For example, if you had to find the square root of a number, you would have to write a rather large, fairly complex routine within a program. Because mathematical operations like finding square roots, using logarithms, and using trigonometric functions are needed so often in programming, FORTRAN includes a set of efficient prewritten routines called built-in functions. **Built-in** functions are subprograms that do common mathematical operations on numeric values. A subprogram is a routine which plays a sub-role in the solution to a problem. It is executed by providing the proper reference to the subprogram name in the main program or another user-written subprogram.

In mathematics the term function refers to a rule for calculating a value from some given value or values called arguments. You may already be familiar with mathematical functions such as the square root, logarithms, and the trigonometric functions of sine, cosine, and tangent.

FORTRAN allows programmers to write their own function subprograms or to use the functions automatically supplied (built-in) in the language. You will learn how to develop user-written functions later on in the text (chapter 15). For now, you need to learn how to use the function subprograms already available to you in the FORTRAN language.

FORTRAN provides certain common mathematical and general functions, such as square root, absolute value, exponential, logarithm, conversion from real to integer mode, conversion from integer to real mode, sine, cosine, and arctangent, in the language itself. These built-in functions are also known as **intrinsics** or **intrinsic functions**. FORTRAN built-in functions are furnished by the computer vendor with the FORTRAN compiler. They are stored in system libraries on magnetic disk or drum storage devices. Hence, they are often referred to as **library-supplied** functions. The terms "intrinsic", "built-in", and "library-supplied" functions are used interchangeably in this text.

Each intrinsic function has a preassigned name. In FORTRAN you direct the computer to use a built-in function by writing the desired function's preassigned name, followed by an appropriate argument (expression) in parentheses. An **argument** is the expression or value supplied to the function to determine the calculated result. A reference to the preassigned name (within a proper FORTRAN statement) directs FORTRAN to invoke (execute) the named function with the value(s) represented by the expression in parentheses. For example, to reference the square root function—named SQRT—and to obtain the square root of the number 17.5, you would write

SQRT (17.5)

The name of the built-in square root function is SQRT. The argument, in this case, is 17.5.

The square root of the variable X would be written as:

SQRT (X)

To compute the square root of $b^2 - 4ac$ (from the quadratic equation), you would write

SQRT(B**2 − 4.0*A*C)

It is important to distinguish between the functions themselves and functional values. For example, SQRT is a function, since it refers to the algorithm which calculates the square root of its argument. The expression—SQRT(X)—is a function-value, the result from the calculation of the square root of X. A function-value is also called a **function reference**, since FORTRAN must refer to the function to compute the needed value.

You can invoke (reference) a numeric function simply by giving its function reference in an arithmetic expression. That is, a function reference may be used any place in an arithmetic expression where a numeric constant could be used in a FORTRAN statement. A function reference is usually given in the Assignment and Logical IF statements.

Examples of using the SQRT function are:

SROOTA = SQRT (A)
Y = Z + SQRT(X) − 5
IF (SQRT(Y + 3.5) .LT. 10.0) STOP

The first statement obtains the square root of A and assigns it to the variable SROOTA. The second statement obtains the square root of X, adds to it the value in Z, and subtracts 5 from the resulting sum. The final result is stored in Y. The third statement tests to see if the square root of the expression Y + 3.5 is less than 10.0. If it is, the program is terminated. Function references may be given in format-free output statements for those FORTRAN compilers that permit this syntax. Standard FORTRAN 66 and FORTRAN IV, however, do not permit function references to be given in its output statements.

Most built-in functions require only one argument. (At least one argument *must* be given in a function reference.) A few functions (like finding the smallest or largest value in a group of values) require more than one argument. You must know the correct number of arguments (i.e., one, two, or two or more) that a function requires to provide the correct statement syntax and to obtain a correct result. Multiple arguments must be separated by commas and given in the proper order.

Each function requires a specific mode for its argument(s). Some functions can take only a real-type argument (like SQRT). Other functions require an integer-type argument (like FLOAT). Some functions require a positive value as an argument (like SQRT and the logarithmic functions). If you tried to take the square root of an integer argument or zero argument, you would get an error message, or perhaps a wrong result. You must be sure to provide the proper mode (real or integer) for arguments, as well as not to supply a negative or zero value as an argument for some functions. Each function returns its calculated value in a specific mode. Different functions may perform the same operation but return results of different types.

The results of providing an argument of the wrong data type or of placing the arguments in the wrong order are generally unpredictable. These errors are some of the hardest to debug. You should be extremely careful in coding the arguments for a function.

An argument of a built-in function may be a constant, a variable, another function reference, or an arithmetic expression containing constants, variables, arithmetic operations, and function references. The argument may also include other built-in function references or may include the same function name. For example, the following Assignment statement invokes the SQRT function which contains an argument having a reference to the SQRT function.

RESLT = SQRT(3.5 * SQRT(X))

An argument expression is evaluated to a single value, which is then passed as a single argument value to the function.

Examples of valid arguments with library-supplied functions are:

C = SQRT(A**2 + B**2)
RES = ALOG(987.4)
V = FLOAT(I + 3)
X = SQRT(A) + ABS(B)
RSLT = SQRT(FLOAT(L))

In the first example, the square root is taken of the expression A**2 + B**2, the formula for finding the length of the hypotenuse of a right triangle. The second example computes the natural (base 2) logarithm of the constant 987.4. The third example converts the sum of I plus 3 to real (floating-point) mode and assigns the result to V. The fourth example adds the square root of A to the absolute value of B and assigns the result to X. In the last example, the variable L is converted to real mode (by the floating-point conversion function FLOAT), and the square root of this real value is obtained and assigned to the variable RSLT.

If other arithmetic operations are included in the arithmetic expression, the function reference is always performed first. That is, a function reference has a higher precedence than any arithmetic operator in the hierarchy of arithmetic operations. A recap of the hierarchy of arithmetic operators which includes a function reference is:

first   — function reference
second   — raising to a power (**)
third   — unary minus sign
fourth   — multiplication and division (* and /)
fifth   — addition and subtraction (+ and −)

For example, the following statement produces a value of 6.5 for X. The circled numbers indicate the order of evaluation.

③ ① ④ ② ⑤

X = 6. * SQRT(9.) / 2. ** 2 + 2.

Of course, parentheses override any operators in the precedence hierarchy, including function references. The statement

X = 6. * SQRT(9.) / (2. ** 2 + 2.)

would produce a value of 3.0 for X.

Since it is difficult for the beginning student in programming to figure out how to use many of these valuable library functions, section two explains each of the built-in functions in ANSI FORTRAN 66 that are available on most FORTRAN compilers.

7.2 FORTRAN BUILT-IN FUNCTIONS AND THEIR USAGE

There are two main categories of built-in functions. First, there is a general set of library functions used for business and scientific problems. Second, there is the collection of trigonometric functions used for mathematical problems involving trigonometry. Let's look first at the general library functions. The FORTRAN preassigned function name will be given, along with its purpose and an explanation of its use.

The names of the functions presented are found in standard FORTRAN compilers. Some of the names may be different on various compilers—e.g., Burroughs 6000 FORTRAN uses the function name LN for the natural logarithm, while standard FORTRAN uses the name ALOG. You must confirm the built-in function names and the available library functions on your machine.

SQRT—Returns the Square Root of an Argument

The **SQRT** function must be given one real-mode argument. The function calculates the square root of the number and returns the result as a real-type value. You must not provide a negative value for the argument; if you do, the program may abort (since the square root of a negative number is not a real number). Some computers, however, will provide the square root of a positive number if a negative argument is given (the computer takes the square root of the absolute value of the argument). An example of calculating the square root of the variable ANUM and storing the result into the variable ASQRT is:

ASQRT = SQRT(ANUM)

If the value of ANUM is 9.61, then a value of 3.1 is returned from the function and stored in ASQRT. An example of computing the square root of the variable A plus 7.3 and storing the result into the variable Y is:

Y = SQRT(A + 7.3)

If the value of A is 8.7, then a value of 4.0 is returned from the function and stored into Y.

ABS and IABS—Returns the Absolute Value of an Argument

The **ABS** and **IABS** functions must be given one argument. The argument may be negative, zero, or positive. The function ABS is used to obtain the absolute value of a real value; therefore, it must be given a real-type argument, and it will return a real-type value. An example of taking the absolute value of X plus 1.5 and storing the result into the variable XABS is:

$$XABS = ABS(X + 1.5)$$

If the value of X is 3.0, then a value of 4.5 is returned. If the value of X is -4.2, then a value of 2.7 is returned. When the value of the argument is greater than or equal to zero, the returned value is the value of the argument. If the value of the argument is less than zero, then the value returned is the complement (additive inverse) of the expression, that is, the absolute value.

The **IABS** function obtains the absolute value of an integer value; it must be given an integer-type argument, and it will return an integer-type result. An example of taking the absolute value of the variable N1 and storing the result in M is:

$$M = IABS(N1)$$

If the value of N1 is 31, a value of 31 is returned by the function reference and stored in M. If the value of N1 is -18, a value of 18 is returned by the function and then the value is stored in M.

AINT and INT—Returns the Integer Part of the Given Argument

The **AINT** and **INT** functions both require one real-type argument. These functions are used to eliminate the fractional part of a real-mode argument and to return the integer (whole number) portion of the number.

The **AINT** function returns a real-type result. An example of obtaining the integer part of the number 37.567, then adding 15.0 to the result and storing this value in ARESLT is:

$$ARESLT = AINT(37.567) + 15.0$$

A value of 52.0 is stored in ARESLT.

The **INT** function returns an integer-type result. An example of obtaining the integer part of the variable X and storing the result into the variable IRESLT is:

$$IRESLT = INT(X)$$

If the value of X is 87.981, then a value of 87 is returned from the function reference and stored in IRESLT.

The INT function is widely used in Monte Carlo techniques for game playing when a pseudo-random number is used to simulate a situation. Since most pseudo-random number generators return a value between .0 and .9999999, you must multiply this value by a certain number and then use the INT function to obtain an integer number which falls within the desired integer range. An example of obtaining the integer results from the argument RNDNR multiplied by 100.0 and storing the results into INTNR is:

$$INTNR = INT(RNDNR * 100.0)$$

The function would return an integer result from the expression RNDNR * 100.0 to provide an integer value for INTNR. If the value of RNDNR is .3610227, then the integer portion of 36.10227 is returned by the function, and the value 36 is assigned to INTNR.

ALOG—Returns the Natural Logarithm of the Given Argument

The **ALOG** function requires one real-type argument. The natural logarithm (Naperian or base "e") of the argument is returned as a real value. The given argument must be a positive number. An example of taking the natural logarithm of the argument X - 2.0 and storing the result in RLOGE is:

$$RLOGE = ALOG(X - 2.0)$$

If the value of X is 15.0, then a value of 2.564949 is returned and stored in RLOGE. A common algorithm to obtain the base ten logarithm of a number using the natural log (ALOG) function is:

$$B10LOG = ALOG(X) / ALOG(10.0)$$

ALOG10—Returns the Base Ten Logarithm of the Given Argument

The **ALOG10** function requires one real-type argument. The common (or log to the base 10) logarithm is returned as a real value. The given argument must be a positive number. An example of taking the base 10 logarithm of the argument X and storing the result in XLOG10 is:

$$XLOG10 = ALOG10(X)$$

If the value of X is 1000, then the value of 3.0 is returned and stored into XLOG10.

EXP—Returns the Value of the Natural Number "e" Raised to the Power of the Argument

The **EXP** (exponential) function requires one real-type argument. A real-type value is returned which is 2.718281 (the value of the natural number "e", that is also the base of natural logarithms) raised to the power of the given argument (in base 10). Thus, the EXP function finds the exponential of the argument, that is, $EXP(x) = e^x$. An example of obtaining the exponential value of the variable X and storing the result in the variable RESULT is:

$$RESULT = EXP(X)$$

If the value of X is 2.0, then a value of 7.3890561 is returned and stored in RESULT.

FLOAT—Returns the Floating Point Value of an Integer Argument

The **FLOAT** function requires one integer-type argument. The value returned is the real-type value of the integer argument. This function is frequently used in arithmetic expressions to avoid a mixed mode expression. An example of multiplying 4.0 times the floating point value of the variable I and storing the results into VAL is:

$$VAL = 4.0 * FLOAT(I)$$

If the value of I is 2, then the results stored in VAL is 8.0.

IFIX—Returns the Integer Value of a Real Argument

The **IFIX** function requires one real-type argument. The function converts the real argument to an integer number. Truncation will occur if the real argument contains a fraction. The function returns an integer-type value. This function is frequently used in arithmetic expressions to avoid a mixed mode expression, for example:

$$INTX = IFIX(X) * 3$$

The function would return an integer value for X to provide integer-mode arithmetic for the arithmetic expression. If the value of X is 32.7409, then a value of 32 is returned by the function and the value 96 is assigned to INTX. The statement

$$INTX = IFIX(-24.73)$$

would produce a value of -24 for the variable INTX.

SIGN and ISIGN—Returns a Value which Represents the Algebraic Sign of the Argument

The **SIGN** and **ISIGN** functions both require one argument. These functions return a value which represents the algebraic sign of the argument. Thus, a programmer uses these functions if he/she wishes to know whether the value of an argument is negative, zero, or positive.

The **SIGN** function returns a value of -1.0 if the argument is negative, a value of 0.0 if the argument is zero, and a value of 1.0 if the argument is positive. For example, if you wish to terminate execution when the argument X is negative, you would write:

$$IF (SIGN(X) .EQ. -1.0) STOP$$

If the value of X is less than zero, a value of -1.0 is returned from the function, and the condition is true.

The **ISIGN** function requires one integer-type argument. An integer value of -1, 0, or 1 is returned if the value of the argument is negative, zero, or positive, respectively. If you wish to obtain the sign of the argument IARG and store the result into ISTORE, you would write:

$$ISTORE = ISIGN (IARG)$$

The following table illustrates the values returned by the SIGN and ISIGN functions:

Argument Value	Result	Example
Zero	0	ISIGN(0)
Positive	1	ISIGN(37)
Negative	-1	ISIGN(-4)

Next, several built-in functions which require more than one argument will be discussed.

AMOD and MOD—Returns the Remainder from the Division of Two Numbers in which the First Argument Is Divided by the Second

The **AMOD** function is used to obtain the remainder (in real mode) from the division of two real-type values. Both the AMOD and MOD functions require two arguments that are separated from each other by a comma. When more than one argument is required for a function, the arguments must be separated by a comma. The comma tells the compiler that one argument has ended and that another argument follows. The closing parenthesis indicates the end of the last argument. To obtain the remainder of 25.0 divided by 6.0 and place the results into the variable REM you would write

$$REM = AMOD(25.0, 6.0)$$

The value of 1.0 would be stored in REM. If either or both of the arguments are negative quantities, the remainder will have the same sign as the sign of the first argument.

The **MOD** function is used to obtain an integer remainder from the division of two integer-type values. Assuming a value of 17 for N1 and a value of 3 for N2, a remainder of 2 is obtained when 17 is divided by 3. If the result is stored in NREM, you would write

$$NREM = MOD(N1, N2)$$

The names AMOD and MOD come from the term ''Modulo'' that is the name of the mathematical operation which yields the remainder function of division. The modulo functions are used frequently in scheduling programs. For example, a dental application program might print dental examination notices every 180 days (6 months) to the dental patients. Another example of the modulo functions is to convert a decimal number to another number base (base 2, 8, or 16). The remainder is used to form a digit in the converted number.

DIM and IDIM—Returns the Positive Difference between Two Arguments

The **DIM** function requires two real-type arguments. The function subtracts the second argument from the first and returns the positive difference as a real value. An example of obtaining the positive difference between the arguments A and B and storing the results in DIFAB is:

$$DIFAB = DIM(A, B)$$

If the values of A and B are 10.0 and 5.0, respectively, a value of 5.0 is obtained for DIFAB. If the values of A and B are 5.0 and 10.0, respectively, a value of 5.0 is stored in DIFAB. If the values of A and B are -10.0 and 5.0 respectively, a value of 15.0 is obtained from the function. If the values of A and B are 10.0 and -5.0, respectively, a value of 15.0 is stored in DIFAB. If the values of A and B are -10.0 and -5.0, respectively, a value of 5.0 is returned from the function DIM and stored in DIFAB.

The **IDIM** function requires two integer-type arguments. The second argument is subtracted from the first and an integer-type positive difference is returned. An example of obtaining the difference between the arguments I and J and storing the results into IDIFIJ is:

$$IDIFIJ = IDIM (I, J)$$

The IDIM function works the same way as the DIM function, except that an integer value is returned instead of a real-type value.

AMAX0, MAX0, AMAX1 and MAX1—Returns the Largest Quantity from a Group of Two or More Arguments

The **AMAX0** and **MAX0** functions require two or more integer-type arguments. These functions return the largest quantity from the set of integer arguments.

The **AMAX0** function returns a real-type value. An example of obtaining the largest item from the variables I, J, K, and L is:

$$RESULT = AMAX0 \ (I, J, K, L)$$

If the values of I, J, K, and L are 35, 18, 41, and 5, respectively, then a value of 41.0 is returned and stored in RESULT.

The **MAX0** function returns an integer-type result. If you wish to obtain the largest item in integer form from the same values of I, J, K, and L and store the result in IRESLT, you would write:

$$IRESLT = MAX0 \ (I, J, K, L)$$

Assuming the same values for the arguments (as in AMAX0), a value of 41 is returned and stored in IRESLT.

The **AMAX1** and **MAX1** functions require two or more real-type arguments. These functions return the largest item from the set of real arguments.

The **AMAX1** function returns a real-type value. An example of finding the largest item from the variables A, B, C, and D, plus the constant 10.0 is:

$$RESULT = AMAX1 \ (A, B, C, D, 10.0)$$

If the values of A, B, C, and D are 6.3, 7.21, 3.5, and 4.802, respectively, then a value of 10.0 is returned and stored in RESULT.

The **MAX1** function returns an integer-type result from the set of real-type arguments. An example of obtaining the largest item from the variables A, B, C, and D, plus the constant 5.0 is:

$$IRESLT = MAX1 \ (A, B, C, D, 5.0)$$

If the same values are used for the variable arguments as in AMAX1, then a value of 7 is returned from the function and stored in IRESLT.

AMIN0, MIN0, AMIN1, and MIN1—Returns the Smallest Quantity from a Group of Two or More Arguments

The **AMIN0** and **MIN0** functions require two or more integer-type arguments. These functions return the smallest quantity from the set of integer arguments.

The **AMIN0** returns a real-type result. An example of obtaining the smallest item from the variables I, J, K, and L is:

$$RESULT = AMIN0(I, J, K, L)$$

If the values of I, J, K, and L are 35, 18, 41, and 50, respectively, then a value of 18.0 is returned and stored in RESULT.

The **MIN0** function returns an integer result. If you wish to obtain the smallest item in integer form from the variables I, J, K, and L and store the result in IRESLT, you would write:

$$IRESLT = MIN0(I, J, K, L)$$

Assuming the same values for the arguments as in the AMIN0 example, a value of 18 is returned and stored in IRESLT.

The **AMIN1** and **MIN1** functions require two or more real-type arguments. These functions also return the smallest item from a set of real arguments.

The **AMIN1** function returns a real-type result. An example of finding the smallest item from the variables A, B, C, D, and the constant 10.0 and storing the result into RESULT is:

$$RESULT = AMIN1 \ (A, B, C, D, 10.0)$$

If the values of A, B, C, and D are 6.3, 7.21, 3.5, and 4.802, respectively, then a value of 3.5 is returned and stored in RESULT.

The **MIN1** function returns an integer-type result. An example of finding the smallest item from the variables A, B, C, D, and the constant 10.0 and storing the result into IRESLT is:

IRESLT = MIN1(A, B, C, D, 10.0)

Assuming the same values for the variables A, B, C and D as given in the AMIN1 example, a value of 3 is returned and stored in IRESLT.

Table 7.1 provides a handy reference of the Library-supplied functions commonly used in business and scientific problems. The Number-of-Arguments column indicates the proper number of input arguments to the function. The Type-of-Arguments column indicates the required type of the input argument to the function. The Type-of-Returned-Value column indicates the type of value returned (real or integer).

Table 7.1 Library Functions Used in Business and Scientific Problems

User Reference Name	FORTRAN Name	Mathematical Definition	Number of Arguments	Type of Arguments	Type of Returned Value
Square Root	SQRT	$\sqrt{a}$	1	Real	Real
Absolute Value	ABS	$|a|$	1	Real	Real
	IABS	$|k|$	1	Integer	Integer
Exponential	EXP	e^a	1	Real	Real
Conversion from integer to real	FLOAT	change integer mode argument to real mode.	1	Integer	Real
Conversion from real to integer	IFIX	change real mode argument to integer mode.	1	Real	Integer
Modulo Arithmetic (Real remainder)	AMOD	$y = \text{Modulo}(a,b)$	2	Real	Real
Modulo Arithmetic (Integer remainder)	MOD	$y = \text{Modulo}(i,j)$	2	Integer	Integer
Natural Logarithm	ALOG	$\log_e(a)$	1	Real	Real
Common Logarithm	ALOG10	$\log_{10}(a)$	1	Real	Real
Largest Value	AMAX0	$\max(a_1,...,a_n)$	≥ 2	Integer	Real
	MAX0			Integer	Integer
	AMAX1			Real	Real
	MAX1			Real	Integer
Smallest Value	AMIN0	$\min(a_1,...,a_n)$	≥ 2	Integer	Real
	MIN0			Integer	Integer
	AMIN1			Real	Real
	MIN1			Real	Integer
Truncation	AINT	eliminate the fractional portion of the argument.	1	Real	Real
	INT			Real	Integer
Transfer of sign	SIGN	sign of a × 1.0	1	Real	Real
	ISIGN	sign of a × 1		Integer	Integer
Positive Difference	DIM	$|a_1 - a_2|$	2	Real	Real
	IDIM			Integer	Integer

Now let's look at the built-in trigonometric functions which are available in standard FORTRAN. The arguments of trigonometric functions must be expressed in radian measure and not in degrees of an angle. If you have a value given in an angular measurement of degrees, then this value may be converted into radians by multiplying the degrees value by the constant .0174533 (which is π divided by 180, since 2π radians are equal to 360 degrees, or π radians are equal to 180 degrees). A radian value may be converted to degrees by multiplying the value by 57.29578 (which is 180 divided by π; 3.1416 or 3.14159 may be used for π), since one radian is equivalent to 57.29578 degrees.

SIN—Returns the Sine of the Argument Expressed in Radians

The **SIN** function requires one real-type argument. The argument must be expressed in radians (and not in degrees of an angle). The function returns a real-type value. An example of computing the sine of the argument X (given in radians) and storing the result into XRESLT is:

$$XRESLT = SIN(X)$$

If the value of X is 0.5235988 (30°), then a value of 0.5 is returned from the function and stored in XRESLT.

An example to test whether the sine of the variable ANGLE (given in degrees) is equal to 0.0 and to print a message of "HORIZONTAL" if this condition is true is written as follows (3.1416 is used as the value for π):

```
     IF (SIN(3.1416 / 180.0*ANGLE) .EQ. 0.0) WRITE (6,299)
299  FORMAT (1H0,10HHORIZONTAL)
```

COS—Returns the Cosine of the Argument Expressed in Radians

The **COS** function requires one real-type argument that must be expressed in radians. A real-type value is returned. An example of using the COS function to find the cosine of the variable RADIAN and to store the result into COSRAD is:

$$COSRAD = COS(RADIAN)$$

If the value of RADIAN is 1.0471976 (60°), then the value 0.5 is returned and stored into COSRAD.

The cosine of a real number may also be computed by using the SIN function and the identity:

$$COS(x) = SIN(x + \frac{\pi}{2})$$

ATAN—Returns the Arctangent of the Argument Expressed in Radians

The **ATAN** requires one real-type argument. The function returns a real-type value in radians. An example of using ATAN to calculate the arctangent of the argument Y and to store the result in YATAN is:

$$YATAN = ATAN(Y)$$

If the value of Y is 0.7853982 (45°), then the value of 1.0 is returned and stored into YATAN.

The ATAN function may be used to compute other inverse trigonometric functions by using simple identities. The arcsin and arccosine may be obtained with the ATAN function.

TANH—Returns the Hyperbolic Tangent of the Argument Expressed in Radians

The **TANH** (hyperbolic tangent) function requires one real-type argument expressed in radians. The function returns a real-type value. An example of calculating the hyperbolic tangent of the argument X is:

$$HTANX = TANH(X)$$

If the value of X is 1.0, then a value of 0.7615942 is returned and stored into HTANX.

TAN—Returns the Tangent of the Argument Expressed in Radians

Some FORTRAN compilers do not include the built-in function TAN to calculate the trigonometric tangent. Since not all implementations of FORTRAN have a built-in function to compute the tangent of an angle, a trigonometric identity can be used to accomplish this calculation. The trigonometric identity that can be easily calculated for a tangent is (the variable A represents the angle):

$$\tan A = \frac{\sin A}{\cos A}$$

If the value of the angle (A) is expressed as X (in radians), then the FORTRAN statement would be:

$$\text{TANVAL} = \text{SIN(X)} / \text{COS(X)}$$

For those versions of FORTRAN which provides a tangent (TAN) function, this function must be given one real-type argument expressed in radians. A real-type value is returned.

Other Trigonometric Functions

Many FORTRAN dialects do not include built-in trigonometric functions to compute the cotangent, arcsine, arccosine, hyperbolic sine, and hyperbolic cosine. If your dialect of FORTRAN does not include these functions, their values may be derived from simple trigonometric identities. For example, the cotangent may be derived from the following identity (the variable A represents the angle):

$$\cot A = \frac{\cos A}{\sin A}$$

FORTRAN 77 includes the built-in functions of ASIN (arcsine), ACOS (arccosine), SINH (hyperbolic sine), and COSH (hyperbolic cosine), but not the cotangent function. ANSI FORTRAN 66 does not include any of these functions. FORTRAN IV compilers vary as to the inclusion of these functions.

Normally there are no built-in functions to calculate the Secant and Cosecant of angles. These trigonometric values may be derived from single identities as follows (A represents the angle):

$$\sec A = \frac{1}{\cos A}$$

$$\csc A = \frac{1}{\sin A}$$

Table 7.2 provides a list of the Library-supplied trigonometric functions.

There are also built-in functions for double-precision and complex arguments in the FORTRAN functions library.

Table 7.2 Library of Trigonometric FORTRAN Functions

User Reference Name	FORTRAN Name	Mathematical Definition	Number of Arguments	Type of Arguments	Type of Returned Value
Trigonometric Sine	SIN	sin(a) a in radians.	1	Real	Real
Trigonometric Cosine	COS	cos(a) a in radians.	1	Real	Real
Arctangent	ATAN	arctan(a) a in radians.	1	Real	Real
	ATAN2	$\arctan(a_1/a_2)$ a in radians.	2	Real	Real
Hyperbolic Tangent	TANH	tanh(a) a in radians.	1	Real	Real
*Trigonometric Tangent	TAN	tan(a) a in radians.	1	Real	Real
*Trigonometric Cotangent	COTAN	cotan(a) a in radians.	1	Real	Real
*Arcsine	ARSIN	arcsin(a) a in radians.	1	Real	Real
*Arccosine	ARCOS	arccos(a) a in radians.	1	Real	Real
*Hyperbolic Sine	SINH	sinh(a) a in radians.	1	Real	Real
*Hyperbolic Cosine	COSH	cosh(a) a in radians.	1	Real	Real

*Indicates nonstandard ANSI function, but included since they are found in most FORTRAN Libraries.

7.3 TECHNIQUES FOR DEBUGGING COMPILATION (SYNTAX) ERRORS

One of the most frustrating aspects of learning programming is being unable to eliminate all the syntax errors found during the compilation of a program. Everyone wants to see output results when a program is run. After spending many hours planning, coding, and entering the program into a computer medium, a student eagerly anticipates a successful run. Yet, one small clerical error, such as a missing comma, can prevent the program from executing. This section discusses various methods and techniques for locating syntax errors detected during program compilation.

Compiler error messages vary in severity and fall into two general categories:

1. **Fatal diagnostic messages.** This level of syntax error is so severe that the compiler cannot translate your source statement(s) into its machine language form. The language translator will continue to check for syntax errors throughout the entire program, but it will not generate the object program needed by the computer to execute the program. No execution of your program is attempted when these types of syntax errors are detected during compilation. Syntax errors causing fatal diagnostic messages might be misspelled keywords or missing delimiters, such as commas and matching parentheses.

2. **Warning diagnostic messages.** This second type of syntax error is not severe enough to prevent the generation of an object program. The computer will attempt to execute the program, but correct results are not guaranteed. One example of syntax errors of this level would be placing a statement number on the END statement or not having a statement number on the statement following a GO TO statement. All warning messages should be corrected, even though the computer will compile and execute the job.

First, you must convince yourself that it is to your advantage and benefit to make an honest effort to locate syntax errors by yourself, before seeking help from others. The more experience you have in identifying syntax errors, the easier it becomes to find and correct them. If you always turn to your instructor or someone else to find your syntax errors for you, you gain no experience in this area. When you find a syntax error on your own, it makes such an impression that you will always remember that particular type of mistake.

Common Syntax Errors Detected During Compilation

You must follow the rules of the FORTRAN language when constructing your FORTRAN statements and other elements (such as variable names). The compiler or language translator is a system program that checks your statements for correctness in accordance with these rules. If a statement has correctly formed elements in the proper order, then the machine language instructions for that statement can be generated. Otherwise, a syntax error is detected and flagged by the compiler.

The method of flagging syntax errors varies among different computers and FORTRAN compilers. Most systems flag an error and print a diagnostic message as close to the error as possible (just beneath the statement in error). Some compilers, however, may list all syntax errors at the end of a program. You should look at the end of your source program as well as in the source program for compilation diagnostic messages. Some compilers print an error code (number) plus a short description of the error as their diagnostic message. These error codes may be looked up in the appropriate system manual for a more descriptive explanation of the error. Most diagnostic messages, however, are descriptive enough to make this unnecessary.

Following are some of the common compilation errors detected by the FORTRAN compiler. Understanding these errors will help you avoid them in your program.

1. Error in a keyword spelling. The keywords at the beginning of FORTRAN statements must be spelled correctly. For example, the statement

WIRTE (6,99) A, B, C

contains a spelling error in the keyword **WRITE**. This transposition spelling error would cause an illegal statement syntax error.

2. Variable names that do not start with an alphabetic letter or are too long. Remember the rules of forming names. They must be six characters or less and start with a letter. An error of omitting the comma to separate variables would also produce this type of error.

3. Missing comma or parenthesis. Commas must be used to separate variables, format codes, and other elements. The specifications in a FORMAT statement must be enclosed within a pair of parentheses. All parentheses used within the Assignment statement must have matching beginning and ending parentheses.

4. FORMAT statement without a statement number. All FORMAT statements must have a statement number in order to be referenced by an I/O statement.

5. Duplicate statement numbers. Each statement number in a program must be unique. That is, the same statement number may not be used with more than one FORTRAN statement (this includes the FORMAT statement).

6. Invalid statement layout. Each statement typed onto cards or at a terminal must have its parts beginning at specific locations. Statement numbers must be punched between positions 1 and 5; position 6 must be used for continuation only; and the statement must begin in position 7 or later and end at or before column 72. The FORTRAN compiler is sensitive to these positions on a statement layout. Starting the statement portion in position 6 would normally result in an illegal statement syntax message.

7. Illegal syntax. All statements must be formed according to their syntactical format. You must follow this form precisely and not make up your own. Check the syntactical construction diagrams to make sure you have included the necessary parts, such as parentheses and commas.

8. Not including a non-blank or non-zero character in column 6 for continuation statements. All continuation statements must be clearly identified by a character in position 6; otherwise, the compiler will interpret the line as a new beginning statement.

9. Too many continuation statements. Most FORTRAN compilers have a limit on the maximum number of continuation statements allowed. The limit normally ranges from five to nineteen.

10. Missing statement number. There must be a statement number on a FORTRAN statement if it has been referenced by a control statement.

11. No END statement in program. Every FORTRAN program must have an END statement as its last physical statement. Otherwise, the compiler does not know where a source program unit ends. The compiler may attempt to compile data cards as part of a program.

12. END statement with a statement number. The END statement must never be given a statement number, since it cannot be referenced by a control statement.

13. Using illegal characters to form a FORTRAN element. Since the numeric "zero" and alphabetic "O" are close to each other on the keypunch and terminal keyboards, they are often mistaken for each other. You may have used the letter O for a zero in a statement number or the digit zero in place of the letter O in a keyword such as GO TO. This error is often difficult to find, but experience in noticing the shape of the characters is helpful in locating this type of error. On most printers the letter "O" is squared at the top and bottom; the digit "0" is more rounded at the top and bottom, like an egg. (An exception is Honeywell printers, in which the reverse is the case.)

14. Unclosed DO loops. The end of a DO statement is indicated by a statement number. Failure to include this statement number will produce the syntax error "unclosed DO loop."

15. Errors in dimensioning (this will be explained in more detail when arrays are discussed). In order to refer to array items with subscripted variables, you must provide a DIMENSION or other appropriate specification statement at the beginning of your program. Failure to do so will cause a syntax error when referencing an array item. When an array item is referenced in a statement, and a DIMENSION (or Type) statement was not given for the array, the compiler translates the array reference as a function reference. A syntax error is produced which says "missing function." The DIMENSION declaration is the only way the compiler can distinguish an array item from a function reference, since both a subscript and the argument(s) for a function are enclosed within parentheses.

16. Specification statements out of order. In order to provide various information to the compiler you may have several specification statements at the start of your program. These multiple specification statements must generally be given in a specific order to provide the necessary specifications to the compiler clearly.

These identified types of syntax errors should help you understand some of the typing and other clerical errors you can make in coding and entering a FORTRAN program in a computer input medium. Other types of syntax errors exist, but these are the ones that occur repeatedly.

Procedures to Follow in Debugging Compilation Errors

A set of procedures to follow in debugging syntax errors flagged during program compilation is given as follows:

1. Use the compiler diagnostic messages as much as possible. The compiler tries to be as helpful as it can and to identify as much as possible what the syntax errors are, but it can only help you so much. A diagnostic message usually pertains to the statement immediately before the error message. However, there may be times when the error really lies in the statement *prior* to the one before the error message (i.e., two statements above the diagnostic message). For example, consider the following syntax error of a missing ending parenthesis for the FORMAT statement.

READ (5, 199) A, B
199 FORMAT (I5, 5X, I4
SUM = A + B
$ invalid format specifications [from the compiler]

The diagnostic message is given after the Assignment statement, although it is actually the FORMAT statement that has the error (no ending parenthesis). Since the format specifications could be continued on a new line, the compiler cannot detect this error until the next statement is looked at. Because the compiler did not find another format code or ending parenthesis, the error message is printed beneath the Assignment statement. The compiler may produce a false error message by expecting a correct syntax and misunderstanding the error. Remember, the compiler was written by a human being; so it is not perfect.

You should always examine closely the diagnostic information printed. A $ or some identifying information is usually printed near the error. Some compilers print the part of the statement that the compiler could not understand, starting with the unintelligible elements.

2. Desk-check the program to carefully review the statements. Examine each statement for spelling errors, proper punctuation, typing errors, and so forth. Make sure you haven't used a numeric zero for an alphabetic "O" and vice versa.

3. Carefully check each statement for its syntactical construction. Be sure to have your textbook with you, and review the syntactical form (general notation) of any statement in question.

4. Make sure the correct columnar positions are used to contain the parts of each FORTRAN statement. Be sure to check that the FORTRAN statement begins in position 7 or later. Also check to make sure the statement does not go past position 72, since any information past position 72 is ignored by the compiler.

5. Repunch or retype the statement or error. This technique often corrects clerical errors, such as using the numeric zero for an alphabetic "O" or vice versa. When a statement is retyped, the correct syntax is often entered, which clears up the error.

6. Another useful technique for finding errors is to put the program aside for a while. "Sleep on it for a night"; then re-examine the error. Putting your program aside for a short period helps you to get the problem out of your mind. Perhaps a new view of how to attack the problem will occur to you. Often you may be in a rut and "cannot see the forest for the trees."

7. After exhausting all possible means of locating the syntax error yourself, turn for help. Seek the advice of your friends or fellow classmates. When all else fails, turn to your instructor for help. Be sure to save and bring your program listings with you to aid in debugging your syntax errors.

After a program compiles, it may still contain logic errors that occur during the execution of a program. The next section explains techniques to locate run-time errors.

7.4 TECHNIQUES FOR DEBUGGING EXECUTION (LOGIC) ERRORS

Programmers are not infallible. The existence of program bugs is almost guaranteed, especially with large and/or complex programs. The programmer must devise ways to verify output results and to locate errors in the program when they occur. Only infrequently is an error caused by hardware or system software errors; they are not infallible, but almost so. You should prove that any program execution error is not the fault of your program before approaching the computer center staff to complain of hardware or compiler error.

Most logic errors result from program design. Trying to develop a program without adequate planning and solution design will nearly always lead to numerous logic errors. Planning the solution and stepping through the associated design logic to ensure its correctness will often produce a program that works correctly the first time.

You should, therefore, make every attempt to plan the solution thoroughly before writing your program. Too often we are in a hurry just to get something on the computer. Remember two important things:

1. Very few programs with more than a dozen statements compile and run the first time. It usually takes four to ten **shots (turnarounds)** on the computer to produce a correct program. Be sure you allow time for correcting **bugs** (logic errors) in your programs. Few programs work perfectly on their first execution.

2. Incorrect answers are produced as a result of bugs in your program, not because something is wrong with the computer. The computer does only what it is told, nothing more. Accept the fact that errors are produced by the logic in your program, and proceed to locate and correct them. Do not blame the computer for errors you can't figure out.

Debugging can be the most frustrating part of the programming task. This section discusses various techniques for locating execution errors. After determining what caused a logic error you must carefully plan how to correct it in order to produce a correct, workable program.

Execution errors usually fall into two categories. The first consists of **logic errors**—the output results are not correct. The computer produces some output, but not what was expected. The second type of error results when a computer is told to do something that it cannot do, and the program "blows up." Such an error is called a **system-fault error** and is caused by some illegal operation, such as dividing by zero.

First, never assume your output to be correct. Always carefully check the output results. As mentioned in chapter 5, the best way to verify the answers is to make hand calculations of some of the input values and determine what the results should be. When your program has several paths it can take in the logic, an input value should be used for each alternative path. If the calculations for the input values involve fractions and are highly complex, prepare some simple numbers and test data. Then, run the program with the simple set of input values and compare the results with the easy-to-calculate values.

Locating the Logic Error

Once you have discovered that a bug exists in your program, there are numerous techniques that may be used to help locate the logic error. Among these are:

1. Desk-check the program.
2. Echo-check the input data.
3. Print intermediate values from calculations.
4. Include check-point messages as temporary WRITE statements.
5. Rewrite the segment of code in error.
6. Use debug facilities and trace packages.
7. Use various control card (JCL) options, such as a program cross-reference of variables.

Desk-Check the Program

You are probably already familiar with the desk-checking technique to locate logic errors. But remember, you ought to have solved the problem in your design step; the computer can only do what it is told. You play the role of the computer and manually trace the execution path through the program. As you follow the logic, jot down the computed values and see if you have told the computer the proper order and way to solve the problem. When an error is discovered, the logic can be corrected. You should not stop as soon as you have found the first error. Continue through the program and correct as many errors as you can find. Resist the temptation to rush back to the computer after finding only one error. Sometimes you can't figure out why the computer doesn't give the same answers as in the desk-check. In that case, you need to turn to other techniques to locate the error.

Echo-Check the Input Data

Too often the beginning programmer assumes that the error is in the program and spends fruitless hours trying to find the bug, when in reality the error lies in the data. A data field may be punched in the wrong columns, in the wrong format, or have incorrect values. The computer does not question the values given to it. It simply reads the data as told. Perhaps you should be using an F7.2 format code when you are actually using an F6.2 specification. Maybe you should be skipping only three blank positions when you are actually skipping four.

During the first test run you should echo-check (print) your input items to verify their validity. Echo-checking your input data means to print the input values you have just read. You simply include a WRITE statement with the same variables, immediately following the READ statement. This way, you can be certain that the input values were read correctly and that you have the proper values stored in memory. After you are certain that the input values are read correctly, the WRITE statements can be removed from your program.

Input data errors may fall into one of the following categories:

1. Specifying the wrong columnar positions for a data item. Perhaps you are reading an item from positions 7 through 10 when the data item actually appears in positions 17–20.
2. An input field specification is too narrow for the data. You may be reading an item from positions 7 through 10 when the data item appears in positions 6 through 10 or 7 through 11.
3. An input field specification is too wide for the data item. You may be reading an item from positions 7 through 11 when the data item is typed in positions 7 through 10. Data fields are usually run together, since a blank position to separate the data items is not needed with formatted data. You should draw a vertical line on your data record to delineate the data fields, to help visualize their correct record positions.
4. Often data fields are punched in the wrong sequence, or the variable names to which they are assigned may be given in the wrong order. Echo-checking the input data items should locate this error.
5. An invalid character is read in a data item. Perhaps you should be reading a numeric field, but an alphabetic character is read instead. This generally causes the program to "blow up." This error may be caused by a typing error in the data or by not reading the correct field positions for an item. Always review your data records as well as your program during desk checking.
6. Failure to include the data records or placing them at the wrong location in the job deck results in no output.
7. The end-of-file JCL statement may be placed at the wrong point (e.g., before all or part of the data records). This may cause no data records to be read or an incorrect number of data records to be read.
8. An infrequent, but frustrating error is specifying the wrong file unit number in the formatted READ statement. Students sometimes specify unit number 6 for the input file unit number when this is really the default output file unit number. Naturally, no input will be read, and no syntax error message is produced. Likewise, students make the mistake of using file unit number 5 for the formatted WRITE file unit number, when this is actually the default input file unit number. No output results are produced, and no syntax message is given. Be sure you have given the correct file unit numbers in the formatted READ and WRITE statements.

Print Intermediate Values from Calculations

Sometimes a long list of values or a long, "hairy" formula such as the computation for a linear regression is calculated. It is best to break up long formulas into shorter ones. When the correct output is not produced, print the resulting values from each of the Assignment statements. Each computed value can be examined to see where the calculations went wrong.

Let's examine the following example in printing intermediate calculated results. The formula used for calculating the value of b in a linear regression is:

$$b = \frac{n\sum XY - \sum X \sum Y}{n\sum x^2 - (\sum X)^2}$$

This is a pretty "hairy" formula to code in FORTRAN in one statement and get it correct. Can you spot the errors in the following invalid coded FORTRAN statement?

$$B = FLOAT(N) * XYSUM - XSUM * YSUM / FLOAT(N) * XSQSUM - XSUM **2$$

No parentheses were used to override the normal precedence of arithmetic operations. An example of breaking this formula into intermediate calculations and printing the results in order to validate the calculations is:

```
      BNUM = FLOAT(N) * XYSUM - XSUM * YSUM
      WRITE (6,99) BNUM
   99 FORMAT (1H0, 7HBNUM = ,F8.2)
      BDEN = FLOAT(N) * XSQSUM - XSUM **2
      WRITE (6,98) BDEN
   98 FORMAT (1H0, 7HBDEN = ,F8.2)
      B = BNUM / BDEN
      WRITE (6,97) B
   97 FORMAT (1H0, 4HB = ,F8.2)
```

The calculations were broken down into three parts. First, the numerator portion is calculated; second, the denominator; then the value of B. Printing the result from each separate portion of the calculations helps determine where the error may be, if one occurs. You could go even farther and break each portion down more. For example:

```
      PART1 = FLOAT(N) * XYSUM
      WRITE (6,99) PART1
   99 FORMAT (1H0,F8.2)
      PART2 = XSUM * YSUM
      WRITE (6,99) PART2
      BNUM = PART1 - PART2
      WRITE (6,99) BNUM
      PART3 = FLOAT(N) * XSQSUM
      WRITE (6,99) PART3
      PART4 = XSUM ** 2
      WRITE (6,99) PART4
      BDEN = PART3 - PART4
      WRITE (6,99) BDEN
      B = BNUM / BDEN
      WRITE (6,99) B
```

In this code the calculations are broken up into very minute portions of the overall formula. The results from the calculations for the sum of X (XSUM), sum of Y (YSUM), sum of X times Y (XYSUM) and the sum of X^2 (XSQSUM) should be printed earlier to check the correctness of their values. Displaying the immediate results from a short expression helps locate any incorrect calculation that might be coded. This may be an example of "overkill," but sometimes you need to use this detail level to find out where the error is.

Include Checkpoint Messages as Temporary WRITE Statements

Temporary WRITE statements (checkpoint messages) may be inserted in a program to trace the flow of execution. You may wonder how you got to a certain statement and how you could possibly get the output results you did. Perhaps you thought a certain condition would be met, but you failed to take into account a special situation. Maybe you have an arithmetic truncation error that always produces a false condition in a comparison.

Checkpoint messages inserted throughout your program will allow you to follow the execution sequence and see exactly what paths the computer is taking. Checkpoint messages also tell you exactly how far the computer got in your program before blowing up, in case you encounter a system-fault error.

Suppose your program is "blowing up," and you can't figure out which statement is causing it. You could code, for example:

```
      . . .
      WRITE (6,99)
   99 FORMAT (1H0,5HCHECK)
      . . .
      . . .
```

```
              WRITE (6,99)
              . . .
              . . .
              WRITE (6,99)
              . . .
              END
```

After running the program again, two "CHECK" messages were printed. Thus, you know that the statement causing the program to "blow up" lies between the second and third checkpoint WRITE. You could then insert other checkpoint WRITE's between the second and third ones. Keep narrowing down the remaining statements until you have a checkpoint WRITE after each statement. This way you can isolate the error.

Different messages must be printed to follow the flow of execution if GO TO's are used in the program. Consider the following example.

```
              . . .
        1     . . .
              WRITE (6,99)
        99    FORMAT (1H0, 7HCHECK 1)
              . . .
              . . .
              . . .
              IF (I .EQ. 10) GO TO 2
              WRITE (6,98)
        98    FORMAT (1H0, 7HCHECK 2)
              . . .
              . . .
        2     WRITE (6,97)
        97    FORMAT (1H0, 7HCHECK 3)
              IF (J .EQ. 0) GO TO 1
              WRITE (6,96)
        96    FORMAT (1H0, 7HCHECK 4)
              . . .
```

With different checkpoint messages as illustrated in this example, you can accurately trace the flow of execution in the program to see what branches are taken in the logic. If the computer is taking a branch that you did not expect, examine the input data or IF statement to find out why.

Debugging statements may be left in place in a program and a variable used to control their printing. This technique allows the debug messages to be used when the program is modified or tested again later. For example, the logical variable SWT is used to determine whether the debug statements are to be printed in the following routine.

```
              LOGICAL SWT
              SWT = .TRUE.
        1     . . .
              IF (SWT) WRITE (6,99)
        99    FORMAT (1H0, 7HCHECK 1)
              . . .
              . . .
              . . .
              IF (I .EQ. 10) GO TO 2
              IF (SWT) WRITE (6,98)
        98    FORMAT (1H0, 7HCHECK 2)
              . . .
              . . .
        2     IF (SWT) WRITE (6,97)
        97    FORMAT (1H0, 7HCHECK 3)
              IF (J .EQ. 0) GO TO 1
              IF (SWT) WRITE (6,96)
        96    FORMAT (1H0, 7HCHECK 4)
              . . .
```

The assignment of the logical constant ".TRUE." to the variable SWT causes the debug messages to be printed. To turn off the printing of the debug messages, you would change the logical constant to ".FALSE." for SWT. Thus, the debug messages may be left in an operational program for later use.

You may also combine the use of checkpoint messages and the output of intermediate values for certain variables to provide useful trace routines. When the program is free of errors, at least in certain segments, these WRITE statements are easily removed. The combination of printing checkpoint messages and desired variables is perhaps the best technique for a beginning student to use in finding logic errors in complex programs.

Rewrite the Segment of Code in Error

When all else fails, rewrite the routine in which the error occurs. Sometimes rewriting the same statements reveals the hidden error. Perhaps the formula was coded incorrectly in the Assignment statement. Maybe an extra set of parentheses is needed to change the order of computations. Perhaps a needed variable or constant was overlooked in the formula. Maybe the condition in the IF statement was given incorrectly. If rewriting the same routine does not work, try a different approach in the logic of the routine. Often a different algorithm or method of attack will correct the problem.

Debug Facility and Trace Packages

A debug facility is a programming aid that enables a user to locate errors in a FORTRAN source program. The IBM G and G1 FORTRAN compilers include such a debug facility. This facility provides for tracing the flow of logic within a program and between program units, displaying the values of variables and arrays, and checking the validity of subscripts for subscripted variables. Debug statements include keywords such as DEBUG TRACE, DEBUG SUBTRACE, AT statement number, TRACE ON, TRACE OFF, and DISPLAY list.

Debug and trace packages are available on other computers. Burroughs 6000 FORTRAN has a DEBUG MONITOR statement to monitor the changes in value of simple variables and array elements within a program unit. Each time the values of designated variables change, their new value is displayed. Many timesharing systems have on-line debugging tools for interactive debugging.

Use Various Control Card (JCL) Options (Cross-Reference Listing)

Most compilers allow the use of certain control card options to provide extra information from the compilation. One common option on IBM compilers is the MAP option to provide the type and location in memory of each variable name used by the program. The XREF option is used on many computers to produce a cross-reference listing. The **cross-reference listing** (frequently referred as an XREF) shows all the variables used in a program and lists all the statements that referenced each variable. The XREF listing is a good debug tool. The generated machine language may also be obtained, but it will have little value for the beginning student (and may cause volumes of output).

System-fault Errors That Cause Program Aborts

The second type of execution error is one that causes the computer to abnormally terminate a program. An arithmetic calculation may result in an attempt to compute a number exceeding the maximum value that a specific computer can hold. This type of error is called an **overflow**. The calculated value may be too large for a storage location, which may be caused by a logic error in the program. For example, on IBM compilers, if a student reads a data value under an integer format code and stores it at a real variable, with a subsequent multiplication, an overflow error will occur. The reverse of an overflow error is an **underflow** error. This means that you tried to compute a number smaller than the smallest value allowed.

Other types of program-abort errors may be caused by a divide-by-zero calculation, an invalid operator, an invalid subscript, or trying to read input data with the wrong type of format specifications. The computer aborts the program and prints an associated system error message as to what caused the termination. With the error messages and printed results produced up to program termination, you may have a clue as to the statement or area of your program that caused the error. Otherwise, you may have to resort to some of the previously discussed debugging techniques. The best way to find program-abort errors is the use of checkpoint messages.

A memory dump can be taken on many computers when a program aborts. The **memory dump** displays the entire contents of memory used by the program and the machine language instructions. This dump can be extremely helpful in finding the most obscure errors. However, you usually must have a thorough knowledge of the computer's machine language and addressing procedures in order to profit from a memory dump. System programmers are quite familiar with a memory dump and can provide assistance in determining the nature and location of the error that caused the abnormal termination. Beginning programmers will waste their time trying to comprehend the large output generated from such a dump.

The WATFOR and WATFIV compilers are extremely helpful in locating program-abort errors. In addition to a clear execution fault error message, a message saying "PROGRAM WAS EXECUTING LINE n IN ROUTINE M/PROG WHEN ERROR OCCURRED" will be printed. The line number n in this message refers to the line sequence number assigned to the statements in your program by the compiler. You may still have to echo-check the variable used in the statement to find which value caused the error. These compilers can also detect many logic errors, such as undefined variables, invalid subscripts, changing the index variable and indexing parameters in a DO loop, and many more.

7.5 SAMPLE DEBUGGING PROBLEMS

This section presents several debugging problems to illustrate the techniques of finding errors in a program. First, a syntax debugging problem will be examined.

A Syntax Debugging Problem

Figure 7.1 lists a program with 16 statements. Each statement in the program has one or more syntax errors. There are 24 errors in all in the program. Try to find all the syntax errors before reviewing the identified errors. The card column positions for a FORTRAN card are given at the top of the program to aid in finding the errors.

Now let's play computer and examine each error by the given line number.

1. Line 1 has one error. The C to identify a comment card is in column 2; it must be in column 1.
2. Line 2 has one error. There is no C in column 1 to identify the card as a comment.
3. Line 3 is a blank card. A blank card is not allowed in a program with most FORTRAN compilers. You must at least include the letter C in position 1.
4. The keyword INTEGER is misspelled. This is a common error because of many people's pronunciation of the word.
5. There are two errors in line 5. The slash (/) between the 5 and 99 should be a comma. A comma is missing after the second variable name NUM2.

```
        card col: 1         2         3         4         5
        12345678901234567890123456789012345678901234567890123456789
 1.     C--- SAMPLE FORTRAN PROGRAM WITH SYNTAX ERRORS
 2.          WRITTEN BY J W COLE
 3.
 4.          INTERGER NUM1, NUM2, NUM3
 5.          READ (5/99) NUM1, NUM2 NUM3
 6.     99   FORMAT ( 3I2
 7.          NRESULT = NUM1 * -NUM2 + NUM3
 8.          A = SQRT (NUM1)
 9.        B = IABS (NUM2)
10.          IF NUM1 EQ 0    STOP
11.          IF (NUM2 .GTR. NUM3) GO TO 10
12.          WRITE (6 98) NUM1, NUM2, NUM3
13.     98   FORM (1X, I4,3X, I4,3X, I4)
14.          WRITE 6, 97, NRESULT, A
15.     97   FORMAT (1X, F5,2,3X, F5.2)
16.          STP0

                  1         2         3         4         5
        12345678901234567890123456789012345678901234567890123456789
```

Figure 7.1 FORTRAN program with syntax errors

6. The ending parenthesis is missing from the FORMAT statement.
7. Line 7 has two errors. The variable NRESULT exceeds six characters. The asterisk (for multiplication) and the unary minus are adjacent to each other. The $-$NUM2 must be enclosed within parentheses to avoid this error.
8. You cannot take the square root of an integer value.
9. The Assignment statement starts in column 6.
10. Two errors exist in line 10. The parentheses are missing for the logical expression. Also the relational operator (.EQ.) does not have the required periods.
11. There are two errors in line 11. The relational operator is wrong and must be given as .GT. to be correct. There is no statement number 10 in the program.
12. A comma is missing between 6 and 98 in the WRITE.
13. The keyword FORMAT is misspelled.
14. Line 14 has three errors. There is no beginning parenthesis. The comma after the 97 should be an ending parenthesis. The variable NRESULT exceeds six characters.
15. Line 15 has two errors. The comma between F5 and 2 should be a period. Since NRESULT is an integer variable, its format code should be an I, not an F.
16. The keyword STOP is misspelled.
       There is no END statement in the program. One must be included after the STOP statement.

How did you do? If you found most of the syntax errors, you should have little trouble finding syntax errors in your program with diagnostic messages. Now let's look at a logic error in a flowchart.

Debugging a Logic Error in a Flowchart

The problem definition is to read ten integer numbers. If a number is less than or equal to 50, then compute the square of the number and print the number and its calculated square. If the number is greater than 50, return to read another number, but also count it as one of the ten input numbers. That is, a number greater than 50 counts as one of the ten input numbers. Figure 7.2 gives the flowchart for this problem. Hint: the error involves processing a number greater than 50.
       The error lies in the action to return to the top of the loop to read a new number and not incrementing the counter for a number greater than 50. If the tenth number read was greater than 50, the counter gets incremented to 11 and an endless loop would occur. The counter is not checked for the tenth number (which is greater than 50); so the condition in the decision symbol would never be met because the tenth number was not checked in this decision. That is, the counter might go from 9 to 11 for a number less than or equal to 50. It would be best to use the "greater than or equal to" relational operator in the counter test.

Debugging a Logic Error in a Program

The problem definition is to read and accumulate the sum of ten integer numbers. A counter (COUNTR) is used to keep count of the numbers read. Can you find the logic error? Play computer and step through the program with ten numbers. Figure 7.3 (p. 230) gives the program with a logic error.
       The error is in the relational operator (.GT.). It should be changed to "greater than or equal to" (.GE.). A .GT. causes the loop to be executed 11 times. You could also initialize COUNTR to 1 to correct the error or change the test value to 9. However, the loop structure is poorly constructed. It would be best to increment the counter immediately after the READ to follow the counter operations better. Another change would be to include the test at the bottom of the loop and implement a REPEAT UNTIL construct.

7.6 OTHER CONSIDERATIONS IN DEBUGGING LOGIC ERRORS

This section discusses two types of logic errors which you should understand and avoid. These two errors can cause nightmares for the beginning programmer because they are so difficult to find. The two errors are: 1) machine truncation (round-off) of numeric values and 2) the "not equal" relational operator (.NE.) used with the ".OR." logical operator.

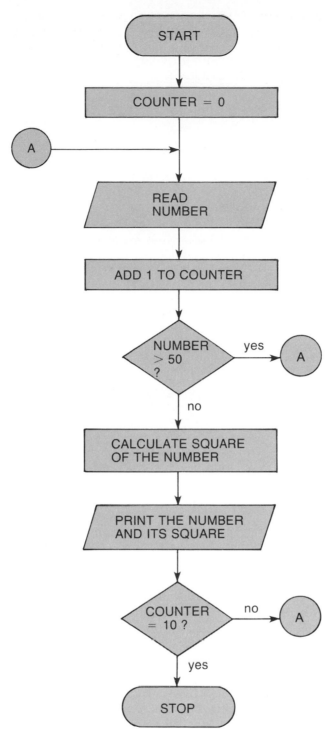

Figure 7.2 Flowchart with logic error

```
C --- SAMPLE FORTRAN PROGRAM WITH LOGIC ERRORS.
C --- OBJECTIVE OF THE PROGRAM IS TO READ AND SUM TEN
C --- NUMBERS. THE VARIABLE COUNTR IS USED TO KEEP
C --- COUNT OF THE NUMBER OF VALUES READ AND SUMMED.
C --- WRITTEN BY J W COLE
C
      REAL NR
      INTEGER COUNTR
      COUNTR = 0
C
100   READ (5, 99) NR
      IF (COUNTR .GT. 10) GO TO 200
      SUM = SUM + NR
      WRITE (6, 98) NR
      COUNTR = COUNTR + 1
      GO TO 100
200   WRITE (6, 97) SUM
      STOP
99    FORMAT (F5.2)
98    FORMAT (1X, F5.2)
97    FORMAT (1X, F6.2)
      END
```

Figure 7.3 FORTRAN program with logic error

Truncation Considerations with Numeric Values

Two types of truncation errors were discussed in chapter 4. The first type results from the division of two integer values in an expression. The second type of truncation results from a real quantity being assigned to an integer variable. The entire decimal fraction is truncated, and only the whole-number portion is stored at the integer variable. You must be constantly mindful of these two types of truncation operations when writing a program.

Another type of truncation occurs in the representation of real quantities. This type of truncation, known as **round-off,** results from the form and limitation of real numbers used in computations or stored in variables. A storage location can hold a maximum of approximately seven digits on some computers (IBM, Amdahl, 32-bit minicomputers, and others). For example, the value of one-third is stored as .3333333. Since the fraction contains a nonending repetition of 3's and is chopped off after seven digits, the exact value of one-third (1./3.) can never be represented in a memory location. The same is true for other decimal fractions such as 2./3., 1./9., or 4./3. that have a repeating fractional digit.

Second, some quantities cannot be exactly represented by the computer. A decimal fraction does not always convert to an exact internal binary (base 2 number system) representation. The numbers .1, .01, .001, and so on, cannot be exactly represented in such a system. The decimal fraction of .1 (and the other numbers of 1 to various powers of minus ten) is represented internally as a series of repeating binary digits, with the result that .1 times 10 does not exactly equal 1.0. You must be very careful when testing for these numbers and never use just the "equal" (.EQ.) relational operator. Always use the "greater than or equal to" (.GE.) or "less than or equal to" (.LE.) relational operators, depending on the required condition.

The comparison of these values, therefore, may never be equal to what you might expect if the calculations were performed by hand. For example:

$$A = 1./3.$$
$$IF (A * 3.0 .EQ. 1.0) \; GO \; TO \; 33$$

The Logical IF statement would never obtain an equal comparison since A * 3.0 would be .9999999. The condition would never be true, and a branch would never be made to statement number 33.

To avoid such errors with the round-off of real quantities, you must use relational operators which include both the equal condition and either a "less than" or "greater than" condition. If you wish to branch to the statement numbered 33 whenever A * 3.0 is less than or equal to 1.0, you would code:

$$IF (A * 3.0 .LE. 1.0) \; GO \; TO \; 33$$

Now you have been warned about the possibility of fractional truncation errors and can take the proper course of action. This type of truncation may cause such subtle errors that the student thinks the computer is playing tricks or is wrong. The next type of error is also very confusing to the beginning programmer.

The Not Equal (.NE.) Relational Operator Used with the .OR. Logical Operator

You may want to form a compound condition that tests whether a variable is not equal to any of several values; if the test is true, then a specific action will be taken. For example, a code of 1 may be used for an inventory receipt, and a code of 2 may be used for an inventory issue. If the variable containing the input code value is not equal to a 1 or a 2, a branch should be made to an error routine. The following incorrect FORTRAN statement is often written without thinking about its illogical construction.

IF (KODE .NE. 1 .OR. KODE .NE. 2) GO TO 300

Believe it or not, this statement will always cause a branch to statement number 300, no matter what value is in the variable KODE.

Why does this statement always cause a branch to statement number 300? What is wrong? The statement looks correct. Wrong! Remember the .OR. logical operator says that if any one condition of a set of compound conditions is true, then the overall condition is true. If a value of 1 is stored in the variable KODE, then the first half of the condition is false (KODE .NE. 1). But, what about the second half of the condition "KODE .NE. 2?" The value in KODE is not equal to a 2 (it has a value of 1), so this half of the condition is true. If any part of a compound "OR" condition is true, then the entire condition is evaluated as true.

What if the variable KODE contains a value of 2? The first half of the condition is true, since the value in KODE is not equal to a 1 (even though the second half of the condition is false). Again, one true part of a compound "OR" condition makes the entire condition true. What if the value in KODE is a 0, a 3, or any value not equal to a 1 or a 2? Then both halves of the "OR" condition are true, and a branch is made to statement number 300.

How do you trap the invalid values of KODE (when KODE is not equal to a 1 or a 2) and let the valid values of 1 and 2 pass through? The answer lies in using the .AND. logical operator instead of the .OR. logical operator. That is, the invalid values must be identified by not being equal to a 1 **AND** not equal to a 2. Remember, in an "AND" compound condition all the relational expressions must be true for the overall condition to be true. If one part of the compound "AND" condition is false, then the entire condition is false.

The correctly coded statement would be:

IF (KODE .NE. 1 .AND. KODE .NE. 2) GO TO 300

If the value of KODE is a 2, then the first half of the compound "AND" condition is false. Likewise, if the value of KODE is a 1, then the second half of the compound "AND" condition is false. With either a 1 or a 2 value in KODE, a branch would never be made to the error routine at statement number 300. But, if an invalid inventory code value is found in KODE, then both halves of the compound "AND" condition would be true. Thus, the entire condition would be true and the branch would occur.

In summary, the rule is to use the .AND. logical operator to compound conditions that individually use the .NE. relational operator. This makes the overall condition true only when you have a value that is not one of the values used in the parts of the compound conditions.

7.7 GUIDELINES TO AID IN DEBUGGING LOGIC ERRORS

The following suggestions are given as aids to debugging execution errors and also to help you prevent these types of errors.

1. Know the program. Know where each routine that performs a particular function is in the program. This can save considerable time in determining what the program was doing when an error occurred.
2. Assign meaningful symbolic names. Don't be afraid to use all six characters to form a symbolic name. This is especially helpful with variables, where the name helps identify the value being used. Never use the same variable name to represent different values in the same program, just to save space. This can cause a debugging nightmare. Use the Explicit Type statements (INTEGER, REAL, and so forth). Even the author of a program may experience difficulty in remembering what a variable represents if its name has little or no mnemonic (memory aid) meaning. A nice technique in remembering the purpose of variables is to include a table with the name and function as internal documentation (comment statements) at the beginning of the program.

3. Check to see if the input items are read correctly. Were they correctly selected from the input record, specified in the correct order, and given the correct names? Did you use the proper input file unit number?

4. Check to see if you have specified the correct variables in the various statements. Was a wrong variable used? Sometimes the close spelling of variable names causes the wrong variable to be specified.

5. Check the initial values of variables. Programmers often fail to initialize a variable to the proper beginning value. It is then difficult to understand why a routine does not work. Make sure all counters and variables are initialized to their proper values. Make sure all variables used in an expression to the right of the equals sign have been defined. Make sure that index variables that are used later are reinitialized to the necessary values.

6. Plan for errors. The old saying "an ounce of prevention is worth a pound of cure" is certainly true in programming. You must realize that errors will occur and plan to avoid them. Some suggestions are:

   a. Write your program in a structured form, so that errors can be localized to certain modules. Use subprograms where feasible.

   b. Check for all possible conditions in your program. If there are three possible valid input values for an item and three possible resulting conditions, don't check for two and assume the third. Check for all three and execute an error routine if the condition is not valid.

   c. Use straightforward logic so that everything you are doing is clear and obvious—not tricky, hidden, and difficult to debug.

   d. Plan for debug traces and printouts in the development of the program. Assume that you will eventually need them and include these precautionary measures from the start, in order to avoid additional compiles and test runs. The debug statements can be removed after the routines have been proven correct.

   e. Save all test decks and tests results. Rerunning these same test decks can save considerable programmer check-out effort if any modifications are made to the program.

7. Check the values of constants in the statement, especially those with more than seven digits. Also consider the possibility of truncation or rounding errors.

8. Check the variable names for misspelling or for type. Output values of zeroes are often the result of conflicting format specifications on some compilers.

9. Check the order of computations in the Assignment statement. You may need an extra set of parentheses in the expression to cause one arithmetic operation to take place before another.

10. Check for truncation errors. Was integer division involved in calculations? Was a real value assigned to an integer variable? These operations may produce a truncated result that leads to a wrong value in a variable.

11. All FORMAT statements should be placed at the beginning or end of the program (preferably the end). This facilitates the search for a particular FORMAT statement that is used by several I/O statements in the program. The FORMAT statements should be placed in a sequential order by their statement number. Thus, one has merely to flip back to the beginning or forward to the end of the source listing to find any FORMAT statement. The removal of the FORMAT statements from the coded logic also improves the readability of the program. A technique may be adopted to number the input-associated FORMAT statements beginning with 199 and work down (198, 197, and so on) and to number the output-associated FORMAT statements beginning with 299 and work down (298, 297, and so on).

12. Check the subscript value and array dimensions for a subscripted item. A subscript value less than one or greater than the dimension size can produce addressing errors.

13. Make sure that the arguments passed between program units are correct and agree in number, order, and mode. Upon entering a subprogram, print a checkpoint message indicating entry into the subprogram and the values of dummy arguments. This ensures that the correct values are passed for the arguments and prevents the hard-to-find errors resulting from incorrect arguments' being used.

14. After you have found the error in a routine, check the entire program to make sure that you did not make the same error elsewhere.

Always try to locate the error yourself, first by trying one or a combination of the debugging techniques discussed here. If you are finally unable to locate the bug, then consult your instructor. Bring the results of the debugging attempts with you, as your instructor will often need them to find your problem.

7.8 SUMMARY

FORTRAN provides the capability to reference prewritten subprograms that evaluate certain mathematical functions. Such built-in functions provide common business and scientific functions for use in problem solving. Trigonometric library functions are also available for trigonometric applications.

A function is the mathematical relationship that defines the value of a dependent variable (the returned results) based on the value of one or more independent variables (the arguments). Examples of built-in functions are SQRT and ABS, which obtain the square root and absolute value of an argument, respectively. An argument is an expression used to provide the value for the function. The argument is enclosed within a set of parentheses following the function name.

To reference a built-in function, you give the function name followed by its argument(s). The function reference is only legal where you would use an arithmetic expression in a FORTRAN statement. The Assignment statement and Logical IF are the two most common statements in which function references are used.

Each function requires a certain type of argument (e.g., integer, real) and returns one value which must also be a specific type. Tables 7.1 and 7.2 were given to show the number and type of arguments and the type of value returned with each function.

Section 7.3 discussed various techniques for finding syntax errors flagged during compilation of a program. There are two primary levels of severity in compilation errors. Fatal errors detected during compilation prevent the generation of the needed object program, and thus no execution of the program is attempted. Warning errors are minor errors that still allow the program to execute. Sixteen types of syntax errors were discussed to make you aware of some of the more common types of compilation errors flagged by the compiler. Finally, a set of seven procedures was given to assist you in finding and correcting these errors.

Section 7.4 discussed various debugging techniques for finding errors which occur in the execution of a program. These errors are of two types. The first is called a logic error and results from the failure of the program to perform the correct actions at the proper time. The second type of run-time error is called a system-fault error, which results in a program "blowing up" (aborting). A system-fault error is caused by an invalid operation that the computer cannot handle, such as dividing by zero, or an underflow or overflow error.

Logic errors are often difficult to find in a program. Seven techniques were discussed to aid in locating them:

1. Desk-check the program.
2. Echo-check the input data.
3. Print immediate values from calculations.
4. Include check-point messages with temporary WRITE statements.
5. Rewrite the segment of code in error.
6. Use debug facilities and trace packages.
7. Use various control card (JCL) options.

When all else fails, a memory dump is used to locate errors.

Section 7.5 presented several problems to illustrate the techniques of debugging various types of errors. Section 7.6 discussed two subtle types of errors which are difficult for the beginning programmer to detect: First, rounding errors occur because the computer cannot precisely represent certain values such as non-ending fractions. The most common problems are with the decimal fractions of .1, .01, and so on, which, in the internal binary notation of the computer, are non-ending. Conditions using "not equal" relational operators with compound "OR" conditions are illogical to the computer. The overall condition is always true. The logical .AND. operator must be used in compound conditions with the .NE. relational operator.

Finally, section 7.7 provided a set of guidelines to aid in detecting and avoiding common types of execution errors. A check list of fourteen items was given to help you avoid various errors commonly encountered in programming.

You should make a habit of trying to debug all errors in your program. This habit provides the experience that will enable you to find even the remotest bug. Do not be discouraged in the effort required. Some professional programmers have spent days and even weeks trying to find the cause for program bugs. You are lucky; you have your instructor to turn to when all your other efforts fail.

7.9 TERMS

Terms and concepts you should become familiar with in this chapter are:

argument	function reference	precision error
built-in functions	function-value	radians
checkpoint message	general built-in functions	round-off error
cross reference listing	library-supplied function	subprogram
debug facility	intermediate values	system error
desk-checking	intrinsic function	trace package
echo-checking input	invoke a function	trigonometric functions
fatal diagnostic message	memory dump	truncation error
function	modulo	warning diagnostic message

7.10 REVIEW QUESTIONS

1. Define a mathematical function.
2. What is a built-in or library-supplied function in FORTRAN?
3. If you wish to take the square root of an expression, what built-in function would you use?
4. What is an argument?
5. How is a built-in function invoked in FORTRAN?
6. What is meant by providing the proper type of argument to a function?
7. Why is it important to know the type of value returned from a function?
8. How many values are returned by a function?
9. What built-in function would be used to convert an integer value to real-mode?
10. What built-in function would be used to obtain the sine of an angle?
11. The arguments to most trigonometric functions must be expressed in what type of measurement?
12. What are the differences between the two main levels of severity in compilation errors?
13. Define the term ''syntax error.''
14. List five causes of syntax error.
15. List the seven steps to follow in locating and correcting compilation errors.
16. Name the two types of errors that can occur during the execution of a program.
17. The process of manually following the logic in a program to determine its operations is called _____ _____ .
18. The printing of input values as they are read to verify their correctness is known as an _____ .
19. How would the display of intermediate calculations help in locating a logic error?
20. The various messages displayed to trace the flow of execution through a program or through various segments are called _____ messages.
21. What are debug facilities and trace packages?
22. Name the three types of errors that may cause a program to abort.
23. Name five things that could cause a logic error in a program.
24. What are round-off errors?
25. Why is it important to assign meaningful variable names in a program?
26. List five things you can do to check for logic errors in a program.

7.11 EXERCISES

1. Identify the syntax error in the following statements:

    a. SINEX = SINE(X)
    b. SQRX = SQR(X)
    c. REAL ISQD ICUBE

    d. ALOG(X) = XLOG2
    e. COUNT = KOUNT + 1
    f. READ (6, 199) X, Y, Z

2. Identify the syntax error in the following statements:

    a. COSINX = COSIN(X)
    b. ABSX = JABS(X)
    c. INTERGER A, B, C

    d. COUNTER = COUNTER + 1
    e. GO TO 199999
    f. WRITE (5, 299) X, Y, Z

3. Identify the logic error in the following statements:

    a. Y = 0.0
       RESLT = (X + 3.5) / Y
    b. ISQRT = SQRT(I)

    c. X = 1./3.
       IF (X * 6.0 .EQ. 2.0) GO TO 50

4. Identify the logic error in the following statements:

    a.   READ (5, 99) PRNCPL, RATE, TIME
       99 FORMAT (F6.2, F4.3, I2)
           RNTRST = PRNCPL * RATE * TIME

    b. XSQRT = SQRT(−X)
    c. X = .1
       IF (X * 100.0 .EQ. 10.0) GO TO 60

7.12 PROGRAMMING PROBLEMS

1. Write a program which uses the built-in function SQRT to compute the square root of 103.46.
2. Write a program to calculate ln x (natural log of x) and $\log_{10}$ x (log base ten of x) for the integral values from 1 to 10. Print the ten values for ln x and the ten values for the $\log_{10}$ x on double-spaced lines.
3. Write a program to compute the sine and cosine of a 90 degree angle.
4. Write a program that uses a built-in function to compute the arctangent of π. (Use 3.1416 for the value of π.)
5. Write a program to convert the decimal-based number 25 to a base-two (binary) number.
6. Write a program to convert the decimal-based number 100 to a base-eight (octal) number.

8 More Details on Reading/Writing Numeric Formatted Data

8.1 INTRODUCTION TO THE USE AND IMPORTANCE OF FORMATTED INPUT/OUTPUT STATEMENTS

If a program consists of a number of calculations using only one set of quantities those quantities could easily be set up as a single list of constants. This is seldom written right into the program itself. In such cases, however, you could probably get the result more quickly on a calculator than on a computer. Most of the time, programs have to deal with *multiple* sets of data over time, and the most efficient way to do this is to *read* the quantities as sets of input data. Constants are coded only for those values that remain fixed throughout the program. The program reads a set of quantities into the named variables, manipulates them according to the proper formulas, outputs the results, and loops back to repeat the same processes for another set of input fields.

Input/output statements provide the programmer with much power and flexibility. After calculating and outputting the results for one set of variables, new values can be read into the same variables and the procedures repeated for the new set of values. Any time a new value is read for a variable, it replaces the old one at that storage location. The READ and WRITE statements are widely used in programs to input and output new sets of values, especially for those variables used in calculations and decision making.

The input/output (I/O) statements in FORTRAN allow the programmer to control the peripheral input/output devices connected to the computer system and to transfer data between memory and the various I/O units. The term **I/O** is an abbreviation for input/output, and it is used by programmers to talk about input/output operations or storage media. I/O may be used to refer only to an input operation, only to an output operation, or to both input and output operations.

Let us review the terms used in connection with the organization of data. Some terms used regarding the organization of input and output data are field, record, and file. A **field** is the smallest division of data and identifies a single item of information. Examples of a field are name, sex, unit cost, radius of a circle, test score, and so on. A field can consist of a single character or multiple characters. A **record** is a complete unit of information, usually about a person or transaction. It consists of a collection of related data fields; examples are: a personnel pay record, an accounts receivable record, an inventory control record, or a student's registration record. This type of record is also referred to as a **logical record.** A record is usually one punched card or a single print line. A **file** contains all the related records for one data processing application. For example, a payroll file contains all the employee pay records for persons employed by a company; an inventory file contains all the stock records maintained by a firm; a student grade file contains grade information on a group of students.

A card file is a collection of records on punched cards. Card files are known as sequential data files. In a **sequential file** the records are read in a serial manner. That is, record one is read, then record two, then record three, and so on. Before the tenth record can be read, the first nine must have been read previously. The data cards are read in the order in which they are arranged in the deck. The first READ statement executed in a program reads the first data card, the next reads the second card, and so on. Sequential files are also written in a serial manner, i.e., record one followed by record two, and so forth. Magnetic tape files, like punched card files, are inherently sequential files. Magnetic disk files are often organized as sequential files; however, they may be organized to allow direct access to any record.

Multiple cards can be read with a single READ statement, depending on how the list of variables is established in the statement and on how the format specifications are organized in the FORMAT statement. The same is true with the WRITE statement and its output operations. This chapter will cover the finer points of the READ, WRITE and FORMAT statements with the input and output of numeric data. A large percentage of the errors (roughly 40 percent) made by students are in the area of I/O specifications. It is very important to try to understand the material covered in this chapter. You will use this information in every program you write. The better the understanding you acquire now of I/O operations, the fewer mistakes you will make in writing programs.

An in-depth discussion of the rules which govern the use of the FORMAT statement and I/O lists with READ/WRITE statements is provided to explain their operation. These rules explain what will happen if you include more variables in an I/O list than you have format codes in the FORMAT statement. Study these rules well, and you will be able to answer many of the questions that students often have on this subject.

8.2 RULES FOR USING THE FORMAT STATEMENT AND THE I/O LIST OF VARIABLES

The FORMAT statement is used in conjunction with the I/O list of variables in the READ and WRITE statements to specify the location and form of data fields within the records. A FORMAT statement must be provided for each READ and WRITE statement that uses format specifications with input and output fields.

A **format code** is used to describe the form and size of each data field transferred to or from memory. These format codes are included in the FORMAT statement in parentheses following the keyword FORMAT. A comma must be used to separate each code.

Some examples of card input FORMAT statements are:

25 FORMAT (I2, I3, F7.2)
98 FORMAT (5X, F5.2, I3, 2X, I4)
359 FORMAT (F6.1, 3X, 2I5, 1X, F4.2)

Some examples of printer output FORMAT statements are:

97 FORMAT (1H1, I4, 5X, F6.2)
186 FORMAT (1H0, F5.1, 3X, I6)
73 FORMAT (1X, I3, 2X, I3, 2X, F4.1)

Remember, a carriage control specification must always be given as the first format code in the FORMAT statement for line printer output, in order to control the movement of the paper. This is also true for terminal output results on many timesharing systems. That is, on these systems, any output results displayed at a terminal must also include a format code for line spacing in the FORMAT statement. The standard format codes for line spacing, and their functions, are given as follows:

Format Code	Line Printer Function	Terminal Function
1X	single spacing	single spacing
'b' or 1Hb (b = a space)	single spacing	single spacing
'0' or 1H0	double spacing	double spacing
'1' or 1H1	page eject; new page	top of screen
'+' or 1H+	suppress spacing (same line)	suppress spacing (same line)

(Note: the single quote to enclose a format code is nonstandard ANSI FORTRAN 66.)

The following rules explain the function of the FORMAT statement and the relationship between the statement and the format specifications contained.

Rule 1. FORMAT statements are not executed; their function is to supply format information concerning I/O specifications to the program. FORMAT statements, therefore, should only be referred to by an I/O statement (READ or WRITE).

Rule 2. FORMAT statements may be placed anywhere before the END statement in a source program, except between continuation statements. Some programmers may place all FORMAT statements at the beginning or end of a program for easy reference, while others place them before or after their related I/O statements. Compilation is easier if all FORMAT statements appear prior to their reference in the input/output statements, since their addresses can be resolved earlier in the process.

Rule 3. When defining a record with a FORMAT statement, the programmer must consider the maximum size of the record allowed for that I/O medium. For example, the maximum size of a card record is 80 characters; the maximum length of a line on a CRT screen is normally also 80 characters; the maximum size of a printer output line is 132 characters (although some have a maximum of only 120).

Rule 4. It is not necessary to specify blanks (X format code) to fill out the remaining positions of a record. For example, to read five items of 4 columns each from a punched card (columns 1–20), the format specifications need only be:

9 FORMAT (5I4)

and not:

9 FORMAT (5I4, 60X)

Format specifications for a record end when the closing (rightmost) parenthesis is reached in the FORMAT statement.

To print a double-spaced line using only the first 70 print positions for seven fields of ten-position integer numbers on a line printer, you need only code:

10 FORMAT (1H0,7I10)

and not:

10 FORMAT (1H0,7I10,62X)

The ending (rightmost) parenthesis indicates the end of a record for both input and output operations.

Rule 5. When formatted records are prepared for printing or output to a terminal, the first character of the format specifications is used as a carriage control character. A carriage control character controls movement of the paper in the printer and specifies how the device is to move the paper (i.e., to the top of the next page, one line, two lines, or no movement). The carriage control character is specified as the first format character of each printer output line. For example:

299 FORMAT (1X,I5,5X,F5.2)
98 FORMAT (5X, F6.2,5X,I4)
80 FORMAT (1H1,5X,I3,5X,I7)

The first example single-spaces the output line and prints two items. In the second example, one of the five initial blank positions is used for single-spacing, the other four blank positions are printed, and two output items are printed, separated by five spaces. In the third example, the output line is printed at the top of a new page (page eject), five blank positions are printed, followed by two output items that are separated by five spaces.

For output media other than the line printer or remote terminals, the first character of the record is treated as data, and no carriage control character is used. If a carriage control specification is not provided for a line printer or terminal output line, the first character in the first data field will be used by the system for carriage control operations. If an invalid carriage control character is generated, one of two things may occur. On some computers a default character of a single space control is provided; on others a ''runaway'' printer (i.e., continuous paper feed) may result.

The remaining rules for using the FORMAT statement relate to the variables in the I/O list.

Input/Output List Rules

The following rules are presented to help you understand the relationship between the I/O list variables and the FORMAT statement specifications. These rules pertain to ANSI FORTRAN 66 and may not be enforced in all FORTRAN IV compilers.

Rule 1. The I/O list can contain any type of variable names.

Rule 2. The I/O list must not include any constants or arithmetic expressions. (This rule is not enforced by FORTRAN IV compilers that provide format-free output statements. Some FORTRAN IV compilers also allow constants, arithmetic expressions, and function references in the I/O list.)

Rule 3. Variable names in the I/O list must be separated by commas.

Rule 4. For each variable that appears in the I/O list, one field (value) is transmitted to or from memory. (Note: an array name without subscripts in the I/O list will cause all the items for the entire array to be read or written.)

Rule 5. A one-to-one relationship exists between the names in the I/O list and the format codes (except the X, H, T, and ') in the associated FORMAT statement. (Note: format codes may be reused if a group repetition factor is used and additional variables in the I/O list remain to be transmitted.)

Rule 6. The order of names in the I/O list must be consistent with the left-to-right order of the data fields in the I/O record and also with the order of the format codes specified in the FORMAT statement. For example:

READ (5, 98) A, I, Z
98 FORMAT (2X, F8.2, I6, 5X, F5.1)

The variable A corresponds to the F8.2 format code, the variable I corresponds to the I6 format code, and the variable Z corresponds to the F5.1 format code. Remember that the X format codes do not relate to a variable or data field, but are used to specify how many positions are to be skipped; thus, there is no corresponding variable in the I/O list for the X format codes. You may think of the X format code as merely printing so many spaces beween data fields.

Rule 7. The types of names assigned, format codes used, and data fields used must all agree with the types of I/O data. For example, an integer (I) format code must be used with an integer variable to read an integer data field. A real variable must be assigned to a numeric field with a decimal point (or an implied decimal point) and be transmitted under an F format specification.

Rule 8. If there are fewer names in the I/O list than there are format codes, the remaining format codes are ignored. The system checks to see whether additional names are present in the I/O list before selecting the next format code. For example:

READ (5,87) X, Y, J
87 FORMAT (F3.1, F4.0, I5, F8.2, I7)

The use of format codes and transmission of data terminate with the code I5 and variable J. The remaining format codes F8.2 and I7 are not used.

Rule 9. If there are more names in the I/O list than there are format codes in the FORMAT statement, the system will automatically supply additional format codes by reverting back to the format code following the last (rightmost) left parenthesis. Put another way, the format specifications are repeated beginning with the specification following the left parenthesis that corresponds to the next-to-last right parenthesis. The system will also cause a new data record to be read at that time. That is, each time the last (rightmost) parenthesis is reached and additional items are to be transferred in the I/O list, a new record is automatically read. The same principle also holds true for output records. For example:

READ (5,40) A, B, C, D, E
40 FORMAT (F4.1, F5.2)

One record will be read with the fields A and B transferred as F4.1 and F5.2 specifications. Since the end of the FORMAT statement is reached but more items need to be transmitted, the system will read a new record and transfer the field C as an F4.1 (positions 1–4 of new record) specification and field D as an F5.2 (positions 5–9) specification. The end of the FORMAT statement is once more encountered with one item remaining to be read. A third record will be read and the field E transferred as an F4.1 (positions 1–4 of new record) specification. A total of three records would be read by the illustrated READ and FORMAT statements.

A more complex example, using group format specifications, would be:

READ (5,198) N1,N2,X,N3,Y,N4,N5,Z
198 FORMAT (I3, 2(I2,F5.3),I4)

The variable N1 would be read with the I3 format code. The variables N2 and X would be read with the I2 and F5.3 format codes, respectively. The variables N3 and Y would be read with I2 and F5.3 format codes, respectively, because of the repeat factor of 2(I2, F5.3). The variable N4 would be read with the I4 format code. The variables N5 and Z would be read with the I2 and F5.3 format codes, respectively, because the system returns to the format specification following the left parenthesis corresponding to the next-to-last right parenthesis whenever the end of the format specifications is reached (the final closing parenthesis) before the I/O list has been completely read. The values for N5 and Z would, of course, be read from a new record. (Group format specifications are discussed in section 9.4).

Rule 10. If the I/O list is omitted from the READ statement, at least one record is still read, but no data items are transferred.

Rule 11. The I/O list may be omitted from the WRITE (or PRINT) statement to print Hollerith (character) data from a FORMAT statement.

Rule 12. The same FORMAT statement may be referenced by different I/O statements in the program as long as the format specifications are the same for the I/O list of variables in each I/O statement.

8.3 DETAILED EXPLANATION OF THE INTEGER (I) AND FLOATING-POINT (F) FORMAT CODES

Integer (I) Format Code

The **integer (I) format code** is used in transmitting integer data fields only. This format code consists of the capital letter I followed by an integer constant, which represents the width (size) of the data field. The general form of the integer format code is:

$$nIw$$

where:

n represents an optional repetition factor that specifies the number of times the format code is to be used. If n is omitted, the default value is 1. The value of **n,** when used, must be an unsigned positive integer constant whose value is less than or equal to 255. **w** specifies the number of record positions in the field. **w** must be an unsigned positive integer constant with a value less than or equal to 255. The specified width includes the sign, if present.

Examples are:

18 FORMAT (I3,I7,I2)
47 FORMAT (I6,2I4,I9)

Input Considerations. On input, any leading, embedded, and/or trailing blanks in the data field are interpreted as zeroes. The sign, if present, must appear in the leftmost position of the field (prior to the first digit). The input value must be right-justified in its field.

Examples to illustrate the input rules when using the I format code for input fields are as follows (b̸s represent blank positions in the field):

Field Size and Value	I Format Code
123	I3
+ 123	I4
+ b̸123	I5
b̸ − 123	I5
− 123	I4
b̸b̸123	I5
b̸ + 123	I5

Output Considerations. On output, the **w** represents the total number of positions in the output field. A sign is printed to the immediate left of the first digit only for negative values. However, students should leave an extra space in **w** for the sign, even if they expect it to be positive (because it might not be), i.e., **w** should be the number of output digits plus one. If the number of digits (and minus sign whenever the quantity is negative) that represents the quantity in memory is less than **w**, the leftmost output positions are filled with blanks. If the output quantity plus the minus sign (when negative) is greater than **w**, asterisks are generally printed on most computers in place of the output value. As many asterisks will be printed as the width specification. All output values will be right-justified in the output field.

Examples to illustrate the output rules when using the I format code for output fields are as follows (b̸s represent blank positions):

Value in Memory	I Format Code	Output Field
123	I3	123
123	I5	b̸b̸123
123	I2	**
− 123	I4	− 123
− 123	I5	b̸ − 123
− 123	I3	***

Floating-point (F) Format Code

The **floating-point (F) format code** specifies the number of record positions in a field to be transmitted as real data. Whole numbers or decimal fields may be read as input. The general form of the F format code is:

nFw.d

where:

    n represents an optional repetition factor that specifies the number of times that the format code is to be used. The value of **n**, when used, must be an unsigned positive integer constant whose value is less than or equal to 255. **w** specifies the number of record positions in the input or output field, which includes any sign or decimal point given in an input field. **w** must be an unsigned positive integer constant with a value less than or equal to 255. The decimal point (.) is a necessary separator between the **w** and **d** parameters. **d** represents the number of digits in the fractional part of the number (i.e., number of digits following the decimal point). **d** must be an unsigned integer constant between 1 and 255, inclusive.

    Examples are:

107 FORMAT (F5.2,I3,F7.1)
96 FORMAT (2F4.1,F8.3,4F3.0,F4.3)

    Input Considerations. On input, any leading, embedded, or trailing blanks in the field are interpreted as zeroes. The sign if present, must appear prior to the first digit. Additional input rules include:

1. The width of the field must include a position for the decimal point, if present, and a position for the sign, if present.
2. If the position of the decimal point in the data field is different from the position specified by the **d** parameter in the F format code, the actual position of the decimal point in the input data item overrides the **d** specification and determines the value of the item. For example:

READ (5,99) A
99 FORMAT (F5.1)

23.45

The value is stored as 23.45 and not 234.5.

3. Since the position of the actual decimal point in the data overrides the **d** specifications, the quantity technically does not have to be right-justified in the field, but normally it is and should be right-justified.
4. If the decimal point is omitted in the field, the **d** specification determines the position of the decimal point in the quantity and, thus, the true value of the number. In business applications the decimal point is normally not punched in the numeric data fields, since business programming languages like COBOL and RPG cannot read numeric input fields containing decimal points. Since you can specify the placement of the implied decimal point in the data field in FORTRAN (as is done in the business applications programming languages), there is no problem. For example:

READ (5, 99) HRS, RATE
99 FORMAT (F3.1, F4.2)

605 675

The value stored for the variable HRS is 60.5 since the format code F3.1 designates a field three positions wide with one implied decimal position. The value stored for the variable RATE is 6.75 since the format code F4.2 designates a field of four positions (the first a blank) with two implied decimal positions.

5. Any permissible form of constructing an integer or real constant may be read by the F format code. No commas are included in a data field. For example, a data field like 43,276.5 is illegal.

Examples to illustrate the input rules when using the F format code for input fields are as follows (ƀs represents blank positions):

Field Size and Value	F Format Code	
12.34	F5.2	
− 12.34	F6.2	
+ 12.34	F6.2	
ƀƀ12.3	F6.1	
ƀ − 12.3	F6.1	
+ ƀ12.3	F6.1	
12.34	F5.0	(Value of 12.34, format code overridden by field value)
1.234	F5.2	(Value of 1.234, format code overridden by field value)
1234	F4.2	(Value of 12.34)
123	F3.0	(Value of 123.)

Output Considerations. On output fields, the following rules apply:

1. A decimal point will always appear in the field followed by as many fractional digits as given in the **d** parameter.
2. The output quantity will always be right-justified in the output field.
3. The width specifications must provide sufficient spaces for the integer digits of the value, the decimal point, the number of fractional digits specified by **d**, and a sign if the output quantity is negative. As in the case of the output specifications for the I format code, students should always allow room for the sign. It is also a good practice to provide room for one integer digit position in the width specifications even though a total fractional value is expected.
4. If insufficient output field positions are provided by **w**, asterisks instead of digits are writen by most computers. The number of asterisks written is equal to the **w** specification.
5. If excessive output field positions are provided (quantity does not fill the total output positions), the leftmost excessive positions are filled with blanks.

If an output quantity is a total fraction (i.e., contains no whole number or no significant digit to the left of the decimal point), and excessive output positions are provided, a single zero will be included before the decimal point. Examples are:

1. Given the value of .934 in memory to be output under an F5.3 format code, the output field would appear as 0.934.
2. Given the same value to be output under an F7.3 format code, the output field would be ƀƀ0.934 (where the ƀs represent blank positions).
3. Given the same value to be output under an F4.3 format code, the output field would appear as .934.

In some compilers the output field specifications for a real quantity must always allow room for at least one integer position. Otherwise, the output field size is not considered wide enough, and asterisks will be printed. For example, a field specification of F4.3 would not allow room for an integer position, even though the quantity in memory may be a total fraction. A field specification of F5.3 would have to be coded to allow the output of three fractional digits. This is true with the WATFIV and Honeywell 6000 compilers.

If the output requirements specified by the **d** parameter truncate any fractional digits of the quantity, FORTRAN provides automatic rounding of the output results. When the first digit to be dropped in the fraction is 5 or greater, the system will automatically round the next left position up (increase) by one. Rounding could continue into the integer positions if the fraction digits are 9's. If the beginning digit of the fractional part that is truncated is less than 5, no rounding up occurs. That is, the output digits remain as they are. Examples to illustrate the **rules of rounding** are:

1. Given the value in memory of 3.8916 to be output under an F5.3 format code, the output value would be 3.892.
2. Given the same value in memory to be output under an F4.2 format code, the output field would appear as 3.89.

3. Given the value 3.98 in memory to be output under an F3.1 format code, the output field would be 4.0.
4. Given the value 29.99 in memory to be output under an F3.0 format code, the output field would appear as 30.; thus, rounding can extend into the integer position digits to the left of the decimal point.

Output examples of the F format specifications to illustrate the output rules are as follows (ƀs represent blanks):

Value in Memory	F Format Code	Output Field
87.153	F7.2	ƀƀ87.15
87.153	F7.4	87.1530
87.153	F7.6	*******
87.153	F7.1	ƀƀƀ87.2
−15.483	F6.3	******
−15.483	F6.0	ƀƀ−15.
−15.483	F6.1	ƀ−15.5
−3.967	F5.2	−3.97
3.967	F8.5	ƀ3.96700
.9348	F7.4	ƀ0.9348
.9348	F4.3	.935

Now let us illustrate the use of these rules with some examples of reading and writing numeric data.

8.4 READING NUMERIC FORMATTED DATA

Each variable in the I/O list must have a corresponding format code to transmit data fields to memory. The type format code must also match the type variable established. The variables are matched up with the data transferring format codes in a one-to-one, left-to-right order.

To begin reading input data fields, the programmer must know four things: (1) the location (record position) of the field, (2) the type of the data field, (3) the size (width) of the field, and (4) the location of the decimal point for decimal data fields. With this knowledge, the proper type variables can be set up, the proper format codes established, and the correct FORMAT statement constructed.

As a first step, a sample record layout is established with field positions given as follows (the record layout of input fields applies to disk input records as well as punched cards):

Card Columns	Field
1–7	Student registration number in the form NNNNNNN)
8	Blank
9	Classification of student (form = N)
10–14	Blank
15–21	Tuition fee (form = NNNN.NN)
22–23	Semester hours enrolled (form = NN)
24–80	Blank

The first field consists of an integer item of seven positions. The proper format code would be I7. An integer variable name must be chosen to represent the storage location into which the value can be read. Let us use the name NRSREG. Card column eight is blank, so we select a format code of 1X to skip that position. No variable is assigned to the X format code, since no data is transferred. The second data field is the student's classification in coded form (i.e., 1 = freshman, 2 = sophomore, 3 = junior, and 4 = senior). Since only one integer digit is coded as the input field, the format code of I1 is used to read the field and store it at the integer variable LVLCLS. Columns 10–14 are blank, so a format code of 5X is needed to skip those positions.

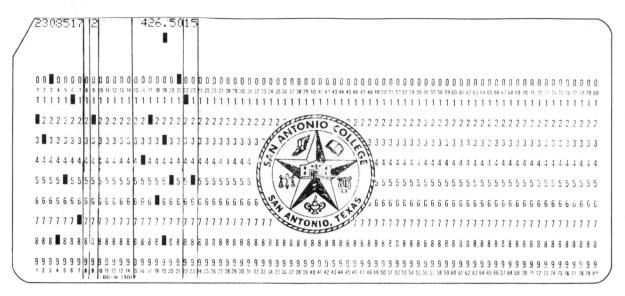

Figure 8.1 Sample card record one

The third data field is a real quantity occupying seven positions with two fractional digits. A field specification of F7.2 is established to read that field. A real variable name of TFEE is suggested for the item of tuition fee. The fourth data field, "semester hours enrolled," consists of two integer positions. A format code of I2 is established to read this field and an integer variable name of NRSHRS assigned to the field. Since the remainder of the card is blank, no further field specifications are needed.

These fields would be punched in a card as illustrated in figure 8.1.

Using the assigned variables and a FORMAT statement (number 99) containing the established format codes, the READ statement and related FORMAT statement appear as follows:

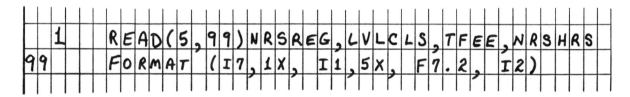

This READ statement would normally be executed repeatedly in a program loop to read many data records. The values in the input fields would not, of course, all be the same, but the arrangement of the fields on the records would have to be the same. This concept of having the data fields located in the same positions as those of the same type record is known as a **record layout design**.

To understand flexibility in reading data fields, study the data card in figure 8.2. Its field layout specifications are represented by vertical lines on the card. These vertical lines (along with the assigned variables written on the card) are solely for your benefit; the computer interprets the data only by the holes and the field specifications that the programmer provides.

If you wish to read and store all the numbers on the card, the following READ statement and its associated FORMAT statement could be used.

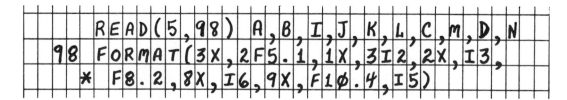

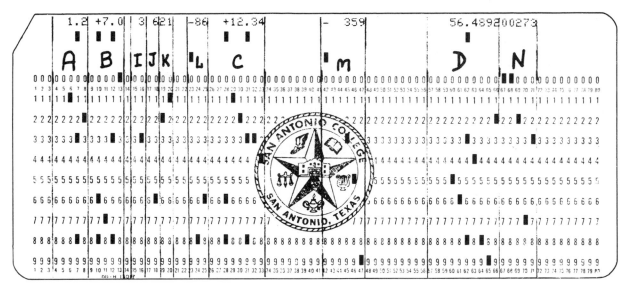

Figure 8.2 Sample card record two

If you wish only to transfer the second field (B), third field (I), and the sixth field (L) to memory, the following READ statement and its associated FORMAT statement could be used.

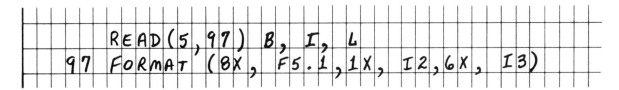

```
      READ(5,97) B, I, L
97    FORMAT (8X, F5.1,1X, I2,6X, I3)
```

If you wish to transfer the third field (I), fourth field (J), seventh field (C), and the tenth field (N), the following READ statement and its associated FORMAT statement could be used.

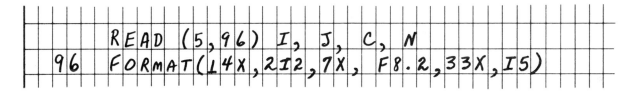

```
      READ (5,96) I, J, C, N
96    FORMAT(14X,2I2,7X, F8.2,33X,I5)
```

There may be situations in which you want the system to read a new record automatically, without specifying multiple READ statements. That is, when the end of the FORMAT statement is reached and there are still additional items in the I/O list, the system will cause a new record to be read. The system will also return to the first encountered left parenthesis in a right-to-left scan (i.e., rightmost left parenthesis) to find new format codes for the remaining variables to be transferred. For example:

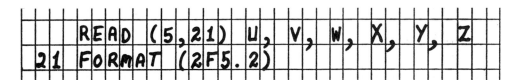

```
      READ (5,21) U, V, W, X, Y, Z
21    FORMAT (2F5.2)
```

This READ statement and associated FORMAT statement cause three records to be read. First, the items U and V are transferred from the first record under the field specifications of 2F5.2. Since no more format codes exist in the FORMAT statement for the remaining variables, the system will cause the next record to be read and will return to the beginning of the FORMAT statement for additional format codes.

The items W and X are read from the second record under the field specifications of 2F5.2. Once again, the end of the FORMAT statement is reached and additional items exist in the I/O list. The system again causes a new record to be read and returns to the first format code to use it.

The items Y and Z are transferred from the third record under the field specifications of 2F5.2. At this point the end of the FORMAT statement is reached, but there are no remaining items to be transferred. Execution of the READ statement is therefore terminated, and control of execution continues with the next instruction in sequence.

8.5 WRITING NUMERIC FORMATTED DATA

Output statements are widely used because they provide the key for the programmer to see the results of his hard labor. Numeric data may be output in the form of printed results, punched cards, magnetic tape, magnetic disk, or other output media. This section will discuss the output of numeric data in the form of the printed page, since it is the most common form of output, especially for the student programmer.

If many data fields are to be printed, the programmer should first construct the output field locations on a printer layout form. It is from this sheet that the output field specifications can begin to take place. Instead of using a printer layout form here, we will describe the values in memory with their assigned variables and the desired output field locations. The values read from the student registration card record given in figure 8.1 will be printed.

Desired Print Line Position	Value in Memory	Assigned Variable
5–11	2308517	NRSREG
17	2	LVLCLS
25–26	15	NRSHRS
30–36	426.50	TFEE

If you wish to print these values on a double-spaced line, you could print them using the WRITE statement as follows:

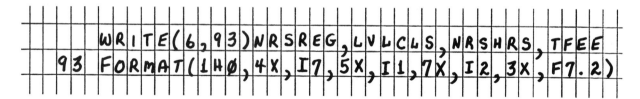

The first character of data in the output record specifications is a carriage control specification of 1H0 to provide a double-spaced line feed. Next, four blank positions are specified as 4X to start the first output field at print position 5. The data item NRSREG is output under an I7 field specification. The data item will be right-justified in the field positions 5–11. We wish to print LVLCLS starting at print position 17, so five blank positions (5X) must be specified to align the field at position 17. The item LVLCLS is transferred under an I1 field specification.

The next field is to begin at position 25. Seven blank positions (7X) must be specified so that we are located at this position when the data field is printed. The item NRSHRS is transferred under an I2 field specification. The last field is to start at column 30, so three blank positions (3X) are specified to align the field at this print column. The item TFEE is transferred under an F7.2 field specification. The item will be right-justified in the output field. The output field will consist of any integer digits present, a decimal point, and two fractional digits.

The printed results for the given output statement are:

```
print                  1         2         3         4
positions:    12345678901234567890123456789012345678 90
              2308517        2        15       426.50
```

You can print any item in memory at any print position and in any sequence. Just because data fields are input in a certain order does not mean that you must output them in that order.

The type of format code used to output a data field must agree with the type of variable with which it is associated (the same type as input requirements). The size need not agree, but the output format codes must agree with the output list in a one-to-one, left-to-right order.

To further illustrate the printing of numeric data, some of the values read from the data card given in figure 8.2 will be printed. The desired output specifications are:

Desired Print Line Position	Value in Memory	Assigned Variable
1–5	1.2	A
9–10	6	J
14–15	21	K
20–22	−86	L
26–35	56.4892	D

If you wish to print these items on a single-spaced line, you would code the WRITE and FORMAT statements as follows:

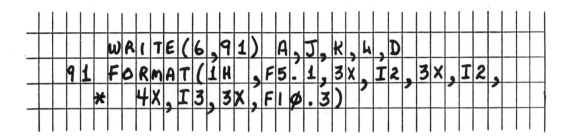

```
      WRITE(6,91) A,J,K,L,D
91 FORMAT(1H ,F5.1,3X,I2,3X,I2,
   *  4X,I3,3X,F10.3)
```

The first character of data in the output record specifications is a carriage control specification of 1Hƀ to provide a single-spaced paper feed. The first item is to be printed at position 1, so you do not have to provide any blank positions before the first field. The item A is transferred under an F5.1 format code. Next, three blank positions are given so that the item J is transferred under an I2 field specification starting at print column 9. Three blank positions are provided with the format code 3X to align the next field at position 14. The field K is transferred as an I2 field specification. Four blank positions are specified to start the field L at position 20. The item L is transferred under an I3 format code. Three blank positions (3X) are specified to start the last field at position 26. The field D is output under an F10.3 field specification. No more items are to be output, so the FORMAT statement ends with the close parenthesis.

The printed results for this output statement are:

```
print                    1         2         3
positions:      1234567890123456789012345678901234567890123456789
               ┌───────────────────────────────────────────────
               │  1.2   6  21    -86       56.489
```

The same results could be obtained by eliminating the X format codes and expanding the width of the other format codes. (Remember that when the width of the output field specifications exceeds the number of output characters, the excessive high-order positions are filled with blanks.) It is considered a better practice, however, to use the X format code to separate data fields, to maintain more accurate internal documentation.

8.6 USING THE SLASH (/) TO SELECT RECORDS WITH READING AND WRITING OPERATIONS

Usually, one record is read with the execution of a READ statement, and one print line is written with the execution of the WRITE statement. There are occasions when a programmer may wish to read multiple input records or skip some records in a file. It is also highly desirable to be able to print multiple lines of output with only one WRITE and its associated FORMAT statement. The slash (/) specification can accomplish all these tasks.

A slash in the FORMAT statement indicates the end of one data record and causes a new one to be read or written. Slashes at the beginning or end of a FORMAT statement and/or consecutive slashes in the middle of a FORMAT statement are used to skip input or output records. Rules governing the use of slashes in the FORMAT statement are:

Rule 1. Slashes may be used instead of (or with) commas to separate format codes.

Rule 2. Whereas a comma separating two format codes indicates that the next field is contained on the same record, a **slash** separating two format codes indicates that the next field is contained on a new record.

Rule 3. If there are **n** (where **n** is the count) consecutive slashes at the beginning or end of the FORMAT statement associated with a READ statement, then **n** input records are skipped and no data fields are transferred from them.

Rule 4. If there are **n** consecutive slashes at the beginning or end of the FORMAT statement associated with an output statement, then **n** blank records are produced as output.

Rule 5. If **n** consecutive slashes appear other than at the beginning or end of a FORMAT statement associated with a READ statement, then **n − 1** (n minus one) input records are skipped.

Rule 6. If **n** consecutive slashes appear elsewhere (other than the beginning or end) in a FORMAT statement associated with an output statement, then the number of blank output records is **n − 1**.

Input Considerations

Examples of using slashes to skip input records are as follows:

Example one:

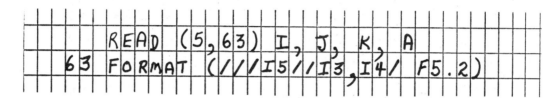

The first three slashes at the beginning of the FORMAT statement indicate that the first three records are to be skipped (read without transferring any data fields). The item I is transferred from the fourth record under the I5 field specification. The next two consecutive slashes indicate that one (**n − 1**) record is to be skipped, so the fifth record is bypassed. The items J and K are transferred from the sixth record under the format codes of I3 and I4, respectively. The slash after the I4 format code indicates that the next field is to be taken from a new record. Consequently, the item A is read from the seventh record.

A total of seven records is read in storing the four data fields in memory. Whenever the number of variables in the I/O list agrees in count with the number of format codes in the FORMAT statement, you may calculate the total records read by counting the number of slashes encountered and adding one. More difficulty occurs when more or fewer variables are given in the I/O list than there are format codes in the FORMAT statement.

Example two:

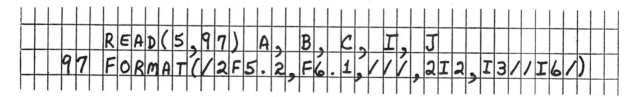

This is an example in which there are fewer variables than format codes; so some of the format codes will be ignored. The one slash at the beginning of the format specifications indicates that the first record is skipped. The three items A, B, and C are transferred off the second record under the format codes 2F5.2 and F6.1, respectively. The commas before and after the next three slashes have no significance and are ignored. The three slashes cause the next two (**n − 1**) records, numbers three and four, to be skipped. The items I and J are transferred from the fifth record under the two integer field specifications of the format code 2I2. No more items exist in the I/O list, so the remaining part of the FORMAT statement is ignored.

A total of five records was read and five data fields transferred to memory. Note that four slashes had been encountered—four plus one equals five records read.

Example three:

This is an example of having more variables in the I/O list than format codes. The first two slashes indicate that records one and two are skipped. The item I is transferred from the third record under the format code I2. The next slash following the I2 format code instructs that the next field be taken from a new record. The items J and K are transferred from record four under the field specifications of I3 and I1, respectively. The next two slashes instruct that one record ($n - 1$) be skipped (record five). The items A, B, and C are transferred from record six under the format codes 2F5.1 and F4.0, respectively. The three slashes at the end of the FORMAT statement command that records seven, eight, and nine be skipped.

Since more items exist in the I/O list, the system reverts to the first left-hand parenthesis in the right-to-left scan to find additional format codes. The two slashes at the beginning of the FORMAT statement imply that the two records, numbers ten and eleven, are skipped. The item L is transferred from record twelve under the I2 format code. The next slash implies that a new record is to be read. The item M is transferred from record thirteen. Since the I/O list has been exhausted, data transfer ends. A total of thirteen records is read and eight data fields are stored in memory.

Output Considerations

Now let's examine the use of slashes in output records. Suppose you want to print the values of A, B, and C on one line and the values of I and J on a new line. The slash could be used in the format specifications to produce these two lines of output with only one WRITE statement. The coded statements would be

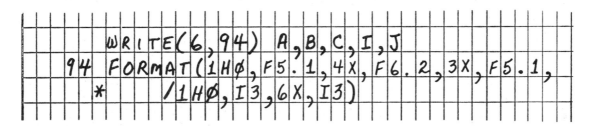

The values of A, B, and C are printed beginning in positions 1, 10, and 19, respectively, on the first line. The slash says to start the next values on a new line, so the values of I and J are printed on a new line beginning in positions 1 and 10, respectively. Note the carriage control specification given after the slash for the second line of output. (Remember, you must include a carriage control specification for each line of printer output. Thus, a carriage control character must be provided in the format specifications for any set of values to be printed on a new line.)

The slash specification provides a simple way of making the printer paper produce blank lines. Each slash moves the paper one line. Suppose you want to triple-space the output lines. This can be done by including the slash as follows:

WRITE (6,98) A, B, C
98 FORMAT (/1H0,3F8.2)

The slash moves the paper one line, and then there is a double-space carriage control specification. Thus, the values of A, B, and C will be written on the third line below the last one.

It is often more convenient to place the slash at the end of the format specifications. You could also provide triple-spacing between output records as follows.

WRITE (6,97) A, B, C
97 FORMAT (1H0,3F8.2/)

First, the output line is double-spaced to write the three values. Then the slash causes the paper to be moved one more line. If the next output record is written as a double-spaced line, it will be printed on the third line below the last one. Terminal output operations follow the same rules as the line printer when slashes are used in format specifications.

8.7 A SAMPLE PROGRAM TO PREPARE A STUDENT TUITION REGISTER

A listing of the records in a file, called a register or roster, is often used for quick reference by clerical personnel. It is a handy reference for checking the status of a person or an item of information. Examples are: payroll registers, leave registers, grade registers, registration registers, inventory registers, and others. To illustrate further the techniques of reading and writing numeric data, let us write a program to prepare a tuition register.

The input records as described in figure 8.1 will be read and the items will be printed as follows:

Field Description	Print Positions
Student registration number	1–7
Classification	12
Semester hours enrolled	20–21
Tuition fee	30–36

Each record will be printed double-spaced.

Let us add the logic to count the number of records printed on a page and print a maximum of only twenty-five per page. The logic to control the number of lines printed per page is called **line counter logic**. We will use a counter (LINECT) and increment it by one each time a new record is printed. When the counter gets to twenty-five we will perform a page eject and write the next record beginning at the top of a new page. We must, of course, reset the line counter to zero when the page eject operation is performed. A sentinel record with a value of 9999999 for student registration number will be used to terminate the processing. The flowchart for the program logic is given in figure 8.3, the pseudocode for the program logic is given in figure 8.4 (p. 252), and the coded program is given in figure 8.5 (p. 252).

The line counter is initialized to 25 to force a page eject before the first detail record is printed. A test is made at the top of the loop for a student number of 9999999 to detect the sentinel record which indicates an end of file. If the line counter is less than 25, a detail record is printed, the line counter is incremented by one, a new student record is read and control returns to the top of the loop. When the line counter is equal to 25, a page eject is performed and the line counter is reset to zero. The current detail record is printed, the line counter is incremented, a new record is read, and control returns to the top of the loop. You may wonder why a WRITE statement for the page eject was not included at the beginning of the program with line counter logic as follows:

```
99 FORMAT (1H1)
98 FORMAT (I7, 1X,I1, 5X,F7.2, I2)
97 FORMAT (1H0, I7, 4X,I1, 7X,I2, 8X,F7.2)
   INTEGER STUNR, STUHRS
10 WRITE (6, 99)
   LINECT = 0
   READ (5, 98) STUNR, LVLCLS, TFEE, STUHRS
20 IF (STUNR .EQ. 9999999) STOP
   WRITE (6, 97) STUNR, LVLCLS, STUHRS, TFEE
   LINECT = LINECT + 1
   READ (5,98) STUNR, LVLCLS, TFEE, STUHRS
   IF (LINECT .EQ. 25) GO TO 10
   GO TO 20
   END
```

You do not want to write the program this way, because it contains a subtle logic error. This logic would cause a blank page to be printed at the end (with headings if they were included in the page eject operation) when the total number of input records to be processed was a multiple of 25. The logic causes a new page to be printed in anticipation of each new page of output. When the total number of input records to be processed is a multiple of 25, there would be one last page eject, with headings, but it would not contain any detail print records. This last blank page might not seem so bad, but what would a user think when there were headings on the page but no output? The user wouldn't know whether there were output records missing, or what had happened. This is an example of some of the subtle points you must remember when developing program logic.

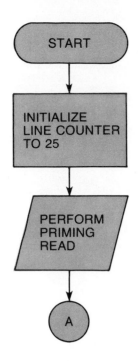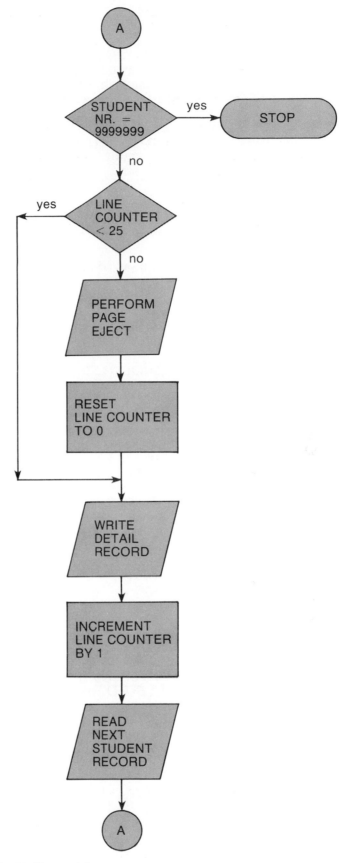

Figure 8.3 Flowchart of logic to prepare student tuition register

```
START ANALYSIS.
   INITIALIZE LINE COUNTER TO 25.
   PERFORM PRIMING READ OF FIRST RECORD.
   DO WHILE STUDENT REGISTRATION NUMBER NOT EQUAL TO 9999999
      IF LINE COUNTER IS EQUAL TO 25 THEN
         PERFORM PAGE EJECT.
         RESET LINE COUNTER TO 0.
      END IF.
      PRINT DETAIL LINE WITH STUDENT FIELDS.
      INCREMENT LINE COUNTER BY 1.
      READ NEXT STUDENT RECORD.
   END DO
END ANALYSIS.
```

Figure 8.4 Pseudocode of logic to prepare student tuition register

```
C --- PROGRAM TO PREPARE STUDENT TUITION REGISTER
C --- WITH LINE COUNTER LOGIC, MAX 25 LINES/PAGE
C
   99 FORMAT (1H1)
   98 FORMAT (I7, 1X,I1, 5X,F7.2, I2)
   97 FORMAT (1H0, I7, 4X,I1, 7X,I2, 8X,F7.2)
C
      INTEGER STUNR, STUHRS
C --- INITIALIZATION OF LINE COUNTER AND PRIMING READ
      LINECT = 25
      READ (5, 98) STUNR, LVLCLS, TFEE, STUHRS
C
C --- LOOP TO PROCESS RECORDS
   20 IF (STUNR .EQ. 9999999) STOP
C ---    CHECK LINE COUNTER FOR PAGE EJECT
         IF (LINECT .LT. 25) GO TO 30
         WRITE (6, 99)
         LINECT = 0
   30    WRITE (6, 97) STUNR, LVLCLS, STUHRS, TFEE
         LINECT = LINECT + 1
         READ (5, 98) STUNR, LVLCLS, TFEE, STUHRS
      GO TO 20
C
      END
```

Figure 8.5 Sample program to prepare student tuition register

8.8 LANGUAGE EXTENSIONS IN FORTRAN DIALECTS (THE END = OPTION WITH THE FORMATTED READ, THE SPECIFIC READ, PRINT, AND PUNCH STATEMENTS)

A very useful option included with the READ statement on some compilers is the **END =** parameter. This parameter may be included in the READ to check for the end of a data file. The general form of the READ with the **END =** option is:

READ (unit, n, END = a) list

The **END =** parameter is included after the format statement number and separated from it by a comma. The "a" represents a statement number assigned to an executable statement to which control is transferred whenever an end-of-file is encountered by the computer on a given file unit.

A JCL card marking the end of a data file is normally used to invoke the **END** = option. That is, when the computer attempts to read another data card, but reads the end-of-file JCL card, the **END** = option is then taken. The use of the **END** = option in a READ statement eliminates the need for a trailer (sentinel) record at the end of the data file and a check for this record. Thus, both the trailer record and Logical IF statement can be omitted in the program. For example:

```
99 FORMAT (I5,1X,3I3)
10 READ (5,99,END=20) ID, NTEST1, NTEST2, NTEST3
   . . .
   . . .
   GO TO 10
20 . . .
```

A loop is formed to read and process multiple sets of data until an end-of-file (EOF) condition is encountered on unit 5. When an EOF conditon is found, control will be transferred to the statement labeled 20.

An abnormal program termination occurs when the programmer tries to read past the end-of-file of a data deck and no provision has been made to detect this condition. That is, if neither the trailer card technique nor the **END** = option is included in the READ, and you try to read a data card when no more are present, the computer will abort the program. The error termination message given on the IBM G compiler is:

217 END OF DATA SET ON UNIT x

where **x** is the file unit number. This means that the programmer tried to read another data record when none was available and when no provisions were included to handle the end-of-file condition.

CDC compilers allow the testing for an end-of-file condition by the following statement:

IF (EOF(unit).NE.0) s

where **unit** is the file unit and **s** is an executable statement. **EOF** (unit) is a call to a system routine to see whether an end-of-file has been encountered on the specified unit. If an end-of-file has **not** been reached, a value of zero is returned. Thus, the IF statement tests for a value other than zero to detect an end-of-file condition and executes the given statement when the condition is true. Examples are:

IF (EOF(5).NE.0) STOP
IF (EOF(5).NE.0) GO TO 100

The **END** = option is available on some compilers and is widely used by programmers. It would be nice to have had the option included in ANSI FORTRAN 66, but it isn't. Therefore, programs in this text will use the sentinel/trailer record technique whenever an undetermined number of data records is read and processed.

The Specific READ Statement

The specific READ statement is available on many FORTRAN IV compilers to read card files. No unit number is supplied, since usually only punched card files are to be read for input. (The specific READ statement may also be used to read from a data file (terminal input) in a timesharing mode.) The statement number of an associated FORMAT statement, which describes the locations and form of the input fields, follows the keyword READ. The variable and array names assigned to each input field follow the FORMAT statement number. Commas are used to separate the FORMAT statement number and each of the variables. The general form of the specific READ statement is given in figure 8.6 (p. 254).

Valid examples of the specific READ statement are:

READ 89, A, B, C, I, J
26 READ 132, IDENT, SCORE1, SCORE2

The first example reads the five fields A, B, C, I, and J as described in the FORMAT statement numbered 89. The second example reads the three fields IDENT, SCORE1, and SCORE2 as defined in the FORMAT statement numbered 132.

```
┌─────────────────────────────────────────────────────────────────────────┐
│                  Specific READ Statement—General Form                     │
├───────────────────────────────────────────────────────────────────────────┤
│                                                                           │
│        READ  n, list                                                      │
│                                                                           │
│  where:                                                                   │
│                                                                           │
│        n       —     is the statement number of the associated FORMAT    │
│                      statement which describes the attributes of the      │
│                      input data.                                          │
│        list    —     is an I/O list which may include one or more variable│
│                      and/or array names separated by commas.              │
│                                                                           │
└───────────────────────────────────────────────────────────────────────────┘
```

Figure 8.6 General notation of the specific READ statement

```
┌─────────────────────────────────────────────────────────────────────────┐
│                      PRINT Statement—General Form                         │
├───────────────────────────────────────────────────────────────────────────┤
│                                                                           │
│        PRINT  n, list                                                     │
│                                                                           │
│  where:                                                                   │
│                                                                           │
│        n       —     is the statement number of the associated FORMAT    │
│                      statement which describes the attributes of the      │
│                      output data.                                         │
│        list    —     is an optional I/O list which may include one or more│
│                      variable and/or array names separated by commas.     │
│                                                                           │
└───────────────────────────────────────────────────────────────────────────┘
```

Figure 8.7 General notation for the PRINT statement

The PRINT Statement

The PRINT statement is available on many FORTRAN IV compilers to provide the capability for printing data on the line printer. This statement does not include a unit number, since only the printer can be used. The statement must have an associated FORMAT statement to describe the output data specifications. An optional list of variables and array names separated by commas follow the associated FORMAT statement number. A comma is used to separate the FORMAT statement number from the first variable, if an I/O list is included. The general form of the PRINT statement is given in figure 8.7.

Valid examples of the PRINT statement are:

PRINT 53, S1, S2, S3
87 PRINT 12, TOTAL
PRINT 174

The first example prints the three fields S1, S2, and S3 according to the output specifications in the FORMAT statement numbered 53. The second example prints the variable TOTAL according to specifications in FORMAT statement 12. The third example prints the data specified in FORMAT statement 174. The last example illustrates the use of the PRINT statement to print only headings that are specified as literal constants inside the FORMAT statement.

```
 ┌─ ── ── ── ── ── ── ── ── ── ── ── ── ── ── ── ── ── ── ┐
 │                    PUNCH Statement—General Form                    │
 ├─ ── ── ── ── ── ── ── ── ── ── ── ── ── ── ── ── ── ── ┤
 │                                                                     │
 │        PUNCH n, list                                                │
 │                                                                     │
 │   where:                                                            │
 │                                                                     │
 │        n      —    is the statement number of the associated FORMAT statement that │
 │                    describes the attributes of the output data.     │
 │        list   —    is an optional I/O list which may include one or more variable and/or │
 │                    array names separated by commas.                 │
 └─────────────────────────────────────────────────────────────────────┘
```

Figure 8.8 General notation for the PUNCH statement

The PUNCH Statement

The PUNCH statement is available in many FORTRAN IV compilers to provide the capability for outputting data in the form of punched cards. Like the other specific I/O statements, no unit number is provided, since this statement always refers to the card punch. This statement must have an associated FORMAT statement to describe the form of the output fields. An optional list of variables and/or array names, each separated by commas, follow the FORMAT statement number. A comma must separate the FORMAT statement number and the first variable, if present. The general form of the PUNCH statement is given in figure 8.8.

Valid examples of the PUNCH statement are:

PUNCH 98, TEST1, TEST2
97 PUNCH 74, XSQ, YSQ, XYSQ

The first example punches the fields TEST1 and TEST2 into a punched card according to the format specifications in statement number 98. The second examples punches the fields XSQ, YSQ, and XYSQ into a punched card according to the specifications in the FORMAT statement numbered 74.

Unexpected Output Results

When an incorrect numeric format code is specified to output a certain type variable (for example: an integer variable under an F format code or a real variable under an I format code), the value normally written with the IBM "G" level compiler is zeroes for the field. If an improper format code is specified with a type variable in **WATFIV**, an execution error will occur with the diagnostic message of:

"FORMAT SPECIFICATIONS AND DATA TYPE DO NOT MATCH"

If the programmer has not stored a value into a variable or has misspelled the name in the output I/O list, unpredictable output results will be printed with the IBM "G" level compiler. WATFIV, when this situation occurs, will print U's ("undefined") in the output field. As many U's as specified in the field width are printed.

Arithmetic Expressions in an Output I/O List

Some compilers, like WATFIV and the B6700, allow arithmetic expressions to be included in the I/O list for the WRITE. For example:

WRITE (6,99) A, B, 10.0, A + B + 10.0
99 FORMAT (1H0, 4F10.2)

This capability comes in very handy when you want to obtain a required answer quickly, or to debug something. Many other FORTRAN IV timesharing systems include this capability.

The J Format Code

The **J** format code is unique to the Burroughs 6700 and 7700 compilers. On input fields, the **Jw** specifications function identically to the Iw specifications. On output, the **Jw** specifications cause the integer value to be printed in the minimum field necessary to contain the value, without exceeding the width specification. That is, any high-order blanks are eliminated. If the output value requires more than **w** positions, then **w** asterisks are printed.

8.9 SUMMARY

Professional FORTRAN programs in real-world applications read input data under format control, i.e., FORMAT statements are used to describe the input fields in a record. Output results are also printed or displayed in precise locations with format specifications given in the FORMAT statement. The capability of a FORTRAN programmer to handle the reading and writing of formatted data is very important. This chapter discussed the finer points of reading and writing numeric formatted data so that you will have an indepth knowledge of how to perform formatted I/O with numeric fields. Many academic institutions teach only formatted I/O (instead of format-free) to ensure that students learn professional programming techniques.

Three important terms in this area are *field, record* and *file*. A field is one item of data, such as age, grade, hours worked, hourly wage, and so forth. It may consist of only one character or multiple characters to provide a value for the item. The characters must be logically related. For example, no letters would be included in a field for hours worked. Thus, a common definition for a field is a logical collection of one or more related characters that represents the value for a data item.

A record is a logical collection of related fields for a person, event, or transaction. When we refer to a record's being a logical collection of related fields, we mean that they are used together to identify all the needed information about a transaction in an application area. Thus, a part number is not included in a payroll record, since it is clearly not related to that application. A record is often referred to as a logical record, which is the unit of data obtained on a READ or WRITE operation.

A file consists of all the logical records for a specific application. It is the entire collection of records to be read and processed when preparing a report or updating a file. A file is analogous to the drawers in a filing cabinet that contain all the records for an application such as payroll, student registration, purchase orders, or inventory. Most files are organized in a sequential fashion. That is, the records in the file must be accessed in a serial manner—record one, record two, record three, and so on.

The reading and writing of formatted data require careful construction of the FORMAT statement and its associated format codes. Many mistakes can be made in a FORMAT statement if you don't pay close attention to the details of the layout of each data field and its related format code.

A format code describes two characteristics of a data field. First, it identifies the type of data, such as integer, floating point, alphanumeric, and so on. Second, it identifies the size or length of the field. The location of a field within the record is determined by the compiler. The compiler starts at position one in a record and sums the length of the previous fields (including the spaces designated by the X format code) to arrive at the beginning position for the field to be transmitted.

Each printer and terminal output line may be spaced differently. That is, you may want to start the output at the top of a new page (page eject) or top line on a video screen, doublespace the line beneath the previous line, and so forth. A carriage control character must be given at the beginning of the format specifications in a FORMAT statement for printer and terminal output. A 1X or literal character of a space (1Hb or 'b', where b represents a space) is used for single line spacing control; the literal of 0 (1H0 or '0') is used for doublespacing a line beneath the previous line; the literal character 1 (1H1 or '1') is used to perform a page eject action (to start the output at the top of the next page). A literal character of + (1H+ or ' +') is used when you want to print a new line *on* the previous line. (Note: the use of the single quote is not allowed in ANSI FORTRAN 66.)

There are many rules for correctly using the FORMAT statement, format codes, and other format specification characters, such as the slash. Five rules were given for the general use of the FORMAT statement. Twelve rules were given for input/output formatting considerations.

The integer (I) and floating point (F) format codes are the primary format codes used for formatting numeric data in business applications. Section 8.3 discussed these two format codes and gave various examples of their use. You should understand the use of these format codes in their input and output operations. For example, the floating point format code will provide the position of an implied decimal point in numeric input fields punched without decimal points. A decimal point punched in an input field overrides the decimal point specification given in the floating point format code. Section 8.4 gave two formatted card records and various format specifications to illustrate the reading of numeric formatted data. Section 8.5 illustrated the writing of numeric formatted data fields.

Section 8.6 discussed the use of the slash to select records and to skip lines with reading and writing operations. Six rules were given concerning the use of the slash in format specifications. Illustrations were included to explain the various input and output considerations when using the slash in the FORMAT statement. Section 8.7 presented a sample program to prepare a student tuition register to illustrate the reading and writing of formatted I/O. Line counter logic was included in the program.

8.10 TERMS

Terms and concepts you should become familiar with in this chapter include:

card file	format specifications	logical record
carriage control character	formatted data	page eject
field	implied decimal point	record
file	I/O	record layout design
file organization	input/output	right justified
floating point format code (F)	integer format code (I)	sequential file
format code	line counter logic	

8.11 REVIEW QUESTIONS

1. What capability do the various I/O statements provide in FORTRAN?
2. A collection of related data fields is called a _____ .
3. A collection of related characters to represent one item of information is a _____ .
4. A collection of related records for a specific application is called a _____ .
5. The FORTRAN I/O statement to read data into the computer is the _____ statement.
6. The FORTRAN I/O statement to write output data onto many different types of media is the _____ statement.
7. What purpose does the FORMAT statement serve in FORTRAN?
8. The format code to read numeric data in integer form is _____ .
9. The format code used to read numeric data in decimal form with a decimal point is _____ .
10. The format code to skip positions on input or to insert blanks on output is the _____ format code.
11. The integer constant which follows the format code letter is used to specify the field's w _____ .
12. Where are carriage control specifications used?
13. FORMAT statements must always have a unique statement number assigned to them. (True/False)
14. FORMAT statements may or may not be executed by the program. (True/False)
15. FORMAT statements may generally be placed anywhere in a program as long as they appear before the END statement. (True/False)
16. Constants and/or expressions may appear in the I/O list of a READ or WRITE statement. (True/False)
17. There is a one-to-one relationship between the names in the I/O list, data fields in the record, and format codes in the FORMAT statement. (True/False)
18. The type format code used must always match the type variable name assigned to an item. (True/False)
19. Numeric data fields are constructed in I/O records in much the same way as numeric constants in FORTRAN statement. (True/False)
20. Can decimal points and/or commas be included in integer data fields that are read by the I format code?
21. Leading, embedded, and/or trailing blanks in an integer input data field are ignored. (True/False)
22. If an integer quantity in memory is too large to be output under the width specifications for the output field, what values will be printed by most computers?
23. If an integer quantity in memory requires fewer positions then specified in the **w** parameter, what values will be printed in the excessive positions?
24. The width specifications for the F format codes must include a position for the decimal point, if present, in an input field. (True/False)

25. On output fields, as many digits as specified in the **d** parameter will be output behind the decimal point. (True/False)
26. Any permissible form of an integer or real numeric field may be read by an F format code. (True/False)
27. All numeric output quantities are left-justified in their output fields. (True/False)
28. FORTRAN provides automatic rounding by the system if the first digit of the truncated fractional part is equal to or greater than _____ .
29. What four things must a programmer know about a field before the proper type variable and field specifications can be constructed?
30. Where must the carriage control specification be given in the FORMAT statement for printer output?
31. The use of commas to separate format codes indicates that the next field comes from the _____ record.
32. The use of slashes to separate format codes for input specifications indicates that the next field comes from a _____ record.

8.12 EXERCISES

1. Construct a READ and its associated FORMAT statement to read the input values of J, K, and L from a punched card in card columns 1–3, 6–8, and 10–12, respectively. Use a statement number of 95 for the FORMAT statement.
2. Construct a READ and associated FORMAT statement to read the two variables N and X from a punched card. The variable N is punched in columns 2–4; the variable X is punched in columns 10–13 in the form NN.N. Use a statement number of 78 for the FORMAT statement.
3. Construct the WRITE and its associated FORMAT statement to print the input values read in exercise one. Use statement number 89 for the FORMAT statement. Output the variables as a double-spaced line with the following field positions.

Field Description	Print Positions
J	3–5
K	10–12
L	15–17

4. Construct the WRITE and its associated FORMAT statement to print the input values of N and X read in exercise two. Use statement number 17 for the FORMAT statement. Output the variables on a single-spaced line with N in print positions 5–7 and X in positions 10–13.
5. Give the required format codes (I or F) to read the following numeric input fields into memory. A ƀ indicates a blank position.

Data Field Value	Required Format Code
12	
ƀ123	
− 12	
+ 12.34	
12.345	
− ƀ1.23	
ƀƀ123.	

6. Give the required format codes (I or F) to read the following numeric input fields into memory. (ƀ = a blank.)

Data Field Value	Required Format Code
1234	
ƀ12	
+ 123	
ƀƀ12.	
ƀ + 1.2	
+ 012.3	
− 12.3	

7. Show the output values printed for the following values in memory with their associated format codes. Include a ƀ to represent a blank position.

Value in Memory	Format Code	Printed Value
-567	I4	
-1819	I4	
0	I5	
21	I3	
0.	F3.2	
0.	F3.1	
49.925	F7.2	
-49.925	F7.1	
49.925	F7.0	
49.925	F7.5	
49.925	F8.4	
.6347	F6.4	
.6347	F4.3	
.6347	F4.1	
.6347	F3.0	
-.6347	F7.4	
-.6347	F8.4	
-.6347	F6.4	
-.6347	F10.6	

8. Show the output values printed for the following values in memory with their associated format codes. Include a ƀ to represent a blank position.

Value in Memory	Format Code	Printed Value
-1234	I3	
-1234	I6	
1234	I4	
0	I3	
0.	F3.0	
12.563	F5.1	
12.563	F5.3	
12.563	F5.0	
12.563	F7.2	
-12.563	F7.2	
.1256	F6.2	
.1256	F5.1	
.1256	F2.1	
.1256	F7.5	

9. How many input records will be read with the following READ statements? Count all records read, whether data fields are transferred from them or not.

a. **READ (5,81)M,N,O,P**
   81 FORMAT (I4//I2///F6.2/F4.2/////)

b. **READ (5, 82)I,J,K,A,B**
   82 FORMAT (//I5,I7///I3,F4.2/2F5.0///)

10. How many input records will be read with the following READ statements? Count all records read, whether data fields are transferred from them or not.

a. **READ (5, 83)X,Y,Z,L,M,N**
   83 FORMAT (///F6.0,2F5.1,I3////2I5/)

b. **READ (5, 84)I,J,A,K,L,B,M**
   84 FORMAT (/I6,I7//F6.2)

11. How many lines of output values will be printed with the following WRITE statement?

WRITE (6, 93)A,B,J,X,K,Y
93 FORMAT (1H0,2F5.2,I3/1X,F4.1/1X,I2/1X,F6.2)

12. How many lines of output values will be printed with the following WRITE statement?

WRITE (6,92)X,Y,Z,I,J,K,G,H
92 FORMAT (1H0,2F6.2/1X,F5.1,I2/1X,I2/1X,I3/1X,F5.2)

8.13 PROGRAMMING PROBLEMS

1. Write a program to read a data record with values of X and Y punched in columns 1–5 and 6–10, respectively. The form of each number is NNN.N. Sum the two numbers and print the following output results beginning on a new page.

Field Description	Print Positions	
X	1–5	
Y	10–14	
SUM	20–25	(Form = NNNN.N)

2. Write a program to read a file of employee labor records with the following values.

Record Positions	Field Description
1–5	Employee number (Form = NNNNN)
6–9	Blank
10–14	Hours worked (Form = NNN.N)
15–19	Hourly pay rate (Form = NN.NN)

Compute the gross pay of each employee. Print each employee record on a double-spaced line with the following specifications. Use a trailer record with 99999 for employee number to indicate the end of the data file.

Field Description	Print Positions
Employee number	5–9
Hours worked	15–19
Hourly pay rate	25–29
Gross pay	40–47

3. Write a program to perform the same function as problem 1, but with multiple data records. Double-space each output line. Use a trailer card with a value −99.9 for X to indicate the end of the data file.

4. Write a FORTRAN program to read a weekly payroll transaction file and list the data in each record. Record layout is as follows:

Record Positions	Field
1–6	Employee number (Form = NNNNNN)
7–19	Blank
20–24	Hourly wage rate (Form = NN.NN)
25–30	Hours worked (Form = NNN.NN)

Write the output values in the following print positions.

Field Description	Print Positions
Employee number	6–11
Hourly wage rate	20–24
Hours worked	33–38

Use a trailer record with a value of 999999 for employee number to indicate the end of the data file.

5. Write a FORTRAN program to read an inventory file and extend (compute) the total value of each item in stock. The input values are to be read from a data record in the following form:

Record Positions	Field Description
1–4	Item number (Form = NNNN)
5–7	Quantity on hand (Form = NNN)
8–13	Unit price (Form = NNN.NN)

As each record is read, compute the total value of each stock item by multiplying quantity on hand by unit price. Print the input values from each card and computed item-worth on a double-spaced line according to the following print positions.

Field Description	Print Positions
Item number	5–8
Quantity on hand	15–17
Unit price	24–29
Item worth	36–44

Use a trailer record with a value of 0000 for item number to indicate an end of the data file. You may use a blank card for the trailer record, since a blank field is read as zeroes for numeric items.

9 Writing Literal Data and Manipulating Character (Alphanumeric) Data

9.1 INTRODUCTION TO LITERAL CONSTANTS AND THE HOLLERITH (H) FORMAT CODE

When only numeric values are written for output, determining which value belongs to a variable is often confusing. One of the most important requirements for output results is clarity; otherwise, the values serve little use. Most reports and printed output include column headings or some textual information to identify the output values. This textual output is known as literal data. The **literal data** is simply a string of characters used to make the output more readable. Literal data is used to:

1. provide report headings, which appear at the top of the output pages to identify the report.
2. provide column headings, which are printed above each column of output values to identify the columnal values.
3. provide any type of titles or textual information to identify output results.

Literal data is usually not read and stored into variables. Since the report heading, column headings, and other textual information are known, the values can be written as **literal constants**. This is not to say that we cannot read alphabetic and other characters and use them in the program. We do this with the alphanumeric (A) format code and can read any character string we wish. This type of format capability will be discussed later in the chapter. At this point, though, we are interested only in including literal data in the output results.

Literal data is specified by the Hollerith (H) format code. This format code is named after Dr. Herman Hollerith, who first devised the coding scheme for representing characters in the punched card. Thus, literal data is often referred to as **Hollerith strings**. The H format code identifies a literal constant. A **literal constant** is a string of literal data in character form that is preceded by the H format code. The letter H used to identify a constant must be preceded by a count of the number of characters in the string. The general form of the H format code is:

$$wH$$

where:

w is an integer constant that represents the width or number of characters in the literal constant. **w** may range from 1 to 255.

Examples of valid literal constants are:

        32HINVENTORY REPORT FOR XYZ COMPANY
        16HPAYROLL REGISTER
         5HTEST1
         8HX-SQUARE
         6HSUM =   (one blank follows the =)
        11HJOHN'S DATA

All characters immediately following the H and through the last character in the string must be counted. Each space is also counted as a character. One must be extremely careful in providing the *exact* count of the characters, since one less or one greater than the actual length will usually result in a syntax error. For example:

        4HTOTAL   (w is too short)
        8HAVERAGE   (w is too long)

What do you do when a long literal constant exists, and continuation cards must be used? You could break the literal constant into several parts and code each part on a different card. This is probably the easiest way, since the beginning of a second literal constant is placed immediately after a prior literal. If the literal is not broken up, but continued onto a new card, the character in card column 7 is included in the literal string immediately after the character in card column 72 of the previous card.

Now let's see how to include these literal constants in our output.

9.2 WRITING LITERAL CONSTANTS

The literal constant is included in the FORMAT statement specifications at the location where you want the literal to be printed. Since the literal is a constant that was formed, rather than stored at a variable in memory, there is no variable name associated with it in the I/O list of the WRITE. A variable name *must never* be associated with a literal constant or the H format code.

A **report heading** beginning on a new page and starting in print position 14 could be coded as follows:

WRITE (6,99)
99 FORMAT (1H1,13X,20HSTUDENT GRADE REPORT)

The 1H1 tells the computer to do a page eject to begin the output on a new page. The carriage control operations such as 1H1, 1H0, 1Hb, and 1H+, that you have been using all along, have been specified as literal constants with the H format code. The 13X means to skip the first 13 positions. Then the literal constant of STUDENT GRADE REPORT, which is 20 characters in length, is printed starting at print position 14. Note that there are no variables in the I/O list of the WRITE, since only the literal constant is printed.

Column headings are printed the same way. Suppose you wish to have headings to identify columns of output values as follows:

Print Positions	Literal Constant
1–7	STUT-ID
10–14	TEST1
17–21	TEST2
24–28	TEST3
32–36	TOTAL
40–46	AVERAGE

See figure 9.1 (p. 264) for a PRINT LAYOUT sheet showing the report and column headings and the technique for showing the columns of data values.

The headings to identify the columns of output values derived from the expanded student grade problem in chapter 5 could be printed as follows:

WRITE (6,98)
98 FORMAT (1H0,7HSTUT-ID,2X,5HTEST1,
* 2X,5HTEST2,2X,5HTEST3,3X,5HTOTAL,
* 3X,7HAVERAGE)

These literal constants would be printed over the corresponding columns of output values to identify the output results clearly. Report and column headings, as described above, are usually printed on every output report. Otherwise, the report would have little value to the users, unless they were very familiar with the locations of the output values.

Now consider how literal data and numeric output fields can be interspersed in the output. That is, a literal constant can be followed by a numeric value, or vice versa. Suppose you want to print the values of X, Y, and SUM with a literal constant before each value to identify which value goes with which variable. The output specifications are:

WRITE (6,96) X, Y, SUM
96 FORMAT (1H0,4HX = ,F4.1,3X,
* 4HY = ,F4.1,4X,6HSUM = ,F5.1)

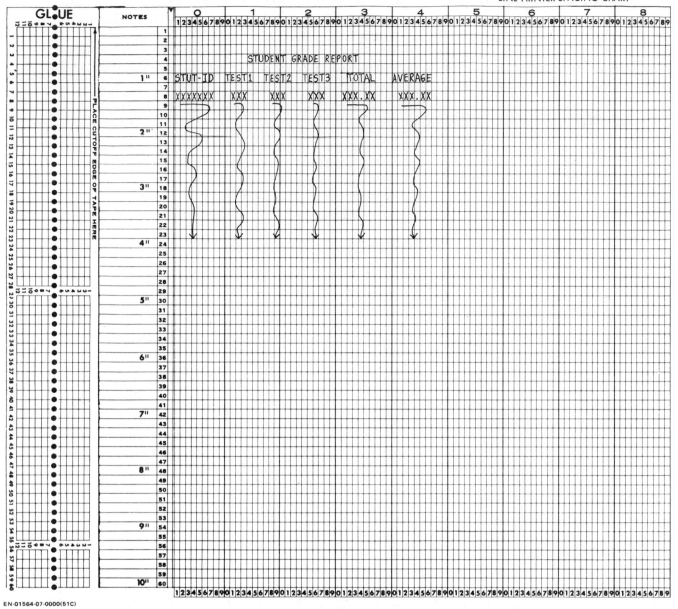

Figure 9.1 Student grades with report and column headings

The first literal constant is followed by the value of X, the second by the value of Y, and the third by the value of SUM. Assuming the values of 7.2, 11.4, and 18.6 for X, Y, and SUM, respectively, the output results would appear as follows:

```
print            1         2         3         4
positions:  123456789012345678901234567890234567890
          │  X = 7.2   Y = 11.4    SUM =  18.6
```

When a literal constant is written as the first output value on a line, many programmers will include the carriage control character as the first character in the literal. For example:

WRITE (6,91) I, N
91 FORMAT (5H0I = ,I2,3X,4HN = ,I4)

This provides a double-spaced line with the literal constant, I = , beginning in position one. It is highly recommended, however, that you code the carriage control characters as a separate literal to avoid forgetting to include them, and for better documentation.

Literal data may be written to punched cards, terminals, magnetic tape, and magnetic disk, as well as to printer output. Now let's see how to use the slash specification in writing various textual headings on printed products.

9.3 USING THE SLASH (/) TO WRITE MULTIPLE HEADINGS

The slash specification is frequently used to produce multiple lines of literal data. That is, multiple headings can be written using only one WRITE statement by separating the literal headings with a slash. For example, a report heading and column headings can be written in the same WRITE statement as follows:

> **WRITE (6,92)**
> **92 FORMAT(1H1,10X,24HSTUDENT GRADES FOR DP101,**
> *** //1H0,7HSTUDENT,5X,5HTEST1,5X,5HTEST2,**
> *** 5X,5HTEST3,5X,5HTOTAL,5X,7HAVERAGE)**

The literal constant, STUDENT GRADES FOR DP101, is printed as a report heading beginning in position 11. The first slash says that the line of output is complete, and that any other data will appear on a new line. The second slash moves the paper one line. The carriage control of 1H0 moves the paper two more lines; so the column headings are printed triple-spaced below the report heading.

The slash is frequently used to place new literals and their respective values on a new line. Assume the values of 36.87, 12.34, and −2.59 for the variables A, B, and C, respectively. Each literal title, followed by its value, can be printed on a new line as follows:

> **WRITE (6,93) A, B, C**
> **93 FORMAT (1H1,4HA = ,F6.2/**
> *** 1H0,4HB = ,F6.2/**
> *** 1H0,4HC = ,F6.2)**

The values would be printed as follows:

```
print                    1
positions:   12345678901234567
           ┌─────────────────
           │  A =  36.87
           │
           │  B =  12.34
           │
           │  C = -2.59
```

Writing multiple lines of headings and literal values with the slash specification proves a shorter and more efficient means of outputting multiple print lines. The longer the format specifications, the more chance for error. Hence, you should use discretion when using the slash for multiple output lines and not attempt to write dozens of lines this way. The simpler the format specifications, the fewer errors you will encounter.

9.4 REPETITION OF GROUP FORMAT SPECIFICATIONS

We often wish to print a group of values that requires a set of repeating format specifications, such as I3, 2X, F5.2, I3, 2X, F5.2, I3, 2X, F5.2. As you can see, there is a group pattern to the format specifications of I3, 2X, F5.2 that is repeated three times. The **group format repetition** is a short-cut notation for repeating a *group* of format codes. The group of format codes to be repeated is enclosed within a set of parentheses. A repetition factor is specified before the beginning parenthesis to denote the number of times the codes are repeated. The general form of the group format repetition is:

$$n(fc_1, . . ., fc_n)$$

where:

n specifies the number of times the group of format codes within the pair of parentheses is to be used. (**fc₁,. . .fcₙ**) represent the group of format codes to be repeated. Any combination of FORTRAN format codes may be used in the group.

Examples of the group format repetition are as follows:

31 FORMAT (I6,2X,3(I4,1X))	(input specifications)
86 FORMAT (4(I2,2X,F6.2),4X,2(1X,I7))	(input specifications)
95 FORMAT (1H0,5I4,4(5X,I3),5X,F7.2)	(output specifications)
91 FORMAT (1H0,16HINPUT VALUES ARE/	(output specifications)
* 10(1H0,3(I5,5X)/))	

Example one inputs a six-digit integer field in columns 1–6; columns 7 and 8 are skipped. Then three groups of four-digit integers, each followed by a blank column, are read. The group format specification of 3(I4,1X) is another way of saying I4,1X,I4,1X,I4,1X. Example two reads four groups of two fields. Each group consists of a two-digit integer, followed by two blank columns, and then by a floating-point field of six positions. The two-digit integer of the first group begins in card column 1; the two-digit integer of the second group begins in column 11; the two-digit integer of the third group begins in column 21; the two-digit integer of the fourth group begins in column 31. Then four columns are skipped, and two groups of a blank column followed by a seven-digit integer are read.

The third example writes five four-digit integer fields. Beginning in print position 21, four groups, each consisting of five spaces followed by a three-digit integer, are written; then five positions are skipped, and a seven-position floating-point field is written in positions 58–64. The fourth example writes a literal heading on one printer line. The group format specification writes ten double-spaced print lines, each containing three groups of five-digit integers, followed by five spaces on the same line. Thus, a total of 30 integer values is printed, three per line.

Group format repetition may be nested to a depth of two. That is, we can have a group format repetition within one other group format specification, as shown in the fourth example. Consider another example:

96 FORMAT (I6,2(3(I2,F5.2),3X))

This format specification says to read a six-digit integer followed by two groups, each containing three groups of a two-digit integer followed by a five-position floating-point field. Three columns are to be skipped at the end of each of the two groups. The equivalent format specification in expanded form would be:

96 FORMAT (I6,I2,F5.2,I2,F5.2,I2,F5.2,3X,I2,F5.2,I2,F5.2,I2,F5.2,3X)

In order to use the group format specifications, the format codes must have a consistent pattern; then the format codes can be grouped according to this pattern and the group format repetition used. All too many students believe that each format code is repeated the specified number of times before the *next* format code is used. Remember the entire group of format codes must be used before they are repeated. Thus, 2(A1,I3) means A1,I3,A1,I3 and *not* A1,A1,I3,I3.

An abbreviated form of the group format repetition is handy for repeating various literal constants. The specification 100 (1H*) would cause 100 asterisks to be formatted. For example:

WRITE (6,98)

98 FORMAT (1H0,100(1H*))

The specifications 40 (3H − * −) would cause 40 groups of hyphen, asterisk, hyphen to be printed. For example:

WRITE (6,97)

97 FORMAT (1H0,40(3H − * −))

The group format repetition is permitted with single format codes but does not provide anything that the normal repetition factor does not do. For example, 3(I4) does the same thing as 3I4, but the 3I4 is much simpler to code. For sake of clarity, always use the simple repetition factor for single format codes.

9.5 A SAMPLE PROGRAM TO ILLUSTRATE THE USE OF HEADINGS AND LITERAL CONSTANTS

To illustrate the use of literal data and output headings, let us develop a FORTRAN program to read an inventory file and prepare a listing of the items in stock. The input records will contain the following items.

Record Positions	Field Description
1–7	Item number (Form = NNNNNNN)
8–9	Blank
10–13	Quantity on hand (Form = NNNN)
14	Blank
15–21	Unit cost (Form = NNNN.NN)
22–28	Unit price (Form = NNNN.NN)

Let's extend the unit cost and unit price of the item in inventory by multiplying these values by the quantity on hand. Also, accumulate the total of the extended unit cost and unit price for all items in inventory. The accumulated totals will be printed at the end of the report with a literal that identifies these values.

The output will contain a report heading to identify the inventory of items in the ABC WAREHOUSE COMPANY. Report headings are normally centered over the other output values. Column headings will be included to identify the output values of each record. Each record will be printed as follows.

Field Description	Print Positions
Item number	1–7
Quantity on hand	14–17
Unit cost	26–32
Unit price	38–44
Extended unit cost	51–58
Extended unit price	65–72

The printer layout form should be used to identify the location of the output requirements in order to supply the correct format specifications. The print layout form is illustrated in figure 9.2.

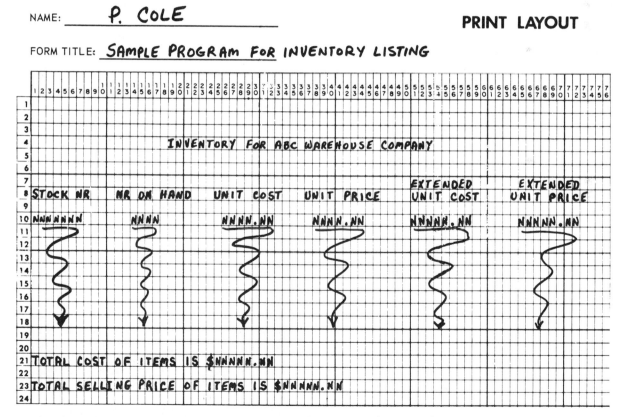

Figure 9.2 Print layout form for sample program

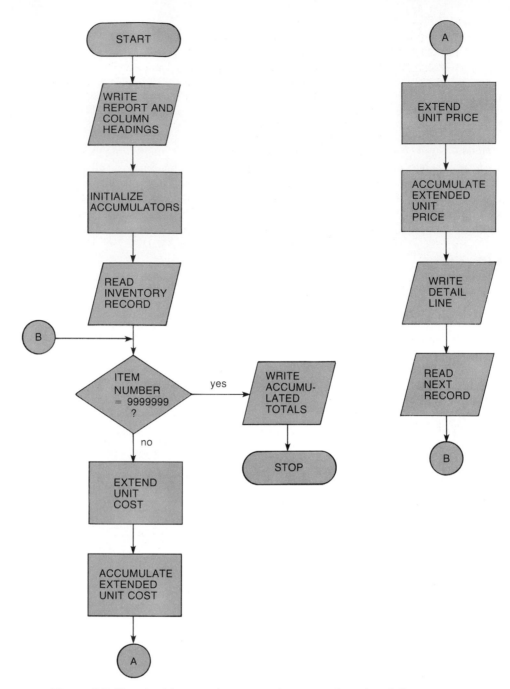

Figure 9.3 Flowchart for sample program to prepare inventory listing

The developed logic would be to print the headings first; then create a loop to read an inventory record, do the calculations, and print the output results until all records have been processed. Remember, be careful not to include the printing of the headings inside the loop. The output results would hardly be readable if a line of headings was printed between each line of stock items. Yet, this mistake is often made by beginning students. The accumulated totals are printed at the end of the report. The developed flowchart is presented in figure 9.3, the pseudocode in figure 9.4, and the coded program in figure 9.5. Assuming five inventory records in the input file, the printed results would appear as illustrated in figure 9.6 (p. 270).

The use of literal constants in output products make them more readable and "fancy." That is, literal constants enable you to make your reports very attractive and pleasing to the eye of the user. Some people refer to this as *"bells and whistles."* You can get carried away; some programmers go overboard and place a border of asterisks around certain values or output. Keep your output simple and use literal constants only when it helps the user to understand the report.

```
          START ANALYSIS.
             WRITE REPORT AND COLUMN HEADINGS.
             INITIALIZE ACCUMULATOR FOR TOTAL COST TO ZERO.
             INITIALIZE ACCUMULATOR FOR TOTAL PRICE TO ZERO.
             PERFORM PRIMING READ OF FIRST INPUT RECORD WITH DATA
                FIELDS OF ITEM NUMBER, NUMBER ON HAND, UNIT COST
                AND UNIT PRICE.
             DO WHILE ITEM NUMBER IS NOT EQUAL TO 9999999
                CALCULATE EXTENDED UNIT COST.
                ACCUMULATE EXTENDED UNIT COST.
                CALCULATE EXTENDED UNIT PRICE.
                ACCUMULATE EXTENDED UNIT PRICE.
                WRITE DETAIL REPORT LINE WITH ITEM NUMBER, NUMBER
                   ON HAND, UNIT COST, UNIT PRICE, EXTENDED
                   UNIT COST, AND EXTENDED UNIT PRICE.
                READ NEXT RECORD WITH ITEM NUMBER, NUMBER ON HAND,
                   UNIT COST AND UNIT PRICE.
             END DO
             WRITE SUMMARY LINE WITH TOTAL ACCUMULATED EXTENDED
                COST AND TOTAL ACCUMULATED EXTENDED PRICE.
          END ANALYSIS.
```

Figure 9.4 Pseudocode for sample program to prepare inventory listing

```
C --- PROGRAM TO LIST THE ITEMS IN INVENTORY FOR THE ABC
C --- WAREHOUSE COMPANY. THE REPORT ALSO INCLUDES THE EXTENDED
C --- UNIT COST AND EXTENDED UNIT PRICE OF EACH ITEM. THESE
C --- CALCULATED ITEMS ARE SUMMED IN ACCUMULATORS WHICH ARE
C --- PRINTED AT THE END OF THE REPORT.
C
C --- AUTHOR: J W COLE
C --- DATE WRITTEN: 3/12/82
C
99    FORMAT (1H1, 18X, 35HINVENTORY FOR ABC WAREHOUSE COMPANY//
      *        1H0,50X, 8HEXTENDED, 6X, 8HEXTENDED/
      *        1H , 8HSTOCK NR, 3X,10HNR ON HAND, 3X,9HUNIT COST,
      *        3X, 10HUNIT PRICE, 4X,9HUNIT COST, 4X,10UNIT PRICE)
98    FORMAT (I7, 2X, I4, 1X, 2F7.2)
97    FORMAT (1H0, I7,6X, I4,8X, F7.2,5X, F7.2,6X, F8.2,6X, F8.2)
96    FORMAT (/1H0,24HTOTAL COST OF ITEMS IS $, F8.2/
      *        1H0,33HTOTAL SELLING PRICE OF ITEMS IS $, F8.2)

C
      WRITE (6,99)
      TOTCST = 0.0
      TOTPRC = 0.0
      READ (5, 98) ITEM, NOHND, UNTCST, UNTPRC
C
10    IF (ITEM .EQ. 9999999) GO TO 20
         RNOHND = NOHND
         EXUNTC = UNTCST * RNOHND
         TOTCST = TOTCST + EXUNTC
         EXUNTP = UNTPRC * RNOHND
         TOTPRC = TOTPRC + EXUNTP
         WRITE (6, 97) ITEM, NOHND, UNTCST, UNTPRC, EXUNTC, EXUNTP
         READ (5, 98) ITEM, NOHND, UNTCST, UNTPRC
      GO TO 10
C
20    WRITE (6, 96) TOTCST, TOTPRC
      STOP
      END
```

Figure 9.5 Sample program to prepare inventory listing

STOCK NR	NR ON HAND	UNIT COST	UNIT PRICE	EXTENDED UNIT COST	EXTENDED UNIT PRICE
123456	10	20.00	30.00	200.00	300.00
235678	5	156.75	199.95	783.75	999.75
238796	100	7.60	19.50	760.00	1950.00
239032	250	3.25	9.99	812.50	2497.50
316738	51	10.33	25.50	526.83	1300.50

TOTAL COST OF ITEMS IS $ 3083.08

TOTAL SELLING PRICE OF ITEMS IS $ 7047.75

Figure 9.6 Printer output results from sample program

9.6 INTRODUCTION TO CHARACTER (ALPHANUMERIC) DATA AND FORMAT SPECIFICATIONS

Most data read and processed by FORTRAN programs is numeric in form, but frequently the need to read alphanumeric data arises. The term **alphanumeric** is used to describe data in which the characters may be alphabetic, numeric, special characters, or a combination of the three types. Alphanumeric data is treated as character or string data and must not be used in computations. That is, digits read as alphanumeric characters are treated differently in the computer from numeric digits read with an I or F format code.

Data items such as name, part number, item description, course number, and address are typical alphanumeric values used in computer programs. Alphanumeric data must be read with the alphanumeric (A) format code. Any attempt to read alphabetic letters or special characters with any of the numeric-type format codes will normally cause an execution error.

The Alphanumeric (A) Format Code

The A format code allows character (alphanumeric) data to be read or written. Any character acceptable to the computer can be read with the A format code. This format code is used to read data items such as names, titles, and other values containing alphabetic letters and special characters. Data items such as student number and part number, which may contain a mixture of alphabetic letters and numeric digits *must* be read with the A format code. A pure numeric field may be read with the A format code, but any item read with the A format code must *not* be used later in any computations.

The general form of the A format code is:

$$nAw$$

where:

n represents an optional repetition factor that specifies the number of times the format code is to be used. The value of **n,** when used, must be an unsigned positive integer constant whose value is less than or equal to 255. **w** specifies the number of card columns or positions in the input or output field. **w** must be an unsigned positive constant with a value less than or equal to 255. Examples are:

```
    READ (5,36) NAME1,NAME2,NAME3,NAME4,NAME5,NUMBR,RATE
 36 FORMAT (5A4,2X,I3,F6.2)
    READ (5,287) DESC1,DESC2,DESC3,DESC4,ID,UNITPR
287 FORMAT (4A4,A3,10X,F8.2)
```

The first example reads the 20 characters in card columns 1–20 as alphanumeric characters. The character field is broken down into five groups of four characters. The second example reads the first nineteen characters of an input record as four groups of 4 characters, plus a group of 3 characters. The need for dividing an alphanumeric field into groups of 4 or fewer characters is explained below.

We learned that a numeric value must be less than eleven digits (i.e., 2147483647) for it to be read and stored with the I format code on IBM mainframe computers. An integer number must be five digits or less, i.e., less than 32767, to be read with the I format code on 16-bit word minicomputers (such as the DEC PDP-11 series). Likewise, only so many characters can be read and stored as a field with the A format code. The maximum number of characters that can be read and stored as a field is related to the size of a computer word. A computer **word** refers to the size of a storage location that determines the amount of data which can be stored. The size of a computer word varies by type of computer. Since ANSI FORTRAN does not provide specifications for a word size, we will assume that a computer word can hold a maximum of 4 characters.

The following table gives the word size (in number of characters) for some of the more widely known computer systems.

Table 9.1 Word Size of Various Computer Systems

Computer System	Word size in bytes (characters)
Amdahl	4
Burroughs 6000	6
Control Data 6000/Cyber	10
DEC PDP-11	2
DEC VAX-11	4
Honeywell 60/6000	6
HP 3000	2
IBM	4
Micros (8-bit word)	1
Univac 1100	6
Your system	

Normally one item or field of information is stored at a given location. Each numeric value read with a format code is placed at a unique memory cell/word. Remember, the format code tells the form and size of the input data or output field. It does not indicate the size of the computer word, which is always a fixed size in a given computer system.

If a storage location can hold only 4 alphanumeric characters, then alphanumeric input fields must be broken into groups of 4 or fewer characters. Suppose a name field has 16 characters. It could be broken into four groups of 4 characters each. But what if the name field contains 15 characters? The character string could be broken down into three groups of 4 characters, plus a group of 3 characters; or, it could be broken down into five groups of 3 characters each.

Remember that a variable name must be assigned to each group of characters being read to designate their storage location. There must be a different variable for each format code that transmits data to memory. If there are four groups of 4 characters each, you must have four format codes, to designate the format of the fields, and four different variables. If there are five groups of 3 alphanumeric characters, you must have five format codes and, likewise, five different variables.

The type of variable and array names assigned to store alphanumeric data may be either integer or real. Since no computations should ever be performed with variables containing data in alphanumeric form, the computer will properly process alphanumeric data no matter which type of variable name is used. Integer variable names are preferred in most cases.

Input Considerations

The above discussion concerning the storage of alphanumeric characters may have lead you to believe that a field of more than 4 characters could not be read with an A format code. This is not true; an alphanumeric field of up to 255 characters can be read with a single A format code. The number of characters *stored* from the input field, however, cannot exceed four. If a 15-character field was read with an A15 format code, only the rightmost 4 characters would be stored.

If the field width specification (**w**) is greater than the maximum number of characters that can be stored at the memory location, then the excess leftmost characters in the field are skipped and the remaining characters read and stored in the variable. Thus, if we read the field DK123C under an A6 format code, only the rightmost 4 characters, 123C, would be stored in memory.

If the field width specification (**w**) is less than the maximum number of characters that can be stored at a memory location, then **w** characters are read and stored in memory. The characters will be stored left-justified in the memory location with the rightmost characters filled with blanks. Suppose the 3-character field, ABC, was read with an A3 format code. The three characters would be stored in the leftmost three positions in the computer word and the fourth position filled with a blank.

If the field width specification (**w**) is equal to the maximum number of characters that can be stored at a memory location, then **w** characters are read and stored to fill the memory word. The 4-character field, COLE, read with an A4 format code would fill a variable with the four characters, COLE.

The following rules sum up these input considerations. (**w** represents the width specification in the A format code.)

1. If **w** > variable (word) size, the rightmost characters that can be stored are placed in the memory word. The remaining leftmost characters are lost.
2. If **w** < variable (word) size, the characters are stored left-justified and the remaining positions filled with blanks.
3. If **w** = variable (word) size, then **w** characters are stored in the memory word.

The field width specification of 4 is recommended for optimum storage utilization because four characters is the maximum number that can be stored in a memory word in many systems. (Two characters is the maximum number of alphanumeric characters that can be stored in a word on many minicomputers.) You will use a different value depending on the word size of your computer. You must not fall into the trap of thinking that all alphanumeric fields should be read as a multiple of four characters. Only as many characters as make up the field should be read. If a 15-character field is used, do not specify a 4A4 field specification. That would read sixteen columns and get into the next field of data. You should specify a 3A4, A3 or some combination that would read only the 15 characters of data that comprise the total field size.

Output Considerations

Since the example computer word holds a maximum of four characters, you can output from 1 to 4 characters from the storage word. You do not have to output all the characters contained in the word, but you should know that the output characters are selected from the word in a left to right order. For example, if you output a variable containing the 4 characters, COLE, with an A2 format code, you would get the high-order 2 characters, CO, printed.

The following rules apply to the output of alphanumeric data under the A format code.

1. If the width specification (**w**) is less than the maximum number of characters that can be stored at a variable, the leftmost **w** characters will be printed. For example, the variable NAME containing the 4 characters, JOHN, written with an A3 format code would produce the output results JOH.
2. If the width specification (**w**) is greater than the maximum number of characters that can be stored at a variable, the output field will contain the contents of the variable right-justified in the output field. High-order blanks will be inserted in the leftmost positions to make up the size of the output field specifications. For example, the variable NAME containing the 4 characters, JOHN, written with an A7 format code would produce the output results of ƀƀƀJOHN (where ƀ represents a blank).
3. If the width specification (**w**) is equal to the maximum number of characters that can be stored at a variable, then the output field will contain the contents of the variable. For example, the variable NAME containing the 4 characters, JOHN, written under an A4 format code would be printed as JOHN.

The main thing to remember in outputting alphanumeric data is to write the data with the same format specifications that the data was read with. Suppose a 15-character field was read as follows:

READ (5,99) N1,N2,N3,N4,N5
99 FORMAT (5A3)

the values would be stored in memory as:

N1	N2	N3	N4	N5
SMIØ	THØØ	MARØ	YØLØ	OUØØ

Suppose the five variables were written as follows:

WRITE (6,98) N1,N2,N3,N4,N5
98 FORMAT (1H0,5A4)

The printed output results would be:

SMI TH MAR Y L OU

The entire contents, including the padded blanks, would be included in the output field. Data printed as such is hardly legible. What you want to do is to write the variables with the same format specifications that put the characters into memory. The output statement should be:

WRITE (6,98) N1,N2,N3,N4,N5
98 FORMAT (1H0,5A3)

Now the printed results would be:

SMITH MARY LOU

This output looks pretty good. If only 3 characters are put into a word during the input operation, then only the high-order 3 characters must be selected on the output specifications.

Let us look at a sample program that illustrates the reading and writing of alphanumeric data. Assume again the problem of computing student grades, but instead of a student number, let us include the student's name. The input items are:

Record Positions	Field Description
1–18	Student name
21–23	Test 1 (Form = NNN)
24–26	Test 2 (Form = NNN)
27–29	Test 3 (Form = NNN)

We wish to compute the sum of the three test scores and their average. A header record will be read which gives the number of students in the class. This value is typed in columns 1–2. The header record will also contain the course number typed in columns 10–21. A page heading containing the course number will be written. The individual student output results will be printed as:

Field Description	Print Positions
Student name	1–18
Test 1	25–27
Test 2	33–35
Test 3	41–43
Total	49–54 (Form = NNN.NN)
Average	58–63 (Form = NNN.NN)

Column headings will be printed over each column of data.

```
C --- PROGRAM TO ILLUSTRATE THE READING AND WRITING OF
C --- CHARACTER DATA. THE PROGRAM FIRST READS THE NUMBER OF RECORDS TO
C --- PROCESS AND THE REPORT TITLE. IT THEN READS AND PROCESSES RECORDS
C --- WITH STUDENT NAME AND THREE TEST SCORES.
C
C --- AUTHOR: J W COLE
C --- DATE WRITTEN: 3/12/82
C
99      FORMAT (1H1, 25X,  19HSTUDENT GRADES FOR,  3A4/)
98      FORMAT (1H0, 7X, 4HNAME,12X, 22HTEST 1   TEST 2   TEST 3,
        *               3X, 5HTOTAL,4X, 7HAVERAGE)
97      FORMAT (I2, 7X, 3A4)
96      FORMAT (4A4, A2, 2X, 3I3)
95      FORMAT (1H0, 4A4,A2, 6X, 3(I3,5X), F6.2, 3X, F6.2)
C
        INTEGER RCDCNT, TEST1, TEST2, TEST3
        READ (5, 97) NRRCDS, TITLE1, TITLE2, TITLE3
        WRITE (6, 99) TITLE1, TITLE2, TITLE3
        WRITE (6, 98)
        RCDCNT = 0
C
10      READ (5, 96) NAM1,NAM2,NAM3,NAM4,NAM5, TEST1,TEST2,TEST3
        TOTAL = TEST1 + TEST2 + TEST3
        AVE   = TOTAL / 3.0
        WRITE (6, 95) NAM1,NAM2,NAM3,NAM4,NAM5, TEST1, TEST2,
        *               TEST3, TOTAL, AVE
        RCDCNT = RCDCNT + 1
        IF (RCDCNT .LT. NRRCDS) GO TO 10
C
        STOP
        END
```

Figure 9.7 Sample program to illustrate the reading and writing of character data

The logic involved is basically the same as that for the student grade problems already worked. A flowchart and pseudocode, are therefore, not included. The program is shown in figure 9.7.

Now let us discuss decision making (testing) with alphanumeric data.

9.7   COMPARING CHARACTER (ALPHANUMERIC) DATA

The question arises, "How do you test a variable for a certain alphanumeric value in FORTRAN?" Of course, the Logical IF statement must be used. But a literal constant cannot be used in the Logical IF statement. That is, you cannot say

IF (CODE .EQ. 'A') GO TO 8

since this syntax is not permitted in ANSI FORTRAN 66 and many FORTRAN IV compilers. It would be nice if you could assign alphanumeric values to a variable in an Assignment statement such as

LETA = 'A'

but this also is not permitted. (Note: The use of a literal constant is permitted on many timesharing systems, such as Burroughs, CDC, and Univac.)

Suppose you wish to process input data with different routines depending upon a code field in the input record. Maybe you wish to charge different tuition fees depending upon whether the student is a resident or nonresident. The input code field might contain the value "R", for resident students and the value, "N", for nonresident students. How can the input code field be tested to see what alphanumeric value it contains?

The secret in testing variables for certain alphanumeric values is to compare two variables. One variable contains the value being sought and the other variable contains the input value. Then you can use the Logical IF statement such as

IF (KODE .EQ. LETA) GO TO 8

where the variable LETA, contains the value against which you wish to compare the input value (in variable KODE).

An alphanumeric value can be stored in a variable by reading the value with the A format code. Then the variable containing the alphanumeric value being looked for can be compared to the input variable. The statements to determine the tuition rates for resident and nonresident students might be coded as follows.

```
C ***   READ ALPHANUMERIC VALUES FOR LATER COMPARISON
        READ (5,99) LETR, LETN
99      FORMAT (2A1)
C ***   READ INPUT RECORD
1       READ (5,98) ID, KODE, SEMHRS
98      FORMAT (I6,3X,A1,F4.2)
        IF (ID .EQ. 999999) STOP
        IF (KODE .EQ. LETR) GO TO 10
        IF (KODE .EQ. LETN) GO TO 20
        WRITE (6,97) ID, KODE
97      FORMAT (1H0,21HINVALID TUITION CODE, I6 ,3X,A1)
        GO TO 1
10      . . .
        . . .
20      . . .
```

One important input rule must be remembered when comparing variables containing alphanumeric values on many computers. The variable names for both variables must be of the same type. Otherwise, an equal condition can never occur in the comparison, even if the contents of the variables are the same. That is, if one name is an integer variable, the other name must be an integer variable; the same holds true for real variable names. This rule does not hold true for all FORTRAN compilers, but is a must for many (especially IBM). You should always try to use integer variable names for alphanumeric data that will be used in comparison operations, since they are more efficient. That is, it takes less time for the computer to compare integer variables than real.

The order of alphanumeric characters as to which ones come before others is determined by their **"collating sequence"** (internal representation). The collating sequence of alphanumeric characters is blank ¢ . (+ & ! $ *) : − / , % ? # @ ' = " A thru Z and 0 thru 9 on IBM and Amdahl Systems. This means that any letter is less than any digit. The special characters in the collection are less than both letters and digits. The order of the specific character, as to which is less than another, relates to their prescribed order above. That is, a blank is less than a " − "; a " + " is less than a " , ". (Note: Collating sequences vary among systems.)

Don't confuse this collating sequence order with an algebraic comparison. When variables and constants are compared with numeric values, the order is by their algebraic value. When you compare character data, the order is by their internal representation or collating sequence. Whenever variables containing multiple alphanumeric characters are compared, the comparison proceeds from left to right, as you would expect. For example "AACD" is less than "ABCE" and "A + " is less than "A*".

See Appendix O for the collating sequence of ASCII characters for computers using this internal representation of characters. Appendix P gives the collating sequence of characters for EBCDIC based Computers (IBM and Burroughs).

9.8   THE DATA STATEMENT FOR COMPILE-TIME INITIALIZATION

Up to now you have learned two statements that put values into memory locations—the Assignment statement and the READ statement. Both of these statements are executed during run time of the program. The DATA specification statement tells the FORTRAN compiler to place certain values at the indicated variables during the compilation of the program.

The initial value for a variable is placed within a set of slashes (/) following the variable. There are three acceptable methods of giving initial values to a group of variables. The most common method is to write the initial value for a variable immediately after writing the variable itself. For example:

DATA X/1.0/, X1/2.5/

DATA name₁/con₁/, . . ., nameₙ/conₙ/

or

DATA name₁, . . ., nameₙ/con₁, . . ., conₙ/

where:

name — any **name** represents a variable or subscripted array element (subscripts must be integer constants).

con — any **con** represents any type of valid constant used to assign initial values to the variable or array element. Any **con** can be preceded by **i*** where **i** is an unsigned integer constant that indicates the **constant (con)** is to be specified **i** times.

Figure 9.8 General notation of the DATA statement

The variable X is given the initial value of 1.0, and the variable X1 is given the value 2.5. The second method is to list the variables and follow them with the corresponding values given within a pair of slashes. There is a one-to-one, left-to-right correspondence between the list of variables and the list of values. For example:

$$\text{DATA A, B, I / 1.0, 0.0, 7/}$$

The variable A is given the value 1.0, B is given the value 0.0, and I is given the value 7. The third method is to use any combination of the first two methods. For example:

$$\text{DATA A/1.0/, B, I / 0.0, 7/,X/1.0/}$$

Note the placement of the commas used to separate the variables and the given initial values in all three methods.

The DATA statement may be used to initialize variables with literal (character) values. If fewer than 4 characters are given in the H format specifications for the literal value, the characters will be left-justified and the rest of the storage location filled with blanks.

The general form of the DATA statement is given in figure 9.8.

Examples of the DATA statement are:

```
DATA  A/1.0/,B/2.0/,C/3.5/,K/3/
DATA  D,E/4.0,5.0/,F/6.0/
DATA  A,B,C,D/1.0,2.0,3.5,4.0/,L/1/
DATA  LETA/1HA/,LETB/1HB/
DATA  X,Y,Z/3*0.0/
```

The first example places the values of 1.0, 2.0, 3.5, and 3 in the variables A, B, C, and K, respectively. The second statement places the values 4.0, 5.0, and 6.0 in the variables D, E, and F, respectively. The third example places the values 1.0, 2.0, 3.5, 4.0, and 1 in the variables A, B, C, D, and L, respectively. The fourth example initializes the variable LETA with the character A and the variable LETB with the character B in their Hollerith notation. The last example initializes the three variables X, Y, and Z to zero. The * says to repeat the constant that follows the * as many times as the constant given before the *.

The sole function of the DATA statement is to establish initial values in variables and array elements at compile time. Thus, run time statements can be eliminated, and a saving in run time can be realized.

The DATA statement is very useful when input items must be compared with alphanumereic values. Suppose that various transaction codes in some input records are alphanumeric values. You must decide what routine to use based on the alphanumeric transaction codes. For example, an input code of "A" might mean to add the transaction quantity to the balance on hand and the code of "D" might mean to subtract the transaction quantity from the balance. You must use either the READ or the DATA statement to get an alphanumeric value in a variable. The DATA statement is by far the easiest way to go. For example:

```
        INTEGER CHAR
        DATA LETA/1HA/, LETD/1HD/
        . . .
        . . .
        READ (5,99) CHAR, NQTY
     99 FORMAT (A1,I4)
        IF (CHAR .EQ. LETA) GO TO 10
        IF (CHAR .EQ. LETD) GO TO 20
        . . .
     10 . . .
        . . .
     20 . . .
```

If the input value read under the variable, CHAR, were an "A", a true condition would result in the first Logical IF statement, and a transfer would be made to statement number 10. The DATA statement cannot precede any other specification statement that refers to the same variable such as an Explicit Type statement. Therefore, any DATA statements should be placed in a program just before the first executable statement. DATA statements for initializing array elements are discussed in chapter 11.

Now let's look at the programming technique of including control breaks in programs for business reports. (Section 9.9 may be skipped without loss in continuity if control-break concepts and logic are not required in your lab problems.)

9.9 SINGLE-LEVEL CONTROL BREAKS FOR BUSINESS REPORTS

Many business reports are prepared with all the information (related records) relating to a specific business entity such as department number, shop, manager, sales person, and so forth printed on the same page. That is, when a new department number, shop, manager, or sales person number data record is read, a page eject is performed, and the information for the new business entity is printed beginning on a new page. This method of report generation has all related information for a business entity together for easy reference and totals. Reports produced in this manner are said to be written with **control break logic**.

A **control break** occurs during the processing of records from an input file when the data value in a specific input field, called the control field, of the current record is different from the data value in the same control field of the previous record. When the value in this field changes between records, a control break is taken. Various actions, such as printing a summary total line or page ejecting to begin the new output on the next page, are performed for the control break. Consider the list of daily sales records given in figure 9.9.

The records in the input file must be sorted on the control field so that all related records with the same data value for that field are together in the input file. Notice that in figure 9.9 there are two control breaks in the list of seven records. The sales person number field changes in value twice from the first value. The first three records contain the same value of 123 for the sales person number field; the fourth record contains a new value of 124 for the control field. Hence a control break is found. The next control break occurs when a change in value is found from the last control break value of 124. Record six contains a new value of 125 for the control field; therefore, a control break occurs on this record.

SALES PERSON NUMBER	INVOICE	SALES DATE	AMOUNT
123	MW11001	811202	39.50
123	MW11002	811202	78.36
123	MW11003	811203	245.75
124	MW11260	811202	381.00
124	MW11261	811203	94.18
125	MW11418	811202	133.19
125	MW11419	811203	401.37

Figure 9.9 List of daily sales records by sales person number

If you wished to give each sales person a copy of their daily sales records for a given period of processing (e.g., daily, weekly, or monthly), then the control breaks can be used as the indicator to start printing the current record with the change in its control field value on a new page. This way records with the same control field value can be isolated and the information printed on the same page or pages. It is an easy operation to separate the pages at the **perforation** (broken at the page fold) and to distribute the proper pages to the various sales people. Otherwise, one might be required to cut the pages with scissors, which is a bothersome and time consuming task.

To perform control break logic in a program, the control field value of the previous data record needs to be retained. This value is saved (stored) in a variable with the Assignment statement. The variable used to save the value of the control field from the previous record is sometimes called a **hold variable** or variable for comparison. The assignment operation must be done before the next data record is read; otherwise, the control field value would be lost when the next record is read. After a new record is read, it becomes the current record in memory for processing. The value in the control field of the current record is compared with the value stored in the hold variable to see if they are equal. If they are equal in value, a control break (change in value) is not found, and the current record is printed on the same page. If they are not equal, a control break is found, and the new record is printed starting on a new page.

The order of processing steps is summarized as:

1. Move the value of the control field in the current record to a selected hold variable to save this value for later comparison. This value represents the control field value of the previous record when the next record is read for processing.
2. Read a new record, which now becomes the current record for processing.
3. Compare the control field of the current (present) record with the value of the previous record control field (which is in the hold variable). The result of this comparison shows whether there is a control break. If the current record control field is not equal to the previous record control field, the required operations will be performed in the control break logic. These operations normally include printing a summary line of totals and performing a page eject with new report and column headings, so that the current record will be printed on a new page.
4. The current record is then processed in the normal way (calculating, printing, and so on).

Totals are usually accumulated for each control break and printed as a summary line after the last record for the set of records with the specific value for the particular control field. That is, the summary line of totals is printed just before the page eject for a new set of related records. The accumulator for the control break must, of course, be reset to zero between control breaks. For simplicity the process of accumulating totals for a control break and printing a summary will be delayed until after this first problem.

Sample Program with a Single-Level Control Break

Let us develop a program to list the daily sales records for each sales person on a separate page. The program name is Daily Sales Report. A sentinel (trailer) record with a sales person number of 999 is used after the last valid data record. This sentinel record will signal the end-of-file condition on the input file, i.e., it indicates that all records have been processed.

The input record description with its field locations are:

Field	Record Position
Sales Person Number	1–3
Invoice Number	4–9
Sales Date	10–15
Sales Amount	16–21 (includes four integer positions and two implied decimal positions)

The flowchart for the program design is given in figure 9.10, the pseudocode for this program design is given in figure 9.11 (p. 280), and the program is given in figure 9.12 (p. 280).

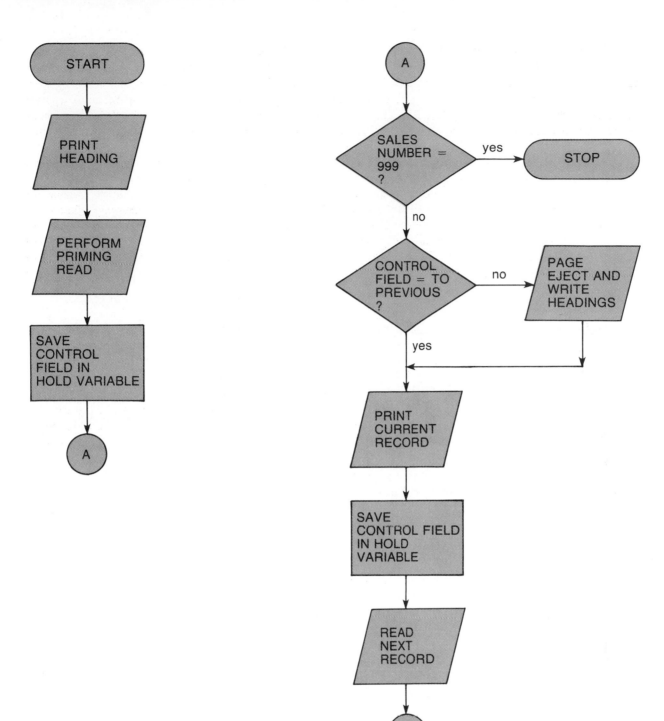

Figure 9.10 Flowchart for daily sales report program

```
        START ANALYSIS OF DAILY SALES REPORT.
            PRINT REPORT AND COLUMN HEADING FOR FIRST PAGE
            PERFORM PRIMING READ OF THE FIRST INPUT RECORD.
            SAVE THE CONTROL FIELD INTO THE VARIABLE PREVNO.
            DO WHILE SALES PERSON NUMBER NOT EQUAL TO 999
                    IF THE CURRENT RECORD'S CONTROL FIELD IS NOT EQUAL TO
                        THE PREVIOUS RECORD'S CONTROL FIELD THEN
                            PAGE EJECT AND PRINT REPORT AND COLUMN
                            HEADING ON THE NEW PAGE.
                END IF
                PRINT THE CURRENT RECORD.
                MOVE THE CURRENT RECORD CONTROL FIELD TO PREVNO.
                READ A NEW RECORD.
            END DO
        END ANALYSIS.
```

Figure 9.11 Pseudocode for daily sales report program

```
C ---   FORTRAN PROGRAM TO PRODUCE DAILY SALES REPORT
C ---   WRITTEN 12/16/81 --- BY PERRY COLE
C
        INTEGER SALNO, INVC1, INVC2, DATE, PREVNO
    99  FORMAT (1H1, 14X, 18HDAILY SALES REPORT, / /
       *           1H0, 12HSALES PERSON, 5X, 7HINVOICE, 5X, 5HSALES,/
       *           1H , 12H    NUMBER   , 5X, 6HNUMBER, 6X, 4HDATE, 7X, 6HAMOUNT)
    98  FORMAT (I3, A4,A2, I6, F6.2)
    97  FORMAT (1H0, 4X, I3, 10X, A4,A2, 5X, I6, 5X, F6.2)
C
C ---   PERFORM THE NECESSARY INITIALIZATION OPERATION SUCH AS:
C ---   PRINT THE REPORT AND COLUMN HEADINGS, PRIMING READ,
C ---   AND SAVE THE CONTROL FIELD.
C
        WRITE (6,99)
        READ (5, 98) SALNO, INVC1, INVC2, DATE, AMOUNT
        PREVNO = SALNO
C
C ---   SET UP DO WHILE LOOP TO READ AND PROCESS RECORDS
C
    10  IF (SALNO .EQ. 999) GO TO 20
C ---       PERFORM CONTROL BREAK ACTIONS WHEN FIELDS ARE NOT EQUAL
            IF (SALNO .NE. PREVNO) WRITE (6, 99)
C ---       PRINT THE CURRENT SALES RECORD
            WRITE (6, 97) SALNO, INVC1, INVC2, DATE, AMOUNT
C ---       SAVE SALES PERSON NUMBER FOR PREVIOUS CONTROL FIELD COMPARISON
            PREVNO = SALNO
C ---       READ NEXT RECORD WITH SALES PERSON DATA FIELDS
            READ (5, 98) SALNO, INVC1, INVC2, DATE, AMOUNT
        GO TO 10
    20  STOP
        END
```

Figure 9.12 Program for daily sales report

```
                      DAILY SALES REPORT

        SALES PERSON      INVOICE      SALES
          NUMBER          NUMBER       DATE        AMOUNT

            123           MW11001      811202       39.50
            123           MW11002      811202       78.36
            123           MW11003      811203      245.75
```

Figure 9.13 Output from program for page one

Three pages of output will be produced from the program processing of the seven daily sales records. The first page of sales information will contain the three records for sales person 123, the second page will show the two records for sales person 124, and the third page will have the two records for sales person 125. See figure 9.13 for the output produced for page one.

Now let us look at how a summary total line would be included with each control break.

Control Breaks with Summary Total Lines

A summary line showing the total sales amount for each sales person would be handy to have in the report. Why should a user have to sum the total sales for each sales person, when the computer can do it much better? Calculations are certainly one thing the computer can do much faster and more accurately than we can. Therefore, why not include the accumulation of the sales amount for each sales person in the control break logic and print the total beneath the last data record when a control break is taken? Such a line with one or more accumulated totals is called a **summary line** or **total line.**

A summary line requires an accumulator for each field to be totaled. The accumulator must be reset to zero between control breaks to accumulate correctly the totals for a new control field value. The summary line must be printed before the accumulator is reset to zero.

The order of the logic steps in accumulating totals for a summary line is:

1. Initialize the accumulator to zero at the beginning of the program.
2. Test each record to be processed to see if a control break is found.
3. If a control break is found, then perform the following actions:
   a. Write the summary line with the accumulated total.
   b. Reset the accumulator to zero for the next set of control break records.
   c. Write the headings beginning on a new page.
4. Add the field to be accumulated to its respective accumulator variable for the new record.
5. Repeat steps 2 through 4 for each record being processed.

Forcing the Last Control Break

When the end-of-file condition is reached on the input file you must include a statement to print the last summary line of accumulated totals. This action is needed after the processing loop because there is no control break with the last data record. There are no more records to compare the control fields with as the basis for a control break. This action is known as **forcing the last control break.** The word "forcing" means that logic must be included after the processing loop to perform the control break; the control break will not occur with the logic inside the processing loop. You need only to print the last summary line. There is no need to reset the accumulator variable to zero or to print new headings.

The Grand Total Line

An overall total for a designated field(s) is normally accumulated for all records. The overall total is printed at the end of the report. This summary line is known as the **grand total line.** The operation is often called the **grand break.** The grand total line may be printed beneath the last summary line or on a new page. This grand total line is useful to a manager in knowing the overall total such as the total sales amount for all sales persons.

Now, let's revise the original Daily Sales Report to include summary lines and a grand total line.

Sample Program With Summary and Grand Total Lines

We will take the same problem and revise the program to include a summary line for each sales person on the report. The summary line will be printed triple spaced beneath the last detail print record for each sales person. A grand total for all sales amounts will be accumulated for all sales persons. The grand total summary line will be printed on a separate page at the end of the report.

The flowchart for the revised program is given in figure 9.14, the pseudocode for the revised program in figure 9.15, the program for the revised Daily Sales Report in figure 9.16, and the first page of output for the revised Daily Sales Report is shown in figure 9.17 (p. 284).

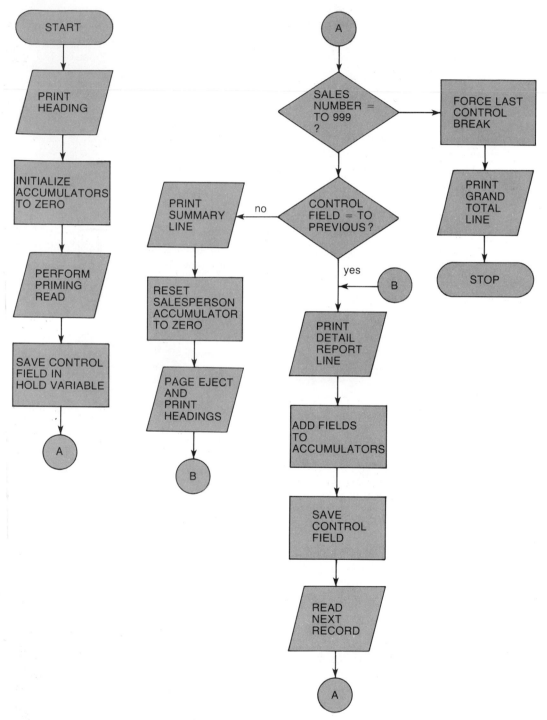

Figure 9.14 Flowchart for daily sales report program with summary lines and grand total line

START ANALYSIS OF DAILY SALES REPORT.
   PRINT REPORT AND COLUMN HEADING FOR FIRST PAGE.
   INITIALIZE SALES PERSON ACCUMULATOR (SALTOT) TO ZERO.
   INITIALIZE TOTAL SALES ACCUMULATOR (GRDTOT) TO ZERO.
   PERFORM PRIMING READ OF THE FIRST INPUT RECORD.
   SAVE THE CONTROL FIELD INTO THE VARIABLE PREVNO.
   DO WHILE SALES PERSON NUMBER NOT EQUAL TO 999
            IF THE CURRENT RECORD'S CONTROL FIELD IS NOT EQUAL TO
               THE PREVIOUS RECORD'S CONTROL FIELD THEN
                  PRINT THE SALES PERSON SUMMARY LINE.
                  RESET SALES PERSON ACCUMULATOR (SALTOT) TO ZERO.
                  PAGE EJECT AND PRINT REPORT AND COLUMN
                     HEADING ON THE NEW PAGE.
            END IF
            PRINT THE DETAIL REPORT LINE.
            ADD SALES AMOUNT TO SALES PERSON ACCUMULATOR.
            ADD SALES AMOUNT TO TOTAL SALES ACCUMULATOR.
            MOVE THE CURRENT RECORD'S CONTROL FIELD TO PREVNO.
            READ A NEW SALES RECORD.
   END DO
   FORCE THE LAST CONTROL BREAK BY PRINTING SALES PERSON
      SUMMARY LINE.
   PRINT THE GRAND TOTAL SUMMARY LINE ON A NEW PAGE.
END ANALYSIS.

Figure 9.15 Pseudocode for daily sales report program with summary lines and grand total line

```
C --- FORTRAN PROGRAM TO PRODUCE DAILY SALES REPORT WITH SUMMARY LINES
C --- WRITTEN 12/16/81 --- BY J W COLE
C
   99 FORMAT (1H1, 14X, 18HDAILY SALES REPORT,/ /
      *         1H0, 12HSALES PERSON, 5X, 7HINVOICE, 5X, 5HSALES,/
      *         1H , 12H    NUMBER  , 5X, 6HNUMBER, 6X, 4HDATE, 7X, 6HAMOUNT)
   98 FORMAT (I3, A4,A2, I6, F6.2)
   97 FORMAT (1H0, 4X, I3, 10X, A4,A2, 5X, I6, 5X, F6.2)
   96 FORMAT (/1H0,3X,31HTOTAL SALES FOR SALES PERSON:  ,I3,6H IS:  ,F9.2)
   95 FORMAT (//1H0, 3X, 30HGRAND TOTAL OF ALL SALES IS:  , 6X, F10.2)
      INTEGER SALNO, INVC1, INVC2, DATE, PREVNO
C
C --- PERFORM THE NECESSARY INITIALIZATION OPERATIONS, SUCH AS:
C --- INITIALIZE THE ACCUMULATORS TO ZERO,
C --- PRINT THE REPORT AND COLUMN HEADINGS, PRIMING READ,
C --- AND SAVE THE CONTROL FIELD.
C
      SALTOT = 0.0
      GRDTOT = 0.0
      WRITE (6, 99)
      READ (5, 98) SALNO, INVC1, INVC2, DATE, AMOUNT
      PREVNO = SALNO
C --- SET UP DO WHILE LOOP TO READ AND PROCESS RECORDS
C
   10 IF (SALNO .EQ. 999) GO TO 20
         IF (SALNO .EQ. PREVNO) GO TO 15
C ---       PERFORM THE CONTROL BREAK ACTIONS
            WRITE (6,96) SALTOT
            SALTOT = 0.0
            WRITE (6, 99)
```

Figure 9.16 Program for daily sales report with summary lines and grand total line (cont. on next page)

Figure 9.16 (cont.)

```
C ---      PROCESS THE CURRENT RECORD BY PRINTING THE RECORD AND ADDING
C ---      AMOUNT TO THE ACCUMULATORS
    15     WRITE (6, 97) SALNO, INVC1, INVC2, DATE, AMOUNT
           SALTOT = SALTOT + AMOUNT
           GRDTOT = GRDTOT + AMOUNT
C ---      SAVE SALES PERSON NUMBER FOR PREVIOUS CONTROL FIELD COMPARISON
           PREVNO = SALNO
C ---      READ NEXT RECORD
           READ (5, 98) SALNO, INVC1, INVC2, DATE, AMOUNT
           GO TO 10
C
    20     CONTINUE
C ---      PRINT THE LAST CONTROL BREAK SUMMARY LINE
           WRITE (6, 96) SALTOT
C ---      PRINT THE GRAND TOTAL SUMMARY LINE ON A NEW PAGE
           WRITE (6, 99)
           WRITE (6, 95) GRDTOT
           STOP
           END
```

```
                      DAILY SALES REPORT

          SALES PERSON      INVOICE     SALES
             NUMBER         NUMBER      DATE      AMOUNT

               123         MW11001      811202      39.50
               123         MW11002      811202      78.36
               123         MW11003      811203     245.75

        TOTAL SALES FOR SALES PERSON 123   IS:     363.61
```

Figure 9.17 Output from program with summary lines for page one

9.10 LANGUAGE EXTENSIONS IN FORTRAN DIALECTS (T, ', :, and $ FORMAT CODES AND THE CHARACTER TYPE STATEMENT)

Tabulation (T) Format Code

It is often very time-consuming to count the number of blanks between input and output fields. A special format code is available in most compilers to eliminate the need for this operation. The Tabulation (T) format code is used to indicate the starting position of input and output fields. That is, you can specify the input positions on the input record of the various fields to be read. Or you can specify various print positions for the beginning of the output fields. This format code is very useful when many columns or positions are to be skipped on input and output records.

The general form of the T format code is:

$$Tw$$

where:

w specifies the position in the input or output record where the transfer of data is to begin. **w** must be an unsigned integer constant with a value less than or equal to 255.

The T format code does not correspond to any variable in an I/O list, since it does not cause any data to be transferred. The T format code simply specifies the beginning position of a field in the input or output record. Thus, the T format code is always followed by the format code of the data item to be transferred.

Examples in using the T format code are:

99 FORMAT (T10, I2, T25, I5)	(input specifications)
98 FORMAT (I3, T11, I4, 2X, F6.2)	(input specifications)
97 FORMAT (1H0, T4, I4, T31, I3)	(output specifications)

The first example says that the first input field begins in card column 10 and is transferred as a two-digit integer field. The next field begins in column 25 and is transferred as a five-digit integer field. The second example illustrates an input field of three integer digits beginning in implied card column 1, in the conventional manner of expressing a field position. The second field of four integer digits begins in card column 11, followed by two skipped columns and a floating-point field of six positions beginning in column 17. The third example tells you to double-space the print line and to output a four-digit integer field beginning in print position 3. A three-digit integer field is also printed beginning at print position 30. The output positions are confusing. Why did we start at a position one less than was given? The reason is that the starting position for T specifications on **printer output** is always one less than what is given, for reasons that will be explained later.

On input the specification given in the T format code indicates the high-order (beginning) position of the field on the input medium. The T format code does not have to precede each of the data-transferring format codes. Any format code not preceded by the T specifications begins at the next card column where the last data transferring format code left off. For example:

98 FORMAT (I2,3X,I3,T20,I5,F5.1)

The first field begins in card column 1 and the second field begins in card column 6, just as we have always indicated the start of each field. The T20 indicates the third field begins in column 20 and goes through column 24. The fourth field then begins where the third field ends, in column 25.

The same specifications apply for output results written to cards, tape, or disk. The T specifications indicate the beginning position of the next field to be written. But for printer output, the T specifications must be *one greater* than the desired position of the printed field. If you wish to begin printing at print position 50, specify a T51 format code. The reason for this different specification is that the computer will always strip off (remove) one position for carriage control. You do not have to supply a carriage control character when using the T specification for the printed line. One position is stripped off and used for single-spacing control. If a carriage control character *is* supplied for the print line, it is stripped off and provides the normal control for the movement of the paper. However, one position is *still* stripped off for all T format code specifications on printer and terminal output. Consider the following examples:

WRITE (6,99) N1,N2
99 FORMAT (T11,I2,T21,I2)
WRITE (6,98) N3,N4
98 FORMAT (1H0,T11,I2,T21,I2)

The first WRITE and FORMAT statements will cause the variable N1 to be printed at position 10; a carriage control operation of single-spacing is obtained from the T11 format code. The second variable, N2, is printed at position 20. The second WRITE and FORMAT statements cause the variable N3 to be printed at position 10 and the variable N4 to be printed at position 20. Since the carriage control character of 1H0 is given, the line will first be double-spaced.

The T format code does not have to indicate field positions in ascending order on the input record. For example, you could specify:

READ (5,99) N1, N2, N3, N3DIG
99 FORMAT (T1,I1, I1, I1, T1,I3)

Thus, the T format code can be used to provide a reread capability of a record, and to reformat the same record under different format codes. The example allows three integer digits to be read as separate fields and then to reread the same three digits as one three-digit integer field. The same capability is permissible with output values, but this operation provides no advantages, inasmuch as the last character formatted at a print position is the character printed.

The T format code is a simple way of skipping certain positions on an input or output record. It really accomplishes the same purpose as the Blank (X) format code. If there is a long gap between fields, you may make a mistake by counting the columns and using the X format code. The T format code saves you time and permits less opportunity for error by allowing you to specify the exact position in which the field starts. The T and X format codes, however, may both be used in the same FORMAT statement. FORTRAN 77, IBM, Honeywell, Burroughs, and WATFIV compilers all allow the T format code.

Single Quote (') Format Code to Express Literal Constants

Most compilers (IBM, DEC, Burroughs, and WATFIV) also provide the single quote (') format code to represent literal constants. The single quote is the 5/8 multipunch character on IBM and Burroughs machines. When the single quote is used to represent a literal constant, the character string is enclosed within quotes. That is, a ' is used to designate the beginning of the literal and a ' is used at the end of the string. (Note: the ending single quote is the same character as the beginning single quote.) If you wish to include a single quote symbol within the literal constant, two consecutive quotes must be used.

For example:

> 'SUM = '
> 'LEAVE REGISTER'
> 'X = '
> 'JOHN''S DATA'

The quote is usually preferred by most programmers, since they then do not have to count the number of characters in the literal. Thus, the mistake of specifying too short or too long a literal, especially in long strings, is avoided. For example:

> **WRITE (6,99)**
> **99 FORMAT (1H1, 20X, 'GRADE REPORT FOR DP101')**

The use of the H format code, however, usually provides clearer documentation and helps prevent exceeding the maximum number of characters allowed on a print line. It is usually easier to modify programs that use the H format code to represent literals, since the number of characters in each string will not have to be recounted. The main advantage of using the H format code over the single quote is that the expression of literals with the H format code is standard on all compilers.

Not all compilers allow the single quote. CDC uses an asterisk (*) to represent literal constants in addition to the H format code. DEC and Burroughs compilers allow both the single quote and the double quote (") to be used to represent literal constants, in addition to the H format code. Honeywell and Hewlett Packard compilers allow the double quote (") to represent literal constants, in addition to the H format code. Following is a table with some of the major computers and the character(s) allowed for enclosing literal constants:

Table 9.2 Permissible Characters for Enclosing Literal Constants

Computer system	Character(s) allowed to enclose a literal
Amdahl	'
Burroughs 6000	' or "
Control Data 6000/Cyber	' or *
DEC PDP-11	' or "
Honeywell 60/6000	"
HP 3000	"
IBM (and WATFOR/WATFIV)	'
Univac 1100	'
Your system	

Colon (:) Format Descriptor for Termination of Format Control

FORTRAN 77, VAX-11 FORTRAN, and other FORTRAN dialects include the colon (:) descriptor for format specifications. The colon (:) descriptor appearing in a format specifications causes the termination of format control if there are no more items to be transferred in the I/O list of the output statement. If there are remaining items in the I/O list, the colon has no effect.

For example, the following statements (using the formatted PRINT statement):

```
          PRINT 99, 5
       99 FORMAT (1X, 'N1 = ', I2, 3X, 'N2 = ', I2)
          PRINT 98, 3
       98 FORMAT (1X, 'N1 = ', I2: 3X, 'N2 = ', I2)
          PRINT 98, 1, 7
```

would print the following three lines:

```
          N1 = 5   N2 =
          N1 = 3
          N1 = 1   N2 = 7
```

Notice that the second line of output does not include the literal "N2" because the colon (:) is included in FORMAT statement 98 after the first I2 format code. The third line of output prints the literal "N2", since there was another item in the I/O list of the third PRINT statement. This format descriptor allows the same FORMAT statement to be used with different output statements in which the number of variables varies in the I/O list.

Dollar Sign ($) Format Descriptor for Line Control Operation

The dollar sign ($) format descriptor is included in FORTRAN 77, VAX-11, DEC PDP-11, and other FORTRAN compilers for output line control operation. The dollar sign ($) is used as a specific carriage-control character in format specifications to modify the carriage-control character specified by the first character in the output format specifications. It advances one line before printing the output record and suppresses a carriage return at the end of the record.

The $ format descriptor is intended primarily for interactive I/O on timesharing systems. The dollar sign descriptor causes the terminal's print position to be left on the same line of output, so that a typed response will appear on the same line after the displayed message. For example, the statements

```
          PRINT 99
       99 FORMAT ($, 3X, 'ENTER A VALUE FOR RADIUS', 2X)
```

would print the text "ENTER A VALUE FOR RADIUS" and then allow the input value to be typed on the same line as the displayed literal.

Assignment of Literal Constants

The B6000 and CDC 6000 compilers permit the assignment of literal constants in an Assignment statement. On the B6000 compiler one may assign a literal constant to a variable by using the H format code or the quote. For example:

```
          LIST1 = 3HSUM
          LIST2 = 'TOTAL'
```

The result is the same as if the literal was read with an A format code. That is, the literal is left-justified in the computer word. If fewer characters are assigned than the size of the word, the remaining low-order positions are filled with blanks.

On the CDC 6000 compilers one may assign a literal to a variable with the H format code as follows:

```
          LIT1 = 3HSUM
```

One may also assign a literal to a variable with the R (Hollerith Right-justified) format code. For example:

LIT1 = 3RSUM

With the R format code on the CDC compilers, the data is stored right-justified with octal (base 8) zeroes in any excessive high-order positions.

The Character (C) Format Code

On the B6000 and H6000 compilers alphanumeric data may be read with the C format code. The C format code stores the input alphanumeric field *right-justified* in a computer word. Any excessive high-order positions are padded with hexadecimal (base 16) zeroes on the B6000 or octal (base 8) zeros on the H6000. The general form of the C format code is:

nCw

where **n** is an optional repetition factor from 1 to 255. **w** represents the width of the input or output field. For example, a data field containing the two letters AB read under a C2 format code would store the two letters "AB" in the two low-order positions in a word and fill the excessive high-order positions with hexadecimal (or octal) zeroes.

You may wonder why we need the C format code in addition to the A format code? The reason lies in being able to compare alphanumeric data in FORTRAN on these computers, as is discussed below.

Comparing Alphanumeric Data on B6000 and H6000 Computers

When alphanumeric data is read with an A format code on the B6000 and H6000 computers, the data affects the sign bit in the word. The sign bit is a special bit in the high-order position of the word to determine the sign of the value contained in the word. If alphanumeric data is compared for an "equal" or "not equal" condition, there is no problem. But if you are comparing for a "less than" or "greater than" condition with alphanumeric data, then you will not get a correct result.

To avoid setting the sign bit incorrectly in the computer word, alphanumeric data must be read with the C format code to store the data right-justified in the word. Also, you must store one less character than can be held by the computer word to avoid filling the entire word with alphanumeric characters. Since the length of a computer word on the B6000 and H6000 is 6 characters, the maximum number of characters read with the C format code should be 5, i.e., C5.

This restriction of reading alphanumeric data with the C format code pertains only to alphanumeric data used in comparison operations. If you do not need to compare the alphanumeric data for a "less than" or "greater than" condition, use the A format code to read and store the data.

The Right-justified (R) Format Code

The Right-justified (R) format code is used on the CDC 6000 to transmit alphanumeric data. The basic difference between the R and A format codes is that the R format code causes character string data to be right-justified in a variable. The general form of the R format code is:

nRw

where **n** is an optional repetition factor from 1 to 255. **w** represents the width of the input or output field.

On *input* **w** characters are read from the data field. If the **w** specifications exceed the maximum number of allowed characters in a variable, the high-order characters are truncated. If **w** is less than the maximum number of characters allowed, the characters are right-justified in the variable and *high-order zeroes* are added to the left. Remember that the A format code causes the data to be left-justified, and blanks are added to the right for a "short" character string.

On *output*, if the **w** specifications exceed the number of characters stored in a variable, blanks are added in the high-order positions. If the number of characters in a variable exceed **w**, then the rightmost **w** characters are printed. Remember that the A format code extracts the characters from the left in a variable on output.

CHARACTER * len name₁ * varsize (dim) /val/ , . . ., nameₙ * varsize (dim)/val/

where:

*	— is a necessary character unless the length is given as a * **varsize** following all names in the list.
len	— is a positive integer constant (less than or equal to 511) which defines the maximum length, in characters, of all variables and arrays in the statement list unless overridden by the * **varsize** parameter.
name	— is a variable, array, or FUNCTION subprogram name whose type and value length are defined by this statement.
* **varsize**	— is an optional parameter which may be used to override the len parameter and define the length of individual variables. **varsize** must be less than or equal to 511.
(dim)	— is an optional parameter to supply dimension information to allocate storage for arrays.
/val/	— is an optional parameter to provide an initial value to the variable or array element at compile time.

Figure 9.18 General notation of the CHARACTER Type statement

The CHARACTER Type Statement

The CHARACTER Type statement is a very useful Explicit typing statement implemented on FORTRAN 77, VAX-11, Honeywell, Univac, and other FORTRAN IV compilers to declare a variable as type character. The CHARACTER Type statement tells the compiler to treat all variables in the statement list as type character, at which an alphanumeric data field is stored. An important function of this Explicit Type statement is that an alphanumeric data field does not have to be divided into groups of characters to match the computer's word size. Also, multiple variables do not need to be formed as required in the normal partitioning of the alphanumeric data field. The CHARACTER Type statement allows one variable name to be used for the alphanumeric data field regardless of its length (i.e., when its length, in number of data characters, exceeds a computer's word size).

The general form of the CHARACTER Type statement is given in figure 9.18.

Examples of the CHARACTER Type statement are:

CHARACTER * 20 NAME
CHARACTER * 18 ADDRS1, ADDRS2
CHARACTER MSG1 * 10, MSG2 * 15
CHARACTER * 12 LIT1, LIT2, LIT3 * 8, LIT4

The first example declares the variable NAME to be of type character with a length of 20. The second example declares the two variables ADDRS1 and ADDRS2 to be 18 characters in length. The third example declares the variable MSG1 to be 10 characters in length and the variable MSG2 to be 15 characters in length. This statement also could have been written as:

CHARACTER * 10 MSG1, MSG2 * 15

The fourth example declares the variables LIT1, LIT2 and LIT4 to have a length of 12 characters; the variable LIT3 has a length of 8 characters, since it overrides the general length parameter.

A variable declared in the CHARACTER Type statement cannot contain more characters than specified in its length parameter. If fewer characters are stored in a variable declared as a CHARACTER type, then the right most remaining bytes (character positions) are filled with spaces (blanks).

A short program which reads and prints an inventory file with records containing a 10-character part number, an 18-character part description, and a five-digit quantity on hand is given as follows. A part number with all zeroes is used to determine an end-of-file condition.

```
        INTEGER QTYOH
        CHARACTER * 10 PARTNO, EOFRCD /0000000000/
        CHARACTER * 18 DESCRP
    10  READ (5, 99) PARTNO, DESCRP, QTYOH
        IF (PARTNO .EQ. EOFRCD) STOP
        WRITE (6, 98) PARTNO, DESCRP, QTYOH
        GO TO 10
    99  FORMAT (A10, A18, I5)
    98  FORMAT (1H0, A10, 5X, A18, 5X, I5)
        STOP
        END
```

The CHARACTER Type statement may also be used with arrays. The discussion of typing array items as CHARACTER is presented in section 11.11.

9.11 SUMMARY

This chapter introduced you to literal constants and alphanumeric data fields. The DATA statement, which assigns initial values to variables at compilation time, was presented. A discussion of control breaks in report generation was also presented.

Literal constants are widely used in programs to:

1. Provide report headings
2. Provide column headings
3. Provide textual information

A report heading is a line printed at the top of the first page of output (or every output page) to identify the report. Column headings are one or two lines of output printed at the top of every page to identify the columns of information on the page. You should have a column heading to identify each output field on a detail line of values. Textual information is simply some title or description to identify output values or provide some descriptive message.

Literal constants (e.g., titles, messages, and so forth) are formed with the Hollerith (H) format code. The length of the literal constant is specified before the H format code, which precedes the literal string of characters. No variable name is associated with a literal constant in the FORMAT statement, since it is a constant and is not assigned to a variable.

The most common use for literal constants is on a report or output file. Literal constants may be read into a FORMAT statement, but this is bad practice and is seldom done. No discussion, therefore, was given on reading literal constants. If literal data is to be read, it should be read with variables and the alphanumeric (A) format code within the FORMAT statement.

The slash (/) is frequently used with literal constants to produce multiple lines of literal data. The use of the slash format specifications to advance to a new line of output saves us the trouble of having to write separate WRITE and FORMAT statements for each line of output. Each slash at the beginning and end of a FORMAT statement produces one new line of output. Multiple consecutive slashes other than at the beginning or end of the FORMAT statement result in n − 1 new lines of output (where n is the number of consecutive slashes given).

Format codes may be given as a group of format codes to be repeated. This technique is known as group format repetition. This capability provides a shortcut notation for repeating a group of identical format codes, rather than having to list them two or more times. The group of format codes to be repeated are given in parentheses, and the repetition factor is given before the open parenthesis. Group format repetition may be nested to a depth of two.

Section 9.6 introduced you to the input, output, and manipulation of character data fields. Character data is referred to as alphanumeric data, since it includes any character acceptable to a computer system. An alphanumeric data field must never be used in calculations. Alphanumeric data items are read and written with the A format code. The important thing to remember when reading or writing alphanumeric data is that the word size of your computer determines the maximum number of characters that can be stored at a variable. An alphanumeric data field, therefore, must be broken into multiples of your computer's word size to determine the number of associated variables needed to store the entire data field. A unique variable name must be assigned to each memory word composed of characters partitioned from the data field. Characters are stored left-justified (aligned from the left) in a word. It is important that alphanumeric data be written in the same format specifications as those in which they are read, in order to maintain the proper character alignment on output.

Alphanumeric data items are also used in comparisons within the Logical IF statement. ANSI FORTRAN 66 and many FORTRAN IV compilers do not permit alphanumeric comparison between a variable and a literal constant; a comparison of two variables must be performed instead. The literal string must be read or established in a DATA statement in order to be stored at a variable. It is best to use integer variable names to store alphanumeric data items to be used in comparison operations. A comparison of alphanumeric data items is performed in a bit (binary digit) representation known as its collating sequence. The collating sequence of characters determines the order in the internal (bit) representation within the computer.

The DATA statement is used to assign values to variables at compile time. No READ or Assignment statement is required to assign values to these variables at execution. The initial value to be given a variable at compile time is placed within a pair of slashes following the variable name. Several methods were discussed for providing the initial values for variables in the DATA statement. If a variable appears in both an Explicit Type statement and a DATA statement, the Explicit Type statement must precede the DATA statement in the program.

Section 9.9 discussed control breaks for business reports. A control break occurs when a value changes in a control field. A control field is simply a selected data field used for report breaks. Some action is taken, such as printing a summary line of totals for the records with the previous (old) value, or page ejecting and printing the record with the new value on a new page. Control breaks are very common operations in business reports. They provide an efficient means of separating and distributing reports to different people or departments without having to cut up the report with a pair of scissors.

9.12 TERMS

Terms and concepts you should become familiar with in this chapter are:

accumulator	control break logic	literal constant
alphanumeric data	DATA statement	literal data
bells and whistles	forcing the last control break	printer page perforation
character data	grand break	report heading
comparing alphanumeric data	grand total	slash format specifications
collating sequence	grand total line	summary line
column heading	group format specifications	summary total
compile time initialization	high order position in a word	total line
control break	hold variable	word
control break field	Hollerith string	word size

9.13 REVIEW QUESTIONS

1. How is a literal constant expressed in FORTRAN?
2. Name three uses of literal constants.
3. A space is not counted in a literal constant. (True/False)
4. What normally happens when the width count does not match the length of a literal constant?
5. Literal constants may be written only on printer output files. (True/False)
6. What is the advantage of using the group format repetition?
7. The group of format codes to be repeated must be enclosed within a pair of _____ .
8. How many levels deep can the group format repetition be used?
9. To use the group format repetition the groups of format codes must have the same pattern. (True/False)
10. A valuable tool used to display the location of literal constants on output is the _____ _____ form.

11. The term alphanumeric refers only to letters. (True/False)
12. All characters acceptable to a computer may be read with the A format code. (True/False)
13. The maximum number of alphanumeric characters that may be stored at a variable or array element is determined by the size of a storage location (word) on different computers. (True/False)
14. If more characters are read than can be stored in a word of storage, the excess rightmost characters are lost. (True/False)
15. The comparison of alphanumeric data must be done with two variables. (True/False)
16. What is the primary function of the DATA statement?
17. Where are DATA statements placed in a FORTRAN program?
18. The initial value for a variable given in the DATA statement must be enclosed within a set of _____ .
19. What are the three methods of supplying variables with initial values in a DATA statement?
20. Explain the term ''control break''.
21. Briefly explain the order of processing steps that must occur in a program with a single-level control break.
22. Explain the term ''summary line''.
23. Why must you force the last control break when including summary lines in control breaks?
24. Explain the term ''grand total line''.
25. What is the function of the T format code?
26. What is the function of the quote in format specifications?
27. What is the function of the CHARACTER Type statement?

9.14 EXERCISES

1. Construct the FORMAT statement for the following output specifications.
   a. Write a report heading of STUDENT REGISTRATION ROSTER to begin on a new page in print position 50.
   b. Write column headings as follows (double-spaced):
      EMPLOYEE NUMBER   beginning in position 1.
      HOURS   beginning in position 20.
      RATE   beginning in position 28.
   c. Write output values that produce the following line of print (single-spaced):
      the literal X = b in positions 1–4,
      the value of X as NN.N in positions 7–10,
      the literal X − SQD = b in positions 15–22, and
      the value of XSQD as NNN.N in positions 25–29.

2. Construct the FORMAT statement for the following output specifications.
   a. Write a report heading of FOOTBALL TEAM ROSTER to begin on a new page in print position 45.
   b. Write column headings as follows (double-spaced):
      BOOK NUMBER   beginning in position 1.
      QTY IN STOCK   beginning in position 15.
      COST   beginning in position 30.
   c. Write output values that produce the following lines of print:
      the literal A = b in positions 1–4 (b represents a blank),
      the value of A as NN.NN in positions 8–12,
      the literal J = b in positions 1–4 (double-spaced on a new line; b represents a blank), and
      the value of J as NNN in positions 7–9.

3. Use the group format repetition to shorten the following format specifications. Also use the simple repetition factor where possible.
   a. **37 FORMAT (I2,I2,3X,I3,3X,I3)**
   b. **86 FORMAT (F6.2,I3,F6.2,I3,F6.2,I3)**
   c. **97 FORMAT (5X,I6,I6,F5.2,2X,F5.2,2X)**
   d. **94 FORMAT (I4,I3,2X,I3,2X,5X,I4,I3,2X,I3,2X,5X)**
   e. **89 FORMAT (1H0,I3,3X,I3,3X,I3,3X,F8.2)**

4. Use the group format repetition to shorten the following format specifications. Also use the simple repetition factor where possible.
   a. **56 FORMAT (I7,3X,F6.2,I7,3X,F6.2)**
   b. **58 FORMAT (I4,I4,I4,3X,F6.2,2X,F6.2,2X)**
   c. **64 FORMAT (5X,I3,I1,1X,I1,1X,I3,I1,1X,I1,1X)**
   d. **76 FORMAT (F6.2,F6.2,5X,F5.2,I3,I1,I3,I1)**
   e. **84 FORMAT (1H0,5X,F6.2,4X,F6.2,4X,F6.2,4X)**

5. Determine the proper A format codes to read the following data fields. Assume all fields begin with the first given letter. The symbol "ƀ" is used to indicate blanks at the end of the field. Assume a maximum of 4 characters per word.
   a. **COLE J W PERRYƀƀƀ**   d. **60 WATT BULBSƀ**
   b. **GO**   e. **SAN ANTONIO, TEXAS**
   c. **L602M3**

6. Determine the proper A format codes to read the following data fields. Assume all fields begin with the first letter. The symbol "ƀ" is used to indicate blanks at the end of the field. Assume a maximum of 4 characters per word.
   a. **JONES JERRY T, JR.ƀƀƀƀ**   d. **HEAVY DUTY BATTERIES**
   b. **STOP HERE**   e. **COLORADO SPRINGS, COƀ**
   c. **K0329M7**

7. Construct a DATA statement to initialize the variables A, X, and M to the values 3.75, 8.6, and 12, respectively.
8. Construct a DATA statement to initialize the variables Y1, Y2, and J to the values 0.0, 8.5, and 0, respectively.
9. Construct a CHARACTER Type statement to declare the variable CITY as a 22-character length variable.
10. Construct a CHARACTER Type statement to declare the variable STATE as a 2-character length variable.

9.15 PROGRAMMING PROBLEMS

1. Write a program to write your initials in block form as presented below. For example, the initials "PC" would appear as:

```
XXXXXX        XXXXX
XX    XX      XX      X
XX    XX      XX
XXXXXX        XX
XX            XX
XX            XX      X
XX            XXXXX
```

   The first initial should begin in print position 20. The second initial should begin in print position 35. Each character should be 7 units (lines) high.

2. Rewrite programming problem 10 in chapter 5 to include identifying literals as follows.
   the literal FAHRENHEIT TEMPERATURE = ƀ beginning in position 1,
   the value of F (fahrenheit) as NNN.N in positions 30–34,
   the literal CENTIGRADE TEMPERATURE = ƀ beginning in position 1, and
   the value of C (centigrade) as NNN.N in positions 30–34.

3. Rewrite programming problem 1 in chapter 6 to include appropriate column headings.
4. Rewrite programming problem 2 in chapter 6 to include appropriate column headings.
5. Rewrite programming problem 4 in chapter 6 to include appropriate column headings.
6. Rewrite programming problem 6 in chapter 6 to include a report heading of "STUDENT REGISTRATION REGISTER" and appropriate column headings.
7. Write a program to read a single data record with your name in columns 1–25 and your date of birth in columns 30–46. Your date of birth should be entered as month, day, year (example, December 16, 1937). Print these two values on a double-spaced line with your name beginning in position 10 and date of birth beginning in position 50.

8. Write a program to read and list an inventory control file. The input values are punched in the following format:

Record Positions	Field Description
1–7	Part number (Form is alphanumeric)
10–35	Description (Form is alphanumeric)
40–43	Quantity on hand (Form = NNNN)
44–50	Unit cost (Form = NNNN.NN)

List the input file according to the following print positions.

Field Description	Print Positions
Part number	3–9
Description	15–40
Quantity on hand	46–49
Unit cost	55–61

Terminate the read loop with a sentinel record containing a value of 9999999 for part number. Include a report title and appropriate column headings.

9. Write a program to prepare a list of employees who have had 30 or more years of service with XYZ Company. The data for each employee is contained in a record in the following layout.

Record Positions	Field Description
1–20	Employee name
21–30	Department (Form is alphanumeric)
31–32	Years of service (Form = NN)

All employees who have had 30 or more years of service with the company will be recognized at the company's annual employee awards banquet. Select all employee records containing a value in the years-of-service field with 30 or greater.

Print the selected records double-spaced according to the following print specifications.

Field Description	Print Positions
Employee name	1–20
Years of service	30–31
Department	40–49

Terminate the loop with a sentinel record containing the value 99 for Years of Service. Include a report title and appropriate column headings.

10. Write a program to prepare a list of blood donors with a specific type of blood. The program should read a header record containing the type of blood in columns 1–4 that is compared with each of the donors in the card file. (Examples: APOS—A Positive; ANEG—A Negative; OPOS—O Positive; ONEG—O Negative; ABPO—AB Positive; and ABNE—AB Negative.)

The donor record is laid out in the following fields.

Record Positions	Field Description
1–6	Donor number (Form = NNNNNN)
7–26	Donor name
28–31	Donor blood type (Form is alphanumeric)
32–39	Telephone number (Form is alphanumeric)

Read the donor file and compare the blood type of each donor with the blood type specified in the header card. Prepare a list of donors with the specified blood type. The roster will be used to call donors when the supply for that type of blood runs low.

The list of donors with the specified blood type should be printed double-spaced according to the following specifications.

Field Description	Print Positions
Donor number	3–8
Donor name	14–33
Telephone number	40–47

Include a report title indicating the type of blood donors. Include appropriate column headings.

11. Write a FORTRAN program to compute the total and average, of five test scores for a class of ten students. The input data will be read in the following specifications.

Record Positions	Field Description
1–18	Name
19–20	Blank
21–25	Test 1 (Form = NNN.N)
26–30	Test 2 (Form = NNN.N)
31–35	Test 3 (Form = NNN.N)
36–40	Test 4 (Form = NNN.N)
41–45	Test 5 (Form = NNN.N)
46–80	Blank

Compute the total and average for each student's five test scores. Print output results as follows:

Field Description	Print Positions
Name	1–18
Test 1	21–25
Test 2	29–33
Test 3	37–41
Test 4	45–49
Test 5	53–57
Total	61–66
Average	71–76

Print each output record double-spaced. Include appropriate column headings.

12. Write a program to draw a specific symbol depending upon the specified type read from an input record. The type of symbols to be drawn will be a line, a square, a rectangle, and a triangle. Each input record will include what symbol to draw as follows:

Field Description	Card Columns	Input Values
Type symbol	1–4	LINE
		SQUA
		RECT
		TRIA

For example, if the value "LINE" is read, you will draw a line such as **********. If the value "TRIA" is read, you will draw a triangle such as

```
            *
          *   *
        *       *
      *           *
    *               *
  *********
```

Use a READ statement to read a record with the four-character literals that are used in the Logical IF statement to be compared with the input variable. For example:

```
     INTEGER LINE, SQUARE, RECTNG, TRIANG, SYMBOL
     READ (5, 99) LINE, SQUARE, RECTNG, TRIANG
  99 FORMAT (4A4)
     . . .
     . . .
     . . .
  10 READ (5, 98) SYMBOL
     IF (SYMBOL .EQ. SQUARE) WRITE (6, 96)
     . . .
     . . .
     . . .
```

The output results will denote the symbol being drawn followed by the drawn symbol. For example (the value "RECT" is read):

RECTANGLE

```
            ***************
            *             *
            *             *
            *             *
            ***************
```

The denoted type symbol will begin in print position 1. The drawn symbol will begin in print position 20. The dimensions of the printed symbols will be:

Symbol	Dimension
line	15 units long
square	7 units long by 5 units high
rectangle	15 units long by 5 units high
triangle	base will be 9 units long, and the height will be 5 units

Triple-space between each drawn symbol.

13. Rewrite problem 12 using a DATA statement to specify the initial values for the four-character literals to be compared in a Logical IF statement with the input variable.

Program Looping with the DO Statement

10

10.1 INTRODUCTION TO COUNTER LOOP LOGIC WITH THE DO STATEMENT

Program looping (as previously explained) consists of a branch to a previous statement, thereby causing a series of instructions to be reexecuted. This looping concept is one of the most powerful and frequently used techniques in programming. To read 1,000 data records requires only one READ statement executed within an input-bound loop 1,000 times. To compute the sum of the integers from 1 to 100 could be accomplished with an Assignment statement executed in a counter loop 100 times. To build a table of compound interest for so many periods of time requires only the computation of the value for one period and then reexecution of the relevant statements for the desired number of periods. Thus, the technique of looping greatly reduces the size of a program that involves repetitive operations. For these reasons most programming languages include a control statement that simplifies loop control and implementation.

Counter loops are frequently used in programs and result in a large number of errors. The biggest problem lies in trying to cycle through the loop the correct number of times. The last pass through the loop usually causes the most problems. The index variable is incorrectly tested, which causes the loop to be executed either one more or one less than the correct number of times.

It would be convenient to have one specific FORTRAN statement to tell the computer to repeat a group of instructions a certain number of times. The DO statement provides this convenience. Not only can you specify in one statement how many times a group of instructions is to be repeated, but an index variable is available for use inside the loop if desired. The specific initial value of the variable, the test value, and the increment value are all given in the DO statement. The computer carries out the operations required in a counter loop using the parameters found in the DO statement.

Figure 10.1 illustrates the simplicity of the DO statement compared to the long method of writing a counter loop. The loop is executed ten times.

The DO loop includes all statements down through statement number 100 (the range statement). The index variable K (used for the counter) is initialized to one before the start of the loop. After each pass of the loop, the index variable K is incremented by one. The loop is repeated until the value of K exceeds ten. When the index variable exceeds ten, the loop is exited, and the statement following the last statement in the loop is executed.

So let us turn our attention to the DO statement—a powerful command to provide counter loop operations with a single statement.

Normal counter loop with
separate statements

Counter loop with a DO statement

```
      K = 1
100 . . .
      (loop body)
      K = K + 1
      IF (K .LE. 10) GO TO 100
```

```
      DO 100 K = 1, 10, 1
         . . .
         (loop body)
100 CONTINUE
```

Figure 10.1 Comparing a normal counter loop with a DO loop

DO n ivar = m_1, m_2, m_3

or:

DO n ivar = m_1, m_2

where:

n	— is the statement number of the last statement to be included in the range of the DO loop.
ivar	— is called the index variable and is an integer variable used by the computer in the initializing, incrementing, and testing functions.
=	— is a necessary separator.
m_1	— is an unsigned positive integer constant or variable used as the initial value of the index variable. A negative or zero value is not allowed.
m_2	— is an unsigned positive integer constant or variable used as the test value by the system to determine when the loop has been completed the necessary number of times. A negative or zero value is not allowed.
m_3	— is an unsigned positive integer constant or variable used by the system to increment the index variable. A negative or zero value is not allowed. m_3 is optional if the index variable is to be incremented by one. If the m_3 parameter is omitted, the preceding comma must also be omitted.

Figure 10.2 General notation of the DO statement

10.2 THE DO AND CONTINUE STATEMENTS

The DO statement is a command to execute a series of statements one or more times. It is a control statement that allows a series of statements to be executed repeatedly while the value of an index variable varies between specified limits. The number of loop iterations is dependent on the value of the index variable and the limits parameter given for the test value. The statements that physically follow the DO statement, down to and including the indicated end (range statement) of the loop, are repeated as specified in the DO. The three operations required in loop control—initialization of an index variable, the increment, and the test of the variable value—and the exit point in the loop are all specified in the DO statement. The DO statement is thus a shorthand version of a counter loop. The general form of the DO statement is presented in figure 10.2.

The index variable is established as the control variable or index to be initialized, incremented, and tested. The parameters m_1, m_2, and m_3 are called **indexing parameters** and specify the respective values for initializing, testing, and incrementing the index variable.

The index variable is frequently used as an index or subscript reference to an array (table) element; it is also widely used as a counter to keep track of the number of iterations in a loop. Thus, the term ''index'' has the double meaning of both index and counter usage.

Examples of the DO statement are:

$$\text{DO 10 KTR} = 1, 10, 1$$
$$\text{DO 76 N} = 1, 100, 2$$
$$168 \text{ DO 33 INDEX} = 1, 53$$
$$\text{DO 24 K} = 1, \text{N}$$
$$\text{DO 43 JJ} = \text{L, NMAX, M}$$

The first example uses KTR as the index variable and repeats a loop through statement number 10 ten times. The second example uses N as the index variable, starts at 1, and increments by 2 until N exceeds 100; thus, the series of statements through 76 are executed 50 times. The third example (with assigned statement number 168) uses INDEX as the index variable, starts at 1, and increments INDEX by 1 until INDEX is greater than 53; thus, the series of statements through statement number 33 are executed 53 times. Remember, the increment is understood to be by 1 if this parameter is not included. The fourth example uses K as the index variable, starts at 1, and increments K by 1 until it is greater than the value of N; the series of statements through 24 are executed the same number of times as the value in N. The last example uses JJ as the index variable, starts JJ at the value in L, increments it by the value in M, and tests JJ against the value in NMAX. Statement number 43 is assigned to the last statement in the loop.

A **DO loop** consists of all the statements included within the loop (range of the DO). The range of a DO statement is defined from the first executable statement following the DO statement through the statement whose label is specified in the DO statement. The DO statement sets up the loop but is not included in it. All the statements in the range of the DO are repeated in execution as long as the value of the index variable is less than or equal to the test parameter (m_2).

The first time the sequence of statements contained in the DO loop is executed, the index variable has the value of m_1. The second time through the loop the index variable has the value of $m_1 + m_3$, the third time $m_1 + 2m_3$, and so on, until the value in the index variable exceeds m_2. The total number of times the DO loop is executed can be quickly calculated by the formula:

$$((m_2 - m_1) / m_3) + 1$$

If the increment value, m_3, is one, the loop will be repeated $m_2 - m_1 + 1$ times. If the value of m_2 is less than or equal to m_1, the loop is executed once.

Following is an example to illustrate the range of a DO in a program to compute the squares and cubes of the numbers from 1 to 100.

```
    DO 11 K = 1,100
    KSQ = K * K ──────────┐
    KCUBE = KSQ * K        ├ DO loop
 11 WRITE (6, 95) K, KSQ, KCUBE ┘
 95 FORMAT (1H0, I3, 3X, I6, 3X, I8)
    STOP
    END
```

The WRITE command with statement number 11 assigned to it is the **range statement** or end of the loop. All statements following the DO down to and including the range statement are in the loop. Remember, the range statement must be an executable statement. The above example also shows how the index variable may be used inside the DO loop.

The DO loop is repeated until the index variable is greater than the test value. When the loop is completed, transfer of control (the exit) is made to the next executable statement immediately following the range statement.

The DO loop does not have to be fully completed the specified number of times. An IF statement may be included in the loop to test for a certain condition. If the condition is met, a transfer may be made out of the loop. Consider the following example:

```
    SUM = 0.
    DO 76 K = 1,100,1
    READ (5,99) X
 99 FORMAT (F5.2)
    IF (X .EQ. 0.0) GO TO 19
 76 SUM = SUM + X
    . . .

    . . .
 19 XK = K - 1
    AVE = SUM / XK
```

Other statements, such as the Computed GO TO, may also be used to transfer control out of the DO loop.

The DO statement provides a structured approach to program loops; therefore, it should be used in place of the Assignment and IF statements whenever possible.

Another helpful technique in following the program logic is the indentation of all statements in a DO loop. This indentation quickly identifies the statements inside the loop and the end of the loop. For example:

```
        SUM = 0.0
        READ (5, 97) N
        DO 10 I = 1, N
            READ (5, 95) X
            WRITE (6, 94) X
10          SUM = SUM + X
        WRITE (6, 93) SUM
        STOP
97      FORMAT (I3)
95      FORMAT (F5.2)
94      FORMAT (1X, F5.2)
93      FORMAT (/ 1X, F7.2)
        END
```

You can readily see the three indented statements that make up the loop.

You may have observed that this program example incorporates header-card logic. The use of variables for indexing parameters provides considerable flexibility in the use of the DO statement. The header-card value read from an input record is used for the value of the test variable. This value then indicates how many times to repeat the loop and also how many data records to read. Variables should be used for many of the indexing parameters where feasible to provide increased flexibility in program looping.

The CONTINUE Statement

The CONTINUE statement is a "do nothing" statement that may be placed anywhere in the source program where an executable statement may appear. The CONTINUE statement acts as a "dummy statement" and does not affect the sequence of execution in any way. Its sole function is to provide a label that can be referenced by an instruction. In other words, the CONTINUE statement causes no action to take place; when it is encountered the computer merely continues its execution. Its main use is to show the end of a DO loop. The general form of the CONTINUE statement is given in figure 10.3.

If the CONTINUE statement is used to end a DO loop, its assigned statement number is, of course, the range statement specified in the DO. For example:

```
        ISUM = 0
        DO 34 INT = 1, 1000, 1
            ISUM = ISUM + INT
            IF (ISUM .GT. 9999) GO TO 7
34      CONTINUE
7       WRITE (6,90) ISUM, INT
90      FORMAT (1X,I8,5X,I5)
```

The above example finds the sum of the integers (starting at 1) that first exceeds 9999.

CONTINUE Statement—General Form

---

n CONTINUE

where:

    n   —   is the statement number assigned to the **CONTINUE** statement.

Figure 10.3 General notation of the CONTINUE statement

The use of the CONTINUE statement is highly recommended for ending all DO loops. Using the CONTINUE statement allows greater flexibility for inserting additional statements at the end of the DO loop or removing the statement normally thought of as the end of the loop. It also serves as an aid in identifying the end of a DO loop. Therefore, most instructors prefer students to use the CONTINUE statement as the range statement in a DO loop. The CONTINUE statement will be used to end all DO loops in this text.

The CONTINUE statement is normally aligned with its respective DO statement to show the end of a DO loop. Some programmers prefer to indent the CONTINUE statement and align it with the other statements in the DO loop. The CONTINUE statement will be aligned with the DO statement in this text.

The CONTINUE is not restricted to use with DO loops. Since it is considered an executable statement, it can be placed at almost any location in a program and used as the target of a branch command to identify the location of the next instruction to be executed.

The DO statement and DO loops have some unique requirements which must not be violated by the programmer. These rules are presented in the next section.

10.3 RULES FOR USING THE DO STATEMENT AND FORMING DO LOOPS

The DO loop created by the programmer must be handled differently from the conditional counter loop with a Logical IF statement. Two common mistakes made by students are: (1) attempting to branch from outside the DO loop to a statement in the middle of the DO loop, and (2) not allowing the system to control the incrementing and testing of the index variable. The rules which must be followed are summed up below. These rules pertain to ANSI FORTRAN 66 but may not apply to all FORTRAN IV compilers.

Rule 1. A DO loop may not be *entered* in the middle. The middle is defined as any statement after the DO, including the range statement. The loop must always be entered from the top (DO statement). For example (the partial box represents the DO loop):

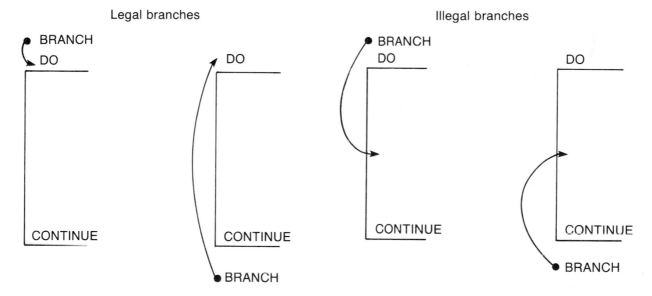

Rule 2. Whenever the DO statement is executed, the index variable is always initialized, and the execution of the loop begins. In a normal pass of the loop, the DO statement itself is not reexecuted; so the index variable retains its incremented value. A common error made by many students is to transfer to the DO statement from inside the loop's range. This causes an infinite loop, since the DO loop is restarted. Reference Rule 13 for the proper way to skip statements in the loop and still allow the next pass of the loop to be performed.

Rule 3. A transfer within the loop to another statement inside the loop is always permissible. For example:

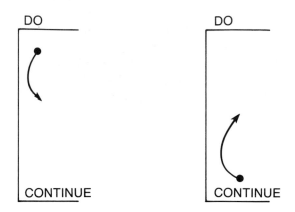

Rule 4. A transfer *out* of the range of any DO loop is permissible at any time. You do not have to complete all the passes of the loop. For example:

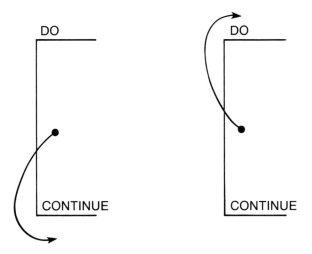

Rule 5. If the DO loop was not completed the specified number of times (because a transfer was made out of the loop), then the index variable has the same value as it had when it was last incremented.

Rule 6. If the DO loop is completed the specified number of times, the value of the index variable is unpredictable and should not be used until assigned another value. The reason for this is that once a DO loop has been completed, no attempt is made by the compiler to retain the last value of the index variable. Do not expect, therefore, that the index variable will retain its value after the exit from the DO loop.

Rule 7. The first statement immediately following the DO statement must be an executable statement. For example, a FORMAT is not permitted as the first statement following the DO statement.

Rule 8. The last statement in a loop must be an executable statement. For example, a FORMAT statement must not be specified as the range statement in the DO loop. The best technique is always to use the CONTINUE statement for the range statement.

Rule 9. The last statement in the range of a DO loop cannot be a control statement that includes

a.   A GO TO statement of any form
b.   A STOP, PAUSE, or RETURN
c.   A Logical IF with a GO TO that provides transfer of control
d.   Another DO statement

Again, the best technique is always to terminate the DO loop with a CONTINUE statement.

Rule 10. Each indexing parameter must be a positive integer constant or variable. (This rule is not true for all FORTRAN IV compilers. Burroughs, for example, permits real constants and variables to allow fractional values for incrementing and decrementing. See the nonstandard language extensions section.)

Rule 11. The index variable and any of the indexing parameters of the DO statement may be used in the range of the DO, but they must not be *changed* by a statement in the range of the DO. This means that they cannot appear as the assignment variable in the Assignment statement or in the input list of a READ statement. An example of an **illegal** routine is:

$$\text{DO } 10 \text{ I} = 1,20$$
. . .
. . .
. . .
$$\text{I} = \text{N}$$
. . .
. . .
. . .
$$10 \text{ CONTINUE}$$

Rule 12. The DO loop will always be executed at least once. The test is not made until the system completes a pass of the loop. The order in which the parameters are handled in the loop in ANSI FORTRAN 66 and FORTRAN IV is:

a. The index variable is initialized.
b. A pass of the loop is made.
c. The increment value is added to the index variable.
d. The test is made between the index variable and the test value.
e. If the index variable is greater than the test value, the loop is complete and control resumes at the next statement after the range statement.
f. If the index variable is *not* greater than the test value, the loop is repeated.
g. Steps c) through f) are repeated until either step e) is satisfied or a transfer is made out of the loop.

Remember, at the end of each pass through the loop the increment is added, and then the test is made (in ANSI FORTRAN 66 and FORTRAN IV compilers.)

In ANSI FORTRAN 77 the test is made *before* the loop is executed. Therefore, no pass of the loop is made if the index variable is greater than the test value. This change in ANSI FORTRAN 77 will affect programs developed on ANSI FORTRAN 66 and FORTRAN IV compilers and subsequently converted to ANSI FORTRAN 77. The converted programs may not produce correct results.

Consider the following DO loop:

$$\text{DO } 20 \text{ INDX} = \text{M1, M2, M3}$$
. . .
. . . } loop body
. . .
$$20 \text{ CONTINUE}$$
$$30 \text{ . . .}$$

The equivalent order of execution in counter-loop form is given for FORTRAN 66 and FORTRAN 77.

FORTRAN 66
```
      INDX = M1
10 . . .
   . . . } loop body
   . . .
      INDX = INDX + M3
20 IF (INDX .LE. M2) GO TO 10
30 . . .
```

FORTRAN 77
```
      INDX = M1
10 IF (INDX .GT. M2) GO TO 30
   . . .
   . . . } loop body
   . . .
      INDX = INDX + M3
20 GO TO 10
30 . . .
```

Note: On the normal termination of the loops, the index variable will not necsesarily have the same value in both versions.

Rule 13. The range statement must be executed in order for the computer to know when to attempt the next pass of the loop. A mistake frequently made by beginning FORTRAN programmers is to test the index variable and branch back to the DO statement. If this is done, the loop is reinitialized and begins anew. Thus, in most cases an endless loop will be formed. If some statements are to be skipped in the loop and the next pass begun, the programmer should branch to the range statement. For example,

```
              DO 12 I = 1, 50
                  . . .
                  . . .
                  . . .
              IF (C1 .EQ.0.0) GO TO 12
                  . . .
                  . . .
                  . . .
          12  CONTINUE
```

10.4 EXAMPLES OF CONSTRUCTING DO LOOPS

The following examples are presented to illustrate the many forms and uses of DO loops.

Example 1:

```
     C *** READ 100 CARDS WITH VALUES IN CARD
     C *** COLUMNS 1–5 AND SUM THESE VALUES.
           SUM = 0.0
           DO 10 ICOUNT = 1, 100
               READ (5, 99) VALUE
      99       FORMAT (F5.2)
               SUM = SUM + VALUE
      10       CONTINUE
```

Example 2:

```
     C *** ADD ALL THE ODD INTEGERS FROM 1–999
           ISUM = 0
           DO 15 INTEGR = 1, 999, 2
               ISUM = ISUM + INTEGR
      15       CONTINUE
```

Example 3:

```
     C *** ADD ALL THE INTEGERS FROM −25 TO ZERO
           ISUM = 0
           NEGINT = −25
           DO 8 K = 1, 26
               ISUM = ISUM + NEGINT
               NEGINT = NEGINT + 1
       8       CONTINUE
```

Example 4:

```
     C *** ADD THE NUMBERS FROM 0 TO 5
     C *** IN ONE-QUARTER INCREMENTS
           SUM = 0.
           XNCREM = 0.
           DO 12 L = 1, 21, 1
               SUM = SUM + XNCREM
               XNCREM = XNCREM + .25
      12       CONTINUE
```

Example 5:

```
C *** DECREMENT J BY 1
C *** FROM 9 DOWN TO 1
      DO 76 I = 1, 9
          J = 10 - I
          . . .

          . . .
76    CONTINUE
```

10.5 FLOWCHARTING AND WRITING THE PSEUDOCODE FOR DO LOOPS

There are many techniques used to flowchart the DO statement and its accompanying DO loop. The symbol normally used is the **preparation symbol.** The preparation symbol is a new flowcharting symbol—a hexagon. It is divided into three areas to depict the three operations of the indexing parameters.

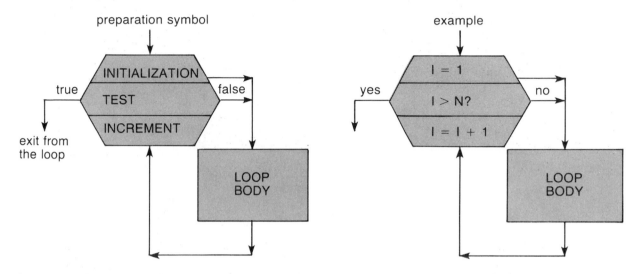

Each of the three areas represents one of the three functions—initialization, increment, and testing—of the loop. If the test is true—i.e. the index variable exceeds the test variable—an exit is made to the next executable statement following the loop. If the test is false, repetition of the loop continues until a true condition is realized or a branch is made out of the loop. Notice the line from the initialization to the loop body, which shows that the test is not made on the first pass of the loop.

Figure 10.4 (p. 306) presents a flowchart of the past program example. The logic of the program is to read a header record to determine how many data records to read and then to sum the input value of X on each record. Note the technique of flowcharting the DO loop.

The DO loop may be flowcharted using other conventions. Some programmers prefer to use the operations symbol (rectangle) divided into three areas as follows:

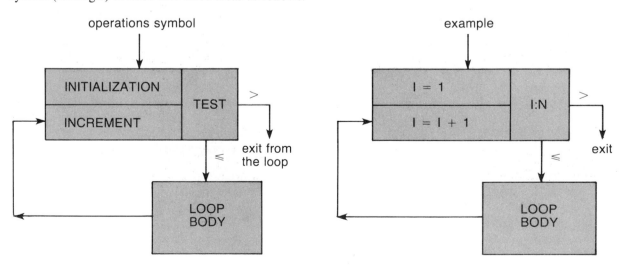

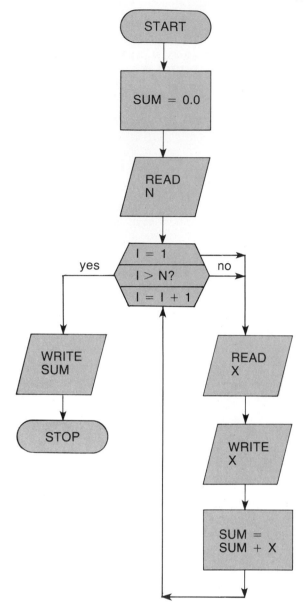

Figure 10.4 Flowchart to illustrate a DO loop and header-card logic

Some programmers divide the operation symbol (rectangle) or preparation symbol (hexagon) into three areas as shown below.

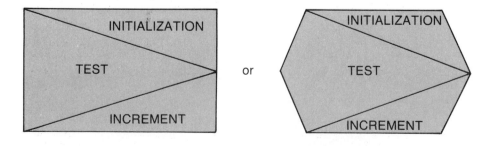

Still other programmers prefer to use a decision symbol at the end of the loop. Inside the decision symbol, a question is asked to determine whether the loop is completed, e.g., $I > N$. The choice of symbols and techniques used in flowcharting the DO statement and accompanying DO loop is up to you or your instructor.

Pseudocode For the DO Statement

The DO loop in FORTRAN 66 is really a REPEAT UNTIL control structure, since the test for exit is at the bottom of the loop. The loop, therefore, may be written in pseudocode as follows (assuming K as the index variable and N as the test value):

DO UNTIL K > N

. . .

. . . (loop body)

. . .

END DO

The REPEAT command is commonly used to form loops in pseudocode. A form of the REPEAT command that is easily understood may be written as follows:

REPEAT FOR index variable = initial value TO test value

For example:

REPEAT FOR K = 1 TO N

. . .

. . . (loop body)

. . .

END REPEAT

You may include a BY option after the test value on the REPEAT command if you wish to show the increment value. Your instructor should inform you of the desired method for implementing DO loops in pseudocode. See figure 10.5 (p.308) for an example of pseudocode with a DO loop.

The DO loop in FORTRAN 77 is a DO WHILE loop, since the test for the exit is made at the top of the loop. Thus, the pseudocode for a DO loop should be shown as a DO WHILE control structure.

Many problems require loops within loops, called nested loops. The next section discusses nested DO loops.

10.6 NESTED LOOPS WITH NESTED DO'S

When loops occur within other loops, they are referred to as **nested loops.** The outside loops are called **outer loops**. The loops inside the outer loops are called the **inner loops**.

A DO loop within a loop may be controlled by a Logical IF statement or included within other DO loops, resulting in **nested DO loops**. The DO loops may be nested in any number of ways, as in the following examples:

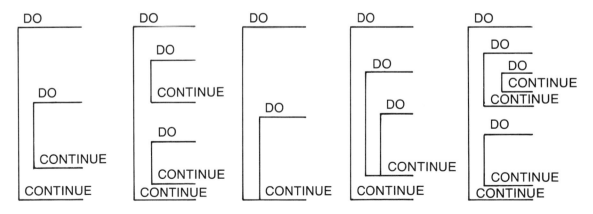

```
START ANALYSIS.
        INITIALIZE ACCUMULATOR SUM.
        READ VALUE FOR N.
        REPEAT FOR I = 1 TO N BY 1
                READ VALUE FOR X.
                WRITE VALUE OF X.
                ADD X TO ACCUMULATOR SUM.
        END REPEAT
        WRITE VALUE OF SUM.
END ANALYSIS.
```

Figure 10.5 Pseudocode with a DO loop

DO loops may be nested to any practical level (number) unless the specific compiler limits their number (e.g., IBM Basic FORTRAN IV limits nested DO loops to 25).

Each inner loop must be completed or exited before the next pass of the outer loop is attempted. When the next pass of the outer loop is executed, and the inner loop is encountered again, the full iteration of the inner loop will be performed. That is, the inner loop is executed in its entirety upon each pass of the outer loop.

The concept of nested looping is analogous to walking around a park and riding the merry-go-round. For each trip around the park you take so many rides on the merry-go-round. The trip around the park is analogous to the outer loop. Going around on a merry-go-round inside the park is analogous to the inner loop. As you can see, a certain number of rounds on the merry-go-round will be completed for each trip around the park. Suppose five rounds on the merry-go-round are made for each trip around the park. If five trips were made around the park, twenty-five rounds on the merry-go-round would be completed.

Following is an example to illustrate nested DO loops.

$$DO\ 7\ I = 1,\ 10$$
$$\cdot\ \cdot\ \cdot$$
$$\cdot\ \cdot\ \cdot$$
$$DO\ 5\ J = 1,\ 5$$
$$\cdot\ \cdot\ \cdot$$
$$\cdot\ \cdot\ \cdot$$
$$5\ CONTINUE$$
$$7\ CONTINUE$$

The outer loop is executed ten times. Since the inner loop is repeated five times for each pass of the outer loop, the inner loop is repeated a total of fifty times.

Nested DO's can get rather involved. Section 10.7 presents the rules that should be followed when using them.

10.7 RULES IN USING NESTED DO LOOPS

As with single loops, certain precautions should be taken when forming nested DO loops. All of the rules which apply to a single DO loop also apply to nested DO loops. In addition, these rules apply to using nested DO loops:

Rule 1. All statements in the range of the inner DO must be in the range of the outer DO. For example, consider the following illegal construction:

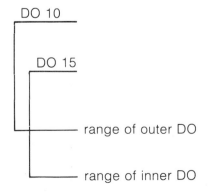

The end of the inner loop is outside the end of the outer loop; therefore, this is not a loop within a loop. It is permissible in most cases, however, (except in rule 6) for the range statement of the inner loop to be the *same* range statement as that of the outer loop. For example:

DO 10 I = 1, 5

· · ·

· · ·

DO 10 J = 1, 10

· · ·

· · ·

· · ·

10 CONTINUE

DO

DO

CONTINUE

This construction is perfectly legal. In fact, many levels of nested DO loops can end on the same range statement. I strongly recommend, however, that different CONTINUE statements be used for the range statements to provide a clearer definition of the DO loops. Ending nested DO loops on the same range statement is a very dangerous practice. Execution errors can occur or incorrect results may be obtained when a transfer (GO TO) is made to the range statement, because the transfer (GO TO) is always treated as a transfer to the range of the inner loop.

Rule 2. You may not branch *into* the middle of an inner or outer DO loop from an outer level loop. For example:

Illegal

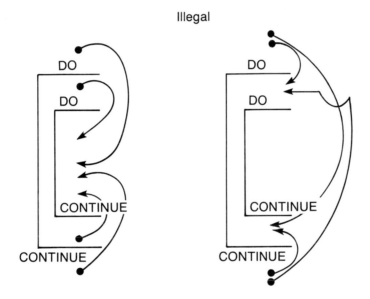

Rule 3. It is permissible to branch around an inner DO loop or to the beginning of the inner DO statement from within the outer loop.

Legal

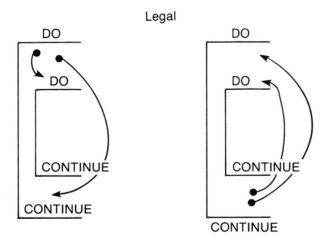

Rule 4. The index variables must be unique in all nested DO statements. For example:

$$\text{DO 20 K} = 1, 10$$

$$\cdot \ \cdot \ \cdot$$

$$\cdot \ \cdot \ \cdot$$

$$\text{DO 10 J} = 1, 10$$

$$\cdot \ \cdot \ \cdot$$

$$\cdot \ \cdot \ \cdot$$

$$\text{10 CONTINUE}$$

$$\cdot \ \cdot \ \cdot$$

$$\cdot \ \cdot \ \cdot$$

$$\text{20 CONTINUE}$$

If K had been used as the index variable for both the outer and inner DO's, the loops would not be repeated the correct number of times. This is really a violation of rule 11 with single loops.

Rule 5. You may branch *out* of any inner level DO loop to any outer level DO loop at any time. Consider the following legal examples:

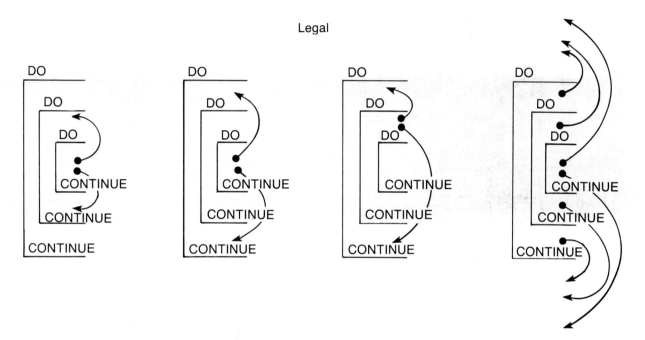

Legal

Rule 6. If the same range statement is used to end nested DO loops, the range statement number may be used in a GO TO or IF statement only in the innermost loop. That is, a branch to the range statement number used to end multiple nested DO loops is only valid from the most deeply nested DO loop. A branch to the range statement ending more than one DO loop from any of the outer DO loops will produce invalid results (i.e., the incrementing to the next pass of that respective loop). For example, the following FORTRAN statements violate this rule.

$$\text{DO 13 I} = 1, \text{N}$$

$$\cdot \ \cdot \ \cdot$$

$$\cdot \ \cdot \ \cdot$$

$$\text{DO 13 J} = 1, \text{M}$$

$$\cdot \ \cdot \ \cdot$$

$$\cdot \ \cdot \ \cdot$$

$$\text{IF (J .GT. I) GO TO 13}$$

$$\text{DO 13 K} = 1, 10$$

$$\cdot \ \cdot \ \cdot$$

$$\cdot \ \cdot \ \cdot$$

$$\text{13 CONTINUE}$$

Since the Logical IF statement is not inside the innermost loop, the branch to the range statement will not provide the correct increments of these DO loops. To overcome this restriction, you must use a different CONTINUE statement to end each DO loop. For example,

```
        DO 30 I = 1, N
        . . .
        . . .
        DO 20 J = 1, M
        . . .
        . . .
        IF (J .GT. I) GO TO 20
        DO 10 K = 1, 10
        . . .
        . . .
10      CONTINUE
20      CONTINUE
30 CONTINUE
```

Summary of Nested DO Loop Rules

The rules for branching into or out of nested DO loops are summed up in the following diagrams.

Legal

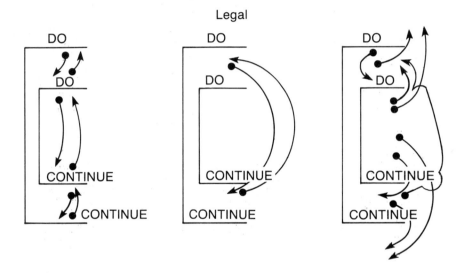

Extended Range of a DO

A question often asked by the student is "Can I jump out of a DO loop, perform some actions, and then branch back into the DO loop where I left off?" Yes, but only from the innermost DO. This concept is referred to as the extended range of the DO.

The **extended range of the DO** is defined as those statements that are executed between the transfer out of the innermost DO (of a set of nested DO's) and the transfer back into the range of this innermost DO. The index variable and indexing parameters must not be changed in the extended range of the DO. The extended range of the DO must not contain another DO statement that also has an extended range in it.

However, this is not a useful feature of FORTRAN, since many variations and quirks exist among FORTRAN compilers. The student is strongly advised not to use this feature in DO loops. A call to a subroutine is a better technique to use (once you have learned how to write subprograms).

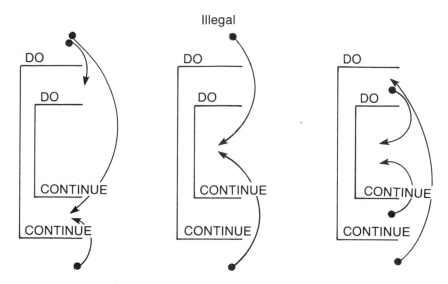

Illegal

10.8 A SAMPLE FORTRAN PROGRAM TO ILLUSTRATE NESTED DO LOOPS

Let us develop a FORTRAN program that demonstrates the use and flexibility of DO loops. Suppose we take the problem of producing a table to show a savings balance and the amount of compounded interest earned on savings each year. Assume a certain amount of money is deposited into a savings account at a specified interest rate and compounded so many times per year. How much interest will be earned and what will the account balance be at the end of five years?

Banks and credit unions advertise that they pay so much interest compounded at given intervals during the year. Tables of earned interest and the account balance with the various parameters can be computed. These tables will permit a comparison of the various interest rates and number of compounding periods, and thus show which method pays the most interest. They would tell you, for example, whether to invest your savings in a bank that pays 6 percent interest compounded annually or in another bank that pays 5.95 percent interest compounded quarterly.

The formula to compute the new balance and compounded interest is balance $= p(1 + r / n)^n$, where p represents the invested principal, r represents the percentage interest rate, and n represents the number of times per year that the interest is compounded or computed. For example, if you invest \$100 at .06 interest, compounded semiannually (2 periods), what would be the earned interest at the end of one year? Plugging these parameters into the formula, you would have balance $= 100 (1 + .06 / 2)^2$. After carrying out the computations, the end-of-year balance will be \$106.09, and \$6.09 interest will be earned.

Program Specifications

We wish to include nested loops and header-record logic in our program to demonstrate these techniques. Based on the requirement to produce multiple tables of compounded interest for various interest rates and different compounding periods, the program specifications are:

1. Produce a desired number of tables to show invested principal, accumulated balance, and earned interest according to these formulas: new balance $= p(1 + r / n)^n$, and interest $=$ new balance $-$ principal.
2. A header record will be read to specify the number of tables to build, and thus the number of data records to read.
3. Each data record read will specify the parameters of each table to be produced. The input parameters are principal of original investment, interest rate, number of compounding periods, and length of years for investment.
4. Computations will be made to produce the new balance and earned interest for each year of investment.
5. Each output table will begin on a new page with a page heading that specifies the various parameters used.
6. Column headings will be used to identify the columns of the output results.
7. Each detail print line will contain the year, beginning balance, new balance, and earned interest for that year.

Using these specs (specifications), let us develop the input and output record formats.

Input and Output Specifications

The input records and their field descriptions are as follows:

Data Record 1 (Header)

Record Position	Field Description	Variable Name
1–3	Number of tables to produce	NTABLE

Detail Data Records

Record Position	Field Description	Variable Name
1–8	Beginning principal (Form = NNNNN.NN)	PRNCPL
10–14	Rate (Form = .NNNN)	RATE
16–17	Number of times interest is compounded per year (Form = NN)	NTIMES
20–21	Number of years principal is left in savings (Form = NN)	NYEARS

A separate data record is used for each table to be built. If three tables are to be built, three data records will follow the header record.

The output specifications for a single table is presented in printer layout form in figure 10.6.

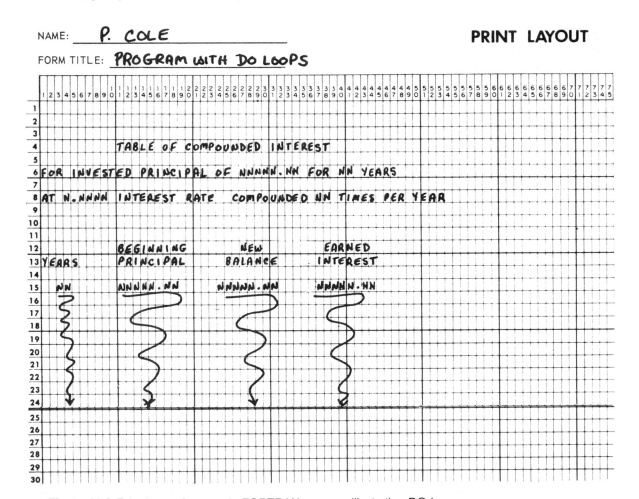

NAME: P. COLE   **PRINT LAYOUT**

FORM TITLE: PROGRAM WITH DO LOOPS

TABLE OF COMPOUNDED INTEREST
FOR INVESTED PRINCIPAL OF NNNNN.NN FOR NN YEARS
AT N.NNNN INTEREST RATE COMPOUNDED NN TIMES PER YEAR

YEARS	BEGINNING PRINCIPAL	NEW BALANCE	EARNED INTEREST
NN	NNNNN.NN	NNNNN.NN	NNNNN.NN

Figure 10.6 Print layout for sample FORTRAN program illustrating DO loops

Flowchart and Coded Program

The problem involves header-record logic to read the first data record and determine how many tables to produce. The value in NTABLE will be used as the test variable in the first DO statement (outer loop). Each data record thereafter sets up the test value NYEARS for the second DO statement (inner loop) and provides the needed parameter values to produce each table.

Since the factor for computing the balance remains the same, it will be calculated only once, outside the inner loop. This saves the computer from having to recompute it each time through the loop and thus produces a faster-running program.

The flowchart of the problem logic is presented in figure 10.7, the pseudocode for the program logic in figure 10.8, the coded program is presented in figure 10.9, and a page of one table of output results is presented in figure 10.10 (p. 316).

The example program illustrates some of the power and flexibility of the DO statement in program loops. Probably the most powerful use of the DO statements is in table manipulation. Table manipulation involves storing values in a table form and accessing the items by the use of indexes or subscripts. The use of tables (arrays) and the DO with table operations is discussed in the next chapter.

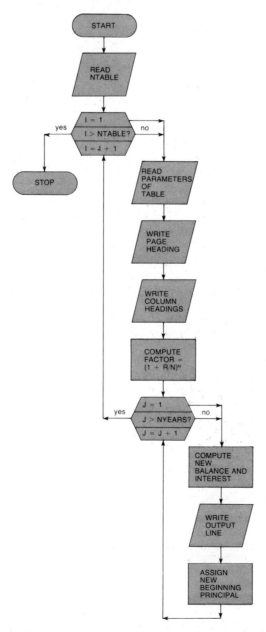

Figure 10.7 Flowchart of program logic to illustrate nested DO loops

```
          START ANALYSIS.
               READ VARIABLE FOR NUMBER OF TABLES TO BUILD.
               REPEAT FOR 1 TO NUMBER OF TABLES
                    READ PRINCIPAL, RATE, COMPOUNDED PERIODS PER YEAR,
                         AND NUMBER OF YEARS.
                    WRITE TABLE HEADING WITH PARAMETERS.
                    WRITE COLUMN HEADINGS.
                    COMPUTE THE FACTOR FOR THE TABLE AS
                         (1 + r/n)ⁿ.
                    REPEAT FOR 1 TO NUMBER OF YEARS
                         COMPUTE BALANCE = PRINCIPAL TIMES FACTOR.
                         COMPUTE INTEREST = BALANCE − PRINCIPAL.
                         WRITE DETAIL LINE FOR TABLE WITH
                              VALUES OF PRINCIPAL, BALANCE AND INTEREST.
                         SET PRINCIPAL TO BALANCE.
                    END REPEAT
               END REPEAT
               TERMINATE PROGRAM.
          END ANALYSIS.
```

Figure 10.8 Pseudocode for program logic to illustrate nested DO loops

```
C *** PROGRAM TO COMPUTE TABLES OF COMPOUNDED INTEREST ON DIFFERENT
C *** PRINCIPALS, INTEREST RATES, AND COMPOUNDING PERIODS.
C
  99      FORMAT (I3)
  98      FORMAT (F8.2,1X,F5.3,1X,I2,2X,I2)
  97      FORMAT (1H1, 10X,28HTABLE OF COMPOUNDED INTEREST/
     1   1H0,26HFOR INVESTED PRINCIPAL OF ,F8.2,5H FOR ,I2,6H YEARS
     2   /1H0,3HAT , F6.4,27H INTEREST RATE COMPOUNDED ,I2,
     3   15H TIMES PER YEAR//)
  96   FORMAT(1H0,10X,9HBEGINNING,7X,3HNEW,7X,7H, EARNED/1H ,
     1            5HYEARS,5X,9HPRINCIPAL,5X,7HBALANCE,5X,8HINTEREST)
  95      FORMAT (1H0,2X,I2,6X,F8.2,5X,F8.2,5X,F8.2)
C
         READ (5,99) NTABLE
C *** OUTER LOOP TO BUILD THE NUMBER OF DESIRED TABLES
         DO 80 I = 1, NTABLE
            READ (5,98) PRNCPL,RATE,NTIMES,NYEARS
            WRITE (6,97) PRNCPL,NYEARS,RATE,NTIMES
            WRITE (6,96)
            RTIMES − NTIMES
            FACTOR = (1.0 + RATE/RTIMES ) ** RTIMES
C *** INNER LOOP TO BUILD EACH TABLE
            DO 70 J = 1, NYEARS
               BALNCE = PRNCPL * FACTOR
               XINTRS = BALNCE − PRNCPL
               WRITE (6,95) J, PRNCPL, BALNCE, XINTRS
               PRNCPL = BALNCE
  70        CONTINUE
  80     CONTINUE
         STOP
         END
```

Figure 10.9 Sample FORTRAN program to illustrate nested DO loops

```
                    TABLE OF COMPOUNDED INTEREST
              FOR INVESTED PRINCIPAL OF   100.00 FOR 10 YEARS
              AT 0.0595  INTEREST RATE   COMPOUNDED  4 TIMES PER YEAR

                       BEGINNING        NEW        EARNED
              YEARS    PRINCIPAL      BALANCE      INTEREST

                 1      100.00        106.08         6.08

                 2      106.08        112.54         6.45

                 3      112.54        119.39         6.85

                 4      119.39        126.65         7.26

                 5      126.65        134.35         7.71

                 6      134.35        142.53         8.17

                 7      142.53        151.20         8.67

                 8      151.20        160.40         9.20

                 9      160.40        170.16         9.76

                10      170.16        180.51        10.35
```

Figure 10.10 One table of output results from sample program to illustrate nested DO loops

10.9 LANGUAGE EXTENSIONS IN FORTRAN DIALECTS (OPTIONS WITH THE DO STATEMENT INDEXING PARAMETERS)

In FORTRAN 77, VAX-11, and other modern structured FORTRAN dialects, any or each of the indexing parameters for the DO (initialization, test, and increment) may be integer or real expressions. That is, the indexing parameters are not restricted to an integer constant or variable as in ANSI FORTRAN 66 and many FORTRAN IV compilers. Therefore, many powerful variations can be formed with the indexing parameters in the DO statement, such as using arithmetic expressions for any of the indexing parameters or using decimal constants or variables for the indexing parameters.

Expressions as Indexing Parameters

An arithmetic expression (integer or real) may be given for any of the indexing parameters in the DO statement. For example, consider the following program with a DO loop to sum the odd integers from one to N minus one. The value of N is read as input:

```
        INTEGER SUM
        READ *, N
        SUM = 0
        DO 10 INDX = 1, N-1
            SUM = SUM + INDX
    10  CONTINUE
        PRINT *, SUM
        STOP
        END
```

Examples of integer expressions as indexing parameters are:

```
        DO 10 I = J + 1, K
        DO 20 INDX = 1, N*2, 2
        DO 30 K = N/2 + 1, MAX-1, INC1 + INC2
```

Decimal Expressions as Indexing Parameters

Decimal indexing parameters can be specified to provide fractional initializing, testing, and incrementing of the index variable. That is, you can increment by .5, 1.5, .02, and so forth. This capability allows the specification of decimal indexing parameters in the DO statement, so that additional statements do not have to be established in the loop. Also, you do not have to figure out how many times to cycle through the DO loop.

You must always use a real variable for the index variable, so that the index variable can take on decimal values. You must not use an integer variable for the index variable, since an integer index variable can take on only whole numbers.

Suppose you want to establish a counter loop that starts with an index variable value of 1.5, increments the index variable in steps of .5, and exits the loop when the index variable exceeds 7.5. The DO loop, using the variable X as the index variable, might be set up as follows:

DO 33 X = 1.5, 7.5, .5

. . .

. . .

. . .

33 CONTINUE

If you wanted to establish a counter loop that went from 0.0 to 2.5 in increments of .001, you might write the following statements:

DO 44 C = 0.0, 2.5, .001

. . .

. . .

. . .

44 CONTINUE

Negative values may be given for the initialization and test indexing parameters. Suppose you want to initialize the index variable Z to -3.5, step by increments of .1 and test for a terminal value of -3.0. You would code the DO loop as follows:

DO 55 Z = -3.5, -3.0, .1

. . .

. . .

. . .

55 CONTINUE

You must be extremely careful in specifying negative indexing parameters. If the test value is not greater than the initial value, an endless loop will result.

FORTRAN 77 and other vendor dialects of FORTRAN (even some FORTRAN IV compilers, such as Burroughs) provide great flexibility in implementing DO loops. You must remember, however, that ANSI FORTRAN 66 and many FORTRAN IV compilers do not allow such flexibility. Conversions to ANSI FORTRAN 66 of FORTRAN programs developed with compilers that permit this flexibility may be difficult to do.

10.10 SUMMARY

Counter loops are widely used in programs. Problems are sometimes experienced with normal counter loops in cycling through the loop the proper number of times. The test for the exit from the loop may be given incorrectly, which causes the loop to be repeated one time more or less than is needed.

The DO statement is the solution to implementing counter loops correctly. The DO statement is used to execute a series of statements one or more times. In the DO statement, you can specify the initialization, increment, and test parameters for the loop. The end of the loop (range statement) is also given in the DO statement. Remember, the range of a DO statement is composed of all the statements from the first executable statement following the DO statement down to and including the statement whose label (statement number) is specified in the DO statement. The FORTRAN translator will generate the proper machine language instructions to execute the loop as given in the DO statement parameters. You can feel assured that the loop will be executed the proper number of times if the correct indexing parameters have been given.

An index variable is given in the DO statement to be used as the control variable in the DO loop. The initial value (m_1), the test value (m_2), and the increment value (m_3) are given in the DO statement to provide the parameters for the counter loop. The increment value may be omitted if the increment will be in steps of one. The indexing parameters may be integer constants or variables. Variables should be used where possible to provide more flexibility in the loop parameters. When constants are used as indexing parameters, the program is "locked" into a specific number of loop iterations. Having to change the constants when you want to change the indexing parameters might require much work in modifying a program.

The CONTINUE statement is an executable statement that really is a "no operation" command. It is used as a dummy statement that contains a statement label (number) and provides a branch label (location). Thus, a CONTINUE statement is normally used to end each DO loop to provide better readability and flexibility. The CONTINUE statement number is specified as the range statement in the DO statement. For example, a DO loop to process all statements down through statement number 200 ten times might be implemented as follows:

$$DO\ 200\ L\ =\ 1,\ 10$$
$$.\ .\ .$$
$$.\ .\ .$$
$$.\ .\ .$$
$$200\ CONTINUE$$

There are various requirements and rules you must follow when using DO loops. For example, you cannot branch into the middle of a DO loop from an outer level loop; you must always enter a DO loop from the top (at the DO statement). You must not change any of the indexing parameters or the index variable within the DO loop; and so on. Thirteen rules were given to correctly implement DO loops.

Section 10.4 presented five examples of how one might write DO loops to solve various tasks. Section 10.5 discussed the methods used in flowcharting and writing pseudocode for DO loops.

Many problems require loops within loops, called nested loops, as part of their solution. Nested loops can vary from two deep to as many as the problem requires. Nested DO loops are widely used to implement nested counter loops within a program.

There are certain rules and precautions you must be aware of when implementing nested DO loops. For example, an inner loop must end before an outer loop. That is, the range of an inner loop must not extend beyond the range of an outer loop. Many of the same rules for branching within single DO loops apply to nested loops. Six rules were given for implementing nested DO loops.

You can gain much power and flexibility in solving problems by using DO loops. The DO statement is a widely used statement in many FORTRAN programs to implement counter loops. DO loops are frequently used with table (array) operations, which is the subject of chapter 11.

10.11 TERMS

Terms, statements, and concepts you should become familiar with in this chapter are:

CONTINUE statement	index variable	nested loops
counter loop	indexing parameters	outer loop
DO loop	initialization parameter	preparation symbol
DO loop rules	inner loop	range of the DO
DO statement	iteration symbol	range statement
flowcharting a DO loop	loop exit	test parameter
increment parameter	nested DO loops	

10.12 REVIEW QUESTIONS

1. What is the function of the DO statement?
2. List the indexing parameters included in the DO statement and explain their use.
3. If the increment parameter is not included on the DO statement, its value is understood to be _____ .
4. Name the two ways that you may exit from a DO loop.

5. What is the advantage of using variables for the indexing parameters of a DO?
6. Describe the construction of the iteration flowcharting symbol.
7. One may transfer out of a DO loop even though it has not been repeated the specified number of times. (True/False)
8. When is the value in the index variable available for use in calculations outside the loop?
9. What statement is often used as the range statement in a DO loop, especially if a Logical IF statement is needed at the end of the loop?
10. What does the term "nested loops" mean?

10.13 EXERCISES

1. Form a DO statement that will start the index variable II at 5, increments by 5, and stop when II exceeds 500. The range statement is number 56.
2. Form a DO statement that will start the index variable M at 3, increment by 3, and stop when M exceeds 99. The range statement is number 38.
3. How many times will the following DO loops be executed, and what are the values that the index variable will take on?

a. **DO 7 I = 1,8**
   . . .
   . . .
   . . .
   7 CONTINUE

b. **DO 13 J = 2,7,3**
   . . .
   . . .
   . . .
   13 CONTINUE

c. **DO 14 K = 4,9,2**
   . . .
   . . .
   . . .
   14 CONTINUE

4. How many times will the following DO loops be executed, and what are the values that the index variable will take on?

a. **DO 10 J = 1,20**
   . . .
   . . .
   . . .
   10 CONTINUE

b. **DO 27 L = 2,11,4**
   . . .
   . . .
   . . .
   27 CONTINUE

c. **DO 18 M = 3,14,2**
   . . .
   . . .
   . . .
   18 CONTINUE

5. How many times will the following inner DO loops be repeated?

a. **DO 6 K = 1,3**
   DO 5 J = 1,4
     . . .
     . . .
     . . .
   5 CONTINUE
   6 CONTINUE

b. **DO 9 I = 2,6,2**
   DO 8 J = 1,5,3
     . . .
     . . .
     . . .
   8 CONTINUE
   9 CONTINUE

6. How many times will the following inner DO loops be repeated?

a. **DO 17 J = 1,5**
   DO 15 I = 1,4
     . . .
     . . .
     . . .
   15 CONTINUE
   17 CONTINUE

b. **DO 10 MM = 1,9,3**
   DO 11 JJ = 2,7,2
     . . .
     . . .
     . . .
   11 CONTINUE
   10 CONTINUE

7. Locate the errors in the following DO statements.
   a. **DO 20 K = 1,K,1**
   b. **DO 30, I = 1,10,1**
   c. **DO 40 ICOUNTER = 1, L**

   d. **DO 50 J = 1,N,J + 1**
   e. **DO 60 M = 1,20, -1**

8. Locate the errors in the following DO statements.
   a. **DO 10 A = 1,5**
   b. **DO 20 K = 0,5,.5**
   c. **DO LOOP = 2,20,2**

   d. **DO 30 MAXIMUM = 100, 500, 10**
   e. **DO 40 N = 1, N, 2+J**

10.14 PROGRAMMING PROBLEMS

1. Write a FORTRAN program to sum the integers from 1 through 100. Write a literal title that says 'SUM OF INTEGERS 1–100 =' followed by the accumulated sum. Use a DO statement.

2. Write a FORTRAN program to sum the odd integers from 1 through 99. Write a literal title that says 'SUM OF ODD INTEGERS 1–99 =' followed by the accumulated sum. Use a DO statement.

3. Write a FORTRAN program to sum the even integers from 2 through 50. Write a literal title that says, 'SUM OF EVEN INTEGERS 2–50 =' followed by the accumulated sum. Use a DO statement.

4. Write a program to prepare a table of simple interest according to the formula i = prt. Let principal = 45000 and rate = 8.5 percent. Use a DO statement to vary time from 1 to 20 years. Write the output results on double-spaced lines with field specifications as follows:

Field Description	Print Positions
Time	1–2 (Format code of I2)
Principal	6–13 (Format code of F8.2)
Rate	17–21 (Format code of F5.3)
Interest	25–32 (Format code of F8.2)

5. Write a program to prepare a table of squares and cubes of the integers 100–110. Use a DO statement to vary the integer number. Write double-spaced output lines with field specifications as follows:

Field Description	Print Positions
Number	5–7 (Format code of I3)
Square	10–14 (Format code of I5)
Cube	20–26 (Format code of I7)

Include appropriate column headings.

6. A student borrows $200.00 at an interest rate of 1½ percent per month on the unpaid balance. If the student pays $10.00 at the end of each month, what is the remaining balance at the end of one year?

   Write a program that includes a DO loop to solve this problem. The mathematics involved is as follows: The interest for the first month is the balance ($200) times .015 = $3.00. Since $10 is paid each month, the balance after the first payment is $200 plus $3.00 less $10.00 = $193.00.

   Write output results with appropriate literal titles for the original loan, interest rate, payment, and balance at the end of the year.

7. Write a program to perform the same function as problem six, but also to build a table of balance, amount paid, and interest paid. The interest rate will be 1½ percent per month on the unpaid balance. Read input values for the original loan amount and payment amount in the following record positions:

Record Positions	Field Description
1–7	Loan amount (Form = NNNN.NN)
8–12	Payment amount (Form = NN.NN)

In addition to computing the new balance, accumulate the total interest paid for the year. Use a DO loop.

   Write each output line double-spaced with the following values:

Field Description	Print Positions
Month (1–12)	3–4
Balance at beginning of the month	10–16
Interest	22–27
Payment	33–37
Balance at the end of the month	43–49

Print the total interest paid and the total amount of payments at the end of the table. Include appropriate column headings.

8. Write a program to compute grades for a class. The first data record serves as a header with the number of students in the class contained in record positions 1–3. The remaining student data records are laid out as follows:

Record Positions	Field Description
1–5	Student ID (Form = NNNNN)
6–8	Score 1 (Form = NNN)
9–11	Score 2 (Form = NNN)
12–14	Score 3 (Form = NNN)
15–17	Score 4 (Form = NNN)
18–20	Score 5 (Form = NNN)

Compute the average grade for each student. Also compute the average score for each of the five test scores. Perform these calculations in the DO loop to read multiple data records.

Print student output records double-spaced as follows:

Field Description	Print Positions
Student ID	2–6
Score 1	10–12
Score 2	16–18
Score 3	22–24
Score 4	28–30
Score 5	34–36
Sum	40–45 (Form = NNN.NN)
Average	50–55 (Form = NNN.NN)

After all student records have been output, print the average of each of the test scores beneath the respective scores of each student. Include appropriate column headings.

9. Write a program to compute the sum of the reciprocal of the integers from 1 through 10. The reciprocal of a number is simply the number 1 divided by that number. For example, the reciprocal of 2 is ½. The sum of the reciprocals from 1 to 3 is $\frac{1}{1} + \frac{1}{2} + \frac{1}{3}$. Use a DO loop and also real arithmetic. Write the output result preceded by the literal title, 'THE SUM OF THE RECIPROCALS FROM 1–10 IS'.

11 Subscript Operations and One-dimensional Arrays

11.1 INTRODUCTION TO THE CONCEPTS OF ARRAYS

In reading, processing, and outputting data we are often concerned with groups of related items. For example, earlier in the text, programs were developed to compute student grades. Unique variable names were assigned to each test score and used when needed to refer to that particular score. Variables that contain a single value are known technically as **scalar variables**. It often becomes convenient to refer to related items by relative position numbers in a group of variables rather than by unique variable names. For example, you could refer to the first test score as NTEST(1), the second as NTEST(2), the third as NTEST(3), and so on. These types of variables are known as **subscripted variables**.

Some programs are written to store large quantities of related data that must be retained in memory for manipulation. This technique of using subscripted variables becomes much more convenient as the list of related items gets longer. Say, for example, that you had 20 test scores that you wanted to read, compute the sum and average, and output the input values and results. It would take a great deal of time coding the variable names for the READ, Assignment, and WRITE statements if unique names were assigned to each test score. It would certainly be convenient if one common name could be assigned to all the test scores and if some shortcut could be found to refer to each of the scores.

FORTRAN allows you to do this with subscripted array elements, which specify a common name for a group of related items and enclose a numeric value within a set of parentheses following the common name. The numeric value within parentheses indicates which item we are referring to—the first, second, third, and so forth. Say you have four test scores of 100, 86, 79, and 90, to which the common name, NTEST is assigned. This concept of referring to the values of NTEST(1), NTEST(2), NTEST(3), and NTEST(4) is illustrated below.

storage locations

100	86	79	90
(1)	**(2)**	**(3)**	**(4)**

NTEST

These are four memory locations containing the four test scores. The group of related storage locations is called an **array**. An array containing a collection of values in this manner can be thought of simply as a linear **list** or a **row** of items. In mathematical terms, an array such as this is called a **vector**.

The name NTEST refers to the entire array or collection of the four test scores previously described. Each storage location or item within the array is referred to as an **array element**. Each array element can be referenced by the array name, followed by its element number enclosed within parentheses. For example, to refer to the third element or item in the array, you would specify NTEST(3). (Read as "NTEST sub 3".)

Array element numbers simply relate to the position of the elements in the array. The element number is referred to as a **subscript**. Thus, a subscript value identifies the position of an element within an array, or the particular array element you are referencing.

The term **subscript** in FORTRAN has the same meaning as the subscripts 1, 2, and 3 in the set of mathematical terms X_1, X_2, and X_3. In FORTRAN, however, subscripts are placed in parentheses following the variable name to which they apply, i.e., X(1), X(2), X(3). Remember in FORTRAN, you must code all characters at the same level on a line; you cannot represent subscripts slightly below and to the right of the array name, the way you can in a mathematical notation; so parentheses are used in FORTRAN to indicate that a subscript value follows.

In math you can refer to a subscripted item of array X as X_i, where "i" can take on any numeric value within the total number of items. If there are ten items in a group, the "i" can take on a value from 1 to 10. The same concept can be used with array items in FORTRAN.

A subscript in FORTRAN can be a variable as well as a constant. For example, you could refer to NTEST(I). If the variable I had a value of 2, then you would be referring to NTEST(2). If the value of I is altered to contain a 4, then NTEST(I) would refer to NTEST(4). The use of variables as subscripts is the means to achieving brevity, flexibility, and power in using arrays.

To sum twenty test scores in a 20-element array called NTEST could be done in a DO loop as follows:

```
          NSUM = 0
          DO 7 I = 1,20
             NSUM = NSUM + NTEST(I)
        7 CONTINUE
```

Each pass through the DO loop, the value of I is incremented by 1; so the element of the array that I is pointing to is added to the variable, NSUM. This method is much more concise than adding twenty unique variable names in an Assignment statement and certainly takes far less time to code and keypunch.

You should now begin to see the power and flexibility to be obtained by using arrays. Suppose you had two 1,000-element arrays called ITEMNR and ITMQTY. ITEMNR contains the part number of 1,000 items in inventory. The array, ITMQTY, contains the quantity on hand for each of the corresponding part numbers. That is, ITMQTY(1) contains the quantity on hand for ITEMNR(1), and so on.

Now, if you wanted to see if any part number had a depleted quantity on hand (balance of zero), you could do this very easily with the use of arrays. The following statements will check for the quantity-on-hand balance for all part numbers. If a part number has a zero quantity-on-hand balance, that part number will be printed so a reorder requisition can be issued.

```
          DO 8 I = 1, 1000
             IF (ITMQTY(I) .EQ. 0) WRITE (6,99) ITEMNR(I)
       99    FORMAT (1H0,I7)
        8 CONTINUE
```

Can you guess what you would have to do if you had stored the 1,000 part numbers and their quantities on hand under unique variable names? Yes, you would need 1,000 Logical IF statements to accomplish the same task. Not counting the input and output operations, you would have lots of coding to do. By using arrays, this can be a very simple operation requiring very few statements.

To permit the operation of subscripting (or indexing, as it is sometimes called), all the elements in an array must be in adjacent memory locations. The DIMENSION statement in FORTRAN tells the compiler to establish an array for the given name and to set up the elements in contiguous storage locations.

An array representing a list of related items is called a **one-dimensional array**. In a one-dimensional array, only one subscript value is needed to locate any array element.

Arrays have become a very powerful tool in computer programming. Using them can make writing an otherwise long, unwieldly program both feasible and easy. Arrays are often confusing at first for beginning programmers. Don't get frustrated; many others have had to cross this barrier before. Simply reread the chapter and contemplate on the concept being presented. It will help if you draw boxes for the array elements and keep track of the values in each element as you step through some of the examples. It is also important to jot down the beginning value of the subscript used and to alter its value as the value in the examples changes. In that way, you can keep track of what is really happening when working with array items.

First, let us see how the DIMENSION statement tells the computer that an array is being used.

DIMENSION arrayname₁(size₁),. . ., arraynameₙ(sizeₙ)

where:

arrayname — is a symbolic name assigned to an array and must be consistent with the type of data contained in the array (unless the Explicit Type statement is used).

size — is a list of up to three unsigned integer constants. Each constant represents one dimension of the array and the maximum number of elements for that level of dimension. If more than one constant is used, they are separated by commas.

Figure 11.1 General notation of the DIMENSION statement

11.2 THE DIMENSION STATEMENT

The DIMENSION statement is a specification statement to the FORTRAN compiler to establish arrays. An array name must be assigned for the collection of items. The compiler must know the size (number of elements) of the array in order to set up that many adjacent memory locations. These specifications are given in the DIMENSION statement as illustrated below.

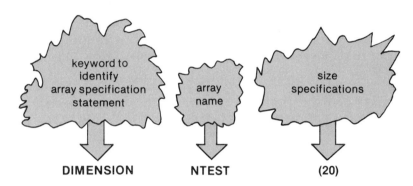

keyword to identify array specification statement

array name

size specifications

DIMENSION　　　　**NTEST**　　　　**(20)**

The general form of the DIMENSION statement is given in figure 11.1.
Examples of the DIMENSION statement are:

DIMENSION X(10), Y(10)
DIMENSION LISTA(25)

The first example establishes the array X as a 10-element, one-dimensional array and the array Y as a 10-element, one-dimensional array. The second example establishes the name LISTA as a 25-element, one-dimensional array.

If more than one array is used in a program, all may be listed in the same DIMENSION statement, or several DIMENSION statements may be given. Commas must be used to separate each of the array specifications whenever multiple arrays are given in the same DIMENSION statement. The allowance of multiple DIMENSION statements in a program provides the flexibility needed if new arrays are to be added later. Suppose there are three arrays: A, B, and C. You could specify:

DIMENSION A(5), B(7), C(3)

or

DIMENSION A(5)
DIMENSION B(7), C(3)

or any arrangement you wish. The three arrays could be coded either as three separate DIMENSION statements or as one combined statement.

Arrays may also be declared and dimensioned with the Explicit Type statement. For example:

REAL X(10), Y(10), L(10)
REAL TABLE (250)
INTEGER LIST(25)
INTEGER J(5), K(17), TAB(40)

The first example dimensions the three real arrays X, Y, and L with ten elements each. The second example declares TABLE to be a real array with 250 elements. The third example declares LIST to be an integer array with 25 elements. The fourth example declares J, K, and TAB to be integer arrays. Array J will contain 5 elements, array K 17 elements, and array TAB 40 elements.

An array may not be declared in *both* a DIMENSION statement and an Explicit Type statement in ANSI FORTRAN 66, WATFOR, or WATFIV. Some FORTRAN IV compilers, however, permit an array to be declared in both statements. The common rule is to declare an array in the DIMENSION statement unless you want to override the standard FORTRAN naming convention in specifying the array type.

Array names are formed like any other variable name in FORTRAN. The type of array name assigned must always agree with the type of the data to be stored in the array. Thus, an integer array name must be used when the array contains integer values. Likewise, a real array name must be used to store real numeric values. (Again, the Explicit Type statement may be used to override the predefined naming convention.) All elements in an array must contain the same type of data, e.g., integer or real.

Dimension information in a "mainline" program must always be given as a numeric integer in FORTRAN. You cannot give a dimension value as a variable and expect to assign a value to the variable at execution to denote the size of the array. For example, the following specification is **illegal:**

DIMENSION X(N)   (Note: this is illegal)
READ (5,99) N
99 FORMAT (I2)

An integer value must be provided for each dimensional value so the compiler will know what size array to establish at compile time.

Since the DIMENSION statement is a nonexecutable specification statement, it must precede any executable FORTRAN statement. No statement number should be assigned to the DIMENSION statement.

Before we look at the operations with one-dimensional arrays, let us discuss subscripts in more detail.

11.3 SUBSCRIPTS

A **subscript**, as defined above, is an integer quantity enclosed in parentheses and used to identify an array element. A subscript may also consist of a *set* of integer quantities separated by commas to identify an array element in a multidimensioned array. The subscript must be written immediately after the name of the array containing the data item being referenced.

Do not confuse the term **subscript** with dimension specifications. Dimension specifications are provided within the set of parentheses with the DIMENSION statement. Subscripts are references to subscripted variables (array items) in executable statements within a program.

The number of values contained in the subscript reference must be the same as the number of dimensions of the referenced array. That is, if A is a one-dimensional array, only one value can be specified in the subscript. The reference A(I,J), for example, would be invalid.

The value of any subscript must always lie between one and the number of elements declared in the dimension of the array, inclusively (i.e., 1 through n). If a one-dimensional array X is dimensioned as X(10), then the value of the subscript must range between 1 and 10, inclusive.

What happens if a programmer accidentally gives an invalid value to a subscript? This can easily happen when a subscript is a variable or an arithmetic expression. If the value of the subscript is zero or negative, most computer systems will detect the error. An error message will be printed and the program terminated. If the subscript is larger than the largest permitted element number, however, many FORTRAN compilers will use an address past the end of the array and keep on executing, with the invalid results.

Finding the invalid subscript is a very difficult problem. You may use erroneous values both from accessing storage locations past the array and from storing values past the array elements. A printout of all the subscript values and their corresponding array elements is usually the best way to debug the invalid subscript problem. Section 11.8 explains this method.

Subscript values may also be other than an integer constant or variable. They may contain arithmetic expressions such as:

$$\text{ITEM } (K + 5)$$
$$\text{LIST } (2*I - 1)$$

The following table illustrates the seven different forms that a legal subscript may take in ANSI FORTRAN 66:

Seven General Forms of a Subscript	Example
Constant	7
Variable	J
Variable + constant	I + 2
Variable − constant	K − 1
Constant * variable	3 * INDEX
Constant * variable + constant	4*I + 3
Constant * variable − constant	2*N − 1

The restrictions regarding valid subscript forms can easily be circumvented by performing the computations in an Assignment statement just before the statement containing the subscript reference. For example, the subscript reference $A(I/M + N)$ is invalid, but you could compute $J = I/M + N$ and then use $A(J)$ as a valid reference.

The use of arithmetic expressions to specify a subscript value often provides much flexibility in programming techniques. If you wish to compare an array element with the next element, you could write (using array A):

$$\text{IF } (A(I).GE.A(I + 1)). . .$$

You are now ready to tackle some problems that use arrays. We shall begin with the manipulation of one-dimensional arrays.

11.4 MANIPULATING ONE-DIMENSIONAL ARRAY ITEMS

You can manipulate the values in array elements in many different ways. Array items can be used in various computations, arrays can be searched for specific values, and the values in any or all array elements can be changed. Arrays can also be initialized or loaded with values that are computed in Assignment statements. There are so many things you can do with arrays that only some of the more common techniques can be covered.

Initializing Array Elements

Array elements are often loaded by reading and storing input values into them. Sometimes it is required that all or selected items in an array be initialized (given a value) to the same current value. This is especially true with work arrays in which values are added to various elements. The value of each element is usually set to zero. The routine to initialize the 100 elements in array X to zero is:

$$\text{DIMENSION X(100)}$$
$$\text{DO 25 I = 1,100}$$
$$\text{X(I) = 0.0}$$
$$\text{25 CONTINUE}$$

Many FORTRAN compilers automatically initialize array elements to zero, but this is not done on all machines (such as IBM). Therefore, it is good programming practice to initialize all arrays before their use.

Let us take another example of generating values for a one-dimensional array. A routine will be written to fill a five-element array named K with values that are two times that of the subscript-number containing them. That is, the value 2 will be stored at K(1), the value 4 stored at K(2), and so on. The routine is:

```
INTEGER ELEMNR
DIMENSION K(5)
DO 20 ELEMNR = 1, 5
    K(ELEMNR) = 2 *ELEMNR
20 CONTINUE
```

There are five values generated by the DO loop index variable ELEMNR, which represents the five element numbers in the array K. The index variable ELEMNR is multiplied by two, and the resulting value is stored at the element number being referenced. The filled array contains the following values:

Array K

2	4	6	8	10

element number   1   2   3   4   5

Summing Array Elements

A common operation with arrays is to sum the values in all the elements. Suppose you sum the ten elements in the array NTEST, containing ten test scores. The array items could be easily summed in a DO loop as follows:

```
DIMENSION NTEST(10)
. . .
. . .
DO 25 I = 1, 10
    NSUM = NSUM + NTEST(I)
25 CONTINUE
```

The index variable I varies from 1 through 10 and allows each array item to be added to the variable NSUM.

To understand how an array element of NTEST is referenced, put ten values in the array and step through the execution of the loop. Write three titles on a sheet of paper as follows:

I   NTEST(I)   NSUM

Fill in the values under the respective columns for each pass of the DO loop. The variable I (used as the subscript) will have the values 1 through 10 listed under its column. Then list the value in the element number pointed to by the subscript I under the NTEST(I) column. The value of NSUM will increase as each new element number of NTEST is referenced and its value added to NSUM. You may prefer to write the element number beside each value in NTEST for easy reference.

Creating Duplicate Arrays

There are times when the contents of one array need to be stored into another array. A duplicate array may be necessary to retain the values from the original array while performing manipulations that change its values. The routine for storing the contents of one array into another is as follows:

```
DIMENSION A(50), AHOLD(50)
. . .
. . .
DO 85 I = 1,50
    AHOLD(I) = A(I)
85 CONTINUE
```

It would be nice simply to code

AHOLD = A

but you can't. Any time an array is used in an Assignment statement, a subscript must be included to refer to a specific element in the array. You cannot reference all values in an array in an assignment operation. Each value must be referenced individually.

Suppose you wish to store the contents of array A into another array, B, in reverse sequence. This can easily be done as follows:

```
          DIMENSION A(100), B(100)
          . . .

          . . .
          DO 95 I = 1,100
              B(101-I) = A(I)
      95  CONTINUE
```

The subscript value of 101-I allows you to reference the upper position of array B and work backwards. That is, A(1) is stored in B(100), A(2) in B(99), and so on down to where A(100) is stored into B(1).

Simple Operations with Selected Array Elements

You do not have to manipulate all of the items for an array in a routine. Individual array elements may be referenced as needed. Consider the following examples.

An array element may be used in a calculation to produce a new value for a variable.

$$RESULT = A * X(3) - 5.6 / R$$

A single array item may be changed by a computation in a routine.

$$X(K) = R + S / 7.5$$

An array element may be used in an IF statement to make a decision.

$$IF\ (X(J)\ .LT.\ 0.0)\ GO\ TO\ 82$$

In other words, selected array elements may be used in various FORTRAN statements in any way the program design dictates. Now let us look at input/output operations with one-dimensional arrays.

11.5   INPUT/OUTPUT OPERATIONS WITH ONE-DIMENSIONAL ARRAY ITEMS

There are three ways you can load (fill) an array with data items or write the items in an array. First, you can specify a subscripted variable as an item in the I/O list of the READ or WRITE statements; second, you can read and write an entire array of items by specifying just the array name by itself in the I/O list; third, you can use a special option called the implied DO loop in the I/O list to specify as many subscripted variables as desired.

Array Input Operations

Let us examine the first technique: reading individually subscripted variables in the I/O list. Assume that seven test scores are punched in columns 1–3 on separate data cards. A DO loop could be written to load the array, NTEST, as follows:

```
          DIMENSION NTEST(7)
          DO 10 I = 1,7
              READ (5,99) NTEST (I)
      99      FORMAT (I3)
      10  CONTINUE
```

The subscript, I, will take on a value of from 1 through 7 from the index variable in the DO statement, and each new test score will be placed in the next element number of the array.

You can also manipulate each subscripted variable as it is read into memory. Suppose you wish to sum all the test scores under the variable NSUM. The following statements show how you could accumulate this sum inside the same DO loop that is used to load each array item.

```
          DIMENSION NTEST(7)
          NSUM = 0
          DO 10 I = 1,7
              READ (5,99) NTEST(I)
```

```
99      FORMAT (I3)
        NSUM = NSUM + NTEST(I)
10 CONTINUE
        AVE = NSUM / 7
```

After the DO loop is completed, the sum of the seven array items is in the variable NSUM. Thus, you can compute the average of the seven scores under the variable AVE.

You are not limited to reading only one subscripted variable in the I/O list. You can include as many as desired. They can also be interspersed with nonsubscripted variables whenever the need occurs. Consider the following two examples:

```
        DIMENSION X(10), Y(10)
        DO 20 I = 1,10
            READ (5,98) X(I), Y(I)
98          FORMAT (F5.2,3X,F5.2)
20 CONTINUE

        DIMENSION A(15), B(15)
        J = 1
 1 READ (5,97) NR1, A(J), NR2, B(J)
97 FORMAT (I3,F4.2,I3,F4.2)
        IF (NR1 .EQ. 999) GO TO 30
        J = J + 1
        . . .

        . . .
        GO TO 1
30 . . .
```

The first of these examples shows how a subscripted variable of array X and Y are read from the same data record. The second example shows how nonsubscripted and subscripted variables can be intermixed in the I/O list. The variables NR1 and NR2 store the firsts and third data fields as nonsubscripted variables; the second and fourth data fields, however, are loaded into the Jth element of arrays A and B, respectively.

The second example also illustrates the technique of loading a variable number of items into an array. The variable J is used to count the number of items loaded into arrays, so that you can keep track of how many data items are in the array. That is, you do not have to load the complete array. Any portion of the array elements can be loaded.

The second technique for loading arrays is the easiest of all. You can read and store all items in an array simply by giving the array name *without* any subscript references in the I/O list. Some instructors refer to giving only the array name in the I/O list as the "short list" option. Let us assume the same problem as in example 1; we wish to load seven test scores contained on separate data records into the array NTEST. You could simply code:

```
        DIMENSION NTEST(7)
        READ (5,99) NTEST
99 FORMAT (I2)
```

Remember, when the end of a FORMAT statement is reached, the computer reads a new data record if the I/O list has not only been completely exhausted.

Using only the array name to load an array is simpler. It also produces far more efficient object code than the first technique. The computer begins loading the first data item at the first array element and continues loading subsequent data items at the next higher array element until the array is completely loaded.

The array name used by itself in this way acts as a reference to the entire array. It is very important to remember that the array name by itself can only be included in the I/O list of a READ or WRITE statement. You cannot use the array name by itself to manipulate all array items in a single Assignment statement, such as LISTA = 0, where LISTA is an array name. In all other FORTRAN statements array items must be referenced as individually subscripted items (except with subprograms, which will be discussed in chapters 13 and 15).

The only drawback to using the array name by itself to load array items is the fact that all items in the array must be loaded. If you wish to load only some of the items in an array you cannot use the array name by itself. Use of the array name in the I/O list causes the computer to try to load as many items into the array as are specified in the DIMENSION statement specifications.

Now let us discuss the third technique. Assume seven test scores are contained in the same data record as follows:

89 92 78 86 97 83 90

The test scores are to be read into a ten-element array NTEST. You could not use a DO loop with a READ as in example 1 to read the scores. Each time the READ statement is executed, at least one input card must be read.

To read the seven test scores as subscripted variables as in technique one, you would have to code the input operations as follows:

```
        DIMENSION NTEST(10)
        READ(5,96) NTEST(1), NTEST(2), NTEST(3), NTEST(4),
     *           NTEST(5), NTEST(6), NTEST(7)
     96 FORMAT(7I3)
```

If this is to be the case, then you might as well go back to nonsubscripted variables. Nor can the array name technique be used, since you are not loading the entire array. Is the long way, as shown in the previous example, the only way out? No, it is not. There is another technique that can be used especially for situations like this.

The third technique used for reading and loading array elements incorporates one or more DO loops in the I/O list. A DO loop in the I/O list is referred to as an **implied DO**. An implied DO can only be used in the I/O list of READ and WRITE statements.

The implied DO option is the most flexible method of reading and loading array items. Array items are treated as subscripted variables; yet all or any portion of the array can be loaded. Input values may be on separate data records or combined onto one or more data records.

The function of the implied DO is to provide multiple subscripted variable names in an I/O list. A variable is used as the subscript value of an array reference, and the subscript value is varied in the implied DO to reference as many or as few subscripted variables as desired. Not only is this a very powerful means of referencing multiple array elements in an I/O list, but it also provides a very concise way of doing so.

The implied DO is formed very much like the DO statement, except that the keyword DO and a range statement number are omitted. An index variable, an initialization value, a test value, and an optional increment value are specified along with a subscripted array name. All these parameters are enclosed within a set of parentheses. A comma must separate the subscripted array name from the index variable.

Now back to the problem: to read seven test scores into the first seven elements of the 10-element array NTEST. This can be accomplished easily by using the implied DO in the I/O list as follows:

```
        DIMENSION NTEST(10)
        READ (5,96) (NTEST(I),I=1,7)
     96 FORMAT (7I3)
```

In the READ statement:

READ (5, 96) (NTEST (I), I = 1, 7)

implied DO

notice how the indexing parameters in the implied DO correspond to those in the DO statement. The same rules which govern the indexing parameters in a DO statement govern the indexing parameters in the implied DO. Remember, the index variable must always be an integer variable.

There are many variations of the implied DO that can be used in an I/O list. More examples of the implied DO with one-dimensional arrays are as follows:

READ (5,98) (A(I),I=1,N), B, C
READ (5,97) W, (X(J),J=N1,N2,N3), V
READ (5,96) (Y(I),I=1,5), (Z(I),I=1,3)
READ (5,95) N, (A(I), I=1,N)

The first example illustrates how to read N number of values into the array A, followed by the nonsubscripted variables B and C. The second example first reads the nonsubscripted variable W; then a certain number of data values are read into array X beginning at the position indicated by the variable N1 until the variable of J is greater than the variable N2. J is incremented by the variable N3; finally, a value is read into the variable V. The third example reads five data values into the array Y and then reads three data values into the array Z. Of course, the associated FORMAT statements (which are not given) dictate how the items will be read off the input records. The fourth example reads the value of N, which determines how many array items to read for the array A. The value of N may be included on the same data record as the array items.

All items in the implied DO must be read before continuing on in the I/O list. In the third implied DO example above, all of the values of array Y are read before the values of array Z. The index variable I varies from 1–5 inside the first implied DO, so the five subscripted variables of Y are loaded. In the second implied DO of the same example, the index variable I is reset to 1 and is incremented by one to read the first three values of the array Z.

You are not limited to only one subscripted variable within an implied DO. Assume that there are twenty values for an array X and twenty values for an array Y. A value of X is typed in columns 1–5 followed by a value of Y typed in columns 10–14. Each value of X (along with a value of Y) is contained in a separate record. To load the twenty values of array X and Y, the implied DO would be as follows:

DIMENSION X(20),Y (20)
READ (5,95) (X(I),Y(I),I=1,20)
95 FORMAT (F5.2,4X,F5.2)

The index variable I is used for each subscripted variable in the implied DO before it is incremented. Thus, X(1), Y(1), X(2), Y(2),. . .,X(20), Y(20) are read in that order.

Let us proceed to the output operations with arrays. The same three techniques used to load array elements can be used to write array elements.

Array Output Operations

To write the seven test scores on separate print lines, you could use a subscripted variable. Using the first technique of individual subscripted variables, the routine is:

DIMENSION NTEST(7)
. . .
. . .
DO 35 I = 1,7
    WRITE (6,99) NTEST(I)
99   FORMAT (1H0,I3)
35 CONTINUE

The subscript I will take on a value from 1 through 7 from the index variable in the DO statement. Thus, each test score will be taken from the referenced array element and written on a separate double-spaced print line.

The array name technique could be used to accomplish the same output. Using the array name to output an array is easier and also more efficient. The output routine is:

DIMENSION NTEST(7)
. . .
. . .
WRITE (6,99) NTEST
99 FORMAT (1H0,I3)

The implied DO technique to output array items could also be used. The output routine using the implied DO is:

```
          DIMENSION NTEST(7)
          . . .

          . . .
          WRITE (6,99) (NTEST(I), I = 1,7)
       99 FORMAT (1H0,I3)
```

But what if you needed the seven test scores to be printed on the same line? Could you use the subscripted variable technique? Yes, you could. But you would also need to use integer subscripts as follows:

```
          DIMENSION NTEST(7)
          . . .

          . . .
          WRITE(6,98) NTEST(1), NTEST(2), NTEST(3), NTEST(4),
        *            NTEST(5), NTEST(6), NTEST(7)
       98 FORMAT(1X,7I6)
```

Again, this technique is very awkward and time-consuming.

The best method is to use the array name technique, and write the entire array. The routine is:

```
          DIMENSION NTEST(7)
          . . .

          . . .
          WRITE (6,98) NTEST
       98 FORMAT (1X,7I6)
```

Or, you could use an implied DO to produce the same output. The implied DO routine is:

```
          DIMENSION NTEST(7)
          . . .

          . . .
          WRITE (6,98) (NTEST(I), I = 1,7)
       98 FORMAT (1X,7I6)
```

Notice that the format specifications specify the form of the output results in both the array name and implied DO techniques.

But what if you had a ten-element array to hold the test scores and you only wanted to output the first seven? The array name could not be used, inasmuch as you do not wish to output all the array items. In this case, you must use the implied DO. The routine is:

```
          DIMENSION NTEST(10)
          . . .

          . . .
          WRITE (6,98) (NTEST(I), I = 1,7)
       98 FORMAT (1X,7I6)
```

The array name is the easiest to use and the most efficient of the three output techniques. Remember, you can use it only to output **all** the elements in an array. As many items will be written as given in the DIMENSION statement specifications.

Nonsubscripted variables may be included in the I/O list along with subscripted variables, array names, and/or the implied DO loop. The format specifications are of the utmost importance, since they control the formatting of the output results. Consider the following two examples:

```
          DIMENSION NTEST(7)
          . . .

          . . .
          DO 45 J = 1,7
          WRITE (6,97) J, NTEST(J)
       97 FORMAT (1H0,I1,3X,I3)
       45 CONTINUE
```

This routine writes the value of J along with its associated array element (test score) on each line. The second example is:

```
          DIMENSION X(10), Y(10)
          . . .

          . . .
          WRITE (6,96) X,Y
       96 FORMAT (11H0X ARRAY = , 10F8.2/
        *          11H0Y ARRAY = , 10F8.2)
```

This routine writes the ten values of the array X on a line followed by the ten values of Y on a new double-spaced line. Each set of array values is preceded by a literal to identify the array.

The real power and flexibility in writing array values with or without nonsubscripted variables are found in the implied DO. You must use the implied DO whenever you wish to dump (output) portions of an array. Consider the following examples using the implied DO.

Suppose you want the values in array X to be printed first, followed by the values in array Y. The routine is:

```
          DIMENSION X(7), Y(5)
          . . .

          . . .
          WRITE (6,94) (X(I),I=1,7), (Y(I),I=1,5)
       94 FORMAT (1X,7F8.2,5X,5F8.2)
```

Since there are two implied DO loops, the first one will be completed before the second is started.

You can include nonsubscripted variables—and even the index variable itself—inside the implied DO loop to be printed. For example:

```
          DIMENSION X(10), Y(10)
          . . .

          . . .
          WRITE (6,95) (I,X(I), Y(I),I=1,10)
       95 FORMAT (1X,I2,3X,F5.2,3X,F5.2)
```

This routine writes the value of I followed by the referenced element of array X and Y on the same line. That is, 1, X(1), and Y(1) are written on the first line; 2, X(2), and Y(2) on the second line; and so on.

Nonsubscripted variables may be included in the I/O list with any implied DO loops. For example:

```
          DIMENSION X(10)
          . . .

          . . .
          WRITE (6,94) A, (X(I), I=1,10)
       94 FORMAT (1X,F5.2,3X,10F8.2)
```

This routine writes the value of A only once, since it is outside the implied DO. Then the ten values in the array X follow on the same line.

There are many variations of the examples covered to illustrate the techniques of array I/O operations. There is no one correct technique to use all the time. The technique chosen depends upon the format of your input data and the desired output results.

Now let's look at some other operations in which the entire array is manipulated. Section 11.6 discusses some of the searching operations performed with arrays.

11.6 SEARCHING OPERATIONS WITH ONE-DIMENSIONAL ARRAYS

There are times when you may want to find the smallest or largest item in an array or to look for a particular value or even count how many times a certain value occurs in an array. All these routines require a search of the items in an array.

Searching is the process of examining each of the items in an array according to some specific criterion. The criterion may be to find the smallest or largest value, or some other specific value. All of the elements in the array are normally tested during the search operation. Only when you wish to find the first item that matches a specific value is the searching process terminated without going through the entire array.

The simplest search technique is the straight **sequential search**. This search method is also referred to as a **serial** or a **linear search.** You simply start at position one and proceed in a sequential manner through the array. The search is over when a specific item is found or when the end of the array is reached, depending upon the problem requirements.

When the DO loop is used, the sequential search is a very easy routine to write. The initialization parameter is set to one, the test parameter is set to the number of items in our array, and the value one is used for the increment parameter. The array item pointed to by the index variable is, therefore, evaluated on each pass of the loop.

Searching an Array for a Specific Value

Looking for a specific value in an array is a very common requirement in many programs. An array is often searched to locate a specific pay grade, part number, account number, and so on. You may just want to verify its validity or to use the value's element number in accessing other array elements in later processing.

Assume you want to search a 100-element array, X, for a match on the value contained in the variable SPECVL. If the value is found, a branch to the routine at statement number 40 will be made. Otherwise, an error message is printed.

The routine to search array X for a match of the value in SPECVL is:

```
DIMENSION X(100)
. . .
. . .
DO 5 I = 1,100
    IF (X(I) .EQ. SPECVL) GO TO 40
 5 CONTINUE
   WRITE (6,99) SPECVL
99 FORMAT (1H0, 10HTHE VALUE ,F10.2, 10H NOT FOUND)
   GO TO 50
40 WRITE (6,98) SPECVL, I
98 FORMAT (1H0, 10HTHE VALUE ,F10.2, 18H FOUND AT POSITION , I3)
50 . . .
```

If the value of SPECVL is found, the location of X(I) is still retained in I, since a transfer is made out of the loop.

Counting the Number of Times a Specific Value Appears in an Array

Frequently you need to know how many times a certain value occurs in an array. The entire array must then be searched and each item compared to a specific value. If a hit (match) is found, one is added to a counter. Assume the value to be found is in the variable SPECVL. The variable KNT will be used to keep count of the number of occurrences of SPECVL in the array. The routine to count the occurrences of SPECVL in a 100-element array X is:

```
DIMENSION X(100)
. . .
. . .
KNT = 0
DO 75 I = 1,100
     IF (X(I) .EQ. SPECVL) KNT = KNT + 1
75 CONTINUE
```

Selecting the Smallest Value in an Array

Suppose your kind instructor announced that he or she is going to eliminate your lowest test score. You would probably be overjoyed.

There are many ways you can go about finding the smallest value in an array. You might rearrange all the test scores in a descending order, so that the last one would be the lowest score. This technique would involve sorting, which is the subject of the next section. At this point, we want to learn how to perform a search operation on an array to locate the smallest value.

The array search for the lowest score is begun by assuming that the first test score is the lowest and storing its position (element number) in a hold variable named **LOW**. Then each of the array items for the test scores is compared against the array value whose position is pointed to by the subscript **LOW**. If the test score being used in the comparison is less than the score pointed to by the subscript **LOW**, that test score's position is placed into the variable **LOW**. This process is continued (in a loop) until all test scores have been compared to **TEST** **(LOW)**. When the array search is finished, the lowest test score's position (element number) will be in **LOW**. Since the first test score is assumed to be the lowest, its position (1) is stored in **LOW**, and the search is begun with the second array item. Assuming an array name of **TEST**, containing ten test scores, the search routine is given as follows:

```
INTEGER TEST (10), SBSCRP
. . .
. . .
LOW = 1
DO 55 SBSCRP = 2, 10
       IF ( TEST(SBSCRP) .LT. TEST(LOW) ) LOW = SBSCRP
55 CONTINUE
```

How can the computer be programmed to drop the lowest test score from the calculated average? You simply code an IF statement to tell the computer to bypass the accumulation operation when the index variable is equal to **LOW**. The routine to eliminate the lowest test score from the sum and compute the average of the remaining nine scores is:

```
INTEGER TEST(10), SUM, AVE, SBSCRP
. . .
. . .
SUM = 0
DO 60 SBSCRP = 1, 10
       IF (SBSCRP .EQ. LOW) GO TO 60
       SUM = SUM + TEST(SBSCRP)
60 CONTINUE
AVE = SUM / 9
```

When a match of the index variable is found with the variable **LOW**, a transfer is made around the accumulation operation; thus, the lowest score is not added to **SUM**.

The flowchart for the program logic to read the ten test scores, find the smallest score, and compute the average of the nine highest scores is presented in figure 11.2 (p. 336). The program for this problem is given in figure 11.3 (p. 337).

The sequential search technique is very slow for large arrays. If there are "N" items in the array, the average number of comparisons needed to find an item is: $(N + 1) / 2$. A more efficient technique is the **binary search**. This technique eliminates half of the items from the search after each comparison in the loop. However, all the items in the array must be arranged in an ascending (or descending) order for the binary search to work. Your instructor may give you the algorithm for a binary search if he or she feels that you should be familiar with it.

Now let's look at the subject of sorting.

11.7 SORTING ONE-DIMENSIONAL ARRAY ITEMS

Sorting is the process of arranging items into an ordered sequence. The items can be sorted in either an **ascending** order, with the smallest item appearing first, or a **descending** order, with the largest item appearing first.

Alphabetic as well as numeric items may be sorted, but we will discuss only the sorting of numeric data. All items to be sorted must be items in an array, since we will only cover sorting of data items in memory. This process is referred to as **internal sorting**. Long strings of items and files containing many data records are normally sorted using magnetic tape and disk media. This type of sorting is known as **external sorting**, which is beyond the scope of this text.

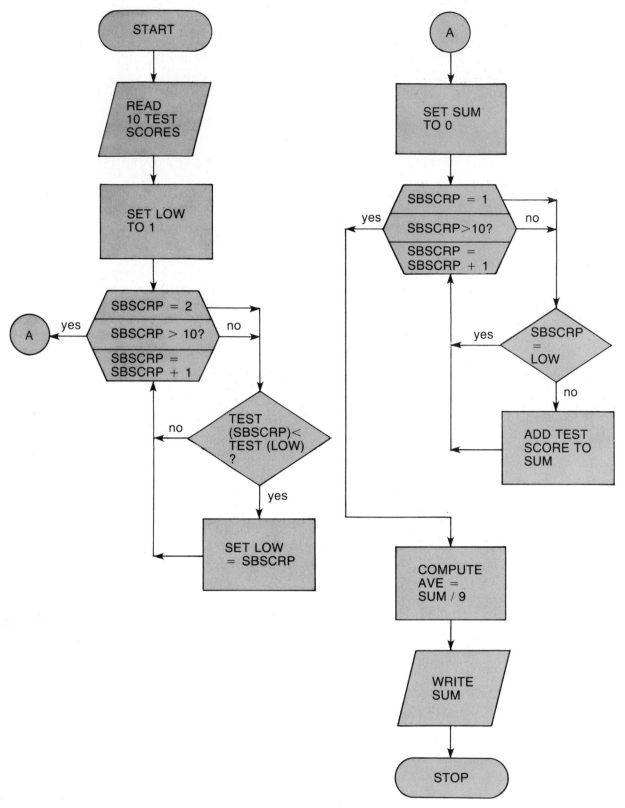

Figure 11.2 Flowchart for program to illustrate searching an array

```
C - - -      PROGRAM TO COMPUTE THE SUM AND AVERAGE OF THE
C - - -      THE HIGHEST NINE OUT OF TEN STUDENT TEST SCORES
C
  199        FORMAT (10I3)
  299        FORMAT (1H0, 10HAVERAGE = , I3)
             INTEGER TEST(10), SBSCRP, SUM, AVE
             READ (5, 199) TEST
             LOW = 1
             DO 55 SBSCRP = 2, 10
                 IF ( TEST(SBSCRP) .LT. TEST (LOW) ) LOW = SBSCRP
  55         CONTINUE
C
             SUM = 0
             DO 60 SBSCRP = 1, 10
                IF (SBSCRP .EQ. LOW) GO TO 60
                SUM = SUM + TEST(SBSCRP)
  60         CONTINUE
C
             AVE = SUM / 9
             WRITE (6, 299) SUM
             STOP
             END
```

Figure 11.3 Sample program to illustrate searching an array

To illustrate the sorting process, let us assume an array, LIST, containing four items. The values of the items are as follows:

LIST(1)   10
LIST(2)   5
LIST(3)   7
LIST(4)   3

The items are in an unsorted sequence. We wish to rank (sort) the items in an ascending order so the results arc 3, 5, 7, and 10 in array elements 1–4, respectively.

Three basic operations are needed in the sorting operation:

1. A comparison of the items with one another.
2. An interchange of the items if they are not in the desired order.
3. Multiple passes/searches through the array to order all the items correctly.

The comparison operation is necessary to determine whether the two items used in the comparison are in order. If the two items are already in order, nothing needs to be done. If they are not, however, then they are placed in order (relative to each other) by the interchange operation.

There are several ways to do the comparison operation. The first item could be compared to all the others, the items could be compared to each other in pairs, and so on. Since there are many ways to do the comparison, there are many types of sorting techniques. We will discuss only two—the **paired interchange** and the **selection-with-interchange** sort techniques.

In the **paired interchange**, you simply compare one array item to the next one. An IF statement in a DO loop is used, much like a search routine. For example:

```
             DO 25 I = 1, 3
                IF (LIST(I) .LE. LIST (I + 1) GO TO 25
                . . .
                . . .
          25 CONTINUE
```

When I is 1, you are comparing LIST(1) to LIST(2). If the quantity in LIST(1) is less than or equal to the quantity in LIST(2), then the items are already in ascending order. The first two items, however, are not in ascending order, so you need to interchange the two items to put them into the correct sequence.

The interchange operation simply switches or exchanges the two items. But you cannot code:

$$LIST(1) = LIST(2)$$
$$LIST(2) = LIST(1)$$

This would result in the quantity 5 being placed into both LIST(1) and LIST(2), since the original value of LIST(1) would be lost. A temporary variable is needed to hold one item and allow you to interchange the two items properly. See the diagram below (LTEMP is used for the temporary variable).

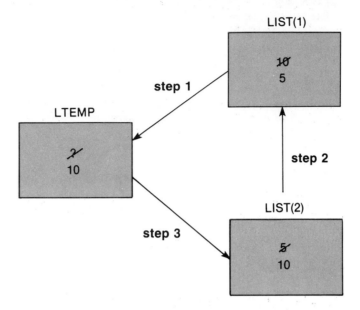

The top numbers in the boxes (crossed out) represent their original value before the interchange operation. The bottom number is the value after the interchange operation. The step numbers indicate the order of the operations. The value of LIST(1) is first stored into LTEMP; then LIST(2) is stored into LIST(1); finally, the value retained in LTEMP is stored into LIST(2).

The interchange operation must apply to any two items interchanged in the loop, so we use the index variable for the subscript. The coded interchange operation is:

$$LTEMP = LIST(I)$$
$$LIST(I) = LIST(I+1)$$
$$LIST(I+1) = LTEMP$$

If the two items in the comparison are not in order, the interchange operation is performed. Thus, the interchange statements are coded in the original DO loop as follows:

```
        DO 25 I=1,3
           IF (LIST(I) .LE. LIST(I+1)) GO TO 25
           LTEMP = LIST(I)
           LIST(I) = LIST(I+1)
           LIST(I+1) = LTEMP
     25 CONTINUE
```

If LIST(I) is greater than LIST(I+1), we "fall through" into the interchange statements and exchange the two items.

The comparison loop is processed only three times, since all items would have been compared in pairs. The results of these three loops are:

	LOOP 1		LOOP 2		LOOP 3	
	Before	*After*	*Before*	*After*	*Before*	*After*
LIST(1)	10	5	5	5	5	5
LIST(2)	5	10	10	7	7	7
LIST(3)	7	7	7	10	10	3
LIST(4)	3	3	3	3	3	10

The arrows indicate the two items involved in the comparison on each loop.

The items still have not been completely sorted in ascending order. That brings us to the third necessary operation. Another loop must be included outside the comparison loop to perform additional passes through the list of array items and to get them in final sorted order. This loop is normally performed n − 1 times (where n is the number of items being sorted).

The complete sort routine is as follows:

```
                  DIMENSION LIST(4)
                     . . .
                     . . .
        C ***** PAIRED INTERCHANGE SORT FOR ASCENDING ORDER
        C ***** FIRST THE LOOP TO CONTROL NUMBER OF PASSES
                  DO 35 L = 1,3
        C ***** NOW THE LOOP TO CONTROL NUMBER OF COMPARISONS
                     DO 25 J =1,3
                        IF (LIST(J) .LE. LIST(J + 1))GO TO 25
        C ***** THE INTERCHANGE OPERATION
                        LTEMP = LIST(J)
                        LIST(J) = LIST(J + 1)
                        LIST(J + 1) = LTEMP
        25         CONTINUE
        35      CONTINUE
```

The following diagram shows the order of items after each pass of the outer loop through the list. The "before" values on passes two and three are the same as the "after" values on the previous pass.

	PASS 1		*PASS 2*	*PASS 3*
	Before	*After*	*After*	*After*
LIST(1)	10	5	5	3
LIST(2)	5	7	3	5
LIST(3)	7	3	7	7
LIST(4)	3	10	10	10

Finally the items are arranged in ascending order. I encourage you to follow the interchange operation through each loop for each pass through the list to see more clearly what is happening.

The paired interchange sort is a very inefficient technique to use, especially if the items are already in a partially sorted order. You must always make the maximum number of passes and comparisons loops (unless a technique is used to terminate the sort when no interchange is made in a pass). This technique was discussed first mainly because it more clearly illustrates the operations that take place in a sort. There are many more efficient sorting techniques. Let us now look at a better sort technique called "selection-with-interchange."

Selection-with-Interchange Sort Technique

This method searches the array for the smallest value (or largest) and places it in the first element. Then the next smallest value is found and placed in the second element, and so on. The routine is:

```
        C *** SELECTION WITH INTERCHANGE SORT FOR ASCENDING ORDER
        C *** NUMBER OF PASSES IS N − 1 ITEMS
                  NMIN1 = N − 1
                  DO 35 J = 1, NMIN1
                  JPLUS1 = J + 1
        C *** NUMBER OF COMPARISONS TO INCLUDE LAST ITEM
                     DO 25 I = JPLUS1,N
                        IF (LIST(J) .LE. LIST(I)) GO TO 25
        C *** INTERCHANGE OPERATION
                        LTEMP = LIST(J)
                        LIST(J) = LIST(I)
                        LIST(I) = LTEMP
        25         CONTINUE
        35      CONTINUE
```

Notice the use of the different subscripts in the comparison. One subscript (J) is held constant during the inner loop and indicates which array element is being used to store the smallest item. The other subscript (I) is used to search the remaining items in the list.

The order of the four items in the array LIST after each pass is as follows:

	PASS 1			PASS 2		PASS 3
	Loop 1	Loop 2	Loop 3	Loop 1	Loop 2	Loop 1
LIST(1)	5	5	3	3	3	3
LIST(2)	10	10	10	7	5	5
LIST(3)	7	7	7	10	10	7
LIST(4)	3	3	5	5	7	10
Subscript	$J=1$	$J=1$	$J=1$	$J=2$	$J=2$	$J=3$
Values are:	$I=2$	$I=3$	$I=4$	$I=3$	$I=4$	$I=4$

The selection-with-interchange reduced the number of comparisons by one-third. After the smallest value is found on the first pass, it is placed in element one, and element one is never referenced again. On each succeeding pass the next smallest element is found and moved up to its position. After $n - 1$ (3 in the problem) passes, all items will be in order. If the first $n - 1$ items are in order, the last item is bound to be in order.

After the sorting operation is completed the items in the array are rearranged according to the type of sort (ascending or descending) performed. The original array order is lost. If you are to maintain the original array, the items must be assigned to a duplicate array in which the sorting is performed.

More Efficient Sorting Techniques

When sorting a small number of array items (perhaps twenty or fewer) you should not worry too much about efficiency (the time required to sort the items). When sorting arrays with hundreds or even thousands of items, you must be concerned with time. There are vast time differences among various types of sorting techniques. Sorting time can be reduced in two ways:

1. Reducing the number of passes through the array
2. Reducing the number of exchange operations

One technique to eliminate unnecessary passes through the array is by using a **switch** variable. A switch is analogous to the common light switch. It has two positions—off and on. A variable is established which may be assigned two values (normally 0 for off and 1 for on). A certain action is taken when the variable has one value, and another action when the switch variable has the other value. A switch is often referred to as a **flag**, since its value signals which action is to be taken.

The switch variable is set off (to zero) before the inner loop that cycles through the array in making comparisons. The switch is set on (to one) inside the inner loop when an exchange operation is performed. The switch is tested after the completion of the inner loop to see whether an exchange operation was performed. If no exchange operation was performed, this indicates that the array items are in order (depending upon the type of sort). Therefore, the process of recycling through the array (with the outer loop) can be eliminated by branching out of the sort routine. There is no need to recycle through the outer loop when the array items are already in order. Normally $N - 1$ passes of the loop are made (N is the number of items in the array). Perhaps only a few items were not already in order, and you only need to recycle through the outer loop several times, rather than the maximum number set up in the outer loop DO statement.

A sort example using a switch variable to end the outer loop when the items become sorted is given in figure 11.4. The array LIST with seven items is sorted in the sample program.

With the switch variable, the outer loop (which controls the number of passes through the array) is exited when the items become correctly ordered. Therefore, the maximum number of passes through the array does not need to be performed. If the array items are already sorted (and sometimes they may be), then the switch variable is never set on, and only one pass of the array is needed. A logical variable is a better choice for the switch usage. The logical variable can be set to .FALSE. instead of the true numeric digit 0 for the "off" condition; it can be set to .TRUE. instead of the numeric digit 1 for the "on" condition.

```
C - - -    AN ASCENDING SORT USING A SWITCH VARIABLE
           INTEGER SWITCH
           DIMENSION LIST (7)
C - - -    LOAD THE ARRAY
           READ (5, 99) LIST
C - - -    PRINT THE UNSORTED ARRAY
           WRITE (6, 98) LIST
C          OUTER LOOP TO CONTROL THE NUMBER OF ARRAY PASSES
           N = 7
           NMIN1 = N - 1
           DO 30 L = 1, NMIN1
C              SET THE SWITCH OFF
               SWITCH = 0
C              INNER LOOP FOR COMPARISONS
               DO 20 J = 1, NMIN1
                   IF ( LIST(J) .LE. LIST(J+1) ) GO TO 20
                   EXCHANGE THE TWO ITEMS
                   LTEMP = LIST(J)
                   LIST(J) = LIST(J+1)
                   LIST(J+1) = LTEMP
C                  SET THE SWITCH VARIABLE ON IF EXCHANGE OCCURS
                   SWITCH = 1
   20          CONTINUE
C              WHEN THE SWITCH IS 0 THE SORTING IS FINISHED
               IF ( SWITCH .EQ. 0 ) GO TO 40
   30      CONTINUE
C
C - - -    PRINT THE SORTED ARRAY
   40      WRITE (6, 98) LIST
           STOP
   99      FORMAT (7I3)
   98      FORMAT (1H0, 7(I3, 5X) )
           END
```

Figure 11.4 Sample program with a sort routine using a switch variable

There are other sorting techniques more efficient than using a switch variable. Dozens of internal sorting techniques exist. Some are highly efficient, but complex to understand and write. Three classifications of sorting techniques and some of sorting methods are:

1. Insertion sorts
   a. Linear insertion
   b. Binary insertion
   c. Shellsort
2. Exchange sorts
   a. Bubblesort
   b. Shakersort
   c. Quicksort
3. Selection sorts
   a. Straight selection
   b. Tree selection
   c. Heapsort

Combinations of these sorting techniques are often formed to produce efficient sort routines. Your instructor may explain some of these sort methods. Entire books are available on sorting if you are interested in acquiring more information on this subject.

You should pick the one sort routine you understand and like best, code it, and run it with some test data to prove to yourself that it works. When you need to implement a sort routine, simply take your already-proven routine and change the array name, dimensional values, and indexing parameters in the DO statements that control the sort loops.

Section 11.8 discusses the subject of debugging array problems.

11.8 DEBUGGING WITH ARRAYS

Logic errors in reading, manipulating, and writing array items are usually more difficult to find than with scalar variables. All the items in an array must be verified, not just a few variables. The best way to correct array problems is to avoid them. Rigorous design and desk-checking are a must with complex problems. Clear writing and structuring of code helps improve the understandability of problem solutions that use arrays.

The best technique to use when array logic problems occur is to print the subscript and the value of the array element for all items in the array. You may also want to print any associated value produced by using an array item. This way you can make sure that the subscript is pointing to the correct element number, and that the correct array value is being used by the subscript reference.

Consider the following program with an array logic problem. The program simply reads and sums the values of seven array items. The seven input values to be read and summed are 5, 10, 20, 30, 40, 50 and 60.

```
INTEGER SUM
DIMENSION ITEM(7)
SUM = 0
DO 22 I = 1, 7
    READ (5, 99) ITEM(I)
    SUM = SUM + ITEM(1)
22 CONTINUE
WRITE (6, 98) SUM
STOP
99 FORMAT (I2)
98 FORMAT (1H0, 11HTHE SUM IS , I3)
END
```

When the program is run the output result produced is:

THE SUM IS 35

The sum of 5, 10, 20, 30, 40, 50, and 60 is certainly not 35; it should be 215. Where did we go wrong in the code? First, the program should be desk-checked to see if the error is obvious. Perhaps you spotted the error right away. But maybe a poor printer listing was received (you may have often encountered a faint or blurred listing), and the logic error still cannot be detected. At this point, a temporary WRITE statement should be included at the top of the program to print a line of column headings, and a temporary WRITE statement should be included after the assignment statement to accumulate the sum of the array items (SUM = SUM + ITEM(I)). The second temporary WRITE statement will print the values of I, ITEM(I), and SUM. The revised program is:

```
INTEGER SUM
DIMENSION ITEM(7)
SUM = 0
WRITE (6, 100)
100 FORMAT (1H0, 20H  I     ITEM(I)     SUM)
DO 22 I = 1, 7
    READ (5, 99) ITEM(I)
    SUM = SUM + ITEM(1)
    WRITE (6,97) I, ITEM(I), SUM
97     FORMAT (1H , I3, 5X, I3, 5X, I4)
```

```
      22 CONTINUE
         WRITE (6, 99) SUM
         STOP
      99 FORMAT (I2)
      98 FORMAT (1H0, 11HTHE SUM IS , I3)
         END
```

The output results with the two temporary WRITE statements to help debug the problem appears as:

I	ITEM(I)	SUM
1	5	5
2	10	10
3	20	15
4	30	20
5	40	25
6	50	30
7	60	35

THE SUM IS 35

The printed results show that the proper values were read into the correct array elements. Thus, the READ statement is all right. However, the value of SUM is incremented by fives. The only statement that accumulates the sum of the items is the Assignment statement. So the problem must be with the Assignment statement in summing each of the array items. After carefully examining the Assignment statement

$$SUM = SUM + ITEM(1)$$

you should find that the digit "1" was coded instead of the letter "I" for the subscript. The temporary WRITE statements helped "zero in" on the statement that is causing the error. After carefully examining the Assignment statement, the invalid subscript problem was located. The statement can be corrected, the temporary WRITE statements removed, and the program rerun with the correct results.

What if the original program had been coded as follows:

```
         INTEGER SUM
         DIMENSION ITEM (7)
         SUM = 0
         DO 22 I = 1, 7
            READ (5, 99) ITEM(1)
            SUM = SUM + ITEM(I)
      22 CONTINUE
         WRITE (6, 99) SUM
         STOP
      99 FORMAT (I2)
      98 FORMAT (1H0, 11HTHE SUM IS , I3)
         END
```

The program might "bomb out" when it was run with some compilers (IBM, WATFOR and WATFIV), since no value was ever read into ITEM(2), and there would be garbage at that storage location. The WATFOR and WATFIV compilers would give a descriptive error message saying: "VARIABLE NOT DEFINED." The output results with the debug WRITE statements would have looked like:

I	ITEM (I)	SUM
1	5	5

*** ERROR *** VARIABLE NOT DEFINED

This would be your clue that nothing was ever stored in the second array element; so you should look at the READ statement to find out why the second input value was never stored into element two.

With some FORTRAN IV compilers the array values would have been filled with zeroes, since many computers clear the memory space allocated for a program to all zeroes before the program is loaded for execution. The output from these computers would have been:

I	ITEM(I)	SUM
1	5	5
2	0	5
3	0	5
4	0	5
5	0	5
6	0	5
7	0	5

THE SUM IS 5

The output results show that the array items were never loaded correctly. The last input value is read into element one, and the remaining elements have a zero value. The accumulator variable SUM has an invalid total, but this is a result of not loading the array correctly. The problem must lie in the READ statement. After examining the READ statement, you find that the digit ''1'' was coded for the subscript value instead of the variable ''I''. This explains the output results. So you know how to fix the problem once the error has been pinpointed.

Since the digit ''1'' and the letter ''I'' look very similar, it may be a good practice (and your instructor might require it) *not* to use the variable I for a subscript or even as the index variable on the DO statement. Many programmers, however, prefer to use the variable I as a subscript and the index variable on the DO, since the letter ''i'' is so frequently used for the array subscript in mathematics and statistics.

Subscript-Out-of-Range Error

A common array subscripting problem is the **subscript-out-of-range error**. This error is caused by using a subscript value that is less than one or greater than the number of elements dimensioned for the array. In other words, you are trying to reference an array element that does not exist. This error often occurs when an arithmetic expression is used for the subscript, and the arithmetic expression calculates an illegal subscript value. This error is referred to as an **invalid index** on Burroughs computers.

Some computers (CDC) will provide a memory address outside the bounds (lower or upper limits) of the array and use the value at this address. The program will continue executing with bad values until it gets so ''fouled up'' that a system-fault error normally occurs. WATFOR and WATFIV compilers will abort the execution of the program and provide a descriptive error message to the effect that a subscript was given referencing an item outside the limits of the array. The best way to debug the subscript-out-of-range error is to print the subscripts used to reference the array items.

The next section discusses the use of the DATA specification statement with arrays. A sample program is given that uses arrays and the DATA statement.

11.9 THE DATA SPECIFICATION STATEMENT WITH ARRAYS

In ANSI FORTRAN 66, you cannot initialize values for the entire array by giving only the array name in the DATA statement. Each array element, with an integer constant subscript, and its initial value, must be specifically indicated. Some FORTRAN IV compilers do allow for an entire array or beginning portions to be initialized by giving only the array name, but not ANSI FORTRAN 66. In this example, array T is dimensioned as 3 elements; array X is dimensioned as 5 elements; and array Y is dimensioned as 7 elements, respectively:

```
DATA T(1)/0.0/, T(2)/0.0/, T(3)/0.0/
DATA T(1), T(2), T(3)/3*0.0/
DATA X(3)/1.333333/
DATA X(1)/1.0/, X(2), X(4), X(5)/1.2, 1.4, 1.5/
DATA Y(1)/1HA/, Y(2)/1HB/
```

The first example assigns the value of 0.0, 0.0, and 0.0 to the array elements T(1), T(2), and T(3), respectively. The second example is an alternate shortcut method of assigning the same values to the same array elements as example one. Example three assigns the value 1.333333 to only element 3 in array X. The fourth example assigns the value 1.0 to element 1 in X, and the values 1.2, 1.4, and 1.5 to elements 2, 4, and 5, respectively, in array X. The fifth example assigns the letter A to element 1 in array Y and the letter B to element 2 in array Y. Elements three through seven of array Y are undefined. Section 11.10 covers the technique of assigning a value to all elements in an array by giving the array name only, with FORTRAN IV compilers that permit this operation.

Let us look at a sample FORTRAN program containing the DATA specification statements and illustrating array manipulation. The program will read the number and suit of a playing card (poker card, to any gamblers) and interpret its respective rank and suit.

The rank of the playing card is read as a two-character alphanumeric field from card columns 1 and 2. The suit of the card is read as a single alphanumeric character in column 3. For example, a two of hearts would be punched as a 2ƀH. The ten of clubs would be punched as a 10C. A jack of diamonds would be punched as a JƀD. The ace of spades would be punched as a AƀS. For example:

We will interpret the playing card and print its rank and suit on a single print line. If a K, blank, and a C had been read, then we would print, beginning in print position one:

RANK AND SUIT OF INPUT CARD IS THE KING OF CLUBS

The coded program is given in figure 11.5 (p. 346).

11.10 LANGUAGE EXTENSIONS IN FORTRAN DIALECTS (NON-ANSI 66 SUBSCRIPTS AND CHARACTER ARRAYS)

One-dimensional arrays are standard features in every FORTRAN compiler, but one of the nonstandard features is the construct of subscripts. Most compilers allow a more general subscript expression than does ANSI FORTRAN 66.

Extensions to Subscript Expressions

Many FORTRAN compilers allow any permissible arithmetic expression that results in either an integer or real value. For example, a subscript reference to array A could be:

$$R = A(K/N * L - (5 + 3*M))$$

If a real quantity results from an arithmetic expression, it is converted to an integer form by truncating the fractional part.

The value provided as a subscript to an array may also contain a subscripted variable. That is, the values of an array can be used to identify elements in another array. For example, you could write

$$LIST (KTR(J))$$

where the subscripted variable, KTR(J), provides a resulting subscript value for the array, LIST. This is a very complex technique to understand, but it can prove very useful in accessing arrays. Even though ANSI 66 and IBM Basic FORTRAN do not allow a subscripted variable reference for a subscript, many other compilers do.

You should stick to subscript expressions of the ANSI standard forms. This will insure compatibility among FORTRAN compilers and generally result in more efficient object coding. If a complicated subscript such as: (K − M) * N / 3 + 1 is needed, it can be achieved easily by computing the subscript value in a prior Assignment statement as follows:

$$INDEX = (K - M) * N / 3 + 1$$
$$HOLD = LIST(INDEX)$$

```
          INTEGER RANKIN,RANK (13), SUIT (4), SUITIN
          INTEGER CR1(13),CR2(13),CSUIT1(4),CSUIT2(4)
          DATA RANK(1)/1H2/,RANK(2)/1H3/,RANK(3)/1H4/,RANK(4)/1H5/,
        *      RANK(5)/1H6/,RANK(6)/1H7/,RANK(7)/1H8/,RANK(8)/1H9/,
        *      RANK(9)/2H10/,RANK(10)/1HJ/,RANK(11)/1HQ/,RANK(12)/1HK/,
        *      RANK(13)/1HA/
          DATA CR1(1)/3HTWO/,CR1(2)/4HTHRE/CR1(3)/4HFOUR/,CR1(4)/4HFIVE/,
        *      CR1(5)/3HSIX/,CR1(6)/4HSEVE/,CR1(7)/4HEIGH/,CR1(8)/4HNINE/,
        *      CR1(9)/3HTEN/,CR1(10)/4HJACK/,CR1(11)/4HQUEE/,
        *      CR1(12)/4HKING/,CR1(13)/3HACE/
          DATA CR2(1)/1H /,CR2(2)/1HE/,CR2(3)/1H /,CR2(4)/1H /,CR2(5)/1H /,
        *      CR2(6)/1HN/,CR2(7)/1HT/,CR2(8)/1H /,CR2(9)/1H /,
        *      CR2(10)/1H /,CR2(11)/1HN/,CR2(12)/1H /,CR2(13)/1H /
          DATA   SUIT(1)/1HC/,SUIT(2)/1HD/,SUIT(3)/1HH/,SUIT(4)/1HS/
          DATA CSUIT1(1)/4HCLUB/,CSUIT1(2)/4HDIAM/,CSUIT1(3)/4HHEAR/,
        *      CSUIT1(4)/4HSPAD/,CSUIT2(1)/1HS/CSUIT2(2)/4HONDS/,
        *      CSUIT2(3)/4HTS /,CSUIT2(4)/4HES  /
       99 FORMAT (A2,A1)
       98 FORMAT (1H0,19HINVALID INPUT RANK ,A2)
       97 FORMAT (1H0,19HINVALID INPUT SUIT , A1)
       96 FORMAT (1H0,35HRANK AND SUIT OF INPUT CARD IS THE ,A4,A1,
        *          4H OF ,2A4)
      105 READ (5,99) RANKIN, SUITIN
          DO 10 I = 1, 13
               IF (RANKIN .EQ. RANK(I) ) GO TO 20
       10 CONTINUE
          WRITE (6,98) RANKIN
          STOP
       20 DO 25 J = 1, 4
               IF (SUITIN .EQ. SUIT(J) ) GO TO 30
       25 CONTINUE
          WRITE (6,97) SUITIN
          STOP
       30 WRITE (6,96) CR1(I),CR2(I),CSUIT1(J),CSUIT2(J)
       40 STOP
          END
```

Figure 11.5 Sample program to illustrate the DATA statement with arrays

DATA Statements with Arrays

With many FORTRAN compilers (IBM, Burroughs, and CDC, for example), all the elements in an array can be initialized by giving only the array name (instead of individual array items) in the DATA statement. Consider the following examples (assuming that array X contains five elements and array L contains seven elements):

DATA X /1.0, 2.0, 3.0, 4.0, 5.0/
DATA L /7 * 0/

The first example initializes element one in array X to 1.0, element two to 2.0, element three to 3.0, element four to 4.0 and element five to 5.0. The second example initializes all seven elements in array L to 0.

CHARACTER Arrays

A few FORTRAN compilers (including FORTRAN 77, Honeywell, and Univac) allow character arrays to be declared with the CHARACTER type statement. Consider the following examples:

CHARACTER * 18 MSG (5)
CHARACTER * 40 TITLES (7)

The first example declares the name MSG to be a five element array in which each element consists of 18 characters. The second example declares TITLES to be a seven element array in which each element consists of 40 characters.

11.11 SUMMARY

The use of arrays is a powerful and efficient technique for solving computer problems. Problems that are table-oriented and require table searching or internal sorting operations require the use of arrays. Whenever you must refer to all the input items or to groups of related items, arrays are the most efficient structures to use.

An array is a group of related items stored under a common name. Each item within the array is referred to as an array element. An individual item in an array is referenced by a subscripted variable. That is, the array name is given, followed by a subscript value in parentheses. The subscript points to the position of the value within the array. A subscript must be a positive integer whose value is greater than or equal to one and less than or equal to the maximum number of elements dimensioned for the array. Subscript values must be integer constants, integer variables, or integer arithmetic expressions. The arithmetic expression may only be one of seven legal forms presented in section 11.3.

An array must be dimensioned in either the DIMENSION statement or an Explicit Type statement (but not in both). The statement that declares the array must be given before the array is referenced in the program. In ANSI FORTRAN 66 the declaration statement must be given at the beginning of the program before any executable statements.

The DIMENSION statement is a specification statement to the compiler to declare the number of dimensions in an array and each dimension size in number of elements. The dimension size must be given as an integer constant.

There are many operations that may be performed with arrays and array elements. Some of these operations are:

1. Summing array elements
2. Initializing array elements
3. Creating duplicate arrays
4. Calculation and assignment of an array item
5. Comparison with an array item
6. Input operations with array items
7. Output operations with array items
8. Searching arrays
9. Internal sorting of arrays

Section 11.5 discussed the methods you can use in reading and writing array items. The entire array may be read or written by using only the array name. As many items are read or written as are given in the array dimension specifications, when only the array name is used. Specific array items may be read or written as subscripted variables with specific subscript references. The implied DO is an important feature for reading and writing specific array items; it is given in parentheses on the READ or WRITE statements and must follow the array name(s) to which it applies.

Searching operations with arrays are frequently used in programs to locate or calculate specific values. A search operation examines each array item according to a specific criterion. For example, you may want to find the smallest or largest value in an array, or the value that matches a certain constant or variable, or the number of occurrences of certain values within the array.

Internal sorting of array items is a common technique to put the items in a specific sequence. Usually the array items will be sorted in ascending sequence (lowest value first) or descending sequence (highest value first). Internal sorting is performed in memory. External sort operations are performed with data files stored on disk or magnetic tape. There are many sorting techniques for ordering array items, and there are many variations to these techniques. Combinations of various sorting techniques are often used to gain efficiency.

The first sorting technique discussed was the paired-interchange sort. This is the most inefficient type of internal sorting, but it was presented for its simplicity and clarity in illustrating the sorting process. The selection-with-exchange sort was presented next to show how to reduce the number of exchange operations. A switch variable was included in the paired-interchange sort to provide a more efficient sort. The switch variable technique eliminates unnecessary passes in the sort after the items are arranged in order.

Internal sorting consists of three basic operations.

1. A comparison between two array items to determine their order.
2. An exchange of the two items to reorder them in the array, if needed.
3. Multiple passes through the array to obtain the desired order of items.

The exchange operation uses a temporary variable to hold one of the exchange items while the other item is switched. Then the temporary variable is stored into the other position to complete the exchange.

Section 11.8 discussed a common method of debugging array logic problems. The best technique is to print the values of the subscript, array item, and any associated variable produced from using the array item.

Section 11.9 discussed the DATA specification statement used to initialize array elements at compile time. ANSI FORTRAN 66 requires that values be assigned to individual elements in the DATA statement; that is, all elements cannot be assigned a value by giving the array name only.

The real power of a computer can be appreciated once the use of arrays has been mastered. Arrays have many applications, and the ability to use arrays in dealing with a large collection of related data items not only enhances the computer's computational power, but provides greater ease in program development. The use of arrays is one of the most powerful techniques in programming. Learn to use them well, and they can save you much work and time.

11.12 TERMS

Terms and concepts you should become familiar with in this chapter are:

array	initializing arrays	sequential search
array declaration	internal sorting	sorting array items
array element	loading an array	subscript
creating a duplicate array	one-dimensional array	subscript reference
dimension specification	paired-exchange sort	subscripted variable
exchange operation	scalar variable	summing array items
external sorting	searching an array	switch
implied DO	selection-with-exchange sort	vector

11.13 REVIEW QUESTIONS

1. What is an array?
2. Why is the use of arrays so important to programmers?
3. The statement used to tell the FORTRAN compiler to establish an array and provide the specification information is the _____ .
4. How is an array name formed?
5. The type of array name chosen must agree with the type of values it contains. (True/False)
6. The dimension specifications given in the DIMENSION statement may be in the form of variables. (True/False)
7. Only one array name is allowed in each DIMENSION statement. (True/False)
8. During program execution, a _____ is used following the array name to designate a specific array element.
9. Subscript values may be integer constants, integer variables, or special forms of an arithmetic expression. (True/False)
10. Negative subscript values are permitted in FORTRAN. (True/False)
11. Name the three techniques that may be used to control reading and storing values into arrays.
12. The nonsubscripted array name allows you to read/write any portion of an array that you wish. (True/False)
13. The implied DO used in an I/O list allows you to read/write as many or as few array items as you wish. (True/False)
14. The implied DO is always contained in parentheses when used in an I/O list. (True/False)
15. Only one subscripted variable (array name) may be contained in an implied DO. (True/False)
16. The process of examining the items in an array according to some specified criterion is called _____ .
17. The process of arranging the items in an array into a specified order is known as _____ .
18. How does the FORTRAN compiler know that a given symbolic name is an array name?
19. Is it possible to have an array with only one element?
20. What is the importance of DO loops to arrays?
21. Where must the DIMENSION statement be placed in a program?
22. Describe a technique you might use to debug an array error.

11.14 EXERCISES

1. Provide the DIMENSION statements for the following specifications.
   a. A group of twelve items called GROUP.
   b. A group of forty items called LISTX.
   c. A group of sixty items called LISTA, and a group of fifty items called LISTB.

2. Provide the DIMENSION statements for the following specifications.
   a. A group of twenty items called K.
   b. A group of two hundred items called XHOLD.
   c. A group of ten items called XARRAY, a group of thirty items called YARRAY, and a group of ten items called ZARRAY.

3. Locate the errors in each of the following statements.
   a. **DIMENSION A(10) B(10)**
   b. **READ (5,99) (LIST(X),X = 1,10)**
   c. **READ (5,98) (A(I),I = 1,7) (B(I),I = 1,5)**
   d. **WRITE (6,97) (GROUP(J,J = 1,8)**
   e. **WRITE (6,96) (HOLD(2*N),N = 1,K,2)**

4. Locate the errors in each of the following statements.
   a. **DIMENSION X(TEN)**
   b. **READ (5,99) (LIST(N)N = 1,20)**
   c. **READ (5,98) ITEMS(J),J = 1,N**
   d. **WRITE (6,97) (ARYZ(Z),Z = 1,9)**
   e. **WRITE (6,96) XARRAY, YARRAY ZARRAY**

5. Complete the following exercises on the I/O of array items. Use ARRAY as the array name and use the implied DO.
   a. Write a routine to read eleven data items with the format specifications of 11F5.2.
   b. Write a routine to write the first ten items on a double-spaced line under the specifications 10F7.2.

6. Complete the following exercises on the I/O of array items. Use ARRAY as the array name and use the implied DO.
   a. Write a routine to read sixteen data items with the specifications of 16F4.2.
   b. Write a routine to output the array items read in a) four per each double-spaced line under the specifications 4F7.2.

7. How many data records will be read by each of the following group of statements?
   a. **DIMENSION X(10)**
      READ (5,99) X
      99 FORMAT (2F5.2)
   b. **DIMENSION X(10)**
      READ (5,98) X
      98 FORMAT (10F5.2)
   c. **DIMENSION X(10)**
      READ (5,97) (X(I),I = 1,10)
      97 FORMAT (2F5.2/F5.2)

8. How many data records will be read by each of the following group of statements?
   a. **DIMENSION X(10)**
      READ (5,99) X
      99 FORMAT (4F5.2)
   b. **DIMENSION X(10)**
      READ (5,98) (X(I),I = 1,10)
      98 FORMAT (F5.2)
   c. **DIMENSION X(10)**
      READ (5,97) X
      97 FORMAT (F5.2/F5.2)

9. Complete the following exercises on the manipulation of array items.
   a. Write the routine to zero out the first fifty elements of a one hundred-element array named A.
   b. Write the routine to sum all the items stored in odd element numbers of the sixteen-element array called L16.
   c. Write a routine to move all the items in a twenty-element array called X20 down one position. That is, X20(1) is replaced by X20(2), X20(2) is replaced by X20(3), . . . and X20(20) is replaced by X20(1).

10. Complete the following exercises on the manipulation of array items.

    a. Write the routine to initialize a fifty-element array called L50 with the values of its respective array element numbers. That is, element one contains a 1, element two a 2, . . . , and element fifty the value 50.
    b. Write the routine to sum all the items stored in even element numbers of the sixteen-element array called L16.

c. A group of high school seniors (509) recently took a college entrance exam. The scores on the exam ranged from one to one hundred. Write a routine that will use a one hundred-element array called NEXAM and create a frequency distribution on each exam score. That is, determine the number of students who made each score. For example, if a student made a score of 76, then add one to the array element 76. Read the student scores from data records typed in columns 1–3 as I3. Name the input variable NSCORS. Use a trailer record containing the value of 000 for NSCORS to indicate an end of file. When an end of file is reached, branch to statement number 30.

11.15 PROGRAMMING PROBLEMS

1. Write a program to load a twenty-element array called K20 from a single data record. The format specifications for the input items are 20I3.

    Reverse the items in the array. That is, exchange item 1 with item 20, item 2 with item 19, and so on. A duplicate array may be used, but this can be done with the same array by including an interchange operation.

    Write out the original array items on a single print line with format specifications 20I6. Then write out the reversed array items with the same format specifications.

2. Write a program to read the items for two ten-element arrays named I1 and I2. The items for array I1 will be read with a 10I2. The items for array I2 will be read from a separate data record under the same format specifications.

    Multiply the items in array I1 by their corresponding item positions in array I2. That is, I1(1) is multiplied by I2(1), I1(2) is multiplied by I2(2), and so on. The resulting products are to be stored in the corresponding item positions in a ten-element array called I3.

    Write out the items for each array on the same print line under the specifications 10I6. Each array will be on a new line.

3. Write a program to find the largest item in a one-dimensional array called NRS. The array NRS is a 20-element array and is loaded from a single data record under the format specifications 20I3.

    Write the twenty array items on a single line under the format specifications 20I5. Then perform the search. When the search is completed, write a message that says:

    THE LARGEST ITEM IN ARRAY NRS IS mmm
    AND IS LOCATED IN POSITION nnn

where mmm is the largest item in the array and nnn is its element number.

4. Write a program to perform a searching operation on a one-dimensional array called NUMBRS. The array NUMBRS is a 20-element array that is loaded from a single data record under the format specifications 20I3. A three-digit integer is read from columns 1–3 on the second data record and is used in the search operation. The search operation consists of matching the three-digit input value with one of the array items; the search will begin with the first element. Before the search is begun, write the twenty array items on a single line under the format specifications 20I5.

    As soon as a match is found between the input value and an array item, write a message that says:

    THE VALUE mmm WAS FOUND IN POSITION nnn

where mmm is the input value and nnn is the array element number. Then terminate the program.

    If the input value is not found in the array, write a message that says:

    THE VALUE mmm WAS NOT FOUND IN THE ARRAY

5. Expand the problem in number 4 to continue searching the array for additional occurrences of the input value. Each time a match of the input value is found, write the message containing the value and the element number at which the value was found.

6. Write a program to perform a descending sort on ten test scores contained in a ten-element array called NTEST. The values will be read off a single data record in the form 10I3.

    Write the unsorted test scores on a single print line in the form 10I6; then write the sorted test scores with the same format specifications.

7. Write a program to read twenty two-digit integer numbers and compute their mean and standard deviation. The input values will be read from a single data record in the form 20F2.0 and stored in the twenty-element array called X.

Their mean will be computed according to the formula:

$$\overline{X} = \frac{\displaystyle\sum_{i=1}^{N} X_i}{N}$$

The symbol "Σ" means "the summation of"; the mean is represented by the symbol $\overline{X}$. Thus, the formula says that the mean is equal to the summation of the array elements X_i, where i goes from 1 to N (N is 20 in our case) divided by the number of elements (N).

The standard deviation is calculated from the formula:

$$\sigma = \sqrt{\frac{\displaystyle\sum_{i=1}^{N} (X_i - \overline{X})^2}{N-1}}$$

This formula says to first square each of the differences between each element in the array (i.e., X_i) and the computed mean. Each of these differences squared is added to a variable to accumulate their sum. Then this summation is divided by the number of items (N) minus one. Finally, take the square root of the results to find the value of σ.

For output results write the following:

a. The twenty values in the array X, on one print line.
b. The computed mean ($\overline{X}$) on a new line, preceded by the literal "MEAN =".
c. The computed standard deviation (σ) on a new line, preceded with the literal "STANDARD DEVIATION = ".

12 Two-dimensional and Three-dimensional Arrays

12.1 INTRODUCTION TO THE CONCEPT OF TWO-DIMENSIONAL ARRAYS

The concept of one-dimensional arrays is indeed a very powerful tool for the manipulation of a group of related items. There are times, however, when multiple groups of related items can be more conveniently handled by using two-dimensional arrays. A two-dimensional array may be thought of as a **matrix** or **table** of values.

A two-dimensional array consists of a number of horizontal lists of elements called **rows** (or row vectors), and a number of vertical lists of elements called **columns** (or column vectors). Any item can be referenced by using a row vector and column vector coordinate as normally done with tables of data.

An illustration of a two-dimensional array with 2 rows and 3 columns is as follows:

	column 1	column 2	column 3
row 1	79	83	76
row 2	91	78	86

A reference to row 1, column 3 would give the value of 76. If you wished to obtain the item with a value of 91, you would refer to row 2, column 1.

This is the same concept as that used in mathematics. If you had a matrix X_{ij} with i rows and j columns and you wanted to refer to the item in the second row and third column, you would specify X_{23}.

You are exposed to two-dimensional arrays (tables) in many aspects of daily life. Airline schedules, bus schedules, tax tables, and so forth are two-dimensional arrays. You read down an airline schedule until you find the desired city and then read across that line to obtain the flight number, departure time, and arrival time. You read down a tax table until you find your taxable income bracket and then read across that line to find the tax amount and percentage. The common checkerboard and BINGO card can be viewed as two-dimensional arrays. You can visualize them as being divided into rows and columns.

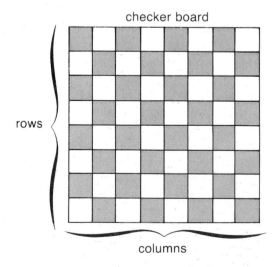

checker board

rows

columns

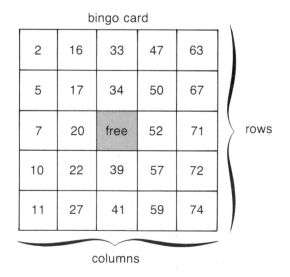

bingo card

2	16	33	47	63
5	17	34	50	67
7	20	free	52	71
10	22	39	57	72
11	27	41	59	74

rows

columns

Consider the problem of computing the grade averages of five students for three tests. The averages could be calculated using nonsubscripted variables or a one-dimensional array, provided that the test scores did not need to be kept in memory for later reference. Suppose, however, you do need to retain the test scores for all the students in memory for some later operation, such as searching or sorting. You could have five separate one-dimensional arrays—one for each student—but handing each of these arrays separately would be very lengthy and time-consuming.

If the test scores for all students could be handled in a matrix-like arrangement, the process of manipulating this two-dimensional array becomes quite easy. When the number of students increases, say to thirty, the program remains essentially the same. But if you were to use thirty one-dimensional arrays, they would become quite a burden. The program would really expand with individual routines to handle each student.

Let us illustrate the concept of two-dimensional arrays by establishing a 5-row by 4-column matrix containing the data for five students. Each row in the matrix will contain all the information about one student—an identification number and three test scores. Thus, column one will relate to the identification number; column two to the first test score; column three to the second test score; and column four to the third test score.

The proposed matrix would look like this:

	column 1	column 2	column 3	column 4
row 1	121	79	83	76
row 2	148	91	78	86
row 3	137	98	87	94
row 4	126	81	66	74
row 5	135	72	75	80

Thus, student number 121 has the three test scores 79, 83, and 76; the second student with an identification of 148 has test scores of 91, 78, and 86; and so on.

A two-dimensional array must be identified in the DIMENSION statement or appropriate Explicit Type statement. Two dimensions are indicated by providing two constants in the dimension specifications. For example:

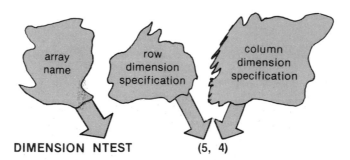

DIMENSION NTEST   (5, 4)

array name   row dimension specification   column dimension specification

The dimension specifications follow the array name and are enclosed in parentheses, just as they are in one-dimensional arrays. Each dimension specification is separated by a comma. The first specification indicates the number of rows, and the second specification indicates the number of columns. Thus, the DIMENSION statement example says there is a two-dimensional array, NTEST, with 5 rows and 4 columns. By multiplying the size of each dimension specification by the others, the compiler determines the total size of the array (number of elements) and how many storage locations to reserve. ($5 \times 4 = 20$, in the example.)

When referring to any array item of NTEST during the execution of the program, two subscript values must be provided after the array name. For example:

NTEST (1,3) (i.e., row 1, column 3)

or

NTEST (I,J) (i.e., Ith row, Jth column)

The first subscript denotes the row vector, and the second subscript denotes the column vector for a specific element. Each subscript may be any of the seven permissible forms allowed for one-dimensional arrays. One subscript may take one form and the other subscript may take another form. For example:

NTEST (3,J + 1)

or

NTEST(I,1)

Giving one subscript a constant value and the other a variable value can be very handy in some operations.

The same general rules that apply to one-dimensional arrays and their subscripting operations apply also to two-dimensional arrays, but the number of dimension references is two, to provide the form of a matrix. To be consistent, let us use the variable I for the row subscript and J for the column subscript when variables are used as subscripts in examples. Of course, you can use any integer variable that you want to, but the variables I and J are frequently used in algebra with references to a matrix, such as X_{ij}. Now let us discuss the manipulation of items in two-dimensional arrays.

12.2 MANIPULATING TWO-DIMENSIONAL ARRAY ITEMS

Calculations, search operations, and sorting with two-dimensional array items are performed just as they are with one-dimensional arrays. Two-dimensional array operations are a little more involved, since there are two subscripts to take into account.

Since two subscript values must be used to reference a two-dimensional array element, the normal procedure is to control the two subscript values with nested DO loops. The inner DO loop normally controls the column vector subscript, and the outer DO loop controls the row vector subscript.

Initializing Array Elements

Two-dimensional arrays are often used for work arrays. Thus, the elements must be initialized to some value, usually zero. The routine to initialize a two-dimensional array X to zero is:

```
        DIMENSION X(10,5)
        DO 25 I = 1,10
            DO 15 J = 1,5
                X(I,J) = 0.0
    15      CONTINUE
    25  CONTINUE
```

The preceding example sets the elements of array X to zero in row order, i.e., the column subscript changes more rapidly. If you wish to access the array in column order (with the row subscript varying more rapidly), the order of the DO loops is simply reversed. For example:

```
        DIMENSION
        X(10,5)
            DO 30 J = 1,5
                DO 20 I = 1,10
                    X(I,J) = 0.0
    20          CONTINUE
    30  CONTINUE
```

Accessing the elements in a two-dimensional array in column order, as shown above, is usually more efficient than row order, but there are times when you need to access the elements in row order, as in the grade computation examples. For small arrays, the difference in efficiency is usually very minor. So the choice is left to you. If you feel more comfortable in accessing the array elements in row order, then do it that way. Remember, **row order** means accessing elements in different columns of the same row. **Column order** means accessing the items in different rows in the same column vector.

Let us take another example of generating values for a two-dimensional array. We will write a routine to fill a three-row, four-column array named NARRAY with consecutive numbers starting at one. That is, the value 1 will be stored at NARRAY(1,1), the value 2 will be stored at NARRAY(1,2), and so on. The routine is as follows.

```
        INTEGER ROW, COL
        DIMENSION NARRAY (3,4)
        NUMBER = 0
        DO 30 ROW = 1,3
            DO 20 COL = 1,4
                NUMBER = NUMBER + 1
                NARRAY (ROW,COL) = NUMBER
20      CONTINUE
30 CONTINUE
```

There will be twelve numbers (from 1 through 12) generated by the counter and stored at the twelve array elements in row order. After the routine is finished, the array will be filled with values as follows:

	column 1	column 2	column 3	column 4
row 1	1	2	3	4
row 2	5	6	7	8
row 3	9	10	11	12

You may want to follow through this example by writing down the values of the index variables from the two DO loops as each value of NUMBER is stored in the array. This will help you visualize how the subscripts are working, and how the values are being stored.

Summing Array Elements

Suppose we sum the three test scores and compute their average for each of five students. The same array, NTEST, with 5 rows and 4 columns is used to illustrate this technique. There must be two nested DO loops to control the subscripts and reference all the test scores. The routine is:

```
        DIMENSION NTEST (5,4)
        . . .
        . . .
        DO 20 I = 1,5
            NSUM = 0
            DO 10 J = 2,4
                NSUM = NSUM + NTEST(I,J)
10      CONTINUE
            AVE = NSUM / 3
            WRITE (6,98) (NTEST(I,J),J=1,4), NSUM, AVE
98      FORMAT (1H0,5I7,F6.2)
20 CONTINUE
```

The inner DO loop begins at 2 to pick up the first test score and goes through 4 to add in the second and third test scores. The variable NSUM must be initialized to zero outside the inner loop to reset the counter between each grade calculation. After the average of each student is calculated, the four array items, with their sum and average, are printed. The outer loop is executed five times to compute the average for each student. The number of test scores and/or students processed may easily be expanded by changing the upper limit of the proper DO statements.

If the sum and average values need to be retained for later array operations (searching, sorting), these values could easily be stored in unused columns of the array. For example:

```
          DIMENSION NTEST(5,6)
          . . .
          . . .
          DO 20 I = 1,5
             NTEST(I,5) = 0
             DO 10 J = 2,4
                NTEST(I,5) = NTEST(I,5) + NTEST(I,J)
     10      CONTINUE
             NTEST(I,6) = NTEST(I,5) / 3
     20 CONTINUE
```

The sum is stored into column 5 of each row, and the average is stored into column 6.

Calculated values can be stored from one array into another array. Suppose you want to store the total from each row into a one-dimensional row total array. Assume that there is a three-row, four-column array named X, and that you want to store the total of the values in each row into another array named XROW, which is a one-dimensional array with three elements. You must have as many elements in the one-dimensional array as there are rows in the two-dimensional array. The routine is:

```
          INTEGER R, C
          DIMENSION X(3,4), XROW(3)
          . . .
          . . .
          DO 30 R = 1,3
             XROW(R) = 0.0
             DO 20 C = 1,4
                XROW(R) = XROW(R) + X(R,C)
     20      CONTINUE
     30 CONTINUE
```

Another common practice is to sum the values in each of the columns of a two-dimensional array and store the column totals into a one-dimensional array. This routine will be left for you to write. (Hint: you must vary the column subscript more slowly than the row subscript.)

Creating Duplicate Arrays

There is often a need to retain the original values of an array for later output if the values are changed in processing. A routine for storing the values in array X into a duplicate array called Y is as follows:

```
          DIMENSION X(10,5), Y(10,5)
          . . .
          . . .
          DO 25 I = 1,10
             DO 15 J=1,5
                Y(I,J) = X(I,J)
     15      CONTINUE
     25 CONTINUE
```

Simple Operations with Selected Array Elements

Single array elements can be referenced in Assignment and IF statements. Consider the following examples.

An array item is used in calculating a value for a nonsubscripted variable:

$$RESULT = A*X(I,6) + 3.2/T$$

A single array item may be calculated in an Assignment statement:

$$X(I,7) = A - B*8.7$$

An array item may be used in an IF statement to make a decision:

IF (X(I,J) .GT. 100.0) GO TO 90

or

IF (X(I,J) .EQ. 0.0) Y = 0.0

Now let us turn our attention to input/output operations with two-dimensional array items.

12.3 INPUT/OUTPUT OPERATIONS WITH TWO-DIMENSIONAL ARRAY ITEMS

You can use the subscripted variable method to read/write individual items, or you can use the implied DO. Use of these techniques can become even more complex, in that you may use the index variable in a DO loop to vary one subscript and the implied DO to vary the other.

Input Operations with Two-dimensional Arrays

Let us examine each of these two techniques in reading the five students' identification numbers and three test scores. In loading two-dimensional arrays, all the data items for one row are often contained in the same record. So let us assume each student's data is punched in a separate record as follows:

Record Positions	Input Field
1–3	Student ID (3-digit integer)
4	Blank
5–7	Test Score 1 (3-digit integer)
8–10	Test Score 2 (3-digit integer)
11–13	Test Score 3 (3-digit integer)

You certainly would not want to read the array items as subscripted variables using constants for both subscript references. This would require five separate READ statements in the form:

READ (5,99) NTEST(1,1), NTEST(1,2), NTEST(1,3), NTEST(1,4)
READ (5,99) NTEST(2,1), NTEST(2,2), NTEST(2,3), NTEST(2,4)
and so on

To provide flexibility in expanding the number of student grade cards that can be read, you should vary the row subscript in a DO loop. The routine is:

```
       DIMENSION NTEST(5,4)
       DO 10 I = 1,5
           READ (5,99) NTEST(I,1), NTEST(I,2), NTEST(I,3), NTEST(I,4)
99         FORMAT (I3,1X,3I3)
10 CONTINUE
```

This is a long way to load the array. What if there were ten test scores to store in each row? Rule this technique out when reading many items stored in the same row vector.

A better technique to use is the implied DO. All the parameters for subscript control could be placed inside the implied DO as follows:

```
       DIMENSION NTEST(5,4)
       READ (5,99) ((NTEST(I,J), J = 1,4), I = 1,5)
99 FORMAT (I3,1X,3I3)
```

With the implied DO technique, one implied DO can be nested within another. Examine the following illustration of the READ.

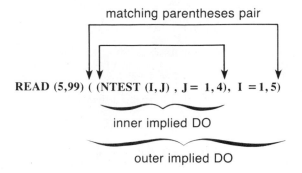

This statement produces the same result as the previous example. The inner implied DO (with index variable J) will vary from 1 to 4, while the outer implied DO (with index variable I) holds constant until the index variable J is completed. Then I is incremented by one, and the looping is performed again with J varying from 1 to 4. When I is 5, and the inner loop with J is finished, both implied DOs are completed.

The rules for nested implied DO loops are as follows:

1. Each set of implied DO parameters must be enclosed within a pair of parentheses. Hence, in the example two pairs of parentheses are needed. One pair will set off the subscripted array name and the end of the parameters for the index variable J. The second pair will include the inner implied DO and set off the subscripted array name and the end of the parameters for the index variable I.
2. A comma must separate each implied DO. (Note the comma after the inner implied DO.)
3. The implied DO closest to the subscripted array name will be performed first. That is, the subscript corresponding to the innermost implied DO will change more rapidly. Then the next closest implied DO will be performed, and so on until the outermost implied DO is performed. When the outermost implied DO is completed, the implied DO is finished.

The best technique for reading two-dimensional array values contained in a record this way is to include a DO loop to control the row subscript reference, and an implied DO to control the column subscript reference. The revised routine to read the input fields with one implied DO is as follows:

```
        DIMENSION NTEST(5,4)
        DO 10 I = 1,5
            READ (5,99) (NTEST(I,J), J = 1,4)
99          FORMAT (I3,1X,3I3)
10 CONTINUE
```

This routine produces the same results as the nested implied DO, but you can see more clearly what is happening in the subscript references. The subscript I will change only when a pass in the DO loop is completed. The subscript J is varied and completed in the implied DO on each pass in the DO loop.

Suppose the array NTEST is dimensioned as a 30-row by 7-column array, but, you only want to load the first four columns of each row. The number of students (rows vectors) is read as a header record. The routine becomes:

```
        DIMENSION NTEST(30,7)
        READ (5,199) N
199 FORMAT (I3)
        DO 10 I = 1,N
            READ (5,99) (NTEST(I,J), J = 1,4)
99          FORMAT (I3,1X,3I3)
10 CONTINUE
```

When array items are punched one value per data card or entered at a terminal one at a time, nested DO loops can be used to load (fill) the array. Suppose there are twelve values, each typed on separate data records, and you wish to read them into a two-dimensional array named MATRIX with four rows and three columns.

Using the index variable R for the row subscript and C for the column subscript, the routine with nested DO loops would be:

```
          INTEGER R,C
          DIMENSION MATRIX (4,3)
          DO 20 R = 1, 4
              DO 10 C = 1, 3
                  READ (5,99) MATRIX (R, C)
     10       CONTINUE
     20 CONTINUE
     99 FORMAT (I3)
```

This routine would load the twelve input values in row order.

The implied DO could also be used in substitution for the inner loop. A format specification of I3 would cause a new data record to be read for the next value (since reaching the end of the format specifications signals the end of a record in the implied DO). The routine with an implied DO to read twelve values on separate records would be:

```
          INTEGER R, C
          DIMENSION MATRIX(4,3)
          DO 20 R = 1, 4
              READ (5,99) (MATRIX(R,C), C = 1, 3)
     20 CONTINUE
     99 FORMAT (I3)
```

Two-dimensional arrays can also be read with just the array name, as with one-dimensional arrays. The array elements are read, however, with the first subscript changing more rapidly (i.e., in column-major order instead of row-major order as we have been doing). This means you must either reverse the row-column dimension specifications to column-row order or prepare the input data in column-major order. This technique of using just the array name for I/O operations with two-dimensional arrays is less flexible and tends to produce more errors than the techniques discussed above.

Now let's look at the routines used for writing two-dimensional array items.

Output Operations with Two-dimensional Arrays

The same two techniques for loading the two-dimensional array NTEST can be used to write the array elements. Two-dimensional array items are normally written in row-order fashion. That is, all the items for a row vector are written on the same print line.

When writing subscripted variables in the I/O list, you should use a DO loop to control the row subscript. The routine is:

```
          DIMENSION NTEST(5,4)
          . . .

          . . .
          DO 20 I = 1,5
              WRITE (6,98) NTEST(I,1), NTEST(I,2), NTEST(I,3), NTEST(I,4)
     98       FORMAT (1H0,4I7)
     20 CONTINUE
```

In the I/O list of the WRITE, the implied DO can be used in the same manner as with the READ statement. You can have nested implied DO's or a DO loop to control the row subscript value and an implied DO on the WRITE to control the column subscript value.

The routine using nested implied DO loops in the WRITE is as follows:

```
          DIMENSION NTEST(5,4)
          . . .

          . . .
          WRITE (6,98) ((NTEST(I,J), J = 1,4), I = 1,5)
     98 FORMAT (1H0,4I7)
```

The nested implied DO's on the WRITE statement work the same as on the READ. The innermost implied DO is completed first, and then the outermost implied DO is incremented.

The recommended way to write the array items with an implied DO is to have a single implied DO on the WRITE inside of a DO loop. The routine is:

```
              DIMENSION NTEST(5,4)
              . . .

              . . .
              DO 20 I = 1,5
                    WRITE (6,98) (NTEST(I,J), J = 1,4)
        98          FORMAT (1H0,4I7)
        20 CONTINUE
```

This technique is fairly easy to understand and allows greater flexibility.

Let us return to the problem that established a 30-row by 7-column dimension specification for the array NTEST. Only the first four columns were loaded and the number of students (row vectors) was determined by the value N read from a header record. You want to write only those array items that were loaded. Thus, the implied DO must be used. The routine is:

```
              DIMENSION NTEST(30,7)
              . . .

              . . .
              DO 20 I = 1,N
                    WRITE (6,98) (NTEST(I,J),J = 1,4)
        98          FORMAT (1H0,4I7)
        20 CONTINUE
```

The implied DO references only the first four columns, even though seven column vectors are available.

You can also write all the elements in an array by using only the array name, but the first subscript will change more rapidly, to give the same problem (column-major order) as reading two-dimensional arrays with just the array name.

You may sometimes need to print only the items in a single row or column, or even just a particular element. This is easily done by specifying the desired row or column subscript as a constant and the other subscript as a variable that is varied in a DO loop. For example, the routine to print the second row of a two-dimensional array named X would be:

```
        C *** PRINT ROW 2 OF ARRAY X
              DIMENSION X (10,5)
              . . .

              . . .

              . . .
        99          FORMAT (1H0,F5.2)
              DO 30 J = 1,5
                    WRITE (6,99) X (2,J)
        30          CONTINUE
```

The routine to print the items in column 3 of array X would be:

```
        C *** PRINT COLUMN 3 OF ARRAY X
              DIMENSION X (10,5)
              . . .

              . . .
        99          FORMAT (1H0,F5.2)
              DO 20 I = 1,10
                    WRITE (6,99) X(I,3)
        20          CONTINUE
```

An implied DO could also be used to print all the items on the same print line. If the items for row 2 or column 3 were to be printed on the same line, you would have to change the FORMAT statement and use an implied DO in the WRITE.

To print a particular element such as row 4, column 1, the statement would be:

C * PRINT A SINGLE ELEMENT OF ARRAY X**
WRITE (6,99) X(4,1)

There are many variations in reading and writing two-dimensional array items. It all depends on what is needed. We now turn our attention to the techniques used to search and sort two-dimensional arrays.

12.4 SEARCHING OPERATIONS WITH TWO-DIMENSIONAL ARRAYS

Often you need to find the smallest or largest value, or some other particular value, in a two-dimensional array. The same sequential search technique used for one-dimensional arrays can be used. The main difference is that now you must search each column in every row.

Suppose you wish to count the occurrences of the items in the array X that match the quantity in the variable SPECVL. The routine is:

```
DIMENSION X(10,5)
. . .
. . .
KNT = 0
DO 25 I = 1,10
   DO 15 J = 1,5
      IF (X(I,J) .EQ. SPECVL) KNT = KNT + 1
15    CONTINUE
25 CONTINUE
```

The outer loop controls the selection of a row vector, and the inner loop controls the column vector being searched.

Suppose you wish to find the largest item and its location in the array X. The routine is:

```
DIMENSION X(10,5)
. . .
. . .
ILOC = 1
JLOC = 1
DO 25 I = 1,10
    DO 15 J = 1,5
        IF (X(I,J) .LE. X(ILOC,JLOC)) GO TO 15
        ILOC = I
        JLOC = J
15      CONTINUE
25 CONTINUE
```

The item in X(1,1) is assumed to be the largest value. Its row and column element numbers are placed into the variables ILOC and JLOC. Then you search the array and compare each item to the quantity pointed to by the subscripts ILOC and JLOC. Whenever a larger value is found, its indices are placed into ILOC and JLOC.

12.5 SORTING TWO-DIMENSIONAL ARRAY ITEMS

A sorting operation with a two-dimensional array is usually based on the values in one specific column. The main difference between sorting a two-dimensional array and sorting a one-dimensional array is in the interchange operation. All items in the two rows must be exchanged, not just the two items in the comparison. Thus, a third loop must be included to exchange all the items in the two rows.

Suppose the averages of the five students used in the previous discussion are to be sorted. Assume that the sum and average have been stored in the fifth and sixth columns of the array NTEST, respectively. The routine to produce a descending sort in average order using the selection-with-interchange sorting technique is:

```
            DIMENSION NTEST (5, 6)
            N = 5
C --- OUTER LOOP TO CONTROL THE NUMBER OF PASSES IN THE SORT
            NMIN1 = N - 1
            DO 45 I1 = 1, NMIN1
                IPLUS1 = I1 + 1
C ---           LOOP TO CONTROL THE NUMBER OF COMPARISONS
                DO 35 I2 = IPLUS1, N
                    IF (NTEST(I1,6) .GE. NTEST(I2,6)) GO TO 35
C ---                   LOOP TO CONTROL THE EXCHANGES BETWEEN ROWS
                        DO 25 J = 1, 6
                            NHOLD = NTEST(I1, J)
                            NTEST(I1,J) = NTEST(I2,J)
                            NTEST(I2,J) = NHOLD
25                      CONTINUE
35              CONTINUE
45          CONTINUE
```

Three DO loops must be used. The innermost loop is used to exchange all the items (one through six) in the two rows (referenced by I1 and I2). The index variable J varies from 1 through 6 to exchange the six column values between the two rows. The outer loop controls the number of passes, as in one-dimensional array sorting. The second loop controls the number of comparisons. The best way to understand fully what is happening is to play computer. Step through each of the loops and change the values in the array as called for in the sort routine.

To help you understand two-dimensional arrays, the next section presents a calendar problem.

12.6   A SAMPLE PROBLEM WITH TWO-DIMENSIONAL ARRAYS

The manipulation of two-dimensional array items and their subscripts is a difficult concept to grasp. This section presents a problem with two-dimensional arrays, which should increase your understanding of multiple-dimensional arrays. The problem involves the input and manipulation of daily temperature values for a calendar month (February). Various calculations are performed on the data to help you better understand how the array items are referenced.

A Month of Daily Temperatures

This problem emphasizes the input of two-dimensional array items and the calculation of selected array items. It involves the calendar month of February, which has 28 days. The first day begins on a Sunday. The entire month is laid out as follows:

S	M	T	W	T	F	S
1	2	3	4	5	6	7
8	9	10	11	12	13	14
15	16	17	18	19	20	21
22	23	24	25	26	27	28

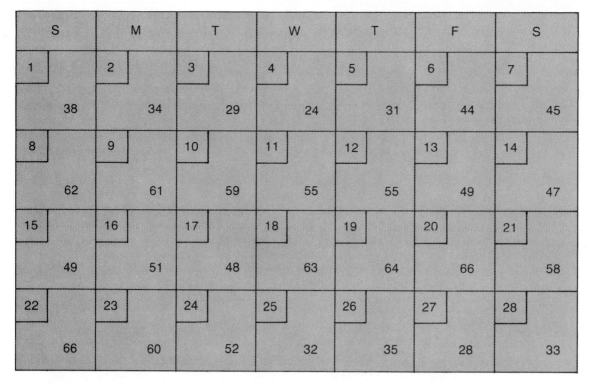

Figure 12.1 Monthly planning calendar with daily average temperatures

Now, assume a planning calendar for this month, in which the date is in the upper left-hand corner of each 'day' box, and there is space left over in which to enter information. The average daily temperature is entered for each day of the month. The resulting planning calendar is given in figure 12.1. The first day (Sunday) has the average temperature value of 38, the second day (Monday) has the average temperature value of 34, and so on.

You should be able to visualize these data items as a two-dimensional array. The array can be viewed as four rows of weeks. You can view the seven days as columnar elements of each week, or subsets of a week. If you wanted to refer to the temperature for the third Wednesday, it could be viewed as position (3, 4), or the third week and fourth day. If you talked about temperature on the fourth week and the first day, it could be found at position (4, 1).

Now let us write some program segments to manipulate the array items. The array name will be MONTH and will consist of four rows and seven columns. The DIMENSION statement would be:

DIMENSION MONTH(4, 7)

The first exercise is to write a program segment to read the average daily temperatures and store them in row order. Four data records are to be read. Each data record contains seven temperatures written as three digit integers in columns 1–21. The variable WEEK is used as the row subscript, and the variable DAY is used as the column subscript. The program segment is:

```
      INTEGER WEEK, DAY
      DIMENSION MONTH(4, 7)
   99 FORMAT (7I3)
      DO 5 WEEK = 1, 4
          READ (5, 99) (MONTH(WEEK, DAY), DAY = 1, 7)
    5 CONTINUE
```

The second exercise is to write a program segment to calculate the average temperature for all the days in the month. The program segment is:

```
INTEGER WEEK, DAY, TOTTMP, AVETMP
DIMENSION MONTH(4, 7)
. . .
. . .
TOTTMP = 0
DO 20 WEEK = 1, 4
    DO 10 DAY = 1, 7
        TOTTMP = TOTTMP + MONTH(WEEK, DAY)
10      CONTINUE
20 CONTINUE
AVETMP = TOTTMP / 28
```

The third exercise is to calculate the average temperature for the second week in February. In this exercise the week subscript is given as the constant 2. The program segment is:

```
INTEGER WEEK, DAY, TOTTMP, AVETMP
DIMENSION MONTH(4, 7)
. . .
. . .
TOTTMP = 0
DO 10 DAY = 1, 7
    TOTTMP = TOTTMP + MONTH(2, DAY)
10 CONTINUE
AVETMP = TOTTMP / 7
```

The fourth exercise is to calculate the average daily temperature for the weekdays (Monday through Friday). This exercise involves nested loops, but all columns are not referenced in the array (only the second through the sixth). The program segment is:

```
INTEGER WEEK, DAY, TOTTMP, AVETMP
DIMENSION MONTH(4, 7)
. . .
. . .
TOTTMP = 0
DO 20 WEEK = 1, 4
    DO 10 DAY = 2, 6
        TOTTMP = TOTTMP + MONTH(WEEK, DAY)
10      CONTINUE
20 CONTINUE
AVETMP = TOTTMP / 20
```

The fifth exercise is to calculate the average daily temperature for the weekends (Saturdays and Sundays). This exercise involves nested loops, but only the first and seventh columns are referenced in each row of the array. The program segment is:

```
INTEGER WEEK, DAY, TOTTMP, AVETMP
DIMENSION MONTH(4, 7)
. . .
. . .
TOTTMP = 0
DO 20 WEEK = 1, 4
    DO 10 DAY = 1, 7, 6
        TOTTMP = TOTTMP + MONTH(WEEK, DAY)
10      CONTINUE
20 CONTINUE
AVETMP = TOTTMP / 8
```

The sixth exercise is to calculate the average weekly temperature for each of the four weeks and determine which week had the highest average temperature. For this exercise we will use a two-dimensional array named WKLYAV which contains four rows (one for each week) and two columns. One column will be initialized to the values one through four to represent the week number. The second column will contain the weekly average temperatures. This set of weekly average temperatures will then be sorted in descending order, and the first row of values from the WKLYAV array will tell us the week with the highest average. A message will be printed with this information. The program segment is rather long; so, it is given in figure 12.2.

These exercises should help you better understand subscript operations and how two-dimensional array items can be manipulated.

```
            INTEGER WEEK, DAY, WKLYAV (4, 2), WTEMP
            DIMENSION MONTH (4, 7)
            . . .
            . . .
            . . .
C
C ---    GENERATE THE WEEK NUMBER IN COLUMN 1 OF THE WKLYAV
C ---    ARRAY WITH THE SUBSCRIPT WEEK
            DO 5 WEEK = 1, 4
                WKLYAV (WEEK, 1) = WEEK
    5       CONTINUE
C
C ---    CALCULATE THE TOTAL WEEKLY TEMPERATURES IN COLUMN
C ---    TWO OF THE WKLYAV ARRAY
            DO 20 WEEK = 1, 4
                WKLYAV (WEEK, 2) = 0
                DO 10 DAY = 1, 7
                    WKLYAV (WEEK, 2) = WKLYAV (WEEK, 2) + MONTH (WEEK, DAY)
    10          CONTINUE
    20      CONTINUE
C
C ---    CALCULATE THE AVERAGE WEEKLY TEMPERATURES BACK INTO
C ---    COLUMN TWO OF THE WKLYAV ARRAY
            DO 30 WEEK = 1, 4
                WKLYAV (WEEK, 2) = WKLYAV (WEEK, 2) / 7
    30      CONTINUE
C
C ---    NOW SORT THE WKLYAV ARRAY IN DESCENDING ORDER ON THE
C ---    SECOND COLUMN USING A SELECTION-WITH-INTERCHANGE SORT
            M = 3
            N = 4
C ---    OUTER LOOP FOR NUMBER OF PASSES
            DO 60 L = 1, M
C ---        NOW THE INNER LOOP TO DO COMPARISONS
                LP1 = L + 1
                DO 50 J = LP1, N
                    IF (WKLYAV (L, 2) .GE. WKLYAV (J, 2) ) GO TO 50
C ---                NOW THE EXCHANGE LOOP TO SWITCH THE ITEMS
                    DO 40 K = 1, 2
                        WTEMP = WKLYAV (L, K)
                        WKLYAV (L, K) = WKLYAV (J, K)
                        WKLYAV (J, K) = WTEMP
    40              CONTINUE
    50          CONTINUE
    60      CONTINUE
C ---    PRINT THE WEEK NR AND HIGHEST AVERAGE WEEKLY TEMPERATURE
            WRITE (6,98) (WKLYAV (1, N), N = 1, 2)
    98      FORMAT (1H0, 5HWEEK, I3, 26H HAD THE HIGHEST AVERAGE,
        *15HTEMPERATURE OF , I3, 9H DEGREES.)
```

Figure 12.2 Exercise six for monthly temperature problem

12.7 INTRODUCTION TO THE CONCEPT OF THREE-DIMENSIONAL ARRAYS

Often there is a need to refer to a group of matrices in an array arrangement. That is, you can shorten a program by using a third subscript reference to indicate which matrix you are referencing. Such an array is called a three-dimensional array, which can be thought of as two or more related two-dimensional arrays. A **row** subscript is used to denote the row vector, a **column** subscript is used to denote the column vector, and a **level** subscript is used to indicate which level number or matrix you are referencing.

For example, consider a program to play BINGO on the computer. Suppose you decided to play with three BINGO cards. This would be an ideal situation for using a three-dimensional array. The first two subscripts would indicate the row and column coordinates on a single card. The last subscript would tell which card was being played.

The specifications in the DIMENSION statement tell the compiler when a three-dimensional array is to be used in the program. The DIMENSION statement to provide the array specifications for three 5-row, 5-column matrices for the BINGO program would be:

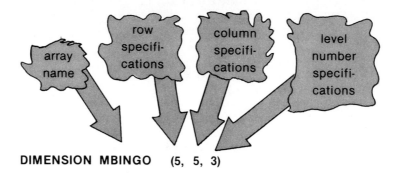

DIMENSION MBINGO   **(5, 5, 3)**

Whenever an element in the array MBINGO is needed, three subscripts must follow the array name. Consider in figure 12.3, the three BINGO cards used with the array MBINGO. A subscript reference of MBINGO(4,2,1) gives the value 22. If you wanted to get the value in the second row and first column of the third card, you would use a reference of MBINGO(2,1,3).

You could write a program to play BINGO as three two-dimensional arrays. But, there must be a separate routine to search each card for a match with a called number (generated from a random number routine) and to check for a BINGO. By using a three-dimensional array, you need only one routine with three nested loops. The inner loop would control the column subscript, the middle loop would control the row subscript, and the outer loop would control the level or card number.

bingo card 1

2	16	33	47	63
5	17	34	50	67
7	20	free	52	71
10	22	39	57	72
11	27	41	59	74

bingo card 2

1	16	32	46	62
3	18	34	48	65
4	21	free	51	68
8	23	38	55	70
13	27	42	58	73

bingo card 3

1	17	31	47	63
2	19	33	49	65
6	24	free	51	70
10	27	41	53	72
14	28	43	57	75

Figure 12.3 Three sample bingo cards

Three-dimensional arrays are generally even more involved than two-dimensional arrays. But the use of a three-dimensional array can shorten a program and make the job of programming less tedious and time-consuming. The one-dimensional and two-dimensional arrays are much more frequently used in programming, and you should concentrate your learning efforts on them. You may never have the need to use three-dimensional arrays.

12.8 LANGUAGE EXTENSIONS IN FORTRAN DIALECTS (LEVELS OF DIMENSION)

Various FORTRAN dialects provide different levels of dimension capabilities. Two-dimensional arrays are standard on all FORTRAN compilers. Basic ANSI FORTRAN 66 allows only two levels of dimension; full ANSI FORTRAN 66 provides up to three levels. FORTRAN 77, VAX-11 FORTRAN, IBM G-level FORTRAN, WATFIV, and other FORTRAN compilers allow up to seven levels of dimension. Some FORTRAN compilers provide more than seven levels (e.g., 64 levels), while a few compilers allow an unlimited number of dimension levels for an array.

Why would anyone ever want to use more than three levels of dimension in a problem? Multi-dimensional levels are convenient when you think in logical groupings. You might want to have a four-dimensional array to represent telephone extension numbers for individuals. Each of the four digits in the number could be used as an element number and the name of the individual placed into the array element. For example, the array reference NRTELR(2,4,4,1) might contain the name COLE.

Suppose someone wished to index the keywords in several volumes of manuals. (Imagine the work!) He might use one subscript for the line number on a page, one for the page number, and one each for the section number, manual number, volume number, and so on.

Suppose an agricultural research station wanted to perform a study on different varieties of seed corn. They might divide a plot of land into 4 quadrants, which are in turn divided into 4 smaller quadrants. This division process might continue for two more levels, ending with very small quadrants in each of which five rows of corn are planted. The data results from the different varieties of seed corn could be stored in array form in which each dimension represented a different quadrant or section of land. The results could then be evaluated from a multi-dimensional array (such as SECTN(4, 4, 4, 5)). So you see that having access to a number of dimension levels can be very useful in some applications.

12.9 SUMMARY

You may sometimes encounter problems where a multi-dimensional array is needed for the solution. Using a two-dimensional array provides far more flexibility and efficiency than using multiple one-dimensional arrays. A two-dimensional array is thought of as a matrix or table of related values. A two-dimensional array consists of a number of horizontal lists of elements, called rows, and a number of vertical lists, called columns. The common checkerboard and BINGO card may be thought of as two-dimensional arrays.

Two subscripts must be used to reference an item in a two-dimensional array. One subscript (usually the first one) is used to identify the row vector, and the second subscript is used to identify the column vector. Thus, the intersection of the row and column vectors as identified by the two subscripts yields the array element being referenced.

A two-dimensional array may be declared in the DIMENSION statement or in the Explicit Type statement, but it must not be declared in both. The array name is given in the declaration statement, and the upper bounds of each dimension are given in parentheses. The upper bounds of the dimensions are separated by a comma. As a rule, the first dimension specification provides the number of row elements, and the second dimension specification provides the number of column elements. The upper bound for each dimension must be given as a constant. Thus, the subscripts for the array elements for each dimension may range from one through the upper bound value.

The forms of the subscript values are the same as for one-dimensional arrays. Either or both the subscripts may be constants, variables, or allowed arithmetic expressions. It is often convenient to give a variable as one subscript and a constant as the other.

Manipulation operations with two-dimensional arrays are the same as with one-dimensional arrays. Two loops are normally needed to reference the array items; one loop controls the row subscript, the other the column subscript.

Section 12.3 discussed input/output operations with two-dimensional arrays. Two-dimensional arrays are usually read and written in row order, which means that all the items in the same row are processed before proceeding to the next row. In other words, the column subscript is varied faster than the row subscript. The implied DO is frequently used to control the column subscript for reading and writing two-dimensional array items.

The various types of searching operations performed on one-dimensional arrays are also performed on two-dimensional arrays. Again, two loops must usually be used in searching arrays. One loop (usually the outer) is used to vary the row subscript, and the other loop (inner) is used to vary the column subscript.

When sorting two-dimensional array items, a third loop is needed for the exchange operations, because all the related items in a row must be swapped along with the array item used as the basis for the sort.

Section 12.7 gave a brief introduction to the concept of three-dimensional arrays, since many FORTRAN compilers provide at least three dimensions of array reference. The third subscript represents a third dimensional reference, which is called a level or plane vector.

Two-dimensional arrays are often difficult for the beginning programmer to grasp. Their use, however, in solving various complex problems, is invaluable. Two-dimensional arrays can shorten the amount of code required to solve a problem. They may also provide greater flexibility and efficiency in problem solving with the computer.

12.10 TERMS

The terms and concepts which you should become familiar with in this chapter are:

column	multi-dimensional array	row subscript
column order	nested implied DO loops	row vector
column subscript	plane or level vector	table
column vector	row	three-dimensional array
matrix	row order	two-dimensional array

12.11 REVIEW QUESTIONS

1. What advantage does the use of a two-dimensional array have over the use of multiple one-dimensional arrays?
2. How is an item referenced in a two-dimensional array?
3. How does the FORTRAN compiler know that a two-dimensional array is used in a program?
4. How does the FORTRAN compiler determine how many storage locations to reserve for a two-dimensional array?
5. When using nested implied DO's, the innermost implied DO is always completed first. (True/False)
6. Each implied DO in nested implied DO's must be enclosed in parentheses and separated by a comma. (True/False)
7. When should three-dimensional arrays be used instead of two-dimensional arrays?

12.12 EXERCISES

1. Provide the DIMENSION statements for the following specifications.
   a. A matrix of 7 rows by 5 columns named MATRIX.
   b. A matrix of 20 rows by 11 columns named TABLE.
   c. Four groups of matrices with 6 rows and 4 columns named CLASS.

2. Provide the DIMENSION statements for the following specifications.
   a. A matrix of 11 rows by 6 columns named X.
   b. A matrix of 30 rows by 4 columns named MATX.
   c. Five groups of matrices with 10 rows and 7 columns named SALES.

3. How many data records will be read by each of the following groups of statements?

    a.   **DIMENSION Z(3,12)**
          DO 10 I = 1,3
             READ (5,99) (Z(I,J),J = 1,12)
       99   **FORMAT (6F5.2)**
       10 CONTINUE

    b.   **DIMENSION L2(5,30)**
          READ (5,99) (L2(I,J),J = 1,30),I = 1,5)
       99 FORMAT (15I2)

4. How many data cards will be read by each of the following groups of statements?

    a.   **DIMENSION B(6,20)**
          DO 10 I = 1,5
             READ (5,99) (B(I,J),J = 1,10)
       99   **FORMAT (10F4.1)**
       10 CONTINUE

    b.   **DIMENSION MM(11,40)**
          READ (5,99) ((MM(I,J),J = 1,40),I = 1,11)
       99 FORMAT (20I1)

5. Complete the following exercises on the I/O of two-dimensional arrays. Use X as the array name and use at least one implied DO in the READ/WRITE statements. Assume X is dimensioned as a 6-row by 10-column array.
   a. Load the array X from six data records with ten items per record under the specifications 10F6.2.
   b. Write the first eight items in each row under the specifications 8F10.2.

6. Complete the following exercises on the I/O of two-dimensional arrays. Use Y as the array name and assume dimension specifications of 8 rows and 12 columns. Use at least one implied DO in the READ/WRITE statements.
   a. Load the first nine columns of each row in the array Y from eight data records. Each data record contains nine values under the specifications 9F4.0.
   b. Write the first five values in each row double-spaced under the specifications 5F7.0.

7. Complete the following exercises on the manipulation of two-dimensional array items.
   a. Write the routine to initialize the elements in a 9-row by 30-column array named K to one.
   b. Write the routine to sum all the items stored at odd-numbered rows in a 6-row by 6-column array named NN.
   c. Write a routine to search a 50-row by 7 column array named D for the value 76.5. As soon as the value is found, branch to statement number 77.

8. Complete the following exercises on the manipulation of two-dimensional array items.
   a. Write the routine to add one to each element in a 4-row by 20-column array named HOLD.
   b. Write the routine to create a second array named B2 from an array named B1. The arrays contain 12 rows and 3 columns.
   c. Write the routine to count all the occurrences of a quantity stored in K with the items in a 40-row by 20-column array named KARY.

12.13 PROGRAMMING PROBLEMS

1. Write a program to find the smallest item in a two-dimensional array named XDATA. The array XDATA is a 5-row by 5-column array and is loaded from five data records under the format specifications of 5F5.0.
      Write the array in row-order fashion under the output specifications of 5F5.0. Then search the array. When the search is completed, write a message that says:

            'THE SMALLEST ITEM IN ARRAY XDATA IS' mmm

   where mmm is the quantity of the smallest item in the array.

2. Expand problem 1 to include the row and column location at which the smallest item was found. When the search is over, write a message that says: 'THE SMALLEST ITEM IN ARRAY XDATA IS' mmm 'AND WAS FOUND AT ROW' ii 'AND COLUMN' jj where mmm is the smallest item in the array, ii is the row location, and jj is the column location.

3. Write a program to search a two-dimensional array named M and count all the occurrences of the items that match the value in a variable MVAL. The array, M, is a 3-row by 10-column array loaded from three data records with the format specifications 10I2. The variable MVAL is read from a fourth data record with its value in columns 1–2.
      Write the array M in row-order fashion under the format specifications 10I5. Then search the array. After the search operation is completed, write a message that says: 'THE VALUE' mmm 'OCCURRED IN THE ARRAY M' nnn 'TIMES', where mmm is the quantity in MVAL and nnn is the count of occurrences.

4. Write a program to compute a biweekly gross pay report using a search operation on a pay grade table. A biweekly payroll record is prepared for each employee, containing his employee number in columns 1–4 (integer form), his hours worked (form = NNN.NN) in columns 7–12, and his pay grade (form = NN.) in columns 15–17. The pay grade field is used to search a pay grade table to locate the hourly wage rate. By using the hourly wage rate from the table and the number of hours worked from the payroll card, the employee's gross pay can be calculated.

The pay grade table is a 9-row by 2-column array named PAYGRD. Nine data records are used to load the table in row order, with each record containing the pay grade in columns 1–3 (form = NN.) and the hourly wage rate in columns 5–9 (form = NN.NN).

Next, nine employee payroll records are read and processed against the pay grade table to compute gross pay. As each payroll record is read, a search is performed in the array, PAYGRD, to match the pay grade (column one) in the payroll record. Then the column two quantity (hourly rate) is multiplied by the hours worked (from the payroll record) to produce gross pay.

As the gross pay is calculated for each employee, write a print record as follows:

Field Description	Print Positions
Employee number	7–10
Pay grade	14–16
Hourly wage rate	20–24
Hours worked	30–35
Gross pay	40–46

Also accumulate a running total of the gross pay calculated for all employees.

The last payroll record (record 10) read will contain a value of 9999 for the employee number field. This data record is used as a trailer record to signal the end of the payroll transaction file. Print the accumulated gross pay after the last printed employee record, with an appropriate literal. Also include appropriate column headings to identify each column of output values.

5. Write a program to process transactions for an inventory control application. The file of ten inventory items is read into a two-dimensional array named INVCTL. The array INVCTL is a 10-row by 3-column array loaded in row order from ten data records in the following format:

Record Positions	Field Description
1–5	Item number (Form = NNNNN)
10–12	Quantity on hand (Form = NNN)
13–15	Quantity on back order (Form = NNN)

After the file containing the ten records is loaded into the array INVCTL, write the array in row order under the output specifications 3I10. Include column headings to identify each column of data. The next eight data records represent transaction records that are processed against the items in INVCTL. The transaction records are typed according to the following format.

Record Positions	Field Description
1–5	Item number (Form = NNNNN)
7	Transaction code
	(1 = Receipt of items,
	2 = Shipment of items)
10–12	Quantity involved (Form = NNN)

As each transaction record is read, search the array, INVCTL, for a match on the item number (column one). When a match is found, update the quantity-on-hand vector (column two) and/or the quantity-on-back-order vector (column three) according to the following requirements.

a. If the transaction code is a receipt of items (code of 1), you should add the quantity in the transaction record to the quantity-on-hand column for that item number.

b. If the transaction code is a shipment of items (code of 2), then subtract the quantity in the transaction record from the quantity-on-hand column for that item number. However, you must first check to see if there are any items on hand. If there is a sufficient quantity, do the subtraction. If there is not a sufficient quantity on hand to satisfy the shipment request, then ship as many items as are on hand and add the difference (between shipment request and quantity on hand) to the quantity-on-back-order column. If the difference is added to the back-order column, be sure to set the quantity-on-hand column to zero.

Assume that the inventory item numbers in the transaction records are valid, and that the transaction codes are also valid. You should always program for possible error conditions in the transactions for "real-world" applications. To shorten the problem, however, we will assume that they are correct.

A ninth transaction record will be included as a trailer record to indicate the end of the transaction records. This data record will have 99999 punched as its item number. When this record is read, print the updated array under the same output specifications as before. Also include column headings.

13 Subroutine Subprograms

13.1 INTRODUCTION TO THE USE OF SUBROUTINE SUBPROGRAMS

Programs often include routines repeated at various locations. It would be convenient if a routine could be written only once and called whenever needed in a program. A subprogram allows you to do just that. You can write a routine as a subprogram and refer to it whenever you wish in a program. This has the same effect as writing the routine at each appropriate location in the program.

A **subprogram** may be defined as a set of instructions contained in a separate program that performs a specific task under the direction of another program. The subprogram is executed when its name is used in a calling program. The subprogram is designed to solve only one small part of a problem, such as sorting, searching, calculations, output operations, or some other operation. It is a complete program in itself and plays a subrole in the problem solution. Hence, the name *subprogram* is very appropriate.

There are two basic types of subprograms in FORTRAN:

1. SUBROUTINE subprograms
2. FUNCTION subprograms

This chapter is concerned solely with subroutine subprograms, which can be used for any type of routine needed. Function subprograms are used primarily to compute mathematical functions in which a single resulting value is produced; they are covered in chapter 15.

Each type of subprogram must have at least four statements. These statements are:

1. A SUBROUTINE or FUNCTION statement to identify the type of subprogram.
2. At least one executable statement (e.g., READ, WRITE, Assignment).
3. A RETURN statement.
4. An END statement.

An END statement must be included as the last statement in every subprogram to inform the FORTRAN compiler where the subprogram ends. Thus, each subprogram is a separate and complete program within itself. It may contain any number of source statements. A subprogram may also contain any statement that a main program does, with the exception of another subprogram statement (i.e., SUBROUTINE or FUNCTION).

Whenever the term *subprogram* is used in this chapter, it refers to both types of subprograms in general. When the term *subroutine* is used, it refers to the specific type of subroutine subprograms.

The program that creates the whole program and normally calls the subprograms is referred to as the **main program** or **mainline program**. Only one main program is allowed in a FORTRAN job. One or more subprograms may be combined with a main program to form the whole program designed to solve a given problem. The subprograms are usually placed in the job deck after the main program.

The term **calling program** refers to the program unit that is invoking (using) a subprogram. The term **program unit** means any type of program (i.e., main program or a subprogram).

The CALL statement in the calling program makes a subroutine subprogram available for use. Whenever the subroutine is referenced, control of execution is directed to the subprogram. After the execution of the subroutine is completed, control is turned back to the calling program. The compiler automatically provides the necessary transfers of control and communication links. You need only specify the subprogram name, the information you want passed to the subprogram, and the information you want returned.

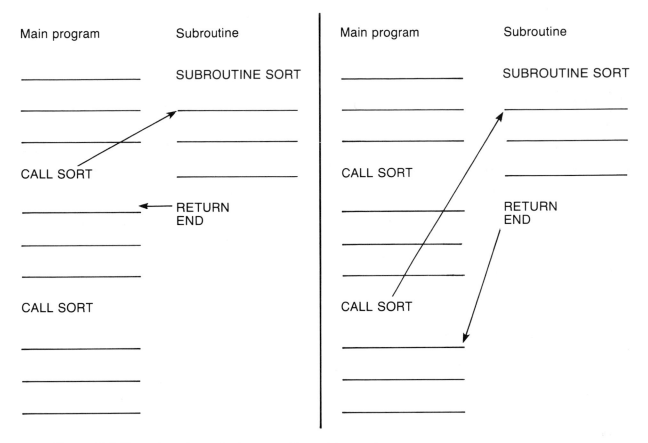

Main program	Subroutine	Main program	Subroutine
	SUBROUTINE SORT		SUBROUTINE SORT

Figure 13.1 Illustration of transferring control to and from subprograms

Assume you have a program that needs a sorting routine at several different locations. The sorting routine will be written as a subroutine named SORT. The concept of transferring control to and from the subprogram is illustrated in figure 13.1. The arrows indicate the transfer of execution.

Control is transferred to the first statement in the subroutine whenever its name is referenced in the CALL statement. Control is turned back to the calling program at the statement after the CALL.

Let us define the problem in a little more detail. Suppose you want to read the arrays X, Y, and Z and sort the items in each of these arrays. The following "skeleton" programs in figure 13.2 (p. 374) illustrate the two methods that might be used to produce the desired operations.

If the program is coded in the typical in-line (sequential) fashion, you would have to write the sort routine three times. The subprogram approach keeps you from having to rewrite long or complex program segments. You can simply write the sort routine, SORT, one time and include it in your source program as a subroutine subprogram. Whenever you need to use it, you simply call it by its assigned name. The savings in coding and typing time becomes increasingly important as the number of references to the subroutine increases.

The beginning of our subroutine subprogram is identified as follows:

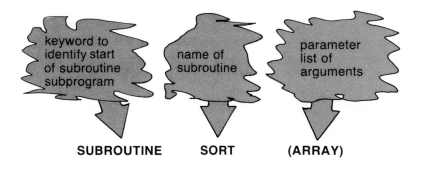

keyword to identify start of subroutine subprogram   name of subroutine   parameter list of arguments

SUBROUTINE   **SORT**   **(ARRAY)**

	Conventional in-line coding		Using the subroutine subprogram approach
	DIMENSION X(10),Y(10),Z(10)		DIMENSION X(10),Y(10),Z(10)
99	FORMAT (10F5.2)	99	FORMAT (10F5.2)
	READ (5,99) X		READ (5,99) X
C ***	ROUTINE TO SORT ARRAY X		CALL SORT (X)
	. . .		READ (5,99) Y
	. . .		CALL SORT (Y)
	READ (5,99) Y		READ (5,99) Z
C ***	ROUTINE TO SORT ARRAY Y		CALL SORT (Z)
	. . .		. . .
	. . .		. . .
	READ (5,99) Z		STOP
C ***	ROUTINE TO SORT ARRAY Z		END
	. . .		SUBROUTINE SORT (ARRAY)
	. . .	C ***	ROUTINE TO SORT AN ARRAY
	STOP		. . . . . .
	END		. . . . . .
			RETURN
			END

Figure 13.2 Illustration of two approaches to providing a SORT routine

A subroutine name is formed the same way as other names in FORTRAN (i.e., 1–6 characters, beginning with a letter). The type of name chosen does not have to conform to the integer/real convention, since no values are ever associated with the name. A variable or array, however, must not have the same name as any subroutine name used by the program.

You may wonder how to sort different arrays with the same routine. The answer lies in the ability to pass different values, called **arguments,** to the subprogram to use. The subprogram is written in a general fashion and sorts whatever array is passed to it. The arguments, as shown in the example, are placed in parentheses following the subprogram name. Thus, the values (X), (Y), and (Z) are the different arguments in the calls to the subroutine SORT. The SUBROUTINE statement receives each array and places the items into its own array, named ARRAY. The sorted items in ARRAY are returned to the array that was passed to the subprogram.

The calling program is usually the main program, but it may also be another subprogram. The CALL statement invokes (starts execution of) the subroutine identified by its name in the CALL.

Consider the following illustration of the CALL statement.

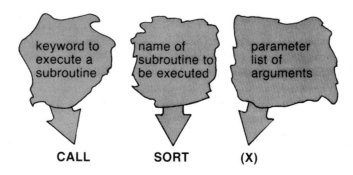

This statement calls the subroutine named SORT and passes the array X as an argument to the subprogram. A subprogram may call other subprograms, but it cannot call itself. If a subprogram called itself, an endless loop would result on many computers. Neither can two subprograms call each other. With these two restrictions, subroutines may include calls to other subroutines to practically any desired depth.

A RETURN statement in the subprogram tells the computer when to turn control back to the program that called it. A RETURN statement must be used, not a STOP statement. The STOP statement would tell the computer to terminate processing the job altogether.

The use of subprograms provides many advantages in designing and developing of programs to solve various problems. These advantages are:

1. Reduction in the amount of required work. Since the routine is included at only one location in the program, there is a substantial reduction in the amount of coding and keypunching performed.

2. Modular programming techniques can be incorporated. Each task can be coded as a different subroutine. Each subroutine can be thought of as a different module in the development of the program. This module technique provides a highly structured program approach to problem solving.

3. Debugging is easier. It is usually far easier to debug an individual subprogram than it would be to debug a routine in the main program. There are fewer statements to look at, thus the logic can be more easily understood.

4. Division of work is simplified. Suppose a program must be developed by three people. The major tasks can be identified and coded as subprograms. Thus the tasks can easily be divided among the programmers. In contrast, the development of one main-line program by more than one person can be quite a hassle.

5. Number of required storage locations reduced. Every executable statement in a program requires a certain amount of memory. By using a subprogram instead of repeating a routine in a program, fewer statements are required and thus, less memory.

6. Once written and debugged, the subroutine can be used repeatedly. Programming errors in the reuse of the same routine are reduced.

7. Incorporation of library-supplied subprograms. Those subprograms used by many programmers may be included in a library of subprograms. The library of subprograms is usually included with the FORTRAN compiler and is available during compilation of the program. The programmer does not have to code the subprogram, but merely calls it into his program. The subprogram is then copied from the library and included in the program.

The statement numbers, variable names, and array names are completely independent of the statement numbers and symbolic names used in the other program units. They may be duplicated between program units without any conflict. Statement numbers and variables/arrays are assigned unique locations within each program unit. Thus, the variable X in a subprogram refers to a different storage location from the variable X in another program unit. This is why you must pass arguments in a parameter list when communicating values between program units.

Subprograms are one of the most powerful tools available to the programmer. Knowledge of their use and capability will greatly increase your competence in programming. Now that the basic concepts of subprograms have been discussed, let us examine the subroutine-related statements in detail.

13.2 THE SUBROUTINE, RETURN, AND CALL STATEMENTS

The SUBROUTINE statement identifies the beginning of a subroutine subprogram. Thus, this statement must be the first one in the subroutine. The SUBROUTINE statement begins with the word SUBROUTINE, followed by its assigned name. A parameter list, if used, is enclosed in parentheses and follows the subroutine name. Figure 13.3 presents the general form of the SUBROUTINE statement.

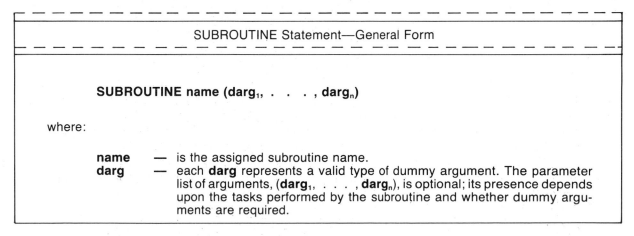

SUBROUTINE Statement—General Form

SUBROUTINE name (darg₁, . . . , dargₙ)

where:

name — is the assigned subroutine name.

darg — each **darg** represents a valid type of dummy argument. The parameter list of arguments, (**darg₁, . . . , dargₙ**), is optional; its presence depends upon the tasks performed by the subroutine and whether dummy arguments are required.

Figure 13.3 General notation of the SUBROUTINE statement

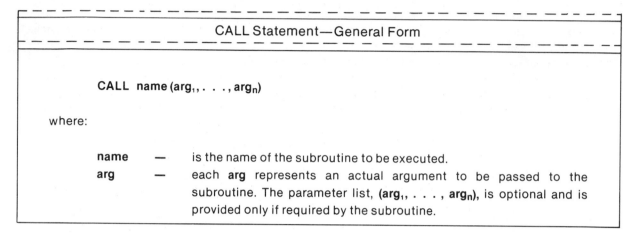

RETURN Statement—General Form

RETURN

Figure 13.4 General notation of the RETURN statement

CALL Statement—General Form

CALL name (arg$_1$, . . ., arg$_n$)

where:

name — is the name of the subroutine to be executed.

arg — each **arg** represents an actual argument to be passed to the subroutine. The parameter list, (**arg$_1$, . . ., arg$_n$**), is optional and is provided only if required by the subroutine.

Figure 13.5 General notation of the CALL statement

The RETURN statement terminates execution of the subprogram and returns control to the calling program. There can be more than one RETURN statement in a subprogram, just as there can be more than one STOP statement in the main program. The RETURN statement consists solely of the keyword RETURN. Figure 13.4 gives the general form of the RETURN statement.

A subroutine is called into use by the CALL statement. This statement contains the word CALL followed by the subroutine name. A parameter list of arguments, if required, is enclosed in parentheses and follows the subroutine name. The CALL statement may be included in the main program or in any subprogram that requires use of the subroutine. Figure 13.5 gives the general form of the CALL statement.

13.3 PASSING ARGUMENTS IN A PARAMETER LIST

A **parameter list** is defined as a list of variables, constants, and/or arrays which communicates values between a subprogram and a calling program. Each variable, constant, or array name in the list is called an **argument,** which either passes a value to another program unit or takes on a value passed from a program unit. Some programmers refer to the list of arguments as an **argument list** instead of a parameter list.

The parameter list of arguments is the way of communicating values between program units. If a subroutine requires a certain number of arguments to be used in calculations, both the SUBROUTINE and the CALL statements must include corresponding arguments in their parameter lists. If a subroutine returns some calculated results, arguments must also be included in both parameter lists for the returned values.

The parameter list is an optional part of the SUBROUTINE and CALL statements. That is, if no arguments need to be passed between the subroutine and the calling program, then the parameter list is omitted. For example, you may have a subroutine named NEWPAG, which simply performs a page eject operation for which no arguments need be passed.

The arguments included in the parameter list of the CALL statement are refered to as **actual** or **formal arguments.** The variables and array names contained in the parameter list of the subprogram are called **dummy arguments.** Dummy arguments may be thought of merely as placeholders for the actual arguments. The first dummy argument holds a place for the first actual argument, and so on. So whenever the term **dummy argument** is used, it refers to an argument in the subprogram parameter list; the term **actual argument** refers to an argument in the CALL.

Dummy arguments may be one of three types:

1. input arguments—that furnish values for the subroutine to use in its operations and are not modified by the subroutine.
2. output arguments—that the subroutine calculates and returns to the calling program.
3. input/output arguments—that furnish values to the subroutine, are modified in the subroutine, and are passed back to the calling program. Input/output arguments are also known as mixed arguments.

When a subroutine is called by a program unit, the values are placed in the input arguments; then the execution of the subroutine begins. When execution is finished, the calculated or redefined values are placed in the output arguments, and control is returned to the calling program.

The name of an actual argument can be the same as that of its corresponding dummy argument, or it can be different. For the sake of clarity and documentation, it is wise to use the same names whenever feasible. If, however, different programmers write different program units, no difficulty is encountered in using different names.

Arguments in the parameter list may include values other than numeric constants or variables. They may include literal constants or even various types of expressions. Following is a list of the different types of values that may be included as actual arguments in a parameter list.

1. A numeric constant of any type
2. A logical constant
3. A literal constant
4. Any type of nonsubscripted variable
5. Any type of subscripted variable
6. Any type of array name
7. Any type of arithmetic expression
8. Any type of logical expression
9. The name of a subprogram

If an array is passed as an argument, then the associated argument in both parameter lists is an array name. The array dimensions *must be included* in both programs. If a single item in an array is to be passed, then it is passed as a subscripted variable by specifying the element number after the array name.

Constants and expressions are used only as actual arguments. It makes no sense to include constants or expressions as dummy arguments. Dummy arguments may only be a variable, array name, or a subprogram name. A subprogram must not change the value of any dummy argument having as its corresponding actual argument a constant or expression. An example of a CALL containing constants, an expression, and a subscripted variable is as follows:

CALL SUBR(10,8.7,3HCAT,2*5 + N,RESULT(1))

The first two arguments (10,8.7) are numeric constants. The third argument is a literal constant. The fourth argument is an arithmetic expression that yields an integer value. The last argument is an example of a subscripted variable, which passes the first value in the array RESULT. The use of subprograms themselves as arguments will be discussed in chapter 15, when some of the more exotic subprogram statements are covered.

All arguments in the parameter list of the calling program must agree with the arguments in the subprogram's parameter list in four ways. These four ways are:

1. In number (that is, by count in the parameter list)
2. In order (that is, in a left-to-right progression)
3. In type (that is, integer, real, literal, and so on)
4. In length (that is, single precision or double precision)

The same number of arguments must be included in both parameter lists. If the SUBROUTINE statement contains three arguments, then the CALL statement must contain three arguments in its parameter list.

The arguments must agree in a one-to-one, left-to-right order in both lists. If a subroutine expects to receive a certain value as the first argument in its list, then you must ensure that the corresponding value appears first in the list of the CALL. The positional relationship of all corresponding arguments must be maintained in each list.

Suppose you have a subroutine CALC that sums the items in each of two arrays named A and B. The variables ASUM and BSUM are used to return the sum of arrays A and B, respectively. Assume the SUBROUTINE statement is coded:

SUBROUTINE CALC (A,ASUM,B,BSUM)

Array A is considered to be the first array (one-dimensional containing ten items), and B is the second array (one dimensional containing twenty items).

You wish to pass two arrays named X and Y to the subroutine to calculate the sum of their items and receive these sums back under the variables XSUM and YSUM, respectively. Array X is a ten-element, one-dimensional array, and array Y is a twenty-element, one-dimensional array. The CALL statement must be coded as follows:

CALL CALC (X,XSUM,Y,YSUM)

Thus, the order of the actual arguments placed in the parameter list agrees with the order of the corresponding dummy arguments in the SUBROUTINE list.

The relationship between the arguments in the CALL and SUBROUTINE statements is illustrated as follows:

CALL CALC (X,XSUM,Y,YSUM)

SUBROUTINE CALC (A,ASUM,B,BSUM)

The array names A and B in the subroutine take on the values in the arrays X and Y, respectively. The arguments XSUM and YSUM in the CALL take on the values in ASUM and BSUM, respectively. Remember, it is the position of the arguments in the CALL, not their names, that determines their use in the subroutine.

The arguments may be included in the parameter list of the SUBROUTINE statement in any order you wish. But the order of arguments in the list of the CALL must be arranged to agree with the order of arguments in the subroutine list. Suppose the subroutine list is written as follows:

SUBROUTINE CALC (A,B,ASUM,BSUM)

The CALL statement must be coded as:

CALL CALC (X,Y,XSUM,YSUM)

The positional relationships of the corresponding arguments are still maintained.

The common practice is to include the input arguments first in the subroutine parameter list, and the output arguments last. This is only a recommended procedure. The main thing is that the arguments between the two lists agree with one another in the order in which they are put into their lists.

Agreement by type and length means that the corresponding arguments in the two lists should agree in their mode of data. If a dummy argument is type integer, the actual argument must be an integer type also. If the dummy argument is a real type array, then the corresponding actual argument must be a real type array. Agreement in length means that the corresponding arguments must agree in precision. If a dummy argument is double precision, then its corresponding actual argument must also be double precision.

If an actual argument is intended to be different from the type implied by the first letter of its name, then the argument must be declared in an Explicit Type statement. For example:

Mainline	Subroutine
REAL INCH	**SUBROUTINE CONVRT (RINCH,FEET)**
. . .	. . .
. . .	. . .
CALL CONVRT (INCH,FEET)	. . .

Likewise, an Explicit Type statement must be used in a subprogram if a dummy argument is intended to be a type different from that implied by the first letter of its name.

There is generally no limit on the number of arguments in a parameter list. Thus, the maximum number of arguments is the number that can be contained on allowed continuation cards.

Now to some sample programs.

13.4 SAMPLE SUBROUTINE SUBPROGRAMS

To illustrate the concepts and statements discussed in section 13.3, let us examine three subroutine subprograms: first, a subroutine that uses no arguments; next, a subroutine that has both input and output arguments in its parameter list; finally, a subroutine that uses an array.

You may need to print a page heading and column heading at various points in a long program. This operation can be very easily done by a subprogram, which makes your work easier and less prone to coding errors in complex format specifications.

Let us assume a grading program that needs a page header that reads "GRADES FOR DATA PROCESSING 101." Column heading for a student number, test 1, test 2, test 3, test 4, test 5, and average also will be printed. The coded subroutine name HDGS is:

Subroutine	Main Program
SUBROUTINE HDGS	——————
WRITE(6,99)	——————
99 FORMAT(1H1,30X,	——————
*30HGRADES FOR DATA PROCESSING 101)	CALL HDGS
WRITE(6,98)	——————
98 FORMAT(/1H0,5X,4HNAME,14X,	——————
*6HTEST 1,3X,6HTEST 2,3X,6HTEST 3,3X,	——————
*6HTEST 4,3X,6HTEST 5,3X,7HAVERAGE)	CALL HDGS
RETURN	——————
END	END

To illustrate the use of a parameter list, let us examine a subroutine that computes the sum, difference, product, and quotient of any two values passed to it. The subroutine is named CMPUTE and is:

Subroutine	Main Program
SUBROUTINE CMPUTE(X,Y,S,D,P,Q)	READ(5,99) A,B
S = X + Y	99 FORMAT (2F5.2)
D = X − Y	CALL CMPUTE(A,B,S,D,P,Q)
P = X * Y	WRITE(6,98) A,B,S,D,P,Q
Q = X / Y	98 FORMAT(1H0,6F10.2)
RETURN	READ(5,99) G,H
END	CALL CMPUTE(G,H,A1,A2,A3,A4)
	WRITE(6,98) G,H,A1,A2,A3,A4
	CALL CMPUTE(8.3,5.71,S,D,P,Q)
	WRITE(6,98) S,D,P,Q
	STOP
	END

The subroutine CMPUTE receives the two input values under the arguments X and Y. The sum, difference, product, and quotient are computed and passed back under the arguments S, D, P, and Q, respectively.

The main program first reads the two variables A and B and passes them to the subroutine. The results are received back under the variables S, D, P, and Q. The same variable names are used for the actual arguments in the CALL parameter list as the dummy arguments in the subroutine parameter list. This is fine, and is recommended where feasible. However, the variable names do not have to be the same. In the second CALL the variables A1, A2, A3, and A4 are used to receive the computed values. The third CALL passes two numeric constants as the input values to the subroutine.

To illustrate a subroutine that uses an array, let us consider a subroutine named SUMARY, which sums the items in variously sized one-dimensional arrays. The array name and number of elements are passed to the subroutine as the first two arguments, respectively. The subroutine is:

Subroutine
```
SUBROUTINE SUMARY(X,N,TOT)
DIMENSION X(20)
TOT = 0.0
DO 10 I = 1,N
     TOT = TOT + X(I)
10 CONTINUE
RETURN
END
```

Main Program
```
   DIMENSION A(10),B(20)
   READ(5,99) A
99 FORMAT (10F4.2)
   CALL SUMARY(A,10,SUM)
   WRITE (6,98) A,SUM
98 FORMAT(1H0, 10F7.2/
  *1H0,11HSUM OF A = ,F7.2)
   READ(5,97) B
97 FORMAT (20F3.1)
   CALL SUMARY(B,20,SUM)
   WRITE(6,96) B,SUM
96 FORMAT(1H0,20F6.1/
  *1H0,11HSUM OF B = ,F7.2)
   STOP
   END
```

The main program passes the array to be summed as the first argument. The second argument is a numeric constant specifying the number of items in the array. The sum of the array items is received back under the variable SUM. The subroutine receives the values of the array under the array named X. The array X is dimensioned in the subroutine as twenty elements; so the items can be summed in any one-dimensional array up through twenty elements. The size of the array is received under the variable N. The total of all items in the array is accumulated under the argument TOT.

These sample programs should help you understand the many ways in which subroutines can be used. Subprograms are very powerful tools to make your job of programming easier. They should be used wherever feasible, to provide a modular approach to programming and to make your program more understandable and easier to debug.

The next section discusses how to flowchart subprograms.

13.5   FLOWCHARTING SUBPROGRAMS

The **predefined process symbol** is used in a flowchart to indicate a subprogram. This one symbol refers to the entire subprogram, so a separate flowchart must be developed to specify all the logical steps that are included in the subprogram. The predefined process symbol is:

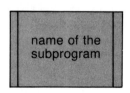

name of the
subprogram

This symbol is simply the rectangular operations symbol with a vertical line drawn down each side. Figure 13.6 illustrates the use of this symbol in a flowchart. We will flowchart the third sample program in section 13.4, which calculated the sum of the elements in a one-dimensional array.

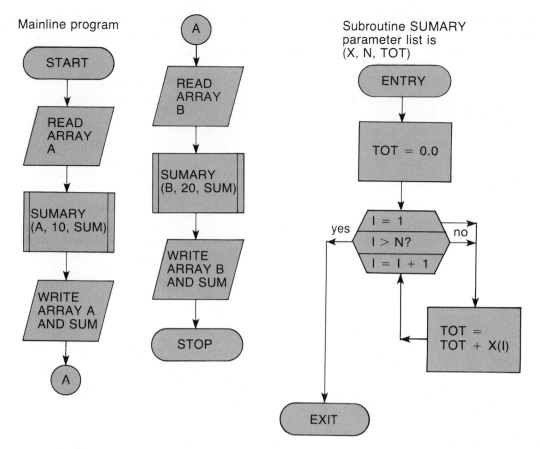

Figure 13.6 Sample flowchart of program using subprograms

The predefined process symbol in the main program indicates that the subroutine is called at that point in the program. The symbol includes the name of the subroutine called, since there can be more than one subroutine. The parameter list is optional but is helpful for documentation purposes. The subroutine itself is flowcharted in detail on a separate page.

13.6 JOB SETUP FOR SUBPROGRAMS

Subprograms may be included in a job deck either before or after the main program. In fact, you can have some subprograms before and some after the main program. The recommended way is to include all subprograms after the main program. A good technique for locating subprograms is to put them in alphabetical order. Figure 13.7 (p. 382) illustrates the setup of a job that includes subprograms. No matter how the subprograms are arranged in the job deck, execution is always begun at the mainline program.

Subprograms must be developed as separate files on some timesharing systems. They must be compiled and linked to the main program unit before the execution of the main program is begun. This process of linking subprograms with the main program unit is performed by a special program known as a link editor or linkage loader. Subprograms may be included in the same file as the main program on some timesharing systems, such as Burroughs.

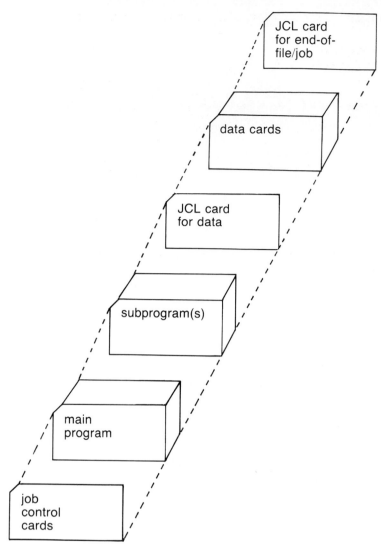

Figure 13.7 Job deck setup for subprograms

13.7 LANGUAGE EXTENSIONS IN FORTRAN DIALECTS (MULTIPLE RETURN N OPTION, ENTRY, AND SAVE STATEMENTS)

Control of execution ordinarily returns from the RETURN statement in a subroutine to the next executable statement following the CALL in the calling program. An extra option is available in the IBM "G" level compiler, WATFIV, and other FORTRAN IV compilers to allow the return of program control to other statements in the calling program as well.

Returns to Alternative Points in a Program (RETURN n)

The alternate return points in the calling program are specified in the CALL statement parameter list by an actual argument of "&n", where the "&" identifies a statement label as an actual argument, and the "n" represents a valid statement number. The statement number must, of course, be assigned to an executable statement. Since the arguments in both parameter lists must be the same number, an asterisk (*) is included as a dummy argument in the subroutine parameter list, to be matched with each alternate return point.

A number is included in the RETURN statement to indicate the point to which control should return in the calling program. That is, RETURN 1 indicates a return of control to the first alternate statement number given in the parameter list, RETURN 2 indicates a return to the second point, and so on. The regular RETURN statement, by itself, still indicates a return of control to the statement after the CALL.

The following routines illustrate the use of the alternate return point option.

Calling Program	Subroutine
CALL ASUB(X,Y,&40,&50,&60)	SUBROUTINE ASUB(X,Y,*,*,*)
ADD = X + Y	IF (X.GT.Y) GO TO 4
. . .	IF (X.EQ.Y) GO TO 5
. . .	IF (X.LT.0.0) GO TO 6
40 SUB = X − Y	RETURN
. . .	4 RETURN 1
. . .	5 RETURN 2
50 XMUL = X * Y	6 RETURN 3
. . .	END
. . .	
60 DIV = X / Y	
. . .	

The calling program provides three alternate return points by using the actual arguments &40, &50, and &60 (i.e., statements numbered 40, 50, and 60, respectively). Three asterisks must be placed in the subroutine parameter list to match these three alternate return point arguments.

The subroutine evaluates each of the Logical IF statements and makes the proper return of control. If the quantity in X is greater than the quantity in Y, control is returned to statement number 40 in the calling program. The RETURN 2 returns control to statement number 50, and the RETURN 3 returns control to statement number 60. If the value of X is less than Y, but not less than zero, the normal RETURN is taken. The integer constant included on the RETURN statement must not exceed the number of alternate return points given in the parameter list. (Note: the RETURN n statement could also have been given on the Logical IF.)

The ENTRY Statement

There are times when you may wish to enter a subprogram at a point different from the first statement. You can do this by using the ENTRY statement. The purpose of the ENTRY statement is to provide entry points at different locations in a subprogram. The IBM, WATFIV, and other FORTRAN IV compilers provide this capability.

The ENTRY statement begins with the keyword ENTRY, followed by an assigned name. This name is constructed like any other subprogram name, and a parameter list in parentheses may follow this ENTRY statement name. For subroutines, the parameter list with the ENTRY statement is optional. Figure 13.8 gives the general form of the ENTRY statement.

If the subprogram is a subroutine, the ENTRY statement name is treated the same as a subroutine name. There is no data type associated with it, since the values are returned under the dummy arguments in the parameter list of the ENTRY statement.

ENTRY Statement—General Form

ENTRY name (darg₁, . . ., dargₙ)

where:

name — is the name of the entry point into the subprogram.

darg₁, . . ., dargₙ — represent a parameter list of dummy arguments. This parameter list is optional for subroutines.

Figure 13.8 General notation of the ENTRY statement

Suppose you want to enter a subprogram at the beginning the first time you call it in order to initialize some variables or an array, but you want to enter the subprogram at a different point whenever it is called after that. The following example illustrates this technique on a subroutine named BEGPAG.

Subroutine	Mainline
SUBROUTINE BEGPAG	_____
NP = 0	_____
ENTRY NEWPAG	CALL BEGPAG
NP = NP + 1	_____
WRITE (6,99) NP	CALL NEWPAG
99 FORMAT(1H1,120X,4HPAGE,I6)	_____
RETURN	_____
END	CALL NEWPAG

The first time the subroutine is called (CALL BEGPAG), it is entered at the top (beginning). The variable NP is initialized to zero. Control continues at the statement: NP = NP + 1. The variable NP is incremented by one, and a "1" is the page number resulting from the print operation of the subroutine. The succeeding times that the subroutine is called (CALL NEWPAG), it is entered at the point named NEWPAG, the page number counter is incremented by 1, and the next page number is printed at the top of a new page.

Now, consider the following program segment with a subroutine, containing a parameter list.

```
            . . .
            . . .
            . . .
        CALL CALC (A, B, C)
            . . .
            . . .
            . . .
        CALL CALC1 (B, C)
            . . .
            . . .
            . . .
        END
        SUBROUTINE CALC (A,B,C)
        A2 = A + A
        ENTRY CALC1 (B, C)
        B2 = B + B
        C = A2 * B2
        RETURN
        END
```

The first time the subroutine is called (as CALC), it is entered at the top. The value of A2 is calculated from the argument A. Then, the variables B2 and C are calculated, and the value of C returned to the calling program. The second time the subroutine is called (as CALC1), it is entered at the entry point CALC1. The variable B2 is calculated from the passed argument of B. The variable C is calculated from the previous value of A2 and the new value of B2; then the value of C is returned to the calling program.

From this example you can see that the parameter list of an ENTRY statement does not have to agree with the parameter list of the SUBROUTINE statement. Neither do any two ENTRY statement parameter lists have to be the same. Dummy arguments in an ENTRY statement parameter list need only agree with the actual arguments in the parameter list of the corresponding calling/invoking statement in the calling program.

The ENTRY statement is considered a specification statement; thus, it is nonexecutable. As such, it does not affect the execution sequence of the statements in the subprogram when entry is made at the beginning. An ENTRY statement, however, must not be placed within the range of a DO loop. The use of an ENTRY statement is one exception to the rule that all specification and statement functions in the subprogram must appear at the beginning, before any executable statements; any number of ENTRY statements may be used in a subprogram.

Retaining Values in Subroutines With the SAVE Statement

As an extension of ANSI FORTRAN 66, most dialects of FORTRAN (IBM, CDC, Honeywell, and others) permit the retention of values passed to, read, or calculated in subprograms (at the end of execution of the subprogram). Thus, when a subroutine is entered again (at the top or an entry point), it retains the values it had at the end of its last execution (in most dialects of FORTRAN IV).

A few FORTRAN IV dialects prohibit the retention of such values unless special options are included (e.g., a compiler directive) to save values at the completion of execution. With Burroughs's FORTRAN IV compiler, for example, you must direct the computer to retain any such values. This option is set for subroutines with the following compiler control statement:

$$\$ \text{ SET OWN}$$

You must place the $ SET OWN statement before the first subprogram in the source deck or timesharing file. You may put it at the beginning of the source program or before the first subroutine if all subroutines are to retain their values.

FORTRAN 77, VAX-11 FORTRAN, and other modern dialects of FORTRAN provide the SAVE statement to retain the values in a subroutine after execution. The form of the SAVE statement is:

$$\text{SAVE [a [,a] ...]}$$

where "a" is one of the following entities: a variable name, an array name, or a named COMMON block name. The named COMMON block name must be preceded and followed by a slash. (Named COMMON will be discussed in chapter 15.) The brackets ([and]) represent optional parameters for the statement; if this optional parameter list is not used, all entities in the program unit in which the SAVE statement resides will be saved. That is, a SAVE statement that does not explicitly contain such a list is treated as though it contained a list of all allowable items for the subprogram in which it appears. Dummy arguments and subprogram names may not appear in the SAVE statement.

Consider the following examples:

SAVE X, Y, Z
SAVE /COM1/, BARRAY
SAVE

In the first example, the variables X, Y, and Z will retain their values in a subprogram after it is executed; in the second example, the named COMMON name COM1 and the array BARRAY will retain their values after execution of a subprogram; in the third example, all values will be retained by the subprogram after execution.

A SAVE statement in the main program unit has no effect. You must place the SAVE statement in each subprogram for which you wish to retain all or some of the values after execution. The SAVE statement is included in a subprogram after the subprogram statement (SUBROUTINE or FUNCTION statement).

The reason for not automatically retaining all values after the execution of a subprogram has to do with modern structured programming practices. Chapter 14 will address the subject of "data hiding", in which items in a subprogram are established as local entities. Local entities are restricted to use within a specific subprogram and should normally go away (not be retained) after the execution of that module.

Except for FORTRAN 77 dialects, most FORTRAN IV compilers (except Burroughs) retain the values in subprograms after execution, so that they are available for the next execution of the subprogram. If you are using a FORTRAN IV compiler and do not get correct output results after repeated executions of subprograms, the compiler probably does not retain the values after execution. This has caused many debugging headaches for both beginning and advanced programmers.

13.8 SUMMARY

Programs will often use the same routine at different points in execution. Subprograms may be called at these required points to eliminate the need for coding redundant routines. Using subprograms to design and develop programs and systems provides many advantages, such as:

1. Reduction in coding
2. Incorporation of modular programming
3. Ease in debugging
4. Division of work among programmers

5. Reduction in program memory requirements
6. Reuse between programs
7. Incorporation into program libraries

A subprogram is defined as a set of instructions contained in a separate program that performs a specific task or function. The subprogram is executed under the direction of another program unit by giving the subprogram name in the appropriate calling statement. A subprogram may be called by the main program unit or by another subprogram. A subprogram must not call itself.

A subprogram is a self-contained unit which must include four statements:

1. A SUBROUTINE statement to identify the subprogram
2. At least one executable statement
3. A RETURN statement
4. An END statement

A subroutine may contain any FORTRAN statement except another SUBROUTINE (or FUNCTION or BLOCK DATA) statement. A subroutine must not call itself directly (within the same subroutine) or indirectly (by calling another subprogram that then calls the subroutine).

A subroutine is called by another program unit with the CALL statement. The name of the subroutine is given following the CALL keyword. A parameter list of arguments may be included in parentheses following this subroutine name. The parameter list of arguments is used to pass values to and from the subroutine.

Control is passed to the first statement in the subroutine. The RETURN statement is used in the subroutine to indicate the point at which control of execution returns to the calling program. Control is returned to the next executable statement following the CALL statement.

A subroutine name is formed in the same way as a variable or array name in FORTRAN. It must begin with a letter and can consist of from one to six characters. Only letters or digits may be used for the second through the sixth characters. There is no data type associated with the subroutine name.

Data items may be passed to and returned from a subroutine by arguments in a parameter list, which is a list of variables, constants, arrays, and so forth that communicates between the two program units. An argument is a data item used or produced by the subroutine and passed back to the calling program. Arguments in the parameter list on the CALL statement must agree with the arguments in the parameter list on the SUBROUTINE statement in four ways:

1. By number (count)
2. In a left-to-right order
3. By data type (integer, real, and so on)
4. By data item length

Arguments in the parameter list of the CALL statement are referred to as "actual" or "formal" arguments. The arguments in the parameter list of the SUBROUTINE statement are referred to as "dummy" arguments. The term "dummy arguments" is used because these arguments serve as holders for the actual arguments passed to them. Dummy arguments may be categorized as input arguments, output arguments, or input/output arguments. The names of the dummy arguments may be the same names as their corresponding actual arguments, or they may be different. For sake of clarity and documentation, you should use the same names. Actual arguments may be any of nine different kinds as listed in section 13.3.

Section 13.5 illustrated the method used to flowchart subroutines and the reference to a subroutine. A predefined symbol is used to indicate a call to a subroutine or subprogram.

Subroutines may be placed before the main program, after the main program, or any combination of the two. The compiler will recognize the subroutines by the SUBROUTINE statement and correctly separate them from the main program. On timesharing systems, subroutines must often be developed as separate files, compiled separately, and then linked to the main program in a process known as linking or link editing.

Subroutines provide a modular approach to programming, making for a more structured discipline in program design and development. Chapter 14 discusses the use of structure charts for illustrating the modules or routines identified for a problem solution. Subroutines can then be used to implement this modular, structured design.

13.9 TERMS

Terms, statements, and concepts with which you should become familiar in this chapter are as follows:

actual argument	input argument	program segment
argument	input/output argument	program unit
argument list	main program	RETURN statement
CALL statement	mainline program	subprogram
calling program	modular programming	subroutine
dummy argument	output argument	subroutine name
formal argument	parameter list	SUBROUTINE statement

13.10 REVIEW QUESTIONS

1. List three advantages in using subroutine subprograms in programming.
2. How is a subroutine subprogram identified in a program?
3. What four statements must be included in every subroutine subprogram?
4. The statement used in a subroutine subprogram to return control of execution to the calling program is the _____ statement.
5. How is a subroutine subprogram referenced in the calling program?
6. How are values passed to and returned from a subroutine subprogram back to the calling program unit?
7. Where is control of execution returned to in the calling program?
8. What is the minimum number of arguments that can be passed to or from a subroutine subprogram?
9. What are the four ways that the arguments in a subroutine reference must agree with the arguments in the SUBROUTINE statement?
10. What symbol is used to identify a call to a subroutine in a flowchart?

13.11 EXERCISES

1. Determine the error in each of the following pairs of statements.

Main Program	Subroutine
a. CALL MPY(A,B,C)	SUBROUTINE MPY(X,Y)
b. CALL CAL(3,X)	SUBROUTINE CAL(A,B)
c. CALL PAGERT	SUBROUTINE PAGERN

2. Determine the error in each of the following pairs of statements.

Main Program	Subroutine
a. CALL CAT(X(1),Z)	SUBROUTINE CAT(X(1),Z)
b. CALL DOG(G)	SUBROUTINE DOG(5.7)
c. CALL MOUSE	SUBROUTINE MOUSE(M)

3. Write the SUBROUTINE statement for each of the following requirements.
   a. A subroutine named PAGE that prints page and column headings. No arguments are passed.
   b. A subroutine named PAGELN that performs a line count operation and prints a page heading. The dummy argument is named LINCNT.

4. Write the SUBROUTINE statement for each of the following requirements.
   a. A subroutine named CALC that produces the sum of three input arguments named A, B, and C. The computed sum is passed back under the dummy argument T.
   b. A subroutine named COUNT that counts the number of occurrences of an item in an array argument named X. The computed count is returned under the dummy argument KNT.

5. Write the CALL statement for each of the following requirements.
   a. Call a subroutine named SUBRTN that prints column headings. No arguments are needed.
   b. Call a subroutine named SUB1 that performs a line count operation and prints a page heading. The argument to be passed is named LINCNT.

6. Write the CALL statement for each of the following requirements.
   a. Call a subroutine named COUNT that counts the number of occurrences of a value in the array argument named A. The computed count is received back under the argument K.
   b. Call a subroutine named SUM to compute the sum of the four arguments named A, B, C, and D. The computed sum is received back under the argument named TOT.

7. Given the following statements:

   Mainline Program
   ```
   X = 3.0
   CALL SUB1(X,XSQ,XCUBE)
   . . .
   . . .
   ```

   Subroutine
   ```
   SUBROUTINE SUB1(Y,YS,YC)
   YS = Y * Y
   YC = YS * Y
   RETURN
   END
   ```

   a. What is the value of Y in the subroutine?
   b. What is the returned value of XSQ?
   c. What is the returned value of XCUBE?

8. Given the following statements:

   Mainline Program
   ```
   A = 2.0
   B = 3.0
   CALL CALC (A,B,C,D)
   . . .
   . . .
   ```

   Subroutine
   ```
   SUBROUTINE CALC (W,X,Y,Z)
   Y = W * X + 1.0
   Z = (Y + 1.0) / 4.0
   RETURN
   END
   ```

   a. What is the value of X in the subroutine?
   b. What is the returned value of C?
   c. What is the returned value of D?

13.12 PROGRAMMING PROBLEMS

1. Write a FORTRAN subroutine named SQR that will square each item in a one-dimensional array named M. The subroutine must also accumulate the total of all newly squared items. This total is to be returned to a main program under the argument MSUM.

   A mainline program will read the values of a twenty-element, one-dimensional array named M20 under the format specifications 20I2. The main program will first write the array M20 under the format specifications 20I5. Then the array will be passed to the subroutine SQR for the squaring of each item. Upon return of control to the main program, the updated items will be written under the specifications 20I5. The total of the updated items will be printed with an appropriate literal.

2. Write a subroutine named SORT to sort the items in a one-dimensional array into ascending sequence. Include a mainline program to read ten values under the format specifications 10F4.1 and load them into a ten-element array named A. Write the array A under the format specifications 10F7.1. Then pass the array A and the number of items to be sorted to the subroutine SORT. After the items are sorted and control returned to the main program, write the sorted array under the specifications 10F7.1.

3. Write a subroutine named SMALL to find the smallest value in a two-dimensional array. Include a mainline program to read twenty values under the format specifications 20I2 and load them into a four-row by five-column array named MATRIX. Pass the array, the number of rows, and number of columns to the subroutine SMALL. After the subroutine has returned the smallest value, write the array SMALL (in row-order) and the smallest value found.

4. Write a subroutine named MATADD to perform a matrix addition operation on two symmetrical two-dimensional arrays. The two input arrays, named A and B, each contain five rows and five columns. The output matrix is named C and is also a 5 by 5 two-dimensional array. Matrix addition is accomplished by adding corresponding elements in the two input arrays and storing the sum at the same location in the output array. That is, A(1,1) is added to B(1,1) and stored at C(1,1); A(2,1) is added to B(2,1) and stored at C(2,1), and so on.

Include a mainline program to read the values of A under a 25F3.1 specification and the values of B from a second data record under the same specification. After the subroutine has performed the matrix additon, write each of the three matrixes in row-order fashion under a 5F6.1 specification. Include a title over each output matrix to identify the matrix.

5. Write a subroutine named MATSUB to perform a matrix subtraction operation on the two input arrays described in problem 4. Matrix subtraction is performed by subtracting corresponding elements in the second array (B) from the first array (A) and storing the sum in the same location in the output array (C). That is, B(1,1) is subtracted from A(1,1) and stored in C(1,1), and so on. Include a mainline program to read and print the arrays as described in problem 4.

6. Write a subroutine named QUAD to solve a quadratic equation of the form $ax^2 + bx + c = 0$. Two real roots are possible. The formulas for computing the roots are:

$$R_1 = \frac{-b + \sqrt{b^2 - 4ac}}{2a}$$

$$R_2 = \frac{-b - \sqrt{b^2 - 4ac}}{2a}$$

Include a mainline program to read the values of A, B, and C under a 3F5.2 format specification. After the two roots are returned, print the values of A, B, C, ROOT1, and ROOT2 under the specifications 5F10.2. Include column headings to identify each printed value.

7. Select any FORTRAN program that you have previously written and convert it into a subroutine subprogram. Include a main program to read the input values and pass them to the subroutine by a parameter list. Return any computed values by arguments in the parameter list and output these values in the main program.

14 Top-Down Modular Design and Structured Software Development

14.1 INTRODUCTION TO THE NEED AND IMPORTANCE OF STRUCTURED SOFTWARE DEVELOPMENT

In your programming class you have written programs that increased in size and complexity as your problem-solving and programming skills increased. Just as a baby starts out being fed milk, then carefully selected and easily digested food, and then more solid food, you have been assigned problems of increasing difficulty. You may have wondered whether you would be able to complete some of the problems assigned. Hopefully, you learned and used the top-down structured methodologies explained in chapter 3 in developing your design solution and program. If you used these methodologies, then completing the problem assignments should not have been too frustrating or distasteful; if you didn't use these top-down structured methodologies, you may have spent more hours completing an assignment than classmates who did use them.

Chapter 3 discussed the methodology of top-down problem decomposition using flowcharts. This design tool may be all right for smaller, less complex problems, but you have advanced to the point where you are able to write larger, more complex programs using arrays, subroutines, and so forth. A better program design tool is available to aid in developing the program structure for a problem. This chapter discusses two widely-used, top-down problem decomposition and design tools—structure charts and HIPO diagrams.

The overall structure of a program is important in producing software that is reliable, easily maintainable, and modifiable. Top-down design is a methodology for designing the overall structure of a program or system from a top-down view. The overall structure of a program is represented by a collection of functional modules required to solve a problem, and by their relationship to each other. Flowcharts tend to hide the structure of a complex program, since they are primarily used to visualize the control flow of program execution. A structure chart or hierarchy chart is an invaluable design tool for developing and depicting the overall structure of a program. Control flow is not shown in a structure or hierarchy chart, but the structural parts of the program-design solution and their interface (relationship) to each other are identified.

Chapter 3 discussed the software crisis that sparked the software revolution taking place across the country and world today. The increased use of computers and automated systems reflects the need for increased programmer/analyst productivity. This chapter presents some improved programming techniques, such as chief programmer teams, structured walk-throughs, and development support libraries. These techniques provide a more organized approach to software development, which allows on-time implementation, and robust (fail-safe) and reliable systems.

Top-down implementation and testing are two techniques that provide a structured "piecemeal" development of programs. A program is developed, implemented, and tested in a top-down, modular manner. This approach allows for the coding, verification, and implementation of the higher-level functions prior to the coding of the subordinate lower-level functions. The correctness of the program can be verified as you proceed down the hierarchical structure with additional modules. This way the program can be built in stages (as recommended in chapter 3) and in a highly modular form. Consideration for later program maintenance is inherent in the process. Interface errors and other costly design problems can be detected at an early stage.

Software errors are no laughing matter in operational programs. Errors have occurred in aerospace programs that resulted in an abort of space missions, as you may have read or heard on the news. Errors have caused much embarrassment to management. Errors such as incorrect billings and credit notices have caused undue harassment of people. The tools and techniques presented in this chapter help produce software that contains fewer errors and, thus, increases the reliability of programs and systems.

Section 14.2 discusses the concepts of top-down modular design.

14.2 TOP-DOWN MODULAR DESIGN AND FUNCTIONAL DECOMPOSITION

Coding must not be the first step in developing a program; it must be preceded by careful, rational design. There are two completely different aspects to designing a program. The first is concerned with the design of the program structure, i.e., how the functional components are built and their relationship with one another. The second aspect is the control logic for the individual routines and the overall program. Chapter 3 dealt with the aspect of logic design and explained flowcharting and pseudocode as two logic design tools. This section and several of the later sections deal with the first aspect of program design—the program structure.

Before beginning the design of a program, you should make sure that you understand the problem as well as possible. If a problem specification is provided, you should read it thoroughly and make sure that you understand every part of it—output requirements, input data, and the processing rules in decision making and manipulating data. If there is anything you do not understand, ask for clarification. Do not be afraid of appearing stupid— you may have thought of things that no one else considered. If some of the specifications are imprecise, or incomplete, or not written down at all, you should determine your own precise specification and seek confirmation that it is correct.[1]

Figure 14.1 (p. 392) presents a "swing" cartoon depicting assumptions made by many people in the problem-solving process. No one seemed to grasp just what the problem requirements asked for and what the user really wanted.

The lesson to be learned from this cartoon is that you should always make sure you understand what the user wants. The user is not always familiar with programming terms, and a programmer does not always understand user terminology, so be sure to use layman's terms and describe to the user what you think he is saying. Many programmer/analysts make sure they record all agreed-on specifications to prevent disagreements later.

You should also understand how a new program or system fits in with the other systems within its application. You must understand the purpose of the new program and how it interacts with other programs. Learn why the user really wants the new program, and how it will be used. By obtaining a complete view of how a new program fits into an application system, you will have a better perspective of how to design and develop it. You can determine the relative priorities of the problem requirements and get a feel for what is crucial to the success of a properly working program; then you are ready to begin work on the program design.

Mastering Complexity

Mastering complexity is the key to successful software design and development. If the complexity of a program can be overcome, the finished software should be a workable, reliable system. Programmers need better methods and tools to master and manage the complexity of developing large, sophisticated software. The terms "large" and "complex" are relative to each programmer. A file-maintenance program to update six data files, consisting of two-thousand lines of code, may be considered large and complex by many programmers. An on-line, interactive order-entry system consisting of a thousand lines of code may be thought of as a large, complex program by its programmer. The author once worked on a FORTRAN application program with over 37,500 lines of code. Just to print the source listing took over a half an hour on a high-speed line printer. Some application systems have been implemented that required over a million lines of code. The point is that most operational programs will be large and complex compared to most academic problems. So, how does one master this level of complexity?

The only way to deal effectively with complexity is to break the problem into "chunks." Divide the problem into manageable pieces that can be understood and solved. Remember the rule, **DIVIDE and CON-QUER.** One important consideration is how to split up the parts to the problem. You must use a top-down, hierarchical approach to partition the problem solution correctly. A carefully planned design that "looks down from the top" will produce an effective solution.

Functional Decomposition

A programmer cannot create a large program in a single leap because of the large number of details that must be dealt with. The hierarchical approach, decomposing a problem into functional modules, partitions a problem into related components dealing with ever-lower levels of detail.

---

1. Brian Meek and Patricia Heath, *Guide to Good Programming Practice* (Chichester: Ellis Horwood Limited, 1980), p. 15.

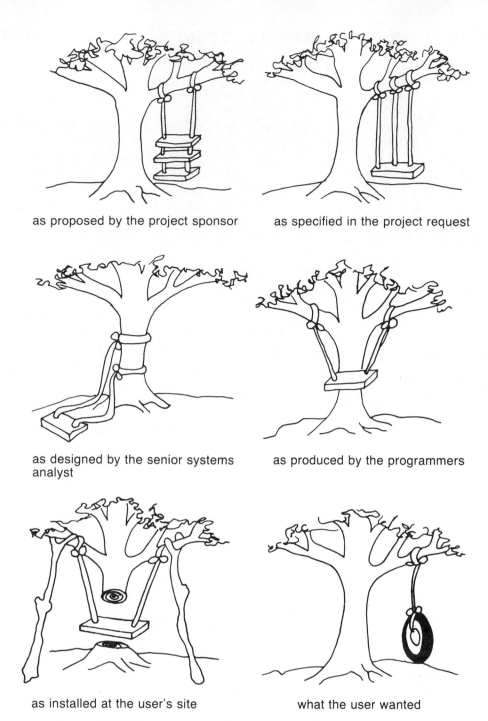

as proposed by the project sponsor

as specified in the project request

as designed by the senior systems analyst

as produced by the programmers

as installed at the user's site

what the user wanted

Figure 14.1 Swing cartoon (author unknown)

Functional decomposition may be viewed as moving from the abstract statement of a problem to a concrete representation of the actions to be implemented on a computer. The problem is attacked at the abstract level and recursively refined into more detailed levels. Beginning with a high-level design and proceeding to lower and lower levels of detail is a natural way of intellectually tackling a large, complex problem. As you move from a high level of conceptualization to a lower level, you gain more insight into the intricacies of the problem solution.[2] The generic term *top-down design* has been given to this process. Dividing a program into appropriate functional components is thus crucial to designing the program structure.

2. Randall W. Jensen and Charles C. Tonies, *Software Engineering* (Englewood Cliffs, N.J.: Prentice-Hall, Inc., 1979), p. 72.

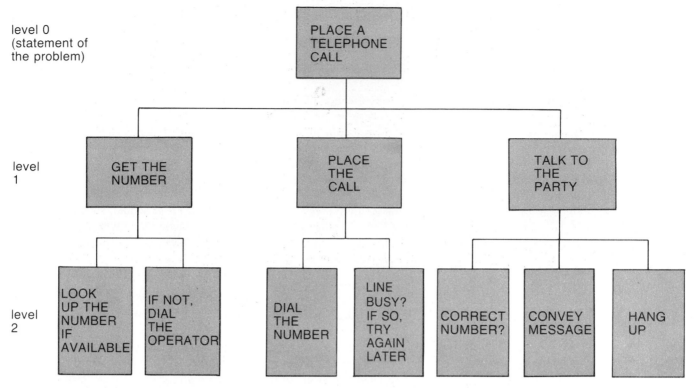

Figure 14.2 A structure chart showing the different levels of problem definition for placing a telephone call

Modularity

The module is the primary unit of a program structure. A **module** may be defined as a collection of statements that solve a part of the program requirements. The term *module* is synonymous with terms such as *components, chunks, parts,* and *pieces* that have been used to denote the partitioning of a problem. The **well-designed module** consists of functionally-related statements that solve a single specific task in a program. The term *functionally-related* means that the statements in the module are directly related to each other as elements of the solution to one specific function (task) in the program.

Consider the decomposition and structure of a non-computer-oriented problem. Figure 14.2 presents a structure chart of the components or modules in placing a telephone call. The top-level module (level zero) states the problem requirement. Observe the three primary modules given at the first level in abstract terms. These modules are decomposed into another, lower, level of detail. The level of detail at level two is sufficient to understand the actions required in the problem solution. If the decomposition of modules at level two were not detailed enough, then this level would have to be decomposed into another level. Decomposition of the modules continues until there is enough detail to fully understand the solution to the problem.

The decomposition and structure chart for a non-computer-oriented problem is constructed the same way as for a computer-oriented problem. You can use this technique and tool to analyze, plan, and organize many projects totally unrelated to computer programming.

A module should be described by its function—what it does—and not by a description of its logic. The phrase "edit-control module", for example, is a description of logic, not function. When defining a function, use a verb/object form.[3] Describe the module as doing something to something. Examples would be "Read the next transaction record" or "Sort the master file by account number". The functional description should be given in a phrase as short as possible.

---

3. Glenford J. Myers, *Composite/Structured Design* (New York: Van Nostrand Reinhold Company, 1978), p. 13.

Modularity offers many valuable benefits in the design and development of programs. Some of these benefits are summarized as follows:

1. The overall problem is broken down into manageable pieces that can be understood. You can then evaluate these pieces to determine whether they actually represent the major functions required of the program.
2. Modularity aids in the debugging and correction of program errors. It is fairly easy to trace an output error back to the specific routine (module) that produced it.
3. Modularity is especially important in program enhancement. New user requirements and changes to a program can be made with little difficulty because of the built-in flexibility of modular routines. The entire program does not have to be modified to incorporate these new enhancements. You can usually isolate the changes to one or more specific modules and not have to reverify the logic of the entire program.
4. You can use an already existing routine from another program. You can lift a module, such as a search or sort routine, from an existing operational program and insert it in a new program with few or no changes. Many common routines exist in subroutine libraries. These can save you considerable time by not having to rewrite and test already debugged routines.

Documentation should always be done as you proceed through the stages in the development of a program. Structure or hierarchy charts help you do this, since they are constructed before the detailed logic design. After the problem is decomposed into its functional modules, as shown in the structure chart, each module can be designed and documented with a design tool such as pseudocode. Additional remarks—such as more precise specifications or logic techniques used in the solution—can easily be added at any point along the way. Finishing the complete documentation package at the end of the project will thus not be a burdensome task, since much of it will already have been created as an integral part of the top-down design process.

In summary, do not begin program coding until you have a complete understanding of the problem and a general plan of attack. The design of a program should be accomplished in two stages: First, identify the functional modules and their relationship to each other in the overall program structure (program structure and module interface design); second, design the control logic for each module (module logic design).

The next section discusses the construction of structure charts to accomplish the first stage in the design of complex programs.

14.3   STRUCTURE CHARTS AS A PROGRAM DESIGN TOOL

The **structure chart** is a graphic design tool that provides a graphic overview of the functional parts of a program and the relationship of those parts to one another. Structure charts illustrate program structure by showing the hierarchical modules in the design solution and the relationship of each sub-part to the larger parts of the problem. They are invaluable for organizing and documenting the thought process leading to the design and solution of a problem. The structure chart can be used at any level of design to divide the solution into simpler, more manageable components.

Symbols

A structure chart consists of two basic graphic symbols—the **module symbol** and **hierarchical lines. The module symbol,** a rectangle, represents a functional component of the solution at a specified level of detail. The **hierarchical lines** connect the modules to show subordination to higher level modules in the overall solution design. Hierarchical lines between rectangle symbols represent "calls." A line coming from the bottom edge of a rectangle represents a call from that module. A line coming to the top edge of a rectangle represents a call to that module.

Two types of modules may be used in a structure chart. One type is the **yet-to-be-developed module,** which has yet to be written, and the other is the **predefined module,** which already exists. The undeveloped module is represented by a simple rectangle symbol. A brief description (several words) of the function of the module is included in the rectangle to describe what the module does. For example, the functional module to perform **housekeeping** (initialization of variables, printing of headings, and other start-up actions) might be drawn as follows:

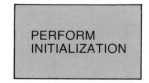

Yet-to-be-developed module

The predefined module symbol is a rectangle with extra lines down the two sides. Predefined modules may be library subroutines, such as an internal sort routine or a specific calculation. A predefined sort module might look like this:

Predefined module

The structure chart is composed of these two types of modules (mostly the yet-to-be-developed modules) interconnected by hierarchical lines to show the hierarchical relationship to one another. The hierarchical lines may be drawn as **diagonal lines** or as **perpendicular straight lines.** An arrow head may be included at the end of a line to show the direction of control. Consider the example shown in figure 14.3:

In this example, module A controls the execution of modules B and C; that is, modules B and C are subordinate to module A. For module A to perform its identified function, it must cause module B and module C to be performed in some combination. In other words, the control of execution for modules B and C is in module A. Somewhere in module A is a control statement (a CALL) that transfers control of execution to module B. After module B is finished, control returns to module A, where the transfer originated, and the next statement in A is executed. Module A also contains a reference to module C that causes C to perform some function. This is described as a **normal connection** and is read as "A calls B" and "A calls C."

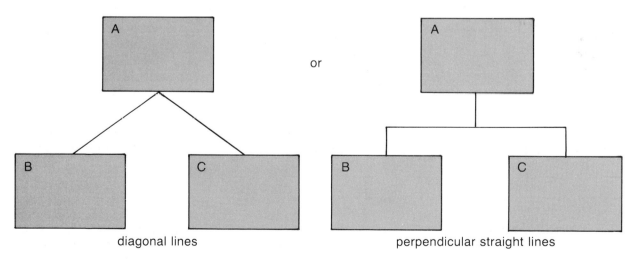

diagonal lines   perpendicular straight lines

Figure 14.3 Illustration of hierarchical lines

A Structure Chart Does Not Show Logic

It is important to remember that **a structure chart does not show logic.** Do not confuse the structure chart with a flowchart. This is perhaps the most common mistake made by students trying to construct structure charts. The structure chart shows *what* needs to be done in the solution, not *how* it needs to be done.

No specific order of execution for lower-level modules is shown in the structure chart. The left-to-right placement of the modules does not always indicate a left-to-right execution of these modules in the program. In figure 14.3 there are no clues as to the order of execution of modules B and C from module A. Neither is there any indication as to the number of times they are called, or if one or both modules are called each time module A is executed. Module C could be called before module B. Suppose that B was a module to edit input data fields for their validity and that C was a module to display an error message. Module B might be called many times (once for each input field), but module C would be called only if an input field were invalid.

Again, logic is not shown in a structure chart. You are simply identifying the parts (components) of a problem solution. These parts are successively refined to show the relationship between each level of detail. The module symbols show what major functions are involved in the solution, and their purpose. The hierarchical lines show the relationship of control between modules and which modules execute others.

Construction of a Structure Chart

The construction of a structure chart begins at a very general, abstract level. At the higher levels of modules you should not concern yourself with details. In fact, one rule in developing structure charts is to postpone the details as long as possible so that you do not lose sight of the major parts of the solution. This is known as **judicious postponement.** At each level the modules are refined into further components of detail. This process is known as **stepwise refinement.** You continue refining the modules into smaller parts at each step (level) until you can see all the parts to the solution. At the bottom/lowest level you have the details of the specific actions needed for the problem solution.

Details should be "hidden" until the end. Always put them off until they can no longer be avoided. This prevents you from losing sight of what you are trying to accomplish. Defining the parts and subparts to a problem in a hierarchical manner also helps you keep the purpose of the problem more clearly in mind.

You cannot see or understand the solution to a complex problem at the top levels. But as you continue to refine each of the higher-level modules into smaller pieces, you begin to see pieces of the solution. Take the problem of putting a person on the moon—a mind-boggling problem. As the problem is refined into smaller pieces, however, such as a propulsion system, a control system, and a life-support system, you begin to understand the components of the solution. The same principle holds true for computer-related problems, such as a payroll program, which includes the functional components of input, edits, gross pay calculations, deductions, and others.

A structure chart begins with a single module symbol at the top (usually centered on a page). Inside the top module you give a general statement of the problem. This level is known as level zero. The problem is then divided into the major parts that involve large functional aspects of the solution. This is known as level one. Next, these major parts are decomposed into more detailed modules, referred to as level two. The recursive process in decomposing the modules continues until all the modules have been worked out in sufficient detail to understand the problem solution. The structure or organization of the pieces to the problem solution is easily seen in the final structure chart. A basic structure chart might appear as shown in figure 14.4.

Notice that the predefined module H is called by both modules C and D. This is known as **module sharing.** That is, a module is called by more than one module at a higher level. Many people consider this a dangerous practice, since a change in module H would affect both modules C and D. Module sharing can make a program more difficult to debug or to modify later, but it is often found with common routines such as sorts and page counter logic (with new report and column heading). One of the great advantages of structured design is the clearly-understood use of common modules.

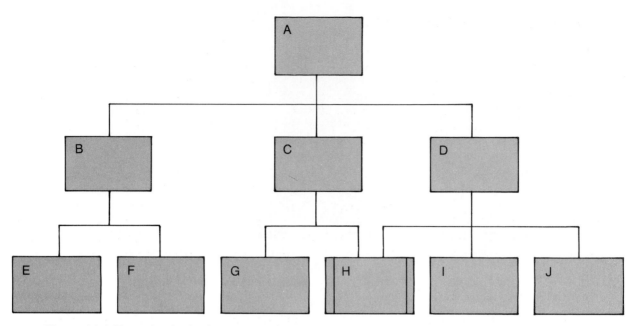

Figure 14.4 Example of a basic structure chart

It is often difficult to draw a structure chart on a narrow sheet of paper such as typing or notebook paper, because of the fan-out pattern towards the bottom of the chart. One way of avoiding this is to show the module hierarchy in a vertical arrangement. For example:

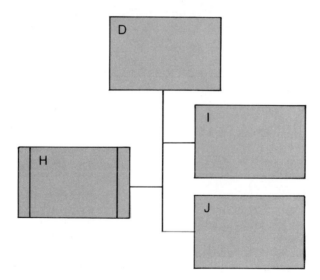

This technique still shows the modules H, I, and J under the parent module D. Do **not,** however, draw the modules in a vertical-line hierarchical manner such as this:

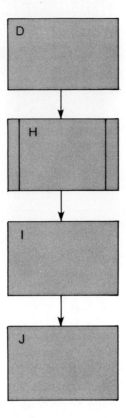

This does not show the modules H, I, and J under the parent module D, as you might think. It shows module H called by D, module I called by H, and module J called by I, which is not the intended hierarchical arrangement.

Models for Structure Charts

There are two basic models or approaches to developing a structure chart. They are known as:

1. The Transaction Model
2. The Event Model

The transaction model shows the main, first level modules as input, processing, and output, since these are the main functions performed on data in a transaction. The first level of the transactional model structure chart is shown in figure 14.5.

The event model shows the main, first-level modules as start-up (initialization), processing, and wrap-up, since these are the main functions performed when you think of the program as an event taking place in time. There must be some initial actions performed, some processing done during the middle of the program, and some wrap-up actions performed at the end. The first level of the event model structure chart is shown in figure 14.6.

The event model structure chart provides an easy and practical approach to most student computer problems. Under the start-up module, you include any initialization actions, such as initializing counters and accumulators, opening external disk files (if required), and performing a priming read for the first data record. The process module may be broken down into calculations, decision-making logic, formatting and writing the output results, and reading a new data record. Edit routines, when needed, are also shown under the process module. The wrap-up module consists of any final actions, such as writing final summary lines, closing external disk files (if required), and so on. I recommend the use of this structure chart model over the transaction model to provide a clear, top-down structured design of your computer lab assignments.

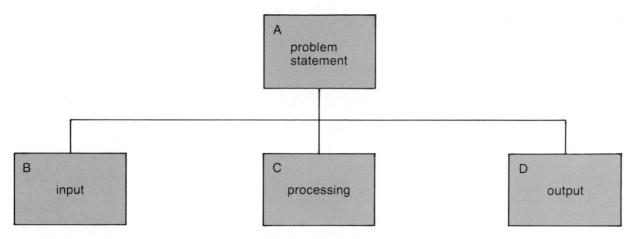

Figure 14.5 The transaction model structure chart

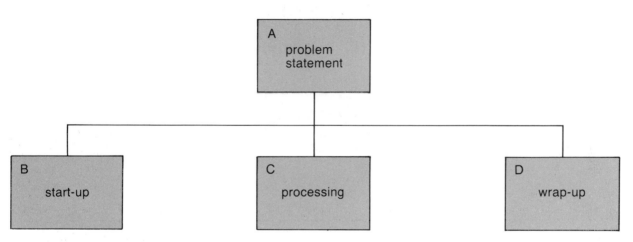

Figure 14.6 The event model structure chart

Showing Partial Logic with Structure Charts (Procedural Annotation)

Structure charts are not intended to show logic, but rather the functional modules of a problem solution and their relationship to each other. There are provisions, however, for showing a certain amount of logic, such as decisions and iterations. The symbols to show decisions and iterations are not widely used, however, because they clutter up the design and add little to the understanding of the logic of a program.

A **small diamond** is used to show a decision, such as a conditional call to a module. A **counter-clockwise, semicircular line** is used to indicate a loop or iteration of execution of a module. See figure 14.7 (p. 400) for an illustration of the two symbols for these operations in a structure chart.

In figure 14.7 module A calls module B based on some decision. Module A also contains a loop which calls module C some number of times.

If a module is to be executed (called) a specific number of times, this number may be included in the higher level module symbol. An annotation symbol may also be included with a module to provide additional explanation of the use or function of the module. An **annotation symbol** is a rectangle with an open right side (just as in flowcharting) attached with dashed lines to a module. See figure 14.8 for an illustration showing these additional features of a structure chart.

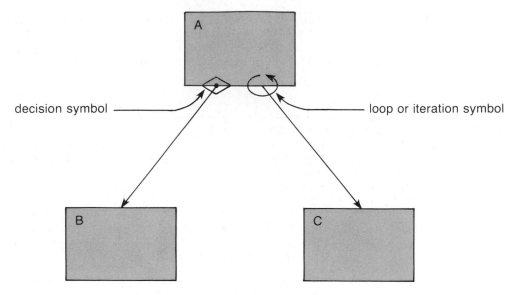

decision symbol ——————————— loop or iteration symbol

Figure 14.7 Showing logic in a structure chart

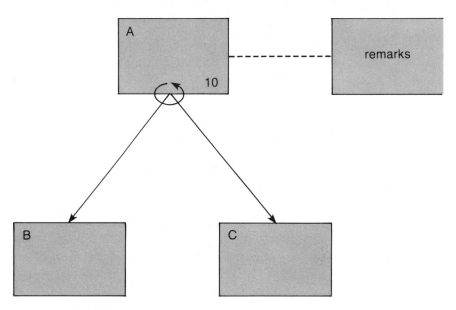

Figure 14.8 Showing loop count and remarks in a structure chart

Figure 14.8 shows that module A calls both modules B and C in a loop which is executed ten times. The annotation symbol provides additional comments about module A.

Some organizations use a modified structure chart that includes the use of pseudocode above the modules to explain when a module is executed. Your instructor may show you other variations in constructing a structure chart. It is a tool to be used as a guideline in program-structure design. One of my students constructed his chart with the detailed pseudocode beneath each lowest-level module to combine the program logic design with the program structure design (to aid in developing his programs). It is important to use an educated application of a tool rather than a blind adherence to conventions. Use what serves you best in developing the functional structure of your programs.

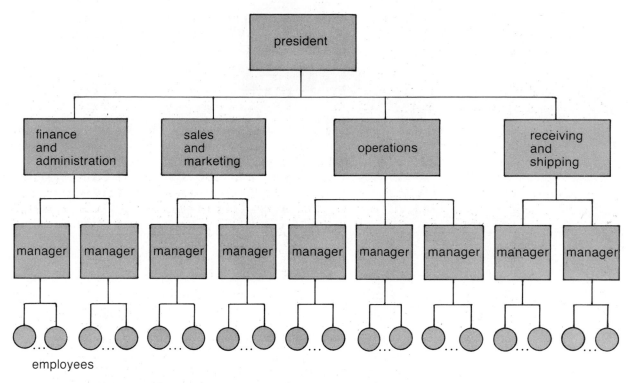

employees

Figure 14.9 A typical business organization chart

Other Aspects of Structure Charts

You may have noticed that a structure chart resembles an organizational chart. A typical organizational chart of the parts or make up of a business organization might appear as shown in figure 14.9.

Just as an organizational chart shows the structure of an organization, a program-structure chart shows the structure of a problem solution. The functional modules shown provide a clear picture of the parts of the solution. The detail logic for solving the problem with a program will be shown later in a proper logic-design tool. The logic within each module can be depicted in pseudocode or another chosen logic-design tool. When the functional components have been identified in enough detail for you to fully understand the pieces to the solution, you can start putting these pieces in order and create the detail design of the program with the logic-design tools.

One of the most common and difficult problems in software development is that of interface control—passing the proper data items in the correct order between programs in a system. Passing data items between routines within the same program, known as module interface or module coupling, is also difficult. Problem specifications may be changed but not communicated to all the people involved in the program development. Sometimes programmers just do not develop correct logic in a straightforward manner to perform the actions needed.

Structure charts help manage interface control by encouraging programmers to think in terms of how modules will interface (communicate) with other modules. You can see the hierarchical structure of the module relationships and know what data needs to be passed to which modules. A structure chart can also show the communications between modules by indicating data flow. The normal data flow (referred to as **direct**) is illustrated in figure 14.10. Module A passes data item "X" to module B, and module B returns control information named "Y" to module A. The symbol ○→ indicates data flow, and the symbol ●→ indicates control information flow. The distinction between "data" and "control" type information is determined by the primary purpose of the data item.

Some people attempt to draw their modules in the structure chart to reflect a left-to-right order of execution in the program. In fact, it is highly recommended that you use this approach to placing the modules in the structure chart. Nonetheless, you should never assume that this technique is always used in a structure chart. There is no rule specifying that it must be used.

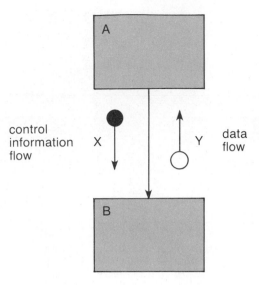

Figure 14.10 Illustration of control and data information flow

Usually five or six is the maximum number of levels you should use in a structure chart. Using more than six levels tends to distract from the overall understanding of the design solution.

The structure chart changes much less from its earliest design than does the coding logic in the program. Thus, a structure chart is very useful in program documentation. The chart can be used to supplement the source program listing to allow a new programmer to grasp the overall program design.

Some people prefer to use the IBM-developed design tool of HIPO (Hierarchy plus Input-Process-Output) charts. The HIPO design tool includes a VTOC (Visual Table of Contents), which shows the modules and their hierarchical structure for a problem solution. The VTOC (pronounced "vee-tock") is often referred to as a hierarchy chart and is very similar to a structure chart. The graphics involved in the HIPO VTOC diagram and the structure chart are very similar, differing only in regard to their labelling schemes, and users can mix or match features of both to create a useful tool. HIPO also includes other diagrams known as overview and detail diagrams to depict the input, processing, and output operations of each function for specific levels. HIPO is a popular design tool to show design in a highly detailed and documentary form. It is described in the next section.

This discussion of structure charts should provide you with enough information to attack complex problems and to break them down into their functional modules. This subdivision of a problem into its various functional parts allows you to better understand the requirements and parts needed in the problem solution. A structure chart is an invaluable tool for illustrating the segments of a program design. A better designed program provides greater reliability and modifiability in the final software.

Section 14.4 presents an overview of HIPO and hierarchy charts, which are intended to serve the same purpose as structure charts, plus a more detailed description of each function.

14.4 HIERARCHY (HIPO) CHARTS AS A PROGRAM DESIGN TOOL

Good documentation is essential to the success of a program development effort. Most documentation, under the traditional bottom-up programming approach, was prepared late in the program development, since many programmers wait until they have produced an operational program before completing the final documentation. Documentation was also often shortchanged because of tight project completion dates. In the past, documentation usually consisted of a program flowchart plus various narratives, but flowcharts reflect only program logic. What was lacking in program documentation was a description of the function of the program—what the program did, rather than how it did it.

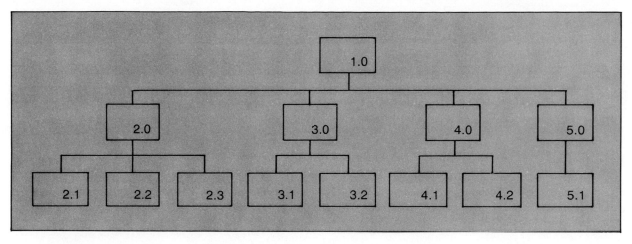

Figure 14.11 Example of a visual table of contents diagram

Hierarchy plus Input-Process-Output (HIPO) is a technique originally conceived at IBM as a program documentation tool. Some IBM personnel believed that documentation that emphasized the program's functions could contribute to the maintenance effort; so they developed the HIPO technique of documenting the functional aspects of a program. Later HIPO was used to express program specifications. Today HIPO is used by many programmers and analysts as both a design aid and documentation tool.

A HIPO package consists of a set of diagrams that graphically describe a program's functions from the general to the detailed level. Each major function is identified and then subdivided into lower-level functions as performed in the top-down design process. Thus, HIPO diagrams may be used from the design phase to the implementation phase of a program or system. They are also used in program maintenance to help identify sections of program code needing changes.

The major objectives of HIPO as a design and documentation technique are: [4]

1. To provide a structure by which the functions of a program can be understood.
2. To state the functions to be accomplished by the program, rather than to specify the program statements to be used in the logic.
3. To provide a visual description of input to be used and output to be produced by each function for each level of diagram. HIPO graphically illustrates the transformation of input data to output data.

A typical HIPO documentation package consists of three kinds of diagrams—a visual table of contents, overview diagrams, and detail diagrams. A more detailed explanation of these three diagrams is as follows: [5]

1. **Visual Table Of Contents (VTOC) diagram.** Like a structure chart, the VTOC diagram provides a pictorial overview of the functional modules in the program. It contains the names and identification numbers of all the overview and detailed HIPO diagrams in the documentation package. It also shows the structure of the program functions and the hierarchical relationship of these functions, which is why it is also known as a hierarchy chart (see figure 14.11). The VTOC may also serve as an index to the individual diagrams of the functions.

   A hierarchy chart (VTOC diagram) differs from a structure chart primarily in two ways. A hierarchy chart assigns an identification number in addition to the name for each module. The identification number relates to the overview or detail diagram that shows the input, processing, and output operations for a function. The second difference between a hierarchy chart and a structure chart is that the hierarchy chart is intended to be a tree structure in which a box (function) has only one parent. Most programs are not tree structures, in that an individual module may be repeated in several

4. International Business Machines Corporation, *HIPO—A Design Aid and Documentation Technique* (GC20–1851) (New York: IBM Technical Publications/Systems, 1975), pp. 1–3.
5. Ibid., p. 3.

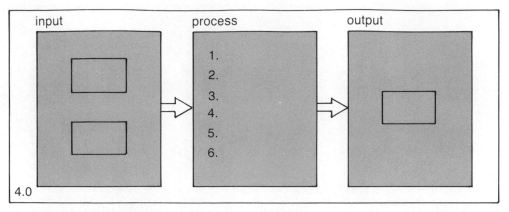

Figure 14.12 Example of an overview diagram

places. This is accomplished in a VTOC by representing the same function box several times, under each of its "parents".[6] A structure chart, on the other hand, represents a specific function only once— since it is coded only once in the program—and connects it by hierarchical lines to each of its "parents".

2. **Overview diagrams.** These are high-level HIPO diagrams. They describe the major functions given in the VTOC and reference the detail diagrams when needed to explain the functions in greater detail. The overview diagram is divided into three sections, which depict the inputs, processes, and outputs in general terms. The input section identifies the input files, records, and tables used by the function. The process section contains a series of numbered steps that describe the major processing activities in the function. These steps are usually restricted to five or six major processing actions. The output section reflects the data files, records, and other data items that are created or modified by the process steps. One or more arrows connect the input items to the process steps and the process steps to the output items. See figure 14.12 for an illustration of the overview diagram. An extended description area may be used to describe in more detail the process steps and the input and output items.

3. **Detail diagrams.** The lower-level HIPO diagrams are called detail diagrams. They represent the functions at the detailed level and show the actual operations in these functions. These diagrams describe specific functions that will be coded as modules in the program. They show the specific input data items (fields or tables), the specific processing steps, and the specific output data items produced by the function. The detail diagrams also refer to other detail diagrams by a solid black arrow coming into and going out of the diagram. An extended description section is contained on the detail diagram to amplify the process steps and refer to other logic tools, record layouts, and so forth. See figure 14.13 for an illustration of the detail diagram.

The general and detail diagrams are often referred to as IPO (Input-Process-Output) charts, since they reflect the input items, processing steps, and output items for a function.

Let's use a payroll problem of calculating an employee's pay to examine these diagrams in more detail. The VTOC diagram is shown in figure 14.14.[7] Notice the identification numbers given in the lower right corner of each function.

The VTOC shows only the calculation of gross and net pay as the level-one modules. The reading of input records and writing of output results are not shown as separate modules. These I/O operations will be performed within the detail-level modules wherever needed.

6. Myers, *Composite/Structured Design,* p. 17.
7. IBM, *HIPO,* p. 2.

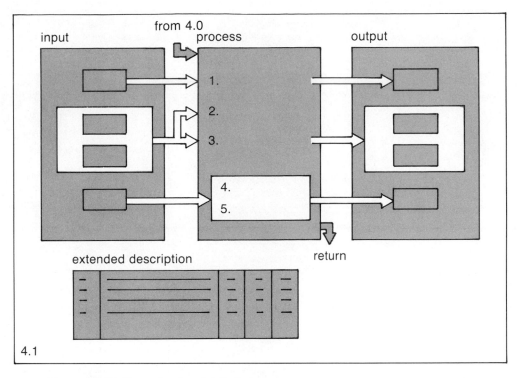

Figure 14.13 Example of a detail diagram

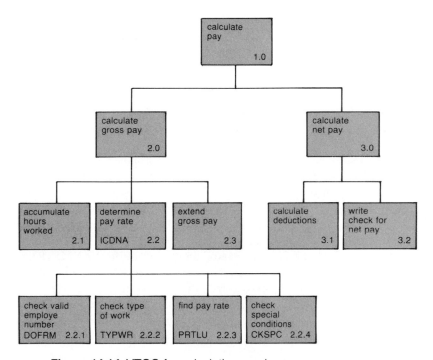

Figure 14.14 VTOC for calculating employee pay

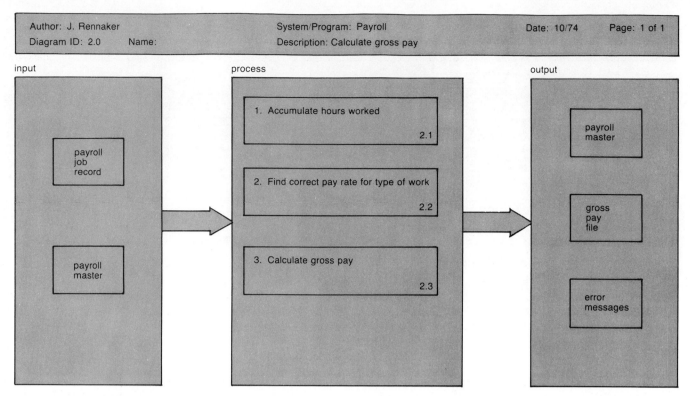

input

process

output

payroll
job
record

1. Accumulate hours worked

2.1

2. Find correct pay rate for type of work

2.2

payroll
master

3. Calculate gross pay

2.3

payroll
master

gross
pay
file

error
messages

Figure 14.15 Overview diagram for calculating gross pay

The overview diagram for module number 2.0, to calculate gross pay, is shown in figure 14.15.[8] The Payroll Job file with employee transaction records is read to obtain the employee number, hours worked, and type of work for each job performed by an employee. The employee Payroll master file is read to obtain the employee's record, containing employee number, number of exemptions, year-to-date gross pay, miscellaneous deductions, and other items. Gross pay is calculated according to the sum of the hours worked and appropriate pay rate for the type of work on all jobs performed by an employee. The Payroll master file is updated with the new gross pay data, a record is written to the Gross Pay file (from which the payroll register will be later printed), or an appropriate error message is printed if an error is found. Thus, the overview diagram for module 2.0 reflects the major actions (in an abstract form) to calculate an employee's gross pay.

The detail diagram for module number 2.2, to determine pay rate, is shown in figure 14.16.[9] Two types of flowlines are used in the detail diagram. The wide black flowlines at the top and bottom of the diagram represent control flow. Control was passed to the module from the module with identification number 2.0. Control is returned to the same module (2.0). The wide white flowlines depict data movement. That is, these flowlines show the input and output of data.

The detail diagram shows the fields from the Payroll master record (file PAYMSTR), the Payroll Job record (file PJR), and the Rate Table (RATETAB) used to determine the correct pay rate for the type of work performed by the employee. The Payroll Job record is updated with the pay rate if the employee number is found and the type-of-work codes are correct. If an error is found (invalid employee number or type-of-work code), an error message is printed and the job records for the employee are bypassed. Thus, the detail diagram shows the detailed actions of how to determine the pay rate for the job an employee performs.

Kinds of HIPO Packages

There are three major kinds of HIPO packages. The **initial design package** is prepared by a design group at the start of a project. This package describes the overall functional design of the project in general terms and is used as a design aid for the structure of a program or system. The initial design package is used primarily in design reviews for managers and users.

8. Ibid., p. 3.
9. Ibid., p. 6.

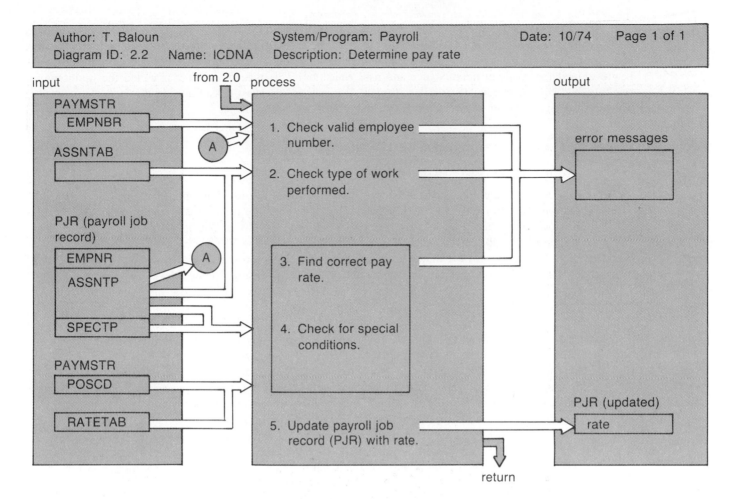

| Author: T. Baloun | System/Program: Payroll | Date: 10/74 | Page 1 of 1 |
| Diagram ID: 2.2   Name: ICDNA | Description: Determine pay rate | | |

input

PAYMSTR
EMPNBR

ASSNTAB

(A)

PJR (payroll job record)
EMPNR
ASSNTP

(A)

SPECTP

PAYMSTR
POSCD

RATETAB

from 2.0

process

1. Check valid employee number.

2. Check type of work performed.

3. Find correct pay rate.

4. Check for special conditions.

5. Update payroll job record (PJR) with rate.

return

output

error messages

PJR (updated)
rate

Extended description

Notes	Module	Segment	Ref.
1. If invalid, job records are bypassed and error message is printed.	ICDNA	DOFRM	2.2.1
2. If type of work is incorrect, job records are bypassed and error message is printed.	ICDNA	TYPWR	2.2.2
3. Use pay rate table (RATETAB) to find correct rate.	ICDNA	PRTLU	2.2.3
4. Check for overtime, shift pay, or holiday pay and add to rate.	ICDNA	CKSPC	2.2.4

Figure 14.16 Detail diagram for determining pay rate

The second type of design package is called the **detail design package**. It is prepared by the programmers and analysts. They use the initial design package as a base and provide more details. Additional levels of detail HIPO diagrams may be added to provide a complete, accurate design document. An optional third package may be developed for program maintenance and user education. This type of package is called the **maintenance package** and is used to educate users and to make corrections, changes, or additions to the program or system. The detail design package often serves as the maintenance design package.

Order of Steps in Preparing a HIPO Package

The order of steps usually followed in preparing a HIPO package is:

1. Make a complete and detailed statement of the user's requirements. The initial planning is done by a small group of users and analysts who define the functions to be performed by the program and their interrelationship. Then the data items needed by the lower-level functions are identified.
2. Create the visual table of contents (VTOC). This step creates the VTOC diagram showing the hierarchical structure of the major functions performed by the program and their relationship to each other. The top-level box states the overall function of the program. The next level breaks those functions into logical subfunctions. The lower-level boxes break down each of the higher-level functions into detailed subfunctions as needed. A functional description and identification number should be included in each of the boxes. It may be impossible to identify all the lower-level functions at this point, since all the detail tasks in the higher-level functions may not yet be fully understood. As the overview and detail diagrams are completed, the VTOC is refined.
3. Create the overview diagrams for the major functions. These diagrams will usually consist of the boxes at the first and second levels of the functions as shown in the VTOC. The overview diagrams serve as a general introduction to the function and a guide to the lower-level functions. All major input items, processing steps and output items are identified in each overview diagram.
4. Create the detail diagrams for the lower-level functions. Usually the third- and lower-level functions are shown in detail diagrams. Detail diagrams may be constructed for second-level functions if the details are sufficient at that level. The purpose of the detail diagram is to provide all the information necessary to understand the function given in the next higher-level (parent) function.

The HIPO process has been used formally, modified drastically, and even applied in totally piecemeal fashion by many organizations since its introduction. In the vast majority of cases, the users have experienced positive results, even with highly modified versions and usage. Again, you should adopt those features of this design tool that can aid you in program and system development. For example, the VTOC and general diagrams provide an excellent tool for gross project estimation of new system development.

A detailed explanation of HIPO may be found in IBM manual GC20-1851, *HIPO—A Design Aid and Documentation Technique*. A description of HIPO may be found in many computer reference books in your library.

The next section discusses several design considerations for the strength of modules in terms of intra- and inter-relationships.

14.5 TOP-DOWN MODULAR DESIGN CONSIDERATIONS AND MODULE INDEPENDENCE

The most important consideration in top-down, modular design is the idea of high module independence. Module independence involves the partitioning of a problem into hierarchical structures so that each module is as independent from all other modules as possible.[10] Two main types of module independence will be discussed— module cohesion and module coupling.

Module Cohesion

The first measure of module independence is module strength or cohesion (also referred to as cohesiveness). **Module cohesion** is a measure of the relationship of the elements or instructions within a module. Cohesion is the inner strength of a module. A design goal is to maximize this strength so that high cohesiveness is achieved. The stronger the relationship of the module's instructions, such as to perform a single functional task, the more likely that the module can be viewed as a single unit.

10. Myers, *Composite/Structured Design*, p. 23.

There are six levels of module cohesion. The scale from the highest strength to the lowest is: [11]

1. Functional
2. Sequential
3. Communicational
4. Temporal
5. Logical
6. Coincidental

Each category of module strength will be discussed in more detail:

Functional. A functional strength module is one that performs a single, well-defined function. All the statements are directly related, and only one function is accomplished by the module. The module is considered a single unit and stands alone for a specific function. This is the highest level of strength for a module, since it is easy to follow, modify, and maintain.

Sequential. Sequential strength implies that modules are executed in a sequential or linear fashion, one after the other. There is a tendency to structure modules sequentially, since doing so makes it easier to conceptualize the program in terms of procedural operations. Sequential strength is not the highest level of strength, since a sequential strength module tends to contain multiple functions or partial functions.

Communicational. Communicational strength implies a common usage of data. A communicational strength module performs multiple sequential functions and exhibits data relationships among all the functions. For example, a module which displays an error message to a terminal for an invalid transaction and also copies the transaction to an error file would be a communicational strength module. This level of strength represents a fairly high level of cohesion.

Temporal. Temporal strength implies that the statements in the module are related in time. A temporal strength module performs multiple functions at a fixed point in time. For example, a start-up or initialization module may open files, print headings, initialize variables, and so on at the beginning of a program. This level of strength is not too bad, since this type of module is fairly simple, and all statements are executed at a common point in time with no intervention of other modules.

Logical. Logical strength implies that different logical processes are contained in the same module. A logical strength module contains a set of multiple functions, each one of which is explicitly selected by a control code from the calling module. For example, the first time a logical module is called, it may only initialize a table. In subsequent calls the module may manipulate items in the table. This type of module is reasonably bad, since it has a single interface for multiple functions. The shared module defeats the purpose of good modular design.

Coincidental strength. Coincidental strength implies no functional relationship among the multiple functions performed by the module. This type of module contains a collection of statements that perform unrelated functions. An example of a module with coincidental strength is the arbitrary partitioning of statements to make up a module. In other words, you may place the first fifty statements of a program in module one, the next fifty statements of the program in module two, and so on. A coincidental strength module may be worse than no program partitioning at all. It would be extremely difficult to modify such a program. [12]

There is some disagreement among educators and computer professionals as to the terminology, definition, and labelling of the levels of module strength and complexity. Various texts may describe the levels of module strength with different terms and provide a slightly different definition. This is an ongoing but relatively minor disagreement in this area of top-down, modular design.

Modules should be designed so that each accomplishes a clearly defined function in the program. It may not be possible to develop a functional strength module for each function of the program. The higher categories of intra-modular strength may be acceptable, depending on the application problem to be solved.

Module Coupling

The second measurement of module independence is module coupling. **Module coupling** is a measure of the relationships that exist between modules. In other words, it is the interrelationship of a module with other modules. The strength of module coupling is measured by the type of connection and the types of data communications. The amount and type of data passed to the module indicates the measure of coupling. The design goal is to minimize module coupling, so that each module is completely independent of all others.

11. Jensen and Tonies, *Software Engineering*, p. 176.
12. Myers, *Composite/Structured Design*, p. 29.

Minimizing module coupling is the process of eliminating the communication or relationship among modules. The design objective is to obtain modules that are **loosely coupled**. Loosely coupled modules have no direct relationship with other modules. That is, the module stands by itself and is called only from a single higher-level module (its parent). The module receives only those data elements essential to its operations.

The data items used are local (within or restricted) to its respective module. These local variables (and arrays) go away when the execution of the module ends. The objective in module coupling is to have a data-coupled module in which only the data that the module needs in order to perform its function is passed to it. The data items should not be global (available to all program units). Restricting a module to only the required data items helps ensure the integrity and reliability of a program.

Other Structured Design Objectives for Modules

Although maximizing module strength (cohesion) and minimizing module coupling are two important objectives in designing a program structure, there are other guidelines in designing a top-down structured program. These additional guidelines are:

Restrict module size. A module should not exceed a page of code—about 50 statements. This size allows all the statements for the module to be contained on a single printed page. A programmer can usually retain the logic on a single page in his or her head because of the visual span of eye contact. Multiple pages distract from eye contact, since one has to flip the pages to follow the logic.

There will be many occasions when a module has fewer than 50 statements. A program function may need only several lines of code. However, too many small modules will produce too small an attention-to-program-logic span. Jumping too often to new small modules interrupts the continuity of the overall logic. On the other hand, large-sized modules will produce too many simultaneous thoughts to follow the module logic.

The 50-statement-module-size rule is only a guideline. The number of statements for a module size will vary with the program complexity and overall size. You may want to combine several small modules if the statements are related; or you may want to divide a large module into several smaller ones if there is a logical separation.

Modularize I/O routines. The reading of data items and the writing of the results should be contained in individual modules. If the format of an input record is changed, then only the input module is affected. If the output format is modified, then only the output module is affected. If you need to echo check the input data, then the required statements can easily be inserted and removed in the input module. If a program is converted to another machine or compiler with different I/O features and statement syntax, the I/O modules can easily be changed.

One important aspect of using subroutines to help modularize the logic in a program is to promote portability between computers. The nonstandard features of a language, such as format-free I/O and random file I/O (reading and writing randomly organized disk files), can be placed into separate subroutines. If a program must be converted to run on a different computer, the nonstandard features implemented within separate subroutines are relatively easy to convert.

Pass only necessary data items to a module. For the sake of reliability, only the data items required by a module should be passed to it. Do not pass the entire data record unless it is needed. A module might have a logic error and "clobber" (destroy) some of the other data items in the record.

Data items should be passed as parameters to and from subprograms to provide restricted access to the data on a need-to-know basis. This enforces the concept of **information hiding,** that is, only the information needed by the subprogram is passed to it. All data items not needed by the subprogram are "hidden", i.e., not available to it. Data items being processed at a given time should not be global to all modules in the program. Information hiding provides greater reliability and data integrity (security) in a program or system.

Some programmers feel that the data flow is easier to handle if all modules have access to all data items, i.e., to make them global variables. Every data item may be made available to each module via named or blank common. Named or blank common are memory locations shared between program units (covered in chapter 15). Sharing all data items with every module, however, can be disastrous over the life of a program if the organization of the data is misunderstood or changed for a program modification.

Use recognized control-flow structures to present the logic. The design of control logic within the individual modules should be presented in a top-down fashion using only the recognized restricted control-flow structures of SEQUENCE, SELECTION (IF-THEN and IF-THEN-ELSE), ITERATION (DO WHILE and REPEAT UNTIL), and SELECT CASE. Pseudocode is an excellent structured design tool to use for presenting the logic in each module.

Use indentations to emphasize logical structures. Statements should be indented three to four spaces within the Selection and Iteration control-flow structures to emphasize these logical structures. Be sure to assign all logical structures at the same level to the same starting position, e.g., two consecutive, unrelated IF statements should be aligned in the same starting position. The logical relationships in the coding then correspond to the physical position on the program listing. A pictorial representation of the logical structure is implied by the indentations.

Section 14.6 explains the process of top-down implementation and testing, in which subroutines play an important role.

14.6 TOP-DOWN PROGRAMMING AND IMPLEMENTATION WITH SUBROUTINES

Traditional software development has evolved as a bottom-up procedure in which the lowest level of details is coded first. Data definitions (type and length of data items) and interfaces tend to be simultaneously defined by more than one person and are often inconsistent. During program and system testing, these problems of definition are discovered. Program testing is delayed while the data definitions and interfaces are corrected and the program revised to accomodate the changes.

The concept of modular programming has long been recognized and used as an invaluable technique for developing programs that are easier to read, maintain, and modify. **Modular programming** means that a program is built from segments of code that solve a specific functional task. The concept of decomposing a problem into functional segments goes hand in hand with modular programming. If all the pieces related to the solution of a particular problem can be kept together in the same module of code, the module lends itself to easy modification. If a change needs to be made in a program, you can usually make the necessary changes to one or more specific modules without affecting the rest of the logic (code).

Program logic that has not been segmented into functional modules usually is very difficult to modify. The logic for a functional task may be tied together throughout the entire program like a bowl of spaghetti. A change in one part of the program logic may cause a **"ripple effect"** throughout the rest of the program. The ripple effect can be devastating when changes are required in a program. Modularized programs lessen this ripple effect and provide easier-to-make changes and more reliability in program modifications. Thus, modular programming is a way of implementing top-down, structured design.

Top-down programming (or implementation) is patterned after the top-down design process. The technique requires that programming proceed from developing the control architecture (interface) statements and initial data definitions downward to developing and testing the functional units. Top-down programming is an ordering of program development to allow for the continual integration of new parts (modules) as they are developed. This process provides for interfaces prior to the parts being developed; thus, the interface problem is minimized. At each stage, the code already tested drives the new code, and only external data is required.

The top-down programming process provides a vehicle for maintaining the integrity of the program/system step by step. Control (interface) code is produced before the functional code, and no checking of detail logic in the lower modules occurs until needed. A top-down approach provides the benefits of giving the critical top-level modules the most testing, giving earlier warnings of module interface problems, and spreading the testing and debugging over a greater part of the development cycle.

In top-down programming, the program is organized into a tree structure of modules. The top-level module contains the highest level of control logic within the program and passes control to the next level (level 1) of modules for execution of these functions. This level (level 1) of modules may contain either the required coded statements, or what is called a *stub*.

A **stub** is a dummy or stand-in statement for the code needed for the module to perform its function. A program stub is simply one or two lines of code to indicate the module was entered, even though the code for it has not yet been developed. The stub usually displays a message to the effect that the module was entered, and this message is eventually replaced by the required code. While it is recognized that such stubs are eventually discarded, the effort involved in writing them is much less than that required to produce stand-alone test programs and to pass data to a module for module testing. The process of replacing successively lower-level stubs with the required processing code continues for as many levels as required until all functional modules within the program or system are defined in executable code.

The top-down programming and implementation approach allows the program to evolve in a manner that maintains the characteristic of always being operable, extremely modular, and available for successive levels of module integration and testing. The quality and reliability of a program produced using this approach is increased, resulting in fewer logic errors in the coding process. Structuring the logic requires more forethought, but the modularization of the structured code contributes to a reduction in program errors. Because of the segmented nature of top-down programming, the resulting program is extremely modular in function and logic structure. This approach minimizes the effect of requirement changes on already-developed code.

Conceptually, top-down programming and implementation proceeds from a single starting point, while the traditional bottom-up approach proceeds from as many starting points as there are major routines. The single starting point does not imply that the top-down implementation must proceed down the hierarchy in parallel. Some modules in a level may be developed into their lower-level detail modules before other modules on the same level. In many applications, requirements for some types of processing become fixed before the requirements in other areas. The areas defined by known requirements can be developed while the requirements for the other areas are still being developed. In fact, a program may become operational and still include stubs in modules intended for long-range implementation. This allows the overall design to be completed, and the stubs serve as a guide if and when the module is needed. The stubs in these uncompleted modules may simply reflect that the modules have not been implemented.

The beauty of top-down implementation is that a program can be developed that performs some part of its function very early in the project. The input, essential processing, and the output routines, for example, may be developed in a quick implementation plan. Later the edit routines and more sophisticated decision-making and processing routines can be added to meet the full requirements of the program. By implementing the most useful functions first, a user can get an idea of how valuable the program will be before investing any more resources in the difficult or esoteric functions. You also ensure that the required functions are handled as simply as possible, which usually leads to greater efficiency and readability in the end.

Top-down implementation provides the capability for building a program in stages. The idea is to select a small, manageable piece of the program and make it work. If the original design is well-planned, the later pieces should fit smoothly. Debugging and testing are easier to perform on the individual pieces rather than the entire program. If you find the design will not work and decide to scrap the program at some point, you are only scrapping that fraction developed so far.

There is a lot of merit in developing a program incrementally. You can get the program to accomplish something useful in a minimal amount of time. There is a morale boost in having something working early. Managers and supervisors are pleased, since they can see some early results to an assigned project. The remaining routines can be added one at a time. This process divides a big job into smaller, more manageable pieces.

Another advantage in developing a program incrementally is that the user can confirm the usefulness of the results. It is very foolish to develop the entire program before revealing any part of it. Users are famous for getting others' suggestions in the output requirements and changing their minds. Users usually know how they want to use a product but may not get this across to the programmer/analyst. You may learn that what the user really wants is quite different from what you thought.

Often you will learn that what the user wants is less elaborate than what you imagined was described to you. Remember the "swing cartoon." A user's review of limited program output may provide vital feedback to evaluate the functions that already exist. Review of a preliminary report may cause the user to reevaluate the needs or requirements of the product, thus saving unnecessary work and time.

A goal of top-down programming is to be able to test each module independently from the other. The next subsection explains the process of top-down testing.

Top-down Testing

You should test and "check out" code as it is written, rather than leaving the entire program to be debugged after it is finally coded. Modules may be tested to confirm their correctness as they are developed, rather than relying on a final testing-and-debugging "binge" at the end to correct everything. Besides, designing and writing code are the fun parts of programming. The testing and debugging phase is often very frustrating and not much fun. Performing the testing and debugging in an incremental fashion helps spread this activity across the development process.

Top-down testing is the process of testing new modules as they are integrated into the program. It is common to test the highest levels of code first, since most bugs are detected at this integration level. This also allows the programmer to start testing as soon as possible, before most of the modules are even written. This top-down testing technique goes hand in glove with top-down implementation.

Top-down testing helps to reduce **computer saturation** (when the computer is filled with scheduled jobs) by spreading the required computer time for testing purposes over a greater time span. The computer may be available for programmer use at the start and middle of a project, but it may become overloaded towards the end of a project when everyone wants a lot of computer test time.

You can expect problems in testing your code and should prepare for them. It is virtually certain that you will have coding and design errors in your programs. Testing the early developed part of a program is easier because it is smaller. Debugging is a less painful process, since there is less code to examine and correct. If the design is good, the later modules can be added incrementally with little impact on the resulting program. The already tested and debugged code is usually error free. Thus, you can concentrate on the newly integrated module(s) if an error appears. The problem of proving the program's correctness is reduced to proving the correctness of only the newly integrated modules.

The next subsection explains the use of subroutines in top-down implementation and testing.

Top-down Implementation and Testing with Subroutines

The intelligent use of subroutines is useful in modular programming. A separate subroutine can be written to solve each functional task of a program, thus effectively modularizing the whole program. The program will include calls to the proper subroutines to achieve its overall objective and output. Subroutines are an easy way of providing modules to serve as building blocks in the development of a program.

A big advantage in using subroutines to modularize the logic of a program is better readability. A lengthy program that consists solely of one main program (with or without many GO TO statements) is usually difficult to follow. The normal amount of code you can retain (in your head) is limited to about one page. Most FORTRAN compilers will list each subroutine starting on a new printer page. Thus, subroutines help in understanding the logic of a program by breaking the code into small, digestible modules.

In top-down implementation, the main program structure is implemented as a series of CALL statements to the first-level modules, which are coded as subroutines. The main program serves as a "driver" to the execution of the hierarchical modules. CALL statements are included in the first-level modules, where needed, to execute the second-level modules. The second-level modules include CALL statements to the third-level modules, and so on.

The lowest-level modules (under their first-level modules) become the detailed FORTRAN statements to perform the functional task. In other words, the lowest-level modules of each hierarchical path are not subroutines; they represent the details of how the module accomplishes its function. Any undeveloped module may be implemented as a subroutine containing only a stub, displaying a message to the effect that the module was executed. An example of this process is given in the following subsection.

Example of a Student Grade Roster and Class GPA Problem Developed with Subroutines

A problem to produce a student grade roster and class GPA (Grade Point Average) is used to illustrate top-down development and implementation with subroutines. The problem specifications are:

1. Develop a roster of student grades for the course CS100—Introduction to Computer Programming.
2. A maximum of thirty students can be enrolled in the course.
3. Each input record contains the student ID (4 digits), name (20 characters), and five test scores (3 digits each). A trailer record with a student ID of 9999 is used to indicate the end of the student records.
4. Calculate the sum of the five test scores for each student.
5. Determine the appropriate letter grade earned by each student as follows:
   a. A grade of A is assigned for 92%–100% of the 500 possible points.
   b. A grade of B is assigned for 80%–91% of the 500 possible points.
   c. A grade of C is assigned for 70%–79% of the 500 possible points.
   d. A grade of D is assigned for 60%–69% of the 500 possible points.
   e. A grade of F is assigned for less than 60% of the 500 possible points.
6. Print a double-spaced detail line with the student ID, name, five test scores, total points, and assigned letter grade.
7. Calculate the overall class GPA. The points for each letter grade are:

> Each A grade earns 4 points
> Each B grade earns 3 points
> Each C grade earns 2 points
> Each D grade earns 1 point
> Each F grade earns 0 points

The formula for calculating the class GPA is:

$$GPA = \frac{A*4 + B*3 + C*2 + D*1 + F*0}{A + B + C + D + F}$$

where A represents the number of A grades assigned,
B represents the number of B grades assigned,
C represents the number of C grades assigned,
D represents the number of D grades assigned, and
F represents the number of F grades assigned.

8. Print the class GPA triple-spaced after the last student detail record. Include an appropriate message, such as "CLASS GPA IS".
9. Include line counter logic to print a maximum of twenty detail records per page.
10. Include an appropriate report and column heading.

The structure chart for the program design solution is given in figure 14.17. An event-model structure chart is used to establish the first level of modules.

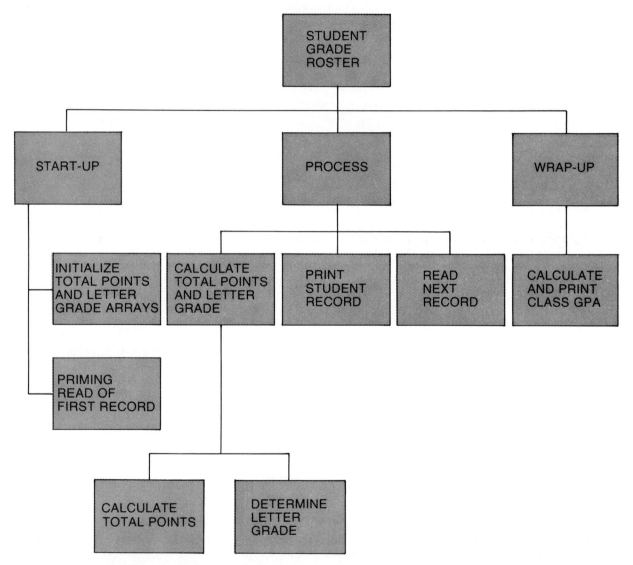

Figure 14.17 Structure chart for student grade roster problem

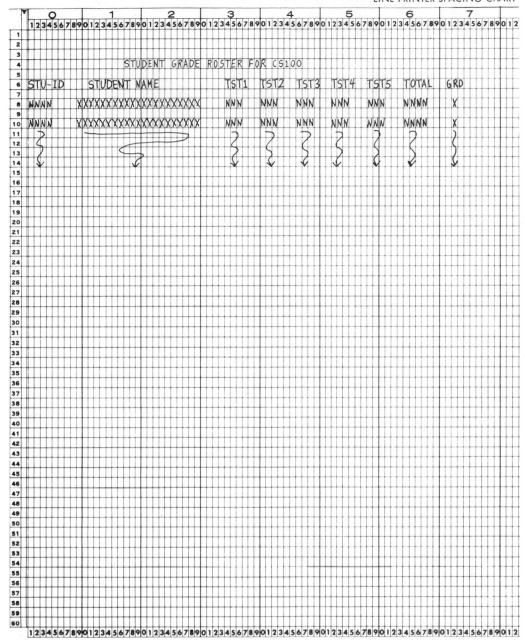

Figure 14.18 Print layout form for student grade roster

The Print Layout chart for the report is shown in figure 14.18.

Since the logic for various student grade problems has been previously presented, a flowchart or pseudocode is not given. Seven data records are constructed to test the program. The test records are shown in figure 14.19 (p. 416).

The program will be developed in stages using top-down implementation and testing techniques. Only the modules necessary to build the program skeleton, which implements the first-level modules and the reading and writing of the data records, will be written first. Subroutine stubs will be used to incorporate the second-level modules. The stubs will contain the code to initialize any yet-to-be-calculated values to zero and print a message that the called module was executed. Figure 14.20 (p. 416) shows the resulting main-line and subroutine program units for the first stage of implementation. The subroutines are placed in alphabetic order to help find their location in the overall program.

```
        3028MARY B. SMITH              98  87 100 93 96

        1876BILLY R. ANDERSON         74  91 89 82 77

        3879DEBORA N. ADAMS           92  89 94 86 99

        2954JOHN HANKS                70  62 78 68 75

        5721SALLY C. POWELL           65  80 71 66 62

        5047STEVEN K. BERRY           51  63 48  0  0

        4135KIRK R. WILLIAMSON        67  82 74 72 76

        9999 -- END OF FILE --
```

Figure 14.19 Test data for student grade roster program

```
C ---   TOP-DOWN MODULAR IMPLEMENTATION OF FORTRAN PROGRAM TO
C ---   CALCULATE STUDENT GRADES AND CLASS GPA
C
C ---   AUTHOR: J. W. COLE
C ---   DATE WRITTEN: 3/6/82
C
C ---   STAGE 1 OF PROGRAM DEVELOPMENT
C
        INTEGER STUID, STUNAM (10), SCORES (5)
        INTEGER LTRGRD (5), POINTS, STUGRD
C
        CALL STRTUP (STUID, STUNAM, SCORES, LTRGRD, LNECNT)
C
C ---   DO WHILE LOOP TO PROCESS STUDENT RECORDS
C
  10    IF (STUID .EQ. 9999) GO TO 20
            CALL GRADES (SCORES, POINTS, LTRGRD, STUGRD)
            CALL PRTRCD (STUID, STUNAM, SCORES, POINTS, STUGRD, LNECNT)
            CALL READRD (STUID, STUNAM, SCORES)
        GO TO 10
C
  20    CALL CALGPA (LTRGRD)
        STOP
        END
C
C ---   SUBROUTINE CALGPA TO CALCULATE THE CLASS GPA
C
        SUBROUTINE CALGPA (LTRGRD)
        INTEGER LTRGRD (5)
        WRITE (6, 299)
  299   FORMAT (1H0, 29H*** ENTERED MODULE CALGPA ***)
        RETURN
        END
```

Figure 14.20 First stage of program development (cont. on next page)

Figure 14.20 (cont.)

```
C
C ---      SUBROUTINE GRADES TO CALCULATE TOTAL POINTS AND LETTER GRADE
C
           SUBROUTINE GRADES (SCORES, POINTS, LTRGRD, STUGRD)
           INTEGER SCORES (5), POINTS, LTRGRD (5), STUGRD
           DATA A/1HA/, B/1HB/, C/1HC/, D/1HD/, F/1HF/
           POINTS = 0
           WRITE (6, 299)
  299      FORMAT (1H0, 29H*** ENTERED MODULE GRADES ***)
           RETURN
           END
C
C ---      SUBROUTINE PRTRCD TO PRINT A DETAIL STUDENT RECORD
C
           SUBROUTINE PRTRCD (STUID, STUNAM, SCORES, POINTS, STUGRD, LNECNT)
           INTEGER STUID, STUNAM (10), SCORES (5), POINTS, STUGRD
           DATA NOGRD/1HN/
           STUGRD = NOGRD
           IF (LNECNT .GT. 20) WRITE (6, 299)
  299      FORMAT (1H1, 17X, 30HSTUDENT GRADE ROSTER FOR CS100/
          *          1H0, 6HSTU-ID, 4X,12HSTUDENT NAME, 10X,4HTST1, 2X,4HTST2,
          *             2X, 4HTST3, 2X,4HTST4, 2X,4HTST5, 2X,5HTOTAL, 2X,3HGRD)
           IF (LNECNT .GT. 20) LNECNT = 0
           WRITE (6, 298) STUID, STUNAM, SCORES, POINTS, STUGRD
  298      FORMAT (1H0, I4, 4X,10A2, 4X,5(I3,3X), I4, 4X,A1)
           LNECNT = LNECNT + 1
           RETURN
           END
C
C ---      SUBROUTINE READRD TO READ A STUDENT RECORD
C
           SUBROUTINE READRD (STUID, STUNAM, SCORES)
           INTEGER STUID, STUNAM (10), SCORES (5)
           READ (5, 199) STUID, STUNAM, SCORES
  199      FORMAT (I4, 10A2, 5I3)
           RETURN
           END
C
C ---      SUBROUTINE STRTUP TO PERFORM INITIALIZATION FUNCTIONS
C
           SUBROUTINE STRTUP (STUID, STUNAM, SCORES, LTRGRD, LNECNT)
           INTEGER STUID, STUNAM (10), SCORES (5), LTRGRD (5)
C
           DO 10 NR = 1, 5
              LTRGRD (NR) = 0
   10      CONTINUE
           LNECNT = 99
           CALL READRD (STUID, STUNAM, SCORES)
           RETURN
           END
```

*** ENTERED MODULE GRADES ***

STUDENT GRADE ROSTER FOR CS100

STU–ID	STUDENT NAME	TST1	TST2	TST3	TST4	TST5	TOTAL	GRD
3028	MARY B. SMITH	98	87	100	93	96	0	N

*** ENTERED MODULE GRADES ***

1876	BILLY R. ANDERSON	74	91	89	82	77	0	N

*** ENTERED MODULE GRADES ***

3879	DEBORA N. ADAMS	92	89	94	86	99	0	N

*** ENTERED MODULE GRADES ***

2954	JOHN HANKS	70	62	78	68	75	0	N

*** ENTERED MODULE GRADES ***

5721	SALLY C. POWELL	65	80	71	66	62	0	N

*** ENTERED MODULE GRADES ***

5047	STEVEN K. BERRY	51	63	48	0	0	0	N

*** ENTERED MODULE GRADES ***

4135	KIRK R. WILLIAMSON	67	82	74	72	76	0	N

*** ENTERED MODULE CALGPA ***

Figure 14.21 Output results from first stage of program development

The main-line program calls five subroutines to perform the needed functions. The start-up function is performed by subroutine STRTUP, which initializes the array for counting the number of different letter grades to zero and performs a priming read of the first data record. The processing function calls three subroutines. The subroutine GRADES will calculate the sum of the test scores and the earned letter grade. The subroutine PRTRCD will print the student detail record. The subroutine READRD reads a new student record. (The student name is read as ten two-character fields to be compatible with minicomputers.) The wrap-up function calls the subroutine CALGPA to calculate and print the class GPA.

The level-one modules and their interface will be tested to ensure a proper flow of control through the program. The modules to perform the start-up function, read a student record, and print a student record will be written to allow the program to read and write the data records. The modules to calculate grades and class GPA will contain only stubs to reflect their execution. The output produced in testing the first stage of the program development is shown in figure 14.21.

Next, the module to calculate the students' total points and letter grade is developed. The stubs are deleted from the subroutine GRADES and replaced with the proper code. Note that the boxes under the "calculate total points and letter grade" module in the structure chart do not get implemented as subroutines. These boxes represent detail actions at the lowest-level of the hierarchy; thus, they are coded as statements in the "calculate letter grades" module. The program, with the revised GRADES module, is shown in figure 14.22.

```
C ---   TOP-DOWN MODULAR IMPLEMENTATION OF FORTRAN PROGRAM TO
C ---   CALCULATE STUDENT GRADES AND CLASS GPA
C
C ---   AUTHOR: J. W. COLE
C ---   DATE WRITTEN: 3/6/82
C
C ---   STAGE 2 OF PROGRAM DEVELOPMENT
C
        INTEGER STUID, STUNAM (10), SCORES (5)
        INTEGER LTRGRD (5), POINTS, STUGRD
C
        CALL STRTUP (STUID, STUNAM, SCORES, LTRGRD, LNECNT)
C
C ---   DO WHILE LOOP TO PROCESS STUDENT RECORDS
C
  10    IF (STUID .EQ. 9999) GO TO 20
            CALL GRADES (SCORES, POINTS, LTRGRD, STUGRD)
            CALL PRTRCD (STUID, STUNAM, SCORES, POINTS, STUGRD, LNECNT)
            CALL READRD (STUID, STUNAM, SCORES)
        GO TO 10
C
  20    CALL CALGPA (LTRGRD)
        STOP
        END
C
C ---   SUBROUTINE CALGPA TO CALCULATE THE CLASS GPA
C
        SUBROUTINE CALGPA (LTRGRD)
        INTEGER LTRGRD (5)
        WRITE (6, 299)
 299    FORMAT (1H0, 29H*** ENTERED MODULE CALGPA ***)
        RETURN
        END
C
C ---   SUBROUTINE GRADES TO CALCULATE TOTAL POINTS AND LETTER GRADE
C
        SUBROUTINE GRADES (SCORES, POINTS, LTRGRD, STUGRD)
        INTEGER SCORES (5), POINTS, LTRGRD (5), STUGRD
        INTEGER A, B, C, D, F
        DATA A/1HA/, B/1HB/, C/1HC/, D/1HD/, F/1HF/
        POINTS = 0
        DO 10 NR = 1, 5
            POINTS = POINTS + SCORES (NR)
  10    CONTINUE
        MAXPTS = 500
        IF (POINTS .GE. .92 * MAXPTS) GO TO 90
        IF (POINTS .GE. .80 * MAXPTS) GO TO 80
        IF (POINTS .GE. .70 * MAXPTS) GO TO 70
        IF (POINTS .GE. .60 * MAXPTS) GO TO 60
        STUGRD = F
        LTRGRD (5) = LTRGRD (5) + 1
        RETURN
  60    STUGRD = D
        LTRGRD (4) = LTRGRD (4) + 1
        RETURN
  70    STUGRD = C
        LTRGRD (3) = LTRGRD (3) + 1
        RETURN
```

Figure 14.22 Second stage of program development (cont. on next page)

Figure 14.22 (cont.)

```
 80      STUGRD = B
         LTRGRD (2) = LTRGRD (2) + 1
         RETURN
 90      STUGRD = A
         LTRGRD (1) = LTRGRD (1) + 1
         RETURN
         END
C
C ---    SUBROUTINE PRTRCD TO PRINT A DETAIL STUDENT RECORD
C
         SUBROUTINE PRTRCD (STUID, STUNAM, SCORES, POINTS, STUGRD, LNECNT)
         INTEGER STUID, STUNAM (10), SCORES (5), POINTS, STUGRD
         IF (LNECNT .GT. 20) WRITE (6, 299)
299      FORMAT (1H1, 17X, 30HSTUDENT GRADE ROSTER FOR CS100/
        *         1H0, 6HSTU-ID, 4X,12HSTUDENT NAME, 10X,4HTST1, 2X,4HTST2,
        *             2X,4HTST3, 2X,4HTST4, 2X,4HTST5, 2X,5HTOTAL, 2X,3HGRD)
         IF (LNECNT .GT. 20) LNECNT = 0
         WRITE (6, 298) STUID, STUNAM, SCORES, POINTS, STUGRD
298      FORMAT (1H0, I4, 4X,10A2, 4X,5(I3,3X), I4, 4X,A1)
         LNECNT = LNECNT + 1
         RETURN
         END
C
C ---    SUBROUTINE READRD TO READ A STUDENT RECORD
C
         SUBROUTINE READRD (STUID, STUNAM, SCORES)
         INTEGER STUID, STUNAM (10), SCORES (5)
         READ (5, 199) STUID, STUNAM, SCORES
199      FORMAT (I4, 10A2, 5I3)
         RETURN
         END
C
C ---    SUBROUTINE STRTUP TO PERFORM INITIALIZATION FUNCTIONS
C
         SUBROUTINE STRTUP (STUID, STUNAM, SCORES, LTRGRD, LNECNT)
         INTEGER STUID, STUNAM (10), SCORES (5), LTRGRD (5)
C
         DO 10 NR = 1, 5
             LTRGRD (NR) = 0

 10      CONTINUE
         LNECNT = 99
         CALL READRD (STUID, STUNAM, SCORES)
         RETURN
         END
```

STU–ID	STUDENT NAME	TST1	TST2	TST3	TST4	TST5	TOTAL	GRD
3028	MARY B. SMITH	98	87	100	93	96	474	A
1876	BILLY R. ANDERSON	74	91	89	82	77	413	B
3879	DEBORA N. ADAMS	92	89	94	86	99	460	A
2954	JOHN HANKS	70	62	78	68	75	353	C
5721	SALLY C. POWELL	65	80	71	66	62	344	D
5047	STEVEN K. BERRY	51	63	48	0	0	162	F
4135	KIRK R. WILLIAMSON	67	82	74	72	76	371	C

*** ENTERED MODULE CALGPA ***

Figure 14.23 Output results from second stage of program development

The output produced from testing the stage two development of the program is shown in figure 14.23.

Finally, the module to calculate the class GPA is developed. The program stubs are removed and replaced with the proper calculations. The program with the revised CALGPA module is shown in figure 14.24 (pp. 422–23). The output produced from testing the final program version is shown in figure 14.25 (p. 424).

The value of well-structured modular programs is especially apparent during program maintenance. Imagine how program maintenance might be carried out for the modular-designed and developed grade roster program. If the calculation of grades is changed to a new percentage of points, the only module affected is the GRADES module. If the format of the output reports needs to be changed, only the PRTRCD module is affected. Extensive use of subroutines is recommended to modularize code and to implement top-down design and testing techniques.

Section 14.7 discusses some of the additional structured programming techniques used to increase the productivity of programmers and analysts.

14.7 IMPROVED PROGRAMMING TECHNIQUES

Top-Down Structured Programming (TDSP) techniques constitute a methodology that provides a systematic approach to problem solving and software development. The TDSP methodology uses a combination of techniques and tools, which includes:

1. Top-down design
2. Top-down implementation
3. Top-down testing
4. Program design language (PDL)
5. Structured coding (SC)
6. Top-down documentation
7. Chief programmer team (CPT)
8. Structured walk-throughs
9. Development support library (DSL)

Techniques seven through nine are discussed in this section.

```
C --- TOP-DOWN MODULAR IMPLEMENTATION OF FORTRAN PROGRAM TO
C --- CALCULATE STUDENT GRADES AND CLASS GPA
C
C --- AUTHOR: J.W. COLE
C --- DATE WRITTEN: 3/6/82
C
      INTEGER STUID, STUNAM(10), SCORES(5)
      INTEGER LTRGRD(5), POINTS, STUGRD
C
      CALL STRTUP (STUID, STUNAM, SCORES, LTRGRD, LNECNT)
C
C --- DO WHILE LOOP TO PROCESS STUDENT RECORDS
C
  10  IF (STUID .EQ. 9999) GO TO 20
          CALL GRADES (SCORES, POINTS, LTRGRD, STUGRD)
          CALL PRTRCD (STUID, STUNAM, SCORES, POINTS, STUGRD, LNECNT)
          CALL READRD (STUID, STUNAM, SCORES)
      GO TO 10
C
  20  CALL CALGPA (LTRGRD)
      STOP
      END
C
C --- SUBROUTINE CALGPA TO CALCULATE THE CLASS GPA
C
      SUBROUTINE CALGPA (LTRGRD)
      INTEGER LTRGRD (5), GRDPTS, TOTGRD
      GRDPTS = 0
      TOTGRD = 0
      DO 10 NR = 1, 5
          GRDPTS = GRDPTS + LTRGRD (NR) * (5-NR)
          TOTGRD = TOTGRD + LTRGRD (NR)
  10  CONTINUE
      GPA = FLOAT(GRDPTS) / FLOAT(TOTGRD)
      WRITE (6, 299) GPA
 299  FORMAT (/1H0, 13HCLASS GPA IS , F5.2)
      RETURN
      END
C
C --- SUBROUTINE GRADES TO CALCULATE TOTAL POINTS AND LETTER GRADE
C
      SUBROUTINE GRADES (SCORES, POINTS, LTRGRD, STUGRD)
      INTEGER SCORES(5), POINTS, LTRGRD(5), STUGRD
      INTEGER A, B, C, D, F
      DATA A/1HA/, B/1HB/, C/1HC/, D/1HD/, F/1HF/
      POINTS = 0
      DO 10 NR = 1, 5
          POINTS = POINTS + SCORES(NR)
  10  CONTINUE
      MAXPTS = 500
      IF (POINTS .GE. .92 * MAXPTS) GO TO 90
      IF (POINTS .GE. .80 * MAXPTS) GO TO 80
      IF (POINTS .GE. .70 * MAXPTS) GO TO 70
      IF (POINTS .GE. .60 * MAXPTS) GO TO 60
      STUGRD = F
      LTRGRD(5) = LTRGRD(5) + 1
      RETURN
```

Figure 14.24 Final student grade roster program (cont. on next page)

Figure 14.24 (cont.)

```
60      STUGRD = D
        LTRGRD(4) = LTRGRD(4) + 1
        RETURN
70      STUGRD = C
        LTRGRD(3) = LTRGRD (3) + 1
        RETURN
80      STUGRD = B
        LTRGRD(2) = LTRGRD(2) + 1
        RETURN
90      STUGRD = A
        LTRGRD(1) = LTRGRD(1) + 1
        RETURN
        END
C
C --- SUBROUTINE PRTRCD TO PRINT A DETAIL STUDENT RECORD
C
        SUBROUTINE PRTRCD (STUID, STUNAM, SCORES, POINTS, STUGRD, LNECNT)
        INTEGER STUID, STUNAM(10), SCORES(5), POINTS, STUGRD
        IF (LNECNT .GT. 20) WRITE (6, 299)
299     FORMAT (1H1, 17X, 30HSTUDENT GRADE ROSTER FOR CS100/
        *          1H0, 6HSTU-ID, 4X,12HSTUDENT NAME, 10X,4HTST1, 2X,4HTST2,
        *            2X,4HTST3, 2X,4HTST4, 2X,4HTST5, 2X,5HTOTAL, 2X,3HGRD)
        IF (LNECNT .GT. 20) LNECNT = 0
        WRITE (6, 298) STUID, STUNAM, SCORES, POINTS, STUGRD
298     FORMAT (1H0, I4, 4X,10A2, 4X,5(I3,3X), I4, 4X,A1)
        LNECNT = LNECNT + 1
        RETURN
        END
C
C --- SUBROUTINE READRD TO READ A STUDENT RECORD
C
        SUBROUTINE READRD (STUID, STUNAM, SCORES)
        INTEGER STUID, STUNAM(10), SCORES(5)
        READ (5, 199) STUID, STUNAM, SCORES
199     FORMAT (I4, 10A2, 5I3)
        RETURN
        END
C
C --- SUBROUTINE STRTUP TO PERFORM INITIALIZATION FUNCTIONS
C
        SUBROUTINE STRTUP (STUID, STUNAM, SCORES, LTRGRD, LNECNT)
        INTEGER STUID, STUNAM(10), SCORES(5), LTRGRD(5)
C
        DO 10 NR = 1, 5
          LTRGRD (NR) = 0
10      CONTINUE
        LNECNT = 99
        CALL READRD (STUID, STUNAM, SCORES)
        RETURN
        END
```

STUDENT GRADE ROSTER FOR CS100

STU-ID	STUDENT NAME	TST1	TST2	TST3	TST4	TST5	TOTAL	GRD
3028	MARY B. SMITH	98	87	100	93	96	474	A
1876	BILLY R. ANDERSON	74	91	89	82	77	413	B
3879	DEBORA N. ADAMS	92	89	94	86	99	460	A
2954	JOHN HANKS	70	62	78	68	75	353	C
5721	SALLY C. POWELL	65	80	71	66	62	344	D
5047	STEVEN K. BERRY	51	63	48	0	0	162	F
4135	KIRK R. WILLIAMSON	67	82	74	72	76	371	C

CLASS GPA IS 2.29

Figure 14.25 Output results from final program version

Chief Programmer Team

The chief programmer team, introduced in 1969, is a technique for managing the software development process. Its basic idea is to organize a small number of highly competent people according to their special and complementary skills. The newly emerging structured programming technology provides the vehicle by which the team members communicate and function.

The team consists of approximately four to six members responsible for various parts of the assigned project. The chief programmer team consists of the following experienced personnel:

1. A chief programmer
2. A senior backup programmer
3. A program librarian
4. Several other programmers with specialized experience

A senior programmer, known as the chief programmer, acts as the team head. The chief programmer is a highly skilled individual in system design, development, and technical supervision. He or she is responsible for the design of all programs and is vested with the complete technical project responsibility. The chief programmer writes the high-level modules, the critical code of the system, and defines the other lower-level modules, which are written by the other programmers. The management function of directing and supervising the team members is performed by the chief programmer. A chief programmer is often referred to as a "super programmer."

A second senior programmer is normally included in the team to serve as a backup to the chief programmer. The backup programmer works closely with the chief programmer and may assume the duties of the chief programmer if the need arises. The backup programmer may be responsible for supervising the structured walkthroughs performed by the other programmers and for the testing phase of the project. This member's functions are almost as critical as those of the chief programmer. He or she acts as a sounding board for the chief programmer, contributes to design solutions and implementation techniques, writes significant portions of the code, and provides guidance to the other members.

The program librarian is an integral team member who relieves the programmers of the time-consuming clerical duties necessary in a programming project. This person is responsible for maintaining the status of programs and test data in such a form that the programmers can work more effectively. The librarian manages the Development Support Library containing the source and object programs, test data files, and source listings. The program librarian also arranges for the compilation and testing of programs and may compile management statistics for the project. The librarian may be a junior programmer or a clerical person but must possess administrative skills.

The other members of the team are experienced programmers with various expertise. One member may be highly skilled in Job Control Language, another may have in-depth experience in Data Base Management or a specific high-level language. These programmers are responsible for writing the detailed modules. They also serve as reviewers in structured walk-throughs.

With this combination of people and structured programming technology, the chief programmer can attain an overall comprehension of a fairly complex design and implementation. When he or she designs and supervises an entire system in this manner, significant advantages in improved system reliability and increased programmer productivity can be achieved. The "New York Times project" was the first reported instance of this software management technique. The New York Times project was an on-line information system designed by IBM to provide access to past articles in that newspaper. Under the guidance of Harlan Mills and Terry Baker, a large, complex system (over 83,000 lines of code) was produced in an unusually short time period with very few errors.

Many organizations are using a more informal team concept, which simply involves a committment to put the necessary people together at the same time to maximize project effectiveness. This requires far fewer resources and is applicable to small groups.

Now let's look at the technique of structured walk-throughs.

Structured Walk-throughs

Management realized that chief programmer teams needed a scheduled review to determine the project status at a given time and to evaluate design progress. Recognizing this need, IBM developed the concept of structured walk-throughs as part of its chief programmer team approach to project organization. Other programming organizations have used this concept for a long time under different names, such as "team debugging", "design reviews", and other terms.

When programming teams use structured programming techniques, one of the benefits is the ease of communication among individuals on the team. Any programmer on the project team can readily comprehend the code of the other programmers. This fact serves as the basis for the structured walk-through or peer review. These reviews should be conducted at significant points (accomplishments) throughout the software development, to eliminate design and logic errors before they affect the project.

A **structured walk-through,** then, is an informal, systematic, technical examination of a programmer's design, logic, or procedures by his or her peers. Its purpose is best served by reviewing the proposed design of a module, program, or system before the logic is "hard" coded. As mentioned in chapter 3, paper changes are much less costly than changes to already implemented code. Structured walk-throughs are also held for coding, implementation, and testing reviews.

The structured walk-through consists of the person developing the design or procedure (the reviewee) and his or her peers (reviewers). Two to five fellow programmers/analysts are selected to attend the review. A qualified user may be invited to the meeting to aid in the review process. A copy of the proposed design or procedure is given to the attendees several days prior to the scheduled meeting. This allows the reviewers time to study the problem and proposed design. No managers should attend the review. This avoids their forming an opinion of the reviewee's ability or productivity, which could be reflected later in the reviewee's evaluation.

A walk-through should be brief and concise, and reviewers should concentrate on error detection rather than error correction. The review should last for an hour or so. To avoid mental fatigue, it should not last longer than several hours. Any accomplishments made after several hours of technical review are minimal.

Again, the main objective of the structured walk-through is to detect errors, not to correct them. This approach of not providing corrections at the meeting is intended to save time. One of the reviewers is chosen as a recorder to take down comments and note errors. Several days after the meeting, the reviewee should provide the reviewers with a memorandum or report on how the errors will be corrected. A later walk-through may be scheduled, if needed, to review the changes and new design.

Programmers have continually been urged to perform extensive desk-checking before developing the code or running their program on the computer. This was seldom actually done, since the programmer was usually anxious to get some code developed for testing. Again, the need for more reliable and maintainable programs helped bring about the practice of structured walk-throughs in many programming organizations.

Structured walk-throughs tie in nicely with top-down design and implementation. At a very early stage in a project, the programmer should be able to provide the overall design of a program. Much of the details of logic may still be in program stubs (dummy modules), but the overall design structure is present. In fact, the reviewing team members should concentrate their efforts, at the beginning of a project, on reviewing the high-level program structure rather than worrying about the low-level modules. This process allows any major design flaws to be identified early in the project.

In summary, structured walk-throughs provide the following advantages: 1) problems are discovered early, 2) the designer is more confident that his or her design is complete, 3) managers know that design issues are resolved and 4) they serve as a learning experience for new team members. Structured walk-throughs are being held more and more frequently within programming organizations across the country. Most programmer/analysts welcome the idea of other knowledgeable people helping find flaws in their design or code (this is known as **egoless programming**). The benefits gained from this invaluable technique are seeing programs produced today that are much more reliable and maintainable. You may wish to perform a walk-through on a lab problem with some of your classmates. Be sure you also do your own work in design and coding, though, or else the exams will find you out.

Finally, let's look at the development support library.

Development Support Library

The development support library serves as a central repository of all data, relevant to the project, in both human-readable and machine-readable form. The library is used to organize and control the software development and is the focal point of information exchange, both managerial and technical. The development support library is also known as a program support library or a programming production library.

The program support library concept is used to separate the clerical tasks in program development from the actual design and coding functions. In many projects, the library is maintained by the program librarian of the chief programmer team. By using procedures furnished by the programmers, the librarian performs any of the library operations, such as compiling modules, storing the object code, or backing up the libraries. The programmers then interface directly with the computer only occasionally.

The development support library consists of two entities. One is the internal library, which is maintained on magnetic disk files. The **internal library** contains all the source and object programs, the job control language modules for running the programs, and test files. The second entity is the external library, which is in human-readable form. The **external library** consists of all the source program listings, the results of test runs, the listing of job control language modules, a listing of the test records, and related items.

The use of development support libraries and the program librarian has alleviated much clerical work and allowed a greater percentage of the programmers' time to be dedicated to designing and writing programs, thus increasing programmer productivity.

The next section presents eight considerations and techniques to aid in developing well-designed programs.

14.8 CONSIDERATIONS AND TECHNIQUES FOR BETTER DESIGNED PROGRAMS

The design of a program is often built around various techniques used to make a program more understandable and readable. Eight rules recommended for a more readable FORTRAN program are:[13]

1. Comment cards should be used freely, but wisely. Each program and subprogram should include an initial group of comments that completely describes the program, what it does, what the inputs are, and what outputs are produced. Comments should be used at the beginning of "logical blocks," that is, the logical groupings of statements for major tasks in the program. Several blank comment cards should be used to set off the logical sections so that they will stand out as such.

   Comment cards should normally include a few special characters such as dashes (-) or asterisks (*), at the beginning, so the cards will not be confused with the FORTRAN statements. Remarks contained in the comment card should tell *what* is logically being done, not *how* it is being done, as given in the FORTRAN statement. For example, writing a comment that says "add 1 to K" before the statement K = K + 1 is no particular help. Use a remark like "bump records-processed counter by 1." Again, tell what is being done in terms of the problem, not in terms of the statement. Express your comments in a way that will help the reader know what the logic is doing.

---

13. Daniel D. McCracken, and Gerald M. Weinberg, "How to Write a Readable FORTRAN Program," *Datamation* 18, no. 10 (October 1972), pp. 73–77.

2. Eliminate unnecessary GO TO's. The GO TO statement should be used sparingly. Programs containing excessive GO TO's are difficult to follow, understand, and maintain, since they are heavily interlocked. Situations that may require the heavy use of GO TO's may be better written as subprograms. In some cases, the excessive use of GO TO's can be avoided by the use of multiple Logical IF statements. For example:

$$\textbf{IF (N .EQ. 1) K = 0}$$
$$\textbf{IF (N .EQ. 1) A = B + C}$$

3. Every DO statement should have a CONTINUE as the range statement in the loop. Each DO statement should also refer to a separate CONTINUE statement. The statements contained in the DO loop should be indented several spaces under their respective DO. Consistent indentation enhances readability; so the finished program will indicate visually the relationships among the statements.

4. When an IF statement contains compound conditions, place each simple condition within a set of parentheses to make the order of the logical operators (.AND., .OR., and .NOT.) crystal clear. When there are three or more simple conditions, use continuation cards to put each simple condition on a separate card, and align the conditions vertically for better readability.

5. Assign statement numbers in some systematic order that will facilitate better understanding of the program flow. For example, assign the statement numbers in an ascending sequence in some increments, such as tens. This facilitates inserting new statement numbers between the existing ones. A program thus becomes easier to follow when a later reference is made to a statement number that occurs elsewhere in the program. FORMAT statement numbers should be assigned a number beginning with the digit 9 or some chosen pattern to indicate this type of statement. All FORMAT statements should be placed at the beginning or end of the program, whatever your preference.

6. Assign meaningful symbolic names. Don't be afraid to use all six characters to form a symbolic name. This is especially helpful with variables, where the name helps identify the value being used. Use the Explicit Type statements to aid in the formation of symbolic names. Never use the same variable to represent different values in the same program, just to save space. This can cause a debugging nightmare.

7. Show logical structures by indenting all statements within the control-flow structure. That is, all statements within the Selection, Iteration, and Select Case control structures should be indented three to four spaces. This technique improves the readability of program logic and aids in understanding the intended meaning of a logical structure.

8. Do not use tricks or "clever" programming techniques that are difficult to follow and understand. Do not use a complicated algorithm (such as for efficiency) when a simple one will work.

The use of these suggested techniques can help you write better-designed programs that are more readable and meaningful to other people. You should, of course, use top-down design, top-down implementation, and structured programming methodologies in the development of a program.

14.9 SUMMARY

This chapter provides an explanation of some of the design methodologies and tools used to solve more advanced, complex problems. The functional structure of a program is an important consideration in its design. Decomposing a problem into functional modules is an effective way to design and develop reliable and easy-to-maintain programs.

Section 14.2 discussed the top-down approach to a modular designed program. First, you must understand the purpose and function of a new program and how it will be used. Then, you should prepare a structure or hierarchy chart showing the functional modules required for a properly working program.

Controlling complexity is essential in computer programming. As human beings, we are limited by the relatively small number of details and logical relationships we can keep in our heads. The development of programs must be simplified to make them easier to understand and to keep their complexity within manageable limits. The best way to master the complexity of an assigned problem is to divide it into smaller parts that can be understood and dealt with. The top-down, hierarchical decomposition process divides problems into logical parts called modules. A functional module should ideally be a separate entity of related statements that perform a single program function. A module should not be a tangle of multiple statements tied together with spaghetti-like code or lumped together in an arbitrary fashion.

The major functions involved in a problem should first be determined to gain a proper perspective of the major modules needed in the solution. General abstractions of these modules should be developed at the highest level of decomposition. You should state what is to be done in abstract terms and not worry at this point about how the functions will be carried out by the program. There should be a gradual change at the intermediate level from a description of *what* the program is to do to *how* the program will do it.

One of the main reasons for decomposing a problem in a top-down manner is to create a well-designed program structure. A checklist for good program structure would include positive answers to these questions:[14]

1. Is the organization of your program modular?
2. Does each routine and subroutine perform a well-defined, complete function?
3. Is the program's flow straightforward?
4. Does it go from top to bottom instead of jumping around?

Section 14.3 discussed structure charts, a graphic design tool that presents a pictorial overview of the functional modules of a program and their relationship. Symbols are used to denote yet-to-be-developed and predefined modules. The module symbol shows the functions at various hierarchical levels in a decomposed problem. Hierarchical lines are used to show the relationships among modules.

The structure chart is not intended to show logic. It shows the functional modules required to solve a problem at various levels of detail. A structure chart may also be used to decompose any problem into manageable pieces. You may be able to use this tool in some of your non-computer-related classes.

Section 14.4 described HIPO (Hierarchy plus Input-Process-Output) diagrams, a graphical technique for showing what a program does and what data it uses and creates. HIPO is used as both a design aid and a documentation tool. A HIPO package consists of three types of diagrams.

1. Visual Table Of Contents (VTOC) diagram
2. Overview diagrams
3. Detail diagrams

The VTOC, or hierarchy chart, is similar to a structure chart. It shows the hierarchical structure of the functions required in the program structure. The first level of functions represents the major functions performed by the program. These high-level functions are decomposed into lower-level functions until a sufficient amount of detail is reached.

The overview and detail diagrams are divided into three sections—input, process, and output. A detail diagram may include an extended description section to provide additional information regarding the function.

There are three kinds of HIPO packages. An initial design package is used by managers and users when reviewing the overall design of a program or system. The detail design package is developed by the programmer to document the details of the program functions. The maintenance package is used by new users and programmers to learn the functions of a program or system.

Section 14.5 discussed aspects of the top-down design process for developing modules. The measure of a module's independence is important to good program design. This independence is measured by its cohesiveness and coupling strength.

Module cohesion is a measure of intra-modular strength, a measure of the relationship of the instructions within the module in performing a function. High module cohesion is a major design objective. There are six levels of module cohesion. In descending order of module strength, they are:

1. Functional
2. Sequential
3. Communicational
4. Temporal
5. Logical
6. Coincidental

The highest level, functional cohesiveness, characterizes a module in which all instructions perform a single, well-defined task, all the statements are directly related so that the module stands alone as a single functional unit.

14. Charles B. Kreitzberg and Ben Shneiderman, *The Elements of FORTRAN Style, Techniques For Effective Programming* (New York: Harcourt Brace Jovanovich Inc., 1972), p. 13.

Module coupling is a measure of inter-modular strength, a module's relationship to the other modules. The design objective is to minimize module coupling, so that a module is independent of all other modules. Such a module is said to be loosely coupled and communicates only with its parent module to receive the data items needed to perform its function.

There are several other considerations a programmer should follow in developing the program structure design and logic design for a module. A module's size should be restricted to no more than 50 statements. This allows the programmer to retain the logic in his or her head and to better comprehend the function of the module. Input/output routines should be modularized for debugging purposes or later conversion of the program to a new computer or compiler. Only the necessary data items required by a module should be passed, rather than an entire data record. This maximizes data integrity (information hiding). You should develop the detail logic for a module using only the recognized control-flow structures to enforce top-down coding. The statements within the selection and iteration control-flow structures should be indented to emphasize their logical relationship.

Section 14.7 described the improved programming techniques of chief programmer teams, structured walk-throughs, and the development support library. These techniques provide a more organized approach to software development and help ensure a more economic cost to programs which are readable, reliable, and maintainable.

Section 14.8 presented eight considerations and techniques to provide better designed FORTRAN programs.

This chapter emphasizes the importance of top-down design and implementation to produce well-structured programs. Experience in using these techniques will help provide the skill needed to develop the large, complex programs required in an operational environment. The goals of high programmer productivity, easier-to-read programs, more reliable systems, and more easily modifiable programs can be achieved by using these techniques.

14.10 TERMS

Terms and concepts you should become familiar with in this chapter are:

chief programmer team	hierarchy chart	predefined modules
detail diagrams	HIPO	program structure
development support library	HIPO package	ripple effect
function	local variables	structure chart
functional decomposition	loosely coupled module	structured walk-through
functional module	module	top-down decomposition
functional strength	module cohesion	top-down design
global variables	module coupling	top-down implementation
hierarchical lines	module sharing	Visual Table Of Contents (VTOC)
hierarchical structure	overview diagrams	yet-to-be-developed module

14.11 REVIEW QUESTIONS

1. Why is the program structure important to a well-designed program?
2. Why should you be concerned about software errors?
3. Why is it important to understand a problem fully before beginning its design?
4. What is the best way to master the complexity of a problem?
5. What is meant by functional decomposition of a problem?
6. Explain the process of functionally decomposing a problem.
7. Define the term *module*.
8. List four benefits of program modularity.
9. What is a structure chart?
10. What is the purpose and importance of a structure chart in developing a computer program?
11. What graphic symbol represents a module in a structure chart?
12. A structure chart is intended to show program logic. (True/False)
13. How is a normal connection between modules represented?
14. Define judicious postponement.
15. Define stepwise refinement.

16. What does the acronym HIPO stand for?
17. What are the three diagrams in a HIPO package?
18. Which HIPO diagram can be used as a hierarchy chart?
19. What is the purpose of the VTOC?
20. What are the three sections in an overview or detail diagram?
21. What are the three kinds of HIPO packages?
22. List the four steps (in order) for preparing a HIPO package.
23. Define module cohesion.
24. What is the highest strength category of module cohesion?
25. Define module coupling.
26. What is meant by a loosely coupled module?
27. What is meant by a tightly coupled module?
28. Why should you restrict the size of a module to 50 statements?
29. Why are subroutines important to top-down program implementation?
30. What is a stub? Give an example of its use.
31. Define the term *chief programmer team*.
32. Describe the members usually comprising a chief programmer team.
33. Define the term *structured walk-through*.
34. Explain the procedure for conducting a structured walk-through.
35. Define the term *development support library*.
36. Describe the function or purpose of a system flowchart.

14.12 EXERCISES

1. Draw a structure chart for chapter 10, programming problem 7.
2. Draw a structure chart for chapter 11, programming problem 7.
3. Draw a structure chart for chapter 12, programming problem 4.
4. Draw a structure chart for chapter 12, programming problem 5.

14.13 PROGRAMMING PROBLEMS

1. Rewrite programming problem 7 in chapter 10 using a top-down, modular implementation with subroutines.
2. Rewrite programming problem 7 in chapter 11 using a top-down, modular implementation with subroutines.
3. Rewrite programming problem 3 in chapter 12 using a top-down, modular implementation with subroutines.
4. Rewrite programming problem 4 in chapter 12 using a top-down, modular implementation with subroutines.

User-Written Function Subprograms and Additional Subprogram Statements

15

15.1 INTRODUCTION TO FUNCTION SUBPROGRAMS

User-written function subprograms serve the same purpose as subroutines in FORTRAN programs. That is, they provide a subprogram that can be coded once and executed at different locations in other program units. **Function subprograms** are used where a single calculated value is needed.

In mathematics the term **function** refers to an operation or rule for computing a quantity from a set of values called arguments. For example, you may want to compute the function of Y according to the formula: $Y = X^2 + Z$. The values X and Z are input arguments to the function of Y. The value of Y is computed by plugging the input arguments into the given formula. If $X = 3$ and $Z = 1$, then Y is calculated as 10.

The concepts of function subprograms closely match those of mathematical functions. One or more arguments are passed to the function subprogram, which calculates a single resulting value. The value returned by the function subprogram is known as the **function value**.

A user-written function subprogram is a separate program unit, just as a subroutine is. Since a function subprogram is compiled as a separate program unit, there is no conflict between duplicate variable names and statement numbers in other program units. There must be at least four statements in a function subprogram just as in a subroutine, except that the first statement is the FUNCTION statement to identify the start of the subprogram.

A function name is assigned to the subprogram and follows the keyword FUNCTION. A parameter list is *always* included after the function name. For example:

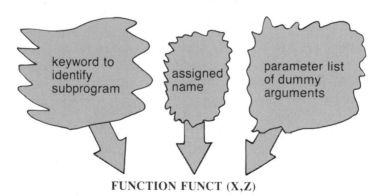

FUNCTION FUNCT (X,Z)

A function subprogram must contain at least one executable statement, which usually includes an Assignment statement that assigns a value to the function name. The RETURN and END statements serve the same purpose as in subroutines.

The function subprogram name is formed the same way as other symbolic names. The initial letter of the function name, however, determines the type of value returned, unless the function is specified as a given type. That is, if you assign a real symbolic name as the function subprogram name, a real value is returned. Likewise, an integer value is returned if an integer symbolic name is assigned. A type option may be given before the keyword FUNCTION to declare the function value to be a specific type (see section 15.2).

The function subprogram can contain any number or kind of statements except another FUNCTION, SUBROUTINE, or BLOCK DATA statement, so in many respects a function subprogram is constructed and operates like a subroutine. The three major differences are:

1. The way it is invoked (i.e., called).
2. The number of values that may be returned and the method used for returning them.
3. The location in the calling program to which control is returned.

A function subprogram is invoked, not by a CALL statement, as in a subroutine usage, but by using its name in an arithmetic expression. The term **invoke** or **reference** will be used to indicate the way a function subprogram is executed—not the term "called"—to prevent confusion with subroutine execution. (Even though many people use the term "call" to refer to the execution of either a subroutine or a function subprogram.) Basically, however, a user-written function is invoked the same way as a built-in function.

The function subprogram reference is usually made in an Assignment statement, such as:

$$\text{RESULT} = \text{FUNCT(X,Z)}$$

where FUNCT is the name of the subprogram and X and Z are arguments. A function subprogram reference, however, may be used at any place in an expression where a variable or constant of the same type could be used. For example:

$$\text{IF (FUNCT(X,Z).GT.0.0) GO TO 20}$$

Here the function subprogram is invoked to obtain a value that is used to determine a logical condition in an IF statement.

The second major difference in function subprograms is the argument list and the way the computed value is returned to the calling program. Only one value is returned from the function subprogram, and it is returned under the subprogram name. The calculated value is placed in the function name by an Assignment statement such as:

$$\text{FUNCT} = \text{X ** 2 + Z}$$

where FUNCT is the function subprogram name.

In ANSI FORTRAN 66 the function subprogram may return more than one value by assigning new values to any of the dummy arguments. If any dummy argument is modified, the values of corresponding actual arguments in the calling program are also changed. In many other compilers it is forbidden in a function subprogram to modify any of the variables representing the dummy arguments. That is, the dummy arguments may be used in calculations, decision making, or whatever, but they must not be given a new value in the function subprogram. The modification of a dummy variable in a function subprogram is not a good programming practice. This technique often results in hard-to-find errors during debugging.

The function subprogram must *always* include a parameter list, and that list must always contain at least one argument. Most FORTRAN compilers allow an unlimited number of dummy arguments. Some smaller compilers, like Basic FORTRAN IV, limit the number of dummy arguments to fifteen.

The parameter list of a function subprogram and the parameter list of the invoking statement may contain any type of argument that can be used with subroutine parameter lists. However, the actual arguments must agree with the dummy arguments in the same four ways—number, order, type, and length. Actual arguments may or may not have the same name as their corresponding dummy arguments. They must always keep positional correspondence in a left-to-right order. For example:

mainline
function
reference: Y = FUNCT (A,B)

FUNCTION
statement: FUNCTION FUNCT (X,Z)

If an array name is passed as an argument, then the array must also be dimensioned in the function subprogram.

The third major difference in using function subprograms is the location in the calling program to which control is returned. Control is returned to the *same* statement that invoked the function subprogram. It is *not* returned to the next statement, as with the CALL and subroutines. The reason for this is that the execution of the statement that invoked the subprogram has yet to be completed. For example:

$$VALUE = FUNCT(X,Z) + 3.7 * S$$

The reference to the function subprogram named FUNCT supplies only one value in the expression. The rest of the expression must be completed before the one resulting value is assigned to the variable VALUE. The same principle holds true even if you have an Assignment statement such as:

$$VALUE = FUNCT(X,Z)$$

Control must be returned to the same statement to check for additional operations and to assign the computed value to the assignment variable.

In an arithmetic expression that contains a function subprogram reference, the function reference takes precedence over any arithmetic operator and is, therefore, performed first. Of course, parentheses can be used to override this hierarchy and cause other operations to be performed before the function reference. For example:

$$Y = (3.0 + R) * FUNCT(X,Z) - T$$

R is added to 3.0 first, because of the parentheses. The function FUNCT is invoked second, because it takes precedence over arithmetic operations. Next, the result of the function is multiplied by the result of the first step. Lastly, T is subtracted from the result in step three to obtain the final value for Y.

The value returned from the function subprogram can never be accessed by using the subprogram name, except where an expression is allowed. For example, it is forbidden in ANSI FORTRAN 66 to write:

$$WRITE (6,98) FUNCT(X,Z)$$

where FUNCT is a function subprogram reference. The value returned from the subprogram must be assigned to a new variable in an Assignment statement if the calculated value is to be printed or used in later calculations. Many FORTRAN timesharing systems, however, permit function references in the I/O list of the PRINT or WRITE statements.

Function subprograms may invoke other function subprograms or call subroutines. But a function subprogram must not invoke itself or invoke another subprogram that references it in turn. Basically the same concepts that apply to subroutine subprograms hold true for function subprograms, except for the three noted differences.

To illustrate the operation of function subprograms, let us code the problem of computing the function of $Y = X^2 + Z$. The program units are as follows:

Function Subprogram	Mainline Program
FUNCTION FUNCT(X,Z)	99 FORMAT(2F5.2)
FUNCT = X ** 2 + Z	98 FORMAT(1H0,F7.2)
RETURN	READ (5,99) X,Z
END	Y = FUNCT(X,Z)
	WRITE (6,98) Y
	READ (5,99) A,B
	Y = FUNCT (A,B)
	WRITE (6,98) Y
	STOP
	END

In the mainline program, two values are read under the variables X and Z. The function subprogram is invoked using these input values. The subprogram FUNCT receives the input values X and Z under the dummy arguments of X and Z, respectively. The function is computed according to the formula $X^2 + Z$, and the calculated value is placed in the function subprogram name. Control is returned to the mainline program, where the calculated value is assigned to the variable Y and printed. This same process is also performed with two more input variables, A and B.

Table 15.1 (p. 434) summarizes the differences between function and subroutine operations. Study this table carefully to avoid confusing the two types of subprograms.

You may now wonder when to use a function subprogram rather than a subroutine. You can always use a subroutine subprogram to perform any type of operation. Function subprograms should be used when a single calculated value is needed from a routine.

Function subprograms are flowcharted using the same symbols and technique as for subroutines. The job setup for programs that include function subprograms also remains the same as for subroutines. Whenever

Table 15.1 Comparison of Function and Subroutine Subprograms

Function	Subroutine
Invoked by using its name in an expression.	Invoked by means of a CALL statement.
Name takes on a value and may be used in an expression. Dummy arguments may be modified if more than one value is returned.	Name does not take on a value. All values are returned through the arguments.
The type of the value returned depends upon the type name assigned.	Subroutine names are not typed. The type of values returned depends upon the type of the arguments.
Must have at least one dummy argument.	Does not require any dummy arguments.
Control is returned back to same statement.	Control is returned to the next executable statement after the CALL.

function subprograms are used in conjunction with subroutines, it makes no difference which type of subprogram is included first. In fact, you may have a subroutine followed by a function subprogram, followed by another subroutine, and so on.

There are two kinds of function subprograms available in FORTRAN:

1. Function Subprograms—complete subprograms similar to subroutines.
2. Statement Functions—one-statement functions represented in an arithmetic Assignment statement.

First, we will continue to discuss the function subprogram.

15.2 THE FUNCTION STATEMENT AND A SAMPLE SUBPROGRAM USING ARRAYS

The FUNCTION statement identifies the beginning of a function subprogram. It normally begins with the word FUNCTION followed by the assigned function name. A parameter list in parentheses follows the function subprogram name. A type option may be given before the keyword FUNCTION if you want to explicitly type the resulting value of the subprogram name. For example:

INTEGER FUNCTION FSUB(I,K,M)

Even though the function subprogram is assigned a real type name (FSUB), the resulting value will be an integer when the Explicit INTEGER type option is used. The type specification can be INTEGER, REAL, DOUBLE PRECISION, LOGICAL, or COMPLEX to explicitly type the resulting value in the function subprogram name.

Figure 15.1 gives the general form of the FUNCTION statement.

Now let us examine a function subprogram that uses an array as a dummy argument. Suppose a function subprogram named NSUM is written to sum the elements in a one-dimensional integer array. The dummy

---

FUNCTION Statement—General Form

type FUNCTION name (darg$_1$,. . ., darg$_n$)

where:

type — is an explicit type specification which denotes the type value of the function name. **Type** may be REAL, INTEGER, DOUBLE PRECISION, LOGICAL, or COMPLEX. Its inclusion is optional.

name — is the assigned function name.

(darg$_1$,. . ., darg$_n$) — represents a parameter list of dummy arguments.

Figure 15.1 General notation of the FUNCTION statement

arguments will include an array name for a one-dimensional array and the number of elements to sum. The coded program units are:

Function Subprogram	Mainline Program
FUNCTION NSUM(LIST,N)	DIMENSION L1(10),L2(20)
DIMENSION LIST(20)	99 FORMAT (10I3)
NSUM = 0	98 FORMAT (20I2)
DO 10 I = 1,N	97 FORMAT (1H0,10I5,I6)
NSUM = NSUM + LIST(I)	96 FORMAT (1H0,20I4,I5)
10 CONTINUE	READ (5,99) L1
RETURN	L1SUM = NSUM(L1,10)
END	WRITE (6,97) L1,L1SUM
	READ (5,98) L2
	L2SUM = NSUM(L2,20)
	WRITE (6,96) L2, L2SUM
	STOP
	END

The mainline program first reads a ten-element array named L1. The array name and the number of elements are passed as actual arguments when the subprogram is invoked by the statement

$$L1SUM = NSUM(L1,10)$$

The subprogram receives the input arguments under the dummy arguments LIST and N. The sum of the ten items is computed and assigned to the function subprogram name. The calculated sum is returned under the function name NSUM and assigned to the variable L1SUM in the main program. Then the array L1 and its sum are printed.

Next, the mainline program reads a twenty-element array named L2. The array and its number of elements are passed in the statement

$$L2SUM = NSUM (L2,20)$$

Again the array and number of elements are received under the dummy arguments LIST and N. The sum of the items is calculated and returned under the function name. The mainline program assigns the returned value to the variable L2SUM; then the array L2 and its sum L2SUM are printed.

The next section discusses another type of function that is not a subprogram—the statement function—which is coded as a single statement using a form of the Assignment statement.

15.3 THE STATEMENT FUNCTION

A statement function consists of a single statement that defines a function. This statement definition can then be invoked by other statements in the program, just like any other subprogram. It is not, however, coded as a separate subprogram in the same way that subroutines and regular function subprograms are. There is no keyword to identify the statement function, nor are any RETURN and END statements associated with it. The statement function can compute only one value.

A "modified" arithmetic Assignment statement is used to define the mathematical function (hence the term **statement function**). The modified Assignment statement that defines the statement function looks like this.

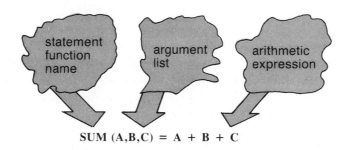

SUM (A,B,C) = A + B + C

To the left of the equal sign is the statement function name, followed by its parameter list of dummy arguments. The right-hand part of the statement contains the arithmetic expressions that define the calculations. The statement function must not be assigned a statement number.

The statement function name is formed the same way as a function subprogram name. Its initial letter determines the type of value returned. Of course, the chosen name of the statement function must not be the same as another variable or array name in the program.

You may have any number of dummy arguments in a statement function, but it must contain at least one. (Basic FORTRAN limits the number of dummy arguments to 15.) The same dummy arguments may be used in more than one statement function and may be the same as other variable names used in the program. A dummy argument may not be a subscripted variable; however, subscripted variables may be used as actual arguments passed from an invoking statement elsewhere in the program to the statement function. The same rules for arguments that apply to function subprograms also apply to statement functions. The same rules for arguments that apply to function subprograms also apply to statement functions. The actual and dummy arguments must always agree in number, order, type, and length.

The arithmetic expression appearing to the right of the equal sign may contain

1. numeric constants
2. numeric variables
3. built-in functions
4. other user-defined function subprograms
5. other statement functions

The expression must *not* contain any subscripted variables. The variables may be the same as the dummy arguments or as additional variables that do not appear in the argument list. Those variables used in the arithmetic expression, but not appearing in the argument list, contain their current values in the program. When variables of this nature are used, their values may be changed between references to the statement function. The expression must contain all of the dummy arguments.

This one-statement function is often called the **statement function definition.** The statement is nonexecutable and only defines the statement function; thus, it does not cause any computation to take place. It is limited to one statement and can return only one value.

The statement function must immediately precede the first executable statement in the program. It must also be placed **after all** specification statements. Thus, its position in a program is between the last specification statement and the first executable statement.

The general form of the statement function is:

$$\text{name (darg}_1, \ldots, \text{darg}_n) = \text{expression}$$

where:

name	—is the name assigned to the statement function.
darg₁, . . . ,dargₙ	—represent a parameter list of one or more nonsubscripted dummy arguments.
expression	—is an arithmetic expression involving the dummy arguments and optional additional constants, variables, various types of function subprogram references, and/or another statement function.

Following are valid examples of statement function definitions.

$$\text{DIF(X,Y)} = \text{X} - \text{SQRT(Y)} * 2.0$$
$$\text{TOT(A,B,C,D)} = \text{A} * (\text{B} - \text{C}) / \text{D} + \text{E}$$
$$\text{IRSLT(J,K,L)} = \text{IFUNCT(J,K)} / \text{L} - 3 * \text{L}$$

A statement function is invoked in the same way as a function subprogram by statements elsewhere in the program. Its name may be used in any form of arithmetic expression. To invoke the statement function named SUM which computes the sum of three arguments, you could code:

$$\text{RESULT} = \text{SUM(A,B,C)}$$

or:

$$\text{IF (SUM(A,B,C) .LE. 0.0) RSLT} = 0.0$$

The actual arguments are passed in a left-to-right correspondence to the dummy arguments. For example:

$$\text{SUM (X,Y,Z)} = X + Y + Z$$

$$R = \text{SUM(A,B,C)}$$

The statement function must not refer to itself. The statement,

$$\text{SUM(A,B,C)} = A + B + C * \text{SUM(A,B,C)}$$

would be invalid. A statement function may, however, include another statement function as part of its arithmetic expression. When this is true, the statement function included in the arithmetic expression must appear before the definition of the statement function in which it is used.

Since this type of function appears in the program and is not a separate program unit, it is compiled along with the program unit it is in. Therefore, the statement function can only be referenced by the program unit it is in and not by any other program unit. Any program unit, however—mainline, subroutine, or function subprogram—can contain its own statement functions.

Now let us construct a sample program to illustrate the use of statement functions. The same example given in section 15.1 for the function subprogram—to compute $Y = X^2 + Z$—will be used.

The program is:

```
C *** MAINLINE WHICH INCLUDES A STATEMENT FUNCTION
      FUNCT(X,Z) = X ** 2 + Z
99    FORMAT (2F5.2)
98    FORMAT (1H0,F7.2)
      READ (5,99) X,Z
      Y = FUNCT(X,Z)
      WRITE (6,98) Y
      READ (5,99) A,B
      Y = FUNCT (A,B)
      WRITE (6,98) Y
      STOP
      END
```

The statement function, in combination with the mainline program, achieves the same results that were produced by the sample function subprogram in section 15.1. Statement functions are very useful when you have complex calculations that are used many times in a program.

The remaining sections discuss the additional statements and concepts that may also be used with function and subroutine programs.

15.4 THE EXTERNAL STATEMENT AND SUBPROGRAM NAMES PASSED AS ARGUMENTS

You learned in section 13.3 that a subprogram name can be used as an actual argument in the parameter list of a program calling or invoking another subprogram. The subprogram name can be passed as an actual argument in one of two ways: (1) as a function subprogram name followed by its required parameter list or (2) as a function or subroutine subprogram name by itself.

When the actual argument is a function subprogram name followed by its required parameter list, the subprogram is executed, and its resulting value is passed to the invoked/called subprogram as an actual argument. For example:

$$\text{CALL SUBR (A,FUNCT(X,Z),RESLT)}$$

A and RESLT are variables, and FUNCT is the name of a function subprogram. However, since the function FUNCT has its arguments included after its function subprogram name, FUNCT is executed *before* the arguments are passed to the subroutine SUBR. The resulting value of FUNCT(X,Z) is then passed as the second actual argument along with A and RESLT.

Suppose the function subprogram FUNCT and subroutine SUBR are:

Function	Subroutine
FUNCTION FUNCT(X,Z)	SUBROUTINE SUBR(A,F,R)
FUNCT = X ** 2 + Z	R = A + F
RETURN	RETURN
END	END

If the value of A is 10.0, the value of X is 3.0, and the value of Z is 5.0, then the statement

CALL SUBR (A,FUNCT(X,Z),RESLT)

would produce a value of 24.0 for the argument RESLT. When a function subprogram name with its required parameter list is passed as an actual argument, there is no problem.

When you pass just the subprogram name as an actual argument, it presents the name of a subprogram that is to be executed *during* the execution of the called/invoked subprogram. That is, the subprogram name by itself is used as an actual argument to specify which subprogram is to be executed when the corresponding dummy argument is used in the called/invoked subprogram. This gives you the flexibility of being able to change the subprogram that is executed within another subprogram simply by using a subprogram name as an actual argument. No matter what subprogram name you pass in the actual argument list, the called subprogram logic remains the same.

Suppose we have a function subprogram called MINMAX. If you pass it the built-in function AMIN1, then the subprogram will use the function AMIN1 in its calculations. If you pass it the built-in function AMAX1, then the subprogram will use the function AMAX1 in its calculations. The coded function subprogram is:

```
      FUNCTION MINMAX (SUBPGM)
      READ (5,99) A,B,C
   99 FORMAT (3F5.2)
      MINMAX = SUBPGM(A,B,C)
      RETURN
      END
```

Suppose you invoked the subprogram MINMAX with the following statement.

RESLT = MINMAX (AMIN1)

Since the built-in function AMIN1 is passed as an actual argument, the function subprogram MINMAX would return the smallest value among the three input variables.

Now suppose you invoked the subprogram MINMAX with the following statement.

RESLT = MINMAX (AMAX1)

Since the built-in function AMAX1 is passed as an actual argument, the function subprogram MINMAX would return the largest value among the three input values. Thus, the statement in the subprogram MINMAX that was coded

MINMAX = SUBPGM (A,B,C)

could be used to execute *any* function subprogram that used three arguments.

A problem arises when you pass just the function or subroutine subprogram name by itself. How does the computer know that the actual argument is a subprogram name and not a variable or an array name? It would know that it is not an array name if it was not dimensioned in a proper dimensioning statement. Otherwise, the computer assumes that the actual argument is a variable.

When only the subprogram name is used as an actual argument, the computer has no way of knowing that it is a subprogram name and not a variable, unless you tell it somehow. The statement needed to tell the computer that an actual argument is indeed a subprogram name is the **EXTERNAL** statement. When you code:

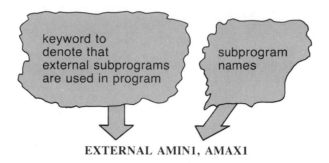

EXTERNAL AMIN1, AMAX1

then the computer knows the symbolic names AMIN1 and AMAX1 to be names of subprograms that are external to this program unit.

The EXTERNAL statement, therefore, specifies that a symbolic name is to be regarded as the name of a subprogram, rather than as a variable, when it is included as an actual argument in a parameter list. The general form of the EXTERNAL statement is given in figure 15.2.

The EXTERNAL statement is a specification statement and should not be assigned a statement number. It must precede any statement function subprograms and executable statements in the program unit.

You may use either a single EXTERNAL statement to contain all the names of external subprograms or multiple EXTERNAL statements to declare the same information.

To make the program correct when a subprogram name is used as an actual argument, you must include the EXTERNAL statement with the names of all subprograms used as actual arguments. The program unit that invokes the function subprogram MINMAX should be:

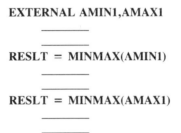

EXTERNAL AMIN1,AMAX1

———

———

RESLT = MINMAX(AMIN1)

———

———

RESLT = MINMAX(AMAX1)

———

———

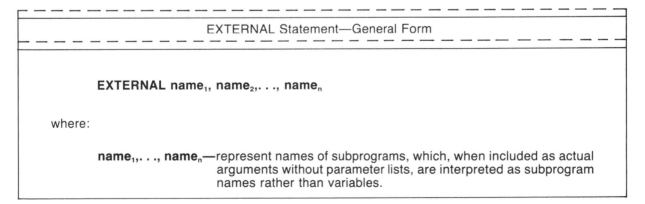

EXTERNAL Statement—General Form

EXTERNAL name₁, name₂,. . ., nameₙ

where:

name₁,. . ., nameₙ—represent names of subprograms, which, when included as actual arguments without parameter lists, are interpreted as subprogram names rather than variables.

Figure 15.2 General notation of the EXTERNAL statement

The same concepts hold true when subroutines are called. An actual argument may be the name of a function or subroutine subprogram. For example:

Mainline	Subroutine
EXTERNAL SQRT,SIN	**SUBROUTINE SUBF (X,FX,R)**
. . .	**R = FX(X)**
. . .	**RETURN**
CALL SUBF (20.5,SQRT,R)	**END**
. . .	
. . .	
CALL SUBF (3.14,SIN,R)	

The first time the subroutine SUBF is called, the built-in function SQRT is passed; so the subroutine calculates the square root of the input value in X. The second time SUBF is called, the built-in function SIN is passed; so the subroutine calculates the trigonometric sine of the input value in X.

Although the examples have shown only function subprogram names, subroutine names may also be passed as actual arguments. In the CALL statements you have the same flexibility for changing any subroutine that is called as one of the actual arguments.

15.5 OBJECT TIME DIMENSIONS IN SUBPROGRAMS

Object time dimensions allow you to postpone declaring the dimension size of arrays used in subprograms until execution time. As you will recall from chapter 11, you must specify the dimension size of arrays in the main program as a numeric constant, so that the proper amount of adjacent storage locations are assigned during compilation. Within subprograms, however, you can say:

$$\text{DIMENSION X(N)}$$

where the value of N is not provided until the execution of the subprogram.

The dimension size of an array provided by the value of variables must be equal to or less than the actual size specifications of the array passed as an actual argument. That is, if a fifty-element, one-dimensional array named A is passed as an actual argument, then the size of the corresponding dummy array argument must never exceed fifty. For example (assume the arrays A and B have been read),

Main Program	Subprogram
DIMENSION A(50),B(30)	**SUBROUTINE SUBR(X,N,S)**
. . .	**DIMENSION X(N)**
. . .	**S = 0.0**
CALL SUBR(A,50,SUM)	**DO 10 I = 1,N**
. . .	**S = S + X(I)**
. . .	**10 CONTINUE**
CALL SUBR(B,30,SUM)	**RETURN**
. . .	**END**

A COMMON or a DATA statement must not be used by the subprogram to assign a value to the variable of the DIMENSION statement specifications.

Object time dimensions may also be used with two- and three-dimensional arrays, but extreme caution is advised when doing so. Serious problems have been encountered because of the way the storage locations are assigned for multidimensional arrays and passed to subprograms.

When a two-dimensional array is used as a dummy argument, the first (row) subscript must have the same dimension as the corresponding actual array argument in the main program. The size of the second (column) subscript in the subprogram need not agree with the size of the second subscript in the main program. The same principle holds true for three-dimensional arrays. For object time dimensions of three-dimensional arrays in a subprogram, the first two (row and column) subscripts must be the same size as the array being passed by the calling program. The general rule is that the first n − 1 (n minus 1, where n is the number of dimensions) subscripts of the subprogram's DIMENSION statements for object time dimensions must correspond to the dimensions in the main program.

Section 15.6 discusses the EQUIVALENCE statement, which allows multiple variables to be assigned the same memory location.

EQUIVALENCE (name$_1$,. . ., name$_n$), (name$_1$,. . ., name$_n$)

where:

name—any name represents a variable or subscripted array element. All names within the same set of parentheses refer to the same storage location.

If name represents an array name, the subscript must be given as an integer constant.

Figure 15.3 General notation of the EQUIVALENCE statement

15.6 THE EQUIVALENCE STATEMENT

Suppose a large program were divided among three programmers. One programmer might code the input operations and editing of the input data; the second might code part of the calculation routines; the third might code the rest of the computations and output operations. When the three programmers attempt to put their routines together, they might discover that they have used different variables to represent the same data. For example, one programmer may have used L, another LNG, and the third the variable LENGTH to represent the variable for the value of length.

What should they do to make the variables represent the same location in memory? Should they agree on one variable and recode the other two to agree with the first? To do so might be very time-consuming. No, they do not have to perform this operation. There is an easy solution—use the EQUIVALENCE statement.

The EQUIVALENCE statement allows the programmer to equate two or more corresponding variables to the same memory location; so no matter which variable is used, you are still referring to the same location in memory. The general form of the EQUIVALENCE statement is given in figure 15.3.

Examples of the EQUIVALENCE statement are:

EQUIVALENCE (L,LNG,LENGTH)
EQUIVALENCE (B,BLK,BLOCK), (A,RA)
EQUIVALENCE (A(1),A1), (B(5),B5), (C(1),D(1))

The first example assigns the variables L, LNG, and LENGTH to the same memory location. The second example assigns the variables B, BLK, and BLOCK to the same memory location and the two variables A and RA to the same memory location. The third example equates the first element in array A with the variable A1, the fifth element in array B with the variable B5, and the start of the two arrays C and D to the same memory location, so that these two arrays share the same locations.

Remember, equivalence between variables implies storage sharing only, and not mathematical equivalence. The storage location value will change any time a new value is assigned to any one of the equated variables. The EQUIVALENCE statement is used to override the compiler in assigning unique storage locations to each new variable encountered in the program.

A programmer may develop a long program and unconsciously change a variable name at some point in the program. Whenever this mistake is found, the programmer simply uses the EQUIVALENCE statement to correct it. You may also use the EQUIVALENCE statement to conserve memory requirements in a large program. The programmer may have used the variables A, B, and C earlier in the program. These variables may cease to be used in later segments of the program. Thus, the variables X1, T2, and S1, which are used in the latter parts of the program, may be equated to A, B, and C to save three memory cells.

The saving in memory locations can be significant if large arrays are equated to each other. Suppose that the first part of a program used array A of 200 memory cells, which was not needed in the latter part of the program, and that array B of 100 memory cells is used only in the latter part of the program. If these arrays are equated so that they occupy part of the same locations in memory, 100 storage locations are saved.

When using the equivalence statement with elements in multiple arrays, you must be careful that array elements do not extend to the left of the beginning element in the other array. For example:

DIMENSION A(10), B(7)
EQUIVALENCE (A(1), B(3))

This is bad, since the first two elements in the array B—B(1) and B(2)—would extend to the left of the first element in array A; it could be disastrous.

You, as a student, may not have the need to use the EQUIVALENCE statement to conserve memory, but on small computers and with large FORTRAN programs, the EQUIVALENCE statement might mean the difference between fitting the program into memory or not.

The EQUIVALENCE specification statement must be placed at the beginning of a program unit ahead of any executable statements and must not be assigned a statement number. This statement must appear after the DIMENSION statement if any array elements are placed in equivalence.

Since the majority of the specification statements have been introduced, you may be confused as to their placement in a FORTRAN program. What happens if you use several specification statements in the same program; which one should come first? Following is a list of the FORTRAN statements that have been covered so far and their general sequence in a program unit.

Explicit Type statements
DIMENSION
EQUIVALENCE
DATA
Statement functions
all other executable statements
END

The next section discusses the COMMON statement, which allows the same memory locations to be shared among program units.

15.7 THE COMMON STATEMENT

Up to this point you have passed arguments between a calling program and subroutines in a parameter list. FORTRAN has the capability, however, to set aside a number of storage locations to be shared among program units. The shared storage locations are referred to as "COMMON" storage, meaning common to a number of program units. Arguments assigned to the Common storage locations need not be passed in a parameter list. The group of common storage locations is often referred to as a **Common Block.**

The COMMON statement is used to establish these common storage locations and to identify the variables and/or arrays assigned to them. A COMMON statement must be included in *every* program unit that is to share the assigned variables and arrays.

Suppose you want to assign the three variables X, Y, and Z to the common storage area and have them share these locations among different program units. The COMMON statement

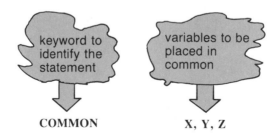

COMMON   **X, Y, Z**

would be included in each program unit that needs to reference these variables. Three storage locations are set aside in the Common storage area. These locations contain the quantities of X, Y, and Z, respectively, and these locations are accessible to every program unit that contains this particular COMMON specification statement. The last value assigned to any of the three variables by a program unit becomes its current value. That is, if the main program last assigned the value of 3.5 to X, that would be the current value of X when it is used by a subprogram. If the subprogram altered the value of X to 7.8, then that would be the current value of X when control is returned to the calling program.

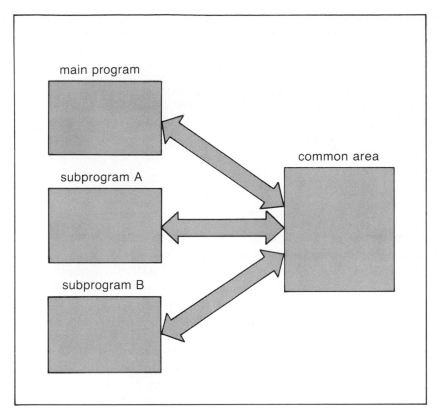

Figure 15.4 Communications between program units using COMMON

This type of Common memory area is called **Blank Common** or **Unlabeled Common,** since no name is assigned to the Common Block. Only one Blank Common Block can be established in a FORTRAN program.

The communication among program units using a COMMON statement is illustrated in figure 15.4. Any program unit using the COMMON memory may share variables with any number of other program units.

Use of the COMMON statement not only eliminates the necessity of establishing a parameter list but is also a more efficient technique. The number of storage locations is reduced by at least 50 percent, since there is no need for redundant locations in each program unit. Program units process faster during execution because values do not have to be passed between them. The addresses of the variables in the Common area are established during compile time for each program unit.

A subroutine may receive or pass an argument via the parameter list *or* via the COMMON statement, but the argument must not be passed by both methods. That is, a dummy argument used in a parameter list must not appear in a COMMON statement.

Variables and/or array items are assigned to Blank Common cumulatively in the order of their appearance within the COMMON statement. That is, the first variable found in the COMMON statement is assigned to the first storage location, the second variable is assigned to the second location, and so on. If multiple COMMON statements are used, the variables/arrays in the second and successive COMMON statements are appended to the end of the Common Block in which the other variables leave off. For example:

COMMON A,B
COMMON D,E,F
COMMON G

The variables A and B are assigned to the first and second locations; variables D, E, and F are next assigned to the third, fourth, and fifth locations; the variable G is assigned to the sixth location in Common memory.

The same variable may not be placed in a Blank Common Block more than once. For example, the following statements are illegal:

COMMON A,B,C
COMMON I,J,A

The variable A appears in two COMMON lists, which is illegal.

The variables in the COMMON statements between program units need not be the same variable/array names. The concept works the same as with the actual arguments in a calling program and the dummy arguments in the subprogram. The variables/arrays in COMMON statements within *each* program unit are assigned beginning with the first location in the Common Block. For example:

Main Program:	**COMMON A,B,C**
Subprogram:	**COMMON X,Y,Z**

These variables are assigned to Common memory as follows:

main program:	A	B	C
common block:			
subprogram:	X	Y	Z

The variables X, Y, and Z in the subprogram correspond to the variables A, B, and C in the main program.

It is best to use the same symbolic names and identical COMMON statements in all program units that make use of the Common Block. You must take extreme care when a change is made to a COMMON statement to ensure that the corresponding changes are made in all program units using COMMON.

A Blank Common Block does not have to be the same length (i.e., contain the same number of variables) in all program units. A programmer must ensure the proper arrangement of arguments in Common storage by maintaining agreement as to (1) order, (2) type, and (3) length of variables. A COMMON statement may include "dummy" (extra) variables/arrays in order to provide the desired arrangement for the locations of arguments.

Just as the position of arguments is important in a parameter list, so the positional correspondence of variables/arrays is important in COMMON statements. If positional correspondence is violated, confusing results as well as hard-to-locate errors may occur.

Whenever the types of arguments are of different length, it is good practice to list the arguments in descending order of length; so double-precision variables and arrays should precede single-precision variables and arrays in the COMMON statement. This ensures proper "boundary" alignment of storage locations.

Whenever array names are contained in the COMMON statement, they may be supplied with dimension specifications in the COMMON statement itself. For example:

COMMON A,B(10),C(5,3)

where B is a ten-element one-dimensional array, and C is a five-row by three-column two-dimensional array.

Alternatively, the dimension specifications may still be given in the DIMENSION statement and only the array names given in the COMMON statement. For example,

DIMENSION B(10),C(5,3)
COMMON A,B,C

These statements provide the same specifications as the previous example. Either way to provide dimension specifications for arrays in the Common memory area is correct, but the preferred way is to supply the dimension specifications within the COMMON statement itself. This provides clearer documentation and requires fewer statements. If the dimension information is given in a DIMENSION statement, it must precede the COMMON statement containing the array names.

In situations where Common storage is needed, it is often useful to divide the Common area into subdivisions of smaller blocks. Labels (names) are assigned to these subdivisions to identify the "labeled" Common Block. Whereas there can be only one Blank Common Block, multiple **Labeled Common Blocks** can be established.

COMMON Statement—General Form

COMMON /comnam/var$_1$, . . ., var$_n$

where:

comnam	—	is an optional Common area name. If no name is used, the variables are assigned to a Blank Common area. If this option is used, the name identifies the labeled Common area.
var$_1$, . . ., var$_n$	—	are variable or array names which identify the locations assigned to a Common area.
		Multiple labeled Common areas may be included on the same COMMON statement.

Figure 15.5 General notation of the COMMON statement

The name of a Labeled Common Block is enclosed within slashes following the keyword COMMON. The names of the variables and/or arrays to be included in the block are given after the block name. For example:

name assigned to a Labeled Common Block

list of variables/arrays assigned

COMMON/LIST1/ A,B,C(10)

A Labeled Common Block name is formed the same as other symbolic names in FORTRAN. No type meaning is given to the first letter of the name (i.e., integer or real), since different types of data may be assigned to a single Labeled Common Block. The name used as a label in the COMMON statement must not be used as a variable/array name elsewhere in the program.

Breaking up the Common area into labeled blocks makes it possible for specific program units to communicate with each other directly without concerning the other program units. For example:

Main Program:	**COMMON /LIST1/A,B,C/LIST2/X,Y,Z**
Subprogram 1:	**COMMON /LIST1/A,B,C**
Subprogram 2:	**COMMON /LIST2/X,Y,Z**

Thus, the Labeled Common Block named LIST1 is used only between the main program and subprogram 1. The Block named LIST2 is used only between the main program and subprogram 2.

The general form of the COMMON statement is given in figure 15.5.

The COMMON statement is a specification statement. It must appear before any executable statements and must not be assigned a statement number. Any other specification statement referring to variables or arrays listed in the COMMON statement must precede the COMMON statement.

Both Blank Common items and Labeled Common Blocks may be listed in the same COMMON statement. For example:

COMMON A,B/COM1/X,Y,Z

If the Labeled Common Block is given first, two consecutive slashes must be used to indicate the end of a Labeled Common Block and the beginning of Blank Common items. For example:

$$\text{COMMON /COM1/X,Y,Z //A,B}$$

A Labeled Common Block may appear more than once in the same or additional COMMON statements. For example:

$$\text{COMMON /COM1/ X,Y /COM1/ Z}$$

or:

$$\text{COMMON /COM1/ X,Y}$$
$$\text{COMMON /COM1/ Z}$$

Additional items in the same Labeled Common Block are appended to the end of the list. This has the same effect as if the Labeled Common Block had been coded as:

$$\text{COMMON /COM1/ X,Y,Z}$$

The FORTRAN compiler will continue to assign items at the end of a Blank Common Block or Labeled Common Blocks as it translates each COMMON statement.

The same block size must be maintained in all program units using the same Labeled Common Block. That is, the number of storage locations assigned to a Labeled Common Block must be the same in all program units. The names assigned to a Labeled Common Block may be different in each program unit, but the block name and the total number of locations in the block must agree. For example:

Main Program:	**COMMON /GRP1/ A,B,C**
Subprogram:	**COMMON /GRP1/ A1,B1,C1**

The variables A1, B1, and C1 equate to the same locations in the Labeled Common GRP1 as A, B, and C, respectively.

The EQUIVALENCE statement must *not* be used to declare two variables or arrays that appear in COMMON statements within the same program unit equivalent to each other. It is permissible to declare a quantity in COMMON equivalent to another variable that does not appear in a COMMON statement. This has the effect of placing the second variable into Common storage also, at the same location as the first.

No values can be predefined in a DATA or Explicit Type statement for any value in a Blank Common Block. The DATA and Explicit Type statements can be used to preassign values in a Labeled Common Block, but this preassignment of values to Labeled Common must be done in a special program unit called a BLOCK DATA subprogram. Section 15.8 will cover the construction of BLOCK DATA subprograms.

The COMMON statement can provide quite a shortcut when many calls are made to subprograms. It also eliminates the tedious construction of a long parameter list, which can often cause difficult-to-find errors arising from misarranged arguments. But the COMMON statement must be used with caution to ensure that the proper storage location contains the value you think it does.

To illustrate the use of a COMMON statement, let us recode the second sample program in section 13.4 using Blank Common. This sample program computed the sum, difference, product, and quotient of two values. The subroutine and main program with a Blank COMMON statement are:

Subroutine	Main Program
SUBROUTINE CMPUTE	COMMON A,B
COMMON X,Y,S,D,P,Q	COMMON A1,A2,A3,A4
S = X + Y	READ (5,99) A,B
D = X − Y	99 FORMAT (2F5.2)
P = X * Y	CALL CMPUTE
Q = X / Y	WRITE (6,98)A,B,A1,A2,A3,A4
RETURN	98 FORMAT (1H0,6F10.2)
END	READ (5,99) A,B
	CALL CMPUTE
	WRITE(6,98)A,B,A1,A2,A3,A4
	STOP
	END

The subroutine CMPUTE used six variables in Blank Common to compute and store its results. The main program also used the first six variables in Blank Common to store the input values and write the output results.

There are several important features of this program that must be examined closely. First, the variables in the COMMON of the main program did not have the same names as the COMMON of the subroutine. The same basic rules hold true for variables in the COMMON as for arguments in the parameter list. They must agree in order, type, and length. That is, the variables in COMMON statements within each program unit are assigned at the beginning of the Common area. The variables in COMMON between the program units share memory illustrated as follows:

Blank COMMON

subroutine CMPUTE variables	X	Y	S	D	P	Q

storage locations

main program variables	A	B	A1	A2	A3	A4

You could use the same variable names in the COMMON statements for both program units, but it is not necessary. The variables will be matched in a one-to-one, left-to-right order as they are assigned to Blank Common. It is recommended, however, that you use the same variable names assigned to Common memory, for better documentation and easier-to-follow programs.

The second thing to notice in the program is that there were no variables G and H used to read the values from the second data card. These variables could be used if you had equated them by an EQUIVALENCE statement to the locations used for A and B. This statement would be:

EQUIVALENCE (A,G),(B,H)

Thus the locations for G and H would be the same for A and B, respectively. A third COMMON statement that included the variables G and H would not work, since G and H would have been placed at the end of Blank Common after the variable A4.

Sometimes it is advantageous for you to include part of the arguments in COMMON and pass part of them via a parameter list. Normally, those variables that do not change should be put into Blank Common or even Labeled Common; those arguments that have different names and should not be equated to other variables are passed in a parameter list. This technique would have to be used in the sample program if the values in the variables A and B needed to be saved and not equated with G and H. That is, the input values should be placed in a parameter list and the calculated variables put into a COMMON statement to provide the flexibility we need.

The EQUIVALENCE statement cannot be used to extend a Blank Common Block to the left. That is, you must not equivalence (equate) the first variable in a Common Block with other than the first element of an array. For example, this would be an invalid use of the EQUIVALENCE statement:

DIMENSION X(10)
COMMON A
EQUIVALENCE (A,X(5))

Blank Common Blocks may, however, be extended to the right with the EQUIVALENCE statement. The following example is a valid use of the EQUIVALENCE statement.

DIMENSION A(10),B(20)
COMMON A
EQUIVALENCE (A(5),B(1))

The next section discusses a special type of subprogram called BLOCK DATA.

15.8 BLOCK DATA SUBPROGRAMS TO INITIALIZE LABEL COMMON BLOCKS

A BLOCK DATA subprogram has as its sole purpose the assigning of initial (compile time) values to storage locations in Labeled Common Blocks. It is the only way you are permitted to initialize variables and array elements in Labeled Common Blocks. The BLOCK DATA subprogram, however, may not be used in ANSI FORTRAN 66 to provide initial values for variables/arrays assigned to a **Blank Common** Block.

The BLOCK DATA subprogram begins with the BLOCK DATA statement and ends with the END statement. No executable statements are included in the subprogram. The only statements allowed in the subprogram are specification statements that assign compile time values to storage locations and provide declaratory information. The statements are limited to the COMMON, DIMENSION, EQUIVALENCE, DATA, and Explicit Type statements. The subprogram may also include comment cards.

Only the DATA statement may be used in ANSI FORTRAN 66 to assign initial values. Other FORTRAN compilers also allow the Explicit Type statements to be used to assign initial values. The COMMON statements must precede any DATA statements in the subprogram.

When the elements of an array are to be initialized in a BLOCK DATA subprogram, each element must be listed individually with its subscripted name. Some compilers permit the use of the array name followed by a constant with the "*s" specification to initialize the entire array.

An example of a BLOCK DATA subprogram is as follows:

```
BLOCK DATA
INTEGER R,T
REAL K,L,L2
DIMENSION A(5),B(3)
COMMON /LIST1/SUM,A,R,K
COMMON /LIST2/T,L,B
EQUIVALENCE (L,L2)
DATA SUM/0.0/,R,T/1,2/
DATA A(1),A(2),A(3),A(4),A(5)/5*0.0/,L/3.5/
DATA B(1),B(2),B(3)/3*1.0/
END
```

This BLOCK DATA subprogram initializes two arrays and four variables in two Labeled Common Blocks. Note the fact that all variables in a Labeled Common Block must be included in the COMMON statement whether or not they are initialized. For example, the variable K in our sample subprogram is not given an initial value.

Initial values may be assigned to more than one Labeled Common Block in a single BLOCK DATA subprogram. For example, the sample program includes two Labeled Common Blocks, LIST1 and LIST2. All values in a single Common Block that are to be initialized must be located in the same BLOCK DATA subprogram.

15.9 LANGUAGE EXTENSIONS IN FORTRAN DIALECTS (THE ENTRY STATEMENT WITH FUNCTIONS AND THE INTRINSIC STATEMENT)

The construction of the ENTRY statement and its use with subroutines were covered in section 13.7. The general form and basic rules in the use of the ENTRY statement were also covered in that section. This section will present an example of a function with multiple entry points. Remember, the ENTRY statement is not available in FORTRAN 66, but it is available in FORTRAN 77 and other FORTRAN IV compilers.

The ENTRY statement name, when used with functions, takes on the resulting value, just as the function subprogram name would. Thus, the chosen ENTRY statement name must be the same type as the returned value. The ENTRY statement must include a parameter list with one or more arguments.

Consider the following function subprogram and its references.

Function Subprogram	Mainline Program
FUNCTION FSUM(A, B, C)	. . .
D = B + C	. . .
E = B * C	T = FSUM(X, Y, Z)
ENTRY FSUM2(A)	. . .
FSUM = A + D + E	. . .
RETURN	T = FSUM2(X)
END	. . .

The first time the function FSUM is invoked, it is entered at the top with the input arguments of A, B, and C. The input arguments B and C are used to calculate D and E. The variables D and E will retain their values after the execution of the function FSUM. Any variable that is not a dummy argument will retain its last assigned value automatically on most FORTRAN compilers. The sum of A, D, and E is calculated and stored under the function name FSUM.

The next time the mainline program invokes the function, it is entered at the first executable statement following the ENTRY point named FSUM2. Only the argument A is passed to the function and used to calculate a new sum. The new value of A and the previous values of D and E are used to compute the new sum. The resulting sum is passed back in both the names of FSUM and FSUM2. Since the invoking Assignment statement referenced FSUM2, the value is obtained from that function name.

The parameter list of the ENTRY statement does not have to agree with the parameter list of the FUNCTION statement. Neither do any two ENTRY statements' parameter lists have to be the same. Actual arguments in the parameter list in the invoking program need only agree with the dummy arguments' parameter list for the corresponding ENTRY statement.

The INTRINSIC Statement

The INTRINSIC statement is used to identify a symbolic name in a parameter list as representing a built-in (intrinsic) function. This statement is not available in FORTRAN 66 and most FORTRAN IV compilers. These compilers allow a built-in function name to be passed as an argument to either a subroutine or a function, without any special instructions to the compiler. FORTRAN 77, VAX-11 FORTRAN, and other modern FORTRAN compilers include the INTRINSIC statement, which must be used to identify built-in functions passed as actual arguments to either a function or a subroutine.

An intrinsic function is one available to the FORTRAN compiler (SQRT, EXP, SIN, and others) but not written by the programmer. A function or subroutine written by a programmer is known as an external subprogram. Since all subroutines are programmer-defined (there are no intrinsic subroutines in FORTRAN), any subroutine name passed as an actual argument must be declared in the EXTERNAL statement. The same rule holds true for programmer-defined functions.

The form of the INTRINSIC statement is:

INTRINSIC funct-name [, funct-name] . . .

where:

each **funct-name** is an intrinsic function name.

The beginning ([) and ending bracket (]) indicate optional use. The three ellipses (. . .) signify that additional function names may be included.

If the specific name of an intrinsic function is passed as an actual argument in a program unit, it must appear in an INTRINSIC statement in the program unit. The names of intrinsic functions for type conversion and for choosing the largest or smallest value must not be used as actual arguments.

Only one appearance of a symbolic name for an intrinsic function is permitted in all the INTRINSIC statements of a program unit. The same symbolic name must not appear in both an EXTERNAL statement and an INTRINSIC statement in the same program unit.

15.10 SUMMARY

Functions are separate program units that can be coded once and executed at different locations in other program units. They are useful when only one resulting value is needed from a subprogram. This chapter discussed user-written functions and some of the additional statements and features related to FORTRAN subprograms.

Functions are similar to subroutines. A function must be identified by a FUNCTION statement at the start of the subprogram. There must be at least one executable statement in the function subprogram. The RETURN statement is used to return control back to the invoking statement. The END statement must be the last physical statement in a function, since it is a separate program unit.

Functions differ from subroutines in the following ways:

1. A function is invoked (executed) by using its name in an expression.
2. A function must include a parameter list with at least one argument. More than one argument may be used if needed.
3. Only one value is returned from a function. The value is returned under the FUNCTION name. The type of value returned depends on the FUNCTION name.
4. Control is returned from the function back to the same statement that invoked it.

The type of value returned depends upon the name of the function given in the FUNCTION statement. A function name may be typed with the INTEGER, REAL, or other keyword preceding the keyword FUNCTION. A function may contain any number of statements and any kind of statement except another FUNCTION, SUBROUTINE, or BLOCK DATA statement.

The parameter list of the invoking statement may contain any type of argument that could be used in the parameter list of a CALL statement for a subroutine. The dummy arguments must agree with the actual arguments in the same four ways as in subroutines (number, order, type, and length).

A function may invoke another function or call subroutines. A function must not invoke itself directly (by a statement with a reference to the same function) or indirectly (by executing a subprogram that in turn invokes the original function itself).

Section 15.3 discussed the statement function, a single statement that defines a function. It is not coded as a separate program unit, but as a single statement at the beginning of a program unit. It must appear before any executable statements in the program unit. The statement function itself is not an executable statement, but defines the expression to be used in calculation.

The statement function is written as an Assignment statement. Arguments may be passed to it. The expression may contain numeric constants, variables, built-in functions, other user-defined functions, or another statement function. The expression cannot contain any subscripted variables.

A statement function is invoked the same way as a user-written function. Its name may be given in any statement where an arithmetic expression may be used. The statement function must not refer to itself in its expression.

Section 15.4 discussed the EXTERNAL statement, which must be used to identify all programmer-defined subprogram names that are given as actual arguments in a parameter list.

Section 15.5 explained object time dimensions, which allow arrays to be dimensioned with variables, rather than constants, in subprograms. The dimension size is provided by a dummy argument to which the value of an actual argument is passed during execution, rather than at compile-time. This technique is quite handy for performing calculations with arrays or searching and sorting arrays, but you must be extremely careful when using object time dimensions with multi-dimensional arrays.

Section 15.6 explained the EQUIVALENCE statement, which is used to assign different symbolic names to the same memory location. It is used to compensate for misspellings of variable names referring to the same value, and can also be used to conserve memory by making large arrays share the same memory locations. The EQUIVALENCE statement is a non-executable specification statement that should be placed at the beginning of a program unit before any executable statements. It must not be assigned a statement number.

Section 15.7 discussed the COMMON statement, which is used to share memory locations among program units. One advantage of this statement is in the saving of memory locations, but it is used mainly to avoid having to pass arguments in a parameter list.

There are two types of Common areas in FORTRAN. Blank (or unlabeled) Common is not given a name. There can only be one Blank Common area in a FORTRAN program. Labeled (or named) Common is a shared area of memory with a specific name. There can be multiple labeled Common areas in a given program.

Section 15.8 presented a new type of subprogram called BLOCK DATA. Its sole purpose is the assignment of initial values at compile time to Labeled Common blocks, and it is the only way to accomplish this task. In FORTRAN 66 you are only allowed to use the DATA statement to initialize items in Labeled Common. In many FORTRAN IV compilers you can also use the Explicit Type statements in the BLOCK DATA subprogram to initialize these areas.

15.11 TERMS

Terms, concepts, and statements you should become familiar with in this chapter are:

blank Common	function value	reference a function
BLOCK DATA subprogram	INTRINSIC statement	statement function
common block of storage	intrinsics	statement function definition
COMMON statement	invoke a function	subprogram names as arguments
EQUIVALENCE statement	labeled Common	typing function names
EXTERNAL statement	named Common	unlabeled Common
FUNCTION statement	object time dimensions	user-written function
function subprogram	programmer-defined function	

15.12 REVIEW QUESTIONS

1. When do you normally include a function subprogram in the design of a program?
2. How is a function subprogram identified in a program unit?
3. How is a function subprogram referenced by a program unit?
4. What is the minimum number of arguments that must be included in the parameter lists to communicate between a function subprogram and an invoking program?
5. What is the usual number of values returned from a function subprogram to its invoking program?
6. How is the value usually returned from a function subprogram to its invoking program?
7. What determines the type of value returned from a function subprogram?
8. How is a value generally assigned to the name of a function subprogram?
9. Where is control of execution returned to in the invoking program?
10. Arguments in a function subprogram reference must agree in what four ways with the dummy arguments in the FUNCTION statement?
11. What is the advantage of using a statement function?
12. Must a statement function have dummy arguments?
13. What is the difference between a statement function and a function subprogram?
14. Where must the statement function subprogram be placed in a program?
15. How is a statement function subprogram referenced?
16. Where does control of execution return to from a statement function reference?
17. What is the purpose of the EXTERNAL statement?
18. What is the advantage of object time dimensions in a subprogram?
19. What is the purpose of the EQUIVALENCE statement?
20. What is the purpose of the COMMON statement?
21. Name the two types of Common areas.
22. What is the purpose of a BLOCK DATA subprogram?
23. Can any executable statements be included in a BLOCK DATA subprogram?

15.13 EXERCISES

1. Write the FUNCTION statement for each of the following:
   a. FUN1 with arguments consisting of the variables A, I, and P.
   b. FY with only one dummy argument consisting of the array named Y.
   c. CALC with the following arguments: variables X, Z, and TOTAL.

2. Write the FUNCTION statement for each of the following:
   a. CAT with arguments consisting of the variables MOUSE and RAT.
   b. FUN with the array named GRP1 and the variables S, T, U, and V as arguments.
   c. PLOT with the arguments X, Y, and K.

3. Find the error in each of the following statements.
   a. **FUNCT1 = FUNCT1(X + Z)**
   b. **AFUNCT = FUNCT2/A/**
   c. **FUNCTION FOFX**

4. Find the error in each of the following statements or group of statements.
   a. **FUNCT(X,Z) = Y**
   b. **FUNCTION CALC /X,Y,Z/**
   c. **FUNXYZ = (FUNCT)X,Y,Z**

5. Given the following statements:

Mainline Program	**Function Subprogram**
EXTERNAL SQRT	**FUNCTION FUNCTX (X,FX)**
A = 25.0	**FUNCTX = FX(X)**
R = FUNCTX(A,SQRT) + 7.2	**RETURN**
. . .	**END**

   a. What is the value of X in the subprogram?
   b. What is the returned value in FUNCTX?
   c. What is the value of R?

6. Given the following statements:

Mainline Program	**Function Subprogram**
EXTERNAL SQRT	**FUNCTION FUNCTS (X,FX)**
X = 7.0	**FUNCTS = FX (X + 2.0)**
XS = FUNCTS (X, SQRT) + 3.4	**RETURN**
. . .	**END**

   a. What is the value of X in the function subprogram?
   b. What is the returned value in FUNCTS?
   c. What is the value of XS?

7. Determine whether a function or a subroutine is the best type of subprogram to accomplish the following operations:
   a. Initialize an array to zeroes.
   b. Locate the smallest value in an array.
   c. Count the occurrences of an item in an array.
   d. Sort an array into descending sequence.

8. Determine whether a function or a subroutine is the best type of subprogram to accomplish the following operations:
   a. Find the largest value in an array.
   b. Square all the items in an array.
   c. Perform a matrix addition operation on two matrices.
   d. Compute the value of $2.0 * X^3 + Y$.

9. How many storage locations are reserved in Blank Common by each of the following sets of statements?
   a. **COMMON A,B**
      COMMON C,X,Y
   b. **COMMON G,H(11),I,J**
   c. **DIMENSION Z(15),N(5,5)**
      COMMON R,S,Z
      COMMON N
   d. **DIMENSION B1(100),B2(50,2)**
      COMMON T,V
      EQUIVALENCE (B2(1,1),B1(1),V)

10. How many storage locations are reserved in Blank Common by each of the following statements or sets of statements?
    a. **COMMON A,B,C,D**
       COMMON I,J,R
    b. **COMMON X,Y(5),Z(7),W**
    c. **DIMENSION G(10)**
       COMMON G,H,I
    d. **DIMENSION X(75),Y(30)**
       COMMON X,Z
       EQUIVALENCE (X(1),Y(1))

11. Write a BLOCK DATA subprogram to initialize the items of A, X, and J in a Labeled Common Block named GROUP1 to 5.3, 8.7, and 3, respectively.

12. Write a BLOCK DATA subprogram to initialize the items of X, Y, and Z in a Labeled Common Block named SET1 to 1.7, 86.5, and 3.87, respectively. Also initialize the four elements of a one-dimensional array named KNT to zeroes.

15.14 PROGRAMMING PROBLEMS

1. Write a FUNCTION subprogram named NSUM to find the sum of the integers from 1 to N. The value of N is read in a mainline program under the specifications I3 and passed to the subprogram via a parameter list. Upon return from the subprogram, write the following output:

    'SUM OF THE INTEGERS FROM 1 TO ' n ' IS' nn

    where n is the input value and nn is the computed sum.

2. Many mathematical and statistical solutions are derived for problems using a factorial series. N factorial (represented by N!) is derived from the product of all the integers from 1 through N. That is, 3! means $3 \cdot 2 \cdot 1 = 6$ (or $1 \cdot 2 \cdot 3 = 6$). However, 1! and 0! are both equal to one.

    Write a function subprogram named NFACTL to compute the factorial of the value contained in the variable N. A mainline program will read the value of N under the specification I2. The variable N will be passed to the subprogram and the value of N! returned. Then the value of N and N! are to be printed under the specification 2I10. Include the appropriate column headings.

    The following algorithm is given to describe the calculation of N!.

    a. **Set NFACTL to 1.**

    b. **If N ≤ 1 RETURN**

    c. **For values of I from 2 to N multiply NFACTL by I.**

    d. **RETURN**

3. Write a Function subprogram named LARDIV that computes the largest common divisor of the number N. Include a mainline that reads the value of N under the specification I3.

    Write an output line that reads 'THE LARGEST COMMON DIVISOR OF ' n ' IS ' m where n is the input number and m is the computed largest common divisor of N returned from LARDIV.

    Hint: Use the built-in function MOD in the Function subprogram and check for a remainder of zero. Include a DO loop that varies I from 1 to N. Use N as the first argument of MOD and N-I (N minus I) as the second argument of MOD.

4. Write a FORTRAN function subprogram named MEDIAN to compute the median score in a group of n number of test scores. A mainline program is used to read the value of N and the array of test scores named NTEST. The variable N and array NTEST will be passed to the subprogram named MEDIAN. The returned median score is printed upon the return of control to the main program.

    The value of N is read from the first data record under the specification I2. The array NTEST is read from the remaining data records under the specification 10I3.

    After the array NTEST is read, print the message:

    'THE ARRAY NTEST WITH ' n ' VALUES IS'

    where n is the input value of the variable N. Next print the items in the array NTEST on a new line with the specification 10I5. When the median score is returned to the mainline, print the calculated median score on a new line preceded by a literal that reads:

    'THE MEDIAN SCORE IS ' m

    where m is the computed median score.

    Hint: The median value of a group of items may be calculated as follows:

    a. First, sort the items into an ascending sequence.

    b. Next, determine if the value of N is an even or odd value. This may be determined by the formula:

    $$N / 2 * 2 - N$$

    If the resulting value is zero, then the value of N is an even number. If the resulting value is -1, then the value of N is an odd number.

c. 1. If N is an odd number, the median value is the middle item and is located at the position $N/2 + 1$.
   2. If N is an even number, the median value is the average of the two middle items. This median value may be obtained by adding the item at location $N/2$ to the item at location $N/2 + 1$ and taking the average of the sum.

Object time dimension may be used in the problem if you so desire.

5. Write a function subprogram named NBINRY to convert an integer to its corresponding binary integer. The decimal integer is positive and is less than 100. Read the decimal integer under the variable INT with an I3 format specifications. After the decimal integer is converted to its equivalent binary number, print a message that reads:

'DECIMAL NUMBER ' dn ' IS = TO BINARY NUMBER ' bn

where dn is the input decimal number, and bn is the converted binary number.

Hint: A decimal number is converted to a binary number by repetitive division by 2. The remainder after each division is used to form the binary number. The first remainder becomes the first binary digit, the second remainder becomes the second binary digit, and so on. The division process is complete when a quotient of zero is obtained.

6. Write a function subprogram to accomplish any problem you have previously programmed. Use a mainline program to read any input values and to print the output results.

7. Write a statement function named AVE to compute the average of three variables passed to it. The three input values will be read under the specifications 3F5.2 and named A, B, and C, respectively. The dummy arguments A1, B1, and C1 will be used in the statement function subprogram.

   After the computed average is returned, print the three input values and the computed average on the same line. Include appropriate column headings.

8. Rewrite programming problem 3 in chapter 11 using a function subprogram. Eliminate the requirements to print the element position. That is, just return the largest item in the array NR under the function name.

9. Rewrite programming problem 4 in chapter 11 using a function subprogram to perform the array-searching operation.

10. Rewrite programming problem 7 in chapter 11 using function subprograms. Write a function that will return the average of the twenty numbers and a second function to return the standard deviation.

11. Rewrite programming problem 1 in chapter 12 using a function subprogram to find the smallest item in the array XDATA.

12. Rewrite programming problem 3 in chapter 12 using a function subprogram to count the number of occurrences of the variable MVAL in the array M.

Additional Types of FORTRAN Constants, Variables, and Format Specifications

16

16.1 INTRODUCTION TO THE ADDITIONAL TYPES OF FORTRAN CONSTANTS, VARIABLES, AND DATA

The types of data that we have been manipulating in programs so far have been restricted to numeric values of type integer and single-precision floating point, and to alphanumeric values. Most FORTRAN compilers, however, have the capability to work with other forms of data. You may wonder what other types of data there can be. Business and social science applications use numeric and alphanumeric data as the basic forms of data. Math and engineering, however, use several other types of data.

A primary form for representing numeric constants is exponential notation. The **exponential notation** uses an exponent appended to a numeric value to represent the position of the decimal point and thus, the true value of the number. The exponential form of constants is patterned after the **scientific notation** for expressing numeric values. **Appendix D** explains the scientific notation and the basic exponential form for expressing numbers for those unfamiliar with it.

You may express numeric quantities to the compiler in an exponential form by using the E or D symbol preceding the exponential value. Numeric data fields expressed with an exponential value can also be read or written in FORTRAN with the E and D format codes. Sections 16.2 and 16.3 explain the use of these format codes for the input/output of numeric values.

Mathematicians also represent data in a boolean form. A boolean type constant may have only a value of either true or false. Boolean type constants are also widely used by engineers in expressing inputs and outputs to logic circuits. In FORTRAN, boolean values are referred to as logical data. Section 16.4 discusses this type of data.

In mathematics the use of complex numeric values is very important. The use of complex type data, which consists of a real part and an imaginary part, is discussed in section 16.5. A Generalized (G) format code for reading and writing any type of numeric value is explained in section 16.6. The use of a P scale factor to override the decimal point location in an input or output value is explained in section 16.7.

System programmers, those who work with compilers and operating systems, often need to display data in a number base other than base 10. The Octal (O) and Hexadecimal (Z) format codes are used to read and write data in base 8 and base 16, respectively. These format codes are explained in section 16.8, since they are not standard format codes. Their availability in a FORTRAN compiler depends on the number base used by a computer to represent its data internally in memory.

Business and social science students studying FORTRAN may never need to use any of these other data types. They are, however, extremely useful in specialized applications and programs.

16.2 SINGLE-PRECISION EXPONENTIAL TYPE CONSTANTS AND THE E FORMAT CODE

The precision of most real quantities can be expressed by six digits or less. Based on this consideration, computers have been designed to allow internal floating-point calculations with numbers having at least seven decimal digits and an exponent. Externally, a floating-point number may be constructed with or without the exponent. The use of a single memory word (normally one to seven digits) to represent a real constant is known as **single-precision** mode. The basic decimal form (i.e., a string of decimal digits with a decimal point) is the way most of us represent numbers with fractions in our everyday life. This is the form you have been using thus far in the text to express real constants.

A single-precision real constant may also be represented as a real or integer number followed by a decimal exponent. The **exponent** consists of the letter E followed by a signed or unsigned 1- or 2-digit integer constant. The exponent represents a power of 10 by which the number is multiplied to obtain its true value. The exponent can range from a power of -78 to $+75$ on IBM mainframe computers. Other computers may have a different range. Thus, extremely large and small numbers may be represented in an abbreviated form.

Single-precision examples of *real* constants expressed with a decimal exponent are:

432.1E+00	(Has a value of 432.1)
$-8769.2E-2$	(Has a value of -87.692)
65.423E3	(Has a value of 65423.)
$-24.638E-01$	(Has a value of -2.4638)

Single-precision examples of *integer* constants followed by a decimal exponent are:

$-87E+0$	(Has a value of -87.)
147E−03	(Has a value of .147)
2E4	(Has a value of 20000.)

The real type variables that you have been using all along may be used to store single-precision real constants expressed with exponents. The same Assignment statement used to compute and assign real values is also used with this exponential form of real constants. For example:

PI = .31416E01
R = 7203E−2
HAREA = (PI * R ** 2) / .25E+1

Data fields may be read or written with their values in exponential form. The F format code may be used to *read* input values expressed with an exponent. The E format code may also be used to *read* data with exponents and *must* be used to *write* data in an exponential form.

The Exponential Floating-point (E) Format Code

The E format code is used to transmit numeric fields, normally represented in scientific notation, that contains a numeric quantity with an appended exponent. The numeric data fields, expressed in scientific notation, are formed in exactly the same way as numeric constants expressed with an exponent.

The general form of the E format code is:

nEw.d

where:

n represents an optional repetition factor that specifies the number of times the format code is to be used. The value of **n**, when specified, must be an unsigned positive integer constant whose value is less than or equal to 255. **w** specifies the number of card columns or record positions in the input or output field. **w** must be an unsigned positive integer constant with a value less than or equal to 255. The decimal point (.) is a necessary separator between the **w** and **d** parameters. **d** represents the number of digits in the fractional part of the number. **d** must be an unsigned integer constant between 1 and 255.

All input rules for the F format code apply for the E format code. Any permissible form of constructing an integer or real constant may be read by the E format code.

Input examples to illustrate the input rules when using the E format code are as follows (bs represents blanks):

Field Size and Value	E Format Code to Be Used
12.345E+2	E9.3 (Value of 1234.5)
1234.5E−03	E10.1 (Value of 1.2345)
$-123.45E00$	E10.2 (Value of -123.45)
ƀƀ+12.3E1	E9.1 (Value of 123.)
12.34	E5.2 (Value of 12.34)
12345	E5.3 (Value of 12.345)
123E01	E6.0 (Value of 1230.)
+12.3E3	E7.1 (Value of 12300.)

The E format code is normally used to read data fields expressed in scientific notation with an appended exponent, such as 1.0E04. The above examples show that this format code can also read numeric quantities that we normally express in our everyday decimal form.

Consider the following input example:

READ (5,99) V1,V2,V3,V4
99 FORMAT (E7.2,1X,E6.2,1X,E8.2,1X,E9.1)

```
12.34E5  − 56.27 18735.10  − 438.1E − 2
```

The values *written* with an E format code will always contain an appended exponent. The following paragraphs discuss the format of the output fields printed with the E format specifications.

Output Considerations. The output rules which apply to the F format code also apply to the E format code. Data fields output under the E format are, however, formatted in a different manner from those formatted with the F format code.

An output field specified with an E format code will consist of an optional sign (required if negative), a decimal point, the number of digits specified by **d**, and an exponent part that denotes the power of 10 to be multiplied with the numeric quantity to obtain the true value of the number. The exponent part always consists of the four positions given as follows:

1. the letter E
2. the sign of the exponent (a blank is output if the exponent is positive or zero)
3. a two-digit integer constant representing the exponent as a power of 10.

The numeric quantity is expressed in a pure fractional form (called **normalization**). That is, a decimal point is placed before the first significant (nonzero) digit. As many digits are included in the fraction as are specified by the **d** parameter of the E format specification.

Examples of the E format code to illustrate the output form of the data fields are as follows (bs represents blanks in the high order field positions):

Value in Memory	E Format Code	Output Field
12.345	E10.5	.12345E 02
12.345	E10.4	0.1235E 02
12.345	E9.5	*********
12.345	E10.3	b0.123E 02
− 12.345	E10.6	**********
− 12.345	E12.4	b − 0.1235E 02
− 12.345	E10.4	− .1235E 02
.0001	E9.3	0.100E − 03

Real constants expressed with an exponent are normally used by mathematicians and engineers, because they are accustomed to expressing quantities in a scientific notation. The main advantage comes from being able to represent extremely large or small numeric values in a shorthand form.

16.3 DOUBLE-PRECISION CONSTANTS AND VARIABLES AND THE D FORMAT CODE

Seven digits are hardly enough for accumulating large sums and solving problems that use values containing a substantial quantity. Thus, most computers allow for an extended precision of the basic single-precision seven-digit numbers. This extended form of precision is called double-precision, since the number of significant digits is more than double those in single-precision real numbers. A double word (two adjacent memory words) is used to store double-precision values.

A **double-precision** floating-point number can contain eight through sixteen digits on most computers. A sign, if present, is an allowable character beyond the maximum possible length of sixteen digits. A double-precision floating-point constant in decimal form is formed the same way and must adhere to the same rules as a single-precision real number in basic decimal form. The double-precision constant must, however, contain more than seven decimal digits, or the quantity will be formed in memory as a single-precision number. Examples of valid double-precision floating-point numbers in basic decimal form are:

$$245.467193$$
$$-.546683207$$
$$+468902043.$$

Double-precision *real* constants may also be expressed with an appended decimal exponent. The exponent may be represented with the letter D followed by a signed or unsigned one- or two-digit integer constant. The value of the exponent can range from -78 to $+75$ on IBM mainframe computers. The range of the exponent value varies on different computer systems.

Examples of double-precision floating-point constants represented with an appended exponent are:

$$.1234567892D+00$$
$$-991.257643D9$$
$$.8765428312D-3$$

A double-precision real constant may also be represented as an *integer* number followed by a decimal exponent. The exponent normally consists of the letter D followed by a signed or unsigned one- or two-digit integer constant. Valid examples of double-precision real constants, each formed as an integer constant and each followed by an exponent are:

$$-47D-3$$
$$93D+06$$
$$1D-9$$

While double-precision numbers have the advantage of greater precision, they have a negative effect on computer storage and processing speed. Use of double-precision numbers over single-precision has two main disadvantages. First, double-precision numbers occupy twice as much computer storage space as do single-precision numbers; second, double-precision numbers take more time to process. For these reasons, the programmer should specify double-precision constants and variables only where they are mandatory.

Double-precision Variables

Variables that may be assigned double-precision real values are referred to as double-precision variables. A double-precision variable may be any valid symbolic name, but must be declared a type double-precision in an Explicit Type statement. The general form of the DOUBLE PRECISION Type statement is given in figure 16.1.

An example of the DOUBLE PRECISION specification statement to declare double-precision variables and array elements is:

DOUBLE PRECISION A,I,X(10),Y(5,3)

where the variables A and I are declared to be double-precision variables; the array named X is declared to be a one-dimensional array with ten double-precision elements; the array named Y is declared to be a two-dimensional array with fifteen double-precision elements (five rows and three columns).

Array dimensions may be specified in the DOUBLE PRECISION statement or may be declared in a separate DIMENSION statement that precedes the DOUBLE PRECISION statement. The DOUBLE PRECISION statement cannot specify initial values for variables or array elements.

Double-precision Expressions and Assignment Statements

A double-precision expression is one that assigns a resulting double-precision value to a double-precision variable. The expression may contain double-precision constants, variables, and array elements. Following are examples of double-precision expressions:

$$10.89D17$$
$$A$$
$$3.5D12 + A * (B - .8671D-7)$$

where the variables A and B are declared as double-precision variables.

DOUBLE PRECISION name₁,. . ., nameₙ

where:

name₁,. . ., name ₙ—each **name** represents a variable, array, or function subprogram name. If the **name** is an array name, the dimension information may be specified following the array name.

Figure 16.1 General notation of the DOUBLE PRECISION statement

The Assignment statement is used to assign double-precision values to variables. The general form of this Assignment statement is:

double-precision variable = double-precision expression

Examples of the double-precision Assignment statement (the variables W, X, and Y are assumed to be double-precision variables, and Z is assumed to be a double-precision, one-dimensional array) are as follows:

$$W = 1.345876924$$
$$X = .1D - 12$$
$$Y = W + X * 10.0D + 14$$
$$Z(1) = Y / (345.672983 + W)$$

Input/Output of Double-precision Fields with the D Format Code

The D format code is used to transfer numeric fields expressed as double-precision quantities. Like the E format code, the numeric fields read with the D format code are normally represented in scientific notation. The appended exponent part normally contains a D to denote double-precision floating-point values.

The general form of the D format code is:

nDw.d

where:

n represents an optional repetition factor that specifies the number of times the format code is to be used. The value of **n,** when specified, must be an unsigned positive integer constant whose value is less than or equal to 255. **w** specifies the number of card columns or record positions in the input or output field. **w** must be an unsigned positive integer constant with a value less than or equal to 255. The decimal point (.) is a necessary separator between the **w** and **d** parameters. **d** represents the number of digits in the fractional part of the number. **d** must be an unsigned integer constant between 1 and 255.

Examples in the use of the D format code are:

18 FORMAT (D12.8,2X,2D14.9)
21 FORMAT (1H0,5X,3D24.16)

The first example reads a 12-position double-precision numeric quantity in columns 1–12 and two 14-position double-precision values beginning in column 15. The second example (an output specification) prints three 24-position, double-precision fields beginning in print position 6.

All input and output rules that apply to the E format code apply to the D format codes. Output fields written with the D format specification will be printed in the same form as with the E format specifications, except that the letter D will be used in place of the letter E.

One unexpected thing happens when single-precision variables are printed with the D format code. If the variable is single-precision, then the computer prints the output results as expressed with an E format specification, even if the D format code is used. The same principle holds true for double-precision variables written with the E format code. The computer prints the output results as expressed in the E field descriptor, but replaces the E with a D.

Double-precision Function Subprograms

Many double-precision built-in functions are available to manipulate double-precision values. For example, the built-in function DSQRT takes the square root of a double-precision value. Double-precision built-in functions included in FORTRAN are (all functions require one real double-precision argument unless otherwise indicated):

Function Name	Function Description
DABS	Absolute Value
DEXP	Exponential
DLOG	Natural Log
DLOG10	Common Log
DSQRT	Square Root
DMAX1	Maximum Value (more than one argument)
DMIN1	Minimum Value (more than one argument)
IDINT	Truncation
DMOD	Modulo Arithmetic (2 arguments)
DSIGN	Transfer of Sign
DBLE	Precision Increase
DSIN	Sine
DCOS	Cosine
DATAN	Arctangent
DATAN2	Arctangent (2 arguments)

Each of these functions returns one double-precision value.

You may also write double-precision-valued function subprograms by specifying the type option to be DOUBLE PRECISION. For example:

DOUBLE PRECISION FUNCTION SUM (X,N)

Thus, the resulting value via the function name SUM will be a double-precision value. User-supplied or built-in double-precision function subprograms must always have their names declared in a DOUBLE PRECISION statement in the invoking program, to inform the compiler that the referenced function subprogram is to return a double-precision value.

16.4 LOGICAL DATA AND THE LOGICAL (L) FORMAT CODE

Logical constants and variables were discussed in section 6.6. Now we want to look at the reading and writing of logical data. This section discusses the logical (L) format code, which is used to provide the format specifications for logical input data items and printing logical values.

The Logical (L) Format Code for Reading and Writing Logical Data

The Logical (L) format code is used to read and write logical data. The general form of the L format code is:

nLw

where **n** represents an optional repetition factor from 1 to 255, which may be used to repeat the same width logical data fields in adjacent card columns. The letter **w** is an unsigned integer constant specifying the number of characters in the field width. **w** must be an unsigned integer constant between 1 and 255.

On input fields the first T or F encountered in the **w** characters causes a value of .TRUE. or .FALSE., respectively, to be assigned to a variable. If the input field contains all blanks or does not contain a T or F, the value of .FALSE. is assigned. Consider the following input example:

LOGICAL X1,X2,X3,X4,X5,X6,X7
READ (5,99) X1,X2,X3,X4,X5,X6,X7
99 FORMAT (L4,L5,1X,L3,1X,L4,1X,L3,1X,L1,L2)

```
TRUEFALSE CAT FROG DOG T
```

The variable X1 is assigned a value of .TRUE. from the four characters TRUE. The variable X2 is assigned a value of .FALSE. from the input field FALSE. The variable X3 is assigned a value of .TRUE. from the input field CAT read with an L3 format specification, because of the "T" in the word. The variable X4 is assigned a value of .FALSE. from the input field FROG, because it contains an "F." The variable X5 is assigned a value of .FALSE. from the input field DOG, since no letter T or F is found. The variable X6 is assigned a value of .TRUE. from the input field T. The variable X7 is assigned a value of .FALSE., since two blanks are read under an L2 format code.

On output a T or F is inserted in the output field depending upon the value of the output variable. The single character is right-justified in the output field and is preceded by **w** − 1 blanks. For example,

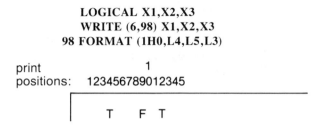

The values of X1, X2, and X3 were assumed to contain the values .TRUE., .FALSE., and .TRUE., respectively, from the input example.

Logical Function Subprograms

A function subprogram that returns a logical value can be written by the user. The FUNCTION statement must include the LOGICAL type option to specify a logical function subprogram. For example:

LOGICAL FUNCTION CHECK(N)

If a program unit invokes a Logical type function, a LOGICAL statement must also be given in the invoking program. This LOGICAL statement must include the name of the Logical type function subprogram, so that the compiler will know that the referenced function subprogram is to return a logical value.

The use of logical type constants and data are very helpful to mathematicians, engineers, and logisticians. Logical data can be useful in boolean algebra, hardware circuitry design, scheduling problems, and a wide variety of other applications.

16.5 COMPLEX FLOATING-POINT CONSTANTS AND VARIABLES

Complex numbers, used mainly in mathematical applications, consist of a pair having two values. The first value in the pair represents the **real part** of the complex number; the second value represents the **imaginary part** because of the result when the term is reduced to its simplest value. For example, the second term may be $\sqrt{-25}$. Since it is impossible to take the square root of a negative number, this item must be replaced with $\sqrt{-1} \cdot \sqrt{25}$ which would then give us 5i. (The term $\sqrt{-1}$ is known as i.)

In math textbooks, complex numbers are often written in the form a + bi, where a and b are real numbers and i = $\sqrt{-1}$. Complex numbers are also written in vector form as (a,b), where a represents the real part and b represents the imaginary part. The latter form is used in FORTRAN. Thus, a complex constant is represented in FORTRAN as an ordered pair of signed or unsigned real constants separated by a comma and enclosed in parentheses. For example:

(4.6, − 1.37)	(Has the value 4.6 − 1.37i)
(− 8.91,6.2)	(Has the value − 8.91 + 6.2i)
(14E + 02, − 1.6E − 1)	(Has the value 1400 − .16i)
(.27E − 2,.86E + 1)	(Has the value .0027 + 8.6i)

Illegal forms of complex constants are:

(A,3.29)	a variable must not be used
(5,7)	integer constants must not be used

┌───┐
│   COMPLEX Statement—General Form   │
├─ ─┤

COMPLEX name$_1$,. . ., name$_n$

where:

name$_1$,. . ., name$_n$ — each **name** represents a variable, array, or function subprogram name. If the **name** is an array name, the dimension information may be specified following the array name.
└───┘

Figure 16.2 General notation of the COMPLEX statement

Either of the two real constants in a complex number may be a positive, zero, or negative quantity. If either of them is unsigned, it is considered positive. Each of the two must be a valid real constant formed from any of the permissible types. Both parts, however, must occupy the same number of storage locations (i.e., single-precision or double-precision).

Complex Variables

A variable that may be assigned a complex number is considered to be a complex type variable. A complex variable can be any valid symbolic name, but it must be declared a complex type variable. This declaration is accomplished in an Explicit Type statement with the keyword COMPLEX. Figure 16.2 shows the general form of the COMPLEX statement.

An example of the COMPLEX type statement is:

$$\text{COMPLEX A,X(10),J}$$

The variables A and J are declared to be complex variables, and X is declared to be a one-dimensional array of ten complex elements.

Complex Expressions and Assignment Statements

An expression that produces a complex resulting value is said to be a complex expression. Any arithmetic operator may be used with complex expressions, and the established rules of operator precedence apply.

A complex variable can be assigned a value using the Assignment statement. Its form is:

$$\textbf{complex variable} = \textbf{complex expression}$$

Following are examples of complex Assignment statements and expressions.

```
COMPLEX A,B,C,D(5)
A = (3.5, -7.24)
B = (-8.21,5.67)
D(1) = A + B
C = D(1) * (3.6,9.2) - A / B
```

Format Specifications for the Input/Output of Complex Numbers

You must remember that a complex number always consists of two parts, so when you read or write a complex value, two format codes must be given. The first format code is used for the real part, the second for the imaginary part.

There is no special format code for reading or writing complex numbers. The F, D, or E format codes may be used, depending on the precision of the input values or the output form of the printed values. An example of reading a complex number is:

COMPLEX N
READ (5,99) N
99 FORMAT (2F7.2)

3214.738610.92

An example of writing a complex number is:

COMPLEX N
WRITE (6,98) N
98 FORMAT (1H0,2F10.2)

Complex Function Subprograms

Many built-in function routines are available to manipulate complex numbers. For example, CSQRT(A) will compute the square root of the complex argument A. The result is a complex number. Of course, the argument A must be declared a complex variable.

Complex built-in functions include:

Name	Mathematical Definition
CABS	Absolute value
CEXP	Exponential
CLOG	Natural Log
CSQRT	Square Root
CMPLX	Convert two real values to complex
REAL	Obtain real part of complex number
AIMAG	Obtain imaginary part of complex number
CONJC	Obtain conjugate of a complex number
CSIN	Sine
CCOS	Cosine

A user may write complex function subprograms that return a complex value. The type option in the FUNCTION statement must be used to specify a complex type function. For example:

COMPLEX FUNCTION CMPLX(A)

The Complex type function name (CMPLX) must be declared in a COMPLEX statement in the invoking program unit. Any user or built-in complex function subprogram invoked by a program must have its name declared in a COMPLEX statement, to inform the compiler that the function subprogram returns a complex value.

16.6 THE GENERALIZED (G) FORMAT CODE

The G format code is a generalized field specification that can be used to read and write numbers expressed in a decimal (F) or exponential (E) form. The general form of the G format code is:

nGw.d

where **n** represents an optional repetition factor that may range from 1–255. The **w** specifies the width of the field being read or written. The **d** indicates the number of digits to be included in the fractional part of an input field or the number of significant digits to be printed for an output field. The . is a necessary separator. **w** and **d** must be unsigned integer constants between 1 and 255.

On **input fields** the form of the transferred value to memory depends on how it is represented in the data record.

Consider the following input example:

READ (5,99) A,B
99 FORMAT (G7.2,1X,G5.1)

```
12.31E3 543.2
```

Since the input value for A has an exponent, it will be stored as if read with an E7.2 format code. The variable B is stored as if read with a F5.1 format code.

On **output fields** the computer will select the most suitable format specifications (i.e., E or F) depending on the size of the number. The **d** specification in the format code determines the number of digits to be printed and, thus, the form of the output value. If the absolute value of an output variable, say X, is in the range $.1 \leq |X| < 10^{**}d$, then the F form is used. If the absolute value of X is outside this range, the E form is used.

Thus, the **Gw.d** format code, when used to output real values, says to use w output positions for the field, which includes **d** positions for the number, one position for a decimal point, and four positions for an exponent. The **d** specifies the number of significant digits that are to be printed; they may be on *either* side of the decimal point, depending on the output value and its form. The number will appear in F or E form depending on its magnitude (i.e., within the range of $.1 \leq |value| < 10^{**}d$).

The location of the value in the output field depends on the output form used. Values written in the E form will be right-justified in the field and formatted as if written with an E format code. Values written in an F form will be printed with the four rightmost positions left blank, since there is no exponent. There will be **d** significant digits printed, with the location of the decimal point determined by the value of the number.

Consider the following output examples:

A = −.103E02
B = −.005
C = 485.7263
D = 391285.7E10
WRITE (6,99) A,B,C,D
99 FORMAT (4G11.4)

```
print               1         2         3         4         5
positions:  12345678901234567890123456789012345678901234567890
```
```
     -10.30     -0.5000E-02   485.7      0.3913E 16
```

The G format specifications of G11.4 says to output four significant digits in an eleven-position field, with four spaces used for an exponent. Since **d** is 4, the output value will be printed in F form if its absolute value is in the range $.1 \leq |value| < 10^{**}4$ or $.1 \leq |value| < 10000$. Since the value of A is -10.30, and its absolute (positive) value is 10.30, A is within the range $.1 \leq |10.30| < 10000$; so the value of A is printed in F form. The absolute value of B (.005) is not within the range $.1 \leq |B| < 10000$; so B is printed in E form. Note the rounding result in D caused by the truncation operation.

Additional output examples are as follows (b̶ represents a blank):

Memory Value	G Format Code	Printed Value
99.	G10.2	b̶b̶b̶99.b̶b̶b̶b̶
25.3	G11.4	b̶b̶25.30b̶b̶b̶b̶
−1.396	G11.3	b̶b̶−1.40b̶b̶b̶b̶
.4873	G9.3	0.487b̶b̶b̶b̶
87645.29	G11.4	b̶0.8765Eb̶05

To sum up the output form used by the G format code, the computer attempts first to output the value in F form, if it can be represented in **d** positions. Otherwise, the E form is used. If the magnitude of the values to be printed is not known, it is wise to make the **w** specifications at least seven larger than the **d**, so that sufficient positions are available should the E form be used.

16.7 THE P SCALE FACTOR SPECIFICATIONS

You learned in chapter 8 that the decimal point in the input data field overrode any fractional specifications given by the **d** parameter in the **Fw.d** format code. It is sometimes desirable to override this decimal point location in the data field and specify a new location that gives a new value. The P scale factor allows you to move the decimal point to the left or right a specified number of positions.

The P scale factor is specified as the first part of a D, E, F, or G format code. The number of positions that the decimal point is to be moved is expressed as a signed or unsigned integer constant before the letter P. For example:

97 FORMAT (F7.2,3PF6.1, −2PF5.3)

On input the P scale factor affects the value of the data field as follows.

1. A positive scale factor causes the decimal point to be moved to the left. For example:

READ (5,99) RATE
99 FORMAT (2PF4.1)

7.5

The value stored at RATE is .075, since the decimal point is moved two positions to the left. If the P scale factor had not been used, the value would have been stored as 7.5.

2. A negative scale factor causes the decimal point to be moved to the right. For example:

READ (5,98) HOURS
98 FORMAT (−3PF5.4)

.1605

The value stored at HOURS is 160.5, since the decimal point is moved three positions to the right. If the P scale factor had not been used, the value would have been stored as .1605.

The P scale factor is ignored when reading a number with an exponent. Once a P scale factor is established for any field, it applies to all subsequent D, E, F, or G format codes in the same FORMAT statement unless a new scale factor is encountered. A P scale factor of 0 (zero) must be used to discontinue the effect of the previous established scale factor. Consider the following example:

READ (5,97) A,B,C,D
97 FORMAT (−2PF6.2,1X,F7.3,1X,E8.3,1X,0PF5.2)

<pre>
                         1   2   3
         12345678901234567890123456789 0
card
columns   72.583 123.456 4.572E01 82.39
</pre>

The value for A is stored as 7258.3. The scale factor is still in effect for B so the value for B is stored as 12345.6. C remains unchanged, since the number has an exponent. The value of Z is stored as 82.39, since the scale factor is discontinued with the use of 0P.

On output the effect is basically the same except that the decimal point is moved in the opposite direction. For output the effects are:

1. A negative scale factor causes the decimal point to be moved to the left.
2. A positive scale factor causes the decimal point to be moved to the right.

Once the P scale factor is established for an output field, it applies to all subsequent fields in the same FORMAT statement until a new scale factor is encountered. A 0P scale factor must be used to discontinue the effect of a previous scale factor.

The form of the output value affected by a P scale factor varies as to the format code used. For F format codes, the decimal point is moved the specified number of positions in the output value. For G format codes, the effect of the scale factor is suspended when the number is printed in F form. Thus, the scale factor affects a G format code only if the value is written in E form. For E and D format codes the decimal point is not moved, but the exponent is adjusted to reflect the new value. If the decimal point is to be moved to the left, then the exponent is decreased by the number given in the P scale factor. If the decimal point is to be moved to the right, then the exponent is increased by the number for the scale factor. A repetition code may also precede the D, E, or F format codes when the P scale factor is used. For example, 2P3F6.3 is valid.

The P scale factor can be very useful in converting input and output numbers to represent a new value. It can be used to convert decimal values to percentages, grams to kilograms, and so on. This capability of moving the decimal point in data fields during the reading and writing of variables saves you from having to compute the new values and also allows you to retain the original values.

16.8 LANGUAGE EXTENSIONS IN FORTRAN DIALECTS (HEXADECIMAL AND OCTAL CONSTANTS AND DATA)

This section discusses addition forms of constants and format codes found on the IBM, CDC, Honeywell, and Burroughs compilers. The ability to output the internal representation of values in a number base corresponding to the base used by the computer is put to considerable use by system programmers. The two most common number bases for internal data representation are hexadecimal (base 16) and octal (base 8).

Hexadecimal Constants and Data

The hexadecimal number base consists of sixteen digits ranging from 0–F. These hexadecimal digits and their equivalent decimal and binary values are:

Hexadecimal Digit	Decimal Number	Binary Number	Hexadecimal Digit	Decimal Number	Binary Number
0	0	0000	8	8	1000
1	1	0001	9	9	1001
2	2	0010	A	10	1010
3	3	0011	B	11	1011
4	4	0100	C	12	1100
5	5	0101	D	13	1101
6	6	0110	E	14	1110
7	7	0111	F	15	1111

Hexadecimal constants and data fields are available only on base 16-oriented computers, such as the IBM mainframe and the Burroughs 6000 and 7000. The number of hexadecimal digits that can be stored in a variable depends on the computer and the length of the variable used. For a full word the IBM mainframe computers can hold eight hexadecimal digits. The Burroughs 6000 and 7000 word size can hold twelve hexadecimal digits. Different length variables affect the maximum allowed digits. Each byte (8 bits) contains two digits. A **byte** is the collection of continuous bits used to represent a character.

A **hexadecimal constant** is a string of hexadecimal digits preceded by the letter Z. Hexadecimal constants may only be given as data initialization values in a specification statement. They cannot be used in expressions in the Assignment statement. An example of providing a hexadecimal constant is:

DATA V1/ZC3D6D3C5/, V2/Z0000FFFF/

The variable V1 is given the value C3D6D3C5. The value 0000FFFF is stored in the variable V2. A four-byte word is assumed, since the constants consist of eight digits.

The hexadecimal digits are stored right-justified in the word. If the hexadecimal constant is greater than the maximum allowed digits, the high-order digits exceeding the word size are truncated. If the hexadecimal constant has fewer than the maximum allowed digits, high-order hexadecimal zeroes are added to the left to fill the word. Any type of variable name may be used to hold hexadecimal constants and data.

The Hexadecimal (Z) Format Code

The Z format code is used to transmit hexadecimal data fields. The general form of the Z format code is:

nZw

where **n** is an optional repetition factor that can range from 1 to 255. **w** specifies the width of the field being read or written and must be an unsigned integer constant between 1 and 255. Each hexadecimal digit uses one card column record position.

On **input** the data field is scanned from right to left. Any leading, trailing, or embedded blanks in the field are treated as hexadecimal zeroes. If the number of digits in the field is greater than the maximum allowed, the leftmost hexadecimal digits are truncated. If the number of digits is less than the maximum allowed, hexadecimal zeroes are added on the left.

Consider the following input example (assume a four-byte word that can contain a maximum of eight hexadecimal digits):

READ (5,99) A,B,C
99 FORMAT (Z2,1X,Z8,1X,Z10)

```
FF  D45EC102  B7205E6000
```

The values 000000FF, D45EC102, and 205E6000 are stored at the variables A, B, and C, respectively.

On **output**, if the number of hex digits stored in a variable is greater than **w**, then the leftmost print positions of the field are filled with blanks. If the number of digits in a variable is greater than **w**, then only the rightmost **w** digits are printed. If **w** is equal to the maximum number of digits that can be stored in a variable, then **w** hexadecimal digits are printed.

Consider the following output example (assume the same values as used in the input example):

WRITE (6,98) A,B,C
98 FORMAT (1H0,Z4,1X,Z8,1X,Z11)

```
print                     1          2
positions:   12345678901234567890123456578

             00FF D45EC102     205E6000
```

Octal Constants and Data

The octal number base consists of eight digits ranging from 0–7. These octal digits and their equivalent decimal and binary values are:

Octal Digit	Decimal Number	Binary Number
0	0	000
1	1	001
2	2	010
3	3	011
4	4	100
5	5	101
6	6	110
7	7	111

Octal constants and data fields are only available on base 8-oriented computers, such as the CDC 6000, Honeywell 6000, Univac 1100, and Burroughs 6000 and 7000. The number of octal digits that can be stored in a variable depends on the computer and the length of the variable used. On the CDC 6000 a maximum of twenty octal digits may be stored in a word. On the Honeywell 6000 and Univac 1100 a maximum of twelve octal digits may be stored in a word. On the Burroughs 6000 and 7000, a maximum of sixteen octal digits may be stored in a word. Different length variables affect the maximum allowed digits. Each byte (6 bits) contains two octal digits.

An **octal constant** is a string of octal digits preceded by the letter O. Octal constants may be given only in compile time initialization statements such as the DATA statement. They cannot be used in expressions in the Assignment statement. For example:

DATA V1/O23363325/,V2/O07777/

The octal digits are stored right-justified in the word. If the octal constant is greater than the maximum allowed digits, the high-order digits exceeding the word size are truncated. If the octal constant is less than the maximum allowed digits, high-order octal zeroes are added to the left. Any type of variable name may be used to hold octal constants and data.

The Octal (O) Format Code

The O format code is used to transmit octal data fields. The general form of the O format code is:

nOw

where **n** is an optional repetition factor from 1 to 255. **w** is the width of the field and must be an unsigned integer constant between 1 and 255. Each octal digit uses one card column.

On **input**, any leading, trailing, or embedded blanks are treated as octal zeroes. If the number of digits in the field is greater than the maximum allowed, the leftmost digits are truncated. If the number of digits is less than the maximum allowed, octal zeroes are added to the left. The input operations for octal values are the same as for hexadecimal data, except that octal digits are read.

On **output**, if the number of octal digits in a variable is less than **w**, then the leftmost print positions of the field are filled with blanks. If the number of digits in a variable is greater than **w**, then only the rightmost **w** digits are printed. If **w** is equal to the maximum number of digits that can be stored in a variable, then **w** octal digits are printed. The output operations for octal values are the same as for hexadecimal values, except that an octal digit is printed.

Complex Constants

On IBM, Burroughs, and other compilers, complex constants and variables may also be double-precision in length. Each constant part of a complex number is expressed in double-precision decimal form or exponential form. Complex variables may be specified to be double-precision by using the DOUBLE PRECISION or REAL *8 type statements.

16.9 SUMMARY

This chapter discussed the additional types of constants and variables available in FORTRAN. The format codes for reading and writing these new types of values were presented. Business and liberal arts students normally use the integer, decimal, and character form of constants and types of variables in their problem solving. The logical (boolean) form of values are often used for switches and flags. The other forms of representing data, such as exponential, complex, hexadecimal, and octal are often used by mathematics, engineering, and other scientific-oriented students.

Section 16.2 explained the exponential form of representing single-precision constants, which is very much like the scientific notation for representing numbers. The basic number is followed by the letter E, a sign (optional if the exponent is positive) and a one- or two-digit exponent. The exponent represents the power of ten that the basic number is multiplied by to obtain the actual value of the number.

The single-precision exponential format code (**E**), for reading and writing data in this form, was discussed. The **E** format code has the same form—**Ew.d**—that the **F** format code has. The form of the output value given with the E format code is normally a total fraction, the letter **E**, the sign of the exponent (blank if the exponent is positive), and a two-digit exponent. Basically, all rules that apply to the **F** format code, apply to the **E** format code when reading and writing numeric values.

Section 16.3 discussed double-precision constants, variables, and the **D** format code. A double-precision constant is a numeric value that exceeds the normal size of a single-precision constant—usually around eight digits on many computers, but the size varies among systems. A double-precision constant or expression cannot be stored in a regular variable (a storage location that is only one word in length); it must be stored in a double-precision variable, which occupies two adjacent memory locations (words). A double-precision variable must be declared in the DOUBLE PRECISION type statement, to inform the system that a double word is being used for the variable.

Double-precision values must be read and written with the **D** format code. Its form—**Dw.d**—is similar to the **E** format code. The rules for reading and writing double-precision fields are the same as for the **E** format code. Double-precision built-in functions exist to compute values for double-precision constants, variables, and expressions. A double-precision user-written function must be identified by the keyword DOUBLE PRECISION before the FUNCTION keyword.

Section 16.4 covered the Logical (**L**) format code for reading and writing logical data. The form of the logical format code is **Lw**, where **w** gives the length of the input or output field. The first **T** or **F** in the input field determines the stored value (of TRUE or FALSE). If no **T** or **F** is encountered in the input field, a value of FALSE is stored at the variable. On output a **T** or **F** is printed, depending on the stored value in the specified variable.

Section 16.5 discussed complex constants and variables. A complex number has two parts. The first part represents the **real** part of the complex number, and the second part represents the **imaginary** part. The imaginary part is a number times the value of the square root of minus one. Complex numbers are frequently used in mathematics—for example, in root equations. Complex built-in functions exist for performing operations on this type of numeric value. A complex function may be written by preceding the FUNCTION keyword with the keyword COMPLEX.

Section 16.6 explained the generalized (**G**) format code, which is used to read and write values in a decimal (F) or exponential (E) form. The form of the output results depend on whether the value can be printed in a decimal form. If the number cannot be printed in a decimal form, then the output result is given in exponential form. This format code is not used very often in professional programming.

Section 16.7 presented the **P** scale factor format code, which is used to override the actual decimal point location in a value. It moves the decimal point position to the left or right a specified number of positions. You must be careful in using the **P** scale factor, since it must be "turned off" when it is no longer needed for reading or writing values.

Section 16.8 discussed hexadecimal (base 16) and octal (base 8) constants and data. The representation and I/O of these number base values are not part of FORTRAN 66 or some FORTRAN IV compilers. This capability is useful, especially for system programmers who need to express and display the internal representation of items. The internal representation of values in a system depends on whether the system uses a six-bit or eight-bit byte for data representation. A system using a six-bit byte will use an octal base representation; a system using an eight-bit byte will use a hexadecimal representation.

The hexadecimal (**Z**) format code is used to read and write base 16 numbers. Each hex digit occupies one position in a record; thus, the width part of the format code specifies how many positions of hexadecimal digits are to be read or written. The octal (**O**) format code is used to read and write base 8 numbers. Likewise, each octal digit occupies one position in a record, and the width part of the format code specifies the number of octal digits in the field.

16.10 TERMS

Terms, concepts, and statements you should be familiar with in this chapter are:

complex constant	double-precision variable	octal number base
COMPLEX Type statement	exponential notation	real number
complex variable	hexadecimal number base	scale factor
double precision	imaginary number	scientific notation
double-precision constant	logical data	single precision
DOUBLE PRECISION Type statement	normalization	

16.11 REVIEW QUESTIONS

1. The E format code is primarily used to read and write what type of numeric fields?
2. Describe the general form of a constant in exponential form.
3. Describe the general form of the output field printed with an E format code.
4. How does the computer recognize a double-precision constant?
5. A double-precision variable must be declared in a _____ type statement.
6. The D format code is primarily used to read and write what type of numeric fields?
7. What are the two logical constants available in FORTRAN?
8. A logical variable must be declared in a _____ type statement.
9. The _____ format code is used to read and write logical data.
10. What are the two parts of a complex number?
11. How is a complex constant represented in FORTRAN?
12. A complex variable must be declared in a _____ type statement.
13. What format codes may be used to read and write complex values?
14. The G format code is used to read and write what type of data?
15. The computer attempts to output data written with a G format code in decimal (Fw.d) form unless the **d** specifications are too small. (True/False)
16. What is the purpose of the P scale factor?
17. How is the P scale factor specified with a format code?

16.12 EXERCISES

1. Construct the E format codes necessary to read the following input fields.

Value	E Format Code
12.3E2	
123E − 1	
1.23E + 2	
123	

2. Construct the E format codes necessary to read the following input fields.

Value	E Format Code
.1E − 5	
45.6	
456.E + 3	
45.6E1	

3. Show the output results produced when printing the following values with their respective E format code. Show all blank positions with the symbol ƀ.

Memory Value	Format Code	Output Results
12.345	E10.3	
−12.345	E12.5	
123.45	E14.6	
123.456	E14.5	
−12.3456	E14.5	
−.0012	E12.4	

4. Show the output results produced when printing the following values and their respective E format code. Show all blank positions with the symbol ƀ.

Memory Value	Format Code	Output Results
4.5126	E10.4	
4.5126	E10.3	
−4.5126	E15.7	
−4.5126	E14.4	
.45	E10.3	
−.00016	E11.3	

5. Determine the logical value resulting from each of the following logical expressions. Assume A and B to be .TRUE. and C to be .FALSE.

a. .NOT. C
b. .NOT. C .AND. A
c. .NOT. A .OR. .NOT. C

d. B .AND. C .OR. A
e. .NOT. (A .AND. B)

6. Determine the resulting logical value from each of the following logical expressions. Assume A and B to be .TRUE. and C to be .FALSE.

a. A .AND. .NOT. C
b. A .AND. B .AND. C
c. .NOT. (A .AND. C) .AND. B

d. A .OR. B .OR. C
e. A .OR. .NOT. (B .OR. C)

7. Show the output results produced when printing the following values with the given Gw.d format code. Show all blank positions with the symbol ƀ.

Memory Value	Format Code	Output Results
99.0	G9.2	
.1	G9.2	
146E − 10	G10.3	
−574.3E − 1	G10.3	

8. Show the output results produced when printing the following values with the given Gw.d format code. Show all blank positions with the symbol ƀ.

Memory Value	Format Code	Output Results
−99.1	G10.3	
1.2E − 1	G9.2	
+67.3E − 07	G11.4	
3.1416	G12.5	

9. Give the P scale factor to change the following input fields to the new value.

Input Field	New Value	P Scale Factor and F Format Code
8.75	.0875	
.31416	3.1416	
125.0	.1250	
1.	1000000.	

10. Give the P scale factor to change the following input fields to the new value.

Input Field	New Value	P Scale Factor and F Format Code
873021.	873.021	
.1	.000001	
34.8762	3487.62	
.1	1000.0	

16.12 PROGRAMMING PROBLEMS

1. Write a program to read the value of RADIUS and to compute the volume of a sphere. The input value is contained in exponential form in columns 1–8 and should be read with an E format code.

   After reading the value for RADIUS, compute the volume of its associated sphere according to the formula (use 3.14 as π):

   $$V = \frac{4}{3}\pi r^3$$

   Print the value of RADIUS in positions 1–12 and the computed volume in positions 20–34. Output values are to be written using the E format code. Include appropriate column headings.

2. Write a program to read and sum two complex variables named X and Y. The two complex numbers are to be read with 4F6.2 format specifications. Write the variables X, Y, and SUM under a 6F10.2 format specification. Use column headings to identify each number.

3. Write a logical-valued function subprogram named EVEN to determine whether a numeric integer input value is odd or even. If the input value is an even number, the function EVEN returns a logical value of .TRUE.; the function returns a value of .FALSE. if the input value is an odd number.

   A mainline program is used to read the input value and print the results. The input value must be a positive integer between 1 and 100, and it is read with the variable name INTGR under a I3 format specification. After the function EVEN has determined whether the number is even or odd, write an output message as follows:

   'THE NUMBER ' n ' IS ' I

   where **n** is the value of the input number, and **I** is the literal 'ODD' or 'EVEN', depending on the evaluation of the number.

   Hint: Determine if the number is even or odd by the formula:

   INRSLT = INTGR/2*2 − INTGR

   If the result in INRSLT is 0, then the variable INTGR contains an even integer. If the result is − 1, then the input value is an odd integer number.

4. A real estate agency wants a listing of all property sold during the year. The agency also wants a total of the sale prices and commissions on all the properties sold. The totals are to be stated by the type of property sold.

   Write a program to read a file containing real estate transactions for the Smiley Cole Real Estate Agency. Each transaction record is punched according to the following record layout:

Record Positions	Field Description
1–6	Sales number (Form = NNNNNN)
7–15	Sales price (Form = NNNNN.NN)
16–23	Commission (Form = NNNNN.NN)
24	Type property (P = Private residence, C = Commercial)

Accumulate the amount of sales and earned commissions by each of the two types of properties. Also compute what percentage of the sale price is commission (i.e., total of commissions divided by total of sale prices).

For output results:

a. Write a report heading, beginning on a new page.

b. Write appropriate column headings.

c. Write double-spaced detail records with the proper information in columns as described below:

Print Positions	Field Description
3–8	Sales number
15–23	Sales price of private residence
31–38	Commission from private residence
46–54	Sales price of commercial property
62–69	Commissions from commercial property
77	Type property
85–91	Commission percentage of sales price (Form = NNN.NNN)

d. Write the accumulated totals beneath their respective columns (Form = NNNNNNNNNN.NN).

Also use a DATA statement to initialize the letters P and C. Use double-precision variables for sales price and the four counters for

a. the accumulated sales price for private residences,

b. the accumulated sales price for commercial property,

c. the accumulated commissions for private residences, and

d. the accumulated commissions for commercial property.

17 Magnetic Tape Statements and Operations

17.1 INTRODUCTION TO THE USE AND CONCEPTS OF MAGNETIC TAPE

The ever-faster internal speeds of computers call for high-speed input and output devices to ensure that program execution is not held back by having to wait for input or by an inability to get processed data to an output medium. Magnetic tape units, with their dual capability for input and output, provide a very high data transfer rate into and from computer memory. Modern tape drives can transfer data at the rate of several hundred thousand characters per second. This means that a full reel of data can usually be read in several minutes, whereas the equivalent 800,000 punched cards would take more than thirteen hours to read through a card reader.

Another prime virtue of magnetic tape is its ability to store an enormous amount of data on an easy-to-handle reel at a very low cost. The equivalent of about 800,000 fully punched cards can normally be stored on one 2,400-foot reel of magnetic tape—over 64,000,000 characters of data. When large data files are processed, magnetic tape is often used as the storage medium.

The techniques of magnetic tape recording are very much like those used in the making of tape recordings in the home. A long thin ribbon, usually one-half inch wide and made of a plastic base coated with a metallic oxide, is wound on a reel. This reel is referred to as the **file reel** or **data reel**. A take-up reel, known as the **machine reel**, is used to hold the tape that is unwound from the data reel. The machine reel and file reel are mounted on the tape unit. The tape from the file reel is threaded through the transport mechanism (see figure 17.1).

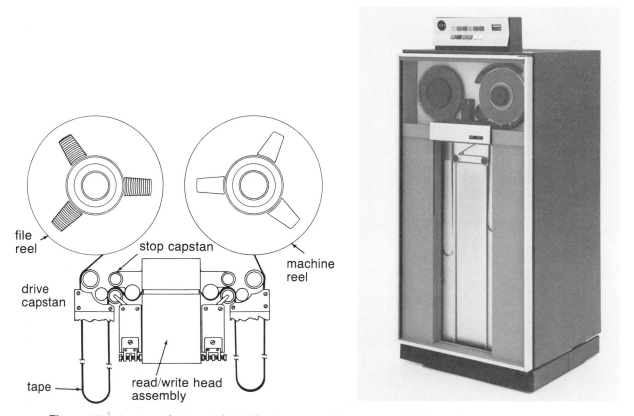

Figure 17.1 A magnetic tape unit and its operation. (Courtesy of IBM)

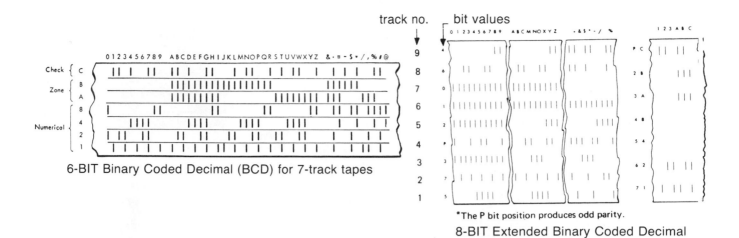

track no.   bit values

6-BIT Binary Coded Decimal (BCD) for 7-track tapes

*The P bit position produces odd parity.

8-BIT Extended Binary Coded Decimal Interchange Code (EBCDIC) for 9-track tapes

Figure 17.2 Magnetic tape coding schemes. (Courtesy of IBM)

The recording of data onto the tape takes place by moving the tape under a stationary **read/write head**. Data from the computer memory is transferred to this read/write head, which magnetizes spots in parallel tracks along the length of the tape to record the proper information. A coded pattern of 0 and 1 bits across the width of the tape represents data received from the computer. This data is coded according to coding schemes that vary by computer and vendor. A different coding scheme is also used depending on whether a 7- or 9-track tape unit is used (see figure 17.2). Modern tape units use a phased-encoded recording method different from that used for 7- or 9-track tapes. Data previously recorded on the tape is automatically destroyed by overwriting it with new data. As with the home tape recorder, reels of magnetic tape may be used hundreds of times for recording data.

Data that has been recorded onto the tape may be read by passing the tape over the read/write heads, but with the tape unit instructed to read data instead of to write or record it. Reading is nondestructive; the same information can be read time and again from a reel of tape.

Magnetic tape must have some blank space at both the beginning and the end of the reel to allow threading through the feed mechanism of the tape unit. Markers, called **reflective strips**, are placed on the tape (about twenty feet from each end) to enable the magnetic tape unit to sense the beginning and end of the usable portion of tape. Photoelectric cells in the tape units sense these markers and stop the tape.

The reflective strip at the beginning of the tape is known as the **load-point marker** and indicates where reading or writing of the first record of data is to begin. The tape must be located at this point at the start of processing before the tape unit can begin the reading or writing of data correctly. A computer operator, after mounting the reel of data, will press the proper buttons on the tape drive to position the tape at **load point**. This load point is also referred to as the **beginning-of-tape (BOT) marker**.

The reflective strip at the end of the tape is known as the **end-of-reel marker** or **end-of-tape (EOT)**. If this reflective marker is sensed during a write operation, the last record will continue to be written, and then the tape will be rewound.

Older tape drives require the operator to thread the tape through the read/write head assembly, around the various capstans, and onto the take-up reel. Modern tape drives are self-loading and only require the operator to mount the data reel. Upon depressing the load button, self-loading mechanisms will automatically thread the tape and position it at load point. See figures 17.3 and 17.4 for an IBM 3420 self-loading tape drive and a Digital Equipment Corporation TU-77 self-loading tape drive.

The tape unit does not recognize the end-of-reel marker (reflective strip) as the end of a data file when reading the tape. To indicate the end of the valid data belonging to the last recording, an end-of-file record is written on the tape. The **end-of-file record** is simply a special character that is written in a separate record after the last block of recorded data on the tape. This end-of-file mark (also known as a **tapemark**) is a must when reading the tape, to make sure that you stop at the end of your data set. Without this marker, you may continue reading data past the last record in the file. A technique of writing a record with all 9's, or some other chosen character, might be used as an alternative to the system's end-of-file record. You would have to check for this special record after reading each record to determine an end-of-file condition.

Figure 17.3 An IBM 3420 self-loading tape drive. (Courtesy of IBM)

Figure 17.4 A DEC TU-77 self-loading tape drive. (Courtesy of Digital Equipment Corporation)

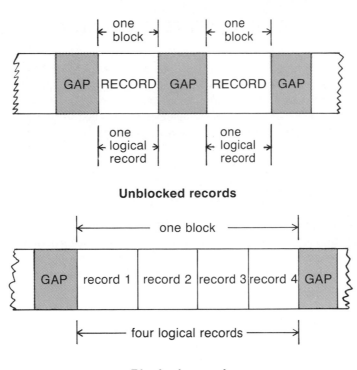

Figure 17.5 Unblocked *vs.* blocked magnetic tape records

The recording of data onto magnetic tape is performed in physical records. We refer to a **physical record** as a tape block or simply a **block**. Magnetic tape records are not restricted to any fixed record size as are punched cards. Records may be any practical size within the limits of internal storage capacity. A physical record can consist of a single logical record or a multiple of logical records grouped together. The number of logical records in each physical record is called the **blocking factor**.

Each physical record is separated on the tape by an inter-block gap (referred to as an **IBG**). The **inter-block gap** is a length of blank tape, which varies from 0.60 to 0.75 of an inch, depending on the model of tape drive used. This inter-block gap is automatically produced by the computer system at the end of each block of records during a write operation. During reading, the block begins with the first character sensed after the inter-block gap and continues without interruption until the next gap is reached. The entire block of data is read into internal memory for use in processing. Thus the inter-block gap allows for starting and stopping the tape between blocks of physical records.

Figure 17.5 illustrates the concept of unblocked and blocked records.

The tightness at which data can be recorded onto magnetic tape is referred to as its **density**. Modern tape units record data at 800, 1,600, or 6,250 characters per inch. Since characters are recorded in a pattern of parallel vertical bits, the terms **bits per inch (BPI),** bytes per inch, and characters per inch are synonymous. If one 80-character logical record is recorded on a tape block at a density of 800 BPI, only 0.10 of an inch would be required to hold the 80 characters of data. You can see that for unblocked logical records on tape, most of the tape is blank, since so much of the tape is used by the IBGs to separate the records. Both for economy in storage saving and for efficiency in I/O operations, records should normally be blocked in production processing of magnetic tape files.

Not only must you be able to read and write magnetic tape files, but you also need to be able to perform operations such as rewinding the tape, putting an end-of-file marker on the tape, and backspacing to previous records. The seven FORTRAN statements that provide I/O operations on magnetic tape are (1) formatted READ, (2) unformatted READ, (3) formatted WRITE, (4) unformatted WRITE, (5) REWIND, (6) END FILE, and (7) BACKSPACE. Let's look at the construction of these statements.

17.2 FORMATTED READ/WRITE STATEMENTS WITH MAGNETIC TAPE FILES

Magnetic tape is considered a sequential storage medium. Records are written in a serial manner, usually in sequence according to a certain **key**, such as SSAN, account number, stock number by warehouse, or some other sequencing field. To get to a specific record, all records falling before the desired one must be read. For example, to retrieve the sixth record, the first five records must be read first.

The sequential formatted READ and WRITE statements explained in chapters 5 and 8 apply to magnetic tape files as well as to card and printer files. The general form of the formatted READ statement is the same as for the READ statement you have been using throughout the text.

Valid examples of the formatted READ statement for tape files are:

3 READ (8,97) A, B, C, D
READ (9,84) ITEMNR, NRONHD, NRONBO

Any file unit other than 5 (and the standard output units of 6 and 7) may be used, provided that it is an acceptable unit number on the system. When these other file units are used for magnetic tape or disk files, they must be included in the JCL (Job Control Language) to identify which physical peripheral units are actually being used.

The general form of the formatted WRITE statement for tape operations is also the same as the WRITE statement you have been using all along. The output file unit must be other than a 5, 6, or 7. The appropriate JCL card must be included in your job deck to assign the chosen file unit to a tape unit. Valid examples of the formatted WRITE statement for tape files are:

15 WRITE (10,37) I, X, Z
WRITE (8,77) NAME, NUMBER, GRADE

The formatted WRITE statement for magnetic tape functions the same way as the formatted WRITE statement for printer output files. However, no carriage control specification is required in the FORMAT statement for data written to tape.

The data generally transmitted to tape by one WRITE statement is called a **logical record** or simply a record. The size of a record is determined by the number of list items and the format specifications. If the number of transmitting format codes in the format statement agrees with the number of list items in the WRITE statement, one logical record is written. If the number of format codes is less than the number of list items in the WRITE statement, multiple logical records are written. Records are written onto tape under the control of the FORMAT statement in the same way that format codes control the generation of printer lines. The same principle is true for reading records on tape. An entire record is read or written each time the computer scans from the beginning left parenthesis to the last (ending) right parenthesis in a FORMAT statement. The following I/O statements illustrate the number of characters and records that are read/written with their respective FORMAT statement.

READ (8,78) X,Y,X	(One record with 3 fields of data is read)
78 FORMAT (2F6.1,F4.2)	
READ (10,20) A,B,C	(Three records, each with 7 characters, are read)
20 FORMAT (F7.2)	
WRITE (9,30) X,Y,Z	(One record with 3 fields totalling 30 characters is written)
30 FORMAT (3F10.3)	
WRITE (10,40) I,J,K	(Three records, each with 50 characters are written. Note
40 FORMAT (I5,45X)	the last 45 characters in each record are blanks)

In addition to reading/writing magnetic tape records with the formatted READ and WRITE statements, unformatted READ and WRITE statements are available for reading and writing magnetic tape files.

17.3 UNFORMATTED READ/WRITE STATEMENTS WITH MAGNETIC TAPE FILES

Occasionally, a tape file may need to be read several times by a program or by different programs, or a tape file may be created by a FORTRAN program to be read by another FORTRAN program in a later processing run. Reading and writing of formatted records in FORTRAN is a very slow operation, since individual input fields must be converted from an external form to an internal binary word form in memory, and vice versa on output.

Unformatted READ Statement—General Form

READ (unit) list

where:

    unit   —   represents the file unit being read.
    list   —   represents the I/O list of variables, array names, and/or subscripted
                         variables.

Figure 17.6 General notation of the unformatted READ statement

To overcome the inefficient speed of the formatted READ and WRITE operations, two FORTRAN statements are available to allow you to perform unformatted I/O operations. Using unformatted READ and WRITE statements, data is transmitted to and from memory at a highly increased speed. No conversion of the data from an external to an internal form, or from an internal to an external form takes place. Data is read and written in machine word format, as it is required to look in internal storage. In addition to the efficient speed of unformatted I/O operations, a secondary advantage is the elimination of writing a FORMAT statement with each I/O statement.

The unformatted READ statement, therefore, allows efficient speed in reading input records already in machine word format. The general form of the unformatted READ statement is given in figure 17.6.

Valid examples of the unformatted READ statement are:

    24 READ (8) NRSTUD, GRADE1, GRADE2, GRADE3
    READ (10) T, U, V

The unformatted READ statement allows data to be read and transmitted to memory without any character or field conversion. Data already in binary word format is stored in word locations in the identical form it had when it previously resided in memory. Each data record read with an unformatted READ statement must have been *previously recorded* by an unformatted WRITE statement.

Since data fields are transmitted in word form under nonformat control, each data field represents one full word. The following READ statement causes one record composed of five words to be read from a magnetic tape and transferred to memory.

    READ (8) A, B, C, D, E

When the unformatted READ statement is used, the number of words comprising the tape record being read must be equal to the number of variables and/or array elements given in the list portion of the statement. An unequal match causes a program abort. Special care must also be taken to ensure that the type and length of the variables and/or array elements located in the list of the READ statement are the same type and length as the variables and/or array elements located in the list portion of the WRITE statement that wrote the record on magnetic tape.

Data may be written to tape in a binary word form with the unformatted WRITE. The general form of the unformatted WRITE statement is given in figure 17.7 (p. 480).

Valid examples of the unformatted WRITE statement are:

    7 WRITE (9) DATA1, DATA2, DATA3, DATA4
    WRITE (3) A, B, C, D, SUM, AVE

No conversion of data fields occurs. A tape written with an unformatted WRITE statement must be read with an unformatted READ statement when it is used for an input file.

Let us now look at the three statements used in manipulating magnetic tape files other than reading and writing records.

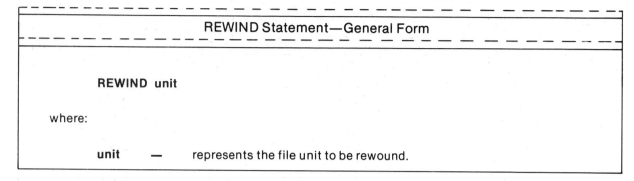

```
------------------------------------------------------------------------
                    Unformatted WRITE Statement—General Form
- - - - - - - - - - - - - - - - - - - - - - - - - - - - - - - - - - - -
|                                                                      |
|        WRITE (unit) list                                             |
|                                                                      |
|  where:                                                              |
|                                                                      |
|        unit   —    represents the file unit being written.           |
|        list   —    represents the I/O list of variables, array names,|
|                    and/or subscripted variables.                     |
|                                                                      |
------------------------------------------------------------------------
```

Figure 17.7 General notation of the unformatted WRITE statement

```
------------------------------------------------------------------------
                        REWIND Statement—General Form
- - - - - - - - - - - - - - - - - - - - - - - - - - - - - - - - - - - -
|                                                                      |
|        REWIND unit                                                   |
|                                                                      |
|  where:                                                              |
|                                                                      |
|        unit   —    represents the file unit to be rewound.           |
|                                                                      |
------------------------------------------------------------------------
```

Figure 17.8 General notation of the REWIND statement

17.4 THE REWIND, END FILE, AND BACKSPACE STATEMENTS

REWIND Statement

The REWIND statement is used to position a magnetic tape file back to the load point in such a way that the first record of the file is ready to be read or written. This operation may be needed after a tape file has been written, so that the operator will not have to manually cause the tape to rewind. The general form of the REWIND statement is given in figure 17.8.

Valid examples of the REWIND statement are:

REWIND 8

39 REWIND 2

REWIND JTAPE

Only one file unit may be rewound with a single REWIND statement. The statement REWIND 8, 9 would be invalid in attempting to rewind both units 8 and 9 in one REWIND statement.

END FILE Statement

The END FILE statement defines the end of a file by causing an end-of-file record to be written to the tape. The general form of the END FILE statement is given in figure 17.9.

Valid examples of the END FILE statement are:

END FILE 10

200 END FILE 8

END FILE INTAPE

```
┌─────────────────────────────────────────────────────────────────┐
│               END FILE Statement—General Form                     │
├─────────────────────────────────────────────────────────────────┤
│                                                                   │
│        END FILE unit                                              │
│                                                                   │
│   where:                                                          │
│                                                                   │
│        unit    —    represents the file unit to which the         │
│                     end-of-file marker is written.                │
└─────────────────────────────────────────────────────────────────┘
```

Figure 17.9 General notation of the END FILE statement

```
┌─────────────────────────────────────────────────────────────────┐
│              BACKSPACE Statement—General Form                     │
├─────────────────────────────────────────────────────────────────┤
│                                                                   │
│        BACKSPACE unit                                             │
│                                                                   │
│   where:                                                          │
│                                                                   │
│        unit    —    represents the file unit being repositioned.  │
└─────────────────────────────────────────────────────────────────┘
```

Figure 17.10 General notation of the BACKSPACE statement

Only one file unit may be used with each END FILE statement. The statement END FILE 8, 10 would be invalid in attempting to place an end-of-file mark on both units 8 and 10 with a single END FILE statement. If the end-of-file record has been written on the tape file and is checked for in the READ statement by the END option (for those compilers that allow this option), then the end-of-file record, when read, will cause the transfer of control to the statement number indicated by the END option.

BACKSPACE Statement

The BACKSPACE statement is used to position the tape file back one logical record, i.e., to the beginning of the previous record. If the file is already positioned at the load point, the statement has no effect. The form of the BACKSPACE statement is given in figure 17.10.

Valid examples of the BACKSPACE statement are:

> **BACKSPACE 9**
> **27 BACKSPACE 8**
> **BACKSPACE IFILE**

Only one file unit may be backspaced with a single BACKSPACE statement. The statement BACKSPACE 8, 10 would be invalid in attempting to backspace both units 8 and 10 with a single BACKSPACE statement. If you wish to backspace more than one logical record, separate BACKSPACE statements must be given for each logical record. For example, if it is desired to back up to the third previous record on unit 9, you would code three separate statements as follows:

> **BACKSPACE 9**
> **BACKSPACE 9**
> **BACKSPACE 9**

The BACKSPACE statement is intended for input files only, to provide a reread capability of an input record. You must not use the BACKSPACE statement on an output file to rewrite a record. Using the BACK-SPACE statement on an output file may produce unpredictable results. On input files a backspaced record can only be reread; it must not be rewritten to the input file. To update a tape file, the output records must be written to a different file.

```
C --- PROGRAM TO ILLUSTRATE THE CREATION AND READING
C --- OF A SEQUENTIAL TAPE FILE
C
C --- AUTHOR: J W COLE
C --- DATE WRITTEN: 3/23/82
C
      INTEGER RECORD
      DIMENSION RECORD(20)
      DATA NINES /4H9999/
C
C --- LOOP TO READ CARD FILE AND CREATE A TAPE FILE
   10 READ (5, 199) RECORD
      WRITE (9, 299) RECORD
      IF (RECORD(1) .NE. NINES) GO TO 10
C
C --- WRITE END OF FILE MARK AND REWIND THE TAPE
      END FILE 9
      REWIND 9
C
C --- LOOP TO READ THE TAPE FILE AND PRINT THE RECORDS
   20 READ (9, 199) RECORD
      IF (RECORD(1) .EQ. NINES) GO TO 30
      WRITE (6, 299) RECORD
      GO TO 20
C
C --- REWIND THE TAPE AND TERMINATE THE PROGRAM
   30 REWIND 9
      STOP
  199 FORMAT (20A4)
  299 FORMAT (1H0, 20A4)
      END
```

Figure 17.11 Sample program to create a magnetic tape file

The following example is to read a record under one set of format specifications and then to reread the record under a different set of specifications.

```
      DIMENSION TREC(20), SCAN(66), PGMID(2)
      READ (8, 91) TREC
   91 FORMAT (20A4)
      BACKSPACE 8
      READ (8, 90) ISEQNR, CONT, SCAN, PGMID
   90 FORMAT (I5, A1, 66A1, 2A4)
```

Now let us look at a complete program to see how you program magnetic tape files.

A Sample Magnetic Tape Program

Figure 17.11 presents a sample program to illustrate the concepts and various statements used in magnetic tape manipulation. The program reads a card file and puts it on tape. The tape file is then rewound, read, and printed.

17.5 USE OF SEQUENTIAL TAPE FILES IN BUSINESS APPLICATIONS

Magnetic tape is a widely used storage medium for sequential files in business data processing. Sequential file processing on magnetic tape is most desirable when the file size is large and the activity (number of transactions against the master file) is considerable. Business files may relate to personnel, payroll, accounts receivable, accounts payable, inventory control, and other applications.

The primary file of related records belonging to a specific function is known as the **master file**. The master file contains information of a relatively permanent type, relating to the function, as, for example, customer accounts, inventory items, and personnel data. The master file may be read by retrieval systems and various application programs to produce periodic reports. This master file must be updated at certain intervals or periods of time to reflect the latest data. The updating of the master file is known as **file maintenance** or **file update**. A majority of computer time in business applications is normally spent in file maintenance.

File maintenance involves two input files of information. One is the master file; the other is known as a transaction file. The **transaction file** contains current and changing information about the records on the master file. The transaction file records are applied against the master file to update the master file with the latest information.

Sequential file update requires the input transactions to be batched together and sorted into the same sequence as the master file. The master file records will be sequenced by social security, account number, stock number, customer account number, or some other field, depending on the application. By having the records sorted in the master and transaction files according to specific items selected as **sort keys**, the computer does not have to waste time in searching for the desired record. A record is read from the master file and compared with the transaction record. Various decisions are made depending whether the master key is less than, equal to, or higher than the transaction record key. Thus the master file is completely read only once during the file maintenance operation.

File maintenance of the master file involves the updating of information in selected records. In an accounts receivable application, the transaction file would contain payments and also new charges against a customer's account. The customer account number would be included in a transaction record with other fields of data. Both the master file and transaction file would be read until the account number in the transaction record matched the account number in a master file record. Then the payment amount field in the transaction record would be subtracted from the account balance in the master file record, or the new charge amount field in the transaction record would be added to the account balance in the master file record, depending on the type of transaction. After the transaction had been applied against the proper master file record, the master file would then reflect the latest data on that particular record. The customer's billing might also have been produced at the time his record was updated.

New customers may be added to the accounts receivable master file and old customers removed or deleted from the master file. Thus, in addition to updating a record with current information (normally known as a **change** transaction), new records may be **added** and old records may be **deleted** from the master file.

Errors in a transaction record (such as an invalid account number or amount field) may result in not being able to properly update the master record. **Editing** (checking for invalid fields) should always be performed in order to reject those transaction records with an error. These rejected transaction records are usually written to an error file, which is later printed. You review the error listing, locate the cause of the reject, and correct the record, which is later resubmitted for processing.

File maintenance with sequential files is illustrated in figure 17.12. Note the output file labeled "Updated Master Tape." In sequential file maintenance, the updated master file is always written to a new tape file. Additions and deletions of records prohibit the writing of records back to the old master file.

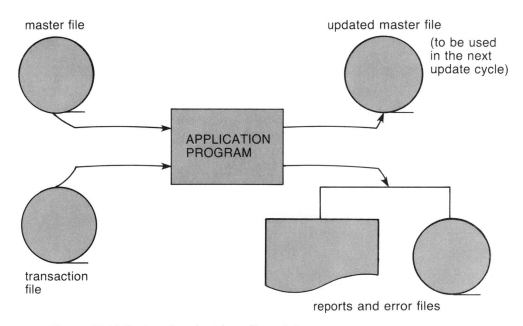

Figure 17.12 System flowchart for a file maintenance

The general procedures for updating a master file are as follows:

1. Compare the key in the master file record with that of the transaction file record.
2. If the key in the master file record is less than the key in the transaction file record, then no action is taken against that master record. The current master record is written to the new master file; the next master file record is read, and return to step 1 to repeat the comparison.
3. If the key in the master record matches the key of the transaction record, apply the required operation indicated in the transaction code. If the transaction code is a change, the appropriate fields in the master record are updated, and the updated master record is written to the new master file. A new master record and transaction record are read, and you return to step 1. If the transaction code is a delete, read a new transaction record and return to step 1. The old master record is thus not written to the new master file. If the transaction code is not a change or delete, the transaction record is in error.
4. If the key in the master file record is greater than the transaction record key, check the transaction code. If the transaction code is an add, the current transaction record is written to the new master file, a new transaction error is read, and you return to step 1. If the transaction code is not an add, the transaction record is in error, and an error message is written.

These procedures are continued until all transaction records have been processed. The above type of update does not allow for multiple transaction records with the same key. If multiple transaction records with the same key are allowed, the updated master record is not written, nor is another master record read, until a "less-than" condition is found against the transaction record key.

17.6 LANGUAGE EXTENTIONS IN FORTRAN DIALECTS AND ADDITIONAL REMARKS (THE ERR = OPTION)

ERR Option in the READ Statement

IBM "G" level, WATFIV, FORTRAN 77, VAX-11 FORTRAN, and most other FORTRAN compilers include the ERR = option in the sequential READ statement. This option is available for use in both the formatted and unformatted READ statements.

The ERR = option allows the programmer to check for parity errors. A **parity error** means that an invalid read operation occurred during the I/O of a record. That is, the various checks in the computer system indicate that the data was not read correctly—a bit may have been dropped or an extra bit picked up in transmitting the characters.

The general form of the READ statement that allows the ERR = option is:

READ (unit, n, END=a, ERR=b) list

where **b** represents a statement number to which control is transferred whenever a parity error occurs.

Occasionally dust or smoke particles stick to the recording surface of the tape, or the ferric oxide has flaked away. The area of tape where these problems occur cannot be read by the tape unit. An I/O error (i.e., a parity error) occurs. If the tape unit cannot read the area on tape after several retries, the program will be terminated by the system. The **ERR** option, when available in the READ statement, can be used to prevent an abort and allow the programmer to code his own error routine in his program. The following statements illustrate use of the **ERR** option that can be of value in tape processing.

```
16 READ (8, 37, END=52, ERR=94) A, B, C
37 FORMAT (3F6.2)
   . . .
   . . .
94 WRITE (6, 76) A, B, C
76 FORMAT (21H0PARITY ERROR ON TAPE , 3F10.2)
   GOTO 16
   . . .
52 . . .
```

There is usually no way to get around parity errors. You simply try to interpret the data in the record containing the error and reconstruct it in a later update operation. If an abort of the program can be prevented, the remaining records in the file can be read and are available for use, but the record with the parity error cannot be used and must be skipped.

Additional Remarks

There are other aspects of magnetic tape files to be aware of in a production environment. Tapes may have system header and trailer labels that provide identifying and other useful information about the file. FORTRAN tape files, however, generally do not have these labels. Multiple files can be put on one reel of tape. These files are called a multifile reel tape. Tape units may record data in an "even" or "odd" parity mode, and this mode serves as the basis for detecting parity errors. Tapes may be protected against accidental erase by removing the file protect ring, which is used to allow writing on a tape.

Many details in hardware operation and systems programming involving sequential tape files are left unmentioned here, since they are beyond the scope of this text. Many of these details usually do not need to be known by the student programmer.

17.7 SUMMARY

Chapter 17 introduced you to magnetic tape operations and the statements available to manipulate tape files. Magnetic tape is a valuable secondary storage medium. Over 50 million characters can be stored on a single 2,400-foot reel of magnetic tape. The entire reel of data can be read in minutes, which makes magnetic tape a fast I/O medium for reading and writing data. When large sequential files are processed, magnetic tape is often the preferred medium.

There are two reels involved on a tape unit: the data or file reel, which contains the data file, and the take-up reel. The tape is moved under a read/write head, which reads or writes data on the tape, depending on the desired operation. Different recording schemes are used to encode the data depending on the type of tape unit (7-track, 9-track, or phased encoded). A data file on magnetic tape can be read numerous times during the life of the tape, and new files may be recorded on a previously used tape.

A reflective marker, placed approximately 20 feet from the beginning of the tape, is known as the load-point or BOT (beginning of tape) marker. A tape must be positioned at this load point to be processed. Modern tape drives will automatically load the data reel at the load point.

Data is recorded on magnetic tape in blocks. A tape block may be a single data record or a combined number of data records. Each tape block is separated by an inter-block gap (IBG). The IBG is used not only to separate the tape blocks, but also to allow space for the tape to get up to speed before, and to slow down after, reading/writing a block.

Seven statements are available in FORTRAN for manipulating tape files: 1) the formatted READ, 2) unformatted READ, 3) formatted WRITE, 4) unformatted WRITE, 5) REWIND, 6) END FILE and 7) BACK-SPACE. One important point to remember about processing tape files is that the file is either an input file or an output file. The same file cannot be read from and then written to in the same processing loop.

The formatted READ and WRITE statements function the same way with tape files as with other I/O files. Magnetic tape is a sequential storage medium, which means that prior records must be read before the next one in sequence can be read. You must select a file unit number other than 5, 6, or 7 to be designated for the file unit, since those numbers are predefined symbols for card reader/terminal, line printer/terminal, and card punch.

In unformatted READ and WRITE statements with magnetic tape files, an unformatted file is written in binary form, the data fields are not formatted in an external manner as they are in card files or printer files, but in the same form as their internal memory representation. This form allows much greater speed in reading and writing unformatted (binary) files, since the translation from an internal mode to an external mode, and vice-versa, is eliminated. No format statement is needed for an unformatted READ or WRITE statement, since no external formatting takes place.

The REWIND statement is used to reposition a tape file back to its load point, to allow the reading of a newly created file or to save the operator from having to wait for the tape to rewind. The END FILE statement is used to write an end-of-file record on the record file; it can be sensed by the computer with the END = option in the READ statement (a non-FORTRAN 66 feature). The BACKSPACE statement is used to position the tape file back one logical record, to the previous record. If the tape is at load point, the BACKSPACE statement has no effect.

Magnetic tape is a widely used storage medium in business applications, especially for large sequential files. A data file that contains relatively permanent data for an application is known as a master file. A transaction file is used to store temporary records of current events. The master file is updated from the transaction file on a periodic basis in a process known as file maintenance (or update). Reports should be prepared from the latest data to provide up-to-date information. Thus, a file maintenance operation may occur daily to keep the master file updated with the latest data.

File maintenance involves reading both the master file and transaction file as input. The records in the transaction file are matched against the records in the master file according to a specific "key" field or fields. Different operations are performed depending on whether the key in a record of one file is less than, equal to, or greater than the key in the corresponding record of the other file. Transaction codes must be included in the transaction records to indicate which of three update operations (add, change, or delete) are desired. This not only ensures the correct update operation is performed, but also allows the programmer to catch update errors.

17.8 TERMS

Terms, concepts, and statements you should be familiar with in this chapter are:

addition of a record	END FILE statement	machine reel
BACKSPACE statement	end-of-file mark	master file
binary record	end-of-file record	physical record
beginning of tape (BOT)	end of tape (EOT)	read/write head
bits-per-inch (BPI)	file maintenance	REWIND statement
block	file reel	take-up reel
blocking factor	file update	tapemark
change of a master record	inter-block gap (IBG)	transaction file
data reel	key	unformatted I/O
deletion of a master record	load point	unformatted READ
density	load-point marker	unformatted WRITE

17.9 REVIEW QUESTIONS

1. Give two advantages of using magnetic tape as a storage medium.
2. The most common size reel of magnetic tape contains _____ feet of tape.
3. The reel of tape containing the data to be read is called the _____ reel.
4. Data is recorded onto tape or read from tape by moving the tape under a _____ _____ .
5. A magnetic tape must be positioned at its _____ _____ for the first record to be read/written.
6. Recorded data may be read from a magnetic tape many times. (True/False)
7. A magnetic tape may be used to record data over and over again. (True/False)
8. The last record on a reel of tape to indicate an end-of-file condition is called an _____ record.
9. The collection of logical records that form a physical record is also called a _____ .
10. Each tape block is separated by an _____ _____ .
11. Formatted READ and WRITE statements used with magnetic tape files work the same way as with sequential card and printer files. (True/False)
12. Unformatted READ and WRITE statements read and write data in a pure binary form and, thus, provide a much *slower* I/O operation. (True/False)
13. No FORMAT statement is required with unformatted READ or WRITE statements. (True/False)
14. The unformatted WRITE statement should be used to create an output tape file when the output file is to be read by the same or different programs. (True/False)
15. The statement used to position a magnetic tape back to the load point is the _____ .
16. The statement that causes an end-of-file record to be written is the _____ .
17. The statement that causes the tape unit to position the tape file back one logical record is the _____ .
18. The BACKSPACE statement may be used successfully on both input and output files. (True/False)
19. The data file in a business application that is used to contain all the records relating to a specific function is known as the _____ file.
20. The data file containing various transactions in a business function is known as a _____ file.
21. The process of updating a master file from a given transaction file is known as _____ _____ .
22. Sequential file update requires the records in a master file and its associated transaction file to be sorted in a specified sequence according to certain keys. (True/False)
23. List the three types of update actions that a transaction file may contain.

17.10 EXERCISES

1. Construct the following READ statements.
   a. Construct a READ statement to read the variables X, Y, and Z according to the format specifications provided in a FORMAT statement numbered 98. File unit 11 is used to denote a tape file.

   b. Construct an unformatted READ statement to read the same data in a binary form as specified in 1a.

2. Construct the following READ statements.
   a. Construct a READ statement to read the variables I, J, G, and H according to the format specifications given in a FORMAT statement numbered 97. Use 10 as the file unit number.

   b. Construct an unformatted READ statement to read the same variables in a binary form as specified in 2a.

3. Construct the following WRITE statements.
   a. Construct a WRITE statement to write the variables M, N, and O according to the specifications given in a FORMAT statement numbered 96. Use 11 as the file unit number.

   b. Construct an unformatted WRITE statement to write the same data in a binary form as specified in 3a.

4. Construct the following WRITE statements.
   a. Construct a WRITE statement to write the variables A, B, and L according to the specifications given in a FORMAT statement numbered 95. Use the variable NOUT as the file unit designator.

   b. Construct an unformatted WRITE statement to write the same data in a binary form as specified in 4a.

5. Construct the following statements.
   a. Write the statement to rewind a tape on unit 12.
   b. Construct the statement to write an end-of-file record on unit NTAPE.

   c. Construct the statement to backspace the file on unit 3 to the previous record.

6. Construct the following statements.
   a. Write the statement to rewind a tape on unit INF.
   b. Construct the statement to write an end-of-file record on unit 4.

   c. Write the statements to backspace the file on unit 8 two previous records.

17.11 PROGRAMMING PROBLEMS

1. Create a Master Student Directory on magnetic tape: Prepare a data deck with the following record layout:

CC 1 20	Student Name (Last, First, Middle Initial)
CC 21–36	Student Street Address
CC 37–49	City (Alphanumeric)
CC 50–51	State Code (Alphanumeric)
CC 52–56	ZIP Code (Form = NNNNN)
CC 57–59	Area Code (Form = NNN)
CC 60–66	Telephone Number (Form = NNNNNNN)
CC 67–78	Major area of study (Alphanumeric)
CC 79–80	Reserved

   The card deck is arranged in student name sequence. The card deck will contain a trailer card with a value of 99999 for ZIP code to indicate an end-of-file trailer record.

Write a program that reads the data deck, writes it onto a tape with the same format specifications, rewinds the tape, and prints it (double-spaced) for verification. This tape, which we will call the Student Directory Master File, has a record for each student and is in student-name sequence.

The printer output specifications are:

Print Positions	Field Description
1–20	Student name
25–40	Student street address
47–59	City
65–66	State code
70–74	ZIP code
80–82	Area code
84–90	Telephone number
99–110	Major area of study

Include appropriate column headings and a report heading.

2. Write a program that reads the Student Directory Master File created in problem 1 and prepares an output listing of all out-of-state students. An out-of-state student will be one with a state code other than the one chosen to represent an in-state student (e.g., not equal to TX). Use the DATA statement to provide the value for the variable used to identify an in-state student. Use the same printer output specifications as given in problem 1.

3. Write a program to read the Student Directory Master File created in problem 1 and to prepare an output listing of all students majoring in a specific area of study such as COMP SCI (Computer Science). Read the major study area from a punched card in the form 3A4. Use the same printer output specifications as given in problem 1.

4. Suppose a student changes his address or telephone number. Prepare a program to read data change cards (in student-name sequence) that also have all the same fields as the master records. When a match in student name is found on the Master File, replace the current record on the Master File with the values in the new change record. If a change record does not match a record on the Master File (change record name will be less than Master File name due to being out of sequence or not being in the master file) write the change record on a printer file as an error and halt processing.

Use only the first four characters of the name field to determine a match. Also use a trailer card with the value of 99999 for ZIP Code in the card update file to signal an end-of-file. Print the card update records as each is processed, to maintain a listing of processed card changes. To verify the correct changes, write the new master file to the printer. Use the same printer output specifications as given in problem 1. Note: A new file must be written for the updated Student Directory Master File.

5. Write a program to read a transaction file of changes to the Student Directory Master File and to update the Master File. Transaction data cards will be punched in the same format as the original master data deck cards but will carry a type transaction code punched in CC 80. If a "1" is punched in CC 80, the transaction record is to be added to the Master File. If a "3" is punched in CC 80, the transaction record is to replace the corresponding record on the Master File. If a "2" is punched in CC 80, the corresponding student record is to be deleted from the Master File. Use only the first four characters in the name field to determine a match.

Write the transaction update records to the printer as each is processed. Write the new Master file to the printer. Use the same printer output specifications as given in problem 1. Remember, a new tape file must be written for the updated Master file.

Magnetic Disk Statements and Operations

18

18.1 INTRODUCTION TO THE USE AND CONCEPTS OF MAGNETIC DISK

Today, nearly all computer systems have magnetic disk units to store required system and application program modules, compilers, and data files. The primary value of magnetic disk is that programs and data files may be kept on-line to the computer system and accessed in a fraction of a second. This random-access approach allows direct access to records without extensive searching through a data file. Access time to retrieve any record ranges from 20 to 50 milliseconds.

Modern disk packs may contain over 300 million characters of data. Data transfer rate is double that of the fastest tape unit. Over 800,000 characters of data can be transferred to and from memory in a second.

High capacity, randomly accessible disk storage devices make real-time (or on-line) processing feasible. Real-time processing provides the capability for processing an event as soon as it occurs. Intermixed and nonsequential input data can be processed as it becomes available and does not have to be batched and sorted, as it does in sequential processing. The latest up-to-date information is available at a moment's notice. Remote devices can be hooked into the computer through data communication networks and, with the use of large on-line direct-access storage units, make teleprocessing possible. A good example of an efficient on-line teleprocessing system is the airlines reservation system.

Disk storage is extremely effective in a high-activity application with a relatively small master file (for example, 5000 records) involving a comparatively small number of records updated frequently. An on-line disk file is commonly used with applications that require an immediate response. For timesharing systems, magnetic disk is essential; main storage could not hold all the various users' programs at the same time. Magnetic disk, therefore, is used to store programs temporarily until others have finished execution.

Magnetic disk units are thus known for their ability to provide random access (or direct access) to on-line files. Random access processing is characterized by being able to skip around within a file and by being able to read or write specific data records with no particular regard to the sequence.

Disk units may contain only one or more disk drives. See figure 18.1 for an example of a disk storage unit with multiple drives. A magnetic **disk pack** is mounted on each **drive** (or **spindle,** as it is sometimes called). See figure 18.2 for a picture of an individual disk pack (with a protective plastic case). Different disk packs containing various application files may be switched on a disk drive by using removable packs. This capability allows a more economical and efficient use of the disk drive.

Magnetic disk consists of thin circular, metal plates coated on both sides with a ferrous oxide recording material much like that used on magnetic tapes. This circular disk looks very much like an LP record used on a stereo. Normally, eleven circular plates, called **platters,** are mounted on a spindle to form a disk pack. Data is stored along **circular tracks** on both sides of each platter by magnetic fields recorded by a read/write head. Information is represented by a coding scheme of magnetic spots (the same as used on magnetic tape) placed by the read/write head. Read/write heads are mounted on movable access arms that move them in and out among the platters to the desired track (see figure 18.3).

All the tracks available for reading or recording data at one position of the access arm are said to make up a cylinder. A **cylinder** on magnetic disk, therefore, consists of all the tracks in a vertical line through the disk pack. See figure 18.4 for the concept of a cylinder.

Figure 18.1 A magnetic disk unit with multiple disk packs. (Courtesy of IBM)

Figure 18.2 A magnetic disk pack with a protective plastic cover. (Courtesy of IBM)

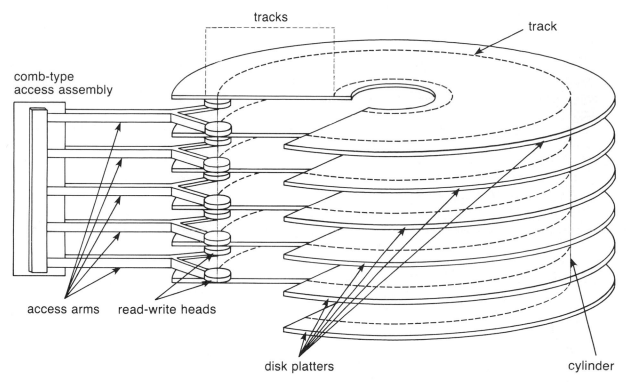

Figure 18.3 Operation of a magnetic disk drive. (Courtesy of IBM)

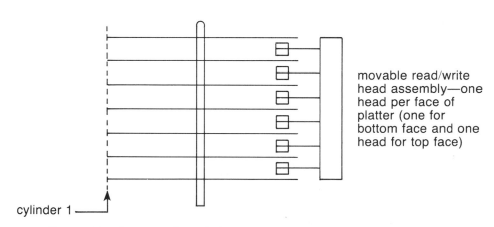

Figure 18.4 Concept of a cylinder on a magnetic disk pack

Data may be read/written as unblocked or blocked logical records, just as on magnetic tape. Again, JCL is used to describe the construction of a block or physical record in FORTRAN. Interblock gaps are also used to separate physical records on disk. There is no minimum-size record that can be written on disk. If desired, a single-character record can be recorded and read. Disk files are normally retained on disk storage until they are "purged" by the programmer or data base administrator.

Older disk drives use a removable pack for the storage of data. Modern disk units use a so-called "Winchester" technology, in which the read and write mechanisms and the recording disks are sealed in a unit. The sealed unit protects the disk from contaminants that can cause malfunctions. Winchester disks for large systems are 14-inch diameter platters. Winchester disks of 8-inch and 5.25-inch diameters have been developed for use in small business and word processing systems. These rigid disk systems are expected to become competitive with the "floppy" diskettes currently in widespread use on microcomputers and word-processing systems.

A popular Winchester disk used today on IBM systems is the 3340 Direct Access Storage Facility, which provides large storage capacity, high performance, and increased data reliability and flexibility. These units combine the access arms, read/write heads, and disk within the disk unit. Combining these components into a single integrated unit results in greater data reliability, because the read/write head alignments between drives are eliminated. Since the units are contained in a sealed cartridge, they operate in a clean-air environment, thus guarding against airborne contamination. See figure 18.5 for a picture of the IBM 3340 Direct Access Storage Facility.

Digital Equipment Corporation manufactures several Winchester disk drives. One of their first Winchester drives is the RM80, which can store over 300 million characters of data. See figure 18.6 for an illustration of the DEC RM80 disk unit.

With the presentation of the basic concepts of magnetic disk units, let us proceed to examine the FORTRAN statements for manipulating disk files.

Figure 18.5 An IBM 3340 Direct Access Storage Facility. (Courtesy of IBM)

Figure 18.6 A DEC RM80 Winchester disk unit.
(Courtesy of Digital Equipment Corporation)

18.2 FORTRAN STATEMENTS USED WITH SEQUENTIAL MAGNETIC DISK FILES

Even though magnetic disk storage provides for the direct access of records, disk is often used to store sequentially organized files. Sequential file organization is still the best design for files when there is a large volume of activity, such as updating of transaction records, or when most of the file must be read. Sequential disk files provide on-line access to the file and eliminate certain setup operations for the job, such as mounting and dismounting tape files.

The same FORTRAN statements available in processing sequential magnetic tape files can be used in processing sequential disk files. The form and a brief explanation of each statement are as follows:

1. Formatted READ statement:

   READ (unit ,n) list
   or
   READ (unit, n, END = a, ERR = b) list

   The file unit used for disk files can be any integer constant or variable (except 5, 6, or 7) that is accepted on the computer system. The formatted READ statement uses a related FORMAT statement to describe the form of the input data fields. All other elements in the statement function just as they do in sequential card or tape input files.

2. Unformatted READ statement:

   READ (unit) list
   or
   READ (unit, END = a, ERR = b) list

   The elements of an unformatted READ statement serve the same function as with tape files. Input data is read in binary word format.

3. Formatted WRITE statement:

   WRITE (unit, n) list

   The formatted WRITE statement uses a related FORMAT statement to describe the form of the output fields. No carriage control specification is needed in an output record. The elements in the formatted WRITE statement function the same as with tape files.

4. Unformatted WRITE statement:

   WRITE (unit) list

   The elements of the unformatted WRITE statement function the same as with unformatted records on tape. Data is transmitted to disk in the same word format as when the fields resided in internal storage.

5. REWIND statement:

   REWIND unit

   The REWIND statement allows you to reposition the disk to the beginning of a file. There is no reflective strip to indicate the beginning of a file on disk. Each disk pack maintains a **directory** of the starting address of each file stored on that disk pack. The REWIND statement for magnetic disk files, however, serves the same purpose as for tape files—to allow us to start processing at the first record in the file. The address of the first record in the file is obtained as the location of the next record to be read or written.

6. END FILE statement:

   END FILE unit

   The END FILE statement causes an end-of-file record to be written after the previously recorded record. It is used in conjunction with the ''END'' option in the READ statement to sense an end-of-file condition.

7. BACKSPACE statement:

   BACKSPACE unit

   The BACKSPACE statement allows the programmer to access the previous logical record. As with magnetic tape operations, the BACKSPACE statement is used with read operations on input files only.

Magnetic Disk Statements and Operations   493

The concepts of sequential file processing with records on magnetic disk are the same as for processing sequential files on tape. The records are read and written in a serial manner. To access the tenth record, the first nine must have been previously read. File maintenance with sequential disk files also remains the same. A new disk file must be created as the newly updated master file.

Following is a program to build a sequential file on disk. A blood donor file with blood donor number, blood type, and telephone number is read from cards and created on file unit 3. The file is written without format control. An input sentinel record with a donor number of 9999999 signifies the end of the input file.

```
C  ***  PROGRAM TO BUILD A BLOOD DONOR FILE
C  ***  ON SEQUENTIAL DISK IN UNFORMATTED FORM
   99      FORMAT (I7,A4,I7)
   10      READ (5,99) NRDONR, TYPEBD, NRTELE
           WRITE (3) NRDONR, TYPEBD, NRTELE
           IF (NRDONR .NE. 9999999) GO TO 10
           END FILE 3
           STOP
           END
```

Now, let's see how random (non-sequential) files are processed.

18.3 RANDOM FILE PROCESSING ON MAGNETIC DISK

Files may be organized in a random manner to allow the system to go directly to the desired record instead of having to search for it sequentially. Devices that provide this capability of reading a specific record at random are known as **direct-access devices.** The capacity for locating records directly on these devices depends on being able to assign addresses to storage locations. On magnetic tape, however, no storage address is associated with a given record, which is why magnetic tape does not have a direct-access capability.

Think of a file as consisting of a given number of records. Each record in the file has an address or index associated with it to make a direct reference to that record possible. In FORTRAN, this index pointer indicates the relative position of the record in the file. The first record has index 1, the second record has index 2, and the last record has index n, where n is the maximum number of records on the file. By using the proper index pointer, any record can be located and read into memory in a few milliseconds.

FORTRAN files that are set up in this manner are said to be in **random organization** and are known as **direct-access files.** These files must be created and processed using direct-access I/O statements, which differ slightly from the sequential I/O statements used to create and process sequential files.

ANSI FORTRAN 66 does not provide specifications for random access statements because of the wide variety of statements and techniques used by different compilers. Therefore, this text explains the statements used for IBM "G" level FORTRAN compiler and WATFIV. Section 18.8 gives the syntax and procedures in using random-access statements for CDC, Honeywell, Burroughs, Univac, HP, and DEC PDP-11 compilers.

The six direct-access I/O statements in FORTRAN are: (1) DEFINE FILE, (2) formatted random READ, (3) unformatted random READ, (4) formatted random WRITE, (5) unformatted random WRITE, and (6) FIND. Each of these statements and their syntax construction will be discussed in detail.

18.4 THE DEFINE FILE STATEMENT

The DEFINE FILE statement is used to identify random organized direct-access files in FORTRAN and to specify their characteristics. Any file specified in a DEFINE FILE statement is considered to be a random organized file. You must use the random READ and WRITE statements when these files are used in I/O operations.

In addition to informing the FORTRAN language that a file is to be used as a random-organized, direct-access file, you must indicate the maximum number of records allowed in the file, the size of each record, and whether you are using format statements to describe the data in the records. You must also provide the system with the name of the index pointer to be used when referring to records in the file. All this information is provided in the DEFINE FILE statement whose syntax is given in figure 18.7.

Valid examples of the DEFINE FILE statement are:

```
DEFINE FILE 2(50, 80, L, INDEX)
DEFINE FILE 3(10000, 25, U, IREC), 10(10, 35, E, KTR)
```

DEFINE FILE unit (r,s,f,v)

where:

unit	—	is an integer constant that represents the file unit.
r	—	is an integer constant specifying the maximum number of records in the file.
s	—	is an integer constant specifying the maximum size of each record. Record size is measured in bytes or words depending upon specifications for **f**:
f	—	is established from one of the following selections:

> **L** — either with or without format control; maximum record size is measured in bytes.
>
> **E** — with format control; maximum record size is measured in bytes.
>
> **U** — without format control; maximum record size is measured in words.

v	—	is a nonsubscripted integer variable called an associated variable; it is set to a value which points to the next record to be transmitted.

Figure 18.7 General notation of the DEFINE FILE statement

The first example describes a file on unit 2 to contain a maximum of 50 records. The maximum size of each record is 80 bytes. A byte is equal to one character. The option "L" indicates that the records may be read/written with or without format control, but the record length is measured in bytes (80). The variable, INDEX, is established as the associated variable for the file and can have a range of 1 to 50. The second example defines two files as being type random organization (unit 3 and unit 10). The file on unit 3 is written/read without format control. The file consists of a maximum of 10,000 twenty-five word records. IREC is identified as the associated variable to be used in accessing the records on file unit 3. The file on unit 10 is always written/read with format control. There can be only ten records on the file; each record can be a maximum of 35 characters in length. The associated variable is KTR.

The **f** parameter in the DEFINE FILE statement defines whether the records will be transmitted under format or nonformat control, and whether the record size is measured in byte or word count. The "**L**" option indicates that the record size is measured in bytes and that the record may be read/written either under control of a FORMAT statement or under nonformat control. When you use the "**L**" option, you have the choice of: (1) reading/writing all records in the file under format control, (2) reading/writing all records in the file under nonformat control or (3) a mixture of the two forms. If you mix the forms of the records on the file, you must remember in what form each record was written, in order to use the proper form of the READ statement (formatted READ or unformatted READ) in accessing the records. When the "**E**" option is specified, all records must be written and read under format control. When the "**U**" option is specified, all records must be written and read without format control.

A direct-access file on disk can have only one associated variable assigned to it. The associated variable given for the file unit in the DEFINE FILE statement must always be used whenever the relative record to be read or written to the file is indicated by an integer variable in the random I/O statements. That is, if INDEX has been identified as the associated variable in the DEFINE FILE statement, only the variable INDEX can be used as the associated variable in the related READ, WRITE, and FIND statements. The value in the associated variable is automatically incremented by one to point to the next record in the file after execution of each random READ or WRITE statement.

The DEFINE FILE statement must be present for all FORTRAN files that are organized randomly. Since the DEFINE FILE statement is considered to be a specification statement, it should appear in the program before any executable statement. The DEFINE FILE statement describes the characteristics of a direct-access file and dictates, to a large degree, the form of the random READ and WRITE statements.

```
            READ (unit ' v, n, ERR = b) list

where:

    unit      —   represents the file unit being read.
    '         —   is a necessary separator.
    v         —   is an integer constant, expression, or associated variable used by the
                  system to locate the record to be read.
    n         —   is the number of the format statement used to describe the input
                  record.
    ERR = b   —   b is a statement number to which control is transferred in case of a
                  parity error. This is an optional parameter.
    list      —   is an I/O list.
```

Figure 18.8 General notation of the formatted random READ statement

18.5 THE FORMATTED AND UNFORMATTED RANDOM READ STATEMENTS

The formatted random READ statement permits the direct reference and reading into memory of the record (*from direct-access storage*) indicated by an integer expression or the associated variable (index pointer). The general form of the formatted random READ statement is given in figure 18.8.

Valid examples of the formatted random READ statement are:

> **READ (9 ' 34, 53, ERR = 86) A, B, C**
> **12 READ (8 ' INDX, 87) ACCTNR, UNITS, PRICE, AMT**
> **76 READ (3 ' 2*L/3, 40) X**
> **READ (10 ' JREC + 3,66) I, M, P, Q**

The formatted random READ uses an integer constant, an expression, or the value in the associated variable to locate the relative record and read it into internal storage. A FORMAT statement is used to describe the external form of the input record being read.

In the example below

> **IREC = 23**
> **READ (9 ' IREC, 39) J, K, L, M**
> **39 FORMAT (4I5)**

the twenty-third record is read and four fields stored at the variables J, K, L, and M.

An integer constant or expression may be used to indicate a specific record to be read. The statement

> **READ (2 ' 20, 98) STDNR, GRADES**

would read the twentieth record in the file. Whenever this statement is executed, the twentieth record would always be read. The statement

> **READ (8 ' 3*2 + 1, 95) STDNR, GRADES**

would always cause the seventh record in the file to be read. Even though an integer constant expression is used to denote the desired record, the associated variable will always be changed by the system to point to the next record after the desired relative record has been calculated. For example, in the READ statement above, the associated variable would have a value of 8 after the statement had been executed. Nonetheless, if this statement were read repeatedly in a loop, it would still always cause the seventh record to be read.

The value of the associated variable is also automatically incremented by one when used in the READ statement. Thus, if you wanted to read an entire file or a portion of records with ascending position numbers, you would have only to initialize the associated variable to the desired starting location. Following is an example to read the first twenty records on a random file and dump them to the printer.

```
     DEFINE FILE 8(50, 80, E, NRREC)
     DIMENSION NAME (5), GRADES (10)
  98 FORMAT (5A4, 10F5.1)
  97 FORMAT (1H0, 10X, 5A4, 10F7.1)
     NRREC = 1
   5 READ (8 ' NRREC, 98) NAME, GRADES
     WRITE (6, 97) NAME, GRADES
     IF (NRREC .LT. 21) GO TO 5
     STOP
     END
```

A check is made for NRREC to be less than 21, since the associated variable NRREC is incremented by one after each execution of the random READ statement.

Data may also be read from random disk without format control, i.e., in internal word form. The form of the unformatted random READ statement is as follows:

READ (unit ' v, ERR = b) list

The programmer-supplied elements are the same as the formatted random READ, except that there is no associated format statement number.

Valid examples of the unformatted random READ statement are:

```
     READ (8 ' INDX) A, B, C
  26 READ (3 ' JREC, ERR = 37) I, J, Z
  18 READ (2 ' 17) M, N, P
     READ (9 ' MRCD + 5) K, X, Y
```

The unformatted random READ statement functions the same as the formatted random READ in all respects except that the transfer of data is in internal word form and not under the control of any FORMAT statement. For data to be transferred without format control, the U or L option must be specified in the DEFINE FILE statement. The unformatted random READ can only be used on files that have been *written* without format control (i.e., an unformatted random WRITE).

18.6 THE FORMATTED AND UNFORMATTED RANDOM WRITE STATEMENTS

The formatted random WRITE statement directs the computer to transfer data from memory to a direct-access file on disk. Data is transferred under control of a related FORMAT statement and is written to the relative disk record as indicated by the integer constant, expression, or associated variable. The general form of the formatted random WRITE statement is given in figure 18.9 (p. 498).

Valid examples of the formatted random WRITE statement are:

```
  16 WRITE (3 ' INDX, 98) A, B, C
     WRITE (8 ' 36, 39) I, X, J, Y
```

The first WRITE statement writes the values of A, B, C to the relative record indicated by INDX on file unit 3. The second WRITE statement writes the values of I, X, J, and Y as the thirty-sixth record on file unit 8. The file unit being written must have been previously defined by a DEFINE FILE statement.

Formatted Random WRITE Statement—General Form

WRITE (unit ' v, n) list

where

unit	—	represents the file unit.
'	—	is a necessary separator.
v	—	represents an integer constant, expression, or associated variable used by the system to indicate the desired record position to be written.
n	—	is the number of the format statement used to describe the output record.
list	—	is an optional I/O list.

Figure 18.9 General notation of the formatted random WRITE statement

The value in the associated variable is automatically incremented to the next record in the file by the system after execution of each WRITE statement. Thus, if you wanted to write an entire file, you would have only to initialize the associated variable to the desired starting location. Following is an example of creating a random file of 50 records with record addresses of 1–50.

```
    DEFINE FILE 8(50, 80, E, K)
    DIMENSION NAME(5), GRADES(10)
98  FORMAT (5A4, 10F5.1)
    K = 1
5   READ (5,98, END=200) NAME, GRADES
    WRITE (8 ' K, 98) NAME, GRADES
    GO TO 5
200 STOP
    END
```

The unformatted random WRITE statement is used to transfer data from memory in word form to a direct-access disk file. The general form of the unformatted random WRITE statement is as follows:

WRITE (unit ' v) list

The programmer-supplied elements are the same as for the formatted random WRITE, except that there is no associated format statement number.

Valid examples of the unformatted random WRITE statement are:

```
   WRITE (3 ' 14) A,B,C
86 WRITE (9 ' JREC) D,E,F
```

The first example writes the three fields A, B, and C as the fourteenth record on file unit 3. The second example writes the three fields D, E, and F as the relative record indicated by the associated variable JREC on file unit 9.

The unformatted random WRITE statement functions the same as the formatted random WRITE statement in all respects, except that the transfer of data is in word form and not under control of any FORMAT statement. For data to be transferred without format control, the "U" or "L" option must be specified in the DEFINE FILE statement.

```
┌─────────────────────────────────────────────────────────────────────┐
╎                      FIND Statement—General Form                      ╎
├─────────────────────────────────────────────────────────────────────┤
│                                                                       │
│         FIND (unit ' v)                                               │
│                                                                       │
│    where:                                                             │
│                                                                       │
│         unit   —     represents the file unit.                        │
│         '      —     is a necessary separator.                        │
│         v      —     is an integer constant, expression, or associated variable used by the │
│                      system to locate the desired record position.    │
│                                                                       │
└─────────────────────────────────────────────────────────────────────┘
```

Figure 18.10 General notation of the FIND statement

18.7 THE FIND STATEMENT

The FIND statement is used to speed up execution of a program by reducing the time it takes the computer to locate and address a record position on magnetic disk. The function of the FIND statement is to position the read/write heads over the proper track in which a desired record is to be read or written. The general form of the FIND statement is given in figure 18.10.

Valid examples of the FIND statement are:

> **20 FIND (3 ' 26)**
> **FIND (4 ' IREC + 1)**
> **17 FIND (10 ' INDEX)**

The first example positions the read/write heads over the track containing relative record number 26 in the file designated by unit 3. The second example positions the read/write heads over the track containing the relative record indicated by IREC plus 1 for file unit 4. The third example positions the heads over the track containing the relative record indicated by the associated variable, INDEX, for file unit 10.

The FIND statement does not transfer any data to memory; it simply positions the read/write head over the proper track as indicated by the integer constant, expression, or associated variable. A delay is encountered when reading/writing disk records in a random file to allow the mechanical action of moving the heads in or out among the disk platters to locate the proper track. If the read/write heads are positioned at the proper track, a READ or WRITE statement need only to wait for the disk to revolve to the proper record to transfer data. Thus, the FIND statement often allows the programmer to speed up I/O operations by not having to wait for the horizontal delay in positioning the read/write heads over the desired track. The following example illustrates this concept.

> **DEFINE FILE 8(750,50,U,N)**
> **DIMENSION REC (50)**
> **N = 1**
> **5 READ (8 ' N) REC**
> **FIND (8 ' N)**
> **. . .**
> **. . .**
> **IF (ISWT .EQ. 0) GO TO 5**

When control is transferred back to the READ statement, the FIND statement has already caused the read/write heads to be positioned over the proper track of the next record to be read. Data can be transferred as soon as the proper record rotates under the read/write heads. A random READ or WRITE statement immediately following a FIND statement does not provide any benefits in speeding up the accessing of a record. Rather, as above, the FIND should follow a READ or WRITE in a loop.

A Sample Program

The following program illustrates the use of the FORTRAN statements available with random disk files. A disk file of 100 eighty-character records is created on file unit 8 under format control. A student number (within the range from 1–100) is used to specify the address at which the record is written. After the disk file has been created, the records are read, beginning at record one, and written to the printer.

```
         DEFINE FILE 8(100,80,E,NRSTD)
         DIMENSION NAME(5), GRADES(10)
      98 FORMAT (I3,5A4,10F5.1)
      97 FORMAT (5A4,10F5.1)
      96 FORMAT (1H0,I3,5X,5A4,5X,10F7.2)
         NRREC = 0
      10 READ (5,98,END=15) NRSTD,NAME,GRADES
         NRREC = NRREC + 1
         WRITE (8 ' NRSTD, 97) NAME, GRADES
         FIND (8 ' NRSTD)
         IF (NRREC .LE. 100) GO TO 10
      15 NRSTD = 1
      20 READ (8 ' NRSTD, 97) NAME,GRADES
         FIND (8 ' NRSTD)
         WRITE (6, 96) NRSTD, NAME, GRADES
         IF (NRSTD .LT. 100) GO TO 20
         STOP
         END
```

18.8 LANGUAGE EXTENSIONS IN FORTRAN DIALECTS (RANDOM I/O ON VARIOUS SYSTEMS AND THE OPEN AND CLOSE STATEMENTS)

Nearly every FORTRAN compiler handles random access files in a different fashion. The earlier sections in this chapter described their use on IBM "G" level and WATFIV compilers. This section will briefly discuss the conventions, procedures, and statements used for random access files on the CDC 6000, Honeywell 6000, Burroughs 6000 and 7000, Univac 1100, HP 3000, and DEC PDP-11 series computers. This section will also explain the OPEN and CLOSE statements available on some systems.

CDC 6000/Cyber

Random access files on a CDC 6000/Cyber system may be read/written to mass storage units (disk, drum, or other) or to Extended Core Storage (ECS). The subroutine call:

CALL OPENMS (parameters)

is used to open a mass storage file and inform the computer that it is a random access file.

Some of the random access statements for direct I/O operations on the CDC 6000 are:

CALL READMS (parameters)
CALL READEC (parameters)
READ MS (parameters)
CALL WRITEMS (parameters)
CALL WRITEEC (parameters)
WRITE MS (parameters)
WRITE ECS (parameters)

THE CALL STINDX statement performs the same function as the FIND statement on IBM compilers.

H6000

On the Honeywell 6000 a subroutine named RANSIZ permits the user to specify the record for a random access file. This subroutine must generally be called before any I/O operation is made to the random file. The general form of this subroutine call is:

CALL RANSIZ (unit, recsize, file-indicator)

The **"unit"** parameter is a file unit number, such as 10. The **"recsize"** parameter is the record size in number of words (variables). H6000 random files must have a constant record size that is read or written on each I/O operation. The third parameter, **"file-indicator"**, is optional. When this parameter is not supplied, the random file is processed as a standard system format file.

Random files are read with the random READ statement, general form for which is:

READ (unit ' v, ERR = b) list

Random files are written on the H6000 with the random WRITE statement. Its general form is:

WRITE (unit ' v, ERR = b) list

The random READ and WRITE statements are used with strictly unformatted (binary) files. The data cannot be formatted as with the IBM compilers. Note the ERR = option on the random WRITE statement to allow an error routine to be executed if a write parity error is encountered. Otherwise, the random READ and WRITE statements on the H6000 are formed the same as the unformatted random READ and WRITE statements with the IBM compiler.

B6000 and B7000

Data may be written to and read from a random file in either a formatted or unformatted form. No DEFINE FILE statement or subroutine call is necessary to establish a random access file on the B6000 and 7000 systems.

Random files are read with the random READ statement. Its general forms are:

READ (unit = v, n, ERR = b) list

or

READ (unit = v, ERR = b) list

The first form is for a formatted read. The second form is for an unformatted read. The " = " is a necessary separator denoting a random READ. The single quote (') may be used in place of the " = " if you so desire.

Random files are written with the random WRITE statement. Its forms are:

WRITE (unit = v, n, ERR = b) list

or

WRITE (unit = v, ERR = b) list

The first form is for data written under format control. The second form is for an unformatted write. **"unit"** represents the file unit number used. " = " is a necessary separator denoting a random WRITE. The single quote (') may be used in place of the " = " if desired.

The FIND statement may be used to position a random file at a designated record. The general form of the FIND is:

FIND (unit = v)

where " = " is a necessary separator to indicate a random file. The single quote (') may be used in place of the " = " if you desire.

When a disk file is created on the B6000 and B7000 computers, the operating system will automatically allocate disk storage space for the file. To retain the newly created disk file, a LOCK statement must be executed. For example:

LOCK 8

would save the created disk file written on unit 8 and put the file name in the disk directory. If the LOCK statement is not executed, a disk output file will be considered a temporary file and automatically purged at the end of the job.

Univac 1100

Data may be written to and read from a random disk file in either a formatted or unformatted form. Any random file must have been previously defined in a DEFINE FILE or OPEN statement as a direct-access file.

The form of the Univac 1100 DEFINE FILE statement is similar to the IBM format given in section 18.4, but Univac provides two more letters for the **f** (third) parameter in addition to the L, E or U. These two additional letters are: 1) the letter **M,** which is the same as L except that the file is always skeletonized and 2) the letter **F,** which is the same as E, except the file is always skeletonized.

The form of the Univac 1100 direct-access READ statement is:

$$READ\ (u'\ r\ [,f]\ [,ERR=s]\ [,IOSTAT=ios]\ )\ [iolist]$$

or

$$READ\ ([UNIT=]\ u\ [,[FMT=]f],\ REC=r\ [,ERR=s]\ [,IOSTAT=ios])\ [iolist]$$

where:

[ ]	represent an optional element.
UNIT =	is an optional clause; when used, it identifies the file unit.
u	is the same file unit number as for the associated DEFINE FILE or OPEN statement. The file number must be followed by an apostrophe for the first form. The UNIT = clause is optional for the second form. The UNIT = and FMT = must either both appear for formatted I/O statements, or neither must appear.
'	is a necessary separator signifying a direct-access file for the first form.
r	is an integer constant, nonsubscripted integer variable, integer expression, or parameter variable that represents the relative position of a record within the file. The REC = clause must be present for the second form of the READ. The REC = , UNIT = , and FMT = clauses must not be present in the first form of the READ.
FMT =	is an optional clause; when used, it identifies the FORMAT statement.
f	is a format specification. Both UNIT = and FMT = must appear for formatted READ statements, or neither must appear.
ERR = s	is an optional clause that will cause control to be transferred to statement label **s** if an error is detected in the execution of the READ statement.
IOSTAT = ios	is an optional I/O status clause specification; **ios** is an integer variable or integer array element that may indicate, for example, the successful completion of input.
iolist	is an ordered list of variables that are to receive the record read.

The form of the Univac 1100 direct-access WRITE statement is:

$$WRITE\ (u'\ r\ [,f]\ [,ERR=s]\ [,IOSTAT=ios])\ [iolist]$$

or

$$WRITE\ ([UNIT=]\ u\ [,[FMT=]f],\ REC=r\ [,ERR=s]\ [,IOSTAT=ios])\ [iolist]$$

where:

[ ]	represent an optional element.
UNIT =	is an optional clause.
u	is the same file unit number as for an associated DEFINE FILE or OPEN statement. The file number must be followed by an apostrophe for the first form. The UNIT clause is optional for the second form. Both the UNIT = and FMT = must appear for formatted I/O statements, or neither must appear.
'	is a necessary separator signifying a direct-access file for the first form.
r	is an integer constant, nonsubscripted integer variable, integer expression, or parameter variable that represents the relative position of a record within the file. The REC = clause must be present for the second form. The REC = , UNIT = , and FMT = clauses must not be present in the first form of the WRITE.

FMT =	is an optional clause; when used, it identifies the FORMAT statement.
f	is a format specification. Both FMT = and UNIT = clauses must be present, or neither may be used.
ERR = s	is an optional clause that will cause control to be transferred to statement label **s** if an error is detected in the execution of the WRITE statement.
IOSTAT = ios	is an optional I/O status clause specification; **ios** is an integer variable or integer array element that may indicate, for example, the successful completion of output.
iolist	is an ordered list of variables that are to be written. This element must be present if field f is not present.

The general form of the FIND statement is:

$$\text{FIND } (u' \ r \ [,\text{ERR} = s] \ [,\text{IOSTAT} = ios])$$

or

$$\text{FIND } (\ [\text{UNIT} =] \ u, \ \text{REC} = r \ [,\text{ERR} = s] \ [,\text{IOSTAT} = ios] \ )$$

where:

[ ]	represent an optional element.
UNIT =	is an optional clause; when used, it identifies the file unit.
u	is a file unit number.
r	is an integer constant, a simple integer variable, or an integer expression specifying the relative position of a record within the file. The apostrophe must appear for the first form. The REC = and UNIT = clauses must not be present in the first form of the FIND.
ERR = s	is an optional clause that will cause control to be transferred to statement label **s** if an error is detected in the execution of the FIND statement.
IOSTAT = ios	is an optional I/O status clause specification; **ios** is an integer variable or integer array element.

If the UNIT = clause appears in any of these statements, the other specifiers may appear in any order in the second form of the statement.

HP 3000

There is no DEFINE FILE or FIND statement in HP 3000 FORTRAN, but both formatted and unformatted (binary) disk files may be manipulated. The direct READ and WRITE statements, however, are restricted to files on direct-access devices with fixed-length records.

The general form of the HP 3000 direct READ statement is:

$$\text{READ (unit-no @rec-no, format, END} = sn_1, \text{ ERR} = sn_2) \text{ iolist}$$

where:

unit-no	is the file number.
@rec-no	the @ is a required symbol to specify a direct-access file; **rec-no** is an integer constant, integer variable, or integer expression whose integer value is taken as the record number to be read.
format	is a required statement number of the FORMAT statement for a formatted read. This parameter is omitted for an unformatted read. If the format parameter is omitted, a binary transfer of data takes place.
END =	is an optional parameter. When used, control is transferred on the end-of-file condition to sn_1, which is the statement number of an executable statement.

| ERR = | is an optional parameter. When used, control is transferred on a parity-error to sn_2, which is the statement number of an executable statement. |
| iolist | is the input list of variables to be read. |

The general form of the HP 3000 direct WRITE statement is:

WRITE (unit-no @rec-no, format, END = sn_1, ERR = sn_2) iolist

where:

unit-no	is the file unit number.
@rec-no	the @ is a required symbol to specify a direct access file; **rec-no** is an integer constant, integer variable, or integer expression whose integer value is taken as the record number to be written.
format	is a required statement number of the FORMAT statement for a formatted write. This parameter is omitted for an unformatted write. If the format parameter is omitted, a binary transfer of data takes place.
END =	is an optional parameter. When used, control is transferred on the end-of-file condition to sn_1, which is the statement number of an executable statement.
ERR =	is an optional parameter. When used, control is transferred on a parity-error to sn_2, which is the statement number of an executable statement.
iolist	is the output list of variables to be written to disk.

DEC PDP-11

DEC PDP-11 FORTRAN allows both formatted and unformatted direct-access I/O of magnetic disk files. Both the DEFINE FILE statement and the FIND statement are available.

The general form of the DEC PDP-11 DEFINE FILE statement is:

DEFINE FILE u (m,n,U,v) [,u (m,n,U,v)] . . .

where:

[ ]	represents optional additional file specifications.
u	is an integer constant or integer variable that specifies the file unit number.
m	is an integer constant or variable that specifies the number of records in the file.
n	is an integer constant or variable that specifies the length, in words, of each record.
U	specifies that the file is unformatted (binary). The letter U is the only acceptable entry in this position. (Note: If formatted I/O is used, the OPEN statement must be used in place of the DEFINE FILE.)
v	is an integer variable, called the associated variable of the file. At the conclusion of each direct-access I/O operation, the record number of the next higher numbered record in the file is assigned to **v**.

The general form of the DEC PDP-11 direct-access READ statement is:

READ (u′ r [,f] [,ERR = s]) [iolist]

where:

[ ]	represent optional specifications.
u	is the file unit number.
′	is a necessary separator signifying a direct-access file.
r	is the record number. The record number may be given as an integer constant, integer expression, or associated variable given in the DEFINE FILE statement.
f	is the statement number for a formatted read. If this parameter is omitted, an unformatted (binary) read is performed.

| **ERR =** | is an optional parameter for parity errors. Control is transferred to statement number **s** if a parity error occurs. |
| **iolist** | is the list of input variables to be read. |

The general form of the DEC PDP-11 direct-access WRITE statement is:

WRITE (u′ r [,f] [,ERR = s]) [iolist]

where:

[ ]	represent optional specifications.
u	is the file unit number.
′	is a necessary separator signifying a direct-access file.
r	is the record number. The record number may be given as an integer constant, integer expression, or associated variable given in the DEFINE FILE statement.
f	is the format statement number for a formatted write. If this parameter is omitted, an unformatted (binary) write is performed.
ERR =	is an optional parameter for parity errors. Control is transferred to statement number **s** if a parity error occurs.
iolist	is the list of output variables to be written.

The general form of the DEC PDP-11 direct-access FIND statement is:

FIND (u′ r)

where:

u	is the file unit number.
′	is a necessary separator signifying a direct-access file.
r	is the record number. The record number may be given as an integer constant, integer expression, or associated variable given in the DEFINE FILE statement.

An important thing to remember about the DEC PDP-11 random read and write operations is that the first record in a file begins with record number 0 (zero). The maximum number of records in a PDP-11 direct-access file cannot exceed 32767 (since this is the maximum integer that can be stored in a PDP-11 memory word). If a record number is used that is greater than 32767, the system wraps around the record. For example, if a record with record number 32768 is written, the system will write the record as record number 0.

The OPEN Statement for PDP-11 FORTRAN

The OPEN statement is used to connect an existing file to a logical file unit or to create a new file and to connect it to a logical file unit. The statement may also contain specifications for file attributes that will direct the creation and/or subsequent processing. The OPEN statement is preferred over the DEFINE FILE statement to describe direct-access files.

The general form of the PDP-11 OPEN statement is:

OPEN (p [,p] . . .)

where:

p is a specification in one of the following forms:

key	key is a keyword.
key = e	e is a numeric expression.
key = s	s is an executable statement label.
key = lit	lit is an alphanumeric literal of special significance.
key = v	v is an integer variable name.
key = n	n is an array name, variable name, or array. element name, or alphanumeric literal.

The keywords and specifications for the PDP-11 OPEN statement are given in Table 18.1.

Table 18.1 Keywords in the PDP-11 OPEN Statement

Keyword	Function	Values
UNIT	logical file unit number	e
NAME	file specification	n
TYPE	file type	'OLD' 'NEW' 'SCRATCH' 'UNKNOWN'
ACCESS	access method	'SEQUENTIAL' 'DIRECT' 'APPEND'
READONLY	read-only file access	
FORM	file format	'FORMATTED' 'UNFORMATTED'
RECORDSIZE	direct-access record length	e
ERR	error condition transfer label	s
BUFFERCOUNT	number of buffers	e
INITIALSIZE	file allocation size	e
EXTENDSIZE	file extension increment	e
NOSPANBLOCKS	unspanned records	
SHARED	shared file access	
DISPOSE	file disposition	'SAVE'
or		'KEEP'
DISP		'PRINT' 'DELETE'
ASSOCIATEVARIABLE	associated variable name	v
CARRIAGECONTROL	carriage control type	'FORTRAN' 'LIST' 'NONE'
MAXREC	number of direct-access records	e
BLOCKSIZE	physical block size	e

where:

e	is a numeric expression.
n	is a variable name, array name, array element name, or an alphanumeric literal.
s	is an executable statement label.
v	is an integer variable name.

You should consult the DEC PDP-11 FORTRAN Language Reference Manual (AA-1855D-TC), for a detailed explanation of these options.

Examples of the PDP-11 OPEN statement with its associated DEFINE FILE statement are:

```
C – – – EXAMPLE # 1. CREATING A NEW FILE FOR OUTPUT.
C
        DEFINE FILE 2 (1, 1600, U, NXX)
        OPEN (UNIT = 2,NAME = 'ACT.TAB',TYPE = 'NEW',ACCESS = 'DIRECT',
      *      RECORDSIZE = 300)


C – – – EXAMPLE # 2. USING AN ALREADY CREATED FILE.
C
        OPEN (UNIT = 2,NAME = 'ACT.TAB',TYPE = 'OLD',ACCESS = 'DIRECT',
      *      RECORDSIZE = 300)
```

```
C - - - EXAMPLE # 3. USING AN ALREADY CREATED FILE FOR INPUT.
C - - - FILE IS OPENED IN SHARED MODE SO OTHER USERS CAN ACCESS
C - - - THE FILE AT THE SAME TIME.
C
        DEFINE FILE 1, (ITOT,256,U,IPTR)
        OPEN (UNIT=1,NAME='PHONE.DAT',TYPE='OLD',ACCESS='DIRECT',
      *      RECORDSIZE=128,SHARED)

C - - - EXAMPLE # 4. SEQUENTIAL DISK OUTPUT FILE FOR A REPORT FILE.
C - - - FILE CONTAINS CARRIAGE CONTROL CHARACTERS IN THE RECORDS,
C - - - SINCE THE FILE IS BUILT AS A REPORT FILE (TYPE FORTRAN).
C - - - NO DEFINE FILE IS NEEDED SINCE THIS IS A SEQUENTIAL FILE.
C
        OPEN (UNIT=1,NAME='REPORT.FIL',TYPE='NEW',
      *      CARRIAGECONTROL='FORTRAN')
```

The PDP-11 CLOSE Statement

The CLOSE statement disconnects a file from a file unit number. The file is no longer available to the program unless it is reopened. A system abort error will occur if you attempt to read or write a file that has been closed (or not opened).

The general form of the PDP-11 CLOSE statement is:

CLOSE (UNIT=u [,DISPOSE=p] [,ERR=s])

where:

[ ]	represent optional specifications.
u	is the logical file unit number.
p	is a literal that determines the disposition of the file. The possible values are: 'SAVE', 'KEEP', 'DELETE', and 'PRINT'. 'SAVE' and 'KEEP' are synonyms; if either are specified, the file is retained after it is closed. If 'DELETE' is specified, the file is deleted after it is closed. If the 'PRINT' value is used, the file is printed by the system line printer after it is closed. If the DISPOSE parameter, p, is omitted, default values are provided. The default value for a file opened as a 'SCRATCH' file is 'DELETE'. The default value for all other files is 'SAVE'.
s	is an executable statement label.

Examples of the PDP-11 CLOSE statement are:

```
C --- EXAMPLE # 1. THE FILE ON UNIT 3 IS CLOSED AND PRINTED.
C
      CLOSE (UNIT=3,DISPOSE='PRINT')

C --- EXAMPLE # 2. THE FILE IS DELETED AFTER IT IS CLOSED.
C --- IF AN ERROR OCCURS DURING THE CLOSE, CONTROL IS
C --- TRANSFERRED TO STATEMENT LABEL 200.
C
      CLOSE (UNIT=KFILE,DISPOSE='DELETE',ERR=200)
```

IBM Requirements for File Retention

A temporary disk file may be created on IBM computers by including only a proper Data Definition (DD) JCL card. To retain a created disk file on IBM computers, however, a special utility program called IEFBR14 must be run to allocate the required space and assign a directory name.

Your instructor will assist you in constructing any required JCL statements you might need to use disk files on your computer system.

18.9 SUMMARY

This chapter exposed you to magnetic disk operations and the statements used to manipulate disk files. Magnetic disk is widely used on computer systems for the on-line storage of programs (both system and application) and data files. Magnetic disk units can store over 300 million characters on each unit. Some disk units can store up to as much as 650 million characters. Data transfer between memory is also very high. Most drives can transfer over 800,000 characters per second.

A disk is comprised of one or more circular plates called platters, which are made of highly polished metal and covered on both sides with a magnetic oxide coating for the data recording. Data is stored on these platters in concentric circles known as tracks. Tracks in the same vertical plane on different platters constitute a cylinder. The cylinder concept in storing data is very important, because it reduces the movement of the read/write heads and thus reduces the access time for retrieving data.

Many disk drives, especially the older ones, use removable packs for the data storage; so disk packs can be kept in a library like magnetic tapes and used when needed. That is, a pack does not have to be mounted all the time; so drives can be shared by various application files between their use. Modern disk drives use a "Winchester" technology, in which the read/write heads, recording mechanisms, and disks are contained in a sealed unit. This provides greater data reliability because of less exposure to contaminated air.

Section 18.2 presented an overview of the sequential READ/WRITE and other I/O statements that can be used to manipulate sequential disk files. Section 18.3 discussed random file processing on magnetic disk. Random file processing means that a file is organized in a random manner, so that a record may be directly accessed without searching the file in a linear manner. Random-accessed files must be stored on a direct-access device. There are six direct-access I/O statements in FORTRAN: 1) the formatted random READ, 2) unformatted random READ, 3) formatted random WRITE, 4) unformatted random WRITE, 5) DEFINE FILE, and 6) FIND statements.

Section 18.4 explained the DEFINE FILE statement. This statement must be used with IBM, Univac, WATFIV, DEC PDP-11, and a few other systems to identify a random organized disk file and its characteristics. The DEFINE FILE statement specifies the maximum number of records, the size of each record, whether formatted or unformatted data is being used, and an associated variable that serves as an index (record) pointer to a record.

Section 18.5 discussed the formatted and unformatted random READ statements used with random organized disk files. These statements are similar to the formatted and unformatted sequential READ statements, but the record number of the data record to be read/written must be given after the file unit number. The desired record number may be given as an integer constant, integer expression, or with the associated variable identified in the DEFINE FILE statement. Each time a random READ statement is executed, the system automatically increments the associated variable by one. A random organized file contains N number of records, each of which has a record number (from 1 to N) depending on its relative location in the file.

Section 18.6 discussed the formatted and unformatted random WRITE statements. As with the random READ statements, the random WRITE statements must include an integer constant, integer expression, or associated variable after the file unit number to identify the record number of the desired record to be written. The associated variable is automatically incremented by one by the system after each execution of the random WRITE statement.

Section 18.7 explained the FIND statement. This statement simply locates the indicated record and causes the read/write heads to be positioned at the track for that record. No data is read or written with the FIND statement. It is used to speed up execution by having the read/write heads pre-positioned at the next record to be read or written when control returns to the READ or WRITE statement in a processing loop.

Section 18.8 presented the format of the random READ and WRITE statements for the CDC 6000/Cyber, Honeywell 6000, Burroughs 6000 and 7000, Univac 1100, Hewlett Packard 3000, and DEC PDP-11 series computer systems. This section also discussed the OPEN and CLOSE statements used on DEC PDP-11 series systems.

18.10 TERMS

Terms, concepts, and statements you should become familiar with in this chapter are:

access time	disk drive	random file organization
associated variable	FIND statement	random READ statement
cylinder	on-line access	random WRITE statement
DEFINE FILE statement	platters	spindle
direct-access device	random access	Winchester drive
direct-access file		

18.11 REVIEW QUESTIONS

1. What is the primary value of magnetic disk?
2. Random access files must be read in a sequential manner. (True/False)
3. All the tracks in the same position on different platters constitute a _____ .
4. Magnetic disk may be used to store sequential files as well as random files. (True/False)
5. The statement used to position a sequential disk file back to the beginning of the file is the _____ .
6. The statement used to define a random access file and its characteristics on an IBM 360/370 is the
   _____ .
7. When reading/writing to a random access file, an index value must be given to denote the position of a specific record. (True/False)
8. Random access files may be written only under format control. (True/False)
9. The statement used to speed up the access of a particular record by prepositioning the read/write heads over the proper track is the _____ .

18.12 EXERCISES

1. Write a DEFINE FILE statement to identify a random disk file written on file unit 3. The associated variable is to be KPTR. Data is to be transferred under format control only. The maximum number of records is 175 and the maximum size of each record is 110 bytes.
2. Write a DEFINE FILE statement to identify a random disk file written on file unit 10. Data may be transferred with or without format control. The file will contain a maximum of 90 records, each to contain 80 bytes. The variable JRCD is the associated variable.
3. Write the READ statement to read the 26th record from a random disk file on file unit 10 and transfer the variables X, Y, and Z without format control.
4. Write a READ statement to read the 35th record from a random disk file on file unit 3 and transfer the variables A, B, and C without format control.
5. Construct a WRITE statement to transfer the values of the variables I, J, K, and L to record position N under format control. Each variable is to be written as a three-digit integer on file unit 9 set up as a random file. Use statement number 99 as the FORMAT statement number.
6. Construct a WRITE statement to transfer the values of the variables A, B, C, and D to record positions K-1 (K minus 1) under format control. Each variable is to be written under an F6.2 format specification on file unit 8 set up as a random file. Use statement number 99 as the FORMAT statement number.
7. Write the statement to find record K on file unit 2, which is set up as a random file.
8. Write the statement to find record N on file unit 4, which is set up as a random file.
9. How many records will be read with the following READ?

READ (4 ′ 14, 98) I,J,K,L
98 FORMAT (I3)

10. How many records will be read with the following READ?

READ (8 ′ 21, 97) W,X,Y,Z
97 FORMAT (2F6.2,F5.1)

11. How many records will be written with the following WRITE?

WRITE (8 ′ J, 87) I,J,K,L,M
87 FORMAT (2I5)

12. How many records will be written with the following WRITE?

WRITE (9 ′ K, 96) W,X,Y,Z
96 FORMAT (F7.1,F6.3)

18.13 PROGRAMMING PROBLEMS

1. Write a program to read a card file containing records of student data as follows:

Record Positions	Field Description
1–20	Name
21–29	Social security number
30–33	Student number (Form is NNNN)
34–39	Class (Form is alphanumeric)
40–42	Section (Form is NNN)
43–44	Blank
45–47	Grade 1 (Form is NNN)
48–50	Grade 2 (Form is NNN)
51–53	Grade 3 (Form is NNN)
54–56	Grade 4 (Form is NNN)
57–59	Grade 5 (Form is NNN)
60–62	Grade 6 (Form is NNN)
63–80	Blank

Create a sequential disk file. Assume that the records are in sequence by name within section within class. Write the input record to disk in the same format specification as read for input. Use a trailer card with a value of 999999999 for SSAN to indicate an end-of-file on the card input file.

2. Write a program to read the sequential disk file created in problem 1 and compute each student's grade average. Print the student data along with the computed average.

The printer output specifications are:

Print Positions	Field Description
1–20	Name
26–34	SSAN
39–42	Student number
47–52	Class
57–59	Section
70–72	Grade 1
79–80	Grade 2
86–88	Grade 3
94–96	Grade 4
102–104	Grade 5
110–112	Grade 6
118–123	Average

Include an appropriate report heading and column headings.

3. Write a program to read a card file with records of student data as described in problem 1. Create a random disk file using Student Number as the key (disk address) for each record. Assume a maximum of 300 student records with student numbers from 1–300. Write a disk record that is formatted in the same specifications as the card input record.

4. Write a program to read a card file with only the student numbers to serve as the keys to access the desired records in the random file created in problem 3. The student number will be read as an I4. Read the proper disk record and then compute each student's grade average. List each record with the newly computed average under the same printer specifications as given in problem 2. Use a trailer card with a value of 9999 for student number to indicate the end of file for the card input file.

5. Read an employee file of 50 card records and load them to sequential disk. The card records are laid out as follows:

Record Positions	Field Description
1–25	Name
26–30	Employee number (Form is NNNNN)
31–32	Age (Form is NN)
33–34	Department (Form is NN)
35–36	Years with company (Form is NN)
37–39	Pay grade (Form is NNN)
40–46	Monthly salary (Form is NNNN.NN)

Write the disk records in an unformatted (binary) form.

6. Read the sequential disk file created in problem 5 and prepare a company roster of all employees with more than 30 years of service with the company.

The printer output specifications are:

Print Positions	Field Description
1–25	Name
31–35	Employee number
41–42	Age
48–49	Department code
55–56	Years with company
62–64	Pay grade code
70–76	Salary

Include an appropriate report heading and column headings.

7. Read a file containing records with information on the status of the different buildings on a military installation. Each record will contain the following data:

Record Positions	Field Description
1–4	Building number
5–30	Type of activity/function utilizing the building (alphanumeric)
31–34	Telephone extension of building monitor
35–40	Type structure (alphanumeric)
41–80	Misc. information (alphanumeric)

A trailer record with a value of 9999 for building number is used to indicate the end of file. Create a random disk file using the building number as the disk record key address. Write the file in an unformatted (binary) form. Assume a maximum of 500 buildings.

8. Using the unformatted random disk file created in problem 7 and a transaction file with building number in columns 1–4, prepare a status report for those buildings included in the transaction file. A trailer record with a value of 9999 for building number is used to indicate the end of the input file.

The printer output specifications are:

Print Positions	Field Description
1–4	Building number
10–35	Type of activity/function
41–44	Building monitor telephone extension
50–55	Type of structure
61–100	Misc. information

Include an appropriate report and column headings.

Additional FORTRAN Statements and Features

19

19.1 INTRODUCTION TO ADDITIONAL FORTRAN STATEMENTS AND FEATURES

The additional statements and features in ANSI FORTRAN 66 that have not been discussed are included in this chapter to provide complete coverage of the language. Although the student programmer may find little use for these statements and features, they do serve an important role in many specialized and production applications.

The PAUSE statement permits the programmer to stop the program temporarily when certain specific actions need to be taken before continuing. The ASSIGN and ASSIGNED GO TO statements are additional control statements to selectively transfer control of execution in a program. The Arithmetic IF provides a three-way branch based on an arithmetic expression. Object time format specifications provide a great deal of flexibility in the reading of the same data file under different format specifications. These specifications can be provided during the execution of a program, thus eliminating the need to change and recompile the program.

There are several additional nonstandard FORTRAN 66 statements with which you should be familiar. The NAMELIST statement is a convenient way to read and write a list of variables without an accompanying FORMAT statement. It is often used in scientific applications where little I/O is required. The DECODE and ENCODE statements allow memory-to-memory formatting of items. The IMPLICIT statements allow a programmer to specify the type of variables based on the initial letter of their symbolic names.

19.2 THE PAUSE STATEMENT

The PAUSE statement is used to stop the program execution temporarily, allowing the computer operator to set a sense switch (a switch on the computer) or to mount a magnetic tape or a disk pack. An octal number (consisting of the digits 0–7) is usually included after the keyword to communicate the desired operations to the operator. This coded number is displayed on the operator console along with the word "PAUSE", so that it can be seen by the operator. If the operator is not familiar with the coded number, he can refer to the job "run book", which describes the required operation to take for specific numbers. After the desired operation is accomplished, the operator presses the start button or sends a message that causes the computer to resume execution. Execution of the program then continues at the next statement after the PAUSE. Figure 19.1 gives the general form of the PAUSE statement.

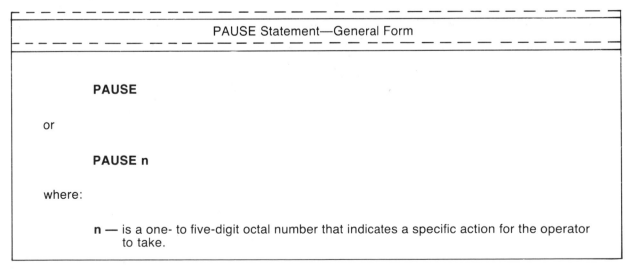

PAUSE Statement—General Form

    PAUSE

or

    PAUSE n

where:

    n — is a one- to five-digit octal number that indicates a specific action for the operator
        to take.

Figure 19.1 General notation of the PAUSE statement

Following is an example of the use of the PAUSE statement.

READ (5,99) NUM,A,B
99 FORMAT (I5,2F5.2)
IF (NUM .EQ. 1) PAUSE 134

The octal number 134 might mean that the operator is to mount a tape file needed by the program when the variable NUM is equal to one. Some FORTRAN compilers allow a literal constant to be displayed after the word PAUSE to provide a more meaningful message.

Student programmers usually do not require any operator intervention during the running of their job; so the PAUSE statement should not be used in your program. In fact, the WATFIV compiler ignores (skips) any PAUSE statement in a program and continues at the next statement.

19.3 THE ASSIGN AND ASSIGNED GO TO STATEMENTS

The Assigned GO TO statement is very similar to the Computed GO TO; control is transferred to one of several alternative statements in the program. However, control is transferred to a specific statement based on the **statement number** assigned to an integer variable. The ASSIGN statement is used in conjunction with the Assigned GO TO to assign a statement number to the integer variable. Figure 19.2 gives the general form of the ASSIGN statement.

Examples are:

ASSIGN 46 TO K
27 ASSIGN 238 TO NSTMT

The ASSIGN statement must be executed (to assign the desired statement number to the variable) before the Assigned GO TO statement is executed. The Assigned GO TO causes a conditional transfer of control to the statement number last assigned to the integer variable by an ASSIGN statement. Figure 19.3 gives the general form of the Assigned GO TO statement.

Examples are:

GO TO K, (10,5,147)
83 GO TO NSTMT, (20,40,30,10)

Note the syntax requirement of a comma to separate the integer variable and the beginning left parenthesis.

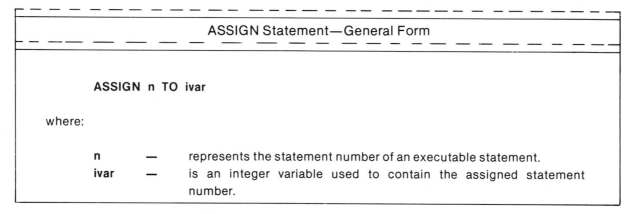

Figure 19.2 General notation of the ASSIGN statement

GO TO ivar, (n₁,n₂,. . .,nₙ)

where:

> **ivar** — represents an integer variable containing the statement number assigned by the ASSIGN statement.
>
> **(n₁,. . .,nₙ)** — are statement numbers of executable statements in the program.

Figure 19.3 General notation of the Assigned GO TO statement

An example of using these two statements is:

ASSIGN 37 TO K

_____

_____

GO TO K, (18,56,37,3)

The statement number 37 is assigned to the variable K. After executing the Assigned GO TO, control is transferred to statement number 37, and processing will resume at that statement. The statement number assigned to the integer variable must be for an executable statement. The position of the statement numbers in the Assigned GO TO is not important, unlike the Computed GO TO.

You cannot use the arithmetic Assignment statement to assign a statement number. For example:

K = 37
GO TO K, (18,56,37,3)

is invalid. Assigning a statement number with the ASSIGN statement is not the same thing as an arithmetic assignment. The statement number must be assigned with the ASSIGN statement.

Normally, more than one ASSIGN statement is used in conjunction with the Assigned GO TO statement. Suppose you wish to sum two variables if an input code is equal to 1, but you wish to compute the product of the two variables if the input code is equal to 2. (Otherwise, a value of zero is assumed.) A sample routine, which uses the ASSIGN and Assigned GO TO statements to perform this logic, is:

```
   READ (5,99) K,X,Y
99 FORMAT (I2,2F5.2)
   RESLT = 0.0
   ASSIGN 30 TO LOC
   IF (K .EQ. 1) ASSIGN 10 TO LOC
   IF (K .EQ. 2) ASSIGN 20 TO LOC
   GO TO LOC, (10,20,30)
10 RESLT = X + Y
   GO TO 30
20 RESLT = X * Y
30 CONTINUE
```

Once the integer variable has been assigned a statement number by the ASSIGN statement, the variable cannot be used in any arithmetic expression. The variable can be used only in an Assigned GO TO statement. The statement number assigned to the integer variable must be one of the statement numbers tested in the Assigned GO TO. If the variable is assigned a statement number other than one of those given in the Assigned GO TO, control continues at the next statement. This statement immediately following the Assigned GO TO should have a statement number, since otherwise it can never be referenced in the program, and a syntax warning message will result.

The only advantages in the use of the Assigned GO TO over the use of the Computed GO TO are small savings in execution time and storage locations. However, the Computed GO TO is more popular and more in accordance with structured programming. The Computed GO TO is usually simpler, more convenient, and allows more flexibility, since the value read for an input variable can be used directly by the computer to make the test of which statement to transfer.

19.4 THE ARITHMETIC IF STATEMENT

The Arithmetic IF statement is used to test an arithmetic expression and to provide branching to one of three possible program statements. The Arithmetic IF has an arithmetic expression in parentheses following the keyword IF. Three statement numbers follow the closing parenthesis to provide the statements that control can be transferred to, based on the evaluation of the arithmetic expression. If the resulting value of the expression is negative, a branch is made to the first statement number; if the value is zero, the branch is made to the second statement number; if the value is positive, the branch is made to the third statement number. The general form of the Arithmetic IF statement is illustrated in figure 19.4.

Examples of the Arithmetic IF are:

$$\textbf{IF (R) 100, 200, 300}$$
$$\textbf{IF (KOUNT} - \textbf{10) 1,1,2}$$
$$\textbf{28 IF (A / T} - \textbf{S), 3,5,3}$$
$$\textbf{IF ((N / 2) * (J} - \textbf{6)) 7,34,34}$$

From these examples you see that the statement numbers may either all be different or any two can be the same. The logic required determines which form you use. For example, if you wish to execute a loop ten times, you would probably construct the Arithmetic IF statement according to the second example. A counter would be kept and 1 added to it each pass through the loop. If the counter was less than or equal to 10, you would get a negative or zero result and branch back to statement number 1. When the counter is greater than 10, statement number 2 would be executed next.

Arithmetic IF Statement—General Form

IF (arith exp) n_1, n_2, n_3

where:

arith exp — represents any arithmetic expression permitted in FORTRAN.

n_1 — is a statement number assigned to an executable statement to which control will be transferred if the value of the arithmetic expression is less than zero (negative).

n_2 — is a statement number assigned to an executable statement to which control will be transferred if the value of the arithmetic expression is equal to zero.

n_3 — is a statement number assigned to an executable statement to which control will be transferred if the value of the arithmetic expression is greater than zero (positive).

Figure 19.4 General notation of the Arithmetic IF statement

You may wonder why the Arithmetic IF is available in addition to the Logical IF statement. The Arithmetic IF can provide branching for up to three different statements, is sometimes easier to use, and is often more efficient. However, it is not usually accepted in structured programming; so the Logical IF is recommended over the Arithmetic IF unless a need exists for a three-way branch.

The Arithmetic IF is flowcharted as follows when a three-way branch is used.

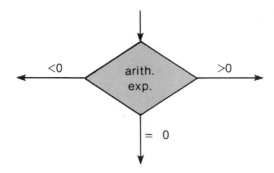

CDC also has a two-way branch on the Arithmetic IF statement. Its form is:

IF (arithmetic expression) n₁,n₂

where n_1 and n_2 are statement labels. If the arithmetic expression is not equal to zero, a branch is made to statement label n_1. If the arithmetic expression is equal to zero, a branch is made to statement label n_2. For example,

IF (M − 100) 30,40

If M is not equal to 100, and the resulting expression is unequal to zero, control is transferred to statement label 30. If M is equal to 100, and the resulting expression is equal to zero, control is transferred to statement label 40.

19.5 OBJECT-TIME FORMAT SPECIFICATIONS

Sometimes a user will change the location or even the form of data fields in input records, which will require you to change the program format specifications accordingly. When you change the program, you must also recompile it, so that the program execution will contain the new changes. It would be nice, however, to have the flexibility to change format specifications for new forms of data without having to recompile the program.

What is needed is a way to give the format specifications to the computer at execution time. **Object-time format specifications** provide this capability. The format specifications are read as alphanumeric data and used to provide the form of the input or even output data with no modification of the existing program. Object time format specifications are also known as **variable formats** or **execution time formats**.

To accomplish object time format specifications, a one-dimensional array must be established to hold the format declarations. The specifications are then read from a data record into this array. The format specifications are punched in the data record, with the first character being the beginning left parenthesis. The statement number and the keyword FORMAT are not included in the record. The entire format specifications that would normally be included within the required pair of parentheses are punched into the data record and read into the array with the alphanumeric (A) format code.

Suppose the input specifications of the input record are:

A punched in card columns 1–5 in the form NN.NN
B punched in card columns 6–9 in the form NN.N
K punched in card columns 13–14 in the form NN

The input specifications, therefore are:

F5.2,F4.1,3X,I2

These specifications would be included within the normal set of parentheses and punched in a data record as follows:

$$(F5.2,F4.1,3X,I2)$$

Now the specifications need to be read from the data record into the array, which we shall call FARRAY. There are seventeen characters in the format specifications, so FARRAY must be declared to be at least five elements. That is, if each alphanumeric element can contain a maximum of four characters, then five array elements are needed. It is recommended that the array be established with more than five elements, to allow for reading longer object-time format specifications later under the same array name. So let us establish FARRAY as a twenty-element array, which allows the reading of an entire card of format specifications. Since the remainder of the data record is blank, there is no harm in having more elements than needed.

The statements to dimension FARRAY and load the format specifications in it are:

DIMENSION FARRAY(20)
READ (5,99) FARRAY
99 FORMAT (20A4)

Execution of the READ statement would load the specifications from the data record into the array FARRAY, which can now be used to provide object-time format specifications. The array FARRAY would have the following values in the array elements:

F(1) would contain (F5.
F(2) would contain 2,F4
F(3) would contain .1,3
F(4) would contain X,I2
F(5) would contain)

and elements 6 through 20 would contain blanks.

To use the format specifications loaded into the array, the array name is substituted for the FORMAT statement number in the READ or WRITE statement. That is, the array name takes the place of the usual format statement number and supplies the format specifications. For example:

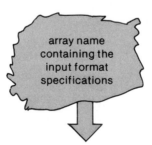

array name
containing the
input format
specifications

READ (5, FARRAY) A,B,K

The array name FARRAY contains the input format specifications and tells the computer how to read the three variables A, B, and K.

An array name must be used to store the format specifications, even if the array consists of only one element. The array name must not be subscripted in the READ or WRITE statements when used to refer to object-time specifications. For example:

READ (5, FARRAY(I)) A,B,K

would be invalid and cause a syntax error.

Object-time format specifications allow you to write programs of a very general nature. They can be quite powerful and timesaving where the same program is used to process data with different format specifications. A program can even be made to selectively modify parts of a format statement by reading in parts of the format statement through specific array elements. Thus, the arrays used to hold the object-time format specifications can be altered element-by-element.

NAMELIST Statement—General Form

```
    NAMELIST /listname₁/ varlist₁, . . ., /listnameₙ/ varlistₙ
```

where:

        listname   —   each **listname** represents a NAMELIST name which refers to a group of variables and/or array names.

        varlist   —   each **varlist** represents a list of variables and/or array names each separated by commas to be used in NAMELIST input/output operations.

Figure 19.5 General notation of the NAMELIST statement

19.6   LANGUAGE EXTENSIONS IN FORTRAN DIALECTS (THE NAMELIST, DECODE, ENCODE, AND IMPLICIT STATEMENTS)

The NAMELIST Statement and Operations

Perhaps you have wished that a name could be assigned to a list of variables so that the list name could be used to represent the group of variables. This would certainly provide a shorter means of supplying the list of variables, much to be preferred over the use of an I/O list in READ and WRITE statements that continually refer to the same variables. The NAMELIST statement provides this ability.

The NAMELIST Statement. In addition to representing a group of variables by one name, the NAMELIST statement also provides other advantages. The variable name is printed as a literal title preceding the output value of each variable. This capability greatly simplifies the identification of the output results. The input values for the list of variables are also read without having to describe the data fields with FORMAT statements. Thus, the NAMELIST statement provides an input and output capability that is virtually format-free.

The NAMELIST statement declares a name to represent a particular list of variable or array names. The list name is formed in the same way as other symbolic names and is enclosed in a pair of slashes. The general form of the NAMELIST statement is given in figure 19.5.

Examples of the NAMELIST statement follow:

$$\text{NAMELIST / LIST1/ A, B, C, I, J}$$
$$\text{NAMELIST / L1/ X, Y, Z, / L2/ M, N}$$

In the first example the variables A, B, C, I, and J are assigned to the list name of LIST1. In the second example the variables X, Y, and Z are assigned to the list name of L1, while the variables M and N are assigned to the list name of L2.

The NAMELIST statement is a specification statement. It should precede all executable instructions and any statement functions in the program. DIMENSION statements, if used, must precede the NAMELIST statement. A single NAMELIST statement (which could include continuation cards) or multiple NAMELIST statements may be used in a program.

The variable or array names in the list may be any symbolic name allowed in FORTRAN, but the variable or array names may not be used for any other I/O operations in the program, only for NAMELIST use. That is, a variable or array appearing in a NAMELIST list must be used only in a NAMELIST read or write operation and cannot be used to read or write data under format control. The following paragraphs explain and illustrate how the NAMELIST statement is used in a FORTRAN program.

NAMELIST Input Operations. The syntax of the READ statement is different from the normal construction of the READ statement you have been using. The statement number used to reference a FORMAT statement is replaced by the NAMELIST name. Also, no I/O list is included on the READ statement. The syntax of the READ statement used with NAMELIST input operations is:

READ (unit, listname)

An example of this type of READ is:

READ (5, LIST1)

The input data records must include the NAMELIST name and the variable names and/or the array elements in the NAMELIST that are being read. Each variable is separated from its corresponding value by an $=$. An &END must follow the last value to signal the end of the input variables. The NAMELIST name, preceded by an &, must appear at the beginning of the first data record.

The READ statement gives the name of a list, which must correspond to the name of a list in the data record. If the list names do not agree, an error message will be given and the program discontinued.

A short FORTRAN program to illustrate the I/O operations of the NAMELIST capability follows.

```
C *** EXAMPLE OF NAMELIST INPUT AND OUTPUT
      DIMENSION K(3)
      NAMELIST /GROUP1/ A, B, K, SUM1, SUM2
      READ (5, GROUP1)
      SUM1 = A + B
      SUM2 = K(1) + K(2) + K(3)
      WRITE (6, GROUP1)
      STOP
      END
```

The input data records might be:

```
&GROUP1 A = 15.6,  B = 7.83,  K(1) = 10,  K(2) = 85,
K(3) =  - 12 &END
```

When the data records are read, the input values will be stored at the variables shown on the card, provided that those variable names have been defined as part of the NAMELIST list. Not all the variables or arrays in the NAMELIST statement need to appear in the input data.

The input data must be in a special form in order to be read using a NAMELIST. The rules which pertain to the format of the NAMELIST input data are:

1. The first character in each record to be read must be blank.
2. The second character in the first record must be an & (ampersand), immediately followed by the NAMELIST name.
3. The NAMELIST name must be followed by a blank and must not contain any embedded blanks.
4. This name is followed by data items separated by commas.
5. The form of the data items in an input record is:

    Symbolic name = constant   For example: **AVAL = 13.79**

    The symbolic name may be an array element or a variable name. Subscripts must be integer constants. The form of the constant must be consistent with the type of variable. The constants may be integer, real, literal, complex, or logical. (If constants are logical, they may be in the form: T or .TRUE., and F or .FALSE.).
6. Two forms may be given for the values of arrays. The array name may be specified, followed by the set of constants (each separated by a comma) for the array. The number of constants must be less than or equal to the number of elements in the array. Successive occurrences of the same constant can be represented in the form **i*** constant, where **i** is an integer value specifying the number of times the constant is to be repeated. The second form for specifying array values is to list each array element, followed by its respective value.
7. The variable and array names specified in the input data set must appear in the NAMELIST list, but the order is not significant.

8. Each data record must begin with a blank followed by a complete variable, array name, array element, or constant (that is, they cannot be split between cards).
9. Embedded blanks are not permitted in names or constants. Trailing blanks after integers and exponents are treated as zeroes.
10. Within a data record, it is not mandatory to include values for all variables/array names that appear in the NAMELIST statement.
11. The end of a data group is signaled by &END.

Now let us look at the output operations of the NAMELIST.

NAMELIST Output Operations. The syntax of the WRITE statement is also different from that of the normal WRITE statement using format control. The NAMELIST name replaces the statement number used to represent a FORMAT statement. The I/O list is eliminated. The syntax of the WRITE statement used with NAMELIST output operations is:

WRITE (unit, listname)

An example of this type of WRITE is:

WRITE (6, GROUP1)

The output results from our sample NAMELIST program would appear as:

```
&GROUP1
A = 0.14600000E 02, B = 0.78300000E 01, K = 10, 85, - 12, SUM1 = 0.23430000E 02,
SUM2 = 0.83000000E 02
&END
```

The format of the values for NAMELIST output operations is as follows:

1. The first output record will contain only the &(starting in position 2) and the NAMELIST name.
2. Subsequent records will contain the variables and array names followed by their values for all the items in the NAMELIST list.
3. All variables and array names specified in the NAMELIST list and their respective values are output, each according to its type. Real values are written in an exponential form.
4. The last record will contain only &END starting in position 2.

The above description of the NAMELIST statement and operations pertains solely to the IBM, WATFOR, WATFIV, and B6000 compilers. The Control Data 6000, Univac 1100, Honeywell 6000, and Digital Equipment PDP-10 FORTRAN compilers use a dollar sign ($) instead of the & to denote namelist data.

The DECODE Statement

Sometimes you may want to change data read under one format specification into different format specifications with new variables. For example, suppose a record was read as all characters (maybe a 20A4), and you wish to break it apart into different fields, such as treating the first five positions as an integer variable. Is there a way it can be done? Yes. The DECODE statement allows you to reformat character data stored in memory. This is often referred to as "memory-to-memory formatting." The Honeywell 6000, Univac 1100, and DEC PDP-11 DECODE and ENCODE statements will be explained in this subsection. The DECODE statement is not available on FORTRAN 66 and FORTRAN 77 compilers.

Honeywell 6000 DECODE Statement. The DECODE statement causes the characters in a character string to be converted into the specified data items. The general form of the Honeywell DECODE statement is given as follows:

DECODE (a, f) iolist

where:

a	is a character variable, character array element, or an array of any type. **a** provides the data item(s) to be converted into numeric form.
f	is the statement label of a FORMAT statement that contains the format specifications for the form of the new numeric items.
iolist	is the list of data items at which the converted values are to be stored.

The DECODE statement takes a character variable, character array element, or array and converts the characters into other format specifications according to a given FORMAT statement. The format specifications and items in the DECODE I/O list should not require more characters than given in the character variable or array. Let's look at two examples. The first example using a character variable is:

```
        CHARACTER * 2 VARX
        VARX = ' 3'
        DECODE (VARX, 97) K
    97  FORMAT (I2)
        . . .
```

The DECODE statement converts the value of VARX (the character string of ' 3') into a two-digit integer (format code of I2) and assigns the numeric value of 3 to the variable K. The value of the variable VARX is not changed.

The second example is to read a FORTRAN statement on a card-image record as all characters and then break it into the different FORTRAN statement fields. An array will be used to store the record in character form.

```
        CHARACTER * 4 CRDREC(20)
        CHARACTER CONT*1, STMT*66, ID*8
        INTEGER SEQNR
        READ (5, 99) CRDREC
    99  FORMAT (20A4)
        DECODE (CRDREC, 98) SEQNR, CONT, STMT, ID
    98  FORMAT (I5, A1, A66, A8)
        . . .
```

This example reads a card-image record representing a FORTRAN statement format as a twenty-element array named CRDREC. (The record could have been read as an 80-character length variable, but an array is used for illustration of decoding an array.) The DECODE statement divides the eighty characters in the array CRDREC into four new variables. The sequence number in positions 1–5 is stored in the variable SEQNR as a five digit integer; the single character in position 6 is stored in the variable CONT; the next 66 characters, representing the FORTRAN statement, are stored in the variable STMT; and the last eight characters are stored in the variable ID.

The Honeywell ENCODE Statement. The ENCODE statement works in just the reverse of the DECODE statement. The ENCODE statement is used to convert numeric data items into character-type items. The character item (character variable or character array element) into which the numeric data is to be converted is given within the ENCODE statement. A FORMAT statement number is given after this character item to indicate the format specification for encoding the numeric item. The general form of the ENCODE statement is given as follows:

ENCODE (a, f) iolist

where:

a	is a character variable, character array element, or an array of any type. **a** specifies the storage location(s) at which the converted items are to be stored.
f	is the statement label of a FORMAT statement that contains the format specifications for encoding the data item(s).
iolist	is the list of numeric data items in memory to be converted into character data items.

An example of the ENCODE statement is:

```
        CHARACTER * 4 VARX
        K = 3
        ENCODE (VARX, 98) K
    98  FORMAT (I4)
        . . .
```

The numeric value of K (the value 3) is converted into a character value of ƀƀƀ3 (where ƀ is a blank) and stored in the variable VARX.

Univac 1100 and DEC PDP-11 DECODE and ENCODE Statements. The general form of the DECODE and ENCODE statements on the Univac and DEC PDP-11 compilers are different from the Honeywell general form but basically similar to each other. They are:

$$\text{DECODE (c, f, b [,ERR = s]) iolist}$$

and

$$\text{ENCODE (c, f, b [,ERR = s]) iolist}$$

where:

[ ]	represents an optional specification.
c	is an unsigned integer constant or expression whose value specifies the number of characters (bytes) that are to be converted or that are to result from the conversion.
f	is the statement label of a FORMAT statement that contains the format specifications. If the format specifies more than one record, an error condition arises.
b	is the name of a variable, array element, or array. In the DECODE statement, **b** *contains* the characters that are to be converted into internal format. In the ENCODE statement, **b** *receives* the characters once they have been converted into a character format.
s	is an executable statement label. Control will be transferred to the statement label if an error is detected in the execution of the statement.
iolist	is the list of variables, array elements, or array. In the DECODE statement, the **iolist** *receives* the data that has been converted from characters to a different internal format. In the ENCODE statement, the **iolist** *contains* the data that is to be converted to characters.

Univac 1100 allows one extra parameter after the **b** parameter (before the ERR = parameter). The parameter is the **t** parameter; it must be an integer variable or array element that, upon completion of the DECODE or ENCODE operation, will contain the number of characters actually scanned or generated during the execution of the DECODE or ENCODE statement, respectively.

Examples are:

```
        CHARACTER *4 X(3)
        INTEGER K(3)
        DATA X(1)/'1234', X(2)/'5678'/, X(3)/'9009'/
        DECODE (12, 99, X) K
    99  FORMAT (3I4)
        . . .
```

Execution of the DECODE statement causes the 12 characters in array X to be converted to integer format (according to FORMAT statement number 99) and stored in array K as follows:

$$K(1) = 1234$$
$$K(2) = 5678$$
$$K(3) = 9009$$

The next example decodes character items into real variables.

```
        CHARACTER *5 A(3)
        DATA A(1)/'001.2', A(2)/'0034.5', A(3)/'0067.8/
        DECODE (15, 98, A) X, Y, Z
    98  FORMAT (3F5.1)
        . . .
```

Execution of the DECODE statement would cause the following values to be stored in X, Y, and Z.

$$X = 1.2$$
$$Y = 34.5$$
$$Z = 67.8$$

An example of the ENCODE statement for Univac 1100 and PDP-11 FORTRAN is:

DIMENSION X(3)
A = 1.2
B = 23.4
C = 56.7
ENCODE (15, 98, X) A, B, C
98 FORMAT (3F5.2)
. . .

Execution of the ENCODE statement would cause the following results to be stored in the array X.

X(1) = '1.2 '
X(2) = '23.4 '
X(3) = '56.7 '

The DECODE statement is frequently used by many programmers. Its value lies in being able to read an input record as all characters to avoid a system I/O error. (Such errors are often caused when reading a numeric field that contains an illegal character, such as a letter or a special character.) Once the data has been input in character form, the programmer can decode it into numeric fields and variables.

IMPLICIT Statement

Another specification statement, available on many compilers, allows you to declare the type of variables and arrays by specifying that names beginning with certain letters be of a certain type. This statement is called the IMPLICIT statement. The individual letters are given in parentheses. A range of letters can be specified by giving the first and last letters separated by a minus sign ($-$). The general form of the IMPLICIT statement is given in figure 19.6.

Examples of the IMPLICIT statement are:

IMPLICIT INTEGER (A-D,S)
IMPLICIT REAL (J,M)
IMPLICIT REAL (K-N), INTEGER (R-W)
IMPLICIT INTEGER (E,H-J,T), REAL(N)

The first example declares all variables that begin with the letters A, B, C, D, and S to be type integer. The second example declares the variables that start with the letters J and M to be type real. The third example declares the variables that begin with K, L, M, and N to be type real, and the variables that begin with the letters R through W to be type integer. The fourth example declares the names beginning with the letters E, H, I, J, and T to be type integer and the variables starting with the letter N to be type real.

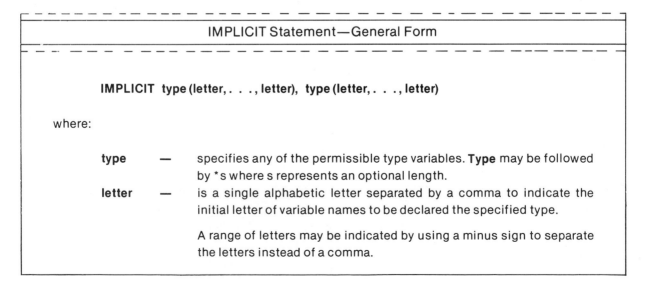

```
                    IMPLICIT Statement—General Form


            IMPLICIT  type (letter, . . ., letter),  type (letter, . . ., letter)

   where:

            type     —   specifies any of the permissible type variables. Type may be followed
                         by *s where s represents an optional length.
            letter   —   is a single alphabetic letter separated by a comma to indicate the
                         initial letter of variable names to be declared the specified type.

                         A range of letters may be indicated by using a minus sign to separate
                         the letters instead of a comma.
```

Figure 19.6 General notation of the IMPLICIT statement

Only one IMPLICIT statement is allowed in a FORTRAN program or subprogram. When the IMPLICIT statement is used, it must be the **first** statement in the program. The symbol $ is considered to be the last letter in the alphabet (i.e., after Z) on compilers that allow the $ to be used as a letter.

The IMPLICIT statement provides a fast and simple way of overriding the standard type and length of FORTRAN variables. But what if a programmer forgets that he or she has declared a certain letter to be a different type variable than established by the predefined convention of the FORTRAN language? The results could be disastrous and cause much time-consuming debugging effort. The IMPLICIT statement, therefore, is not recommended for changing the type of specific variable names based on the initial letters; use the Explicit Type statements to specifically identify the variables that are to be a certain type. When an IMPLICIT statement and an Explicit statement contradict each other in the case of specific first letters or variables, the Explicit statement overrides the specifications and determines the type of the variable.

Length Options and Initial Values with the Type Statements

Certain compilers permit the programmer to specify different length options and to include initial values of variables/arrays given in the Type statements. The length option refers to different size storage locations, such as a half-word or double-word, which can be specified for variables on some compilers. The initial values refer to assigning values to the given variables at compile time as performed in the DATA statement.

The IMPLICIT statement may also specify different length storage locations, but initial values cannot be specified in the IMPLICIT statement, since it only denotes the type of variables/arrays by their initial letter.

19.7 SUMMARY

Chapter 19 presented the remainder of the statements and features available in FORTRAN 66 and some of the additional statements available in FORTRAN IV. The FORTRAN 66 statements and features discussed were the PAUSE, ASSIGN, ASSIGNED GO TO, Arithmetic IF, and object-time format specification. The nonstandard FORTRAN 66 statements discussed were the NAMELIST, DECODE, ENCODE, and IMPLICIT statements.

Section 19.2 explained the PAUSE statement. Its function is to stop execution temporarily while the operator performs some function, such as setting a sense switch or mounting a tape or disk pack. This statement is rarely used with modern computers, since most of them do not use sense switches, and there are enough tape and disk drives available to preclude the need for operator intervention.

Section 19.3 discussed the ASSIGN and ASSIGNED GO TO statements. These statements are similar to the Computed GO TO statement, in that control is transferred to one of several alternative statements in the program. In the ASSIGN/Assigned GO TO, however, a statement label, rather than an integer value, must be assigned to a variable. These statements are rarely used by programmers.

Section 19.4 covered the Arithmetic IF statement, which is a carryover from FORTRAN II, where it was the only statement available to perform decision-making. The Logical IF statement was later introduced in FORTRAN IV. The Arithmetic IF statement tests a numeric expression for one of three possible results—negative, zero, or positive—and transfers control to one of three statement labels on the basis of that result. The Arithmetic IF statement is hardly used any more, since it violates top-down, structured programming principles, which express decisions as having one of two paths—true or false. You may, however, find the Arithmetic IF used in many older existing FORTRAN programs.

Section 19.5 explained object-time format specifications. Sometimes a programmer needs the flexibility to change the specifications in a FORMAT statement. Object-time format specifications eliminate the need to set up many different statements to handle alternative formats. They also enable the programmer to establish these specifications in an array that can be easily modified at execution time by assigning new values to the format specifications in the array elements. The array name that contains the format specifications is given in the READ or WRITE statements in place of the FORMAT statement number. Object-time format specifications are also known as variable formats or execution-time formats.

Section 19.6 discussed the remaining major statements used in FORTRAN IV. The NAMELIST statement is a handy statement to provide a name for a group of variables that may be read or written together. The system will display the variable or array name prior to printing the output value. This statement is not used frequently any more, since the modern dialects of FORTRAN, such as FORTRAN 77, allow literal strings in the format-free output statements.

The DECODE and ENCODE are two powerful statements available on a few FORTRAN IV compilers such as Honeywell, Univac, and Digital. It is not available in FORTRAN 66 or 77. The DECODE statement allows a programmer to convert character items in memory to a numeric form. The ENCODE statement provides the capability to convert numeric items in memory to a character form. This internal translation or conversion capability is known as memory-to-memory formatting, since the conversion of the items takes place in memory.

The IMPLICIT statement allows a programmer to declare the types of variables and arrays by the first letter of the symbolic name, making all variables and arrays beginning with a specified letter to be of a specific type. Most programmers, however, prefer to use the Explicit Type statement to type each individual variable or array name. The use of the IMPLICIT statement can be very dangerous, since a programmer often forgets that all names that begin with the specified letters will be a certain type and misuses a name for the wrong type of data.

All of the statements in ANSI FORTRAN 66 have now been covered in this text, providing complete coverage of this dialect. Most of the new features and statements in FORTRAN 77 have also been discussed. You will find a few new features on various computer systems dialect(s) of FORTRAN. With the knowledge of the statements covered in this text, however, you should have no problem in understanding existing programs and writing new ones.

19.8   REVIEW QUESTIONS

1. The PAUSE statement is used to permanently terminate the processing of a job. (True/False)
2. The Assigned GO TO statement causes a transfer of control to one of several statements based on the _____ _____ assigned to an integer variable.
3. The ASSIGN statement must be used before the Assigned GO TO to assign a statement number to the integer variable. (True/False)
4. The Arithmetic IF is used to provide a three-way branch based on the resulting value of an arithmetic expression. (True/False)
5. What is the main advantage of using execution-time formats?
6. The NAMELIST statement can be used to read data with or without format specifications. (True/False)
7. In addition to the output values, the NAMELIST feature also displays the variable name preceding its value. (True/False)
8. The NAMELIST name must be enclosed within a pair of _____ .
9. The single character _____ must be attached to the NAMELIST name on the first input record to indicate that Namelist data is being read on IBM computers.
10. On Namelist input operations the variable/array name followed by an = must be given prior to the input value. (True/False)
11. The DECODE statement is used to convert numeric items into character items. (True/False)
12. The ENCODE statement is used to convert numeric items into character items. (True/False)
13. What is the purpose or function of the IMPLICIT statement?
14. What is the danger of using the IMPLICIT statement?

19.9   EXERCISES

1. Find the errors in the following statements (or group of statements).
    a. **PAUSE NOW MOUNT A TAPE**
    b. **ASSIGN 83 FOR K**
    c. **GO TO (33, 46, 92, 131, 7)**
    d. **NAMELIST A,B,C**
    e. **IF (SUM .LT. 10) 13,14,15**
    f. **IF KNT 10,11,10**
    g. **ASSIGN 10.0 TO M**
       GO TO M, (20.0,10.0,7.0)

2. Find the errors in the following statements (or group of statements).
    a. **PAUSE 573246**
    b. **ASSIGN 145763 TO K**
    c. **GO TO K (45,8,17,65)**
    d. **NAMELIST GROUPA /X,Y,Z/**
    e. **IF (N − 10) STOP**
    f. **IF (SUM − 100) 9,8,8**
    g. **J = 7**
       GO TO J, (5,19,3,7)

3. Determine which statement number control will be transferred to upon executing the following groups of statements.

    a. **ASSIGN 56 TO M**
       GO TO M, (31,89,56,5)

    b. **ASSIGN 5 TO N**
       L = 10
       IF (L/2.GE.4) ASSIGN 17 TO N
       GO TO N, (4,5,17,90)

4. Determine which statement number control will be transferred to upon executing the following groups of statements.

    a. **ASSIGN 13 TO L**
       GO TO L, (13,15,8,43)

    b. **ASSIGN 7 TO M**
       X = 10/3
       IF (X .GT. SQRT(9.0)) ASSIGN 3 TO M
       GO TO M, (7,3)

5. Write the Arithmetic IF statements to accomplish the following actions.
    a. If the expression $3.5 * A + C$ is negative, zero, or positive, then branch to statement labels 10, 20, or 30, respectively.
    b. If the expression $N / 2 * 2 - N$ is zero, then branch to statement label 33; otherwise, branch to statement label 12.
    c. If the value of SUM is negative or zero, then branch to statement label 46; otherwise, branch to statement label 18.

6. Write the Arithmetic IF statements to accomplish the following actions.
    a. If the value in K is zero, then branch to statement label 39; otherwise, branch to statement label 66.
    b. If the expression $X + Y / (3.7 - Z)$ is positive, then branch to statement label 46; otherwise, branch to statement label 71.
    c. If the expression $100 - KTR$ is negative, zero, or positive, then branch to statement labels 13, 86, and 53, respectively.

7. Prepare the Namelist input data formats for the following specifications: A NAMELIST name of LIST2 with the variables A, K, and L containing the values 31.8, 17, and 43.

8. Prepare the Namelist input data formats for the following specifications: A NAMELIST name of HOLD with the variables M, X, and Z containing the values 14, 89.72, and 56.073.

19.10 PROGRAMMING PROBLEMS

1. Write a program that reads two values and computes their sum. The input values are read with the variables X and Y under the format specifications 2F6.2. Either variable may contain a negative quantity.

    If the sum of the two variables is greater than zero, transfer to a WRITE statement that writes the two variables, their sum, and a message to the effect that the sum is a positive quantity. If the sum of the two variables is equal to zero, transfer to a WRITE statement that writes the variables, their sum, and a message to the effect that the sum is zero. Likewise, transfer to a WRITE statement that writes the variables, their sum, and a message that the sum is negative when the sum is less than zero. Use the ASSIGN and Assigned GO TO statements to accomplish this action.

    Print the variable X in positions 5–10, the variable Y in positions 15–20, the computed sum in positions 25–31, and the literal message starting in print position 40. Include appropriate column headings.

2. Write a program that computes the sum and average of ten items. Each item is read from separate data records. The first five items are contained in columns 1–5 of each record in the form NNN.N. The remaining five items are contained in columns 10–14 in the same form. Use object-time format specifications to read each group of input values.

    Print the input values in the print positions 5–9. Include an appropriate column heading. Print the sum and average on a double-spaced line with appropriate literal constants to identify each value.

3. Write a program that computes the product of the two variables X and Y. The input values are to be read using a NAMELIST data format. The input values and the computed product are to be written with a NAMELIST data format.

20

Case Studies

20.1 INTRODUCTION

This chapter presents two case studies that provide more complex problems for you to solve. The case studies present larger problems to provide you with experience in solving problems that require careful planning of the solution. You should first develop a structure or hierarchy chart to plan the program structure. You should also develop the logic in a modular form using subprograms. The two case studies are: a simulation of a soft drink machine and a linear regression and correlation problem.

20.2 CASE STUDY #1: SIMULATION—A SOFT DRINK MACHINE

Simulation is the technique of modelling some portion of the physical world. Computer simulation is an economical method of simulating an event without the expense or time-consuming effort needed to make decisions. It is often done prior to building a physical system in order to anticipate problems or to estimate cost. Many times, simulation is used to model an event when the real occurrence would not be feasible. For example, to find out how destructive a 50-megaton nuclear blast on Colorado Springs, Colorado would be, you would certainly not set off a bomb. This event can be simulated with a computer, however, to provide the desired information.

This case study simulates a soft drink machine. It is intended to illustrate top-down, structured design, development, and testing of a problem. The use of modular programming techniques, arrays, and so forth is recommended to provide a well-designed solution.

The soft drink machine to be simulated accepts three denominations of coins—nickels, dimes, and quarters. Any other coin will be returned as a "slug." Each can of soda costs 40 cents. The machine will dispense four types of soda—cola, orange, grape, and root beer. The machine will also deliver change in a "highest denomination first" order. Thus, if the change is 10 cents, it would try to return a dime. If there are no more dimes available, it would return two nickels. If there were only one nickel left to make change, only 5 cents would be returned (you would be cheated out of 5 cents, such as often happens with some machines). Coins which are inserted in the machine are immediately available to make change.

Input/Output Requirements

The output of the simulation consists of two parts. First, you should print what, if any, change is returned. Second, you should print an announcement that the requested soda has been delivered, or that it could not be delivered (and to make another choice). Certain other messages will also be printed when required, such as "ENTER EXACT CHANGE."

To aid in the simulation's testing, the number of each coin and soda type in the machine should be displayed. A prompt will be displayed to indicate the time to enter a coin. A single coin is entered for each prompt. The input values must be in the form of the numbers 5, 10, or 25, indicating the denomination of the coin inserted in the machine. The program will continue to prompt for a coin until at least 40 cents has been entered. One of the numbers 1, 2, 3, or 4 will be entered to indicate which of the four types of soda is chosen (1 = cola, 2 = orange, 3 = grape, and 4 = root beer). An entry of "−1" for any prompt will be used to terminate the program.

"Exact Change Only" Analysis

Under what circumstances should you display the 'exact change only' message? If there is insufficient change to deliver, regardless of what coins are entered, you must give this warning by displaying the message.

The most change that can be returned at any one time is 20 cents. This would occur when 35 cents had been entered, followed by a quarter (35 cents + 25 cents = 60 cents, 20 cents more than the price of a soda).

A table is given listing all cases where change would be returned, i.e., where the amount deposited is greater than 40 cents. In some cases, some of the same coins which are used in the deposit may be used to return change. For example, if seven nickels and then a quarter are deposited, four of these nickels could be used to return the 20 cents change. In other cases, however, the coins in the deposit are insufficient to make the required change. This deficit must be made up with coins from a reserve in the machine. The minimum level of the reserve defines the decision point for displaying the "exact change only" message.

The table of all cases where change would be returned is given as follows:

Table 20.1 All Cases Where Change Would Be Returned

| Deposit | | | | | Change Used | Extra | Extra Coins |
N	D	Q	Total	Change	From Deposit	Required	Required
7	0	1	60	20	Yes		
5	1	1	60	20	Yes		
3	2	1	60	20	Yes		
2	0	2	60	20	Yes	10	2 nickels or 1 dime
0	1	2	60	20	Yes	10	2 nickels or 1 dime
6	0	1	55	15	Yes		
4	1	1	55	15	Yes		
2	2	1	55	15	Yes		
1	0	2	55	15	Yes	10	2 nickels or 1 dime
5	0	1	50	10	Yes		
3	1	1	50	10	Yes		
1	2	1	50	10	Yes		
0	0	2	50	10		10	2 nickels or 1 dime
7	1	0	45	5	Yes		
5	2	0	45	5	Yes		
3	3	0	45	5	Yes		
2	1	1	45	5	Yes		
0	2	1	45	5		5	1 nickel
4	0	1	45	5	Yes		

The extra coins required for the simulation may be stated as the intersection of all cases. The intersection is expressed as (n ≥ 1) and (n ≥ 2 or d ≥ 1), or by applying the Distributive Law, (n ≥ 2) or (n ≥ 1 and d ≥ 1).

Minimum Test Requirements

The following minimum tests must be conducted to verify that the simulation performs according to the problem specifications:

1. You must show that change is delivered correctly, according to the "highest denomination first" rule.
2. You must show that the required soda is delivered when available, and display a message when the soda is not available.
3. An "EXACT CHANGE ONLY" message must be displayed if the machine would be unable to deliver change under all circumstances. This message is displayed unless there are two or more nickels, or if there are one or more nickels and one or more dimes left in reserve in the machine.

Initial State of the Machine

The initial state of the machine is the number of cans of soda and the amount of change for each denomination in reserve in the machine. The initial state of the simulated machine will be:

1. There will be four cans each for each type of soda (i.e., four cans of cola, four cans of orange, four cans of grape, and four cans of root beer).
2. There will be two dimes and three nickels available in the machine to make change.

Display of Sample Execution

Following is a display of output from the execution of the author's program. You may design the prompts and output requirements to your desires.

```
        NICKELS = 3    DIMES = 2    QUARTERS = 0

        COLAS = 4    ORANGES = 4    GRAPES = 4    ROOT BEERS = 4

        ENTER COIN
        25

        ENTER COIN
        25

        CHANGE—DIME

        SELECT SODA
        1

        COLA DELIVERED

        NICKELS = 3    DIMES = 1    QUARTERS = 2

        COLAS = 3    ORANGES = 4    GRAPES = 4    ROOT BEERS = 4

        ENTER COIN
        25

        ENTER COIN
        5

        ENTER COIN
        5

        ENTER COIN
        25

        CHANGE—DIME

        CHANGE—NICKEL

        CHANGE—NICKEL

        SELECT SODA
        3

        GRAPE DELIVERED

        NICKELS = 3    DIMES = 0    QUARTERS = 4

        COLAS = 3    ORANGES = 4    GRAPES = 3    ROOT BEERS = 4

        ENTER COIN
        25

        ENTER COIN
        25
```

CHANGE—NICKEL

CHANGE—NICKEL

SELECT SODA
2

ORANGE DELIVERED

NICKELS = 1   DIMES = 0   QUARTERS = 6

COLAS = 3   ORANGES = 3   GRAPES = 3   ROOT BEERS = 4

ENTER EXACT CHANGE

ENTER COIN
25

ENTER COIN
50

SLUG

ENTER COIN
10

ENTER COIN
10

CHANGE—NICKEL

SELECT SODA
4

ROOT BEER DELIVERED

NICKELS = 0   DIMES = 2   QUARTERS = 7

COLAS = 3   ORANGES = 3   GRAPES = 3   ROOT BEERS = 3

ENTER EXACT CHANGE

ENTER COIN
−1

END OF SODA MACHINE PROGRAM

20.3 CASE STUDY #2: STATISTICS—LINEAR REGRESSION AND CORRELATION

The instructor of a FORTRAN Programming course believes there is a strong correlation between the number of hours students study in preparation for an exam and their resulting exam grade. He wishes to confirm that the more time a student studies for an exam, the better the grade achieved. To perform this study and to give his students experience in programming a statistical problem, the instructor assigns the problem to the class. They are to design, code, and test a program that will accept a given number of data pairs and perform a linear regression analysis.

The first number in the data pair represents the number of hours studied (range of 0.0 to 99.9) to the nearest tenth of an hour. The second number of the data pair represents the resulting exam score (an integer between 0 and 100, inclusively). The program will prompt for the data pair of study hours and exam score. A value of -9.9 for study hours and -99 for exam score will be entered to terminate the loop for input items. An example of the input procedure is:

ENTER PAIR OF NUMBERS   **1**
5.0,100

ENTER PAIR OF NUMBERS   **2**
0.0,50

ENTER PAIR OF NUMBERS   **n**   (where n is the last prompt
-9.9,-99   number for the input pair)

The responses are given on the line after the prompt message.
The recommended output format is:

REGRESSION ANALYSIS OF nnn SAMPLE PAIRS

MEAN OF THE X VALUES IS nnn.nn
MEAN OF THE Y VALUES IS nnn.nn

VARIANCE OF THE X VALUES IS nnnn.nn
VARIANCE OF THE Y VALUES IS nnnn.nn

CORRELATION COEFFICIENT IS nn.nnnn

THE LINEAR REGRESSION EQUATION HAS:
    A SLOPE OF nnnn.nnnn
    AN INTERCEPT OF nnnn.nnnn

The first "nnn" is the count of the number of data pairs entered on input. The remaining "nnn.nnn," "nnnn.nn," and so on are the calculated values from the program.

The students are supplied with a list of definitions and formulas for use in solving the problem. The definitions and formulas are given as follows:
Number of cases (samples):

$$n$$

Mean X, the average of the X values (study hours):

$$\overline{X} = \frac{1}{n} \sum_{i=1}^{n} x_i$$

Mean Y, the average of the Y values (exam scores):

$$\overline{Y} = \frac{1}{n} \sum_{i=1}^{n} y_i$$

Variance of the X values:

Method 1

$$\sigma_x^2 = \frac{1}{n-1} \sum_{i=1}^{n} (x_i - \overline{X})^2$$

Method 2

$$\sigma_x^2 = \frac{1}{n-1} \left[\sum_{i=1}^{n} x_i^2 - \frac{1}{n} \left(\sum_{i=1}^{n} x_i \right)^2 \right]$$

Variance of the Y values:

Method 1

$$\sigma_y^2 = \frac{1}{n-1} \sum_{i=1}^{n} (y_i - \overline{Y})^2$$

Method 2

$$\sigma_y^2 = \frac{1}{n-1} \left[\sum_{i=1}^{n} y_i^2 - \frac{1}{n} \left(\sum_{i=1}^{n} y_i \right)^2 \right]$$

Correlation coefficient is a number that ranges between -1.0 and $+1.0$. If the correlation coefficient is close to 1.0, this value implies there is a strong positive relationship between X and Y, i.e., as X increases, the observed Y values increase and vary little from their predicted value. A value of -1.0 indicates a strong negative relationship, i.e., as X increases, the observed values of Y decrease and vary little from their predicted value. A value of 0.0 (or close to 0.0) indicates no apparent relationship between the X and Y values. Normally a correlation coefficient of .80 or higher (or $-.80$ or lower) is desirable before extrapolating (predicting) a future value of Y based on a value of X. The formula for finding the correlation coefficient is:

Method 1

$$C_{x,y} = \frac{\frac{1}{n-1} \sum_{i=1}^{n} (X_i - \overline{X})(Y_i - \overline{Y})}{\sqrt{\sigma_x^2 \, \sigma_y^2}}$$

Method 2

$$C_{x,y} = \frac{\frac{1}{n-1} \left[\sum_{i=1}^{n} X_i Y_i - \frac{1}{n} \sum_{i=1}^{n} X_i \sum_{i=1}^{n} Y_i \right]}{\sqrt{\sigma_x^2 \, \sigma_y^2}}$$

Linear regression formula is the line that best predicts the Y value of a given X value. This line always passes through the point—mean X, mean Y. This formula requires two calculations to provide the values of "m" and "k" for the predictive formula of:

$$\hat{Y} = mX + K$$

"m" is the slope of the line. "K" is the intercept of the y-axis. $\hat{Y}$ is referred to as Y-hat. The formula for "m" is:

Method 1

$$m = \frac{\sum_{i=1}^{n} (x_i - \overline{X})(y_i - \overline{Y})}{\sum_{i=1}^{n} (x_i - \overline{X})^2}$$

Method 2

$$m = \frac{n \sum_{i=1}^{n} x_i y_i - \sum_{i=1}^{n} x_i \sum_{i=1}^{n} y_i}{n \sum_{i=1}^{n} x_i^2 - \left(\sum_{i=1}^{n} x_i \right)^2}$$

The formula for "K" is :

$$K = \overline{Y} - m\overline{X}$$

The **mean** and the **line of regression** are measures of centrality. The **variance** and the **correlation coefficient** are expressions of dispersion. The **standard deviation** (σ), which is the square root of the variance, is another expression of dispersion.

You may have noticed there are often two different ways to calculate certain expressions (such as variance, correlation coefficient, and "m" in the linear regression formula). Although the second method of expressing the equation looks more complicated, it is actually easier to calculate than the first method. The first method of expressing the equation requires that the data be kept in an array for later reference. For example, in the variance formula:

$$\sigma_x^2 = \frac{1}{n-1} \sum_{i=1}^{n} (x_i - \overline{X})^2$$

the mean, $\overline{X}$, is determined, and then each of the data elements must be used to calculate the sum of the squares of the difference between the data item and the mean.

The second method of expressing the equation does not require a pre-calculated value of the mean. It merely requires that, as each item is read, the value and its square (X_i and X_i^2) are accumulated. Thus, the second method of expressing the equation (which does not use $\overline{X}$ and $\overline{Y}$) is the recommended formula to use in your program.

As part of the next class exam, the instructor requested that each of his ten students write on his or her exam paper the number of hours spent in studying for the exam. The noted hours of studying, with the resulting exam score, were:

Study Hours (X)	Exam Score (Y)
5.0	100
0.0	50
3.2	85
2.5	80
4.2	90
1.5	65
2.6	75
3.4	80
0.5	85
4.2	95

The students were given this data with the program assignment for use in the linear regression analysis program. They were asked first to plot the study hours and the resulting exam scores on an X-Y axis to show that a linear relationship existed before writing the program. The hours of study should be plotted along the horizontal X-axis, and the resulting exam scores should be plotted on the vertical Y-axis of the graph. Plotting the data items on a graph of this type should be done to prove (visually) that a linear relationship, instead of a curvilinear relationship, exists between the two items.

For the case study, you should:

1. Plot the study hours (X-axis) and corresponding exam scores (Y-axis) to show that a linear relationship exists.
2. Develop the program to perform the linear regression analysis using the ten pairs of numbers given in the case study. Prepare the output in the recommended format.

Appendixes

Features of the WATFIV and WATFIV-S Compilers

Appendix A

A.1 INTRODUCTION TO THE IMPORTANCE AND USE OF THE WATFIV COMPILER

The WATFIV (pronounced "wat five") FORTRAN compiler developed by the University of Waterloo, Ontario, Canada in 1969 for the IBM 360, plays an important role in teaching students the FORTRAN language. Hundreds of junior colleges and universities across the nation use this outstanding compiler. The speed of the WATFIV provides faster turnarounds than other FORTRAN compilers. The WATFIV compiler also helps the instructor, since students using WATFIV understand the error messages more easily and thus can correct the errors themselves. All in all, the WATFIV compiler can make life easier for anyone concerned with the development of FORTRAN programs.

The two main advantages of the WATFIV compiler, then, are:

1. Its amazing speed in the compilation and execution of small and average-size programs.
2. Its effective and efficient debugging capabilities.

The WATFIV compiler compiles source programs much faster than other compilers, for two reasons: First, the WATFIV compiler is an in-core or in-memory compiler. That is, the compiler stays in memory during the compilation of many WATFIV jobs, while other FORTRAN compilers have to be brought back into memory for each job, which means that only one FORTRAN program can be compiled at a time. Second, the WATFIV compiler takes less time to translate a source program into object code. This design efficiency results in WATFIV compilations being many times faster than those of other compilers.

The WATFIV compiler is also superior to other FORTRAN compilers in its debugging abilities. The diagnostic error messages are much more intelligible than those of most compilers and are consequently a greater help to the student struggling to locate specific errors. WATFIV provides a clear explanation as to what the error is and also prints characters surrounding the error. WATFIV also has the ability to detect many kinds of *execution errors,* such as undefined variables, changing the indexing parameters in a DO loop, invalid subscript values, and others—an ability that many compilers do not have. WATFIV can also identify the statement being executed at a point of program blowup.

WATFIV is designed after the IBM "G" FORTRAN IV compiler described in IBM Form C28–6515. However, WATFIV does not include all the features in the IBM "G" compiler and has additional extensions to the "G" compiler. The WATFIV compiler is also written in accord with ANSI standards and will run on ANSI compilers when the standard subset of statements is used.

Following is the control cards setup for a WATFIV job.

```
$JOB
        FORTRAN source statements are inserted here
$ENTRY
        Data cards, if used, are inserted here
```

An IBM job card is required before the $JOB card. Some installations may require an end-of-file (/*) card after the last data card. The $JOB and $ENTRY cards are punched beginning in column 1 with no embedded blanks. The $ENTRY card is required even if no data cards are used, since this card signifies that execution is ready to begin. No input data card may have a $ in column 1, because the dollar-sign symbol is used to indicate a control card.

A.2 WATFIV EXTENSIONS TO THE FORTRAN IV LANGUAGE

WATFIV contains many features that are extensions to the ANSI standard and IBM "G" level FORTRAN compilers. The more important extensions are discussed in this section.

A-1

Format-free Input-output

Perhaps the most important of the additional features is the format-free input/output capability. With it, the students need not worry about the complex data field specifications of the input/output records and can concentrate more on the basic principles of programming concepts.

The WATFIV compiler permits two format-free READ statements that eliminate the need for a related FORMAT statement.

The form of the specific READ statement to provide format-free I/O in WATFIV is:

READ, list

The form of the general READ statement to provide format-free I/O in WATFIV is:

READ (unit, *, END = a, ERR = b) list

where **unit** may be any valid file unit specified as an integer constant or variable. The * is coded as such to denote the use of a free-form format. The parameters "END = " and "ERR = " are optional. The parameters **a** and **b** are supplied by the programmer and represent assigned statement numbers when either of the two optional parameters are used; **list** indicates an I/O list of variables and/or array elements.

Valid examples of these two forms of format-free READ statements are:

READ, X, Y, Z
READ, N, (X(I), I = 1,N)
16 READ (5,*) D1, D2
2 READ (5,*, END = 76) N1, N2, N3

The input data fields may be punched one per card, or many per card. If multiple fields are punched in the same card, each field must be separated by a comma and/or one or more blanks. The first data field does not have to start in card column 1. A data field may not be continued across two cards, since the end of a card acts as a delimiter (separator).

Successive cards are read until enough fields have been found to satisfy the requirements of the I/O list. Any fields remaining on the last card read for a particular READ statement will be ignored, since the next READ statement executed will cause a new card record to be read.

Data fields may be signed or unsigned and may consist of the following type data: integer, real (in F, E, or D form), complex, logical, and alphanumeric. The type of input data field must match the type of variable used in the I/O list. Whenever **alphanumeric data** is read under format-free I/O, the characters must be enclosed within a set of **single quotes.** If a quote is required as input in the string, two successive quotes must be punched. Complex values must be put in parentheses, with each number separated by a comma. A duplication factor may be given in the data card to avoid punching the same constant many times. For example:

DIMENSION A(50)
READ, A

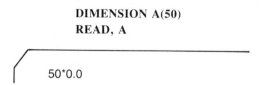

50*0.0

It is permissible to use both the general READ and format-free READ statements in the same program.

Three forms of format-free output statements are available—the PRINT, PUNCH, and WRITE statements.

The form of the format-free PRINT statement is:

PRINT, list

The form of the format-free PUNCH statement is:

PUNCH, list

The form of the format-free WRITE statement is:

WRITE (unit, *) list

where **unit** is a valid file unit specified as an integer constant or variable. The * must be used in place of a format statement number to denote format-free output. **list** represents an I/O list of variables, array elements, constants, and/or expressions.

Valid examples of format-free output statements are:

> **PRINT, A,B,C**
> **2 PRINT, K**
> **PUNCH, SUM, N**
> **WRITE (6,*) I, J, TOT**
> **WRITE (6,*) (X(J), J = 1,10)**

Data output under the format-free I/O statements is formatted as follows:

Type Fields	Format Code Specifications
Integer	I12
Real*4	E16.7
Real*8	D28. 16
Complex*8	'(' E16.7 ' , ' E16.7 ')'
Complex*16	'(' D28.16 ' , ' D28.16 ')'
Logical	L8
Character * n	An (where n represents the length of the character string)

An additional blank character is included to separate each field. Ten integer data fields can be output to a line; seven real*4 fields can be output to a line. Any combination of type fields can be output on the same line. It is permissible to use both the general WRITE and format-free output statements in the same program.

Expressions in Output Lists

WATFIV permits the use of constants and expressions in output lists. The one resulting value of an expression is printed. Function subprogram references may also be included in the output list. For example:

> **PRINT, 12, A + B**
> **PRINT, 'I = ', I**
> **WRITE (6,*) X, SQRT(X)**
> **WRITE (6,99) Y**2 + Z − 4, 500.37**

The first example illustrates the use of an integer constant and an expression in the output list. Example two illustrates the use of a literal constant and a variable in the list. Example three uses a variable and a built-in function reference in the output list. Example four shows a compound expression and a real constant in the list. The use of constants and expressions in an output list provides a very powerful and flexible way of debugging programs.

One restriction must be observed in forming the output list. The first value in the list must not begin with an open left parenthesis, since this is used as a signal to denote an implied DO. That is, the expression

> **PRINT, (K + J)/2**

would be invalid. The expression could be written as

> **PRINT, +(K + J)/2**

to avoid the beginning left parenthesis. Parentheses other than the first character in the I/O list pose no problems. Real values are output in exponential form.

Character Type Variables

A primary weakness of FORTRAN lies in its capability for handling input/output character strings. As you know, the character string must be broken up into groups, usually of four or fewer characters. This restriction is understandable because of the intended nature of FORTRAN for scientific applications. WATFIV, however, in response to the wide use of FORTRAN for many business applications, has included capabilities for handling character type variables and constants.

Variables that take on character values can be declared in the CHARACTER type statement. Unless specified in the provided length option of the statement, each character type variable has a length of one.

The general form of the CHARACTER type statement is:

CHARACTER * s name$_1$*s, . . . , name$_n$*s

where ***s** is optional and provides the length of the character string contained in the variable. The length option may be from *1 through *255. If the length option is omitted, the default length is one. The **name$_1$, . . . , name$_n$** represent a list of variable and/or array names. As indicated in the general form notation, the length option may be specified after the keyword CHARACTER and/or after each individual name. The length option after each name overrides any length specification given after the keyword. Dimension specifications may be included for array names. Initial data values may also be included after the name by coding the character values as a literal constant and enclosing the value within a set of slashes. This syntax is basically the same for the other Explicit type statements.

Consider the following examples.

> **CHARACTER X, Y*3**
> **CHARACTER * 7 VAL1, VAL2**
> **CHARACTER * 5 R1, S1 * 6/ 'TOTAL = '/**
> **CHARACTER MONTH*3(12) / 'JAN', 'FEB', 'MAR'/**
> **CHARACTER * 4 A/1HA/, BB/2HBB/, T/'ABCDE'/**
> **CHARACTER * 25 NAME**

In the first example, the variable X is by default assigned a length of one. The variable Y is capable of storing three characters because of the *3. In example two, the length attribute of *7 applies to both variables VAL1 and VAL2 and allows them to store up to seven characters. In the third example, the variable R1 has a length of 5, while the variable S1 has a length of 6. The content of S1 is also initialized to the characters 'TOTAL = '. In example four, MONTH is declared to be a one-dimensional array of twelve elements; each element is of length three. The first three elements are also initialized to 'JAN', 'FEB' and 'MAR'.

In the fifth example, the three variables A, BB, and T are each declared to be four characters in length. The variable A is initialized to the one symbol 'A'. Since A is of length four, three blanks are added to the right of the constant 'A' to provide an initial value of 'A   '. The same holds true for the variable BB. Two blanks are added to the right to provide the initial value 'BB '. Five characters are coded for the initial value of T. Since the length of T is only four, one character must be dropped. As with the input of alphanumeric data, the leftmost characters in excess of the variable's length are truncated. Thus, the symbol 'A' is dropped, and the initial value of T is 'BCDE'. A warning message is always printed whenever initializing constants contain too many characters and some must be truncated. Example five allows a 25-length character string to be stored at the variable NAME.

The character type variables can conserve memory requirements whenever character-string processing is needed for individual characters. For example:

> **CHARACTER * 1 CARD(80)**
> **READ (5,99) CARD**
> **99 FORMAT (80A1)**

Only one byte is used to hold each character, as opposed to one word when character variables/arrays are not used.

An initially defined character variable or array element must not appear in Blank Common. Otherwise, character type variables and/or arrays may appear in

1. DIMENSION statements
2. COMMON statements.
3. NAMELIST statements
4. DATA statements
5. CALL statements
6. FUNCTION references
7. Dummy arguments
8. I/O statements
9. Assignment statements
10. Logical IF statements

WATFIV also permits character data to be assigned to a variable in a CHARACTER Assignment statement. The syntax of this statement is the same as the regular Assignment statement and is:

Character type Variable = Character value

The character value on the right of the = symbol may be either a character variable or a character constant. If the receiving variable to the left of the = symbol is longer than the assigned variable length, blanks are padded in the rightmost positions. If the receiving variable is shorter than the assigned variable length, truncation takes place. A warning message is given whenever the lengths of the two variables are not the same.

Character constants may be assigned to a character variable by coding them as literal constants. For example:

$$CHARA = 'A'$$
$$STRING = 6HSUM =$$
$$R(1) = 'SUM OF X + Y IS'$$

This allows execution time assignment of character values instead of compile time initialization.

Character variables may be used in a Logical IF statement as operands of relational operators, provided both operands are of type CHARACTER. For example:

$$CHARACTER\ K,\ L,\ KODE(5)$$
$$IF\ (K\ .EQ.\ L)\ CALL\ SUBL$$
$$IF\ (K\ .EQ.\ KODE(1))\ GO\ TO\ 30$$
$$IF\ (K\ .NE.\ 'C')\ GO\ TO\ 40$$

Thus, character variables, array elements, and constants can be used as either operand in the relational expression. If the operands are not the same length, the shorter operand is padded on the right with blanks to match the length of the longer operand.

Extended Assignment Statement

The extended Assignment statement feature permits a value to be assigned to more than one variable in a single statement. For example:

$$A = B = C = 0.0$$
$$K = N = I = J = 1$$
$$RESULT = X = SQRT(Y) + 5.\ *\ R$$

The first statement assigns the value of zero to the variables A, B, and C. The second example assigns the value of one to the variables K, N, I, and J. The third example assigns the resulting value of the arithmetic expression to the two variables RESULT and X.

Extreme care must be taken when mixing types of variables in this statement. In the statement

$$A = I = W = 7.5$$

the compiler assigns the values beginning with the rightmost variable and works left. This statement is equivalent to the following three statements:

$$W = 7.5$$
$$I = W$$
$$A = I$$

Since I is an integer variable, the value 7 is assigned to I. Thus, A is assigned the value 7.0 rather than 7.5.

Precision may also be lost when an integer value is assigned to a real variable in this type of statement. For example:

$$K = X = J = 872164359$$

J is assigned the value 872164359. If X is a single-precision variable, only about seven significant digits are retained. Thus, X would be assigned the value 8721643, and K would be assigned the value 8721643 also.

Multiple Statements Per Card

This feature permits several FORTRAN statements to be punched on the same card, thus condensing the size of the source deck. For those statements without statement numbers, a semicolon is used to separate successive statements. No semicolon is placed after the last statement. For example, the card:

$$READ,X,Y;\ SUM = X+Y;\ PRINT,X,Y,SUM;\ STOP;\ END$$

is equivalent to the following statements:

$$READ,\ X,Y$$
$$SUM = X + Y$$
$$PRINT,\ X,\ Y,\ SUM$$
$$STOP$$
$$END$$

When statement numbers are used, they must either appear in columns 1–5 as usual, or they must be separated from the FORTRAN statement by a colon. For example, the card:

1 READ,N; K = 0; DO 10 I = 1,N; K = K + I; 10:CONTINUE

is equivalent to the following cards:

1 READ, N
K = 0
DO 10 I = 1,N
K = K + I
10 CONTINUE

Only columns 7–72 of a card can be used, since the compiler ignores columns 73–80. The continuation column may still be used to indicate the continuation of the last statement. Comment cards must still be punched in the conventional manner with a C in column one.

Comments on FORTRAN Statements

WATFIV is written to terminate the left-to-right scan by the compiler on a card when the "ZIGAMORPH" character is encountered; so comments may be included after this character. For example:

AREAC = 3.14 * R ** 2 Ż COMPUTE AREA OF CIRCLE

where Ż represents the "ZIGAMORPH" character. The "ZIGAMORPH" symbol is punched as a 12/11/0/7/8/9 multipunched character. It is not, however, printed on the source listing.

Carriage Control Characters

WATFIV will, without warning, replace invalid carriage control characters with blanks. In addition to the standard set of carriage control characters, WATFIV also permits the use of '-' to provide triple spacing.

Transfer Statements as the Object (Range) of the DO

WATFIV allows the last statement (range) of a DO loop to be an Arithmetic IF or a Logical IF. The Logical IF may contain a GO TO statement of any form, a PAUSE, or a STOP statement. In a subprogram, the Logical IF may contain a RETURN statement. If the condition expressed in the Logical IF is false, control is transferred back to the beginning of the loop to reexecute the statements in the DO loop. If the condition is true, the action statement on the Logical IF is executed.

Initializing Common Blocks

WATFIV allows the programmer to initialize Labeled Common Blocks in other than BLOCK DATA subprograms. Thus, variables and arrays in Labeled Common may be initialized by the DATA and Explicit type statements in the mainline program. Blank Common may also be initialized with the DATA and/or Explicit type statements.

Error Messages

Error messages may be produced by WATFIV during program compilation and/or execution. Three types of diagnostic messages may appear from the compilation phase. They are:

1. **Extension.** These messages flag the use of language extensions that may not be found in other compilers, such as the use of an implied DO in a DATA statement using arrays, or the use of multiple Assignment statements.
2. **Warning.** These messages flag statements that contain ambiguous syntax but can nevertheless continue to generate object code. For example, a variable name containing more than six characters is flagged with a warning message, but the first six characters are used as the variable name, and compilation continues. Other examples are "missing END statement" and "this statement should have a statement number."
3. **Error.** These messages flag FORTRAN statements that cannot be translated by the compiler, such as misspelled keywords or missing operators. The error message generally appears after the statement in error, gives a description as to the type of error and provides information about it.

Execution error messages that identify programmer blunders and prevent hard-to-detect bugs are an outstanding feature of the WATFIV compiler. Some examples of error messages that may be produced at execution time are:

a. Attempt to redefine a DO-loop parameter within the range of the loop.
b. Format code and data type do not match. For example, reading a real variable with an integer format code.
c. Attempt to use a subprogram recursively (i.e., calling itself).
d. Subscript is out of range. That is, it is less than one or greater than the dimension size.
e. Subscript is undefined. No initial value has been assigned to the subscript variable.
f. Variable is undefined. For example, coding $N = N + 1$ where the variable N has never been assigned an initial value.

Any attempt to print an undefined variable will result in an output value of **U**'s. For example:

$$A = 10.0$$
$$B = 20.5$$
$$SUM = A + B$$
$$WRITE\ (6,99)\ A, B, SUMM$$
$$99\ FORMAT\ (1X,F4.1,5X,F4.1,5X,F5.1)$$

will result in the following values being printed.

$$10.0 \quad 20.5 \quad UUUUU$$

As many **U**'s will be printed as will fill out the format code width specifications. This is a highly useful feature for catching the misspelling of variables used in the output list or for variables that have never been assigned a value. The U's in the above output result from the spelling of the variable SUMM with two M's instead of one.

Since the diagnostic messages are highly descriptive and would also be verbally the same, the available list of WATFIV error messages is not included in this text.

A.3 HOW WATFIV DIFFERS FROM THE IBM FORTRAN IV "G" LEVEL COMPILER

Features of the IBM "G" compiler not found in WATFIV and major differences are as follows:

1. The concept of the extended range of a DO loop is not supported in WATFIV.
2. The service subprograms named DUMP and PDUMP are not supported in WATFIV.
3. The Debug Facility is not supported in WATFIV.
4. The name of a Labeled Common Block must be unique. That is, the name may not also be used as the name of a variable, array, or statement function in WATFIV.
5. The number of continuation cards, as well as the use of operator messages with the STOP and PAUSE statements, are installation options in WATFIV.
6. In WATFIV the character string "FORMAT(" is a reserved character sequence when used as the first seven characters of a statement. For example,

$$FORMAT(I) = 7.3$$

will result in an error message, whereas

$$A = FORMAT(I)$$

is legal, assuming that the name FORMAT is an array or Function name.

7. Since WATFIV is a "one-pass" compiler, the ordering of specification statements is highly important. Specification statements referring to variables used in NAMELIST or DEFINE FILE statements must precede those NAMELIST or DEFINE FILE statements. COMMON or EQUIVALENCE statements referring to variables used in data or initializing type statements must precede the DATA or initializing Explicit Type statements. A variable may appear in an EQUIVALENCE statement and then in a subsequent Explicit Type statement only if the type statement does not change the assumed length of the variable.

WATFIV incompatibilities with the IBM FORTRAN IV G and H level compilers other than those extensions described in section A.2 are as follows:

1. WATFIV allows any number of contiguous comment cards.
2. Comment cards may be intermixed between continuation cards.
3. Commas are not required between format codes in WATFIV, if their omission does not cause ambiguity.
4. WATFIV does not allow group format repetition or format code repetition field counts to be expressed as a zero.
5. DO loops may be nested to any depth in WATFIV. A maximum of 255 DO loops are allowed in a program unit.
6. Negative values may not be exponentiated (raised to a power).
7. The name SORT may not be used as a variable name. That is, it must be used as a function subprogram reference only.
8. REAL *4 values are printed with a maximum of seven significant digits.
9. The use of the T format code in WATFIV, which does a backward tab in an output buffer, does not cause the existing characters in the buffer to be blanked out.

Now let us look at the control options that may be included on the WATFIV $JOB control statement and as additional job control cards in a FORTRAN source deck.

A.4 WATFIV JOB CONTROL STATEMENTS

In a WATFIV job any card containing a "$" in card column 1 is regarded as a job control card. Every WATFIV job must contain a "$JOB" and a "$ENTRY" control card (unless the control card requirements have been changed on your system). The $JOB card must precede your FORTRAN source program. The $ENTRY card must precede your data cards and must be included whether data cards are present or not. Other job control cards to cause page eject in source listings, to insert a blank line in the source listing, and other tasks may also be included in a source deck.

The $JOB card has $JOB punched in columns 1–4, WATFIV in columns 8–13 and an account number beginning in column 16. Various job options may follow this account number. When any of the options are used, a comma must follow the account number. If more than one option is present, a comma is used to separate each one. A comment composed of any combination of symbols may follow the first blank column after column 16.

Following are ten job options that may be included on the job card. Any or all of these options may be used. The items in each pair of braces indicate the alternatives, of which you must, in each case, choose one. The underlined option is usually the default value, which will be used unless you change it.

Application	Options	Description
Keypunch model	$KP = \left\{ \begin{matrix} \underline{29} \\ 26 \end{matrix} \right\}$	The chosen number indicates which keypunch model is used for the source program. The keypunch used determines the encoding of the special characters.
Execution time limit	TIME = n or T = n	This option limits the amount of computer time allowed for execution of the program. n is represented by one of the following forms: "m";"(m,s)"; or "(,s)" where "m" denotes the number of minutes and "s" seconds.
Execution time limit on number of pages of printed output	PAGES = p or P = p	p denotes the maximum number of pages printed before the job is terminated.
Limit of number of lines printed on each page	LINES = n	n denotes the maximum number of lines printed per page before a page eject is performed.
Execution time processing with error conditions	RUN = $\left\{ \begin{matrix} \underline{CHECK} \\ NO\ CHECK \\ FREE \end{matrix} \right\}$	The "RUN = " is optional. See the paragraph on execution time error checking for the CHECK and NOCHECK options. RUN = FREE or simply FREE causes program execution to be attempted even though there are compile-time errors.

Printer listing of source program	$\left\{ \begin{array}{l} \underline{LIST} \\ NOLIST \end{array} \right\}$	This option controls the listing of the source program. "NOLIST" is useful when listings are not desired, especially with long programs.
Printer listing of library subprograms	$\left\{ \begin{array}{l} \underline{LIBLIST} \\ NOLIBLIST \end{array} \right\}$	This option controls the listing of library subprograms called/invoked in the program.
Printing of warning messages	$\left\{ \begin{array}{l} \underline{WARN} \\ NOWARN \end{array} \right\}$	This option permits or suppresses the printing of warning messages during program compilation.
Printing of extension messages	$\left\{ \begin{array}{l} \underline{EXTEN} \\ NOEXTEN \end{array} \right\}$	This option permits or suppresses the printing of compiler extension messages during program compilation.
Library mainline program	PGM = **name**	"**name**" is the name of a library program to be used as the mainline program.

All 80 columns of the $JOB card may be used. The options may be punched in any order. If a given option is invalid (e.g., misspelled), this option and all options that follow it are ignored. If an option is included more than once, the last specification will be used in the job.

Compile Time Control Cards

The following WATFIV control cards may be used to control output of the source listing produced during program compilation. The "$" must appear in column 1.

$PRINTON—All source statements that follow this control card will be listed by the compiler.

$PRINTOFF—All source statements that follow this control card will not be printed by the compiler. This card may be used in conjunction with the $PRINTON control card to selectively turn on and off the printing of source statements by the compiler.

$EJECT—This card causes a page eject to occur in the source listing and is useful for starting subprograms or special routines on a new page.

$SPACE—This card causes a blank line to appear at its location in the source listing.

$WARN—This card causes compiler WARNING messages to be printed. If NOWARN is set in the $JOB card, and the $WARN card is used, this card overrides the option in the $JOB card.

$NOWARN—Compiler WARNING messages will not be printed on the source listing.

$EXTEN—This card causes compiler EXTENSION messages to be printed.

$NOEXTEN—This card causes compiler EXTENSION messages not to be printed on the source listing.

Execution Time Error Checking

Two control cards are available concerning undefined variables during program execution. These two cards are:

$CHECK—This card causes a check to be made during execution to insure that each variable has been assigned a value before it is used in a computation. An error message is produced if the variable is undefined.

$NOCHECK—When this control card is used, no error message is produced if an undefined variable is used in a computation.

Execution Time Tracing of Statements

Two control cards are available to trace the execution of statements during processing.

$ISNON—This control card turns the trace feature on. When this feature is used, statement numbers are listed in the order in which they are executed in the program. This feature is especially useful in debugging to see the flow of execution in a program. At least one executable statement must precede the $ISNON control card.

$ISNOFF—This card turns the trace feature off. This control card can be used in conjunction with the $ISNON card to limit the trace to specific portions of a program.

A.5 WATFIV-S FEATURES

WATFIV-S is a FORTRAN IV programming language that includes extensions to the WATFIV compiler. The "S" in WATFIV-S stands for "structured" and means that the extensions in WATFIV-S are designed to include features to make it easier to write structured programs. WATFIV-S includes several new statements and block structures, such as IF-THEN-ELSE and WHILE-DO, which provide structured control blocks in the WATFIV language. These new extensions, therefore, allow you to develop better top-down, structured programs, which are more easily read and understood. Many of these extensions in WATFIV-S are included in the new standard FORTRAN 77 set of specifications.

The new statements in WATFIV-S produce a block structure, or simply a block. A block structure is a group of consecutive FORTRAN statements that begins with a new special statement—such as IF (logical-expression) THEN DO, or WHILE (logical-expression) DO—and ends with a special END statement—such as END IF or END WHILE. These block structures may be wholly contained within another block structure, but must not overlap, just as nested DO loops must not overlap. For example, an IF-THEN-ELSE block could be contained within a WHILE-DO block of statements.

IF-THEN-ELSE:END IF Block

This new block structure is an extension to the Logical IF statement. This block permits more than one statement to be executed if the logical expression being tested is true. Remember, the Logical IF statement permits only a single statement to be given after the logical expression. This certainly makes structured programming difficult in the current FORTRAN language. The new block structure also permits an optional ELSE DO capability to the IF-THEN-ELSE block, to include statements to be executed whenever the logical condition is false. The general form of this new block structure is as follows:

```
              IF   (logical-expression) THEN DO
                   . . .
                   . . . statement(s) to be executed
                   . . . when the condition is true
                   . . .
block         ELSE DO
structure          . . .
                   . . . statement(s) to be executed
                   . . . when the condition is false
                   . . .
              END IF
              . . . ◄——— (continue execution of program here)
```

When the logical-expression is true, the statements following the IF (logical-expression) THEN DO statement and preceding the ELSE DO statement are executed. Control of execution is then transferred to the statement following the END IF statement. When the logical expression is false, the statements following the ELSE DO statement and preceding the END IF statement are executed. Control of execution is then transferred to the statement following the END IF statement. Consider the following example.

```
              IF (N .LT. 0) THEN DO
                   NNEGSM = NNEGSM + N
                   NNEG = NNEG + 1
              ELSE DO
                   NPOSSM = NPOSSM + N
                   NPOS = NPOS + 1
              END IF
```

This block adds N to a specific counter and also increments another counter by one, depending on whether N is negative or not.

The ELSE DO statement is optional. When this statement is omitted, and the logical expression is false, control of execution is simply transferred to the statement following the END IF statement. For example:

IF (X .GT. 0.0) THEN DO
XSUM = XSUM + X
N = N + 1
END IF

This block adds X to a counter and increments the counter N by one only if the value of X is positive.

The ELSE DO and END IF statements are nonexecutable. If a branch is made to a statement inside the block structure, execution proceeds in a sequential manner with the ELSE DO (if present) and END IF statements being ignored. Control of execution may be transferred to a statement ouside the block structure at any time. When this is desired, a GO TO statement is normally included immediately before the ELSE DO or END IF statements. The IF (logical-expression) THEN DO statement cannot be the range statement in a DO loop, nor can it be the statement given in a regular Logical IF statement.

WHILE-DO: END WHILE Block

This block structure implements the WHILE-DO control structure in structured programming. The WHILE-DO block permits the repeated execution of a group of statements while a given expression is found to be true (that is, until the expression becomes false). The general form of this block structure is:

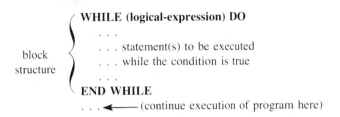

If the logical expression is true, then the statements following the WHILE (logical expression) DO statement and preceding the END WHILE statement are executed. Control of execution then returns to the WHILE (logical expression) DO statement and retests the logical expression. This flow of execution continues repeatedly until the logical expression becomes false or until another test statement inside the block causes a transfer out of the block structure. When the logical expression is false (which includes the first test), control of execution resumes at the statement following the END WHILE. For example:

99 FORMAT (F5.1)
98 FORMAT (1H0,F8.2,5X,I3)
N = 0
XSUM = 0.0
WHILE (N .LE. 100) DO
READ (5,99) X
IF (X .EQ. −99.9) GO TO 10
XSUM = XSUM + X
N = N + 1
END WHILE
10 WRITE (6,98) XSUM, N

The loop would be reexecuted until 100 cards were read or a value of −99.9 for X is read.

When a WHILE-DO control structure is used in a program, a particular variable is normally identified as the **loop-control variable**. The loop-control variable is that variable whose value is continually tested in the logical expression. This variable must be correctly initialized prior to entering the WHILE DO block in order for the loop to be executed the correct number of times. The value of the loop-control variable should be updated within each loop execution. Otherwise, the logical expression may never become false and the loop exit may never occur. The updating of the loop-control variable is usually the last executable statement in the WHILE loop.

The END WHILE statement is a nonexecutable statement. If control of execution is transferred to a statement inside the block structure, the statements are executed in a sequential manner, and the END WHILE statement is ignored. Control of execution may be transferred to a statement outside the block structure at any time. The WHILE (logical-expression) DO statement cannot be the range statement in a DO loop nor the given statement in a Logical IF.

DO CASE: END CASE Block

The DO CASE block implements the Select Case i of $(S_1, S_2, \ldots, S_n)$ control structure. This block structure provides capabilities similar to those of a Computed GO TO statement. The general form of the DO CASE block is:

```
           ⎛  DO CASE index-variable
           ⎜  CASE
           ⎜      .
           ⎜      . statement(s)
           ⎜      .
           ⎜  CASE
           ⎜      .
           ⎜      . statement(s)
   block  ⎨      .
structure  ⎜      .
           ⎜      . (additional cases)
           ⎜      .
           ⎜  IF NONE DO
           ⎜      .
           ⎜      . statement(s)
           ⎜      .
           ⎝  END CASE
              . . . ◄——— (continue execution of program here)
```

The "index-variable" must be an integer variable whose value is used to select the proper CASE and its related statements. That is, if the value of the index-variable is 1, then the statements belonging to the first CASE statement are executed; if the value of the index-variable is 2, then the statements belonging to the second CASE statement are executed; and so on. After the statements belonging to the selected CASE statement are executed, control of execution resumes at the statement immediately following the END CASE statement (unless a GO TO statement was encountered).

If the value of the index-variable is negative, zero, or greater than the number of CASE statements, then the statements following the IF NONE DO statement and preceding the END CASE statement are executed. Control of execution is then resumed at the statement following the END CASE statement. The IF NONE DO statement acts like an "else" option to cover all invalid values of the index-variable.

The IF NONE DO statement is optional. If this statement is omitted, control of execution resumes at the next statement after the END CASE whenever the index-variable is negative, zero, or greater than the number of cases. If the IF NONE DO statement is used, it must follow the statements associated with the last case. Only one IF NONE DO statement is allowed in a DO CASE block structure.

An example of the use of a DO CASE is as follows:

```
99 FORMAT (I2)
98 FORMAT (1H0,31HINDX IS NOT A 1,2, OR 3, BUT = ,I4)
   READ (5,99) INDX
   DO CASE INDX
       CASE
           I1S = I1S + 1
       CASE
           I2S = I2S + 2
       CASE
           I3S = I3S + 3
       IF NONE DO
           WRITE (6,98) INDX
   END CASE
```

When a value of 1 is read for INDX, a 1 is added to a special counter named I1S. If the value of INDX is 2, a 2 is added to a special counter named I2S. A 3 is added to a special counter named I3S when INDX has a value of 3. If the value of INDX is not a 1, 2, or 3, then a message is written to this effect.

The CASE, IF NONE DO, and END CASE statements are nonexecutable statements. Control may be transferred to a statement inside the block structure from a statement outside the block. If such a transfer of control is made, any CASE statement, the IF NONE DO, and END CASE statements are ignored; thus, control of execution continues in a sequential manner from the statement to which the transfer is made. Control of execution may be transferred from a statement inside the block to a statement outside the block at any time.

The DO CASE statement must not be the range statement in a DO loop or the statement given on a Logical IF statement. The first CASE statement immediately following the DO CASE statement is optional. If the first CASE statement is omitted, correct logic is performed as if it were present. A CASE statement may be followed immediately by another CASE statement. This allows a value of the index-variable to be ignored, and control of execution resumes at the statement after the END CASE. A comment may be added after the keyword "CASE" on the CASE statement. Care should be taken in this capability since an " = " symbol in the comments may be taken as an Assignment statement.

EXECUTE Statement

The EXECUTE statement causes a REMOTE BLOCK structure to be executed. The general form of this statement is:

EXECUTE name

where **name** is the name assigned to the REMOTE BLOCK as given in the REMOTE BLOCK statement.

Control of execution resumes at the statement following the EXECUTE statement after execution of the REMOTE BLOCK named in the EXECUTE statement. An EXECUTE statement may be in the range statement of a DO loop, or it may be the statement given in a Logical IF statement.

REMOTE BLOCK: END BLOCK Structure

This block structure identifies a group of consecutive statements that are preceded by the REMOTE BLOCK statement and terminated by an END BLOCK statement. The REMOTE BLOCK structure can be executed only by using an EXECUTE statement in a program unit. Thus, the use of REMOTE BLOCK structures provides a parameterless, subroutine-like capability within a program unit. Since no arguments or parameter list is used, the current value of a variable is used upon entering a REMOTE BLOCK. Any variable modified within the REMOTE BLOCK retains its new value upon exit from the block.

Each REMOTE BLOCK structure is assigned a symbolic name, which is formed from the rules for choosing other FORTRAN variable names. Each REMOTE BLOCK must be assigned a unique name. This name, however, may be the same name as a variable, array, or subprogram used in the same program unit. The general form of the REMOTE BLOCK structure is:

block structure
$\Bigg\{$

REMOTE BLOCK name
. . .
. . . statement(s) to be executed
. . . when the remote block is referenced
. . .
END BLOCK

REMOTE BLOCK structures may be located anywhere in a program unit. However, a GO TO or a transfer of control statement must immediately precede the REMOTE BLOCK statement to prevent sequentially "falling into" the block structure. The first executable statement (not belonging to another REMOTE BLOCK structure) following the END BLOCK statement should have a statement number assigned to it; otherwise, it could never be executed. It is recommended that you place all REMOTE BLOCK structures at the end of a program unit between a STOP or RETURN and the END statement, in order to avoid placement errors. A maximum of 255 REMOTE BLOCK structures may be used in a program unit.

The REMOTE BLOCK and END BLOCK statements are nonexecutable. A comment may be included on the END BLOCK statement. Care should be taken to avoid certain special characters in the comment, since a " = " symbol may be taken as an Assignment statement.

Consider the following example.

```
99 FORMAT (1H0,I7)
   I = 7
   EXECUTE X
   WRITE (6,99) XRSLT
   I = 11
   EXECUTE X
   WRITE (6,99) XRSLT
   STOP
   REMOTE BLOCK X
        XRSLT = (I*3) / (I-1)
        END BLOCK OF X
   END
```

A REMOTE BLOCK structure must not be nested (defined) within another REMOTE BLOCK structure. No statement in a REMOTE BLOCK structure may transfer control from within a REMOTE BLOCK to another statement in the program unit (a compiler error will occur). Otherwise, any WATFIV or WATFIV-S statements and block structures may be used in a REMOTE BLOCK structure. Subprograms may be called/invoked from within a REMOTE BLOCK structure. A REMOTE BLOCK may contain an EXECUTE statement that causes another REMOTE BLOCK structure to be executed. As with subprograms, a REMOTE BLOCK structure must not call a subprogram, execute itself, or execute another REMOTE BLOCK that results in a loop.

A REMOTE BLOCK may be entered only by means of an EXECUTE statement. The BLOCK execution is terminated by executing the statement immediately preceding the END BLOCK statement. Transfers or loops may be performed by statements within the block as long as control of execution is maintained within the block. Any attempt to transfer control to a statement inside a REMOTE BLOCK from a location outside the block will result in an execution error.

WHILE-EXECUTE Statement

The WHILE-EXECUTE statement causes a REMOTE BLOCK structure to be executed repeatedly while a specified condition in a logical expression is true. The general form of the WHILE-EXECUTE statement is:

WHILE (logical expression) EXECUTE name

If the logical expression is true, the REMOTE BLOCK identified by **"name"** is executed, and control of execution returns to the WHILE statement. When the logical expression is false, control of execution resumes at the next executable statement after the WHILE. For example:

WHILE (KNT .LE. 50) EXECUTE RB1

The REMOTE BLOCK named RB1 will be repeatedly executed while KNT is less than or equal to 50. If the REMOTE BLOCK named RB1 does not assign a value greater than 50 to KNT, the program will loop indefinitely (until execution time is exhausted). The WHILE-EXECUTE statement must not be the range statement in a DO loop or the given statement in a Logical IF statement.

AT END DO: END AT END Block

The AT END DO block structure is used to specify the processing to be done when an end-of-file condition is encountered by a READ statement. The general form of this block is:

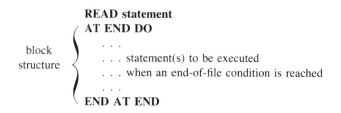

The AT END DO statement must immediately follow a READ statement.

If an end-of-file condition is encountered by the READ statement, the statements following the AT END DO statement and preceding the END AT END statement are executed. Control of execution then resumes at the statement following the END AT END statement. If an end-of-file condition is not encountered by the READ statement, control of execution is transferred to the statement immediately following the END AT END statement.

The AT END DO and END AT END statements are nonexecutable. Control of execution may be transferred to a statement inside the block from a statement outside the block. When such a transfer is made, the END AT END statement is ignored, and execution continues in a sequential manner. Control of execution may be transferred to a statement outside the block from a statement inside the block at anytime. An example is:

99 FORMAT (F5.2)
98 FORMAT (1H0,15HEND OF DATA SET)
READ (5,99) X

```
              AT END DO
              N = N − 1
              WRITE (6,98)
              GO TO 20
          END AT END
                . . .
                . . .
                . . .
          20 CONTINUE
```

When the end-of-file is encountered on unit 5, one will be subtracted from the variable N, an end-of-data-set message is printed, and control of execution is transferred to statement number 20.

The READ statement associated with an AT END DO block cannot be 1) the range statement in a DO loop, 2) the statement given in a Logical IF statement, 3) used with direct access files or "core-to-core" read operations, or 4) used when the "END =" option is included in the READ statement.

WATFIV is indeed a highly versatile, efficient compiler. The rapid compilation for fast turnarounds and the outstanding error diagnostics for student independence in program debugging make this an attractive FORTRAN compiler for academic institutions.

The 80-Column Punched Card   Appendix B

A common medium to input programs and data to the computer in a student environment is the punched card. It contains 80 vertical columns, each of which holds one character, and twelve horizontal rows. A particular character is encoded by punching holes in the proper rows for the respective column.

You should be familiar with these terms about the punched card:

Character—A character is a single alphabetic letter, numeric digit, or special character encoded in one vertical column on the card.

Column—A column is one vertical area on the card, used to contain one character. Each column contains twelve horizontal rows.

Column 1—Column 1 is the leftmost column in the card.

Column 80—Column 80 is the rightmost column in the card.

Row—A row is one horizontal area across the card. There are twelve rows on a card. The top two rows are the 12 and 11 rows. These two rows are not labeled (printed with digits). The remaining ten rows are labeled 0–9.

12 Edge—The 12 edge is the top edge of the card, the edge nearest the 12 row.

9 Edge—The 9 edge is the bottom edge of the card, the edge nearest the 9 row.

Zone rows—The top three rows (12, 11, 0) of the card are known as the zone rows. The top two zone rows are not labeled.

Digit rows—The bottom ten rows (0–9) of the card are known as the digit rows. Note that row 0 is considered both a zone and a digit row. The character contained in the column (letter or digit) determines which type of row the 0 row is used as. The ten digit rows have their corresponding digit printed in each of the 80 columns.

Field—A field is one or more adjacent columns used to contain an item of information. For example, the nine-digit Social Security number is a field requiring nine adjacent columns to encode. If an item such as a name consists of twenty characters, a twenty-column field is required to encode it.

Face—The face of the card is the front side with the printed information.

Interpreting—Interpreting is the translating of the punched code into a form readable by people. The interpreting of encoded characters is printed at the top of the card. Each character is interpreted at the top of the column in which it is punched. The interpreting is done automatically by the keypunch machine as the card is punched, provided that the print switch is on. If the print switch is off, the characters are not interpreted. The interpreted characters along the top edge of the card mean nothing to the computer; they are solely for your benefit, to read the encoded information; the card reader reads and translates only the punched holes.

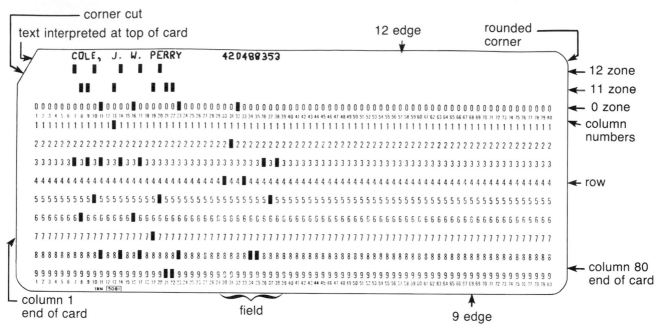

Figure B.1 Features of the 80-column punched card

These features of the punched card are illustrated in figure B.1.

The standard 80-column card is 3¼″ high by 7⅜″ long. Punched cards come in a variety of colors. The color is of no significance to the computer; to the computer operator, however, different colors represent different types of cards. For example, one color might be used to identify the beginning job card. Punched cards come with and without printed fields on them. The printed information is needed in many production environments and means something to the user. The punched card normally used in the student environment is the standard card without any identifying fields printed on it. A punched card may have the upper left or the upper right corner cut off. Different types of corner-cuts identify different types of cards, such as the beginning or ending card in a deck of cards. For example, you may be required to use a right-handed corner cut card for the first card in your card deck, while all the remaining cards have a left-handed corner cut. This procedure helps the computer operator separate individual decks when multiple card decks are loaded together in the card reader. The rounded corner cut helps reduce wear and tear on a card and also helps reduce the chance of card jams in the card reader.

Holes are punched for the various characters in accordance with the following special coding scheme:

Numeric digits. A numeric digit is coded in a column by a single hole in the respective row for the desired digit. For example, the digit 2 would be coded by punching a hole in row 2 in a specific card column; the digit 7 would be coded by punching a hole in row 7.

Alphabetic letters. An alphabetic letter is coded by punching two holes in a column. One hole is punched in the zone area (either row 12, 11, or 0), and one hole is punched in the numeric area (one of the rows 1 through 9). For example, the letter A would be represented by a punch in the 12 row and 1 row; the letter M would be coded by a hole in the 11 row and the 4 row.

Special characters. Special characters (characters other than numeric digits and alphabetic letters) are coded as one, two, or three punches. For example, the minus sign ($-$) is represented by a single hole in row 11. The plus sign ($+$) is represented by three holes in rows 12, 6, and 8. The decimal point (.) is coded as three holes in rows 12, 3, and 8.

It is not necessary to memorize the code for the different characters in the punched card. The holes are punched into a card by a machine called a keypunch, which has a keyboard very similar to that of the typewriter. By typing the proper character on the keyboard, the correct holes are punched.

Different computer systems, however, may require a different punched card code to encode the special characters. For example, a " + " sign is encoded as the combination 12-6-8 punches for an IBM system, while it is encoded as a 12 punch for a CDC computer. The IBM 029 keypunch code configuration is used for some computers; the IBM 026 or Univac 1710 keypunch configuration is used for others. Figure B.2 shows the 029 Keypunch codes for Amdahl, Burroughs, and IBM computers.

A card punched with the various characters available on the 029 keypunch is shown in figure B.3. Note that all alphabetic letters are punched as capital letters.

All computers use the same punched card code for the alphabetic letters and numeric digits. The special characters "-", "/", "*", "$", "." and "," are also punched with the same card code on all computers. The other special characters are encoded with different punch combinations on various computers. Special care must be taken when punching the other special characters on an 029 keypunch for a computer that requires the 026 keypunch code configurations.

Alphabetic letters	EBCDIC (029) card punch code	Numeric digits	EBCDIC (029) card punch code
A	12–1	0	0
B	12–2	1	1
C	12–3	2	2
D	12–4	3	3
E	12–5	4	4
F	12–6	5	5
G	12–7	6	6
H	12–8	7	7
I	12–9	8	8
J	11–1	9	9
K	11–2		
L	11–3		EBCDIC (029) card punch code
M	11–4	Special characters	
N	11–5		
O	11–6		
P	11–7	space	no punches
Q	11–8	+	12–6–8
R	11–9	–	11
S	0–2	/	0–1
T	0–3	*	11–4–8
U	0–4	=	6–8
V	0–5	(	12–5–8
W	0–6	)	11–5–8
X	0–7	.	12–3–8
Y	0–8	,	0–3–8
Z	0–9	$	11–3–8
		'	5–8
		&	12
		"	7–8
		:	2–8
		@	4–8
		%	0–4–8
		#	3–8
		;	11–6–8
		?	0–7–8

Figure B.2 Punched card codes for Amdahl, Burroughs, and IBM computers using the 029 keypunch code configurations

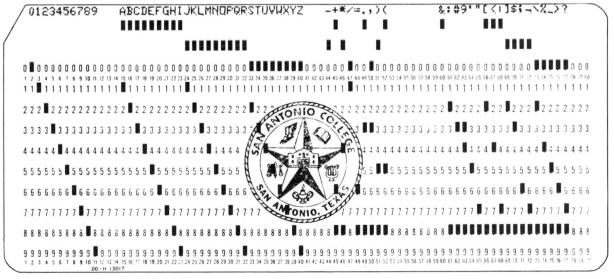

Figure B.3 Coding scheme of the characters available on the 029 keypunch

Special characters	Hollerith (026) card punch code	Your system
+	12	
=	3–8	
(	0–4–8	
)	12–4–8	
'	11–5–8	
&	0–7–8	
"	4–8	
:	2–8	
@	5–8	
%	6–8	
#	0–6–8	
;	12–7–8	

Figure B.4 Punched card codes for various computers using the 026 keypunch code configurations

Depending on the card reader, Univac, CDC, DEC, and Honeywell may use the punched card codes given in figure B.4. If your system uses a different punched card code, you should write its codes in the column labeled "Your System."

Punched cards are used because of their flexibility. If you want to correct a card in a program or data file, you can simply locate the card, repunch it, and replace the corrected card into the deck. Punched cards also provide a permanent record, which can be used repeatedly. However, they do have their limitations. Their record size is limited to 80 characters. Punched cards cannot be folded, spindled, mutilated, or stapled and are sensitive to high humidity and cold temperatures. They also are a very slow medium for input and output of data compared to other media.

IBM 029 Keypunch Operations   Appendix C

In a student environment, FORTRAN jobs may be submitted to the computer on punched cards. The FORTRAN statements, JCL, and data cards are all punched onto the 80-column punched card by using a special machine known as a **keypunch machine.** (Some people also refer to this machine as a card punch machine.) Consequently, students using punched cards must learn how to operate the keypunch. Even though your computer center may keypunch your source program, you must still punch your corrections.

There are several types of keypunch machines available for punching the 80-column card. Univac has a very efficient keypunch known as the model 1710. IBM produces several models—the 026, 029, and 129. The 026 model may be used at some installations, especially those having CDC computers. The machine most commonly used is the 029, which is used to keypunch programs for IBM, Honeywell, and Burroughs computers. The main difference between the two machines (026 and 029) is in some of the special characters. The purpose of this Appendix is to provide an overview to the operations of the most frequently used features of the IBM 029 keypunch machine.

The four stations on the keypunch machine are:

1. Input card hopper—in which the blank cards are loaded to be fed into the machine.
2. Punch station—at which a card is positioned for punching.
3. Read station—to which the punched card is advanced after being punched. The read station may be used for duplicating a card or portions of it, in case of errors.
4. Output card stacker—at which the cards are stacked after leaving the read station.

Each punch card usually passes through each of these stations in the machine operation. That is, a card is fed from the input hopper into the punch station, where it is punched. It is then released to the read station and then to the output stacker. However, a card may be duplicated or corrected by inserting it directly into the read station. Figure C.1 presents a picture of the IBM 029 keypunch machine and the location of these four stations. Note that the card hopper is located in the upper right-hand portion of the machine. The read and punch stations are located at the middle of the machine behind the keyboard. The card stacker is located in the upper left-hand portion of the machine.

Figure C.1 also shows the location of other important features of the keypunch. The mainline power switch is a red toggle lever located beneath the keyboard and to the far right. You flip the switch up to turn the machine on and down to turn it off. The keyboard for typing is located towards the right-hand side on the reading board (table top). The other features you will use are the column indicator and backspace button. These are located in the center of the machine above the read station.

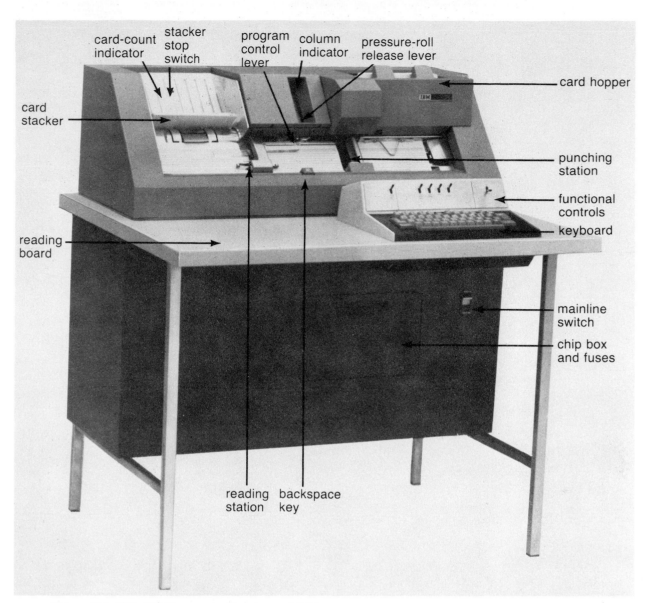

Figure C.1 IBM 029 Keypunch. (Courtesy of IBM)

The Keyboard. The keyboard is used to type the characters to be punched and to control the movement of the cards through the four stations. The position of the alphabetic characters is identical to their position on the typewriter keyboard. The location of the digits and the special characters is different. The numeric digits are all located on the right side of the keyboard. Since most input data is numeric, the location of all the digits on the right of the keyboard allows a keypunch operator to control the coding sheets with the left hand and to punch the digits with the right hand. The space bar which moves the card forward one position each time it is depressed is located at the bottom of the keyboard, as on the typewriter. Study the location of these keys on the keyboard, as shown in figure C.2, before you proceed to learn the control keys.

The light or gray-colored keys are for punching characters. The dark or blue-colored keys are control keys for special purposes, such as feeding cards, registering cards at a station, shift selection, and other functions.

Three main control keys you will use all the time are the feed (FEED), register (REG), and release (REL). These are located towards the far right of the keyboard and are used to control the movement of the cards. The FEED key feeds a card from the card hopper down to the punch station but normally does not engage it at the station. The REG key must be depressed to register the card at the punch station before you are able to begin typing. If you depress the FEED key twice, the machine will feed two cards from the hopper and automatically register the first one at the punch station. You must never feed more than two cards down to the punch station; otherwise a card jam will occur.

Figure C.2 Keyboard on an IBM 029 keypunch. (Courtesy of IBM)

The REL key releases a card to the next station. If a card is in the punch station it is moved to the read station. If the machine is in auto feed mode, the card will be automatically registered at the read station. Otherwise you must depress the REG key to register the card at the read station. Again, depressing the REL key followed by the REG key will move the card at the read station into the stacker. If the machine is in auto feed mode, the cards will be automatically registered at the next station when the REL key is depressed.

Notice the NUMERIC shift key at the lower left corner of the keyboard and the ALPHA shift key at the lower right. These are similar to the shift keys on the typewriter, but there are only capital letters on the keyboard; so these two keys allow you to shift from alpha mode to numeric, and vice versa. The alphabetic letters, comma, period, and some special characters are in alpha mode. The numeric digits and other special characters (indicated above the letters) are in numeric shift.

The standard mode of the machine is ALPHA shift. To punch the characters indicated on the lower half of the key, you simply type the proper key. But, to punch a digit or some special characters indicated on the upper half of the key, you must depress the NUMERIC shift key. Releasing the NUMERIC key returns the machine to alpha mode. You can place the machine so that it will be in numeric mode all the time by using the program control feature (which will be discussed later) and lowering the "starwheels" control mechanism. Then, when alpha mode characters are needed, you must depress the ALPHA shift key. The student does not always use the program control feature; so we will assume the alpha shift mode to be the normal setting. If, however, you get special characters or numeric digits when you depress a key, look to see if the "starwheels" control mechanism is engaged. This switch is located above the backspace button and can be disengaged by flipping it in the opposite direction.

The DUP key is located in the center of the top row of keys. When depressed it will duplicate the information in the card at the read station into the same card columns of the card at the punch station. This key gets considerable use in making corrections. You simply insert the card to be corrected into the read station, feed and register a blank card into the punch station, and duplicate the information up to the column in error. Then you can type in the correct character or information and duplicate the rest of the card.

If you attempt to depress two keys at the same time, the keyboard will lock, and you will be unable to type a character. To free the keyboard, depress the ERROR RESET key located on the far left side of the keyboard; then resume typing. The MULT PCH key located at the upper left corner of the keyboard allows you to punch multiple punches into a column on a card. When this key is depressed, the card is locked at the punch station, and any number of characters can be typed into the same column. Of course, this usually produces an invalid character, but that is sometimes desired. Releasing the MULT PCH key then causes the card to move to the next column in the punch station.

Switches. Located immediately above the keyboard are six switches. Starting from the right, these switches and functions are:

CLEAR switch—Flipping this switch upward will clear the cards in both the punch and read stations and stack them in the card stacker. This provides a shortcut way of retrieving a punched card without having to go through the procedure of repeatedly depressing the REL and REG keys. This switch is spring loaded, so that it automatically returns to the down position.

LZ PRINT (left-zero print) switch—Is used to print high-order zeroes in a field and should be set on (up).

PRINT switch—Causes the characters to be printed across the top of the card. When turned off, the printing operation is not performed. This switch should always be set on (up).

AUTO FEED switch—Provides for the automatic feeding of cards. If you wish to have the cards continuously fed in an automatic mode, then set this switch up. When you are duplicating individual cards, however, you usually want to feed and register them individually. Therefore, set the switch off (down).

PROG SEL (Program select) switch—Is used in conjunction with the program control feature. Since the student does not use this feature, it is normally set down. However, the setting of this switch has no effect if the program control feature is not engaged.

AUTO SKIP DUP (auto skip/duplicate) switch—Is also used in conjunction with the program control feature.

Column Indicator and Backspace Button. The location of the characters on the card is important. For example, the FORTRAN statement must begin in column 7 or later. When the card is registered at the punch or read stations, it is positioned at card column 1. You can advance the card to column 7 by depressing the space bar six times. However, it is impractical to keep mental track of the current position of the card. So the **column indicator** is used to show the column at which a card is positioned.

Above the read station is a window through which can be seen a red pointer and a dial indicating the current position of the card. The dial has hashed marks like a ruler to indicate the current position (card column). The odd positions have a long hash mark, and the even positions have a short hash mark with the indicated position number. Thus, you can read the current position of a card from the dial by noting the column indicated by the red pointer.

The backspace button is a large, protruding, light-colored button located beneath the center of the read station. Each time you depress this button the cards in the read and punch stations are moved backwards one position. Of course, it is impractical to backspace more than a few positions. Simply feed a new card and use the DUP key to help make the desired corrections.

Loading Cards into the Hopper. Many computer centers provide cards for the students. Others expect the students to provide their own. In either case, the student must know how to properly load the cards into the hopper when it is empty.

A spring-loaded pressure plate is provided in the card hopper to force the cards to the front of the hopper. When this plate is pushed to the rear of the hopper, a catch will retain it in this position. The cards can now be inserted into the hopper. You should take extreme care to ensure that the cards are loaded in straight. Pat them down gently to make sure that the tops of the cards are even and inserted correctly. Next, depress the flat metal button on top of the spring-loaded plate to cause it to move up against the cards. Should the cards fail to feed, it usually means that the front card is bent at the bottom. Push the plate back and remove the bent card(s).

Clearing a Card Jam. When more than one card is registered at the punch or read station, a card jam occurs. The cards will not move when you type, depress the REL key, or flip the CLEAR switch. Depressing the FEED key will only jam more cards. **DO NOT** attempt to pull the cards out with brute force, since this will damage the punch dies and the machine.

The top center portion of the machine, which houses the window to the column indicator, will fold down. Simply pull upwards and forward on this portion. The metal portion will fold out and lie down against the read station, exposing the column indicator. Located at the lower right of the column indicator is a silver-colored, metal lever called the pressure-roll release lever. By depressing this metal lever towards the back of the machine, the pressure is removed from the punch dies. It usually takes a great deal of force to depress this lever, since it has a heavy spring. Fully depress this lever first; then you can pull out the jammed cards without damaging the machine. If you are uncertain of this operation, contact someone in the computer center who knows how to remove the cards. Remember, do not attempt to pull out the cards physically without fully depressing this lever. If you are unable to clear the card jam, put a note on the keypunch as to the problem and find a new machine.

Summary of Operations. Assuming that cards are in the card hopper, the following rules summarize the operations of the keypunch machine.

1. Make sure the red power switch is on, i.e., in the up position.
2. Press the FEED key.
3. Press the REG (Register) key.
4. Punch the card. Watch the column indicator as to current position of the card to make sure that you punch the characters in the desired columns.
5. Press the REL (Release) key to move the card from the punch to the read station.
6. If more cards are to be punched, repeat steps 2–5. Otherwise, flip the clear switch or press the REG and REL keys alternately until the card is placed into the stacker.
7. If the AUTO FEED switch is on (up), you need only to depress the FEED key twice. This will cause the machine to automatically feed and register the cards for you.
8. The NUMERIC shift key must be depressed when punching digits and most special characters.
9. The backspace key may be used to move a card backwards in the station.
10. Corrections cannot normally be made by backspacing and repunching. A character punched over another character in the same column usually produces an invalid character, which cannot be read by the computer. Corrections are normally made by releasing the current card at the punch station, duplicating the correct portion of the old card, and punching the correction onto the new card.

The Program Drum and Program Card

The keypunch program drum is used to aid people in punching large numbers of cards (a program or data), with the same format. The program drum allows tabulation, skipping, and duplication of card fields automatically. This greatly reduces the time required to punch a large deck of cards.

Each keypunched card usually consists of several fields. For example, FORTRAN statement cards have the statement number field, continuation column, statement field, and the sequence number/identification field. Data cards may have multiple fields, depending on the record format. Each field may have one of three operations performed when it is punched. It may be skipped, duplicated from the previous card, or manually punched.

There is a card called a program card, which is divided into a similar set of fields. Each field will control the operation to be performed on the corresponding field in the punched card (source program or data card). A program card is punched with the proper codes and placed on the program drum. The program card is activated by the program-control lever. This lever lowers a set of starwheels onto the program card for the keypunch machine to sense the punched codes in the program card.

Every program card field is made up of two elements:

1. A start code in the first column.
2. A definition code in the remaining columns of the field.

The start code for manual entry of the punched field is a blank. Punching will be continued until the end of the field is reached or until the SKIP key is pressed.

The start code for automatic skipping is the 11 punch. The 11-row punch causes an automatic skip to the end of the field. That is, skipping will continue until the beginning of the next field (as defined by a start code) or until the end of the card is reached. The AUTO SKIP/DUP switch must be set on (up position) for the automatic skip operation to work.

The start code for automatic duplication is the 0 punch. The 0-row punch causes automatic duplication to the end of the field. That is, duplication of the data card field (from the previous data card) will continue until the beginning of the next program field (as defined by a start code) or until the end of the card is reached. The AUTO SKIP/DUP switch must be on (up position) for automatic duplicating to work.

The field definition code is a 12 punch. The 12-row punch must appear in every column of the field except the first position. This 12-punch code, therefore, defines the length of the field. It causes a skip or duplication operation (begun in that field) to continue through the end of the field.

In addition to the start and field definition codes, it may be necessary to include the alphabetic shift code. The alphabetic shift code is a 1 punch. The 1-row punch is required in a manual entry field when alphabetic characters or special characters under the alphabetic shift are punched. If this code is omitted, the effect is as if the NUMERIC shift key were locked down, i.e., the ALPHA shift key must be depressed for the proper alphabetic characters. If the alphabetic shift code is included, the effect is as if the ALPHA shift key were locked down; you must press the NUMERIC shift key for numeric digits or special characters under the NUMERIC shift key. Only those characters in a data field that are to be used for alphabetic data need the alphabetic shift code. Normally the alphabetic shift code is included in every column for an alphabetic data field. If the alphabetic shift code is included with another code, such as the field definition code, it is multipunched with the other code. The character "A" consists of the 12 and 1 punches and may be punched for a field requiring both the 12-punch field definition code and the 1-punch alphabetic shift code.

There are two program card codes for IBM 029 and IBM 129 keypunch machines. The program code previously discussed was for PROG ONE codes. Following are the drum card program codes for both PROG ONE and PROG TWO.

Function	PROG ONE Code	PROG TWO Code
field definition	12	4
start AUTO SKIP	11	5
start AUTO DUP	0	6
punch alphabetic	1	7

Let us look at two examples of a program drum card. The first example allows the following operation on the punched cards.

> skip columns 1 to 30
> duplicate columns 31 to 35
> skip column 36
> punch manually columns 37 to 40 (alphabetic shift)
> punch manually columns 41 to 80 (numeric shift)

Following are the codes punched in the program card using the PROG ONE code. A "-" represents an 11 punch, an "&" represents a 12 punch, a "0" represents a 0 punch, a "1" represents a 1 punch, and an "A" represents the combination of 12 and 1 punches.

```
                    1                   2                   3                   4         7 8
card columns:  1 2 3 4 5 6 7 8 9 0 1 2 3 4 5 6 7 8 9 0 1 2 3 4 5 6 7 8 9 0 1 2 . . . 9 0
               - & & & & & & & & & & & & & & & & & & & & & & & & & & & & & 0 & & & & - 1 A A A   & . . . & &
```

The example below shows a program card that could be used for punching a FORTRAN source deck. The operations would be:

> punch manually columns 1 to 5 (numeric shift)
> punch manually column 6 (numeric shift)
> punch manually columns 7 to 72 (alphabetic shift)
> skip columns 73 to 80

Following are the punched codes in the program drum card.

```
                    1                   2                   3       6   7               8
card columns:  1 2 3 4 5 6 7 8 9 0 1 2 3 4 5 6 7 8 9 0 1 2 3 4 5 6 7 8 9 0   1 . . . 8 9 0 1 2 3 4 5 6 7 8 9 0
               & & & &   1 A  AA AA AA AA AA AA AA AA AA AA AA   A . . . AA AA A - & & & & & &
```

Following is a summary of the codes for punching various types of fields:

Punch a NUMERIC field	— First column is blank, followed by a 12-punch for each column in the remainder of the field.
Duplicate a NUMERIC field	— First column is a 0 punch, followed by 12-punches for the remainder of the field.
Punch an ALPHABETIC field	— First column is a 1 punch, followed by letter A's (12 and 1 punches)
Duplicate an ALPHABETIC field	— First column is a / (slash), followed by letter A's. (A slash is a 0 and a 1 punch.)
Skip a field	— First column is an 11 punch (a "-"), followed by 12-punches for the remainder of the field.

Operation of the Program Drum and Program Card

The following instructions are given for installing and removing the program drum and program card:

Program drum removal. The program-control lever must be switched off (to the right) to remove the program drum. Turn the program-control lever to the right to raise the sensing mechanism (starwheels). Do **NOT** attempt to remove the program drum with the starwheels down. This will damage the starwheels so that the machine cannot read the program card. Remove the program drum by pulling in a direction parallel to the sensing mechanism. It is housed on a steel shaft, so do not pull to one side. If another program card is already on the drum, it must be removed before you insert your program card.

Program card removal. Turn the clamping strip handle (at the top of the drum) to the center position and remove the column-1 end of the card from beneath the clamping strip. Next, turn the handle fully counter-clockwise and remove the column-80 end of the card from the drum. A new card may now be inserted on the program drum.

Program card insertion. Turn the clamping strip handle fully counter-clockwise to release pressure on the drum. Insert the column-80 end of the card under the smooth edge of the clamping strip. The 9-edge of the card should be flush with the metal rim of the drum. Make sure the column-80 end of the card is flush with the metal edge under the strip. Two alignment check holes in the clamping strip are available to ensure this alignment visually. With the column-80 of the card inserted under the clamping strip, turn the handle to the center position. This tightens the smooth edge of the clamping strip and loosens the toothed edge. Wrap the card tightly around the drum (with a smoothing twist of the hand) and insert the column-1 end of the card under the toothed edge of the clamping strip. Then turn the handle clockwise as far as it will go. This fastens the toothed edge of the clamping strip. The drum with its program card is now ready to be inserted in the machine.

Program drum insertion. With the program sensing mechanism raised (program-control lever to the right), place the drum on the mounting shaft of the program drum unit. Be sure to position the drum so that the aligning pin (on the drum) falls in the aligning hole in the column indicator dial. Make sure the drum is firmly seated in its housing, by giving a gentle downward push. To activate the program drum, turn the program-control lever to the left. This lowers the sensing mechanism (starwheels) on to the program card. Press the release key. Note: an empty program drum should not be inserted in the program unit, and the sensing mechanism must never be lowered when no program drum is in place.

If any duplication is to be done, insert a "master" card in the read station. Set the AUTO SKIP/DUP, PROG SEL, and AUTO FEED switches on. Press the FEED key twice. The keypunch with the program drum should be ready to use.

Practice is usually the best teacher in learning how to use the keypunch machine. Take time to learn the many control keys and their functions. Punched cards have been with us for a long time in data processing; so you should learn how to use the keypunch machine to punch the cards for your various needs. For a complete discussion on the full use and capabilities of the IBM 029 keypunch machine, refer to Reference Manual IBM 029 Card Punch, A24–3332-5.

The Scientific Notation and Exponential Form for Representing Numeric Values   Appendix D

Mathematicians, engineers, and other people engaged in scientific work often represent numeric quantities in a shorthand notation referred to as a **Scientific Notation**. A constant is represented as a decimal value followed by a power-of-ten value, such as 1.678×10^{15} or 42.3×10^{-12}. The decimal value is multiplied by the power-of-ten value to obtain the true value of the constant. The advantage of the scientific notation is the ease and brevity with which very large and very small numbers can be represented. For example $.871265 \times 10^{20}$ takes less space and time to write and is easier to read than

$$87126500000000000000.$$

Likewise, $.1265 \times 10^{-11}$ is shorter and easier to read than

$$.000000000001265$$

The power-of-ten value is known as the exponent part. Since a power of ten involves moving the decimal point one position, the exponent tells us how many positions left or right the decimal point in the number is to be moved to obtain the true value of the number. If the power of ten is a positive number, then the true value of the constant is found by moving the decimal point that many positions to the right. When the power of ten is a negative number then we have the reciprocal of a positive power. That is: $10^{-2} = \dfrac{1}{10^2}$. Therefore, a division by the power-of-ten value takes place, and you must move the decimal point that many positions to the left to find the true value of the constant.

In FORTRAN there is no way to raise characters a half line to indicate a superscript or exponent value. The number 10 is not written, since it is understood that the exponent always indicates a power of ten. To indicate the end of the decimal value and the beginning of the exponent, the letter E is used. For example, 1.234E09. Thus, the letter E may be interpreted as "times 10 to the power of."

The exponent value must be a one- or two-digit integer. A sign may precede the integer exponent value to denote the value, e.g., E + 10, E − 2, E − 03, E + 5. The exponent values from 0 to 9 may be represented by a single digit or as two digits, however you wish. The maximum and minimum values (range) of the exponent vary by computer and must not be exceeded. For example, the largest positive exponent value on the IBM mainframe computers is + 75 and the smallest negative exponent is − 78. The decimal portion of the constant must be formed in accordance with the rules of the basic real constants.

Examples of scientific formed constants with an exponent in FORTRAN are:

147.34E+ 1	(value of 1473.4)
23.5E7	(value of 235000000.)
.1E05	(value of 10000.)
1.0E0	(value of 1.0)
1.E−06	(value of .000001)
.1E−5	(value of .000001)

The true value of an exponential constant is determined as follows. If the exponent value following the E is positive, you must move the decimal point that many positions to the right. For example,

$$93.0E+06$$

means to move the decimal point 6 places to the right to give the true value of 93000000. If the exponent value following the E is negative, you must move the decimal point that many positions to the left. For example,

$$1.5E−03$$

means move the decimal point 3 places to the left to give the true value of .0015. If the exponent value following the E is zero (0 or 00), you do not move the decimal point at all. For example,

$$12.34E+00$$

represents the true value of 12.34.

Numeric input values may also be formed with an exponent. They can be read with the F format code or with the E format code discussed in chapter 16.

Floating-point values in a program may be written with an exponent by using the E format code. Since some compilers print the output values written with format-free I/O in exponential form, let us briefly discuss this output form.

All output values written in exponential form appear as a normalized number. That is, the decimal number is written as a total fraction with the decimal point appearing before the first (leftmost) digit. The exponent value is adjusted accordingly to represent this operation. A maximum of seven fractional digits are written, followed by the exponent. The exponent part consists of the letter E followed by a sign and two digits. A blank is replaced for the sign if the exponent is positive.

Consider the following examples as they will be written by WATFIV and some other compilers using format-free output:

Value	Output Form
1.34	0.1340000E 01
.1234	0.1234000E 00
− 12.34	− 0.1234000E 02
.00123	0.1230000E-02
− .0003456	− 0.3456000E-03

For mathematicians and engineers the scientific notation is a very common and widely used form for the expression of numerical constants.

Digital Equipment Corporation (DEC) RSTS/E Usage and the EDT Text Editor

Appendix E

E.1 INTRODUCTION

This appendix discusses the log-on procedure, the RSTS/E operating system, RSTS/E file naming conventions, Peripheral Interchange Program (PIP) utility, EDT text editor, and FORTRAN language execution for the PDP-11 series computers (PDP 11/34, 11/40, 11/60, 11/70, and so on). RSTS/E stands for Resource Sharing Timesharing System/Extended. It is one of the most popular operating systems, used on many PDP-11 minicomputers because of its versatility in a timesharing environment.

To turn on the Decwriter II or Decwriter III terminals, flip the switch in the upper left hand corner of the terminal keyboard to the right (ON(1)). Other key settings in the upper left corner of the Decwriter should be set as follows:

LINE/LOC—up
FDX/HDX—up
110 key—up
300 key—down
All four keys on the bottom row are up

Let us first look at the log-on procedure for a PDP-11 system using RSTS/E.

E.2 LOG-ON AND LOG-OFF PROCEDURES FOR A PDP-11 USING RSTS/E

DEC PDP-11 series computer users are assigned an account number consisting of two parts—a project number and a programmer number, separated by a comma. For example, the account number with project number 52 and programmer number 17 would be given as 52,17. The user account number is referred to as a PPN (Project-Programmer Number). A one- to six-character password is also assigned to each account. A password may be any combination of letters and digits, but no special characters are allowed.

The procedure for logging on to a PDP-11 system with RSTS/E consists of the following steps:

1. Once the terminal is on-line, enter the command

HELLO

and depress the RETURN key. This tells the system you wish to log on to the computer.

2. The system responds by typing an identification message and then a new line with the message "User:" in the left margin. This is the system prompt for you to enter your account number. For example:

RSTS/E V7.1-11 UCCS JOB 12 KB6 12-Jul-82 11:26 AM
User:

3. Type your assigned account number after the "user:" prompt:

User:52,17

4. The system responds with a message to enter your password:

Password:

5. Type your assigned password on the same line and transmit it to the system by depressing the RETURN key. Your password is not echoed (displayed) back to the terminal. A message specified by the system manager is then printed. The system manager message provides you with changes or additions to the system and may change on a day-to-day basis. The Ready messsage is displayed at the terminal if the password is valid.

If you enter an invalid account number or password, the message

Invalid entry—try again

is printed. You must repeat steps 3 through 5 by reentering your account number and password if either was invalid. You are allowed a maximum of five tries to enter a correct account number and password before you are denied access to the system. After five invalid attempts the message

Access denied

is displayed on your terminal. You either have the wrong account number or have not entered the correct password.

The command **LOG** may also be used in place of the HELLO to log on. The account number may be given after the HELLO (or LOG) command to avoid the system identification message and the user prompt. A slash may be used instead of the comma to separate the project number and the programmer number. For example:

HELLO 52/17

This is known as a fast log-on, since the system bypasses the system identification message and user: prompt.

Following is an illustration of the complete log-on procedure.

HELLO

RSTS V7.1-11 UCCS Job 14 KB6 15-Jul-82 11:17 AM
User:52/17
Password: XXXXX   (The Xs represent a valid password)

Ready

After the Ready message, you may begin work at your terminal.

Log-off Procedure

There are several optional forms of the basic **BYE** command for logging off the system. The **BYE/F** command is given to terminate a session and to log off the system; this form of the BYE command is called a fast log-off, since the number of disk blocks in use is not confirmed. The BYE command may be transmitted and then the option (F); or the option may be given after the BYE command (following the slash).

The **BYE/Y** command logs you off, but also prints several lines of text, which confirm the number of disk blocks saved in your account. The **BYE/N** command cancels the log-off procedure (the N option is normally given after the command BYE). That is, you could transmit the BYE command and then change your mind about logging off; you would then type the N option to remain on the system.

The **BYE/I** (for inspect) allows you to inspect the names of the permanent files under your account. Each permanent file name is printed on a separate line. As each file name is listed, you have the option of killing (purging) the file or retaining it. If you wish to kill (delete or purge) the file from your account, type the letter **K** (for **kill**) and transmit it. If you wish to keep the file, strike the RETURN key, and the next permanent file name will be listed on a new line.

If you forget the options available during log-off, you may type **BYE/?** to display the various options available. The option may then be entered as a separate line. That is, you may type only the command BYE, in which case the system will respond with the message—"confirm?". You may then enter any of the options—Y, N, I, or F.

E.3   RSTS/E FILE NAMES

An RSTS/E file name consists of two parts—the **filename** and an **extension**. The **filename** may consist of one to six alphabetic or numeric characters; it does not have to begin with an alphabetic letter as required by other operating systems. The **extension** may consist of zero to three alphabetic or numeric characters. These two parts are separated by a period (referred to as a "dot"). RSTS/E allows an extension part to provide unique file names that still have the first part of each identical to the others. For example:

LP1.FOR
LP1.BAK
LP1.DAT

Since the extensions are different, the three files are unique and are stored as three distinct files. The extension **FOR** is chosen to stand for a FORTRAN source program; **BAK** is chosen to stand for a "backup" copy of a file; **DAT** is used to represent the extension part of the name of a data file for lab problem one (LP1). This method of assigning file names and extensions allows great flexibility later when displaying the disk directory of all files beginning with a specific name or ending with a specific extension.

Listing the Names of Permanent Files

You may wish to see the list of permanent files you have stored on disk. The system command to see the complete list of all permanent disk files is **DIR** (directory). This command shows the file names, their block size, protection code, and date of creation. A summary message is given at the end of the list with the total number of disk blocks of storage.

The attributes of a single file or a category of files may also be listed with the DIR command. To list the name, disk block size, protection code, and creation date of a single file, you type the command DIR, followed by the file name. For example (to see the attributes of the file named LP1.FOR):

DIR LP1.FOR

The **CATALOG** (abbreviated CAT) command may also be used to list the names of the permanent files under your account. No column heading line or summary line with the number of blocks in use are printed. Simply type:

CATALOG

Another way of getting an abbreviated listing of permanent file names is with the **DIR/W** command. The switch, /W, stands for WATCH. Only the file names are printed, six per line. The command **DIR/F** prints only the file names, one per line. This is a fast way of listing all the file names if you do not wish to see the block size, protection code, and creation date of each file.

The command **DIR/S** may be given if you want to see the time of file creation along with the other information regarding the file. This command is useful when you want to confirm the last date and time of day the file was updated.

Wild Card File Names

A wild card version of file names may be used to see the list of attributes for a whole category of files. An asterisk (*) is used on either side of the period to stand for all files for that part of the file name. For example:

DIR LP1.*

would tell the system to list all files with the file name of LP1, regardless of the extension. The command

DIR *.FOR

would list all files with the extension **FOR**, regardless of their file names.

A question mark (?) can be used to mask a portion of a file name in order to list all files with any character in that position. For example:

DIR LP?.FOR

would list all files with three-letter file names beginning with LP and with the extension FOR. Since RSTS/E file names can be six characters in length, it would be best to use enough question marks to make the file name six characters. For example:

DIR LP????.*

would list all files beginning with the two letters LP, regardless of the number of characters used in the file name.

E.4   PERIPHERAL INTERCHANGE PROGRAM (PIP) USAGE

The DEC PDP-11 general purpose file utility program named PIP is used to manipulate files in your account. PIP may be used to:

1.   List your directory, using the switch /LI.
2.   List the contents of your program or file.
3.   Copy files.
4.   Rename files, using the switch /RE.
5.   Delete files, using the switch /DE.

The following subsections describe the use of PIP in these operations. Wild card file names may be used with any of these options. A space is required after the word PIP; do not include a space before the slash that indicates a switch option is being used. These commands apply to all files (data, BASIC, etc.), not only FORTRAN.

Listing Permanent File Names in Your Directory

The PIP command may be used to list the names of permanent disk files. To list all file names in your directory, enter:

PIP /LI

The /**LI** option (for LIST) tells the system to LIst all the permanent file names in your account. This command is usually faster than the DIR command. The switch option /**F** may also be used with the PIP command to list the file names only, without the accompanying information. For example:

PIP /F

would list the names of the files in your directory without their creation date or other attributes.

Listing the Contents of a File

The PIP command may be used to print or list a file. To print the file on your terminal, type the command PIP, followed by the file name and extension:

PIP PROB1.FOR

To print your file at a printer you would give the device name (assume KB15: for a fast Decwriter III), an equal sign (=), and file name and extension:

PIP KB15: = PROB1.FOR

Copying Files

You may copy a disk file to a new disk file with a different name using the **PIP** command. Give the command PIP, followed by the new file name, an equal sign (=), and the old file name. A switch may be included after the old file name to cause certain additional actions. For example, the switch name **WATCH** (**W** for short) may be given to have a message printed to verify that correct copy took place. A slash must be given between the old file name and the switch name to tell the system you are including a switch. For example:

PIP PROB1A.FOR = PROB1.FOR/W

The switch **/I** (for Inspect) may be included to tell the system to display the account number and file name of the file being used. This allows you to decide whether you want the command to be performed for the particular file. For example:

PIP PROB1A.FOR = PROB1.FOR/W/I

The system would display the message (assuming account number [52,17] is being used):

[52,17]PROB1.FOR?

Type Y (for Yes) for the operation to be performed, or type N (for No) to abandon the command. If a Y is entered, the system will copy the file and display the following messages.

[File PROB1.FOR copied to [52,17]PROB1A.FOR]

Ready

The inspect (/I) switch option is useful if you want to be sure that you specified the file names correctly. Remember, the *new* file name is given first. You could wipe out a file if you gave the old (existing) file name first. After the command is executed, the file exists under both the old and the new names. This technique is valuable if you want to maintain a backup copy of the existing version of a file.

Renaming Files

A file may be renamed (given a new name) with the PIP command. The format is the same as for copying an existing file to a new file, except that the **/RE** (RENAME) switch is given after the old file name. For example, to rename the file PROB1.FOR to LP1.FOR you would enter:

PIP LP1.FOR = PROB1.FOR/RE

The old file name PROB1.FOR would then no longer exist, since it has been renamed LP1.FOR. This command may also be used to change the protection code of files to allow other accounts to read them.

Deleting (Purging) Permanent Files on Disk

PIP may be used to delete permanent files from disk storage. To delete a file, type the word **PIP** followed by a space, the file name, a slash (/), and the word **DELETE** (or **DE**). For example, to delete the file named PROB1.FOR, type:

PIP PROB1.FOR/DE

The rules governing wildcard file names may also be used to delete multiple files. For example, to delete all the files with the file name of PROB1, you would type:

PIP PROB1.*/DE

To delete all backup files with the extension of .BAK you would enter:

PIP *.BAK/DE

Files may also be purged from disk storage by the **UNSAVE** and **KILL** commands. Type the command UNSAVE, followed by the file name and extension of the file you want to delete. For example:

UNSAVE PROB1.FOR

When using the KILL command you must put the file name and extension in quotes. For example:

KILL "PROB1.FOR"

Files may also be deleted from your account with the BYE/I command discussed in section E.2.

RSTS/E has no FORTRAN subsystem to allow you to create or modify FORTRAN source programs. You must use a text editor (EDT, EDIT, TECO, or others) for this purpose. Section E.5 explains the use of the DEC EDT standard text editor for creating new files and modifying existing files.

E.5   THE DEC EDT STANDARD TEXT EDITOR

The DEC Editor (EDT) allows you to create a new file or make modifications to an existing file. It can be used to edit programs or to create and modify text. Although it is designed to run on many operating systems, this appendix will be confined to its use on the RSTS/E operating system on the DEC PDP-11 series. For other operating systems, consult the system reference or user's manual.

The DEC EDT standard Editor is invoked by typing **EDT**, followed by the name of the program or file you want to create or modify. This file name will be used as both the input and output file. For example:

EDT PROB1.FOR

If you are creating a new file, the message ''Input file does not exist'' will be displayed. If you wish to specify a different name for the output file, you should type in the name of the output file immediately after the EDT command, followed by an equal sign and the name of the input file. For example, if the input file to be edited is PROB1.FOR, and the desired output file for the edited results is PROB1A.FOR, you type:

EDT PROB1A.FOR = PROB1.FOR

The editor will then prompt you for the next command with an asterisk (*). Commands are entered by typing the appropriate command, followed by a range, which shows the line number or numbers to be operated on. All commands are transmitted by depressing the RETURN key.

In the remainder of this section, commands are shown with their abbreviations in parentheses following the name. The abbreviations may be used in place of the full command name.

The EDT editor creates a text buffer, which is a temporary on-line storage area. If the file name you specified already exists, the editor will copy the contents of that file into the text buffer. If it does not exist, the text buffer will be created with nothing in it. All the commands that you enter while in the EDT editor will be processed on the contents of this buffer.

A range specification is allowed on most of the commands (DELETE, FIND, SUBSTITUTE, and so on) to permit the use of the command on more than the first occurrence of text in a file. If no range option is given, the command terminates after performing its function on the first occurrence in the text. A range specifies the lines where the editor command is to work. Following are the formats of the range options allowed in EDT.

Range formats		Comments
n	—	A single line number. No line number given after the command represents the current line.
'string' or ''string''	—	First line that contains the characters between the quotes (single or double).
%BE	—	First line in the buffer (file).
%E	—	Last line in the buffer (file).
%BEF	—	All lines from the current line back to the beginning of the buffer (i.e., search backwards).
%R	—	All lines from the current line to the last line in the buffer (i.e., search forward).
%WH	—	All lines in the buffer (i.e., the entire file).

Compound range formats specify groups of lines. The code "sr" represents any range format given above. The code "i" represents any integer number.

sr1:sr2	—	All lines between and including sr1 and sr2.
sr1,sr2,sr3	—	Lines sr1, sr2, and sr3 . . .
sr + i	—	The "i"th line after line sr.
sr − i	—	The "i"th line before line sr.

Getting out of the EDT editor. In order to save the contents of this buffer when you are finished with the edit, you must get out of the editor by using the **EXIT** (abbreviated **EX**) command. This will copy the contents of the text buffer into the specified output file. If you use the **QUIT** command, the entire contents of the text buffer will be erased, that is, the results of the edit session are not saved.

While in the editor, you should never type a Control-C (ˆC). If you do, all the work that you have done during that entire editing session may be lost. If you make an error in typing while you are editing, you can delete the last character typed by depressing the DELETE (on DEC terminals) or the SHIFT and RUB keys (on Hazeltine and LSI terminals). You may delete the entire line you are entering by typing the CTRL and O keys (remembering not to transmit the line first).

E.5.1 Save and Restore

While you are in the editor, EDT creates a temporary file on disk, which is available to back up the contents of your text buffer. It is a good idea to periodically save the contents in case of a system crash or other problem, in which you might lose all the edits made during the current editing session. You may do this by typing the command **SAVE** (abbreviated SA), followed by the switch /FI: and then your file name, where your file name is the name supplied by you for this temporary disk file. This command will copy the entire contents of the text buffer into the specified temporary file, without exiting from EDT. For example:

SAVE/FI:PROB1.SAV

If you should need to access this file, it can be accessed only by use of the **RESTORE** (abbreviated REST) command, and only when the following two conditions exist:

1. EDT must be invoked without specifying an input or an output file.
2. All the text buffers must be empty.

For example:

REST/FI:PROB1.SAV

Automatic Backup File Protection. Whenever you go into the editor, EDT will automatically copy the contents of your existing file into a disk file and rename it file name.BAK (where file name is the file name portion of your file). You will, therefore, maintain a copy of your file exactly the way it was before you entered the editor. After finishing your editing session and exiting from EDT, you will have two files in your directory instead of one. For example, if you start out with PROB1.FOR, you would have PROB1.FOR and PROB1.BAK when you are finished. The next time you enter the editor, your current (edited) version of PROB1.FOR would be copied into PROB1.BAK to create a backup of that version. At that time, the original version would no longer be available to you. Therefore, if you wish to always keep your original version available, you should rename it and keep it in your file before entering EDT. For example, using the PIP command, you would type:

PIP PROB1.OLD = PROB1.BAK/RE/W

The /**RE** switch renames the file. The /**W** switch confirms the change for you.

If the system crashes while you are editing a file, it may be recovered with the REC (for RECOVER) option. When the system comes back up, you would type:

EDT/REC file name.ext

This would cause the system to load the file with the name file name.ext from the system journaling file, which is automatically kept by the system.

E.5.2 Adding a New Program

Because there is no run-time system for FORTRAN, new programs must be added through the editor. To add a new program through EDT, you simply type in EDT followed by the file name and extension. For example:

EDT NEWFIL.FOR

The system responds with the message "[Input file does not exist]" and an asterisk (*) on a new line. When the editor comes back with the asterisk(*) prompt, type in the **INSERT** (abbreviated **I**) command and Return. EDT will not prompt you for any more inputs while in the INSERT mode. You then begin to type your FORTRAN program, including statement numbers where needed. You do not type in the line numbers; these will be put in automatically by EDT when you EXIT (EX) from the editor. The line numbers will start at 1 and proceed in increments of one (1, 2, 3, and so on). (Note: on the old version of EDT, line numbers are given in increments of ten.) Just type:

INSERT

or **I**

You may specify a different line number sequencing by using the **/SEQ** switch, followed by the initial line number desired and the increments you want the numbers to be increased by. The format of this switch is: INSERT [range] /SEQ:initial number:increment. In the case of adding a new program, you would not specify a range. For example, if you wanted to start numbering the lines in your program at 100 and proceed in increments of 100, the command would look like this:

INSERT/SEQ:100:100

or **I/SEQ:100:100**

When you have added your program, type a CONTROL-Z (printed as ˆZ) to get out of the INSERT mode and back into the command mode. This is done by pressing the CTRL (or CNTL) key and typing the letter Z. Exit from the editor and save your program by typing the **EXIT** command.

When you exit the editor, a new output file with the name specified when you invoked EDT will be created. The entire contents of the text buffer will be written to this output file.

E.5.3 Listing Your File

Listing the Whole File. After entering EDT, the editor positions the pointer at the beginning of the first line. EDT automatically assigns line numbers, beginning with 1 and proceeding in increments of 1. If you want to list line 2 on your terminal, just depress the RETURN key. The contents of line 2 will be displayed. If you want to have the next line (3) displayed to your terminal, depress the RETURN key again. This will move the pointer down to line 3 and list the line. To keep advancing one line at a time and displaying the lines, just keep depressing the RETURN key. If you wanted to list the entire file, though, this would be a very slow way of doing it. A much quicker and easier way to list the whole file is to issue the command **%WH.** For example:

%WH

This would list every line number in the file and end with an [EOB] to show that you had reached the end of the file.

Listing a Specific Line Number. If you want to list only one line number, type that line number and depress the RETURN key. For example, to list line 50:

50

Listing a Range of Line Numbers. To list a range of line numbers, for instance lines 10 through 20, simply type the first line number, followed by a colon and the last line number. For example, to list lines 10 through 20, type:

10:20

E.5.4 Deleting a Line

You may use the **DELETE** (abbreviated **D**) command to delete one or more lines from your file. This is done by typing DELETE, or D, and the line number, or range of line numbers, to be deleted. For example, to delete line 30, type:

DELETE 30

or **D30**

This will automatically delete the line and show you that one line has been deleted. It will also display the line number of the next remaining line. Note: a space is not required before the line number.

To delete a range of line numbers, type in the DELETE command followed by the first line number to be deleted, colon, and the last line number to be deleted. For example:

DELETE 30:40

or **D30:40**

This will delete line 30 through line 40 and will show that 11 lines have been deleted (30, 31, 32, and so on). The line number of the next remaining line will be shown.

After exiting from EDT, and re-entering, the line numbers will be automatically resequenced. There will not be an 11-number sequence gap after the file is saved.

E.5.5 Adding New Lines

The **INSERT** (abbreviated **I**) command is used to add new lines to a file. The format for INSERT is as follows:

Insert [range] /SEQuence:initial #:increment [/UNsequenced]

When the INSERT command is used in conjunction with a range, the lines to be added are placed immediately ahead of the first line in the range. For example, to insert new lines of text before line number 30, type:

I30

If no range is specified, the new lines are added immediately ahead of the current line. For example, if you were at line 20 and wanted to insert new lines before this line number, all you would do is type:

I

If you want to add new lines at the bottom of your file, simply go to the end of the buffer by typing %**E**. This will move the pointer beyond the last line in the text buffer, and you can add the new lines by using the INSERT command. For example:

> %**E**
> [EOB]
> **I**
> (add the desired lines)
> ˆZ (to get out of the INSERT mode)

New lines are inserted with line numbers of x.1, x.2, and so on, where x is the last line number or given line number of insertion. For example, if the line pointer is at 35 and the insert command is given, the line number of the first inserted line would be 35.1. When the [/UNsequenced] switch is used, the new lines are inserted without having line numbers assigned.

Use of the INSERT command automatically puts you into insert mode. Once in this mode, the editor does not prompt for inputs. Simply begin entering text. When you are finished adding new lines, exit from Insert mode by typing a CTRL/Z (ˆZ). This returns you to the command mode, and you may then continue with additional editing commands.

E.5.6 Text and String Searching

You may not always know which line number contains the text you want to modify. To locate certain words or character strings, enclose the strings in double (" ") or single (' ') quotes. By doing this and entering the command with the RETURN key, EDT will begin to look for an exact match to the characters within the quotes. It will begin searching at its current position and will proceed toward the bottom of the buffer. If you place a minus sign (−) before the object strings, EDT will start at its current position and search backwards, toward the top of the buffer. If you are in the middle of the file and would like to start at the beginning of the file and search from there, you can get back to the beginning of the buffer by first typing %**BE**. For example, to get back to the beginning of the buffer and search for the word "YESTERDAY", type the following:

> %**BE**
> **1**   (contents of line 1 displayed)
> **"YESTERDAY"**

EDT will search until it matches the object string YESTERDAY, and when found, will display that line to your terminal. If the text you are searching for is in lower case (for example, in a data file), make sure the string to be matched is typed in lower case. Note: the ending quote is not required.

Find Command. The **FIND** (abbreviated **F**) command works basically the same as the character string search described above. The only difference is that when the match is made, the line is not automatically displayed. The editor just stops at the line position, and if you want the line to be listed, you must enter the **TYPE** (abbreviated **T**) command. The FIND command is used in the following format: FIND "character string". For example, to locate the word "TODAY":

FIND"TODAY"
T
(contents of line number)

Once again, either the double (" ") or single (' ') quotes can be used to enclose the text to be found. You may specify a range of line numbers to be searched or, to find all occurrences in the entire file, you may include the range option **%WH** after the target text.

E.5.7 Modifying Existing Lines

The **SUBSTITUTE** (abbreviated **S**) command is used to replace one string with another within a certain range. The format is:

SUBSTITUTE/string1/string2/ [range]

String1 is the character, or series of characters, that you want to find and replace. String2 is the character, or series of characters, that you want to replace it with. The range is optional; if no range is specified, EDT will substitute String2 for String1 for the first occurrence it encounters in the current line. If a single line number is given as the range, EDT will change String1 to String2 every time it appears in that particular line. If multiple lines are indicated in a range, the strings will be substituted at each occurrence on every line in the specified range.

For example, assume a typing error was found in line 5 in the spelling of the keyword DIMENSION:

5   DIMENSOIN X(10,5)

To correct this error, you would type:

*S/DIMENSOIN/DIMENSION/5

If you wanted to go through the whole file and substitute all occurrences of "DIMENSOIN" with "DIMENSION", you could do this by including the **%WH** option after the last delimiter:

*S/DIMENSOIN/DIMENSION/%WH

The SUBSTITUTE command with the %WH range option will search the entire buffer for all occurrences of String1 and replace it with the String2 text.

Moving Lines to a New Location. Lines can be moved to new locations within a file by using the **COPY** and **MOVE** commands. The format of the **COPY** (abbreviated **CO**) command is:

COPY range1 %TO range2

When this command is used, the text specified as range 1 will be copied to the position immediately ahead of the first line in range2—i.e., it will be inserted *between* this range 2 line and the line immediately preceding it. However, the text that has been copied will remain in its original position. This can be extremely useful if certain lines of code must be duplicated elsewhere in a program. For example, if you begin with:

1   DIMENSION X(20), Y(20)
2   READ (5,95) (X(I), Y(I), I = 1,20)
3   95 FORMAT (F5.2, 4X, F5.2)

And if you typed the following COPY command:

COPY 3 %TO 1

The result would be:

1   95 FORMAT (F5.2,4X,F5.2)
1   DIMENSION X(20), Y(20)
2   READ (5,95) (X(I), Y(I),I = 1,20)
3   95 FORMAT (F5.2, 4X, F5.2)

The **MOVE** (abbreviated **M**) command works the same way as the COPY command, with the difference that once the text in range1 has been moved to its new position, the old lines no longer exist. Rather than copying the text, the MOVE (M) command transfers the lines in range1 to the position immediately ahead of range2. Using the same example:

MOVE 3 %TO 1

would produce the following results:

.1	95 FORMAT (F5.2, 4X, F5.2)
1	DIMENSION X(20), Y(20)
2	READ (5,95) (X(I), Y(I),I = 1,20)

E.5.8 Getting Out of the Editor

There are two commands which will get you out of the editor—**QUIT** and **EXIT**. If you use the **QUIT** command, the entire text buffer will be erased, and control will be returned to the operating system. None of the changes you made while in EDT will be saved or written to disk. The QUIT command is useful if you have made a serious error while in EDT, such as inadvertently erasing part of your file. By using QUIT, your file will be exactly the way it was before entering the editor. Just enter:

QUIT

The **EXIT** (abbreviated **EX**) command will save all the contents of the text buffer and write them out to the output file. It will also return control to the operating system. The EXIT command should always be used to get out of the editor if you want to save the changes you made while in the editing session. For example:

EXIT

After entering your FORTRAN program with the EDT editor, you are ready to compile and execute it. The next section discusses the procedure to obtain a compilation and how to link and execute a program with the DEC FORTRAN compiler.

E.6   RUNNING A DEC PDP-11 FORTRAN PROGRAM UNDER RSTS/E

Assume a short FORTRAN source program has been created on a file named EX.FOR by the text editor. The program is:

TYPE *,
TYPE *, 'HI COMPUTER'
TYPE *, 10, 20
STOP
END

The **TYPE** statement is the format-free output statement in PDP-11 FORTRAN. Let us discuss the procedures for running the program to obtain the output results.

Program Compilation

First, you must compile the program by entering the command

RUN $FORTRAN

This command executes the FORTRAN compiler (in the $ account with the name FORTRAN), which translates the source program into object code. A file with the extension name **OBJ** is needed to hold the resulting object code. A second file is also needed with the extension name **LST** to store a copy of the compiled source listing with any syntax diagnostic (error messages). The compiler will print an asterisk (*) for you to enter the file name for the object file, the file name for the source listing file, and the file name of the source program. The object file name is separated from the source listing file name with a comma. The source listing file name is separated from the source program file name with an equal sign (=). After the asterisk prompt, type:

EX.OBJ,EX.LST = EX.FOR

The compiler then prints the message

.MAIN.

After the source program is compiled, the compiler responds with another asterisk (*) prompt to let you know that it is finished. Then enter a CTRL/Z or a CTRL/C to exit the FORTRAN compiler:

`^Z`

The system moves down two lines and prints a Ready message. This entire compilation process looks like this:

RUN $FORTRAN
*EX.OBJ,EX.LST = EX.FOR
.MAIN.
*^Z

Ready

Preparing the Program for Execution

You must next prepare the compiled program for execution with the **LINK** command. The object code from the compilation is not in a suitable form to be executed; the LINK command must be given to prepare an executable file in loadable form for later execution. Any subprograms to be used during this step must also be linked. Type only the word LINK to call in the Linkage-Loader program:

LINK

The Linkage-Loader program requires you to type the file name for the loadable code file (with an extension name of **SAV**) and the name of the compiled object file. It prints an asterisk (*) prompt for you to enter this information. After the asterisk (*) prompt, enter the name to be used for the linked loadable code file and the file name of the object file, and separate them by an equal sign. For example, after the asterisk prompt, type:

EX.SAV = EX.OBJ

When the Linkage-Loader process is completed, the program prints an asterisk (*) to let you know it has finished. Then, type a CTRL/Z or a CTRL/C to get out of the Linkage-Loader program. The system responds with a Ready message. The entire step looks like this:

LINK
*EX.SAV = EX.OBJ
*^Z

Ready

The executable program with the extension name of .SAV is now ready to be run. Enter the command **RUN**, followed by a space and the name you gave the Linkage-Loader file. For example:

RUN EX.SAV

The computer executes the linked program and prints the output results. After the last line of output, the computer prints the message

STOP—

and then prints the Ready message. For example:

RUN EX.SAV

HI COMPUTER
      10   **20**
STOP—

Ready

The entire compile, link, and execute process is illustrated as follows:

```
RUN $FORTRAN
*EX.OBJ,EX.LST = EX.FOR
.MAIN.
*^Z
```

Ready

```
LINK
*EX.SAV = EX.OBJ
*^Z
```

Ready

```
RUN EX.SAV
```

HI COMPUTER
          10   20
STOP—

Ready

It is not necessary to include the extension names on the files that will be created, if you do not wish to do so. The system automatically assumes these extension names. However, if you use any other extension names, you must include this extension name as part of the given file name. Thus, you may accomplish the compile, link, and execute steps by giving only the file names without their extension. For example (assuming a file name of EX with an extension of FOR):

```
RUN $FORTRAN
*EX,EX = EX
.MAIN.
*^Z
```

Ready
```
LINK
*EX = EX
*^Z
```

Ready
```
RUN
```
HI COMPUTER
          10   20
STOP—

Ready

If a syntax error occurs in your source program, the output results will not be what you expect. The FORTRAN compiler will print a message during compilation if any error or warning (nonfatal) diagnostics are detected. Suppose, for example, that the comma was not included after the TYPE * in the last TYPE statement, and that the statement appeared as

TYPE * 10,20

in your source program. The results from the RUN $FORTRAN command would be:

```
RUN $FORTRAN
*EX,EX = EX
.MAIN.
?FORTRAN-I-[.MAIN.] Errors: 1, Warnings: 0
*^Z
```

Ready

You must print the compiled source listing file with the extension name of LST to find out what the errors are. The source listing file may be printed with the **PIP** command. For example:

PIP EX.LST

FORTRAN IV   **VO2.1-1   Tue 13-Jan-82 23:03:39**   **PAGE 001**

0001   TYPE *,
0002   TYPE *, 'HI COMPUTER'
0003   TYPE * 10,20
0004   STOP
0005   END

FORTRAN IV   Diagnostics for Program Unit .MAIN.

In line 0003, Error: Syntax error

Ready

The compiled program identifies an error in line 3 (0003). The source program must be corrected and recompiled.

After you have learned about subroutine and/or function subprograms, you will need to link these subprogram files during the linkage-loader step. The form of the information given after the LINK command is:

PM = PM,SP

where ''PM'' represents the main program and SP represents the name of a compiled subprogram file. A maximum of six subprograms (each separated from the other by a comma) may be linked into one resulting file. If more than six subprograms are used, you may link some of them into a file and then link that file with the remaining unlinked subprograms. Let us look at an example where S1, S2, S3, S4, S5, S6, S7, S8, and S9 each represents a file containing a subprogram. The procedure is given as follows (the asterisk is the system prompt):

LINK
***SP = S1,S2,S3,S4,S5,S6**
***^Z**

Ready
LINK
***PM = PM,SP,S7,S8,S9**
***^Z**

Ready

You should now be able to compile and execute your FORTRAN programs on a PDP-11 system. Your instructor will inform you of any differences from the discussed procedures if your system is set up differently.

E.7 SUMMARY OF RSTS/E COMMANDS

A partial summary of the commands available on a PDP-11 RSTS/E system is as follows:

Command	Function	Example
HELLO	To log on the system	HELLO 52,17
LOG	Same as HELLO	LOG 52,17
DIR	Lists permanent files	DIR
CATALOG	Same as DIR	CATALOG
PIP	To list files, copy files, rename files, and delete files	PIP file name PIP file name$_1$ = file name$_2$/RE PIP file name/DE
UNSAVE	To purge a file	UNSAVE file name
KILL	Same as UNSAVE	KILL ''file name''
BYE/option	To log off the system	BYE/F

E.8 SUMMARY OF DEC EDT EDITOR COMMANDS

A summary of the EDT text editor command and their functions are as follows:

Command	Abbrev	Description
COPY	CO	Copies lines in range1 to a position ahead of the first line of range2.
DELETE	D	Deletes one or more lines.
EDT	EDT	To get into the EDT editor.
EXIT	EX	Terminates EDT and writes the contents of the buffer to the specified file name and extension.
FIND	F	Finds the first line of text in the given range.
INCLUDE	INC	Locates a file name and copies it to the position in the buffer.
INSERT	I	Insert mode. Allows insertion of text in the buffer ahead of the first line of the given range or before the current line position. A CTRL/Z must be typed to get out of insert mode.
MOVE	M	Transfers lines in range1 to a position ahead of first line of range2.
PRINT	PR	Generates a new file with the given filename.ext including the EDT line numbers. Switch /FI:newfile.ext is used.
QUIT	QUIT	Terminates EDT without making any changes to the file.
REPLACE	R	Deletes all lines specified by the range option and leaves user in insert mode at last line deleted.
RECOVER	REC	To recover an edited file after a system crash.
RESEQUENCE	RES	Assigns new line numbers to the lines in the buffer or in the given range.
RESTORE	REST	Finds the file created with the SAVE command and uses it to restore the contents of the text buffer.
SAVE	SA	Creates a backup file containing a copy of the text buffer in use.
SUBSTITUTE	S	Changes string1 to string2 for all occurrences of the string for the specified range. If no range option is given, the first occurrence in the current line is used.
TYPE	T	Displays the lines specified.
[range]		Displays the range of lines specified. A single integer number will display only that line. A colon (:) may be used to specify a range of lines.
WRITE	WR	Creates an output file from the contents of the lines in the specified range. If no range is given, the entire file is written. You must use the /FI:file.ext switch to provide the name of the new output file.
XEQ	X	Executes EDT commands contained in the specified range. This allows a file to contain EDT commands to provide the flexibility of not having to repeatedly type the same commands.

E.9 EXPLANATION OF DEC FUNCTIONAL KEYS AND COMMANDS

This section explains the many functional keys and commands that perform various operations in a DEC RSTS/E timesharing environment. A combination of the CTRL (control) functional key, when depressed with certain other keys, causes certain actions to be taken by the timesharing system. For example, you can cancel a line, terminate an operation/command being performed, and so on. These capabilities provide great flexibility and aid in developing, manipulating, and running your programs. First, let us look at the line transmission keys that cause a line of information (or a command) to be transmitted to the computer.

Line Transmission Keys

DEC terminals have two keys that may be used to transmit a line of information (e.g., a command or program statement) to the computer system. These two keys cannot be used interchangeably, since they perform different functions. These keys and their functions are as follows:

Key	Explanation of Use
RETURN key	The **RETURN** key enters a typed line to the system. This key results in a carriage return/line feed operation at the terminal. This is the normal and most frequently used key to transmit a line of information. This key is located on the far right side of the second row of keys.
ESCape key or **ALT MODE** key	The **ESC**ape (or ALT MODE) key enters a typed line to the system, echoes on the terminal as a $ character, and does not cause a carriage return/line feed operation. In other words, it performs the same function as the RETURN key but does not move down to a new line nor reposition the cursor back to position one. You would use this key if you wish to prevent line scrolling (rolling up lines) to keep as much information as possible on the screen of a CRT terminal. This key is located on the far left side in the top row of keys.

Now, let us look at the various control characters you can send to the computer to cause special actions to be performed.

Special Control Characters

Depressing the combination of the Control (CTRL) key and certain other letter keys at the same time provide a special function/request to a DEC system. The following special functions are performed when holding down the CTRL key and depressing the letter key.

CTRL/C — Returns to the Ready level (monitor) and awaits further commands. This function will stop any operation in progress. It is frequently used to stop execution of a program or any command. Warning: if the CTRL/C is used while in any editor, it may wipe out any program or file created up to that point.

CTRL/H — Provides a backspace operation for underlining or overstriking (must not be used for deleting).

CTRL/I — Simulates a horizontal TAB on a CRT. Tab stops are 8 spaces apart.

CTRL/J — Provides a line feed (new line) operation.

CTRL/L — Provides a form-feed (page eject) operation.

CTRL/M — Provides a carriage return operation.

CTRL/O — Stops printing and returns to the monitor. To resume printing, the CTRL/O keys must be depressed a second time. All output between the first and second time the function keys are depressed is lost.

CTRL/Q — Resumes the interrupted printing at point of interrupt caused by the CTRL/S.

CTRL/R — Shows all commands waiting to be processed. Useful if you have "typed ahead" or deleted characters.

CTRL/S — Interrupts printing until a CTRL/Q is typed. The output still remains in the buffer and is not lost.

CTRL/T — Displays keyboard number and current status of your job.

CTRL/U — Cancels (deletes) the current line being typed (before the line is transmitted).

CTRL/Z — End-of-file operation. Used to get out of insert mode with the EDT text editor program.

NOTE: To use these functions, first hold down the CTRL key with the left hand and then strike the other key with the right hand. The CTRL key normally prints at your terminal as an up-arrow (^). Thus, the CTRL/C keys when depressed will print as:

^C

This appendix has explained many of the features of a DEC minicomputer using the RSTS/E operating system to provide an effective timesharing environment for developing and running FORTRAN programs. Good luck and happy programming.

Hewlett Packard (HP) 3000 Timesharing Procedures and the EDIT/3000 Text Editor

Appendix F

F.1 INTRODUCTION

This appendix explains how to use an HP 3000 computer in a timesharing environment. First, the log-on procedure is discussed. Second, the use of the HP EDIT/3000 text editor is explained. Finally, you will be shown how to execute a FORTRAN program using the HP MPE/3000 operating system commands.

A common terminal used with the Hewlett Packard (HP) 3000 timesharing system is the HP 2640A or 2645A. Turn on the terminal and set the on-line mode. On-line mode means that the signals generated from typing at the keyboard are routed to the computer rather than used to control the terminal itself (local mode). To set the on-line mode, depress the REMOTE function key in the second row of functional keys located in the upper left corner of the keyboard.

If you are using an HP 2640A terminal, you should set the following functional keys to these control settings:

BLOCK MODE	Off
AUTO L.F. (Line feed)	Off
CAPS LOCK (Upper cases)	On
DUPLEX	FULL
PARITY	NONE
BAUD RATE	2400 (If you are using a modem, set to 300)

If your terminal is not directly connected to the HP 3000, make the proper connections over the telephone. Then, proceed to the log-on procedure.

If the terminal is already on line, someone else may be using it. The screen should be blank, or the final words on it (from the previous log-off) should be **END OF SESSION**. Test to see if someone else is signed on the terminal by depressing the RETURN key twice. If "ERR 0" appears, the terminal is free. If "ERR 1" appears, the terminal is in use.

F.2 LOG-ON AND LOG-OFF PROCEDURES

The HP 3000 requires a user name and account name (separated by a period) for log-on identification. The form is "user-name.account-name." **PERRY.EDP** will be used as an example identification. PERRY is the user name, and EDP is the account name. You may also be assigned a password to enter during the log-on identification. If a password is used, it may consist of one to eight alphanumeric characters, beginning with an alphabetic letter.

The first action taken during the log-on procedure is to press the RETURN key. A colon will appear in position one. The colon (:) is the prompt used at the system level. You must log on within a few minutes, or the computer will disconnect you. Log on by typing (after the colon):

1. The word HELLO
2. A space
3. Your log-on identification
4. Press the RETURN key

The log-on procedure would look something like the following (the colon [:] is the system prompt):

:HELLO PERRY.EDP

If your log-on is correct, the computer responds with a standard welcome message giving the session number, date, time, and so on. For example:

SESSION NUMBER = #S37
FRI, JANUARY 2, 1981, 10:30 AM
HP 32002A.00.05

:

The final colon indicates that you are logged on successfully and is the prompt character for the next command. If a mistake is made in the log-on identification, you will receive an error message such as:

:HELLO PERRY,EDP
ERR 20,2
:

which means that the punctuation was incorrect (note the erroneous comma); or an error message such as:

:HELLO PERR.EDP
ERR 8
:

meaning that the log-on identification is invalid (the user name or account name does not exist or is incorrect, or the password is incorrect). The repeated colon means you must reenter the correct log-on identification. Assuming a valid log-on identification is given, you may proceed to enter and manipulate a FORTRAN program.

Log-off Procedure

Type the command **BYE** to log off the system and to terminate the session:

BYE

The system prints four lines of messages. Line one tells how many seconds of CPU (computer) time you used. Line two tells how many minutes you were connected to the system. Line three gives the date and time of ending the session. Line four is a message that says **END OF SESSION.**

The usual sequence of operations to develop and execute a FORTRAN program is:

1. Write a source program using EDIT/3000.
2. Compile this program using the FORTRAN/3000 compiler.
3. Execute the object program using MPE/3000 Operating System commands.

So, let's begin by learning the basic operations of using the HP EDIT/3000 text editor for developing a FORTRAN source program.

F.3   HEWLETT PACKARD EDIT/300 TEXT EDITOR

The **EDIT/3000** Editor must be used to enter a new FORTRAN source program on the HP 3000. The Editor reserves the first ten positions on a line for the line number. After printing the line number, the cursor stops at position 11 on the line. This position is column 1 to the user. It is the actual beginning point of the record. The Editor stores the line number at the end of the record on disk files to make the disk records look like card images to the computer.

A FORTRAN statement uses the first five positions for statement labels (numbers), each of which can have up to five digits (1–99999). Column 6 is reserved for a continuation indicator. If these first six positions are not used, you must space over them. Column 1 may also be used to indicate a comment card or a compiler command. A "C" in column 1 indicates that the entire line is to be used for remarks. A "$" in column 1 indicates that the record is a compiler command.

You are now ready to invoke the Editor program, which allows a program to be entered. Enter the Editor by typing the word "EDITOR" after the colon prompt and waiting for the slash prompt. For example:

:EDITOR
HP 322001A.5.01 EDIT/3000 FRI, January 2, 1980, 10:10 AM
/

When the Editor has been invoked, a header line with date, time, and other information is printed. The slash (/) is printed in position 1. The slash is the prompt character for the EDIT/3000 editor.

F.3.1 Adding a New Program

To use the Editor's "add" mode, type the command **ADD** and press RETURN. The terminal prints the line number, spaces over five positions, and waits for you to begin typing. You may then type new lines into your program as follows:

```
/ADD
    1$CONTROL USLINIT
    2        SUM = 100 + 76 + 83
    3        AVE = SUM / 3.
    4        DISPLAY SUM, AVE
    5        STOP
    6        END
    7
```

To exit the "add" mode, press the CTRL (or CNTL) key and strike the Y key. The Control-Y combination terminates the ADD command, prints out three periods, and prints a new slash prompt for a new command. For example:

```
    7 . . .
  /
```

The first statement in a FORTRAN program should be:

$CONTROL USLINIT

The statement should begin in column 1. This insures that the object (USL for User Subprogram Library) file receiving the output from the FORTRAN compiler is initialized to an empty condition before compilation starts.

If file unit numbers are used, you should use the standard input unit number 5 and the output unit number 6. Unit 5 is the terminal keyboard, and unit 6 is the terminal's output device (printer or display).

HP FORTRAN/3000 allows free-field format input with the ACCEPT statement and free-field output with the DISPLAY statement. This capability allows you to enter data from your terminal and display it without having to use file unit numbers and format statements.

A typing mistake may be corrected in one of two ways.

1. To correct part of a line (backspacing):
   a. Hold down the CTRL key.
   b. Strike the H key once for each character position to back up. This combination is called the Control-H.
   c. Resume typing the correct characters.
2. To retype the whole line when the error is far back in the line.
   a. Hold down the CTRL key.
   b. Strike the X key. The computer immediately prints out a triple exclamation mark (!!!) and returns the cursor to character position 1 on the next line. The computer has erased that entire line from your work area, although it is still visible to you. This character combination is called Control-X.

Don't use the "edit" keys (DELETE LINE, DELETE CHAR, and others) that are available on some terminals such as the HP 2640A. These keys are not available for use with the HP Editor. You should have five records (statements) in your work area from the previous ADD command. The LIST commands allows you to see what is in your work area.

F.3.2 Listing Your File

To list the contents of the entire work area, type the command **LIST ALL** after the slash prompt. The command

LIST ALL

will list all records in your work area. For example:

```
/LIST ALL
    1$CONTROL USLINIT
    2        SUM = 100 + 76 + 83
    3        AVE = SUM / 3.
    4        DISPLAY SUM, AVE
    5        STOP
    6        END
```

Listing A Partial Program. A program might be quite lengthy, and you may not want to list all the lines (as performed with the LIST ALL). To list a portion of a file, type the **LIST** command followed by the beginning and ending line numbers you want to see. Separate the two line numbers with a slash. For example, to list the records with line numbers 2 through 4, type:

LIST 2/4

and all statements in the range of 2 and 4 will be listed.

If you are satisfied that the work area is correct or you want to store the contents on disk, type the command **KEEP**, followed by the name under which you wish to save the file. For example, to save the contents of the work area under the file name PROB1, type:

KEEP PROB1

The Editor proceeds to create a new file with the name PROB1 and stores the contents of the work area into that file. This process may take a few seconds. When a new slash prompt appears, you know that the file exits and contains a copy of whatever is in the work area. The records in the work area still exist and are available for manipulation or processing.

If you attempt to save a file under a name that already exists, the system will print a message that says:

PROB1 ALREADY EXISTS
—RESPOND YES TO PURGE OLD AND THEN KEEP
PURGE OLD?

Answer NO if you do not wish to purge the old file on disk with the same name (perhaps you did not realize a file with the same name existed). Answer YES if you want to destroy the old file and replace it with a new file having the new contents.

Actually, any answer other than YES (carriage RETURN or anything) cancels the KEEP command. If you do not type a YES, the Editor prints the message

PURGE OF OLD FILE NOT CONFIRMED—TEXT IS NOT KEPT

followed by a new slash prompt. This gives you a chance to rectify your error. To keep both the old file and the new one, type a new KEEP command with a different filename, e.g.,

KEEP PROB1A

Now, let's see how a permanent file is retrieved from disk.

F.3.3 Retrieving a Permanent File From Disk

The command **TEXT** followed by a space and the old file name, is used to retrieve an existing file on disk and bring it into your work area. For example, to retrieve an old file named PROB1, type:

TEXT PROB1

If there is anything in the work area, the Editor will ask if it is all right to clear the work area. The TEXT command always erases (clears) the work area before bringing in a file. For example, after the slash prompt, type the command TEXT:

/TEXT PROB1
IF IT IS OKAY TO CLEAR RESPOND "YES"
CLEAR?

You will usually answer YES, but if you want to keep the contents of the work area, you are given the opportunity. Any response other than YES to the CLEAR? message will cancel the TEXT command.

F.3.4 Deleting Lines From Your Work Area

The **DELETE** command is used to delete one or more lines from the work area. To delete a single line, type DELETE, followed by a space and the number of the line you wish to delete. For example, to delete line 6, type:

DELETE 6

The system will print the contents of the deleted lines for you, to confirm that the line was actually deleted.

To delete multiple lines from a work area, type the command **DELETE**, followed by a space and the range of line numbers to be deleted. The range is specified by a beginning line number separated by a slash from the ending line number. For example, to delete lines 4 through 6 in the work area type:

/DELETE 4/6
4   DISPLAY SUM, AVE
5   STOP
6   END

The deleted lines are printed for your inspection.

The **DELETEQ** (Q stands for quiet) command may be used to delete one or more lines without having the system print them. The system responds with a message telling you how many lines were deleted. For example:

/DELETEQ 3/4
NUMBER OF LINES DELETED—2
/

This command deleted lines three and four. The system message informs you that two lines were deleted. The deleted lines are not printed out at the terminal.

If you want to clear the work area and start over again, type the command:

DELETE ALL

The **DELETE ALL** command will delete all records in the work area. The Editor will ask you if it is all right to clear the work area, to make sure that you positively want to delete all the records. Answer YES to the system message if you really want to clear the work area.

F.3.5. Adding New Statements to a File

If you want to add new statements (records) to the program in your work area, you may do so with the ADD command.

Adding New Records at the End of the File. The **ADD** command by itself will insert new records starting at the end of the work area. Suppose you have to go to class and don't have time to finish typing in your entire program. You could save what you have already typed with the KEEP command and return later to type the remainder of the program. To start entering statements where you left off, get into the Editor and type

ADD

The Editor will then type the line number that follows in sequence the last line number in your work area. If line 30 was the last line in the work area, the Editor would display line number 31 as the prompt for you to begin entering your new lines. The **Control-Y keys** are typed to get you out of the **ADD** command.

Inserting New Lines in the Middle of a File. You may need to insert new statements in the middle of your program. You can also use the ADD command to insert new lines in a file at places other than the end, but you must specify where you want the lines inserted.

As seen from the previous discussion, in creating a new file the **ADD** command increments the line number by 1 for each added line. However, smaller increments of .1, .01, or even .001 are available for line numbering. If you need to add some lines (fewer than 10) between existing line number 5 and 6, type:

ADD 5.1

The Editor would acknowledge this command by typing the prompted line number 5.1. You would then be automatically prompted for lines 5.1, 5.2, 5.3, and so on. Similarly, if you needed to add more than 10 lines, but fewer than 100, you could type:

ADD 5.01

The system would then prompt you for lines 5.01, 5.02, 5.03, and so on. To add more than 100 lines, type:

ADD 5.001

The **Control-Y keys** are typed to terminate the **ADD** command.

F.3.6. Modifying a Line of Information

You may need to change a statement in your program. This can be accomplished with the **MODIFY** command without having to delete the line and add a corrected line. You may delete or insert characters in a line with the MODIFY command.

Suppose, for example, that you want to change the FORTRAN keyword "DISPLAY" in line 4 to "WRITE (6,99)". Type the command **MODIFY**, followed by the line number of the statement to be changed. The Editor will print out a message confirming the line to be modified and print that line of information. For example, after the slash prompt, you type the command MODIFY 4:

> /MODIFY 4
> MODIFY   4
>   DISPLAY SUM, AVE

The Editor waits for you to enter the modifications. You type a **D** under the first and last characters of the text to be deleted. Thus, to delete the word DISPLAY, you would type a **D** under the letter D and another **D** under the letter Y. For example:

> /MODIFY 4
> MODIFY   4
>   DISPLAY SUM, AVE
>   D   D

Then press the RETURN key. The word DISPLAY is deleted from the line.

After the deletion of characters occurs, the Editor will print the revised line for your inspection. The Editor remains in the "modify mode" until you are satisfied by the line. You can continue making modifications to the line, because the cursor (or carriage) returns to column 1 after printing the modified line and waits for your next action. To exit the modify mode, press RETURN. A new slash prompt will appear.

You may delete a single character with one **D** under the particular character. The remaining characters shift to close the space formerly occupied by the deleted character. A space (or blank) counts as a character.

To insert characters, type an **I** under the character where the insertion is to begin. To insert the characters "WRITE (6,99)", you would type the command MODIFY 4 (after the slash prompt):

> /MODIFY 4
> MODIFY   4
>   SUM, AVE
>   IWRITE(6,99)

Note that the space before the variable SUM is still there. The letter **I** typed under the space (followed by the text WRITE(6,99) says to insert the new text before that character (above the I). After this line is transmitted, the new line would be:

> /MODIFY 4
> MODIFY   4
>   SUM, AVE
>   IWRITE (6,99)
>   WRITE (6,99) SUM, AVE

Then press RETURN once more to get out of the modify mode.

F.3.7 Moving Lines to a New Location

You may need to move one or more lines of code to a new location in your program. To avoid excessive retyping, you may move a block of lines to a new location with the **GATHER** command.

Suppose you want to move lines 15 through 17 to come after line 7. You would type:

> **GATHER 15/17 TO 7.1**

The Editor responds by performing the command and typing (after the entered command of GATHER 15/17 TO 7.1):

> /GATHER   15/17 TO   7.1
>   15   ⇒   7.1
>   16   ⇒   7.2
>   17   ⇒   7.3

You can avoid printing the old/new line numbers by typing the command **GATHERQ** instead of GATHER. The lines previously at 15 through 17 will no longer exist, since they have been moved to lines 7.1 through 7.3.

You may want to resequence the line numbers in your program. The **GATHER ALL** command will resequence all the lines in the work area starting at sequence number 1, in increments of 1.

Suppose you need to duplicate some lines of code at several places in your program. This can be done with the **HOLD** or **HOLDQ** command. The Editor will store the indicated statements in a hold file with the HOLD (or HOLDQ) command while you use the ADD command to add the lines from the hold file.

Let us move lines 11 and 12 to locations 17.1 and 24.1. First, lines 11 and 12 will be stored in the hold file by typing (after the slash prompt):

> **/HOLDQ 11/12**
> **HOLD FILE LENGTH IS 2 RECORDS**
> /

A hold file message is printed by the Editor to let you know how many lines are stored in the hold file. Then, to add the lines from the hold file to your program beginning at line 17.1, type:

> **ADD 17.1,HOLDQ**

You will then be prompted for line 17.1. Respond by typing a Control-Y. The Editor prints several lines that look like the following:

> **17.1 . . .**
> **. . .**
> **LAST LINE =   17.2**
> /

Repeat the same procedure to add the lines at line number 24.1. That is,

> **ADD 24.1,HOLDQ**

The hold file still contains the records stored in it. If you attempt to store other lines in it, you will be asked whether you want the hold file cleared. The original lines at 11 and 12 still remain in the work area, since they were only stored in the hold file and not removed.

F.3.8. Getting out of the Editor

The **END** or **EXIT** command is used to get out of the Editor and return to the system level. For example, after the slash prompt, type the command **EXIT**:

> **/EXIT**
> **IF IT IS OK TO CLEAR RESPOND "YES"**
> **CLEAR? YES**
>
> **END OF SUBSYSTEM**
> :

The END or EXIT command not only takes you out of the Editor, but clears the contents of your work area. You may then run your program or perform any other command available at the system level.

F.4 PURGING EXISTING FILES ON DISK

The **PURGE** command followed by a space and a file name will purge that file from disk. You must be in system mode and not the Editor for this command. For example:

> **PURGE PROB1A**

Any unwanted or unneeded files should be purged from disk to avoid cluttering your account with numerous files.

F.5 LISTING PERMANENT FILES IN YOUR ACCOUNT

The command **LISTF** will list all the files in your account. If the list runs too long, you may terminate it anytime with the **BREAK key**. You must be in system mode, not the Editor, to use this command. For example, after the colon prompt, type the command **LISTF**:

:LISTF
FILENAME
PROB1
:

In this example there is only one permanent file, named PROB1, stored on disk.

F.6 RUNNING A FORTRAN PROGRAM ON AN HP3000

Assuming that you have built a FORTRAN source program with the HP text editor, let us examine the procedures to compile and execute the program to obtain the output results.

To compile and execute a FORTRAN source program, you type the command **FORTGO**, followed by the name of the file containing the source program. For example, assuming a source file named PROB1, you would enter:

FORTGO PROB1

You must be at the system level with the colon prompt to enter this command.

The output results (printed at your terminal) will consist of:

1. A four-digit page number followed by the FORTRAN/3000 revision identification number.
2. A display of the source program. Each source line is preceded by a special eight-digit line number format with the line numbers assigned by the Editor.
3. A display of a set of statistics about the compilation. The message **PROGRAM UNIT COMPILED** means that the compilation was successful. If the compile is unsuccessful, the message **PROGRAM UNIT FLUSHED** is displayed.
4. The messages **END OF COMPILE** and **END OF PREPARE**.
5. The output results from executing the program.
6. The message **END OF PROGRAM** and a new colon prompt.

You may save the runnable version of the program if you wish to avoid having to recompile it for later executions. The runnable version (or prepared program) is in a temporary system file called **$OLDPASS**, which can be saved into a permanent file with the SAVE command. For example, to save the prepared program under the name PROB1PREP, type:

SAVE $OLDPASS,PROB1PREP

System file names must begin with a letter and must be no longer than eight characters. To run the prepared program version, simply type the command RUN followed by the file name. For example:

RUN PROB1PREP

If you wish, you can divide the compile, prepare, and execute processes into individual steps. Following are the commands to accomplish individual steps of compiling, preparing, and running the program.

1. **FORTRAN**—compiles only. The object file may be saved with the SAVE command.
2. **PREP**—prepares the object file only. This prepared file may be saved with the SAVE command.
3. **RUN**—executes the prepared program file only.
4. **FORTPREP**—compiles and prepares the object file. This prepared file may be saved with the SAVE command.
5. **PREPRUN**—prepares and executes the prepared file.

Remember, the FORTGO command will compile your source program into an object file, prepare the resulting object file for execution, and then execute (RUN) it.

If you desire an alphabetic listing of all symbolic names used in your program, include a $CONTROL MAP statement in the program. This option may also be combined with the other $CONTROL parameters. For example:

$CONTROL USLINIT,MAP

F.7 EDIT/3000 AND HP3000 SUMMARY

The program EDIT/3000, commonly known as the Editor, is used as a text editor to enter FORTRAN source programs on the HP3000. A slash is the Editor's prompt character to inform you that it is ready for an edit command. Many Editor commands may be abbreviated to their first letter. For example, K may be given for KEEP, E may be typed for EXIT or END, and so forth.

Following is a summary of the EDIT/3000 and system commands available on an HP3000 computer system. The first command and the last three commands are system commands, not Editor commands. The colon (:) and slash (/) prompts are given before the commands to remind you of the proper level (system or Editor) at which you give these commands. Remember, you do not type the colon or slash.

COMMAND	FUNCTION
:HELLO user-name, account-name	Logs you on to the system.
:EDITOR	Gets you into the Editor subsystem.
/ADD	Allows you to insert next text into the work area.
Control-Y keys	Terminates the ADD mode.
/LIST ALL	Lists the contents of your work area.
/KEEP filename	Saves your work area into a permanent disk file.
/TEXT filename	Retrieves the contents of an existing permanent disk file and brings it into your work area.
/END	Gets you out of the Editor subsystem. This command also clears your work area.
/DELETE	Deletes one or more lines from the work area.
/MODIFY	Allows modification of a line of information.
/GATHER	Moves a block of lines to a new location.
/GATHER ALL	Resequences the line numbers, starting at 1 and in increments of 1.
/HOLD	Stores a block of lines into the hold file.
/JOINQ	Joins the contents of a file to the end of the work area.
:PURGE filename	Purges (eliminates) an old existing file on disk.
:LISTF	Lists the names of all existing files on disk (in your account). This command can be terminated with the BREAK key.
:BYE	Terminates your session and signs you off the system.

This appendix has shown how to develop a FORTRAN source program on an HP3000 system using the EDIT/3000 text editor. You should also have learned how to compile and execute FORTRAN programs on the HP3000. Good luck in your programming assignments.

International Business Machines' (IBM) Time Sharing Option (TSO) Timesharing System and Text Editor

Appendix G

G.1 INTRODUCTION

International Business Machines' (IBM) timesharing system is called **TSO (Time Sharing Option)**. TSO provides text editing and the ability to perform on-line interactive programming.

This appendix discusses the basic commands for large IBM computer systems (S/360, S/370, S/303X, and others) using OS/VS2 TSO. The commands for creating and manipulating files with the EDIT text editor and running a FORTRAN program are explained.

G.2 LOG-ON AND LOG-OFF PROCEDURES

IBM systems use a user identification (userid) number and a password for logging on to its timesharing system. On some IBM timesharing systems, a terminal identification is also used. The exact procedure may vary from installation to installation. The normal procedure for logging-on to TSO is as follows:

1. Type the command:

   logon

2. The system responds with a message for you to enter your userid.

   USERID?

3. Enter your assigned userid. For example:

   USERID? tw0029

4. If your userid is accepted, the system then prompts for your password. The message PASSWORD? is typed followed by a six-character blackout mask.

   PASSWORD? XXXXXX

   Enter your assigned password. The password is typed over the blackout mask to prevent the password from being compromised.

5. If your password is correct, the system responds with a message confirming the log-on, time, and date. A second line with a READY message is also printed. For example:

   TW0029 LOGON IN PROGRESS AT 10:15:03 ON JUNE 2, 1981
   READY

You are now logged on to TSO and may manipulate and run your programs.

The entire log-on procedure is illustrated as follows:

logon
USERID? tw0029
PASSWORD? XXXXXX
TW0029 LOGON IN PROGRESS AT 10:15:03 ON JUNE 2, 1981
READY

The userid may be given after the ''logon'' command to eliminate the prompt for USERID. For example:

logon tw0029

The password may also be included by separating it from the userid by a slash(/). This fast log-on eliminates the prompt for password. For example:

logon tw0029/candy

Three tries at entering a valid userid or password are allowed before the system terminates a log-on.

Log-off Procedure

To terminate a TSO session, you give the command **logoff.** The system responds with a message giving the time and date you logged off. For example:

logoff
TW0029 LOGGED OFF TSO AT 10:30:01 ON JUNE 2, 1981+

TSO does not have a FORTRAN subsystem for you to create or modify FORTRAN source programs. Therefore, you must use the text editor named **EDIT** to create and manipulate FORTRAN source programs.

G.3 TSO EDIT TEXT EDITOR

IBM uses the term **data set** for a file. Thus, a data set is a collection or a set of data records.

There are three modes of operation under TSO. These are:

1. **READY Mode**
2. **EDIT Mode**
3. **INPUT Mode**

You must always make sure that you are in the proper mode of operation when entering your commands or program statements. That is, some commands are valid only when you are in the READY mode (after the READY message has printed). Other commands are only valid when you call the EDIT program and are in EDIT mode. You can only be in INPUT mode when you are already in the EDIT program. It is essential to understand the differences between these three modes and to enter the correct command according to the system mode you are in. TSO and EDIT commands (and subcommands) may be typed in upper case or lower case letters.

You cannot type a new command until the last issued command is finished. A teleprinter terminal connected to an IBM system will go into a "lock state" during the time that a command is being processed. "Lock state" means the terminal will not accept any new command until the current command is finished. When the command is finished, the terminal will unlock and allow you to enter a new command. If you do not get any results when typing at your terminal, do not think that it is broken or the system is down. Merely wait for a command to finish before entering new information.

G.3.1 The Edit Command to Begin an Editing Session

The **edit** command is used to create or modify a data set in the system. The edit command (abbreviated **e**) is followed by the name of the data set to be edited. A slash (/) and assigned password are given after the data-set name, if a password is used. After the password, the keyword "new" or "old" is given, depending on whether a new data set is to be created or an existing data set is to be edited. If the key word "new" is given (to create a new data set), the data set type (such as asm, cobol, fortgi, forth, pli, plif, basic, vsbasic, text, data, or other parameters of the data set) is also given. For example, to create a new data set for a FORTRAN G1 program named PROG1 (and password of super), type:

edit prog1/super new fortgi

To edit the existing FORTRAN G1 source program with a data set name of PROG1 (and password of super), type:

edit prog1/super old

The "new" option to create a new data set with EDIT automatically puts you into the **input** mode. You begin adding statements to the data set. Everything is considered data; that is, you can include JCL statements along with source statements. To get out of the input mode, you must transmit a null statement (a line with nothing typed on it). The system will not recognize any commands until you exit from the input mode. Typing commands before exiting input mode is a common procedure error made by many students. The commands are added to the data set, and must be deleted.

G.3.2 The End Subcommand to Exit the Editor

The **end** subcommand is given to terminate the operation of the edit command. The key word **save** is given after the subcommand to save the results from the current editing session. The key word **nosave** is given after the end subcommand if you do not want to save the results from the editing session. For example, to terminate the edit operation and save the results, type:

end save

To terminate the edit operation and not save the edited results, type:

end nosave

The **end** command will exit you from the editor and take you back to TSO.

G.3.3 The Input Subcommand to Add New Lines of Text

The **input** subcommand (abbreviated **i**) puts the system into input mode, so that you can add or replace data in the data set being edited. The system automatically provides five digit line numbers beginning at 00010. You enter the data (text) by typing the line of input to the right of the line number and pressing the RETURN key. For example:

input
00010

You may specify the beginning line number and increment value by providing these parameters after the input command. For example, to begin the line numbers at 00005 and in increments of 5, type:

i 5 5

You must enter a null line (a line with nothing typed on it) to exit the input mode. A hyphen at the end of an input line indicates a continuation of the line.

G.3.4 The Insert Subcommand to Add New Lines of Text

The **insert**, abbreviated **in,** command is used to insert (add) new lines of text (or data) into the data set being edited. Giving the **insert** command automatically puts you in **input** mode. The current line pointer must be set to the proper line position at which you want to insert new text. That is, the **insert** command allows the insertion of new text at the location of the current line pointer. The operations for the insert subcommand are the same as for the input subcommand. Just type:

in

The current line pointer may be set by the subcommands **top, bottom, down, up, find,** and **list.** The **insert** subcommand is exited by transmitting a null line.

G.3.5 The List Subcommand to Display One or More Lines of Data

The **list** subcommand, abbreviated **l,** is used to display one or more lines of the data set being edited. The subcommand by itself displays the entire data set. Additional operands such as line-number, line-number-1, line-number-2, and *[count] may be used to display a single line, a range of lines, the current line, or a count of lines beginning with the current line number. For example, to display the entire data set, type:

l

To display the text from line number 100 through 200, type:

l 100 200

The asterisk (*) operand after a subcommand indicates the line pointed to by the current line counter. A count (integer number) may be given after the * to indicate a count of lines (which includes the current line). For example, to list the current line plus the next four (a count of 5 lines), type:

l *5

To list the current line, type:

l *

G.3.6 The Delete Subcommand to Delete Records From a Data Set

The **delete** subcommand, abbreviated **del,** removes one or more records from the data set being edited. If no operand is given, the record pointed to by the current line pointer is deleted. The operands line-number, line-number-1, line-number-2, or *[count] may be given after the subcommand to delete a specific line, a range of lines, or a count of lines beginning with the current line. Upon completion of the subcommand, the current line pointer points to the line before the line that was deleted. The current line pointer will be shown on the terminal if the **verify** subcommand has been activated (previously set on). To delete the current line, type:

del

or

del *

To delete the record with line number 100, type:

del 100

To delete the records starting with line number 100 and going through line number 200, type:

del 100 200

To delete the current line plus the next six lines, type:

del *7

G.3.7 The Insert/Replace/Delete Function of Edit

A line number may be given to insert, change, or delete a line of text without specifying a subcommand name. For example, to delete a specific line in the data set, type only the line number. To replace a specific line in the data set, type the line number followed by the new text. To insert a line of text, type the new line number followed by the new text.

G.3.8 The Change Subcommand to Modify One or More Lines of Text

The **change** subcommand, abbreviated **c**, is given to modify a character string in a line of text or multiple lines of text. If no line number is given after the subcommand, only the character string in the current line is modified. The character strings must be delimited by a slash (/). For example, to change the string "DIMNESION" to "DIMENSION" in the current line, type:

c */DIMNESION/DIMENSION/

The single quote may also be used to delimit the character string. For example, to replace the string "WRITE (10," with the string "WRITE (5,", type:

c * 'WRITE (10,' 'WRITE (5,'

The count operand may be given to change a string in a specified number of lines. However, only the first occurrence of the string will be changed unless the **all** option is also included. For example, to replace all occurrences of the string "DIMENSION" with the string "INTEGER" in the current line, plus the next two lines, type:

c *3 'DIMENSION' 'INTEGER' all

G.3.9 The Find Subcommand to Locate a Specific Character String

The **find** subcommand (abbreviated **f**) is used to locate a specific character string in the data set being edited. The search for the character string begins at the current line pointer and searches forward until the character string is found or the end of the data set is reached. If no operand is specified with the subcommand, the system uses the operands as specified in the last usage of the subcommand. For example, to find the character string "READ", type:

f 'READ'

G.3.10 Subcommands to Position the Line Pointer

Certain subcommands are available to reposition the line pointer value. The **top** subcommand repositions the line pointer to the beginning of the data set (value of zero). The **bottom** subcommand positions the line pointer to the last line in the data set. The **up** subcommand positions the line pointer to the previous line (i.e., one line nearer the beginning of the data set). The **down** subcommand positions the line pointer to the next line after the current line (i.e., one line closer to the end of the data set). A count operand may be given with the **up** and **down** subcommands to reposition the line pointer a specified number of lines up or down, respectively.

G.3.11 Subcommands to Execute a Program

Several subcommands are available to process your FORTRAN program. The **SCAN** subcommand (abbreviated **sc**) may be used to initiate syntax checking for the statements in the data set. This way you can make sure that all source statements are constructed correctly before executing the program. If no operand is specified after the command, all statements in the data set are checked for correct syntax. Just type:

sc

A line number or range of line numbers may be given after the command to check the syntax for specified statements. For example, to check the syntax for the statements from line number 100 through 200, type:

sc 100 200

The SCAN subcommand may be set on during the edit operation to perform syntax checking as each statement is typed:

sc on

The **run** subcommand (abbreviated **r**) is used to compile, load, and execute the source program in the data set being edited. The program is executed in an interactive mode with the output results displayed to the terminal. Just type:

run

The **submit** subcommand (abbreviated **sub**) is used to submit the data set being edited as a remote batch job for conventional (batch) processing. Job Control Language (JCL) statements must be included in the data set submitted for remote batch processing. Just type:

sub

The installation manager must authorize the use of the **submit** command for a user. Therefore, you will not be able to perform remote batch processing unless your userid is authorized to use this command.

G.3.12 Additional Subcommands of Edit

Many other subcommands exist under the EDIT mode. Some of these subcommands are: 1) **copy**—to copy one or more records to a new location in the data set and retain the records at the old positions, 2) **move**—to move one or more records to a new location in the data set and delete the records at the old position, 3) **renum**—to number or renumber the lines within the data set, 4) **save**—to retain the data set being edited as a permanent (new or existing) data set, 5) **send**—to send a message to another terminal user or to the system operator, and 6) **help**—to get an explanation (syntax and function) of the EDIT subcommands.

The **renum** subcommand (abbreviated **ren**) is used to number or to renumber (resequence the line numbers) the data set being edited. The default increment is 10 unless a new beginning line number and increment value are given with the subcommand. The **save** subcommand (abbreviated **s**) is used to save the editing operations performed since the last **save** or entry of the editor. The **save** subcommand saves the contents of the data set without exiting the editor or returning to TSO.

G.4   OTHER TSO COMMANDS

Obtaining a List of Permanent Data Sets

The **listcat** (list catalog) command is used on TSO to obtain a listing of all the permanent data sets stored in userid. The system responds with a message that it is in the process of obtaining the names of all your data sets. Then the list of data sets is printed. You must be in the READY Mode to give this command. For example:

> **READY**
> **listcat**
> **IN-CATALOG: tw0029**
> **PROB1.FORT**
> **PROB2.DATA**

Purging Permanent Data Sets

Permanent data sets can be deleted from disk storage by giving the command **delete.** After the command, you enter the name and type of the data set to be deleted. For example, to delete the FORTRAN data set named PROB1, type:

delete prob1.fort

You must be in READY mode to give this command.

Listing a Data Set

A data set may be listed whether you are in READY or EDIT mode. To list a permanent data set or a portion thereof, you use the **list** command. To list the entire data set, type the command **list** followed by the data set name. For example, to list the contents of the data set named PROB1.FORT, type:

list prob1.fort

A portion of a data set may be listed by giving a sequence range of statements. For example, to list lines 50 through 120 in the data set named PROB1.FORT, type:

list prob1.fort 50 120

A space separates the first line number from the second.

Changing the Name of a Permanent Data Set

The name of an old (existing) data set may be changed to a new name with the **rename** command. After the command, give the old data set name and then the new data set name. For example, to change the name of PROB1.FORT to LP1.FORT, type:

rename prob1.fort lp1.fort

The HELP Command

The **help** command (abbreviated **h**) may be used to get information about the function, syntax, and operands of commands and subcommands. This command may also be used to get information on VSBASIC messages. You give the command name or subcommand name following the command. For example, to get information on the **rename** command, type:

h rename

To get information about the function of a command (or subcommand), you include the word "function" after the command name (or subcommand name). To get information about the syntax of a command (or subcommand), you include the word "syntax" after the command name (or subcommand name). If an operand is not given after the **help** command, you get information on all commands.

G.5 RUNNING A FORTRAN PROGRAM WITH TSO

Assume that you have a FORTRAN source program on a disk named PROB1. This program is executed with a **run** command. The command **run** is followed by the name of the file and the file type (fort for FORTRAN). A space must separate each of these items. For example:

run prob1 fort

If there are no syntax errors in the source program, the program will be executed. You must use logical unit 5 to read formatted data from terminal input and logical unit 6 in the WRITE statement to display formatted output results at your terminal. You may also use the format-free input/output statements. The form of the format free **read** statement is:

read *, I/O list

where **I/O list** is the list of input variables to be read. The form of the format-free **print** statement is:

print *, I/O list

where **I/O list** is the list of variables to be printed.

The FORTRAN IV version used by IBM's TSO system is called G1. The G1 FORTRAN compiler may also be run under the EDIT text editor.

G.6 SUMMARY OF TSO COMMANDS

The IBM TSO is a powerful on-line, conversational system for timesharing work. A partial summary of commands available in TSO is as follows:

Command	Function
logon	To log on to the system
logoff	To log off the system
edit	To create or modify a data set in the system.
run	To execute a program
listcat	To list the names of permanent data sets
delete	To delete/purge a data set
list	To list a data set
rename	To change the name of a data set

This appendix has presented an overview of the IBM timesharing system known as TSO and its text editor. A complete description of TSO may be found in IBM manual GC28–0645 and GC28–0646. Good luck and happy programming.

Burroughs 6000 Command and Edit Language (CANDE) Time-sharing System and Editor

Appendix H

H.1 INTRODUCTION

Burroughs 6000 Computers use a powerful text editor known as **Command And Edit Language (CANDE)** for manipulating files. CANDE is used not only to create and modify files, but also to provide a run-time system to compile and execute programs. Thus, CANDE is a complete run-time system for various programming languages in a timesharing environment.

This appendix describes the log-on and log-off procedures for a Burroughs 6000 computer system and its file naming conventions. The CANDE timesharing system is discussed, and the procedure for running a FORTRAN program is explained. The Burroughs B 7000/B 6000 CANDE Users' Manual may be referenced for a complete description of capabilities.

H.2 LOG-ON AND LOG-OFF PROCEDURES

Burroughs' users are assigned a **usercode** to identify their account. The usercode is a combination of letters and digits that uniquely identify each user. A password may also be assigned to a usercode if desired.

Log-on procedure may vary depending on the particular installation. Following is the general procedure for logging on to a Burroughs 6000 series system:

1. Assuming that your terminal is turned on and that CANDE is available, type the command HELLO and depress the XMT (transmit) key (or RETURN key depending upon the available terminal).

HELLO

The command HELLO starts a new session with a new usercode.

2. CANDE responds with a prompt for you to enter your usercode. For example:

#ENTER USERCODE PLEASE

3. Type your assigned usercode (on the new line) after the system message prompt. For example:

#ENTER USERCODE PLEASE
ABC1234

If you have been assigned a password, type a slash after the usercode and then your password. For example:

#ENTER USERCODE PLEASE
ABC1234/SUGAR

If the usercode or password is invalid, the system will respond with the message:

#INVALID USERCODE/PASSWORD; ENTER USERCODE PLEASE

You must reenter your usercode (and password if used). You will be logged off the system if a correct usercode is not entered after several attempts. If this happens, you should see your instructor for help.

4. If you are using a CRT terminal, the system will clear the screen and place the cursor in the home position (upper left corner). The computer also responds with a log-on message giving the session number, time and date, terminal number, and other miscellaneous information. For example:

#SESSION 3910   12:38:49   12/31/80

You are now logged-on to CANDE and may proceed with your session. You may have noticed that CANDE will prefix all messages sent to the user with the pound-sign symbol (#).

A shortcut sign-on may be used, which combines steps one and three. Enter the command HELLO followed by a space and then your assigned usercode. This eliminates the prompt for your usercode. For example:

HELLO ABC1234

The system then clears the screen and places the cursor in the home position.

Another shortcut sign-on procedure exists, which may be helpful to you if CANDE crashes and you do not want to lose the data on your screen when the system comes back up (and you sign on again). This procedure is simply to type your usercode:

ABC1234

The system signs you on but does not clear the screen or move the cursor.

Following is an example of the complete log-on procedure (without using a password):

HELLO
#ENTER USERCODE PLEASE
ABC1234

The CRT screen is cleared, and the following log-in message appears on the first line:

#SESSION number time date

where number, time, and date are an assigned session number, the current time, and date.

You are automatically in CANDE after you have logged-on and can create, manipulate, and run programs.

Log-off Procedure

The command **BYE** is given to log off the system. The computer prints a message giving the session number, time and date that your session terminated, the elapsed time during the session, the total amount of processor time used, the amount of I/O time used, and another message giving charges for the session. An example of the messages displayed by the system at log off is as follows:

BYE
#END SESSION 3910 ET = 39.2 PT = 4.8 IO = 2.3 12:54:02 12/31/80
PARTIAL CHARGES: ET $0.05 PT $0.02 IO $0.02 12:54:02 12/31/80

H.3 B6000 FILE NAMING CONVENTIONS

Burroughs file names consist of one or more "identifiers," each of which may have up to 17 characters. A maximum of 11 identifiers is allowed in a file name. Identifiers may begin with a letter or a digit. Each new identifier is separated from a previous one with a slash, i.e., identifier1/identifier2/identifier3/etc. Valid examples:

> **PROB1**
> **PROB1/FIRST**
> **PROB1/SECOND**
> **A/B/C/D**
> **A/B/E**

The left-most identifiers are called directories to the right-most identifiers. Directories identify files as belonging to larger sets of files, which enables those sets to be referred to as a unit. The use of the slash to include additional identifiers provides a hierarchical file-naming structure. A group of files under directories may be deleted or copied as a group instead of individually. This hierarchical use of identifiers for naming files also provides an orderly manner of naming related files. For example, the three file names

> **LABPROB1/FORTRAN**
> **LABPROB1/FORTRAN/VERSION2**
> **LABPROB1/DATA**

is an orderly approach to naming all three files that relate to lab problem one.

H.4 B6000 CANDE COMMANDS

Most major programming languages, such as FORTRAN, COBOL, ALGOL (Algorithmic Language), PL/I (Programming Language One), and BASIC (Beginner's All-purpose Symbolic Instruction Code) are available for writing and compiling programs on a Burroughs 6000 timesharing system. Before you can create a program or data file you must inform the system to make you a workfile. Burroughs uses the term **workfile** to identify the temporary work area used by CANDE to create and manipulate your current file. Only one workfile is permitted in CANDE to be worked on at a time.

H.4.1 Listing the Names of Permanent Files

You may list the names of permanent files in your account with the **FILES** or **FILE** command. For example, the command

> **FILE**

would cause the system to list all permanent disk files under your usercode. For multiple level file names, the additional levels of a file name will be displayed with an offset under each directory.

H.4.2 Creating a New Workfile and Retrieving a Permanent File

The **MAKE** or **CREATE** command is used to inform the system that you want to create a new workfile. You must give it a name and specify its type such as DATA or FORTRAN. For example, to create a new workfile named EXER2 that is a FORTRAN-type file, enter:

> **MAKE EXER2 FORTRAN**

The computer will respond with a message that a workfile named EXER2, which is type FORTRAN, has been established.

Now you can proceed to enter your FORTRAN statements (program). You must include a **sequence number** (also called a line number) before each statement. The system uses these sequence numbers to keep your statements in a specific order. Also, the sequence numbers are used to delete statements, add new statements, change existing statements, list portions of your workfile, and so on. Therefore, these sequence numbers are of the utmost importance to the computer. The sequence numbers are kept in columns 73 through 80 of a statement but are printed before the information in column 1 for your convenience. You should use some increment, such as by 10's or even 100's, for the sequence numbers. A sequence number may consist of a maximum of eight digits.

For example, a FORTRAN program to compute the sum of two numbers and print the results, might be:

```
100      A = 10.0
200      B = 20.5
300      C = A + B
400      WRITE (6,99) A, B, C
500   99 FORMAT (1X, 3F7.1)
600      STOP
700      END
```

This program in your workfile can now be modified or run to obtain the output results. How can a permanent file be retrieved from disk and loaded into your workfile to manipulate?

Retrieving a Permanent File. Either of the two commands **GET** or **LOAD** followed by the file name will load a permanent disk file into your workfile. For example, to load a permanent file named EXER2 into your workfile, enter:

GET EXER2

or

LOAD EXER2

Either of these commands would retrieve the permanent disk file named EXER2 and load it into your workfile. The GET command is more frequently used. The workfile is ready to be edited and to produce a final program for execution.

H.4.3 Listing a File

To list a file or certain portions of a file, the **LIST** command is used. For example, the following LIST commands allow you to look at all or portions of a workfile:

LIST
LIST 100–300
LIST 100,300,500
LIST 100–300,500
LIST END

The first example will cause the entire file to be listed. A hyphen is used between two sequence numbers to indicate a range of statements to be listed. The second example will thus list the statements with sequence numbers 100 through 300. A comma is used to indicate individual statements to be listed. The third example will list the three individual statements with sequence numbers 100,300, and 500. The fourth example will list all statements starting at line number 100 and ending with line number 300 and the individual statement with line number 500. The keyword **END** represents the last sequence number in a file. Thus, the fifth example lists the last line in your workfile.

H.4.4 Deleting Lines in a Workfile

You may delete individual lines in a workfile by typing the line number and transmitting it. For example, you could delete line number 500 by typing

500

Be sure you do not include a space after the line number; else, the line number, with a blank line, will remain in your workfile.

You can also delete a statement from your file by typing the command **DELETE**, followed by the statement number. For example:

DELETE 100

Or you can delete an entire range of statements by using the hyphen between the beginning and ending sequence numbers. For example, the command

DELETE 200–400

would delete all statements with sequence numbers in the range 200 from 400. Multiple individual lines may be deleted by separating them by a comma. For example, the command

DELETE 100,300,500

would delete the statements with line numbers 100, 300, and 500 from your workfile.

H.4.5 Adding Statements to a Workfile

To add new statements to an existing file, you simply give the new statements a sequence number, which will be merged into the proper order. For example, to add a statement between sequence numbers 200 and 300, you would assign a sequence number of 210 or 250 or whatever, as long as it falls between 200 and 300. This is why you assign sequence numbers in increments of 10 or 100, for the flexibility of inserting new statements in a file.

H.4.6 Modifying Statements in a Workfile

You may need to correct a mistake or want to change portions of your program. To correct a statement, simply type in the corresponding sequence number and the new statement. The computer will automatically replace the old statement with the new one.

CANDE also allows you to edit a file. That is, you can replace certain characters with new ones, find statements containing certain characters, fix portions of a line, and so on. These commands are **REPLACE, FIND, FIX,** and others. They can save you much time in modifying statements in your workfile.

Finding Text. The command **FIND** is used to search for text within a workfile. The command FIND is followed by a beginning delimiter (normally a slash [/]), the text to be found, and an ending delimiter (which must be the same character as the beginning delimiter). Any special character except a semicolon (;), a comma (,), an "at" sign (@), a colon (:), or a percent (%) may be used for a delimiter. The delimiter marks the beginning and end of the text field. For example, to find all occurrences of the word READ in a workfile, enter:

FIND /READ/

This command would search your workfile and list the sequence number of all statements containing the word "READ". The search can be restricted to a range of specific sequence numbers by including a sequence range list after the ending delimiter. For example, to search between sequence numbers 100 and 700 for the text READ, enter:

FIND /READ/ 100–700

This form of the FIND command will locate only text that is bounded by spaces or special characters; so you must use another option to search for a string of characters which appear embedded in the middle of words. The **LITERAL** option (abbreviated **LIT**) is included in the FIND command to locate a string of text at any location in a workfile, i.e., an exact match of the text, including non-essential blank spaces. The LIT option is given after the word FIND. For example, to search a file for the string of characters "RES" you would enter:

FIND LIT /RES/

With the LIT option you can find any string of text, no matter where it appears in your workfile. The sequence range list can also be included with this option. A count option may be included after the command (or LIT, if used) to limit the search to a specific number of occurrences. There are several other options that may be used with the FIND command.

Replacing Text. The **REPLACE** command is used to modify text in a workfile. It allows you to delete and insert text in statements in the workfile. Give the command REPLACE, followed by a delimiter, the old text to modify (the target text), another delimiter, a space, a new beginning delimiter, the new text to replace the old text, and an ending delimiter. For example, to replace all occurrences of the variable RESLT with the new text RESULT, enter:

REPLACE /RESLT/ /RESULT/

This would replace RESLT with RESULT in all statements where the old word RESLT appeared. The old (target) text RESLT must be bounded by spaces in the text. To replace a string of characters appearing in some portion of a word (beginning, middle, or end), you must include the **LITERAL** (abbreviated LIT) option. For example, to replace the string of text SLT with SULT, enter:

REPLACE LIT /SLT/ /SULT/

A sequence range list can be included with the REPLACE command to restrict the replacement of text to a specific range of statements. For example, to replace the text I2 with the new text of I3 between sequence numbers 300 and 800, enter:

REPLACE /I2/ /I3/ 300-800

Two options are available after the new text (or sequence range list, if used), to list the sequence number of each line in which a replacement was done and to display the lines changed by replacement. A colon (:) must be entered after the ending delimiter for the new text (or sequence range list, if used) to indicate the addition of new options. The option **SEQUENCE** (abbreviated **S**) is used to list the sequence numbers of changed lines. The option **TEXT** is used to list the statements in which a replacement was performed. These are good options to verify that the replacement operation was performed on the proper statements.

The rules for the delimiters used to enclose the target text and the new text are the same as for the FIND statement. The REPLACE command may be abbreviated REPL. There are additional options available with the REPLACE command.

Fixing a Line of Text. The FIX command may be used to modify a line of text in your workfile. A sequence number is given after the command to identify the line to be changed; then a beginning delimiter, the old text, an ending delimiter, and the new text are given. For example, to change the text "RESLT" in line 300 to "RESULT", enter:

FIX 300 /RESLT/RESULT

The keywords **BEFORE** and **AFTER** may be used to insert new text in a line before or after certain text. For example, to insert the text "MR. " before the text "ROBERT" in line 200, enter (the line 200 is listed to show the text before and after the FIX command is given):

LIST 200
200 JONES, ROBERT T.

FIX 200 BEFORE /ROBERT/MR.

LIST 200
200 JONES, MR. ROBERT T.

To add text after some other text, the **AFTER** command is used. For example, to add the text " PROGRAMMER" after the text "T.", enter:

FIX 200 AFTER /T./ PROGRAMMER

The FIX command includes additional options that are not discussed here.

H.4.7 Moving and Copying Lines in a Workfile

You may wish to move statements within your file. You may want to move a statement or block of statements to a new location, or you may want to duplicate a statement or block of statements at another location in the file. These operations are easily performed with the MOVE and INSERT commands.

Moving Text to a New Location. The **MOVE** command is used to move a sequence range list of statements to a new location in a file. The MOVE command is followed by the sequence range list, the keyword TO, and the base of the new location (beginning sequence number of the new location). Consider the following examples:

MOVE 100 TO 710
MOVE 300–500 TO 1920
MOVE 270–310 TO 1001 + 1

The first example moves the statement at sequence number 100 to a new location with sequence number 710. The sequence number 710 will be placed in order with the normal range of sequence numbers appearing in the file. That is, if the sequence numbers in the workfile appear in increments of 100, then 710 would be placed after 700 and before 800. The second example moves the block of statements with sequence numbers 300 through 500 to a new location starting with sequence number 1920. Sequence number 1920 must not previously have existed in the workfile. The sequence range list may not overlap the destination sequence numbers, nor may the new sequence numbers overlap unaffected lines within the workfile. The third example moves the lines with sequence numbers 270 through 310 to a new location starting with sequence number 1001; each statement at the new location is incremented by 1. Assuming sequence numbers in increments of 10's in our workfile, line number 270 is moved to 1001, line number 280 is moved to 1002, line number 290 is moved to 1003, and so on. The increment option is useful to avoid overlapping any existing sequence numbers when you move a large block of statements.

Copying Text. The **INSERT** command copies lines from your workfile to new locations in your workfile. The command INSERT is followed by a sequence range list, the keyword AT, and the base sequence number of the new location. Consider the following examples:

INSERT 200 AT 820
INSERT 200–400 AT 950
INSERT 490–530 AT 802 + 2

The first example inserts a copy of the statement at line 200 into a new location at line 820. The original statement at line 200 is unchanged. The second example inserts the range of statements at 200 through 400 at a new location starting with sequence number 950. The third example inserts a copy of the statements at line number 490 through 530 at the new location beginning with sequence number 802. Each additional statement is assigned a new sequence number in increments of 2.

The INSERT command may be abbreviated IN. Lines from permanent files may also be inserted into a workfile with the INSERT command.

H.4.8 Saving a Workfile as a Permanent File

What happens if you have not finished work on a program, and it is time to go to class? You can save your workfile as a permanent file and later retrieve it and continue working where you left off. To save a workfile you simply enter the command **SAVE.** This command will preserve your workfile as a permanent file with the name you gave it when it was created. Just type:

SAVE

This saves your workfile as a permanent file named EXER2. If you already had a permanent file named EXER2, it would be destroyed and replaced with the contents of this workfile. CANDE will respond with a message that it is updating the workfile and another message that the file has been saved.

Perhaps you retrieved a permanent file and want to save it under a new name (if you are not sure of the results). If you want to save it as EXER2TEST, you would type:

SAVE AS EXER2TEST

Now let us look at how to purge or remove a workfile in order to create a new workfile and how to purge a permanent file from disk.

H.4.9 Purging a Workfile and Permanent Files

The **REMOVE** command is used to purge a workfile and permanent disk files. To purge your workfile, type:

REMOVE

This will delete the contents of your workfile and allow you to create a new one. CANDE will not let you log off until you have removed or saved an existing workfile. A message is displayed telling you to do this.

To purge a permanent file from disk, you type the command REMOVE, followed by the permanent file name. For example:

REMOVE EXER2TEST

This would purge the permanent file named EXER2TEST from disk. It is no longer available to you.

H.5 RUNNING A PROGRAM UNDER CANDE

Assume you are ready to compile and execute a program. You use the command **RUN** to cause the workfile to be compiled and executed. Separate commands such as **COMPILE** and **EXECUTE** are available for separately compiling or executing a program. If a program does not compile, the system will provide syntax error messages to the terminal. The computer will list each statement in error, followed by the syntax message. You must correct the mistake and recompile the program. Your output results may be displayed to the terminal or sent to a line printer in case of voluminous output.

Following is a FORTRAN program created with CANDE and executed.

```
MAKE PROB1 FORTRAN
#WORKFILE PROB1:FORTRAN

10$RESET FREE
20        SUM = 10.5 + 11.5
30        PRINT /, SUM
40        STOP
50        END
SAVE
#UPDATING
#WORKSOURCE PROB1 SAVED
RUN
#COMPILING 0967
#DONE ELAPSEDTIME=4.1 PROCESSTIME=0.8 PROCESSIOTIME=0.3
#RUNNING 0967
22.0
#DONE ELAPSEDTIME=1.4 PROCESSTIME=0.1 PROCESSIOTIME=0.1
```

The lines beginning with the number sign (#) are printed by the system. The statement at line 10 is a **compiler control statement,** which terminates the free-form source statement option and requires the standard FORTRAN statement columns to be used. A compiler control statement must start with a $ in column 1. You may turn off the source listing and cause other options to be in effect throughout the program by using various compiler control statements.

A Common Error in Running a Program

A very frequent error is committed by students in running a program with CANDE. Once the object program is produced, it remains until it is deleted or until a new compiled version replaces it. Thus if you give the RUN command and a current copy of the object program already exists in your account, CANDE will not recompile the program; instead, it executes the existing object program. Students are baffled that they get the same output results as from a previous execution. To prevent this, you must either REMOVE the object program or use the **COMPILE** command (abbreviated C) to recompile the workfile. An object program is always given a first identifier of OBJECT in the file name. To remove the object file you may enter REMOVE OBJECT/program name (where program name is the name of the workfile). All object files may be removed by the command REMOVE OBJECT/=.

Resequencing Lines in a Workfile

Lines in your workfile may be resequenced with the **RESEQUENCE** command (abbreviated **RESEQ**). The RESEQUENCE command assigns new sequence numbers to lines in your workfile without changing their order. This command is very helpful when you have inserted or added many new lines and there is no room to add more statements between two lines. The form of this command is the word RESEQ, followed by a base (new beginning sequence), a plus sign, and an increment. For example, to resequence the lines in your file starting at 100 and in increments of 20, enter the command:

RESEQ 100 + 20

The default base of 100 and increments of 100 can be used by giving the command:

RESEQ

This is the faster method of resequencing your lines in increments of 100.

You may limit the range of sequence numbers that you want to resequence with the sequence range option, which would be included after the command. For example, if you only want to resequence the lines betwen 300 and 399 in increments of 5, enter the command:

RESEQ 300-399 300 + 5

Remember the END option when using certain pertinent commands. You could resequence lines 720 through the end of your file and begin the new sequence at number 800 by using the following command:

RESEQ 720-END 800

The default increment of 100 would be used, or you can supply an increment.

H.6 SUMMARY OF CANDE COMMANDS

CANDE is a very powerful text editor. Many more commands exist, which take an entire manual to describe. Your instructor will inform you of any additional commands you might need.

The following is a partial list of system commands that are available in CANDE to create, manipulate, and run FORTRAN programs (or any other type of files). The word "filename" represents the name you have chosen to identify a new or existing file. The word "type" represents the type of file (FORTRAN, BASIC, DATA, and so on).

Command	Function	Example
HELLO	Starts a new session with a new usercode.	HELLO
BYE	Logs you off the system.	BYE
MAKE filename type	Creates a new file in your work area.	MAKE PROB1 FORTRAN
CREATE filename type	Same function as MAKE.	CREATE PROB1 FORTRAN
GET filename	Retrieves a permanent file from disk storage and loads it into your work area.	GET PROB1
LOAD filename	Same function as GET.	LOAD PROB1
REMOVE	Removes the file from your work area.	REMOVE
REMOVE filename	Removes the permanent file from disk storage.	REMOVE PROB1
LIST	Lists the contents of your workfile.	LIST
	Individual lines of the workfile may be listed by separating line numbers with a comma.	LIST 10,50,95
	A range of line numbers may be listed by inserting a hyphen between the two line numbers.	LIST 30-80
	The last line in the file may be listed with the option END.	LIST END
SAVE	Saves the workfile as a permanent disk file. Any existing file with the workfile name is replaced.	SAVE
	The **AS** option saves the workfile under a new name.	SAVE AS PRO1A
RUN	Executes the object program with the name of the workfile. If no object program exists with the workfile name, the source program is first compiled to produce an object program.	RUN
FIND	Searches a workfile for specified text.	FIND /PI/
REPLACE	Modifies text in a workfile.	REPL/2.5/2.6/
FIX	Modifies a line of text in a workfile.	FIX 200 /A/I
RUN filename	Executes a permanent file from a disk.	RUN PROB1

EXECUTE	Same function as RUN.	EXECUTE
COMPILE	Compiles the workfile and produces an object program when written with the word OBJECT plus a slash and the workfile name.	COMPILE
RESEQUENCE	Resequences a workfile with new line numbers.	RESEQ
DELETE line number	Deletes specified line numbers from a workfile.	DELETE 35
	A range of line numbers may be deleted by using a hyphen to specify a range.	DELETE 50–70
FILES or FILE	Lists the names of your permanent files stored on disk.	FILES
TITLE	Retitles a permanent disk file with a new name.	TITLE LP1 TO LPIV2

CANDE allows you to give commands to the operating system. Such commands include:

?STATUS — Displays the status of your terminal or the status of the current CANDE command being processed.

?DS — Terminates any command in process.

?CS — Displays the status of a compilation.

?END — Signals an end-of-file condition of a program that has a file open for input from your terminal.

?TIME — Displays the current time, date, and day of the week.

?WRU — Displays the identity of your station.

This appendix has presented the basics of the B6000 timesharing system known as CANDE (which includes a powerful text editor). You should learn its capabilities well to assist you in developing your FORTRAN programs. Good luck and happy programming.

Honeywell 60/6000 FORTRAN Timesharing System

Appendix I

I.1 Introduction to the Honeywell FORTRAN Timesharing System

Honeywell 60/6000 systems include a FORTRAN subsystem under timesharing. You may create, manipulate, and execute programs while in the FORTRAN timesharing system. This appendix explains the log-on and log-off procedures, file naming conventions, and the FORTRAN timesharing subsystem for the Honeywell 60/6000 computers. You should consult Honeywell FORTRAN manual DD02 for a complete description of the FORTRAN timesharing capabilities.

Log-on Procedure

After turning on the terminal and making any necessary connection to the computer, press the RETURN key. A system identification message is usually printed to indicate that you are connected to the computer. For example:

HIS SERIES 6000 SYSTEM ON (date) AT (time) CHANNEL (nnnn)

This message gives the date, time and channel number that you are connected to with the timesharing system. You may now begin the log-on procedure.

1. Following this connect message, the system asks for the user's identification:

USER ID– –

2. You respond (on the same line) with the user-ID assigned by your instructor or by the timesharing computer center management. The user-ID uniquely identifies a particular user, known to the system, for the purposes of locating the programs and files and accounting for resources used during the TSS session. A response might be:

USER ID– –P.COLE

The entry must be transmitted to the computer by typing the RETURN (or appropriate) key. The entered response must not contain any spaces (i.e., must be one word).

3. After you respond with your user-ID, the system asks for your password (which was assigned to you with your user-ID):

PASSWORD

On teleprinter terminals a new line will be printed with a "strikeover" mask below the request message PASSWORD. The "strikeover" mask is an overstrike of twelve characters, which insures that the password, when typed, cannot be read by another person. On CRT terminals, the typed password is not echoed (displayed) on the screen.

4. Enter your password and depress the RETURN key to transmit the message to the system:

PASSWORD
XXXXXXXXXXXX

User numbers and passwords are assigned to each user (or perhaps to an entire class section) and must be correctly entered to gain access to the computer. If your log-on is incorrect, the computer will respond with a message such as

INVALID USER NUMBER

or INVALID PASSWORD. You are given another opportunity to enter the correct user number or password. After two or three invalid attempts to log on, the system will disconnect you from the computer. In some cases, you might receive other types of messages at this point. If the dollar limit in your account has been exceeded, you will receive a message

RESOURCES EXCEEDED—CANNOT ACCEPT YOU

and you will be disconnected from the system. If there is a limited amount of disk space available, you will receive the message.

nn BLOCKS FILE SPACE AVAILABLE

where nn is the number of disk blocks available. This message will not affect log-on, but may restrict the number of permanent files you can create.

5. Assuming that you responded with a valid user-ID and password and that you have not over-extended the money limit in your account, the system asks you to select the processing system (FORTRAN, BASIC, and so forth) to be used. This is called the system-selection request:

SYSTEM?

Two subsystems—FORTRAN and BASIC—are available to create and run programs on a Honeywell timesharing system. IF you want to work with a FORTRAN program, type the word FORTRAN:

SYSTEM? FORTRAN

followed by a carriage RETURN. Now the computer knows what programming language to use, and it can select the proper computer systems programs/resources.

6. Next, you are asked whether you want to enter a new program (NEW) or to retrieve and work with an existing program stored on disk (OLD). The system request message is:

OLD OR NEW− −

If you want to start a new program (i.e., create a new source program), type NEW. If you want to recall an old source program from disk, type OLD followed by a space and the name of the file to be retrieved from disk.

For example, if you want to build a new program file, type

OLD OR NEW− −NEW

and depress the RETURN key.

If you want to copy an existing file from disk into the current file, respond with OLD, followed by the file name. These user-chosen file names must not exceed six characters and must be given when a file is saved. It may be a combination of letters (A–Z) and digits (0–9) in any order you wish, as long as it does not exceed six characters. Assuming an existing file named PROB1, type:

OLD OR NEW− −OLD PROB1

The system copies the file named PROB1 off disk and into your current file, where it is then available to be manipulated.

After you respond to the OLD OR NEW message, the computer has all the information it needs to begin work and responds with the message

READY

At this point, you may begin typing a new FORTRAN program or modifying an old one (if an old file was chosen). Sometimes the computer may respond with the message:

WAIT

instead of the response READY. WAIT means that the computer is busy. You must wait a few minutes for the computer to service your request. When the computer is available, the READY message will be displayed on your terminal.

The complete log-on sequence of commands to build a new FORTRAN program is as follows:

USER ID− −P.COLE
PASSWORD
XXXXXXXXXXX
SYSTEM? FORTRAN
OLD OR NEW− −NEW
READY
      *

The asterisk (*) indicates build mode, and you may begin entering a statement on the same line.

The complete log-on procedure of commands to recall an existing program named PROB1 from disk is as follows:

USER ID− −P.COLE
PASSWORD
XXXXXXXXXXX
SYSTEM? FORTRAN
OLD OR NEW− −OLD PROB1
READY
      *

Some systems or installations may use a "short log-on" procedure. With this option, after you enter your user number and password, you are not queried by the system; instead you immediately indicate whether you wish to create a NEW program or retrieve an OLD file by giving the command NEW or OLD.

Log-off Procedure

The log-off procedure is quite simple. Type the command **BYE,** and the computer will terminate your session. The computer responds with an appropriate message indicating that the session has been terminated. An accounting message containing the amount of time spent on the system and the charges is displayed. For example:

```
BYE
**COST:  $     0.54 TO DATE     $     54.00 = 27%
**ON AT 14.100 – OFF AT 14.205 ON 02/16/80
```

If any temporary files are open when the BYE command is typed, you are given the opportunity to save them. You must be at the subsystem level and not in build mode to give the BYE command. You may return to the subsystem level with the **DONE** command.

I.2 FILE NAMING CONVENTIONS AND BUILD MODE PROMPT

A file name can consist of up to six characters, which can be any combination of letters and digits. No special characters are allowed.

A file can be placed under a subcatalog if desired. The subcatalog string (referred to as cat file string) is separated from the file name with a slash. To access a file that also includes a cat file string, all levels of the cat file string must be given. A file name does not, however, have to have a cat file string. A direct access file consists only of the file name and resides directly beneath the User Master Catalog (user-id) level. Students in academic institutions will usually use a direct access file.

When you are in build mode, i.e., creating or modifying a file, the system will display an asterisk (*) to let you know when to enter a new statement. You may then enter other timesharing commands to run your program, terminate your session, or accomplish other tasks.

On the Honeywell system, the work area used to hold your file is known as the current file. You may create a new file or modify an existing permanent file brought into your current file. Only one current file may be used at any given time. A line number in a current file may consist of up to eight digits.

Listing the Names of Permanent Files

All the names of permanent files you have stored on disk may be listed with the **CATALOG** (abbreviated CATA) command. Suppose you have the three files SUM, SUM2, and AVE saved on disk. These permanent file names will be listed when you transmit the CATALOG command. For example:

```
CATALOG
AVE
SUM
SUM2
```

I.3 THE FORTRAN TIMESHARING SYSTEM COMMANDS

After your log-on is complete, you may proceed to use the timesharing commands to perform desired system operations and create and manipulate a file. Let us look at some of the available commands.

I.3.1 Creating a New Program and Retrieving an Existing Program

The log-on procedure included the way to create a new program. When the "OLD or NEW—" message is printed, give the command NEW. The system responds with the READY command and a new line with an asterisk (*). You are now in build mode and may type a new program.

Typing Your Program. You must include a line number before each statement. The system uses these line numbers to keep your statements in a specific order. Also, the line numbers are used to delete statements, list portions of your current file, and other operations. These line numbers are of the utmost importance to the computer. You should use some increment, such as 10's or 100's, for the line numbers, to provide flexibility in adding new lines. The timesharing system recognizes a FORTRAN statement by the beginning line number. Any line beginning with a letter is taken as a command.

Suppose you want to type in a program to compute the sum of two numbers and print the result. The typed program might be:

*10	A = 10
*20	B = 20.5
*30	C = A + B
*40	PRINT, A, B, C
*50	STOP
*60	END

The "PRINT, I/O list" is the form of the Honeywell format-free output statement. Real (decimal) values are printed in exponential format, and integer values are printed in integer format. Character strings (literal constants) may be printed by including them in the PRINT statement, bounded by quotes (" or ').

What if an error is made in typing a line of information? Is there an easy way to correct typing errors?

Correcting Typing Errors and Cancelling a Line. Everyone makes typing errors when using a terminal. You might misspell a word or make a mistake in typing a statement. Errors may be corrected in one of several ways; the way you choose usually depends on how many characters have to be corrected.

To correct one or two incorrect characters while you are still close to them on the same line, you may delete the invalid characters and resume typing. To delete a character you depress the key(s) which move you back one space. (Hopefully this will be the ← key, back/left arrow). This has the effect of deleting the character or space immediately preceding the cursor. If the ← key is pressed N times, the characters or spaces in the N preceding positions are deleted. That is, depressing the ← key once deletes the last character; depressing the ← key twice deletes the last two characters, and so on. Continue this process until you have cancelled the first incorrect character and then type the rest of the line with the correct information. For example, suppose you have typed

40   PIRN

before discovering that the command PRINT is misspelled. You could depress the ← key three times to delete the characters N, R, and I. You would then begin typing with the letter R to correctly type the PRINT statement.

You may have typed a complete or almost-complete line before realizing that a mistake was made near the beginning of the line. You could transmit the line and retype it correctly, since a new line with the same line number replaces the previous statement with the identical line number. You may delete an entire line, however, by depressing the CONTROL key (labeled CTRL) in conjunction with the X key. Depressing these two keys causes the whole line to be deleted. The characters DEL are then printed by the system to indicate deletion. For example:

*40   PRINT, X CTRL/X DEL

Some terminals have a break key, which, when depressed, causes a deletion of the line being typed.

Retrieving an Existing Permanent File. You retrieve an existing file from disk by typing the command OLD, followed by the file name, when the system prints the message prompt "OLD OR NEW– –". For example, to retrieve the permanent file LP1 and bring it into your current file, type:

OLD OR NEW– –OLD LP1

The system responds with a READY message and the asterisk-prompt for build mode. You may then modify your program to prepare it for execution. The procedures for correcting typing errors and cancelling lines are the same as those used in new programs. The procedures for modifying a file are discussed in section I.3.5.

I.3.2 Listing Lines in a Current File

To list the contents (already typed statements) of a current file, use the **LIST** command. Type the command LIST, and all statements stored in the current file will be listed in line number order. For example:

LIST	
10	READ, X, Y
20	S = X + Y
30	PRINT, X, Y, S
40	STOP
50	END

If you want to see the name of the current file and the date and time it was created, use the **LISTH** (List with Header) command. For example:

LISTH
PROB1   1/28/80   10:02 PM
10   **READ, X, Y**
20   **S = X + Y**
30   **PRINT, X, Y, S**
40   **STOP**
50   **END**

The **LIST i,j** (where i and j are line numbers) is used to list a range of line numbers in a current file. For example,

LIST 10,80

would list lines with numbers 10 through 80. The form **LIST i** would list from line number i through the end of the current file. The form **LIST ,j** would list from the first line in the current file through line number j. For example:

LIST 150
LIST ,200

The first example would list from line number 150 through the end of the current file. The second example would list from the beginning of the current file through line number 200. The previous two forms may also be used with the LISTH command.

Where three or more individual numbers are desired to be listed, you may use the form **LIST a,b,c,d,...** (where a, b, c, and d are line numbers). For example,

LIST 10,50,175

would list lines 10, 50, and 175 from the current file.

Frequently you wish to know the last line number in the file. You can find this out by the command

LIST 99999999

This command would cause the highest-numbered line in the current file to be displayed.

I.3.3 Changing, Deleting, and Adding Lines in a Current File

Correction or modification of a program in the current file is done on the basis of line numbers. The following rules are given regarding modification to a program.

1. **Changes/Replacement.** A numbered line will replace any identically numbered line previously entered in the current file. Note: the last line entered with line number nnn (where "nnn" represents a specific line number) will replace line number nnn and be the only line so numbered in the file.
2. **Deletion.** A line consisting of only the line number (with no spaces after the line number) will delete the line with the identical line number.
3. **Addition/Insertion.** A line with a number falling between the line-number values for two existing lines will be inserted in the file between those two lines.

Let us examine these procedures in more detail.

Changing or Replacing a Line. When syntax or logic errors exist in a program, you often need to retype a line with its correction. To replace a line in your program with a new line containing a change, simply type the same line number with the complete new statement. For example, you may need to add parentheses to override the hierarchy of arithmetic operations in an Assignment statement. The old statement in error may be:

40   **R = K + 3/M**

Suppose you need to add 3 to K before doing the division by M. You would type the correction with the same line number. For example:

40   **R = (K + 3)/M**

After typing and transmitting the statement, the computer would delete the old statement with line number 40 and replace it with this new statement.

Thus, the last statement typed with a given line number becomes the current statement with that line number in the program. You must be extremely careful not to type a statement with a line number of a statement already in the program, unless you mean to replace it. If you do, and it is transmitted, say goodbye to the old statement. A student often makes this mistake and wonders why he/she does not then get correct output results.

Deleting a Line. To delete or remove a line from a program, type and transmit just the line number. Make sure that there are no blanks after the line number, since that would merely replace the line with a blank statement. Transmitting only the line number tells the computer to delete that line from the program.

An alternate method of deleting one or more lines from a program is to use the **DELETE** command, followed by the line number you want to delete. For example, to delete line number 70 from a program, type:

DELETE 70

The DELETE command may be used to delete multiple single statements or a range of statements in a current file. To delete multiple single statements, separate each line number with a comma. To delete a range of line numbers, give the first line number followed by a hyphen (-) and the last line number. For example:

DELETE 30,50,75
DELETE 45-80

The first example would delete the three statements with line numbers 30, 50, and 75 from the current file. The second example would delete the range of statements with line numbers 45 through 80 from the current file.

Combinations of single statements and a range of statements may also be used. For example:

DELETE 20,60-85,110

would delete the single statement with line number 20, the range of statements with line numbers 60 through 85, and the statement with line number 110 from the current file.

The hyphen (-) can be used to indicate the first or last line in a file. That is, the form **DELETE-n** (where n is a line number) would delete all lines from the beginning of the current file through line number n. For example,

DELETE -110

would delete all lines from the beginning of the current file through line number 110. The form DELETE n- would delete all lines from line number n through the end of the current file. For example,

DELETE 230-

would delete all lines, beginning at 230, through the end of the current file.

Adding New Lines. To add a line in a program, select a line number that is between those of the two statements where you want the new line placed. Suppose you have the two statements

20	READ, X, Y
30	S = X + Y

and want to print the values of X and Y after they have been read. You would have to add a PRINT statement between lines 20 and 30. You could select a line number of 25 for the PRINT statement and type the new line after line 30 as follows:

20	READ, X, Y
30	S = X + Y
25	PRINT, X, Y

Since the line number 25 falls between line numbers 20 and 30, the three statements would be automatically arranged in your workfile as follows:

20	READ, X, Y
25	PRINT, X, Y
30	S = X + Y

You could have picked any number (21, 22, 23, and so on) that fell between 20 and 30 for the new line number, but what if you used 21 for the line number and later needed to add a new statement (perhaps to print a blank line) between the READ (line 20) and the PRINT (line 21) statements? There would be no room. In this case you would have to change the line number of either the READ or the PRINT statement to allow a line to be inserted between them. The best method is to pick a line number that falls halfway between the line numbers at which you want to add a new statement. This will leave room for new statements to be added if the need arises.

I.3.4 Resequencing Line Numbers to a New Sequence

Sometimes you may use all available line numbers in a certain range, as a result of adding new statements to a program. If a need arises to add a new statement in this range, there will be no available line numbers. For example, suppose you want to add a PRINT statement after the READ statement in the program given below. What do you do?

```
1        PRINT, "ENTER 3 NUMBERS"
2        READ, A, B, C
3        S = A + B + C
4        X = S / 3.0
         . . .
```

You could retype the two Assignment statements with higher line numbers, but that would be tedious.

The best solution is to use the **RESEQUENCE** (abbreviated **RESE**) command, which resequences all line numbers in the program. The resequence operation begins with line number 10 for the first statement and continues to renumber the statements in increments of 10. If the previous program is resequenced, you would have:

```
RESEQUENCE
LIST
10       PRINT, "ENTER 3 NUMBERS"
20       READ, A, B, C,
30       S = A + B + C
40       X = S / 3.0
         . . .
```

Now there is room between the READ and first Assignment statements to enter a PRINT statement. So, you could type

```
25       PRINT, A,B,C
```

and it would be inserted after the READ statement.

You can also give the computer the beginning line number you want to start with and the increments between line numbers. You provide this information after the RESEQUENCE command. For example:

```
RESEQUENCE 100,20
```

The program would be resequenced beginning with line number 100 and continued in increments of 20 (120, 140, 160, and so on).

I.3.5 Changing Systems—The DONE Command

The **DONE** system command is given to cause an exit from the Timesharing FORTRAN system. The system-selection question, SYSTEM?, will then be typed, giving you the option of selecting any other system you desire. Any temporary files created under timesharing FORTRAN would be retained.

One useful purpose of this command might be to switch to another subsystem, such as **ACCESS** (the On-line Permanent File System) or **SCAN**. The subsystem ACCESS allows you to create a permanent file or a catalog file string (directory levels for a multiple-level file). The subsystem SCAN allows you to create a permanent file for user output results and later examine them.

I.3.6 Running Your Program

After all the statements in your program have been typed, you are ready for the computer to "run" or execute the program. Type the command **RUN**. The computer will proceed to execute the program. The **READY** message is displayed after the output to indicate that the command is completed.

Consider the following program to read the values of X and Y, print the input values, and compute and print their sum. First, the source program is listed before running it.

```
LIST
10       READ, X, Y
20       PRINT "X = ", X, "Y = ",Y
30       S = X + Y
40       PRINT, "S = ", S
50       STOP
60       END
```

```
READY
RUN
=
10.5,35.73
X = 0.105000E 02   Y = 0.357300E 02
S = 0.462300E 02
```

READY

The equal sign (=) is the system prompt to tell the timesharing user when to begin typing the input values. A better technique would be to print a message in the program to tell the user what data items to enter and when to enter them. In this example, the values 10.5 and 35.73 were then typed in by the user to be read by the system as values for X and Y.

The command **RUNH** will cause the program to be run with a date and time header printed before the first line of output.

If a misspelled word or illegally formed statement is found in the attempted execution of the program, an error message will be printed on the terminal. This message will describe the type of error and the line number in which it occurred. Find the error, correct it, and retype the statement. Then, type the RUN command again.

When your program is free of syntax errors (statement construction errors), it will be executed. The output results will be transmitted to your terminal. Check these results carefully to see if they are what you expected. If the output results are incorrect, you have a logic error in your program. That is, you have not told the computer the correct operations or given the statements in the correct sequence in order to solve the problem correctly. Review your program and locate the logic error. Correct your program accordingly and then reenter the RUN command.

Now that you have typed your program, run it, and obtained the required output values, you must decide whether you want to keep the program for future use or get rid of it.

I.3.7 Saving and Purging Files

Saving and purging a current file or permanent files are common operations in an interactive programming environment. You may not have time to complete a program at one sitting (if you had to go to class, for example). So, save it on disk and recall it later to continue work on it. When you have finally produced a workable program with the correct solution, you should then remove it from the system, to help alleviate the problem of insufficient disk storage.

You may retain or purge (delete) your current file or any previously created permanent disk file. First, let us see how to handle a current file.

Saving a Current File. To retain a newly built current file for future use, give the command **SAVE**, followed by a space and the file name you want to save it under. The SAVE command will store the current file as a permanent file under the assigned name on magnetic disk. For example, say you have created a NEW file and want to save it under the name PROB1.

SAVE PROB1

The system responds with the message DATA SAVED—, followed by the name of the file (if there is sufficient space on disk). For example:

SAVE PROB1
DATA SAVED—PROB1

What about saving permanent files?

Saving A Permanent File. You resave OLD files back under their previous file name with the **RESAVE** command followed by the file name. Thus, the RESAVE command will save the contents of the current file on the previously existing permanent file. For example,

RESAVE PROB1
DATA SAVED—PROB1

Remember, if you recalled an OLD permanent file merely to run it, and never made any modifications to your current file, there is no need to resave the current file.

Remember also, the SAVE command can be used only to save a new file, one with a file name that did not previously exist under your user-ID. If you recall an OLD file, modify it, and wish to save it under the same name, you **cannot** use the SAVE command. You must use the RESAVE command to resave an existing file back under the same name. If you make a mistake and try to save a file that already exists on disk, with the SAVE command, the system will print the message

FILE ALREADY EXISTS

to let you know that it will not perform this action.

You may, however, save an OLD file under a *new* name by giving the SAVE command followed by a different file name. For example,

SAVE PROB1A
DATA SAVED—PROB1A

The new file name, of course, must be a unique, not previously existing name. This technique is used to save backup (secondary) copies when you want to have more than one version of the same program.

Purging a Current File. If you have no further use for a new current file, you should remove it from the system. You should never arbitrarily save all current files, since they occupy valuable disk space. On most computer systems, disk space is highly limited. You remove a current file with the command **REMOVE** (abbreviated **REMO**), followed by the file name. For example, to remove the current file named LP1, type:

REMOVE LP1

On Honeywell timesharing, if you sign off and do not save any temporary files, they will be automatically purged by the system.

Purging Permanent Files. As previously mentioned, disk space usually is at a premium on a computer system. You may hear your instructor plead with the students to please remove all the OLD unneeded permanent files before the system runs out of disk storage space.

The **RELEASE** (abbreviated **RELE**) command removes a file from the permanent file system. Type the command RELEASE, followed by the name of the file. For example, to purge the permanent file named PROB1, type:

RELEASE PROB1

Removing a File from the Available File Table. An **Available File Table (AFT)** is provided for each user on a Honeywell timesharing system. This table holds approximately 20 file names, which are entered into the AFT when the files are initially accessed. The advantages of the AFT are:

1. Files requiring passwords or long cat/file descriptions may be referenced by the file name alone.
2. Frequently-used files remain readily available, which reduces the overhead time of accessing the file each time.

Because the AFT can only hold a limited number of file descriptions, it can become full. If this happens, and you try to access a new file name to be placed in it, the subsystem will print an error message indicating that the AFT is full. You must then remove any unneeded file from the AFT in order to continue. The **STATUS FILES** command produces a list of all the files in the AFT. The **REMOVE** command is used to remove specified files from it. The files are not purged or altered in any way. Only the name is removed from the AFT, and the file is set not-busy.

To remove the single file named PROB1 from the AFT you would type:

REMOVE PROB1

Multiple files may be removed by separating each filename from another by a semicolon. For example:

REMOVE PROB1;PROB2;PROB3

removes the three files PROB1, PROB2, and PROB3 from the AFT. All files may be simultaneously deleted from the AFT by the command **REMOVE CLEARFILES.**

If a user has a file in his/her AFT, the file is set "busy", and no one else may access it. If you are sharing a common file, you should remove it from your AFT, so that the file can be accessed by others.

I.4 SUMMARY OF HONEYWELL TIMESHARING COMMANDS

Following is a summary of the basic commands available in the Honeywell timesharing system. Filename represents an assigned file name.

Command	Function
FORTRAN	To enter the FORTRAN subsystem
OLD filename	To retrieve an existing permanent file from disk
BYE	To log off the system
CATALOG	To list the names of permanent files
LIST	List all or a portion of a file without a header identification
LISTH	List all or a portion of a file with a header identification

DELETE	To delete one or more lines in a file
RESEQUENCE	To resequence lines in a file
DONE	To exit a subsystem
RUN	To execute a program, without a header identification
RUNH	To execute a program, with a printed header identification
SAVE	To save a current file on disk, with a new name
RESAVE	To resave a current file on disk, under an existing name
REMOVE	To remove a current file from the AFT
RELEASE	To purge a permanent disk file
STATUS FILES	To list all files in the AFT

The Honeywell timesharing system also includes a Text Editor known as the Editor, for modifying lines in a file. You should consult the Honeywell Time Sharing Text Editor manual number DD18 if you are interested in using it.

Univac 1100 FORTRAN Timesharing System and CTS Text Editor

Appendix J

J.1 INTRODUCTION

This appendix discusses the sign-on procedure, file naming conventions, CTS text editor, and FORTRAN language execution for the Univac 1100 series computers. Univac has long been noted for its computing capabilities in a timesharing environment. First, let's look at the sign-on and sign-off procedures for a Univac 1100 system.

J.2 SIGN-ON AND SIGN-OFF PROCEDURES FOR A UNIVAC 1100 SERIES COMPUTER USING CMS

Univac 1100 series computer users are assigned a user ID, an account number, and a project ID to allow access to a Univac 1100 timesharing system. The user ID may be from one to six characters. A one- to six-character password is also assigned to each user ID.

The procedure for signing on to a Univac 1100 series system using CMS consists of the following steps:

1. Once the terminal is on-line, enter the command.

DEMAND

and depress the XMIT (transmit) key. This tells the system that you want to sign on to the computer.

2. The system responds by typing an identification message that you are connected to CMS and a message to enter your user ID and password. Then a new line with an SOE (start of entry) character is displayed in the left margin. The SOE character is the system prompt for you to enter your user ID and password. For example:

>**CMS/DEMAND MODE**
>ENTER USERID/PASSWORD:
>

3. Type your assigned user ID and password after the > prompt as follows:

>COLE/PERRY

The entry COLE is the user ID, and PERRY is the password. If you enter an invalid user ID or password, the message:

>ID NOT ACCEPTED
>ENTER USERID/PASSWORD

is printed for you to reenter the user ID and password.

4. If your user ID and password are accepted, the system clears the screen and responds with the message:

>   >*DESTROY USERID/PASSWORD ENTRY
>   >UNIVAC 1100 OPERATING SYSTEM LEV. 37R2A*CCS*02(RSI)*
>   >ENTER ACCOUNT NUMBER
>   >

You must now enter your account number. The account number signifies the account of the user or the project the user is currently working on. An example of an account number would be:

>   >CS9999

5. The system then responds with the message:

>   >ENTER PROJECT-ID:
>   >

The project ID, like the account number, will vary from installation to installation. The project ID is used to uniquely identify your files from other users' files. It may consist of your initials, but it doesn't have to.
An example of a project ID would be:

>   >PC

The project ID signifies the qualifier part of a file name to be assumed for all referenced files, unless it is specified for files outside your account.
The system responds with three lines of messages identifying the run number, last run information, and current date and time. For example:

>   >RUN NUMBER 139
>   >LAST RUN AT: 120181 103459
>   >DATE: 120281   TIME: 111553
>   >

Following is an illustration of the complete sign-on procedure.

>   >**CMS/DEMAND MODE**
>   >ENTER USERID/PASSWORD:
>   >COLE/PERRY
>   >*DESTROY USERID/PASSWORD ENTRY
>   >*UNIVAC 1100 OPERATING SYSTEM LEV. 37R2A*CCS*02 (RSI)*
>   >ENTER ACCOUNT NUMBER
>   >CS9999
>   >ENTER PROJECT-ID:
>   >PC
>   >RUN NUMBER 139
>   >LAST RUN AT: 120181 103459
>   >DATE: 120281   TIME: 111553
>   >

After the run number messages and date/time line are displayed, you are ready to begin work at the terminal.

Sign-off Procedure

The @FIN and @@TERM commands are given to terminate a session and to sign off the system. For example:

1. Enter the command

>   >@FIN

The system responds with ten lines of accounting information reflecting the run ID, account number, project ID, computer usage statistics, and start and stop times on the system.

2. Then enter the command

>@@**TERM**

This command frees the line between the terminal and the computer. The computer signs you off the system and displays the message:

>***CMS/DEMAND MODE TERMINATED***

J.3 UNIVAC FILE NAMING CONVENTIONS

A Univac file name may consist of three parts—the **qualifier**, the **file name**, and an **element name**. The qualifier is similar in nature to the project ID but is always followed by an asterisk. The file name is then given and followed by a period (referred to as a "point"). The element name is optional and, when used, follows the point. The format of these three parts is:

qualifier*filename.elementname

Each part—the qualifier, filename, and elementname—may consist of one to twelve characters. They may consist of alphabetic characters, numeric digits, and the two special characters "dollar sign" ($) and "hyphen" (-). They do not have to begin with a letter. An example of a three-part file name is:

PC*SOURCE.PROG1

The qualifier*filename.elementname format has sometimes been compared to a filing cabinet. The qualifier tells the computer which filing cabinet you are talking about. The file name tells the computer which drawer of the filing cabinet you want, and the element name tells the computer the manila folder that you want in the drawer. The element name can be an entire source program, raw data file, or JCL file.

As in an office, a drawer of a filing cabinet (qualifier*filename.) does not have to contain any manila folders (element names). It might merely contain one large "glob" of papers with no manila folders. In computer terms, a file can be a program, a set of raw data, a set of JCL statements, or any combination of these. Examples are:

PC*SOURCE.PROGRAM1

PC*PROGRAM1.

The first example gives a complete "qualifier*filename.elementname." The second example gives only a "qualifier*filename.", in which the file is a program and cannot contain any elements. This latter format is used basically for system data files and not for programs. Programs are usually made into elements. We will assume that a program is an element in this appendix.

Listing the Names of Permanent Files and Elements

You may want to see the list of permanent files you have stored on disk. You may list all the file names under a qualifier, or you may list all the element names of a particular file.

Listing all your file names is accomplished by the @**MFD** (Master File Directory) command. The format of the @MFD command to list all the file names under your qualifier is:

@MFD,Q qualifier

where qualifier is the qualifier part of your file names. For example, to list all the file names under the qualifier PC you would enter:

>@**MFD,Q PC**

To list all the element names of a particular file you must use the @**PRT** command. For example, to list all the elements in the file name SOURCE and under the qualifier name PC you would enter:

>@**PRT,T PC*SOURCE.**

Now, let's see how to delete, copy, and create elements and files.

J.4 DELETING, COPYING AND CREATING ELEMENTS AND FILES

Deleting Elements and Files

The @**DELETE** command is used to delete elements and files. The format of the @DELETE command to delete a specific element from a specific file is as follows:

@DELETE,S qualifier*filename.elementname

For example, to delete the element PROGRAM1 under the file name SOURCE and qualifier PC, enter:

>**@DELETE,S PC*SOURCE.PROGRAM1**

The format of the @DELETE command to delete a file under your qualifier is:

@DELETE qualifier*filename

For example, to delete the file named SOURCE. under the qualifier PC, enter:

>**@DELETE PC*SOURCE.**

Copying Elements and Files

The @**COPY** command is used to copy an element of a file to a new element or to copy one file to another. The format of the @COPY command to copy an element of a file to a new element is:

@COPY,S qualifier1*file1.element1,qualifier2*file2.element2

For example, to copy the element PROGRAM1 under file name SOURCE. and qualifier PC to the new element name PROGRAM2 under the same filename and qualifier, enter:

>**@COPY,S PC*SOURCE.PROGRAM1,PC*SOURCE.PROGRAM2**

(Note: the numbers 1 and 2 do not have to be used in the actual element names.)

To copy a file (whether it contains elements or not) to another file, you must use the @COPY command with the following format.

@COPY qualifier1*file1.,qualifier2*file2.

For example, to copy the file named SOURCE. to the file named HOLD., you would enter:

>**@COPY PC*SOURCE.,PC*HOLD.**

Creating a New File Name and Element Name

In order to manipulate a file with the previous JCL timesharing commands and with the Univac text editor (explained in the next section), the file must already have been created. The @**ASG** (stands for ASSIGN) command is used to create a new file. The format of the @ASG command is:

@ASG,UP qualifier*filename.

An example of creating a new file named PROG1 under the qualifier PC is:

>**@ASG,UP PC*PROG1.**

Elements in a file are created by either the @COPY command or by the Univac text editor.

There is no true FORTRAN subsystem to create or modify FORTRAN source programs on the Univac 1100. You must use its text editor (CTS or ED) to enter and manipulate your FORTRAN source program. CTS does include a PRESCAN mode for FORTRAN, but it is time-consuming to use if you do not know it well. Section J.5 explains the use of the Univac CTS text editor for creating new files and modifying existing ones.

J.5 THE CTS TEXT EDITOR

CTS (Conversational Time Sharing) is one of the text editors available on Univac 1100 systems. It is similar to the Univac **ED** text editor, but it is somewhat easier to learn and to use. The CTS text editor allows you to create a new file or make modifications to an existing one. (Remember, the new file name must already have been created with the (@ ASG command). It can also be used to create and edit programs or data files.

CTS can be used either for elements or for files that do not have elements (but have the data stored directly in them). The CTS commands are the same whether you are manipulating an element or a file. When you are manipulating a file, you simply omit the element-name reference in the command. For a complete description of CTS you should consult the Programmer Reference manual UP-7940.

The Univac CTS text editor is invoked by typing:

@CTS

The system will respond with three lines of information. The first line gives the date and time; the second line indicates the assumed mode; the third line gives the CTS prompt for your first command. For example:

>CTS   8R1   20 NOV 81 at 14:41:11
>THE ASSUMED MODE IS ASCII
>−>

The >−> symbol is the CTS prompt. CTS will always prompt you with the ">−>" for your next command. CTS, like most text editors, works with a temporary work space in which your element or file is created or manipulated.

Creating and Saving a New Element or File. If you are creating a new program (or JCL or data file), you must specify the qualifier*filename.element by using the **NEW** command. The format of the NEW command is:

NEW qualifier*filename.element

For example, to create a new element named PROG1 in the file SOURCE and under the qualifier PC, enter:

>−>NEW PC*SOURCE.PROG1

When you are finished creating your new element or file in the temporary work space, you must save the contents of the work area onto permanent disk storage. The **SAVE** command is used to save the contents of the work space into a new element or file. Simply type

>−>SAVE

This causes the contents of the work space to be saved under the qualifier, file name, and element that were given in the NEW command to create this new element or file.

Retrieving and Replacing an Existing Element or File. If the element you want to work with already exists, you must use the **OLD** command. The format of the OLD command to retrieve an existing element is:

OLD qualifier*filename.element

For example, to retrieve the element LABPROB2 in the file SOURCE and under the qualifier PC, you would enter:

>−>OLD PC*SOURCE.LABPROB2

When you are finished modifying the existing element in your temporary work space, you must copy the modified element or file back to permanent disk storage. The **REPLACE** command is given to replace the contents of the old permanent element or file with the contents of the work space. Remember, you **do not** use the SAVE command. The SAVE command is used only to save a new element or file, initially. An element or file can only be saved one time, and that is when it is first created. The replacing of an old element can only be done with the REPLACE command. To retain the modifications to an existing element that was retrieved, enter:

>−>REPLACE

The contents of your work space replace the contents of the existing element under the file and qualifier given in the OLD command. The work space still exists after the SAVE or REPLACE command.

Exiting from the CTS Text Editor. When you are finished with the editing of a new or old file, you must exit the editor. The **XCTS** (for e**X**it **CTS**) command is given to get out of the CTS text editor:

>−>XCTS

If you want to save the created work space or replace the modified work space into a permanent element or file, you must give the appropriate SAVE or REPLACE command. If you exit from the CTS editor without first giving the SAVE or REPLACE command, you will lose the contents of the temporary work space. If you do not want to save or replace an element or file on permanent disk storage, then you give only the XCTS command. Giving the XCTS command without having saved or replaced your element should be done only when you have decided not to retain the contents of your work space.

CTS Work Space. CTS creates its work space with line numbers. Each line of text (program, JCL, or data) contains a line number. These line numbers are visible only to CTS and not to any other Univac processor. Most CTS commands require a line number or a line number range to manipulate lines of text. The line number or line number range given on a CTS editing command may have any of the following forms:

Form	Definition of Use
A	All lines in the work space
NUM	Specific line number desired
*	The line following the current line number
+	The current line number and all following lines
*+	All lines following the current line
*I	I lines following the current line
−	The current line and all preceding lines
*−	All lines preceding the current line
*−I	I lines preceding the current line
NUM1,NUM2	All lines from NUM1 through NUM2
NUM+I	NUM plus the next I lines
NUM−I	NUM plus the preceding I lines
!−1	The last line of the text
!−I	The last I lines of the text

Basically, if no range is given after the command, the current line is assumed.

Now, let's look at some of the CTS editor commands to manipulate text in an element or file.

J.5.1 Entering New Lines of Text

As stated earlier, every line of text must have a line number. To enter a line of text in your work space, type a line number and the text you want to enter. The line number indicates where the line of text is placed in the work space. For example, to enter the first two lines of text in a new file with the line numbers 10 and 20, you might type:

>−>**10 THIS IS THE FIRST LINE OF TEXT.**
>−>**20 THIS IS THE SECOND LINE OF TEXT.**

You should always select line numbers in some increments of 10s, 20s, 50s, 100s, and so on to provide the flexibility for adding new lines between existing lines at some later time. Do not select line numbers in increments of ones, i.e., 1, 2, 3, and so on, since this sequence of line numbers would make it difficult to add new lines later.

To add a new line of text between existing lines, select a line number between the numbers of the two lines where the new line is to be added. For example, if you wished to add a new line of text between line numbers 10 and 20, you would select a line number that falls between 10 and 20 (exclusively), and enter the new text. A good rule to follow is to select a line number that falls halfway between the two line numbers. That way you allow for more new lines to be added later, before or after the newly added line of text.

Suppose you wanted to add a new line of text between lines 10 and 20. It would be best to select 15 as the line number. You type:

>−>**15 THIS IS A NEW LINE BETWEEN LINES 10 AND 20.**

The editor would place this new line into its proper order in the file, by line number. If you listed the contents of the work space, it would contain:

>−>**10 THIS IS THE FIRST LINE OF TEXT.**
>−>**15 THIS IS A NEW LINE BETWEEN LINES 10 AND 20.**
>−>**20 THIS IS THE SECOND LINE OF TEXT.**

As you can see, entering new lines of text is relatively simple. When you enter a new line, it is automatically placed in ascending sequence with the other lines of text according to line numbers.

J.5.2 Replacing a Line of Text

Replacing a line of text in your work space is easy to accomplish. All you need to do is to type the line of new text with the same line number that you want to replace. Suppose you want to replace the text at line number 15 with the new text: THIS TEXT REPLACES THE OLD TEXT AT LINE NUMBER 15. You would type:

> >–>15 **THIS TEXT REPLACES THE OLD TEXT AT LINE NUMBER 15.**

If you then listed the first three lines of text in the file, you would have:

> >–>10 **THIS IS THE FIRST LINE OF TEXT.**
> >–>15 **THIS TEXT REPLACES THE OLD TEXT AT LINE NUMBER 15.**
> >–>20 **THIS IS THE SECOND LINE OF TEXT.**

J.5.3 Deleting Lines of Text

You may delete one or more lines of text from your program by using the **DELETE** command, followed by the line number or range of line numbers you want to delete from the file:

DELETE range

For example, to delete line number 15 from your file, type:

> >–>**DELETE 15**

To delete a range of lines, give the first line number, a comma, and the last line number, following the DELETE command. For example, to delete all lines of text from line number 15 through 20, type:

> >–>**DELETE 15,20**

Other forms of the range option may be given to delete multiple lines of text from your element or file. Now let's look at how to list the contents of your work space to see what lines of text are in it.

J.5.4 Listing Your Element or File

Listing All Lines in the Work Space. Listing the contents of an element or file is accomplished with the **PRINT** command. You give the desired range option following the command to list all or portions of your work space. The format of the PRINT command is:

PRINT range

The range option **A** is used to list the entire contents of the work space. For example:

> >–>**PRINT A**

This would list the contents of the work space, starting with the first line number and ending with the last.
Listing A Specific Line Number or Multiple Line Numbers. If you want to list only one line of text, you give its line number following the PRINT command. For example, to list line number 20, enter:

> >–>**PRINT 20**

To list a series of consecutive lines, you give the PRINT command, the first line number to be listed, a comma, and the last line number in the series. For example, to list the text at line numbers 50 through 120, you would enter:

> >–>**PRINT 50,120**

Other forms of the range option allow you to list various lines of text in your work space. Now let us look at some of the other available commands that provide efficiency and flexibility in manipulating text in a work space.

J.5.5 Searching the Element for a Specific Text String

You may not always know which line number contains the text that you want to modify. CTS editor provides the **LOCATE** command to search the work space for a specific text or string of characters. The format of the LOCATE command is:

LOCATE string range (column1,column2)

"String" represents the string of characters that you want to find in the work space. If the string includes a space, you must enclose the character string within a set of single quotes ('). The range option can be the entire work space (A), a range of line numbers, or any form given in the range format table in section J.5. The columns option is an optional part that limits the search to certain column positions.

Take the following example:

> – >LOCATE 'THIS IS' A

This example would find every occurrence of the string 'THIS IS' in the work space. The single quotes around the string of characters are needed, since the string contains a space. The letter A (for All) after the text string specifies the search of the entire file. No column limits were included in the command; so every column will be checked. If the command

> – >LOCATE 'THIS IS' A (1,10)

were typed, then only columns 1 through 10 of every line would be checked for a match with the string.

J.5.6 Modifying Existing Lines of Text

The **CHANGE** command is used to replace one string with another within a certain range. The format is:

CHANGE /string1/string2/ range (column1,column2)

String1 is the character or series of characters that you want to find and replace. String2 is the character or series of characters that you want to replace it with. The range is optional. If no range is specified, the current line is assumed. The slash is a delimiter that bounds the character strings. Any character may be used as a delimiter, as long as the same character is used for all the delimiters in a command and that delimiter does not appear in either of the two strings. The range and column options serve the same function as for the LOCATE command.

For example, suppose a typing error was found in line 50.

50 DIMENSOIN X(10,5)

To correct this error, you could replace this line of text by typing a complete new line with line number 50. An easier way to correct this error would be to use the CHANGE command as follows:

> – >CHANGE /SOIN/SION/ 50

If you wanted to go through the whole file and substitute all occurrences of "SOIN" and "SION", you could do this by including the A range option after the last delimiter. Note: the entire word would be given, to ensure that no variables containing the string "SOIN" would be changed. For example:

> – >CHANGE /DIMENSOIN/DIMENSION/ A

If you wanted to change line numbers 10 through 90 for this type of error, enter:

> – >CHANGE /DIMENSOIN/DIMENSION/ 10,90

If you wanted to change the string "THIS" to "THAT" in columns 1 through 10 for all lines from 15 through the end of the text, enter:

> – >CHANGE @THIS@THAT@ 15+ (1,10)

Notice that the @ character is used here for the string delimiter. The slash is probably the most frequently used character as a delimiter, since it makes the strings more easily understood.

J.5.7 Moving Lines to a New Location

Lines can be moved to a new location within your work space by using one of two commands. The **MOVE** command moves the specified lines of text to the new range and deletes the old lines of text. The **DITTO** command moves the specified lines of text to the new range but does not erase the old lines of text. Their formats are:

MOVE oldrange newline#[,increment]

DITTO oldrange newline#[,increment]

The **oldrange** option gives the lines to move or duplicate at a new location in the work space. The **newline#** parameter gives the new line number to which the line(s) is to be moved or copied. The [,increment] parameter is optional and gives the increment value of the new line numbers for the moved or copied lines of text. If the **increment** parameter is not given, an increment value of 10 is assumed.

An example of the MOVE command is:

> >–>**MOVE 10,50 101,1**

This example will copy lines 10 through 50 to line 101 and increment the new lines by 1. Therefore, line 10 becomes line 101, line 20 becomes line 102, and so on. Lines 10 through 50 will be deleted from the work space.

An example of the DITTO command is:

> >–>**DITTO 20 305**

This example makes a copy (a ditto) of line 20 at line number 305. The original line of text at line 20 is unchanged.

J.5.8 Miscellaneous CTS Commands

Two additional CTS editor commands, which are used quite frequently, are the **RES** (for resequence) and the **GO** commands. The **RES** command is used to resequence the line numbers in your work space. This is an invaluable command when you have used all the available line numbers within a certain range and need to add new lines in it. The format of the RES command is:

> RES I,J

The option I is the number you want for the first line in the work space, and the option J is the increment you want to use. For example, suppose you wanted to resequence the lines in a program. You want to begin with line number 100 and resequence the lines in increments of 50. You would enter:

> >–>**RES 100,50**

The **GO** command moves the line pointer according to the given range. If no range is given, the pointer is moved to the top of the work space (first line). This command can be used to compensate for the fact that the line pointer moves forward through your work space on various commands, such as LOCATE. If you do not reset the line pointer, then pertinent lines may be skipped, since the line pointer is already past them. The format of the GO command is:

> GO range

The line pointer is moved to the line number given in the command. The range may be an earlier line in the work space or a later line number. The GO command without the range option is frequently given to reset the line pointer back to the beginning of the file, so that the entire file will be used in a command. For example, if you want to reset the line pointer back to the beginning of your program, simply enter:

> >–>**GO**

The **ALL** option on various editing commands always sets the line pointer back to the top of the file before an operation is performed.

A concise summary of the CTS text editor commands discussed is given below.

J.5.9 Summary of CTS Text Editor Commands

A summary of the CTS text editor commands and their functions is given as follows:

Command	Abbrev	Description
CHANGE	C	Changes string1 to string2.
DELETE	D	Deletes a given range of lines.
DITTO	DIT	Makes a duplicate copy of the specified lines.
GO	GO	Moves the line pointer.
LOCATE	L	Finds a string of characters.
MOVE	MOV	Moves lines of range1 to range2.
PRINT	P	Prints the specified lines.
REPLACE	REP	Replaces an element into the permanent file of existing elements.
RESEQUENCE	RES	Resequences the line numbers.
SAVE	SAV	Places a newly-created element in your permanent file.

After you have entered your FORTRAN program with the CTS editor, you are now ready to compile and execute it. The next section discusses this procedure.

```
@RUN              COLE,CS9999,PC
@DELETE,C         PGMPRT.
@ASG,UP           PGMPRT.
@BRKPT            PRINT$/PGMPRT
@FTN              ,TPF$.PROGRAM1
         PRINT *, 'HI COMPUTER'
         PRINT *, 10, 20
         STOP
         END
@MAP,S            ,PC*ABS.PROGRAM1
   IN FORLIB.
@EOF
@BRKPT            PRINT$
@FIN
```

Figure J.1 Sample runstream for a Univac FORTRAN compilation

J.6 COMPILING AND RUNNING A UNIVAC FORTRAN PROGRAM

Compiling and executing a FORTRAN program is done in three separate steps—the compilation of the source program, the linking or tying together of all the relocatable program addresses in the object program and modules, and the execution of the resulting module of code. At least three JCL commands must be provided to accomplish these three steps: @FTN, @MAP, and @XQT. Following is a brief description of these commands.

JCL Command	Function Description
@FTN	The @FTN JCL command calls the FORTRAN compiler to compile your source program.
@MAP	This command calls the processor, which is used to gather and interconnect all the necessary relocatable elements to produce one final program unit in a form ready to be loaded into memory for execution. This processor is known as the linkage loader (on some computer systems). It performs the task of linking (tying) all program modules together (library routines, user subprograms, and others) and loading the one resulting module into memory in a form ready for execution.
@XQT	This JCL command causes the computer to execute your compiled and linked program.

Compiling Your Program and Preparing it for Execution

Figure J.1 presents an example of a runstream to compile a program with the name PROGRAM1 and to prepare it for later execution. The program consists of four statements. Output consists of the literal 'HI COMPUTER' and the two integer numbers 10 and 20.

The JCL commands in this runstream are explained as follows:

JCL Command	Explanation of Use
@RUN	This must be the first JCL command in every JCL deck (runstream). It tells the computer the name of the run (COLE), the account number (CS9999), and the qualifier (PC).
@DELETE	This command deletes the file "PGMPRT". In the illustrated runstream the file "PGMPRT" will contain the compilation listing of the source program. If this file does not previously exist, the runstream just proceeds to the next JCL command. The reason for deleting any existing file with this name is that we want to put our new compiled source program listing on the PGMPRT file.
@ASG	This JCL command assigns the file name "PGMPRT" to our new compiled listing. The option ",UP" signifies that this is a new file. This is why we had to delete any existing file with the name "PGMPRT". If the file already exists, and you attempt to assign a new file (with the same name) by the "@ASG,UP" JCL command, your runstream will abort with an error.

@BRKPT	This JCL command stands for BReaKPoinT. This command directs all of the forthcoming print into the file name after the slash. In our example, the compilation listing will be placed in the file named "PGMPRT". All printer output is directed into this file until another "@BRKPT" JCL command is encountered in the runstream. If this JCL command is not included, the compiled listing would be printed along with the rest of the JCL runstream command. That is, this command directs the forthcoming printer output to a file, rather than directly to the printer. Using this operation allows you later to look at the file containing the results of the compilation (using CTS) and to check for errors. If syntax errors have occurred in the program compilation, you can file them via CTS and do not have to get a printed source listing (which might be costly and time consuming for large programs). If the compilation did not contain any syntax errors, then the file can be printed with the @SYM command.
@FTN	This command stands for ForTraN and calls the FORTRAN compiler to compile the source program.
@MAP	This command collects all the relocatable program units for the overall load module and resolves all the various address references. You must perform this operation on the object program produced from the FORTRAN compiler before you can execute the program. The "IN FORLIB." command, which appears with the @MAP command, tells the MAP processor where to find all the FORTRAN library routines, such as FORTRAN built-in intrinsics and subroutines. The name of the FORTRAN library will vary at different installations.
@EOF	The @EOF command signifies the end of the file for the preceding processor. Any @ JCL command will also signify an end of file.
@FIN	This JCL command terminates your run. This command should always be the last command in a JCL runstream.
@SYM	This command sends a report file to the printer. The format of this command is:

@SYM filename.,copies,printername

For example, to print our compiled source program file we would construct a JCL command as follows:

@SYM PGMPRT.

This command would direct the computer to print the report file with the name PGMPRT., (the name of the file onto which our compiled listing was written). Since the "copies" option was not used, one copy of the report file is assumed. Since no "printername" option was specified, the system's main line printer is assumed.

Let us now look at the procedures for running these JCL runstream commands to achieve the compilation of a program. A compile runstream may be run in either remote batch mode or on-line.

Running the Compile Runstream in a Remote Batch Mode

You must use the **@START** command to run your JCL compile runstream in a remote batch mode. The format of the @START command is:

@START qualifier*filename.elementname

An example of using the runstream commands and program in the element named PROGRAM1 in the file named SOURCE. and under the qualifier PC is:

>@START PC*SOURCE.PROGRAM1

The source program would be in PC*SOURCE.PROGRAM1, along with the JCL compile runstream commands. After starting the job with the @START command, the job is turned over to the batch monitor to schedule the execution of the runstream commands and to compile your program as the work load permits. You could continue to edit other elements or files during this process, since the job is actually detached from your terminal access. You must be signed onto a terminal under the **DEMAND** mode in order to start a batch job.

Running the Compile Runstream On-line to a Terminal

You must be signed onto a terminal under **DEMAND** mode to run your JCL compile runstream on-line (with the job attached to your terminal). If you are running the runstream on-line to your terminal, you are in control of the job and can monitor its progress. The system will inform you when the job is finished. You can then check the compiled listing file to see if any syntax errors were found, and proceed accordingly.

You must use the **@ADD** command to run your compile runstream on-line. The format of this command is:

@ADD qualifier*filename.elementname

For example, to execute the runstream commands under the same qualifier (PC), filename (SOURCE.) and elementname (PROGRAM1), enter:

>**@ADD PC*SOURCE.PROGRAM1**

This request will be run on-line to your terminal, so that you can monitor its results. The @FIN command in the runstream is not executed when a JCL runstream is run on-line.

Now, let us see how to execute a successfully compiled and prepared program. You can execute a program either in remote batch mode or on-line.

Executing the Program in Remote Batch Mode

A runstream file with the following three JCL commands should be built in order to execute the program in a remote batch mode. These three JCL commands are:

```
@RUN    COLE,CS9999,PC
@XQT    PC*ABS.PROGRAM1
@FIN
```

The **@RUN** command contains the same information as for the compile runstream. The **@XQT** causes the prepared program under the given qualifier*filename.elementname to be loaded and executed. The @XQT command must reference the same qualifier*filename.elementname as used on the @MAP command. The @MAP command creates the prepared program code for the element name given on the command. The @FIN command terminates the run. Data records would be inserted after the @XQT command, if they are used.

This execution runstream can be started in remote batch mode with the @START command. Suppose these three execution runstream commands were in an element named PROGRAM1 in the file named EXEC. and under the qualifier PC. You would enter the following command to start the runstream in batch mode:

>**@START PC*EXEC.PROGRAM1**

The START command sends the job to the Batch Scheduler in the operating system to schedule the job for execution.

Executing the Program On-line

You use the **@ADD** command to run your execution runstream on-line. The format of the @ADD command is the same as given for running a compile runstream on-line. For example, to execute the runstream commands under the same qualifier (PC), filename (EXEC) and elementname (PROGRAM1), enter:

>**@ADD PC*EXEC.PROGRAM1**

The @ADD command takes over the terminal, which causes all output results to be displayed to the terminal.

A disk data file may be specified in the @ADD command. For example, to give the input file name PC*DATA.PROGRAM1 with the @ADD command, you would type:

@ADD,E PC*DATA.PROGRAM1

You may also execute a prepared program on-line by simply entering the **@XQT** command. For example, the command

>**@XQT PC*ABS.PROGRAM1**

would cause the prepared program in the element PROGRAM1 to be run on-line. Input data is typed as required by the program, the same as in interactive mode. Either of these two methods may be used to execute a prepared program on-line to your terminal so that you can monitor its results.

Printing a Copy of an Element (Runstream Commands and Source Program)

You may get a printed copy of an element that contains your JCL runstream commands and source program. The JCL commands needed are given as follows (the output goes directly to the line printer):

```
@RUN      COLE,CS9999,PC
@PRT,S    PC*SOURCE.PROGRAM1
@FIN
```

Combining the Compile, Prepare, and Execute Steps

These @XQT commands could be placed in the compile runstream to achieve a compile, preparation, and execution process all in the same job. That is, if the program compiled successfully, then it would be prepared and executed in the same job. This is the procedure frequently used in an academic environment. In an operational environment, however, the execution step is usually performed separately from the compilation step, because of the time and cost of printing the compiled source listing for large programs each time they are compiled.

The JCL runstream commands for a combined compilation, preparation, and execution process are given in figure J.2. The source listing and output results go directly to the line printer. The JCL runstream command for a combined compilation, preparation, and execution process, with the output results going to a disk file is given in figure J.3.

This appendix has explained many of the features of a Univac 1100 system and the CTS text editor, to provide an effective timesharing environment for developing and running FORTRAN programs. Good luck and happy programming.

```
@RUN              COLE,CS9999,PC
@FTN              .TPF$.PROGRAM1
       PRINT *,   'HI COMPUTER'
       PRINT *,   10, 20
       STOP
       END
@MAP,S            ,PC*ABS.PROGRAM1
   IN FORLIB.
@EOF
@XQT              PC*ABS.PROGRAM1
@FIN
```

Figure J.2 Sample runstream for a Univac FORTRAN compile, load, and execute, with output results to the line printer

```
@RUN              COLE,CS9999,PC
@DELETE,C         PGMPRT.
@ASG,UP           PGMPRT.
@BRKPT            PRINT$/PGMPRT
@FTN              ,TPF$.PROGRAM1
       PRINT *,   'HI COMPUTER'
       PRINT *,   10, 20
       STOP
       END
@MAP,S            ,PC*ABS.PROGRAM1
   IN FORLIB.
@EOF
@BRKPT            PRINT$
@FREE             PGMPRT.
@SYM              PGMPRT.
@ASG,UP           TEMPFILE.
@BRKPT            PRINT$/TEMPFILE
@XQT              PC*ABS.PROGRAM1
@BRKPT            PRINT$
@FREE             TEMPFILE.
@SYM              TEMPFILE.
@FIN
```

Figure J.3 Sample runstream for a Univac FORTRAN compile, load, and execute, with output results to a file

Control Data Corporation (CDC)
FORTRAN Timesharing System

Appendix K

K.1 INTRODUCTION

Control Data Corporation (CDC) 6000/Cyber systems include a FORTRAN subsystem under timesharing. You may create, manipulate, and execute FORTRAN programs while in the FORTRAN timesharing system. This appendix explains the log-on and log-off procedures, file naming conventions, and the system commands available under the FORTRAN timesharing system.

K.2 LOG-ON AND LOG-OFF PROCEDURES

Log-on Procedure

A CDC 6000 or Cyber user is assigned a user identification, a password and a project number for access to the system. You must know these three items before attempting a log-on. These items must be correctly entered to gain access to the computer. The procedure for logging-on to a CDC 6000 or Cyber system consists of the following steps:

1. After turning on your terminal, insuring that the necessary switches are set to the correct position, and making connection with the computer, depress the RETURN key once or twice. The system will respond with a message indicating the status of the system. For example:

    6000 system up

    (or Cyber system up)

    If the message is unreadable, type the BREAK or NUL key and repeat this step. If the message reads

    System down

    then the computer is currently not available. Any message from the operator is also printed at this connect time.

2. Depress the RETURN key once after the "up message" is received. The computer will respond with a header identification message and will request entry of your User ID, by printing a message such as:

    81/12/26. 20.36.08. CYBER USER ID:

3. Type your user ID on the same line and depress the RETURN key. For example (using a user id of S839),

    81/12/26. 20.36.08. CYBER USER ID:S839

    The entry (S839) after the colon represents a typical user ID. The user ID usually consists of four characters, the first character being a letter. A user ID is normally assigned to you by your instructor or the computer center management. The user ID uniquely identifies a particular user known to the system, for the purpose of accounting for resources used during the timesharing session and for locating a user program and other files in the account.

4. After you respond with your user ID, the system requests entry of your password. On teleprinter terminals, a "strikeover" mask is printed on the line after the prompt for your password. The "strikeover" mask is an overstrike (blackout) of nine characters, which ensures that your password, when typed, cannot be read by another person. On CRT terminals no "strikeover" mask is shown, since the typed password is not echoed (displayed) on the screen. The printed prompt would look like this on a teleprinter terminal:

    PASSWORD
    XXXXXXXXX

    After typing the row of blackout characters, the typing position is moved back to the first position in the blackout mask.

5. Type your assigned password and hit the RETURN key. A unique password is assigned to each user as an additional security item to identify your access to the system. With the user ID and password the system can now verify you as a valid system user. If your user ID or your password is not acceptable (from being typed incorrectly or not currently on the system), the system responds with the messages:

    INVALID USER ID, TRY AGAIN
    USER ID:

You must restart at step 3 and reenter your user ID and password. If you are unsuccessful at logging-in four times in succession, the system issues the message:

TOO MANY LOG-ON FAILURES

and disconnects the terminal from the system.

6. After the system validates the password, it prompts for a project number

PROJECT:

to which the user enters a valid project number. For example (using project number PDJZ):

PROJECT:PDJZ

The project number PDJZ is typed immediately after the colon. You must not have a space before or embedded in the project number. A common project number is usually assigned to an entire class. If the user is not authorized to run on the given project (from typing an incorrect project number), the system will respond:

INVALID PROJECT, TRY AGAIN
PROJECT:

You are allowed four attempts to enter a correct project number. After four unsuccessful attempts, the system will print the message:

TOO MANY LOG-ON FAILURES

and disconnect you.

7. If the project number is accepted, the computer responds with the two messages:

TERMINAL: nnn,iii
SYSTEM:

where nnn is the terminal number that the system uses as part of the unique identifier for each active user; iii is an identifer that describes the type of terminal. For example, TTY describes an ASCII code terminal with standard print. Following is an example of a typical system response:

TERMINAL: 27,TTY
SYSTEM: HHAALLFF

The second prompt message asks what system you want to work with. This is called the system-selection request. Many timesharing computers have several programming languages in which you can create and run programs. Before selecting the FORTRAN system you must set the mode of operation. Many CDC systems will echo back your typed characters, which has the effect of printing duplicate (two) characters of what you type. To avoid these redundant characters you must type HALF (for half-duplex). For example:

SYSTEM: HHAALLFF

You are only typing the world HALF. The redundant letters are from the system, but the HALF command will eliminate these duplicate characters.

If the number of users logged into the system has reached the maximum allowed, you may receive the message:

SYSTEM CLOSED, SORRY

8. The computer responds to the command typed in response to the system prompt with the message "READY.". Now you can enter the system (FORTRAN, BASIC, BATCH, and so on) of your choice. You type the command FORTRAN to select the FORTRAN subsystem:

FORTRAN

9. The system responds to the FORTRAN entry with the prompt:

OLD OR NEW,FILE:

The system wants to know whether you want to select an old (existing) program file from disk or whether you want to create a new FORTRAN source program. If you want to select an existing program, you would type the word OLD, a comma, and the name of the program. For example, to select an existing program named LP1, type:

OLD,LP1

Note the required comma separating the word OLD and the program name. No blanks are allowed before or after the comma.

If you want to start (create) a new program, you type the word NEW, a comma, and the name you have selected for the new program. For example, if you want to create a new FORTRAN source program named LP1, type:

NEW,LP1

The comma is required, and no blanks are allowed.

A shortcut may be used both to select the FORTRAN subsystem and the old or new file by entering this information on one line:

FORTRAN,OLD,LP1

or

FORTRAN,NEW,LP1

Following is an illustration of an actual sign-on to the Cyber system at the University of Colorado at Boulder from a dial-up at the University of Colorado at Colorado Springs. After the log-on procedure is completed, a new FORTRAN source program file named DEMO is indicated to be entered.

Cyber system up

81/12/26. 20.36.44. CYBER USER ID:S839
PASSWORD
XXXXXXXX
PROJECT:PDJZ
TERMINAL: 27,TTY
SYSTEM: HHAALLFF
READY.
READY.
FORTRAN
OLD OR NEW, FILE: NEW,DEMO

READY.

File names on a CDC or Cyber system may be from one to seven characters in length. Only letters and digits are allowed in a file name; no special characters are permitted. The first character of the file name must be a letter.

Log-Off Procedure

The log-off procedure is quite simple. You type the command **BYE** or **GOODBYE**, and the computer responds with an appropriate message and terminates your session. Two accounting messages containing the charges for the session and account balance are displayed. For example:

BYE

JOB COST S839027   PDJZ/S839 81/05/18   21.32.14 $ 0.06 (LOW)
ACCOUNT BALANCE $ 610.13

You may receive other messages if you have permanent files on the system when you log off. You will get a message as to the PF (Permanent File) Accumulation Rate per day for your permanent files storage charges.

On a CDC timesharing system, any temporary current file is purged from memory when the BYE command is given. On some systems you will be automatically logged off a terminal if no entry is made during a certain time period (usually 10 minutes).

If another user is waiting to use the terminal, the logged-in user may log off by typing **HELLO** or **LOGIN** to keep the terminal connected to the system:

HELLO

(or LOGIN)

The system logs the current user off the system, issues the normal log-off messages, retains the connection to the terminal, and automatically initiates a new log-on sequence. The new user would proceed from Step 2 as given in section K.2.

Now, let us look at the timesharing commands to manipulate and run a FORTRAN source program on a CDC timesharing system.

K.3 CDC FORTRAN TIMESHARING SYSTEM COMMANDS

After your log-on is complete, you may proceed to use the timesharing commands to perform the desired operations, or you can enter your FORTRAN statements (program). Remember, you must include a line number before each statement. A line number may be from one to five digits. The system uses these line numbers to keep your statements in a specific order. Also, the line numbers are used to delete statements, list portions of your current file, and other operations. These line numbers are of the utmost importance to the computer. You should use some increment, such as by 10's or even 100's, for the line numbers to provide flexibility in adding new lines.

K.3.1 Typing (Entering) Your Program

Suppose you want to type in a program to compute the sum of two numbers and print the results. The typed program might be:

```
10      X = 10
20      Y = 20.5
30      S = X + Y
40      PRINT *, X, Y, S
50      STOP
60      END
```

The "PRINT *, variable list" is the form of the CDC FORTRAN format-free output statement. Real (decimal) values are printed in decimal format or in exponential format if a number exceeds six digits, and integer values are printed in integer format. Character strings (literal constants) may be printed by including them in the PRINT statement itself, bounded by single quotes (').

What if you make an error in typing a line of information? Is there an easy way to correct typing errors?

K.3.2 Correcting Typing Errors and Cancelling a Line

Everyone makes typing errors when using a terminal. Suppose you misspelled a word or made a mistake in typing a statement. You may correct the error in one of several ways. The way you choose usually depends on how many characters have been typed in error.

To correct one or two incorrect characters while you are still close to them on the same line, you may delete the invalid characters and then resume typing. To delete a character, you depress the key(s) which move you back one space. (Hopefully on a CRT this will be the ← key—back/left arrow; it may be the BACKSPACE, SHIFT/DEL, or SHIFT/RUB keys). This has the effect of deleting the character or space immediately preceding the cursor. On a teleprinter terminal you depress the BACKSPACE key (or CNTRL/H keys on terminals that do not have a backspace key). You continue this process until you have cancelled out the last incorrect character and then continue typing the rest of the line with the correct information. For example, suppose you typed

```
40      PIRN
```

before discovering that you have misspelled the command PRINT. You would depress the ← key (or BACKSPACE key) three times to delete the characters N, R, and I and then begin typing with the letter R to correctly type the PRINT statement.

You may have typed a complete line or almost a full line before realizing that a mistake was made near the beginning of the line. You could transmit the line and retype it correctly, since a new line with a certain line number replaces the previous statement with the same line number. You may delete an entire line, however, by depressing the BREAK key (or CNTRL @). The message *DEL* is then printed by the system to indicate the deletion of the line. For example:

```
40      PRINT *, X *DEL*
```

This would prevent this line from being entered into the current file. You must **not** depress the RETURN key before typing the BREAK key. That is, you type only the BREAK key at the end of the line, not the RETURN key.

Now, let's see how to modify, delete, and add lines in a program.

K.3.3 Changing, Deleting, and Adding Lines in a Current File

Corrections or modifications to a program in the current file are done on the basis of line numbers. The following rules are given for modifications to a program.

1. **Changes/Replacement.** A numbered line will replace any identically numbered line previously entered in the current file. Note: the last line entered with line number nnn, where "nnn" represents a specific line number, will replace the previous line nnn and be the only line numbered nnn in the file.

2. **Deletion.** A line consisting of only the line number (no spaces after the line number) will delete the line with the identical line number. A line number followed by a comma and a higher line number will delete all lines in that range from a file.
3. **Addition/Insertion.** A line with a number falling between the line-numbers for two existing lines will be inserted in the current file between those two lines.

Let us examine these procedures in more detail.

Changing or Replacing a Line. When syntax or logic errors exist in a program, you often need to retype a line with its correction. To replace a line in your program with a new line containing a change, type the same line number with the complete new statement. For example, you may have an error in an assignment statement and need to add parentheses to override the hierarchy of arithmetic operations. The old statement in error might be:

$$40 \qquad R = K + 3/M$$

Suppose you need to add 3 to K before doing the division by M. You would type the correction with the same line number:

$$40 \qquad R = (K + 3)/M$$

After you type and transmit this statement, the computer would delete the old statement with line number 40 and replace it with the new statement having the same line number.

Thus, the last statement typed with a given line number becomes the current statement with that line number in the program. You must be extremely careful not to type a statement with a line number of a statement already in the program unless you mean to replace it. If you do, and it is transmitted, you can say goodbye to the old statement. A student often makes this mistake and then wonders why he or she is not getting correct output.

K.3.4 Deleting a Line

To delete or remove a line from a program, simply type and transmit just the line number. Make sure there are no blanks after the line number, or you would be replacing the old line with a blank statement. Transmitting only the line number tells the computer to delete that line from the program. For example, to delete the statement with line number 50 from your current file, type:

$$50$$

To delete a range of line numbers from a file, type the first line number, a comma, and the last line number in the range you want to delete from the file. For example, to delete line numbers 20 through 50 from your file, type:

$$20,50$$

Some time sharing systems include a DELETE command to delete multiple single lines and a range of line numbers from a file. There is no DELETE command, however, on the CDC FORTRAN timesharing system.

K.3.5 Adding/Inserting a Line

To add a line in a program, select a line number that is between the line numbers of the two statements at which you want the new line to be placed. Suppose you have the two statements:

$$20 \qquad READ *, X, Y$$
$$30 \qquad S = X + Y$$

and want to print the values of X and Y after they have been read. You will have to add a PRINT statement between line numbers 20 and 30. You could select a line number of 25 for the PRINT statement and type the new line after line number 30 as follows:

$$20 \qquad READ *, X, Y$$
$$30 \qquad S = X + Y$$
$$25 \qquad PRINT *, X, Y$$

Since the line number 25 falls between line numbers 20 and 30, the three statements would automatically be arranged in your current file as follows:

$$20 \qquad READ *, X, Y$$
$$25 \qquad PRINT *, X, Y$$
$$30 \qquad S = X + Y$$

You could have picked any number—21, 22, 23, and so on—that fell between 20 and 30 for the new line number, but what if you used line number 21 and later needed to add a new statement (perhaps to print a blank line) between the READ (line number 20) and the PRINT (line number 21) statements? There would not be any room. In this case you would have to change the line number of either the READ or the PRINT statement to insert a line between them. The best method is to pick a line number that falls halfway between the line numbers at which you want to add a new statement. This will leave room for you to add statements later if the need arises.

K.3.6 Listing a Program in a Current File

To list the contents (already typed statements) of a current file you use the **LIST** (abbreviated **LIS**) command. You simply type LIST, and all statements stored in the current file will be listed in line number order. For example:

```
LIST
  12/26/80. 20.37.44.
PROGRAM  DEMO

10        READ *, X, Y
20        S = X + Y
30        PRINT *, X, Y, S
40        STOP
50        END
READY.
```

Two header messages are printed after the LIST command. The first message gives the date and time the program is listed; the second message lists the name of the current file.

If you do not want to display date/time and file name messages before the name of the current file before the contents of the file, you may use the **LNH** (List with No Header) command. For example, if you typed the command LNH, the displayed results would be:

```
LNH

10        READ *, X, Y
20        S = X + Y
30        PRINT *, X, Y, S
40        STOP
50        END
READY.
```

A "READY." message is printed at the end of the program by the timesharing system, to let you know that it has completed the command and is ready for a new one.

If you do not want to list the entire file, you may list only a portion of the file with the "LIST,line number" or "LNH,line number" command. "Line number" represents the line number of the statement at which the display is to begin. That is, the system will list the portion of the file starting at the specified line number and going through to the end of the file. For example, the command

LIST,50

would begin listing the contents of the current file starting at line number 50 and would continue to the end of the file.

What if you only want to list one line in the file or do not want to list through the last line in the file? You would have to enter the command to list the entire file and then hit the break key to interrupt the listing after the last line you wanted to see. You may use one of the CDC system text editors, such as EDIT or SCRIBE, in order to be more selective about which lines in a file are to be displayed back to your terminal. These text editors are also very helpful for creating and manipulating lines in a program, such as adding a new line, deleting a line, or correcting portions of the contents of a line.

After hopefully entering a correct program, you are now ready to run it to obtain the output results.

K.3.7 Running Your Program

After you have typed in all the statements in your program, you are ready for the computer to "run" or execute the program. Simply type the command **RUN**. The computer will proceed to execute the program. A **"RUN COMPLETE."** message is displayed after the output to indicate that the command is completed.

For example, consider the following program, named PROB1, which reads the values of X and Y in format-free form, prints the input values, and computes and prints their sum. First, the source program is listed before it is executed.

```
            LIST

            12/26/80. 21.16.18
            PROGRAM   PROB1

10          READ *, X,Y
20          PRINT *, 'X = ', X, 'Y = ', Y
30          S = X + Y
40          PRINT *, 'S = ', S
50          STOP
60          END
READY.
RUN

?10.5,34.73
 X  =            10.5000     Y =            35.7300
 S  =            46.2300

CP       0.346 SECS.

RUN COMPLETE.
```

The question mark (?) is the system prompt for you to enter the input items for the format-free READ.

The command **RUN** may cause the program to be run with a date and time header printed before the first line of output. The command **RNH** (run with no header) will cause the program to be run without a date and time header printed before the first line of output.

If a misspelled word or illegally formed statement is found in the attempted execution of the program, an error message will describe the type of error and the line number in which it occurred. You simply find the error, correct it, and retype the statement. Then type the command RUN again.

When your program is free of syntax errors (statement construction errors), it will be executed. The output results will be transmitted to your terminal. Check these results carefully to see if they are what you expected. If the output results are incorrect, you have a logic error in your program. That is, you have not told the computer the correct operations or given the statements in the correct sequence for solving the problem correctly. Review your program and reenter the RUN command.

The form of the format-free output results from the CDC FORTRAN timesharing system is to print integer numbers as integers and decimal numbers as six-digit decimal values. No leading zeroes are printed; however, trailing zeroes are printed in decimal numbers to make a total of six output digits. Zoned output fields are established, each field being 15 positions in width. Thus, a maximum of five fields may be printed on a line. The zone positions start at positions 1, 16, 31, 46, and 61. The first position in each zone is used for the sign of the number. If the number is positive, a space is used.

Let's look at how to retrieve a permanent file stored on disk.

K.3.8 Retrieving an Existing Permanent File

As discussed in the log-on procedure, an existing file from permanent storage may be retrieved with the **OLD** command. This command causes the system to load a copy of the specified permanent file into the local (current) file area. You may then proceed to RUN the program or to make modifications to it. For example, if you wanted to retrieve the permanent file named LP1, type:

                    OLD,LP1

If there was already another file in your current work area, it would be replaced with the copy of the permanent file. The name of your current file, of course, would be the name of the permanent file that was retrieved from disk (in our example above, LP1).

If you do not want to store the copy of the current file back on disk, you do not have to replace it. The next subsection discusses how to retain files on permanent storage and also how to remove (purge) them when you are finished with them.

K.3.9 Saving and Purging Files

Saving and purging a current file or permanent files are common operations in an interactive programming environment. You may not have time to complete a program at one sitting (if you had to go to class, for example). You save it on disk and recall it later to continue work on it. When you have finally produced a workable program with the correct solution, you should then remove it from the system.

You may retain or purge (delete) your current file or any permanent disk file you have previously created. First, let us see how to handle a current file.

Saving a Current File. To retain a newly built current file for future use, give the command **SAVE**. The SAVE command will store the current file as a permanent file under the assigned name on magnetic disk. For example, assume you have created a NEW file with the name PROB1 and want to save it:

NEW,PROB1

. . .

. . .

. . .

SAVE

The system responds with the message "READY." when the file has been written to disk:

SAVE

READY.

You may also save a file on disk by including the current file name after the command SAVE (and a comma):

SAVE,PROB1

READY.

This would save the current file PROB1 in the permanent file system.

Purging a Current File. If you have no further use for a new current file, you should purge (remove) it from the system. You should never arbitrarily save all current files, since they occupy valuable disk space. On most computer systems disk space is highly limited.

On CDC timesharing systems you can purge a current work file with the commands OLD or NEW to enter a new program. To clear the current file, but to keep the same name in effect, you use the command CLEAR. If you sign off and do not save any temporary file, the current file will be automatically purged from the system. The commands BYE, GOODBYE, HELLO, and LOGIN will release any current file and log you off the system.

Now, what about saving and purging permanent files?

Saving Old Permanent Files. The SAVE command can be used only to save a file with a name that did not previously exist under your user-ID. What if you recall an OLD file, modify it, and want to save it back under the same name? You **cannot** use the SAVE command, since it is only for saving new files.

You resave OLD files back under their previous filename with the **REPLACE** command, followed by a comma and the filename. Thus, the REPLACE command saves the contents of the current file on a previously existing permanent file. The system responds with a "READY." message. For example:

REPLACE,PROB1

READY.

Remember, if you recalled an OLD permanent file to run it and never made any modifications to your current file, there is no need to replace the current file.

Purging Old Permanent Files. As previously mentioned, disk space usually is at a premium on a computer system. You may hear your instructor plead with the students to please remove all the OLD unneeded permanent files before the system runs out of disk storage space.

The **PURGE** command removes a permanent file from the system. You type the command PURGE, followed by a comma, and the name of the file to be removed from the permanent file system. For example, to purge the permanent file PROB1, type:

PURGE,PROB1

READY.

The system responds with the "READY." message. Remember, you cannot have any embedded blanks before or after the comma. You may purge multiple permanent files with the PURGE command by adding a comma and the new file name. For example,

PURGE,LP1,LP1A

would purge both the files named LP1 and LP1A from the permanent file system.

Here is an example of purging the permanent file DEMO from disk and clearing the current working file with the PURGE and CLEAR commands.

PURGE,DEMO

READY.
CLEAR

READY.
LIST
 80/12/26. 21.51.27
PROGRAM   DEMO

READY.

The current file name DEMO is still in effect for the name of the current file. However, all statements in the current file DEMO were deleted with the CLEAR command.

Several additional useful system commands are covered in the next section.

K.4 ADDITIONAL FUNCTIONAL SYSTEM COMMANDS

Some timesharing systems include other commands to get you out of a subsystem, to allow you to list the names of all the permanent files you have stored on disk, to resequence the line numbers in a file, and so forth. This section will discuss the commands on a CDC system that allow you to perform these operations.

Changing Systems—The NULL Command

The **NULL** system command is given to cause an exit from the FORTRAN timesharing system. The system-selection question SYSTEM? is typed, and the user has the option of selecting any other system he/she desires. Any current program file created under timesharing FORTRAN is lost. A useful purpose of this command might be to switch to another subsystem, such as BASIC.

Listing the Names of Permanent Files

You may list all the names of permanent files you have stored on disk with the **PFLIST** command. Suppose you have the three files PERRYP1, PROB1, and PROB1A saved on disk. These permanent file names will be listed when you give the PFLIST command. For example:

PFLIST

PFLIST OF   PDJZ/S839   12/26/81 21.15.53.

PERRYP1   PROB1   PROB1A

 3 FILES   3 PRUS $ .01 PER DAY

If you do a PFLIST command and there are no permanent files under your account, the system will print the message **"NO FILES."**

Resequencing Line Numbers

Sometimes you might use all available line numbers in a certain range after adding new statements to a program. The need then might arise to add a new statement in this range. For example, suppose you want to add a PRINT statement after the READ statement in the program given below. What do you do?

1	PRINT *, 'ENTER 3 NUMBERS'
2	READ *, A, B, C
3	S = A + B + C

```
4      X = S / 3.0
5      PRINT *, S, X
6      STOP
7      END
```

You could retype the statements beginning at line number 3 with higher line numbers, but this would be tedious.

The best solution is to use the **RESEQUENCE** (abbreviated **RES**) command, which resequences all line numbers in the program. The resequence operation begins with line number 00100 as the first statement's line number and uses an increment of 10 for each of the following line numbers. For example:

```
RESEQUENCE

READY.
LNH

00100      PRINT *, 'ENTER 3 NUMBERS'
00110      READ *, A, B, C
00120      S = A + B + C
00130      X = S / 3.0
00140      PRINT *, S, X
00150      STOP
00160      END
READY.
```

Then you could insert the new PRINT statement after line number 00110 to print the values of A, B, and C. You may type the line number 00115 or just 115. It is best, however, to type the leading zeroes (00115), so that the line numbers will line up.

You may give the base number at which to start the line number sequence by including a comma and the base line number after the command. For example, to begin the sequence 50, type:

RES,50

Five digit sequence numbers, beginning at 00050 and in increments of 10's, will then be given to your statements. You may also include an increment after the base line number. For example, to begin your line numbers at sequence number 00020 and in increments of 20, enter:

RES,20,20

Again, the line numbers will be given as five digit numbers beginning at line number 00020.

K.5 SUMMARY OF CDC TIMESHARING COMMANDS

The following is a list of commands available in the CDC FORTRAN subsystem for you to create, manipulate, and retain FORTRAN programs. The word "filename" represents the name you have chosen to identify a new or existing (OLD) file.

Command	Function	Example
BYE or GOODBYE	Signs you off the system and disconnects the terminal.	BYE
NEW,filename	Creates a new file.	NEW,LP1
OLD,filename	Retrieves an existing file from disk for manipulation.	OLD,LP1
RUN	Executes the program. A date/time and program name header line is printed before the output is printed.	RUN
RNH	Executes the program, but does not print the date/time and program name header.	RNH
SAVE or SAVE,filename	Saves the current working file as a permanent file onto disk.	SAVE SAVE,LP1
LIST	Lists the current file with a date/time and program name header.	LIST

Command	Function	Example
LNH	Lists the current file without a date/time or program header.	LNH
CLEAR	Clears the contents of the current file. The file name remains in effect.	CLEAR
REPLACE or **REPLACE,**filename	Replaces the permanent file on disk with the copy of the current file.	REPLACE REPLACE,LP1
PURGE,filename	Purges a permanent file from disk storage.	PURGE,PL1
NULL	Clears the subsystem in use. The system responds with the READY message.	NULL
HELLO	Logs the current user off the system and reinitiates the log-on sequence. Your terminal is not disconnected.	HELLO
RENAME,nfn = ofn	Changes the name of the working file to a new name. "nfn" is the new file name, "ofn" the old file name.	RENAME,LP1A = LP1
RESEQUENCE or **RESEQUENCE,**ln,ln	Resequences the line numbers in the current primary file, starting at 00100 and in increments of 10. You may set the base and increment by following the command with a comma, the base, another comma, and the increment.	RESEQ RESEQ,20,20
STOP	Terminates any program currently in execution. You must first strike the BREAK key and receive an *INT* message and a *DEL* message before typing the command STOP. After receiving the STOP command, the system responds with *TERM* to let you know that the operation is terminated.	STOP
PFLIST	Lists the permanent files saved under a particular project and account.	PFLIST

Entry errors in an input line can be corrected before the line is transmitted through the use of the backspace character. The backspace character on a terminal is either the BACKSPACE key or the CTRL/H-keys combination (on terminals that do not have a backspace key). One character (including spaces) is deleted for each backspace character entered.

You can delete the entire current line before transmission by pressing the BREAK key or CTRL/@ keys combination. The system ignores the entire input line and responds by printing *DEL* and positioning the carriage to the beginning of the next line.

This appendix has presented the basics of the CDC FORTRAN timesharing system. You should learn its capabilities well to assist you in developing your programs. Good luck and happy programming.

Job Control Language (JCL) Statements for Various Computers

1. JCL for an IBM OS System/360 or System/370 FORTRAN IV "G" Level compile and execute:

```
Card Columns
          1         2         3         4
1234567890123456789012345678901234567890123
//JWC JOB (110,318,200,01),'NAME',MSGLEVEL=1
//ST1 EXEC FORTGCLG
//FORT.SYSIN DD *
     (FORTRAN source program deck goes here)
//GO.SYSIN DD*
     (Data cards, if present, go here)
/*
```

NOTE: The format of the JOB card varies by installation.

2. JCL for an IBM DOS S/360 and S/370 Basic FORTRAN IV compile and execute:

```
Card Columns
          1         2
12345678901234567890
// JOB JOBNAME
// OPTION LINK
// EXEC FORTRAN
     (FORTRAN source program deck goes here)
/*
// EXEC LNKEDT
// EXEC
     (Data cards, if present, go here)
/*
/&
```

NOTE: The JOBNAME in the JOB card is a unique name assigned to the job by the programmer.

3. JCL for WATFIV compile and execute on IBM 360 and 370 systems:

```
Card Columns
          1         2         3         4
123456789012345678901234567890123456789012345
//INITLS JOB (110,318,200,01,),'NAME',CLASS=W
$JOB
     (FORTRAN source program deck goes here)
$ENTRY
     (Data cards, if present, go here)
/*
```

NOTE 1: The format of the JOB card varies by installation.
NOTE 2: The end-of-file card (/*) must not be present in the job deck at some installations.

4. JCL for an NCR 200 FORTRAN compile and execute:

```
Card Columns
          1         2         3         4         5         6
1234567890123456789012345678901234567890123456789012345678 90
        C         NEXTDO FORT/I  ENN     EN1   2B1N032
        C         STOPRD
000000PPGMNAME    FORT/FN
*       P         AUTHORP COLE
*       F         50002P1108001
*       F         66232P01136               060
        (FORTRAN source program deck goes here)
END$
        (Data cards, if present, go here)
END$
```

NOTE: PGMNAME is a unique name assigned by the programmer.

5. JCL for a Honeywell 6000 FORTRAN IV "Y" Level compile and execute:

```
Card Columns
            1         2
12345678901234567890 1234
$       SNUMB    100
$       IDENT
$       USERID
$       OPTION   FORTRAN
$       LOWLOAD
$       FORTY    NDECK
        (FORTRAN source program deck goes here)
$       EXECUTE
$       DATA     05
        (Data cards, if present, go here)
$       ENDJOB
***EOF
```

NOTE 1: The $IDENT and $USERID cards vary by installation.
NOTE 2: File units 5, 6, and 7 may be used to reference the card reader, line printer, and card punch units respectively. File units 41, 42, and 43 may also be used to reference the card reader, line printer, and card punch units respectively.
NOTE 3: The word FORTRAN may be used in place of FORTY in line six.

6. Work Flow Language (WFL) for Burroughs 6000 and 7000 computer systems FORTRAN compile and execute:

```
Card Columns
            1         2
12345678901234567890 1234

?JOB  "JOBNAME"
?USER Your user code
?BEGIN
?COMPILE PGMNAME FORTRAN
?DATA
FILE  5 = CARDS, UNIT = READER
FILE  6 = PRTR, UNIT = PRINTER
        (FORTRAN source program deck goes here)
?DATA CARDS
        (Data cards, if present, go here)
?END JOB
```

NOTE 1: The ? in card column 1 represents an invalid punch—normally a 1/2/3.
NOTE 2: The JOBNAME and PGMNAME represent a unique name supplied by the programmer. Your user code is substituted in the ?USER card.

7. JCL for Control Data Corporation 6000/Cyber FORTRAN compile and execute:

```
Card columns
          1         2         3
1234567890123456789012345678 90

S839,CM=50000,TL=5,JI=COLE          (Job card with user ID)
ABXYZ.       (password)
PDJZ.        (project ID)
FTN.
LGO.
?
          (FORTRAN source program deck goes here)
?
          (Data cards, if present, go here)
&
```

NOTE 1: The ? in column 1 represents a 7/8/9 end-of-record card.
NOTE 2: The & in column 1 represents a 6/7/8/9 end-of-information card.

8. JCL for a Digital Equipment Corporation PDP-11 FORTRAN compile and execute:

```
Card Columns
          1         2         3
1234567890123456789012345678 90

$JOB/CCL [project nr,prog nr]
$FORTRAN $FORLIB.OBJ/LIBRARY
          (FORTRAN source program deck goes here)
$EOD
$DATA
          (Data cards, if present, go here)
$EOD
$EOJ
```

NOTE: Account number consists of two parts—a project number and a programmer number. These two parts are separated by a comma. For example: [52,17].

9. JCL for a Univac 1100 FORTRAN compile and execute:

```
Card Columns
          1         2         3         4
12345678901234567890123456789 01234567890

@RUN           COLE,CS9999,PC
@FTN           ,TPF$.PROGRAM1
     (FORTRAN source program deck goes here)
@MAP,S         ,PC*ABS.PROGRAM1
  IN FORLIB.
@EOF
@XQT           PC*ABS.PROGRAM1
     (data cards, if present, are inserted here)
@EOF
@FIN
```

NOTE 1: There are no specific card column requirements for the options given on the control cards. At least one space must be left to separate the given options from the control card command.
NOTE 2: Your ID, account number, and qualifier name must be given in the @RUN card. The example uses COLE,CS9999,PC. You must replace these parameters with those assigned to you.

Comparison of FORTRAN
Dialects

Appendix M

This appendix compares the statements and features contained in various FORTRAN compilers. A "Yes" is placed in the column if the statement or feature is available in the version of the FORTRAN compiler identified by the column heading; "No" indicates it is not available. An "N/A" (Not Applicable) is placed in the column for those specifications that relate to a specific computer and, thus, are not described in ANSI FORTRAN 66. An "UKN" indicates a specification unknown to the author.

Four standardized versions of FORTRAN compilers have been specified by the American National Standards Institute (ANSI). The first column on the left-hand pages contains the specifications and features of ANSI Full FORTRAN 66 dialect described in ANSI FORTRAN, X3.9–1966. The second column on the left-hand pages contains the specifications and features for the standard Basic FORTRAN 66 dialect described in ANSI Basic FORTRAN, X3.10–1966. The first column on the right-hand pages contains the specifications and features of ANSI FORTRAN 77 level described in ANSI FORTRAN, X3.9–1978. The second column on the right-hand pages contains the specifications and features for the Subset FORTRAN 77 level described in ANSI Subset FORTRAN, X3.9–1978.

Many computer manufacturers have extended the capability of their FORTRAN compilers to provide additional features to ANSI FORTRAN 66 (often referred to as ANSI FORTRAN IV). The remaining columns list those features contained in many of the FORTRAN compilers from various computer vendors. The IBM Basic FORTRAN IV dialect contains the specifications described in IBM Basic FORTRAN Language C28–6629. The IBM G-level FORTRAN IV compiler is described in IBM System/360 and System/370 FORTRAN IV Language manual GC28–6515. Control Data Corporation Cyberg/6000 series FORTRAN compiler specifications are listed as described in CDC FORTRAN Version 5 Reference Manual 60481300. The Honeywell 60/6000 series FORTRAN compiler specifications are listed as described in their FORTRAN manual DD02.

The Burroughs 6000 FORTRAN compiler specifications are listed as described in their FORTRAN Reference Manual 5000458. The Univac 1100 series systems FORTRAN specifications are listed as described in their manual UP–8244.1. The Digital Equipment Corporation VAX–11 FORTRAN specifications are described in their FORTRAN Language Reference Manual AA–D034B–TE. The Hewlett Packard 3000 FORTRAN specifications are listed as described in their FORTRAN/ 3000 Reference Manual 30000–90040. The Digital Equipment Corporation PDP–11 FORTRAN IV specifications are as described in their reference manual AA–1855D–TC. The last column of each page is left blank for you to enter the specifications of your FORTRAN dialect, in case it is not included in the appendix.

FORTRAN Feature	ANSI 66 Standard Full	ANSI 66 Standard Basic	IBM Basic FORTRAN IV	IBM G-level FORTRAN IV	WATFOR	WATFIV	CDC Cyber/6000	Honeywell 6000	Your FORTRAN Compiler
Character Set:									
A–Z, 0–9	Yes	Yes	Yes	Yes	Yes	Yes	Yes	Yes	
+ – */ = .,()ʰ	Yes	Yes	Yes	Yes	Yes	Yes	Yes	Yes	
$	Yes	No	Yes	Yes	Yes	Yes	Yes	Yes	
' (single quote)	No	No	Yes	Yes	Yes	Yes	Yes	Yes	
" (double quote)	No	No	No	No	No	No	Yes	Yes	
&	No	No	No	Yes	Yes	Yes	No	Yes	
:	No	No	No	No	No	No	Yes	No	
Number of characters	47	46	48	49	49	49	50	51	
Variable name	1–6	1–5	1–6	1–6	1–6	1–6	1–7	1–8	
Statement label	1–99999	1–9999	1–32767	1–99999	1–99999	1–99999	1–99999	1–99999	
Continuation lines	19	5	19	19	No limit	No limit	19	19	
Data types: (constants)									
Integer	Yes	Yes	Yes	Yes	Yes	Yes	Yes	Yes	
Real	Yes	Yes	Yes	Yes	Yes	Yes	Yes	Yes	
Double Precision	Yes	No	Yes	Yes	Yes	Yes	Yes	Yes	
Literal (Hollerith)	Yes	No	No	Yes	Yes	Yes	Yes	Yes	
Logical	Yes	No	No	Yes	Yes	Yes	Yes	Yes	
Complex	Yes	No	No	Yes	Yes	Yes	Yes	Yes	
Hexadecimal	No	No	No	Yes	Yes	Yes	Yes	No	
Octal	No	No	No	No	No	No	Yes	Yes	
Character	No	No	No	No	Yes	Yes	Yes	Yes	
Real Constant Basic real constant followed by E exponent	Yes	Yes	Yes	Yes	Yes	Yes	Yes	Yes	
Integer constant followed by a decimal exponent	Yes	No	Yes	Yes	No	Yes	No	No	
$ may be used as a letter in symbolic name	No	No	Yes	Yes	Yes	Yes	No	No	
Double-precision constant Real constant with "D" in place of "E"	Yes	No	Yes	Yes	No	Yes	Yes	Yes	
Size of computer word (in bytes)	N/A	N/A	4 (32-bit)	4 (32-bit)	4 (32-bit)	4 (32-bit)	10 (60-bit)	6 (36-bit)	
Relational expressions	Yes	No	No	Yes	Yes	Yes	Yes	Yes	

FORTRAN Feature	ANSI 77 Standard FORTRAN	ANSI 77 FORTRAN Subset	Burroughs 6000 FORTRAN	Univac FORTRAN (ASCII)	DEC VAX-11 FORTRAN	HP FORTRAN 3000	DEC PDP-11 FORTRAN IV	Your Second FORTRAN Compiler
Character Set:								
A – Z, 0 – 9	Yes	Yes	Yes	Yes	Yes	Yes	Yes	
+ – */ = .,()b	Yes	Yes	Yes	Yes	Yes	Yes	Yes	
$	Yes	No	Yes	Yes	Yes	Yes	Yes	
' (single quote)	Yes	Yes	Yes	Yes	Yes	Yes	Yes	
" (double quote)	No	No	Yes	Yes	No	No	No	
&	No	No	Yes	Yes	Yes	Yes	No	
:	Yes	No	No	Yes	Yes	No	Yes	
Number of characters	49	47	50	50	49	48	49	
Variable name	1 – 6	1 – 6	1 – 6	1 – 6	1 – 31	1 – 15	1 – 6	
Statement label	1 – 99999	1 – 9999	1 – 99999	1 – 99999	1 – 99999	1 – 99999	1 – 99999	
Continuation lines	19	9	No limit	No limit	No limit	No limit	No limit	
Data types: (constants)								
Integer	Yes	Yes	Yes	Yes	Yes	Yes	Yes	
Real	Yes	Yes	Yes	Yes	Yes	Yes	Yes	
Double Precision	Yes	No	Yes	Yes	Yes	Yes	Yes	
Literal (Hollerith)	Yes	Yes	Yes	Yes	Yes	Yes	Yes	
Logical	Yes	Yes	Yes	Yes	Yes	Yes	Yes	
Complex	Yes	No	Yes	Yes	Yes	Yes	Yes	
Hexadecimal	No	No	Yes	Yes	Yes	Yes	Yes	
Octal	No	No	Yes	Yes	No	Yes	No	
Character	Yes	Yes	No	Yes	Yes	Yes	No	
Real Constant Basic real constant followed by E exponent	Yes	Yes	Yes	Yes	Yes	Yes	Yes	
Integer constant followed by a decimal exponent	Yes	Yes	Yes	Yes	Yes	Yes	No	
$ may be used as a letter in symbolic name	No	No	Yes	No	Yes	No	No	
Double-precision constant Real constant with "D" in place of "E"	Yes	No	Yes	Yes	Yes	Yes	Yes	
Size of computer word (in bytes)	N/A	N/A	6 (48-bit)	6 (36-bit)	4 (32-bit)	2 (16-bit)	2 (16-bit)	
Relational expressions	Yes	Yes	Yes	Yes	Yes	Yes	Yes	

FORTRAN Feature	ANSI 66 Standard Full	ANSI 66 Standard Basic	IBM Basic FORTRAN IV	IBM G-level FORTRAN IV	WATFOR	WATFIV	CDC Cyber/6000	Honeywell 6000	Your FORTRAN Compiler
Logical Operators (.NOT., .AND., .OR.)	Yes	No	No	Yes	Yes	Yes	Yes	Yes	
Mixed mode expressions	No	No	Yes	Yes	Yes	Yes	Yes	Yes	
* in column 1 for a remark	No	No	No	No	No	No	Yes	Yes	
Double exponentiation w/o parentheses (i.e., A**B**C)	No	No	No	Yes	Yes	Yes	Yes	Yes	
Statements:									
ACCEPT	No	No	No	No	No	No	No	No	
ASSIGN	Yes	No	No	Yes	Yes	Yes	Yes	Yes	
BACKSPACE	Yes	Yes	Yes	Yes	Yes	Yes	Yes	Yes	
BLOCK DATA	Yes	No	No	Yes	Yes	Yes	Yes	Yes	
CALL	Yes	Yes	Yes	Yes	Yes	Yes	Yes	Yes	
CHARACTER	No	No	No	No	Yes	Yes	Yes	Yes	
CLOSE	No	No	No	No	No	No	Yes	No	
COMMON									
Blank (un-labeled)	Yes	Yes	Yes	Yes	Yes	Yes	Yes	Yes	
Labeled (named)	Yes	No	No	Yes	Yes	Yes	Yes	Yes	
COMPLEX	Yes	No	No	Yes	Yes	Yes	Yes	Yes	
CONTINUE	Yes	Yes	Yes	Yes	Yes	Yes	Yes	Yes	
DATA	Yes	No	No	Yes	Yes	Yes	Yes	Yes	
DECODE	No	No	No	No	No	No	Yes	Yes	
DEFINE FILE	N/A	N/A	Yes	Yes	Yes	Yes	No	No	
DIMENSION	Yes	Yes	Yes	Yes	Yes	Yes	Yes	Yes	
DISPLAY	No	No	No	No	No	No	No	No	
DO	Yes	Yes	Yes	Yes	Yes	Yes	Yes	Yes	
DOUBLE PRECISION	Yes	Yes	Yes	Yes	Yes	Yes	Yes	Yes	
ELSE	No	No	No	No	No	Yes	Yes	No	
ELSE IF	No	No	No	No	No	Yes	Yes	No	
ENCODE	No	No	No	No	No	No	Yes	Yes	
END	Yes	Yes	Yes	Yes	Yes	Yes	Yes	Yes	
ENDFILE	Yes	Yes	Yes	Yes	Yes	Yes	Yes	Yes	
END IF	No	No	No	No	No	Yes	Yes	No	
ENTRY	No	No	No	Yes	Yes	Yes	Yes	Yes	
EQUIVALENCE	Yes	Yes	Yes	Yes	Yes	Yes	Yes	Yes	
EXTERNAL	Yes	No	Yes	Yes	Yes	Yes	Yes	Yes	
FIND	N/A	N/A	Yes	Yes	Yes	Yes	No	Yes	
FORMAT	Yes	Yes	Yes	Yes	Yes	Yes	Yes	Yes	
FUNCTION	Yes	Yes	Yes	Yes	Yes	Yes	Yes	Yes	
GO TO									
Unconditional	Yes	Yes	Yes	Yes	Yes	Yes	Yes	Yes	
Computed	Yes	Yes	Yes	Yes	Yes	Yes	Yes	Yes	
Assigned	Yes	No	No	Yes	Yes	Yes	Yes	Yes	
IF									
Arithmetic	Yes	Yes	Yes	Yes	Yes	Yes	Yes	Yes	
Block	No	No	No	No	No	Yes	Yes	No	
Logical	Yes	No	No	Yes	Yes	Yes	Yes	Yes	

FORTRAN Feature	ANSI 77 Standard FORTRAN	ANSI 77 FORTRAN Subset	Burroughs 6000 FORTRAN	Univac FORTRAN (ASCII)	DEC VAX-11 FORTRAN	HP FORTRAN 3000	DEC PDP-11 FORTRAN IV	Your Second FORTRAN Compiler
Logical Operators (.NOT., .AND., .OR.)	Yes	Yes	Yes	Yes	Yes	Yes	Yes	
Mixed mode expressions	Yes	Yes	Yes	Yes	Yes	Yes	Yes	
*in column 1 for a remark	Yes	Yes	No	Yes	Yes	Yes	No	
Double exponentiation w/o parentheses (i.e., A**B**C)	Yes	Yes	Yes	Yes	Yes	Yes	Yes	
Statements:								
ACCEPT	No	No	No	No	Yes	Yes	Yes	
ASSIGN	Yes	Yes	Yes	Yes	Yes	Yes	Yes	
BACKSPACE	Yes	Yes	Yes	Yes	Yes	Yes	Yes	
BLOCK DATA	Yes	No	Yes	Yes	Yes	Yes	Yes	
CALL	Yes	Yes	Yes	Yes	Yes	Yes	Yes	
CHARACTER	Yes	Yes	No	Yes	Yes	Yes	No	
CLOSE	Yes	Yes	Yes	Yes	Yes	No	Yes	
COMMON								
Blank (unlabeled)	Yes	Yes	Yes	Yes	Yes	Yes	Yes	
Labeled (named)	Yes	Yes	Yes	Yes	Yes	Yes	Yes	
COMPLEX	Yes	No	Yes	Yes	Yes	Yes	Yes	
CONTINUE	Yes	Yes	Yes	Yes	Yes	Yes	Yes	
DATA	Yes	Yes	Yes	Yes	Yes	Yes	Yes	
DECODE	No	No	No	Yes	Yes	No	Yes	
DEFINE FILE	No	No	No	Yes	Yes	No	Yes	
DIMENSION	Yes	Yes	Yes	Yes	Yes	Yes	Yes	
DISPLAY	No	No	No	Yes	No	Yes	No	
DO	Yes	Yes	Yes	Yes	Yes	Yes	Yes	
DOUBLE PRECISION	Yes	No	Yes	Yes	Yes	Yes	Yes	
ELSE	Yes	Yes	No	Yes	Yes	No	No	
ELSE IF	Yes	Yes	No	Yes	Yes	No	No	
ENCODE	No	No	No	Yes	Yes	No	Yes	
END	Yes	Yes	Yes	Yes	Yes	Yes	Yes	
ENDFILE	Yes	Yes	Yes	Yes	Yes	Yes	Yes	
END IF	Yes	Yes	No	Yes	Yes	No	No	
ENTRY	Yes	No	Yes	Yes	Yes	Yes	Yes	
EQUIVALENCE	Yes	Yes	Yes	Yes	Yes	Yes	Yes	
EXTERNAL	Yes	Yes	Yes	Yes	Yes	Yes	Yes	
FIND	No	No	Yes	Yes	No	No	Yes	
FORMAT	Yes	Yes	Yes	Yes	Yes	Yes	Yes	
FUNCTION	Yes	Yes	Yes	Yes	Yes	Yes	Yes	
GO TO								
Unconditional	Yes	Yes	Yes	Yes	Yes	Yes	Yes	
Computed	Yes	Yes	Yes	Yes	Yes	Yes	Yes	
Assigned	Yes	Yes	Yes	Yes	Yes	Yes	Yes	
IF								
Arithmetic	Yes	Yes	Yes	Yes	Yes	Yes	Yes	
Block	Yes	Yes	No	Yes	Yes	No	No	
Logical	Yes	Yes	Yes	Yes	Yes	Yes	Yes	

FORTRAN Feature	ANSI 66 Standard Full	ANSI 66 Standard Basic	IBM Basic FORTRAN IV	IBM G-level FORTRAN IV	WATFOR	WATFIV	CDC Cyber/ 6000	Honeywell 6000	Your FORTRAN Compiler
IMPLICIT	No	No	No	Yes	Yes	Yes	Yes	Yes	
INQUIRE	No	No	No	No	No	No	Yes	No	
INTEGER (type)	Yes	No	Yes	Yes	Yes	Yes	Yes	Yes	
INTRINSIC	No	No	No	No	No	No	Yes	No	
LOCK	No	No	No	No	No	No	No	No	
LOGICAL (type)	Yes	No	No	Yes	Yes	Yes	Yes	Yes	
NAMELIST	No	No	No	Yes	No	Yes	Yes	Yes	
OPEN	No	No	No	No	No	No	Yes	No	
PARAMETER	No	No	No	No	No	No	Yes	No	
PAUSE	Yes	Yes	Yes	Yes	Yes	Yes	Yes	Yes	
PRINT	No	No	No	Yes	Yes	Yes	Yes	Yes	
PROGRAM	No	No	No	No	No	No	Yes	No	
PUNCH	No	No	No	Yes	Yes	Yes	Yes	Yes	
READ									
format-free	No	No	No	No	Yes	Yes	Yes	Yes	
formatted	Yes	Yes	Yes	Yes	Yes	Yes	Yes	Yes	
unformatted	Yes	Yes	Yes	Yes	Yes	Yes	Yes	Yes	
specific	No	No	No	Yes	Yes	Yes	Yes	Yes	
direct access	N/A	N/A	Yes	Yes	Yes	Yes	Yes	Yes	
REAL (type)	Yes	No	Yes	Yes	Yes	Yes	Yes	Yes	
RETURN									
standard	Yes	Yes	Yes	Yes	Yes	Yes	Yes	Yes	
return n option	No	No	No	Yes	Yes	Yes	Yes	Yes	
REWIND	Yes	Yes	Yes	Yes	Yes	Yes	Yes	Yes	
SAVE	No	No	No	No	No	No	Yes	No	
STOP	Yes	Yes	Yes	Yes	Yes	Yes	Yes	Yes	
SUBROUTINE	Yes	Yes	Yes	Yes	Yes	Yes	Yes	Yes	
TYPE	No	No	No	No	No	No	No	No	
WRITE									
format-free	No	No	No	No	Yes	Yes	PRINT	No	
formatted	Yes	Yes	Yes	Yes	Yes	Yes	Yes	Yes	
unformatted	Yes	Yes	Yes	Yes	Yes	Yes	Yes	Yes	
direct access	N/A	N/A	Yes	Yes	Yes	Yes	Yes	Yes	
Assignment statement:									
var = arith exp	Yes	Yes	Yes	Yes	Yes	Yes	Yes	Yes	
var = logical exp	Yes	No	No	Yes	Yes	Yes	Yes	Yes	
extended assignment statement (multiple replacement)	No	No	No	No	Yes	Yes	Yes	No	
character assignment statement	No	No	No	No	Yes	Yes	Yes	Yes	
DO—extended range	Yes	No	Yes	Yes	No	No	Yes	Yes	
END = option in READ	No	No	No	Yes	Yes	Yes	Yes	Yes	
ERR = option in READ	No	No	No	Yes	Yes	Yes	Yes	Yes	

FORTRAN Feature	ANSI 77 Standard FORTRAN	ANSI 77 FORTRAN Subset	Burroughs 6000 FORTRAN	Univac FORTRAN (ASCII)	DEC VAX-11 FORTRAN	HP FORTRAN 3000	DEC PDP-11 FORTRAN IV	Your Second FORTRAN Compiler
IMPLICIT	Yes	Yes	Yes	Yes	Yes	Yes	Yes	
INQUIRE	Yes	No	Yes	Yes	Yes	No	No	
INTEGER (type)	Yes	Yes	Yes	Yes	Yes	Yes	Yes	
INTRINSIC	Yes	Yes	No	Yes	Yes	No	No	
LOCK	No	No	Yes	No	No	No	No	
LOGICAL (type)	Yes	Yes	Yes	Yes	Yes	Yes	Yes	
NAMELIST	No	No	Yes	Yes	No	No	No	
OPEN	Yes	Yes	Yes	Yes	Yes	No	Yes	
PARAMETER	Yes	No	No	Yes	Yes	Yes	Yes	
PAUSE	Yes	Yes	Yes	Yes	Yes	Yes	Yes	
PRINT	Yes	No	Yes	Yes	Yes	Yes	Yes	
PROGRAM	Yes	Yes	No	Yes	Yes	Yes	No	
PUNCH	No	No	Yes	Yes	No	No	No	
READ								
format-free	Yes	Yes	Yes	Yes	Yes	Yes	Yes	
formatted	Yes	Yes	Yes	Yes	Yes	Yes	Yes	
unformatted	Yes	Yes	Yes	Yes	Yes	Yes	Yes	
specific	Yes	No	Yes	Yes	Yes	Yes	Yes	
direct access	Yes	Yes	Yes	Yes	Yes	Yes	Yes	
REAL (type)	Yes	Yes	Yes	Yes	Yes	Yes	Yes	
RETURN								
standard	Yes	Yes	Yes	Yes	Yes	Yes	Yes	
return n option	Yes	No	Yes	Yes	Yes	Yes	Yes	
REWIND	Yes	Yes	Yes	Yes	Yes	Yes	Yes	
SAVE	Yes	Yes	No	Yes	Yes	No	No	
STOP	Yes	Yes	Yes	Yes	Yes	Yes	Yes	
SUBROUTINE	Yes	Yes	Yes	Yes	Yes	Yes	Yes	
TYPE	No	No	No	No	Yes	No	Yes	
WRITE								
format-free	Yes	Yes	Yes	Yes	Yes	Yes	Yes	
formatted	Yes	Yes	Yes	Yes	Yes	Yes	Yes	
unformatted	Yes	Yes	Yes	Yes	Yes	Yes	Yes	
direct access	N/A	N/A	Yes	Yes	Yes	Yes	Yes	
Assignment statement:								
var = arith exp	Yes	Yes	Yes	Yes	Yes	Yes	Yes	
var = logical exp	Yes	Yes	Yes	Yes	Yes	Yes	Yes	
extended assignment statement (multiple replacement)	No	No	No	No	Yes	Yes	No	
character assignment statement	Yes	Yes	Yes	Yes	Yes	Yes	Yes	
DO—extended range	Yes	No	Yes	No	No	No	Yes	
END = option in READ	Yes	Yes	Yes	Yes	Yes	Yes	Yes	
ERR = option in READ	Yes	Yes	Yes	Yes	Yes	Yes	Yes	

FORTRAN Feature	ANSI 66 Standard Full	ANSI 66 Standard Basic	IBM Basic FORTRAN IV	IBM G-level FORTRAN IV	WATFOR	WATFIV	CDC Cyber/6000	Honeywell 6000	Your FORTRAN Compiler
Memory-to-memory I/O formatting	No	No	No	No	Yes	Yes	Yes	Yes	
Multiple statements per line	No	No	No	No	No	Yes (;)	No	Yes (;)	
Format codes:									
A (Alphanumeric)	Yes	No	Yes	Yes	Yes	Yes	Yes	Yes	
C (Character)	No	No	No	No	No	No	No	No	
D (Dble prec)	Yes	No	Yes	Yes	Yes	Yes	Yes	Yes	
E (Exponential)	Yes	Yes	Yes	Yes	Yes	Yes	Yes	Yes	
F (Single prec)	Yes	Yes	Yes	Yes	Yes	Yes	Yes	Yes	
G (Generalized)	Yes	No	No	Yes	Yes	Yes	Yes	Yes	
H (Hollerith)	Yes	Yes	Yes	Yes	Yes	Yes	Yes	Yes	
I (Integer)	Yes	Yes	Yes	Yes	Yes	Yes	Yes	Yes	
J (Integer)	No	No	No	No	No	No	No	No	
L (Logical)	Yes	No	No	Yes	Yes	Yes	Yes	Yes	
O (Octal)	No	No	No	No	No	No	Yes	Yes	
R (Right just.)	No	No	No	No	No	No	Yes	See C	
S (+ sign)	No	No	No	No	No	No	Yes	No	
T (Tab)	No	No	Yes	Yes	Yes	Yes	Yes	Yes	
X (Blank)	Yes	Yes	Yes	Yes	Yes	Yes	Yes	Yes	
Z (Hexadecimal)	No	No	No	Yes	Yes	Yes	Yes	Yes	
' (single quote)	No	No	Yes	Yes	Yes	Yes	Yes	Yes	
" (dble quote)	No	No	No	No	No	No	Yes	Yes	
: (format term.)	No	No	No	No	No	No	Yes	No	
/ (slash)	Yes	Yes	Yes	Yes	Yes	Yes	Yes	Yes	
$ (mixed)	No	No	No	No	No	No	No	No	
P scale factor	Yes	No	Yes	Yes	Yes	Yes	Yes	Yes	
Carriage Control operations for printer output (space before printing):									
blank or 1X (single line)	Yes	No	Yes	Yes	Yes	Yes	Yes	Yes	
0 (double line)	Yes	No	Yes	Yes	Yes	Yes	Yes	Yes	
1 (new page)	Yes	No	Yes	Yes	Yes	Yes	Yes	Yes	
+ (no advance)	Yes	No	Yes	Yes	Yes	Yes	Yes	Yes	
− (triple line)	No	No	No	No	Yes	Yes	No	No	
Format group replication levels	2	1	1	2	2	2	2	2	
Object time format specifications	Yes	No	No	Yes	Yes	Yes	Yes	Yes	
Number of array dimensions	3	2	3	7	7	7	7	7	
Dimensions may be specified in Type statements	Yes	No	Yes	Yes	Yes	Yes	Yes	Yes	

FORTRAN Feature	ANSI 77 Standard FORTRAN	ANSI 77 FORTRAN Subset	Burroughs 6000 FORTRAN	Univac FORTRAN (ASCII)	DEC VAX-11 FORTRAN	HP FORTRAN 3000	DEC PDP-11 FORTRAN IV	Your Second FORTRAN Compiler
Memory-to-memory I/O formatting	No	No	Yes	Yes	Yes	UKN	Yes	
Multiple statements per line	No	No	No	No	No	No	No	
Format codes:								
A (Alpha-numeric)	Yes	Yes	Yes	Yes	Yes	Yes	Yes	
C (Character)	No	No	Yes	Yes	No	No	No	
D (Dble prec)	Yes	No	Yes	Yes	Yes	Yes	Yes	
E (Exponential)	Yes	Yes	Yes	Yes	Yes	Yes	Yes	
F (Single prec)	Yes	Yes	Yes	Yes	Yes	Yes	Yes	
G (Generalized)	Yes	No	Yes	Yes	Yes	Yes	Yes	
H (Hollerith)	Yes	Yes	Yes	Yes	Yes	Yes	Yes	
I (Integer)	Yes	Yes	Yes	Yes	Yes	Yes	Yes	
J (mixed)	No	No	Yes	Yes	No	No	No	
L (Logical)	Yes	Yes	Yes	Yes	Yes	Yes	Yes	
O (Octal)	No	No	Yes	Yes	Yes	Yes	Yes	
R (Right just.)	No	No	See C	Yes	No	Yes	No	
S (+ Sign)	Yes	No	No	Yes	Yes	(ASCII)	No	
T (Tab)	Yes	No	Yes	Yes	Yes	Yes	Yes	
X (Blank)	Yes	Yes	Yes	Yes	Yes	Yes	Yes	
Z (Hexadecimal)	No	No	Yes	No	Yes	Yes	No	
' (single quote)	Yes	Yes	Yes	Yes	Yes	Yes	Yes	
" (dble quote)	No	No	Yes	No	No	Yes	No	
/ (slash)	Yes	Yes	Yes	Yes	Yes	Yes	Yes	
: (format term.)	Yes	No	No	No	Yes	No	Yes	
$ (mixed)	No	No	Yes	No	Yes	No	Yes	
P scale factor	Yes	Yes	Yes	Yes	Yes	Yes	Yes	
Carriage Control operations for printer output (space before printing)								
blank or 1X (single line)	Yes	Yes	Yes	Yes	Yes	Yes	Yes	
0 (double line)	Yes	Yes	Yes	Yes	Yes	Yes	Yes	
1 (new page)	Yes	Yes	Yes	Yes	Yes	Yes	Yes	
+ (no advance)	Yes	Yes	Yes	Yes	Yes	Yes	Yes	
− (triple line)	No	No	No	No	No	No	No	
Format group replication factor	2	2	2	2	2	2	Yes	
Object time format specifications	UKN	UKN	Yes	Yes	Yes	Yes	Yes	
Number of array dimensions	7	3	31	7	7	255	7	
Dimensions may be specified in Type statements	Yes	Yes	Yes	Yes	Yes	Yes	Yes	

FORTRAN Feature	ANSI 66 Standard Full	ANSI 66 Standard Basic	IBM Basic FORTRAN IV	IBM G-level FORTRAN IV	WATFOR	WATFIV	CDC Cyber/ 6000	Honeywell 6000	Your FORTRAN Compiler
Dimensions may be specified in COMMON statement	Yes	No	Yes	Yes	Yes	Yes	Yes	Yes	
Object time dimensions in subprograms	Yes	No	No	Yes	Yes	Yes	Yes	Yes	
Generalized subscript form	No	No	No	Yes	Yes	Yes	Yes	Yes	
Subprogram types: FUNCTION Statement function SUBROUTINE	Yes Yes Yes	Yes Yes Yes	Yes Yes Yes	Yes Yes Yes	Yes Yes Yes	Yes Yes Yes	Yes Yes Yes	Yes Yes Yes	
Type specification in FUNCTION statement	Yes	No	Yes	Yes	Yes	Yes	Yes	Yes	
FUNCTION subprogram may define or redefine its dummy arguments	Yes	No	Yes	Yes	Yes	Yes	Yes	Yes	
Statement function must precede first executable statement	Yes	Yes	Yes	Yes	Yes	Yes	Yes	Yes	
Actual arguments may be: numeric constant numeric variable/array literal (Hollerith) constant logical constant external subprogram name	Yes Yes Yes Yes Yes	Yes Yes No No No	Yes Yes No No Yes	Yes Yes Yes Yes Yes	Yes Yes Yes Yes Yes	Yes Yes Yes Yes Yes	Yes Yes Yes Yes Yes	Yes Yes Yes Yes Yes	

FORTRAN Feature	ANSI 77 Standard FORTRAN	ANSI 77 FORTRAN Subset	Burroughs 6000 FORTRAN	Univac FORTRAN (ASCII)	DEC VAX-11 FORTRAN	HP FORTRAN 3000	DEC PDP-11 FORTRAN IV	Your Second FORTRAN Compiler
Dimensions may be specified in COMMON statement	Yes	Yes	Yes	Yes	Yes	Yes	Yes	
Object time dimensions in subprograms	Yes	Yes	Yes	Yes	Yes	Yes	Yes	
Generalized subscript form	No	No	Yes	Yes	Yes	Yes	Yes	
Subprogram types: FUNCTION	Yes	Yes	Yes	Yes	Yes	Yes	Yes	
Statement function	Yes	Yes	Yes	Yes	Yes	Yes	Yes	
SUBROUTINE	Yes	Yes	Yes	Yes	Yes	Yes	Yes	
Type specification in FUNCTION statement	Yes	Yes	Yes	Yes	Yes	Yes	Yes	
FUNCTION subprogram may define or redefine its dummy arguments	UKN	UKN	Yes	Yes	Yes	Yes	Yes	
Statement function must precede first executable statement	Yes	Yes	Yes	Yes	Yes	Yes	Yes	
Actual arguments may be: numeric constant	Yes	Yes	Yes	Yes	Yes	Yes	Yes	
numeric variable/array	Yes	Yes	Yes	Yes	Yes	Yes	Yes	
literal (Hollerith) constant	Yes	Yes	Yes	Yes	Yes	Yes	Yes	
logical constant	Yes	Yes	Yes	Yes	Yes	Yes	Yes	
external subprogram name	Yes	Yes	Yes	Yes	Yes	Yes	Yes	

ASCII Character Code Table

The ASCII (American Standard Code for Information Interchange) computer coding scheme, pronounced ''ASK-ee,'' is a 7-bit code used by many computers. Minicomputers and home computers use this coding scheme to represent data in an internal form. This code is also widely used by many timesharing systems. The following table is given to show the ASCII character, the terminal key used to obtain this character, the equivalent forms in binary, octal (oct), decimal (dec), and hexadecimal (hex), and the definition of use for the 128 characters in the ASCII code.

ASCII Terminal		– – – EQUIVALENT FORMS – – –				
char	key	binary	oct	dec	hex	Definition of Use
NULL	CTRL/@	0 000 000	000	0	0	Filler
SOH	CTRL/A	0 000 001	001	1	0	Start of Heading; Home Position
STX	CTRL/B	0 000 010	002	2	2	Start of Text
ETX	CTRL/C	0 000 011	003	3	3	End of Text
EOT	CTRL/D	0 000 100	004	4	4	End of Transmission
ENQ	CTRL/E	0 000 101	005	5	5	Enquiry
ACK	CTRL/F	0 000 110	006	6	6	Acknowledge
BELL	CTRL/G	0 000 111	007	7	7	Bell
BS	CTRL/H	0 001 000	010	8	8	Backspace; ← arrow
HT	CTRL/I	0 001 001	011	9	9	Horizontal Tabulation
LF	CTRL/J	0 001 010	012	10	A	Line Feed; ↓ arrow
VT	CTRL/K	0 001 011	013	11	B	Vertical Tabulation; ↑ arrow
FF	CTRL/L	0 001 100	014	12	C	Form Feed; Clear Screen
CR	CTRL/M	0 001 101	015	13	D	Carriage Return
SO	CTRL/N	0 001 110	016	14	E	Shift Out
SI	CTRL/O	0 001 111	017	15	F	Shift In
DLE	CTRL/P	0 010 000	020	16	10	Data Link Escape
DC1	CTRL/Q	0 010 001	021	17	11	Device Control 1
DC2	CTRL/R	0 010 010	022	18	12	Device Control 2
DC3	CTRL/S	0 010 011	023	19	13	Device Control 3
DC4	CTRL/T	0 010 100	024	20	14	Device Control 4
NAK	CTRL/U	0 010 101	025	21	15	Negative Acknowledge
SYNC	CTRL/V	0 010 110	026	22	16	Synchronous Idle
ETB	CTRL/W	0 010 111	027	23	17	End of Transmission Block
CAN	CTRL/X	0 011 000	030	24	18	Cancel
EM	CTRL/Y	0 011 001	031	25	19	End of Medium
SUB	CTRL/Z	0 011 010	032	26	1A	Substitute
ESC	CTRL/[	0 011 011	033	27	1B	Escape
FS	CTRL/\	0 011 100	034	28	1C	File Separator
GS	CTRL/]	0 011 101	035	29	1D	Group Separator
RS	CTRL/^	0 011 110	036	30	1E	Record Separator
US	CTRL/_	0 011 111	037	31	1F	Unit Separator
space	space	0 100 000	040	32	20	Space; blank
!	!	0 100 001	041	33	21	Exclamation Mark
"	"	0 100 010	042	34	22	Double quote
#	#	0 100 011	043	35	23	Number Symbol
$	$	0 100 100	044	36	24	Dollar Symbol
%	%	0 100 101	045	37	25	Percent Symbol
&	&	0 100 110	046	38	26	Ampersand
'	'	0 100 111	047	39	27	Single Quote; Apostrophe
(	(	0 101 000	050	40	28	Left Parenthesis
)	)	0 101 001	051	41	29	Right Parenthesis
*	*	0 101 010	052	42	2A	Asterisk
+	+	0 101 011	053	43	2B	Plus Symbol
,	,	0 101 100	054	44	2C	Comma
–	–	0 101 101	055	45	2D	Minus Symbol; Hyphen
.	.	0 101 110	056	46	2E	Period; Decimal Point
/	/	0 101 111	057	47	2F	Divide Symbol; Slash; Virgule
0	0	0 110 000	060	48	30	Digit Zero
1	1	0 110 001	061	49	31	Digit One

char	key	binary	oct	dec	hex	Definition of Use
2	2	0 110 010	062	50	32	Digit Two
3	3	0 110 011	063	51	33	Digit Three
4	4	0 110 100	064	52	34	Digit Four
5	5	0 110 101	065	53	35	Digit Five
6	6	0 110 110	066	54	36	Digit Six
7	7	0 110 111	067	55	37	Digit Seven
8	8	0 111 000	070	56	38	Digit Eight
9	9	0 111 001	071	57	39	Digit Nine
:	:	0 111 010	072	58	3A	Colon
;	;	0 111 011	073	59	3B	Semicolon
<	<	0 111 100	074	60	3C	Less Than Symbol; Left Caret
=	=	0 111 101	075	61	3D	Equal Symbol
>	>	0 111 110	076	62	3E	Greater Than Symbol; Right Caret
?	?	0 111 111	077	63	3F	Question Mark
@	@	1 000 000	100	64	40	At Sign
A	A	1 000 001	101	65	41	Upper Case Letter A
B	B	1 000 010	102	66	42	Upper Case Letter B
C	C	1 000 011	103	67	43	Upper Case Letter C
D	D	1 000 100	104	68	44	Upper Case Letter D
E	E	1 000 101	105	69	45	Upper Case Letter E
F	F	1 000 110	106	70	46	Upper Case Letter F
G	G	1 000 111	107	71	47	Upper Case Letter G
H	H	1 001 000	110	72	48	Upper Case Letter H
I	I	1 001 001	111	73	49	Upper Case Letter I
J	J	1 001 010	112	74	4A	Upper Case Letter J
K	K	1 001 011	113	75	4B	Upper Case Letter K
L	L	1 001 100	114	76	4C	Upper Case Letter L
M	M	1 001 101	115	77	4D	Upper Case Letter M
N	N	1 001 110	116	78	4E	Upper Case Letter N
O	O	1 001 111	117	79	4F	Upper Case Letter O
P	P	1 010 000	120	80	50	Upper Case Letter P
Q	Q	1 010 001	121	81	51	Upper Case Letter Q
R	R	1 010 010	122	82	52	Upper Case Letter R
S	S	1 010 011	123	83	53	Upper Case Letter S
T	T	1 010 100	124	84	54	Upper Case Letter T
U	U	1 010 101	125	85	55	Upper Case Letter U
V	V	1 010 110	126	86	56	Upper Case Letter V
W	W	1 010 111	127	87	57	Upper Case Letter W
X	X	1 011 000	130	88	58	Upper Case Letter X
Y	Y	1 011 001	131	89	59	Upper Case Letter Y
Z	Z	1 011 010	132	90	5A	Upper Case Letter Z
[	[	1 011 011	133	91	5B	Left Bracket
\	\	1 011 100	134	92	5C	Back Slash; Back Slant
]	]	1 011 101	135	93	5D	Right Bracket
^	^	1 011 110	136	94	5E	Circumflex; ASCII up arrow (↑)
_	_	0 011 111	137	95	5F	Underscore
`	`	1 100 000	140	96	60	Back Quote; Grave Accent
a	a	1 100 001	141	97	61	Lower Case Letter a
b	b	0 100 010	142	98	62	Lower Case Letter b
c	c	1 100 011	143	99	63	Lower Case Letter c
d	d	1 100 100	144	100	64	Lower Case Letter d
e	e	1 100 101	145	101	65	Lower Case Letter e
f	f	1 100 110	146	102	66	Lower Case Letter f
g	g	1 100 111	147	103	67	Lower Case Letter g
h	h	1 101 000	150	104	68	Lower Case Letter h
i	i	1 101 001	151	105	69	Lower Case Letter i
j	j	1 101 010	152	106	6A	Lower Case Letter j
k	k	1 101 011	153	107	6B	Lower Case Letter k
l	l	1 101 100	154	108	6C	Lower Case Letter l
m	m	1 101 101	155	109	6D	Lower Case Letter m

char	key	binary	oct	dec	hex	Definition of Use
n	n	1 101 110	156	110	6E	Lower Case Letter n
o	o	1 101 111	157	111	6F	Lower Case Letter o
p	p	1 110 000	160	112	70	Lower Case Letter p
q	q	1 110 001	161	113	71	Lower Case Letter q
r	r	1 110 010	162	114	72	Lower Case Letter r
s	s	1 110 011	163	115	73	Lower Case Letter s
t	t	1 110 100	164	116	74	Lower Case Letter t
u	u	1 110 101	165	117	75	Lower Case Letter u
v	v	1 110 110	166	118	76	Lower Case Letter v
w	w	1 110 111	167	119	77	Lower Case Letter w
x	x	1 111 000	170	120	78	Lower Case Letter x
y	y	1 111 001	171	121	79	Lower Case Letter y
z	z	1 111 010	172	122	7A	Lower Case Letter z
{	{	1 111 011	173	123	7B	Left Brace
|	|	1 111 100	174	124	7C	Vertical Bar
}	}	1 111 101	175	125	7D	Right Brace
~	~	1 111 110	176	126	7E	Tilde
DEL	DEL	1 111 111	177	127	7F	Delete; Rubout

EBCDIC Character Code Table   Appendix O

The EBCDIC (Extended Binary Coded Decimal Interchange Code) computer coding scheme, pronounced "eb-c-dic," is an 8-bit code used by many computers. Amdahl, Burroughs, Digital PDP–11 series, Hewlett Packard, IBM, and other computers use this coding scheme to represent data in an internal form. The following table is given to show the EBCDIC character, the internal binary representation, the equivalent forms in hexadecimal (hex) and decimal (dec), and the definition of use for available characters in the EBCDIC code. All of the 256 bit configurations for the EBCDIC coding scheme are not presented; only the bit configurations that form the characters normally used by programmers are given in the table.

EBCDIC   – –EQUIVALENT FORMS – –

char	hex	binary	dec	Definition of Use
space	40	0010 0000	64	Space; blank
¢ or [	4A	0100 1010	74	Cents Symbol on IBM; Left Bracket on Burroughs
.	4B	0100 1011	75	Period; Decimal Point
<	4C	0100 1100	76	Less Than Symbol; Left Caret
(	4D	0100 1101	77	Left Parenthesis
+	4E	0100 1110	78	Plus Symbol
!	4F	0100 1111	79	Exclamation Mark
&	50	0101 0000	80	Ampersand
! or]	5A	0101 1010	90	Exclamation Mark on IBM; Right Bracket on Burroughs
$	5B	0101 1011	91	Dollar Symbol
*	5C	0101 1100	92	Asterisk
)	5D	0101 1101	93	Right Parenthesis
;	5E	0101 1110	94	Semicolon
¬	5F	0101 1111	95	Logical Not Symbol
–	60	0110 0000	96	Minus Symbol; Hyphen
/	61	0110 0001	97	Divide Symbol; Slash
,	6B	0110 1011	107	Comma
%	6C	0110 1100	108	Percent Symbol
_	6D	0110 1101	109	Underscore
>	6E	0110 1110	110	Greater Than Symbol; Right Caret
?	6F	0110 1111	111	Question Mark
:	7A	0111 1010	122	Colon
#	7B	0111 1011	123	Number Symbol
@	7C	0111 1100	124	At Sign
'	7D	0111 1101	125	Single Quote; Apostrophe

char	hex	binary	dec	Definition of Use
=	7E	0111 1110	126	Equal Symbol
"	7F	0111 1111	127	Double Quote
a	81	1000 0001	129	Lower Case Letter a
b	82	1000 0010	130	Lower Case Letter b
c	83	1000 0011	131	Lower Case Letter c
d	84	1000 0100	132	Lower Case Letter d
e	85	1000 0101	133	Lower Case Letter e
f	86	1000 0110	134	Lower Case Letter f
g	87	1000 0111	135	Lower Case Letter g
h	88	1000 1000	136	Lower Case Letter h
i	89	1000 1001	137	Lower Case Letter i
j	91	1001 0001	145	Lower Case Letter j
k	92	1001 0010	146	Lower Case Letter k
l	93	1001 0011	147	Lower Case Letter l
m	94	1001 0100	148	Lower Case Letter m
n	95	1001 0101	149	Lower Case Letter n
o	96	1001 0110	150	Lower Case Letter o
p	97	1001 0111	151	Lower Case Letter p
q	98	1001 1000	152	Lower Case Letter q
r	99	1001 1001	153	Lower Case Letter r
~	A1	1010 0001	161	Tilde
s	A2	1010 0010	162	Lower Case Letter s
t	A3	1010 0011	163	Lower Case Letter t
u	A4	1010 0100	164	Lower Case Letter u
v	A5	1010 0101	165	Lower Case Letter v
w	A6	1010 0110	166	Lower Case Letter w
x	A7	1010 0111	167	Lower Case Letter x
y	A8	1010 1000	168	Lower Case Letter y
z	A9	1010 1001	169	Lower Case Letter z
A	C1	1100 0001	193	Upper Case Letter A
B	C2	1100 0010	194	Upper Case Letter B
C	C3	1100 0011	195	Upper Case Letter C
D	C4	1100 0100	196	Upper Case Letter D
E	C5	1100 0101	197	Upper Case Letter E
F	C6	1100 0110	198	Upper Case Letter F
G	C7	1100 0111	199	Upper Case Letter G
H	C8	1100 1000	200	Upper Case Letter H
I	C9	1100 1001	201	Upper Case Letter I
J	D1	1101 0001	209	Upper Case Letter J
K	D2	1101 0010	210	Upper Case Letter K
L	D3	1101 0011	211	Upper Case Letter L
M	D4	1101 0100	212	Upper Case Letter M
N	D5	1101 0101	213	Upper Case Letter N
O	D6	1101 0110	214	Upper Case Letter O
P	D7	1101 0111	215	Upper Case Letter P
Q	D8	1101 1000	216	Upper Case Letter Q
R	D9	1101 1001	217	Upper Case Letter R
\	E0	1110 0000	224	Back Slash; Back Slant
S	E2	1110 0010	226	Upper Case Letter S
T	E3	1110 0011	227	Upper Case Letter T
U	E4	1110 0100	228	Upper Case Letter U
V	E5	1110 0101	229	Upper Case Letter V
W	E6	1110 0110	230	Upper Case Letter W
X	E7	1110 0111	231	Upper Case Letter X
Y	E8	1110 1000	232	Upper Case Letter Y
Z	E9	1110 1001	233	Upper Case Letter Z
0	F0	1111 0000	240	Digit Zero
1	F1	1111 0001	241	Digit One
2	F2	1111 0010	242	Digit Two
3	F3	1111 0011	243	Digit Three
4	F4	1111 0100	244	Digit Four
5	F5	1111 0101	245	Digit Five
6	F6	1111 0100	246	Digit Six
7	F7	1111 0111	247	Digit Seven
8	F8	1111 1000	248	Digit Eight
9	F9	1111 1001	249	Digit Nine

Answers to Review Questions and Odd-numbered Exercises

CHAPTER 1

Answers to Review Questions

1. People have mixed emotions about computers. Some like them and think that they are great. Others think that they are a threat and are always messing things up.
2. There are many, many application areas. Just a few are: banking, accounting, payroll, tax returns, military, criminology, hospitals, numeric analysis, universities, and many others.
3. Business, scientific, and humanities.
4. A computer is simply a machine that can accept data, manipulate it, store it for later retrieval, and communicate results; it must be told everything that it does; it has occasional breakdowns or failures; it cannot solve a problem unless the problem can be defined in explicit steps.
5. Control unit, arithmetic-logic unit, memory unit, input units, and output units.
6. Control unit and arithmetic-logic unit.
7. To execute the program instructions and to direct all the other components (units) of the system.
8. To perform calculations and decision-making operations.
9. A specific location in the memory unit in which an item of data can be stored.
10. To accept data and transfer it to memory.
11. Visual display (CRT) and teleprinter.
12. Hollerith.
13. A keypunch.
14. To transfer data from memory and display or write it onto a specific medium.
15. Line printer, card punch, magnetic tape unit, magnetic disk unit, paper tape punch, visual display (CRT) terminals, and teleprinter terminals.
16. 132.
17. Discrete values such as numbers and characters. That is, the data does not occur in a continuous form.
18. Speed, accuracy, reliability, and economy.
19. Limited intelligence, limited language capabilities, and subject to failure.
20. Super and mainframe computers, minicomputers, and microcomputers.
21. A set of instructions called a program is stored in the memory unit. It provides the flexibility needed in general-purpose computers to solve a wide variety of problems. That is, different programs for different problems can be stored and executed.
22. Input, output, calculations (arithmetic and assignment), control, and specifications.
23. A complete, unambiguous procedure for solving a problem in a finite number of steps.
24. Program.
25. A flowchart or pseudocode.

Chapter 2

Answers to Review Questions

1. Timesharing.
2. Conversational.
3. Command.
4. Permanent.
5. Current file (or workfile or work area).
6. RETURN.

7. Log on.
8. User ID and password.
9. Cursor.
10. Prompt.
11. No.
12. Backspace and retype the error, or retype the entire line.
13. Insert a new statement with a line number falling between the two statements at which the new statement is to be added.
14. By typing only the line number or using the DELETE command.
15. BYE.
16. True.
17. To allow the creation and manipulation of a file with a system program. A text editor allows easy replacement of text without having to retype an entire line. Also, lines may be moved to new locations and otherwise manipulated with an editor.

CHAPTER 3

Answers to Review Questions

1. For recurring tasks that utilize the computer's ability to calculate, store, and retrieve data.
2. Analyzing the problem specifications and defining the problem requirements, planning and designing the computer solution, writing the computer program, preparing the program in a computer input medium, running the program and correcting statement (syntax) errors, testing and debugging the program with test data for logic errors, implementing the program with live data, and documenting the program and problem solution.
3. These steps provide an organized approach to solving simple and complex problems with a computer.
4. Define the problem requirements, identify the variables involved, identify the relationship between the variables, develop a model or formula using the variables, analyze the model, compute the solution, and check the results.
5. Planning and implementation.
6. You must know how to solve the problem manually. If you do not, then it cannot be solved with a computer. Time spent in adequately planning the solution saves much more time in the testing and debugging phase. It also provides a cleaner design of the problem solution for better understandability and maintainability.
7. You should first determine the requirements for proper output results. Then you determine the processing rules (logic) needed to manipulate the input items to achieve the desired output.
8. You must know what is expected from the program in order to proceed to the rest of the analysis and design work.
9. A print (or printer) layout chart.
10. To clearly illustrate the needed steps and their proper order. You can then step through the solution by hand to see if it will work, before writing the program. If it will not work when you desk check the logic by hand, then it certainly will not work on the computer.
11. A flowchart and pseudocode.
12. A flowchart is a graphic tool using symbols of predefined shapes to represent specific computer operations.
13. Differently-shaped symbols represent different computer operations.
14. Terminal (flattened oval), operation (rectangle), decision (diamond), input/output (parallelogram), flowlines (lines with arrowheads), logic connector (small circle), and annotation (a three-sided rectangle with a connecting dashed line).
15. With batched-card processing, you punch a source program on punched cards and may include the data on punched cards in the job deck. JCL (job control) cards must also be provided to indicate the computer resources required for the run. With timesharing, you provide the program in an interactive, conversational mode and give system commands to process the program.
16. Diagnostics.
17. You should use simple test data with which the results can be easily calculated by hand. You calculate the expected results and run the program with the test data. Then you compare the hand-calculated results with the computer output. If they differ, then you probably have a logic error in your program, which must be corrected before the correct results can be achieved.
18. Debugging is the process of locating and correcting logic errors.
19. After testing and debugging a program with simple test data, you use live data with the program.
20. For continuity in maintaining a program.
21. Internal documentation consists of comments contained within the program itself. It makes a program easier to read and follow. It is usually more current than external documentation.

22. A disciplined approach to software development.
23. The program works, uncomplicated design that provides readability and understandability, lower development costs, less testing time and lower testing costs, ease of modification, lower maintenance costs, and efficiency.
24. Lower programmer productivity from excessive program testing; unreliable software because of an unorganized approach to software design and development; software that is difficult to modify and maintain due to poor readability and understandability; errors in software interface due to poor human communications, interface between program units, and overall design.
25. The bottom-up approach starts with the details and works up to provide the overall program. The top-down approach starts with the overall (big) picture and works down into the details, thus avoiding many design and interface problems.
26. The communication (passing of data) between program units.
27. You begin with the big picture and divide a problem into functional components, usually with a program structure tool such as a structure chart. The main modules are expressed in abstract terms at the higher levels; then you decompose these higher-level modules into successive levels of detail until the problem details are identified.
28. It aids in the top-down decomposition of the problem and provides a graphic picture of the program structure.
29. Macro, semi-detailed, and detailed.
30. It is easier to debug and provide reliable code.
31. For flexibility in case program requirements change.
32. Structured programming is a style of programming using structured techniques. Structured coding is writing logic using the recognized control-flow structures.
33. SEQUENCE (in-line, top-down code), selection (IF-THEN and IF-THEN-ELSE decision making), iteration (DO-WHILE and REPEAT-UNTIL looping), and SELECT CASE (selection of actions from multiple alternatives).
34. An informal English prose for describing logic, using the restricted control-flow structures. It provides a more top-down, structured approach to logic design than do flowcharts.

CHAPTER 4

Answers to Review Questions

1. **FOR**mula **TRAN**slation or **FOR**mula **TRAN**slator.
2. 1957.
3. Input/Output, Arithmetic Assignment, and Logical and Control.
4. 47; 26 letters, 10 digits, and 11 special characters.
5. To identify the operation to be performed by the computer.
6. As the first word in each statement.
7. A known numeric value that represents a fixed quantity.
8. Integer and real.
9. A whole number, i.e., one without a fraction.
10. Floating-point.
11. 7.
12. A symbolic name that refers to the contents of a storage location.
13. 1 to 6 characters.
14. Alphabetic, alphabetic or numeric.
15. I through N.
16. A through H and O through Z.
17. An Explicit type statement, such as INTEGER or REAL.
18. Assign, replace, or store.
19. It is the most widely used statement because it assigns values to variables and calculations.
20. Constants and variables.
21. From highest to lower precedence: ** (exponentiation), * (multiplication) and / (division), and + (addition) and − (subtraction).
22. To override the order of precedence (hierarchy) of the arithmetic operators.
23. a. Two adjacent operators. b. Implied operations; no multiplication operator after the 5 and 7. c. Unbalanced (unmatched) parentheses. d. Missing value for the exponent after the raising-to-a-power operator.
24. The type and length of the items (constants and variables) used in the expression.
25. Integer and real.

26. variable = expression. Two examples are:

$$KOUNTR = 0$$
$$X = 2 + (R - 3) * Z$$

27. Store or Replace.
28. Only one.
29. True.
30. 1 through 5.
31. 1 to 99999.
32. True.
33. 6.
34. Blank or 0 (zero).
35. 7, 72.
36. 73 through 80.
37. C in column 1.
38. True.
39. O, I, Z, S, and B.
40. They may be included or omitted as you desire. They are normally included to improve readability.

Answers to Odd-numbered Exercises

1. a. integer
    b. real
    c. real
    d. real
    e. real
    f. real
    g. real
    h. integer
    i. integer
    j. real

3. a. exceeds six characters
    b. begins with a digit
    c. includes a special character (.)
    d. exceeds six characters
    e. includes a special character (*)
    f. includes a special character (−)

5. a. real
    b. integer
    c. real
    d. integer
    e. real
    f. real
    g. real
    h. integer
    i. real
    j. integer

7. a. includes a comma
    b. sign is at the end of the constant
    c. exceeds seven digits
    d. has two decimal points
    e. decimal point precedes the sign
    f. includes a special character

9. a. 17
    b. 3
    c. 8
    d. 48.4
    e. − 27.0

11. a. Valid
    b. Invalid; DISTAN = RATE * TIME
    c. Valid
    d. Valid
    e. Invalid; CSQD = A * A + B * B
    f. Invalid; GRSPAY = 210.75
    g. Invalid; C = A * (− B)
    h. Valid
    i. Valid
    j. Invalid; T = A * B / Z

13. a. First: (3.0 − C) because of the inner parentheses
    second: first operation * 7.5 because of the parentheses
    third: second operation + 8.3
    b. First: Y ** Z (exponentiation)
    second: 5.2 / first operation
    third: second operation * 2.0
    fourth: X + third operation
    fifth: fourth operation − 1.0
    c. First: (J ** K) because of the inner parentheses
    second: I ** first operation
    third: 3 * 7
    fourth: second operation − third operation

d. First: 4 * M
  second: first operation − 1 because of parentheses
  third: (6 + L) because of inner parentheses of second set of parentheses
  fourth: third operation / 10
  fifth: 8 + second operation
  sixth: fifth operation − fourth operation
e. First: (5 * J)
  second: (3 + L)
  third: first operation ** second operation
  fourth: 4 ** 2
  fifth: third operation + fourth operation

CHAPTER 5

Answers to Review Questions

1. A form identifying the program requirements and the necessary processing rules (logic) for achieving the proper output.
2. To serve as an example of how the printer output should appear and what it should contain.
3. To identify the input fields and their location on a punched card record.
4. Develop the algorithm (logic steps) to be followed in writing the computer program.
5. To provide remarks about the program and logic to make it easier for others to understand.
6. A description of what the program does, the author, the date written, the revision date if it is being revised, and description and function of the variables.
7. It aids in understanding the program for later maintenance or modifications.
8. It allows the programmer to override the predefined FORTRAN naming convention and to establish more meaningful symbolic names for variables.
9. INTEGER.
10. REAL.
11. READ.
12. WRITE.
13. FORMAT.
14. To describe the type and length of each data field.
15. To control the forward movement of the paper.
16. True.
17. False.
18. STOP.
19. True.
20. False.
21. True.
22. True.
23. False.
24. True.
25. Desk-checking (or bench-checking).
26. JCL (Job Control Language)—to specify the needed computer resources for the job; source program—to provide the computer program; data cards—to supply the data values for the program during execution.
27. False.
28. Batch processing is the submission of a program with JCL cards to the operating system. Batch processing may be performed with punched cards or as a job submitted from timesharing. Timesharing is an interactive mode of processing a program.
29. It is checked for syntax (construction) errors and is converted into machine language if there are none.
30. True.
31. Warnings and fatal errors.
32. True.
33. After the statement in error and at the end of the source program.
34. Pay attention to the diagnostics printed by the compiler and desk-check the statements for improper construction.
35. It is loaded into memory, and control is turned over to the control unit, which fetches the indicated instruction (pointed to by the instruction counter) and directs the other hardware units in the execution of the command.
36. Perform a hand calculation of the expected results and compare them with the computer output results.

37. Playing computer and desk-checking the program with some data.
38. Echo-checking the input data, playing computer and desk-checking the logic, and printing the values of specific variables for examination.
39. You do not have to worry about the complex format specifications, which are often a source of errors for beginning programmers.

Answers to Odd-numbered Exercises

1.
   a. READ (5,10) HOURS, RATE   comma missing
   b. 10 FORMAT (F5.2,3X,F4.1)   ending parenthesis missing
   c. GPAY = HOURS * RATE   x used for multiplication
   d. WRITE (6,33) HOURS,RATE,GPAY   unit 5 used for output, missing parenthesis

3.
   a. READ (5,99) X, Y   parentheses missing
   b. 20 FORMAT (2F5.2)   statement number missing
   c. WRITE (6,98) X,Y   unit 5 used for output
   d. XYZTOT = X + Y + Z   variable name too long
   e. 79 FORMAT (3X,F5.2,I2)   incomplete **F** format code specification
   f. STOP   invalid syntax for the STOP statement
   g. WRITE (6,97) A, B   erroneous comma

5. F5.2 with A, I3 with I, I1 with J, and F3.1 with B.

7. Error between format code I5 and the variable A.

9. F4.1 with A, F5.1 with B, F6.2 with C, and I3 with I.

CHAPTER 6

Answers to Review Questions

1. Branching, looping, decision-making, and program termination.
2. A normal ending of program execution.
3. To evaluate a condition and determine the operations, based on the true or false result of the condition.
4. To transfer control of execution to a new location in the program.
5. To repeat a series of statements a given number of times.
6. You test to see whether a certain condition is met.
7. To always branch (transfer control) to a specified statement label when the GO TO statement is reached in execution.
8. To perform a decision-making operation.
9.
   a. .EQ.—equal to   d. .LE.—less than or equal to
   b. .NE.—not equal to   e. .GT.—greater than
   c. .LT.—less than   f. .GE.—greater than or equal to
10. The next executable statement following the Logical IF.
11. .NOT., .AND., and .OR. are the three logical operators.
12. .AND.
13. .OR.
14. .NOT. is performed first, .AND. is performed second, and .OR. is performed last.
15. first: arithmetic operations; second: relational operations; and third: logical operations.
16. An unconditional branch is always taken; a conditional branch is taken only if the condition is true.
17. DO WHILE (test-at-the-top type loop) and REPEAT UNTIL (test-at-the-bottom type loop).
18. Input-bound loop (with a sentinel record), counter loop, and general condition loop techniques.
19. By encountering an end-of-file condition, which is indicated by reading a sentinel or end-of-file record on the file.
20. Initialization, testing, and modification (increment or decrement).
21. When an index variable reaches a specific value.
22. Header.
23. For general expressions that do not require a counter loop.
24. True.
25. Integer variable.
26. Data validation or editing.

Answers to Odd-numbered Exercises

1. GO TO 11

3. a. IF (C1 .GT. C2 .OR. C1 .GT. C3 .OR. C1 .GT. C4) GO TO 76
    b. IF (R .LE. SUM / 2.0) READ (5,99) R
    c. IF (ROOT .EQ. 0.0) STOP
    d. IF (A .EQ. 10.0 .AND. B .GT. 0.0) GO TO 41
    e. IF ((X .EQ. 0.0 .OR Y .EQ. 0.0) .AND. Z .NE. 0.0) KTR = KTR + 1

5. GO TO (32,47,15,53,27), M

7. a. GO TO (2,18,5,162), KNT   missing comma
    b. IF (J .LT. 2*M-3) GO TO 42   missing arithmetic operator
    c. IF (SUM .LT. 10.0) GO TO 13   three-way branch not allowed
       IF (SUM .EQ. 10.0) GO TO 14
       IF (SUM .GT. 10.0) GO TO 15
    d. GO TO (3,1,16), ICODE   real variable used
    e. IF (A .EQ. B) C = A   invalid relational operator
    f. GO TO 19999   statement number exceeds five digits
    g. IF (N.EQ.1 .AND. L.GT.5) STOP   invalid logical operator

---

CHAPTER 7

Answers to Review Questions

1. A rule for calculating a value from some given value or values called arguments.
2. A function supplied with the FORTRAN compiler.
3. SQRT.
4. A value(s) supplied to a function, from which a resulting value is calculated or produced.
5. By giving its name in an arithmetic expression.
6. Each function requires its argument(s) to be a specific type, such as integer or real.
7. To know what type of variable to assign the resulting value to.
8. Only one.
9. FIX.
10. SIN.
11. Radians.
12. Warnings will still allow a program to go into execution. Fatal errors prevent a program from being executed.
13. The invalid construction or forming of a statement.
14. See section 7.3 for a list of possible causes of syntax errors.
15. See section 7.3 for the list of the seven steps.
16. Logic errors and system-fault errors.
17. Desk-checking or bench-checking.
18. Echo-check.
19. To determine where a bad calculation is being made.
20. Checkpoint.
21. Features in a language provided by a vendor to aid in debugging.
22. Divide by zero, overflow, underflow, and invalid subscript reference.
23. Invalid input specification, not initializing a variable, performing an incorrect calculation, using the wrong variable name, improper sequence of statements, missing statements, and others.
24. Truncation of values by the computer because of storage size limitations. Also, the inability of the computer to represent specific decimal fractions in an internal binary representation.
25. For better readability and understandability.
26. Desk-check the program, echo-check the input data, print intermediate values from calculations, include checkpoint messages, use debug facilities, rewrite a segment of code, and use various control card options to provide extra information about the program and its variables.

Answers to Odd-numbered Exercises

1. a. SINEX = SIN(X)   incorrect function name
    b. SQRX = SQRT (X)   incorrect function name
    c. REAL ISQD, ICUBE   missing comma
    d. XLOG2 = ALOG(X)   incorrect statement syntax
    e. KOUNT = KOUNT + 1   changing type of variable
    f. READ (5, 199) X, Y, Z   invalid input unit (6)

3. a. Divide by zero.
    b. Taking the square root of an integer argument.
    c. System round-off error and later use of the variable with an .EQ. relational operator.

CHAPTER 8

Answers to Review Questions

1. To transmit input data from an external medium to memory, and to transmit data from memory to an output medium.
2. Record.
3. Field.
4. File.
5. READ.
6. WRITE.
7. To specify the form, length, and location of data values to be read or written.
8. Integer (I).
9. Real or floating-point (F).
10. Blank (X).
11. Width.
12. To output data records to the line printer (and terminal, on some systems).
13. True.
14. False. They are never executed.
15. True.
16. False.
17. True.
18. True.
19. True.
20. No.
21. False. They are treated as zeroes.
22. Asterisks (*).
23. Blanks.
24. True.
25. True.
26. True.
27. False. They are right-justified.
28. Five.
29. Location of the field, type of data, size or width of the field, and location of the decimal point.
30. As the first format specification code.
31. Same record.
32. New or next record.

Answers to Odd-numbered Exercises

1. READ (5,95)J,K,L
    95 FORMAT (I3,2X,I3,1X,I3)

3. WRITE (6,89)J,K,L
    89 FORMAT (1H0,2X,I3,4X,I3,2X,I3)

5. I2
    I4
    I3
    F6.2
    F6.3
    F6.2
    F6.0

7. −567
    ****
    ƀƀƀƀ0
    ƀ21
    .00
    0.0
    ƀƀ49.93
    ƀƀ−49.9
    ƀƀƀƀ50.
    ****
    ƀ49.9250
    0.6347
    .635
    ƀ0.6
    ƀ1.
    −0.6347
    ƀ−0.6347
    −.6347
    ƀ−0.634700

9. a. 11
    b. 7

11. Four

CHAPTER 9

Answers to Review Questions

1. A character string preceded by the Hollerith (H) format code, which is preceded by an integer constant specifying the number of characters in the string.
2. Report titles, page and column headings, and identifying literals in the data output.
3. False
4. A syntax error occurs
5. False
6. To shorten the format specifications
7. Parentheses
8. Two
9. True
10. Printer layout form
11. False
12. True
13. True
14. False. The excess leftmost characters are lost.
15. True
16. To initialize variables/array elements at compile time.
17. At the beginning of a program prior to any executable statements. A DATA statement must follow an Explicit Type statement or DIMENSION statement if any of the same names are given in both statements.
18. Slashes (/).
19. The value following the variable name; all variables and then all values; any combination of these two methods.
20. A set of actions taken when a change in value occurs for a designated control field.
21. Test for a control break, save the values of the control field in a hold variable, and read a new record.
22. A line containing accumulated totals, which is printed when a control break occurs.
23. There is not another record to cause a control break. Thus, the last control break must be automatically taken, i.e., forced.
24. The summary of the overall total for all control breaks.

25. To position (tab) at a specific column.
26. To enclose literal constants instead of using the H (Hollerith) format code.
27. To declare variables and arrays to be of character type.

Answers to Odd-numbered Exercises

1. a. **WRITE (6,99)**
      99 FORMAT (1H1,49X,27HSTUDENT REGISTRATION ROSTER)
   b. **WRITE (6,98)**
      98 FORMAT (1H0,15HEMPLOYEE NUMBER,4X,5HHOURS,3X,4HRATE)
   c. **WRITE (6,97) X, XSQD**
      97 FORMAT (1H ,4HX = ,2X,F4.1,4X,8HX−SQD = ,2X,F5.1)

3. a. **37 FORMAT (2I2,2(3X,I3))**
   b. **86 FORMAT (3(F6.2,I3))**
   c. **97 FORMAT (5X,2I6,2(F5.2,2X))**
   d. **94 FORMAT (2(I4,2(I3,2X),5X))**
   e. **89 FORMAT (1H0,3(I3,3X),F8.2)**

5. a. **(4A4,A1)**
   b. **(A2)**
   c. **(2A3) or (A4,A2)**
   d. **(3A4,A2)**
   e. **(4A4,A2)**

7. **DATA A,X,M / 3.75,8.6,12 /**
   or
   DATA A / 3.75 /,X / 8.6 / ,M / 12 /

9. **CHARACTER * 22 CITY or CHARACTER CITY * 22**

CHAPTER 10

Answers to Review Questions

1. To execute a series of statements one or more times.
2. Initialization—to supply an initial value to the index variable. Increment—to supply the increment value to the index variable each time through the loop. Test—to supply the test value against which the index variable is tested at the end of each loop.
3. One
4. When the loop is executed the specified number of times, or if a control statement causes a branch out of the loop.
5. Provides greater flexibility.
6. It is a rectangle divided into three areas to show the indexing parameters used.
7. True
8. When a transfer is made out of the loop prematurely. If the loop is completed the specified number of times, the index variable is undefined.
9. CONTINUE
10. Loops contained within another loop

Answers to Odd-numbered Exercises

1. **DO 56 II = 5,500,5**

3. a. 8; 1 through 8
   b. 2;2 and 5
   c. 3; 4, 6, and 8

5. a. 12
   b. 6

7. a. **DO 20 K = 1,N,1**   Illegal test variable
   b. **DO 30 I = 1, 10, 1**   Extra comma
   c. **DO 40 ICOUNT = 1,L**   Variable too long
   d. **DO 50 J = 1,N,K**   Invalid increment parameter
   e. **DO 60 M = 1,20, 1**   Invalid increment parameter

CHAPTER 11

Answers to Review Questions

1. A collection of related items stored in adjacent storage locations under a common name.
2. Provides a flexible and powerful tool, which makes long, unwieldy problems feasible and easy to solve.
3. DIMENSION (Explicit Type statements may also be used.)
4. Like any other symbolic name, i.e., 1 to 6 characters; the first must be an alphabetic letter.
5. True
6. False. They must be constants.
7. False
8. Subscript
9. True
10. False
11. Subscripted variable, array name, or implied DO loop
12. False
13. True
14. True
15. False
16. Searching
17. Sorting
18. It is given in a DIMENSION statement.
19. Yes
20. Provides a powerful means of indexing one's way through an array.
21. Prior to the executable statements
22. Include a WRITE statement in a loop to display the specified items.

Answers to Odd-numbered Exercises

1. a. **DIMENSION GROUP (12)**
   b. **DIMENSION LISTX (40)**
   c. **DIMENSION LISTA (60), LISTB (50)**

3. a. **DIMENSION A(10),B(10)** Omitted comma
   b. **READ (5,99) (LIST(I),I = 1,10)** Invalid subscript/index variable
   c. **READ (5,98) (A(I),I=1,7),(B(I),I=1,5)** Missing comma
   d. **WRITE (6,97) (GROUP(J),J=1,8)** Missing parenthesis
   e. **WRITE (6,96)(HOLD(2*N),N=1,K,2)** Missing comma

5. a. **READ (5,99) (ARRAY (I),I=1,11)**
       99 FORMAT (11F5.2)

   b. **WRITE (6,98) (ARRAY(I),I=1,10)**
       98 FORMAT (1H0,10F7.2)

7. a. 5
   b. 1

   c. 7

9. a. **DO 10 I=1,50**
         A(I)=0.0
      10   CONTINUE

   b. **ISUM=0**
      DO 10 I = 1,16,2
         ISUM = ISUM + L16(I)
      10   CONTINUE

   c. **XHLD = X20(1)**
      DO 10 I = 2,20
         X20(I − 1) = X20(I)
      10   CONTINUE
      X20(20) = XHLD

CHAPTER 12

Answers to Review Questions

1. To provide a more convenient means of handling multiple groups of related items, i.e., a matrixlike arrangement.
2. With two subscripts that provide the row-column coordinates. The first one refers to the desired row element, while the second subscript refers to the desired column element.
3. By specifying two levels of dimension in the DIMENSION statement.
4. By multiplying the size of each dimension specification by the other.
5. True
6. True
7. When an additional level of dimension is added to a matrix arrangement of related data.

Answers to Odd-numbered Exercises

1. a. **DIMENSION MATRIX (7,5)**   c. **DIMENSION CLASS (6,4,4)**
   b. **DIMENSION TABLE (20,11)**

3. a. 6   b. 10

5. a.   **READ (5,99)((X(I,J),J = 1,10),I = 1,6)**   b.   **WRITE (6,98)((X(I,J),J = 1,8),I = 1,6)**
   99 FORMAT (10F6.2)   **98 FORMAT (1H0,8F10.2)**

7. a.   **DO 20 I = 1,9**   c.   **DO 20 J = 1,7**
   DO 10 J = 1,30   **DO 10 I = 1,50**
   K(I,J) = 1   **IF (D(I,J) .EQ. 76.5) GOTO 77**
   10   CONTINUE   **10   CONTINUE**
   20   CONTINUE   **20   CONTINUE**
   b.   **NNSUM = 0**
   DO 20 I = 1,5,2
   DO 10 J = 1,10
   NNSUM = NNSUM + NN(I,J)
   10   CONTINUE
   20   CONTINUE

CHAPTER 13

Answers to Review Questions

1. Reduction in amount of required work, incorporation of modular programming technique, ease in debugging, simplification in the division of work, reduction in memory required, use of library subprograms that are tested and debugged.
2. By the SUBROUTINE statement
3. a. Subprogram (SUBROUTINE or FUNCTION) statement
   b. At least one executable statement
   c. RETURN
   d. END
4. RETURN
5. By using its name in the CALL statement
6. Arguments in a parameter list
7. The next executable statement after the CALL
8. There is no minimum. No arguments need be passed.
9. Number, order, type, and length
10. A predefined operation symbol; a rectangle with striped lines down the two sides.

Answers to Odd-numbered Exercises

1. a. Unequal number of arguments in the two parameter lists.
   b. The first argument in the CALL statements does not agree in type with the first argument in the SUBROUTINE statement.
   c. The name of the subroutine in the CALL is not the same name in the SUBROUTINE statement.

3. a. **SUBROUTINE PAGE**
   b. **SUBROUTINE PAGELN (LINCNT)**

5. a. **CALL SUBRTN**
   b. **CALL SUB1 (LINCNT)**

7. a. 3
   b. 9
   c. 27

CHAPTER 14

Answers to Review Questions

1. To identify the major functions of a program in a top-down, hierarchical manner. This aids in developing a program that is more reliable and easy to maintain.
2. They are costly, in terms of both money and time.
3. If you don't understand what is required, then you cannot design it correctly.
4. By dividing it into smaller pieces that can be comprehended.
5. Dividing a problem into its major functions.
6. You begin by expressing the major functions in general abstract terms and working down into the details. At each level of decomposition you refine the problem into more details.
7. A module performs the actions for a specific function.
8. A problem can be broken down into manageable pieces, aids in debugging errors, aids in program maintenance and enhancements, and may save time by using existing modules.
9. It is a graphic tool to illustrate the functional modules and their decomposition into lower level modules from a top-down view.
10. It provides better guidance in developing the detail logic from a top-down, modular view. It provides a pictorial view of the identified functional modules.
11. A rectangle.
12. False. It is intended to show program structure.
13. By a hierarchical line.
14. Postponing dealing with details as long as possible, i.e., until they can no longer be avoided.
15. Refining a module into lower levels of detail by proceeding down a hierarchical path.
16. Hierarchy Input Processing and Output.
17. Visual table of contents (VTOC), overview diagrams, and detail diagrams.
18. VTOC.
19. Same as a structure chart; to show the functional modules of a program in a top-down manner.
20. Input, processing, and output.
21. Initial design package, detail design package, and maintenance package.
22. Identify the user's requirements, create a VTOC, create the overview diagrams for the first level of modules, and create the detail diagrams for the lower-level functions.
23. A measure of the relationship of the elements or instructions within a module.
24. Functional.
25. A measure of the relationships that exist between modules.
26. Minimizing module coupling by restricting the communication of data items or relationship among modules.
27. High dependence of communication among modules.

28. To fit on one printer page, since that is about the maximum amount of detail logic you can keep in mind and concentrate on at a given time.

29. Subroutines provide a modular programming approach that corresponds to a top-down program structure design.

30. A stand-in statement for the logic in a module. For example, displaying a message that the module was entered for execution.

31. A small programming team headed by a senior programmer and consisting of needed programming specialists for a project.

32. A back-up senior programmer, a program librarian, several other programmers with specialized experience, such as a specific programming language, data base, job control language, and so on.

33. An informal, systematic, technical examination of a programmer's design, logic, or procedures by his or her peers, to identify any errors.

34. Two to five fellow programmers are selected and notified several days prior to a review meeting. They are given a copy of the design or source code to examine for errors. A one-to-two hour meeting is held to review the logic and see if any errors are found. No attempt is made to correct the errors. The programmer responds to the noted errors later, in writing which points out the corrections to the noted errors.

35. Serves as a central repository of all data relevant to a project, in both human-readable and machine-readable form. Assigns the administrative duties of software development to a program librarian.

36. Depicts the flow of data and the sequence of events (operations) that occur within the system to process the data.

Answers to Odd-numbered Exercises

1. Calculate Table of Interest

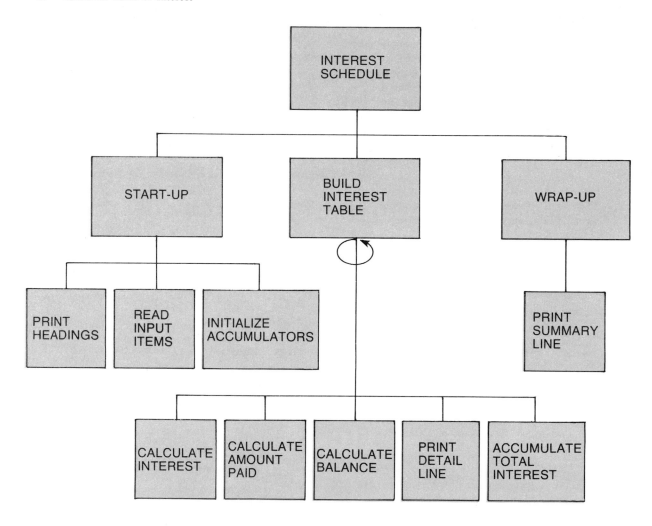

3. Produce Gross Pay Report

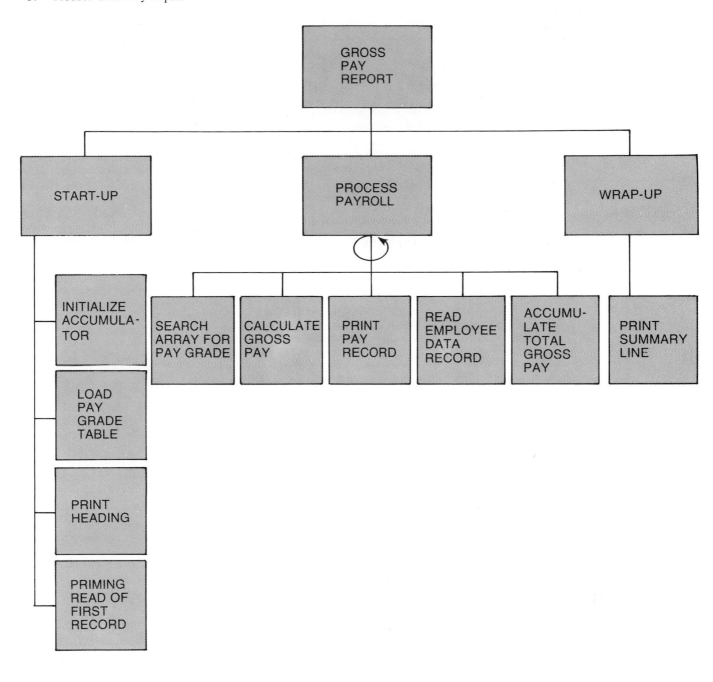

CHAPTER 15

Answers to Review Questions

1. When a single calculated value is needed.
2. By the FUNCTION statement.
3. By using its name in an arithmetic expression, such as in an Assignment or IF statement.
4. One.
5. One.
6. Via the function subprogram name.
7. The type of the function subprogram name.
8. By the Assignment statement.

9. Back to the same statement that invoked the function subprogram.
10. Number, order, type, and length.
11. To perform complex calculations that are repeated many times in a program.
12. Yes, at least one.
13. A statement function is a single Arithmetic-Assignment-like statement belonging to the program in which it appears. A Function subprogram is a separate program unit.
14. After the specification statements and before the first executable statement.
15. By using its name in an arithmetic expression, i.e., the same as a function subprogram.
16. Back to the same statement that invoked the statement function.
17. To identify subprogram names passed as arguments in a parameter list.
18. To provide the dimension specifications of an array at execution time.
19. To provide multiple variables that identify the same storage location.
20. To assign variables and arrays to a common block of memory to be shared among program units.
21. Blank (unlabeled or unnamed) and Labeled (named) Common.
22. To initialize variables and array elements in Labeled Common areas at compilation.
23. No.

Answers to Odd-numbered Exercises

1. a. FUNCTION FUN1(A, I, P)
    b. FUNCTION FY(Y)
    c. FUNCTION CALC (X, Z, TOTAL))

3. a. Function name used both as a variable and a function subprogram name.
    b. Arguments not enclosed in parentheses.
    c. No arguments given.

5. a. 25.0
    b. 5.0
    c. 12.2

7. a. Subroutine   c. Function
    b. Function   d. Subroutine

9. a. 5   c. 42
    b. 14   d. 101

11. BLOCK DATA
    COMMON /GROUP1/ A, X, J
    DATA A/5.3/, X/8.7/, J/3/
    END

CHAPTER 16

Answers to Review Questions

1. Numeric fields represented in exponential form
2. Integer or real constant followed by an exponential value. The exponential value consists of the letter E followed by a one- or two-digit integer constant representing a power of ten. A minus sign may precede the constant when needed to represent a negative power of ten. A plus sign to represent a positive exponent is optional.
3. A total fractional number consisting of the number of digits, as given in the precision portion of the format code, followed by the letter E, followed by a space for a positive exponent or a minus sign for a negative exponent, and ending with a two-digit integer constant for the exponent value.
4. By the constant having more than 7 digits, or by using the letter D in the exponential portion of the constant.
5. DOUBLE PRECISION
6. Double precision numeric values expressed in exponential form
7. .TRUE. and .FALSE.
8. LOGICAL
9. L
10. Real and imaginary

11. Two real constants separated by a comma and enclosed in parentheses.
12. COMPLEX
13. F, D, or E, but two format codes must always be used for each complex variable.
14. Numeric fields expressed in decimal (F) or exponential (E) form.
15. True
16. To override and move the position of the decimal point in the data.
17. The letter P preceding the format code and a positive or negative integer constant preceding the letter P to specify which way to move the decimal point.

Answers to Odd-numbered Exercises

1. a. E6.1
   b. E6.0
   c. E7.2
   d. E3.0

3. a. ƀ0.123Eƀ02
   b. −0.12345Eƀ02
   c. ƀƀ0.123450Eƀ03
   d. ƀƀƀ0.12346Eƀ03
   e. ƀƀ−0.12346Eƀ02
   f. ƀ−0.1200E−02

5. a. .TRUE.
   b. .TRUE.
   c. .TRUE.
   d. .TRUE.
   e. .FALSE.

7. a. ƀƀ99.ƀƀƀƀ
   b. ƀ0.10ƀƀƀƀ
   c. ƀ0.146E−07
   d. ƀ−57.4ƀƀƀƀ

9. a. 2PF4.2
   b. −1PF6.5
   c. 3PF5.1
   d. −6PF2.0

CHAPTER 17

Answers to Review Questions

1. Compact storage of large volumes of data, economic storage, and fast I/O speeds.
2. 2400
3. File or data wheel
4. Read/write head
5. Load-point marker (or BOT marker)
6. True
7. True
8. End-of-file or tape mark
9. Block
10. Interblock gap.
11. True
12. False
13. True
14. True
15. REWIND
16. ENDFILE
17. BACKSPACE
18. False
19. Master file
20. Transaction file
21. File Maintenance (or File Update)
22. True
23. Add, delete, and change

Answers to Odd-numbered Exercises

1. a. **READ (11,98)X,Y,Z**
   b. **READ (11)X,Y,Z**

3. a. **WRITE (11,96)M,N,O**
   b. **WRITE (11)M,N,O**

5. a. **REWIND 12**
   b. **ENDFILE NTAPE**
   c. **BACKSPACE 3**

CHAPTER 18

Answers to Review Questions

1. To provide on-line storage and direct access to a particular record.
2. False
3. Cylinder
4. True
5. REWIND
6. DEFINE FILE
7. True
8. False
9. FIND

Answers to Odd-numbered Exercises

1. **DEFINE FILE 3 (175,110,E,KPTR)**
3. **READ (10 ′ 26)X,Y,Z**
5. **WRITE (9 ′ N,99)I,J,K,L**
7. **FIND (2 ′ K)**
9. 4
11. 3

CHAPTER 19

Answers to Review Questions

1. False.
2. Statement number.
3. True.
4. True.
5. One can define the formats of input/output values at execution time.
6. False.
7. True.
8. Slashes (/).
9. Ampersand (&).
10. True.
11. False.
12. True.
13. To type (as to mode) all variables according to a beginning letter or range of letters.
14. Failure to remember that a beginning letter has been used to declare a type for variables or arrays.

Answers to Odd-numbered Exercises

1.   a. Invalid syntax following the keyword PAUSE; an octal constant must be used.
     b. Word "FOR" should be "TO."
     c. Omitted integer variable and comma after the keyword GO TO.
     d. Missing NAMELIST name within slashes.
     e. Arithmetic operator should be used instead of a relational operator.
     f. Missing parentheses around the variable KNT.
     g. Integer values required.

3.   a. 56
     b. 17

5.   a. IF (3.5 * A + C) 10, 20, 30
     b. IF (N / 2 * 2 − N) 12, 33, 12
     c. IF (SUM) 46, 46, 18

7.   &LIST2 A = 31.8, K = 17, L = 43 &END

Glossary

abnormal termination A program termination caused by a system-fault error, such as a divide by zero or overflow. Contrasted with normal termination.

abort The abnormal termination of a program from a system-fault error or operator intervention.

acronym The use of the first letter or letters of words to form a name. For example, **FORTRAN** is an acronym for **FOR**mula **TRAN**slation. **COBOL** is an acronym for **CO**mmon **B**usiness **O**riented **L**anguage. **CPU** is an acronym for **C**entral **P**rocessing **U**nit.

actual argument A value passed in the parameter list of the statement invoking (calling) a subprogram.

address A location in computer storage. Also referred to as a memory address or disk address.

algorithm The precise steps to be followed in the solution to a problem; a complete, unambiguous procedure for solving a problem in a finite number of steps.

alphabetic Consisting of the letters from an alphabet.

alphameric Contraction for alphanumeric.

alphanumeric The characteristic of data that includes letters, digits, and special characters.

alphanumeric data See character data.

ALU See Arithmetic-Logic Unit.

analysis The study of an activity, procedure, technique, or problem to determine what must be accomplished and how the necessary operations may best be done.

analyst A person skilled in the analysis and design activities of program development.

AND A logical connector that implies that if both elements are true, then the condition is true; if one or both elements are false, then the condition is false.

application A functional area of work to which data processing is applied. May be categorized as business, scientific, or humanities applications. Specific business applications include payroll, inventory control, and so forth.

application program A computer program that solves a problem for a specific application area.

argument An item (constant, variable, or other) used in the calculation of another value.

argument list See parameter list.

arithmetic expression An expression consisting of a single constant or variable, or an expression consisting of any combination of variables and constants, joined by one or more arithmetic operators in such a way that the expression as a whole may be reduced to a single numeric value.

arithmetic-logic unit The part of the central processing unit that performs the arithmetic and logical operations of a computer system.

arithmetic operation The functions of addition, subtraction, multiplication, and division. A mathematical manipulation of constants and variables as given in a specified formula.

arithmetic operator A symbol or character used to denote an arithmetic operation. For example, an asterisk (*) is often used to denote multiplication; a slash (/) is often used to denote division.

array A set of arranged quantities, called elements, having a like characteristic. A list or table of related values. A set of related items.

array declaration A program statement used to identify an array and its dimension specifications.

array element A value in an array identified by its position number.

ASCII American Standard Code for Information Interchange. A coding scheme for representing 128 characters. It is used primarily with timesharing and data communication applications.

assignment statement A statement/instruction used to assign a value to a storage location or to perform calculations and to assign the resulting value to a storage location. A statement used to assign the value of an arithmetic expression to a storage location.

associated variable A variable used to indicate the relative record number to be read/written in a random organized (direct-access) file.

BASIC Acronym for Beginners' All-purpose Symbolic Instruction Code. An algebraic programming language developed at Dartmouth College primarily for a timesharing environment.

batch A collection of data items or records processed during a single computer run.

batch processing The control technique of grouping similar input items for processing during the same machine run. The processing of a stream or batch of tasks, in a general sequential manner, by an operating system that has been initiated by the commands from a timesharing system or control commands on punched cards.

baud The bit rate per second of data transmission.

bench checking See desk checking.

binary The feature of having two distinct states, such as on and off.

binary digit One of the digits zero (0) or one (1). A digit in the binary number base.

binary record A record written in a binary format without format control.

binary search A search routine that reduces the time to locate serial ordered data by continually dividing in half the area in which the data item is located.

bit A contraction of **binary digit**. A single digit in a binary number. A unit of information capacity of a storage device.

blank A space equivalent in length to a character, in which nothing is stored or printed.

blank COMMON A shared area in memory between program units. Blank COMMON does not have a name, and only one blank COMMON area is permitted. Contrasted with labeled (named) COMMON.

block One or more logical records read or written as a physical unit. A group of data treated as a unit.

blocking The technique of combining more than one logical record into a block of data.

blocking factor The number of logical records stored together in a block.

BPI Abbreviation for bits per inch. The measurement of recording density.

branch To jump or transfer control to a designated instruction.

buffer A temporary storage device or circuitry that retains data for transmission between two equipment units. An area in memory used to hold input and output records.

bug A program error; a mistake in a routine. A machine malfunction.

built-in function An intrinsic (function) supplied with a FORTRAN compiler and available for execution by giving its name (and necessary arguments) in an arithmetic expression.

business application A non-scientific use of equipment for processing data, characterized by high volumes of input and output and small amounts of calculations.

byte A unit of data that represents a letter, one or two digits, or a special character. A sequence of bits handled as a unit and usually shorter than a word. A measurable portion of consecutive binary digits, e.g., a 6-bit or 8-bit byte.

call The communication from a program unit to a subroutine to begin its execution.

calling program The program unit invoking (calling) a subprogram.

card See Hollerith card.

card code The combination of punched holes in cards to represent letters, digits, or special characters.

card column A vertical arrangement of holes on a punched card. A card column contains a combination of punched holes representing one character.

card file A data file stored on punched cards.

card image An exact duplication of all the data contained in a punched card.

card punch An output device to record data into punched cards by punching holes to represent the data characters.

card reader An input device to accept data recorded in punched cards and to transfer it to memory.

card row A horizontal arrangement of holes across a punched card.

carriage control specification A character used in the first position of a print record to determine the forward movement of the paper. On many timesharing systems, it is also used to control the line movement on the screen of a CRT terminal.

carriage return The operation (depressing a key or the encoding of a special character) that causes a return to the first position of the next line.

cell A storage location. An element in an array.

central processing unit The collection of hardware units in a computer system that directs the other units and performs the arithmetic-logic operations.

channel A hardware unit that speeds the transfer of data to the CPU from a device by buffering the data into groups. See multiplex channel and selector channel.

character The basic component of a data item; may be a letter, digit, or special character.

character code An ordered pattern of bits assigned to a coding scheme to represent characters. See ASCII, BCD, and EBCDIC.

character data Data read/written as a string of characters. The characters may be letters, digits, and/or special characters.

character set The characters that can be represented by a particular code. The set of characters used in a programming language.

checkout The process of testing programs or equipment.

COBOL Acronym for Common Business Oriented Language. A high-level, procedure-oriented language used primarily for business applications.

code To write instructions for a computer program; to program. A combination of punched holes or bits to represent data.

coding Writing a program. The list of instructions for a program or routine.

coding form A specially designed form used to code statements for a source program in a specific language.

collating sequence The sequence (order) of characters in a coding scheme according to the internal binary representation. Collating sequence of characters is important in character data comparison.

column A position of a character, such as in a punched card, printed line, or line on a CRT. A vertical arrangement of punched holes on a card. The vertical vector designator of a two-dimensional array.

column heading One or more lines of heading above each output field to identify the field of output.

comment Remarks that help identify or explain a particular statement, routine, or program's purpose and logic.

comment card A card/statement in a source program used to include remarks.

compilation The process of translating a high-level source program written in a compiler language into machine language.

compile See compilation.

compile time initialization The initialization of variables, and array items during the compilation of a program.

compiler A language translator used to convert a high-level source program into machine language. Multiple machine commands are normally generated for each source statement.

component A part of the whole; a portion of a process. A basic part. An element.

computer A collection of integrated units of equipment capable of accepting data, processing such data, and communicating the results of such processing. A device capable of solving problems by using programs stored in memory.

computer operator One who manually controls the operations of the computer, mounts and unmounts tapes and disk packs, and services the peripheral equipment, such as the card reader and line printer(s).

computer problem-solving steps The procedure (organized steps) for accomplishing a problem solution with the computer.

concatenate to link data together, primarily alphanumeric string data.

condition An expression used to determine a true or false result.

conditional transfer A jump to a designated instruction when a specified condition is met. Also referred to as a conditional jump or branch.

connector A symbol used to indicate the joining of two points on a flowchart.

console The portion of a computer used for communication between the computer system operator and the CPU.

constant A never-changing value. A fixed, nonvarying value. May be numeric, logical, alphanumeric string, or other type.

control break The comparison of control fields between the current record and the previous record to determine whether a change in value occurs. Various actions, such as printing summary total lines, page ejection, and so forth are taken when a control break occurs.

control break field A field selected for use in control break logic.

control card A JCL card to specify the required computer resources for a job. A punched card containing input data or parameters to provide processing information and control.

control character A character that starts, modifies, and stops an operation, such as displaying or transferring data.

control-flow structure A structured, top-down flow of logic for a specific type of operation, such as sequence, decision-making, or looping.

control statement An instruction used to control the flow of execution in a program.

control unit The unit and circuitry that directs the operations of a computer system. This includes the sequencing of operations, interpretation of instructions, and initiation of execution of instructions.

core A general reference to internal storage or computer memory. Derived from magnetic core, which was used for memory on second- and third-generation computers.

counter A variable used to count a number of occurrences.

counter loop A program loop controlled by a counter.

CPU See central processing unit.

CRT See cathode ray tube.

CRT terminal A terminal device with a video screen for the display of user-entered commands, statements and data, and the display of computer responses.

cursor A symbol (usually a white or green rectangle) displayed on a CRT terminal to indicate the current typing position of a line.

DASD See direct access storage device.

data The collection of values in their raw state (facts); a collection of characters with no readily discernible meaning. A general term used to denote any or all facts, numbers, letters, symbols, and other items that can be processed by the computer. The plural of datum, but in common usage data is often referred to as singular.

data processing The function of creating, manipulating, and reporting data.

debug To identify program errors and their causes with a view to their elimination. To locate and correct any errors in a computer program.

debugging The process of locating and correcting errors in a program.

decision-making The process of evaluating variables and data items to determine alternative operations (logic).

decision symbol A diamond-shaped symbol used in a flowchart to indicate alternative paths of execution based on an evaluated condition. A flowchart symbol whose interior contains the criterion for the decision.

decision table A table divided into four areas that represent the conditions, conditional entries, actions, and action entries upon which decisions and their related actions are based.

delete To remove or eliminate, e.g., to remove a character in a line, to remove a line in a program, or to remove a record from a master file.

desk checking The manual review of a program (or algorithm expressed in a design tool) for syntax and logic errors.

detail flowchart A flowchart reflecting the logic of an algorithm at the lowest practical level of explanation.

detail print line One printer output line of information from a data record.

detail printing See detail print line.

diagnostic A warning or error message from a compilation to denote a mistake in the construction of a statement.

dialect A computer vendor's version of a programming language.

digit One of the possible symbols in a number base.

dimension The declaration of the number of quantities in an array. A level of orientation for arrays.

dimension specification The declaration of the number of dimension levels and the range of elements within each dimension.

direct access The retrieval or storage of data by reference to its specific location on a storage device.

direct-access file A random organized file on a direct-access storage medium, by which records can be read/written directly.

direct-access storage device The units of computer hardware, such as magnetic disk and drum, that permit random (direct) access to a data record.

DO WHILE control structure A restricted control-flow structure for looping, which incorporates a test-at-the-top type loop.

DO WHILE loop A program loop using a DO WHILE control structure.

documentation The collection of information regarding a program development, organized to serve as an aid in understanding the program and/or its use.

documentation package The complete set of documentation for the solution to a problem.

double-precision mode The use of double-precision constants, variables, and so forth in the calculation and manipulation of values.

double-precision number A number using twice as many digits as are normal to represent a quantity.

double-precision variable A variable to which a double-precision value may be assigned.

dummy argument The argument in a parameter of a subprogram.

dump To print the contents of memory or a file. See memory dump and file dump.

EBCDIC Extended Binary Coded Decimal Interchange Code. An eight-bit coding scheme for representing characters.

echo check The printing of input items as a verification of correctly reading these values.

edit A test for the validity checking of input fields. To rearrange or modify data. The insertion of special symbols prior to printing.

element One of the quantities in an array of elements that all have the same characteristics. A component part.

end-of-file A condition that exists when all data records within the file have been read.

end-of-file record A record (normally recorded by the system) identifying the physical end of a file.

endless loop A loop with no exit. A "never ending" execution of a loop. Contrasted with a finite loop.

entry point Any location in a program unit to which control can be passed by another program unit.

error The deviation from a theoretically correct value or logic.

error checking See validity checking.

error message A message displayed from the compilation or execution of a program to denote an illegal syntax or operation.

executable statement A statement in a programming language that causes the execution of some operation. Contrasted with nonexecutable (specification) statement.

execute To interpret a machine instruction and to perform the indicated operation. To carry out a command.

execution The action(s) performed within a computer system to accomplish an instruction (or program).

execution time The time required to decode and perform an instruction. The time required to process a program.

exponent A number written to the upper right of a value, to indicate how many times the value is to be multiplied by itself.

expression A constant, variable, or arithmetic computation involving one or more variables and constants.

external storage The storage housed outside of the CPU, requiring a mechanical operation for the reading and writing of data. Magnetic tape and disk units are examples of external storage devices.

field A logical collection of one or more related characters to represent one item of data.

field length The number of positions or characters used to represent a data item.

file A logical collection of data records pertaining to the same application.

file dump The printing of a file to validate its contents or other use.

file maintenance The process of updating a master file to reflect changes since the last processing cycle.

file organization The organization technique used to store and access records in a file, such as sequential or random.

file update See file maintenance.

fixed record layout The formatting of a data record in which all data fields occupy the same record positions. That is, each field is the same type and length in all records of a file.

flag A variable used to indicate a special condition or status. An indicator used in a later part of the program execution for determining whether some condition has occurred.

floating point An internal form of number representation, in which quantities are represented by one number multiplied by a power of the number base. For example, the number 123.4 might be represented as $.1234 \times 10^3$.

floating-point number A numeric quantity that may have fractional digits. A real number. Contrasted with an integer number.

flow The sequence of events or execution.

flow line A line used to connect flowchart symbols to show the flow of control.

flowchart A graphic presentation of the algorithm for a problem solution using special-shaped symbols to denote specific actions. A pictorial representation of the sequence of operations to be performed by the computer.

flowcharting symbol A graphic symbol used to identify a specific operation to be performed by the computer. For example, a diamond represents a decision.

form A specially designed document used to record data.

format A specific arrangement of data. A predetermined arrangement of the types of characters of which a data item is composed.

format code A format specification designating the type and length of an input or output data field.

format specification The designation of input/output fields' form (type and length) and other special characters used for specifying information about the reading/writing of data items and records.

FORTRAN Acronym for **FOR**mula **TRAN**slation. A high-level, procedure-oriented language used primarily for scientific applications.

FORTRAN program A source program written in FORTRAN.

function reference The identification of a function program name in an arithmetic expression, in order to execute it.

function subprogram A subprogram that returns a single value through its name.

function value The value returned by a function subprogram.

functional decomposition The process of dividing a problem/program into functional modules.

functional module A unit of logic (or code) representing an identified function of a program.

functional strength The strength of a module as related to its performed function.

garbage The unwanted and meaningless information produced from incorrect logic or failure to initialize data items.

general form notation A diagram denoting the syntactical construction of a statement in a programming language.

general problem-solving procedure A set of organized steps for developing the solution to a problem.

grand break The highest-level break of a program, which includes all records.

grand total The overall accumulated totals for selected fields for all records.

grand total summary line A summary line displaying the accumulated grand total values.

group format specification The set of format specifications repeated as a group. Group format specifications are enclosed in parentheses and preceded by the group repetition factor.

hardware The machines, equipment, devices, or units that make up a computer system. The physical components of a computer system.

hexadecimal The base-16 numbering system.

hexadecimal constant A hexadecimal base number.

hierarchical structure The identified program (or system) structure from a top-down view.

hierarchy A specific rank or order of items. The relationship of components in terms of levels of detail or subordination.

hierarchy chart A graphic program structure design tool used to show the hierarchical structure of a program. Also called a VTOC.

HIPO A structured design and documentation tool used in software development.

HIPO package A complete set of structured design and documentation using HIPO charts for software development.

Hollerith card A punched-hole rectangular card of heavy cardboard divided into eighty columns onto which data is recorded.

Hollerith string/literal A string of characters indicated with the H (Hollerith) format code in a FORMAT statement.

housekeeping The administrative operations, such as initialization of variables or printing of headings, that are to be performed before processing can begin.

identifier A symbol, such as a variable, that is used to name or identify data.

IF-THEN-ELSE control structure A restricted control-flow structure for top-down decision making.

index A value used to specify the element in an array. A variable used to keep track of the iterations of a program loop.

index variable A variable used as a counter or index, normally in a loop.

indexing parameters Variables or constants used to specify the initial, test, and increment values in loop control.

information Facts/data converted into meaningful items to be used in decision making and reports.

initialize To set or reset a variable to a specific value, such as zero.

input Data items brought into the storage unit of the computer for further processing. A general term for input media and/or input fields.

input argument A dummy argument in a parameter list of a subprogram, which provides an input value for use in the subprogram.

input-bound loop A program loop in which the number of iterations is determined by the number of input records read. An input-bound loop is terminated upon reaching an end-of-file condition on an input file.

input/output argument An argument in the parameter list of a subprogram, which serves as both an input value to and an output value from the subprogram.

instruction A command to the control unit to direct the operation of its functional units. A command to the CPU to cause some machine action.

integer A whole number. A quantity having no fractional units of value.

integer arithmetic Calculations performed in integer mode.

integer variable A variable to which an integer value may be assigned.

interface The physical connection between two units of equipment. The logical connection between two program units. The feature of making two things compatible.

intermediate-level control break A control break that consists of a collection of records between a major-level and minor-level control break.

intermediate total The accumulated total of a field for an intermediate-level control break.

intermediate values Those values calculated before the final value for a formula or other operation.

internal program documentation The inclusion of comments and remarks about the program variables, logic, or other aspects within the source program, by the use of comment statements.

internal storage The primary storage area (memory) inside the computer. Storage from which instructions are executed. Contrasted with external storage.

interpreter A language translator that decodes and immediately causes the execution of instructions; no machine language is generated.

intrinsic See built-in function.

invoke To cause to be executed, e.g., to invoke a function.

I/O Abbreviation for input/output.

I/O control unit A hardware unit that provides an interface between I/O devices and a channel, for increased control and increased speed of data transfer.

iteration Repetitive execution of a routine.

iteration control structure A control structure for looping. See DO WHILE and REPEAT UNTIL control structures.

iteration symbol A flowcharting symbol used to identify a loop.

iterative The process of repeating a series of instructions until a desired condition is satisfied, i.e., looping.

JCL See job control language.

job A specified unit of work for the computer, in terms of machine accounting. A job consists of a number of job steps (activities or tasks).

JOB card A JCL card that is normally placed at the beginning of a job deck to supply the account number, identify the user, and provide other accounting information.

job control language A language of commands to the operating system to identify the resources needed for a job.

job deck The complete deck of cards for a processing run, which includes the JCL cards, source program, and data, if supplied on cards.

job step A single task or activity, such as a program compilation, execution, or utility.

jump A transfer of control to a designated instruction.

key One or more fields in a record that are used for control information, such as sorting, control breaks, and comparisons in file maintenance operations. A group of characters used to identify a record or unit of information.

keyword The part of a FORTRAN statement that provides the command (action) to the computer. The keyword in a FORTRAN statement indicates which of the functional units of the computer system will be used to carry out the command.

label An external gummed paper label attached to a reel of magnetic tape to identify its contents. A record written as the first data record on tape to identify its contents. An address such as a statement number to which a transfer is made.

labeled COMMON A memory area with an assigned name that is shared among program units. Contrasted with blank (unlabeled COMMON).

language A defined set of instructions with specific rules of grammar, which provides a means of communication between programmers and the computer.

language translator A system program used to convert a source program written in a high-level language or assembly language into machine form for execution.

layout The design or plan for a solution, such as flowcharts and diagrams.

library An organized collection of programs and subroutines stored on tape or disk.

library-supplied function See built-in function.

line printer An output device that prints information on a hard-copy form.

list To print relevant items of data. A related set of items in a one-dimension array.

listing A printed copy of a program, usually one which has already been compiled.

literal A symbol or element in a program that is itself data, rather than a reference to data.

literal constant A character string given as a literal.

load and go The procedure for automatically loading and executing a program if it is compiled successfully.

load point The beginning position of the magnetic tape, at which reading or writing operations can start.

location A storage cell specified by an address in memory.

logic The science that deals with rules and criteria of validity. The process of performing the correct instruction in the proper order.

logic design The logical steps to be performed in the solution to a problem.

logical constant A constant having the value TRUE or the value FALSE.

logical operation The process of comparing two data items to determine their equality or inequality for decision making.

logical operator A symbol or word used to provide compound logical operations.

logical record See record.

logical variable A variable that may be assigned a value of either TRUE or FALSE.

loop A routine that is repeated until a desired result is obtained.

loop body The statements contained/executed within a loop.

loop exit A test (IF statement) to determine when an exit from the loop is accomplished.

looping The iteration (repeating) of a group of program instructions.

macro flowchart A flowchart in which the algorithm is expressed in a high-level general abstraction.

magnetic disk A storage device on which information is recorded on the magnetic surface of a rotating platter.

magnetic drum A magnetic storage device consisting of a revolving cylinder on which data is recorded.

magnetic tape A magnetic storage device using a storage medium consisting of a ribbon of tape much like a home tape recorder.

mainframe The central processing unit and associated internal storage of a computer system. The main part of a computer with its cabinets of electronic circuitry. The class of computers more powerful than minicomputers.

main program The controlling program unit at which execution begins. Contrasted with a subprogram.

mainline program See main program.

maintenance The upkeep of operational programs and correction of any errors. The activity used to keep hardware in a satisfactory working condition.

major-level control break The most inclusive collection of records in a control break.

major totals The accumulated totals from items in a major-level control break.

malfunction The failure of equipment to operate as intended. Pertains to the various devices of the computer, such as card readers, printers, terminals, tape drives, and so forth.

master file A file of records that are relatively permanent by nature. Contrasted with transaction file.

matrix An array of quantities in a prescribed form, usually with two-dimensions.

memory See internal storage.

memory dump See storage dump.

memory unit The component of a computer system that provides internal storage of instructions and data.

microcomputer A small, compact computer used on a small level, such as a small business or personal computer.

microprocessor One or more integrated chips, which provide the functions of a CPU and are used as part of a microcomputer.

microsecond One millionth of a second. ($.000001$ or 1×10^{-6}). Normally expressed as μs.

millisecond One thousandth of a second. ($.001$ or 1×10^{-3}). Normally expressed as ms.

minicomputer A small general purpose computer, more powerful than a microcomputer but less powerful than a large mainframe computer.

minor-level control-break The least inclusive set of records involved in a control break.

minor total The accumulated total for items for a minor-level control break.

mistake A human failing; gross error.

modular Separated into smaller units or subproblems, so that related functional operations may be performed as a unit.

modular programming The technique of dividing a program into functional modules and implementing it in the same fashion.

module A collection of related instructions to perform a functional task.

module cohesion The strength of a module as related to the function of the instructions within the module.

module coupling The strength of a module as related to the data interface between modules.

module sharing The execution of a module by more than one parent module.

modulo A mathematical operation for obtaining the remainder from a division. For example, 25 modulo 4 = 1 as a remainder.

multiple card-layout form A form used to identify the fields (location, size, and type) for a punched card record.

multiple-level control break The use of more than one control field for control breaks.

n A mathematical symbol for an undetermined number, used for illustration purposes.

name A collection of characters (letters and digits) to represent a storage location. See variable.

named COMMON See labeled COMMON.

nanosecond One billionth of a second ($.000000001$ or 1×10^{-9}). Normally expresses as ns.

nonexecutable statement A program statement that provides some specification to the compiler but does not get converted into an executable instruction. Contrasted with executable statement.

normal termination The completion of program execution from a program termination statement, such as the STOP statement.

object language Machine language.

object program A set of computer commands in a machine language. The output produced from compiling a source program.

object time dimensions The language feature allowing the declaration of array dimensions to take place in a subprogram during program execution.

octal A base-8 numbering system.

octal constant An octal base number.

odd-parity check A method of detecting when a bit is dropped or added to a character enforcing an odd count of bits turned on.

on-line Directly connected to the computer.

one-dimensional array An array containing only one level of dimension, i.e., a row of column vector.

operation The process of executing a defined action. A rectangular-shaped symbol used to denote a calculation or assignment operation in a flowchart.

operator One who operates and supervises the equipment in a computer system.

output The results communicated by the computer from the reading and/or processing of data.

output argument The argument in a parameter list of a subprogram, used to transfer an output value from the subprogram back to the calling program unit.

output device/unit The unit of equipment designed to communicate processed data in internal storage onto some output medium.

output requirements The defined results expected from a program.

overview diagram A high-level diagram in HIPO showing the input, processing, and output element for the first level modules of a VTOC (hierarchy chart).

page eject The advancement of a printer (or hard-copy terminal) listing to the top of the next page.

page heading A description of the page content of a report, which appears at the top of each page of output. A page heading normally identifies the report and includes a page number.

parameter list A list of constants, variables, and/or arrays that are communicated between a calling program unit and a subprogram.

parity bit A bit appended to a unit of data bits to make the sum of all bits always an even or odd count, as the basis for parity checking.

parity check A check with an even- or odd-parity system to verify the validity of data.

Pascal A high-level, procedure-oriented, structured language for programming various applications. Named after the French mathematician Blaise Pascal.

password A combination of characters used to identify a valid user for an account on a timesharing system.

peripheral equipment The input, output, and external storage devices normally set up in a periphery around the main frame. Includes card readers, card punches, printers, tape drives, disk units, and other pieces.

permanent file A file stored on an external storage medium such as disk and available for processing by the computer.

physical file The physical storage space used to hold a logical file.

physical record The physical storage space used to hold one or more logical records. Also see block.

platter A magnetic-coated metal disk used as a disk recording medium.

portability The feature of easily converting a program to run on a different computer.

precision The exactness with which a quantity is stated. The number of significant digits is a measure of precision.

predefined module A module that is already written and available for use.

predefined-naming convention The default data type of a variable, based on the first letter in its name.

preventive maintenance The periodic scheduled maintenance of a computer system, which attempts to keep equipment in top operating condition and to preclude failure. Known as **PM.**

print layout chart/form A form used to lay out the format for the printed results from a report, so that you can code the output requirements of a program.

printer See line printer.

problem definition The statement and identification of the problem requirements to be solved.

problem specification form A form used to identify the problem-solution/program requirements.

problem specifications The requirements for the solution to a problem.

procedure The algorithm or step-by-step method for solving a problem.

procedure-oriented language A high-level compiler language with which one solves a problem according to a set of procedures.

processing The skillful manipulation of data to produce desired results.

processor The arithmetic-logic unit of the CPU. Also referred to as processing unit.

program An organized set of instructions to direct the computer in solving a problem.

program design The identification of the modules needed for the program solution to a problem.

program structure The design of a program in terms of its functional components.

program unit A mainline program or subprogram.

programmer One who writes computer programs.

programmer/analyst A person who is familar with programming and skilled in analyzing problems and designing solutions on computers.

programmer-defined function A function subprogram written by a programmer. Contrasted with a built-in function.

programming The development of a program and coding of computer instructions in a programming language to solve a problem.

prompt A timesharing message to a terminal to indicate to the user the completion of a command and/or that the user may enter a new command, data, or statement.

pseudocode A design tool used to express the logic of a design solution in prose-like form. Pseudocode uses the restricted control-flow structures to express the logic design.

punched card The Hollerith card.

queue The order of jobs awaiting input, execution, or output as determined by an order of priority.

radian A mathematical measurement used in measuring angles. One radian is equal to $180 / \pi$ degrees. One degree is equal to .0174533 radian.

radix A number base, such as binary (2), octal (8), decimal (10), or hexadecimal (16).

random access The ability to locate or place data into storage by direct storage address. See direct access storage devices.

random file organization The construction of a file so that records may be accessed directly.

real time The processing of data as close to an event as possible. Coordinating data processing with related external physical events on a timely basis to permit prompt reporting. For example, an airline reservation system must be a real-time system.

record The logical collection of related data fields that represents a unit of information about a person, thing, or event (transaction).

record layout design The identification of the data fields and their order, type, and length to make up a logical record.

record layout form A form used to identify the data fields and their location for a record.

recursive A procedure involving repetitive steps. Finding the factorial of a number would be a recursive procedure.

relational expression An expression that describes the relationship between two values, such as equal, greater than, less than or equal to, and so forth.

relational operator A symbol or combination of characters used to form a relational expression.

reliability The ability to operate without errors or malfunction.

remote batch The submission of a batch job from a timesharing system.

REPEAT UNTIL control structure A restricted control-flow structure for looping with a test-at-the-bottom type loop.

REPEAT UNTIL loop A program loop using a REPEAT-UNTIL control structure.

report heading See page heading.

reserved words The words set in a programming language that cannot be used as variables or identifiers by a programmer.

retrieval Obtaining data from a storage device.

ripple effect The impact of program changes on the rest of a program.

round-off The truncation of the least significant digits due to the word size of storage of a computer. Compared to truncating.

round-off error The extent of error caused by dropping least significant digits.

routine A group of computer instructions to perform a specific function or task.

row, array The horizontal vector designator for a two-dimensional array.

row-major order The reference of two-dimensional array items by all elements in the same row, i.e., the column subscript is varied the fastest.

row subscript The subscript reference denoting a particular row, normally the first subscript of a two-dimensional array item.

run The execution of a program.

running a program The execution of a computer program.

scalar variable A unique variable name identifying one storage location.

search The process of examining data items in order to perform some calculation or to select an item(s) in accordance with a predetermined criterion.

SELECT CASE control structure A restricted control-flow structure that selects an action(s) from a set of alternatives, based on a condition.

selection control structure A restricted control-flow structure that implements decision making in a top-down manner.

sentinel record The last record in a data file, used to denote the termination of data records, i.e., the end of the file. Also known as a trailer record.

sequence control structure A restricted control-flow structure that implements flow of logic in a top-down, linear manner.

sequential access Obtaining items or records in the order in which they are placed.

sequential file A file in which the records are read/written in a serial or linear fashion.

sequential search A serial or linear search of an array, normally to see if a match exits between an array item and a desired value.

serial One at a time; linear.

significant digits A non-zero value in the left-most positions of a number. A zero in the left-most positions of a number is an insignificant digit. A zero in the right-most positions of a fraction is an insignificant digit. That is, a zero in these positions does not change the value of the number.

single-level control break The use of only one control field for control breaks.

single-precision mode The use of constants, variables, and other data whose values are restricted in precision to one memory word.

single-precision number A numeric quantity restricted in precision to the value that can be stored in a single memory word.

software The collection of programs to operate the computer (system programs) and/or to solve application problems (application programs). The totality of programs and routines used to extend the capabilities of a computer.

software engineering The science of a disciplined approach to software development.

sort To arrange items or records according to specific fields in an ascending or descending sequence.

source deck A deck of cards for a source program.

source document A form used to record original data.

source language The original language in which a program is written.

source listing See listing.

source program The program written in a symbolic language by a programmer. Contrasted with object program.

source statement An instruction/statement in a source program.

special character A character other than a letter or a digit.

specification statement An instruction to the language translator to perform some action during the conversion of the program to machine form. A nonexecutable statement, which does not cause any machine language instruction to be generated. Contrasted with an executable statement.

statement An instruction to the computer or language translator.

statement function A one line function expressed as an arithmetic assignment statement.

statement number A number assigned for reference to an instruction.

storage dump The process of printing a portion or all of memory for debugging purposes.

storage location An addressable area of internal memory.

stored program A set of instructions stored in memory for later execution in solving a problem.

string A sequence of characters.

structure chart A graphic program structure design tool used to identify the modules required for a program solution.

structured coding Writing a program by expressing the logic in the restricted control-flow structures.

structured design The organized procedure of constructing an algorithm for a problem solution using structured design tools.

structured programming The systematic development of a program using structured techniques and tools.

subprogram A separate procedure or set of instructions to solve a part of a problem. See function and subroutine.

subroutine A set of instructions to solve a specific aspect of a problem. A subroutine is a closed subprogram.

subscript A value that identifies a specific array element.

subscripted variable An element in an array, identified by means of the array name followed by a subscript value denoting its position within the array.

summary line A printed line of accumulated totals.

summary total An accumulated total for specified control fields.

switch A variable used to denote a special condition. One value of the variable denotes one status, while another value of the variable denotes another status.

symbolic address A symbol, such as a variable or identifier, used to specify a memory storage location.

syntax The rules governing the construction of instructions/statements in a programming language.

syntax error An error in the syntax construction of a program statement.

system A collection of parts, which form an organized whole. An organized activity of input, processing, and output.

systems analysis A study of the various operations and procedures performed within a system.

systems analyst A person skilled in performing systems analysis.

table A collecton of related items represented in an array. Normally a two-dimensional array.

terminal A device capable of sending and receiving information in a timesharing environment.

terminal symbol A flattened-circle symbol, which denotes the beginning and ending point of logic in a flowchart.

test-at-the-bottom type loop A program loop in which the test for the exit is performed at the end (bottom) of the loop. (A REPEAT UNTIL structured loop.)

test data Data developed in order to check a program for reliability and correctness.

test-at-the-top type loop A program loop in which the test for the exit is performed at the beginning (top) of the loop. (A DO WHILE structured loop).

testing The process of checking the output results of a program with known answers in order to determine the correctness of the program. Also known as testing and debugging.

testing and debugging See testing.

text editor An interactive system program to aid in the creation and modification of text in a file.

timesharing The sharing of computer time among multiple users in an interactive environment.

top-down design The design of a program or system in a top-down manner, using a structured design tool such as a structure or hierarchy chart.

top-down implementation The integration of program modules in a top-down manner.

top-down problem decomposition The identification of the problem parts in a top-down analysis and design.

trace A collection of instructions or use of a system command that shows the flow of control in a program.

track A concentric circle on a disk platter, on which data is recorded.

trailer record See sentinel record.

transaction file A file containing records reflecting daily operation and events in a specific application. Transaction files are used to update master files, to reflect their current status.

transfer of control A change in sequential execution flow to a new location in a program.

troubleshoot To search for the cause of a program error in order to correct the logic.

truncation The process of losing or lessening the precision of a number, usually caused by integer division or real assignment to an integer variable.

truncation error An error in calculation or comparison of items, resulting from the truncation of a value.

turnaround time The total elapsed time from submitting a batch job until the return of the output results.

unary operator An arithmetic operator having only one term, such as the negation (−) operator.

unconditional transfer An automatic jumping to a specified instruction. Contrasted with conditional transfer.

unlabeled COMMON See blank COMMON.

update The process of reflecting the latest status of records in a file.

user-written function See programmer-defined function.

utility programs A set of general purpose programs normally supplied by a computer vendor to perform common operations, such as medium-to-medium conversion, dumping files, or labelling tapes. These programs are also referred to simply as **utilities.**

validity checking The process of editing data items for unreasonable input or calculated values.

variable A symbolic name assigned to a storage location. When a variable is used in a statement, it represents the value stored at that location. Contrasted to a constant.

verification The process of checking the results of an operation to validate the answers.

VTOC Acronym for Visual Table of Contents. A hierarchy chart.

warning message A diagnostic message from the compilation of a program, with an error that is not severe enough to prevent execution.

word A unit of storage to hold one numeric value or multiple characters, depending upon the computer's word size. A word may be measured in bits or bytes.

word processing The process of preparing printed material using data processing equipment.

word size The number of bits or bytes that are handled as a unit by the computer.

write To transfer data, usually from memory, to an output medium.

yet-to-be-developed module A module that is not available and needs to be written. Contrasted with a predefined module.

Index